# Some a
# can't be :

GW00702761

Whatever your theatrical speciality, from working independently, to owning a theatre group, or production company, you need dependable financial advice. Without it your high expectations could end with the curtains lowering sooner than anticipated.

Thanks to *Nyman Libson Paul*, it needn't be this way. We're renowned as one of the country's most astute firms of entertainment chartered accountants. For over 60 years, theatre owners, producers, production companies, stage managers, editors, actors ... in fact a complete constellation of stars, have entrusted *Nyman Libson Paul* for shrewd financial, business or personal advice.

Working in partnership for your long-term prosperity, we can do the same for you. Our client list includes winners of the Oscars, Tony, Emmy, BAFTA, Laurence Olivier and Evening Standard awards: Which makes acting on our advice quite an act to follow. For more details, please contact Paul Taiano.

## Nyman Libson Paul
CHARTERED ACCOUNTANTS

Regina House, 124 Finchley Road, London NW3 5JS
Telephone: 0171 794 5611    Fax: 0171 431 1109
E-Mail: entertainment@nymanlibsonpaul.co.uk
Homepage: http://WWW.nymanlibsonpaul.co.uk
DX: 38864 Swiss Cottage

*Accountants to the world of entertainment*

# the original BRITISH THEATRE directory 1999

Editor: Spencer Block
Sales Manager: Lee Rotbart

The British Theatre Directory is published by

Richmond House Publishing Company Ltd
Douglas House, 3 Richmond Buildings, London W1V 5AE
Tel: 0171 437 9556   Fax: 0171 287 3463
Email: sales@rhpco.demon.co.uk

© 1999 Richmond House Publishing Company Ltd.

ISBN 1-870323-25-4

ISSN 0306-4107

Printed in Great Britain by Butler & Tanner Ltd, Frome and London

# APOLLO LEISURE THEATRES

S T A G I N G     T H E     F U T U R E

| | |
|---|---|
| **LONDON** | APOLLO VICTORIA THEATRE |
| | DOMINION THEATRE |
| | LONDON APOLLO |
| | (THE UK'S ONLY VENUE WITH A MAJOR RECORDING FACILITY) |
| | LYCEUM THEATRE |
| **BIRMINGHAM** | ALEXANDRA THEATRE |
| **BRISTOL** | HIPPODROME THEATRE |
| **CARDIFF** | INTERNATIONAL ARENA |
| **DUBLIN** | POINT THEATRE & ARENA |
| **EDINBURGH** | PLAYHOUSE THEATRE |
| **FELIXSTOWE** | SPA PAVILION THEATRE |
| **FOLKESTONE** | LEAS CLIFF HALL |
| **HAYES** | BECK THEATRE |
| **LIVERPOOL** | EMPIRE THEATRE |
| **MANCHESTER** | PALACE THEATRE |
| | OPERA HOUSE THEATRE |
| | MANCHESTER APOLLO |
| | TAMESIDE HIPPODROME ASHTON-UNDER-LYNE |
| **OXFORD** | APOLLO THEATRE |
| | OLD FIRE STATION THEATRE |
| **SCARBOROUGH** | FUTURIST THEATRE |
| **SHEFFIELD** | ARENA |
| **SOUTHPORT** | SOUTHPORT THEATRE (INCLUDES FLORAL HALL) |
| **SWINDON** | WYVERN THEATRE |
| **TORBAY** | PRINCESS THEATRE TORQUAY |
| **YORK** | GRAND OPERA HOUSE THEATRE |

APOLLO
LEISURE
THEATRES

ENTERTAINMENT
EXCELLENCE

For all information and further details please contact:
Sam Shrouder or Nicky Monk

APOLLO LEISURE UK LIMITED
Grehan House, Garsington Road, Cowley, Oxford, OX4 5NQ
Telephone: (01865) 782900 Fax: (01865) 782910

Millennium Countdown!
Whither or Wither?  by Charles Vance    13

*continued on page 7*

*continued from page 5*

## PUBLISHING

## TRAINING AND EDUCATION

## ORGANISATIONS

## SUPPLIERS & SERVICES

*cont.*

**Suppliers & Services**

*Suppliers & Services*

Sadler's Wells, London

*Image by Winona Dot Com*

Sadler's Wells, Auditorium

*Photo by Richard Learoyd*

# MILLENNIUM COUNTDOWN!
# WHITHER OR WITHER?

A theatre producer for 38 years, **Charles Vance** is in his 26th year as Vice Chairman of the Theatres Advisory Council and he is a Patron of the Voluntary Arts Network. He was previously, uniquely, twice President of the Theatrical Management Association. He is also Publishing Editor of Amateur Stage magazine and was the founding editor of the British Theatre Directory.

As the founding editor of this "Bible" of the British theatre, together with John Offord, I would have been proud 30 years ago, had we been able to envisage the extent of the contribution the British Theatre Directory was to make to this great industry.
I am very gratified to welcome this 27th edition which continues to be our constant reference.
Long may she reign!!
But on a more sombre note I turned to the British Theatre Directory of 1973 to compare it with the 1998 edition (the year we now review) exactly a quarter of a century later...

It was a sobering exercise! Taking a random selection of venues from the Provincial Theatre section for comparison it was as though my career of over half a century had been relegated to the history books and no longer part of living memory. The Thorndike Theatre Leatherhead; Playhouse Liverpool; Redgrave Farnham; Playhouse Bournemouth; Pavilion Torquay; Royal Opera House Scarborough; Leas Pavilion Folkestone; Arts Belfast; Knightstone Weston-Super-Mare; Windmill Great Yarmouth; Adeline Genee East Grinstead; Towngate Basildon.. what had this dozen odd got in common? All of them had ceased to be theatres in any shape or form. Despite the superhuman efforts of the Theatres Trust and local lobby groups it was clear that there was little chance of their re-emergence in theatrical form. Not only was there no more central (or local government) funding in either revenue or capital terms but with increasingly larger swathes of Lottery "good causes" money being diverted to bolster the under-funded health and education services, traditionally the responsibility of government expenditure from tax revenues, that source too was rapidly drying up. But then of course this was the age of Cool Britannia — the age of, quote, "No tax increases".
In last year's review I talked of the icy winds of change which I predicted were the tips of icebergs growing to Titanic proportions.
That is now proving to be the understatement of that year!
What I have highlighted in the opening of this review is past history..that dozen examples of lost theatres represents but a quarter of the actual losses. Come up to date and look at to-day's stock as that stooped figure with his scythe turns the page of the calendar to 1999.
What of our stock now? As we go to press we learn that the Palace Theatre Westcliff will close its doors in March (whilst the Southend Council look for a commercial management to take it over); the axe is about to fall on the Wolsey Ipswich; the Festival Paignton is to become a multi screen cinema complex; the Damoclean sword hangs over the Swan Worcester, the Gateway Chester whilst theatres as disparate as the Kings Head in Islington (that house of courage and innovation) and the Chichester Festival lurch from financial crisis to financial crisis.
And these are only illustrative examples of revenue funding crises where the escalating cost of production is not being matched by any appreciable increase in revenue funding and as the country teeters on the brink of recession, despite the sterling work of Colin Tweedy and his Association of Business Sponsorship for the Arts, there are too many

Nicole Kidman in "The Blue Room"                    Photo by Mark Douet

David Suchet as Salieri in "Amadeus"          Photo by Catherine Ashmore

supplicants chasing comparatively too little available sponsorship funding. Thus we have the irony that despite massive Lottery Awards for huge building and rebuilding projects, three years later work grinds to a halt at the Royal Court Theatre, now swathed in scaffolding (whilst their acting company occupies two of the few available playhouses in London's West End) as they struggled to find the required matching funding to trigger the release of the balance of the lottery award. A generous offer of help from the Jerwood Foundation had a condition that the theatre be re-named the Jerwood Royal Court and the resulting outcry from many more Luddite quarters brought that to nothing.

The arts as ever put up a brave public facade but that is being somewhat tarnished as fly on the wall documentaries and tabloid-like reportage give us a more jaundiced view of the state of "play" in our playhouses..and I make no apology for the intended pun! The real truth behind that brave face (which disguises many a tear) is that the arts overall are in a state of bankruptcy - and that bankruptcy is not only material but, sadly, indicative of the state of the creative skills which are withering as the desperate fight for survival drains the very energies of those whose focus should be on innovation rather than their hand to mouth day to day very existence.

I cannot leave this theme without posing the question: what sort of society is it which can allocate œ218 million to the refurbishment of an opera house whilst a dozen or more venues in and out of the capital are being forced into closure, starved of comparatively minuscule revenue and sometimes capital funds which are a minimal fraction of that one elitist project in Covent Garden.

The highly publicised Richard Eyre review of lyric theatre commissioned by the Secretary of State was explicit in its terms of reference which, inter alia, sought "to ensure the maximum public benefit from the use of public money".

Of course our opera houses must be funded and it is imperative that our Royal Opera House is at least on a par with the world's best. But at what cost? Are we to sacrifice a dozen or more companies and venues threatened with closure for the want of a comparative widow's mite when a single opera house is afforded a gargantuan slice of the rapidly crumbling cake — not forgetting that we had already seen another opera house (Sadlers Wells) razed to the ground and rebuilt again with a massive injection of Lottery funding at the same time as the very existence of the D'Oyly Carte Opera Company is in doubt for the want of a pitifully small injection of funding.

It must be said that the "new" Sadlers Wells deserves its pride of place in Rosebery Avenue and the great Dame Ninette de Valois (now in her 101st year) must be overjoyed at the emergence of such a great receiving house for opera and dance. And lest we forget, we have a third London opera house, the London Coliseum, home of English National Opera, also desperately in need (they say) of total refurbishment

I must pose the question: How is it that, in the commercial sector, Cameron Mackintosh can refurbish the Prince Edward Theatre, Andrew Lloyd Webber the Palace Theatre and Apollo Leisure the Lyceum Theatre (all houses capable of housing the lyric arts as well as mega musicals) with the most modest support from bodies like English Heritage and producers like Raymond Gubbay and Harvey Goldsmith mount spectacular productions of opera in huge stadia like Earls Court and make profits with seat prices at half the level of the Opera House with not a penny of subsidy whilst,on the other side of the coin, the flagship state opera house, charging anything upwards of œ100 per seat requires an additional like sum in subsidy per seat?

"Enough" I hear you cry... in the words of the Irish comedian, "There's more" but I'll leave that for a final millennial review in the 2000 edition of this Yearbook.

Now to the year itself.

In the main it was a disappointing year with a lacklustre festival season at Chichester (the first ever, I think, not to boast a single transfer from the main house and only one from the

Minerva, Joe Orton's "Loot", for a short season at the Vaudeville) matched only by the RSC where it was predicted that Adrian Noble would be gone by Christmas — he wasn't! Opera and ballet in the capital fared little better receiving less adulatory press than has been their wont.

The artistic tragedy of the year came just as we went to press — a highly publicised "spat" and falling out between the volatile producer Bill Kenwright and Sir Peter Hall has resulted in the demise of the Peter Hall Company which has been the principal source of quality theatre for the past five or more years leaving a massive void in the provision of drama.

The irony was that this theatrical tragedy coincided with the Special Laurence Olivier Award (the jewel in the crown of all awards) being awarded to Sir Peter Hall for his outstanding contribution to British arts!

In the musical world the news was little less gloomy... the much heralded arrival of the Broadway phenomenon "Ragtime" never happened when the scandal of multi million dollar fraud at production company Livent hit the headlines and its managing director started a long run at a very inaccessible venue!.

A somewhat tired touring production of West Side Story replaced it (now at the Prince of Wales) and will in turn be replaced by the mega ABBA musical "Mamma Mia!" "Whistle Down The Wind", the latest Lloyd Webber offering, staggers on after its debut at the Aldwych but despite all the heavy hype it plays to exceptionally small audiences in the wake of less than euphoric reviews.

But enough of the bad news. Amongst a lot of dross were some delightful gems.

Trevor Nunn's sensational production of "Oklahoma" at the National transferred, en route to Broadway, to the Lyceum keeping the theatre warm for the London debut of "The Lion King" by the knightly duo of Elton John and Tim Rice which has smashed all Broadway records.

The small scale but so refreshing South African musical "Kat and the Kings", acclaimed at the tiny Kilburn Tricycle, transferred to the Vaudeville and deservedly won the American Express Award for the Best New Musical.

Two magnificent plays Michael Frayn's "Copenhagen" (winner of the Evening Standard Award) thrives at the Duchess whilst Conor McPherson's acclaimed "The Weir" (winner of the Laurence Olivier Award) continues to play to packed houses at the Duke of York's, the temporary home of the Royal Court.

Although destined for a comparatively short run at the Duchess, "The Unexpected Man" (a moving new play from Yasmina Reza, the author of "Art") was the vehicle which won for Michael Gambon and Eileen Atkins the Olivier Awards for Best Actor and Actress.

The Evening Standard Award for the Theatrical Achievement of the Year was rightly given to the Almeida Theatre which is now the proud incumbent of the Albery Theatre where the best of their many fine productions transfer from their tiny Islington home for short West End seasons.

It was a year where the quality of performance often exceeded the quality of the vehicle - a year which saw Sinead Cusack win the Evening Standard Best Actress award for "Our Lady of Sligo" and Kevin Spacey the Best Actor for "The Iceman Cometh" (one of the many gems from the Almeida stable) with a special award for the highly publicised appearance of Nicole Kidman in the altogether in "The Blue Room" at the Donmar.

And despite his not winning any of the prizes we cannot forget the brilliant David Suchet as Salieri in Peter Hall's brilliant revival of Amadeus at the Old Vic.

This is the moment for me to give cognisance to the producer whose year it surely was - Peter Wilson. Not only has he two of London's longest running popular and artistic successes still filling the Fortune Theatre (with "A Woman in Black" in its ninth year) and the Garrick ("An Inspector Calls" in its fifth) but it was his inspiration in reviving "Amadeus" which has injected new life into the Old Vic and his inspiration which saw the Royal National Theatre touring "tent" production of "Oh What A Lovely War" re-open the

Camden Town Round House after two decades of virtual dereliction. All this at the same time as his superb hands-on management of the Norwich Theatre Royal and his annual Mobil Tour which was to win for him this year's Barclays Theatre Award for Special Achievement in Regional Theatre.

Before leaving the London scene some of the other highlights must include all that was good in Opera and Ballet. The Welsh National Opera's production of "La Clemenza Di Tito" walked away with the Olivier Award at the Shaftesbury (to be succeeded in that theatre, by the way, by the outstanding American musical "Rent") and Ballet Frankfurt's "Enemy In The Figure" by William Forsythe won the Best New Dance production Olivier Award.

The theatre received its usual share of the accolades in the Honours "lottery" with knighthoods for writers John Mortimer, Tom Stoppard and David Hare and actors Nigel Hawthorne and Ian Holm; a sprinkling of CBE's for Ronald Harwood, Maureen Lipman, June Whitfield and Christopher Bruce of Ballet Rambert and OBE's for Lenny Henry, Wayne Sleep and Terry Pratchett and the veteran theatrical genius Peter Brook was made a Companion of Honour.

And so to the regions where the quality of work, albeit in a diminishing number of production houses, often surpassed their London counterparts.

On the touring circuit the major houses were dominated by Cameron Mackintosh with blockbuster productions of his continuing West End successes playing for seasons of between four to twelve weeks at each venue. The Barclays Awards paid tribute to the outstanding work which enriched both the touring and regional theatre. Bryony Lavery's "Frozen" directed by Bill Alexander at the Birmingham Rep Theatre won the Best New Play Award whilst Caryl Churchill's "Blue Heart" won for Out of Joint the Award for the Best Touring Production.

The Award for the Theatre of the Year was won by Theatre Clwyd whilst the thrice bombed Grand Opera House in Belfast won for Derek Nicholls the Award for the Most Welcoming Theatre.

Welsh National Opera won the Opera Award for "Billy Budd" and "The Coronation of Poppea" whilst David Bintley won the Dance Award for his revival of Ninette de Valois' "The Prospect Before Us" for the Birmingham Royal Ballet.

The West Yorkshire Theatre won the award for Best Musical for Steve Brown's and Justine Greene's "Spend!" (based on the life of pools winner Viv Nicholson) and also staged the third incarnation of Cameron Mackintosh's totally restructured "Martin Guerre" with resounding success for the theatre and the producer.

The Royal Exchange Manchester walked off with acting awards for Tom Smith in "Present Laughter" and Pauline Lockhart in "An Experiment With An Air Pump" whilst Geraldine McEwan was Barclays Best Actress in the Theatre de Complicite/ Royal Court touring co-production of "The Chairs".

Many leading regional theatres found solace in their relationships with commercial producers for whom they mounted, in ever increasing numbers, co-productions enabling them to enjoy high profile star productions en route for tour and West End with appropriate residual income benefits which replaced some, if not all, of their constant shortfall funding.

As the year waned, a glittering Grand Theatre Wolverhampton re-opened after ten months' closure and an œ8 million refurbishment, funded by the Lottery Board, the European Community and the local Council - another feather in the cap of that doyen of regional theatre managers Brian Goddard.

The year ended, yet again, with a brilliant Cirque de Soliel production, "Alegria" at the Royal Albert Hall — as ever a total sell-out enabling me to close, at least, on an up-beat note.

If not particularly a year to remember it was certainly not a year to ignore.

**Venues**

# VENUE FINDER INDEX

Listed below are all the major venues in the British Theatre Directory and opposite each venue is the page number on which it can be found.

# C

# D

# E

# F

# G

# H

# I

# J

# K

# N

# O

# R

# S

# T

# LONDON VENUES

## 100 CLUB
100 Oxford Street London W1N 9FB
Tel 0171 636 0933 Fax 0171 436 1958
Contact: Jeff Horton

## THE ACADEMY
Cleveland Road Uxbridge Middlesex UB8 3PH
Tel 01895 813504 Fax 01895 810477
ADMINISTRATION:
General Manager: Ian Goodwin
Entertainments Manager: Julie Nerney
Capacity: 600

## ADELPHI THEATRE
Strand London WC2E 7NA
Mgmt 0171 836 1166
ADMINISTRATION:
Props: The Adelphi Theatre Company Ltd.
Policy: Large spectacular musicals, revues and plays.
Perfs: Variable according to production; Mats. Wed. and Sat.
Seats: 1,486. Four Bars.
TECHNICAL:
Stage: Proscenium Stage, Flat; Pros. opening 10.97m; Ht. of Pros. 6.50m; Depth of S/Line 14.94m; Ht. of Grid 16.14m; 45 lines, C/W; Scenery Flying Ht. 7.92m; Flying Bars 10.97m-11.58m; W/Widths P.S. 3.05m, O.P. 2.44m; Prompt Cnr. P.S.
Lighting: Switchboard: Dimmers 8 Stms. 3 Perms = 210 dimmers, 7 LD90's.
Sound: Sound Equip; Cue Call.
Other: Dressing Roms 9; Bathrooms 5; Orchestra Pit 40.
Membership: SOLT
"The plan for this venue can be found in the Official London Seating Plan Guide"

## THE ALBANY
Douglas Way, Deptford, London SE8 4AG
Admin 0181 692 0231 BO 0181 692 4446
Fax 0181 469 2253

## ALBERY THEATRE
St. Martins Lane London WC2N 4AD
Mgmt 0171 867 1125  BO 0171 369 1730
SD 0171 867 1125  Fax 0171 240 3478
ADMINISTRATION:
Props: Associated Capital Theatres
General Manager: Hugh Hales
Theatre Manager: Peter Faldon
Policy: Plays & Musicals.
Perfs: Variable according to Production.
Seats: 879 & 21 Standing. Three Licensed Bars.
TECHNICAL:
Stage: Proscenium Stage, Temp c/w avail. Var. speed house tabs. Flat; Pros. opening 9.6m; Ht. of Pros. 6.55m; Depth of S/Line 11.58m; Ht. of Grid 15.85m; 55 lines Hemp, 6 Motor; Scenery Flying Ht. 15.24m; Flying Bars 11.89m; W/Widths P.Ss 1.90m; O.P. 1.90m; Prompt Cnr. as required (normally D.S.L.).
Lighting: Switchboard: 4 CTT Sil 30, 4ADB Fres. Strand MMS, 200 Channel Capacity with special facilities, rear of stalls; circuit distribution F.O.H. 60; Flys 82; Stage 54

F.O.H. Spots 22 Patt. 264, 8 Patt 23.
Sound:  Equip: I/R Hearing. As required, F.O.H. Stereo Amplification System.
Other: Dressing Rooms 16; Bathrooms 5; 1 Shower; Orchestra Pit 28.
Joint Stage Door with Wyndham's Theatre.
Membership: SOLT.
"The plan for this venue can be found in the Official London Seating Plan Guide"

## ALDWYCH THEATRE
Aldwych London WC2B 4DF
Mgmt 0171 379 6736  SD 0171 836 5537
BO Enquiries 0171 379 3367
BO bookings: 0171 416 6000
ADMINISTRATION:
Props: Nederlander Theatres (Aldwych) Ltd
Management: Michael Codron Plays Ltd (0171 240 8291)
Policy: Usual West End policy
Perfs: Variable according to production
Seats: 1,200, 3 Drinks Bars, Coffee facilities.
TECHNICAL:
Stage: Proscenium Stage, Pros. opening 9.65m, height of Pros 6.44m, Rake 1:24. Depth of S.Line 12.09m.
Height of Grid 15.39 D.S., 14.9m U.S. 40 Lines counterweight. Scenery Flying Ht 7.62m, Flying Bars 10.97m. W/Widths P.S. 2.99m, O.P. 2.13m D.S. 0.91m US. Prompt Corner P.S.
Lighting/Sound/Other: Switchboard - Rank Strand Mini Light Palette 90, 146 ways. Dips 10 each side.
Spots bars available. Dressing rooms 12, accom 52, showers. Scene Dock P.S. Dock doors, 4.27m from stage level. 2990mm H x 2590mm W.
Beam Obstruction 200m H x 150mm W Centre Top.
Air conditioned.
"The plan for this venue can be found in the Official London Seating Plan Guide"

## ALEXANDRA PALACE
Alexandra Palace Way Wood Green London N22 4AY
Tel 0181 365 2121 Fax 0181 883 3999
Sales Executive: Sarah Freds
Events Manager: Chris Simpson
Set in 200 acres of parkland this elegant historic venue is ideal for concerts (indoor and outdoor), exhibitions (up to 9300m2), conferences (10-7250 delegates), weddings and banquets (50-5000 guests).  Free on-site parking for 2000 cars.

## ALMEIDA THEATRE
Almeida Street Islington London N1 1TA
Mgmt/SD 0171 226 7432  BO 0171 359 4404
Fax: 0171 704 9581
ADMINISTRATION:
Executive Director: Nick Starr
Artistic Directors: Ian McDiarmid & Jonathan Kent.
Policy: a full-time producing theatre presenting a varied programme of new work, rarely performed classics and international theatre and music.
Seating capacity 299.
TECHNICAL:
Stage: Area 10 x 12m

Lighting: Control: Gemini Memory Board 100 channels, 100 lanterns.
Sound: Apply to theatre for full information.
Other: Air Conditioned

## AMBASSADORS THEATRE
Please see entry for the Royal Court Theatre Upstairs.

## APOLLO THEATRE
Shaftesbury Avenue London W1V 7DH
Mgmt 0171 734 2987 BO 0171 494 5070
SD 0171 437 3435/1872 Fax 0171 434 1217
ADMINISTRATION:
Props: Stoll Moss Theatres Ltd, 21 Soho Square, London W1V 5FD
Tel: 0171 494 5200
Policy: Plays, Musicals, Comedy, Concerts.
Chief Executive: Richard Johnston
Theatre Manager: Martin Floyd.
For all bookings and production enquiries contact Richard Johnston or Nica Burns (Production Directors), Gareth Johnson (General Manager, Production Department), or David Kinsey (Concerts & Hirings Manager).  Facilities may be made available for day time, late night and weekend use for private and press receptions, conferences and meetings - Contact David Kinsey 0171 494 5200 and Fax 0171 434 1217.
Seats: 775
2 Bars, Entertainment Suites.
TECHNICAL:
Stage: Flat; Pros. Opening 9.14m; Ht of Pros. 6.71m; Depth of Stage 7.87m - 8.42m; Ht of Grid 14.63m; 2 Hemp. 36 C/W, Prompt Cnr. P.S.
Lighting: Board: Strand Gemini II, 120 circuits. Situated O.P. Circle Box.
Sound: Please contact venue.
Other: Dressing Rooms: 12.
Membership: SOLT.
"The plan for this venue can be found in the Official London Seating Plan Guide"

## APOLLO VICTORIA
17 Wilton Road London SW1V 1LG
Mgmt 0171 834 6318  BO 0171 828 7074
SD 0171 834 7231 Tech. Mgr. 0171 828 8621
Fax: 0171 630 7716
ADMINISTRATION:
Props: Apollo Leisure UK Ltd.
Theatre Manager: Jamie Baskeyfield
Technical Manager: David Rose
For all booking information and further details please contact Sam Shrouder or Nicky Monk at Apollo Leisure (UK) Ltd., Grehan House, Garsington Road, Cowley, Oxford OX4 5NQ. Tel: 01865 782900; Fax: Oxford 01865 782910.
Policy: Major musicals.
Perfs: 7.45pm. Matinees 3.00pm
Seats: 2,572 (presently seats: 1524). Bars.
TECHNICAL:
Stage: Pros. opening 14.02m; Pros. Ht. 10.06m; Floats to Back Wall 7.32m; PS Wall to O.P. Wall 22.56m; Grid to Stage 21.64m. Flying System: 38 Counterweight Bars: 28 single, 18 double.
Lighting: Switchboard: Impact Lighting Board.
Sound: Pleaee contact venue.
Other: Dressing Rooms: 10 and 2 suites.
Membership: SOLT.
"The plan for this venue can be found in the Official London Seating Plan Guide"

## THE ARTS EDUCATIONAL LONDON SCHOOLS -THEATRES
Cone Ripman House 14 Bath Road Chiswick
London W4 1LY
Tel: 0181 987 6666 Fax: 0181 987 6699
ADMINISTRATION:
Facility Manager: Graham Binghan
Policy: Plays, Dance, Musical Theatre, Rehearsal space, Studio Space, Conference and Seminars, Two Theatres.
Perfs: normally 7.30pm.
Seats: 160 each theatre. Refreshment facilities available.
TECHNICAL:
Full technical staff and facilities. Computerised lighting control and 16-4-2 sound capability. Rehearsal Facilities: available for hire. Dressing Rooms unlimited.

## ARTS THEATRE
6/7 Great Newport Street London WC2H 7JB
Mgmt 0171 379 3280 BO 0171 836 3334 or 836 2132
ADMINISTRATION:
Lessees: Unicorn Theatre for Children (Caryl Jenner Productions Ltd)
Artistic Director: Tony Graham
Admin Director: Chris Moxon
Production Manager: Petrus Bertschinger.
Seats: 340
TECHNICAL:
Stage: Pros. opening 6.17m; Ht. of Pros. 3.96m; Depth of S/Line 6.10m + 2.43 Apron. 6.10m; Ht. of Grid 12.50m; 31 lines, 15 Hemp, 16 C/W; Prompt Cnr. P.S.
Lighting: Switchboard: Arri Image. Soundcraft 2482 Spint Studio.
Sound: Soundcraft Spirit Mixer 16.8.2.  2 x Revox B77, 6 Tannoy Gold Speakers and 4 x EV 580 Main House PA.
Other: Dressing Rooms: 3.
Membership: TMA.

## ASHCROFT THEATRE
Park Lane Croydon CR9 1DG
Mgmt 0181 681 0821 BO 0181 688 9291
SD 0181 688 4555 Fax 0181 760 0835
Fax (Mkt) 0181 686 7944
ADMINISTRATION:
Props: Fairfield (Croydon) Ltd.
Chief Executive: Derek Barr
Head of Artistic Planning: Nick Leigh
Controller of Artistic Planning: Colin May
A registered charity
Capacity: 763.
TECHNICAL:
Stage: Proscenium Stage, Flat; Pros. Opening 8.53m; Ht. of Pros. 5.64m; Depth of S/Line 6.71m; Ht. of Grid 12.19m; 30 lines, C/W; Scenery Flying Ht. 6.10m; Flying Bars 12.19m; W/Widths P.S. 366m, O.P. 3.05m; Prompt Cnr. P.S.
Lighting: Switchboard: Light Palette, 120 cirs. F.O.H. Spots 12 Silhouette 15s, 14 Starlette 1kw, 12 Sil 30s, 10 Starlette 2kw, 24 Thomas 650 Fresnel, 24 Par 64 cans, Cycfloods 24 Iris on 4 cirs. Floats if required; Dips 11 each side. spot Bars.
Sound: 2 Revox Tape Decks with speaker mixing, E. V. speakers, F.O.H. speakers, Amcron Amplifiers, Soundcraft 200, 16-4 mixer, comprehensive patching. Control Room at Rear Stalls, Speakers 3 F.O.H., 4 backstage, mics available. 35mm cinema projection with Dolby stereo and surround sound.
Other: Dressing Rooms: 8; Accom. 60; Orchestra Pit 14.

Membership: TMA.

## BARBICAN - THE PIT
Silk Street, Barbican, London EC2Y 8DS
mgt 0171 628 7123 SD 0171 628 3351
BO 0171 638 8891 Fax 0171 374 0818
Barbican Centre Mgt 0171 638 4141
SD 0171 628 3351 BO 0171 638 8891
Fax 0171 382 7377
ADMINISTRATION:
Artistic Director: Adrian Noble
Executive Producer: Lynda Farran
Theatre Administrator: Graham Sykes
Production Manager: Simon Ash
Status: Producing Theatre. The venue is not self-financing, it is funded by RSC season, ACE, Corporation of London.
Policy: RSC 30 week season of Shakespeare, classics and new writing (Nov-April). Barbican Centre 22 week season includes small-scale contemporary theatre & performance work (May-Oct).
Non-performance activities: Available for hire subject to programming. Willing to premiere shows.
Performance Schedule: No fixed schedule, call box office for details, 0171 638 8891.
Booking Terms: Please contact Theatre Administrator for details.
Seating: 200
Catering: 1 bar and coffee points (see Barbican Centre catering facilities).
Acess: (See Barbican Centre Access facilities).
Facilities for the disabled: 1 wheelchair space.
TECHNICAL:
Stage: Open stage. Performing area 8m X 10m (7.5m with 4th side auditorium) - offstage areas limited. No rake - floor planks, not suitable for dance, crossover to SR at rear normally created by scenery or masking. Average fixed bar height 4.2m. Black masking. Get-in via lorry lift from street level, dock doors 3.1m X 3.1m. Tallescope. Scale stage plan available, 1:25.
Lighting: Strand Gemini II+ board, 144 circuits, operated on platform at back of auditorium - no supply for temporary board - 90 spots, 45 fresnels, 29 parcans, 14 pcs, 11 floods.
Sound: Cadac A series 40:10:10 desk, operated in platform at back of auditorium - one flown 1 floor standing speaker in all four corners of auditorium, plus central cluster - 2 X Denon mini disc players - 1 X Akai s300i sampler - 1 X Amiga sequencer - CD player - 3 effects units - mics shared with Barbican Theatre. Acoustics suitable for music and spoken word.
Stage Mgt: Prompt position on lighting/sound platform at back of auditorium - cue lights, 12 outstations, and headsets, 8 outstations - show relay/Tannoy to dreessing rooms.
Backstage: Dressing rooms shared with Barbican Theatre - green room - band room - 2 quick change rooms - wardrobe as for Barbican Theatre. Refreshments available in green room. Rehearsal facilities as for Barbican Theatre. Staff and security facility shared with theatre. Backstage facilities accessible to disable performers and staff.

Cinema 1
Tel 0171 382 7000
ADMINISTRATION:
Props: Corporation of London,
Programme Planner: Robert Rider.
Policy: Independent film repertory and new releases.
Performances: Usually 2 evening perfs and week-end matinees, Saturday Childrens Cinema Club.

Seats: 280 plus 2 wheelchair spaces.
Full projections, lighting, sound, video, simultaneous interpretation.

Cinemas 2 and 3
Available for conferences, meetings and private screenings. Cinema 2 used for public cinema (see Cinema 1).
Seats: 253 and 153 respectively, plus one wheelchair space in each auditorium.

Other Facilities:
Barbican Art Gallery, Concourse & Foyer Gallery, 1400 sq.m.; open air Sculpture Court; City of London Lending Library; 3 public restaurants; private function rooms; 5 conference rooms; 2 trade exhibition halls, 8000 sq.m. gross; parking for 454 cars.

## BARBICAN CENTRE
Silk Street, Barbican, London EC2Y 8DS
Mgt 0171 638 4141 Fax 0171 920 9648
SD 0171 628 3351 BO 0171 638 8891
ADMINISTRATION:
Managing Director: John Tusa
Arts Director: Graham Sheffield
Director of Public Affairs: Ruth Hasnip
Engineering Director: Mark Chapman
Technical Services Manager: Kim Little
Senior House Manager: Sue Patterson
Press & PR Manager: Valerie Gillard
Head of Box Office Services: Britannia Emson (Miss)
Head of Marketing: Chris Travers
Facilities for the disabled: Barbican Hall, 16 wheelchair spaces plus escorts; Barbican Theatre, 8 wheelchair spaces plus escorts; The Pit, 1 wheelchair space plus escort. Lifts, chairlifts and assistance available, ring box office on 0171 638 8891. Level access and free parking on presentation of disabled car registration certificate.

## BARBICAN HALL
Silk Street, Barbican, London EC2Y 8DS
Mgt 0171 628 7123 SD 0171 628 3351
BO 0171 638 8891 Fax 0171 382 7377
Barbican Centre Mgt 0171 638 4141 SD 0171 628 3351
BO 0171 638 8891 Fax 0171 382 7377
Seating: Barbican Hall 1989, fixed rake, continental style;
TECHNICAL:
Stage: Open Concert Platform. Performing area 20.13m X 12.4m, 10.3m to 6.7m high. No rake - floor beech, unsprung, no crossover, stage heated. Timber surround at rear - drawn. Rear half of stage is a series of mechanical risers. Get-in via goods lift. Scale stage and lighting plans available.
Lighting: ETC Expression 2x board, 168 circuits, operated from control room at rear of stalls . 2 followspots if required.
Sound: Midas XL200 48:8 desk, operated at rear of stalls - Renkus Heinz central cluster speaker system - stocks of AKG, Sennheiser, Shure and Sony Mics. Soundcraft 8000 24:8:8 control room rear of stalls.
Stage Mgt: Prompt corner left, right or centre backstage - cue lights, talkback - show relay to dressing rooms.
Backstage: 21 dressing rooms, access by lifts and stairs - green room - band room. Backstage bar. Rehearsal rooms and pianos, excellent. Advice given on accommodation. Many staff - security, personnel.
"The plan for this venue can be found in the Official London Seating Plan Guide"

## BARBICAN THEATRE

Silk Street, Barbican, London EC2Y 8DS
Mgt 0171 628 7123 SD 0171 628 3351
BO 0171 638 8891 Fax 0171 382 7377
Barbican Centre Mgt 0171 638 4141 SD 0171 628 3351
BO 0171 638 8891 Fax 0171 382 7377
(From Nov-April, managed by the RSC, and from May-Oct, managed by the Barbican Centre)
ADMINISTRATION:
Artistic Director: Adrian Noble
Executive Producer: Lynda Farran
Theatre Administrator: Graham Sykes
Production Manager: Simon Ash
Status: Producing Theatre. The venue is not self-financing, it is funded by ACE, Corporation of London.
Policy: RSC 30 week season of Shakespeare, classics and new writing (Nov-April). Barbican Centre 22 week season of international theatre, opera and contemporary dance (May-Oct). Willing to premiere shows.
Performance Schedule: No Sunday performances, matinees usually Thursday & Saturday.
Booking Terms: Please contact Theatre Administrator for details.
Non-performance activities: Available for hire subject to programming.
Seating: 1,156 and 12 standing.
Catering: 2 private bars , Theatre bars, stalls floor and gallery bar, (also see Barbican Centre catering facilities).
Acess: (See Barbican Centre Access facilities).
Facilities for the disabled: 8 wheelchair spaces plus escorts; infra-red audio system; parking; lifts to all levels; special toilets and assistance available.
TECHNICAL:
Stage: Open Stage. Performing area 15m X 15m - pros opening up to 15m X 9m - wing widths 10m SR, 10m SL, 6m US - Raked stage 1 in 15 (removable), floor surface variable, dance floor available, backstage and understage crossovers, stage heated. Height of grid 30m - 67 powered hoists, 0.2m apart - 500kg permitted on bars - maximum flying height 10m - various masking. 30 X 15A/45A independent circuits. Various stage machinery. Get-in via truck lift, dock doors 4m X 6m. Tallescope. Safety curtain. Scale stage, fly and lighting plans available, 1:25 and 1:50.
Lighting: Obsession 2, 480 ways, 380 X 3kw, 100 X 5kw, operated from control room at rear of stalls - 300 spots, 100 fresnels, Strand - 4 X CSI followspots, operated from No 1 FOH bridge.
Sound: Cadac E Series mixing desk - Beyer, Calrec, Sennheiser, AKG and Neumann mics - Akai sampler, Denon midi disk systems - purpose-built sound editing suite - PA system. Acoustics suitable for music and spoken word.
Stage Mgt: Prompt corner SL and rear of stalls - twin light cue system, 30 outstations - show relay/Tannoy to dressing rooms.
Backstage: 21 dressing rooms, accommodating 88 - green room - band room - quick change rooms - wardrobe on 7th floor, fully equipped. Rehearsal room and piano. Staff (for main Stage and Pit) - 16 stage, 10 lighting, 3 sound, 5 wardrobe - casuals available - security personnel. Backstage facilities accessible to disabled performers and staff. '
Membership: SOLT; TMA.
"The plan for this venue can be found in the Official London Seating Plan Guide"

## BATTERSEA ARTS CENTRE

Lavender Hill London SW11 5TF
Mgt 0171 223 6557 BO 0171 223 2223

Fax: 0171 978 5207
ADMINISTRATION:
Director: Tom Morris
Production Manager: Chris Robinson
Policy: Concentration on the presentation of visual theatre and new writing with an emphasis on the most innovative and challenging new work.
Theatre: Multi-purpose performance space. Seating capacity 170.
Studio One: Seating 48
Studio Two: Seating 60
Seating capacities in the two studios are variable.
TECHNICAL:
Stage (Theatre): The playing area (on floor) is normally 27 feet x 21 feet.
Lighting: 6 X Harmony 1k Fresnels all with Barndoors, 10 X Cantata 1.2k Fresnels all with Barndoors, 10 X Cantata 1.2k Profiles 18/32 with Rotary Gobo Gate, 15 X 650w Prelude Fresnels all with Barndoors, 8 X Thomas Pars all CP 62. LX Desk: ETC Express:- 120 Channels 2k per way Digital
Sound: Soundcraft K1 Sound Desk 16-4, 1 X Denon DCD -425 single C.D. Programmable, 1 X Denon DRM 550 single cassette unit, 2X EV P1250 PWR Amps, 1 X EV XP200 Cross Over, 4 X EV S x 200 Midd and Top Speakers, 2 X EV Sb 120 Bass Speakers, 1 X Alesis Quadravert, Relevant Cables, Patch Bay.
Please contact the Production Manager/Technical Department for further information.
STUDIO 1: (Also available for hire as a rehearsal space).
Flexible rostrad seating - Cap: 50.
Lighting Desk: MX 24 - Man & Computer.
Lighting: 8 X Minim F's, 4 X Minim P.C's, 3 X Minim 23's, 4 X Prelude F's, 2 X Prelude P.C's, 7 X Prelude 28/40 Profiles, 6 x Pars CP 62, 2 X 1k Floods, 2 X 1/2k Floods, LX Desk: ETC Express:- 48 Channels 2k per way, Digital, 2X independents, 2 X Non Dim
Sound: SP.R17 Live 16/3 mixer, 1 X Denon DCD 425 C.D. , ! X Denon DRM 550 Cassette, 1X EV P1250 PWR Amp, 2 X EV S x 200 Top & Mid Speakers.
Please contact the Production Manager/Technical Department for further information.
Arts Cafe: Seating - 64. Fixed stage area 24' x 7'.

## BECK THEATRE

Grange Road Hayes Middlesex UB3 2UE
Mgt 0181 561 7506 BO 0181 561 8371 (3 lines)
Fax 0181 569 1072
ADMINISTRATION:
Props: Apollo Leisure (UK) Ltd.
For all booking enquiries contact Sam Shrouder (Joint Deputy Managing Director) or Nicky Monk (Theatre Bookings Manager) on tel: 01865 782900 or fax: 01865 782910, Grehan House, Garsington Road, Cowley, Oxford OX4 5NQ.
Theatre Manager: Graham Bradbury
MAIN AUDITORIUM: Policy: Major theatre tours and concerts, children's shows, pantomime, films, plus local amateur and daytime conference hirings.
Open 7 days per week.
Seats: Deluxe tiered, fixed auditorium seating: 600.
Seating with orchestra pit/thrust stage: 564.
Second Performance Area: Foyer area seating up to 250 around central performance floor of semi-sprung Canadian maple, dimensions up to 30' x 30'.
Policy: Cabaret performances, dance evenings, folk, jazz, dance workshop, fringe theatre, etc.
Licensed bar, kiosk, bistro restaurant .
Rooms available for private functions and meetings of up to 70; catering by arrangement.
Exhibition areas in foyer and function rooms.

Perfs: Variable, generally 8.00 p.m. for plays and single performance concerts.
TECHNICAL:
MAIN AUDITORIUM:
Stage: Polished Canadian Maple wood flat stage. Proscenium arch - Height: 5.9m; Width: variable opening, either11.6m, 12.8m or 14m; Depth: 9.5m to cyclorama. Stage to Grid: max height 7.5m - NO FULL FLYING FACILITY. Wing Widths: 3.5m to 1m. Walls taper upstage.
Lighting: Arri Imagine 2 console - 100 channels. 5 Rank Strand STM 20-way dimmer racks - includes 18 x 5kw circuits. Tempus 2G - 12 manual lighting board (12-way, 2-preset) for use in the foyer. 2 x 6-way, 10 amp. Tempus dimmer racks for use in the foyer.
Lanterns: 10 Cantata 11/26 - 1200w profile; 15 Cantata 18/32 - 1200w profile; 15 Cantata 26/44 - 1200w profile; 3 Leko 11 - 1000w profile; 2 Leko 18 - 1000w profile; 4 Leko 26 - 1000w profile; 2 Leko 40 - 1000w profile; 5 Prelude 28/40 - 650w profile; 5 Prelude 16/30 - 650w profile; 25 Patt. T.64 - 1000w profile; 25 Cantata P.C. - 1200w prism convex; 5 Prelude P.C. - 650w prism convex; 25 Cantata F. - 1200w fresnel; 5 Prelude F. - 650w fresnel; 35 Patt. 743 - 1000w fresnel; 30 Par Cans - 1000w beamlights (Par 64); 12 Coda 500Mk2- 500w floods; 32 Iris 1 - 625w floods (20 rigged on cyc. LX bar); 2 Patt. 293 Follow Spots - 2000w; 4 LX Stands. Good stock of "Strand" Chromoid and Cinelux colour filters.
Power Supplies: Stage left: 63 Amp 3 phase Cee-Form Socket; 63 Amp 1 phase Cee-Form Socket; (only one socket can be used at a time). 32 Amp 3 phase Cee-Form Socket; 32 Amp 1 Phase Cee-Form Socket; 13 Amp Ring Main (RCD protected). Stage Right: 63 Amp 3 phase Cee-Form Socket; 13 Amp Ring Main (RCD protected). We do not have the facility for 'tailing-in'. All power supplied must be via cee-form or ring main. Special effects: 1 Zero 88 sound-to-light unit. Mirror ball and rotator. 2 Pan-can heads and controllers.
Projection and audio visual: 1 Westrex 35mm film projector with cinemascope. 1 full size cinema screen. 1 Kodak Carousel S-AV2000 slide projector. 2 Kodak Carousel S-AV2000 slide trays. 3 Kodak S-AV2000 lenses 1 x f=100mm; 2 x f=150mm. 1 portable screen 4' x 4'. 1 overhead projector. 1 flipchart/wipeboard. 1 VHS Video recorder and 24" Television (a small hire charge will be incurred for the above items).
Sound: 1 Soundcraft 200SR 24-4-2 mixer desk; 1 Yamaha graphic equaliser - Q2031A, 31 band, 2 channel; 1 BSS frequency dividing system "Series 300"; 2 H/H stereo power amplifiers - VX900 - Mosfet; 1 Pair Martin speaker stacks - 1.8kw total output (Bass - BR125; Mid - MH112; High - HF2R); 1 Yamaha SPX9011 digital effect processor; 1 Technics M222 twin cassette player; 1 Studiomaster monitor mixer Model Stagemaster 24-8 monitor mixer; 2 Yamaha graphic equalisers, Q2031A, 31 band, 2 channel; 3 H/H stereo power amplifiers VX300 - Mosfet; 4 JBL radial wedge speakers, Model 4728P; 2 Martin wedge speakers, Model LE200
Microphones: 5 Shure SM58. 1 Shure 565. 4 AKG 321. 1 AKG 202ES. 1 AKG D12E. 5 AKG D190E. 2 AKG D900 rifle. 4 Sennheiser K30/ME80. 3 Calrec CB20c/CC50/K10. 1 x SM58 radio Freq. 174.5 mHz MPT 1345. Various microphone stands - boom, telescopic, floor, etc.
For use in foyer: Bose sound system - 2 x Bose 302 Bass speakers, 4 x Bose 802 Series II speakers, 2 x Bose speaker stands, Bose 802-C system controller, PA300 Mosfet mixer amplifier (5 inputs), Tascam 225 cassette recorder.

A digital acoustic system is installed in the theatre: S.I.A.P. (System for Improved Accoustic Performance). Other: Equipment: Stage Manager's Desk - with full cue lighting system, 2 intercom circuits and backstage paging system. Desk movable and situated stage left. Two sided (black/white) Harlequin full stage dance floor. Soft plastic (Rosco) white/blue cyclorama. Full soft black box. 12 black wood frame wing flats - 5.5m height, 1.5m width; 15 wood frame rostra - 5 x 18" high; 5 x 36" high 5 x 56" high surface 6' x 4';. 12 metal frame rostra - 12" high, surface 3' x 3'. 1 conductor's "RAT" music stand with lights. 11 "RAT" music stands with lights. 30 lightweight music stands without lights.
Backstage Facilities: 8 Dressing Rooms - including 2 holding 20 each; 4 with private shower facilities. 2 additional shower units. 4 single unit W.C.s. 2 multiple unit W.C.s (1 male/1 female). Laundry facilities , coin operated washing machine and tumble dryer.
Direct access to scene dock through ramp and shutter door. Difficult access for low ground clearance trucks. Parking space for trucks.
Orchestra Pit lift (2.7m deep); 3 positions - as pit; as auditorium floor; as stage apron.
11 bars (14.6m length) winch operated; 3 tab tracks; 7 wipe tracks. 5 lighting bars - including cyc lighting bar. 4 pianos - Steinway 'C' Concert Grand (on stage); Daneman Baby Grand in foyer; Knight Upright; Yamaha PF80 electric piano and stand.

## BLACKHEATH HALLS

23 Lee Road Blackheath London SE3 9RQ
Tel 0181 318 9758 BO 0181 463 0100 Fax 0181 852 5154
ADMINISTRATION:
Artistic Director: Peter Conway
Administrative Director: Sarah Keel
Policy: Flexible concert halls purpose built in 1885.
Policy: Classical, Jazz, Folk, Contemporary, Opera, Musicals, Rock & Pop, Exhibitions, Recordings and Rehearsals. Available for hire, presents own events and co-presents.
Cafe Bar available for hire seating 50 - standing 150.
TECHNICAL:
Recital Room: Capacity 220, 60' x 30', stage 18' x 9' max.
Great Hall: Capacity 700, 1,000 standing, 90' x 60', stage 50' x 25'.

## BLOOMSBURY THEATRE

15 Gordon Street London WC1H 0AH
Mgt 0171 383 5976 Fax 0171 383 4080
BO 0171 388 8822 SD 0171 387 6780
Email: blooms.theatre@ucl.ac.uk
Web Site: www.ucl.ac.uk/bloomsburytheatre/
ADMINISTRATION:
General Manager: Michael Freeman
Chief Technician: Gus Wright
Policy: All-year round programme of visiting Theatre Dance, Concerts, Comedy and Opera, including occasional in-house productions and 12 weeks of Student Productions during October and Spring Terms.
Seats: 515-560. Standing room: 35. Full Catering facilities and Bar.
TECHNICAL:
Stage: Proscenium Stage with two forestage lifts for thrust stage or orchestra pit for 60, Flat; Pros. Opening 9.12m; Ht. of Pros. 7.03m; Stage width: (wall to wall) 24.16m, (stage left wing) 6.6m, (stage right wing) 8.1m; Stage Depth 9.35m (+first forestage 11.97m, + second forestage 14.98m); Stage height: (from stage floor to

underside flying gallery) 6.9m, (from stage floor to top flying dead) 18.29m; 25 d/purchase C/W sets plus 4 Hemps; Flying Bars 11.58m; W/Widths P.S. 7.03m, O.P. 7.63m; Prompt Corner SM desk SR or SL.
Lighting: Control rear of auditorium. Arri Imagine 250 desk. 120 ways of dimming - 112 at 2.5K, 8 at 5K. Luminaires; 14-243, 4 - 2K starlette (fresnel), 10 - 1K Starlette PC, 20 - 743 (1K fresnel), 4 - 5000W Minuette Frenels, 20 - Sil 30 (1K profile), 20 264 (1K profile), 2 - Sil 15 Axial (1K), 2 Sil 15 Followspots(2K), 20 Parcans (C.P.61 or 62 heads), 8 - Berkey 650W 4 compartment battens. 12 Boom arms. 3 I.W.B.'s 10,15 and 18 way. 6 Shin stands. 6 Boom stands (8 feet high), 6 adjustable boom stands (max height 8 feet).
Sound: Soundcraft series 200 SR 16 - 4 - 2. 1 - Revox B77, 1 - A77, 1 - Sony stereo cassette deck TC - RX7OES, 1 -HH Amcron V800 Power amp, 1 - Amcron D60 amp, 2 - Amcron D150 amps. 10 - Bose 802 speakers (8 FOH, & 4 foldback), 2 - Bose 302 (FOH & foldback). 1 - SPX 990 Yamaha effects processor, 1 - Stereo 31 band graphic equalizer. 4 SM57 mics, 4 SM58 mics, 1 - Beyer 300N, 1 - Shure 545SD, 1 -AKG 190, 2 - AKG 1200 E-HB. Various mic stands.
Other: Projection Equipment: 2 x Phillips 35mm FP20 (2 kw Xenon), Cinema Screen, Dolby 'A' Sound System. Steinway Grand Piano. Dressing Rooms: DR 1 accom. 4, DR 2 accom. 4, DR 3 accom. 9, DR 4 accom. 14 (all with showers), Crew room, laundry room, Orchestra Pit 60 players.
Paint Frame: (10.97m x 7.32m drop) and Workshop available for hire.

### BORDERLINE
Orange Yard Off Manette Street London W1V 5LB
Tel 0171 734 2095 Fax 0171 424 1698
Manager: Richard Dutton
Capacity: 275

### BOW THEATRE
Bow House 153-159 Bow Road London E3 2SE
Tel 0181 983 3000  Fax 0181 983 3766
Temporary closed for redevelopment.
Managing Agent for business centre: Raymond Rahimzadeh

### BREAK FOR THE BORDER
8-9 Argyll Street London W1V 1AD
Tel 0171 734 5776 Fax 0171 437 5140
Bar and restaurant available for private hire.
Contact: Craig Brierley
Capacity: 375

### BRITTEN THEATRE ROYAL COLLEGE OF MUSIC
Prince Consort Road London SW7 2BS
Mgt 0171 589 3643 ext 3434 Fax 0171 589 7740
Email: pbritten@rcm.ac.uk
ADMINISTRATION:
Props: Royal College of Music.
Theatre Manager: Prue Britten
Policy: One of London's best-kept secrets, this is an elegant theatre producing Royal College of Music Operas, Concerts, etc. Also available to hire for dance conferences, product launches, concerts, filming etc. Opened in 1986.
Seats: 400 on 3 levels.
TECHNICAL:
Stage: Pros width 9.06m, height 5.18m; Perf area

(without masking) width 10.43m, depth 9.28m; wings widths SR 2.22m, SL 1.82m, US nil; rake flat level standard configuration; floor maple strip on ply; height of grid 12.70m; basic flying details counterweight, single purchase 35 set at 0.23cm spacing no tab track available; max weight on bars 400kg; max flying height 12.35m, basic masking available serge flats, legs, boards, tabs + wipe. Black;Stage power supply 19 X 13amp 240 outlets, stage machinary traps, Forestage dimensions: width 9.35m max, depth 3.58m entrances SL and SR; Orchestra pit dimensions: width 9.35m , depth 9.3m accomodates 80 max.
The stage is suitable for dance and barefoot dance and there is a cross over up-stage. The stage is not heated.
Lighting: Board; Strand 530 consle c/w 400 channels of Genius Pro software, Tracker Moving Light software, Networker System software; dimmers 120 saturated configuration, 100 X 2.4kw, 20 X 5kw, 3 phase, (LD90); operation centre rear dress circle; temporary power supply 3 phase, 63 amp per phase, (USR), Luminaires: 12 X Cantata 11/26 1.2kw, 2 X Cantata 18/32 1.2kw, 22 X Harmony 15/28 1kw, 8 X Patt.264 1kw, 15 X Prelude 16/30 650w, 4 X Prelude 22/40 650kw, 1 X Solo follow spot 2kw, 1 X Cadenza F 2kw, 11 X Cadenza PC 2kw, 12 X Cadenza PC 1.2kw, 6 X Patt. 743 1kw, 1 Prelude F 650w, 24 X Prelude PC 650w, 24 X P.64 240v 1kw (CP61, CP62 only), 8 X Spill Ring for P.64, 2 X P.750, Beamlight 1kw, 12 X Coda 500/3 (3 X 500w), Misc: 2 X 4'6" stands, 4 X turtles, 1 X 16 way internally wired bar, 3 X 14 way internally wired bar, 2 X 6 way internally wired bar (1/2 width); Effect equipment 8 X Scroller Rainbow Pro 8, 33 colours, 2 X Moving Light, Strand Pirouette, 1 X Control for above units.
Sound: 1 X Soundcraft 8-4-2, located SR corner, amplifiers 3 X AGM SC-500, microphones 1 X SM58, 1 X single cassette, house system show relay and tannoy to all dressing rooms, no foyer PA. The theatre is designed with acoustics for music and the spoken word without amplification.

### BRIXTON ACADEMY
211 Stockwell Road, London SW9 9SL
Admin 0171 771 3000 BO 0171 771 2000
Fax 0171 738 4427
Manager: Steve Forster
Stage Manager: Josh Rosen
Seating/Capacity: 4,272 max, including 924 seats in circle. Standing 3,312.

### BROADWAY THEATRE
Broadway Barking Essex IG11 7LS
Mgr 0181 592 4500 extn 3466 BO 0181 591 9662
Fax 0181 591 9662
ADMINISTRATION:
London Borough of Barking & Dagenham
Theatre Manager: Miss C Oatham
Auditorium Seating: 800
Licensed bar & coffee lounge.
TECHNICAL:
MAIN AUDITORIUM - Seats: Auditorium free standing seating, Concert 612, Circle tiered fixed seating 190, Boxing Arena Auditorium free standing seating 480, Circle tiered, fixed seating 190, Dinner Function maximum 350, with dance area/without dance area maximum 425.
Stage: Polished, wooden flat stage with proscenium arch. Variable opening 14.7 m. narrowing to 10.1 mtrs. wide. Height: 6.9 mtrs; depth: 6.75 mtrs. 3 x Footlights; 3 x Lighting Bars; 6 x 100w cans; Reversible black/beige backcloths; reversible black/beige legs; skyblue back

# THE BRITTEN THEATRE

Royal College of Music, Prince Consort Road, London SW7 2BS

ROYAL
COLLEGE
OF
MUSIC

A prestige London venue for opera, dance, corporate entertainment, promotional activities and conferences. The Britten Theatre, opened in 1986, comprises a 402-seat intimate auditorium on three levels, with excellent technical facilities and superb acoustics.

**Details and hire terms from:**
**Special Events Manager**
**Telephone: 0171 589 3643**
**Fax: 0171 589 7740**

cloth; limited flying facilities; access ramp to theatre.
Equipment: 2 Pianos - 1 Bluthner Grand Piano; 1 Berrys Upright; 1 adjustable piano stool; 6 music stands. 1 metal rostra.. Height 7.5 m. Surface 2.45 mtrs x 1.83 mtrs.
Lighting: Axiom 48 channel memory mixer desk controlling lanterns, four side of house and one centre bar incorporating 2 x worklights. 2 follow spots with colour filters. Stock of colour filters.
Special Effects: 1 Sound to light unit; 1 Mirror ball with rotator.
Sound: 1200 watts P.A. including Spirit Folio 4 20 channel COURT SIGNATURE THIRD GENERATION HP400 SERIES mixing desk with full stereo output. Reverberation units. Wedge monitors. Selection of vocal/instrumental microphones with stands.
Other: Communications: Stage - Left and right of stage to control desk and follow spot operators. 3 Station cans. Internal phone system to operational areas throughout theatre. Show call relay to dressing rooms.

## BULL & GATE
389 Kentish Town Road London NW5 2TJ
Tel 0171 485 5358 Booking of Acts and
BO 0171 336 8511 Fax 0171 689 0743
ADMINISTRATION:
Manager: Patrick Lynsky
Seats: 150

## CAMBRIDGE THEATRE
Earlham Street London WC2H 9HU
MGT 0171 240 7664 BO 0171 494 5080
SD 0171 379 0075
ADMINISTRATION:
Props: Stoll Moss Theatres Ltd. 21 Soho Sq. London,

W1V 5FD   Tel: 0171 494 5200  Fax 0171 434 1217.
Policy: Musicals, Comedy, Concerts, Television, Plays.
Chief Executive: Richard Johnston
Theatre Manager: Pauline Loraine
For all bookings and production enquiries contact Richard Johnston or Nica Burns (Production Directors), Gareth Johnson (General Manager, Production Department), or David Kinsey (Concerts & Hirings Manager).  Facilities may be made available for day time, late night and weekend use for private and press receptions, conferences and meetings - Contact David Kinsey 0171 494 5200 and Fax 0171 434 1217.
Seats: 1283
3 Bars Buffet, Entertainment Suite.
TECHNICAL:
Stage: Flat; pros. Opening 9.14m; Ht of Pros. 7.67m; Depth of stage 9.14m; Ht of Grid 16.58m; 43 C/W lines; Prompt Cnr. P.S.
Lighting: Board; Strand Galaxy II, 280 circuits.
Situated rear stalls.
Sound: Please contact venue.
Other: Dressing rooms: 18
Membership: SOLT
"The plan for this venue can be found in the Official London Seating Plan Guide"

## CAMDEN PALACE
1 Camden High Street London NW1 7JE
Tel 0171 387 0428 Fax 0171 388 8850
ADMINISTRATION:
Manager: Lee Hazel
Recently refurbished, the Palace now has an increased capacity (1450) and a custom built 50K JBL sound system.

## CECIL SHARP HOUSE

2 Regents Park Road London NW1 7AY
Tel 0171 485 2206 Fax 0171 284 0534
Contains a number of halls and smaller rooms, available
for hire. Facilities include sprung floors, bar, cafeteria and
garden.

## CENTRAL HALL, WESTMINSTER

Storeys Gate Westminster London SW1H 9NH
Mgt 0171 222 8010 Fax 0171 222 6883
ADMINISTRATION:
Props: Methodist Church.
General Manager: Michael Sharp
Policy: Concerts, Meetings, Conferences, Exhibitions,
Trade Shows, Banqueting & Receptions.
Seats: Great Hall - 2,350, Lecture Hall - 500; Library -
500. Other rooms available.
TECHNICAL:
Open Stage with Choir risers. Thrust Stage Extension:
40' x 60'. 4-manual organ, grand piano on request.
Sound Equipment:24-4-2 Yamaha PM1200 Console
Apogee Speakers. Foldback. 4kW continuous sound
power. New lifts - improved get-in facilities.

## CHARLES CRYER STUDIO THEATRE AND SCENERY WORKSHOP

High Street Carshalton Surrey SM5 3BB
Tel 0181 770 4960 BO 0181 770 4950
Fax 0181 770 4969
Web Site: www.uktw.co.uk/info/charlescryer.htm
ADMINISTRATION:
Props: London Borough of Sutton
Lessees: Sutton Performing Arts Network.
Theatre Director: Keith Lancing
Finance Officer: Teresa Wright
Technical Manager: Graham Weymouth
Marketing and Development Manager: Charlotte Harris
Seating: 80-180, (Average 95 for theatre/dance). Fixed
seats, up to 100 additional loose seats depending on
performance requirements.
TECHNICAL:
Full sound/lighting. Rehearsal Room. Restaurant,Bar.
Policy: Producing, small-scale touring, one nighters,
collaborations. Theatre, music, dance, mime, comedy -
professional and community. Hire, box office splits; fees
sometimes paid. Arts project proposals and co-
production proposals welcomed.
Fully equipped workshop - paint frame, building/welding

## CHAT'S PALACE

Arts Centre & Venue, 42-44 Brooksbys Walk,
London E9 6DF
Tel 0181 986 6714/533 0227 Fax 0181 985 6878
ADMINISTRATION:
Seating capacity: 125-150, Standing: 200
Contact: Shabnam Shabazi

## CHURCHILL THEATRE

High Street Bromley Kent BR1 1HA
Admin/SD 0181 464 7131 BO 0181 460 6677 Marketing
and Publicity 0181 460 1401
Goldcard Hotline 0181 460 5838 Fax 0181 290 6968
ADMINISTRATION:
Props: London Borough of Bromley
Lessees: Theatre of Comedy Co. Ltd.
Theatre Manager: John Short
Theatre Administrator: Dominic Adams
Corporate Hospitality Manager: Alison Carney

Head of Marketing and Publicity: Colin Hilton
Financial Controller: Liz Gentry
Box Office Manager: Zane Rambaran
Production Manager: Digby Robinson
Technical Manager: Chris Nicholls
Technical Stage Manager: Ian Hunter
Company & Stage Manager: Jane Bullock
Policy: Producing theatre, plays, musicals, pantomime,
ballet, Sunday concerts.
Perfs: Evenings Monday-Saturday 7.45. Thursday and
Saturday matinees 2.30.
Seats: 785 (760 when orchestra pit used). Two Bars and
Snack Bar.
TECHNICAL:
Stage: Apron; Flat; Pros. opening 9.15m-13.7m variable;
ht. of Pros. 7.01m; Depth of S/Line 15.09m; Ht. of Grid
14.46m; 50 (47-50 storage only) lines c/w, Scenery
Flying Ht. 5.49m; Flying Bars 16.4m; W/Widths P.S.
10.87m, O.P. 10.67m; Prompt Cnr. P.S. or O.P.
Lighting: Switchboard: Arri Imagine 250 situated rear
stalls. 168 Dimmers 144 x 2.5kW. 24 x 5kW. Patchable
by phase to 380 circuits, F.O.H. 55 profile spots. On
stage 50 Fresnels; 110 parcans, 48 profiles, 6 x IRIS 4
10 x Coda 4 battens.
200A 3 Phase USL, 100A 3 Phase DSR, 200A Single
Phase DSL available for temporary lighting, sound rig.
Sound: Soundcraft Venue 32:8:2 with 8 way matrix. 1
gram 2 Revox 1 cassette 1 CD 24 mic. tielines DSL.
Other: Dressing Rooms 12, accom. 135 inc. Band and
Chorus; 6 Showers; Orchestra Pit :15 plus.

## CLUB JAMMIN

Wkd 18 Kentish Town Road Camden Town
London NW1
Tel/Fax 0171 482 5042
ADMINISTRATION:
Capacity: 400
Contact: Lee H Simba

## THE COCHRANE THEATRE

Southampton Row London WC1B 4AP
Admin 0171 430 2500 BO 0171 242 7040
Fax 0171 831 5476
ADMINISTRATION:
General Manager: Gwen Orr
Technical Manager: Adam Carree
Production Manager: Brendan McEvoy
Receiving Venue. Built in 1963. Central Holborn location.
Self financing.
Local Authority - Camden
The Cochrane Theatre in the heart of London is a wholly
owned subsidiary of the London Institute of Higher
Education Corporation which also owns five other major
art colleges in London. In addition to educational and
exhibition activities presented by the London Institute
colleges, the Cochrane also presents professional
companies working in Dance, Visual and Physical
Theatre Comedy & Drama.
For programming information, availability and rates
please contact Gwen Orr, General Manager on 0171 430
2500.
Seats 314, raked on 1 level.
TECHNICAL:
Stage: Proscenium arch. Performing area 8.8W x 8.00D
- pros opening 8.48W x 4.9H - wing widths 2.3m SR,
3.96m SL. No rake - hardboard over teak floor, suitable
for all dance, grey dance floor available, backstage
crossover, stage heated, stage extract ventilation. Height
of grid 14.64m - 42 counterweight sets, 5 double
purchase, 0.15m apart - 350 kg permitted on bars - no

tab track - black legs and borders - 2 black backcloth - white cyclorama - gold house tabs, flown, 2 x 13A ring circuits, 7 sockets on stage, 2 on each fly floor. Switched independents from control room, 2 on stage, 1 on PS fly floor, 4 FOH. 1 x 60A Cee Form socket SL. Safety curtain. Tallescope Zarges ladder and Access tower. Forestage 8.48m x 2.2m. Orchestra pit accommodates 20. Get in via SL roller door and workshop door 1.68m x 2.88m. Scale stage, auditorium + stage and section plans available.
Lighting: Arri Mirage memory board, 98 circuits @ 2kw - operated from elevated control room at rear of auditorium. 31 profile spots, 47 fresnels, 30 pars, DMX points FOH, stage and flies, 6 CODA Cyc battens.
Sound: Soundcraft live 4 16:4:4'2 desk operated from elevated control room at rear of auditorium. 2 x Yamaha P2700 350W/channel amp. 2 x Harrison X600 300W/channel amp. 4 x Electrovoice S200 speakers + hanging cradles. 2 x Toa 30-SD speakers. 2 x Community LFC215 Bass speakers. 1 x Rane AC22 Crossover. 1 x Yamaha SPX 900 Processor. 2 x Electrovoice EWT 2230 graphic equalisers. 1 x Electrovoice S200 equalising unit. 1 x Denon DN-650F CD player, 2 x Revox B77 (7.5/15ips). 2 x Shure SM58 microphones. 2 x Crown PCC microphones. 1 x Teac W-660R cassette deck. Acoustics suitable for music and spoken word. 1 X Teac P1100 CD Player, 2 X Shur SM57 microphones, 2 X DI boxes.
Other: Stage Management: Prompt corner SL - Technical Research talkback system, 5 units, adequate links all over theatre. 6 cue light system. Show relay/tannoy to dressing rooms. Tannoy to FOH.
Backstage: 2 dressing rooms, accommodating 20 with shower and toilet facilities, access by side of and understage. Paint frame. Workshop. Wardrobe. Upright rehearsal piano, good. Staff - 2 technicians, experienced freelancers available. No security personnel.

## COCKPIT THEATRE
Gateforth Street London NW8 8EH
Admin 0171 262 7907 BO 0171 402 5081
Fax 0171 258 2921
ADMINISTRATION:
Props: City of Westminster College.
Administrator: David Wybrow
Technical Manager: Alistair Thornton
Policy: Incoming companies/shows & exhibitions.
Seats: In the Round 240; Thrust 180; End 120.
Bar, Large dressing rooms, workshop, foyer capacity 240. Large loading dock doors. Hire rates £200-£350 per show day.
Disabled Access at street level to auditorium and disabled toilets.
TECHNICAL:
Stage: Adaptable stage, Round/Thrusts/End.
Lighting: Switchboard: Strand 60 way, 3 x 3 preset; F.O.H. Spots 19 Patt. 223, 27 Patt. 264, 4 Patt. 123, 12 Patt. 23.
Sound: 2 Ferrograph, 1 Garrard in Lighting/ Control Box above stage; Speakers 4 floating 12 in Axion 7 positions.
Other: Dressing Rooms 2; accom. 20; 2 Showers.

## COMEDY THEATRE
Panton Street London SW1Y 4DN
Mgt 0171 839 5522 BO 0171 369 1731
SD 0171 973 0018 Fax 0171 839 3663
ADMINISTRATION:
Props: Associated Capital Theatres,110 St Martin's Lane, London WC2N 4AD

Tel 0171 304 7922  Fax 0171 867 1130
General Manager: Hugh Hales
Theatre Manager: Simon Francis
Policy: Plays.
Seats: 800
TECHNICAL:
Stage: Proscenium Stage, Raked 4%; Pros. opening 7.55m; Ht. of Pros. 5.18m; Depth of S/Line 7.50m; Ht. of Grid 11.76m; 32 lines Hemp; Scenery Flying Ht. 5.49m; Flying Bars 8.53m; W/Widths p.s. 1.68m; O.P. 3.05m; Prompt Cnr. P.S.; Dock Door 3.10m x 1.07m.
Lighting: Switchboard: Strand Gemini 2+ 360 Ways, 120 Dimmers fitted (116 x 2.5kw + 4 x 5kw)
Sound: Please contact venue.
Other: Dressing Rooms 8; 4 Showers; Orchestra Pit 12 approx.
No Scenery Dock; Storage limited.
Membership: SOLT.
"The plan for this venue can be found in the Official London Seating Plan Guide"

## COMMONWEALTH CONFERENCE & EVENTS THEATRE
Commonwealth Institute Kensington High Street London W8 6NQ
Tel 0171 603 4535 Fax 0171 603 9634
ADMINISTRATION:
Enquiries to: Beccy Thorp or Charles Fielder
Availability: seven days a week.
Capacity 460 raked seating. Disabled access for 2 wheelchairs. Theatre foyer with bar, toilets and cloakroom. Resident caterer or list of approved caterers available.
TECHNICAL:
Stage: Total stage area: 140m2. Stage depth: 10.4m. Stage width: 13.4m. Proscenium.
Lighting: 48 channel lighting board, 3 preset, 3 group channel.  50 assorted luminaries, Overhead sunken spotlighting.
2 x 35mm cine projectors with xenon light source and Dolby A and SR sound.  1 x 16mm/Super 16 cine projector with xenon light source. Comopt, Commag and Sepmag (mono and stereo) sound.  "Perlux" cinema screen with 3 fixed ratios: 1.33:1, 1.75:1, 2.35:1.  Full Dolby sound system.
Sound: 16-4-2 sound mixing desk, Bose speakers, cassette and reel to reel tape relay and CD player.  PA system links Foyer to auditorium.
Other: Dressing rooms x 2. Conference audio visual aids available include: Kodak carousel slide projectors with remote control.  Overhead projectors.  Laser pointer. Lectern.  Microphones.
Full colour brochure is available on request.

## CRITERION THEATRE
Piccadilly Circus London W1V 9LB
Mgt 0171 839 8811 BO 0171 369 1737
SD 0171 839 8811 Fax 0171 925 0596
ADMINISTRATION:
Props.: Criterion Theatre Trust
Chief Executive: Sally Greene
Managed by: Associated Capital Theatres, 110 St Martin's Lane, London WC2N 4AD
Tel: 0171 304 7922   Fax: 0171 867 1130
General Manager: Hugh Hales
Theatre Manager: Fiona Callaghan
Policy: Plays, revues, Comedy Venue
Perfs: Variable according to production
Seats: 598. Two licensed bars.

TECHNICAL:
Stage: Proscenium Stage: Pros. opening 7.62m. Ht. of pros. 3.81m. Depth of S/line 6.63m. Ht. of grid 6.71m: 27 lines, Hemp; Scenery flying ht. 6.40m; Flying bars as required; W/Widths P.S.2. 74m; O.P. 3.05m; Prompt Cnr D.S.L.
Please contact theatre for details of lighting and sound facilities.
"The plan for this venue can be found in the Official London Seating Plan Guide"

## CRYSTAL PALACE CONCERT BOWL
Crystal Palace Park London SE20 8UT
Tel 0181 778 7148  Fax 0181 659 8397
ADMINISTRATION:
Capacity: 20,000
Contact Colin Buttery  Tel 0181 460 9955
Also: Peter Beale, Civic Centre Tel: 0181 464 3333

## DOMINION THEATRE
Tottenham Court Road London W1P 0AQ
Mgt 0171 580 1889 BO 0171 416 6060
SD 0171 637 5039 Fax 0171 580 0246
Enquiries for wheelchair and disabled persons access: 0171 636 2295
ADMINISTRATION:
Props: Nederlander/Apollo Dominion
General Manager: Stephen Murtagh
For all booking information and further details please contact Sam Shrouder or Nicky Monk at Apollo Leisure (UK) Ltd., Grehan House, Garsington Road, Cowley, Oxford OX4 5NQ. Tel: 01865 782900; Fax: Oxford 01865 782910.
Policy: Major West End House.
Seating capacity: 2,174, Stalls: 1,372; Circle: 802; Boxes: 2 (12 seats) (retained by house).
TECHNICAL:
Stage: Size: Width 22m (72') wide x 12m (39') deep. Forestage 1.83m (6'). Pros Opening: 15.2m (49'10") width x 9m (29'6") ht. False Pros. Min. Opening: 12m (38') wide x 6m (20') ht. Flying system: 72 Bar, Counterweight 0.05m 0 (2") bars @ 0.2m (6") centres. Height to Grid: 20.42m (67') front, 20m (65'7") back. Stage to Audit. 1.12m (3'8"). Equipment Access: via dock door, off Great Russell Street (street level). Dock Door: 5.64m (18'6") ht. x 2.4m (8'). Hoist: 500kg capacity on 2.5m (8') arm on stage of dock doors. Power Supply: 4 x 400 amp, 3 phase located on 2nd gallery prompt side, 1 x 100 amp, single phase, 240V (sound) with independent earths. F. S. Positions: Located in boxes and upper circle 3 permanent super troupers in upper circle throw upper circle to approx. 28m (92'). Mixer Desk Pos.: Rear stalls 1.78m (5'10") wide x 4.74m (15'6") long (can be extended). Mixer to stage - 35m (110').
Lighting: Board: Located in Royal Box prompt side 36 way 2 preset manual Tempus Desk, 120 dimmable outlets. Prompt Corner: (stage left). Cue light system, full backstage call system. Head sets to flys and spot ops. House Light Controls: Located in Royal Box Prompt side. Front Truss Pos: Located above stage apron. Hanging Points: 13 permanent FOH. 7 above stage apron, 3 above orchestra pit, 3 above stalls row F. 0.5 metric ton SWL per point.
Sound: Please contact venue.
Other: Orchestra Pit: 16.5m (55') long x 2.3m (7'6") wide at centre. Depth from stage 3m (9'8") capacity 30. max. Size with Rows ABCD removed: 16.5m (55') x 7.5m (24'6") wide at centre. Depth from stage : 2.28m (7'6").

"The plan for this venue can be found in the Official London Seating Plan Guide"

## DONMAR WAREHOUSE
41 Earlham Street London WC2H 9LD
Admin 0171 240 4882 BO 0171 369 1732
SD 0171 836 3939  Fax 0171 240 4878
Production Office 0171 379 6342
ADMINISTRATION:
Props: Associated Capital Theatres,
110 St Martin's Lane, London WC2N 4AD
Tel 0171 304 7922   Fax 0171 867 1130
General Manager: Hugh Hales
Theatre Manager: Julia Christie
Seats: 252 & 20 standing.  2 licenced bars.
TECHNICAL: OPEN STAGE THEATRE
Stage Area: 7130 mm x 8280 mm.
Technical Galleries Above Stage 6200mm.
Grid Height 8000mm.  Two dressing rooms.
Lighting: 108 Arri Dimmers & Imagine 250 desk. 150 lanterns. Sound: 24-8-2 (8x8) Desk, 10 speakers, 2 CD players.

## THE DRILL HALL
16 Chenies Street London WC1E 7EX
Admin 0171 631 1353 BO 0171 637 8270
Fax 0171 631 4468
Email: admin@drillhall.co.uk
ADMINISTRATION:
Artistic Director: Julie Parker
General Manager: Mavis Seaman
Seats: 200 max.
Disabled access, licensed bar, vegetarian restaurant on ground floor.
TECHNICAL:
Recently upgraded lighting system and in-house PA system.
Rehearsal rooms and three darkrooms.

## DUBLIN CASTLE
94 Parkway London NW1 7AN
Tel 0171 485 1773
Contact: Tony Gleed, Jim Mattison
Office: Bugbear Promotions,
167A Bermondsey St, London SE1 3UW
Tel: 0171 378 6095  Fax: 0171 378 6104

## DUCHESS THEATRE
Catherine Street London WC2B 5LA
Mgt 0171 379 5717 BO 0171 494 5550
SD 0171 379 0495
ADMINISTRATION:
Props: Stoll Moss Theatres Ltd, 21 Soho Square, London W1V 5FD; Tel: 0171 494 520 and Fax 0171 434 1217.
Policy: Plays, Musicals, Comedy, Concerts
Chief Executive: Richard Johnston
Theatre Manager: Chris Ishermann
For all bookings and production enquiries contact Richard Johnston or Nica Burns (Production Directors), Gareth Johnson (General Manager, Production Department), or David Kinsey (Concerts & Hirings Manager).  Facilities may be made available for day time, late night and weekend use for private and press receptions, conferences and meetings - Contact David Kinsey 0171 494 5200 and Fax 0171 434 1217.
Seats: 470

2 Bars, Entertainment Suite.
TECHNICAL:
Stage: flat; Pros Opening 7.32m; Ht of Pros. 4.27m;
Depth of Stage 7.40m; Ht of Grid 11.58m; 21 lines, plus
tabs, under required; Prompt Cnr. P.S.
Lighting: Board: Strand Gemini II, 114 circuits.
Situated rear of Dress Circle.
Other: Dressing rooms: 8
Membership: SOLT.
"The plan for this venue can be found in the
Official London Seating Plan Guide"

## DUKE OF YORK THEATRE
Please see entry for the Royal Court Theatre Downstairs.

## EARLS COURT ARENA
Warwick Road London SW5 9TA
Tel 0171 385 1200
ADMINISTRATION:
Sales Director: Chris Vaughan
Seating/Capacity: 18,500 max
"The plan for this venue can be found in the
Official London Seating Plan Guide"

## THE EDWARD ALLEYN THEATRE
Dulwich College Dulwich Common London SE21 7LD
Admin 0181 299 9232 Fax 0181 693 6319
Email: drama@dulwich.org.uk
ADMINISTRATION:
Director of Drama: Peter Jolly
Theatre Manager: Susi Hollins
The Edward Alleyn Theatre is a modern multi-purpose
studio theatre producing Dulwich College productions.
The theatre is also available for hire throughtout the year.
The flexible stage and seating areas provide a variety of
layouts for drama, opera and dance. New foyer facilities
make it an ideal venue for conferences and lectures.
Rehearsal facilities: The theatre is available as a
rehearsal space as is the separate drama studio (a
footprint of the stage).
Seats: 150-260
TECHNICAL:
Opening 8.75m, depth 6m, height 4.8m. Fully equipped
with computerised lighting, sound and recording
facilities. Baby grand piano. Workshop, laundry and 3
dressing rooms. Please apply to the theatre for full
specifications.

## ELECTRIC BALLROOM
184 Camden High Street London NW1 8QP
Tel 0171 485 9006 Fax 0171 284 0745
Manager: Brian Wheeler

## ETCETERA THEATRE CLUB
Oxford Arms 265 Camden High Street
London NW1 7BU
Admin Tel/Fax 0171 482 0378 BO 0171 482 4857
ADMINISTRATION:
Director: David Bidmead
Policy: To continue our current successful two shows a
night policy, as well as a Monday night slot for 'one-off'
performances, presenting a popular and varied
programme with an emphasis on new work. To
maintain and enhance the theatre's high media profile
and to continue to provide the opportunity for small
theatre companies, with limited finances, to stage

productions in Central London.
Studio theatre with seating capacity of 50.
TECHNICAL:
Stage: 5.5m x 4.6m.
Lighting: Level 12, Zero 88, 2 preset desk. Fixed
general cover (4 x 743), & 4 x CCT Fresnels, 4 x CCT
profiles and 4 x patt 23.
Sound: Revox B77 1/2 track reel to reel. Teac 6 into 2
mixer and Tascam 122 cassette deck.

## FAIRFIELD HALLS
Park Lane Croydon CR9 1DG
Mgt 0181 681 0821 Stage Door 0181 688 4555
BO 0181 688 9291 Fax 0181 760 0835
Marketing Fax 0181 686 7944
Web Site: www.fairfield.co.uk
ADMINISTRATION:
Props: Fairfield (Croydon) Ltd
Chief Executive: Derek Barr
Head of Artistic Planning: Nick Leigh
Controller of Artistic Planning: Colin May
Policy: Concert Hall, Music, Films, Pop, Jazz, Opera,
Comedy, Conferences, Ballet.
Seats: 1,800
Foyer, Coffee shop, Restaurant, Bars, Banqueting
Rooms.
TECHNICAL:
Stage: Concert Platform, mechanical variable sections.
Lighting: Switchboard: Strand Lightboard 'M'
commanding 120 channels 200amp 3 phase and 60
amp single phase power supplies available for temporary
supply; F.O.H. spots 42 CCT profiles. 2 spot bars
available on electric hoist. Selection of lamps; P.A.R.
cans and fresnels.
Get-in via platform lift, Direct Access & Parking. No flying
facilities, but good grid provision and soft blacks for
upstage masking.
Sound Equipment: 7kw fully integrated Meyer sound
system with permanent mixing position.
Other: Dressing Rooms: 7, accom. 200; 3 showers;
Orchestra Pit 28.90 orch. music stands, 2 Steinway
concert D type Grand Pianos; seating 120 orch. max
250 choir seating.
Staff: 5 Technicians - Casual Crew.
A registered charity.

## FORTUNE THEATRE
Russell Street, London WC2B 5HH
Mgt 0171 836 6260 BO 0171 836 2238
Fax 0171 379 7493
ADMINISTRATION:
Lessees: MAP International Ltd.
Artistic Director: Paul Gane
Seats: 432
TECHNICAL:
Stage: Pros. opening 7.77m; Ht. of Pros. 5.49m; Depth
of S/Line 8.53m; Ht. of Grid 12.80m; 26 lines, 16 Hemp,
10 C/W; Prompt Cnr. P.S.
Lighting: Switchboard: Ovation memory board (64 way).
Paging facilities to backstage and F.O.H.
Sound: Please contact venue.
Other: Dressing Rooms 6 (dress 18).
Membership: SOLT
"The plan for this venue can be found in the
Official London Seating Plan Guide"

## FORUM
9-17 Highgate Road Kentish Town London NW5 1JY

Tel 0171 284 1001 BO 0171 344 0044
Fax 0171 284 1102
Manager: Alan Henehan

## THE FRIDGE
Town Hall Parade Brixton Hill London SW2 1RJ
Mgt/BO 0171 326 5100 Fax 0171 274 2879
Business Manager: Barry Laden
Capacity: 1,100

## GARRICK THEATRE
Charing Cross Road London WC2H 0HH
Mgt 0171 836 9396 BO 0171 494 5085
SD 0171 836 8271
ADMINISTRATION:
Props: Stoll Moss Theatres Ltd, 21 Soho Square,
London W1V 5FD; Tel. 0171 494 5200
and Fax 0171 434 1217.
Policy: Plays, Musicals, Comedy, Concerts.
Chief Executive: Richard Johnston
Theatre Manager: Philip Hawkeswood
For all bookings and production enquiries contact
Richard Johnston or Nica Burns (Production Directors),
Gareth Johnson (General Manager, Production
Department), or David Kinsey (Concerts & Hirings
Manager). Facilities may be made available for day time,
late night and weekend use for private and press
receptions, conferences and meetings - Contact David
Kinsey 0171 494 5200 and Fax 0171 434 1217.
Seats: 694
3 Bars, Small Entertainment Suite.
TECHNICAL:
Stage: raked 1:30; Pros. Opening 8.82m; Depth of
Stage 9.60m. Ht of Pros. 6.10m; Ht of Grid 15.24m; 52
lines; 44 Hemp. 8 moveable counterweights; Prompt
Cnr. as required.
Lighting: Board: Strand Gemini II, 120 circuits.
Situated O.P. Stage Box
Other: Dressing Rooms: 10
Membership: SOLT.
"The plan for this venue can be found in the
Official London Seating Plan Guide"

## G B S THEATRE - ROYAL ACADEMY OF DRAMATIC ART
62-64 Gower Street London WC1 6ED
Mgt 0171 636 7076 Fax 0171 323 3865
ADMINISTRATION:
Royal Academy of Dramatic Art;
At present the building is under construction with
completion scheduled for 2000.

## GEILGUD THEATRE
Shaftesbury Avenue London W1V 8AR
Mgt 0171 439 1912 BO 0171 494 5065
SD 0171 437 6003

## GIELGUD THEATRE
Shaftesbury Avenue, London W1V 8AR
Mgt 0171 439 1912 BO 0171 494 5065
SD 0171 437 6003
ADMINISTRATION;
Props: Stoll Moss Theatres Ltd, 21 Sohc Square,
London W1V 5FD; Tel: 0171 494 5200
and Fax 0171 434 1217.
Policy: Plays, Musicals, Comedy, Concerts.
Chief Executive: Richard Johnston

Theatre Manager: Mike Ockwell
For all bookings and production enquiries contact
Richard Johnston or Nica Burns (Production Directors),
Gareth Johnson (General Manager, Production
Department), or David Kinsey (Concerts & Hirings
Manager). Facilities may be made available for day time,
late night and weekend use for private and press
receptions, conferences and meetings - Contact David
Kinsey 0171 494 5200 and Fax 0171 434 1217.
Seats: 889
3 Bars, Entertainment Suite.
TECHNICAL:
Stage: raked 1: 48; Pros. Opening 9.14m; Ht of Pros.
8.23m; Depth of Stage 10.82m; Ht of Grid 15.70m; 42
C/W sets; Prompt Cnr. P.S.
Lighting: Board: Strand Gemini II, 137 circuits.
Situated Stalls Box P.S.
Other: Dressing rooms: 12
Membership: SOLT
"The plan for this venue can be found in the
Official London Seating Plan Guide"

## GOLDSMITH COLLEGE STUDENTS UNION
Union Hall Lewisham Way London SE14 6NW
Tel 0181 692 1406 Fax 0181 694 9789
Capacity: 800
General Manager: Ms J Courtney

## THE GRACE THEATRE
503 Battersea Park Road London SW11 3BW
Admin/Fax 0171 228 2620 BO 0171 223 3549
Tavern 0171 223 3549
ADMINISTRATION:
Artistic Director: Timothy Sheader
Associate Director & Literary Manager: Richard Hurst
Technical Manager: Leigh Morgan
Seating: 80.
Policy: To present a varied programme of new and
classical work with the accent on quality rather than
following any narrow programming policy. Grace Theatre
Productions is the resident producing company.
Origins: Purpose built above the Latchmere Public
House, the theatre opened in 1982 under the artistic
direction of Lou Stein and the Gate at the Latchmere.
The management changed in 1985 when the theatre
changed its name to the Latchmere and again in 1992
when it became The Grace. Unsubsidised.
Audience: Broad cross-section throughout London and
the South East.
TECHNICAL:
Stage: Raked auditorium seating 80 with end stage on
floor (5.2m x 10m). Permanent lighting grid internally
wired. 3.5m to floor (3.8m ceiling to floor).
Lighting: CCT650W stock 12x minuet fresnels, 6 x
minuet pcs, 6 x minuet TT's and 4 lito profile spots. 24
channel control desk.
Sound: 12 X channel sound mixer, 2 x Twin cassette
decks, stereo amp and 2 speakers.
Other: Recent productions include: Swingers, Fools For
Love, True Colours, Tomfoolery, Dirty Boggers, Loot,
The Double Bass and Owning the Knuckleball.
Disabled facilities: None.

## THE GRAND
21/25 St John's Hill, Clapham Junction,
London SW11 1TT
Tel: 0171 385 0834 Fax: 0171 385 0862
Email: LeopdClubs@aol.com
ADMINISTRATION:

Policy: Live music, nightclub, private hire for events/parties/ conferences, etc.
Event Hire: Contact: Teresa Fowler on 0171 385 0834. Venue available daytime Monday to Sunday, and evenings Sunday to Thursday, for press conferences, receptions, parties, showcases, theatre groups, rehearsals, etc.
Seating/Capacity: Circle raked theatre seating: 300, Gallery raked bench seating: 350. No seating on ground floor - flat with two levels (dance floor + bar) Boxes: 6
Bars: 2 on ground floor, 1 in circle, 1 in gallery
Dressing rooms: 3 with shared shower + toilet.
TECHNICAL:
Stage: Full height fly-tower; 10m x 10m opening to auditorium. Raised performance platform (6ft high) on stage, full width 12m, full depth 10m.
Sound: FOH: 6 x Nexo Alpha E Mid/Hi; 12 x Nexo Alpha E 1*18" Sub Bass. STAGE: 2 x Nexo Alpha E Mid/Hi; 4 x Nexo Alpha E 1*18" Sub Bass. AMPLIFIERS: 3 x Crown MA 5000VZ; 3 x Crown MA 2400; 1 x Crown Studio Reference Monitor. DJ MONITORS: 2 x Nero PS10 1*10". STAGE + CONTROL: 2 x Technics SL1210MK2 Turntables. 2 x Pioneer CDJ500's CD Players; 1 x Rane MM8X Mojo DJ Mixer; 1 x Sony MDSJE500 Mini Disc; 1 x Tascam 202MK2 Twin cassette deck; 2 x Behringer DSP8000 Ultracurve Digital EQ; 2 x Symetrix 402 Compressor; 1 x Zoom 1201 Digital FX Unit; 1 x Soundcraft Spirit Live 6 16/6/2 Mixer; 1 x 12W stage box; 1 x Shure Samson Microphone system; 1 x Shure SM58 Microphone.
Lighting: 8 x Martin Pro918 Robo Scan; 8 x Martin Mac250 Yoke Scan; 2 X Jem ZR22 Smoke Machine; 2 x UV Black gun; 1 x Martin Case 1 Controller; 2 x 48" Mirror Balls.

## GRAND THEATRE
21-25 St. Johns Hill, Clapham Junction
London SW11 1TT
Tel 0171 385 0834 Fax 0171 385 0862
Venue available for hire
Contact: Alexis Billson
Capacity: 1,500

## GREENWICH THEATRE
Crooms Hill London SE10 8ES
Admin 0181 858 4447 BO 0181 858 7755
SD 0181 859 2265 Fax 0181 858 8042
ADMINISTRATION:
Props: Greenwich Theatre Ltd.
Administrative Director: David Adams
Technical Manager: Neil Fulcher
Deputy Technical Manager: Ed Brimley
Policy: Limited runs of New Plays and Classics.
Perfs: Mon-Sat. 7.45; Mat. Sat. 2.30.
Seats: 423. Full Restaurant and Bar facilities.
TECHNICAL:
Stage: Open stage with 3.09m. Thrust, Flat: Depth from S/Line 11.58m; Ht. of Roof 7.62m; Prompt Cnr. in Control Room at rear of Audit.
Lighting: Switchboard: Tempus M24 100 x 2k ways 199 memories rear of audit. 12 CCT MX Colour wheels. Luminaires 25 Patt 53, 18 Patt 243; 40 Patt 264; 2 x Sil 30 2k, 2 x Min. Prof. M 135 500w, 5 Patt 123, 14 Patt 23, 24 AC1001 1k, 12 Berkey Verti-Major 1k, 8 Patt 60, 4 Patt 49, 2 Patt 293, 2 Patt 58, 24 PAR 64 (CP61/2) Long nose, 6 PAR 64 (CP61/2) Short nose.
Sound: 2 B77 15ips, 1 B77 71/2ips, 1 A77 71/2ips, 1 Teac 3440, 1 Denon Cassette Deck M33, Denon CD player 910, Technics SL QX3000 record desk. Yamalia

SPX900 Effects unit: Various graphic equalizers. Trident VPM 16:8:2 desk in control room with 18 way tie line to stage plus 12 speaker line. 4 Quad lines. 4 Quad 405 amps, 2 Quad 303 amps, 7 Bose 802 speakers, 1 Martin BX2 bass bin plus dedicated equalization. 3 SM58 mics, 1 Tandy PZM.
Other: Dressing Rooms 4; accom. 24, 4 Showers. Orchestra Pit removable stage sections to any required size. Very difficult get-in (4.57m off ground, door 3.05m high x 1.52m wide). Only one on-stage actors entrance; auditorium on one rake; working wardrobe in building. Main Stage Thrust removable in triangular 1.98m pieces. 8m diam. revolve.
Membership: TMA.

## HACKNEY EMPIRE
291 Mare Street Hackney London E8 1EJ
Mgt 0181 986 0171 BO 0181 985 2424
SD 0181 986 6128  Fax 0181 985 4781
Email: info@hackemp.demon.co.uk
Web Site: www.hackneyempire.demon.co.uk
ADMINISTRATION:
General Manager: Simon Thomsett
Director: Roland Muldoon
Box Office Manager: Richard Boraman
Head of Press & Marketing: Sharon Duggal
Seating 1,250 raked tiered plus 250 standing.
TECHNICAL:
Stage: Proscenium arch, Performing area 11.59m x 9.75m - 12.2m, pros opening 10.26m x 6.7m, wing widths 3.05m, SR, 3.05m SL, 2.44m US. Stage raked, 1 in 26 floor hardboard on oak tongue and groove, suitable for all dance, backstage crossover, understage heated. Height of grid 15.24m 37 hemp sets, tab track, black felt and drill masking, also used as cyclorama, also white cyclorama - maroon, gold trim house tabs, Flown. 100A 3 phase supply available. 3 traps (no machinery yet), centre stage at 4.27m and 6.1m. Orchestra pit 12.2m x 2.13m, accommodates 15. Get in via rear and SR, dock doors , present door 3.05m x 3.7m. Safety curtain. Scale plans available.
Lighting: Lighting desk; Lighting board M, 60 way 24 submasters.
Lighting racks; 12 x 20A channels, 48 x 10A channels. Power supplies; 100A 3 phase, 100A single phase. 2 x follow spots; 1kw CSI pattern 765, 6 x 1kw Cantata 11/26 spots, 3 x 1kw Sil 30 spots, 2 x 1kw Harmony 15/28 spots, 6 x 1kw Pattern 263 spots, 2 x 2kw Pattern 293 spots, 54 x 1kw Par 64 cans (CP61 + CP62). 8 x 500w Par 64 rays, 8 x 250w 28v Par 64 ACL, 8 x 1kw Prism Convex spots, 14 x 1kw Fresnels, 3 x 2kw Fresnels, 12 x 1kw Cyclorama floodlights.
Sound: TAC 24 channel (into 4 into 2) model X1000 desk operated from rear centre stalls. 4 auxilliary sends for monitors/effects. 4 Hackney cabs on each side of the proscenium arch plus one sub bass cabinet each side at floor level driven by Amcron amps giving approximately 5k out front. Formula Sound 30 band graphic equaliser. Yamaha SPX90 reverb unit. NO ON-STAGE MONITOR DESK. Monitors - 3 x 1k Studiomaster amps, 4 Tannoy Cougar wedges. Yamaha 31 band graphic equaliser on 2 channels only 7 Shure SM58. Sony condenser mic. Sennheiser 451. C Duler. 6 DI boxes. Cassette tape machine with record facility. NO REEL-TO-REEL TAPE MACHINE. 60 amp single phase supply for sound - 32 amp C-form socket. The Hackney Empire has a five-way intercom system.

## HALF MOON

93 Lower Richmond Road Putney London SW15 1EU
Tel 0181 780 9383 Fax 0181 789 7863
Contact: Tony Abis

## HAMMERSMITH & FULHAM TOWN HALL

King Street London W6 9JU
Tel 0181 748 3020 Fax 0181 576 5459
Manager: Dee Little
Functions Coordinator Helen Pennington Ext 2136
Also Direct Telephone Line 0181 576 5008

## HAMPSTEAD THEATRE

Swiss Cottage Centre Avenue Road London NW3 3EX
Mgt 0171 722 9224 BO 0171 722 9301 Production
Office 0171 722 1189 Fax 0171 722 3860
ADMINISTRATION;
Props: Hampstead Theatre Ltd.
Director: Jenny Topper
General Manager: James Williams
Policy: Six-eight week runs of new plays - each
individually cast.
Perfs: Nightly at 8.00. Mats. Sat. 3.30pm.
Seats: 174. Bar (licensed) open 7.00-11.00.

TECHNICAL:
Stage: End Stage, flat; Width 9.7m, depth 7.75m, height
(min) 3.90m; Prompt Cnr. rear of Auditorium.
Lighting: Switchboard: ARRI image + backup/FX,
dimmers; 60 x 10A, 25 Patt 23, 40 Patt 123, 8 Patt 743,
2 Patt 264, 10 x prelude 16/30.
Sound: Equip: 2 Revox A77, Revos B77, 3 Quad 405,
Soundcraft 8-4-2 desk, 4 Tannoy and 2 Visonik 6001
speakers, Cassette and record decks.
Other: Dressing Rooms 3; accom. 18. 2 Showers.
Rehearsal Room (1st floor) 10.95m x 7.75m.
Membership: TMA.
"The plan for this venue can be found in the
Official London Seating Plan Guide"

## HER MAJESTY'S THEATRE

Haymarket London SW1Y 4QR
Mgt 0171 930 5343 BO 0171 494 5400
SD 0171 930 5337
ADMINISTRATION;
Props: Stoll Moss Theatres Ltd, 21 Soho Square,
London W1V 5FD; Tel: 0171 494 5200
and Fax 0171 434 1217.
Policy: Plays, Musicals, Comedy, Concerts.
Chief Executive: Richard Johnston
Theatre Manager: John Fitzsimmons
For all bookings and production enquiries contact
Richard Johnston or Nica Burns (Production Directors),
Gareth Johnson (General Manager, Production
Department), or David Kinsey (Concerts & Hirings
Manager).  Facilities may be made available for day time,
late night and weekend use for private and press
receptions, conferences and meetings - Contact David
Kinsey 0171 494 5200 and Fax 0171 434 1217.
Seats: 1161. 3 Bars, Entertainment Suites.
TECHNICAL:
Stage: Flat; Pros. Opening 10.52m; Ht of Pros. 8.84m;
Depth of Stage 15.09m; Ht of Grid 17.37m; 50 C/W
lines; Prompt Cnr. P.S.
Lighting: Lighting Board: Strand Galaxy II, 350 Circuits.
Situated rear of Dress Circle
Other: Dressing rooms: 18
Membership: SOLT

"The plan for this venue can be found in the
Official London Seating Plan Guide"

## ICA THEATRE

Nash House 12 Carlton House Terrace The Mall London
SW1Y 5AH
Tel 0171 930 0493 BO 0171 930 3647
Fax 0171 873 0051
ADMINISTRATION:
Institute Director: Philip Dodd
Technical Manager: Richard Decordova
Live Arts Co-ordinator: Vivienne Gaskin
TECHNICAL:
Stage: Ply floor 74' x 33' Grid over whole area 14'6".
Seating primarily on four movable bleachers enabling
various endstage traverse thrust and round layouts up to
a maximum capacity of 206 seats.
Lighting: 48 way Micron. Switch patching 3 ways on 12
channels. 174 Grid outlets. Lanterns: 12 x Patt. 23, 12 x
Sil 30, 18 x Cantata Fres., 6 x harmony Fres., 14 x
Parcans (1K), 2 x 15/28 Profiles, 2 x 22/40 Profiles.
Sound: 2 x Revox B77; 1 x Revox A77; 1 x Tascam 8 x
4 x 1 Mixer. Bose Speaker System.

## THE ISLAND

300 High Road Ilford Essex IG1 1QW
Tel 0181 514 5500 Fax 0181 514 0505
Capacity: 2,565

## JACKSONS LANE

Opp Highgate Tube 269a Archway Road
London N6 5AA
Tel 0181 340 5226 BO 0181 341 4421
Fax 0181 348 2424 Tech 0181 341 5581
ADMINISTRATION:
Programme Co-ordinator: John Walmsley
Theatre Technician: Chris Copland
Policy: To provide a programme of music, drama,
dance, mime and cabaret, representing multi-cultural
interests. Training will play a large part in our
programme, and many of our staff are trainees and
volunteers.
Location: Alongside the Archway Road (A1), opposite
Highgate tube. Served by buses 43, 134, X43, 263.
Terms: Hire of theatre (negotiable); box office split.
Seats/Capacity: 129-167 seated, raked; 290 standing.
Bars: one in foyer, one in auditorium.
TECHNICAL:
Stage: semi sprung maple. Width 11m, depth 6.4 -
9.75m, variable. No proscenium. Dance floors available.
Grid height: 6m from stage. Control position: raised at
back of auditorium, 100kva 3 phase supplying 48 x 2.5k
dimmers with 82 circuits.
Lighting: Zero 88 Sirius 48 way computerised lighting
board. Standard dance rig in place, ask for further
details
Sound: Spirit Live 42 24 Channel Mixing Desk, Midiverb
III Fx unit, Denon twin cassette, Tascam DA30 MKII
DAT, twin Denon CD players, Revox, full PA. Upright
piano.
Other: Dressing Rooms: three rooms, backstage, with
showers and toilets.
Get-in 12' high by 4'3" wide, directly from stage to
street. Induction loop in auditorium. All facilities are
accessible to, and usable by, people with disabilities,
including audience, performers and technicians.
For more information contact Chris Copland on 0181
341 5581.

# KENNETH MORE THEATRE

**OAKFIELD ROAD, ILFORD**
**Telephone 0181-553 4466/4464**
**Fax 0181-553 5476**
General Manager: VIVYAN ELLACOTT
Main Theatre Seating 365
Studio Theatre Seating 50

## JAZZ CAFE
5 Parkway Camden Town London NW1 7PG
Admin 0171 916 6060 BO 0171 344 0044
(Ticketmaster)
ADMINISTRATION:
Press Officer: Paul Clarke
Promoter: Adrian Gibson
Promoter's Assistant: Lucy Whitehead
Capacity: 350

## JERMYN STREET THEATRE
16B Jermyn Street London SW1Y 6ST
Mgt 0171 434 1443 BO 0171 287 2875
ADMINSTRATION:
Artistic Director: Neil Marcus
Administrative Director: Penny Horner
Seats: 70
TECHNICAL:
Stage: 12 ft deep, 26 ft wide, 12ft to lighting grid.

## KENNETH MORE THEATRE
Oakfield Road Ilford Essex IG1 1BT
Mgt 0181 553 4464 SD 0181 553 4465
BO 0181 553 4466 Fax 0181 553 5476
Costume hire 0181 553 0444
Email: kmtheatre@aol.com
ADMINISTRATION:
Props: London Borough of Redbridge
Lessees: Redbridge Theatre Co. Ltd
General Manager: Vivyan Ellacott
Assistant Manager: Robert Quarry
Technical Manager: Ralph James Dartford
Lighting Designer: Rob Mitchell-Gears
Box Office Manager: Mark Brock
Policy: Amateur and Professional Productions, Tours,
Exhibitions, Recitals, Conferences, etc. Experimental
productions in Studio, Costume Hire.
Seats: 365 with 3 wheelchair spaces in main auditorium;
Studio Theatre 50 (fixed seating). Licensed bar; hearing-
aid loop.
TECHNICAL:
Stage: Proscenium Stage with 1.83m removable apron
over orchestra pit; Pros. arch 9.14m x 4.42m; S/Line to
back wall 6.71m (with crossover behind wall); Ht. of Grid
12.04m; 28 X 12.08m lines C/W; Scenery Flying Ht.
10.97m; Flying Bars 9.14m; W/Widths 2.44m each side
with direct access to large scene dock and workshop
O.P.; Prompt Cnr. P.S. Counterweighted Trap-Door
Centre Stage. 1:25 plans available.
Lighting: Eurolight Applause & Smart back-up 96 way at
rear of auditorium. 3 F.O.H. bars set in ceiling; 2 F.O.H.
perches; 2 int. wired bars.

Equipment: 14 x Patt. 263, 4 x Patt. 264, 14 x Patt. 743, .
6 x T84, 4 x Sil 15, 6 x Sil 30, 8 x Starlette Fresnel, 10 X
Cantata Fresnel, 23 x Par Cans, 12 x AC1001, 3 x 3
CCT Battens, 2 x C.S.I. Follow Spots.
Sound: Equipment: Soundcraft Delta 24/4/2 situated
rear of auditorium, 8/4/2 Studiomaster mixer situated in
control room, 2 X EAW speakers mounted centre F.O.H,
2 x Pairs Bose 802 mounted left and right F.O.H., 1 x
Pair Rogers RM1Monitors, Denon DR-M33 and
Technics M260 Cassette decks. Denon DCD910 CD
player, 2 x Quad 405 and 1 x Turner B502 amps, 6 x
AKG D2000, 3 x AKG CMS mics, 5 Sennheiser gun
mics, 4 x Shure SM58, 1 X Yamaha SPX 90 effects unit.
Studio Equipment: Strand Mini 2, 36 circuits patched to
12 way board, 6 x Patt. 23, 6 x Patt. 123, 6 x Minim, 6/2
soundmixer, Sharp Cassette, 100 watt P.A., own
dressing room accom.
Dressing Rooms 6 (excl. large green room which can be
used occasionally), accom. 45; 2 x Showers; Orchestra
pit 3.40m x 12.08m.
Membership: TMA

## KENWOOD CONCERTS
English Heritage Concerts Portland House Stag Place
London SW1E 5EE
Tel 0171 973 3428 Fax 0171 973 3425
Capacity: 8,000

## KING'S HEAD (ISLINGTON)
115 Upper Street London N1 1QN
Tel 0171 226 1916/8561 Fax 0171 226 8507

## LA2
165 Charing Cross Road, London WC2H 0EN
Mgt 0171 734 6963 BO 0171 434 0404
Fax 0171 437 1781
Booking Manager Mark Johnson 0171 434 9592
capacity: 1,000

## LE PALAIS
242 Shepherds Bush Road London W6 7NL
Tel 0181 748 2812
Venue being redeveloped not necessarily with another
ballroom.

## LEOPARD LOUNGE
The Broadway Fulham Road London SW6 1BY
Tel 0171 385 0834 Fax 0171 385 0862
Venue available for hire.
Contact: Alexis Billson

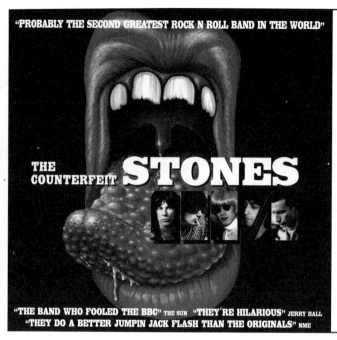
Capacity: 600 standing

## LEWISHAM THEATRE
Rushey Green Catford London SE6 4RU
Mgt 0181 690 2317 BO 0181 690 0002
Fax 0181 314 3144
ADMINISTRATION:
Props: London Borough of Lewisham
Joint General Managers: Martin Costello and Chris Hare.
Technical Manager: Kath O'Sullivan
Policy: Touring, Pantomime, Concerts, Variety, Musical, Opera, etc.
Perfs: variable.
Seats 845. Two Bars.
TECHNICAL:
Stage: Proscenium Stage, slight rake, pros. opening 9.14m. Ht. of Pros 6.10m, Depth of S/line 7.92, Ht. of Grid 5.49m, 9 lines 1 C/W 7 hemp; scenery flying Ht. 5.49m; Flying Bars 9.14m; W/Widths P.S. 1.52m, O.P. 1.52m; Prompt Cnr. P.S.
Lighting: Switchboard: M.24 Control with Back Up F/X Unit, 60 x 2K.W. (14 F.O.H.) Portable. 10 Harmony 16/30, 6 Prelude 15/28, 4 T.Spot, 8 264, 4 CCT Minuette Profile, 2 23, 12 Harmony P.C. 1 K.W. 12 743, 2 Minuette, 4 123, 4  243 (2K.W.) 22 PAR Cans (240v) Medium, 12 Coda 500W. Floods, 4 4 Circuit Code Groundrows. Follow Spots. Pani H.M.I. 1200.
Sound: Equipment: 6.5k Rig - Yamaha PM 3000 40 Channel Mixer - Speakers left and right flown T/R4 clusters by Clair Brothers, Crest Audio amps 2 x 4801 High/Superhigh, 2 x 8001 Meds, 2 x 8001 Lows - crossover unit - programmable equalisers/spectrum analyzer - 5 D.I. Boxes - Effects include equalisers, Compressors and Noise gates - Foldback 4 Clair Brothers Audio 12 am monitors -1 High Speed Revox B77 - 1 Dennon Cassette Deck & CD with remote.

Other: Dressing Rooms 7, accom. 200; 2 Showers; Orchestra Pit 28.
Membership: TMA.

## LILIAN BAYLIS THEATRE
Arlington Way off Rosebery Avenue London EC1R 4TN
Contact Nigel Hives 0171 314 8888

## LITTLE ANGEL THEATRE "HOME OF BRITISH PUPPETRY"
14 Dagmar Passage Cross Street London N1 2DN
Admin 0171 359 8581 BO 0171 226 1787
Fax 0171 359 7565
ADMINISTRATION:
Co founder/Dept. Director: Lindy Wright
Director: Christopher Leith
Policy: Resident & Touring Puppet Theatre.
Perfs: Weekends: Sat. 11.00 and 3.00. Sun. 11.00 and 3.00. Daily School Holidays; some Evenings.
Disabled Access.
Seats: 100
TECHNICAL:
Proscenium Puppet Stage.

## THE LOGAN HALL
University of London 20 Bedford Way
London WC1H 0AL
Admin 0171 612 6401 Admin Fax 0171 612 6402
ADMINISTRATION:
Props: Institute of Education
Administrator: Mrs Sittika Nazim
Senior Technician: John Dobbin
Policy: University multipurpose Hall used for concerts, recitals, films, ethnic variety shows, classical music,

occasional performances, conferences, lectures.
Seats: 933. Bar can be provided in adjoining Crush Hall.
Space available for self-catering.
TECHNICAL:
Stage: Open flat stage; 12 movable rostra.
Lighting: Switchboard: Arri Image Control, Rank Strand
Electric; 12 microphone straight line inputs.
Screen: 20ft x 30ft 60-channel light board/follow spot, 8
rainbow colour changers.
Sound: Equipment: 12 channel mixers, 2 speakers; 1
tape deck; 1 turntable.
Other: Dressing room to accom. 60; 2 Showers. 60
music stands; induction loop for hearing aid users, one
Steinway concert grand piano; one Yamaha 5ft 2in grand
piano.
Seating: 60 max orchestra. By removing cyc, orchestra
and choir can be accommodated.

## LONDON APOLLO

Queen Caroline Street Hammersmith London W6 9QH
Mgt 0181 748 8660 SD 0181 748 2688 BO (Tickets
London) 0171 416 6080 BO Private Line 0181 748 6045
(No Telephone Booking on private line)
Fax 0181 846 9320
ADMINISTRATION:
Props: Apollo Leisure (UK) Ltd
Theatre Manager: Graham Gilmore
For all booking information and further details please
contact Sam Shrouder or Nicky Monk at Apollo Leisure
(UK) Ltd., Grehan House, Garsington Road, Cowley,
Oxford OX4 5NQ. Tel: 01865 782900; Fax: Oxford
01865 782910.
Capacity: 3,485 seated plus 302 standing.
TECHNICAL:
Stage: 24.1m x 9.5m (79ft x 31ft). No rake. Up to 3.7m
(12ft) extension pos. without loss of seats. Permanent
crush barrier. Perm. speaker platforms, each 3.7m x
2.4m (12ft x 8ft). Pros. opening 19.2m wide x 10.7m
high (63ft x 35ft). Safety curtain in use. Ht. to grid 16.8m
(55ft). 22 line double purchase counterweight system.
Stage power supply: 3 phase. 400 amps (lights), 1 phase
100 amps (sound), 3 phase 100 amps various with earth
leakage trip. Stage water supply. Position for lighting
truss in front of pros. arch. Cable run to auditorium
sound control positions; rear stalls, 55m, front circle
73m. Two CS spots.
Other: Dressing Rooms 2 master + 7, accom. up to 42;
Private stage bar. Showers. Catering Space. Get-in (3ft)
ramp direct to stage from car park. Promoter's Office.
Restricted parking.
"The plan for this venue can be found in the
Official London Seating Plan Guide"

## LONDON ARENA

Limeharbour Isle of Dogs London E14 9TH
Tel 0171 538 8880 BO 0171 538 1212
Fax 0171 538 5572
ADMINISTRATION:
General Manager: Alex McCrindle
Commercial Director: Nicky Dunn
Marketing Manager: Ross McDonald
Box Office Manager: Brendan Carroll
Seating/Capacity: 13,500

## THE LONDON BUBBLE

3/5 Elephant Lane London SE16 4JD
Tel 0171 237 4434 Fax 0171 231 2366
Email: admin@londonbubble.org.uk
ADMINISTRATION:

Bubble Theatre Company Ltd.
Artistic Director: Jonathan Petherbridge
Administrator: Helen Chamberlain
Policy: Productions: to tour a variety of productions to
adults and children throughout the Greater London area
in community and traditional venues, and, during the
summer, to London's parks and open spaces. The aim
is to develop a popular theatre style which is bold and
bright, fast and physical, open and accessible.
Seating on average: 250

TECHNICAL:
Stage: 2 trailers, 33', 36' & 40' convertible into dressing
room unit, To carry tent and site equipment. Aluminium
box lighting truss.
Lighting: Celco pathfinder lighting board, 36 ways
Tempus dimming, distribution from generators for both
site and Theatre lighting. Lanterns:- 8 Thomas Par Cans,
4 Sil 30, 6 Prelude 16/30, 12 Prelude F, 6 Prelude P.C.,
10 Patt. 308, 4 Patt. 23, 2 Patt. 23N, 4 ADB 1k, 5 Patt.
123, 1 Patt. 223, 1 Sil 15 Follow Spot.
Sound: Soundcraft 200b 16/4/2. Revox B77, Revox
A77, 6 Bose 802, 2 Turner 302, 1 Quad 405, 2 E.V.
Graphics, Audio Radio Mikes, Asstd. Shure SM58 etc.
All equipment available for hire from September-May.
Other: Rehearsal Room in Rotherhithe available for hire
all year round.

## LONDON COLISEUM

St. Martins Lane London WC2N 4ES
Mgt 0171 836 0111 BO 0171 632 8300
SD 0171 836 1416 Fax 0171 836 8379
Press & Pub Fax 0171 497 9052 Telex 264867 ENOG
ADMINISTRATION:
Director of Human Resources: Mimi Watts
Technical Director: Laurence Holderness
General Director: Nicholas Payne
Executive Director: Russell Willis Taylor
Music Director: Paul Daniel
Financial Controlller: Graeme Wallace
Owners: English National Opera.
Perfs: Normally 7.30.
Seats: 2,358 on four levels. Licensed Bars and Buffets
serving full refreshment on all levels.
TECHNICAL:
Stage: Proscenium Stage: Flat, Proscenium opening
15.24m wide x 8.76m high. False Proscenium adjustable
opening 12.19m - 14.02m, adjustable height usually 7m
- 8.76m, Grid 21.33m high, 63 lines - counter weights,
flying bars 16.76m, scenery 7.62m high. Wing widths PS
3.05m, OP 3.05m. Prompt Corner OP.
Lighting: Switchboard: Rank Strand Galaxy II 360
channels, F.O.H. 100 circuits, 30 x 2KW Sils 10, 12 x
1.2KW Cantata, 6 x 2KW Sils 30, 5 x Cadenza 2KW
9/15.2 x 2KW Sils 15, 12 x 1KW Pars, 12 x 1KW Pars to
12 x Patt. T64, 18 x 1K Fresnels, KUPU followspots x 2.
Stage: 8 x tracked ladders c/w 1KW Pars, 2 x Perch
Assembly - 650W preludes 12 dips per side, 4 circuits
g/row. Spot Bars: 5 Perm Bars, 23 circuits patchable on
4.12 on 1, x Cyc front light 6 x IRIS 4, 1 x Cyc
backlight 6 x IRIS 4. Total dimmers 174 x 2KW, 178 x
5KW, 8 x 10KW.
Sound: 32 input CADAC 'E' type mixer, 2 x OTARI 5050
2B tape decks, seven channel Sennheiser radio mic
system, 6 x Meyer UPA1 speakers, 3 x Meyer amplifier
racks, 5 x Newmann microphones.
"The plan for this venue can be found in the
Official London Seating Plan Guide"

## LONDON GUILDHALL UNIVERSITY
Students Union 2 Goulston Street London E1 7TP
Tel 0171 247 1441 Fax 0171 247 0618
Email: studentunion@lgu.ac.uk
Contact: Meridy Bates

## LONDON PALLADIUM
Argyll Street London W1A 3AB
Mgt 0171 734 6846 BO 0171 494 5020
SD 0171 437 1278
ADMINISTRATION:
Props: Stoll Moss Theatres Ltd, 21 Soho Square,
London W1V 5FD; Tel: 0171 494 5200 and Fax 0171
434 1217.
Policy: Musicals, Comedy, Concerts, Television.
Chief Executive: Richard Johnston
Theatre Manager: Gareth Parnell
For all bookings and production enquiries contact
Richard Johnston or Nica Burns (Production Directors),
Gareth Johnson (General Manager, Production
Department) or David Kinsey (Concerts and Hirings
Manager). Facilities may be made available for day time,
late night and weekend use for private and press
receptions, conferences and meetings - Contact: David
Kinsey 0171 494 5200 and Fax 0171 434 1217.
Seats: 2,286
3 Bars, Café, Entertainment Suites.
TECHNICAL:
Stage: Flat; Pros. Opening 14.48m; Ht of of Grid
16.76m; 60 lines, C/W; Depth of Stage 12.34m;
Revolving Stage 9.75m & 5.45m; Circular Centre Lift
3.66m; Prompt Cnr. P.S.
Lighting: Board: Strand Galaxy II, 298 Circuits.
Situated rear of Royal Circle.
Other: Dressing rooms: 24
Membership: SOLT.
"The plan for this venue can be found in the
Official London Seating Plan Guide"

## LYCEUM THEATRE
21 Wellington Street London WC2E 7DA
Mgt 0171 420 8191 SD 0171 420 8100
BO (Tickets North) 0870 606 3441
BO (enquiries only) 0171 420 8112 Fax 0171 240 4155
ADMINSTRATION:
For all booking information and further details please
contact Sam Shrouder or Nicky Monk at Apollo Leisure
(UK) Ltd., Grehan House, Garsington Road, Cowley,
Oxford OX4 5NQ. Tel: 01865 782900; Fax: Oxford
01865 782910.
General Manager: Debbie Garrick
Deputy General Manager: Lowri Madoc
Technical Manager: Rob Hayden
Seats: 1,800-2,000
TECHNICAL:
Please contact Rob Hayden
"The plan for this venue can be found in the
Official London Seating Plan Guide"

## LYRIC THEATRE
Shaftesbury Avenue London W1V 7HA
Mgt 0171 437 3694 BO 0171 494 5550
SD 0171 437 5443
ADMINISTRATION:
Props: Stoll Moss Theatres Ltd, 21 Soho Square,
London W1V 5FD; Tel: 0171 494 5200 and Fax 0171
434 1217.
Policy: Plays, Musicals, Comedy, Concerts.

Chief Executive: Richard Johnston
Theatre Manager: Alison Heys
For all bookings and production enquiries contact
Richard Johnston or Nica Burns (Production Directors),
Gareth Johnson (General Manager, Production
Department) or David Kinsey (Concerts and Hirings
Manager). Facilities may be made available for day time,
late night and weekend use for private and press
receptions, conferences and meetings - Contact: David
Kinsey 0171 494 5200 and Fax 0171 434 1217.
Seats: 932
4 Bars.
TECHNICAL:
Stage: flat; Pros. Opening 9.14m, Ht of Pros. 7.32m;
Depth of Stage 12.65m; Ht of Grid 15.24m; 25 lines, 7
S.P./19 D.P C/W; Prompt Cnr. P.S.
Lighting: Lighting Board: Strand Galaxy II, 192 circuits.
Situated rear of Upper Circle.
Other: Dressing rooms: 14
Membership: SOLT.
"The plan for this venue can be found in the
Official London Seating Plan Guide"

## LYRIC THEATRE HAMMERSMITH
King Street London W6 0QL
Mgt 0181 741 0824 BO 0181 741 2311
SBO 0181 741 8701 Fax 0181 741 7694
ADMINISTRATION:
Props: Lyric Theatre Hammersmith Trust
Artistic Director: Neil Bartlett
Financial Director: Pam Cooper
Chief Executive: Sue Storr
Administrative Producer: Simon Mellor
Producing and Receiving House.
Policy: Limited runs of new plays and classics, and
international work, live music, youth work.
Seats: 537.
Studio: Visiting small scale companies, predominantly
new plays, classic revivals and international plays.
Seats: 110
TECHNICAL:
Stage: Proscenium Stage, Flat, Pros. opening 8.2mts.
Ht. of Pros. 6.95m; Depth of S/Line 9.1m; Elevator
Forestage 2m; Ht. of Grid 15m; 38 lines, C/W; Flying
Bars 10.5m; Gt-in Goods Lift 1.8m x 3m deep. Ht. 2.5m.
Lighting: Switchboard: Galaxy 100m channel 85 x 2K. 15
x 5K.
Sound: Equipment: DDA 24-8-2 Theatre Matrix Mixer;
F.O.H. speakers 6 Bose 800.
Dressing Rooms 8; Orchestra Pit.

STUDIO THEATRE:
Approx. 11m square; Ht. of Grid 4.8m.
Switchboard: Compact 36 x 2K channels.
Sound Equipment: 1 DDA 16-8-2 Theatre Matrix Mixer, 4
x Tannoy Little Red Speakers.
"The plan for this venue can be found in the
Official London Seating Plan Guide"

## MACOWAN THEATRE
Logan Place London W8 6QN
Mgt 0171 373 6932 BO 0171 373 9883
Fax 0171 370 1980
ADMINISTRATION:
Props: London Academy of Music and Dramatic Art
Technical Director: John MacKinnon;
Policy: Productions by LAMDA, student actors and
technicians. Club licence.
Seats: 130-250. Bar.

TECHNICAL:
Stage: Flexible seating, mainly proscenium. Sprung
wood floor. Pros 13.3m by 5.47m. Depth S/Line 9.2m.
Grid 10.85m. 9 Counterweights, some hemps. Flying
Bars 11.58m DS, 10.15m US. Wings 0.83m PS, 1.47m
OP. PS prompt. Tallescope.
Lighting: Strand 520. 84 2kw dimmers. Position SL FOH.
50 Profiles, 30 Fresnels, 30 Parcans, 2 Follow Spots.
Lantern stocks are varied for teaching requirements.
Sound: Equipment: Yamaha PM1200. Position SRFOH.
Again a wide stock of other equipment for teaching.
Other: Dressing Rooms 2, accom. 30; 5 Showers;
Orchestra Pit 12. Wardrobe department.

**MEAN FIDDLER**
24-28a High Street Harlseden London NW10 4LX
Mgt 0181 961 5490 Fax 0181 961 9238
Contact: Polly Hancock
Capacity: 650

**MERMAID THEATRE**
Puddle Dock Blackfriars London EC4V 3DB
Mgt/SD 0171 236 1919 Fax 0171 236 1819
ADMINISTRATION:
Props: The Mermaid Theatre
General Manager: Gary Nelson
Chief Electrician: Mark Crump
Technical Manager: Alex Walker
For information on conference and rehearsal facilities
contact Gary Nelson Tel 0171 236 1919.
Seats: 610 on one raked level; Loop system for the hard
of hearing. Disabled facilities. Servery and 2 large bars.
TECHNICAL:
End stage, 14.8m wide; 23.8m deep; Dock Door direct
off street, 4.6m high, 4.6m wide; 0.8m drop to stage
level; Revolve manual, 6.1m diam. Trap DSC.
Communications: 1 channel ring intercom; Cue lights
patchable to 14 positions; dressing room paging and
show relay
"The plan for this venue can be found in the
Official London Seating Plan Guide"

**MILLFIELD THEATRE**
Silver Street Edmonton London N18 1PJ
Mgt 0181 807 6186 BO 0181 807 6680
Fax 0181 803 2801
ADMINISTRATION:
Props: Millfield Theatre Ltd.
Theatre Manager: Graham Bennett
Assistant Manager (Technical): Phil Wharfe
Policy: Amateur and professional productions, tours,
concerts and recitals, conferences, trade fairs, etc.
Perfs: Variable.
Seats: Variable 321 to 362.
Theatre bar, light refreshments.
TECHNICAL:
Stage: Complete adjustable performance area. Depth
3.46m-7.63m. Width up to 14.15m Optional Pros.
variable. Width up to 9.1m Depth up to 5.2m. Electrically
operated lowering/mobile grid. 10 hemp sets. 3 tab
tracks. 5 x wipe tracks. Flying bars 11m. Prompt corner
PS, F.O.H. Direct get-in PS. Scene dock OP. Sprung
floor over entire performance area. Control room at rear
of auditorium.
Lighting: Control: Memory control system with manual
back-up. 60 x 2.5kw dimmers and 6 x independants
linked through patch bay to outlets throughout of
performance area. 5 spot bars + 2 F.O.H. side booms +
2 stage side booms with 20 x 1kw Profiles, 24 x 1kw

Fresnels, 30 x Parcans, 12 x 650w Profiles, 12 x 500w
Fresnels, 4 x 500w Profiles, 8 x 500w Floods, 6 x Coda
4 Battens, 4 x 1kw Floods. 2 x 2kw followspot. 5 x 1kw
PC Remote colour-change equipment available.
Sound: Equipment: 24/4/2 Soundcraft desk + Shure
10/2 desk. 30 mic lines, permanent auditorium PA + tie-
lines to other areas. Revox B77 + Tascam 34B Four
Track, + 6 EDC Radio Mics and two cassette decks.
SPX90 effects unit and SPX 900, CD player, 2 Stereo
delays, gate. Shure/AKG/Sennheiser Micro-phones.
Other: Dressing Rooms 8, accom. 65; 2 Showers;
Shallow orchestra pit for up to 30. Full disabled access
and facilities. Car park available.

**MOUNTVIEW THEATRE SCHOOL**
104 Crouch Hill London N8 9EA
Admin 0181 347 3602  BO 0181 347 3601
Tech 0181 347 3612  Fax 0181 348 1727
ADMINISTRATION:
Prop & Lessees: Mountview Arts Centre Ltd
Chief Executive: Peter Coxhead
Principal: Paul Clements
Technical Director: Jacqui Leigh
Registrar: Angela Wharton
Policy: Professional Drama School
Perfs: Week nights 7.30pm Sat. 3.30 & 7.30pm
Seats: Mountview Theatre 112, Judi Dench Theatre 60,
Club Bar.
TECHNICAL:
Mountview Theatre:
Stage: Proscenium Stage, Pros. opening 7.32m; Ht. of
Pros. 3.35m; Depth of S/Line 7.62m; W/Widths P.S.
0.91m; Prompt Cnr. DSR.
Lighting: Equipment: 30 lanterns, 78 Dimmers (72 wired
to 6 pre-wired bars & 6 in mini 2 rack) 96 way Lightboard
M (Rank Strand) Possible further 50 Lanterns (shared
with Judi Dench Theatre).
Sound: Equipment: 2 Revox B77 Tape decks, 1
Cassette deck, 8 into 4 into 2 Mixer, up to 6 Speakers
and assorted microphones (Shared with the Judi Dench
Theatre).
Other: Communications Tech.  Pro ring intercom & show
relay also Q light system.

Judi Dench Theatre:
Stage: Experimental studio acting area, variable.  Overall
size 10.97m x 9.14m.
Lighting: Equipment: 26 Lanterns, 40 patch sockets to
24 dimmers, 24 way action desk (Rank Strand).
Possible further 50 lanterns (shared with the Mountview
Theatre).
Sound: Equipment: 2 Revox B77 Tape decks, 1 cassette
deck, 6 into 4 mixer, up to 6 speakers & assorted
microphones (shared with Mountview Theatre).
Communications: Tech Pro ring intercomm, & show
relay, also Q light system.
Other: Dressing rooms, 2 accom. 30; Green room; 8
Rehearsal studios; 3 workshops; Wardrobe.
Also at RRM5, Kingfisher Place, London N22: 20
Rehearsal Studios; Green room; showers.

Studio 2 Theatre: Lighting Equipment: 12 Lanterns, 40
Patch sockets to 12 dimmers, 24 way tempus board
(Rank Strand).
Sound Equipment: 1 Tascam 32 tape deck, 6 into 4
mixer, 2 speakers.

**NATIONAL CLUB**
234 Kilburn High Road London NW6 4JR
Tel 0171 328 3141 Fax 0171 624 5349

Manager: Jason Carey
Capacity: 2,100

## NETTLEFOLD HALL

West Norwood Library Norwood High Street
London SE27 9JX
Mgt/BO 0171 926 8070  Fax 0171 926 8071
ADMINISTRATION:
Props: London Borough of Lambeth
Manager: Jean Wilson
Policy: General Purpose Hall - Stage Plays, Cinema,
Concerts, Exhibitions, Meetings and Rehearsals etc.
Seats: 213
TECHNICAL:
Lighting, Sound. Cinema; 16mm x 35mm facilities.

## NEW LONDON ASTORIA

157 Charing Cross Road London WC2H 0EN
Tel 0171 434 9592 BO 0171 434 0403/4
Fax 0171 437 1781
ADMINISTRATION:
Globelast Ltd
Total Capacity: 2,000
TECHNICAL:
Stage: Pros. Opening 14.63m; Ht. of Pros. 9.42m;
W/Widths P.S.O. 76m, O.P.O. 76m. Ht. of Grid 14.44m,
Flying Height 14.29m.
Lighting: Switchboard: Rank Strand Compact 120 260
memories. Chase and Sound to light facilities through
matrix system.
Other: Dressing Rooms 6 to accom. 18; bandroom to
accom. 10.

## NEW LONDON THEATRE

Drury Lane and Parker Street London WC2B 5PW
Mgt 0171 242 9802 BO 0171 405 0072
SD 0171 242 9802 Fax 0171 831 5487
ADMINISTRATION:
Props: Really Useful Stage Productions.
Theatre Manager: Callum Cunningham
General Manager: William G. Differ
Maintenance Engineer: Dennis Barthram
Policy: As normal West End Theatre; Conferences.
Perfs: Variable.
Seats: 1,102. Two Bars & One Coffee Bar.
TECHNICAL:
Stage: Proscenium or Round Stage, Flat with 4.88m
diam. revolve; Apron Stage; Front of Apron to Back Wall
11.81m; Pros. opening 17.68m variable; Depth of S/Line
8.53m; Ht. of Grid 16.76m; 39 lines, C/W; Scenery Flying
Ht. 16.15m; Flying Bars 17.68m; W/Widths P.S. 5.33m;
Prompt Cnr. either side or upstage.
Theatre in The Round: 10 Electric Motor Flying Bars.
Lighting: Switchboard: Strand IDM Mk. 2a, rear gallery;
120 ways; F.O.H. Spots 2 Patt. 765, 35 Patt. 773, 65
Patt. 763; Dips 25 circuits.
Sound: Equipment: Stagesound, 6 channel 2 group, 2
Stereo Grams, 2 Stereo Tape rear gallery; 100v line
speakers, 2 Pros. SL/SR. 3 on stage.
Other: Dressing Rooms 9, accom. 40; 12 Showers.
Orchestra Pit 18.
Membership: SOLT
"The plan for this venue can be found in the
Official London Seating Plan Guide"

## THE OLD VIC

The Cut Waterloo Road London SE1 8NB
Mgt 0171 928 2651 BO 0171 928 7616

SD 0171 928 2651 Mgt Fax 0171 261 9161
BO Fax 0171 401 3870
ADMINISTRATION:
Prop: Ed Mirvish
Executive Producer: David Mirvish
Artistic Director: Sir Peter Hall
Director (New Plays): Dominic Dromgoole
Associate Producer: Gillian Diamond
General Manager: Andrew Leigh
Production Manager: Martin Hazlewood
Policy: Subscription Seasons. Own productions: 5
classics and 5 new plays per year, in repertoire.
Perfs: Eves Sun-Sat 7.30pm; Mats Thurs, Sat & Sun
variable  times (check first).
Seats: 1,067. Four Bars.
TECHNICAL:
Stage: Proscenium Stage, Raked 1:22; Pros. opening
8.50m; Depth from iron 10.11m; Perm. Fore-stage
1.50m, Forestage extension 3m; Rear Stage 9.5m x
9.5m; Ht. of Pros. 6.10m; Ht. of Grid 15.60m; 53 double
purchase C/W bars; Flying Bars 11.00m; W/Widths P.S.
7.00m, O.P. 7.00m; Prompt cnr. O. P. or P.S.
Lighting: Control: 2 x ETC Expressions ( identical to ARRI
Imagine 3) with full tracking back up, capable of
supporting 600 channels, 1024 dimmers, with 2
playbacks, 3.5" drive and dual display.  Operated from
control room at rear of the dress circle, with remote
control facility onstage.  Console or remote monitors can
be moved to stalls during production periods.  DMX and
Ethernet patchable to various outlets around the stage.
Electrical: 144 Permus Dimmers installed - 22 x 5K  12
x 2.5K - but facility on SR for additional temporary
installation.  12 switchable 15A independents distributed
around the stage and auditorium.  Auxiliary mains supply
pannel on-stage comprising 2 x 100A three phase
busbars, 3 x 63A C17 three phase sockets, 3 x 63A C17
single phase sockets.  Additional three phase supply on
SL fly floor for motors or stage machinery.
Lighting equipment: 28 x Sil 15 1K Axial 40 x Patt 264.
These are usually FOH, and schematic layout is available
on request, but it is not a fixed rig.  No follow spots but
position for up to four spots available at rear of upper
circle slightly to SL of centre.  NB.  Due to construction
of the circle fronts, no circle front or upper circle front
lighting positions available.
Access equipment: 1 Tallescope, 2 x Focus Bridges and
a selection of ladders, inc 12 rung Zarges.
Sound: The theatre has no sound equipment, but it is
equipped with approx 60 3pin XLR tie lines.  A 6 inch
duct connects the sound mixing position at the rear of
the stalls to the orchestra pit, and a further duct links to
the substage room with position for amplifier racks,
complete with 3 x 32A C17 single phase power supplies
(all on the same phase).  Proscenium boom positions
available for speakers, as well as points for central
overhead cluster and rear auditorium speaker mountings
on all levels.
Communications: RTS two channel headset system
capable of supporting 17 belt packs. 20 outlets
throughout building, 10 belt packs (325's), 16 Beyer
Headsets with master station in prompt desk.
Other: Cue lights - 24 fixed positions, 12 remotable, fully
patchable into 20 way control on prompt desk. Prompt
desk also provides BT ringing supply, either manually
controlled or on a standard pattern, as well as a digital
clock/stopwatch.
CCTV: although the theatre does not supply a camera,
BNC tie lines are provided to a variety of camera
positions, and two 9" monitors are available.
Dressing Rooms for 36 persons; 4 Bathrooms.
Male & Female Band Rooms (pit capacity 24 musicians).

Maintenance, Wardrobe & Laundry Room.
"The plan for this venue can be found in the Official London Seating Plan Guide"

## OPEN AIR THEATRE

Regent's Park London NW1 4NP
Mgt 0171 935 5884 BO 0171 486 2431
SD 0171 486 6991 (BO & SD tels May to Sept. only)
Fax 0171 487 4562
ADMINISTRATION:
Props: Department of Culture, Media and Sport
Lessees: The New Shakespeare Co. Ltd
Artistic & Managing Director: Ian Talbot
Policy: The New Shakespeare Company is a non-profit distributing Company founded in 1962 whose main function is to present Summer Seasons of Shakespeare plays at the Open Air Theatre.
Perfs: Mon/Sat 8.00; Mats. Wed/Thurs & Sat. 2.30; June, July, August and first part of September.
Seats: 1,187. Refreshment; Fully Licensed Bars. buffet (cold) and barbecue available before performance from 6.45. Bar open until 12 midnight.
TECHNICAL:
Technical facilities vary according to production.
The Theatre is leased to the New Shakespeare Company by the Department of Culture, Media and Sport and is not generally available for hire.
Membership: SOLT
"The plan for this venue can be found in the Official London Seating Plan Guide"

## PALACE THEATRE

Shaftesbury Avenue London W1V 8AY
Mgt 0171 434 0088 BO 0171 434 0909
SD 0171 434 0088 Fax 0171 734 6157
ADMINISTRATION:
Props: Palace Theatre (London) Ltd.
Theatre Manager: Mark Hone
Assistant Theatre Manager: Stephen Bush
Catering Manager: Suzanne Hubbard
Chief Electrician: Kriss Buddle
Policy: Usual West End Policy of Commercial Theatre
Seats: 1,400. Bars in all parts.
TECHNICAL:
Stage: Proscenium Stage, Raked; Pros. opening 10.29m; Ht. of Pros. 10.36m; depth of S/Line 12.50m-14.20m; Ht. of Grid 21.03m; 44 lines; Scenery Flying Ht. 9.14m; Flying Bars 14.63m; Prompt Cnr. O.P.
Lighting: Switchboard: Rank Strand Light Palette, situated P.S. Box F.O.H.; F.O.H. Spots various, plus 2 Berkey Colorspot II. Generator.
Sound: Equipment: Sound console in Auditorium; Speakers to all parts.
Other: Orchestra Pit.
Membership: SOLT
"The plan for this venue can be found in the Official London Seating Plan Guide"

## PAUL ROBESON THEATRE

Centrespace 24 Treaty Centre High Street Hounslow Middlesex TW3 1ES
For admin. queries please contact: Arts, Events & Venues Chiswick Town Hall, Heathfield Terrace, Chiswick, London W4 4JN
Admin/Mgt 0181 862 6502  Admin Fax 0181 862 6570
BO 0181 577 6969  BO Fax 0181 572 3758
ADMINISTRATION:
Props: London Borough of Hounslow.

Business Manager: Mary Tennant
Operations Manager: Laurie Woollcott
Senior Technician: Rachel Francis
Press Officer: Nicole Flammer
Policy: Mixed programme of evening performances including theatre, dance, multicultural events, music and children's shows. Daytime activities include youth workshops, children's events and senior citizen events. The theatre is also available for commercial and community hire.
Closed Sundays.
Seats: 280.
Fully licensed bar and Café/Restaurant. Community Room - adjacent to the theatre, can be used as Green Room or as a separate facility.
Dressing Room: 2 - shower facility.
TECHNICAL:
Stage: No actual stage. Performance space same level as row A; Performance Space: 39ft x 18ft (inc. cross over and tab bunching); Performance Area: 25ft x 14ft; Height to Grid: 30ft; Flying Lines: None, 3 x Wipe Tracks D.S./C.S./U.S.; Tabs: Black tabs at rear & mid stage, plus legs and borders; House Tabs: Blue/Green (Motorised); Cinema Screen: Picture Size 18ft x 9ft max (C.S.); Cinema Projector: Elmo Lx 2200 16mm; Slide Projector: Elmo Omnigraphic 552 Xenon; Power Supply: One 32A Cee Form (P.S.) 16 x 13A sockets (S.R.).
Lighting: Lighting Desk: Zero 88, Sirius 48; Dimmers: Electrosonic ES6000 series 2kw/chan also 4 x Non dim circuits (1kw each); Stage Bars: 3, 1 x 12 way, 1 x 10 way, 1 x 6 way (all internally wired); Stage Dips: 4 (U.S.L.), (All stage bars and dips are patchable across 22 circuits); F.O.H. Bridges: 2 each 6 way (both paired and internally wired); Follow Spot: 1 x Strand Solo 1kw CSI; Lanterns: Various types of luminaries are available.
Sound: Sound Desk: Yamaha MC2404 II 24 Chn. Main Amps: Harrison Xi 600 (300w/chn) Mustang 200 (100w/chn); House Speakers: 4 x Tannoy Puma (Flown above pros), 2 x Yamaha S2 15ES (floor level); Foldback System: A basic 2 mix monitor system is available; Yamaha CDX480 CD player. Tape Decks: Revox B77 (1/2 Track 1/4 inch) JVC TD-X502, Denon M12 XR (Cassette Decks); Effect Units: Alesis Midiverb II; EMP100; Yamaha Comp/LIM. Equalisation: Citronic SPX 7-21 Graphic (Pre Set). Mics: Various types of vocal and instrument mics are available along with 5 passive D.I.s.

## PEACOCK THEATRE - SADLER'S WELLS IN THE WEST END

Portugal Street (off Kingsway) London WC2A 2HT
Admin 0171 314 8888 BO 0171 863 8222
ADMINISTRATION:
Managed by Sadler's Wells Trust Ltd
Chief Executive: Ian Albery
Technical Director: Paul Richardson
Chief Technician: Martin Hunt
Seats: 1000
2 Bars, Buffet, Entertainment Suite
TECHNICAL
Stage: Flat stage; pros. opening: 13.9m; pros. height: 5.97m; iron opening: 14.85m; depth of stage: 10.75m; wings, stage left: 2.63m; Dock door get in: 5.1m; Upstage dock opening: 6.09m; Flys: 52 flying bars, grid height: 15.6m;
Dance floor available;
Lighting: Rank Strand Galaxy II control system; 130 dimmers 18 X 5k, 112 X 2k; Foh Rig: advance bar 8 X Sil 19-40° 1kw profiles, bridge 12 X Sil 15-32° 1kw profiles, box booms 3 X Sil 15-32° 1kw profiles (both sides),

proscenium 4 X Sil 15-32° 1kw profiles (both sides),
booms; Stage equipment 12 X Sil 15-32° 1kw profiles,
40 X Sil 19-40° 1kw profiles, 9 X strand P243 2kw
fresnels, 30 X strand P743 1kw fresnels, 10 X CCT
starlette 1kw fresnels, 10 X ADB 1kw fresnels, 10 X CCT
starlette 1kw PC, 16 X 110V Parcans, No 5 medium
flood, 40 X 240V Parcans, assorted heads, Cyclorama:
18 X AC1001 1kw floods, 5 X 4 compartment 1kw
ground rows; Follow spots: 2 X Pani 1200w HMI on
bridge. Powers supplies: 200A 3PN on camlocks fly
floor SR, 63A SPN Ceeform outlet midstage right, 32A
3PN Ceeform outlet upstage centre; Music stands and
conductor's dais available
For futher information please contact the Chief
Electrician on 0181 314 8820.
"The plan for this venue can be found in the
Official London Seating Plan Guide"

## PHOENIX THEATRE
110 Charing Cross Road London WC2H 0JP
Mgt 0171 465 0211 BO 0171 369 1733
Fax 0171 465 0212 SD 0171 465 0211
ADMINISTRATION:
Prop: Associated Capital Theatres,
110 St Martin's Lane, London, WC2N 4AD.
Tel  0171 304 7922 Fax 0171 867 1130
General Manager: Hugh Hales
Theatre Manager: David Lyness
Policy: Plays and Musicals.
Perfs: Variable.
Seats: 1,012. Five Bars.
TECHNICAL:
Stage: Proscenium Stage, Flat; Pros. opening 9.52m;
Ht. of Pros. 7.57m; Depth of S/Line 8.54m; Ht. of Grid
15.39m; 44 lines inc. House Tabs, Scenery flying Ht.
14.63m; Double-Purchase C/W Lift 325lb normal. Flying
Bars 11.28m; W/Widths P.S. 2.74m, P.O. 2.13m;
Prompt Cnr. P.S.   Stage Extension: 2.74 Depth, 11.90
Width, 6.20 Height, Flying Height 5.85, 3 pile Winches
(adjustable positioning).
Lighting: Switchboard: located in O.P. Stage Box Dress
Circle level but position is variable; 120 ways; 6 2kw
Rank/Strand Cadenzas; Dip 6 each side plus Dips for
Ground row and Float. Lighting Control: ARRI 250 120
way in house.
Sound: Please contact venue.
Dressing Rooms 16; 2 Showers; 1 Bathroom plus
Dressing Rooms with Showers. Orchestra Pit 16.
Membership: SOLT
"The plan for this venue can be found in the
Official London Seating Plan Guide"

## PICCADILLY THEATRE
Denman Street London W1V 8DY
Mgt/SD 0171 867 1128 BO 0171 369 1734
Fax 0171 437 5336 Artistes No. 0171 437 2124
ADMINISTRATION:
Props: Associated Capital Theatres,
110 St Martin's Lane, London WC2N 4AD
Tel 0171 304 7922, Fax 0171 867 1130
General Manager: Hugh Hales
Theatre Manager: Carol Gore
Policy: Plays, Musicals, Ballet etc.
Perfs: Variable according to Production.
Seats: Variable capacity auditorium - Small 792 seats;
large 1,132. Licensed Bars.

TECHNICAL:
Stage: Proscenium Flat Unit Stage, removable

completely or in part; Pros. Opening 9.70m; Ht. of Pros.
6.40m; Depth of S/Line 11.58m; Ht. of Grid 16.54m; 40
lines C/W. Hemp as required; Scenery Flying Ht.
15.09m; Flying Bars 11.73m; W/Widths P.S. 3.35m,
O.P. 4.27m; Prompt Cnr. variable.
Lighting: Switchboard: MMS 200 channels, 320
memories. Many special facilities. F.O.H. Spots: 22 T
Spots; 12 Patt. 264; 2 Patt. 765 Follow Spots; 4
Battens, 3 circuit; Floats 3 circuit, if required.
Sound: Equipment: F.O.H. Stereo Amplification System
and as required.
Other: Dressing Rooms 17, accom. 60; Orchestra Pit
28. Fully Air Conditioned Theatre.
Membership: SOLT
"The plan for this venue can be found in the
Official London Seating Plan Guide"

## THE PLACE THEATRE
17 Dukes Road London WC1H 9AB
Mgt 0171 380 1268 BO 0171 387 0031
Fax 0171 383 2003
ADMINISTRATION:
Props: Contemporary Dance Trust.
Director of Admin. & Finance: David Burnie
Theatre Director: John Ashford
Administrator: Colette Hansford
Press & Publicity: Sam McAuley
Technical Manager: Ian Richards
Policy: Indep. Dance Cos. presented for 30 weeks.
Theatre available for hire in remaining 22 weeks.
Perfs: 8.00pm (or by arrangement).
Seats: 300. Bar and Café.
TECHNICAL:
Stage: Open Stage, flat; sprung wooden floor with
grey/black lino covering. Total stage area 15.5m x 11m.
Normal performance area 10.5m x 9m (black legs in
position). Height to grid 6m. White Cyclorama Available.
Lighting: Equipment: Arri Imagine 250, 92 Strand LD90
Dimmers (60 Patchable via 263 outlets), 40 x Patt 743,
30 x Sil 30, 8 x ADB 1 KW PC, 16 x Prelude 16/30
650w, 3 x Patt 243, 16 Patt 23 650w, 8 x AC1001, 20 x
Par 64 (CP62 only) 8 x 3m vertical booms, 6 x colour
Chromatics for Sil 30. Tallescope.
Sound: Equipment: Soundcraft Venue 16:8:2 Mixer,
Tascam DA30 DAT Machine, 2 x Tascam 112 Cassette
Decks, Denon CD Player, Revox B77, (available on
request Denon DN 990 Mini Disc Recorder), Yamaha
SPX 900, 4 Bose 802 Speakers, 2 Bose 302 Speakers,
2 Bose 1800 Amplifiers, 1 x Yamaha P2100 Amplifier, 2
x Crown D60 Amplifiers, 2 Bose Equalisers, 1 x Yamaha
Graphic Equaliser, 4 x Stage Monitors (Purpose Built), 3
x Sure SM58, 2 x AKG 451, 1 x Crown PCC 160, 1 x
AKG D112, 4 x Di boxes, 5 x boom mic stands, Tecpro
intercom system.
Other: Dressing Rooms: 2, accom. 16, show relay &
tannoy.

## PLAYERS THEATRE
The Arches Villiers Street London WC2N 6NG
Tel 0171 976 1307 BO 0171 839 1134
Fax 0171 839 8067
Email: info@theplayerstheatre.co.uk
Web Site: www.theplayerstheatre.co.uk
ADMINISTRATION:
Props: Players Theatre Club
Trustees: Geoffrey Brawn; Dominic Le Foe
Manager: Stephen Grey
Policy: Victorian Music Hall, Melodrama & Pantomime.
Perfs: Tues-Sun 8.15.  Seats: 256

## THE PLAYHOUSE THEATRE
Northumberland Avenue London WC2N 5DE
Mgt/SD 0171 839 4292 BO 0171 839 4401
Fax 0171 839 8142
ADMINISTRATION:
Props: Patrick Sulaiman
Theatre Manager: Dominic Hale
Policy: Varied
Seats: 800. Four Licensed Bars plus 75 seat Restaurant.
TECHNICAL:
Stage: 13.6m x 8.7m Prosc. width 7.88m. Height to
Grid 13.2m. Flying: 34 Counter Weight sets at 200mm
centres. Two advance F.O.H. bars on electric winches
for lighting and loud speakers. Understage: 19th Century
system with traps, bridges and sliders restored to full
working order.
Lighting: Strand Gemini 120-way with disc drive and
memory back-up in control room at rear of circle; 108
2.5kW and 12.5kW Permus Dimmers on 300A TPN
supply. Dimmer circuits are paralleled to up to four
locations.
Touring Power: 160A TPN on stage right fly gallery for
lighting 60A SPN below stage for sound.
Sound and Communication: A basic 'in house' system is
provided, comprising a Soundcraft 200SR 12/4/2 mixer.
6 Bose 402 loud speakers with controllers, 4 Yamaha
loud speaker amplifiers and 1 Revox B77 tape recorder.
The sound control room is located at the rear of the
circle and connected by tie lines to a rack room via
speaker, microphone and communication tie lines.
Other: Box Office: Ticketmaster. Space-Time.
Dressing Rooms: Five with total spaces for 21 artists.
Wardrobe/ Laundry and Company Office.
Stage Manager: Portable Sm desk Stage Right with 12-
way cue lights front of house and dressing room paging,
bar bells and Clearcom compatible communication
system with SM station and six portable belt packs.
"The plan for this venue can be found in the
Official London Seating Plan Guide"

## PRINCE EDWARD THEATRE
Old Compton Street London W1V 6HS
Mgt 0171 437 2024 BO 0171 447 5400
SD 0171 439 3041
ADMINISTRATION:
Props: Delfont Mackintosh Theatres Ltd
General Manager: Peter Austin
Chief Electrician: Gavin McGrath
Master Carpenter: Simon gant
Seats: 1,618. 4 Bars.
TECHNICAL:
Stage: Proscenium Stage Flat 0.25' hardboard surface
on timber floor. Pros. Opening 13.38m; Ht. of Pros.
9.27m; Depth of S/Line 9.75m; Depth of Apron 2.70m;
Ht. of Grid 19.84m; 47 lines C/W single purchase;
Maximum height for Flown Scenery 10.57m; Flying Bars
14.90m average; Distance from Centre of Stage to O.P.
wall 10.62m; Centre of Stage to P.S. wall 11.53m; Ht. of
fly floors 10.87m; Width between Fly floors 19m; Prompt
Cnr. P.S.
Lighting: Switchboard: Control and. Spots. As required.
Sound: Please contact venue.
Other: Dressing Rooms 30, accom. 95; 4 Showers.
Orchestra Pit 25.
Membership: SOLT

## PRINCE OF WALES THEATRE
31 Coventry Street London W1V 8AS
Mgt 0171 930 1867 BO 0171 839 5972/5987

SD 0171 930 1432 BO Fax 0171 930 5108
Mgt Fax 0171 839 3419
ADMINISTRATION:
Props: Delfont Mackintosh Theatres Ltd.
Lessees: Prince of Wales Theatre Ltd.
General Manager: Michael M. Churchill
Chief Engineer: Nick Eglin
Policy: Musical and Plays.
Perfs: Currently Eves. Mon-Sat 8.00pm., Wed and Sat
3.00pm.
Seats: Depends on production - up to maximum of
1,133 otherwise. Stalls Bar (1), Circle Bar, Confectionery
Kiosk. Facilities for hard of hearing.
TECHNICAL:
Stage: Performing area 12.8m x 8.23m (42'1" x 27');
Proscenium opening 12.8m x 6.55m (42'1" x 21'). Stage
has no rake and is constructed of oil tempered
hardboard over wood. Suitable for dance (not barefoot).
No lino available. Stage heated by hot water pipes in
wings and on back wall, assisted by heat exchanger unit
above stage which incorporates air cooling when
required. Grid height 14.78m (48') 33 counter weight
sets, double purchase, 0.2m apart, 300kg permitted on
bars. No tab track. Maximum flying height 14.4m (45'7").
Back wall sometimes used as cyclorama. House tabs -
dark red - flown. Steel safety curtain with drencher.
Descent time 24 secs. Orchestra pit 12.9m x 4.8m
(42'4" x 15'9"). Heated by water pipe. 10 x 10 amp
independent circuits. Seat 20. Stage get-in via dock
door Whitcombe Court 2.59m x 2.74m (8'2" x 8'8")
Tallescope available.
Lighting: Board: Strand Galaxy 3. 378 dimmers -
operated from biograph room over rear circle. STM &
PERMUS 500 amp 3 phase, FOH Lighting Bridge with
followspot position.
Sound: Please contact venue.
Other: Stage management. Prompt corner stage left.
12 light outstations. Show relay/calls to dressing rooms,
calls to F.O.H.
3 followspot positions operated from biograph room.
Backstage: 17 dressing rooms on 5 floors, access via
stage door in Whitcombe Street. 200 amp stage main
available understage. Quick change either side of stage.
Wardrobe on 4th floor with 10 power points. Washing
and drying equipment not supplied.
Rehearsal piano available in front stalls and in stalls bar.
Stalls bar floor suitable for dance.
No auditorium sound equipment available.
"The plan for this venue can be found in the
Official London Seating Plan Guide"

## PURCELL ROOM
The South Bank Centre Belvedere Road
London SE1 8XX
Mgt 0171 921 0600 BO 0171 960 4242
SD 0171 921 0633 Fax 0171 928 0063
ADMINISTRATION:
Props: South Bank Board
Non-Executive Chairman: Elliott Bernerd
Director of Performing Arts: Jodi Myers
Music Management: Vanessa Casey,.0171 921 0952
Non-Music Management: Claire Furey on 0171 921
0936
Head of Halls Programming: Elspeth McBain 0171 921
0843
Head of Dance: Alistair Spalding 0171 921 0833
Head of Audience Development (non-classical music):
David Sefton 0171 921 0634
Conferences & Corporate Entertaining Administrator:
Lisa Bradshaw: 0171 921 0680

Catering Services Manager: Mervyn Shilliday
0171 921 0623
Policy: The space is used for classical concerts, jazz,
world, folk, mime/theatre, dance, talks, conferences,etc.
It is flexible and multi-purpose. When the extended
stage is in, the seating capacity reduces to 300.
Seats: 368. Shares common Buffet/Bar in Foyer with
Queen Elizabeth Hall (Catering Dept. 0171 921 0806).
"The plan for this venue can be found in the
Official London Seating Plan Guide"

## QUEEN ELIZABETH HALL

The South Bank Centre Belvedere Road
London SE1 8XX
Mgt 0171 921 0600 BO 0171 960 4242
SD 0171 921 0796/0633 Fax 0171 928 0063
ADMINISTRATION:
Props: South Bank Board.
Non-Executive Chairman: Elliott Bernerd
Director of Performing Arts: Jodi Myers
Music Management: Vanessa Casey 0171 921 0952
Non-Music Management: Claire Furey 0171 921 0936
Head of Halls Programming: Elspeth McBain
0171 921 0843
Head of Dance: Alistair Spalding 0171 921 0833
Head of Audience Development (non-classical music):
David Sefton 0171 921 0634
Conferences & Corporate Entertaining Administrator:
Lisa Bradshaw: 0171 921 0680
Catering Services Manager: Mervyn Shilliday 0171 921
0623
Policy: Concert Hall used for Chamber Concerts,
Recitals, Films, Exhibitions and performances of Opera,
Dance and Readings.  Large Foyer available as
exhibition area.
Seating/Capacity: 902 (Platform seats by arrangement)
Buffet/Bar in Foyer (Catering Department 0171-921
0806).
TECHNICAL:
Open Stage with Thrust Extension.
Switchboard: Galaxy III, rear of auditorium; 240-ways;
F.O.H. Spots; 24 Harmony Profiles (IK); 36 harmony
fresnels (IK); 2 HMV 2500 Zoom, 2 Nielhammer Follow
Spots.  Plus full stock of lighting equipment.
Sound Equipment: Soundcraft Delta with Court Acoustic
Amp and speakers permanently installed.
Dressing Rooms: 8, accom 98; 5 showers; Orchestra Pit
by arrangement.  Laundry facilities.
Part of the South Bank complex, incorporating the Royal
Festival Hall, The Queen Elizabeth Hall, The Purcell
Room and the Hayward Gallery.
"The plan for this venue can be found in the
Official London Seating Plan Guide"

## QUEEN MARY & WESTFIELD COLLEGE

Students Union 432 Bancroft Road London E1 4DH
Mgt/BO 0171 975 5390 Fax 0181 981 0802
ADMINISTRATION:
General Manager: Laura Younger
Entertainments Manager: Iain Shields
Capacity: 500

## QUEEN'S THEATRE

Shaftesbury Avenue London W1V 8BA
Mgt 0171 734 0869 BO 0171 494 5040
SD 0171 734 1348
ADMINISTRATION:
Props: Stoll Moss Theatres Ltd, 21 Soho Square,

London W1V 5FD; Tel: 0171 494 5200
and Fax 0171 434 1217.
Policy: Plays, Musicals, Comedy, Concerts, Television.
Chief Executive: Richard Johnston
Theatre Manager: Hugh McLeod
For all bookings and production enquiries contact
Richard Johnston or Nica Burns (Production Directors),
Gareth Johnson (General Manager, Production
Department) or David Kinsey (Concerts and Hirings
Manager).  Facilities may be made available for day time,
late night and weekend use for private and press
receptions, conferences and meetings - Contact: David
Kinsey 0171 494 5200 and Fax 0171 434 1217.
Seats: 990
3 Bars, Entertainment Suites.
TECHNICAL:
Stage: Raked 1:24; Pros. Opening 9.14m; Ht of Pros.
6.79m; Depth of Stage 11.72m; Ht of Grid 15.24m; 32
lines; C/W; Prompt Cnr. O.P..
Lighting: Lighting Board: Strand Gemini II, 144 circuits.
Situated O.P. Box Stalls.
Sound: Please contact venue.
Other: Dressing rooms: 12
Membership: SOLT
"The plan for this venue can be found in the
Official London Seating Plan Guide"

## THE QUESTORS THEATRE

Mattock Lane Ealing London W5 5BQ
Mgt 0181 567 0011 BO 0181 567 5184
ADMINISTRATION:
Props: The Questors Ltd
Administrator: Elaine Orchard
Policy: Amateur Theatre Club with Resident Amateur
Company. Regular visits from Professional Companies.
One Playhouse and one studio in which 23 productions
are produced a year, (apply to theatre for technical
details of studio).
Perfs: 7.45.
Seats: 325/450. Buffet and Members Bar and Theatre
Bar. Access for people with disabilities.
TECHNICAL:
Stage: Adaptable; Proscenium Thrust or Arena Stage,
Flat; Pros. opening 7.32m. - 10.97m; Ht. of Pros.
5.49m; Depth of S/Line 7.01m; Ht. of Grid 7.32m;
W/Widths P.S. 6.10m, O.P. 4.88m; Prompt Cnr. P.S.
Max. Scenery Ht. 5.49m; Flying of small items is
possible on purpose-rigged hemp lines.
Lighting: Switchboard: Arri Impulse, 72 dimmer
cassette; Six Bridges and Two side Galleries provide
positions for adaptable rig.
Sound: Equipment: 2 Tape Decks, channels, F.O.H.
Speakers various outlets on 10 circuits.
Other: Dressing Rooms 2, accom. 30; 2 Bathrooms;
Orchestra Pit depends on stage form.
Membership: LTG of Great Britain.

## RAYMOND REVUEBAR THEATRE

Walkers Court Brewer Street London W1R 4ED
Mgt 0171 734 2369  Fax 0171 734 2369
BO 0171 734 1593
ADMINISTRATION:
Props: Sitor Enterprises PLC
Managing Director: Gerard Simi
General Manager: Marc Lamport
Theatre Administrator: Gary Elphick
Policy: Intimate Revue.
Perfs: 2 nightly, Mon-Sat.
Seats: 218. Bar.

TECHNICAL:
Thrust Stage for cabaret-style presentation.
Switchboard: Rank Strand SP80. Sound Equipment.

## RICHMOND THEATRE
The Little Green Richmond Surrey TW9 1QJ
Mgt/SD 0181 940 0220 BO 0181 940 0088
Fax 0181 948 3601
ADMINISTRATION:
Props: Richmond Theatre Trust.
Theatre Director: Karin Gartzke
Marketing Manager: Lucy Dale
Theatre Manager: Simon Pearce
Box Office Manager: Jane Caldwell
Technical Manager: John Young
Policy: Touring Drama, Opera and Ballet, Concerts and
Pantomime.
Perfs: Evenings at 7.45 pm, Matinees Wed and Sat at
2.30 pm.
Seats: 840 on three levels. Three licensed bars and
entertaining suite.
TECHNICAL:
Stage: Proscenium raked 1:24. Pros opening 8.16m. Ht.
of Pros. 7.0m. Depth of Stage 9.1m. Ht. to Grid 14.0m.
Wings 5.5m. P.S. 3.0m O.P. x over stage level. Flying
system 35 sets single purchase counterweight 350kg
S.W.C., bars 10m long. Get-in street level P.S.
Removable rostra (row A) over orchestra pit 10m x 2m
approx.
Lighting: Control: Eurolight Applause at rear of stalls.
Dimmers 168 x 2.5kw and 12 x 5kw. Lanterns. Full
permanent F.O.H. rig - details on application.
Sound & Communications: Full wiring infrastructure for
sound control on stage or by prior arrangement at rear
of stalls. Details of equipment on application. Full
cuelight system, ring intercom and paging to all usual
areas.
Other: Dressing Rooms 9, accom. 26 on 3 floors; 8
Showers; Green Room; Bandroom; Wardrobe and
Laundry.

## RIVERSIDE STUDIOS
Crisp Road Hammersmith London W6 9RL
Mgt 0181 237 1000 BO 0181 237 1111
Fax 0181 237 1001
ADMINISTRATION:
Hires Co-Ordinator: Jon Fawcett
Artistic Director: William Burdett-Coutts
Chief Technician: Kevin Kiely
Opening Times: 7 days a week.
TECHNICAL:
Studio 1: 75' x 75' x 23'H (Stage area: 30' x 68') seating
500.
Studio 2: 65' x 60' x 23'H (Stage area: 30' x 53') seating
400.
Studio 3: 14.3m x 6.6m. (Stage Area 7m x 3.5m) seating
104.
Cinema (with 16/35mm projection facilities) seating 200.
A multi-resource arts centre also including bar,
restaurant, gallery & rehearsal space.
Ex BBC film Studios available for performance or
commercial hire. Easy get-in access from street.

## ROCK GARDEN
6/7 The Piazza Covent Garden LONDON WC2E 8HA
Tel 0171 836 4052 Fax 0171 379 4793
ADMINISTRATION:
Managing Director: Philip Matthews
Entertainments Director: Sean McDonnell

Capacity: 250

## THE ROCKET THEATRE
University of North London 166-220 Holloway Road
London N7 8DB
Mgt 0171 753 3200 Fax 0171 753 3201
ADMINISTRATION:
Venue Director: James Hann
A large Victorian theatre/multi-purpose venue with an
emphasis on music and dance. It accommodates 350
seated and 1000 standing. It is also suitable for
conferences and educational activities.

## RONNIE SCOTT'S
47 Frith Street London W1V 6HT
Tel 0171 439 0747 Fax 0171 437 5081
Capacity: 250

## ROYAL ALBERT HALL
Kensington Gore London SW7 2AP
Mgt 0171 589 3203 Ticket Shop 0171 589 8212
Catering Office 0171 589 8900 Fax 0171 823 7725
ADMINISTRATION:
Chief Executive: David Elliott
Sales & Marketing Executive: Louise Buchan
Sales & Marketing Manager: Simone Pomerance
Box Office Manager: Sarah Howarth
Policy: Concerts - Pop, Rock, Jazz, Classical, Meetings
and Conferences, Sporting Events, Ballet.
Perfs: Varies according to type of show. Evening
concerts normally 7.30pm.
Seats: 5,092. Buffet Bars on each level. Private rooms
available for Receptions, Dinner Parties, etc.
TECHNICAL:
Show Dept. Manager: Rob Flower
Concert platform and arena. 9 rows raised choir stalls
behind concert platform (1-4 removeable/adjustable).
Dressing Rooms: 6 principal, 5 choir for up to 200 each.
"The plan for this venue can be found in the
Official London Seating Plan Guide"

## ROYAL COURT THEATRE
Sloane Square London SW1W 8AS
Mgt 0171 565 5050 Fax 0171 565 5001
Email: royal-court@cityscape.co.uk
ADMINISTRATION:
Artistic Director: Stephen Daldry
Executive Director: Vikki Heywood
NB: The Sloane Square theatre will re-open summer
1999. However, the Royal Court Theatre is still operating
from the Royal Court Theatre Downstairs (Duke of Yorks)
and Upstairs (Ambassadors).

## ROYAL COURT THEATRE DOWNSTAIRS
## (AT THE DUKE OF YORK THEATRE)
St. Martins Lane London WC2N 4BG
Mgt/SD 0171 565 5050 BO 0171 565 5000
Fax 0171 565 5001
ADMINISTRATION:
Props.: Turnstyle Group Ltd., 25 Shaftesbury Avenue,
London W1V 7HA
Tel 0171 240 9891 Fax 0171 379 5748
Lessees: The Royal Court Theatre
Artistic Director: Stephen Daldry
Executive Director: Vikki Heywood
Production Manager: Edwyn Wilson

Seating Capacity: 600
TECHNICAL:
Stage and Lighting: Please contact venue.
Sound: cadac `B` type 16:8 mixer with 8x8 matrix, 4
pre/post mix; Akai S1000 sampler with Macintosh
computer and Vision sequencing; 2 x Denon minidisc; 1x
CD; 1 x cassette; 1 x reverb; 1 x Meyer CP10 parametric
eq; 6 x d&b 902 spkrs as pros/fx; 1 x Cerwin Vega
sunwoofer with crossover; 6 x JBL Control 1+ delay
spkrs via BSS TCS804; many small fx speakers, a few
mics and stands; 10 channels of amplification, of which
4 x channelsdedicated d&b amps; Sennheiser infra-red
hearing assistance; open mix position rear stalls.
"The plan for this venue can be found in the
Official London Seating Plan Guide"

## ROYAL COURT THEATRE UPSTAIRS (AT THE AMBASSADORS THEATRE)

West Street London WC2H 9ND
Mgt/SD 0171 565 5050 BO 0171 565 5000
Fax 0171 565 5001
ADMINISTRATION:
Props.: Turnstyle Group Ltd., 25 Shaftesbury Avenue,
London W1V 7HA.
Tel  0171 240 9891 Fax  0171 379 5748
Lessees: The Royal Court Theatre
Artistic Director: Stephen Daldry
Executive Director: Vikki Heywood
Production Manager: Edwyn Wilson
Seating Capacity (Circle): 130
Seating Capacity (Stage Space): 60
TECHNICAL:
Stage and Lighting: Please contact venue.
Sound (Circle): Soundcraft 8:6 mixer; 2 x Denon
minidisc; 1 x CD; 1 x cassette; 1 x reverb; 4 x JBL
Control 10 main spkrs; 4 x JBL Control 1+ delay spkrs
via BSS TCS804; 2 x Ramsa A80 fx spkrs; 14 x
channels of Quad amps; deaf loop; open mix position
rear auditorium.
Sound (Stage Space): Soundcraft 8:6 mixer, 2 x Denon
minidisc; 1 x CD; 1 x cassette; 1 x reverb; 4 x main
speakers; 6 x channels of amplification; deaf loop; open
mix position rear seating.

## ROYAL FESTIVAL HALL

The South Bank Centre Belvedere Road London SE1
8XX
Mgt 0171 921 0600 BO 0171 960 4242
Fax 0171 401 8834
ADMINISTRATION:
Props: South Bank Board.
Non-Executive Chairman: Elliott Bernerd
Director of Performing Arts: Jodi Myers
Music Management: Vanessa Casey, 0171 921 0952
Non-Music Management: Claire Furey on 0171 921
0936
Head of Halls Programming: Elspeth McBain 0171 921
0843
Head of Dance: Alistair Spalding 0171 921 0833
Head of Audience Development (non-classical music):
David Sefton 0171 921 0634
Conferences & Corporate Entertaining Administrator:
Lisa Bradshaw: 0171 921 0680
Catering Services Manager: Mervyn Shilliday 0171 921
0623
Policy: Concert Hall, used for Concerts, Recitals, Films,
Exhibitions and occasional performances of Opera and
Ballet for which a fit-up Proscenium is erected.
Seats: 2,895 (2,639 without choir seats).

Exhibition and meeting places include the Thames
Pavillion, Waterloo Bar, Hungerford Bar,Sunley Pavilion,
Chelsfield Room. Record shop and book shop. Foyers
are open for free events, exhibitions, etc., from 10am
every day until 11pm.
Self-Service Cafeteria, Bars and buffets and "Peoples
Palace" Restaurant. Part of the South Bank  Centre
complex, incorporating the Royal Festival Hall, the Queen
Elizabeth Hall, Purcell Room and Hayward Gallery.
TECHNICAL:
Stage: Open Thrust Stage 17.25m x 6.76m. Height of
main stage 0.79m. Height of stage with first riser 0.91m.
No proscenium, no rake, no flying, wood floor,
backstage crossover, stage heated. Minimum height to
ceiling 9.3m/10.06m. Choir seating behind stage if
required.
For dance 'proscenium opening' and Orchestra Pit can
be installed by arrangement.
Access to hall: 50m. Flat run to goods lift direct to stage
level or through front of house doors. Scenery lift (limited
in size) available. Backstage facilities accessible to
disabled performers and staff.
Technical Staff: Two Production Technicians available
8am-10pm for set-up, rehearsal and performance.
Normally a Production Manager is allocated to each
project. Get-in/get-out time is by arrangement with SBC
depending on requirements and on venue availability.
Lighting and Sound Equipment: The RFH has restricted
in-house LX equipment and sound system, film
projection equipment for 35mm. P.A.system and Closed
Circuit TV to foyer, talkback, Callboy, Show relay to
dressing rooms.
Detailed stage plans, technical equipment lists and extra
technical information are available on request.
Dressing Rooms: 20, accom. 250; 19 Showers;
Orchestra Pit 53. Prop. Store, Wardrobe.
"The plan for this venue can be found in the
Official London Seating Plan Guide"

## ROYAL NATIONAL THEATRE

Upper Ground South Bank London SE1 9PX
Mgt/Admin 0171 452 3333 SD 0171 452 3333
BO 0171 452 3000 Information 0171 452 3400
Fax 0171 452 3344
ADMINISTRATION:
Director of the National: Trevor Nunn
Company Secretary & Head of Finance:
Lew Hodges
General Manager: Maggie Whitlum
Head of Touring: Roger Chapman
Associate Directors: Michael Bryant, Howard Davies,
Declan Donnellan, Peter Gill, David Hare, Nicholas
Hytner, Sir Ian McKellen, Deborah Warner, Nicholas
Wright.
Associate Designers: Bob Crowley, William Dudley, John
Gunter.

OLIVIER THEATRE
Stage: The stage is open, without a proscenium arch or
safety curtain, facing a fan shaped auditorium spanning
120 degrees. In the centre of the stage is the Drum
Revolve, diameter 11.5m. The stage is generally 850mm
above the level of the seats. There is the possibility of
two actor entrances from under the side intermediate
tiers. The main stage is separated from the rear stage by
three sound reducing fire shutters. Height to grid is
27.1m, under lighting galleries 12.9m.
Machinery: Stage surface of masonite on gurjun strip on
laminboard. 11.5m diameter drum revolve is split in two
semi-circular discs, one of which can be lowered 8.5m

into the service areas below and replaced by a third disc complete with a second setting. The flying equipment consists of 127 scenery hoists providing double purchase single scenery hooks that move below tracks across stage beneath the grid and 20 point hoists which can be positioned anywhere between the tracks. All can be synchronised electrically by the computer controlled cycloconverter drive system. The control panel is situated on the front fly gallery stage left. Hoists can be grouped into groups of no more than 16 at a time and all infinitely controllable at speeds up to 1.8m per second within a repeat accuracy of 6mm.

Lighting: 5 auditorium bridges and 4 hanging "chandeliers" used for both auditorium and stage lighting. Front and rear circle lighting positions. 3 lighting slots, 1 lighting bridge and 3 booms on side walls. Follow-spot positions rear of upper tier and side wall lighting bridges. Projection rear of upper tier and auditorium bridge. Over stage one row of six powered lighting bars (rigged with remote focusable lights) with independent height settings. Over stage bridge spanning fly tower rigged with 138 assorted profile, fresnel and cyc floods. Fly gallery at rear of stage with an additional 106 lighting units. 768 dimmers in total of which 666 combine 2.5kw and 5kw circuits and 75 Non-Dims.

Lighting Control:"Galaxy" at rear of lower tier. Galaxy Nova consisting of 2 channel controllers, 2 theatre playbacks, 6 group masters, 10 preset masters, programmable effects and motion panel controlling 9 PALS and 114, 16 colour scrollers. Also a remote Nova is available in the stalls or circle for technical rehearsals.

Sound: Cadac computer assisted control desk with 36 inputs and 26 outputs, situated at the rear of the stalls. 13 auditorium and 8 paralleled on stage speaker circuits comprising E.V.; S200/S100/S80/1152/GTS 215R auditorium and stage speaker system and E.V. horn and sub bass pros system. Multiple tie lines to stage and auditorium via bantam jack field.

6; broadcast cart machines. 2; 18 megabyte S1000 samplers. 3; effects processors. 1; 4 track tape machine. 8 channels of Micron radio receivers and transmitters.

Other: Stage Management: 25 way, fully patchable into 64 out-station cue light desk. 3 independent comms rings, one with interface to radio communications system.

## LYTTELTON THEATRE

Stage: The proscenium arch framing the scenic stage is adjustable in width from 10.4m to 13.6m. in height from 5m to 9m, in plan up to 1.6m from safety curtain. Variable height stage riser generally set 1.05m above auditorium floor level. Two part safety curtain: one third rising from below to form stage riser. Stage depth 16m from safety curtain to full width sound reducing door between main stage and rear stage. Stage width 11m SR to wall and 11m SL to full width sound reducing door dividing main stage from side stage. Height to grid 23.5m, under fly floors 7.6m.

Machinery: Stage surface of masonite on gurjun strip on laminboard. Main stage elevator 13.6m wide by 12m deep with 1.6m satellite extension variable in rake from flat to 1 in 8. Three front elevators in line across stage total width 13.6m and 1.6m deep capable of being set at orchestra pit, auditorium and stage levels as well as raking in conjunction with main stage elevator. Rear stage wagon 13.6m by 12m incorporates disc revolve 11.5m diameter. This wagon can be set on the main elevator at rakes of up to 1 in 16. Flying equipment consists of 75 single purchase counterweights, except

for proscenium zone at 150mm centres and 6 bars up and downstage for masking. House tabs on a motorised counterweight set.

Lighting: 4 Auditorium bridges+2 back boxes using Cadenza 12/22 Lanterns. 2 x sidewall auditorium slots using Cantata Lanterns. 2 x colour arc 2000 followspots at rear of circle. Onstage adjustable prosc lighting bridge + towers, using Cantata PC's + 18/32 profiles. 5 stage lighting bars using Cantata 18/32 + 26/44, Cadenza PC's, 2kw fresnels + alto 2.5kw fresnels, par 64/5 + rainbow scrollers. 5 ladders aside which are adjustable up and down stage. All above incorporated into the basic focus rig.

Lighting control: Galaxy II at rear of stalls with remote stalls wing controlling 498 circuits wiht 2.5kw + 5kw dimmers.

Sound: Cadac computer assisted control desk with 32 inputs and 36 outputs, situated in a control box at the rear of the stalls.

11 auditorium and 12 paralleled onstage speakers circuits comprising E.V 1152 on stage and pros / E.V S80 surround system. Bose 101 under circle delay line. Multiple tie lines to stage and auditorium via bantam jack field. 3; BSS Varicurve EQ and 3 BSS delay processors. 4; broadcast cart machines. 1; 32 megabyte S1000 sampler. 6 channels of Sennheiser 1036 radio transmitters and receivers. 3; effects processors.

Other: Stage management: Identical to that fitted to the Olivier.

## COTTESLOE THEATRE

Stage: Space holds between 200 and 400 depending on layout. The audience is accommodated on three interconnected levels on three sides of central space which is available to either audience or performer. The whole space can be laid out in a number of different ways including scenic end stage, theatre in the round; thrust end stage and, by raising the auditorium in the central space to stage height a flat floor over the whole space. For promenade area accommodating 247 standing, retractable bleacher seating for 176 at pit level. The whole space is 21m long by 19m wide. The five lighting and access bridges and interconnecting walkways are 7.3m above stage level. The central area between the encircling galleries 9.9m wide and 13.2m long. In scenic end stage form the stage area is 9m deep x 9.9m wide, the stage riser 1m.

Lighting and Sound: Lighting positions on central bridges, on tier fronts and over the end stage areas, where minimal scenic suspension on hemp and winch lines are provided. Lighting control by a memory system, Gemini with 180 dimmers. Sound control desk/SM control and lighting control at rear auditorium 1st level. General Communications: Paging to artistes and staff backstage from stage door, main rehearsal rooms and theatres, incorporating performance priority. Paging from theatres to associated foyers, and paging from foyers to all public areas. Show relay sound and vision to backstage areas and to foyers for latecomers (not Cottesloe). PABS telephone and radio bleep staff location system.

Sound: D.D.A. control desk with 18 inputs and 16 outputs situated in control box at rear of auditorium. 10 onstage and 6 auditorium speaker circuits comprising E.V. S200/S80 and sub bass. Multiple tie lines to stage and auditorium via G.P.O. jack field. 4; broadcast cart machines. 1; 32 megabyte S1000 sampler. 6 channel of Trantec Radio transmitters and receivers. 3; effects processors.

Other: Stage Management: 20 way, fully patchable into 20 out-station cue light desk. Tec-pro comms with

interface to radio communications system.
"The plan for this venue can be found in the Official London Seating Plan Guide"

## ROYAL OPERA HOUSE

Floral Street Covent Garden London WC2E 9DD
Tel 0171 212 9123
Props: Royal Opera House, Covent Garden, Ltd
Closed for redevelopment until late 1999, meanwhile
The Royal Opera & The Royal Ballet will perform in other venues in London, regionally and abroad. For information please phone the above number.

## ROYALTY THEATRE

Renamed The Peacock Theatre See Correct Entry

## SADLER'S WELLS

Rosebery Avenue, Islington, London, EC1R 4TN
BO 0171 863 8000
Capacity: 1,550

## SAVOY THEATRE

Savoy Court The Strand London WC2R 0ET
Mgt 0171 836 8117 BO 0171 836 8888
SD 0171 836 8117 Fax 0171 379 7322
ADMINISTRATION:
Props & Licensee: Savoy Theatre Ltd
General Manager: Thomas Bohdanetzky
Tel 0171 828 0600
Theatre Manager: Kevin Chapple
Seating Capacity: 1,158 (Play), 1,130 (using small orchestra pit), 1,090 (using large orchestra pit)
Membership: SOLT, TMA
TECHNICAL:
Stage: Area: Proscenium opening 9.0m wide x 7.5m high. Depth of stage from back of proscenium ot back wall 9.3m. Depth of rear stage from back wall of stage 5.0m (approx.,). Width of rear stage 7.3m.
Depth of apron from back of proscenium to stage edge 1.2m. Width of apron 8.4m. Width of stage side wall to side wall 18.6m at centre stage. Centre line to stage left wall 9.3m. Centre line to stage right wall 9.3m. Wing space stage left 3.0m (approx) x 9.4m deep. Wing space stage right 2.5m (approx) x 9.4m deep. Height to underside of grid 15.8m. Clearance under fly floors 7.0m. Width of orchestra pit 10.0m. Depth of small orchestra pit 4.0m (25-30 musicians approx.). Depth of large orchestra pit 6.2m (50 musicians approx.). Access to pit from under stage area left and right. Stage floor - Hardboard on plywood on bearers on demountable steel framework. Equipment and scenery access via door in stage right wall at fly floor level. Electric hoist on jib lifts equipment from Carting Lane through trap in fly floor to stage level. Stage access - up left and up right. Pass door - downstage left.
Rigging: 42 No. 450kg single purchase counterweight sets. 40 cross stage sets, 2 up/downstage sets. Typical pipe length - 10.0m; 4 lines. 3 No. 250kg hand winches and pipes in rear dock. 2 No. FOH trusses suspended from electric chain hoists provide support for lighting and sound rigs. Truss capacity - 1000kg.
Drapes: House curtain and border. Black and coloured borders, legs and travellers. Side masking by legs on tracks under fly floors.
Lighting: Strand Galaxy 4 lighting control with tracking back up and printer located in control room at rear of Dress Circle. Designers location at stalls level has colour monitors and ability to connect designers remote. Riggers remote and data lines located throughout stage and auditorium. House lights are controlled from lighting control room or S.M. position stage left. Orchestra pit lights from S.M. position. Dimmers - 244 Strand EC90MD. 214 No. 2.4kW, 30 No. 5.0kW, Spot and Cyc bars - 4. Luminaires - 20 No. Cantata 11/26 1,200 watt, 16 No. Cantat 18/32 1,200 watt, 16 No. Cantata 26/44 1,200 watt, 10 No. Prelude 600 watt, 40 No. Cantata Fresnels 1,200 watt, 10 No. Cadenza Fresnels 2,000 watt, 36 No. Parcans, 4 No. Iris 4 cyc units 1,000 watt, 4 No. Iris 1 cyc units 1,000 watt, 12 No. Nocturne floods 500 watt, 2 No. Solo follow spots.
Sound and Communications: Substantial wiring infrastructure and sound box distribution system. Permanent system of installed BOSE 102 delay loudspeakers set into stalls ceiling. Electro-voice S40 loudspeakers set into auditorium walls at all levels for effects. Portable loudspeakers - 4 No. Electro-Voice 5200, 4 No. Galaxy-Hotspots. Systems complete with associated power amps, graphic equalisers, etc. Small 'in-house' 4-1 sound mixer provided for shows not requiring more sophistication. Larger shows requiring 'in-house' mixing position may use location centre of dress circle level. Outboard equipment includes - DAT, CD, cassette and tape machines. Building wide communications provide paging and show relay signals. Show relay camera on circle front relays video signal to monitors FOH and backstage. SM desk may be located stage left or right. Cue lights and technical intercom connection points location at all key areas. Hard of hearing facilities provided at all levels.
Contact: Julian Courtenay, Savoy Theatre Limited, 1 Savoy Hill, London WC2R 0BP. Tel 0171 836 8117. Fax 0171 379 9403.
Other: Accommodation: Orchestra room and crew room under stage.
Dressing Rooms: 18. Total capacity 60.
"The plan for this venue can be found in the Official London Seating Plan Guide"

## SECOMBE THEATRE

Cheam Road Sutton Surrey SM1 2ST
Mgt/Admin 0181 770 6998 BO 0181 770 6990
ADMINISTRATION:
Props: London Borough of Sutton
Theatre Manager: Shirley Carpenter
(Tel 0181 770 6986)
Press & Publicity: Michael Coventry
Policy: Mixed programme, professional one nighters, drama, tours, variety, dance, cinema, children's shows, pantomime, annual talent show, amateur theatre, lettings.
Seats: 347 (Max. 400). Foyer Bar, Foyer Buffet. Second performance space/letting room available.
TECHNICAL:
Stage: Proscenium stage, flat: Pros. opening 8.50m; Ht. of Pros. 4.57m; Depth of Stage 9.00m; Wing Space 3.00m S.L., 5.00m S.R.; Ht. of Grid 9.00m; 18 hemp sets; House tabs on C/W ; Prompt desk S.L.
Lighting: Control, strand MX 48 plus MX12, 2.5kw/channel; circuits: 42 on stage, 18 F.O.H. and 15 independents; 1 F.O.H. spotbar, 4 F.O.H. vertical booms, 4 overstage spotbars on winches. Lanterns: 16 Silhouette 30, 10 Starlette Fresnel, 3 Starlette PC, 18 Minuette Fresnel, 8 Minuette PC, 24 x 1k Par, 15 Minuette Flood, Le Maitre pyroflash system (2 pods), 2x2K FOH follow spots.
Sound Equipment: Soundcraft series 400B 16/4/2, 400 watts per channel stereo amp into 6 fixed position

F.O.H. speakers (Bose system). 100 watts per channel stereo amp into 2 mobile effects speakers. Revox B77, tape-to-tape Teac cassette 4 radio mics (Trantec), Various Shure and AKG mics and stands.
Other: Communications: Promps desk PS; 9 cue lights; ring intercom, show relay. Dressing Rooms 3, accom. 10 each; 2 Showers; Orchestra Pit 15. Second performance: 11m wide x 11.8m length, small stage at one end; seats 120 max; no stage lighting installation. Can be used for performance or functions, own bar.

## SHAFTESBURY THEATRE
Shaftesbury Avenue London WC2H 8DP
Mgt/SD 0171 379 3345 BO 0171 379 5399
Fax 0171 836 0466
ADMINISTRATION:
Props: The Theatre of Comedy Company
Chief Executive: Andrew Leigh
Theatre Manager: Christopher Flatman
House Manager: Marc Evans
Duty Manager: Frazer Hoyle
Technical Manager: Ben Arkell
Chief Electrician: Peter Goodman
Seating: 1,405
TECHNICAL:
Stage: Proscenium Stage, Flat; Pros. opening 9.75m; Ht. of Pros. 5.99m; Ht. of Grid. 15.69m; Flying height: 15.42m; Depth of S/Line; S.R. 8.83m, S.L. 9.44m Lines; 33 C/W; W/Widths P.S. 5.79m, O.P. 5.48m; Centre area of stage removeable as 4' x 4' modules. Orchestra pit. Prompt Cnr. Stage Left (or Stage Right by arrangement): show relay/calls system, 8 way cuelights, video show relay to prompt corner only.
Lighting: Switchboard at rear Circle, Arri 1250, 2 x connexion output modules + 192 dimmers as 150 x STM 10A, 32 x Permus 10A, 10 x STM 20A.

Sound: Please contact venue.
Other: Seats removeable at rear of Grand Circle to accommodate up to four followspots.
Dressing Rooms accommodating up to 40; Showers 6.
Membership: SOLT
"The plan for this venue can be found in the Official London Seating Plan Guide"

## SHAKESPEARE'S GLOBE
New Globe Walk Bankside Southwark London SE1 9DT
Admin/SD 0171 902 1400 BO 0171 401 9919
ADMINISTRATION:
Artistic Director: Mark Rylance
General Manager: Maralyn Sarrington
Production Manager: Richard Howey
Seats: 1,401, including. 500 standing (Groundlings) in uncovered yard.
TECHNICAL:
Height: 33 ft to the eaves, diameter: 100 ft, circumference: 300 ft.
Stage height: 5ft, length: 44ft, breadth: 25ft.
Theatre season: May-September, the remainder of the year used as an educational resource by Globe Education Department.
"The plan for this venue can be found in the Official London Seating Plan Guide"

## SHEPHERD'S BUSH EMPIRE
Shepherds Bush Green London W12 8TT
Mgt 0181 354 3300 Mgt Fax 0181 743 3218
BO (Tickets sales) 0171 771 2000 BO Fax (Ticket sales) 0171 738 4427 BO (Enquiries only) 0181 743 8081
BO Fax (Enquiries only) 0181 743 5384
Theatre Manager: Bill Marshall

Capacity: 2,000

## SOUTHBANK STUDENTS UNION
Keyworth Street London SE1 6NG
Mgt/BO 0171 815 6060 Fax 0171 815 6061
Contacts: Bill Hanlon
Capacity: 1,200 (approx)

## ST. GEORGES THEATRE
Tufnell Park Road Islington London N7
Mgt 0171 607 7978
ADMINISTRATION:
Artistic & Managing Director: George Murcell
Theatre Coordinator: Suzie Hardie
Policy: Traditional Elizabethan Shakespeare Productions
and Educational Programme.
Ring Box Office for details of performances.
Seats: 600. Licensed Bar. Buffet Snack Bar. Book &
Confectionery Shop.
TECHNICAL:
Stage: Open Thrust Stage, 0.86m high, projecting
10.49m into auditorium. Stage lozenge-shaped, 16.11m
wide and 13.53m deep. The circular auditorium is
25.84m in diameter, and 8 terracotta-tiled columns at
7.60m centres on a circle of 18.24m diameter support
gothic arches and an octagonal clerestorey.
Lighting: Rank Strand SP80, 3 pre-set board with 60 x
2kw channels and 20 x 5kw channels.
Sound Equipment: Teac 6 into 4 mixer fed from tape
machines, in turn fed to Quad control units, 7-way
loudspeaker control panel with outlets positioned around
the auditorium.

## ST. JOHN'S
Smith Square Westminster London SW1P 3HA
Mgt 0171 222 2168 Box Office and Information Centre
0171 222 1061 Fax 0171 233 1618
ADMINISTRATION:
Props: St.John's, Smith Square Charitable Trust
Registered Charity No: 1045390
Registered in England Co.No: 3028678
General Manager: Paul Davies.
Policy: Concert Hall available for hire for concerts,
choral & orchestral recitals, chamber opera, etc.
Perfs: Normally 1.00 or 7.30; all performances end
before 10.00.
Seats: 780 max. Art exhibitions in The Footstool
restaurant gallery. Open for lunch on weekdays and at
all concerts. Fully licensed. Special functions also
catered for.
TECHNICAL:
Unusually-adaptable stage incorporating 6 variable
orchestra/choral risers. Max. no of performers 100, but
also suitable for recitals. Stage-lighting 24 x 1kw
operated by 12-channel fader.
Dressing Rooms: 4 plus changing area.
In addition to public concerts, St. John's is used for
recording and by the BBC and major record companies
on account of its exceptional acoustics.

## ST. MARTIN IN THE FIELDS
6 St. Martins Place Trafalgar Square London WC2N 4JJ
Tel BO & CC Line 0171 839 8362 Mgt 0171 930 0089
Fax 0171 839 5163
ADMINISTRATION:
Concert Manager: Shirley Allcott
Policy: Primarily Baroque music
Capacity: 825

## ST. MARTIN'S THEATRE
West Street London WC2H 9NG
SD 0171 836 1086 BO 0171 836 1443
Fax 0171 379 8699
ADMINISTRATION:
Mousetrap Productions Limited.
General Manager: Thomas Bohdanetzky
Tel: 0171 828 0600
Policy: West End Runs of Plays.
Perfs: 8.00; Tues. 2.45; Sat. 5.00.
Seats: 550. Bars. Air conditioning.
TECHNICAL:
Stage: Proscenium Stage, practically flat; Pros. Opening
7.92m; Ht. of Pros. 7.77m; Depth of S/Line 7.01m P.S.,
7.62m O.P.; Ht. of Grid 15.24m US, 18.29m DS, 28
lines, 23 C/W, 5 Hemp; Scenery Flying Ht. 7.32m; Flying
Bars 10.97m; W/Widths P.S. 4.57m. O.P. 2.44m;
Prompt Cnr. O.P.
Lighting: Switchboard: Strand Electric Compact 80
ways; F.O.H. Spots 26 10 1000w, 16 500w; 4 Battens;
Floats; Dips 11 each side; 4 Spot Bars.
Sound Equipment: Cue Call.
Other: Dressing Rooms 10, accom. 25; Orchestra Pit 8.
Membership: SOLT
"The plan for this venue can be found in the
Official London Seating Plan Guide"

## STANLEY HALLS
12 South Norwood Hill London SE25 6AB
Mgt 0181 653 3630 Fax 0181 771 8788
ADMINISTRATION:
Props: London Borough of Croydon
Manager: Zoe Harris
Policy: Available on Hire
Perfs: As required.
Seats: 320. Bar.
TECHNICAL:
Stage: Proscenium stage, Flat; Pros. opening 6.71m; Ht.
of Pros. 4.57m; Depth of S/Line 6.10m; Scenery Flying
Ht. 6.10m; 6/7 lines, Hemp; W.Widths P.S. 2.44m, O.P.
2.44m; Prompts Cnr. O.P.
Lighting: Switchboard: Strand Master, 24 ways; F.O.H.
Spots 4 Patt. 253; 1 Batten; 1 Float; Dips 2 each side; 2
Spot Bars. Cyc Float and Ground Row.
Sound Equipment: Speakers House P.A. + Amp. Twin
tape deck & microphones available for hire.
Other: Dressing Rooms 3, accom. 36. Orchestra Pit 10.
Available with other room attached as excellent
rehearsal or audition rooms.
Membership: TMA

## STEINER THEATRE
35 Park Road London NW1 6XT
Tel 0171 723 4400 Fax 0171 724 4364
ADMINISTRATION:
Props: Anthroposophical Association Ltd.
Manager: Terry Goodfellow
Policy: Small scale performances of music, theatre and
dance both professional and amateur.
Perfs: usually 7.30pm.
Seats: 250, slightly raked seating.
Light Catering. Suitable for small conferences, AGM's
etc.
TECHNICAL:
Stage: Slightly raked stage. 11 x 8m. Proscenium arch.
Small forestage. Intercom between lighting control,
prompt corner and dressing rooms.
Lighting: Jands ESP 48 channel lighting console. 8 x
CEE22 Powermaster dimmer units, together with 4 x 36

# The Steiner Theatre
## 35 Park Road, London NW1 6XT

250 seat theatre, raked seating and proscenium arch available for hire and new productions.
Five minutes from Baker Street tube and close to Regents Park.

## For further details ring 0171-723 4400

way cord patch panels fitted with 130 patching leads.
Lamps: 36 Fresnels, 8 Lee Colortran Profiles, 6 763's.
Sound: None.
Other: Dressing Rooms 3, with toilet facilities, accom. 30.

### STRAND THEATRE
Aldwych London WC2B 4LD
Mgt 0171 836 9817 BO 0171 930 8800
SD 0171 836 4144 Fax 0171 836 4992
ADMINISTRATION:
Props: Strand Theatre Ltd. - part of the Louis I Michaels Group.
Chairman: Arnold Crook
General Manager: Nigel Everett
Policy: Theatrical productions of all types.
Perfs: No set times.
Seats: 1,069. Bars on each floor.
TECHNICAL:
Stage: Proscenium Stage, slight rake. Pros opening 9.60m(w) x 6.40m(h). Depth of slight line 9.75m. Ht. of Grid 17.37m. 31 lines ets. Scenery flying ht. 9.14m. Flying bars 12.19m D/S, 11.58m U/S. Working widths S/L 3.05m D/S 0.91m U/S; S/R 3.66m D/S with dock 5.49m x 4.27m. Prompt corner S/R. Orchestra Pit: 18-20.
Lighting: Electrics: Gemini lighting board, disk backup, Permus dimmers, 144 ways. Lantern Stock: 8 Sil 30 (1kw axial), 2 Prelude 16/30, 12 Patt. 23, 20 Patt. 743, 12 Patt. 53, 6 Patt. 49, 12 Furse 500w floods. Cue light system. Generator capable of running entire installation.
Other: Dressing Rooms: 16, accom. 44; 2 Showers.
Membership: SOLT
"The plan for this venue can be found in the Official London Seating Plan Guide"

### STUDIO 14
Malet Street London WC1E 6ED
Tel 0171 636 7076 Fax 0171 323 3865
Props: Royal Academy of Dramatic Art
Administration:
Principal: Nicholas Barter
Under Construction.

### SUBTERANIA
12 Acklam Road Ladbroke Grove London W10 5QZ
Mgt/BO 0181 960 4590 Fax 0181 969 6976
ADMINISTRATION:
Manager: Mark Fairclough
Promoters: Sue Humphrey and John O'Sullivan
Tel 0181 961 5490

Fax 0171 961 9238
Capacity: 600

### THE TABERNACLE
Powis Square London W11 2AY
Tel 0171 565 7890 Fax 0171 565 7810
Contact for enquiries: Matthew Philip

### THE HIPPODROME
North End Road, London NW11 7RP
Tel 0171 765 4010
Seats: 520 circle; 180 stage.

### THEATRE ROYAL, STRATFORD EAST
Gerry Raffles Square London E15 1BN
Mgt 0181 534 7374 BO 0181 534 0310
Press Office 0181 534 2178 Fax 0181 534 8381
ADMINISTRATION:
General Manager: Nick Jones
Artistic Director: Philip Hedley
Associate Director: Kerry Michael
Production Manager: Bob Irwin
Policy: The bulk of the year is taken up with own productions of new plays with the occasional classic. No permanent company and a minimum technical and administrative staff. Play choice ranges from family shows like pantomimes, musicals, melodramas and farces through to controversial modern work, particularly with appeal to young audiences.
On Sundays, once a month, run our own Variety Shows or have in guest bands, dance companies or fringe groups.
Seats: 464
TECHNICAL:
Lighting: Equipment: Board; Arri Impulse 2.
Dimmers: 112 x 2K, 12 x 5K. Lanterns: 150 various.
Follows spots: 2 x 1K CSI.
Sound: Equipment: Board; Hill Audio 4400 (24-8-2). Good FOH amplification and speakers and FX. 2 Revox and CDE. Misc. mics and stage speakers.
Musical Equipment: 1 piano.
Other: Limited hemp flying, stock masking including 20' x 20' soft black box, stage braces and weights. Limited video equipment. Two Licensed Bars
Dressing Rooms 5, accom. 20; Showers. Orchestra Pit 6.
Membership: TMA.
Seating Capacity: 446

## THEATRE ROYAL, DRURY LANE
Catherine Street London WC2B 5JF
Mgt 0171 240 0115 BO 0171 494 5550
SD 0171 836 3352 Fax 0171 379 6836
ADMINISTRATION:
Props: Stoll Moss Theatres Ltd, 21 Soho Square,
London W1V 5FD; Tel: 0171 494 5200
and Fax 0171 434 1217.
Policy: Musicals, Comedy, Concerts, TV.
Chief Executive: Richard Johnston
Theatre Manager: Rupert Bielby
For all bookings and production enquiries contact
Richard Johnston or Nica Burns (Production Directors),
Gareth Johnson (General Manager, Production
Department), or David Kinsey (Concerts & Hirings
Manager).  Facilities may be made available for day time,
late night and weekend use for private and press
receptions, conferences and meetings - Contact David
Kinsey 0171 494 5200 and Fax 0171 434 1217.
Seats: 2,196
6 Bars, Restaurant, Entertainment Suites, Theatre Tours.
TECHNICAL:
Stage: Raked 1:24; Pros. Opening 12.95m; Ht of Pros.
7.92m; Depth of Stage 24.69m; Ht of Grid 21.34m; 120
lines,  C/W; Prompt Cnr. P.S.
Lighting: Lighting Board: Strand Galaxy II, 360 circuits.
Situated Rear of Grand Circle.
Other: Dressing rooms: 22
Membership: SOLT
"The plan for this venue can be found in the
Official London Seating Plan Guide"

## THEATRE ROYAL, HAYMARKET
Haymarket London SW1Y 4HT
Mgt 0171 930 8890 BO 0171 930 8800
SD 0171 930 538 Fax 0171 321 0139
ADMINISTRATION:
Props: Crown Estates
Lessees: Theatre Royal Haymarket Ltd,
Chairman: Arnold M. Crook
General Manager: Nigel Everett
Theatre Manager: Mark Stradling
Master Carpenter: Andy Chelton
Chief Electrician: Steve MacGuire
Box Office Manager: Philip Green
Policy: Plays.
Seats: 880. Bars.
TECHNICAL:
Stage: Proscenium Stage, Raked 1 in 20; Pros. Opening
8.23m; Ht. of Pros. 7.62m; Depth of S/Line 8.69m to
12.60m; Ht. of Grid 15.85m; 23 lines, 15 C/W; Scenery
Flying Ht. 7.62m; Flying Bars 11.28m; W/Widths P.S.
2.05m O.P. 4.27m; Prompt Cnr. P.S.
Lighting: Switchboard: Gemini 120 way, P.S. Perch;
F.O.H. Spots 26 Patt. T645, 2 Patt. 23N 500w; 3
Battens; Dips 10 each side, 22 Flys; 1 Spot Bar 16 Patt.
23, 4 Patt. 123.
Sound: Please contact venue.
Other: Dressing Rooms 10, accom. 30-35; 1 Shower;
Orchestra Pit 10 plus extension.
Membership: SOLT
"The plan for this venue can be found in the
Official London Seating Plan Guide"

## TOWER THEATRE
Canonbury Place London N1 2NQ
Mgt 0171 226 5111
BO (afternoons and evenings) 0171 226 3633
ADMINISTRATION:

Props: Tavistock Repertory Co. (London)
Lessees/Licensee: Tavistock Repertory Guarantors Ltd.
Administrator: Abby-Lee Knight
Policy: Amateur Company presenting Repertory of 18
Plays a year; Theatre available for lettings when not in
use by Tavistock Repertory Company. Public Theatre
Licence. Rehearsal rooms available daytime.
Perfs: 7.30.
Licensed Foyer Bar, additional Bar for members only.
TECHNICAL:
Stage: Proscenium Stage with small Flat; Pros. opening
6.10m; Ht. of Pros. 4.19m; Depth of S/Line 7.54m; Ht.
of Grid 4.42m; 10 lines, Scenery Flying Ht. 5.49m; Flying
Bars 4.57m; W/Widths P.S. 1.22m, O.P. 1.22m; Prompt
Cnr. O.P.
Lighting: Sirius 48 board (35 x 1K) (5 x 2K) (6 x 2.5K); 2
F.O.H. bars; Stage bars rigged as needed; 70 lanterns.
Sound Equipment: 12 Channel Mixer with 2 Tape decks,
2 Turntables, 5 Speakers, CD.
Other: Dressing Rooms 3, accom. 20.

## TRICYCLE THEATRE
269 Kilburn High Road London NW6 7JR
Mgt 0171 372 6611 BO 0171 328 1000
Fax 0171 328 0795
ADMINISTRATION:
Props: Tricycle Theatre Co. Ltd
General Manager: Mary Lauder
Artistic Director: Nicolas Kent
Policy: Presentation of new plays. Adult programme
generally for 6-9 week runs. Childrens shows on
Saturdays. Plays both by Tricycle Co. and by other
production companies.
Seats: 225
TECHNICAL:
Open Stage (7.92m x 6.09m) back by small Pros. arch
(6.09m x 3.05m). Full technical information from
management on 0171 372 6611.

## THE UNDERWORLD
174 Camden High Street Camden London NW1 0NE
Tel 0171 267 3939 Fax 0171 482 1955
Contact: Adam Elfin and Jon Vyner
Capacity: 500

## UNICORN THEATRE
Plaese see under ARTS THEATRE

## UNIVERSITY COLLEGE LONDON UNION
25 Gordon Street, London WC1H 0AH
Tel 0171 387 3611 Fax 0171 383 3937
ADMINISTRATION:
Manager: Mike McLeod
Seating/Capacity: 550

## UNIVERSITY OF GREENWICH UNION
Bathway London SE18 6QX
Tel 0181 331 8268 Fax 0181 331 8591
Contact: Justin Goldsack
Capacity: 1,000

## UNIVERSITY OF LONDON UNION
Malet Street London WC1E 7HY
Mgt 0171 664 2000  Mgt Fax 0171 436 4604
BO 0171 664 2030  BO Fax 0171 664 2040
ADMINISTRATION:

General Manager: Lesley Dixon
Entertainments Manager: Steve Keeble
Capacity: 828 max

## VANBRUGH THEATRE
Malet Street London WC1E 6ED
Mgt 0171 636 7076 Fax 0171 323 3865
Props: Royal Academy of Dramatic Art
Administration:
Principal: Nicholas Barter
Under Construction.

## VAUDEVILLE THEATRE
404 Strand London WC2R 0NH
Mgr 0171 836 1820 BO 0171 836 9987
SD 0171 836 3191
ADMINISTRATION:
General Manager: Thomas Bohdanetzky
Tel: 0171 828 0600
Theatre Manager: Alistair Sutherland
Policy: West End Presentation.
Perfs: Times of performances vary according to
production.
Seats: 694; 3 bars.
TECHNICAL:
Stage: Proscenium stage, pros opening 7.26m, height of
pros 5.03m, rake 1:24, depth of stage from pros 9.54m,
forestage 0.54m, height of grid 14.33m, 50 lines, 12
counterweights, 38 hemp, wing widths P/S 1.83m, OP
2.29 D/S, 3.20 U/S.  Prompt corner P.S.
Lighting: Board: Rank Strand Mini Light Palette 90 - 100
ways.
Other: Dressing rooms 9, accom. 27; 9 Showers.
Additional Rooms for Company Manager and Wardrobe.
Air conditioned.
Membership: SOLT
"The plan for this venue can be found in the
Official London Seating Plan Guide"

## THE VENUE
Elstree Way Borehamwood Hertfordshire WD6 1NQ
Tel: 0181 207 2277 Closed for 3 year redevelopment.
All enquiries to to Phil Collins, Director of Leisure
Hertsmere Borough Council

## THE VENUE
2a Clifton Rise New Cross London SE14 6JP
Mgt/BO 0181 692 4077 Fax 0181 694 8208
Promoter: Richard Evans
Capacity: 1,000

## VICTORIA PALACE THEATRE
Victoria Street London SW1E 5EA
Admin/SD 0171 834 2781 Admin Fax 0171 828 6882
BO 0171 834 1317  BO Fax 0171 931 7163
ADMINISTRATION:
Props: Victoria Palace
General Manager: Thomas Bohdanetzky
Policy: Musicals, Variety, Revue, Plays, Sunday
Concerts.
Perfs: Once & Twice nightly.
Seats: 1,515. Five Licensed Bars.
TECHNICAL:
Stage: Proscenium Stage, Raked 12.7mm to 25.4mm;
Pros. opening 10.77m; Ht. of Pros. 9.22m; Depth of
s/Line 9.45m; Ht. of Grid 16.76m; 38 lines; C/W
Scenery Flying Height 7.32m; Flying Bars 12.19m; O.P.

5.49m; Prompt Cnr.; O.P. W/Widths P.S. 12.19m.
Lighting: Switchboard: ARRI, 110 Memories; 140
circuits; 36 F.O.H.; 16 Stage dips, Flys 88, Spot Bars as
required.
Sound Equipment: Details available direct from Theatre.
Dressing Rooms 12, accom. 75; 6 Showers; Orchestra
Pit 24. Easy get-in direct to stage from street level.
Other: Membership: SOLT
"The plan for this venue can be found in the
Official London Seating Plan Guide"

## WALTHAMSTOW ASSEMBLY HALL
Forest Road London E17 4JD
Mgt 0181 527 5544 Ext. 4420 BO 0181 521 7111
SD 0181 527 5394 Fax 0181 531 8642
ADMINISTRATION:
Props: London Borough of Waltham Forest
Entertainments Manager: Eamonn O'Machaill
Hall Manager: Andy Lamarque
Policy: Concert Hall, Music, Pop, Jazz, Opera, Ballet,
Dances, Conferences, Boxing, Exhibitions, Recordings,
Touring Shows.
Seats: 1,150 (Stalls 922, Balcony 228). Two Bars,
Banqueting Facilities.
TECHNICAL:
Stage: Proscenium Stage, Pros opening 11m, Ht. of
Pros. 7.5m, Stage Depth 7.5m. Wings 3m either side;
Stage Extension up to 18 sq.m.(max.).
Lighting: Switchboard: Rank Strand A.M.C. rear of
balcony; 40-ways, F.O.H.: 24 Profile Spots + 2 x 2kw
Follow Spots. Stage: 4 Bars (60 + Floods and Spots) +
Portable Wing Floods.
Sound Equipment: Wilding 16 Channel mixer with
Reverb. Echo, Cassette and Record Decks. Foldback
Facility - output 200 watts feeding 8 x 100 watt
speakers.
Other: Dressing Rooms: 4, accom. 50; 1 Shower.
In addition to public concerts, Walthamstow Assembly
Hall is used for recordings on account of its world
renowned acoustics.

## WATERMANS ARTS CENTRE
40 High Street Brentford Middlesex TW8 0DS
Admin 0181 847 5651 BO 0171 568 1176
Fax 0181 569 8592

## WEMBLEY ARENA
Wembley Middlesex HA9 0DW
Tel 0181 902 8833 BO 0181 902 0902
Fax 0181 903 7930
ADMINISTRATION:
Props: Wembley Stadium Ltd
Director: Paul Sargeant
Sales Manager: John Drury
Technical Manager: Bob Gillett
TECHNICAL:
Stage: Stage - 18.3m wide x 12.2m deep plus up to
3.7m wide x 9.7m deep PA wings (variable height).
Boxing ring - full international world title size.
The ice plant is capable of manufacturing in around 48
hours, ice using water at 65°F to cover an area of
approximately 3,900m sq metres to a depth of
approximately 4.5cm.
Lighting: 180 off 1500-watt lamps capable of producing
up to 1000 Lux over Arena floor, these are installed on
motorised bars with add on capabilities. 14 strong
Supertrouper spotlights fitted with intercom facilities.
Sound: Area served by a single Central Cluster Array of

Constant Directivity Loudspeakers for stage based microphone presentations, event commentary and performance sound. The loudspeakers can be electrically configured to match the various operational modes and audience capacities of the Arena.
Other: Dressing rooms: Fully equipped dressing rooms of varying size run the length of the building on both sides. Superstar dressing room for solo artist.
"The plan for this venue can be found in the Official London Seating Plan Guide"

## WEMBLEY CONFERENCE AND EXHIBITION CENTRE
Grand Hall Wembley Middlesex HA9 0DW
Mgt 0181 902 8833 BO 0181 902 0902
Fax 0181 903 3234
ADMINISTRATION:
Props: Wembley Stadium Ltd.
Director: Paul Sargeant
Technical Theatre Manager: Steven Lee
Technical Manager: Steve Hunter
Policy: Concerts - Classical, Folk, Jazz, Light Entertainment, Dance. Companies and Theatre. Touring One-Night Stands.
Seats: 6-2,700. Variable. Bars. Restaurant and Banqueting facilities.
TECHNICAL:
Stage: Proscenium Stage, 18.24m wide by 12.25m deep; Ht. of Pros. 7.30m; Apron Stage 18.24m wide by 14.44m deep with 12 mechanical variable sections; Depth of S/Line variable, 4.86m on Pros. Stage; No Fly Tower; Orchestra Pit 8.5m x 2.8m and extensions of 4.8m x 2.8m on either side. Get-in access; rear stage hydraulic lift: 10 tonnes load, 5.5m x 2.6m x 3.2m high.
Lighting: ADB Vision 10 with tracking backup, 178 ways 2.5kw. eurodim televison standard 12 ways 5kw eurodim dual electronic with DMX patch system. Spots 72 Patt. 743 lanterns, 30 Patt. T64 lanterns, 24 Patt. 774 lanterns, 30 Parcans. 1000 watts. 12 x Patt 243 2kn, follow spots. Independents on stage - 8; 2 x 200 amp TPN; Supplies 1 Prompt. 1 OP sides; 1 x 600 amp TPN in Grid; 1 x 600 amp TPN Loading Bay; TV connection; 4 Lighting Bars over Stage, 6 Lighting Bars over apron stage; DMX control room at rear of auditorium and 4 other positions.
Sound: F.O.H. speakers and Turbosound Floodlight Concert System. Mixer, 40-8-2 situated in auditorium. Ancillary equipment as required; C.C.T.V. facilities; 35mm and 16mm projection equipment; Projection Screen 13.00m wide x 6.70 deep with facilities for large-screen video colour projector up to 8.00m. Facilities for simultaneous translation in up to 8 languages.
Other: Dressing Rooms: 7, Showers: 5, accom. for 70, with extra rooms available as required.
"The plan for this venue can be found in the Official London Seating Plan Guide"

## WEMBLEY STADIUM
Wembley Middlesex HA9 0DW
Mgt 0181 902 8833 BO 0181 902 0902
Fax 0181 900 1045
ADMINISTRATION:
Props: Wembley Stadium Ltd
Director: Paul Sargeant
Sales Manager: Charles Shun
Technical Manager: John Glasgow
Capacity: Sport 80,000 all seated; Concerts 72,000 end stage.
TECHNICAL:

Stage: Supplied by Promotor - generally built to suit event.
Lighting: supply available as required - equipment provided by Promoter to suit production.
Sound: Wembley has its own in-house multi-purpose PA system.the system can be fully integrated with front of house equipment, providing high quality distributed sound to all areas within the Stadium.
Flooring: The Wembley turf is protected by Terraplas - designed and developed especially for Wembley Stadium providing a clean, safe and comfortable surface to walk on.
Other: Dressing rooms: Full suite of dressing rooms including two luxurious super star suites.
"The plan for this venue can be found in the Official London Seating Plan Guide"

## WEST ONE FOUR
3 North End Crescent North End Road
West Kensington London W14 8TG
ADMINISTRATION:
Orange Promotions
Tel 0171 381 0444  Fax 0171 381 0821
Contact: Phil Brydon or Tom Larkin
Capacity: 300

## WHITEHALL THEATRE
14 Whitehall London SW1A 2DY
Mgt 0171 925 2107 BO 0171 369 1735
SD 0171 867 1129 Fax 0171 839 3462
ADMINISTRATION:
Props: Associated Capital Theatres
110 St Martin's Lane, London WC2N 4AD
Tel: 0171 304 7922 Fax: 0171 867 1130
General Manager: Hugh Hales
Theatre Manager: Craig Prentice
Perfs: Varies according to production.
Seats: 648. Two bars.
TECHNICAL:
Stage: Pros. Stage Flat. Pros. Opening 8.46m; Ht. of Pros. 6.40m; Depth of Setting Line 4.10m; Ht. of Grid 14.93m; No. of Lines 20 C/W; Electric Act Drop; Scenery Flying Ht. 13.72m; Width of Flying Bars 13.72m; W/Widths O.P. 1.52m, P.S. 2.13m; Prompt Cnr. P.S.
Lighting: Switchboard: Dress Circle level, Gemini, Softpatch 180 ways 15 2360 dimmers, disc storage 2 x 100 amp. Special effect on PS perch; 3 x Colour wheel controllers.
Other: Dressing Rooms 8, accom. 30; 2 Showers. Dock Doors 2.40m high x 1.50m wide 3.96m above stage.
"The plan for this venue can be found in the Official London Seating Plan Guide"

## WIGMORE HALL
36 Wigmore Street London W1H 0BP
Mgt 0171 486 1907 BO 0171 935 2141
Fax 0171 224 3800 BO Fax 0171 935 3344
ADMINISTRATION:
Lessees: City of Westminster.
Artistic Director: William Lyne, MBE, Hon FTCL
Registered Charity No. 1024838
Policy: Concerts.
Perfs: Mondays to Saturdays at 7.30pm. Sundays - September & October: 11.30am & 7 pm, November to March: 11.30am & 4pm, April to July: 11.30am & 7pm.
Seats: 540. Restaurant, Sponsors Area and fully licensed bar.

TECHNICAL:
Concert Platform. no Pros. Flat.
Dressing Rooms: 4.
Excellent acoustics - often used for recording sessions
by BBC and all Record Companies. The Hall is equipped
with an induction loop for hearing aid use.

## WIMBLEDON THEATRE
The Broadway Wimbledon London SW19 1QG
Mgt 0181 543 4549 BO 0181 540 0362/3
SD 0181 540 4073 Fax 0181 543 6637
ADMINISTRATION:
Props: London Borough of Merton
Lessees: Wimbledon Civic Theatre Trust Ltd (Registered
Charity)
General Manager: Anthony Radford
Stage Manager: Jem Nicholson
Policy: touring, pantomime, opera, ballet, concerts,
amateur productions, variety and music halls. Also
facilities for use of visiting film and television companies,
and rock group rehearsals.
Perfs: Times vary. Mats. usually Thurs.
Seats: 1,502. four fully licensed bars.
TECHNICAL:
Stage: Proscenium stage raked 1 in 32, pros. opening
10.40m, Ht. of pros. 6.30m. Max Ht House Header
6.00m. Depth of setting line 10.60m. Total depth of
stage 12.45m. Ht. of grid 15.54m, 57 Hemp lines + 4
C/Ws Lines include 9 Help Assistors operated O/P/Fly
Floor. Scenery Flying Clearance Ht. 7.00m. Flying Bars
12m. Ht. to Fly Floor 6.70m U.S. W/Widths P.S. 5.00m,
O.P. 1.60m. Small Scene Dock D.S. O.P. 4.40m x
3.670m. Prop. Room O.P. Prompt Cnr. P.S. 13 ways
cue board with answer headphone intercom system.
Switchboard: Gemini - 240 circuits - control rear stalls.
Lighting: Equipment: Gemini 2b desk with two monitors
In rear stalls position. Designer position in stalls/circle
with monitor and designers control. Riggers control from
positions in auditorium and stage. 240 circuits (inc. 36
5ks) controlled by 2 EC90 dimmers. (56 FOH, 4 in
orchestra pit, 180 backstage). On stage - 300 amp 3
phase, 2 x 60 amp 3 phase and 1 x 32 amp single
phase supplies. Headsets to all positions (and 4 extra on
stage). Cue light to all backstage positions controlled
from moveable prompt desk. Lanterns - 2 x strand solo
follow spots, 40 x patt 743 1ks, 16 x Parcan 1ks, 26 x
Harmony 1ks (FOH) 8 x Sil 30 1ks (FOH/ROH), 6 x 243
1ks, 8 x patt 23's, 6 x Coda 4 (cyc bar), 6 x Coda 4
(ground row). Blues and White working lights backstage.
Sound Equipment: Soundcraft mixing desk 20-4-2, in
rear stalls position. 1 Revox, 1 Teac Cassette.
Auditorium cover - Stalls, 2 Martins; Circle, 2 Martins;
Balcony, 2 Martins; 2 Front Stage fill; 2 Side Stalls fill; 4
Rear Circle fill; 4 Rear Stall fill. All fill speakers are Bose
101's. Backstage - 2 channel, 4 position foldback.
Other: Dressing Rooms 12, accom. 96; 3 Showers;
Orchestra Pit up to 40.

## WYNDHAMS THEATRE
Charing Cross Road London WC2H 0DA
Mgt 0171 304 7925 BO 0171 369 1736
SD 0171 867 1125 Fax 0171 240 3492
ADMINISTRATION:
Props: Associated Capital Theatres
110 St Martin's Lane, London WC2N 4AD
Tel: 0171 304 7922 Fax: 0171 867 1130
General Manager: Hugh Hales
Theatre Manager: William Ingrey
Policy: Plays, Musicals etc.

Perfs: Variable according to production.
Seats: 800. Licensed Bars.
TECHNICAL:
Stage: Proscenium Stage, Flat; Pros. opening 8.31m;
Ht. of Pros. 6.40m; Depth of S/Line 8.00m; Ht. of Grid
14.78m; 30 lines, Hemp; Scenery Flying Ht. 14.02m;
Flying Bars 10.06m; W/Widths P.S. 6.52m; O.P. 3.40m;
Prompt Cnr. as required.
Lighting: Switchboard: Arri Imagine board installed.
Circuit distribution. F.O.H. 42, Flys 54, Stage 34, 60A 3
phase available for additional dimmers. Control Desk
rear of Royal Circle; Remote Terminal Prompt Cnr.
F.O.H. Spots 16 Patt. 264; 3 circuits; Floats & Dips as
required. Air Conditioned (Auditorium).
Sound Equipment: As required.
Other: Dressing Rooms 8, accom. 30
Membership: SOLT
"The plan for this venue can be found in the
Official London Seating Plan Guide"

## YOUNG VIC THEATRE
66 The Cut London SE1 8LZ
Mgt 0171 633 0133 BO 0171 928 6363
Fax 0171 928 1585
ADMINISTRATION:
Artistic Director: Tim Supple
Administrative Producer: Caroline Maude
Production Manager: Richard Howey
Policy: Theatre.
Perfs: Phone or write or see Press for details.
Seats: 400-500; Studio Space: 80-90
Cafe and Wine Bar.
TECHNICAL:
Stage: Thrust/in the round Stage, Flat; Ht. of Grid
8.23m; Prompt Cnr. O.P. audit.
Lighting: Switchboard: Gemini Memory Control System
for 132 and capacity of 192 cues. dips 5 patchable each
side; Spot Bar, Open Grid; 36 Patt. 264, 10 Patt. 23.
Sound: Soundcraft K3, 16-8-2 with 8X8 matrix, Alcai
3000 sampler, 2 Cds, 1 Minidisc, 1 SPX1000, Assorted
microphones, Meyer speaker system.
Other: Dressing Rooms 4, accom. 20; Showers.
Entrance from dressing rooms to S.R. and round back
of auditorium to SL and SR stairs removable to acting
balcony. Bridges to connect balconies.

# FRINGE THEATRES

## AFRICA CENTRE
38 King Street, Covent Garden, London WC2E 8JT
Tel 0171 836 1973 Fax 0171 836 1975
Email: africacentre@gn.apc.org
ADMINISTRATION:
Director: Dr Adotey Bing
Press & Publicity Co-ordinator: Karen Weir
Seats up to 120 depending upon layout and production;
total area 50' x 20'.

## THE ALBANY
Douglas Way, Deptford, London SE8 4AG
Admin 0181 692 0231 BO 0181 692 4446
Fax 0181 469 2253

## THE ANDREW SKETCHLEY THEATRE
189 Whitechapel Road London E1 1DN
Tel 0171 377 8735
Administrator: Judith Reynolds
50 seat, studio theatre stage area 20' x 20'
Not available for hire.

## BATTERSEA ARTS CENTRE
Lavender Hill London SW11 5TF
Mgt 0171 223 6557 BO 0171 223 2223
Fax: 0171 978 5207
ADMINISTRATION:
Director: Tom Morris
Production Manager: Chris Robinson
Policy: Concentration on the presentation of visual
theatre and new writing with an emphasis on the most
innovative and challenging new work.
Theatre: Multi-purpose performance space. Seating
capacity 170.
Studio One: Seating 48
Studio Two: Seating 60
Seating capacities in the two studios are variable.
TECHNICAL:
Stage (Theatre):  The playing area (on floor) is normally
27 feet x 21 feet.
Lighting: 6 X Harmony 1k Fresnels all with Barndoors, 10
X Cantata 1.2k Fresnels all with Barndoors, 10 X Cantata
1.2k Profiles 18/32 with Rotary Gobo Gate, 15 X 650w
Prelude Fresnels all with Barndoors, 8 X Thomas Pars all
CP 62. LX Desk: ETC Express:- 120 Channels 2k per
way Digital
Sound: Soundcraft K1 Sound Desk 16-4, 1 X Denon
DCD -425 single C.D. Programmable, 1 X Denon DRM
550 single cassette unit, 2X EV P1250 PWR Amps, 1 X
EV XP200 Cross Over, 4 X EV S x 200 Midd and Top
Speakers, 2 X EV Sb 120 Bass Speakers, 1 X Alesis
Quadravert, Relevant Cables, Patch Bay.
Please contact the Production Manager/Technical
Department for further information.
STUDIO 1: (Also available for hire as a rehearsal space).
Flexible rostrad seating - Cap: 50.
Lighting Desk: MX 24 - Man & Computer.
Lighting: 8 X Minim F's, 4 X Minim P.C's, 3 X Minim 23's,
4 X Prelude F's, 2 X Prelude P.C's, 7 X Prelude 28/40
Profiles, 6 x Pars CP 62, 2 X 1k Floods, 2 X 1/2k Floods,
LX Desk: ETC Express:- 48 Channels 2k per way, Digital,
2X independents, 2 X Non Dim
Sound: SP.R17 Live 16/3 mixer, 1 X Denon DCD 425

C.D. , ! X Denon DRM 550 Cassette, 1X EV P1250 PWR
Amp, 2 X EV S x 200 Top & Mid Speakers.
Please contact the Production Manager/Technical
Department for further information.
Arts Cafe: Seating - 64. Fixed stage area 24' x 7'.

## BRICK LANE MUSIC HALL
134-146 Curtain Road London EC2A 3AR
Tel 0171 739 9996/7
ADMINISTRATION:
Manager: Zara Kattan
Seats: 250
Full Time Music Hall
Dinner and Show.

## BROADGATE ARENA
Broadgate Estates Exchange House 12 Exchange
Square Primrose Street London EC2A 2BQ
Tel 0171 505 4000 Fax 0171 382 9854
ADMINISTRATION:
Manager: C Purdie
Assistant: M Smith
Open Air Amphitheatre hosting free weekday lunchtime
entertainment, May to September annually.
TECHNICAL:
Performing area 80' diameter max. Canopy available.

## BROMLEY LITTLE THEATRE
North Street Bromley Kent BR1 1SD
Tel/BO 0181 460 3047
ADMINISTRATION:
Props: Bromley Little Theatre Ltd.
Artistic Director: Robert Dilks
Seats: 112
TECHNICAL:
Stage: Proscenium, Flat; Pros. Opening 4.88m; Ht. of
Pros. 2.59m; Depth of S/Line 6.40m; Ht. of Grid 6.10m.
Other: Dressing rooms: 2, accom. 24 approx.
Club Theatre. Resident Company. Established 1937.
Season January to December.

## BUSH THEATRE
Shepherds Bush Green Goldhawk Road London W12
8QD
Mgt 0171 602 3703 BO 0181 743 3388
SD 0181 743 5050
ADMINISTRATION:
Props: Indcoope Taylor Walker
Lessees: Alternative Theatre Company Ltd
Artistic Director: Mike Bradwell
General Manager: Deborah Aydon
Policy: Producing new writing, some receiving of
productions.
Perfs: 8.00 Mon. to Sat.
Seats: Licensed to seat 105. Bar and Buffet in pub.
TECHNICAL:
Lighting: Control: Arri image with Arri connexion and
effects. Green Ginger racks 48 x 2kw patching to 98
outlets in I.W. grid. Approx. 70 Units; 8 parcan 64, 10
1kw Berkey fresnel, 10 650w prel fresnel, 6 650w prel
16/30 assorted 23, 123.
Sound: Control: Studiomaster 16-4-2, 2 quad 405, 1

quad 303, 6 sentry 100 amp speakers, electrovoice graphic, midiverb 11, 2 A77, 1 Awai F350 cass. deck, 1 technics SL1200 turntable. Various hardwired mic, speaker, cue outlets.

## CANAL CAFE THEATRE
The Bridge House Pub, Delamere Terrace,
London W2 6ND
Tel 0171 289 6054 Fax 0171 266 1717
ADMINISTRATION:
Fringe Pub Theatre in cafe-style layout with bar and food. Ali Robertson presents comedy, cabaret, drama.

## CHAT'S PALACE
Arts Centre & Venue, 42-44 Brooksbys Walk,
London E9 6DF
Tel 0181 986 6714/533 0227 Fax 0181 985 6878
ADMINISTRATION:
Seating capacity: 125-150, Standing: 200
Contact: Shabnam Shabazi

## THE CHELSEA CENTRE THEATRE
World's End Place King's Road London SW10 0DR
Tel: 0171 352 1967 Fax: 0171 352 2024
Email: chelseacentre@btinternet.com
Web Site: www.btinternet.com/~chelseacentre/
Artistic Director: Francis Alexander
General Manager: David Micklem
Administrator: Colman Stephenson
Policy: In-house producing and middle scale touring. Committed to the presentation of new writing of high literary value dealing with the issues of today. Also workshops & full youth arts programme..
Seats: 84 - 122

## COCKPIT THEATRE
Gateforth Street London NW8 8EH
Admin 0171 262 7907 BO 0171 402 5081
Fax 0171 258 2921
ADMINISTRATION:
Props: City of Westminster College.
Administrator: David Wybrow
Technical Manager: Alistair Thornton
Policy: Incoming companies/shows & exhibitions.
Seats: In the Round 240; Thrust 180; End 120.
Bar, Large dressing rooms, workshop, foyer capacity 240. Large loading dock doors. Hire rates £200-£350 per show day.
Disabled Access at street level to auditorium and disabled toilets.
TECHNICAL:
Stage: Adaptable stage, Round/Thrusts/End.
Lighting: Switchboard: Strand 60 way, 3 x 3 preset; F.O.H. Spots 19 Patt. 223, 27 Patt. 264, 4 Patt. 123, 12 Patt. 23.
Sound: 2 Ferrograph, 1 Garrard in Lighting/ Control Box above stage; Speakers 4 floating 12 in Axion 7 positions.
Other: Dressing Rooms 2; accom. 20; 2 Showers.

## CORBETT THEATRE
Rectory Lane Loughton Essex IG10 3RU
Admin/BO 0181 508 5983 Fax 0181 508 7521
ADMINISTRATION:
Technical Manager: Geoffrey Dennard
Secretary: Margaret Taylor
Excellent small theatre with extensive parking facilities set in 5 acres of gardens with lake - periodically for hire. 12

miles east from Central London, 4 miles off M25; 1 mile off M11; access also by tube to Debden, Central Line.
Seats 125

## COURTYARD THEATRE
10 York Way, Kings Cross, London N1 9AA
Tel/Fax: 0171 833 0870
Artistic Director: June Abbott
An oasis in busy Kings Cross, a converted stables/carriage block. The resident companies, the Court Theatre Company and the Court Theatre Training Company, together with visting productions present both new and classical works.
Performances usually 8pm. Tuesdays to Sundays.
Seating 70 on rake.

## DANCE ATTIC
368 North End Road Fulham London SW6 1LY
Mgt 0171 385 2460 BO 0171 610 2055
ADMINISTRATION:
Props: Dance Attic Studios
Directors: Dee Dee Wilde, Andrianna Maimaris.
Perfs: Fri., Sat., Sun.
Seats 100
TECHNICAL:
Stage Area 40ft x 40ft
Basic Lighting Rig.

## EMBASSY THEATRE
Central School of Speech & Drama 64 Eton Avenue Swiss Cottage London NW3 3HY
Tel 0171 722 8183 Fax 0171 722 4132
ADMINSTRATION:
Marketing Co-ordinator: Linda Roe, ext.2288
A fully equipped Theatre with a seating capcity of 274, plus the Embassy Studio - adaptable seating with a capacity of up to 100. Both venues are used for public productions of students' work and are available for hire at certain times throughout the year. (Also a further 2 studio spaces available).

## ETCETERA THEATRE CLUB
Oxford Arms 265 Camden High Street
London NW1 7BU
Admin Tel/Fax 0171 482 0378 BO 0171 482 4857
ADMINISTRATION:
Director: David Bidmead
Policy: To continue our current successful two shows a night policy, as well as a Monday night slot for 'one-off' performances, presenting a popular and varied programme with an emphasis on new work.  To maintain and enhance the theatre's high media profile and to continue to provide the opportunity for small theatre companies, with limited finances, to stage productions in Central London.
Studio theatre with seating capacity of 50.
TECHNICAL:
Stage: 5.5m x 4.6m.
Lighting: Level 12, Zero 88, 2 preset desk.  Fixed general cover (4 x 743), & 4 x CCT Fresnels, 4 x CCT profiles and 4 x patt 23.
Sound: Revox B77 1/2 track reel to reel.  Teac 6 into 2 mixer and Tascam 122 cassette deck.

## FAIRKYTES ARTS CENTRE
51 Billet Lane Hornchurch Essex RM11 1AX
Tel 01708 456308

ADMINISTRATION:
Arts Officer: Miss Chris Cole
Supervisor: John Shadwell
Converted Georgian house seating 40, used for many
kinds of arts and crafts activities. Also small studio
theatre seating 100. Spacious garden is suitable for
drama performances if a company tours all its own
equipment.

## GATE THEATRE
Above The Prince Albert 11 Pembridge Road
London W11 3HQ
Admin 0171 229 5387 BO 0171 229 0706
Contact: Phillipe Le Moine
Seating: 110

## GREENWICH & LEWISHAM YOUNG
## PEOPLES THEATRE
Burrage Road London SE18 7JZ
Tel 0181 854 1316/0181 855 4911 Fax 0181 317 8595
ADMINISTRATION:
Administration Director: Bryan Newton
Seating variable. Maximum capacity: 90
TECHNICAL:
Acting space: 27' x 21'.
Lighting Equipment: Details of other equipment available
on application. Studio workshop also available. Access
for wheelchairs.

## HOXTON MUSIC HALL THEATRE
130 Hoxton Street London N1 6SH
Tel 0171 739 5431 Fax 0171 729 3815
ADMINISTRATION:
Director: Chris Bowler
Genuine Victorian Music Hall restored and used as the
heart of a neighbourhood centre.
Seats 120 max
TECHNICAL:
Stage: Variable raked or raised stage. There are various
combination of rostras that can be altered for different
acting spaces. Dimensions of floor space: 26' x 38'.
Dimension of stage space: 11'6 x 16'6.
Lighting: lighting board - Manual Green Ginger microet
20. 3 masters and 9 sub-masters. Dimmer racks - 3 x
Zero 88 6 x 10 amp Betapacks. 1 x Zero 88 3 x 10 amp
Alphapack. Lighting rig - 48 x 16 amp outlet sockets.
Lanterns - 6 x 500w Strand Quartet 22/40 zoom profile.
4 x 1k vision 1200 F Fresnel. 3 x 1K Rank Strand Par-
Blazer parcan. 6 x 500w Strand 123 Fresnel. 6 x 500w
Strand 23 profile. 1 x 500w CCT Minuette TT. 1 x 500w
CCT Minuette zoom profile.
Sound: amplifier - 1 x Peavey 8.5c 550w per channel.
Speakers - 2 x Peavey Hi Sys 2 350w. Reverb - 1 x
Peavey Univerb II. Mixer - 1 x Phonic BK x 8800. Tape
Deck - 1 x Denon DRW 760 twin cassette deck. 1 x
AIWA AD-F410 single cassette deck. Microphones
available on request. 2 Pianos.
Additional facilities: Large spaces for filming,
conferences, rehearsals etc. Centrally situated with
good public transport and unrestricted parking available
outside the Hall. Reasonable hire rates.

## ICA THEATRE
Nash House 12 Carlton House Terrace The Mall
London SW1Y 5AH
Tel 0171 930 0493 BO 0171 930 3647
Fax 0171 873 0051
ADMINISTRATION:

Institute Director: Philip Dodd
Technical Manager: Richard Decordova
Live Arts Co-ordinator: Vivienne Gaskin
TECHNICAL:
Stage: Ply floor 74' x 33' Grid over whole area 14'6".
Seating primarily on four movable bleachers enabling
various endstage traverse thrust and round layouts up to
a maximum capacity of 206 seats.
Lighting: 48 way Micron. Switch patching 3 ways on 12
channels. 174 Grid outlets. Lanterns: 12 x Patt. 23, 12 x
Sil 30, 18 x Cantata Fres., 6 x harmony Fres., 14 x
Parcans (1K), 2 x 15/28 Profiles, 2 x 22/40 Profiles.
Sound: 2 x Revox B77; 1 x Revox A77; 1 x Tascam 8 x
4 x 1 Mixer. Bose Speaker System.

## INTERCHANGE STUDIOS
Dalby Street, Kentish Town London NW5 3NQ
Tel 0171 267 9421 Fax 0171 482 5292
ADMINISTRATION:
Acting Managing Director: Julian Stanley
Bookings Manager: Pamela McCall
TECHNICAL:
2 Halls: 40' x 50' with unfixed seats, theatre equipment,
dance studios, new fully sprung dance floors, music
rooms, catering, good facilities for the disabled. Central
London location for rehearsals or conferences.

## JACKSONS LANE
Opp Highgate Tube 269a Archway Road
London N6 5AA
Tel 0181 340 5226 BO 0181 341 4421
Fax 0181 348 2424 Tech 0181 341 5581
ADMINISTRATION:
Programme Co-ordinator: John Walmsley
Theatre Technician: Chris Copland
Policy: To provide a programme of music, drama, dance,
mime and cabaret, representing multi-cultural interests.
Training will play a large part in our programme, and
many of our staff are trainees and volunteers.
Location: Alongside the Archway Road (A1), opposite
Highgate tube. Served by buses 43, 134, X43, 263.
Terms: Hire of theatre (negotiable); box office split.
Seats/Capacity: 129-167 seated, raked; 290 standing.
Bars: one in foyer, one in auditorium.
TECHNICAL:
Stage: semi sprung maple. Width 11m, depth 6.4 -
9.75m, variable. No proscenium. Dance floors available.
Grid height: 6m from stage. Control position: raised at
back of auditorium, 100kva 3 phase supplying 48 x 2.5k
dimmers with 82 circuits.
Lighting: Zero 88 Sirius 48 way computerised lighting
board. Standard dance rig in place, ask for further details
Sound: Spirit Live 42 24 Channel Mixing Desk, Midiverb
III Fx unit, Denon twin cassette, Tascam DA30 MKII DAT,
twin Denon CD players, Revox, full PA. Upright piano.
Other: Dressing Rooms: three rooms, backstage, with
showers and toilets.
Get-in 12' high by 4'3" wide, directly from stage to
street. Induction loop in auditorium. All facilities are
accessible to, and usable by, people with disabilities,
including audience, performers and technicians.
For more information contact Chris Copland on 0181
341 5581.

## LION & UNICORN PUB THEATRE
42-44 Gaisford Street, London NW5 2ED
Tel: 0171 482 0850 Fax: 0171 388 7329
Manager: David Jubb
The Lion actively seeks out and promotes small scale

new work - with a visual emphasis. Three day periods on 60/40 split for companies experimenting with new ideas or touring work to North London. A very supportive venue.
9.7 x 6.9m space with flexible seating configurations. Good facilities: powered rig, 18 lanterns, Spirit PowerStation 1200, Sherman CObb 400 speakers, CD, Double tape deck, Shure SM58 mic + second basic sound system.

## MAN IN THE MOON
392 Kings Road Chelsea London SW3 5UZ
Admin 0171 351 5701 BO 0171 351 2876
Fax 0171 351 1873
ADMINISTRATION:
Executive Director: Leigh Shine
Associate Director: G. Cooper
General Manager: Nick Eisen
"Shirk Productions" was formed in 1976 by Rob Quirk and Leigh Shine. They found a permanent home at the Man in The Moon in 1981 and started to produce very successful shows, most notably Nigel William's CLASS ENEMY. With the profits from this and after several charitable events they were able to convert the pub's one time cold-store into a usable theatre space. The theatre opened officially in 1982 with John Godber's adaptation of Anthony Burgess' novel A CLOCKWORK ORANGE, under the direction of Godber himself. The success of this production established the high reputation that the theatre still maintains today. Since then it has seen the world premiere of Lanford Wilson's A BETROTHAL starring Ben Kingsley and Geraldine James (Autumn '86) and visits by the Duchess of York (to BREAKFAST, LUNCH AND DINNER, summer '90). Three years ago the theatre instigated its 'WOMEN IN THE MOON REP SEASON', plays written and directed by women performed by one company of actors over a period of three months, this has received across the board praise with an excellent press coverage and has included "The False Count" by Aphra Behn, "Approaching Zanzibar" by Tina Howe, "She ventures and he wins" by Ariadne, "Stories from the National Enquirer" by Jeanne Murray Walker and Cheryl Robson's "The Taking of Liberty". The theatre is also available for hire.
TECHNICAL:
Stage: Fixed seating can accommodate 68, arranged on two sides with an upper gallery. Stage space is 6.5m x 3.5m. height to grid 4.3m. Hardwired trunking system for lighting.
Lighting: Control: 18 way 2 preset dipless crossfade desk; Lanterns: 8 Patt. 23, 8 Patt. 123, 6 Patt. 803, 2 Patt. 137, 2 lito floods 500w, 1 prelude PC 500w, 2 prelude 28/40, 1 harmony 15/28, 1 minim F; 3 nocturne 500w, 5 harmony PC's 1kw, 6 minim 23 profiles 500w. Stock of barn doors, colour frames, masks, etc.
Sound: Equipment: 1 x TEAC 6-2 Mixer, 1 x Revox A77; 1 x JVC cassette deck; 1 Quad 405 stereo amplifier. 1 Tandberg reel to reel recorder. 1 Akai reel to reel recorder. 1 pair Yamaha 100w speakers. 1 pair Pro-Ac 60w speakers.
Other: Complete internal telephone system. Workshop space. Dressing room with toilet and lockers.

## THE MISKIN THEATRE
Miskin Road Dartford Kent DA1 2LU
Tel 01322 629433 BO 01322 629472
Fax 01322 629469
Email: miskintheatre@compuserve.com
Theatre Administrator: Laurajane Lavender

Artistic Director: Robbie McGovan
Seating: 140

## NEW END THEATRE
27 New End Hampstead London NW3 1JD
Admin 0171 794 9963 BO 0171 794 0022
Fax 0171 431 6705
ADMINISTRATION:
Chief Executive/Artistic Director: Brian Daniels
Performance area 5m x 7m
Venue hired out to companies - new plays and revivals, also 50% in-house productions.
seating 77

## OLD RED LION THEATRE CLUB
418 St. John Street Islington London EC1V 4QE
Admin 0171 833 3053 Fax: ring before use.
BO 0171 837 7816
ADMINISTRATION:
Administrator: Ken McClymont
Seats: 60
Performance area approx. 20' square.
Policy: New British writing, London Premieres of North American Plays.

## THE ORANGE TREE THEATRE
1 Clarence Street Richmond Surrey TW9 2SA
Mgt 0181 940 0141 BO 0181 940 3633
Fax 0181 332 0369
ADMINISTRATION:
Director: Sam Walters
Administrative Director: Gillian Thorpe
Marketing Manager: Karen Adams
Stage Manager: Teresa Lyons
Policy: New, classics, revivals, musicals. Schools and children's work.
Perfs: Mon-Sat 7.45pm, Mats Thursdays 2.30pm, Saturdays 4.00pm.
Seats: 160, fully licensed theatre bar.
TECHNICAL:
Theatre-in-the-round. Stage 4.85m X 5.70m, height to grid 4.75m.
Lighting: Tempus M24 + FX panel, 60w of dimmers, 32 X 650w profiles, 16 X 1200w profiles, 15 X 650w Fresnel, 16 X 1200w Fresnel, 16 X Par 64, 32 X Floods.
Sound: Soundcraft Delta 200, 3 poweramps/ 4 JBL1, 2 vocals.
Other: 2 dressing rooms, green room, shower, wardrobe with Iron, washing machine, dryer. Staff: 3 stage, 2 lighting and sound - casuals available.

## OVAL HOUSE THEATRE
52-54 Kennington Oval London SE11 5SW
Admin 0171 735 2786 or 0171 582 0080
BO 0171 582 7680 Fax 0171 820 0990
Email: ovalhouse@dial.pipex.com
Web Site: dspace@dial.pipex.com
ADMINISTRATION:
Props: Christ church (Oxford) Clubs
Lessees: C.C.U.C.
Policy: Seasons of plays e.g. new work, emerging companies, women's, lesbian & gay, black and Asian, work relevant to local audiences.  Performance and Rehearsal space.
New cafe & cabaret space; extra dance studio and rehearsal space.
Primarily Touring. Not usually a producing theatre, but does a number of productions involving workshop

participants and professional performers connected with Oval House and has a Artistic Development Programme. Two performance spaces, upstairs and downstairs 50 and 100 capacity respectively.

## PEOPLE SHOW
St James the Great Institute Pollard Row
London E2 6NB
Tel 0171 729 1841 Fax 0171 739 0203
Administrator: Jane Martin
Seating: 60

## PLEASANCE LONDON
Carpenters Mews 40 North Road London N7 9EF
Tel 0171 700 6877 BO 0171 609 1800
ADMINISTRATION:
Director: Christopher Richardson
Associate Director: Richard Osborne
Administrator: David Cotton
Production Manager: Dan Watkins
Status: National Touring House & Producing Theatre. Designed by Christopher Richardson, this 300 raked, flexible seater is housed in the General Omnibus Company's timber store in Carpenters Mews. Beside a cobbled courtyard and the splendid Shillibeer's Brasserie, the venue is run by the same management team as the Pleasance venue in Edinburgh.
Venue is self financing. RAA LAB.
Policy: Pleasance (meaning Pleasureground). An export of the festive atmosphere of the Edinburgh Fringe. Open all day, for extendable runs, split weeks and a mixed programme of the best of drama, late night comedy, afternoon entertainment and mid morning education. Emphasis on encouraging new work, new performers and new writers. Willing to premiere show. Rehearsal space also available.
Performances: Vary. Morning to late night. Bookings: guarantee and percentage split by negotiation.
1 licenced bar, coffee bar.
Facilities for the disabled.
TECHNICAL:
Stage: Floor. Performing area 9m x 9m. No rake. Sprung wooden floor suitable for dance. Height of grid 4.5m. Maximum flying height 7m (restricted width). Full blacks. First floor get-in doors on to stage plus stairway and lift from ground floor. Scale plans available.
Lighting: Arri mirage. 48 dimmable circuits @ 15A 12 independants at stage level operated from a control room above the auditorium.
Sound: 16-4-2 desks, cd, revox, mic stage boxes, suspended PA. Stage Management, show relay to foh and dressing rooms. Cue light system and comms.
Other: Backstage: 2 dressing rooms, 2 aux. changing rooms, control room and dimmer/store room above auditorium. Production manager, Master carpenter and stage manager.

## POLKA THEATRE FOR CHILDREN
240 The Broadway Wimbledon London SW19 1SB
Mgt 0181 542 4258 BO 0181 543 4888
Fax 0181 542 7723
Email: polkatheatre@dial.pipex.com
Web Site: www.polkatheatre.com
ADMINISTRATION:
Prop: Polka Children's Theatre Ltd.
Artistic Director: Vicky Ireland
Admin: Stephen Midlane
Policy: Children's Theatre Repertoire and visiting Children's Theatre Companies.

Seats: 300. Children's Restaurant, Exhibitions, Playground.
TECHNICAL:
Proscenium stage. Area: 6.77m width, 6.33m depth. Full details on request.

## THE PRINCE REGENT THEATRE
The Centre For Performing Arts 75 Guildford Road East
Farnborough Hampshire GU14 6PX
Mgt 01252 510859 Fax 01252 371112
BO 01252 371112
ADMINISTRATION:
Props: P.R.T.S. Management,
Founder and Artistic Director: Mr. Freddie J. Eldrett
General Enquiries: Jock Mills
Stage Manager: Graham McCarron
Seats: 70-90. Apply to theatre for details.
Available for hire of theatre and costumes.

## ROMFORD CENTRAL LIBRARY
St. Edwards Way Romford Essex RM1 3AR
Tel 01708 772374 Fax 01708 772391
ADMINISTRATION:
Contact: George Saddington
200-seater performance space in Central Reference Library. Used for one man shows, concerts, lectures etc. Simple lighting available.

## TABARD THEATRE
2 Bath Road Turnham Green Chiswick London W4 1LW
Tel 0181 995 6035 Fax 0181 747 8256
Email: cmb@dircom.co.uk
Artistic Director: Kate Bone
Founded 1986.
The Tabard aims to promote new work of contemporary relevance with particular emphasis on multi-media events, cross-art forms, new writing and experimental performance styles.
Seats: 48

## THEATRE MUSEUM
1e Tavistock Street, London WC2E 7PA
Tel: 0171 836 7891 Fax: 0171 836 5148
Head of Museum: Margaret Benton
The Theatre Museum exists to provide the national record of stage performance in Britain and to increase the public understanding and enjoyment of the performing arts through the expert interpretation of its collections. In its main premises in Covent Garden, the Museum houses permanent displays and special exhibitions drawn from its unrivalled collections, together with a souvenir shop and box office for West End shows. It runs a popular events and education programme. A study room is also available for research; please call 0171 836 7891 for an appointment. Both the Paintings Gallery and Studio Theatre are available for corporate hire. The public entrance is in Russell Street and admission charges are: adults £3.50, students, OAPs, UB40 holders and children aged 5 to 14 £2, children under 5 and Friends of the V&A free.
Venue Info:
Events Manager: Malcolm Jones
Studio Capacity: 80 seats, Paintings Gallery: 100 seats
Policy: Studio Theatre used for group workshops. Paintings gallery occasionally used to showcase musicals or playreadings. Both are used for talks, lectures and demonstrations.
Regular events and some performance work. Talks and

seminars.
Occasional 'trade' events and conferences. Available for corporate hire, parties, press launches etc.

## THEATRO TECHNIS
26 Crowndale Road London NW1 1TT
Tel 0171 387 6617
Director: George Evgeniou

## TRICYCLE THEATRE
269 Kilburn High Road London NW6 7JR
Mgt 0171 372 6611 BO 0171 328 1000
Fax 0171 328 0795
ADMINISTRATION:
Props: Tricycle Theatre Co. Ltd
General Manager: Mary Lauder
Artistic Director: Nicolas Kent
Policy: Presentation of new plays. Adult programme generally for 6-9 week runs. Childrens shows on Saturdays. Plays both by Tricycle Co. and by other production companies.
Seats: 225
TECHNICAL:
Open Stage (7.92m x 6.09m) back by small Pros. arch (6.09m x 3.05m). Full technical information from management on 0171 372 6611.

## UPSTAIRS AT THE GATEHOUSE
The Gatehouse, Highgate Village, London N6 4BD
Tel: 0181 340 3488 (B.O.) 0181 340 3477
(Mgr) Fax: 0181 340 3466
Upstairs at The Gatehouse is a large London Fringe Theatre situated in a refurbished Victorian Music Hall. It is administered by Ovation Theatre Ltd (0171 387 2342). Policy is completely open. New plays, revivals and occasional one-off cabaret and comedy nights. Ideal for Festival previews.
Location: Junction of Hampstead Lane and North Road, N6. Nearest tube: Highgate, Buses: 143, 214, 210, 271. Easy street parking.
Terms: Rental, Box office splits or Co-productions.
Seating: Theatre style: 130 (on three sides). Cabaret: 140 using a combination of tiered seating and pub style tables and chairs.

## WAREHOUSE THEATRE CROYDON
Dingwall Road Croydon CR0 2NF
Tel 0181 681 1257 BO 0181 680 4060
Fax 0181 688 6699
ADMINISTRATION:
Director: Ted Craig
Production Manager: Graham Constable
Policy: We are a new playwriting theatre presenting up to six in-house productions per year, building upon a tradition of discovering and nurturing new writers. In addition the Warehouse encourages co-productions and hosts selected touring companies from around the world who share the theatre's commitment to new work.
Origins: Found 1977.
Subsidy: London Borough of Croydon, LBGC, LAB.
Personnel: Artistic director, administrative director, marketing manager, children's programmer, production manager, box office manager, stage manager.
Audience: Seats 100-120.
Productions: 1997
The Servant of Two Masters by Carlo Goldoni, adapted by Ted Craig (Warehouse Theatre Company), The Seal Wife by Sue Glover (Attic Theatre Company), Sea of

Faces by Daniel Jamieson (Theatre Alibi), Fat Janet is Dead by Simon Smith (Warehouse Theatre Company), The Blue Garden by Peter Moffat (Warehouse Theatre Company), The Dreams of Anne Frank by Bernard Kops (Contraband Productions), Coming Up by James Martin Charlton (Warehouse Theatre Company), The Castle Spectre by MG 'Monk' Lewis, adapted by Phil Willmott (Warehouse Theatre Company).
Other Activities: Writer's workshops, youth theatre workshops, Saturday morning children's shows, international playwriting festival, cabaret. Busy bar and restaurant serving lunches. Open Mon-Fri all day, Sat 7-11pm, Sun 4-8pm
Disabled facilities: Induction loop.Until we move to our new theatre we are unable to offer wheelchair access.
TECHNICAL:
Stage: Adaptable to most layouts. Performing area 8.8m x 5.5m LX bars at 3.1m.
Lighting: Sirious Zero 88 LX board - 24 channel, 2 pre-set, 99 programmable memories, 9 level chases + 90 "insert" level memories; 13 x 1/2 K spots, 1 x 1K spot, 18 x 1/2 K fresnels, 14 x 1K frsnels.
Sound: Soundcraft 8 into 3 mixing desk; Tascam 32 reel to reel; Denon twin cassette system; BGW 250w amp; 2 x Bose 802 speakers & 2 JBL control 1 speaker; 2 x EV mics & stands. Piano.

## THE WORKHOUSE THEATRE
242 Pentonville Road London N1 9JY
Tel 0171 278 9783
Contact: Paul Caister
Seating: 80 max. Licensed.

## YAA ASANTEWAA ARTS AND COMMUNITY CENTRE
1 Chippenham Mews, London W9 2AN
Tel/BO 0171 286 1656 Fax 0171 266 0377
Community arts and social centre, providing cultural, artistic, educational and recreational activities relevant to the needs of the local population.

## YORK HOUSE
Richmond Road Twickenham Middlesex TW1 3AA
Tel 0181 831 6109 Fax 0181 940 7568
ADMINISTRATION:
Contact the Lettings Officer,
London Borough of Richmond on Thames,
Leisure Services Department, Langholm Lodge,
146 Petersham Road, Richmond TW10 6UX
Large Hall, with stage facilities.
Seating Capacity: 320

## YOUNG VIC THEATRE
66 The Cut London SE1 8LZ
Mgt 0171 633 0133 BO 0171 928 6363
Fax 0171 928 1585
ADMINISTRATION:
Artistic Director: Tim Supple
Administrative Producer: Caroline Maude
Production Manager: Richard Howey
Policy: Theatre.
Perfs: Phone or write or see Press for details.
Seats: 400-500; Studio Space: 80-90
Cafe and Wine Bar.

# PROVINCIAL VENUES

## ABERDARE, Mid Glamorgan

Pop: 64,500. Newspapers: Western Mail (daily); Cynon Valley Leader (weekly). Local commercial radio: Red Dragon. Local television station: HTV Wales. STD Code 01685

### THE COLISEUM

Mount Pleasant, Trecynon, Aberdare,
Mid Glamorgan CF44 8NG South Wales
Mgt 01685 882380 BO 01685 881188
Fax 01685 883000
Props: Rhondda Cynon Taff County Borough Council
Director of Leisure Services: E. Hitchings
Manager: Adrian WIlliams
Technical Manager: Ioan Wynne
Marketing Manager: Andrea Beecham
Front of House Manager: Ann Mills
Policy: Mixed Programme
Seats: 621
Stage: Proscenium stage, very slight rake. Pros. opening 7.8m; Width (wall to wall 9.9m; Depth (Iron to back wall) 5.85m; Fore-stage Depth 2.85m; Height (below flyfloor) 6.6m. Flying system; 5 x winch bars, 12 x hemp bars.
Lighting: Switchboard: Strand Lightboard (72 way, with 24 submasters, and 199 memories); Strand Act-6 Dimmers - 72 channels in all.
Sound Equip: Desk; Allen & Heath SC series 16:4:2 - feeding Left/centre/right clusters. 1 Denon DRM 510 cassette deck. 1 Yamaha CDX550E CD player.
Other: Dressing Rooms: 3, Accom. seating 27.
2 Showers, orchestra pit 24.
35 mm full projection facilities.
Bar/Function Rooms.
Car parking for 75 cars adjacent to theatre.

## ABERDEEN

Pop 204,000. London 543 miles. Newspapers: Evening Express (ntly); The Press & Journal (dly). Local commercial radio: Northsound. Local television station: Grampian. STD Code 01224

### ABERDEEN EXHIBITION & CONFERENCE CENTRE

Exhibition Avenue Bridge of Don Aberdeen
Scotland AB23 8BL
Tel 01224 824824 Fax 01224 825276
ADMINISTRATION:
Props: Aberdeen Exhibition & Conference Centre Ltd.
Managing Director: Clarke Milloy
Sales Manager: Jim Francis
For bookings contact: Sales Department.
Policy: Modern complex used for concert, sporting and arena events, conferences and exhibitions.
Capacity: 4,700 seated; 7,500 standing.
TECHNICAL:
Electrical: 300, 200 and 100 amp 3 phase supplies .
Also single phase. Access: 5m x 5m shutter door from car park direct into arena. Fork lift on site. Staging, lighting, backstage, arrangements according to requirements. Excellent flying capability.

### HIS MAJESTY'S THEATRE

Rosemount Viaduct, Aberdeen AB25 1GL
Mgt 01224 637788 BO 01224 641122
SD 01224 638677 Fax 01224 632519
ADMINISTRATION:
Props: Aberdeen City Council
Arts and Recreation Department
Operations Manager: Martin Milne
Assistant House Manager: Kenneth Luke
Technical Manager: Lena Dowell
Sales & Marketing Officer: Alison Lubek
Policy: Opera, Ballet, Plays, Summer Revues, Pantomime and Touring.
Perfs: Variable.  Seats: 1,450.  Two Bars.
TECHNICAL:
Stage: Proscenium stage, raked 1 in 34; Depth of S/Line 15.24 from footlights; Pros. opening 9.16m; Ht. of Pros. 7.08m; Ht. of Grid 15.33m downstage; 52 lines C/W, flying bars 11.90m; W/Widths PS 4.88m, OP 2.44m; Prompt Cnr. P.S.
Lighting: Switchboard: Eurolight Ovation 286.240 ways - rear of upper circle.
Sound Equip: Soundcraft 200, rear of auditorium.
(Please apply to theatre for details of lanterns and sound equipment).
Other: Dressing Rooms: 14; Orchestra Pit: variable up to 45 musicians; 2 Bandrooms.
Revolving stage 10.70m diameter, variable speeds.
Powered scenery lift from basement to stage 5.49m x 1.83m; powered paint frame above rear stage 10.50m wide.

### MUSIC HALL

Union Street, Aberdeen AB10 1QS
Mgt 01224 632080 BO 01224 641122
Fax 01224 632400
Email: abzmusichall@dial.pipex.com
ADMINISTRATION:
Props: Aberdeen City Council
Arts and Recreation Department
Operations Manager: Duncan Hendry
House Manager: Julie Sinclair
Senior Technician: Ewan Munro
Sales & Marketing Officer: Alison Lubek
Policy: Multi purpose auditorium, concerts,exhibitions and conferences. Full license and full catering facilities.
Capacity: 1,282 seated; 1507 standing.
TECHNICAL:

Stage: Frontage 13.6m, max 17.8m, depth 10.6m, height 13.6m.

Lighting: Control Celco "Aviator R180" lighting control desk. Strand "Permus" dimmers, 71 X 2.5kw and 10 X 5kw, 2 X zero 88, Demux 48. rig: 3 bars each containing 15 circuits. Advance bar 9 X 2.5kw circuits and 6 X 5kw circuits. All other bars 13 X 2.5kw circuits and 2 X 5kw circuits. 2 X FOH booms on balcony, 6 X 2.5kw circuits per boom. 4 X dips on stage 6 X 2.5kw circuits per dip. All lighting outlets are 15amps. 5kw circuits terminte in the roof space into 32amp Ceeform outlets. Lanterns: 72 X Par can 1kw, 34 X Strand Nocturne flood 1kw, 6 X ADB flood 1kw, 2 X Alto profile 2.5kw, 8 X Cadenza profile 2kw, 8 X Alto fresnel 2.5kw, 9 X Cadenza fresnel 2kw. Follow spots: 2 X Pani HMI 1200. Flying: installed bars 200kg evenly distributed on each spotbar. Points: currently there are no flying points available at the Music Hall. All rigs to be ground supported.

Sound:  control: 1 X Soundcraft 200B 24:4:2 Mixer, 1 X Allen & Heath SR12 (back up). Effects: 1 X Yamaha & Graphic EQ Q2031A, 1 X Ashly Stereo 6 band para Eq.PQ26. 1 X Ashly 4ch. noise gate SG35E, 1 X Denon CD player DCD 1290, 1 X Denon cassette deck DRS810, 1 X Yamaha SPX90 Amplification: 1 X JBL MPA 1100, 4 X C Audio SR707, 3 X C Audio SR606, 1 X C Audio SR404, 2 X C Audio graphic equalisers EQ312, 1 X C Audio graphic equaliser EQ311, 2 X JBL system controller C236A, 1X time corrector - BSS TCS-803. Speakers: 8 X JBL 4892 flown in exploded cluster, 2 X JBL 4892 on stage, 2 X JBL 4893 on floor, 4 X JBL control 1 (spread under rear balcony). Monitors: 2 X Carlsbro wedge (powered), 2 X Toa wedge, 2 X Yamaha wedge, 4 X JBL MR series wedge monitors, 2 X JBL control mirco table top. Foldback Amplification: 3 X Audio RA 3001. A good selection of mircrophones DI boxes etc. incorporating SM58, 87, AKG 401, Boycr etc. EMO DI boxes, EMO microphone splitters, boom and banquet stands. Microphone and speakers patch built into amp racks in control room.

General: Six dressing rooms; 3 large band rooms, 2 star rooms, 1 green room. Ring intercom, technical projects system with 9 outlets. A purpose built Control room is situated above the balcony stage right. lighting and sound systems can be controlled from the rear of centre stalls. Stage manager's desk incorporates paging for dressing rooms and front of house. Induction loop, "Ampetronic" system covering most of the auditorium, microphones positioned on balcony adjacent to stage. Sisco dual-height rostra providing ample risers for choirs and orchestras, includes treads and guardrails.

# ABERGAVENNY, Monmouthshire

Pop: 12,500 (Catchment 30,000). London 147 miles. Nespapers: Abergavenny Chronicle. STD Code 01873

## BOROUGH THEATRE

Town Hall, Cross Street, Abergavenny, Monmouthshire NP7 5HD
Mgt 01873 735830 BO 01873 850805
Fax 01873 858083
ADMINISTRATION:
Manager: Nick Banwell
Technician: Bernard Zavishlock (on 01873 859882)
Status: Bricks and Mortar. Theatre situated on top (3rd) floor of town hall, built late 1800s, renovated 1990, central local.
Venue funded by Monmouth County Council.

RAA Arts Council of Wales
Policy: All forms of music, dance, drama and opera. Can negotiate fees, split, first call etc. Theatre not available for hire to commercial managements. Non-performance activities: Occasional functions, exhibitions and conferences.
Facilities: Seating 338; raked cinema seats. Catering, Bar and light refreshments available. Access car park: adjacent, nearest railway station: 1 mile, nearest coach terminal: 5 mins' walk, bus routes: local buses.
For the disabled 5 wheelchair spaces - deaf loop system - lift - assistance available contact box office- parking - level access - all house facilities fully accessible except bar.

TECHNICAL:
Stage: Proscenium arch with forestage. Performing area 13.72m x 8.12m - pros opening 8.7m x 5m - wing widths 1.58m SR, leading to dock 3.66m x 5.49m, height 3.66m, 1.58m SL. Stage raked - floor lino on plywood on wooden boards, suitable for all dance possible backstage crossover, stage heated. Height of grid 6m - 9 motorised winches, 2 used for LX - 2 tab tracks - 250kg permitted on LX bars, 125kg on others - black side masking on runners, 2 sets black legs and borders - white filled cloth cyclorama - blue/green house tabs, drawn. 8 x 13A independent circuits.  Forestage curved, 9.15m x 0.95m in centre, entrances from stage. Orchestra pit 8.7m x 1.52m, accommodates 15.  Get-in via FOH or rear of stage and stairs - 1 fire door at rear of stage. Scenery lift. Scale stage, fly and lighting plans available.

Lighting: Strand Tempus M24 board, 72 circuits (36 operational), operated from control room at rear of auditorium - 100A 3 phase supply available for temporary board - 12 spots, 16 fresnels, 12 PCs, 4 x 4-circuit battens, Strand - followspots can be acquired, operated from rear of auditorium.

Sound: Alan and Heath GL2 12 channel mixer, 2 x JBL 4716A Loudspeakers, JBL MPA400 amplifier, 4 microphones and 3 stands (2 booms) controlled from lighting box or SR wings.  3 way intercom, S.L. and S.R. lighting box intercom.  Available to 2 dressing rooms.

Other: Stage management: Prompt corner SR - headsets, 3 outstations - show relay.
Good condition upright piano available.
Backstage: 2 dressing rooms, accommodating 32, access by stairs - also space for 32 in The Corn Exchange, a large room on the 1st floor used for rehearsal, dressing and wardrobe purposes - 12.8m x 7.3m, several 13A sockets - used by a dance school Monday, Tuesday, and Wednesday.
Backstage facilities accessible to disabled performers and staff (there is a lift). Technicians and casuals available.
Air conditioned.

# Aberystwyth

Pop: 10,650. London 212 miles. Newspapers: Cambrian News (wed). STD Code 01970

## ABERYSTWYTH ARTS CENTRE

Penglais, Aberystwyth, Ceredigion SY23 3DE
Tel 01970 622882 BO 01970 623232
Fax 01970 622883 Stage Mgr 01970 622892
ADMINISTRATION:
Props: University of Wales, Aberystwyth
Director: Alan Hewson
Administrator: Maris Davies

Stage Manager: Tom Corfield.
Policy: Drama, Ballet, Concerts, Recitals, Exhibitions,
Coures, conferences and Films plus special events.
Touring professionals/local amateurs. Arts Centre
comprises Theatr Y Werin (321 seats) plus Concert Hall
(900 seats), Art Galleries and 100 Seat Studio.
TECHNICAL:
Theatr Y Werin
Stage: open end or proscenium, flat with thrust or
Orchestra Pit. Pros. opening 14.6m/12.7/11.0/9.75m;
Ht. of Pros. and fly floors 6m; distance between fly floors
11m; Depth of Stage from Pros 8.93m (with thrust
12.9m); Ht to Grid 15.4m; 22 lines C/W double
purchases; Bars 9.5m; Prompt Cnr. S.L. or rear
auditorium.
Lighting: Switchboard: Rank Strand Gemini 2 rear
auditorium.
Other: Dressing Rooms 6; Accom. 21; Chorus Room
Accom. 30; 2 Shower suites.
Major refurbishment of venue (£4 millon) taking place
during 1998.

# Aldeburgh

Pop 2,670. London 97 miles. STD Code 01728

## SNAPE MALTINGS CONCERT HALL

(and Britten-Pears School for Advanced Musical Studies)
Snape Bridge, Snape, Near Saxmundham,
Suffolk IP17 1SP
Address for correspondence: Aldeburgh Productions,
High Street, Aldeburgh, Suffolk, IP15 5AX Mgt: 01728
452935 BO: 01728 453543 Fax: 01728 452715 Admin
email: enquiries@aldeburghfestivals.org Box Office email:
boxoffice@aldeburghfestivals.org
ADMINISTRATION:
Chief Executive: Jonathan Reekie
Policy: Concerts, Opera, Ballet, Master Classes,
Jazz/Folk/Dance.
Seating: 827 (280 on level rows A-K; 547 raked rows L-
ZF). Catering: Restaurant overlooking River Alde and
marshes, special parties catered for, full bar. Ticket
outlets: Aldeburgh Box Office, telephone (01728)
453543. Access car park: on site, nearest railway
station: Saxmundham, 2 miles; nearest coach terminal:
Saxmundham, 2 miles; bus routes: 081 Aldeburgh-
London. For the disabled: 6 wheelchair spaces -
parking - level access - at the moment the bar and
restaurant are not accessible. Other facilities: Rehearsal
rooms, practice studios, seminar room.
TECHNICAL:
Stage: End Stage. Performing area 17.68m wide x
12.2m deep x 6.1m (height at sides). Stage can be
raked (jack system for raking stage, understage) - floor
gurjun strip, suitable for dance, lino available, no
crossover, stage heated. No tab track - 1 tonne
permitted on 4 bars - maximum flying height 6.1m -
black and brown masking. 6 single RCD 13A sockets.
Forestage 14.63m x 2.7m, 2 entrances. Orchestra pit
accommodates 50 in forestage and understage area.
Get-in via SL side - dock doors 2.6m x 2.28m.
Tallescope. Scale stage and lighting plans available.
Lighting: Zero 88 Sirius board, 96 circuits, 198
memories - 100 various lanterns.
Sound: Recording room and comprehensive mic.
sockets and tie lines for recording and editing - sound
reinforcement system by prior arrangement. Acoustics
ideally suitable for music.
Stage Management: Show relay/Tannoy to dressing
rooms.

Backstage: 9 dressing rooms, 2 chorus rooms, 1
wardrobe room, access by artist's entrance - green
room/band room - double socket in each dressing
room. Refreshments by arrangement with caterers.
Advice given on accommodation. Staff - 2 stage -
casuals available - no security personnel. Backstage
facilities not fully accessible to disabled performers and
staff. Additional Information: Chamber Organ:
Hindmarsh, built 1971; transposing keyboard (A = 415
and A = 440), tracker action, 6 speaking stops, 1
manual, 336 pipes, very good condition. 2 Steinway D
Grand pianos also available.

# Aldershot

Pop: Rushmoor 81,400. London 36 miles. Newspapers:
Aldershot News and Mail; Star. STD Code 01252

## PRINCES HALL

Princes Way, Aldershot, Hampshire GU11 1NX
Mgt 01252 327671 BO 01252 329155
Fax 01252 320269
ADMINISTRATION:
Props. Rushmoor Borough Council
General Manager: Steven C Pugh
Technicians: Sean Connor, Philip Goddard
Policy: One night stands, concerts - m.o.r., variety,
middle range pop, ballet, opera, amateurs, conferences,
rallies, exhibitions, children's entertainment and
pantomime.
Perfs: Usually 8p.m., but by arrangement.
Seats: 680. Fully licensed bars.
TECHNICAL:
Stage: Proscenium Stage, Flat; Pros. opening variable
up to 15.24m, plus apron 1.22m or 2.44m deep; Ht. of
Pros. 4.57m; Depth of S/Line 6.10m; Ht. of Grid 7.32m;
7 Hemp lines; Scenery Flying Ht. 2.44m only rolled
cloths; Flying Bars 13.72m; W/Widths variable as Pros.
is formed with front tabs; Prompt Cnr. O.P.
Lighting: Switchboard: 48 channel Zero 88 Eclipse; 2 x
Preset Manual; 200 x Cue Memory and Fully
Programmable Chase Facility Giving 2 x 200 Step
Chases. F.O.H. 14 Silhouette 30; 4 Starletts P.C.; 2
Spot Bars; 18 ADB Fresnels; 8 Patt 60; Floats 34
Compartments; Dips 7 P.S. 7 O.P.; 6 Minuette Floods.
Sound Equip: 16 Channel into 4 TOA mixer desk.
Graphic equaliser, Fold back, 4 BOSE 802 speakers.
Tape, Cassette, Gram Deck.
Other: Dressing Rooms: 4; Accom. 20; 2 showers.

# Altrincham

Pop: 41,140. London 178 miles. Newspapers: Sale &
Altrincham Messenger (thurs). STD Code 0161

## GARRICK PLAYHOUSE

Barrington Road, Altrincham, Cheshire WA14 1HZ
Mgt/BO 0161 928 1677 SD 0161 928 2972
Mkt 0161 929 8779
ADMINISTRATION:
Administrator: Peter Coatman and Rita Howard
Marketing Officer: Roger Metcalfe
Policy: Repertory
Perfs: Mon. to Sat. 7.30. Seats 480. Public Bar and
Coffee Bar; Private Bar.
Seats: 471
TECHNICAL:
Stage: Proscenium Stage, Flat; Pros. Opening 9.14m;

Ht. of Pros. 4.57m; Depth of S/Line 7.92m; Ht. of Grid 6.50m; 24 Flying lines; Prompt Cnr. P.S.
Lighting: Eurolight Applause computerised lighting desk. 100 channels of dimming. 3 LX bars over stage. Side & Cyclorama lighting available. 70 Channels on stage. 30 Channels F.O.H. A vast variety of lanterns - in excess of 100. 2 x 1kw F/Spots in control box.
Sound Equip: Seck12:8 mixer. Open Reel, cartridge & cassette machines. Amps 2 x Quad 405. 2 x Quad 202 and others. F.O.H. speakers Martin CX2. Foldback stage Pro-Ac Stabs. 12 mic lines to box. Various mic inc 5 x Sennheiser 803. Beyer M201. AKG D190. Live musicals can be mixed from rear of auditorium.
Studio Theatre: Rear rehearsal room (35' x 25') can double as a 50 seater studio theatre. Please discuss your requirements with the administrators. Any technical queries can be answered by the stage director. Extra equipment can be hired in to suit.
A full size theatre run entirely by amateurs and its membership. Employing professional producers and workshop staff.

# Ammanford

### AMAN CENTRE
Margaret Street Ammanford Dyfed SA18 2NP Wales
Tel 01269 595199
Contact: Cheryl James 01269 826267
Seats: 180

# Andover

Pop: 35,000. London 74 miles. Newspapers: Andover Advertiser (fri); Southern Evening Echo (daily). STD Code 01264

### CRICKLADE THEATRE
Charlton Road, Andover, Hampshire SP10 1EJ
Tel 01264 365698 Fax 01264 332088
ADMINISTRATION:
Theatre Director: Matthew Shepherd
Administrator: Stuart Morris
Theatre Technician: Rob Bartholomew
Policy: The Cricklade Theatre is set within a modern complex housing Cricklade Tertiary College. There is easy access to car-parking, public transport and the nearby shopping precinct. The theatre is community orientated serving as a base for local amateur productions, student Drama work and visiting professional companies. The Theatre welcomes good quality touring shows presenting modern classics and contemporary work. Companies interested in a residency and prepared to contribute workshops and a strong educational input welcomed. Jazz, Folk, Rock bands are also of interest.
Finance: Test Valley Borough Council, Hampshire County Council (County Recreations), Southern Arts, Friends of Cricklade Theatre.
270 fixed seats in raked auditorium (250 if orchestra pit is used).
TECHNICAL:
Stage: 45' x 20'; Pros. opening 35' maximum (usually about 25' to curtain line) x 13'6" high, 14' to lighting grid. Black masking. Control room at rear of auditorium.
Lighting: Eurolite Applause board, 52 channels, with Strand SP40 manual backup, operated from rear of auditorium - 100A 3 phase supply available for

temporary board - 18 spots, 14 fresnels. 4 pcs, Rank Strand and CCT.
Sound: Alice 8:28 desk, operated at rear of auditorium - Alice, Quad 405, Peavey International system - 2 x Shure, 4 X AKG D190 mics - Ferrograph Logic 7 cassette tape system. Accoustics suitable for music and spoken word. 16mm cine, Carousel Slide projector, large film screen; upright piano and yamaha.
Other: Two dressing rooms - capacity 8 - 10 each. Two washbasins in each.
Disabled facilities. Parking for 3 vehicles. Wheelchair access and toilets. Loop system.

# Ashton-Under- Lyne

Pop: 44,032. London 181 miles. Newspapers: Ashton-Under-Lyne Reporter (thurs); Ashton Advertiser (thurs). STD Code 0161

### TAMESIDE HIPPODROME
Oldham Road, Ashton-under-Lyne, Lancashire OL6 7SE
Mgt 0161 330 2095 BO 0161 308 3223
SD 0161 3309256 Fax 0161 343 5839
ADMINISTRATION:
Props: Apollo Leisure (UK) Ltd
For all booking information and further details please contact Sam Shrouder or Nicky Monk at Apollo Leisure (UK) Ltd., Grehan House, Garsington Road, Cowley, Oxford OX4 5NQ. Tel: 01865 782900; Fax: Oxford 01865 782910.
Theatre Manager: Karen Jones
Chief Technician: Pat O'Leary
Stage Manager: Mike Weatherby
Chief Electrician: Shaun Everton
Policy: Varied to include Tours, Pantomime, Variety, Orchestral, Popular, Cultural and Films.
Perfs: Variable.
Seats: 1,262. One fully licensed bar.
TECHNICAL:
Stage: Proscenium Stage, slightly raked; Pros. Opening 10.59m; Ht. of Pros. 7.62m; Depth of S/Line 12.19m; Ht. of Grid 12.80m; 34 C/W, Scenery Flying Ht. 6.20m; Flying Bars 12.80m; W/Width P.S. 4.56m, O.P. 5.41m; Prompt Cnr. P.S.
Lighting: Switchboard: Arri mirage 120 channel, backup 120 way pin matrix (Rank Strand) and pin matrix with effects rack, located rear auditorium; FOH Spots 12, 18/32 cantata, 6, SIL 30's, 9, SIL 15's, 4 Spot Bars each with 12, Starlette Fresnel's and 4 Patt T64, 1 Flood Bar consisting of 4 Iris 3, 2 x HMV 1202 Pani follow Spots.
Sound Equipment: 1 Revox 77 and Tascam cassette deck; AHB System 8 sound mixer 24/2/8; speakers 8 Bose main auditorium, 4 Bose foldback; prompt call system and technical talk-back. Full 35mm film facilities.
Other: Dressing Rooms 8; plus 2 chorus rooms, Orchestra Pit 10.97m x 3.37m.

# Aylesbury

### LIMELIGHT THEATRE
Queen's Park Centre, Queen's Park, Aylesbury, Buckinghamshire HP21 7RT
Mgt Tel 01296 424332 Fax 01296 337363
Artistic Director: Amanda Eels
Capacity: 120

# Ayr

Pop: 50,000. London 390 miles. Newspapers: Ayr
Advertiser (thurs); Ayrshire Post (fri); Ayr Free Press
(thurs). STD Code 01292

## AYR TOWN HALL

New Bridge St Ayr KA7 1LX Scotland
Bookings: Tel 01292 612367 Fax 01292 612143
Town Hall direct line 01292 618222
Leisure Services 01292 282 842 Fax 01292 610650
Bookings Contact: Alison Taylor
Seats: 700. Stalls stack, balcony fixed.

## CIVIC THEATRE

Craigie Road, Ayr KA8 0EZ Scotland
Tel 01292 263755 Admin 01292 264630
ADMINISTRATION:
Props: South Ayrshire Council,
c/o Gaiety Theatre 01292 6174000.
Principal Officer Arts & Entertainments: Gordon Taylor
Technical & Stage Manager: John Seaman
Policy: Repertory (Summer Season) and small scale tour
venue.
Seats: 345. Bar.
TECHNICAL:
Stage: Proscenium Stage, Flat; Pros. opening 6.40m; Ht.
of pros. 4.27m; Depth of S/Line 4.27m; 10 lines, Hemp;
W/Widths P.S. 3.66m O.P. 2.13m; Prompt Cnr. P.S.
Lighting: Switchboard: Rank Strand SP/2, 30 way; Over
Prompt Cnr; F.O.H. Spots 10; Battens 3; Floats 1.
Sound Equip: Prompt Cnr. OHM Amp and speakers, 5
channel input.
Other: Dressing Rooms 5; Accom. 20; Orchestra Pit.

## GAIETY THEATRE

Carrick Street, Ayr KA7 1NU
Admin 01292 617400 BO 01292 611222
SD 01292 262787
ADMINISTRATION:
Props: South Ayrshire Council
Principal Officer for Arts &
Entertainments: Gordon Taylor
Technical & Stage Manager: John Seaman
Policy: Pantomime, Variety, Touring Productions,
Summer Shows.
Perfs: 8.00p.m.; if twice nightly 6.00 and 8.30p.m.
Seats: 584; 1 Stalls Bar, 1 Circle Bar.
TECHNICAL:
Stage: Proscenium Stage, Raked; Pros. opening 7.16m;
Ht. of Pros. 4.57m; Depth of S/Line 7.92m; Ht. of Grid
14.01m; 34 lines, Hemp; Scenery Flying Ht. 6.5m; Flying
Bars 9.14m; W/Widths S.L. 3.58m, S.R. 3.58m; Prompt
Cnr. S.R.; Get-in direct onto stage at street level.
Lighting: Gemini 2+ at rear of circle, FOH-20CCTs,
Flys/perches 60 CCTs, Dips 16 CCTs, 6 non-dim on
stage, 2 non-dim in flys. Equipment: F.O.H. 20 x 1k
profiles, 4 Patt 23; Stage 25 x 1k fresnels, 11 x Patt 23,
4 x Patt 750, 4 x Minim F, 26 x Par 64, 6 x 1k floods (all
these for bars or ladders). CYC. Lighting - 4 X CODA
500/3 + 5 X CODA 500/4; LIMES - 2 x Solo 2K.
Sound: 24Ch Allen & Heath desk, with reverb. Yamaha
and Quad amps, JBL F.O.H. speakers, various foldback
speakers, AKG and Shore microphones. Revox and
Cassette Deck. Dressing room relay.
Other: Dressing Rooms 9; Accom. 35. Orchestra Pit:
approx 8m x 1.7m.
Membership: TMA

## PAVILION BALLROOM

Esplanade Ayr KA7 1DT
Tel 01292 265489 Fax 01292 611614
ADMINISTRATION:
Proprietor: Mrs. C. MacIntyre
Manager: Mr F. MacIntyre
Policy: Concert Venue for all types of music, classical,
popular and dance music.
Seats: 1,000
TECHNICAL:
Stage: Proscenium arch (platform 1.53m high).
Performing area 10.98m x 12.2 to centre of curved back
wall, pros. opening 9.14, stage slightly raked, floor lino
on sprung wood, suitable for all dance. Backstage and
understage crossovers. Height of grid 12.2m max flying
height 6.1m 4 x 13A independant circuits. Get in via
large double doors at street level.
Lighting: 4 Golden scan 1200 MK2 plus various effects,
Par Cans and Stage Lighting controlled by a Pulsar
Masterpiece. 1 x 6 Watt Water cooled Multi-Coloured
laser system. 60A 3 phase and 60A single phase
supplies available.
Sound: 16 Kilowatt JBL Sound Power series sound
system driven by Amcron Machrotech Amps, with 12
Channel Soundcraft Spirit Mixing Desk, Full FOH and
Monitor Mixing Desks plus MICS Engineers and extra
sound available on request.

# Bangor

Pop: 10,700. London 235 miles. STD Code 01248

## JOHN PHILLIPS HALL

University of Wales, Holyhead Road, Bangor,
Gwynedd LL57 2PX Wales
Tel 01248 351151 Fax 01248 370451
Contact: Central Bookings: 01248 382033
Seats: 400

## PRICHARD JONES HALL

University of Wales, Bangor, Gwynedd LL57 2DG
Tel: 01248 351151 Fax: 01248 370451
Contact: Central Bookings: 01248 382033
Seats: Prichard Jones Hall: 632 (inc balcony 126).
Powis Hall: 200

## THEATR GWYNEDD

Deiniol Road, Bangor, Gwynedd LL57 2TL Wales
Admin 01248 251707 BO 01248 351708
Fax 01248 351915
ADMINISTRATION:
Props: University College of North Wales
Director: Dafydd Thomas
House Manager: Sheila Jones
Deputy Director: Ann Evans
Secretary: Beryl Price
Stage Manager: Dylan Rowlands
Chief Electrician: Tony Bailey Hughes
Projectionist: Gwynfor Davies
Assistant Electrician: Sion Gregory
Marketing: Fiona Otting
Policy: Mixed programme of drama, dance, opera, films
and pantomime. Open all year round except for 3 weeks
in June.
Seats: 346. Level access for the disabled to auditorium.
Art exhibitions in upper foyer. Fully licensed bar.
TECHNICAL:

Stage: Open end with or without pros. with apron. Pros width 12.80 max, normal 9.60. Pros height 5.7m Max, 5.2 normal. Stage width 16.10 max wall to wall, Stage Depth 10.30m max (to back wall) Normal 9.25 (cyc). Apron Depth 2.75m. Stage to Fly Floor 5.8m (clearance). Stage to Grid 13.90m (Flying). 15 Single Purchase C/wt sets. Length of Bars 12.20m, 50mm Diam. Cinema Screen on C/wt set between 2 and 3. Selection of Hemp Bars (moveable). Orchestra Pit for approx 35 players. Depth of pit 2.44m. SM desk stage left or rear control room.
Lighting: Set at rear of auditorium. Strand Gemini Board. 104 ways. 100 x 2KW, 4 x 5 KW. Strand + CCT lanterns.
Sound: Control at rear of auditorium. TAC 16-8-2 mixer. 2 Revox tape decks 19 CMS/SEC. 1 stereo disc turntable. 6 stage speakers: 2 fixed on Pros. arch; 4 movable. C.D. Player & Cassette Player.
Other: Projection: Control at rear auditorium. 2 westar 2000 35mm projectors. 1 Fumeo 16mm projector. 1 cinema screen with adjustable masking. 2 Kodak Carousels 2050 slide projectors with dissolve unit, selection of lenses.
Dressing Rooms 2; for 4 artistes, 1 for 5, 1 for 8. Large Green Room for chorus dressing room or wardrobe. 6 showers.
Membership: TMA, W.A.P.A., N.C.A.

# Barnsley

Pop: 224,000. London 172 miles. Newspapers: Barnsley Chronicle (fri). STD Code 01226

## CIVIC THEATRE
Eldon Street Barnsley South Yorkshire S70 2JL
ADMINISTRATION:
Props: Barnsley Metropolitan Borough Council
Theatre closed, expected to reopen in 2002.
For enquiries and further information contact Julie Rodgers on 01226 774467

# Barnstaple

Pop: 32,000. London 195 miles. Newspapers: North Devon Journal - Herald (thurs); North Devon Gazette (wed); North Devon Advertiser (thurs). STD Code 01271

## QUEEN'S THEATRE
Boutport Street, Barnstaple, Devon EX31 1SY
Mgt/Admin 01271 327357 BO 01271 324242
Fax 01271 326412
ADMINISTRATION:
Programming Director: Karen Turner
Operations Director: Tracy Davison
Resident Stage Manager: Glynn Allen
Publicity Officer: Debbie Cooke
Seats: 688
Raked Stalls plus circle.
Traditional theatre design, built 1952. Extensively renovated in 1993. Venue financed by North Devon District Council, RAB SWA, the local authority.
Policy: Varied programme of entertainment including educational and cultural events, with the emphasis on diversity and quality. Willing to premiere show.
Performance schedule: Evening performances start at 7.30-8pm. Booking terms: hire, box office split, guarantee & split, guarantee, co-production, by negotiation. Other activities exhibition,

educational projects.
Café bar, 2 licensed bars, Access car park; adjacent; railway station: 0.75 mile; coach terminal: 0.5 mile. For the disabled up to 8 wheelchair spaces - assistance available - deaf loop system - ramp - all house facilities fully accessible. Lift to all floors.
TECHNICAL:
Stage: Proscenium arch. Performing area 10.6m x 6.7m - pros opening 9.14m x 4.6m - wing widths 2.44m SR, 2.44m SL. No rake - wood floor, suitable for dance, understage crossover, stage heated. Height of grid 10.98m - 16 hemp sets. 0.45m apart, tab track - maximum flying height 5.33m - black basic masking - filled white cotton cyclorama - gold house tabs, drawn. Safety curtain.
Lighting: Gemini MK1, operated from control room at rear of stalls. 200A 3 phase 2 x CSI 1kw followspots operated from roof void.
Sound: 24:4:2 desk, operated from rear of stalls - Shure mics - Yamaha cassette. Acoustics suitable for music and spoken word.
Other: Stage management show relay to dressing rooms. Backstage 4 dressing rooms, accommodate 90, access by stage entrance. Advice given on accommodation. Staff - technician - casuals available. Backstage facilities not accessible to disabled performers and staff.

# Barrow-In-Furness

Pop: 72,635. London 278 miles. Newspapers: North Western Evening Mail (ntly); West Cumberland Advertiser (thurs). STD Code 01229

## FORUM 28
28 Duke Street, Barrow-in-Furness, Cumbria LA14 1HH
Mgt 01229 894752 BO 01229 820000
Fax 01229 894942
ADMINISTRATION:
Business Manager: Neil Ward.
Policy: Multi-purpose theatre.
Seats: 485. Licensed Bars and Restaurant.

# Basildon

Pop: 134,330. London 29 miles. Newspapers: Basildon Standard Recorder (fri); Evening Echo (ntly); Yellow Advertiser (fri). STD Code 01268

## TOWNGATE THEATRE & CONFERENCE CENTRE
St Martins Square Basildon, Essex SS14 1DW
ADMINISTRATION:
All enquiries to Basildon District Council
Tel 01268 533333  Fax 01268 294224
Two auditoriums for hire.
Seating/Capacity: Main Auditorium: 552 seated; 700 standing. Studio: 188 seated; 300 standing.
We provide facilities for Theatre, Conferences, Exhibitions, Receptions, Seminars and Private Parties.
TECHNICAL:
Please contact Basildon District Council for details.

# Basingstoke

Pop. 91,000. London 47 miles. Newspapers: Reading Post (dly); Basingstoke Gazette (mon/wed/fri). STD code 01256

## THE ANVIL

Churchill Way, Basingstoke, Hampshire RG21 7QR
Admin/SD 01256 819797 BO 01256 844244
Fax 01256 331 733
ADMINISTRATION:
Chief Executive: Christine Bradwell
Technical Manager: Simon Spearing
Two licenced bars
Cafe/bistro
Proscenium Format
Seats: 1,060 (without orchestra pit) 992 (with orchestra
pit) 6 wheelchair spaces.
TECHNICAL:
Stage: Demountable Proscenium 10 metres wide x 7
metres high, stage front to setting line 2 metres, setting
line to rear wall 9.5 metres, width at setting line 17
metres, width at rear wall 11 metres, flying height 20
metres, 8 motorised bars (500 kilo SWL), 20 hemp sets.
Four 500 kg. rigging points F.O.H. for advance truss,
flying bar lengths vary from 16m downstage to 10m
upstage.  Prompt corner D.S.L.
Lighting: Equipment: Control desk Strand Mini Light
Palette 90, dimmers 168 x 2.5kw, 12 x 5 kw, Luminaires:
12 2k profiles 9/15, 24 1.2k profiles 10/26, 16 1.2k
fresnels, 16 1.2k P.C, 60 Par cans, 4 4 x 1k cyc floods,
2 Pani followspots.
Sound: Equipment: Soundcraft venue II 32 input mixer,
Revox PR99 high speed 1/4" reel to reel tape machine,
Dennon DN 2000F twin quick start CD player, Tascam
DA30 DAT machine, Tascam 122Mk II cassette
machine, Yamaha SPX 900 multi effects processor,
Rane 1/3 octave graphic equaliser, various mics and
stands, 48 input and 12 return tie lines from
stage/control room.
Loudspeaker System: EV CD Horn & Bin Central Cluster,
with Delay covering all seats. Four large sub woofers,
Front fills.
Powered by Amron Amplifiers via Yamaha D2040.
Programmable controllers, portable loudspeakers; 2 x EV
FM1202 wedge monitors 3xEV S1503 side fill/effects
speakers, 2 x EV S200 speakers.
Other: Dressing room facilities: stage level 3 en suite
rooms and 4 with sinks, visiting managers office with
phone.  First floor level 4 rooms, laundry room and
showers.
Power supplies: Visiting lighting supply 200 amp 3 phase
U.S.L. Buss Bar, visiting sound supply 100 amp 1 phase
D.S.L. Buss Bar, 4 x 32 amp C form sockets, visiting
O.B. supply 300 amp 1 phase.
Communications: Stage Managers Desk D.S.L. c/w cue
lights, ring intercom c/w 10 x headsets and packs,
Induction Loop, 2 channel infra red system, paging &
show relay, video show relay, computer tie lines.
Get In: The get in is all at stage level via loading bay and
corridor minimum width 2.3 metres.
Auditorium: The Auditorium has a variety of different
layouts offering up to 1400 seats.
Orchestra pit: The Orchestra pit is available in the certain
format and is approx. 4 metres x 18 metres. The venue
has 80 RAT music stands.
Stage Equipment: The venue has a complete set of
black masking, half stage of royal blue masking, white
cyclorama, house tabs and cinema screen. Assorted
weights braces, and sand bags.
Film Projection Equipment:
Main Hall: Cinemeccania Victoria 5 B/5000.
35mm Dolby Stereo Film projector - With all ancillary
items.
Small Hall: Cinemeccania Portacine 35mm projector
with screen and DGB 2 x 15 Film Tower
Small Hall Sound and Lighting:

Lighting control: Strand MX 24
Dimmers: 24 x 2.5 kw
Sound: The system for the small hall incorporates 6
ceiling mounted speakers which can be independently
selected depending on the room arrangement, and the
input is derived from either cassette, CD or mics.

## HAYMARKET THEATRE

Wote Street, Basingstoke, Hampshire RG21 7NW
Mgt 01256 323073 BO 01256 465566
ADMINISTRATION:
Management Body & Theatre Lessees: Basingstoke
Theatre Trust
Theatre Director: Alasdair Ramsay
Policy: Producing theatre - up to 8 in house shows +3 or
4 visiting shows.
Season: September to June. Shows run between 1 and
4 weeks. Developing community and education
programme.
Perfs: usually 7.45p.m.
Seats: 460, Circle and Stalls, Licensed & Coffee Bars,
Theatre Restaurant.
TECHNICAL:
Stage: Pros. opening 8970 x 5000; Depth of stage 9480
Width 13200, Height of grid 10200; 29 Hemp sets, 5
Motorised bars Bar length 10000, Orchestra pit elevator
1600 x 9500.
Lighting: Control Strand 520, 180 channels. 144 x 2.5kw
EC90' 24 x 2.5kw ACT 6 temp racks. Lantern details on
application.
Sound and Communications: Soundcraft Delta DLX
24.4.2 Full details on application. Cue lights and ring
intercom. Paging to all areas.
Other: Dressing rooms: 7. 6 showers, Green room,
rehearsal room, Wardrobe and Laundry.

# Bath

Pop. 85,000. London 106 miles. Newspapers; Bath &
West Evening Chronicle (ntly); Western Daily Press (dly);
Evening Post (ntly); Keynsham Weekly Chronicle;
Chippenham News/Wiltshire Times, Somerset
Guardian/Standard, Wiltshire Gazette & Herald (wkly).
STD code 01225

## ASSEMBLY ROOMS

Bennett Street Bath BA1 2QH
Tel 01225 477000 Evenings & Weekends Emergency
Number: 01225 477789
Email: ruth_warren@bathnes.gov.uk
ADMINISTRATION:
Bath & North East Somerset  Council, Heritage Services,
Pump Room, Stall Street, Bath BA1 1LZ
Tel 01225 477782/477786 Fax 01225 477476
Seats: 529

## BATH PAVILLION

North Parade Road Bath BA2 4ET
Tel: 01225 462565 BO: 01225 312121
ADMINISTRATION:
Manager: Tim Ridley
Assistant Manager: Jenny Jacob
Cafe and Bar facilities (unspecified catering)
Seats: 1,000
TECHNICAL:
50' x 26'9" stage, (110A TP & N3 phase supply), 90' x
70' hall.

## GUILDHALL
The High Street Bath BA1 5AW
Tel 01225 477000 Evenings & Weekends Emergency
Number: 01225 477793
Email: ruth_warner@bathnes.gov.uk
ADMINISTRATION:
Bath & North East Somerset Council, Heritage Services,
Pump Room, Stall Street, Bath, BA1 1LZ
Venue Manager: Ian Burns
Tel: 01225 477782/477786 Fax: 01225 477476
Seats: 360

## MOLES CLUB
14 George Street Bath BA1 2EN
Tel/BO 01225 404445 Fax 01225 404447
Studio DL 01225 404446
ADMINISTRATION:
Prop: Philip Andrews; Studio: Jan Brown; Club: Louise
Evans.
Capacity: 175

## PUMP ROOM
Stall Street Bath BA1 1LZ
Tel 01225 477000 Evenings & Weekends Emergency
Number: 01225 477784
Email: ruth_warren@bathnes.gov.uk
ADMINISTRATION:
Bath & North East Somerset Council, Heritage Services,
Pump Room, Stall Street, Bath, BA1 1LZ.
Tel 01225 477782/477786 Fax 01225 477476
Seats: 316

## THE RONDO
St. Saviours Road, Bath BA1 6RT
Tel 01225 444003 BO 01225 448844
ADMINSTRATION:
Props: Rondo Trust for the Performing Arts
Contact: Mrs Leonard
Technical Manager: David Stevenson
Seats: 105
TECHNICAL:
Stage: 7.9m wide to tab line or 5.5m to the audience.
Height is 3.6m to tad line border, approx 4m at side
walls and 6m to ceiling for the centre 4m width of the
stage. A set of soft black borders and legs are available
for masking, and all stage walls are painted black. A
dance floor is available in black..
Lighting: supply 100 single phase. Dimmers: 5 racks
each 6#2kw & 3#1kw for house and control room
lighting. Distribution 42 patch circuits. All outlets at
ceiling height; boxes marked on plan. Desk: Arri Image.
Lanterns: 8 X Patt 743 1kw fresnel, 6 X Berkey 1kw
fresnel, 2 X Cantata PC 1kw PC, 2 X Patt 814 1kw PC, 4
X Patt 764 1kw profile, 4 X Sill 40 1.2kw profile, 4 X Patt
123 500 fresnel, 12 X Patt 23 500 fresnel, 2 X Raylight
1kw, 4 X Cycfloods 1kw, 1 X Sil 12 1kw follow spot.
Sound: 2offNAD 602 cassette, Revox B77, Philips CD
player, 12 into 4 mixer, Quad 303 and Quad 606 amps,
EV 200 speakers front of Tabs, Yamaha rear stage
speakers. Show relay: Stereo mics to control room, with
feed to dressing room. Clearcom intercom headsets 3
sets.

## THEATRE ROYAL
Sawclose St. Johns Place Bath BA1 1ET
Mgt/SD 01225 448815 BO 01225 448844
Fax 01225 444080
ADMINISTRATION:

Props: The Theatre Royal Bath Limited
Director: Danny Moar
Associate Director: Fiona Clark
Membership & Special Events Director: Ann Meddings
Finance Director: Simon Payne
General Manager: Kate Eggleston
Theatre Administrator: Kate Carrol
Stage Manager: Eugene Hibbert
Chief Electrician: Pete Minall
Policy: Touring, Opera, Ballet and Pantomime. Concerts.
Perfs: (usual) Mon-Wed 7.30; Thurs to Sat 8.00; Mats:
Wed 2.30p.m. Sat: 2.30p.m. Restaurant . Private
Catering Suite.
Seats: 950 approx. 4 fully licensed bars.
TABS - ticket selling agency for Local, National, London
Concerts.
TECHNICAL:
Stage: Proscenium stage, flat; Pros. opening 8.35m; Ht.
of pros. 7.70m; Depth of stage 13m; Ht. of Grid 18.30m;
Dist. between Fly Floors 12.6m; Ht. under Fly Floor
7.35m; O.P. 1.95m, P.S. 2.95m; X over understage.
51 Bars (c/w) tabs on Bar 3 diverted. P.Corner P/S on
perch above stage entrance.
Get-in U.S.C. from yard (dock at stage level/tailboard
Ht.)
Lighting: Control: Rank Strand Galaxy Desk with Rate
Playback, Computer back-up, Pin patch, BDU monitor &
Riggers control.
Dimmers and Circuits: Rank Strand permus dimmer inc.
House lights and independents. 174 Circuits 18 at 5kw
and 156 at 2.5kw.
Lanterns: Full permanent F.O.H. Rig of Cantata 11/26
1.2kw; Harmony 15/28 1kw; Prelude 16/30 Zoom 650w;
assorted lanterns for on stage use of P.23, P.64,
A.D.B.s, starlet 1kw fresnel and Iris 4. Full details on
application. 2 Rank Strand Solo CS1 follow spots.
Sound: Crest Century VX 20/8/3 hard wired F.O.H.
system, consisting of 2: pairs Meyers UPA1 speakers
controlled by Meyer AB200 amps and controller and 1
pair: Martin CX1 speakers controlled by a Yamaha
PC2002M amp and a Martin EX2 equaliser. On stage 2
Martin CXW speakers controlled by a Yamaha PC2002M
and a Martin EX2 equaliser. 2 Revox B77 reel to reel.
Denon DN 1000F CD. Denon twin cassette EFX unit.
Control can be from the Sound Room (situated at the
rear of the Gallery), Dress Circle or Stage. This is
serviced by a fully patchable G.P.O. jackfield. Stage
Manager's desk with full cue lights to all usual stations
plus other if required. CCTV monitor, paging R.O.H.
Prompt side operation RTS ring intercom patchable to all
salient parts of the Theatre. N.B. For use of Dress Circle
mixing, prior notice should be given.
Other: Orchestra pit rows A and B on lift with understage area. Rows C, D and E on rostra.
Dressing Rooms 12 accom. 43. M.D.'s room, 2 Band
rooms, Company Manager's office, Wardrobe, Laundry.
Other Control: Temporary 200 amp 3 phase supply
U.S.L., Temporary 100 amp 1 phase supply D.S.R.

USTINOV STUDIO
TECHNICAL:
The studio is fully air coditioned 150 seat space. It is a
non-smoking area. Flat plywood with 6mm hardboard
skin.Width 6.83m Depth S/L 6.39m S/R 7.13m. dreesing
rooms X 2, each with 4 stations and ensuite WC and
shower. Control area at the rear of auditorium on
mezzanine area. Open plan. Option to operate via
facilities panels on stage with prior notice at rear of
auditorium.
Sound: Soundcraft Spirit * 16/4/2/8/2, 2 X Meyer AB
amps, 2 X Martin EM75 plus controller (fixed position)

speakers, 2 X Sherman SH1 (foldback) speakers, 1 X tascam reel to reel (quarter inch), 1 X Teac twin cassette deck, 3 X dynamic mics., 3 X boom stands, 2 X C747 conference style mics (for hire POA), patching is performed via a GPO jackfield located in the control room.
Lighting: Strand LBX console, Strand LBX colour monitor, Strand GSX 75 channel genius software, LD90 dimmer racks 72 ways by 2.5k. Luminaries: 18 X Cantata F, 4 X Cantata PC, 10 X Prelude 16/30, 6 X Prelude 28/40, 1 X Cantata follow spot, 2 X Thomas "Howie Batten".
General: 1 X Stage management desk, 4 X belt packs, 4 X headsets.

# Bedworth

Pop. 40,000 London 99 miles. Newspapers: Tribune (thurs); Coventry Evening Telegraph. STD code 01203

## CIVIC HALL IN BEDWORTH
High Street, Bedworth, Warwickshire CV12 8NF
Mgt 01203 376705 BO 01203 376707
Fax 01203 376730
ADMINISTRATION:
Props: Nuneaton & Bedworth Borough Council
Entertainments & Civic Hall Manager: David Matthews
Policy: Multi-purpose.
Perfs: Variable.
Seats: 813 approx. Bar, Coffee Bar, Small Hall and Meeting Rooms.
TECHNICAL:
Stage: Multi-purpose Proscenium Stage, Flat; Pros. opening 12.19m maximum (variable); Ht. of Pros. 6.10m (adjustable); Stage Depth 7.62m; Ht. of Grid 7.92m; total Stage Width 22.86m.
Lighting: Control: Tempus M24 + Tempus M24 FX. 72 - 2KW Dimmers Bar 1 F.O.H. 12 Cantata Spots, 4 with colour change. F.O.H. Bridge; 8 Cantata PC's, 2 Cantata Spot, 2 Harmony Spot. 8 Par's. Three-Spot Bars on stage. 22 Cantata Fresnals, 12 Prelude F. 12 Prelude Spots 2 Harmony F. Coda/4 Batten, Coda/4 Groundrow. 4 Nocturne 1000W Floods. 2 1000W C.S.I. Follow Spots.
Sound Equip: 16.4.2. Allan Heath Mixer, bose 802, 302 Speakers, Fold Back Tape; Revox 77A Stereo. Sony, Sharp & Aiwa Cassotte Tape Decks. Technics Turntable SL-D202. Mics. - A.K.G.
Other: Film: Elk, Xenon Ex 5000 Projector 16mm. Fumeo 1000 16mm Projector.

# Belfast

Pop. 500,000 Newspapers: Irish News (dly); News Letter (dly); Belfast Telegraph (dly). STD code 01232

## BELFAST CIVIC ARTS THEATRE
41 Botanic Avenue, Belfast BT7 1JG
Mgt 01232 316901 BO 01232 316900
Fax 01232 316906
ADMINISTRATION:
Props: Belfast Civic Arts Theatre Ltd
Administrator: Anthony Stott
Deputy Administrator: Hilary Branson
Technician: Roger Hewitt
Policy: Mixed programme - own productions, including pantomime, touring, variety, dance, amateur musicals, children's shows.

Perfs: Normally Mon - Sat 8.00 pm, frequent Sunday shows.
Seats: 549. Bar and Coffee shop.
TECHNICAL:
Stage: Proscenium Stage with apron. Extensions to apron available. Performing area 8.04m x 8.23m. Pros. opening 8.23m x 4.12m. Wing widths: SL 1.52m, SR 3.64m. Fixed rig at 5.16m downstage to 4.25m upstage. No rake - floor plywood over concrete, crossover via Dressing Rooms - 2 tab tracks - various masking available - house curtain drawn - get in via stairs, get in doors 2.07m x 1.28m. No tallescope. Scale stage and lighting plans available.
Lighting: 120 channels at 2.5kw, 12 channels at 5kw, 1 x Gemini 2 + desk, 10 x 24/4 quartet, 8 x Scrollers, 8 x 32/4 Cantata, 10 x Harmony 15/28, 6 x Silhouette 90, 2 x Silhouette 30, 8 x Harmony pc, 40 x par 64, 10 x Prelude, 10 x Coda, 6 x Starlette, 6 x patt 23, 6 x patt 743.
Sound: 1 x Allen and Heath 32/8/2 live desk. Mic system consisting of 6 channels comprising 4 separate lapels and 2 handheld or lapel. 4 x 4 Ashley graphic EQ, 2 x Bi-amp DL2 Delay, 1 x Ashley Parmetic EQ, 1 x Sabine 701 feedback eliminator. 2 x Ashley comp/limiter, 1 x Ashley 4 channel noise gate, 1 x Yamaha SPX1000, 1 x Yamaha SPX990, 1 x Alesis Quadraverb, 2 x Tascam 112 cassette, 1 x Tascam Da30 DAT. Denon Pro cd player, inductive loop system. 4 x RS220 speakers, 2 x 2 x 18' Bass speakers, 4 x RS JR speakers, 2 x RS220 controller, 2 x RS JR controller, 6 x CSX 38M Wedge monitors. 1 x 8001 Crest amp, 2 x PT1800 Carver power amp, 4 x PM1400 Carver power amp, 3 x Crown PCC 160 mics, 6 x BSS DI boxes, 8 x SM58 mics, 4 x SM57 mics, 4 x SE300 Power modules and Cardioid heads, 2 x Shotgun heads, 6 x Rat stands.

## BELFAST WATERFRONT HALL CONFERENCE & CONCERT CENTRE
2 Lanyon Place Belfast BT1 3WH Northern Ireland
Tel 01232 334400 Fax 01232 334467
Email: kylea@waterfront.co.uk
Web Site: www.waterfront.co.uk
The Belfast Waterfront Hall is designed as a multi-functional venue offering state fo the art facilities for all required uses. Comprises two halls - a main auditorium seating from 450 to 2,235 and the studio seating up to 500.
Contact: Janice Crowe

## GRAND OPERA HOUSE
Great Victoria Street, Belfast BT2 7HR
Mgt/SD 01232 240411 BO 01232 241919
Fax 01232 236842 BO Fax 01232 329606
Web Site: www.gohbelfast.com
ADMINISTRATION:
Theatre Director: Derek Nicholls
Marketing Manager: Mary Trainor
Acting Technical Manager: Anne Muldoon
Policy: No. 1 Touring plus some local productions - Drama, Opera, Ballet, Musicals, Celebrity Shows and Variety, Concerts and Recitals, Pantomime, Children's Shows.
Perfs: Normally Mon to Sat 7.45. Mats. variable. Occasionally twice nightly.
Seats: 1,001 on three levels. Three licensed bars.
TECHNICAL:
Stage: Proscenium Stage, Raked 1:20; Pros. Opening 12.10m, Ht. of Pros. 7.47m; Stage Width; from Centreline, S.L. 9.45m, S.R. 9.45m; Wing Widths; S.L.3.43m, S.R. 3.43m; Depth of Stage: Rear of Pros. to

back wall 13.11m. Forestage and Orchestra lift 4.04m; Ht. to underside of grid: Up-stage 17.99m, Downstage 18.60m; to under fly floors (clear) Upstage 7.32m, Downstage 7.62m; Scenery flying ht. 9.00m; Flying System; 50 sets double purchase counterweights at 0.20m centres. Last line 11.43m from tabs; Bar capacity 380kg; Counterweight Bars 14.63m long, except first three sets 12.80m long; House tabs hand operated from fly floor P.S.; Prompt Cnr; P.S. Storage S.L. 35.3sq.m., S.R. 35.3sq.m. Get-in: Street level O.P; Dock Doors 2.45m wide 5.49m high.

Lighting: Control: Strand Gemini +2. Location: Control Room rear of Gallery R. Dimmer Ways: 120 x 16A  24 x 32A (18 Stage 6 FOH) All Strand EC90

Lanterns: FOH: 16 x Cadenza 9/15 2K (Bridge), 3 x Sil 15, 3 x Sil 10 (each side), 2 x Cantata 18/32 (each side); No.1 Spot Bar: Prewired 16 circuits (normally 16 x 743 1K). Other equipment list available on request.

Sound: Space for mixer desk can be reserved rear stalls.

Other: Artistes' Accommodation: 18 Dressing Rooms accommodate 58 artistes on 3 floors above stage level; 16 Showers, 1 Conductor's Room; 1 Bandroom; Green Room.

Orchestra Accommodation: 60 players.

## GROUP THEATRE
Bedford Street, Belfast BT2 7FF
Tel 01232 323900 Fax 01232 247199
ADMINISTRATION:
Props: Belfast City Council
Administrator: Pat Falls
Stage Technician: Mr P Byrne
Policy: Productions by both professional and amateur companies. Available for hire.
Perfs: Normally Wed-Sat. (incl.)
Seats: 240 (incl. 67 balcony). Refreshment Bar.
TECHNICAL:
Stage: Pros. Stage Width 5.8m plus false pros. add 1.07m; Ht. 3.7m; Depth curtain to back wall 4.8m; Grid Ht. 3.8m; 12 lines Hemp; 3 lines wire. Fly Bars 7m; Fly Tower Ht. 7.4m. 1m stage apron.
Lighting: Switchboard: Strand Tempus 24, 24 2kw circuits; 30 ways, Stage; 1 cyc flood bar 6 ways, 1 spot bar 8 ways; 6 wall socket. F.O.H. 16 spots: Equipment - sufficient for most productions. Separate 6-way board for lunch-time productions.
Sound: House music and sound effects. Amp and decks. Betamax and VHS video recording equipment installed.
Other: Dressing Rooms 3.

## KING'S HALL
Lisburn Road, Balmoral, Belfast, BT9 6GW
Northern Ireland
Tel 01232 665225 Fax 01232 661264
Email: www.kingshall.co.uk
Web Site: www.ruas.co.uk
ADMINISTRATION:
Commercial Director: Philip Rees
Also contains Balmoral Conference Centre.
Contact: Lucy Moore
Seats: 600

## LYRIC THEATRE
55 Ridgeway Street, Belfast BT9 5FB
Mgt 01232 669660/669463 BO 01232 381081
Fax 01232 381395
ADMINISTRATION:
Props: Lyric Players Theatre Trust

Artistic Director: David Grant
Administrator: Patricia McBride
Policy: Subsidised Repertory.
Perfs: 8.00p.m. Monday to Saturday (inclusive). Matinees and Sunday performances optional.
Seats: 304. One Bar, Coffee Bar.
TECHNICAL:
Stage: Semi-thrust, performing area 12m x 7.11m (plus apron of 1.83m). Pros opening 11.28m x 5.49m. No rake - floor wood, backstage crossover, stage heated, height of grid 5.49m - hemp sets; tab track - various masking available. Forestage 11.28m x 1.83m. Get-in via scene dock SR. No tallescope. Moveable scaff tower plus extension ladders. Scale stage and lighting plans available.
Lighting: Rank Strand Gemini Board; FX panel and disc facility; 108 circuits @ 2K each; board operated from rear of auditorium - various silhouettes, starlettes Patt 743, minuettes; Harmony PCs, Patts 123s, 223s, Parcans etc. available.
Sound: Operated from lighting control box. 2 x Quad 405 stereo amps @ 100W each; 2 x mono Audix amps @ 50W each; 2 x FOH speakers (fixed); 2 x onstage spakers; 2 x Aud speakers, 2 x Revox B.77 reel-to-reel tape decks; 1 x Tascam CD, cassette and DAT; 1 x Seck 18/8/2 mixing desk. 1 x CD player.
Stage Management: Prompt corner SL - cuelights, intercom - show relay and tannoy to dressing rooms.
Other: Backstage: 2 x dressing-rooms; one on ground-floor, one upstairs - green room, quick change room, wardrobe at top of building with irons, sewing machines, washing machine in scene dock SR. Limited kitchen facilities available.
Rehearsal room and piano. Advice given on accommodation.
Staff: 4 Stage Management, 2 Technical; casual labour available.
Most backstage facilities accessible to disabled performers and staff.

## QUEEN'S UNIVERSITY CONCERT HALLS
College Park, Belfast BT7 1NN Northern Ireland
Tel 01232 273075 Fax 01232 319943
Seating/Capacity: Whitla Hall 1,250; Harty Room: 250
Contact: Elizabeth Moore

## ULSTER HALL
Bedford Street, Belfast, BT2 7FF Northern Ireland
Tel 01232 323900 Fax 01232 247199
ADMINISTRATION:
Props: Belfast City Council
Administrator: Pat Falls
Stage Technician: Mr. P Byrne
Policy: For Hire
Seats/Capacity: FOH Ground Floor (removable) 824; Balcony 446; Rear stage 309; Choir 143 (removable).
TECHNICAL:
Open Half-moon stage 38ft wide, 23ft depth, 5ft height, 24 channel overhead plus FOH lights and followspots, 6 channel 2.5kw P.A. Mulholland Grand Organ.

# Bexhill-on-Sea
Pop. 40,000. London 65 miles. Newspapers: Bexhill News (wed). STD code 01424

## DE LA WARR PAVILION
Marina, Bexhill-on-Sea, East Sussex TN40 1DP
Mgt 01424 787900 BO 01424 787949

SD 01424 787923 Fax 01424 787940
ADMINISTRATION:
Props: Rother District Council
General Manager: Caroline Collier
Assistant Manager: Linda Lewis
Senior Technician: Tony Williams
Policy: Plays, Conferences, Concerts, Ballet, Opera,
Festivals, Dancing, Variety, One Night Stands, Orchestra
etc.
Perfs: As required.
Seats: 1,016 Lounge and Theatre Bars, Café and Party
Catering.
TECHNICAL:
Stage: Proscenium Stage and Large Apron, Flat floor;
Pros opening 28'; Ht. of Pros. 14', Depth of Apron 8'6"
and removable 3' extension. Depth from setting line to
cyc - 28'. 16 Hemp Set; Flying Ht. 20'; Flying Bars width
30'.
Lighting: Switchboard: Lee Colortran Prestige 1000
located in lighting box at rear of balcony. Lee Colourtran
Status 24/48 located in S.M. Corner. F.O.H. Spots: 8
Windsor 11-26 Profile (1KW), 4CCT Sil 15 (1KW),
Advance Bar: 6 743 Fresnels (1KW), 4 Windsor 24-48
Profiles (1KW). On stage no.1 bar: 8 743 Fresnels (1KW);
On stage no.2 bar: 6 743 Fresnels (1KW); Cyc Bar: 6
1KW Iris Floods; Side lighting FOH 4 1kw Parcan,
Downstage 4 1KW Parcan, Midstage 4 1KW Parcan.
Followspots: 2 Lycian Followspots with integral 6
colourchangers. (In Lighting Box); Additional Lamps 6
Minim PC (500W); Various additional floods, Stands etc.
Sound: Seck 12 into 8 Studio Mixer; Twin Channel 10
Band Graphic Equaliser; Stereo 400W MOS - FET
Amplifier; 4 x 150W Celestion Speakers FOH. Show relay
talkback to six stations.
Other: Dressing Rooms 7; Accom: 60; Orchestra Pit 20.

# Biggar

### BIGGAR PUPPET THEATRE
Broughton Road, Biggar, Lanarkshire
ML12 6HA Scotland
Mgmt: 01899 220521 Box Office: 01899 220631
Fax: 01899 220750
ADMINISTRATION:
Props: Jill Purves, Company Director
Policy: Pantomime, plays, private hiring by negotiation.
Craft fairs, receptions, film, educational projects, in-
service courses, workshops and youth theatre.
Performances: Variable
Facilities: Up to 10 wheelchair spaces, deaf loop system,
assistance available parking - level acces, special toilet -
all house facilities fully accessible.
TECHNICAL:
Proscenium arch. Performing area 6.5m x 4m - pros
opening 4m x 2.5m - wing widths 1m SR, 1m SL. No
rake - floor wood sections, suitable for all dance, lino
available, backstage crossover, stage heated. Height
grid 7.5m - 10 hemp seats, 20cm apart - tab track -
100kg permitted on bars - maximum flying height 4.2m -
black velvet legs and traverse - back wall used as
cyclorama - red velvet house tabs, drawn. Seven 13
amp sockets. Traps in centre of stage. Get-in via rear of
side entrances, 2 steps up, large double doors. Scale
stage, fly and light plans available.
Lighting: Strand Tempus 12 board, 12 circuits, operated
from back-stage or rear of auditorium - no supply
available for temporary board. 12 lanterns.
Sound: Operated from various positions. Music by
arrangement - Revox B7 reel-to-reel; cassette tape

systems - small recording studio. Ascoustics suitable for
music and spoken word.

# Billingham

Pop. 35,900. London 240 miles. Newspapers: Evening
Gazette; Northern Echo (dly). STD code 01642

### FORUM THEATRE
Town Centre, Billingham, Cleveland TS23 2LJ
Mgt 01642 551389 BO 01642 552663
SD 01642 551380 Fax 01642 360656
ADMINISTRATION:
Props: Riverside Leisure  Promotions Ltd
Theatre Manager: Terry Gleave
Theatre House Manager: Dee Hall
Stage Manager: Eric Dunning
Policy: Mixed Programme - touring, Opera, Ballet,
Pantomime, Concerts, Films.
Perfs: 8.00 Evenings. 2.30 Matinee (Saturdays)
Seats: 619 + 4 wheelchair positions. Bar, Cafeteria.
TECHNICAL:
Stage: Proscenium Stage: Width (across upstage edge
of proscenium) 13.41m; Max. working Ht. of opening
5.79m (tabs), 7.01m(pros) Stage Depth U/S Proscenium
edge right to back wall of stage 11.73m; U/S
Proscenium line to front of stage at centre 0.53m; Apron
3.27m; Forestage 5.41m.
Stage Width: Centre line of Proscenium opening to stage
wall left U/S 10.55m, D/S 10.55m; Centre line of
Proscenium opening to stage wall right U/S 10.55m, D/S
10.55m; Width between fly rails 17.05m; Height Pros.
opening 7.01m; Stage Floor to underside of Grid
17.37m; Clear working height under fly gallery stage left
7.01m (min) 8.23m(max); Clear working height under fly
gallery stage right 7.92m; Clear working height under
stage 2.48m. Stage Floor: Rake of stage none; Area of
orchestra pit 31.59 sq.m; Surfacing material Canadian
Maple covered in hardboard, painted dark grey. Stage
front to orchestra pit rail 2.74m (max) 1.52m (min); Stage
level to orchestra pit floor 1.47m; Orchestra pit floor to
front stalls floor 0.51m.
Flying: 13 Hemp sets spotted at variable centres; 1
Single purchase C/W set (house tabs); 23 Double
purchase C/W sets spotted at various centres (including
permanent framed cyc.); length of C/W bars
15.24m.Get-In: Dock space back wall and P.S. nil; Dock
space O.P. 80.8sq.m.
Height of stage above street 0.15m; Access for scenery;
Dock doors in cul-de-sac at rear of theatre.
Lighting: Control: Main board Rank Strand Tempus M24,
199 memories, 118 circuits, back up board Rank Strand
Threeset.
Circuits: F.O.H. 40 (plus 4 cloat circuits. Float not
installed); Fly Floor P.S. 34 (including 4 circuits Paired
across); Fly Floor O.P. 30; Dips P.S. 11 (including 8
circuits paired across); Dips O.P. 11.
Equipment: 2 Patt. 243 (plus barn doors); 36 Patt. 223
(plus barn doors); 16 Patt T64; 30 Patt.264; 18 Patt. 23
(+ 2 x 'N' Lenses); 10 Patt 123 (plus barn doors); 2 CCT
1000W C.S.I. follow spots; 16 Nocturn 1000; 24 Patt 60;
4 Patt. 49; 4 x 4 circuit 1.83m lengths groundrow; 4 x 4
circuit 1.83m lengths batten. Basic Rig: F.O.H. 8 Patt.
264 + 3 Patt. T64 per side upper circle; 4 Patt. 264 each
side prosc. boom. No. 1 spot bar:- 16 Patt.223.
Sound: For full technical specifications available from
stage manager.
Other: Accommodation: 9 Dressing Rooms each
capable of taking 3 artistes if necessary; 3 Chorus
dressing rooms. Showers in 8 main dressing rooms plus

1 each in ladies and gents toilets.
Membership: TMA

# Birkenhead

Pop. 15,743. London 200 miles. Newpapers: Daily Post;
Liverpool Echo (ntly); Wirral Globe (wkly); Wirral
Newspapers (free). STD code 0151

## GLENDA JACKSON THEATRE

Borough Road, Birkenhead, Wirral Merseyside L42 9QD
ADMINISTRATION:
Props: Wirral Metropolitan College
Contact: Sally Boyd (0151 551 7630)
Seating: 494 raked circle; retractable raked stalls.
TECHNICAL:
Stage: Proscenium arch. Performing area 9m x 7.4m -
pros opening 9m x 5.8m - wing widths 4.2m SR, 4.2m
SL, 1.2m US, no rake - floor sprung wood, suitable for
dance, dance floor available, backstage crossover,
height of grid 14m - 12 hemp sets, 0.23m apart - 3 x
winched LX bars - cable track - 250kg permitted on bars
- maximum flying height 13.5m - full set legs, tabs and
borders available in grey - seamless white sharkstooth
cyclorama - maroon house tabs, flown or drawn.
Forestage 9m x 1.5m fixed, entrances via stalls SR & SL,
8.2m x 2.3m removable, entrances via foyer and rear R &
L. Orchestra pit in lieu or part or all of apron. Get-in via
dock doors from loading bay UL stage level, 2.25m x
2.4m. Safety curtain. Scale stage, fly and lighting plans
available. Stage Management - Prompt corner SL (desk
mobile) - show relay to dressing rooms.
Lighting: Strand M24 board, 60 channel, 155 memories
plus M24 FX control, 3 phase, operated from booth at
rear of circle.  Good stock of Lanterns.
Sound: Studio Master Proline Gold 16:4:2 mixer, 2 x
DATS (Sony DTC D3 and TDC P7).  2 x Tape decks
(Yamaha K350 and Hitachi D305), 2 Track Revox B77, 8
Track Fostex A80, CD - AIWA, Dynamic processor,
digital multi-processor, 8 x Bose 802, 2 x H/H MX500
amps ZYDEC monitor, 7 x Shure SM58, 7 x Sennheiser
KU3, 1 x Shure prologue I4L, 1 x AKG D900E.
Other: Backstage: 2 Dressing Rooms, USL via loading
bay scene dock - irons, Sewing machines, Rehearsal
piano, Roland electric. Advice given on accommodation.
Staff - Technical Manager - no casuals or security
personnel. Backstage facilities not accessible to disabled
performers and staff.
Other Facilities: Exhibition space/social function are in
lieu of stalls seating area if seats retracted.
Disabled: 14 wheelchair spaces available by
arrangement (by removing row A of stalls).  All house
facilities except circle accessible.  26 seats.

# Birmingham

Pop. 1,076,760. London 110 miles. Newspapers:
Birmingham Evening Mail (ntly); The Birmingham Post
(dly); Metro News (dly). STD code 0121

## ALEXANDRA THEATRE

Station Street, Birmingham B5 4DS
Mgt 0121 643 5536 BO 0870 607 7544 Group
Bookings Line 0121 643 3168 SD 0121 644 5235
Fax 0121 632 6841
ADMINISTRATION:
Props: Apollo Leisure Group PLC
For all booking information and further details please

contact Sam Shrouder or Nicky Monk at Apollo Leisure
(UK) Ltd., Grehan House, Garsington Road, Cowley,
Oxford OX4 5NQ. Tel: 01865 782900; Fax: Oxford
01865 782910.
Managing Director: Paul Gregg
General Manager: Charlie Ingham
Technical Manager: Andy Thomas
Chief Electrician: Pete Evans
Seats: 1,347
TECHNICAL:
Stage: Proscenium Stage, raked .03m to .91m; Pros.
opening 11.99m; Ht. of Pros. 5.46m to Tabs; Depth of
S/Line 8.84m; Ht. of Grid 16m; 52 counterweights (max.
550lbs each); Scenery Flying Ht. 16.00m; W/Widths P.S.
5.49m, O.P. 4.27m; Prompt Cnr. P.S. S/L.
Lighting: Switchboard: Arri Mk1 "Imagine" 250. 120
ways F.O.H. Rig: Balcony front: 18 Strand 'Cantata'
1200w. 18/32 profiles. 6 'Cantata' 11/26, Circle front: 2
x 243 tab warmers.Follow Spots: 2 x Teatro "Talento"
1200w MSR.
Additional Equipment: 6 x 12 way 20 foot IWB,
terminating in 2 Socapex per bar. 4 x 15m Socapex
multis with plug and socket spiders. 8 x 20m Socapex
multis with plug spider only. FOH advance bar position
over orchestra pit, with five 500kg suspension points and
girder clamps.
Stage Luminaires: 12 x Strand "Cantata F" 1200w
fresnels.  12 x Strand "Cantata PC" 1200w fresnels.  6 x
Strand "Prelude" 650w 28/40 profiles.  20 x 240v Long
Nose PAR 64 CP 62. 10 x "Nocturne" 1k floods.
Sound Equip: Permanent Sound Installation: Allen and
Heath SC plus 12 channel sound mixer situated in
control room in rear stalls. 2 x Revox B77's. 1 x Dennon
twin cassette machine. 14 x Bose 802 in house
speakers, 2 x JBL 6/31 wedge stage monitor speakers.
Citronic amplifiers and graphic equalizers. Yamaha SPX
900 effects processor.
Other: Dressing Rooms 11; Accom. 80; Orchestra Pit
adaptable 7 - 30.
Get-in scissor lift to stage level from street, width 2.26m.
Membership: TMA

## ASTON UNIVERSITY

Students Guild, Aston University, The Triangle,
Birmingham B4 7ES
Tel 0121 359 6531 Fax 0121 333 4218
Entertainments Manager: Martin Colvin
City Centre venue. Hall with stage and capacity of 940

## BIRMINGHAM HIPPODROME

Hurst Street, Birmingham B5 4TB
Mgt 0121 622 7437 BO 0121 689 3000
SD 0121 689 3100 Fax 0121 622 5518 (Mgt)
0121 689 3154 (Tech) Fax 0121 622 6506 (BO)
ADMINISTRATION:
Props: Birmingham Hippodrome Theatre Trust Ltd
Theatre Director: Peter Tod
Head of Sales: Paul Steeples
Theatre Accountant: James Prescott
Theatre Manager: Barry Hopson
Stage Director: Tony Guest
Policy: Touring, Variety, Opera, Ballet, Musicals,
Pantomime and Concerts.
Perfs: As required.
Seats: 1,887; 1,792 Ballet & Opera. Two large bars and
The Leith Restaurant.
TECHNICAL:
Stage: Proscenium Stage: Flat: Lino (covered) Black.
Pros opening 12.79m. Ht. of Pros 8.10m. Depth to
setting line 18.60m. Overall stage depth 20.39m.

Maximum stage depth using forestage 22.42m. Height of grid 22.00m. Flying system comprises of 81 C/W sets, consisting of 75 S/P max. load 500kg and 6 D/P max. load 250kgs. Length of C/W barrels 18.28m. O/D 60mm. Dual get-in of 1 Hymo scissor lift SWL 3000kgs and 1 aluminium ramp SWL not known. Get in point 2.80m above stage level. Prompt corner is stage left.
Lighting: Control is by 240 way Eurolight Ovation with 240 way Applause back-up. 240 dimmers comprising 182 x 2kw, 58 x 5kw. 10 x independent relays. 56 x 1.2kw Cantata front of house. 2 x 2kw Xenon ColorArc follow spots. Working light is area programmable and switchable from prompt desk. Full specification on request.
Sound equipment: No mixer desk available. Sound mixing position is centre rear stalls in lounge area with access to stage via crawl through duct for multicores. A comprehensive and reliable tie line system exists including radio mic aerial links from rear stalls to balcony front and stage. Delay system consists of 2 rows in stalls - 7 x ProAcc Tablette II under front of balcony and 8 x ProAcc Tablette II under rear of balcony. Circle - 5 x JBL cabaret half way up circle and 6 x ProAcc Tablette II at rear of circle. Also 1 x Revox B77 mk II. Full specification on request from Tony Guest.
Other: Dressing Rooms: 17, accommodation for 140 artists, also includes Green Room with vending machines, Company Managers Office, Dressers Room, Laundry and Wardrobe. Backstage canteen.
Orchestra Rooms: 3 with accommodation for 70 musicians.
Membership: TMA
The Birmingham Hippodrome is the home base of The Birmingham Royal Ballet (Tel.No. 0121-622 2555).

## BIRMINGHAM REPERTORY THEATRE
Broad Street, Birmingham B1 2EP
Mgt 0121 236 6771  BO 0121 236 4455
SD 0121 236 6771  Fax 0121 236 7883
ADMINISTRATION:
Props: Birmingham Repertory Theatre Ltd
Artistic Director: Bill Alexander
Executive Producer: John Stalker
Project Manager: Ros Robins
Production Manager: John Pitt
Policy: Repertory
Perfs: Variable
Seats: 898. Cafe Bar/ Brasserie, Four Licensed Bars.
TECHNICAL:
Stage: Proscenium Stage, Flat; Pros. Opening 15m; Ht. of Pros. 8m; Depth of S/Line 15m; Ht. of Grid 23m; Fly 56 C/W sets, Flying Bars 17m; W/Widths P.S. US 4m, DS 10m, O.P. 3.2m DS 6m.
Lighting: Switchboard: Rank Strand Galaxy 3, 216 x 2.5kw dimmers, 48 x 5kw dimmers, spots various including 2 Teatro 1200W followspots, Dips, Spot Bars variable.
Other: Dressing Rooms: 10 plus 2 chorus, accommodation 60; Bathrooms 9; Orchestra Pit 15.

Studio Theatre: Seats 119/140, variable staging.
Lighting: Strand 430 Consul 40 x 2.5kw Dimmers, Spots variable; Sound: Allen and Heath 8 x 4 desk.
Membership: TMA, NCA

## BIRMINGHAM TOWER BALLROOM
Reservoir Road, Edgbaston, Birmingham,
West Midlands B16 9EE
Tel 0121 454 0107  BO 0121 455 7282
Fax 0121 455 9313

ADMINISTRATION:
Manager: Miss Susan Price
Capacity: 1,200
Policy: Multi-purpose venue, suitable for concerts, shows, conferences, exhibitions, dinner dances, etc. Fully licensed with car parking facilities for up to 400 cars.

## BIRMINGHAM TOWN HALL
Victoria Square, Birmingham B3 3DQ
Tel 0121 605 5116 Fax 0121 605 5121
Closed until Summer 1999. For enquiries please write to the above address or call the appropriate telephone or fax number.

## CRESCENT THEATRE
Sheepcote Street, Brindleyplace, Birmingham B16 8AE
Mgt/Admin 0121 643 5859 BO 0121 643 5858
Fax 0121 643 5860
ADMINISTRATION:
General Manager: Jacqueline Green
Administrator: Paul Cooper
Policy: The Crescent Theatre Company stages a wide variety of productions each season, including studio and touring shows, in addition to approximately 10 main productions each year. The Theatre is available for hire by touring groups, conference organisers and others.
Seats: 342
Studio Theatre Max. Cap:120.
TECHNICAL:
For full technical details apply to the Theatre.

## THE DOME II
Horse Fair, Birmingham B1 1DB
Tel 0121 622 2233 Fax 0121 622 2310
General Manager: John Bunce
Entertainments Manager: Pete Sherriff
No 1 UK discoteque also available for private hire.
Capacity: 2,850

## MAC - THE CENTRE FOR BIRMINGHAM
(Midlands Arts Centre), Cannon Hill Park, Birmingham B12 9QH
Admin 0121 440 4221 BO 0121 440 3838
Fax 0121 446 4372
ADMINISTRATION:
Props: Midlands Arts Centre
Director: Dorothy Wilson
Marketing Manager: Shirley Kirk
General Manager: Jaki Booth
Technical Manager: Sebastian Barnes
Policy: Concerts, Films, Visiting Companies, Festivals, Professional Music, Theatre, Literature Events, Education Programmes, Exhibitions.
Perfs: Various, 10.30, 13.00, 14.30, 20.00, 22.30.
Seating: the Theatre: 202 (The Theatre can be adapted to suit particular type of play.); the Hexagon: 86; the Open Air Arena Theatre: 470; the Cinema: 146.
Dressing Rooms: the Theatre: 2, the Hexagon: 2; Showers.
Cafe and Bar.
Membership: TMA

## NATIONAL INDOOR ARENA (NIA)
King Edwards Road, Birmingham B1 2AA
Mgt 0121 200 2202 BO 0121 200 2222
Fax 0121 643 5663

ADMINISTRATION:
Manager: Terry Colton
Bookings Contacts: Terry Colton (General), Richard Callicott and Sally Prudhoe (Sporting Events).
Seats: 13,412

## NEC ARENA
National Exhibition Centre, Birmingham B40 1NT
Tel 0121 605 4141 Fax 0121 767 3850
BO: 0121 780 4133
Director of Arenas: Linda Barrow
Seating Capacity: 12,386: Demountable.

## THE OLD REP THEATRE, BIRMINGHAM
Station Street, Birmingham B5 4DY
Mgt/Admin 0121 605 5116 Fax 0121 605 5121
SD 0121 605 5117 BO 0121 236 5622
ADMINISTRATION:
Manager: Theresa Janssen
378 seat theatre staging professional and amateur theatre productions, stand-up comedy, dance productions and small concerts. Also home to the resident professional theatre company 'Birmingham Stage Company.

## RONNIE SCOTT'S
258 Broad Street, Birmingham B1 2HF
Tel: 0121 454 7020
Managing Director: Barry Sherwin
Marketing Director: Jim Simpson Tel 0121 454 7020
Capacity: 300

## SYMPHONY HALL
International Convention Centre, Broad Street, Birmingham B1 2EA
Mgt 0121 299 2999 BO 0121 212 3333
Fax 0121 212 1982
ADMINISTRATION:
Prop: National Exhibition Centre Ltd.
Director, Symphony Hall: Andrew Jowett
Technical Manager: Michael Rye
Operations Manager: Chris Baldock
Marketing Manager: Mary Coles
Development Manager: Philippa Sherwood
Box Office, ICC: John Finn.
Policy: Broad and varied programme including British and overseas orchestras, solo recitals, contemporary and early music, semi-staged opera, pop, jazz, choral concerts, folk, cabaret, conferences and lectures. CBSO, resident orchestra.
Seating/Capacity: 2,260 on 4 levels, including choir.
Perfs: Normally 7.30 or 8.00pm, matinees as required. Coffee terrace, bar area on each foyer level, shop/sales area. Facilities for people with disabilities including easy access, toilets and infra-red hearing system.
TECHNICAL:
Stage: Semi-circular concert platform, 23m wide x 15m deep. With pit lift raised, depth increased to 18m. Platform height 1.2m. Orchestra/choir risers on air castors for use as required (in left/right and upper/lower sections). No rake - timber floor, suitable for dance.
Access: Flat access to platform area via loading door 8m wide x 4.5m high. Covered loading bay area approx. 24m long, 8m wide, 4.5m high.
Suspension: Approx. 90% of platform covered by movable acoustic canopy, containing dedicated concert lighting (N.B. cannot tilt). Around and to the rear of the canopy provision for point hoists and curved bar set for

masking drapes. Ceiling height 18.75m above platform level. Point hoists can be rigged by ICC staff at various points in auditorium ceiling. Rigging plan available.
Lighting: Concert - Dedicated permanent lighting rig mounted in canopy and ceiling around it, independent of main production lighting. Stage - Arri imagine 250 control with 400 cue capacity, rigging controls, designers remote, full tracking backup. By prior arrangement control can be exchanged for either a Celco 90 Gold with Connexions soft patch to 512 circuits or a Celco 60 major with Connexions soft patch to 512 circuits. Circuits: 222 x 2.5kw and 8 x 5kw. Luminaires: 24 x 2kw profile spots, 30 x 2kw Fresnel PC spots; 12 x 1kw profile spots; 42 x 1kw Lekolites 48 x Par.64; 2 x 2.5kw HMI follow spots and 2 x 1.2kw HMI spots. Full circuit layout and standard rig drawing available.
Sound: Acoustic adjustments within the auditorium rely on physical means and no electronics are used. Reverberation chambers behind auditorium walls contain a volume of approx. 37% of the hall itself. The reverberation time is adjusted by a series of hydraulically operated doors opening onto the chambers. Acoustic banners and curtains can reduce reverberance. Acoustics suitable for live music and amplified sound. Amplification: 3 suspended loudspeaker array's, one central within the acoustic canopy and one on each side of the front of the canopy. All units d + b audiotechnik 402 - 1200A amps 10k. Additional d + b 402 - 1200A amps ground fill 5k. sound consoles; DDA D series 24:8:8 in control room; DDA D series 40:8:8 in FOH cockpit; DDA D series 36:8 foldback console. Cockpit desk can be removed to accommodate artists' own equipment. All consoles supported by comprehensive effect racks. Cassette and open reel tape record/replay facilities available including 4 track open reel and 3 track cassette for AV plus CD player. DAT digital tape recorder/player and record turntable. Comprehensive stock of microphones.
Communications: Hall and foyers covered by main ICC PA system divided into zones as required. Telecommunication and Datacom circuits available. Radio communication system with dialling access to and from telephone system. Performance communications via Clear Com mainstations and hardwired unit with TECHPRO portable outstations. All industry standard audio visual equipment available for hire on request. Temporary Power Supplies: 2 x 250amp TPN & F at rear stage. Permanent power supplies: 200 amp TPN & E stage right (LX), 100 amp TPN & E stage left (Sound). Cable Access: With advance notice, cable pass-through available to link all areas.
Other: Backstage: 4 orchestra rooms, artists lounge, 6 dressing rooms, 2 offices, rehearsal piano. Backstage facilities accessible to disabled performers and staff. Full selection of concert Grand Pianos available (Steinway and Yamaha).

# Blackburn

Pop. 143,000. London 215 miles. Newspapers: Lancashire Evening Telegraph (ntly); The Citizen (thurs). STD code 01254

## FITNESS AND DANCE STUDIOS, KING GEORGE'S HALL
Northgate, Blackburn, Lancashire BB2 1AA
Tel (For Fitness Studio) 01254 264355
For further details please see entry in the Local

Authorities section.

## KING GEORGES HALL
Northgate, Blackburn, Lancashire BB2 1AA
Mgt 01254 582579 BO 01254 582582
Fax 01254 667277
General Manager: Geoff Peake
Entertainments Bookings: Steve Birch
Seating: 1,853; Seating/Standing: 2,000

## RED BRICK THEATRE
Aqueduct Road, Blackburn Lancs BB2 4HT
Mgt 01254 698859
ADMINISTRATION:
Owners: Blackburn Theatre Trust Ltd
Chairman: Miss C Kay
Expected to open in 2000.
The Trust is currently running an appeal for funds to convert and equip the theatre. Policy will be touring, variety shows, opera, ballet, concerts and amateurs.
Seats: 350
TECHNICAL:
The building is being converted from a cinema to a theatre. Please apply to venue for details.

## THE WINDSOR SUITE, KING GEORGE'S HALL
Northgate, Blackburn Lancashire BB2 1AA
Contact King George's Hall.
Seats: 584; Standing: 750

# Blackpool

Pop. 150,000. London 228 miles. Newspapers: West Lancashire Evening Gazette (ntly); Blackpool Herald (fri)

## CENTRAL PIER - SHOWBAR
Promenade, Blackpool Lancs FY1 5BB
Mgt 01253 623422 BO 01253 622522
ADMINISTRATION:
Props: Leisure Parcs Ltd
General Manager: Keith West
Deputy General Manager: Andy Conquer
Assistant Manager: Caroline Reeves
Seats: 306

## GRAND THEATRE
33 Church Street, Blackpool FY1 1HT
Admin 01253 290111 BO 01253 290190
SD 01253 294571 Fax 01253 751767
ADMINISTRATION:
Blackpool Grand Theatre Trust Ltd
General Manager: Stephanie Sirr
Deputy General Manager: Neil Thomson
Finance Director: David Cass
Head of Press & Marketing: Sarah Ogle
Policy: Mixed programme Touring House, Summer Season, Plays, Dance, Musicals, Concerts.
Seats: 1,214. 4 Licensed Bars (coffee lounge and Matchams Bar open during the day).
TECHNICAL:
Stage: Proscenium Stage, rake 1 in 48, Hardwood, Pros. Opening 9.35m; Depth of Stage Safety curtain to rear wall 8.9m; Safety curtain to edge of stage 1.2m; Ht. of Grid 15.24m; 50 line C/W. Flying Bars 11.58m Wing Width P.S. 5.4 - 6.3m O.P. 5.4m; Scene Dock P.S.;

Prompt Cnr. P.S.
Lighting: Switchboard: Avolites QM 500TD. Racks Stm,
112 2 x 5kw, 8 x 5kw. FOH lighting, 6 1kw sil 40's, 6
1kw T84's, 10 Prelude 650w's, 4 1kw 243's.
Sound: Desk, 1 x Trident series 65 32:8:2 with 8 x 8
matrix. Speakers; FOH; Turbosound 6 x TXD 530 2 x
TXD 518 Driven by Crest and Mat Amps. Foldback: 2 x
Turbosound TMW 212 and various small monitors.
Microphones: mainly AKG + Beyer. FOH: 1 x Matamp
Q1000. Stage: 2 x Yamaha P2200. Also Revox and
Cassette facilities.
Other: Dressing Rooms 12; showers: 6; plus wardrobe
with washer and dryer; bandroom and new studio
available for hire.

### NORTH PIER THEATRE
North Pier, Promenade, Blackpool FY1 1NE
Mgt/SD 01253 621456 BO 01253 292029
Fax 01253 752308
ADMINISTRATION:
Props: Leisure Parcs Ltd
General Manager: George Black
Deputy General Manager: Miss M Hutchins
Policy: Summer Show
Perfs: Twice Nightly
Seats: 1,500
TECHNICAL:
Stage: Proscenium Stage: Pros. Opening 10.49m; Ht. of
Pros. 3.86m; Depth of S/Line 9.30m; Ht. of Grid 8.99m;
20 lines Hemp, 9 lines C/W; Scenery Flying Ht. 4.27m;
Flying Bars 12.19m; W/Widths P.S. 2.59m, O.P. 2.59m;
Prompt Cnr. P.S.
Lighting: Switchboard: ETL Lightmaster 500; 60 off 2kw
dimmers fitted, provision for 18 dimmers; 500
cue capacity without disc; Disco facility included.
Sound Equip: Mixer is now Soundcraft 200B 16/4/2;
Turbo Sound Speakers; Stereo sound in auditorium.
Other: Dressing Rooms 16; Accom. 30, 4 Bathrooms.

### OPERA HOUSE
Church Street, Blackpool FY1 1HW
Mgt 01253 625252 BO 01253 292029
Fax 01253 751204
ADMINISTRATION:
Props: Leisure Parcs Ltd
General Manager: Mark Osborne
Theatre Manager: Greg Ormerod
Stage Manager: Duncan Jump
Policy: All types of Productions
Seats: 2,920 Bars + 100 standing
TECHNICAL:
Stage: Proscenium Stage, Raked; Pros. opening
13.72m; Ht. of Pros. 9.14m; Depth of S/Line 13.41m;
Ht. of Grid 21.34m; 94 lines, C/W Scenery Flying Ht.
9.14m P.S., O.P.; Flying Bars 17.68m; W/Widths P.S.
6.10m, O.P. 3.05m; Prompt Cnr. P.S.
Lighting: Switchboard: Galaxie II Rearstalls Control
Room.
Other: Dressing Rooms 16; Accom. 100; 6 Backstage
Showers; Orchestra Pit 22.

### PLEASURE BEACH ARENA
Blackpool Pleasure Promenade, Ocean Boulevard,
Blackpool, Lancs FY4 1EZ
Mgmt: 01253 341033 Arena Office Ext. 1280
Entertainments Dept. ext 280/281
Mgmt: Fax 01253 407609
Arena Office Fax: 01253 405467 BO: 01253 341707
ADMINISTRATION:

Props: Blackpool Pleasure Beach Ltd.
Manager of Arena: Jeremy Smart
Policy: Summer shows, Sunday concerts, Public Ice
Skating.
Seating: 1,800 to 2,400 max.
TECHNICAL:
Stage: Arena 59' 6" x 111'.  Plus flat stage.  Pros
opening 30w x 20h.  Height of grid 48'.  17 single
purchase counterweights.  OP wing 40' x 17', PS wing
18' x 14'.
Lighting: LX switchboard Avolites Sapphire.
Sound: Soundcraft 18/4/2. 8 x Bose 802, 4 x Bose 302,
2 Bose acoustic wave cannons, 4 track, CD, cass.
Other: Dressing rooms - 12, accommodation 45.

# Bletchley

### BLETCHLEY LEISURE CENTRE
Princes Way, Bletchley, Milton Keynes,
Buckinghamshire MK2 2HQ
Tel 01908 377251 Fax: 01908 374094
Manager: Michael Robertson
Seating Capacity: 1,400

# Bognor Regis

Pop. 33,910. London 65 miles. Newspapers: B R
Observer (thurs); Promoter (wed); Journal (wed);
Guardian (thurs). STD code 01243

### THE WATERSHED THEATRE, ARTS &
### EXHIBITION CENTRE
Belmont Street, Bognor Regis, West Sussex PO21 1BL
Mgt 01243 867676 BO 01243 862020
Fax 01243 861010
ADMINISTRATION:
Director: Bill Shields
TECHNICAL:
Stage: Proscenium arch. Performing area 9.14m x
9.14m; Pros. opening 9.14m x 5.49m; wing widths
4.57m S.R., 4.57m S.L., no rake; Floor - plywood on
battens, suitable for dance (not barefoot); backstage
crossover; stage heated; height of grid to lowest block
7.4m; 10 hemp sets at 250 Kg. each, 6 winches at 500
Kg. each, 1 winch at 250 Kg.; 4 sets black legs &
borders; 1 set black tabs; 1 set silver tabs; 1 set
orange/red house tabs. Back wall used as Cyclorama. 7
x 13 Amp. & 8 x 15 Amp. independant circuits.
Forestage entrance in front of Pros. Orchestra pit on
hydraulic lift. Get in via doors from car park. Tallescope.
Safety curtain. Plans available.
Lighting: Eurolight Micron board, 88 x 2 Kw. & 8 x 5 Kw.
circuits + multiphase 423/4 x 2 Kw. effect unit.
Other: Stage management: Prompt corner S.R. cue
lights & headsets; show relays & calls to all rooms. 5
dressing rooms, access by stage door. Iron, washing
machine & tumble dryer available.
Perfs: as required.
Seats: 352-382 depending on use of apron stage or
orchestra pit, 3 wheelchair spaces, induction loop.
Equipment (Theatre and/or Exhibition Centre)
Lighting: Lamps: 24 x T84, 4 x T64, 8 x P264, 4 x 2 Kw.
Sil 15, 4 x Minielipse, 8 x P23, 3 x P293, 2 x 1000W CSI,
2 x 500W CSI, 20 x 803, 6 x P749, 62 x Par cans, 8 x
floor cans, 6 x P76, 2 x minnims, 2 x P282, 6 x P243, 44
x P743, 4 x Iris 4, 5 x 4 way s/batton, 1 x 32 feet 3 way
mag batton.

Sound: Allen & Heath 1 x 24-16-2 desk, 1 x 16-4-2 desk, 1 x 12-2 desk. Amps: 2 x PPX900, 1 x PPX450, 1 x Turner 500W, 2 x Turner 200W, 2 x HHV200 Electrovoice speakers; 2 x SH1202, 2 x SH1512ER, 2 x TL606DX, 1 x 1502, 2 x TL606ARX. 2 x 70W ohm wedges, 2 x Altec N1209/8A. 2 x Bose 802, 2 x Marshall 200W Supadins, 2 x Carlsbro Horns. 2 x Roost 200W cabs., 3 x Denon cassette decks.
Effects: Yamaha SPX90, Art Proverb 200, Boss DE200 delay line. Mics: Beyer and AKG, DI boxes, Disco unit with Citronic mixer, Rane graphics, 70M mobile multicore 24 way and 8 returns, Revox B77s, NAD compact disc.

# Bolton

Pop. 261,000. London 195 miles. Newspapers: Evening News (ntly); Metro News (thurs). STD code 01204

## ALBERT HALLS
Victoria Square Bolton BL1 1RU
Tel 01204 391548 Fax 01204 399928
BO 01204 364333 24 hr hotline 01204 371688
ADMINISTRATION:
Props: Bolton Metropolitan Borough Council
Acting General Manager: Christine Forster
Entertainments Manager: Phil Smith
Technical Manager: Jeanette Mason
Policy: Concert hall used for concerts, recitals, opera, ballet, fashion shows, exhibitions, children's entertainment, pantomime. Booking Terms: Hire, box office split, guarantee and split, guarantee by negotiation.
Seating/Capacity: Maximum 670 concert seating. Variable layouts
TECHNICAL:
Stage: Thrust: Performing area 16m x 6m, wing widths dependant on masking. No rake, floor sprung wood, suitable for all dance, backstage crossover, 6 stage heated. Four Lx Bars 750 Kg Max. permitted on bar, black masking, white cyclorama. Proscenium Arch and black fibre optic starcloth available at extra cost. 13 x 30A ring mains. Piano hoist, centre stage. 2m x 14m Stage extension available. Orchestra pit, dimensions variable according to number of seats removed. Get in via ground floor. Scale stage plans available.
Lighting: Electrosonic Multiway 2 board, 60 circuits 10A, operated from control room rear of hall, 200A 3 phase supply available from temporary board, 36 spots, 12 fresnels, 24 pars, CCT MSR followspots, operated from control room
Sound: Bose 802 and 803, 4 foldback monitors, 3 x 1 K Mos fet amps, graphic equaliser/digital delay AKG, 1 cassette tape deck, basic facilities for recording and editing. Acoustics suitable for music and spoken word.
Other: Stage management: Show relay/Tannoy to dressing rooms. Talk-back system. Backstage: 5 dressing rooms, band room, quick change rooms. Refreshments available, tea/coffee/sandwiches if requested beforehand. Rehearsal piano

## OCTAGON THEATRE
Howell Croft South, Bolton BL1 1SB
Mgt 01204 529407 BO 01204 520661
Fax 01204 380110
ADMINISTRATION:
Props: Octagon Theatre Trust Ltd
Artistic Director: Lawrence Till
Administrator: Amanda Belcham
Production Manager: Jim Niblett
Head of Marketing: Lynn Melville

Policy: Repertory (4-weekly)
Perfs: Evenings 7.30
Seats: 334 - 420, Bar, Coffee Bar
TECHNICAL:
Octagon Theatre:
Stage: Flexible Stage hence variation in seating. Round 7.95m x 5.4m; Thrust 7.95m x 8.00m; Open 17.00m x 7.20m; Ht. of Grid 7.00m; Prompt Cnr. F.O.H. Control Box.
Lighting: Switchboard: Compulite Applause 286 with back-up. 64 x 2.5 Kw Lee Dimmers: Circs 1-20 Patchable: Circs 21-64 Hardwired, Lanterns: 8 x T84, 2 x T64, 10 x 16/30, 6 x 764, 6 x 264, 22 x 23, 2 x Sil 15, 2 x 23N, 10 x Starlette, 10 x MFR, 24 x 123, 4 x 804, 8 Parcans, 2 x Coda 4, 1 x 252, 16 Parcans.
Sound Equip: 16 Way Soundcraft Delta 2 x B77, 1 x A77, 1 x ADC Disc, 2 x H + H M900 AMB, 8 way speaker patch, 10 x 8" Cabs, 2 x JUC 15" Cabs, 1 x SM58, 1 x 14L, 2 x 803 + ME40.
Communications: Full F.O.H. and B/S Paging Relay, 16 way Q Light System (all installed ) 5 Belt Packs.
Bill Naughton Theatre:
Flexible seating for 80-100.
Lighting: Switchboard: Tempus M24 + Tempus 24 Way 2 G: 4 x 6 way Tempus 15A Racks: 56 way 15 amp patch.Lanterns: Shared with main house. Speak to Chief LX.
Sound Equipment: 1 x Revox 377, 1 x Studio Master - 2 - 1, 1 x Stella Amp, 2 x 8" cabs, 8 x XLR TIE Lines, 4 way speaker patch.
Other: Communications: Full F.O.H. and B/S Paging, 3 Belt Packs.
Dressing Rooms 2; Accom. 8; 1 Shower.
Membership: TMA

# Borehamwood

## THE VENUE
Elstree Way Borehamwood Hertfordshire WD6 1NQ
Tel: 0181 207 2277 Closed for 3 year redevelopment.
All enquiries to to Phil Collins, Director of Leisure Hertsmere Borough Council

# Boston, Lincs

Pop. 26,230. London 116 miles. Newspapers; see Lincoln. STD code 01205

## BLACKFRIARS ARTS CENTRE
Spain Lane, Boston, Lincolnshire PE21 6HP
Mgt 01205 363108 BO 01205 363108
ADMINISTRATION:
Props: Blackfriars Arts Centre Ltd
Director: Sam Mason
Outreach & Education Officer: Tracy Simpson
Technical Manager: Justin Clark
Policy: Touring, Amateurs, Outreach and Community Arts Development
Seats: 233 + 2 wheelchair spaces. Fully licensed bar.
TECHNICAL:
Stage: Proscenium Stage with 0.91m apron, Flat: Pros. Opening 7.32m; Ht. of Pros. 3.96m; Depth of S/Line 7.32m; Ht. of Grid 9.14m; 17 lines, 20 stage weights. Scenery Flying Ht. 9.14m; Flying Bars 5.49m; W/Widths P.S. 3.05m, O.P. 2.44m; Prompt Cnr. P.S. Vinyl dance floor.
Lighting: Switchboard: Sirius Board 48 Channels;

Control Box at rear of Auditorium; 12 Patt 23; 10 Patt 123; 10 1000w Profiles; 3 Cyc Floods; 6 Par cans; 8 650 watt Fresnels; 4 650 watt Profiles.
Sound Equipment: 4 F.O.H. Speakers; 8 INTO 2 Mixer Amp; 3 Microphones; Twin Cassette Decks; Revox; Compact Disc, DAT Machine.
Other: Dressing Rooms 3; Accom. 20. Show Relay.

# Bournemouth & Boscombe

Pop. 153,000. London 104 miles. Newspapers: Evening Echo (ntly); Bournemouth Times (fri). STD code 01202

## BOURNEMOUTH INTERNATIONAL CENTRE

Exeter Road, Bournemouth, Dorset BH2 5BE
Tel 01202 456500 BO 01202 456456
Fax 01202 456400 BO Fax 01202 451024
Party Bookings Tel 01202 451865
ADMINISTRATION:
Props: Borough of Bournemouth.
Director: Kevin Sheehan.
Entertainments Mgt: Rob Zuradzki.
Policy: Multipurpose hall used for concerts, summer shows, sporting and special events, conferences and exhibitions.
Seating/Capacity: 3,600 seated, 4,300 standing.
TECHNICAL:
Stage: Proscenium arch 14m wide x 6m high, stage depth 6.75m to safety curtain; 7.6m overall. Portable staging available in unit sizes 2m x 1m.
Lighting: Rank Strand Type AMC (48 way)
Sound: 24:2:8 soundcraft 500. Speaker details; 8 F.O.H. plus foldback. Electrical: Bus bars on 3 sides offering 300 amp 3 phase supply. In addition there is a 200 amp 3 phase supply O.P. of stage, 100 amp 3 phase P.S. of stage. Full technical details on request.

## PAVILION THEATRE

Westover Road, Bournemouth
Mgt 01202 456400 BO 01202 456456
Fax 01202 456500 BO Fax 01202 451024
Paty Bookings Tel: 01202 451865
ADMINISTRATION:
Director: Kevin Sheehan
Entertainments Manager: Rob Zuradzki
Stage Manager: Roger Stares
Policy: Plays, Ballet, Opera, Musicals, Pantomime, Summer Spectaculars, one night stand concerts, pop, rock, MOR.
Perfs: Vary with type of attraction.
Seats: 1,518. Bars and Restaurants.
TECHNICAL:
Stage: Proscenium Stage, Flat; Pros. opening 13.64m; Ht. of Pros. 8.53m; Depth of S/Line 12.19m; Ht. of Grid 14.63m; 50 lines, C/W, 17 Hemp; Scenery Flying Ht. 14.02m; Flying Bars 13.41m; W/Widths P.S. 4.88m, O.P. 6.10m; Prompt Cnr. P.S.; 10.97m dia. revolve electrically driven.
Lighting: Switchboard: M.M.S. 140 ways; F.O.H. Spots 12 Patt. 143 above Orchestra Pit, Circle Spots 6 Patt. 263/264 each side of circle paired across, 3 Patt.764 each side; Spot Bar 12 Patt.743; Flood Bar 12 1kw horizon lamps; Stage Floods 10 Patt.49; Stage Spots 6 Patt. 143, 6 Patt. 243 2kw, 4 Patt.743, Spot Bars 2-7 way 4.27m, 2 4.88m ladders; Limes 3 Zenon arch; 5 Battens of 4 circuits; Floats 4 circuits; Stage Dips 16 each side.

Sound Equip: Bose 802 6 speakers, 1 1800 Bose Amp, H/H 16-channel stereo mixer, 2 speakers each side of pros. opening, all mic. inputs on XLR Canon. AKG C451E rifle microphones, 10 Shure Unidyne MKIII.
Other: Dressing Rooms 17; Accom. 100; 2 Shower Rooms; Orchestra Pit 15.24m x 2.74m.

## PIER THEATRE

Bournemouth
Mgt/SD 01202 456400 BO 01202 456456 Tech.Mgr: 01202 451798 (Mob: 0585 777292) Fax 01202 456500
Email: 101362.261@compuserve.com
ADMINISTRATION:
Director: Kevin Sheehan
Theatre Manager: Mike Cooper
Entertainments Manager: Rob Zuradzki
Technical Manager: Christian Knighton
Policy: Summer Season, farce, variety, conferences, amateurs
Perfs: Vary with type of attraction
Seats: 837. Bar-Cafe in Season
Dressing Rooms: 8 accommodating up to 19 people. 1 x shower.
No orchestra pit, but floor space for 6 musicians with pit rail around.
TECHNICAL:
Stage: Proscenium Stage, Flat; Pros. opening 7.62m; Ht. of Pros. 3.66m; Depth of S/Line 5.40m; Ht. of Grid 8.29m; Lines 16 C/W, 2 Hemp; Scenery Flying Ht. 4.88m; Flying Bars 9.14m; W/Widths P.S. 4.27m, O.P. 4.27m; Prompt Cnr. P.S.
Lighting: Control ETC Express 125. 60 x 2kw Dimmers, FOH 20 1kw zoom profiles & 10 x 650 w Profiles. On stage 2 x spot bars each with 12 1kw fresnels and barn doors. 24 x 1kw Par Cans. 12 x 500w Cyc Floods.
Sound: Soundcraft 16/4/4/2. FOH L.S. JBL M350, Mutiverb LT. 4 x wedge monitors. 5 Beyer Rifle Mics. 3 Shure SM 58 Vocal Mics. 1 AKG D190. 2 x Audio Technica Vocal Mics. 4 EMO Passive D.I. Boxes. 7 x Mic Stands.
C5 speakers F.O.H.; 4 x Bose Foldback on stage.

# Bracknell

Pop. 80,000 (district). Newspapers: Reading Evening Post (dly); Bracknell News; Bracknell Times. STD code 01344

## SOUTH HILL PARK ARTS CENTRE

Wilde Theatre, South Hill Park, Bracknell, Berkshire RG12 7PA
Mgt 01344 427272 BO 01344 484123
Fax 01344 411427
Email: shp@vossmet.co.uk
The Theatre is part of the Arts Centre complex, which also includes a cinema, recital room, gallery, art and craft studios, workshops, rehearsal rooms, 50 seat studio theatre, and two bars.
ADMINISTRATION:
Director: Tim Brinkman
Technical Director: Andrew Wyard
Policy: In-house theatre and music theatre productions, mid-scale theatre, music theatre and dance tours, concerts, amateur companies.
Seats: 330 (plus 70 standing) or 300 (with orchestra pit).
TECHNICAL:
Stage: Width at proscenium: adjustable 10.7m to 8.5m; Max height at proscenium 6.0m, Ht. to Grid 8.0m; Depth of stage 9.2m.

Lighting: 84 channel Strand 430 lighting board; 26
Harmony F(1kw), 16 Prelude F (650kw), 18 Harmony
15/28 (1kw), 10 Prelude 16/30 (650kw), 5 Coda 500/4, 1
Patt.818 follow spot + 16 Par 64 + 12 Iris 1K floods.
Other: Orchestra Pit: Yamaha Baby Grand plus 30
musicians.
Dressing Rooms 3; Accom. 23; Bathroom facilities.
Membership: TMA

# Bradford

Pop. 483,000. London 195 miles. Newspapers:
Telegraph & Argus (ntly). STD code 01274

## ALHAMBRA THEATRE AND STUDIO

Morley Street, Bradford, West Yorkshire BD7 1AJ
Mgt 01274 752375 SD 01274 752375
BO 01274 752000 Fax 01274 752185
ADMINISTRATION:
Props: City of Bradford Metropolitan District Council.
Seats: 1,464. 3 Bars & Bistro
General Manager: John Botteley
Programme Administrator: Laura Wood
Head of Customer Services: Gerry Clifford
Head of Community, Education and Outreach: Iain
Bloomfield
Head of Sales and Marketing: David Warren
Head of Technical Services: Neil Bohanna
Chief Electrician: Caroline Burrell
Policy: Touring Opera, Ballet, Drama, Musicals,
Pantomime and Concerts.
TECHNICAL:
Stage: Proscenium Stage, Flat; Pros Opening 10.8m;
Pros Height 7.5m; Pros Height to bottom of pelment
7.0m; Depth of S/Line to B/wall 15m; Height of Grid
18m; 88 c/w lines plus two up and down bars each side,
flying bars 15.7m; W widths P.S. 4.5m; O.P. 4m;
Orchestra Pit seats 30-60; Scene dock 13.3m x 10.6m.
Technical Workshop facilities, wardrobe facilities
including 4 extra washer/drier points.
Lighting Equipment: Lighting Board - RSE Gemini 2 +
360 way; F.O.H. Lighting Circuits - 38; Stage Lighting
Circuits - 112 (+40 extras). Circuits - 1.132: 2.5kw;
133.150 : 5kw; 151.190 : 2.5kw; 6 internally wired bars -
5 x 18 way; 1 x 12 way. Lanterns - F.O.H. - 8 pairs of
1.2kw optiques. Loose Equipment: 20 x 1k axial sil 15,
10 x 1k sil 15. Harmony 15.28 Profile x 14; Harmony
22.40 Profile x 20; Harmony F Fresnel 1kw x 48;
Cadenza Fresnel 2kw x 2; Iris 1 - 1kw Flood x 26; 4
Circuit Thomas Groundrow x 5; Follow Spots - RSE Solo
x 3; Pan Can 64's x 40, Ancillary Power - 250A TPNE
located on stage level DSR, 400 TPNE Located on fly
floor D.S.R. - Down Stage Right. 12 x 6 way 20m
Multicore. Bradford Centre Theatres will provide within
reason all F.O.H. colour in LEE filter.
Sound: Desk & Stage: A & H Saber Desk with 24 into 8
into 8. 72 Mic inputs around stage area including 2 x 19
way stage-box - All appearing on Jack Field in control
room. 8 Tie line sockets around the stage area plus 24 in
control room - All appearing on Jack Field in control
room. 2 x B77 Revox reel to reel tape machine 15/17.5
i.p.s. 2 x Technics Cassette Machine; 1 x Technics CD
Player 1 x Denon cassette player, 1 x Pioneer CD player
(6 disc), 2 x 31 band graphic equaliser, 1 x spx 1000, 1 x
DMPX; 1 x Yamaha DMD7.
AMPS: Yamaha PZ2002 main amps drive pros left (2) -
right (2) - cluster (2) - sub-bass L&R (1) plus 2 floating for
foldback. Main PA operating with Meyer Limiters.
Speaker System: All Meyer UPA1 (4 x pros. L & R) (4 x
centre top Cluster) with back up re-inforcement on digital

delay in rear Stalls, Circle, Balcony, 2 x Sub bass units
(Meyer) USW/1; Foldback 2 x Yamaha Wedge S2115
HZ; 2 x Yamaha S3115H (general work); 2 x EV Eliminatir
10. 2 x DVB Audiotechnik HON 15 wedger Patchable
Speaker Outlets EP3's; 8 on Stage; 4 Orchesta; 12
Auditorium; 2 Flys; 2 Understage. Apply to the theatre for
further details.
DRESSING ROOMS:
Dressing room accommodation: 72 places, company
office, technical office.

ALHAMBRA STUDIO:
Small performance/ rehearsal area, 15.7m x 25.5m
including 2 dressing rooms (accommodating up to 20
people), which can also be used in conjunction with
those for the main house.  The rehearsal area's
dimensions corresponds with the working area of the
main stage. Seats up to 200 in theatre style.
Technical:
6 x 8m motorised Flying Bars (S.W.L. 300kg each).
Lighting Board R.S.E. Lightboard M; Lighting Circuits: 72
appearing as 12 per electric flying bar or patchable to
floor area; Ancillary Power - 100A TPNE located at stage
level.
Membership: TMA

## ST GEORGE'S CONCERT HALL

Bridge Street Bradford W Yorks BD1 1JS
Mgt 01274 752374 BO 01274 752000
Fax 01274 720736
ADMINISTRATION:
Props: City of Bradford Metropolitan District Council
Manager: Gerry Clifford
Functions Manager: Andrew Burns
Seats. 1,500; Pop. 1,900 (stalls standing, circle seated)
Policy: Classical Concerts; Popular Music, Variety
Concerts, Rock Concerts, Conferences, Exhibitions.
Four bars and Restaurant/Buffet.
TECHNICAL:
Stage: Platform stage flat. 14.75m Wide and 11.90
Deep. 4 flying bars electrically operated. S.W.L. 850kg
evenly distributed. Flying height 15m.
Lighting: Switchboard: R.S.E. Lightboard M Junior 60
way with patch panel M F.O.H. lamps 6 x 1kw profile.
Stage lamps 40 x Par 64 (CP62) and 4 x 1 Iris 1 cyc
floods. 2 x CSI follow spots. Special effects bus bar
chamber stage right. 3 phase 300A each plus single
phase 100A.
Sound: Soundcraft Series 400B; 24 Channel. 4 Bose
1800 Amplifiers. Bose 302/802 Speakers deployed
throughout auditorium with foldback option available.
Revox B77 tape deck and cassette deck. Available are a
selection of microphones and stands. Talkback system
wired to Limes. Sound, lighting at both sides of platform.
Show relay to all dressing rooms.
Other: Dressing Rooms: 8. Accommodation - with
centrally situated showers and W.C. Large
Orchesta/Chorus room accommodates 100. Principal
dressing room with private shower and W.C.
Membership: TMA

## THEATRE IN THE MILL

University of Bradford, Richmond Road, Bradford,
West Yorkshire BD7 1DP
Mgt 01274 233185 BO 01274 233200
Fax 01274 233187
ADMINISTRATION:
Props: University of Bradford
Theatre Manager: Stephen Walker
Policy: Touring, Professional touring groups. Home for

University of Bradford Theatre Group.
Perfs: Variable.
Seats: 100-140. Theatre Bar.
TECHNICAL:
Stage: Great Flexibility of both stage and lighting.
Lighting: Tempus M24 & M24 FX plus Tempus 24 &
Tempus 6-way desks, 4 Patt.23, 12 Patt.123, 4
Patt.743, 3 Battens, 6 flood, 16 minuet fresnels, 2 Sil -
30 profiles, 8 prelude 28/40 profiles, 6 prelude 16/30
profiles, 10 prelude P.C., 4 Patt.264s, 6 Patt.223s.
Sound Equip: Studiomaster 16/4/2 Mixing desk; Teac
0.25 Track Reel to Reel; Revox A77 DENON DRM 400,
Yamaha KX 330 Cassette Deck, Cassette Deck; Garrard
401 Record Deck; 2 Bose 802, 2 Bose 402, 2Bose 101
Speaker; Mosfet 600 W & Mosefet 300 W Amps; 2 Quod
303 Amps; 1 HH Echo & Reverb. Unit; 1 Technical
Projects 2 Circuit Communication System with 3
portable headset stations, and show relay/paging to
dressing rooms and FOH; 6 mics. with flexible Mic. and
speaker line system. Additional equipment available if
requested in advance.
Other: 2 Dressing Rooms, Max. Accom. 12, Showers.

# Brentwood

## THE BRENTWOOD CENTRE
Doddinghurst Road, Pilgrims Hatch, Brentwood,
Essex CM15 9NN
Booking of Hall 01277 261111 BO 01277 262616
Fax 01277 200152
Contact: Steve Allen
Leisure and recreation.
2,000 seater Event Hall, Squash Courts, Health Suite,
Gymnasium, 2 Swimming Pools, 12 Badminton Courts,
Cafeteria, Bar, Exhibition and Conference facilities.

## HERMIT
Shenfield Road, Brentwood, Essex CM15 8AG
Tel 01277 216722 BO 01277 225505
Fax 01277 212770
ADMINISTRATION:
Props: Essex County Council
Contacts: John Maynard and Denny Newman
Capacity: 120.

# Bridgend

## BERWYN CENTRE
Ogwy Street, Nantymoel, Bridgend,
Mid Glamorgan CF32 7SA Wales
Tel 01656 840439 Fax 01656 841393
Seating/Capacity: 300
Valley Arts Project Officer/Manager: Mari Major
Theatre has proscenium arch with sprung stage and
apron. One tier of fixed raked seats.,
Facilities: 6 dressing rooms plus 2 communal.

## BRIDGEND RECREATION CENTRE
Angel Street Bridgend Mid Glamorgan CF31 4AH Wales
Tel 01656 657491 Fax 01656 647886
Contact: Mike Payne
Seating/Capacity: 500
TECHNICAL:
Stage dimensions 35' x 16' (width can be extended with
portable staging units).

2 separate artists changing rooms with en suite facilities.
Lighting: 18 flood lights, 16 spot lights and follow spot.
Catering facilities: licenced bar available.

# Bridlington

Pop. 28,590. London 221 miles. Newspapers:
Bridlington Free Press (thurs); Hull Daily Mail (dly). STD
code 01262

## LEISURE WORLD
Promenade, Bridlington, East Yorkshire YO15 2QQ
Mgt 01262 606715  Fax 01262 673458
Props: East Riding of Yorkshire Council
Senior Facility Manager: Rob Clutterham
Stage Manager: Peter Robson
Policy: Theatre/Revues/Conferences - Exhibitions, etc.
Seats: 700 seated; 1,000 standing.

## SPA ROYAL HALL
South Marine Drive, Bridlington, E. Yorks YO15 3JH
Mgt 01262 678255 BO 01262 678258 BO (Private line)
01262 678257 SD 01262 679582 Fax 01262 401769
ADMINISTRATION:
Props: East Riding of Yorkshire Council
Senior Facility Manager: Rob Clutterham
Stage Manager: Peter Robson
Policy: Musical concerts, amateur operatic productions -
available for hire.
Seats: 2,000, raked circle, linked chairs in stalls. 1
licensed bar.
Access car park: Spa slipway, adjacent, nearest railway
station: 300 yards, nearest coach terminal: 300 yards,
bus routes: local routes.
For the disabled: Wheelchair spaces by arrangement -
assistance available, contact Entertainments Officer -
parking - level access - ramps - all house facilities fully
accessible.
TECHNICAL:
Stage: Platform stage with curved front. Performing area
12.2m x 7.92m (stage front 22m wide). No rake - floor
sprung wood, suitable for all dance, no crossover, stage
heated. Height to girders 6.7m - tab tack - girders can
take 450kg per point - maximum flying height 5.5m
approx - gold tabs - curved black back wall used as
cyclorama - gold house tabs, drawn. Several 13A
independent circuits. Get-in via rear of stage, street level,
large fire doors. Tallescope. Scale stage, fly and lighting
plans available.
Lighting: Strand MX 48 memory control desk - 200A 3
phase supply available for temporary board - 30 various
spots and fresnels, 10 x 3 circuit battens, 6 floods - 5
followspots, operated from balcony.
Sound: Studiomaster 12 way mono desk, operated in
control room - 10 amplifiers - 4 columns of speakers
each - 15 x Shure mics (some available from Spa
Theatre) - reel-to-reel and cassette tape systems -
record deck - PA system - 60A single phase supply
available for sound.  Acoustics suitable for music and
spoken word.
Other: Stage Management: Show relay/Tannoy to
dressing rooms.
Backstage: 4 dressing rooms, accommodating 20,
access by stairs. Rehearsal piano, boudoir grand, good.
Advice given on accommodation. Staff - 1 lighting -
casuals available - security personnel. Backstage
facilities accessible to disabled performers and staff.
Additional Information: Performance pianos available - 1
boudoir grand, 2 baby grands, 1 Bluthner concert gr.

## SPA THEATRE

South Marine Drive, Bridlington,
East Yorkshire YO15 3JH
Mgt 01262 678257 BO 01262 678258
SD 01262 679582 Fax 01262 604625
ADMINISTRATION:
Props: East Riding of Yorkshire Council
Senior Facility Manager: Rob Clutterham
Stage Manager: Peter Robson
Policy: Summer Shows, Touring and Amateur Shows out
of Season + Cinema 35mm. Star Concerts.
Seats: 1,000. Stalls Bar, Restaurant adjoining.
TECHNICAL:
Stage: Proscenium Stage, Raked 1 40; Pros. Opening
9.14m; Ht. of Pros. 5.79m; Depth of S/Line 11.89m; Ht.
of Grid 9.14m; 54 lines, Hemp; Scenery Flying Ht.
4.57m; Flying Bars 10.67m; W/Widths P.S. 3.05m, O.P.
4.88m; Prompt Cnr. P.S.
Lighting: Strand: 1 x MX 48 Memory control desk
complete with memory card and 48 ways of strand
dimmers together with demux units, rear upper circle.
Stage: 4 x 4 Colour Battens, Spot Bar 8 circuits, 6 x
1000w Cyc Floods, 4 x 4 Dip Boxes; FOH 12 1000w
Profile Spots, 16 1000w Fresnels, 2 1000w CSI Follow
Spots.
Sound Equip: Studiomaster 12-2C, Twin 400W. Amps.
Speakers 2 each side. Pit and stage fold back.
Other: Dressing Rooms: 8; Accom. 30. 3 Showers;
Orchestra Pit 16.

# Bridport

London 139 miles. Newspapers: Bridport News (fri). STD
code 01308

## PALACE CINEMA

South Street, Bridport, Dorset DT6 3NY
Tel 01308 422167
ADMINISTRATION:
Manager: Graham Frampton
Policy: Films and 2 shows in January & April, opera &
pantomime.
Perfs: To be arranged with Show.
Seats: 450. Light refreshments.
TECHNICAL:
Proscenium Stage, Raked; Pros. Opening 8.69m; Ht. of
Pros. 4.88m; Depth of S/Line 5.03m;
 Ht. of Grid 6.25m; W/Widths P.S. 1.14m, O.P. 1.37m;
Prompt Cnr. P.S.
Sound Equip: Installed as required.
Dressing rooms 6.

# Brighton

Pop. 163,710. London 53 miles. Newspapers: Evening
Argus (ntly); Brighton & Hove Leader (free wed). STD
code 01273

## BRIGHTON CENTRE

Kings Road, Brighton, East Sussex BN1 2GR
Mgt 01273 290131 BO 0870 900 9100
Fax 01273 779980
Email: b-centre@pavillion.co.uk
Web Site: www.brightoncentre.co.uk
ADMINISTRATION:
General Manager: Stephen Piper
Marketing and Programme Manager: Wendy Walton
Technical Manager: Steve Sillence

Capacity: Main Hall 5127 (Standing/Seated), 4,500 (Fully
Seated), East Wing 600 (Standing), Hewison Hall 600-
800.

## THE DOME

29 New Road, Brighton, East Sussex BN1 1UG
Admin 01273 700747 BO 01273 709709
Fax 01273 707505
ADMINISTRATION:
Props: Brighton & Hove Council
Director of Resort Services: Deborah Grubb
Operations Manager: John Lucas
House Manager: Jenny Lewin-Taylor
Policy: Concerts, Symphony Concerts, One Night
Stands, Summer Entertainments Conferences, Pop, Jazz
Shows, etc.
Perfs: Variable
Seats: 2,091
Licensed Bar and Catering Services. Manager: Maria
Young
TECHNICAL:
Stage: Proscenium Stage, Flat; Pros. opening 9.14m; Ht.
of pros. 7.01m; Depth of S/Line 7.32m; Ht. of Grid
9.75m; 12 lines, Hemp; W/Widths P.S. 4.57m, O.P.
4.57m; Prompt Cnr. P.S.
Lighting: Switchboard: Strand P.S. 96 ways; F.O.H.
Spots 8 preset, 2 CSI 1000w Follow Spots; 4 Battens;
Dips P.S. & O.P.; Spot Bars 2 Bars Fresnel Spots.
Sound Equip: Tape-Disc A & H 24 channel-4-2 mixer
desk; Speakers pros. arch and rear.
Other: Dressing Rooms 7; Chorus Rooms 2; Band Room
1;
Accom 60; Orchestra Pit 15.

## EVENT II

Kingswest, West Street, Brighton, East Sussex BN1 2RE
Tel 01273 732627 Fax 01273 208996
Capacity : 1,920
General Manager: Tony Buck

## GARDNER ARTS CENTRE

University of Sussex, Lewes Road, Falmer, Brighton,
East Sussex BN1 9RA
Tel 01273 685447 BO 01273 685861
SD 01273 696975 Fax 01273 678551
ADMINISTRATION:
General Manager: Sue Webster
Technical Manager: Steve Douglas
Policy: Multi-purpose arts centre providing national and
international concerts, drama, dance, mime and visual
arts.
Perfs: Usually Mon-Sat 7.45p.m.
Seats: 482. Licensed bar and bistro.
TECHNICAL:
Stage: Flexible, usually thrust proscenium, Flat; Pros.
opening 10.67m; Ht. of Pros. 7.01m; Depth of S/Line
13.72m; Ht. of grid 7.62m; 14 lines, Hemp; Flying Bars
variable; W/Widths PS. 1.52m, O.P. 1.52m; Prompt Cnr.
P.S.
Lighting: Gemini 2+ - 80 ways F.O.H. Spots; 6 x cantatat
18 - 32 1.2Kw, 12 x Patt.264, 6 x CCT Sil 30, 23 x
Patt.23, 10 x Patt.243, 17 x Patt 743, 2 x ADB, 2 x CCT
Minuette F with barn doors, 2 x Patt.123, 6 x Harmony
Fresnels, 12 x Thomas Par Cans, 8 x Verti majors
1250w, 7 x Patt.49 1K, 2 x Patt.49 1K, 2 x Patt.60
500w, 2 x Patt.252, 2 x Patt 293 F/S with stands.
Sound Equip: Control F.O.H. 16 into 2 Allan Heath Mixer;
8 Tannoy lynx speakers; 2 x tannoy Cougar Wedges, 1 x
Revox B77 tape recorder, 7/15, 3/7, 1 Teac cassette

# THEATRE ROYAL BRIGHTON

## THE SOUTH COAST'S PREMIER NUMBER ONE TOURING DATE

### Seating Capacity 951

For availability call:
Roger Neil (General Manager) on **01273 327480**

deck; 1 x Yamaha SPX90 Mk2 Effects Unit.
Other: Dressing Rooms 6; Accom. 16 showers.
Single rake auditorium. Centre and two side blocks.

## KOMEDIA
14-17 Manchester Street, Brighton BN2 1TF
Admin 01273 277070 BO 01273 277772
Fax 01273 277010
Email: komedia@brighton.co.uk
Web Site: http://www.brighton.co.uk/komedia
ADMINISTRATION:
Props: Komedia Productions Ltd
Director: Marina Kobler
Artistic Directors: Colin Granger & David Lavender
Administrator: Jathan Granger
Press and PR Officer: Sally Moulsdale
Seats: 90
TECHNICAL:
Stage: Area: 7500mm x 4600mm. Grid height: 2500mm.
Lighting: Zero 88 XLS Lightmaster desk, 36 lanterns.
Sound: Seck 122 desk, Bose 800 amp and speakers,
Revox B77 reel-to-reel, Eclipse CD50 CD player.
Other: 3 dressing rooms accommodating 9.

## PAVILION THEATRE
29 New Road, Brighton East Sussex BN1 1UG
Admin 01273 700747 BO 01273 709709
Fax 01273 707505
ADMINISTRATION:
Props: Brighton & Hove Council
Director of Resort Services: Deborah Grubb
Operations Manager: John Lucas
House Manager: Jenny Lewin-Taylor
Policy: Hall available for hire.
Seats: 255 on level floor or 231 tiered seating. Licensed
bar and Catering Services. Manager: Maria Young
TECHNICAL:
Stage: Proscenium Stage, Flat; Pros. opening 6.40m; Ht.
of Pros. 3.35m; Depth of S/Line 4.27m; Ht. of Grid
4.27m; 3 lines.
Lighting: Switchboard: Strand Tempus 40 way; 3
Battens.
Sound: Speakers F.O.H. - 12 way mixer desk.
Other: 2 Dressing Rooms; Accom. 12 persons.
Hall is used for various other functions - Exhibitions,
Dances, Bazaars, Dinners etc.

## SALLIS BENNEY THEATRE
University of Brighton, Faculty of Art and Design, Grand
Parade, Brighton, East Sussex BN2 2JY
Mgt 01273 643010  Fax 01273 643038
Theatre situated within University of Brighton in the

centre of town near Brighton Pavilion. At the junctions of
Lewes Road (A27) and London Road (A23).
ADMINISTRATION:
Props: University of Brighton
Manager: Bob Clutterham
Policy: Available for hire: fringe, tours, concerts, films,
conferences, exhibitions.
Seats: 370 + 6 wheelchairs. Flat floor. Raised side
galleries.
TECHNICAL:
Stage: Proscenium stage: flat, pros. width 9.2m; depth
5.8m; height to fixed grid 4m. In the round: max. width
9.2m, length: 12.3m.
Lighting: 36 x 10A circuits via hard/soft patch to 24 way
desk, 63A 3 phase + 3 x 32Amp. Zero 88 'Sirius'
Memory control F.O.H. 22 x 500W fresnels, 9 x 1kw
fresnels, 4 1kw Sil 30s, 20 x 500W profiles, 1 x 2kw Sil
15 as follow spot, 10 x Patt.60. Other lighting equipment
available on hire. Film: stage screen.
Sound: 1 x Revox B77, 2 x cassette, GL2 mixer, Fostex
300 stereo amp, 2 x Tannoy Lockwood speakers, 2 X
Peavey 2 way 2kw PA. Other A.V. equipment available
on hire. Other: Video projection.
Piano: Baby Grand (Bluthner)
Dressing Rooms: 2, accommodation 30.

## THEATRE ROYAL
New Road, Brighton, East Sussex BN1 1SD
Mgt 01273 327480 BO 01273 328488
SD 01273 327155 Fax 01273 777156
ADMINISTRATION:
Props: Theatre Royal Brighton Limited
Chairman: Brook Land
General Manager: Roger Neil
Stage Manager: Roy Roe
Chief Electrician: Grant Minshull
Policy: No. 1 Touring
Perfs: Mon-Sat 7.45; Mats. Thurs. 2.30, Sat. 4.00.
Seats: 951. Six Licensed Bars. Corporate entertaining
facilities.
TECHNICAL:
Stage: Proscenium Stage, Raked 1 in 24; Pros. opening
8.99m; Ht. of Pros. 9.14m; Depth of S/Line 8.99m; Ht. of
Grid 15.24m; 60 hemp lines approx. 3 assit; Scenery
Flying Ht. 9.14m; Flying Bars 10.82m; W/Widths P.S.
4.57m, O.P. 4.06m; Prompt Cnr. P.S.
Lighting: Switchboard: Strand Gemini 2 Plus; P.S. Stage;
119 ways; F.O.H. Spots 11 Major; 4 Battens, 4 circuits;
Dips 16 P.S., 16 O.P.; Spot Bars 1 x 12 way Patt.743.
Other: Dressing Rooms: 13; 2 Showers.
Orchestra Pit approx. 20. Large Scene Dock PS. Very
Large Dock O.P. with Street Entrance.
Wardrobe.

## UNIVERSITY OF SUSSEX STUDENT'S UNION
Mandela Hall, Falmer House, Falmer, Brighton,
East Sussex BN1 9QF
Tel 01273 678152 Fax: 01273 678875
Seating: 400, Standing: 600.

## THE ZAP
187/193 Kings Road Arches, Brighton,
East Sussex BN1 1NB
Tel 01273 202407
Policy: Cultural innovation in entertainments and the arts.
Seating/Capacity: seated 200; 400 standing. Disabled
access (6 wheelchairs).

# Bristol

Pop. 376,148. London 126 miles. Newspapers: Evening
Post; Bristol Journal. STD code 0117

## BRISTOL BIERKELLER
All Saints Street Bristol BS1 2NA
Tel 0117 926 8514 Fax 0117 925 1347
Seating/Capacity: 400 seated, 800 standing.
Contact: Austin Mockeridge

## BRISTOL HIPPODROME
St. Augustines Parade, Bristol BS1 4UZ
Mgt 0117 926 5524 BO 0870 607 7500
SD 0117 927 3077 Fax 0117 925 1661
ADMINISTRATION:
Props: Apollo Leisure Group PLC
Managing Director: Paul Gregg
Theatre Manager: John Wood
Technical Director: John Randall.
For all booking information and further details please
contact Sam Shrouder or Nicky Monk at Apollo Leisure
(UK) Ltd., Grehan House, Garsington Road, Cowley,
Oxford OX4 5NQ. Tel: 01865 782900; Fax: Oxford
01865 782910.
Policy: Ballet, Opera, Musicals, Variety, Pantomime,
Major Drama and One Night Stands.
Perfs: 7.30 (6.15 & 8.45 twice nightly); Mat. as required
Wed. and/or Sat.
Seats: 1,981. Stalls and Circle Bar.
TECHNICAL:
Stage: Proscenium Stage; Pros. Opening 14.63m; Ht. of
Pros. 9.14m; Depth of S/Line 18.28m, last line 14.63m;
Ht. of Grid 18.28m; 65 lines including 5 elec., C/W;
Scenery Flying 9.14m; Flying Bars 16.61m; W/Widths
P.S. 8.53m, O.P. 8.53m; Prompt Cnr. Right.
Lighting: Switchboard: Eurolight Ovation. F.O.H. Spots;
2 x Lycian, 12 T84s, 16 T-Spot Box Booms, 8 Patt.263,
Pros. Booms, 2 Battens, 1 Float, Spot Bar 2 x 12
Patt.743s.
Other: Dressing Rooms 20; Accom. 90; Wardrobe and
Band Room. Showers on all floors, Scene Dock with
street entrance.

## BRISTOL OLD VIC
King Street, Bristol BS1 4ED
Mgt 0117 949 3993 BO 0117 987 7877
SD 0117 949 3993 Fax 0117 949 3996
Email: bristol.oldvic@cableinet.co.uk
ADMINISTRATION:
Props: Theatre Royal Trustees
Lessees: The Bristol Old Vic Trust Ltd

Artistic Director: Andrew Hay
General Manager: Sarah Smith
Assistant General Manager: James Taljaard
Production Manager: Derek Simpson
Policy: Repertory, Visting Companies
Perfs: Mon-Wed 7.30p.m. Thurs-Sat 8.00p.m.
Mats: Thurs & Sat 2.30 p.m.
Seats: Theatre Royal 658, New Vic 150/200

## COLSTON HALL
Colston Street Bristol BS1 5AR
Tel 0117 922 3693 Fax 0117 922 3681
BO: 0117 922 3686
ADMINISTRATION:
Props: Bristol City Council.
General Manager: Ken Lovell
Concert Planning and Promotions Manager: Paul
Preager
Publicity Officer: Asif Khan
Policy: Concert Hall available for hire for all musical
events with some joint promotions.
Seating/Capacity: 1,886 or 2,121 with choir and boxes
TECHNICAL:
Stage: Concert platform, performing area 14.9m x
7.62m, floor sprung wood. Variable height grid - 3
tonnes permitted on each of bars 1 & 2, 2 tonnes on bar
3. Get-in via ramped entrance at stalls level. Scale stage
and lighting plans available.
Lighting: Celco major 30 lighting board operated from
front of house or from control room overlooking platform.
41 x 1kw downlighters over platform. 30 x Par 64. 2 x
CSI follow spots.
Sound: TAC Bullet 12:4:2 board operated from control
room or DDA 32:8:2 operated from mid stalls FOH. Stalls
speakers: 2 x Turbosound TXD 580. Balcony speakers:
4 x Turbosound TSE 111, 4 x Turbosound TSE 118.
Central cluster: 4 x Turbosound TSE 111, 2 x
Turbosound TSE 118. Microphones: 11 x Beyer 201, 2 x
AKG 321, 2 x SM 58, 4 x AKG 451 + CK 8, 4 x DI
Boxes. CD and cassette players. Acoustics suitable for
music and spoken word.
Other: Backstage: 6 dressing rooms, band room, irons,
etc. as required. Refreshments available. Advice given on
accommodation. Staff: 2 lighting/sound; casuals
available; security personnel as required. Backstage
facilities available to disabled performers and staff.
Additional information on application.

## NEW VIC
King Street, Bristol BS1 4ED
Contact Bristol Old Vic.
TECHNICAL:
Stage: Studio Theatre, Elongated Hexagonal Space,
Upper Balcony Surround; total seating and (variable)
playing area: 8m x 12.50m; Balcony Width: 2.21m; Ht.
under Balcony 2.19m; Flat Stage. Sound & Electrics;
Control on Balcony level.
Lighting: Control: 84 way Gemini, Fresnels - 40 x 650w,
6 x 1kw; Profiles - 30 x 650w, 3 x 1kw; Permanent
Gantry.
Sound Spirit Live 12-43;2 Revox; 6 speaker outlets.
Other: 3 Dressing Rooms; Accom. 20; 2 showers.

## THE REDGRAVE THEATRE
2 Percival Road, Clifton, Bristol BS8 3LE
Admin 0117 973 0866  Fax 0117 973 6422
BO/SD 0117 974 3384
ADMINISTRATION:
Props: Clifton College

Administrator: CJE Jeffries
Technical & General Manager: Bruno Hunt
Publicity & Box Office: Richard Gourlay
Policy: Educational venue.
Drama, Dance, Film, Lectures, Concerts, Small Scale
Opera, Local & Touring, Amateur and Professional.
Willing to Premiere show.
Seats: 327, disabled access.
Facilities: Licensed foyer bar.
TECHNICAL:
Stage: Proscenium Arch. Pros. opening 10m, tapering to
8.5m x 7.5m. Pros. Arch 10m x 4.1m. Wing width 1.5m.
Height of grid 6.4m. Orchestra pit 5m x 4m on split level.
Dock doors, SL, 1.8m x 3.8m. Green House Tabs, flown.
Lighting: ARRI Mirage with colour monitor, 48ch.
Tempus 36 way, 2 preset, 4 group manual board. 126
Patch channels. Control room at rear of auditorium. 31
spots, 32 Fresnels, 12 PC's, 10 Pars, 5 Cyc battens; All
Strand.
Sound: Soundcraft 200B 16:4:2 Desk. 2 x Bose 802, 2x
Bose 101, 2x ATC Bass Bins, 2x Community CSX 35.
PPX Amps. AKG & Beyer Mics. Tape deck, CD player,
Revox B77. Acoustics suitable for music & spoken word.
Tecpro Talkback system. Foyer & backstage show relay
system.
Other: 2 x Dressing rooms, 1 x Green room. Piano,
upright, reasonable.
2 x Technicians, 1 x Wardrobe, Casuals available.

### ST GEORGE'S BRANDON HILL
Charlotte Street Bristol BS1 5PZ
Admin Tel 0117 929 4929 BO: 0117 923 0359
Fax 0117 927 6537
Administrator: Catherine Freda
Seating/Capacity: 500

### THEATRE ROYAL
King Street, Bristol BS1 4ED
Contact Bristol Old Vic.
TECHNICAL:
Stage: Proscenium width 7.7m, height 6.2m. Playing
area 11m X 11.85m to setting line (plus 2.25m
forestage). Height to fly floor - 7.6m. Height to grid
14.8m.
Lighting: Control: Strand 520 controlling 12 x 5Kw, 40 x
2Kw and 92 x 2.5Kw dimmers. 60 Amp, 3 phase supply
available on stage for special effects etc. Lanterns: 12 x
Alto F, 1 Cadenza F, 6 x 243, 36 x 743, 27 x Cantata
PC, 27 x Cantata 18/32 (20 rigged permanently
FOH),12 x Cantata 26/44 (4 rigged permanently FOH),
20 x Prelude 28/40, 20 x 23, 50 x Parcans (CP62), 10 x
AC1001 1Kw floods, 10 x Coda 1Kw floods, 10 x Coda
3500w floods, 10 X birdies & transformers. Spot Bars: 1
x 24 way, 3 x 12 way, 2 x 18 way, 1 x 3 way flood bar
(5k per way). Special FX: 3 X Bowens flash guns, 1 X Le
Maitre G300 smoke machine, 1 X 12inch mirror ball, 2 X
4ft UV tubes and fittings, 2 X 252 effects projectors, 2 X
3inch 252 lenses, 1 X 2.5inch 252 lens.
Sound: Speakers: 8 X Wharfdale Force 9 250w, 2 X
Whardale Force 10 1200w sub bass, 8 X 250w wedge
monitors, 2 X 100w turbo sound monitors, 2 Tannoy
Lynz, 4 X Control one monitors, 2 X 100 bass bins, 2 X
500w bass bins, 3 X Tannoy Gold 75w, 2 X Tannoy SRM
10, 2 X Fostex powered speakers 150w. Mixers: Spirit 8
32 Channel 2x PSU, Sprirt Live 4 12 Channel,
Soundcraft 500B 16-8-2, Total Audio concepts 16-8-2,
Yamaha Pro-mix 01 16-2, Yamaha MV 802 8-2 rack
mount, DDA 12-4-2 (sound studio). Effects 2 X
Quadraverb reverb + delay, 1 X Lexicon PCM60 reverb,
1 X Klark technics DN3600 graphic, Drawmer DL 24

Dual Auto compressor/limiter, 1 X Helios RE 24
Parametric graphic. Playback: 2 X Sony JE 500 minidisc
players, 2 X CD players, 2 X B77 Revox 3fi - 7 IPS, 1 X
A77, 4 X cassette machines, Pioneer D-05 Dat player,
Sony DA8 portable Dat & power supply, Akai SI000
sampler + midi keyboard, DAC R4000 Hard disc system.
Amps: 1 X MX 300, 1 X MX 500, 1 X MX 250, 1 X PPX
1200, 2 X PPX 900, 2 X PPX 450, 1 X PPX 300, 1 X VX
500, 2 X Quad ST50 + HHIC100L + 10w mini amp.
Microphones: 8 AKG CK77, 6 X SM58, 4 X Beyer 201, 2
X AKG 451 CK1 + CK2 heads swivels + 10db pads, 3 X
PC160, 2 X AKG202, 2 X Sennheiser Rifle mics, 6 X
AKG WMS 3000UHF radio mics with aerial splitter, 1
midi analogue converter.
Misc: 8 X channels passive DI, 1 X 15m multi 26 way
with 6 returns, 1 X 50m multi 28 way with 4 returns +
monitor split, 8 X beyer mic stands, 2 X speaker stands,
1 CD woofer.
General: 6 Dressing rooms acomm 20, 2 showers.

# Bromley, Kent

### CHURCHILL THEATRE
High Street Bromley Kent BR1 1HA
Admin/SD 0181 464 7131 BO 0181 460 6677
Marketing and Publicity 0181 460 1401
Goldcard Hotline 0181 460 5838 Fax 0181 290 6968
ADMINISTRATION:
Props: London Borough of Bromley
Lessees: Theatre of Comedy Co. Ltd.
Theatre Manager: John Short
Theatre Administrator: Dominic Adams
Corporate Hospitality Manager: Alison Carney
Head of Marketing and Publicity: Colin Hilton
Financial Controller: Liz Gentry
Box Office Manager: Zane Rambaran
Production Manager: Digby Robinson
Technical Manager: Chris Nicholls
Technical Stage Manager: Ian Hunter
Company & Stage Manager: Jane Bullock
Policy: Producing theatre, plays, musicals, pantomime,
ballet, Sunday concerts.
Perfs: Evenings Monday-Saturday 7.45. Thursday and
Saturday matinees 2.30.
Seats: 785 (760 when orchestra pit used). Two Bars and
Snack Bar.
TECHNICAL:
Stage: Apron; Flat; Pros. opening 9.15m-13.7m variable;
ht. of Pros. 7.01m; Depth of S/Line 15.09m; Ht. of Grid
14.46m; 50 (47-50 storage only) lines c/w. Scenery
Flying Ht. 5.49m; Flying Bars 16.4m; W/Widths P.S.
10.87m, O.P. 10.67m; Prompt Cnr. P.S. or O.P.
Lighting: Switchboard: Arri Imagine 250 situated rear
stalls. 168 Dimmers 144 x 2.5kW. 24 x 5kW. Patchable
by phase to 380 circuits, F.O.H. 55 profile spots. On
stage 50 Fresnels; 110 parcans, 48 profiles, 6 x IRIS 4
10 x Coda 4 battens.
200A 3 Phase USL, 100A 3 Phase DSR, 200A Single
Phase DSL available for temporary lighting, sound rig.
Sound: Soundcraft Venue 32:8:2 with 8 way matrix. 1
gram 2 Revox 1 cassette 1 CD 24 mic. tielines DSL.
Other: Dressing Rooms 12, accom. 135 inc. Band and
Chorus; 6 Showers; Orchestra Pit :15 plus.

# Buckhaven, Fife
Pop. 6,500. Newspapers: East Fife Mail (wkly); Dundee
Courier (dly); Scotsman (dly). STD code 01592

### BUCKHAVEN PARISH CHURCH THEATRE

Lawrence Street, Buckhaven, Leven,
Fife KY8 1BQ Scotland
Mgt/BO 01592 715577
ADMINISTRATION:
Props: Buckhaven Parish Church
Theatre Director & Administrator: Bryce Calder
Stage Manager: Alan Dingwall
Box Office Manager: Fred Pullar
Policy: Community theatre with commitment to
professional theatre training. Regular professional
productions - own company, ARK - with Christmas
pantomime. Additional touring productions by own
community company, local amateur companies,
professional concerts, youth & children's theatre. Aims to
give training and experience to theatre personnel and to
recreate an 'old-style' repertory theatre within the local
community. Welcomes small professional touring
companies.
Perfs: Mon-Sat 7.30p.m. Mats. Saturday and by
arrangement.
Seats: Auditorium 102 raked plus boxes accommodating
10-30 (depending on staging). Foyer: 30-40, moveable
seating.
TECHNICAL:
Stage: Proscenium width 7.25m opening to 12m with
some restricted view. Stage depth 7.5m within
proscenium width. Forestage: Removeable extension.
Width 7.10m. Depth 2.20m. Overall stage depth 9.80m
Proscenium height 4m, grid height 4.5m, masking height
3.5m. Prompt on stage right. Workshop on stage right
11.1m x 4.2m x 4.9m high. Complete black masking.
Stage Equip: 5 tab tracks plus house tabs. 8 x 3m
braces. 8 x 2m braces. 20 x 28-lb stage weights.
Lighting: Lighting board M24 plus effects panel. 72
circuits. 12 prelude 16/30. 8 prelude 28/40. 18 prelude
F. 10 prelude PC. 5 coda 500/4. 2 Patt.23. 4 T-84. 2 T-
64. 1 Cantata 11/26 (F-Spot). 4 Code 500/1. 35mm
slide projection facilities available. 4 stage stands.
Sound equip: Studiomaster 8 into 4 mixer. 3
Studiomaster Mosfet 500 amplifiers. 2 x 300w OHM
FOH speakers. 2 x 70w Peavey wedges. 3 SM58 mics.
1 Teac cassette deck. 1 Sharp cassette deck. 1 Revox
B77, 2 M69, 1 M201. 1 AKG 451. Headset
communication points throughout auditorium.
Other: Dressing Room call system. F.O.H. call system.
Cue lights x headsets x 6.
Projection: 1 Fumeo HL 2000 16mm projector, with
1800m spool capacity.
Video facilities: Hi8 Sony Camera and playback facilities.
Dressing Rooms: 4 with comfortable accom. for 50
people plus utilitiy room. 6 showers. Orchestra pit for 36
musicians with 24 stands. Green Room.
Non Performance Activities: Conferences, art & craft
exhibitions, youth theatre (Sat. mornings), film club.
Catering: Restaurant & Coffee/snack bar open daily at
lunch time and in the evenings. Suppers/full meals can
be booked in Theatre restaurant.
Access: Own car parks and other free parking spaces
available. Nearest station: Kirkcaldy. Bus service. Free
transport often available for early block bookings.
Facilities for the Disabled: Up to 8 wheelchair spaces; lift;
toilets; auditorium and front-of-house fully accessible.
Other Facilities: Conference rooms, audio/visual equip.,
Yamaha and clavinova, superb condition. Smoke
machine, large costume hire department.

## Builth Wells, Powys

Pop. 1,600. London 173 miles. Newspapers: Brecon &
Radnor Express (wed); County Times and Express (sat);
Mid-Wales Journal (fri). STD code 01982

### WYESIDE ARTS CENTRE

Castle Street, Builth Wells, Powys LD2 3BN Wales
Mgt 01982 553668 BO 01982 552555
Fax 01982 552515
ADMINISTRATION:
Administrator: Debbie Burch
Technical Manager: Chris Sennett
Multi use Arts Centre - 2 Auditoria, Gallery.
Disabled access, symbols for wheelchairs and hard of
hearing (infra red & lift now installed).
Max. seating approx. 258
TECHNICAL:
Market Theatre  Unique performance area 19m x 10m,
flat floor, stone finished interior with alcoves on 3 sides.
Usual use: end stage 7m x 10m with raked seating.
Sprung Stage, suitable for dance.  M24 Lighting Board
into 70 ways hard wired.  6'6" Bechstein Grand.
Castle Theatre/Stereo Cinema End stage 9m x 7m, no
wing space, limited height. Fixed seating max. 212. Two-
level projection/control room auditorium rear - 2 x
Westrex 35mm projectors. Thorn SM40 3-Preset board,
limited lighting facilities. 5'8" Bechstein grand.
Available between 2 theatres:
Lighting: 16 x 1K Profiles; 26 x 1K Fresnels, 10 x 650w
Fresnels.
Sound: 12/2 Studiomaster mixer; 1 x B77 Revox reel-to-
reel tape deck; 1 x Teac Stereo Cassette deck; 1 x HZ
DPX1000 power amp, Driving Kudos, full range cabs
(1/2 k per side approx.).

## Burnley, Lancs

Pop. 94,000. Newspapers: Burnley Express (tue-fri);
Burnley Citizen (wkly); Lancs Evening Telegraph (ntly).
STD code 01282

### BURNLEY MECHANICS

Manchester Road Burnley, Lancashire BB11 1JA
Mgt 01282 430005 BO 01282 430055
Fax 01282 457428
ADMINISTRATION:
Props: Burnley Borough Council
General Manager: David Peirce
Technical Manager: Jon Yull
Policy: Amateur and Professional drama, music and
dance plus resource base for community out-reach
programme.
Seats: 500 standing or 427 fully seated. Two bars,
coffee bar, buffet.
TECHNICAL:
Stage: Proscenium stage, flat floor. Opening 9.1m,
Depth 7.2m, Ht. to Grid 6.25m, 24 Hemp lines, no fly
tower. Prompt corner S.L. back stage & FOH paging.
Orchestra cue. Cue + induction loop system.
Lighting: Switchboard: ARRI impuls 108 CH + ARRI
connexion plus with effects module & connexion remote
control. Demmultiplex: two ARRI connexion modules
USITT D.M.X. 512 (RS 485). Dimmers 120 Strand
Permus, 108 at 10 amps & 12 at 20 amp. Circuits, FOH
48 Flies 52 & Dips 20 lanterns. 6 x C.C.T. sil 15, 6 x
Harmony 15/28, 4 x Harmony 22/40, 10 x Prelude
16/30, 20 x Harmony P.C. 10 C.C.T. PC 6 x Coda 500 x
3, 20 Thomas PAC 64 C.C.T. 500W flood S.R. 2 Strand
Solo 2Kw F/spots.
Sound Equipment: 16 into 2 into 2 mixer. Revox 877 Mk
II L.S., Cassette 1 x Teac 1 x Technics CD player L.A.D.
turntable. 2 x Amcron AMPS E.V. central cluster approx.

2Kw plus foldback. Larger rig available up to 6Kw +
monitor mix. For further details please call.
Other: Dressing Rooms: 4, Accom. 60; 4 Showers.

# Bury St. Edmunds, Suffolk

Pop. 30,000. London 75 miles. Newspapers: Bury Free
Press (fri); East Anglian Daily Times. STD code 01284

### THEATRE ROYAL
Westgate Street, Bury St. Edmunds, Suffolk IP33 1QR
Mgt 01284 755127 BO 01284 769505
SD 01284 755838 Fax 01284 706035
ADMINISTRATION:
Props: The National Trust
Lessees: Bury St. Edmunds Theatre Management
Director: Colin Blumenau
Marketing Manager: Matthew Sanders
Stage Manager: Mark Passey
Policy: Touring, Opera & Ballet, Concerts, Pantomime,
Amateurs
Perfs: (usual) 7.30
Seats: 352. Circle Bar. Foyer Coffee (Restaurant)
TECHNICAL:
Stage: Proscenium Stage, Flat with either Forestage or
Orch. Pit; 1 Mechanical Trap U/SC; Pros. Opening
7.32m; Ht. of Pros. 4.82m (variable); Depth of S/Line
9.75m; Ht. of Grid 6.09m; 18 Hemp sets, 5 Winch sets;
Flying Bars 9.75m; W/Widths P.S. 1.52m, O.P. 1.52m;
Prompt Cnr. P.S.
Lighting: Rank Strand Light Board M, the board has a 3
1/2" disk drive. There are 96 circuits, 78 x 2.5k circuits
17 FOH, 61 onstage, 18 x 5.9k circuits, 3 FOH, 15
onstage.
The control room is located at the back of the gallery.
There is no room for sound equipment in the LX box.
Sound and Lighting are operated from separate
positions and cannot be run by the same person.
Lanterns: 12 x Cantata 18/32, 10 x Silhouette 30, 4 x
Silhouette 40, 4 x Prelude 16/30, 2 x Prelude 28/40, 20
x Patt 743, 6 x Patt 243, 6 x Cantata F 1.2k, 18 x par
can, 8 x patt 123, 4 x Minuete F, 19 x Patt 23, 12 x
Starlette floods 1k, 2 x follow spots 2.5k.
Sound: The Theatre Royal Sound System is operated
from the back of the Grand Circle. The Mixing Desk can
be moved onto the stage if required. Sound Equipment
list: 1 Soundcraft 200b Delta Mixing Desk, 4 Electro
Voice S200 speakers, 2 Electro Voice AXR 606 Bass
speakers, 1 EVT EX18 Crossover, 3 H/H VX 900
amplifiers, 1 Revox B77 reel to reel 7 1/2 15 ips, 1
Tascam 32 reel to reel, 1 Denon DRM 500 cassette
player, 1 Yamaha 32 Band Graphic Equaliser, 1 Yamaha
SPX 1000, 6 Shure SM 57 Microphones, 6 Shure SM 58
Microphones, 2 DI Boxes EMO.
Other: Dressing Rooms 6; Accom. 35 excl Band
accommodation; 1 Shower, Orchestra Pit up to 25.
Get-in limited by gate 1.22m x 2.59m.
Parking difficult.
Membership: TMA

# Buxton, Derbys

Pop. 20,000. London 159 miles. Newspapers: Buxton
Advertiser (thurs). STD code 01298

### OCTAGON THEATRE
Pavilion Gardens, St John's Road, Buxton, Derbyshire
SK17 6XN
Tel 01298 23114 Fax 01298 27622
Seating/Capacity: 1,000 (flexible).

### OPERA HOUSE
Water Street, Buxton, Derbyshire SK17 6XN
BO 01298 72190 SD 01298 71382 Mgt 01298 72050
Fax 01298 27563
Email: admin@buxton-opera.co.uk
ADMINISTRATION:
Props: High Peak Theatre Trust Ltd
Theatre Director: Andrew Aughton
Technical Manager: Guy Dunk
Policy: Professional and Amateur Productions, One Night
Stands, Conferences, Filming, Festival July/August.
Perfs: Variable (usually 7.30p.m.; Mats, Thurs & Sat
1.30p.m.)
Seats: 937. 3 Bars.
TECHNICAL:
Stage: Proscenium Stage, raked with removable
forestage over orchestra pit, to seat 60 Musicians. Pros
opening 9.06m x 6m high. Pros wall to back wall 12m.
Grid Ht. (downstage) 14.75m. Flying; 37 lines, 'Hemp'
from OP flyfloor. 4 lighting winches. Up to 3 pieces of
flying scenery may be counterbalanced assisted. W/widths
PS 3.97m, OP 4.02m. Prompt corner PS. Get in down
13 steps. Get in doors 3m wide x 4.25m high.
Lighting: Strand Lighting Gemini 2+, 360 channels.
Multiplex output to dimmers, Strand D54 protocol.
DMUX unit: 144 channels, of which 120 are controlling
installed dimmers and 24 are available to control
dimmers using a -10v control voltage via 4 Bleecon (8
pin DIN) connectors. Dimmers: 120 Strand STM 2 KW
dimmers with one 15A BESA outlet per dimmer on S.L.
flyfloor. Luminaires: Standard rig: 14 Cantata 11/26
1.2KW Profile on gallery bar; 6 Cantata 18/32 1.2KW
Profile on S.L. Upper Circle Boom; 6 Cantata 18/32
1.2KW Profile on S.R. Upper Circle Boom; 12 Cantata
PC 1.2KW prism convex, with barndoors on winch 1; 12
Cantata PC 1.2KW prism convex, with barndoors on
winch 2; 12 Cantata PC 1.2KW prism convex, with
barndoors, on winch 3; 16 Iris 1KW Floods, (4 washes)
on winch 4. Additional rig (stored understage): 12
Cantata 26/44 1.2KW profile; 6 Harmony 15/28 1KW
Profile; 2 Cantata PC 1.2KW prism convex, with
barndoors; 6 Prelude 28/40 650w profile; 6 Prelude PC
650w prism convex, with barndoors. Also available for
hire: 40 Thomas Parcans PAR 64 240v, 1KW
CP62/61/60; 4 Cadenza F 2KW Fresnels, with
barndoors; 2 Cadenza PC 2KW prism convex, with
barndoors.
Sound: 1 Soundcraft series 400B 16-4-2 mixing console;
3 HH V500 stereo amplifiers, 250 watts per channel; 4
Bose 802 series 11 loudspeakers, 240 watts each, with
1 Bose 802-C system controller, rigged on proscenium
booms; 2HH Pro 200 series 11 loudspeakers, 400 watts
each; 1 Revox B77 Mk.1 half track tape recorder, 33/4
/71/2 i.p.s; 19 way multicore (fifteen sends and four
returns), permanently installed from S.L.
Orchestra pit to seats O,P,Q 11-16 centre rear stalls;
Yamaha SPX-90 digital multi-effect processor; 2 BSS
AR116 Direct Injection Box, 48v phantom powered.
Rear stalls sound re-inforcement: 1 Klark Teknik DN716
digital delay system; HH V500 stereo amplifier, 250 watts
per channel; 4 Bose 101 loudspeakers, mounted under
the front edge of the dress circle of the dress circle. 6
SM58 mics with boom stands.
Other: Orchestra Pit: Large Orchestra Pit available by

removing sections of the forestage; 23 lit music stands; 1 RAT conductors lit music stand.
Wardrobe with automatic washing machine and tumbledryer. 8 Dressing rooms to take 55 artistes, 2 showers.

# Camberley, Surrey

Pop. 44,967. London 30 miles. Newspapers: Camberley Mail (tues); Camberley Courier (fri); Star (thurs); Camberley News (fri). STD code 01276

## ARTS LINK

Knoll Road, Camberley, Surrey GU15 3SY
Mgt 01276 707606 BO 01276 707600
ADMINISTRATION:
Props: Surrey Heath Borough Council
Policy: Pantomime, Variety Shows, Opera, Ballet, One Night Stands, Amateur Productions, cinema and conferences, exhibitions, etc. Full A.V and conference facilities.
Perfs: Variable
Seats: 408 max. Licensed Bar, Cafe/Bar, Full Catering services. 16 x 16m flat floor available.
TECHNICAL:
Stage: Proscenium Stage, Flat; Pros. opening 8.84m plus 1.83m deep apron; Ht. of Pros. 4.27m; Depth of S/Line 6.40m; Full depth 8.5m; Wing width 3m approx.; Stage floor: black; Centre and side steps available; Flying ability: rolled cloths only. Prosc to grid 1m. 11 lines (hemp). Bar length: 11m. 2 E-tracks, mid and stage left. House tabs (Gold, black and blue available), 4 sets of black legs, 4 sets of borders, 1 gauze available.
Lighting: Serius Zero 88 48 way switchboard, 48 Eurorack dimmers, 2 Followspots, 8 FOH profiles, 24 1k fresnels, 12 parcans, 4 x 4 way 1k Flood Batons.
Sound: 5k Mono system. Sound console: Soundcraft Delta DLX 24-4-2. Situated rear of auditorium. 6 auxilarys - 4 way monitor mix. Central cluster: EV deltamax 1122, 2EV TL15 Bass Bins, 4 EV S80 delay speakers. Monitors: JBL control 1`s & 2 SX 200. Processors and playbacks. 2 Denon DRM 540 Tape players, 1 B77 Revox, 1 Dennon CD player. 1 Alesis Quadreverb unit. Microphones: shure SM58s, SM57s, D112, AKG Condensers and Di boxes.
Other: Orchestra: Pit length: 9.2m, width: 1.8m. Depth: 50cm./20cm optional. 4 music stands with lights. Staging: 3 x 4 x 8ft height, variable 2ft - 4ft. 3 x 4 x 8ft height, 1 ft.

Studio: Width: 6.4m. Length: 10.36m. 1 dressing room, stage right. Lighting: Serius Zero 88, 24 way. 8 x 650 watt. 8 x 650 watt fresnels and 4 x 500 watt floods. Sound: mobile sound system available for use in the studio or cafe/bar.
Full lighting and sound details are available from the resident technician.

# Cambridge, Cambs

Pop. 100,250. London 54 miles. Newspapers: Cambridge Evening News (ntly); Cambridge Weekly News (thurs); Town Crier (thurs). STD code 01223

## ADC THEATRE

Park Street, Cambridge Cambs CB5 8AS
Mgt 01223 359547 BO 01223 503333
Fax 01223 300085

Email: info@adc-theatre.cam.ac.uk
ADMINISTRATION:
Props: Amateur Dramatic Club
Lessees: University of Cambridge
Manager & Licensee: Nigel Godfrey
Production & Publicity Managers: Helena Ball & Zoe Spyvee
Policy: Amateur productions by University and local groups, occasional small professional touring groups (no fees given).
Perfs: 8p.m + 11pm. Tues-Sat and late nights
Seats: 227. Licensed Bar.
TECHNICAL:
Stage: Proscenium Stage with flat forestage, stepped apron or orchestra pit. Flat Pros. Opening 6.63m; Ht. of Pros. 3.96m; Depth of S/L 8.53m; Ht. of Grid 12m; 40 lines (26 Hemp, 14 cwt). Flying width 9.5m; W/widths PS 4.27m, OP 2.89m; prompt corner P.S.
Lighting: Switchboard Rank Strand 'Gemini" with effects unit controls 92 fixed 2.5kw & 8 fixed 5kw dimmers & 3 Act 6 dimmer racks located around stage area. Can be expanded to 180 dimmers, space for follow spot in lighting box. Lanterns: 20 1kw Silhouette 30, 2 1kw Silhouette 15, 24 1kw Starlette Fresnels, 8 2kw Patt. 243, 24 120V Par 64, 15 500W Minuette Profiles, various 500W fresnels, 12 Coda 1000, 1 2kw Silhouette 15 follow spot, 6 kw starlette PC, 5 Coda 3 Groudrow, 8 240v par 64.
Sound Equip: Mixers - 1 Allen & Heath SC Plus 24-4-2, Power amps; 1 C Audio RA3000, 1 Bose 1800 dual channel (425w), 1 Quad 606 Dual channel (150w); Speakers: 6 Bose 802, 2 A & R CS62 100w columns; Sources: 1 Ferrograph Logic 7 Reel to Reel, 1 Denon DN990R minidisc, 1 Denon DN770 Twin Casssette Deck, 3 CD players, 1 Yamaha REV100 reverb unit, 1 stereo 30 band EQ; Mics: 3 Shure SM58, 3 AKG D190, 3 Beyer M201.
TecPro Talkback ring (10 station); 2 x 35mm Carousel slide projectors (250w) with dissolve unit.
Scenery and lighting service available during vacations.
Other: Dressing Rooms - 2; Accom. 25; Washing machine, irons and drier; Orchestra Pit 10
Winch motor installed..
Membership CEA.

## CAMBRIDGE ARTS THEATRE

6 St. Edwards Passage, Cambridge Cambs CB2 3PJ
Mgt 01223 578933 Fax 01223 578929
BO 01223 503333
Email: theatre@cambarts.co.uk
ADMINISTRATION:
General Manager: Ian Ross
Head of Operations: Raymond Cross
Technical Stage Manager: Nick Stewart
Marketing Manager: Nicola Upson
Front of House Manager: Rebecca Tullett
Box Office Manager: Vivien Mayne
Status: National Touring House. City centre venue built in 1936, designed by C Kennedy. Reopened in December 1996 after major refurbishment. Currently funded by Eastern Arts Board, Cambridge City Council, South Cambridgeshire District Council. Membership of TMA.
Policy: Drama, Dance, Opera, Music, Film, Pantomime and Revue. Willing to premiere show. Terms by negotiation. Also workshops, conferences, trade shows, lectures, films.
Seating: Raked on two levels. Capacity 671.
Catering: restaurant and bars with new facilities.
Access: Nearby car parks, 20 mins from Cambridge rail station, 5 mins from Cambridge coach station.
Facilities for disabled: fully accessible to audience, staff &

performers. Wheelchair spaces, accessible toilets on every floor, hearing loop, facilities for signed performances and audio description, accessible dressing room space including shower. Lift to all floors.
TECHNICAL:
Stage: Proscenium arch. Performing area 10.2m x 10.2m pros opening 7.72m x 4.8m. wing widths 3.5m SR, 4.5m SL with 12.5m flat scene dock. No rake - floor lino on wood, suitable for dance. Understage crossover, stage heated. Height of grid 14.4m 47 counterweight lines. House tabs flown. Forestage apron extensions 1.5m or 2.5m, entrances in front of pros. Orchestra pit in two sizes, maximum depth 6m, width 11.5m. Get-in via alleyway doors SL. Tallescope. Safety Curtain. Scale stage and lighting plans available.
Lighting and Sound: Please contact venue for details.
Other: Backstage: space for 50 understage. 5 rooms with ensuite facilities. Accessible room at stage level. 15 band changing spaces. Crew changing rooms and kitchens. Wardrobe and laundry.
The Arts Theatre is owned and managed by Cambridge Arts Trust.

### CAMBRIDGE CORN EXCHANGE

Wheeler Street, Cambridge Cambs CB2 3QB
Mgt 01223 457555 BO 01223 357851
Fax 01223 457559
Email: admin.cornex@cambridge.gov.uk
Web Site: www.cambridge.gov.uk/cornex.htm
ADMINISTRATION:
Props: Cambridge City Council
Director: Robert Sanderson
Entertainment and Events Manager: Mick Gray
Marketing Manager: Margaret Levin
Operations Manager: Mark Taylor
Business Manager: Graham Saxby
Box Office Manager: Roberta Gates
Policy: Rock, Jazz, Classical concerts, Theatre Productions, Musicals, Opera, Dance, Spectator Sports. Also lectures and private bookings.
Capacity: 1205 - 1462 seated; 1837 standing.
TECHNICAL:
Stage: Fixed stage 16.5m x 4.5m. 2 stage extensions on 6 ton UDL lifts extending to full stage size 16.5m x 9.5m. Stage ht. 1m. Overstage walkways; 20' clearance, 24' clearance to grid, 6 x 250kg winch.
Front of House Lighting Bridge.
House sound and lighting available.
Lighting: Control Arri Impuls II with reflection back up and connection mux unit. 90 circuits of 2K pulsar dimmers. Lighting Equipment includes 70 x PAR 64, 23 x 1K, 6 x 2K Profile, 28 x 1K Fresnel, 10 x 2K Fresnel, 2 x PANI HMI 1200 Follow Spots. Power 3 Phase 250A available for touring lighting. 3 phase 100A for sound. Some masking available, House Tabs on full stage. Casual crew available.
Sound: Martin Audio, Soundtracs sequel II 40:8:2 Desk.
Other: Dressing Room accommodation up to 50 plus production office and fully equipped kitchen.

### GUILDHALL

The Guildhall, Market Street, Cambridge, Cambs CB2 3QJ
Tel 01223 457000 Fax 01223 457519 Premises Manager: Cambridge City Council Tel 01223 457441
Fax 01223 457039
Contact: Martin Beaumont
Seating/Capacity: 699 seated; 400 standing.

# Cannock

Pop. 63,210. London 31 miles. Newspapers: Cannock Express & Star; Cannock Chronicle; Chase Post; Mercury. STD code 01543

### PRINCE OF WALES CENTRE

Church Street, Cannock, Staffordshire WS11 1DE
Mgt 01543 466453 BO 01543 578762
Fax 01543 574439
ADMINISTRATION:
Theatre Manager: Richard Kay
Technical Manager: Terry Fullwood
Status: Multi-purpose centre. A modern building, situated in the town centre, a multi-purpose entertainments complex, built in 1984. Venue funded by Cannock Chase District Council; Local Authority Cannock Chase District Council. RAA WMA.
Policy: Complete range of entertainment including music (classical, jazz, folk, popular), dance, drama, variety and rock music.
Perfs: Usually open 7 days a week. Booking terms box office split, guarantee & split, guarantee, by negotiation.
Non-performance activities: Snooker, wrestling, darts, exhibitions, craft fairs, sales and conferences.
Seating: 439; half flat floor, half retractable.
Catering: 2 Licensed bars.
Ticket outlets: Box Office only.
Access car park: Adjacent, nearest railway station: Cannock, nearest coach terminal: adjacent, bus routes: adjacent.
For the disabled: Wheelchair spaces provided as required - assistance available, contact Duty Manager - lift - parking - level access - ramp at entrance - all house facilities fully accessible.
TECHNICAL:
Stage: Proscenium arch. Performing area 9m x 6.65m - pros. opening 9m x 5.82m - wing widths 1.83m SR, 1.06m SL. Stage raked, 1 in 50 - floor sprung wood, suitable for all dance, no crossover, stage heated. Height of grid 2m - 16 hemp sets, 10cm apart - tab track - maximum flying height 4.57m - black borders, legs and book wings - white cyclorama - red house tabs, drawn - 8 x 13A, plus 60A independent circuits. Forestage 1m. Orchestra pit can be formed by removing front seats. Get-in via dock doors SL - dock doors 1.9m x 2.1m. Tallescope. Scale stage, fly and lighting plans available.
Lighting: Rank Strand Duet 2 Memory System board, 96 circuits @ 10A, 3 phase, operated from back of auditorium or SL - 28 spots, 32 fresnels, Rank/Harmony - followspots operated from back of auditorium.
Sound: Oval 12:2 series 3 desk, operated from back of auditorium - 4 x 250w output FOH, 2 x 100w output foldback, reverb unit - 3 radio, 5 x Shure, 5 x AKG, 2 x Rifle mics - cassette tape systems. Acoustics suitable for music and spoken word.
Other: Stage Management: Prompt corner SL - Technical Projects cue system, 6 outstations - show relay to dressing rooms.
Backstage: 1 x SR, 2 x SL dressing rooms, access by stage door. No wardrobe, but iron and board available, 4 x 13A sockets. Refreshments available during the day from the cafe until 3.00p.m. Piano, moderate. Advice given on accommodation. Staff - 2 technicians - casuals available - no security personnel. Backstage facilities not accessible to disabled performers/staff.

# Canterbury

Pop. 36,290. London 56 miles. Newspapers: Kentish

Gazette (fri); Adscene (tues); Canterbury Extra (tues). STD code 01227

## GULBENKIAN THEATRE

The University Canterbury, Kent CT2 7BN
Mgt 01227 827677 BO 01227 769075
SD 01227 769565 Mktg 01227827956
Technical 01227 823493 CC 01227 823282
ADMINISTRATION:
Props: University of Kent
Director: Dee Ashworth
Technical Director: Pam Hardiman
Box Office Manager: Jenny Woods
Located on the University Campus, purpose built in 1969. Part of a complex incorporating BFI film theatre, licensed bar cafe and exhibition area.
Policy: Mixed programme, small - middle scale touring, student amateur and in-house productions. Willing to premiere shows. Also concerts, opera, dance and lectures. Vacation conference use.
Seats: 342. Raked auditorium. Licensed bar / cafe with exhibition area. Perf: usually Thursday - Saturday at 7.45pm.
(Nearest BR station: Canterbury West) Public Car Park adjacent.
TECHNICAL:
Stage: Open thrust Flat stage raised 0.6m above auditorium floor - hardboard on sprung wood. No dance floor available. D.S. width of thrust 4.95m widening to 10.97m at max. Depth 10.13m, Ht. of grid 5.64m. W/widths S.L. 6.4m. S.R. NO WING. Prompt corner S.L. No Flying. fixed scaffolding grid. Soft black masking. White cyc available. Hard winched blue house tabs S.L. Get-in dock doors 5m x 3m S.L. at stage level. Scale plans avaiolable. Upright and Bechstein grand pianos available.
Lighting: Strand LBX 75 channel memory board in control room at rear of auditorium. F.O.H: 12 sil 30 1kw, 6 patt 264, 12 patt 743, 4 Prelude 16/30. On stage: 2 patt 243, 18 patt 743, 5 patt 263, 8 patt 23, 6 patt 123, 4 Prelude PC, 6 Iris 1, 4 patt 60, 2 patt 252, 6 par 64 (CP61), 1 2kw Sil 30, 1 patt 293 followspot in control room.
F.O.H. outlets 18 x 2kw. 2 auditorium booms 1 x 1kw and 1 x 2kw per side. Advance bar 16 x 1kw. Overstage 24 x 2kw and 4 x 5kw patchable. Dips 8 x 2kw U.S.I. Open fixed grid. 60A single phase supply SL. Mobile tower.
Sound: adjacent to LX board in control room. Allen & Health SC Plus mixer 16:4:2. 2 Revox B77 (3 & 7.5ips) Quad amps. 3 x Martin CX2 F.O.H. 2 x Goodmans onstage monitors. 2 x EV Sx200 wedges onstage. Technics CD player, Yamaha SPX 900, Denon single cassette deck, Kenwood tuner, Nad turntable, various mikes, 8 mike tie lines to lighting box. Accoustics suitable for music and the spoken word. Mixing position in auditorium - advance notice required.
Other: Stage Management: Techpro show relay and paging system to all areas.
Dressing rooms: 3 accomm. 30. Also one dressing room equipped with washing machine, tumble dryer, iron and board, fridge and microwave. No showers.
Staff: 2 technical. Casuals available.
Disabled access: backstage and F.O.H. areas fully accessible to performers and public.

## THE MARLOWE THEATRE

The Friars, Canterbury, Kent CT1 2AS
Mgt 01227 763262 BO 01227 787787
SD 01227 786867 Fax 01227 781802

ADMINISTRATION:
Props: Canterbury City Council
Theatre Director: Mark Everett
Head of Marketing & Development: Karen Adams
Theatre Manager: Peter Walker
Policy: Touring, Concerts, Pantomime, One-Night-Stands
Seats: 993. 2 Licensed Bars.
TECHNICAL:
Stage: Pros. Opening 13.00m. Ht. of Pros. 6.00m to fixed pelmet. (Width may be reduced to 10.40m by tormentors); Stage width centre line to SR counter-weight frame 10.75m, centreline to SL 9.85m. Distance between fly floors 17.80m; Stage depth, rear of safety curtain to back wall 12.4m, to crossover gallery 11.6m, in front of Safety Curtain 0.75m; Floor flat; Flying: 43 installed sets with capacity in wall frame for 48 single purchase C/W, generally at 200mm centres. Max. bar capacity 453kg, bar length 17m. The most downstage set has restricted travel. The House Curtain is hand-operated at Flys level; Stage Manager working corner SR. Mobile Control Desk with extension cable may also be plugged in SL.
Lighting: Switchboard: Rank Strand 160 way Gemini 2, control room rear of auditorium; Dimmers 30 x 5k (to 32a CEE 17 socket with changeover facility to 4 x 15a 3-pin sockets). 80 x 2.5k (15a 3-pin sockets), 50 x 2k (15a 3-pin sockets) in FOH plus 2 circuits on No.1 Spot Bar. Dimmer room below stage level, SR.
Sound Equipment: DDA Q Series 24-8-2 mixer desk, 47 mic tie lines, 10 return lines, 2 Revox tape decks, 1 Tascam double, 2 cassette deck, full appogee F.O.H. rig, 4 foldbacks. Stage management desk by Electrosonic with paging and show relay, twin ring intercom, cue lights and effects circuits.
Storage: Properties store in SL 19 square metres, access, 3.8m x 3.0m high. Get-in: Tailboard height at stage level, upstage right. Doors 3.2m wide x 4.5m high.
Other: Orchestra Pit: 37.5 sq.metres without loss of seats or side stairways; 51 sq.metres with loss of 1 row (27 seats), 87.4sq. metres with loss of 3 rows (87 seats) and side stairs. Accommodation Band Room 34 sq.metres.
Dressing Rooms: 17, Accom. 56/104. Company Manager's office. 10 Showers (5 each sex); Green Room at stage level. Stage door keeper.
Wardrobe: One dressing room equipped with water supply and drainage for two washing machines (one installed), and Tumble Drier.

# Cardiff

Pop. 278,400. London 154 miles. Newspapers: South Wales Echo (ntly); Western Mail (dly); South Wales Argus (dly). STD code 01222

## CARDIFF INTERNATIONAL ARENA

Mary Ann Street, Cardiff CF1 2EQ Wales
Tel 01222 234500 BO 01222 224488 Group Bookings (10 people+) 01222 234551 Fax 01222 234501
General Manager: Graham Walters
Technical Manager: Adrian Hocking
Props: Apollo Leisure (UK) Ltd
For all booking information and further details please contact Sam Shrouder or Nicky Monk at Apollo Leisure (UK) Ltd., Grehan House, Garsington Road, Cowley, Oxford OX4 5NQ. Tel: 01865 782900; Fax: Oxford 01865 782910.
Main arena facilities: 5,500 Entertainment and Convention Seating Capacity, 2,000 Banqueting Seating

Capacity.
Exhibition Area: 4,000 sq.m.
TECHNICAL:
Stage: Steel deck stage, 2 x 300amp 3 phase stage
power. Exhibition services via floor ducts. 12K Sherman
Performance Sound System. Extensive Conference
Services, Barco 5,000 Projector.
350 Delegate conference suite, 36 executive suites,
press suite with dedicated facilities, function suites for up
to 500 persons.
Also includes: Cardiff World Trade Centre - trade
research, business secretariat and communications
centre, video conference suite, boardrooms, meeting
rooms and offices, private dining rooms, langleys
restaurant and World Trade Centre club lounge.

## NEW THEATRE

Park Place, Cardiff CF1 3LN
Mgt 01222 878787 Mgt Fax 01222 878788
BO 01222 878889 BO Fax 01222 878880
Minicom 01222 878881
Information (24 hrs) 01222 878890 SD 01222 878900
ADMINISTRATION:
Props: Cardiff County Council
Head of Arts and Cultural Services: Judi Richards
General Manager: Giles Ballisat
Marketing & Sales Manager: Michael Grensted
House Manager: Jeff Burns
Technical Manager: Neil Williams
Box Office Manager: Pam Ferguson
Policy: Touring, Drama, Opera, Ballet, Pantomime,
Children's Shows
Perfs: Variable, but usually Mon-Sat 7.30, Sat.Mat. 2.30
or 3.00
Seats: 1159
TECHNICAL:
Stage: Proscenium Stage, cantilevered over orchestra
pit. No traps available. Rake 1 in 24. Dock door R.S.L. at
street level. Understage crossover possible. House Tabs
can be operated from stage or fly floor. Height under fly
floor, downstage 7.5m, upstage 7m. Height under grid
16.15m; Pros. Opening 9.14m; 6.4m to border; Depth of
setting line 12.19m; Wing widths, P.S. 5.18m, O.P.
4.42m; Prompt corner O.P. (stage right); 45 X
counterweight sets, 15 X double purchase @ 300kg, 30
X single purchase @ 400kg, All bars 12.05m. Power on
stgae, 200A TPN bus-bar with RCD set 300mA @
200ms delay; 3 X 125A BS4343 socket outlets; 3 X
200A SPN speed clamps. power on fly floor S.L., 200A
TPN cam-locks with RCD set 300mA @ 200ms
delay.Orchestra Pit/Forestage: On three hydraulic
scissors lifts 3.05 X 9.11m each. Full large pit 9.11 X
9.54m, & extends 5.49m under stage, to accommodate
75 musicians.
Lighting: Galaxy Nova sited in control room at rear of
stalls, with 120 X 10A Permus ways & 12 X 25A Permus
ways. 2 X Theatro 1200w MSR follow spots; 27 X
Cantata F, 13 X Patt 743, 12 X Furse MPR, 4 X Sil 30, 6
X Patt 23, 49 X Parcans, 5 X Iris 4; FOH 24 X Cadenza,
12 X Cantata 11/26, 10 X Cantata 18/32.
Sound: Soundcraft 500 mixer 24-8-2 sited in control
room; Central cluster with Renkus-Heinz speakers fed by
2 X "C" Audio SR 404 amps, Renkus-Heinz speakers at
stalls level fed 1 X "C" Audio RA 2000 amp, BES
speakers in 2 X delay rings for rear stalls & rear circle fed
by 1 X "C" Audio SR 202 amp, Misc. Shure & Kudos
speakers for on stage foldback etc.; Klark- Teknic &
Harrison 1/3 outave graphics, Yamaha SPX1000
processor, Revox B226 CD, Denon DRM-540 cassette,
2 X Revox B77 R-R; 5 X PCC160, Selection AKG mics,
Selection Shure mics.

General: 13 X dressing rooms for 77 people; Wardrobe,
Wig room, & Laundry equipped with 1 X washing m/c &
1 X tumble dryer; Company Office, Visiting Dtage
Manager, Conductor, Band room for 60 persons, Band
room for 10 persons. Telephones in all general &
dressing rooms; fax points in Company Office, Stage
Manager, Dressing room 1 & 1A, & fax m/c at stage
door. Show relay, voice & video communication to all
parts of theatre.
Signed and audio described performances on selected
shows.

## SHERMAN THEATRE

Senghenydd Road, Cardiff, South Wales CF2 4YE
Mgt/SD 01222 396844 BO 01222 230451
Mktg 01222 373446 Fax 01222 665581
ADMINISTRATION:
Props and Lessees: Sherman Theatre Ltd
Artistic Director: Phil Clark
General Manager: Margaret Jones
Policy: Theatre for young people with 2 auditoria
centreing round productions of resident Sherman
Theatre Company. Venue for visiting large and small
scale professional drama, dance, opera and concerts;
also host to local amateur and operatic companies.
Programme includes Saturday morning childrens shows
and touring of own childrens and young people's
productions. Facilities for conferences.
Perfs: Morning, lunchtime, afternoon, evening, late night.
Seats: Sherman main auditorium 472 plus space for 2
wheelchairs. Arena Theatre flexible units giving up to 240
seats depending on arrangement. Public bar, restaurant,
backstage bar.
TECHNICAL:
Main Theatre:
Unstressed proscenium opening 11.66m x 5.53m. Depth
of stage excluding apron 10.64m. Max depth of semi-
circular apron (orchestra lift) 3m Grid Ht. 14.44m; Wing
Space 4m (PS) 7m(OP); Single Purchase Counterweights
34. Bar length 15.85m. Get in door 2.7m x 3.5m, 1.6m
above road level.
Lighting Control: A.D.B Vision 10 plus full tracking
backup.m 250 ways fitted. 3 F.O.H. bridges, and two
side auditorium lighting slots. O.P. and P.S.
Sound: Soundcraft venue 2.36 into 8 into 8 mixer, 8 off
meyer UPA1 B1 amped speakers, 2 stereo tape decks
(half track).
Cinema: Screen overall 11.15m x 5.49m (picture size
31ft x 13.5ft), 2 x 35mm, 1 x 16mm projectors. Stereo
optical sound.
Arena:
Octagonal with all round balcony at 1.98m. Max width of
floor 11.89m. Width of clear floor with seating in the
round 6.4m. Get in doors 1.7m x 1.93m at road level.
Lighting bridges over stage. Arri Image Control, 80 ways
overhead. 12 ways on stage.
Sound Equip: Sound Tracs 16 into 4 mixer, 3 x 100w
stereo amps, 2 stereo tape (half track), 4 fixed and up to
4 mobile speakers.
General:
Communications: Full SM facilities, F.O.H. calls ring
intercom, cue lights, show relay. Closed circuit TV (Main
Theatre only).
Dressing Rooms: 5 on 2 floors accommodating 12, 16,4,
7, 17 Showers
Orchestra Pit: 20 musicians.
Recording Studio:
Soundtracs 24:8:2 mixer; 2 stereo tape decks (half
track), cassette decks. 1 compact disc player. 1 Tascam
DA 30 DAT, 1 Tascam DA 88 DAT, 1 Akai 53200
Sampler. Assorted effects.

To rear of stage is a large paint shop extending the full width of stage including PS and OP wing. Paint frame fitted.
Wardrobe and laundry are situated on the first floor. Rehearsal Room, and Dance Studio are accommodated in the basement.

## ST DAVID'S HALL

The National Concert Hall of Wales, The Hayes, Cardiff CF1 2SH
Mgt 01222 878500 BO 01222 878444
Fax 01222 878599
ADMINISTRATION:
Props: Cardiff County Council
Head of Arts & Cultural Services: Judi Richards
Operations Manager: Tony Williams
Programme Manager: Jennifer Hill
Technical Director: Derek Hawker
Policy: Classical and popular music, conferences, film and fashion shows, lectures.
Seats: 1,956. Film 1,200 approx.
TECHNICAL:
Stage: Open platform in 10 hydraulic lifts, standard platform size 10.8m x 17.3, maximum platform size 16.6m x 17.3m; Suspension facilities over stage.
Lighting: 164 Channel Rank Strand Galaxy control 2.5k 5k and 10k dimmers; 2 x 3kw Xenon Lee Colortran F.S.
Sound System: P.A. 24 channel 8 group mixer, 18 mic points in auditorium, 32 on platform.
Other: Communications: Full S.M. desk facilities, ring intercom and cue light. Dressing room calls and show relay. CCTV system. Loop aerials throughout stalls area for deaf aids and translation.
TV facilities: Power supplies and cable ducts to vehicle parking bay. Auxiliary power supplies available on platform. 1 x 200 amp TPN, 2 x 100amp TPN, 1 x 60 amp SP.
Film Projection: 35mm and 16mm film projectors. Full size roll-up cinemascope screen. 35mm Slide projection facility with dissolve.
Scenery access: Goods lift 2.8m x 2.1m to platform level. Plus direct access via external hoist.
Green Rooms and Dressing Rooms: Green Room with licensed bar and refreshment facilities; one other small rest room. 7 dressing rooms with toilet and show facilities en suite. 8 changing rooms with different capacities and toilet and shower facilities.
Membership: TMA

# Carlisle, Cumbria

Pop. 71,000. London 307 miles. Newspapers: Cumberland News (fri); Courier Gazette (wed); Weekly Group. STD code 01228

## SANDS CENTRE

The Sands, Carlisle CA1 1JQ
Mgt 01228 625208 BO 01228 625222
Fax 01228 625666
ADMINISTRATION:
Props: Carlisle City Council
Centre Manager: Jim Douglas
Promotions Manager: Nicky Appleby
Policy: This extremely versatile venue can house classical and popular music concerts, comedy, opera, ballet, dance, plays, pantomime, spectator sports, conferences, exhibitions.
Seating theatre style variable. Main Hall 1410. Secondary Hall 252. 2 Bars and Mobile bars. Restaurant.

Full disabled facilities. Two licensed bars, restaurant, riverside terrace.
TECHNICAL:
Stage Facilities: Main Hall 36m x 26m Height clearance 9m. Secondary Hall 17m x 17m Height clearance 7m. Upper Foyer. Main Hall Gallery. 4 ton suspension point.
Lights: Zero 88, 60 way Eclipse board, rear of auditorium, 2 Follow spots 440w. Tin Halide colour temp 5500 K, 48 1kw PAR 64 Thomas cans, 20 1kw Colortran 6" Fresnels, 10 1kw CCT Silhouette 15, 90 Way theatre lighting panels, patched to 60 channel, green ginger dimmer rack 2kw per channel.
Sound System: Main Hall.
Stage End:
a) 2 x Bose 302 Bass, 4 x 802 Series 2.
b) Fold Back 2 x Bose 802 Series 2.
Catwalk level (10m) Stereo 24 x Bose 802 Series. 2 x KlarTeknik digital delay units. Formula sound Graphic equaliser. Tascam 34 reel to reel. Tascam 12 Cassette deck. Technics SL 1200 Mk 2 Turntable. Allen and Heath SR series 16 into 4 into 2 sound desk, modified. Total power, 7,000 watts RMS. Microphones available: 4 AKG D330 GT.2, D3105, 1AKG C567E, Lavier, Tie clip. 2 AKG D109 Lavier. 1 Audio Shure SM 78 radio mic. 8 Station talkback system. 2 way radio and transceiver paging system. Control room patch panel connecting 19 tie lines and 36 microphone lines situated around the main hall. Conference sound facilities available for the Secondary Hall.
Sound: 60 amp per phase and lighting 200 amp per phase.
TV and Concert Power Supply: 315amp single phase. 2 Phases at catwalk height (10m), 1 Phase stage right with cable hole to outside.
Other: Access: direct to stage, height 3.70m width 3.50m.
Dressing Rooms: 2 x 20 + buffer room, 2 x star. All with showers, handbasins and toilets.

# Carmarthen

## ST PETER'S CIVIC HALL

Nott Square, Carmarthenshire, Dyfed SA31 1PG Wales
Tel 01267 235199 Fax 01267 221607
Contact: Mrs. Fiona Thomas
Seating/Capacity: 500 (400 downstairs, 100 upstairs).

# Carshalton, Surrey

London 17 miles. STD code 0181

## THE CHARLES CRYER STUDIO THEATRE

High Street, Carshalton, Surrey SM5 3BB
Mgt 0181 770 4960 BO 0181 770 4950
Fax 0181 770 4969
Web Site: www.uktw.co.uk/info/charlescryer.htm
ADMINISTRATION:
Props: Sutton Performing Arts Network
Contact: Keith Lancing
Policy: Producing and receiving small-scale theatre venue. Also programmes dance, mime, cabaret, music. Professional and community programme. Hire, split, sometimes fees. Integral Thai restaurant and bar.
Seats: 80-180
TECHNICAL:
Stage: Open flexible performance space suitable for end on: In the round etc.

Lighting: Zero 88 Sirius 48 desk; 50 lanterns + 12 parcans
Sound: Soundtracs FM 12:4:2 sound desk + revox, cassette, CD + turntable. 12 mics, 7 stands, 2 X mini disc players.
Other: Dressing Rooms: 2. Disabled access to control room. Rehearsal room available. Adjacent scenery workshop with full facilities for building, painting, scenery for hire, commercial & educational projects, tuition, school parties, visits etc. Outdoor paved area for craft, street performers etc.

# Castle Douglas

## CASTLE DOUGLAS, TOWN HALL
5 St. Andrew Street, Castle Douglas, Kirkcudbrightshire DG7 1DE
Tel 01556 502732
For Bookings Contact: Mrs. Sandra McCreadie
(01557 330291 Ext. 320)
Seating/Capacity: 296 (Main Hall).

# Chatham, Kent

Pop. 59,060. London 31 miles. Newspapers: Chatham News; Chatham Stand (fri/tues); Kent Today (mon-fri); Adscene. STD code 01634 (Medway)

## THE CENTRAL THEATRE
170 High Street, Chatham, Kent ME4 4AS
Mgt 01634 848584 BO 01634 403868
Fax 01634 827711
ADMINISTRATION:
Props: Medway Council
Theatre Manager: Tony Hill
Technical Manager: Chris Stevens
Front of House Manager: Andrew Cook
Policy: One night stands and weekly productions
Orchestral, Pop., Folk, Big Band, Jazz, Country, Panto.
Perfs: Varies
Seats: 945. Licensed Bar and full catering services.
TECHNICAL:
Stage: Proscenium (with 3.66m apron stage), Flat; Grid; Width 9.09m; C. Line 7.47m curved back wall; 2 (door width) entrances; Prompt Cnr. O.P.; (apply to management for full technical specification). 15 Hemp Flying Barrels. CCTV to all areas.
Lighting: Switchboard: Jands Event Plus - 250 channels; Rear balcony control room, 2 follow spots 2KW. 6 FOH bars, 3 onstage LX winch; 40 Profile, 40 Fresnels, 50 Parcans, Battens and SP F/X.
Sound Equip: Allen & Heath GL4 32-8-2 with complete effects rack (patchable to Cinema Dolby Stereo).
Projection: 35mm Projector with full Dolby Stereo.
Other: Dressing Rooms 5; Accom. 40 persons: 3 Showers; Band Room for 80 persons.

# Chelmsford, Essex

Pop. 58,000. London 32 miles. Newspapers: Chelmsford Weekly News (thurs); Essex Chronicle (fri). STD code 01245

## CHANCELLOR HALL
Market Road, Chelmsford Essex CM1 1XA
Mgt 01245 606635 BO 01245 606505

Duty Manager 01245 606982
ADMINISTRATION:
Props: Chelmsford Borough Council
Dir. of Leisure Services: Bernard Mella
Arts and Entertainments Mgr: Jim Gillies, M.I.L.A.M.
Policy: Concerts, Cabaret, Dinner Dances, Conferences, Trade Fairs, Dance, Small Scale Drama, Tea Dances.
Events promoted by Chelmsford Borough Council range from Dinner Dances, Rock Concerts, Classical Concerts and Light Entertainment. Available for general hiring, suitable for various functions, i.e. conferences, trade shows etc. Multi-purpose hall.
Capacity: 190 raked seating, 300 standing or dinners.
TECHNICAL:
Stage: Main Hall: 27m x 17m; Stage 9m x 3m Apron and 6 x 2m.
Lighting: 36 x 10A dimmers patchable into 24 channels stand MX24 Board, 2 preset memory board. Permus Demux into 2 Tempus 6 x 10 amp Dimmers. Lamps - various - par cans, fresnels and profiles - available on request.
Sound: Soundcraft Spirit 8 into 2 desk. 2 RA 1000 Audio amps. 4 Toa SL150 2way speakers. 1 Dennon Twin Cassette deck. various mics available by special arrangement.
Other: Facilities: Kitchen, 2 Bars and Buffet Bar.

## CIVIC THEATRE
Fairfield Road, Chelmsford CM1 1JG
Mgt 01245 606635 SD 01245 259167
BO 01245 606505 Duty manager 01245 606950
ADMINISTRATION:
Arts/Entertainments Manager: Jim Gillies
Director of Leisure Service: Bernard Mella
Venue funded by Chelmsford Borough Council
Local Authority Chelmsford Borough Council
RAA EA
Policy: From October to March there is a professional repertory/touring theatre and dance season with occasional opera, ballet, concerts, panto and childrens' shows. April to September - professional concerts, amateur productions, childrens' shows, touring theatre/dance.
Perfs: Open 7 days - evening shows starting at 7.30p.m. and 8.00p.m. Sat.mat. start at 2.30, 3.30 or 5.00p.m.
Booking terms: Hire, Box Office split, guarantee & split, guarantee, co-production, by negotiation.
Non-performance activities: Seminars, workshops.
Seating: 525, raked.
Catering: Coffee, ice cream, sweets etc. available, buffets can be arranged, bar with theatre licence.
Access car park: adjacent, nearest railway station: Chelmsford, adjacent, nearest coach terminal: Chelmsford, adjacent, bus routes: adjacent.
For the disabled: 6 wheelchair spaces available - infra red assistive listening system - level access - all house facilities fully accessible, except balcony.
TECHNICAL:
Stage: Proscenium arch. performing area 12.2m x 7.31m - pros opening 11.73m x 4.11m - wing widths 3.66m SR, 1.83m SL. No rake - wooden floor, suitable for all dance, harlequin dance floor in black available, understage crossover, stage heated. height of grid 10.21m - 18 counterweight sets, double purchase, 7 winch sets, 2 tab tracks, hard and soft black masking, 2 set of black drapes, 1 set of silver satin drapes, white back wall used as cyclorama, red velvet house tabs flown, forestage 1.8m deep, dock doors 1.53m x 4.85m, tallescope and ladders, safety curtain. Scale stage and fly plans available. Motorised Orchestra Pit to accomodate up to 20+ musicians; can be reduced to

accomodate up to 6 musicians.
Lighting: ETC Insight 2X, operated at box rear of stalls, 120 x 10 amp channels, 12 x 25 amp channels, strand EC 90 dimmers situated SR., 12 x switched circuits, plus 36 0 - 10v anaologue outputs for ancillary items.  125 amp per phase 3 phase supply in prompt corner SR, for additional equipment.  Lamps: FOH advance bar; 16 x 743's, 4 x 26/44 1.2k cantatas, No 1 perch 4 par 64's, 1 x 1k starlettes for tab dressing, No 2 perch: 3 x 1k silhouette 15/30, No 3 perch 1 x 2k silhouette. on stage lamps: 26 x 743's; 12 Cantata 18/32 1.2KW; 12 Cantata PC's 1KW; 14 x par 64's, 4 2k starlette f's, 4 x 1.2k cantata 26/44, 6 x starlette f's, 6 x 4 way codas for cyc, 2 x strand solo follow spots with magazines and dimmers.
Sound: 6kw system (ex monitors) featuring C-audio amps and Martin JBL speakers.  48 way multicore at side and rear auditorium. Soundcraft Spirit Live 24:3 desk, FX rack with 2 x stereo graphics, reverb, cassette; CD & DAT.  Revox B77 x 2 on request, up to 6 x wedge monitors + 22 mics.
Other: Stage Management: prompt corner SR - TP comms system, 8 and out stations, 8 cue lights stations, show relay/tannoy to dressing rooms, black and white camera monitor system.
Backstage: 2 x dressing rooms below stage accommodating max 18 each, with showers, access by stairs, WC understage with showers, 1 stage level dressing room accommodating max 3 people with shower and wc, large green room with sink, refeshments from foh bars and kiosks, 1 x Knight upright piano, 1 x Kemble upright piano, staff: 2 technicians plus casuals as required, no back stage security. Backstage accessible to disabled performers and staff, with exception of understage facilities .
additional information: 18 lit stands, workshop facilities, scene dock with additional loading bay.

## CRAMPHORN THEATRE
Fairfield Road, Chelmsford CM1 1JG
Mgt 01245 606635 BO 01245 606505
Duty Manager 01245 606950
ADMINISTRATION:
Props: Chelmsford Borough Council
Policy: Small Scale Touring Theatre & Dance, Concerts and Recitals, Workshops, Cabaret.
Box Office and bar in foyer, plus publicity display space and pay-phone.
Capacity: 145 seats; 182 seats with no stage; seating is raked with a central aisle.  It is strongly advised that in view of sightlines, all productions make use of staging.
TECHNICAL:
Stage: The overall size is 14' deep x 36" wide, made up of modular units of 8' x 4', plus 4 units of 8' x 3'. Please note the maximum playing depth is 14', allowing for 2' of the stage which is lost beneath the projection screen. The stage is 800mm high. Stage Drapes - everything is in a matching matt dark black fabric. There is one set of tabs on tab track running immediately in front of film screen (see plan). Plus two drapes of adjustable height for either masking stage right and left, or midstage or downstage tabs.
Lighting: Fluorescents for working lights. Dimmable spot houselights. Stage lanterns available -6 x Harmony 22/40's, 12 Harmony F's. if requested in advance, further lamps are available. Stage lighting control in control room at rear of auditorium and comprises of a Sirius 48 channel memory board. There is a patch circuiting system comprising of 62 hard wired plugs into 36 dimmer channels. Please note that there is no access to control room via auditorium for any cables from stage

area (window does not open). There are 4 x 13 amp sockets at floor level.
Projection: 35mm + 16mm Cine Projection; 2 x Kodak Carousels with dissolve.
Sound: At present the only sound equipment the venue has is for Dolby stereo 35mm projection. However, the three speakers situated behind the projection screen may be patched in to an 8 channel mixer in the control room or auditorium. Plus Revox B77 reel to reel & Denon Twin Cassette Deck
Other: Dressing Rooms: Male & female dressing rooms each accommodating 10 people, plus toilets and one shower. No wardrobe facilities at present and there is limited backstage storage.  Infra red assistive listening system.

# Cheltenham, Glos
Pop. 85,000. London 98 miles. STD code 01242

## EVERYMAN THEATRE
Regent Street, Cheltenham, Gloucestershire GL50 1HQ
Mgt 01242 512515 PR 01242 236700
BO 01242 572573 Fax 01242 224305
ADMINISTRATION:
Props: Cheltenham Borough Council
Lessees: Gloucestershire Everyman Theatre Co. Ltd.
Chief Executive: Philip Bernays
Policy: Producing and presenting theatre and Saturday childrens shows and Sunday night concerts. Active Outreach department.
Main House capacity: 658, Studio theatre capacity: 60 (variable).
Perfs: (usual) Mon-Fri 7.45, Sat 8.00. Mats. Thurs, Sat 2.00.
Restaurant, Cafe and Bars 01242 255021
TECHNICAL: (Main House)
Flat stage prosc. opening 7.36m, height 8.8m, depth from setting line 9.7m; setting line to apron 1.6m; orchestra pit 2.8m deep x 12.2m wide; hydraulic pit, 20 musicians; height of grid 17.7m; counterweight lines 34, scenery flying height 9m; flying bars 10m + 2m extensions; wing widths SR 8.3m, SL 5.4m; prompt corner SR; LX control room rear dress circle.
Lighting: LX board strand 430, Genius software; 2 FOH follow spots Solo CSIs.
Sound Equipment: 32 into 4 into 2 mixer; 6 FOH tannoy speakers; 2 Revox A77 tape decks; 2 cassette decks.
TECHNICAL (Studio)
Length 9.8m; depth 6m; LX grid height 5m; restricted get in/out; limited suspension; LX board: Strand GSX 24 channels; 12 into 4 into 2 sound mixer; cassette deck; gallery at one end.
Dressing Rooms: 6, accom. 50; 10 showers, 2 baths.

## PITTVILLE PUMP ROOM
Pittville Park, East Approach Drive, Cheltenham, Gloucestershire GL52 3JE
Mgt 01242 523852 BO 01242 227979
Fax 01242 526563
ADMINISTRATION:
Props: Cheltenham Borough Council
Head of Festivals & Entertainment: Jeremy P. Tyndall
Capacity: 400 seated or standing.
Fine Regency building in the grounds of Pittville Park. Available for hire for any suitable function or event. Usually open 7 days a week. Booking terms: hire, co-production, box office split, guarantee and split by negotiation. Full catering facilities, 1 licensed bar,

computerised box office Databox.
Parking adjacent to front doors; level access to all facilities; suitably adapted toilet. Dressing rooms not accessible to wheelchair users. Assistance available. Guide dogs permitted.
TECHNICAL:
Flexible performance area. Flat floor, suitable for dance. Portable staging. 30A 3 phase supply. Basic lighting. House PA. Acoustics suitable for music and speech, if amplified.
Dressing rooms: 2. Upright piano.

### THE BACON THEATRE

Dean Close School, Cheltenham,
Gloucestershire GL51 6HE
Tel 01242 258002 Fax 01242 258007
ADMINISTRATION:
Theatre Administrator: Marian Venn
Policy: To provide a well equipped stage for Dean Close School and local amateur productions, and professional entertainment; small drama groups, small opera and dance companies, mime, touring professional companies.
Seats: 550 Licensed bar/teas/coffees/catering facilities.
TECHNICAL:
Stage: 20m wide x 10m; Scenery flying facilities; Orchestra pit 9m wide x 2.5m; Steinway 9ft grand piano with lift.
Lighting: 48-way Zero 88 SIRUS lighting desk and 8 ZERO 88 beta packs with twin 15 amp outlets. 50 assorted lanterns.
Sound: Sec 12 channel mixer; Carver PM900 amplifier; 2 pairs of Bose 802 speakers/ Tech pro communications systems.
Other: Green room and changing facilities for up to 50.

### TOWN HALL

Imperial Square, Cheltenham,
Gloucestershire GL50 1QA
Mgt 01242 521621 BO 01242 227979
Fax 01242 573902
ADMINISTRATION:
Props: Cheltenham Borough Council.
Head of Festivals & Entertainments: Jeremy P. Tyndall
Entertainments & Marketing Manager: Tim Hulse.
Policy: Concert Hall.
Broad-ranging music and light entertainments programme. Booking terms: hire, box office split, guarantee, co-production by negotiation.
Seating/Capacity: 1,008 seated or standing. Full catering service and licensed bar. Computerised box office Databox. Facilities for the disabled: parking spaces in rear car park; ramped access; suitably adapted toilet and telephone; level access to all facilities, but no lift to balcony. Assistance available. Guide dogs admitted.
TECHNICAL:
Stage: Platform stage, performing area 15.85 x 6.7m. No rake. Floor sprung deck, suitable for dance. 160A 3 phase independent circuits. Orchestra pit/stage lift. Get-in via rear, dock doors 1.83m x 2.13m.
Lighting: CCT lighting desk, 24 circuits operated from SL. 2 Rank Solo CSI followspots operated from rear balcony.
Sound: Soundcraft desk, portable operating position, 2 channel, 16 graphic splits, 2 x time zones, gated system, various mics, cassette tape system, house system. Acoustics suitable for music.
Other: Dressing rooms: 3, green room, band room, quick change room. Steinway "D" concert grand, baby grand and upright pianos. Advice given on accommodation. No

permanent stage staff but casuals available. Backstage facilities accessible to disabled performers and staff.

# Chesham, Bucks

London 28 miles. Newspapers: Chesham Advertiser and Bucks Examiner. STD code 01494

### THE ELGIVA

St. Marys Way, Chesham, Buckinghamshire HP5 1LL
Tel 01494 582902 BO 01494 582900
Fax 01494 582901
ADMINISTRATION:
Props: Chesham Town Council
Theatre Manager: David Roden
Policy: Mixed programme, all touring arts and entertainment, cinema, conferences, exhibitions, banquets.
Seats: variable up to 328, disabled access.
Catering: Legends Bar Cafe in foyer. Fully licensed.
TECHNICAL:
Stage: Proscenium stage with 1m thrust. Pros. opening 10m; height of Pros. 3.835m; depth of sight line 9m; 8 lines, hemp; scenery flying height 4.13m; length of flying bars 10m; wing widths p.s. 2m, O.P. 2m; prompt corner O.P.
Lighting: Switchboard: Zero 88 Sirius Lighting Control 48 way. Control room at rear of auditorium. Luminaires-9 Strand 264, 1 batten at rear of stage, 3 spot bars front and mid-stage, 2 follow spots, Strand 23 and 1 Patten 292, 8 Cantata Profiles, 10 Par Cans, 18 650w Preludes Fresnels. 4 x ADB 1KW Fresnels; 4 Minuettes 650 watt.
Sound: Soundcraft Delta 16-4-2, Yamaha SPX 900 Effects Processor, Denon-CD, Cassette, Tuner amplifier; JBL control 5 monitor speaker; Tecpro intercom system. Onstage/F.O.H.-4 4726 speakers; 2 JBL G731 monitor speakers; 2 HH VX 900 power amplifiers; 1 HH VX1200 power amplifiers; BSS-FDF360 electronic crossover; Yamaha Q203A graphic equalizer; Rene GE14 graphic equalizer; Mustang induction loop amplifier; 1JBL control speaker in Dressing Room. Mics - 2 Sure SM58's; 1 AKG D90; 1 AKG D190E; 1 AKG 125; 2 Zennheiser M60/3KU; 2 DI Boxes; A selection of cables and stands.
Other: Full 35mm cinema equipment.
Yamaha C7 Grand Piano.
Dressing rooms 2; maximum accomodation 26. Two toilets.
Orchestra Pit: 7.93m x 2.32m.
Disabled access; Disabled people welcome, please contact venue for details of facilities.

# Chester, Cheshire

Pop. 62,320. London 182 miles. Newspapers: Chester Chronicle (fri). STD code 01244

### GATEWAY THEATRE

Hamilton Place, Chester, Cheshire CH1 2BH
Mgt 01244 344238 BO 01244 340392
Fax 01244 317277
ADMINISTRATION:
Props: Chester City Council
Lessees: Chester Gateway Theatre Trust Ltd
Artistic Director: Deborah Shaw
Production Manager: Scott Ramsay
Lighting Designer: Alan Jackson
Policy: Repertory, Concerts

Perfs: 7.45 Fri/Sat. 8.00. Mat. 2.30p.m. Wednesday, 3pm Saturday.
Seats: 440. Bar, Cafe Bar (open from 10.00a.m.)
TECHNICAL:
Stage: Proscenium Stage with 3m deep removable forestage. Flat. Pros. opening 9.75m, Ht. of Pros. 4.88m. S/Line to limit of flying 11.17m. Ht. of Grid 12.19m. 30 lines C/W. Flying Bars 10.36m, W/Widths. S.L. Minimal S.R. Dock 4.88m Ht. x 4.5m square. Rear Dock 9.7m x 2.8m x 5.5m Ht. Prompt Cnr. S.L. Get-in 5.4m above ground.
Lighting: Switchboard: Gemini 2+, 132 ways 2 x F.O.H. Bridges Stage Spot Bars variable.
Further details on request.
Sound: AHB 24-8-3 mixer, 2 x Revox, 1 x Cassette, 1 Turntable, 4 x Bose 802, 2 x Bose 302, HH + Harrisson Amps and DDA 20-4-2, 4 x martin (SPX) Bose 1800 amp.
Other: Dressing Rooms 4; Accom. 35; 2 Showers; Orchestra Pit.
Membership: TMA

# Chesterfield

Pop. 95,000. London 149 miles. Newspapers: Derbyshire Times (fri); Sheffield Star (dly). STD code 01246

## POMEGRANATE THEATRE
Corporation Street, Chesterfield, Derbyshire S41 7TX
Mgt 01246 345220 BO 01246 345222
Fax 01246 345224
ADMINISTRATION:
Props: Chesterfield Borough Council
Arts Manager: Ian Whiteside
Stage Manager: Stuart Basson
Chief Technician: Keith Tuttle
Policy: Touring, Pantomime, Plays, Musicals, Variety, Sunday Concerts.
Perfs: to suit production.
Seats: 546. Licensed Bar in Stalls; Coffee bar.
TECHNICAL:
Stage: Proscenium Stage, Raked; Pros. opening 7.92m; Ht. of Pros. 6.71m; Depth of S/Line 9.10m; Ht. of Grid 13.41m; 22 lines; Hemp. Flying Ht. 7.32; Flying Bars 9.14; W/Width 2.44m; Prompt Cnr. O.P.; Get-in Street Level.
Lighting: Switchboard: Rank Strand Duet 2 or 60 x 10, Duet Pin Matrix. remote from rear stalls; FOH Spots 6 T84, 14 Patt.763, 4 Patt.23; Stage 3 Patt.23, 7 Patt.23S, 14 Patt.123, 3 Patt.23N, 6 Patt.223, 7 Patt.243, 2 Patt.252, 10 Iris 1, 2 Patt.43B, 2 Patt 765 Follow Spots.
Sound Equip: 1 Revox B77 Tape deck 2 Tandberg 0.50 track Tape Decks; H/H Amplifier.
Other: Dressing Rooms 7; Accom 25; Orchestra Pit 25.
Membership: TMA

## THE WINDING WHEEL
13 Holywell Street, Chesterfield, Derbyshire S41 7SA
Tel 01246 345333 Fax 01246 345330
Contact: Ms Chris Norcliffe
Seating/Capacity: 1,000

# Chichester, West Sussex

Pop. 21,000. London 163 miles. Newspapers: Chichester Observer (fri); Chichester Promoter (thurs). STD code 01243

## CHICHESTER COLLEGE OF ARTS
Westgate Fields, Chichester, West Sussex PO19 1SB
Tel 01243 786321  Fax 01243 539481
ADMINISTRATION:
Head of Department: M G Seath
Tel 01243 812210  Fax 01243 527884
Studio Theatre (seats 100, retractable) to form large studio or exhibition area. Workshop, Dressing Rooms. 2 Dance Studios - sprung floors, mirrors. 5 Drama Studios - showers, toilets. Lighting and sound control room, recording facilities. Adminstration and box office, coffee bar area.

## CHICHESTER FESTIVAL THEATRE
Oaklands Park, Chichester, West Sussex PO19 1SB
Mgt 01243 784437 BO 01243 781312
SD 01243 784437 Fax 01243 787288
ADMINISTRATION:
Props: CFT Trust Company Ltd
Lessees: CFT Productions Co Ltd
Director: Andrew Welch
General Manager: Paul Rogerson
Administrator: Kate Mosse
Production Manager: Christopher Bush-Bailey
Policy: The main season runs from late Spring to early Autumn. During the rest of the year, performers of renown provide a kaleidoscope of entertainment which includes music, ballet, opera, jazz, pop groups, touring plays and a family show at Christmas.
Perfs: 7.30 Mon-Sat; Mat. Thurs & Sat 2.30.
Seats: 1,374. Three Bars, One Snack Bar.
TECHNICAL:
Stage: Thrust. Performing area 9.34m x 9.65m. No Rake. Floor Canadian Maple (not sprung), suitable for dance. Understage crossover. Stage heated. Height to rods 6.4m, no flying, hanging only - Black flats and soft masking, tab track. 100A 3 phase independent circuit. Forestage entrances and footlights. Get-in via platform lift. Dock door 3.05m x 2.64m. Scenery lift. Talescope. Scale stage and lighting plans available.
Lighting: Strand Galaxy Nova Board, 168 circuits @ 32-10A, 18 circuits @ 25A, 3 phase, operated from auditorium - 100A 3phase supply available from temporary board up centre - 130 spots, 130 fresnels, 60 pars - 2 followspots operated from roof.
Sound: 1 x Amek Langley 501 40:8:4 sound desk, operated from auditorium/FOH - C Audio and D&B amps - D&B, Bose & turbosound speakers - AKG, beyer and Sennheiser mics, 6 x Micron radio mics - 3 x Denon minidisc, 1 x AKAAIS3000 sampler, 2 x Revox B77, 1 x Tascam 4-track reel to reel tape systems - facilities for recording and editing. Acoustics suitable for both music and the spoken word.
Other: Stage Management: prompt corner auditorium/F.O.H. Clearcom and radio cue system, Clearcom 12 outstations, radio 6 outstations and cue lights 10 outstations - show relay/Tannoy to dressing rooms.
Backstage: Various dressing rooms, showers, access by backstage. Green Room. Band Room. Quick Change Room. Wardrobe backstage with laundry facilities and various sockets. Refreshments available include hot drinks, snacks, sandwiches, etc. Piano OK. Advice given on accommodation.
Staff: 4 stage, 4 lighting, 1 sound, casuals available.
Security Personnel. Backstage facilities accessible to disabled performers and staff.

MINERVA THEATRE
at the Chichester Festival Theatre

ADMINISTRATION:
See the Chichester Festival theatre.
Policy: Theatre which offers one of the most adventurous programmes during the year in the south. Season runs in conjunction with the main house. During Autumn, Winter and Spring months, touring productions offer a mixture of drama, comedy, ballet, dance, opera and classical and contemporary music recitals and a season of films with some of the biggest new cinema releases, screen successes, popular and art house movies presented in The Minerva's flexible seating which is altered to give a cinema-type layout. Conference facilities.
Perfs: 7.45 Mon-Sat, Thurs & Sat 2.45.
Seats: 278
Theatre Restaurant (Tel 01243 782219); Society Club Room (Tel 01243 774565); Bookshop; Bar.
TECHNICAL:
Stage: Thrust. Performing area 9.7m x 7.3m. No Rake. Wooden floor. Black flats and soft masking track. Height to lighting bars 5.6m - tab track. No flying, hanging only. Platform lift 4.8m x 2m from get-in to stage level. Scale stage and lighting plans available on request.
Lighting: Gemini 2+ board, 72 ways, 10A per channel - no supply available for temporary board - 42 spots, 48 fresnels, 20 pars.
Sound: Soundcraft 500 16:8:2 desk operated in either control box or auditorium. Bose and EV Speakers - 2 x Revox B77 reel to reel and cassette tape systems; 3 x Denon minidiscs.
Technical projects communication systems, 6 outstations - 6 x TP headsets/belt packs. Show relay and tannoy to dressing rooms.
Backstage: 2 dressing rooms - accommodates 20. (Staffing as main house), showers in toilets, washing machine and tumble dryer.

# Chipping Norton, Oxon

Pop. 5,500. London 74 miles. Newspapers: Oxford Times; Cotswold Standard; Banbury Guardian.  STD code 01608

## THE THEATRE
Spring Street, Chipping Norton, Oxfordshire OX7 5NL
Mgt 01608 642349 BO 01608 642350
Fax 01608 642324
ADMINISTRATION:
Props: Council of Company
Director: Tamara Malcolm
General Manager: Mathew Russell
Policy: Touring Theatre (including Children's), concerts, films, occasional own productions, including yearly pantomime.
Perfs: Variable
Seats: 235. Bar, Art Gallery
TECHNICAL:
Stage: Proscenium Stage, Flat; Width of Pros 5.34m; Ht. of Pros. 3.46m; Depth of Stage 7.9m; W/Widths 1.22m; Ht. of Grid 3.6m. Flying facilities: 16 hemp sets, 4 winched LX bars. Prompt Cnr. P.
Lighting Control: 72 ways. Dressing Rooms 3; Accom. 16.
Membership: TMA

# Cirencester, Gloucestershire

## SUNDIAL THEATRE
Stroud Road, Cirencester, Gloucestershire GL7 1XA
Admin 01285 640994 Fax 01285 654228
Fax 01285 644171
ADMINISTRATION:
Theatre Manager: Eric Richards
Technician: Andy Webb
Marketing Officer: Louisa Davison
Artistic Adviser: Duncan Walthew
Policy: To further the partnership between the professional arts, education and the community.
Status: Arts Centre on the Fosse Way Campus of Cirencester College.
Seats: 244 raked, retractable, fully upholstered One bar, full licence, variable hours College Refectory, variable hours. Disable access and toilet. Car park in College grounds. Nearest station: Kemble.
TECHNICAL:
Stage: Performing area sizes overload. End platform stage. Wings defined by curtains. Entrance via side doors or main entrance. Height of grid from stage 3.92m. Height of grid from floor 4.85m.
Lighting: Strand lighting MX board, 24 channels with Strand lighting Tempus 12 backup operated from control at rear of auditorium. Lanterns: 4 spots, 10 Fresnels, 5 Quartet PCs, 4 Cantata PCs, 4 Parcans, 6 Floods, 4 Coda IIIs, 6 PAR 38s and 1 mini strobe.
Sound: Miscara M1002PD 12 channel (2-4 stereo) including digital effects processor, Behringer compressor/noise gate, Denon cassette, Denon CD, 2 X Audio Technica, 2 X Shure SM58 Vocal mics, and 2 X Shure Prologue condenser mics. 2 X Laney TE600 speakers. Standby PA to dressing rooms and/or bar area. 5-way headset intercom system available, operated from control box at rear of auditorium. Acoustics suitable for music and spoken word. Wooden floor suitable for dance. Broadwood grand piano tuned regularly.
General: Large dressing room with power points and sink. Large workshop area with excellent access to stage. Solid moveable partition between workshop and stage.

# Clacton-on-Sea, Essex

Pop. 50,000. London 69 miles. Newspapers: Clacton Gazette (fri). STD code 01255

## PRINCES THEATRE
Station Road, Clacton-on-Sea, Essex CO15 1SE
Mgt 01255 253208/9 BO 01255 422958 Advance Sales 01255 423400 Enterainments Officer 01255 253298
ADMINISTRATION:
Props: Tendring D.C.
Entertainments Officer: Bob Foster (Tel. 253298)
Policy: All year attractions (mainly One Night Stands), Band and Orchestral Concerts, Dances, Wrestling, Conferences. Also Amateur Operatic and Dramatic Society productions.
Seats: 820. Lounge Bar.
TECHNICAL:
Stage: Rake; Pros. Opening 9.75m; Ht. of Pros. 5.49m; Depth of S/Line 6.10m; 20 lines, C/W; Flying Bars 10.97m.
Lighting: Switchboard: Sirius 48 channel zero 88, 16 Dip Points, 3 Battens, Floats, 10 F.O.H. Spots, 48 Cabaret Floods, Mirror Ball with 4 x 500 Spots; 2 x 2000 Follow Spots.  Full technical talk back system.
Sound Equip: Soundcraft 200SR Mixer Desk 16-4-2. Hill amplifiers LC1200 and LC400. Bose speaker system and fold backs. 12 x Shure SM58 microphones. 4 x

Sennheiser Rifle microphones. 4 x Sennheiser Diversity Clip-on microphones.

## WEST CLIFF THEATRE

Tower Road, Clacton-on-Sea, Essex CO15 1LE
Mgt 01255 474000 BO 01255 421479
ADMINISTRATION:
Props: West Cliff (Tendring) Trust Ltd
Administrator: Mike Grady
Technical Manager: Alan King
Policy: Medium-scale touring productions & concerts, amateur drama and panto; professional summer show July-Sept.
Perfs: vary with event.
Seats: 590 + 3 wheelchairs. Bar/coffee bar. Foyers used for small exhibitions.
TECHNICAL:
Stage: Raked (2°) stage with thrust, 8.5m wide, 9m deep, working height 5.5m, max flying height 7.5m. possible within thrust. Rope flying with 17 barrels.
Lighting: Avolites Pearl 2000 desk, 60 dimmers, plus Eltec Sceptre computer; usual lanterns plus 2 Strand 765 follow-spots.
Sound: Soundcraft Delta SR mixing desk, Quad 606 amp feeds Bose 802 speakers. Cassette, selection AKG & Shure microphones. Yamaha Clavinova 550 electric piano (no grand).
Dressing Rooms: 7, Accom. 30.

# Colchester, Essex

Pop. 145,100. London 54 miles. Newspapers: East Anglian Daily Times; Evening Gazette (ntly); Colchester Express (thurs); Essex County Standard (fri). STD code 01206

## MERCURY THEATRE

Balkerne Gate, Colchester Essex CO1 1PT
Mgt 01206 577006 BO 01206 573948
SM 01206 766739 Restaurant 01206 546645
Fax 01206 769607
ADMINISTRATION:
Lessees: Colchester Mercury Theatre Ltd
Chief Executive: Dee Evans
Artistic Producer: Gregory Sloy
Marketing Director: Philip Bray
Production Manager: John Buckle
Policy: Repertory
Perfs: Mon, Tues, Wed 7.30; Thurs, Fri & Sat 8.00; Mat. Thurs 3.00, Sat 4.00.
Seats: 499 Open Stage. 409 Pros. Licensed Bar, Restaurant, Lift, Wheelchair Spaces, Studio Max. seating 75.
1 signed performance per run.
TECHNICAL:
Stage: Adapatable Proscenium/Open semi-thrust stage flat, hexagonal; Pros. Opening min. 8.53m; Max. open width 12.19m; Ht. of Pros. 5.73m; Working stage depth 8.84m plus 1.52m apron; Ht. of grid 13m; 10 double-purchase C/W lines, 1 single purchase C/W for house tabs; W/Widths P.S. irregular 1.40m min. 4.88m max., O.P. regular 1.40m max. some room in scene dock adjacent P.S. Prompt Cnr. P.S.
Lighting: F.O.H.:- 3 Bridges with catwalks over auditorium, side positions in audit. walls. 50 circuits. On Stage:-Bars spotted from grid as required. 43 circuits on fly floors. 8 circuits at stage level. 16 independents. Eurolight Micron 96 way memory board patched into 101 dimmers. Strand SP 80 as backup. Spacious

LX/Sound Box rear of auditorium. 2 x Sil 15 CID followspots. S/By generator for F.O.H. Offices and Stage/auditorium working lights and 18 stage circuits.
Lantern Stock: 45 x 264; 30 x 743, 11 x 243, 2 x ADB 2k; 10 X Sil 30; 2 x Sil 25; 8 x Sil 15; 12 x 123; 30 x 23; 12 Nocturne 1k Cyc floods. 61 x Par 64.
Studio Equip: Green Ginger 20 way 3 Pre./9 GRP board and racks.
Sound Equip: 3 Revox B77, 2 x Cassette Decks; 1 x L.A.D. 828P Record Deck ; 1 x CD Player; Soundcraft Spirit Studio 16-8-2 Mixer; 22 mic lines to stage; 2 x Bose 802 spkrs F.O.H;1 x Yamaha SPX90 Digital Processor, 2 x JBL Control 5s, various cabs on stage; 2 x Turner Power amps; 2 x Quad Amps to 14 way 100V line patch system. Mics: 6 x AKG CK 451; 5 x CK1; 4 x CK8; 1 x CK9; 1 x D310; 3 x D190; 1 x Electrovoics. Separate loop induction system.3 x SM58.
Dressing Rooms 5; Accom. 23; 2 showers. Orchestra Pit 5 plus.
Membership: TMA

## UNIVERSITY OF ESSEX LAKESIDE THEATRE

Wivenhoe Park, Colchester Essex CO4 3SQ
Mgt 01206 873261 Fax 01206 873702
ADMINISTRATION:
Props: University of Essex
Artistic Director: Jonathan Lichtenstein
Technical Manager: Tim E Hatcher
Arts Officer: Christopher Holden
Policy: To run a season of Wednesday night theatre programming a selection of the best small-scale touring companies. The theatre has a strong commitment to student productions with 12 productions a year. Theatre available for hire during vacation.
Perfs: Variable
Seats: 217. Bars. Coffee Bars and Restaurant available on campus.
TECHNICAL:
Stage: Flexible, normally Proscenium with apron, but licensed and easily used as Open form with small thrust. Stage floor flat. Permanent curved Cyc. Pros. opening 9.38m; Ht. 4.51m; Depth of S/Line 7.74m; Ht. of grid 6.32 - 7.23m; W/Widths P.S. 2.43m; O.P. 2.68m; Prompt Cnr. P.S.
Lighting: Board: Ovation 96 ways fitted, 2 x SP60/III backup. Control room at rear audit; 16 x Patt.264, 6 x Patt.T64, 8 x Sil 25, 9 x Patt.23 ('N' noses available), 15 x Patt. 243, 30 x Patt.743, 7 x Patt.123, 2 x Patt.750, 12 x Parblazer 4, 12 x AC1001L, 5 x Pallas 4, 2 x Patt.230C, 2 x Patt.252, Follow Spot: Sil 10 (2kw); Dips 15 each side; 2 F.O.H. Spot Bars (access via catwalks), 5 Stage Bars, 4 F.O.H. Perches, 2 Pros booms.
Sound Equip: Thorens/SME/V15 Record deck, Revox PR99, Tascam BR20 (7.5/15ips), Denon DN77OR cassette, Panasonic SV3700, Libra 10 modular mixer (12 mic/line in, 10 groups out), 6 x JBL Control 10, 2 x Stagesound ST2/115, 2X Mission 770 speakers with individual associated power amps; Signal Processing: 2 x Roland SDE 3000 Digital Delays, 2 x Dod 31 Band Graphic Equalisers, 6 x Rebis Compressor/Limiters. 8 x Rebis Parametrics, 6 x Rebis Gate/Expanders, G.B.S. Yamaha SPX1000 Reverberation Unit; D.B.X. (Simultaneous) on tape machines, 4 F.O.H., 4 Stage, 2 Foyer speaker outlets. 10 mic inputs P and O.P. 2 mic inputs control room. 5 undedicated tielines P and O.P. to control room. A.K.G. microphones and stands. Show Relay, S.M. Call, ring headsets and cue-lights to all locations.
Dressing Rooms 4, Accom 29 min, 2 showers,

Wardrobe Room. Fully equipped Workshop/Paintshop. Small Rehearsal Room. Get-in at stage/street level, direct access to service road - Dock doors 4.78m x 1.35m. No fly tower, but height and equipment to fly smaller items.
Membership: TMA, ABT.

# Coleraine, County Londonderry

Pop. 25,000. Newspapers: Coleraine Times (wed); Coleraine Chronicle (thurs); Northern Constitution (fri). STD code 01265

### RIVERSIDE THEATRE
The University of Ulster, Cromore Road, Coleraine, County Londonderry BT52 1SA Northern Ireland
Mgt 01265 44141 exts 4683, 4456, or 4459
BO 01265 51388 Fax 01265 324924
ADMINISTRATION:
Arts Development Officer: Terence Zeeman
Tel 01265 324449  Fax 01265 324924
Theatre Manager: Janet Mackle
Technical Supervisor: David Coyle
Policy: Touring, Ballet, Opera, Own Summer Show, Christmas Show
Perfs: Mon-Sat 8.00p.m.; Occasional Schools Mat. 10.30a.m. or 1.30 p.m.
Seats: Thrust 358, Pros. 274, bar, Foyer, Art Gallery.
TECHNICAL:
Variable Auditorium.
Stage: Thrust stage flat; Height of grid 7.60m; 18 lines suspension only. Prompt corner variable P.S. O.P. or Control Box; Pros. stage flat; stage 9.12m depth 8.51m opening; Wings 2.89m max. Flat Height 4.86m Easy get-in 7.60m x 3.65m.
Lighting Equip: Strand Light Board M, 84 way, all circuits 2kw + 45kw; 5 ind. non-dim 2kw circuits; Lamps 14CCT SIL30 profile, 15 strand contata, 30 fresnels; 2 x Sil. 15 follow spots, 2 Pani BP 15, 30 Harmony P.C.S. Lighting bridges wrap around, and centre crossover. Control room rear auditorium.
Sound Equip: 1 Total Audio Concepts 16-8-2 mixer, 2 Amcron DC300A amps, 1 Amcron D150A amp, 4 Profley 200 speakers, 2 foldback wedges, 4 FX speakers, 12 mic lines, 6 speaker lines, all fully patchable via 260-point patch field and local tie lines; 2 Revox B55 track stereo tapes, 1 Garard 401 deck; 1 Technics RST33R cassette. All speaker connections 4 Pin XLR all mics 3 Pin XLR. SM Control 16 out station ring intercom. 10 way patchable Q Light system. 6 x 12 volt AC and DC supplies.
Dressing Rooms: 4; Accom. 30 plus Quick Change room op. (2); 2 showers; 1 large rehearsal room; Orchestra Pit varies 5 to 30.
Membership: TMA

# Colwyn Bay, Conwy

Pop. 25,470. London 221 miles. Newspapers: North Wales Weekly News (thurs); Abergele Visitor (fri); Llandudno Advertiser (fri); Colwyn Bay Pioneer (sat). STD code 01492

### THEATR COLWYN
Abergele Road, Colwyn Bay, Conwy LL29 7RU
North Wales

BO 01492 532668 SD 01492 530892
Fax 01492 533971
ADMINISTRATION:
Events Manager: Philip Batty
Props: Conwy County Borough Council. For promotion or hire information contact Nick Reed on 01492 879771
Policy: Small-scale Tours/Summer Show/Winter Openings Rep. theatre.
Seats: 434 and space for 3 wheelchairs. One Bar.

# Congleton, Cheshire

Pop. 25,000. London 140 miles. Newspaper: The Congleton Chronicle. STD code 01260

### DANESIDE THEATRE
Park Road, Congleton Cheshire
Tel 01260 278481
ADMINISTRATION:
Props: Daneside Theatre Trust Ltd
House Manager: Mrs S A. Hood  Tel 01782 513066
Policy: Multi-use. Mostly amateur, but available for hire by professional companies for shows and rehearsal.
Perfs: Vary according to show
Seats: 300 raked auditorium. Bar.
TECHNICAL:
Stage: Proscenium, Pros. opening 30ft. Height of pros. 14ft, depth of stage 20ft. Stage width 50ft. Loading doors 6ft hight, 8ft wide. Height to grid 18ft. Workshop same size as stage. 6 Minin Fresnel, Sirius 48 Desk.
Lighting: Switchboard: 40 x 2.5Kw; 12 Harmony 22/40, 12 Patt.137, 10 Patt.23, 4 Patt.223, 2 Prelude PC, 24 way cyc. batten.
Sound Equip: Seck 1282 mixing desk, feeds onstage and FOH speakers and dressing room feed, 9 AKG microphones. TEAC 3440 tape deck.
Dressing Rooms 4; accom 40. Orchestra Pit area 2m x 15m.

# Corby

### FESTIVAL HALL
George Street, Corby, Northamptonshire NN17 1QB
Admin 01536 402551 BO 01536 402233
Fax 01536 403748
ADMINISTRATION:
Props: Corby Borough Council
General Manager: Charles L. Sanders
Operations Manager: Ted Blair
Technical Manager: Duncan Mitchell
Catering Manager: Mike Green
Policy: Multi-purpose Arts and Entertainment Centre able to stage arts, entertainment, cinema, conferences, exhibitons, catering events and functions.
Seats: 690 seated + 274 in balcony, unraked. 450 (dances, etc.). Bar and Kiosk at Hall entrance. Also two Lounge Bars.
TECHNICAL:
Stage: 14.6m wide x 5.48m deep x 1.37m high. Front half of stage made of boxes 1.82m x 0.91m x 0.46m, giving multi-shape facility.
Power: 2 x 13 amp points at rear wall of stage, 60A 3 phase supply at stage right, 100A 3 phase supply at stage left (3m from stage).
Lighting: Switchboard: Pulsar MK2 Rock Desk (18 channel) at rear of auditorium. Par blazer lamps and 2 x 1kw CSI follow spots.

Sound Equipment: Peavey 701R Mixer, 32 Bank Eq.,
CS800 & CS1000 power amps with ass. speakers. Also
4 Wedge Fold Backs. RD400 Cassette Desk.
Other: Dressing Rooms: 8, accom. 150; 1 shower.

# Cork, Eire

Pop. 133,000. Newspapers: The Examiner; Evening
Echo. STD code 00 353 21

## CORK OPERA HOUSE

Emmet Place, Cork, Eire
Admin 00 353 21 274308 Admin Fax 00 353 21 276357
Mkt 00 353 21 271168 Mkt Fax 00 353 21 276357
BO 00 353 21 270022 BO Fax 00 353 21 271198
Email: operahousecork@tinet.ie
ADMINISTRATION:
Props: Cork Opera House Plc.
Executive Director: Gerry Barnes
Financial Controller: Aileen Sweeney
Executive Assistant: Verdi Ahern
Marketing Manager: Miriam Hurley
Marketing Assistant: Susan Whealey
Box Office Manager: Catherine Wedgbury
House Manager: David Connolly
Half Moon Theatre Manager: Celine Kenneally
Policy: Used for Musicals, Concerts, Plays, Grand Opera,
Ballet, Conferences and Exhibitions. Front of House
equipped with Bars, Coffee Kiosk & Shop.
Seating Capacity: 1,001
TECHNICAL:
Stage: 40' wide, 30' deep; stage clearance 17' each
side and 15' back of cyclorama; computer Lighting
Board: T.V. Luminaries.
Backstage: Green room with Bar, 9 Dressing Rooms
plus rehearsal rooms.

The Half Moon Theatre which is situated at the rear of
Cork Opera House opened in December 1997 following
redevelopment as a multi-purpose entertainment venue
with an audience capacity from 150 to 450.

# Corwen

## CORWEN PAVILLION

London Road, Corwen, Denbighshire LL21 0DR Wales
Tel 01490 412819
ADMINISTRATION:
Centre Manager: Adrian Roberts Tel: 01490 412600
Bookings (01490 412378)
Seating/Capacity: 1,250

# Coventry, West Midlands

Pop. 336,370. London 92 miles. Newspapers: Coventry
Evening Telegraph; Birmingham Post and Mail;
Leamington Spa Courier. STD code 01203

## BELGRADE THEATRE

Belgrade Square, Corporation Street, Coventry,
West Midlands CV1 1GS
Mgt 01203 256431 BO 01203 553055
SD 01203 227730 Fax 01203 550680
ADMINISTRATION:
Lessees: Belgrade Theatre Trust (Coventry) Ltd;
Theatre Director: Bob Eaton

General Manager: David Beidas
Marketing Manager: Simon Daykin
House Manager: Martin Walker
Production Manager: Eric Hickmott
Associate Producer: Jane Hytch
Policy: Repertory, Pantomime with occasional Tours - 3
weekly Rep, one off concerts, Studio-New Work
Perfs: Mon-Thurs 7.30; Fri 8.00; Sat 8.00; Mat 2.30.
Seats: 866. 2 Licensed Bars, Licensed Restaurant,
Snack and Coffee Bar.
TECHNICAL:
Stage: Proscenium, Flat; Pros. opening to 10.90m; Ht. of
Pros. 5.79m; Depth of S/Line 8.24m; Ht. of Grid 12.50m;
37 lines, C/W; 2 wing bars over aprom W/Widths PS TM
op 1.5m. Scenery Flying Ht. 6.00m; Flying Bars 13.26m;
W/Widths P.S.
Lighting: 120 Way Galaxy 2 Arena, Rear of Stalls 100 x
2kw circuits; 20 x 5kw circuits; 2CCS.S15, 2kw, 20 CCT
S30 1kw, 10 CCT S25 1kw, 18 Patt.264, 20 Patt.223,
10 Patt.243, 29 ADB 1k, 6 Harmony 1, 5 Iris 4, 14 T84,
6 S63 G/rows, 2 CCT CS1 Follow Spots.
Sound Equip: DDA 24/8/2 D Series in Control Room rear
of Stalls, 5HH V500; 4 Amcron D150; 8 Bose 802; 2
Bose 302; and other speakers, various mics; Prompt
Corner PS or Control Room.
Dressing Rooms: 7; Accom. 30 approx; 4 showers;
Orchestra Pit 12-14 max.
Permanent Plaster cyc. white Forestage approx. 2.8m.
Height under Fly Floors approx. 5.9m, Flys Operating
Gallery O.P.
Membership: TMA

## WARWICK ARTS CENTRE

University of Warwick, Gibbet Hill Road, Coventry,
West Midlands CV4 7AL
Admin 01203 523734 Tech 01203 524525
Minicom 01203 524777 Tech 01203 523793
Publicity 01203 523804 Fax 01203 523883
ADMINISTRATION:
Props: University of Warwick
Director: Stella Halt
Deputy Director: Alan Rivett
Technical Director: Howard Potts
Policy: A mixed programme of middle scale touring;
opera; concerts; dance and drama with an independent
film programme. The Arts Centre has five auditoria:
Concert Hall, Theatre, Studio, Conference Room and
Film Theatre, also art gallery, a bookshop, restaurant and
shop.
Theatres:
Perfs: Nightly (theatre) 7.30p.m. Occasional mid-
week/Sat.Mats. 2.30 & 5.00p.m.
Seats: 543/573. Cafe Bar, Restaurant open Mon-Sat
9.00a.m. - 8.00p.m.; two licensed bars, large foyer
accommodating 2,000. Bookshop open Monday to
Saturday.
TECHNICAL:
Stage: Adjustable pros. arch. Performing area 27.32m x
12.2m - pros. opening 10.98m x 5.35m - 6.4m - wing
widths 7.31m SR, 7.31m SL. No rake - floor hardboard
over birch ply/demountable, suitable for dance, lino
available, backstage crossover, stage heated. Grid
height 18.28m - 30 counterweight sets, double
purchase, 0.22m apart - no tab track - 250kg permitted
on bars - maximum flying height 16.75m. Off white
plaster back wall used as cyclorama - blue house tabs,
flown. Forestage 2.74m x 10.98m. Orchestra pit
forestage lift/understage area, accomodates 70. Get-in
via step 0.91m - dock doors 2.28m x 7.01m. Tallescope.
Large paintframe and workshop facilities available.
Lighting: Switchboard: Rank Strand Galaxy III; 100

dimmers; 95 at 2kw, 5 at 5kw. Lanterns: 10 SIL 15, 25 SIL 30, 25 1 kw Fresnels, 6 2kw Fresnels, 20AC 1001 1kw fllods.
Sound Equip: Turbosound speakers with crest amps: 2 Revox tape decks, DDA desk 32/8, 35mm Carousel - 16mm projector: Screen.
Dressing Rooms: 6, plus large chorus room; 8 showers; Orchestra Pit 30-40.
Studio Theatre: nightly 7.45p.m. with flexible bleachers seating (max 200). Lighting switchboard Gemini 2+; 40 2kw dimmers. Sound: DDA desk 16-8, tannoy CPA 15 + CPA 12 speakers, HH Amps.
The Conference Room: seats 250, 35mm Carousel; overhead projector; screen; public address system; cassette/record reply.
Hall: perfs: nightly 8.00p.m. Seats 1,471 (max)
Switchboard: Rank Strand three set 80 ways sited in rear auditorium 70 2kw, 10 5kw all circuits patchable; lighting bars cover length of hall, 115 lanterns; 2 follow spots.
Sound: one Revox B77 tape deck, one Neal cassette deck, Alice 20 into 4 mixer desk, DDA Desk 32-8, JBL. Speakers C-Audio Amps. Various microphones. Fastfold front and rear projection screen. Orchestra platform on 3 levels 63' x 26', with 8' x 4' modules to create greater depth. Choir stalls: 3 (seating 177) at rear. Bleacher seating. 2 star dressing rooms, large band room, chorus room, showers.
Film Theatre: perfs: Mon - Fri 6.30p.m. and 9.00p.m. Sat 4p.m, 6.30p.m, 9 p.m. Sun 4p.m, 7.30 p.m. Seats: 250
Workshop: Fully equipped carpenters workshop; paintframe: 41' x 30' (avail. for hire).
Mead Gallery: 600sq. mtrs. will subdivide into three equal areas.
Membership: TMA. Association of British Concert Promoters.

# Crawley, West Sussex

Pop. 93,000. London 31 miles. Newspapers: Crawley News, Crawley Observer (wed); Evening Argus (ntly). STD code 01293

## THE HAWTH

Hawth Avenue, Crawley, West Sussex RH10 6YZ
Mgt 01293 552941 BO 01293 553636
SD 01293 510022 Fax 01293 533362
ADMINISTRATION:
Props: Crawley Borough Council
Theatre & Arts Manager: Kevin Eason
Promotions & Entertainments Manager: Dave Watmore
House Manager: Dori Watmore
Technical Manager: Chris Wilcox
Publicity Officer: Steve Crane
Policy: Broadmix programme - professional Touring Drama, traditional and contemporary arts, light entertainment, rock, pop, childrens shows and pantomime. Willing to premier show. Film, exhibitions, trade shows, conferences, banquets. Studio - small scale performances including theatre, cabaret, dance, jazz, folk, country, lectures, workshops, exhibitions etc. Summer programme possible in grounds. Amphitheatre available.
Perfs: 7.30p.m. to 8.30p.m. including Sundays 2.30p.m. Usually open 7 days a week.
Seats: Main House: 850 raked. Portable /retractable/ground. Up to 1000 in the round. Studio: Max 146 raked.
Additional Facilities: 5 spaces for wheelchairs, disabled parking area, level access. Induction loop system for the hard of hearing.

TECHNICAL:
Stage (Main House): Variable - proscenium, thrust in the round. Performance area 13m x 12m. Proscenium opening 13m x 8.5m. Flying height 17.5m 49 c/w sets, single and double purchase. Auditorium/Front-stage access S.R. 100 seat choir stalls. Extensive range of rostra units. Tallescope. Steinway grand piano. Yamaha upright piano. 3-phase 200A USL, 100A DSI. 1:25 plans available on request.
Lighting: Strand 550 lighting control. 178 Strand LD90 2.5kw 8 LD90 5kw dimmers. 2 x 1Kw Solo CID Follow Spots with Dimmer shutters and 6-way Colour Magazines. 8 x 2Kw Cadenza 12/22 Profiles with Iris and Gobo holders. 22 x 1.2kw Cantata 11/26 Profiles. 30 x 1.2kw Cantata 18/32 Profiles. 6 x 2kw Cadenza PC's with Barn Doors. 4 x 2kw Cadenza F's with Barn Doors. 24 x 1.2kw Cantata Pc's with Barn Doors. 20 x 1.2kw Cantata F's with Barn Doors. 30 x 1kw Punchlite Parcans. 8 x 1.25kw Iris 3 flood battens. 8 x Coda 4 flood battens/groundrow.
Sound: Allen & Heath Sabre 40-8-8-2 Matrix Mixing Desk. 2 x Shure handheld radio mics. 8 x beltpack radio mics. 11 x Shure SM 58.8 x AKG C 451 EB. 6 x AKG CK 1 Mic. Capsules. 4 x AKG CK 3 Mic. Capsules. 6 x AKG CK 8 Mic. Capsules. 1 x AKG D 112.2 x AKG C 567E Tie-Clip Mics. 2 x AKG VR2 extension tubes. 6 x AKG VR1 extension tubes. 7 x EMO passive DI boxes. 2 x Yamaha SPX 900 effects units. 2 x Yamaha SPX90 II Effects Units. 2 x TOA310D Digital Delay Units, 1 x Peavey Autograph analyser and Equaliser Unit, 4 x Peavey Automate Equalisers Units. 4 x TOA E11 31 Band Graphic Equalisers. 2 Yamaha 2031 Graphic Equalisers. 1 x Bose CSC-1 Cinema Sound Controller, with output to Bose Cannon Bass Units. 1 x Yamaha GC2020B Compressor/Limiter. 1 x Tascam GE20B Graphic Equaliser. 5 x Bose 802C Control Units, 1 x Bose 402C Control Unit.. 3 x Revox B77 Tape Decks. On wheeled stand. 1 x Tascam 122 Cassette Deck. 1 x Tascam 112 Cassette Deck. 1 x TEAC V550X Cassette Deck. 1 x Tascam 388 8-track mixer/recorder. 1 x Revox B226 Compact Disc player. 1 x Denon DCD-1500 Compact Disk player. Sound Effects Discs. 4 x TOA P300D 2-Channel amplifiers. 1 x TOA P75D 2-Channel amplifier. 2 x HILL LC1200 amplifiers. 2 x H.HM900 2-Channel amplifiers. 1 x Quad 306 2-Channel amplifier. 4 x Q.S.C.2 chan. amps1 x LIC Audio XL 2500 Induction-loop amplifier. 6 x TOA 380SE rull-range cabinets. 2 x Bose Cannon Bass Units. 12 x Bose 802 Units. 2 x Bose 402 Units. 1 x Dolby 4-channel sound de-coder. 2 x TOA SM-25M powered monitor speakers. 1 x Fostex self-powered monitors. 10 x TOA F150 speakers in Delay System. 2 x Yamaha NS10M monitors. 2 x JBL control one monitors. 2 x BOJ double-ported monitors. Canford Tecpro Intercom Outstation, 10 way cuelight system. Closed circuit television monitor. Paging to dressing rooms and front of house, script desk and light. 10 x Canford Tecpro Single Muff Headsets. 2 x Canford Tecpro Double Muff Headsets.
Other: Stage-Door paging to dressing rooms. Full show-relay to all back-stage areas. With Stage Manager over-ride. CCTV System: camera focussed on stage, with 6-way video BNC Patchfield to outlets on stage and in the auditorium. Acoustics suitable for music and the spoken word. 7 dressing rooms, Green Room, company office. Rehearsal room by prior arrangement. 2 quick change rooms. Accommodation 70. Full B.T. connection in all dressing rooms and company office.

# Crewe, Cheshire

Pop. 103,164 (Crewe and Nantwich Borough). London

161 miles. Newspapers: Crewe Chronicle (wed); The Guardian (wed). STD code 01270

## LYCEUM THEATRE
Heath Street, Crewe Cheshire CW1 2DA
Mgt 01270 537243 BO 01270 537333
Fax 01270 537322
ADMINISTRATION:
Props: Crewe and Nantwich Borough Council
Head of Leisure Services: Byron Davies
General Manager: Cliff Stansfield
Marketing Manager: Emma McDermott
Technical Manager: Steve O'Brien
Refurbished in 1994 to provide completely new front of house facilities, the Lyceum is now a first class presenting venue. A wide-ranging policy of quality work embraces drama, dance, opera, concerts, children's theatre and a traditional pantomime. The Lyceum is also home to and premieres much of the work of English Touring Theatre.
Perfs: Variable
Seats: 691
Disabled: Seats in stalls, lift and toilets on all floors, infra red hearing system.
Membership: TMA
TECHNICAL:
Stage: Proscenium, Raked (1:18) with removable forestage (1.35m) to reveal orchestra pit to seat 16 musicians. Front three rows of stalls seating also removable to create orchestra space for 35 musicians. Pros opening 8.55m x 5.6m; Depth from front of stage to last fly bar 10.36m (C.L.).Ht of grid (upstage): 13.08m. Fly floor height (u/s) 6.4m. Hemp lines x 24, counterwieght lines 4 + 1 for house tabs, winches x 4 (lx). Hemps & winches grid at 12.8m. Counterweights at 11.4m. Prompt corner.PS comms with outstations & cue lights. Show relay and tannoy to dressing rooms. Get-in DSR through 3 dock doors; outer:H2.7m x W1.8m central:H2.4m x 1.8m inner:H3.5m x 1.55m.
7 Dressing Rooms: to take 17 artistes (1 optional as company office). Green Room/Wardrobe with washer and tumbledryer. Iron/Ironing Board available.
Lighting: LX: Arri Impuls 108 way desk located rear of stalls. 94 x 2.5KW dimmers, 6 x 5KW dimmers. Permanent FOH rig comprises 18 x Cantata 18/32 1.2KW profile & 6 x Cantata 11/26 1.2KW profile on galllery front rail, & 3 x Cantata PC 1.2KW each side on pros booms.
Other equipment: 8 x Patt 264 1KW profile, 12 x Cantata 26/44 1.2KW profile, 6 x Cantata PC 1.2KW, 30 x Cantata F 1.2KW fresnel, 13 x 1KW fresnel, 10 x 2KW fresnel, 16 x 1KW cyc flood, 40 x Par 64 cans, 2 x Patt 793 2KW follow spots.
Sound Equipment: located rear of stalls, Soundcraft Delta 16:4:2. 2 x Crest Audio amps driving 4 x Nexo PS10 central flown cluster & 2 x Nexo PS10 stalls. AVX Systems digital delay and Crest Audio amp drives JBL control 1 speakers at stalls rear.
2 x BSS 30 band system graphics. 2 x HH VX900 amps and 4 x Peavey CL2 speakers available for effects/foldback. System cabled for stereo mix. Temp mixer position available outside control room at rear stalls.

# Cromer, Norfolk

Pop. 5,380. London 133 miles. Newspapers: North Norfolk News (thurs); Eastern Daily Press (dly). STD code 01263

## PAVILION THEATRE
Cromer Norfolk
Mgt 01263 516003 Fax 01263 515113
BO 01263 512495 Pavilion Theatre 01263 512281
ADMINISTRATION:
Props: North Norfolk District .Council
Theatre Manager: Paul Dayson
Press and Publicity: Scott Butler
House Manager: Jane Jardine
Box Office Manager: Emma Traylen
Policy: Home of own produced seaside special. Early-Late season attractions. Sunday Celebrity Concerts, Children's Shows.
Perfs: 8.00
Seats: 443. Licensed Bar, Coffee shop.
TECHNICAL:
Proscenium Stage; Pros. opening 10.06m; Ht. of Pros. 4.57m; Depth of S/Line 6.10m; 12 lines Henderson Tracking.

# Croydon

## FAIRFIELD HALLS
Park Lane Croydon CR9 1DG
Mgt 0181 681 0821 Stage Door 0181 688 4555
BO 0181 688 9291 Fax 0181 760 0835
Marketing Fax 0181 686 7944
Web Site: www.fairfield.co.uk
ADMINISTRATION:
Props: Fairfield (Croydon) Ltd
Chief Executive: Derek Barr
Head of Artistic Planning: Nick Leigh
Controller of Artistic Planning: Colin May
Policy: Concert Hall, Music, Films, Pop, Jazz, Opera, Comedy, Conferences, Ballet.
Seats: 1,800
Foyer, Coffee shop, Restaurant, Bars, Banqueting Rooms.
TECHNICAL:
Stage: Concert Platform, mechanical variable sections.
Lighting: Switchboard: Strand Lightboard 'M' commanding 120 channels 200amp 3 phase and 60 amp single phase power supplies available for temporary supply; F.O.H. spots 42 CCT profiles. 2 spot bars available on electric hoist. Selection of lamps; P.A.R. cans and fresnels.
Get-in via platform lift, Direct Access & Parking. No flying facilities, but good grid provision and soft blacks for upstage masking.
Sound Equipment: 7kw fully integrated Meyer sound system with permanent mixing position.
Other: Dressing Rooms: 7, accom. 200; 3 showers; Orchestra Pit 28.90 orch. music stands, 2 Steinway concert D type Grand Pianos; seating 120 orch. max 250 choir seating.
Staff: 5 Technicians - Casual Crew.
A registered charity.

# Cumbernauld, Strathclyde

Pop. 55,000. Glasgow 12 miles. Newspapers: Cumbernauld News (wkly); Glasgow Herald; Evening Times (dly). STD code 01236

## CUMBERNAULD THEATRE

Kildrum Braehead Road, Cumbernauld, Glasgow
Strathclyde G67 2BN Scotland
Mgt 01236 737235 BO 01236 732887
Fax 01236 738408
ADMINISTRATION:
Artistic Director: Simon Sharkey
General Manager: Debbie Murdoch
Policy: Home productions. Touring Theatre Companies,
Music, Mime, Theatre in Education, Dance, Exhibitions,
Films, Workshops
Seats: 258 (main auditorium): 57 (studio)
TECHNICAL:
Stage: Permanent Thrust Stage, adaptable to be 'in the
round'. Steep Rake: 6.9m wide x 13.5m deep x 5.53m
to grid; Control Room at back of auditorium.
Lighting: Arri Imagine II memory desk, Arri smartracks 96
x 2.5kw; 14 x T64, 6 x T84, 26 x Patt.73, 18 x Patt.23,
19 x Patt.123 12HD; 6 ind. circuits all 2k; All connections
15 amp 3 pin round.
Sound Equip: Revox B77 .DAT. CD., Dennon cass;
Garrard SO25; Mixer:Soundtracks 24:4:2.
Other: Dressing Rooms 2.
Studio: Performing space 7.1m x 4.19m x 2.7m to grid.
Pulsar MS4 72 way board, Racks 2k dimmers. All
connections 15 amp round pin.
Membership: TMA, FST

# Cwmbran, Torfaen

Pop. 48,000. London 147 miles. Newspapers: S.W.
Argus and S.W. Echo (ntly); Western Mail (dly); News and
Free Press (wkly). STD code 01633

## CONGRESS THEATRE

50 Gwent Square, Cwmbran, Gwent NP44 1PL Wales
Admin/BO 01633 868239 Fax 01633 867809
ADMINISTRATION:
Props: Congress Theatre Board.
Contact: Derek Michael
Policy: Touring, Community Theatre, Children's Shows,
One-Night Stands, Jazz and Classical Concerts,
Conferences and Meetings, Amateur Productions,
Seminars, 16mm Cine.
Perfs: As required
Lounge Bar.
Seats: 319
TECHNICAL:
Stage: Fixed timber stage, flat; Opening 12.20m, Ht. to
Lighting Battens 5.18m; Depth of Stage 7.52m; No
Flying Facilities; Prompt Cnr. O.P.; small storage area,
get-in 4.57m above pavement; hand winch/small lift.
Lighting:: 6 Patt.15-28 Harmony, 6 Patt Harmony 'F',  3
Batten, 12 x Patt 264, 2 x Cantata Profiles, 6 x Cantata
Fresnels, 6 x Thomas Profiles, 6 x Thomas Fresnels, 6 x
Par Cans, 2 x ACT 6.
Switchboard: Strand SP60, 3 Preset plus M24 48
Channel.
Sound: 8 mics. Mixer Studiomaster 16-2 Stereo. 3 x 300
watt Marshall Amps. Revox B77.150w RCF Speakers
and Monitors, 1  x Technics Graphic, 2 x Technics
Cassette, 1 x Technics C.D., 1 x Alesis Midi Verb III, 2 x
Record Decks, 4 Foldback Monitors.
16mm Cine Projector, 14' x 10' Cine Screen.
Dressing Rooms: 4; Accom. 21; 2 showers; green room.

# Dalbeattie

## DALBEATTIE, TOWN HALL

High Street, Dalbeattie, Kirkcudbrightshire DG5 4AD
Tel 01557 330291 ext 323
Contact: Mary Kirkpatrick
Seating capacity: 250

# Darlington, Co Durham

Pop. 100,000. London 242 miles. Newspapers: The
Northern Echo (dly); The Evening Gazette; Darlington &
Stockton Times (sat). STD code 01325

## THE ARTS CENTRE

Vane Terrace, Darlington, County Durham DL3 7AX
Admin 01325 483271 BO 01325 486555
Fax 01325 365794
Centre Manager: Peter Cutchie
Stage Technician: Alison Rigby
Theatre seating between 140 and 350 in flexible layouts.
Ballroom for cabaret and functions, Film Theatre with
35mm projector and screen seating 200. Garden Bar
seating 80 to 100 for cabaret, folk, jazz etc. Dance
studio, galleries, foyer, self-service restaurant and bar.
Wide range of meeting rooms and practical workshop
facilities, artists' and craftspersons' studios, sound and
video recording facilities, residential accommodation
available for visiting performers, course participants and
conference visitors, resident theatre companies; also
base for Cleveland Theatre Company. Darlington
Borough Council provides this service.

## DARLINGTON CIVIC THEATRE

Parkgate, Darlington, County Durham DL1 1RR
Mgt 01325 468006 BO 01325 461896
SD 01325 467743 Fax 01325 368278
Visiting Company Manager 01325 461896
ADMINISTRATION:
Props: Borough of Darlington
Head of Theatre & Arts: Peter Cutchie
Theatre Manager: Sarah Richards
House Manager: Stephen Sandford
Marketing Manager: Nick Bagshaw
Technical Manager: Adam Nix
Policy: Major touring of plays, ballet, opera, musicals.
Variety and major pantomime season. Conference
facilities.
Perfs: variable
Seats: 909, 3 Licensed bars and 2 coffee bars. 6
wheelchair spaces at rear of Stalls. Disabled persons
toilet. Infra red hearing system and loop.
TECHNICAL:
Stage: Pros. Stage Raked. Pros width 8.68m. Ht. to
house border 5.5m. Ht. to grid 13.3m. Depth of Stage
8.8m. 30 sets of lines in hemphouse. Flying bars 11m.
Flys working side S/R. W/widths S/L. 3.05m. S/R 2.44m.
Prompt Cnr. S/R.
Lighting: Switchboard: 430 (150 channels) rear of stalls.
Stage 14 x 5kw. 72 x 2.5kw. F.O.H. (via patch panel). 34
x 2.5kw 300 amp TPN supply on stage; F.O.H. lanterns;
16 x 1kw. sil 15; stage lanterns: 30 x starlette 1kw
Fresnel, 6 x sil 30, 11 x Patt.264, 20 Parcans. 12 x Iris 1.
Four electric bars on motorised winches.
Sound Equip: located at rear of Stalls. 2 Revox tape
machines; Hill 18 x 8 x 2 mixer. 6 x float mics. Speakers:
4 x Bose 802 + delays. Full head set system around

theatre.
Dressing Rooms: 11; showers 3; Orchestra Pit. Fire
Curtain. Wardrobe; 8 music stands, plus conductor
stand.
Membership: TMA

### THE DOLPHIN CENTRE
Horse Market, Darlington, County Durham DL1 5RP
Tel 01325 388411 Fax 01325 369400
ADMINISTRATION:
Centre Manager: Terry Collins.
Contact: Customer Services Office
Seating/Capacity: Main Sports Hall: 1,250 seated;
Central Hall: 500 seated (theatre style seating).

# Dartford, Kent

Pop. 76,000. London 17 miles. Newspapers: Kentish
Times Group (thurs); Kent Messenger Group (fri); Kent
Today (dly); News Shopper (wed); Mercury Group (thurs).
STD code 01322

### THE ORCHARD
Home Gardens, Dartford Kent DA1 1ED
Mgt 01322 220099 BO 01322 220000
Fax 01322 227122
ADMINISTRATION:
Props: Dartford Borough Council
Director of Environment & Leisure: Chris Oliver
Publicity Manager: Beverley Davies
Box Office Manager: Nicky Morgan
Policy: Touring plays and musicals, Opera, Ballet,
Concerts (rock, popular and classical), Children's
entertainment, Exhibitions, Conferences and Banquets.
Seats: 950. Two licenced bars; lunchtime catering (Mon-
Sat).
TECHNICAL:
Stage: Proscenium, flat, grey lino covered. Pros. opening
variable max. 13.8m x 10.96m normal; Pros. ht 6.00m;
stage depth 10.60m, forestage/orchestra lift 3.30m
extra; ht. of grid 15.10m; ht. of fly floors 8.00m; 44 single
purchase C/W sets x 200mm centres; length of bars
15.25m, max bar weight 453kg; Prompt Cnr. PS;
Storage 3.45m on OP - get-in direct on stage OP;
tailboard height (covered); width between fly floors
16.00m.
Lighting: Lightboard M120 at rear of stalls circle;
dimmers 107 x 2.5kw, 13 x 5kw, 2 x Pani HMI follow
spot; f.o.h. Bridge 22 x Sil 15 2kw; balcony front 2 x Sil
15 2kw; balcony booms 10 x Harmony 22/40 plus tab
dressing; 30 x Harmony F, 6 x 743, 20 x 240v parcans;
6 x cadenza Iris PC, 6 x Minuette profiles, 14 x Harmony
22/40, 17 x 500w floods, 4 x 1 rise 4, 8 x Pallas 4
ground row, 4 x S64 footlights. 8 stands, 2 booms, 4
moveable IWBs- 1 x 18 way, 1 x 16 way, 1 x 13 way, 1 x
5 way and 4 circuits for cyc.
Sound: 24/8/2 Allen & Heath mixer. Bose PA; 3 Harrison
Xi1000 amps; 6 x Bose 802 portable speakers.
Microphones - 4 x SM58, 4 x Crown PCC 160, 3 x AKG
D224, 3 x AKG D1200, 5 x AKG 451 with 5CKl and
5CK8 capsules, 1 AKG D330, 1 Dl. Revox B77 (3.75,
7.5), twin cassette deck, CD player.
Projection: 2 x 35mm, Dolby Stereo.
Communications: SM desk PS; 12 way cue light system;
paging to dressing rooms, auditorium and foyer areas,
bar bells, ring intercom.
Dressing Rooms: 14; accommodates 60. 2 band rooms,
green room, six shower rooms. Wardrobe at stage level
with washing machine and dryer.

Orchestra Pit: 45, 65 extended. 1 conductor's and 25
music stands.
Membership: TMA

# Derby, Derbys

Pop. 219,910. London 125 miles. Newspapers: Derby
Evening Telegraph (ntly). STD code 01332

### ASSEMBLY ROOMS
Market Place, Derby, Derbyshire DE1 3AH
Mgt 01332 255443 BO 01332 255800
SD 01332 255422 Fax 01332 255788
ADMINISTRATION:
Props: Derby City Council
General Manager: Chris Ward-Brown
Technical Manager: Nigel Palmer
Policy: Multi-use Hall, Stage Shows, Orchestral
Concerts, Recitals, One-Night Stands, Exhibitions,
Conferences, Banquets, Wrestling etc.
Seats: Orchestral Concert (small stage) 1846 max;
Orchestra Concert (full stage) 1694; Proscenium Show
with orchestra pit 1228 max. Standing concerts 2000.
Full bar and catering facilities.
TECHNICAL:
The Great Hall is rectangular, with a balcony all round.
Retractable Proscenium Towers and Side screens
convert the auditorium into theatre form. The Orchestra
lift can be moved to 4 levels; level 1 for get-in, level 2 as
Orchestra Pit, level 3 at auditorium floor level, level 4 at
stage level.
Stage: The main stage is fixed with demountable sides.
Proscenium Opening (width between lowered towers)
11.43m; Top border variable; Depth of Fixed Stage
6.85m; Ht. 7.30m; 12 lines motorised; Demountable
Stage 2m wide each side; No wings, but space under
side balaconies.
Lighting: 144 channel Lightboard M Mk2, (D54, AMX
192, DMX 512 protocols); wide variety of lanterns
including parcans, one and two KW profile spots, floods
and stands etc. 2x1 KW CID floowspots (Patt.765).
Sound Equip:  Soundcraft 500 24/8/2; Court and
Yamaha 1/3 octave graphics; BSS 4 band crossovers;
H+H amplifiers; Marquee/Court Hanging PA speakers;
four wedge monitors; selection of mics, Dls and stands;
CD player, two cassette players/recorders; Yahama SPX
90; Technics SL1200 turntable.
35mm film projection equipment, with four band stereo
playback system. Stage managers desk with full paging
facilities; Canford Tech Pro ring intercom.
Power supplies: 3 phase 300 amp, 3 phase 100 qamp,
single phase 60 amp.
Dressing Rooms 4 and Band room and Production
office. Showers in all dressing rooms.
Pianos: Steinway 'D' type concert grand; Bechstein 10'
grand; Bechstein 7'6" baby grand; Technics electric
piano; Technics electronic organ.

The Darwin Suite, seating 300-400 is available for
conferences, recitals, rock shows, etc. Flat Floor. Own
Sound & Lighting facilities.
The '45 Suite & Reception Suite, seating 150  & 70
respectively, are available for wedding parties, meetings,
etc.Full facilities.

The Guildhall Theatre stage, proscenium, has an opening
of 25', a depth of 18' (22' with forestage), and a grid
height of 15'. The raked auditorium seats 181 plus three
wheelchair spaces, with 62 in the balcony - total capacity
246. It has a licensed bar and coffee bar.

Lighting: Control is by way of a Zero 88, 24 Channel Sirius board controlling a variety of lanterns including Patt.123, 803, 16/30 and T spots.
Sound amplification is by a Teac Tascam 5 8:4 mixer, HH electronic TPA 50D Amps and 4 Millbank 100W amps (on stage) and Carlsbro Speakers. The venue has a Sony stereo cassette deck and a small number of microphones.
The Guildhall Theatre is situated in the centre of Derby and currently stages an expanding programme of alternative comedy, recitals, concerts, an Arts Festival, musicals and small mid/scale theatre companies, this being an area the venue would like to build on.

### DERBY PLAYHOUSE
Theatre Walk, Eagle Centre, Derby Derbyshire DE1 2NF
Mgt 01332 363271 BO 01332 363275
SD 01332 362937 Minicom 01332 292277
Catering 01332 348591 Fax 01332 294412
Press 01332 346841 (Phone/Fax)
Email: admin@derbyplayhouse.demon.co.uk
ADMINISTRATION:
Props: Derby Playhouse Ltd
Lessees: Derby Playhouse Ltd
Executive Director: David Edwards
Artistic Director: Mark Clements
Production Manager: Kit Lane
Stage Manager: Moby Renshaw
Policy: Subsidised Regional Theatre operating own productions for around 40 weeks a year. Special facilities for disabled patrons. Studio presentations in Studio Theatre.
Perfs: Mon-Sat 7.30. Mat as advertised.
Seats: 535 (Main Theatre) 110 max (Studio). Restaurant Seats 60 to 80, plus licensed Bar and Café Bar.
TECHNICAL:
Stage (Main House): Pros opening 10.4m wide x 5.65m high - Wing widths 4.92m SR, 14.68m SL. Performing area 10m x 10m - flat floor, wooden, suitable for all dance. Height of grid 15.25m - 28 counterweight sets, 13 hemp sets, 0.2m apart - max flying height 14.7m. Curved forestage/orchestra pit on elevator 10m x 2.7m max. Accommodates 17. Get in via back of building, 1 floor up in lift, 5.1m high, 1.8m wide, 2.7m deep.
Lighting: Galaxy 2, 152 circuits. 80 profile lanterns, 55 fresnels, 60 parcans and beamlights, cyc flood and S battens, Scrollers, colour wheels.
Sound: Mini disc, CD, DAT, Tape and cassette players. Akai sampler. Soundcraft Megas (32:8:2) and spirit live (12:8:2) mixers. Renkus Heinz and Bose speakers. Sennheiser radio mics. Accessories: smoke and dry ice machines, strobes, mirror balls, UV.

Studio: Performing area 10.6m x 9.9m. Flat wooden floor. Height of fixed grid 3.65m. Get-in 1.8m x 3.6m. Seating capacity 110, layout flexible, on seating rostra. ADB Tango Control System, 48 circuits. 15 Profiles lanterns, 30 fresnels.
Tape and Cassette players. Allen & Heath (8:2) mixer. 2 Bose 901 speakers.

## Dewsbury

### DEWSBURY TOWN HALL
Old Wakefield Road, Dewsbury,
West Yorkshire WF12 8DQ
Tel 01924 324502
Assistant Venue Manager: Mrs Sue Lenton

For bookings contact Gary Ellis or Sue Wood on 01484 221913/221947 or fax 01484 221876
Seating: 685

## Doncaster

### THE DOME
Doncaster Leisure Park, Bawtry Road, Doncaster, South Yorkshire DN4 7PD
Tel 01302 370777 Fax 01302 532239
Events Managers: Michael Hart and Patrick Hone
Capacity: 1,738 seated; 3,264 standing.

## Douglas, I.O.M.

Pop. 72,000. Newspapers: Isle of Man Examiner (tue); Isle of Man Independent (fri); Isle of Man Courier (thurs). STD code 01624

### GAIETY THEATRE
Harris Promenade, Douglas, Isle of Man IM1 2HH
Mgt 01624 620046 SD 01624 673437
BO 01624 625001 Fax 01624 629028
ADMINISTRATION:
Artistic Director: Mervin Russell Stokes
Production Manager: Seamus Shea
Policy: Musicals, straight plays, opera, ballet, concerts - pop, jazz and classical. Performance schedule Open 7 days - no performances Christmas Day - evening shows start at 8.00p.m., matinees on various days at 2.30p.m. Booking terms hire, box office split, guarantee & split, guarantee, by negotiation.
Facilities: Seating 845; raked. Catering Full Carvery dining room, brasserie, 2 licensed bars, 2 private entertaining suites. Facilities for the disabled 27 wheelchair spaces - deaf loop system - assistance available, contact Box Office - level access - toilets at lower stalls level accessible by electric chair lift.
TECHNICAL:
Stage: Proscenium arch. Performing area 8.68m x 12.2m - pros opening 8.68m x 9.4m - wing widths 2.3m SR, 3.96m SL, 6.1m US. Stage raked, 1 in 36 - floor sprung wood covered in lino, suitable for all dance, backstage crossover, stag heated. Height of grid 14.63m - 29 Counterweight, 0.6m apart - tab tracks - 250kg permitted on bars - maximum flying height 13.71m - full set black masking - white linen weave cyclorama - blue house tabs, flown Victorian Act Drop Curtain. Orchestra pit 10.21m x 2.21, accommodates 15. Get-in via dock doors, 2.14m x 3.05m. Safety curtain. Scale stage and fly plans available.
Lighting: G.S.X. Desk. 120 Circuits. Operated from rear dress circle. 100 amp 3 phase supply available on stage. 29 profiles. 45 Fresnels. 10 Parcans. 2 Rank Strand Follow Spots 2kw.
Sound: Soundcraft K2 32ch. Peavey Miniframe 208 Media Matrix control system, Denon mini disc, Denon CD player SPX990, 4 X EV system 200 stage monitors, rev 7 reverb. Various Crown & Sure mics with boom stands. Full Range P.A. System. Cassette decks + Revox reel to reel tape recorders. Operated from rear of dress circle or stalls. Basic recording and editing facilities. Accoustics suitable for music and spoken word.
Backstage: 8 dressing rooms, modern shower rooms access by rear of stage - quick change rooms. No wardrobe, but washer, tumble dryer, spin dryer available, ample power points. Pianos: Stage, new Rehearsal

Piano and 6'8" Danemann Grand (Concert work only)
Orchestra Pit: New Matched Pair of Good Upright
Pianos. Advice given on accommodation. Staff - 4 stage
- casuals available - no security personnel. Backstage
facilities not accessible to disabled performers and staff.
Stage management Prompt corner SL - cueing via
headsets x 6 - show relay to dressing rooms.

## VILLA MARINA ROYAL HALL
Harris Promenade, The Colonnade, Douglas,
Isle of Man IM1 2HP
Mgt 01624 674171 BO 01624 628855
ADMINISTRATION:
Props: Douglas Corporation.
Manager: Martin Blackburn  Tel 01624 623021
Stage Manager: Iain Wylie
Policy: Concerts, Wrestling, Dancing, Conferences,
Exhibitions, Shows
Perfs: 8.00p.m.
Seats: 1,600. Licensed Bar & Restaurant.
TECHNICAL:
Stage: Proscenium Raked; Pros. opening 9.45m; Ht. of
Pros. 5.49m; Ht. of Grid 9.14m; 9 lines, Hemp;
W/Widths P.S. 1.22m, O.P. 1.22m; Prompt Cnr. P.S.
Lighting: Switchboard: Strand, 7 x 4ways; F.O.H.
Spots 2 400w Mercury Iodise; 4 Battens; 1 Float; Dips 3
each side; 4 Spot bars.
Sound Equip: Pan/Tape P.S.; Speakers 350w amplifier
P.S.
Dressing Rooms 9; Accom. 30; Orchestra Pit 12.

# Dublin, Eire
Pop. 1,024,000. Newspapers: Evening Herald (ntly);
Evening Press (ntly); Irish Independent (dly); The Irish
Times (dly); The Irish Press (dly); Sunday Independent,
Sunday Press, Sunday Tribune, Sunday World. STD
code 00 353 1

## ABBEY THEATRE
26 Lower Abbey Street, Dublin 1 Eire
Mgt 00 353 1 874 8741 BO 00 353 1 878 7222
Credit Card Booking 00 353 1 878 7222
Fax 00 353 1 872 9177
ADMINISTRATION:
Props: National Theatre Society Ltd
Managing Director: Martin Fahy
Artistic Director: Patrick Mason
Policy: Irish plays and international classics. Resident
year round Repertory Company.
Perfs: 8.00 nightly except Sunday.
Seats: 638. Bar. Portrait Gallery.
TECHNICAL:
Stage: Proscenium with Thrust, Flat, but with 3 Lifts to
alter levels; Pros. opening 12.19m; Ht. of Pros. 9.75m;
Depth of S/Line 8.53m; Ht. of Grid 18.90m; 39 lines,
C/W; Scenery Flying Ht. 8.53m; Flying Bars 14.63m;
W/Widths P.S. 3.96m, O.P. 3.96m; Prompt Cnr. P.S.
Lighting: Switchboard: Rank Strand Galaxy 240 channel
memory board with automatic back-up system and
ancillary equipment; FOH Spots 55 Patt.264, Dips 12
PS, 17 OP; 4 Spots Bars Patts.223, 264, 243 plus CCT
profile and fresnel spots.
Sound Equip: DDA Q Series Mixer 16/8/2; 2 Revox B77
HS; 1 Sony D.A.T.; 1 Sony CD; 1 ALESS15 MIDIVERB
11; 1 8 track Tascam; 1 Roland W30
Sampler/Sequencer/Keyboard; 1 Roland U110 sound
module; 1 Techniks twin cassette deck; 1 C-Audio RA-
1000 amp; 2 Quad 405 Amp; 8 Loudspeaker positions.

Back Stage; 2 FOH PROS; 2 Back Auditorium.
Dressing Rooms 6; Accom 36; Showers in all.  Orchestra
pit 28.
F.O.H. Light is fixed to ceiling panels which are variable
in height (motorised to suit scenery).
1.52m permanent Forestage with additional forestage
(lifts) 2.74m.

## BANK OF IRELAND ARTS CENTRE
Foster Place, Dublin 2 Eire
Tel 00 353 1 671 1488 Fax 00 353 1 670 7556
Contact: Barry O'Kelly
The Bank of Ireland's Arts Centre stages live
performances as well as exhibitions. It has provided the
first major public platform for many young Irish artistes.

## DAGG HALL
Royal Irish Academy of Music 36-38 Westland Row
Dublin 2 Eire
Tel 00 353 1 676 4412 Fax 00 353 1 662 2798
Seating/Capacity: 160-170; stacking chairs

## DUBLIN GATE THEATRE
Cavendish Row Dublin 1 Eire
Mgt 00 353 1 874 4368  BO 00 353 1 874 4045
SD 00 353 1 874 7483  Fax 00 353 1 874 5373
ADMINISTRATION:
Props: Edwards-MacLiammóir, Dublin Gate Theatre
Productions
Director: Michael Colgan
Deputy Directors: Marie Rooney & Anne Clarke
Theatre Manager: John Higgins
Production Manager: Liam Pawley
Policy: Arts Theatre
Perfs: 8.00
Seats: 371. Cafe serving coffee, minerals and
confectionary; licensed bar.
TECHNICAL:
Stage: Please contact venue for specific details.
Lighting: Control: Strand GSX Genius version 1.2, 72 x
2kw dimmers, 8 cantata 18/32, 6 x P264, 1 x T84, 4 x
T64, 1 x P243, 12 x Prelude 16/30, 8 x Minuette V.B
Profile, 4 x P23, 18 x P223, 5 x P123, 16 x Minuette
Fresnel, 4 x Berkey 6" Fresnel, 8 x Mini Ellispe, 10 x P60,
2 x SP Battens, 25 x Par 64, 9 X Source 36 degrees..
Sound: Sound room at rear of auditorium studiomaster
12:4:2 desk. 3 stereo amps s/master and bose. 1
monitor amp. FOH: 2 EV Motor Vator 2R speakers. 2
bose speakers at rear of auditorium. Stage: 6 speaker
lines. TOA speakers. 2 Revox B77 stereo 1/4 recorders.
1 Tascam tape deck. 1 JVC twin tape deck. 1 Sony CD
player. 1 Yamaha SPX 90 II 1 mixer 31 band graphic
equaliser. 4 AKG rifle mics. 2 Denon Mini Disc players.
Full speaker and amp patch facility. Acoustics suitable
for spoken word. Tannoy to green room and dressing
rooms. Talk back between auditorium, stage and control
room.
Dressing Rooms 4. Full Wardrobe facility.

## GAIETY THEATRE
South King Street, Dublin 1 Eire
Mgt 00 353 1 679 5622 Fax 00 353 1 677 1921
BO 00 353 1 677 1717
ADMINISTRATION:
Executive Director: John Costigan
PA to Executive Director:Lisa Miksch
Marketing Manager: Aine McCann
Public Reations Officer: Geraldine Kearney

# The Isle of Man's Leading Entertainment Venue

## Royal Hall

- The impressive Royal Hall will comfortably seat up to 1500 people

- Theatre Bar can be open to serve drinks and refreshments

- Full PA facilities

- Full lighting facilities

## Garden Room

- The Garden Room provides an alternative, smaller venue to seat 200 – 320 people depending on the arrangement

- Full bar facilities are available and catering can be arranged

- Stage lighting and PA System available

**Villa MARINA**

Subject to availability all venues are bookable all year round

HARRIS PROMENADE • DOUGLAS • ISLE OF MAN
TELEPHONE: (01624) 674 171

Theatre Manager: Gavin Rynne
Retail Manager: James Matthews
Box Office Manager: Alan McQuilian
Administration/Accounts: Barbara Boyle
Stage Manager: Terry Power
Chief Electrician: Liam Daly
Policy: Touring Companies, Musicals, Drama, Opera,
Pantomime, Revue.
Perfs: Nightly 8.00pm, Matinee Sat 3.00pm (may vary).
Seats: 1,166; 4 Fully Licensed Bars; Corporate
Hospitality.
Technical:
Stage: Proscenium Stage - no rake; Pros. opening
8.40m; Ht. of Pros. 7.10m; Depth of s/line 9.50m; Ht of
Grid 14.564; 34 counter weight; 3 hemp lines; Scenery
flying Ht. 6.20m; Flying Bars 10.90m; Scene Docks P.S.
4m X 12m; Prompt Cnr. O.P.; 3 full black curtains; 10
soft black legs; 2 full borders; 10 hark black masking
flats.
Lighting: Switchboard: Strand Gemini 166 Channel
Control; 200 laterns of various types, beams and angles
including 18 FOH, 2 boom bars each side of pros. and 2
CSI follow spots.
Backstage: Green room with bar; Dressing rooms 11,
Accom. 40 (coms and show relay to all); Showers 5.
Other: Orchestra Pit 20.
PLEASE SEE ADVERT ON INSIDE FRONT COVER

### IRISH MUSEUM OF MODERN ART
Royal Hospital, Kilmainham, Dublin 8 Eire
Tel 00 353 1 612 9000 Fax 00 353 1 612 9999
Seating/Capacity: Great Hall 540, Chapel 250

### LIBERTY HALL
Beresforde Place Dublin 1 Eire
Tel 00 353 1 874 9731 Fax 00 353 1 874 9558
Post Room Fax 00 353 1 874 9368
Seating/Capacity: 750

### NATIONAL CONCERT HALL
Earlsfort Terrace, Dublin 2 Eire
Admin 00 353 1 475 1666 Admin fax 00 353 1 478 3797
BO 00 353 1 475 1572 BO Fax 00 353 1 475 1507
Director: Judith Woodworth
Seating/Capacity: Main auditorium 1,200. John Field
Room: 250

### NATIONAL GALLERY OF IRELAND
Merrion Square (West), Dublin 2 Eire
Tel 00 353 1 661 5133 Fax 00 353 1 661 5372
Seating/Capacity: Shaw Room 320; Lecture Theatre 250

### NATIONAL STADIUM
South Circular Road Dublin 8 Eire
Tel 00 353 1 453 3371/454 3525
Fax 00 353 1 454 0777
Manager: Don Stewart
Capacity: 2,200 seated, max

### OLYMPIA THEATRE
72 Dame Street, Dublin 2 Eire
Mgt 00 353 1 677 1020 SD 00 353 1 677 1400
Production Office 00 353 1 478 2153/83
Fax 00 353 1 678 2295/679 9576
BO 00 353 1 677 7744 BO Fax 00 353 1 679 9474
ADMINISTRATION:

Props: Olympia Theatre Ltd
Lessees: Olympia Productions Ltd
Chairman: Kevin Bourke
Managing Director: Gerry Sinnott
House Manager: Tara Sinnott
Policy: Touring Companies, Revue, Drama, Pantomime,
Opera, Musicals, Ballet
Perfs: Nightly at 8.00, Matinee Sat. 3.00
Seats: 1,200; standing cap.: 2,000 (seats removeable).
Bars and Coffee Lounge
TECHNICAL:
Stage: Proscenium, Raked 1 in 48; Pros. Opening
10.46m; Ht. of Pros. 7.32m; Depth of s/line 8.38m; Ht.
of Grid 16.50m 15 Counter weight. 12 Hemp lines.
Scenery Flying Ht. 7.32m; Flying Bars 11.73m; W/Widths
P.S. 3.96m, O.P. 4.09m; Prompt Cnr. O.P.
Lighting: Switchboard: Arri Imagine 150 Channel Control.
Total of 120 various lanterns including 20 FOH, 1 Boom
Bar each side of pros. arch and 2 Follow Spots
CSI/CCT.
Sound Equip: Deltamax 1152 full range system with
delay lines and cluster driven by Amcron Amps. TAC
Scorpion 30. 12 desk FOH and Stage mix. FOH effects
Rack and EV mikes.
Other: Dressing Rooms 8, Accom. 40. 3 Showers.
Orchestra Pit 20 (extendable).
Membership: Irish Theatre Management Assn.

### PEACOCK THEATRE
26 Lower Abbey Street, Dublin 1 Eire
Mgt 00 353 1 874 8741 BO 00 353 1 878 7222
Credit Card Booking 00 353 1 878 7222
Fax 00 353 1 872 9177
ADMINISTRATION:
Props: National Theatre Society Ltd
Artistic Director: Patrick Mason
Managing Director: Martin Fahy
Policy: New Work and Experimental Theatre.
Perfs: Mon-Sat 8.15p.m. Lunchtimes usually 1.10 p.m.
Seats: 157. Bar
TECHNICAL:
Stage: Convertable stage to 6 different positions. Flat in
proscenium; pros opening 8.43m; Ht of pros 3.73m;
depth of S/line 5.79m; ht of grid 12.04m, 20 lines, c/w
double purchase; scenery flying ht 457m; flying bars
8.53m; w/widths P.S. 2.74m, O.P. 4.42m; prompt Cnr.
O.S.
Lighting: Switchboard: Rank Strand Gemini 160 Channel
Dips - P Side 15; O.P. Side 15; Spot Bars - Patt 23, Pat
123, Patt 223, Prelude 16/30, Prelude 28/40 Quartet F.
Sound Equipment: 1 Spirit Auto 16-8-2 and Atari Ste
and Steinberg prog, 2 Revox B77 H.S.; 1 Harrison 6001
Amp; 2 Quad 303 Amps; 6 Loudspeaker positions; 4 on
stage; 2 FOH; 2 Back Aud; 1 Technics twin Cassette
deck. 1 Alesis Quadraverb II, Intercom -4 Channel
Clearcom Headset system.
Other: Dressing rooms 4, Accom 24, showers in all
dressing rooms.
Permanent forestage 1:52m with entrance on at Actors
Left. It is possible to convert to Theatre-in-Round
(almost) in four hours approx. Permanent Forestage
1.52m with entrance on at Actors Left.

### THE POINT DEPOT
Northwall Quay, Dublin 1 Eire
Mgt 00 353 1 836 6777 BO 00 353 1 836 3633
Fax 00 353 1 836 6422
ADMINISTRATION:
For all booking information and further details please
contact Sam Shrouder or Nicky Monk at Apollo Leisure

(UK) Ltd., Grehan House, Garsington Road, Cowley, Oxford OX4 5NQ. Tel: 01865 782900; Fax: Oxford 01865 782910.
Director and Chief Executive: Mike Adamson
Finance Director: Breda Fox
Theatre Manager: Cormac Rennick
Deputy Manager: Barry Walsh
Secretary: Denise Murphy
Please contact venue for further details.

### ROTUNDA PILLAR ROOM
The Rotunda Dublin 1 Eire
Tel 00 353 1 872 2377/872 2729
Seating/Capacity: 250

### ROYAL DUBLIN SOCIETY CONCERT HALL
Merrion Road, Ballsbridge, Dublin 4 Eire
Tel 00 353 1 668 0866 Fax 00 353 1 660 4014
ADMINISTRATION:
The Royal Dublin Society
Seating/Capacity: 1,000 retractable tiered seating

### SFX CENTRE
23 Upper Sherrard Street Dublin 1 Eire
Tel 00 353 1 284 1747 Fax 00 353 1 284 1767
Contact: Darryl Downey
Seating/Capacity: 750

### SIMMONSCOURT PAVILION
Simmonscourt Road, Ballsbridge, Dublin 4 Eire
Tel 00 353 1 668 0866 Fax 00 353 1 660 4014
Royal Dublin Society
Seating/Capacity: Leinster Hall 7,000

# Dudley
Pop. 304,615. London 115 miles. Newspapers: Express and Star (dly); Chronicle (fri). STD code 01384

### DUDLEY TOWN HALL
St James's Road Dudley West Midlands DY1 1HF
Tel 01384 815544 BO 01384 812812
Fax: 01384 815534
ADMINISTRATION:
Props: Dudley Metropolitan Borough Council
Principal Arts Officer: Rosemary Amos
Senior Arts Officer: Stephanie Donaldson (01384 815540)
Hall Manager: Andrew Grimshaw
Technical Manager: Martin Jones (01384 815539)
Box Office Manager: Carole Welding
Multi purpose concert hall, wide range of music, light entertainment, jazz, one night stands.
Seats: 1,060

### NETHERTON ARTS CENTRE
Northfield Road, Netherton, Dudley,
West Midlands DY2 9EP
Mgt 01384 815544 Curator 01384 812846
Fax 01384 815534
ADMINISTRATION:
Props: Dudley M.B.C.
Principal Arts Officer: Rosemary Amos
Senior Arts Officer: Stephanie Donaldson
(01384 815540)
Technical Manager: Martin Jones (01384 815539)

Box Office Manager: Carole Welding
Policy: touring drama, children's theatre, local amateur groups, available for hire.
Seats: 361 (stalls flat, balcony raked)
TECHNICAL:
Stage: Proscenium arch. Performing area 10.97m x 6.87m - pros opening 7.01m x 3.43m - wing widths 1.97 SR, 1.97m SL. Stage very slightly raked - floor wood, suitable for dance (not barefoot), lino not available, no crossover, stage heated. Height of grid 6.7m - 7 hemp sets, 280mm apart - tab track - 35kg permitted on bars - 4 borders, 4 pairs legs, black/grey, 2 sets of tabs in black and blue - gold house tabs, drawn. 12 x 13A independent circuits. Trap, centre stage. Get-in via doors SL or through auditorium - dock doors 1.48m wide. Safety curtain. Scale stage and lighting plans available.
Lighting: Furse 2 present board, 36 circuits @ 10A, 3 phase, operated from control room at rear of stalls - no supply for temporary board - 8 spots, 14 fresnels, 3 floods, Strand - 2 followspots can be operated from rear of balcony.
Sound: Seck 16:8:2 desk - 2 foldback speakers - 4 mics, radio mics by arrangement - 2 cassette tape systems. Acoustics suitable for music and spoken word.
Backstage: 3 dressing rooms, access by SR - quick change room. Refreshments can be provided by prior arrangement. Piano, poor. Advice given on accommodation. Staff - 1 technician - casuals by arrangement - security personnel by arrangement. Backstage facilities not accessible to disabled performers and staff.
Stage management: Techpro headset system. 8 sets, show relay and paging.

# Dundee
Pop. 181,842. London 428 miles. Newspapers: Courier & Advertiser (dly); Evening Telegraph (ntly). STD code 01382

### BONAR HALL
University of Dundee, Park Place, Perth Road, Dundee, DD1 4HN Scotland
Tel 01382 345466 Fax 01382 345467
Seating/Capacity: Main Hall 494, Ustinov Room
Capacity: 180
Contact: Sheena Jack

### CAIRD HALL COMPLEX
City Square Dundee DD1 3BB Scotland
Tel/Fax 01382 434451 BO: 01382 434940/1
ADMINISTRATION:
Props: Dundee City Council Arts and Heritage Department.
Policy: Concert Hall used for concerts, exhibitions, conferences.
Seating/Capacity: Caird Hall 2,400; Marryat Hall 350; Lesser Halls (2) 60.

TECHNICAL:
Further details from above number.

### DUNDEE REPERTORY THEATRE
Tay Square, Dundee DD1 1PB Scotland
Mgt 01382 227684  Fax 01382 228609
BO 01382 223530
ADMINISTRATION:
Props: Dundee Repertory Theatre Ltd

Artistic Director: Hamish Glen
Administrative Director: Joanna Reid
Marketing Manager: Denise Winford
Stage Manager: Linda Kyle
Policy: Repertory, 4 week run interspersed with visiting productions.
Perfs: Tues.-Sat. 7.30; Mats Sat 2.30p.m.
Seats: 450. 2 Bars and Restaurant
TECHNICAL:
Stage: Adaptable Proscenium/Open Flat; Pros. Opening width variable to 13.00m max, Ht. variable 5.00m to 9.00m; Depth, Setting Line to Back Wall 9.60m, Setting Line to front of apron (centre stage only) 1.75m; Width, Centre Line to PS Wall 9.17m, to OP Wall 9.17m; Ht. to underside of grid 15m, to underside of fly floors 6m; Flying equipment 20 Hemp sets (adjustable as required), 8 Double purchase C/W sets 200kg capacity; Length of Bars 13.5m; Prompt Crn. P.S.
Lighting: Switchboard: Rank ARRI Imagine 120 way, situated at rear of auditorium; FOH 40 circuits (patchable), Flys 66 circuits, Dips 14 circuits; 2 FOH Bridges and 2 Slots.
Equipment: 12 CCT 1K Floods. 36 1K SIL 30, 12 Minuette 500W Floods, 3 2K Fresnels, 18 par 64, 48 1k Fresnels, 20 Patt.23, 6 Minuette Fresnels, 10 Minuette Profiles. 1.2 kw SIL15 Follow Spot
Sound Equip: Control situated with lighting control equipment. Soundtracs Solo Live 16:4:2 Mixer; 3 HH V800 Power Amplifier; 2 Revox B77 Tape Decks, 1 Technics Cassette Deck 1 x Sony CD Player, 1 Technics Turntable; FOH P.S. 4 x BOSE 802 Loudspeakers; 2 HH Unit system 3 Effects Speakers; 30 Mic lines, 20 L/S lines. Equipment list available.
Dressing Rooms: 8 with showers to accommodate 26. Green Room.
Orchestra: Front 3 rows of seating removable for orchestra space approx. 30 sq. metres at 600mm below stage level.
Get-in at street level, rear of Stage; clock door 3.00m wide; Door 3.00m wide x 5.5m high.
Membership: TMA. Fed. of Scottish Theatres

### WHITEHALL THEATRE
Bellfield Street, Dundee DD1 5JA
Mgt: 01382 322684 Press/Marketing: 01382 434940
SD: 01382 322738 BO: 01382 434940
ADMINISTRATION:
Chair: Bill Crowe
Production/Technical Manager: George Clark
Marketing Secretary: Jenny Lawrie
Local Authority: City of Dundee District Council
Policy: Touring shows, one-night stands, plus local operatic and musical societies. Willing to premiere show. Built in 1928 as Alhambra Cinema, with a stage for acts between the films; the stage was extended in 1984. Venue is self-financing.
Performance Schedule: Open 20 to 25 weeks a year; evening performances start at 7.30pm, matinees on Saturdays at 2.15pm. Booking terms: hire only.
Facilities: Seats: 750 raked. Coffee bar, licensed bar. Car park adjacent, station: Dundee, coach terminal, bus route: 21. 6 wheelchair spaces for the disabled, deaf loop system - assistance available. Parking & level access. Small rehearsal hall, large workshop and storage area.
TECHNICAL:
Please contact theatre for details.

# Dunstable

### QUEENSWAY HALL
Queensway Hall, Vernon Place, Dunstable, Bedfordshire LU5 4EU
Admin 01582 609620 BO 01582 603326
Fax 01582 471190
ADMINISTRATION:
Props: Sports and Leisure Foods Ltd. For South Bedfordshire District Council.
General Manager: Yvonne Mullens
Policy: Hiring Hall
Seating/Capacity: 900
TECHNICAL:
Proscenium Arch, flat stage, 25 stage feet deep, 30 feet width, 17 feet high.

# East Kilbride
Pop. 85,000. London 397 miles. Newspapers: East Kilbride News (thurs). STD code 01355

### THE VILLAGE THEATRE
Maxwell Drive, East Kilbride, Glasgow G74 4HG
Tel 01355 248669 Fax 01355 248677
ADMINISTRATION:
Props: South Lanarkshire Council
Arts & Entertainments Mgr: Alexander P M McBain
Theatre Manager: Margaret Campbell
Theatre Techical Officer: Carrick McGhie
Policy: Tours, One Night Stands, Hire, Amateur
Perfs: Usually 7.30pm
Seats: 333 (on one raked tier) 318 if orchestra pit used. Rehearsal room with kitchen, bar, Coffee Bar.
TECHNICAL:
Stage: Proscenium, Flat; opening 7.31m; Pros. Ht. 5m; Depth of S/Line 8.08m; W/Widths P.S.4.95m, O.P. 2.89m; Grid Ht. 11.31m; Ht. to under fly floor 6.23m; Flying Bars C/W (16 of) 18.08m, Hemp (6 of) 10.06m. 18 C/W flylines. (3.05m extension available).
Lighting: Switchboard: "Eurolight Micron" Memory System (60 way), plus "Thorn TGM" Manual System (60 way) Control Room is at rear of auditorium. FOH Lighting: 8 @ CCT Sil.30; FOH Alcoves: 2 @ Par 64 and 2 @ Sil. 30 per side. 4 Sils and the 4 Par 64 have "Chromatic" Colour-Wheels; Perches: 2 @ 1kw Fresnels per side; Footlights: 3 Circs (S-Type Battens); No.1 Bar: 12 @ Pat.743; No.2 Bar: 8 @ Pat.743 extra spot-bars can be rigged as required. Flood Bar: 12 @ CCT. 500w Minuette Floods (3 Circs) Flys and stage area have Dips and independent Skts. 10 Non-Dim Skts controlled form Switchboard. Headset/Cue Light Skts in most areas.
Sound Equip: "Electrosonic" 10 channel/3 Group Mixer. 100w per Group. "PAN" Facility (100V Line) 1 Revox A77; 2 @ Cassette Decks; 1C Record Deck. (situated in Control Room); Various monitors available. 24 @ Show Relay/Paging Speakers situated around the Theatre at strategic points. Tech communication - Headset "Ring" system or Cue Lights. Induction Loop System fitted. Land-Line installed for "Live" transmission to local hospital radio network.
Dressing Rooms 6; with comfortable accommodation for 4 in each. 1 auxillary room 4 showers. Orchestra Pit: Front row of seats must be removed. Accommodated 8-10.

# Eastbourne

Pop. 80,000. London 64 miles. Newspapers: Eastbourne Gazette (wed); Eastbourne Herald (sat). STD code 01323

## THE CONGRESS THEATRE

Carlisle Road, Eastbourne East Sussex BN21 4BS
Mgt 01323 415500 BO 01323 412000
SD 01323 410048 Fax 01323 727369
Correspondence to Winter Garden, 14 Compton Street,
Eastborne, East Sussex BN21 4BP
ADMINISTRATION:
Props: Eastbourne Borough Council
Dir. of Tourism & Community Services: Ronald G
Cussons
General Manager: Ian Alexander
Assistant General Manager: Gavin Davies
Sales & Marketing Director: Jakki Hall
Stage Manager: Mark Sayer
Marketing & Publicity Manager: Beverley Ebdy
Box Office Manager: Zoe Gail Bourne
Policy: All Class (Except Rep)
Perfs: Variable, depending on production.
Seats: 1,689. Two Licensed Bars, Licensed Restaurant
(organised party catering).
TECHNICAL:
Stage: Proscenium, Flat; Pros. opening 13.72m; Ht. of
Pros. 6.40m; Depth of S/Line 10.97m; Ht. of Grid
16.00m; 56 lines, 42 C/W, 14 Hemp; Flying Bars
15.24m; W/Widths P.S. 3.96m average (variable), O.P.
9.14m; Prompt Cnr. P.S.
False sprung floor available for Ballet presentation. Direct
on stage Get-in facilities. Electrically operated orchestra
lift. Tallescope.
Lighting: Strand Gemini 2+ 100 Way-in Rear Stalls. FOH.
10 Harmony 22 Circle Front, 6 x 264 each circle side, 4 x
264 on perches paired across. 3 x 4 circuit battens, 2
circuit floats. No. 1 Spot Bar 20 x 743 NO2 10 x 243
Flood Bar 4 x Iris 4 Floods.
Sound Equip: Soundcraft Series 400B mixing desk,
700w proscenium mounted Altec Speakers. Klark Teknik
Graphic Eq. Twin Channel Limiter, Urban Parametric
Equalizer, Stabilizer Frequency Shifter. Monitors: Tannoy
Cougar Wedge x 6.
Tape Machines: Teac C3 Cassette with remote x 1, Teac
A334 4 Track Reel to Reel x 1, B77 MKII Reel to Reel x
2, Technics Turntable. 'Clear Com' Talk Back to all out
stations & belt packs. Cue lights to all out stations.
Dressing Rooms 11; Accom. 100;
5 Showers.
Orchestra Pit 25 (average).
Membership: TMA

## DEVONSHIRE PARK THEATRE

8 Compton Street, Eastbourne East Sussex
Mgt 01323 415500 BO 01323 412000
SD 01323 410074 Fax 01323 727369
Correspondence to Winter Garden, 14 Compton Street,
Eastbourne, East Sussex BN21 4BP
ADMINISTRATION:
Props: Eastbourne Borough Council
Director of Tourism and Community Services:
Ronald G Cussons
General Manager: Ian Alexander
Assistant General Manager: Gavin Davis
Stage Manager: Paul Debreczeny
Marketing & Publicity Manager: Beverley Ebdy
Box Office Manager: Zoe Gail Bourne
Policy: Major Touring Plays
Perfs: Variable, depending upon production

Seats: 936, Licensed Bar.
TECHNICAL:
Stage: Proscenium. Raked 1 in 24; Pros. Opening
8.04m; Ht. of Pros. 4.27m to border; Depth of S/Line
7.32m; Ht. of Grid 10.05m - 30.36m; 26 lines, Hemp. 2
C/W, 4 winch sets; Scenery Flying Ht. 9.75m; Flying
Bars 10.97m; W/Widths P.S. 3.66m, O.P. 3.66m;
Prompt Cnr. P.S.
Direct on stage Get-in facilities, P.S. scene-dock with
4.88m headroom.
Lighting: Switchboard: Strand Duet, 80 ways, sited rear
of dress circle; Lanterns; Grand Circle level 14 x 264's, 2
x T64's; Box 1 Spot Bar; 12 x 743's. Additional
Equipment: 14 x 743's, 10 x Quartet Fresnels, 16 x Par
64's, 4 x 243 (2 ks) 6 x Berkey 1k Floods. 4 x 3-way
ground row, 4 x 4-Way Way cyc. battens; 8 x 4' 6"
stands.
Circuits: 25 x 2kw in O.P. Flys; Stage: 13 x 2kw O.P. 10
x 2kw P.S., plus 4 x 2kw linked across.
Sound Equip: Sound Desk situated rear dress circle.
Soundcraft 200B mixer 16 into 4 into 2 + 2 foldback. 2 x
Revox B77's. 1 Gram Deck. 1 x Cassette. 4 Electrovoice
mid/high cabinets on prosc. - 300 watts each. 6 Shure
SM 58 Microphones, 3 AKG D190 microphone, 6 floor
stands with Boom arms.
Dressing Rooms 9, Accom 25-30. 2 showers. Orchestra
Pit.
Membership: TMA

## ROYAL HIPPODROME

Seaside Road, Eastbourne, East Sussex BN21 3PF
Mgt 01323 415522 BO 01323 412000
SD 01323 410106
ADMINISTRATION:
Props: Mathews Productions Ltd
Cary Point, Babbacombe Downs Road, Torquay, Devon
TQ1 3LU; Contact Colin Mathews Tel 01803 322233 Fax
01803 322244
Theatre Manager: John Pleydell
Stage Manager: Ray Grove
Policy: Summer Variety Shows
Perfs: Evening 8.15p.m., Mats Tues & Thurs 2.30p.m.
Seats: 643, Licensed Bar and Coffee Shop.
TECHNICAL:
Stage: Proscenium, Raked; Pros. Opening 7.62m; Ht. of
Pros. 5.18m; Depth of S/Line 6.71m; Ht. of Grid 14.5m;
25 line; Hemp; 3 C/W. Scenery Flying Ht. 7m; Flying
Bars 9.14m. W/Widths P.S. 2.50m, O.P. 2.50m; Prompt
Cnr. P.S. Scene Dock U/S P.S. 9.75m x 3.66m x 5.49m
high; Prop Room U/S O.P. 5.49m x 3.66m x 2.74m high.
Lighting: Switchboard: Strand Threeset, 40 ways,
situated rear of Grand Circle; Lanterns: Follow Spots 2 x
Patt.293 2kw;
FOH 6 Patt.T84 plus colour wheels, Stage 11 Patt.223,
8 Patt.264, 9 Patt.123, 7 Patt.23; 5 AC1001 Floods. 2
Patt.243, 2 Patt.137; 2 x 4 Circuit Battens; 6 Booms.
Sound Equipment: RH Sound Allen & Heath SR 12 way
mixing desk; PPX 900 Citronic Amplifier; PPX450
Citronic Amplifier;
Denon Cassette machine; Show Relay; Talk Back
System; various microphones.
Dressing Rooms 8 plus
Wardrobe; Accom. 22;
Band facilities below Stage. Orchestra Pit 8.
Membership: TMA

## WINTER GARDEN

14 Compton Street, Eastbourne, East Sussex BN21 4BP
Mgt 01323 415500 BO 01323 412000
Fax 01323 727369

ADMINISTRATION:
Props: Eastbourne Borough Council
Dir of Tourism & Leisure Services: Ronald G Cussons
General Manager: Ian Alexander
Marketing & Publicity Manager: Beverley Ebdy
Stage Manager: Adam Calver
Box Office Manager: Zoe Gail Bourne
Perfs: Variable
Membership: TMA
FLORAL HALL
Seats: 1,100 Theatre, 596 Cabaret, 842
Wrestling, 1,200 Dancing.
2 Licensed Bars.
Lighting: Strand SP 40 Board, 40 circuits, operated from
SR on stage level - 100A 3 phase supply available for
temporary board - various pats, spots and fresnels, 2
follow spots operated from gantry at rear of auditorium.
Dressing Rooms: 3 large dressing rooms near stage level
plus one above, accommodating 24
Backstage facilities not accessible to disabled
performers and staff.

GOLD ROOM:
Above Floral Hall.
Multi-purpose flat-floor hall.
Seats: 400. Licensed Bar.
Stage: 6m deep x 13m wide (variable).
Lighting: Thorn 20/2 switchboard.
Sound Equipment: 12 Channel Sect mixing desk,  twin
cassette deck,  4 x FOH speakers.

# Edinburgh

Pop. 439,721. London 373 miles. Newspapers: Evening
News (ntly); The Scotsman (dly). STD code 0131

## CHURCH HILL THEATRE

33 Morningside Road, Edinburgh EH10 4RR
Admin 0131 447 7597 PCB 0131 447 7582
ADMINISTRATION:
Props: City of Edinburgh Council (For bookings contact
Joyce Sibbald on 0131 529 4147).
Halls Officer: Jo Navarro
Policy: Mostly amateur but professional in Summer and
odd weeks in Winter.
Perfs: Vary according to show
Seats: 360. Coffee Bar and Rehearsal Rooms
TECHNICAL:
Stage: Proscenium, Flat; Pros. opening 8.53m wide by
3.81m high; Depth of S/Line 7.62m; Forestage 1m; Grid
none; 8 Hemp Sets; Paint Dock; Scene Dock; Bars
10.36m wide; Wings P.S. 2.13m, O.P. 2.29m; Prompt
Cnr. P.S.; One Wardrobe Room; Get-in; Dock Doors
3.50m by 1.19m; Difference in level 0.91m.
Lighting: Switchboard: Situated at back of auditorium.
(44 x 1kw, 10 x 2kw); 3 Battens, 4 Patt.263 (with colour
change), 10 Patt.23, 16 Patt.123, 34 Patt.60 3 x 1.83m
Patt. S Groundrow. Can be augmented by equipment
from other theatres (C.S.I.'s etc.)  Rank Strand lightboard
(m)3 Junior. Dimmers (80) way.
Sound Equip: 4 mics and amplifier; Speakers F.O.H.
Tape input.
Dressing Rooms: 4 with Showers and toilets; 24
persons. Orchestra Pit: Area 18 sq.m., rail 1.83m in front
of stage. Disabled toilet - unisex.

## THE EDINBURGH CORN EXCHANGE

Newmarket Road, Edinburgh EH14 1RL Scotland
Tel: 0131 228 2413 Fax: 0131 229 4990

Contact: Paul DeMarco
Stage: 8m x 15m

## EDINBURGH FESTIVAL THEATRE

13-29 Nicolson Street, Edinburgh EH8 9FT Scotland
Mgt 0131 662 1112 Fax 0131 667 0744
BO 0131 529 6000 Fax 0131 662 1199
Email: www.eft.co.uk
ADMINISTRATION:
Props: City of Edinburgh Council
General Manager: Stephen Barry
Operations Manager: Brian Loudon
Theatre Manger: David Todd
Financial Manager: Helen Bates
Marketing Manager: Anne McCluskey
Technical Manager: Alan Campbell
Stage Manager: Iain Gillespie
Chief Electrician: Andy Devenport
Seating Capacity: 1,900
Please contact the theatre for full technical details.

## EDINBURGH INTERNATIONAL
## CONFERENCE CENTRE - EICC

The Exchange, Morrison Street, Edinburgh EH3 8EE
Tel 0131 300 3000 Fax 0131 300 3030 The Cromdale
Exhibition Hall, The Strathblane Hall, The Lomond Suite
and The Galloway Suite, Breakout Rooms & The
Pentland Suite,
ADMINISTRATION:
Sales & Marketing Director: Trevor McCartney
Association Sales Manager: Heather Bell
THE CROMDALE EXHIBITION HALL
750 sq.m.net 1185 sq.m/12 738 sq.ft. gross.  Suitable
for banquets of up to 800, exhibitions & receptions.
TECHNICAL:
Under floor ducts on 6.5m./24ft.centres, including high
powered electrical outlets, telephone points, water &
waste. Closed circuit television and PA systems. Disable
access. A 5000kg capacity goods lift serves all floors.
THE STRATHBLANE HALL
1128 sq.m. net/12 128 sq.ft net.
Capacity 1000.
THE LOMOND SUITE AND THE GALLOWAY SUITE,
BREAK OUT ROOMS AND THE PENTLAND SUITE
Further details available on request.

## EDINBURGH PLAYHOUSE

18-22 Greenside Place, Edinburgh EH1 3AA Scotland
Admin 0131 557 2692 BO 0131 557 2590
Fax 0131 557 6520
ADMINISTRATION:
Props: Apollo Leisure (UK) Ltd.
For all booking information and further details please
contact Sam Shrouder or Nicky Monk at Apollo Leisure
(UK) Ltd., Grehan House, Garsington Road, Cowley,
Oxford OX4 5NQ. Tel: 01865 782900; Fax: Oxford
01865 782910.
Theatre Manager: Andrew Lyst
Stage Manager: Stuart Haldane
Technical Manager: Graham Wade
Policy: Multi-use; Opera, Ballet, Rock and Pop Concerts,
Variety, Cinema, Musicals etc.
Seats: 3,056. 5 Bars
TECHNICAL:
Stage: Proscenium width 14.87m; Pros. height 8.50m;
Full stage width 22.80m; full stage depth P.S. 12.17m;
O.P. 13.60m; width between Fly Floors 18.25m; Flying
width 15.24m; Flying Depth (from Tabs) 10.70m; Ht. to
Grid Front 18.13m; Ht. to Underside Fly Floor, Front

8.50m; Ht. to Bar - out Dead 17.20m; Ht. to Beams in grid 21.54m; No Rake; Prompt Cnr. Stage Right (S.L. possible).

Flys: (operated from Stage Right) Counterweight Sets: Single Purchase 26 (1-22), Double Purchase 26 (27-52); maximum weight loading spread over 4 lines 500kg.

Lighting: Strand Century 'Light Palette' updated with V6E software

Rigging Positions: Both Circle and Balcony fronts have 2" aluminium scaffolding bars running the full length. The Cove bar no longer exists but the circuits can be used if an advance truss is rigged. The Balcony front has 28 T84's permanently rigged along this Bar. The Dome Bridge has 8 Strand 818's permanently rigged along this bar.

On-Stage Rigging Positions: Both the LX gallery and the Fly floor have 2" scaffolding frames running the full length of the stage which can also be used for cross lighting if required.

Stage Lighting Stock: Permanently Rigged FOH: 28 1kw Strand T'84s; 8 2kw Strand 818's; 2 2kw Strand 243's; 2 1kw Strand 803's. 20 1kw Strand 743's; 10 1kw Starlette PC's; 16 1kw Silhouette 30; 13 2kw Mole Richardson's; 46 1kw 240v Par Can's; 10 650w Strand 813's; 6 1kw Iris 4's (unusable at this time); 2 2.5kw Xenon Follow Spots (converted Sunspots); 10 20' 10 circuit Internally Wired Bars.

Orchestra Pit: Basic small Pit: 30 musicians - no seats removed; Medium Pit: 65-80 musicians - rows A,B,C, removed; Large Pit: 110-120 musicians - rows A,B,C,D,E, removed (approx.)

## HERIOT-WATT UNIVERSITY STUDENT'S UNION

The Union, Riccarton, Currie, Edinburgh
EH14 4AS Scotland
Tel 0131 451 5333 Fax 0131 451 5344
Capacity: 500 standing; seated 350
Vice President (Services): Fiona Torrance

## KING'S THEATRE

2 Leven Street, Edinburgh EH3 9LQ Scotland
Mgt 0131 229 4840  BO 0131 220 4349
SD 0131 229 3416
ADMINISTRATION:
Props: City of Edinburgh Council
General Manager: Stephen Barry
Operations Manager: Brian Loudon
Theatre Manger: David Todd
Financial Manager: Helen Bates
Marketing Manager: Anne McCluskey
Technical Manager: Alan Campbell
Stage Manager: Iain Gillespie
Chief Electrician: Andy Devenport
Policy: Touring, Pantomime, etc.
Perfs: Variable depending on production
Seats: 1,340. 4 Bars.
TECHNICAL:
Stage: Proscenium, Raked 1 in 24; Pros. opening 9.75m; Ht. of Pros. 6.55m; Depth of S/Line 15.24m; Ht. of Grid 15.24m; 57 lines, Fly Floor, C/W; Scenery Flying Ht. 14.63m; Flying Bars 12.04m; W/Widths P.S. 3.50m; O.P. 4.27m; Prompt Cnr. P.S. One Wardrobe Room, Dock Door 1.83m from street level; Paint Frame back door; 2 Traps.
Lighting: Switchboard: Strand Galaxy 150 ways (upper circle). Lanterns: 200 Assorted mostly strand, 4 x 4 circuit battens, 4 x 4 circuit footlight/groundrow 4 x 5 way flood bar, 2 x 12 I.W. Spot Bars, 4 x 4 way ladders each side of track. F.O.H. positions on centre front of

both circles and top tier of side boxes.
Sound: Full PA system including 20 way Alice Mixer 2 Revox B77 tape decks and an assortment of microphones. Full sound and lighting details on application to electrics department.
Dressing Rooms 13; Accom. 96; 6 Showers; Orchestra Pit partially under forestage.
Membership: TMA

## THE QUEEN'S HALL

Clerk Street, Edinburgh EH8 9JG Scotland
Mgt 0131 668 3456 BO 0131 668 2019
Fax 0131 668 2656 CC Hotline 0131 667 7776
ADMINISTRATION:
Status: Concert Hall.
General Manager: Paul Gudgin
A converted Georgian church opened by HM The Queen in July 1979. Home of Scottish Chamber Orchestra and Scottish Ensemble and host to professional amateur and popular music. Central location. Venue is self financed.
Local Authority: City of Edinburgh District Council.
Membership Edinburgh Capital Group, Edinburgh Arts & Entertainment.
Policy: No programming policy, some promotions. anything considered - professional, amateur, classical, jazz, folk, rock, children's shows etc. Willing to premiere show.
Performance schedule usually open 7 days. Booking terms hire, box office split.
Other activities: Functions, receptions, conferences, trade exhibitions, contemporary art and photography exhibitions, meetings.
Facilities: Seats, Main auditorium 900; some pews, some moveable. Catering Counter service, wide and varied international menu including vegetarian and wholemeal cooking, full bar service with public house licence serving real ales, beers etc. Open Mon-Sat 10am - 5pm and before concerts.
Access car park: St. Leonard's Street, Crighton Street (NCP 0131 668 4661); station: Edinburgh Waverley; coach terminal: St Andrew's Square; bus routes; 3, 3A, 5, 7, 8, 14, 31, 33, 36, 51, 69, 80, 81, 81A, 82, 87 and 89.
For disabled persons: Up to 299 wheelchair spaces - infra red sound system and induction loop - ramp at entrance - assistance available - all house facilities fully accessible - special toilet, low telephone.
Other Facilities: The Lothian Room, The Hope Scott Room and John Tunnell Room, each seat 150, suitable for meetings and receptions.
TECHNICAL:
Stage: Thrust 0.6m high, flexible. Performing area 9.75m x 7.92. No rake - floor part wood, rest moveable platforms, suitable for dance, no lino available, backstage cross-over, stage not heated. 1 operational set - no tab track - 120kg permitted on bars. Get-in via front or back. Scale stage plans available.
Lighting: 200A 3 phase supply. Also 63A 3 phase supply. Tango 48 Board. 1 x 12 channel front of house bar, 2 x 6 channel side bars, 6 Bresnels, 8 Preludes, 4 Profiles.
Sound: Integrated public address and show relay system with facility for background music in foyers and auditorium. Suitable for speech and small bands. Backdrop bar. A motorised bar with black backdrop. Acoustics suitable for music and spoken word.
Stage Management: Show relay/Tannoy to dressing rooms.
Backstage: 3 dressing rooms, access from front or back - 2 band rooms. Facilities include iron with board and numerous power points. Refreshments available from

FOH. Two Steinway concert grand pianos. Advice given on accommodation. Staff - 2 stage - casuals available - security personnel. Backstage facilities accessible to disabled performers and staff.

## REID CONCERT HALL, UNIVERSITY OF EDINBURGH
14 Bristo Square Teviot Place Edinburgh
EH8 9AH Scotland
Mgt 0131 650 2423 Mgt Fax 0131 650 2425
Hall Tel 0131 650 4367
Seating/Capacity: 300; raked.
Contact: Fiona Donaldson

## ROYAL LYCEUM
Grindlay Street, Edinburgh EH3 9AX Scotland
Admin 0131 248 4800 BO 0131 248 4848
Fax 0131 228 3955
ADMINISTRATION:
Props: City of Edinburgh Council
Lessees: The Royal Lyceum Theatre Company Ltd
Artistic Director: Kenny Ireland
Marketing Manager: Clare Simpson
Assistant Artistic Director: Steve Gale
Theatre Manager: Marcus Ford
Management Accountant: Derek Kennedy
Production Manager: David Butterworth
Chief Electrician: Stella Goldie
Major repertory theatre, built 1883; architect C.J. Phipps. Listed grade A; major refurbishment finished September 1996 base for Royal Lyceum Theatre Company Limited; funded by Scottish Arts Council, The City of Edinburgh Council.
Membership: TMA, Federation of Scottish Theatres, ABTT, SFTTT.
Policy: Repertory seasons of major world classics and production of new Scottish writing. 10/12 productions per year. Willing to premiere show. Occasional visiting productions. Performance schedule: open Tuesday to Saturday; 7:45pm evening performances (8:00pm during summer); 2.30pm matinees (1 or 2 per month).
Non-performance activities: Conferences, receptions, meetings, exhibitions.
Facilities: Seating - Theatre 658. Catering - Restaurant and four bars licensed until 1:00am. Ticket outlets - Waverley Bridge Ticket Centre; Queens Hall, Clerk St. Edinburgh Tourist Board Information Centre Artlink. Access/car park: NCP Castle Terrace; nearest railway station Haymarket/Waverley, nearest coach St Andrew Square. For People with disabilities: Designated orange badge parking within 50m, 9 wheelchair spaces in Stalls level adjacent to other seats, lifts to all areas, level at entrance, induction loop all levels + infra-red system, adapted toilet, low level public telephones, restaurant seating not fixed, staff training. Any speciifc requirements contact Theatre Manager/House Manager.
TECHNICAL:
Stage: Proscenium arch. Pros opening 8.46m x 7.16m, 7.47 pelmet, wing widths 2.44m SR, 112.78 sq m SL, stage raked 1:24, floor hardboard over wood, suitable for dance, no lino available, understage cross-over, stage heated. Height of grid 20m. 55 single purchase counterweight including 2 up/down stage SWL 450kg. Spot hemps as required. Full black masking. White Cyc. Red/gold house tabs flown No. 1 bar. No traps as yet. Removable forestage 12.6m x 1.6m. Orchestra pit 12.6m x 1.5m or 12.6m 3.7m accommodates 12/40. Get-in via lift 4.6m from street, SWL 5000kg. Lift depth 6.8m , width 2.9m, height 3.07m. Tallescopes. Safety Curtain. Scale stage, fly and lighting plans available 1:25.

Lighting: Strand Gemini 2+ board, 180 circuits, 170 @ 2Kw, 10 @ 5Kw, 3 phase, oprated from rear Upper Circle, 100A 3 Phase supply for temp board - 70 spots, 50 fresnels, 6 pars, 15 floods -2 followspots operated from gallery.
Sound: Soundcraft 200B desk, operated from rear Upper Circle - FOH speakers - 2 x Revox B77 tape systems. Acoustics suitable for music and spoken.
Stage Management: Prompt corner SL - headsets, 10 outstations - show relay/tannoy to dressing rooms, backstage work areas and FOH.
Backstage: 10 Dressing rooms accommodating 24, access by stairs - green room - wardrobe on level 5 with iron, laundry. Advice given on accommodation. Staff - 3 Stage, 3LX, casuals available, security personnel.

## ST CECILIA'S HALL
Niddry Street Cowgate Edinburgh EH1 1LJ Scotland
Mgt 0131 650 2423 Mgt Fax 0131 650 2425
Hall Direct Line 0131 650 2805
Seating/Capacity: 200; flat.
Contact: Fiona Donaldson

## TRAVERSE THEATRE
Cambridge Street, Edinburgh EH1 2ED Scotland
Admin 0131 228 3223 BO 0131 228 1404
Fax 0131 229 8443
ADMINISTRATION:
Artistic Director: Philip Howard
Literary Director: John Tiffany
Literary Associate: Ella Widridge
Administrative Producer: Lucy Mason
Marketing Manager: Fiona Sturgeon
Sponsorship Manager: Noelle Henderson
Theatres Manager: Michael Fraser
Production Manager: Mike Griffiths
Chief Electrician: Renny Robertson
Policy: The Traverse produces innovative writing of the highest quality plus visiting companies.
Perfs: Traverse 1 Tues-Sun 8.00pm.
Traverse 2 Tues-Sun 8.00pm (different time if simultaneous events are running)
Seats: Traverse 1 from 216 up to 328 depending on configuration. Traverse 2 up to 120
TECHNICAL:
Stage, (Traverse 1): Flexible seating system, 9 configurations. 3 proscenium, Pros to back wall 7.50, Pros 8.50 wide. 1 U-shaped ,10.70 x 6.20. 3 in round, 6.20 x 6.20. 1 Traverse, 13.60 x 4.70. 1 Thrust, 10.60 x 6.30. Seats from 240 up to 328 depending on configuration. 5 counterweight fly bar in pros arch. 8 hemp fly bars. Height to Grid 6.40. Tab track masking all round the auditorium.
Lighting: Strand light board M - a combined manual/memory control system with 140 memories and integral floppy disk. The manual section consists of a 72 channel, 2 preset with timed dipless crossfades. The board also has 24 submasters to which channels, memories and groups may be assigned. 144 channels and soft patch. Designers remote control. EC90 digital dimmers. There are 120 x 2kw circuits and 24 x 5kw circuits all patchable to 300 outlets in grid and on stage. 12 x 1.2kw narrow profile 11/26 cantata. 16 x 1.2kw medium profile 18/32 cantata. 12 x 1.2kw wide profile 26/44 cantata. 12 x 650w wide profile 22/40 quartet. 6 x 1.2kw prism convex 5/40 cantata. 6 x 650w prism convex 10/55 quartet. 31 x 1.2kw fresnel 10/55 cantata. 16 x 650w fresnel 15/40 quartet. 10 x 1kw par 64 cp60/61.
15 x 500w lcompartment coda flood. 30 x 200w

lcompartment coda flood

Sound: 1 Allen & Heath SC series 16/4/2 sound mixer. 2 H+H mx 1200 amplifiers. 1 Revox B77 mk2 tape recorders 33/4 + 71/2 ips. 1 Revox B77 mk2 HS tape recorder 71/2 + 15 ips. 1 Denon DRM 710 Cassettes deck. 1 London Acoustic Development - GA5942 SP turntable. 1 Denon DCD 660 CD Player + Remote Control. 1 x Sony DTC - P7 Dat Player + Remote Control. 2 x Pair of Bose 802 Speakers + Bose EQ. 40 x mic outlets located in grid and on-stage. 40 x speaker outlets located in grid and on-stage.

Stage (Traverse 2): Flexible 3 row seating in 8 moveable modules. 5 configurations approx. stage space 5m x 5m. Grid height 4.50. No flys. Tab track masking all around perimeter. Get-in door 2.40 x 5.00.

Lighting: Strand Light board m - a combined manual memory control system with 200 memories and integral floppy disk. The manual section consists of 48 channels, 2 preset with timed dipless crossfade. The Designers Remote Control. EC90 dimmers 48 x 2kw circuits. 15 x Patt223 1kw fresnel. 40 x Patt 23 500w fresnel. 15 x Patt23 500w profile. 4 x minuette 650w profile. 10 x minuette 650w P.C.

Sound: Allen + Heath Sc series 12/4/2 Sound mixer. 2 H+H mx 900 amplifiers. 1 x Revox B77 mk 2 tape recorder 33/4 + 71/2 ips. 1 x Revox B77 tape recorder 71/2 + 15 ips. 1 x Denon DRM 700 cassette deck. 2 x pair of Bose 802 speakers. Mic outlets situated in grid and on-stage. Speakers outlets situated in grid and on-stage.

Both Theatres: 6 x AKG microphones. 1 x Shure SM58 microphone. 4 x AKG telescopic mic stand, 3 x pair Bose speaker stands. 2 x Kodak carousel projectors with 1 remote control (but no crossfade).

Induction loop, show relay, ring intercom and FOH + backstage paging system. Stage managers desk with control of cue lights, ring intercom and paging microphone desks can be in control room or in prompt corner for Traverse 1 or below control room in Traverse 2.

Get-in: scenic lift 4m x 2m from Ground floor loading bay. Direct from lift into workshop 14 x 9 through scenic corridor to Auditorium. Workshop suitable to build sets, not fitted out with heavy machinery.

Dressing rooms 4-6 people per room, showers and washbasins in each. There are 3 backstage toilets and a green room with cooking facilities.

## USHER HALL

Lothian Road Edinburgh EH1 2EA Scotland
Tel 0131 228 8616 Fax 0131 228 8848
Manager: Moira McKenzie
Theatre currently undergoing renovation. Expected re-opening date November 2000.
Seating/Capacity: 2,200

# Enniskillen, County Fermanagh

Pop. 15,000. Belfast 90 miles. Dublin 105 miles. Newspapers: News Letter, Irish News (dly); Belfast Telegraph (ntly); Fermanagh Herald; Impartial Reporter (wkly). STD code 01365

## ARDHOWEN THEATRE AND ARTS CENTRE

Dublin Road, Enniskillen, Co Fermanagh
BT74 6BR Northern Ireland
Admin 01365 323233 BO 01365 325440

Fax 01365 327102
ADMINISTRATION:
Props: Fermanagh District Council
General Mgr and Artistic Director: Eamonn Bradley
Technician: Tom Sharkey
Policy: Mixed programme, touring drama, music, opera, dance, films, exhibitions, concerts, pantomimes and amateur productions. Available for private functions, including trade shows and conferences.
Theatre By The Lakes: Seats 300. Two bars, restaurant, lakeview terrace and marina.
TECHNICAL:
Stage: Proscenium, flat and level with optional thrust apron over orchestra pit, pros. 8700 wide, 5300 high to fixed pelmet. c.st-s right 4900, c.st-s left 5900. depth-rear of pros. wall to back wall - 8700, to x-over gallery 7475. Height (beneath fly floors) 4900, beneath roof beams - 7484. Flying: 10 installed sets, (capacity 33), single purchase, 400Kg per bar. Bar length 13000. S.M. sl corner (can be removed to s.r.) scenery store s.l. (capacity 79m2) Orchestra Pit 30m2, 2600m below stage.
Lighting: 120 way Gemini II, with full back-up and disc storage, Dimmers Rank-Strand permus II, (24 5k, 96 2.5k). Additional power 2 200A tpn situated USL. 1 16mm elf film projector, 1 roll drum projection screen.
Sound: 16/4/2 mixer by Audix Ltd., 27 mic inputs, 19 loudspeaker outlets, 1 Revox B77, 1 stereo cassette deck, 1 record desk.
Desk by Audix Ltd., c/w paging, show relay, twin ring intercom, cue lights and effects circuits.
Dressing Rooms: 6 rooms for 50 persons, on 3 floors. S.M. office, green room, showers.

Studio Theatre:
Seats: 45-50
Policy: Rehearsal room and readings. Facility for electrics (24 circuits 2.5k) and sound size: 7900 by 7850.

# Epsom, Surrey

Pop. 70,000. London 19 miles. Newspapers: Epsom Herald; Epsom & Ewell Advertiser (thurs); Epsom Guardian; Epsom News; Epsom Planet. STD code 01372

## EPSOM PLAYHOUSE

Ashley Avenue, Epsom, Surrey KT18 5AL
Mgt 01372 742226 BO 01372 742555
SD 01372 726228
ADMINISTRATION:
Props: Borough of Epsom & Ewell
Playhouse Manager: Trevor Mitchell
Production/Technical Manager: Stan Masters
Chief Electrician: Simon Banks
Policy: Touring - opera, dance, drama, concerts, films pantomime, jazz and rock music, exhibitions and amateur productions, conferences and trade shows.
Perfs: Variable
Seats: Main auditorium 406, studio 80.
Two Bars/Coffee Bar/Restaurant.
TECHNICAL:
Stage: Proscenium, flat with either forestage or orchestra pit. Pros. opening 11.5m; Auditorium raked seating or flat floor; Ht. of Pros. 5.00m; Depth of S/Line 6.70m; Ht. of Grid 10.90m; 20 Hemp sets, 7 winch sets; Flying Bars 10.00m; W/Widths: P.S. 3.85m, O.P. 5.40m.
Lighting: Switchboard: Impression 2 - dimmers, 128 ways at 2.5kw & 6 ways at 5kw. Lanterns; stock of various profiles, fresnels, cyc. battens. 100ATPN touring

outlet.
Sound Equip: Control Room; 16 to 8 Soundcraft 500;  2 x Revox B77; record deck + cassette deck; CD Player, mic lines to stage and aud. L/speaker lines to stage and aud.
Dressing Rooms: 4, accom. 34. Chorus Dressing Room for 40, 4 showers. Orchestra pit 25 max.
Projection Equip: 2 x 35mm projectors and ancillary equipment. Dolby SR + 16mm Projector.
Parking: multi-storey next door to theatre.

# Exeter, Devon

Pop. 105,000. London 170 miles. Newspapers: Express & Echo (dly); Western Morning News (dly). STD code 01392

## EXETER UNIVERSITY GREAT HALL

Stocker Road Exeter Devon EX4 4PZ
Tel 01392 215566 Fax 01392 263512
Bookings Manager: Marilyn Carter
Seating/Capacity: 1,435

## NORTHCOTT THEATRE

Stocker Road, Exeter, Devon EX4 4QB
Mgt 01392 256182 BO 01392 493493
SD 01392 277516 Fax 01392 499641
ADMINISTRATION:
Props: University of Exeter
Lessees: Northcott Theatre and Arts Centre
Artistic Director: Ben Crocker
Administrator and Licensee: John W Clarke
Marketing Director: Sarah Dance
Production Manager: Mike Reddaway
Policy: Repertory
Perfs: Variable
Seats: 433. Licensed Bar and Buttery Bar
TECHNICAL:
Stage: Proscenium, Flat; Pros. opening 15.85m; Ht. of Pros. 6.55m; Depth of S/Line 9.14m; Ht. of Grid 14.33m; 23 lines, C/W Scenery Flying Ht. 7.01m; Flying Bars 16.17m; W/Widths P.S. 2.74m. O.P. 2.74m; Prompt Cnr. mobile P.S. Electrics.
Lighting: Gemini Control System, 114 x 2kw, 6 x 5kw dimmers, 30 Prelude 16/30, 20 Cantata 11/26, 14 Cantata 26/44, 20 Par Can, 30 Harmony, PC, 20 Harmony F, 2 Cadenza PC, 4 Patt. S-battens, 12 Iris Flood.
Sound: 24 way A & H "Sabre" Desk, 4 tape recorders, 6 speakers. Detailed electrics & sound list on request.
Chief LX: Maurice Marshal
Dressing Rooms 4; Accom. 36; 2 Showers; Orchestra Pit Semi-Circle approx. 3.66m radius, 18 persons.

Studio Theatre: Seats: Variable up to 100, variable staging. Lighting: Strand SP40 way 3 preset (manual), Dimmers, Sports, Sound variable.
Policy: Own produced seasons each Spring, limited access for other small scale companies.
Membership: TMA

## THE RIVERSIDE LEISURE CENTRE

The Plaza, Cowick Street, Exeter EX4 1AF
Tel 01392 221771 Fax 01392 499676
ADMINISTRATION:
Props: City Centre Leisure.
General Manager: Phil Roebuck
Operations Manager: Peter Hill

Policy: Large Arena used for Concerts, Theatre Productions, Events and Conferences.
The Studio Function Room; 250 seated, 350 standing.
TECHNICAL:
Arena West: Stage: Platform stage made from units 1.83m x 2.44m. Performing area 9.75m x 7.31m. No rake - Merrick Sico units, not suitable for dance, possible backstage crossover, stage not heated. Height of grid 10m - several fixing points - 1 tonne per point permitted - 2 flats, blue tabs - black screen at rear - back wall panelled. Several 13A independent circuits. Get-in via rear of stage, ground level, drive-in doors 3.5m x 2.6m. Cherry picker. Scale stage and lighting plans available.
Lighting: 16 channel manual board, 16 circuits, operated from rear of auditorium or front of stage area - 1 x 60A 3 phase, 1 x 160A 3 phase, 3 x 32A single phase supplies available for temporary board, 12 spots, 4 fresnels, 12 pars, 4 x 4 circuit battens, 2 x CSI followspots, operated from side balcony.
Sound: Third Generation 24 channel mixer, flexible operating position, 6 speakers - 2 x 1000w amps, 1 x 675w amp - 24 channel graphic equaliser, foldback sound, compensator limiter, 6 x SMB58 mics, 1 x Citronic cassette deck, disco deck, Citronic twin record decks, PA system. Acoustics suitable for music and spoken word.

## ST GEORGE'S HALL

George Street, Exeter, Devon EX1 1BU
Tel 01392 265866 Fax 01392 422137
Seating/Capacity: 500
Managing Director: David Lewis

## WESTPOINT ARENA AND EXHIBITION CENTRE

Westpoint, Clyst St. Mary, Exeter, Devon EX5 1DJ
Tel 01392 446000 Fax 01392 445843
ADMINISTRATION:
Events Manager: Sarah Symons
Policy: Exhibitions and concerts
Seating capacity: 6,000 (including tiered seats)
TECHNICAL:
Stage: Length: 85 metres. Width: 54 metres. Gross usable area: 4,590 square metres. Clear height: Eaves: 7 metres. Apex: 13 metres. Height of goods doors: 6 metres (Direct access to stage). Width of goods doors: 6 metres (Direct access to stage). Floor surface: Asphalt. Floor loading: 100KN/square metre. Roof loading: 2 tonnes per frame evenly distributed, frames at 6.6 metre centres. Power: 400 amp high level bus bar and 600 amp single point supply. House lighting: Adjustable to 500 lux maximum. Heating and ventilation: By air handling units at roof level. Box Office.

# Eye, Suffolk

## EYE THEATRE

Broad Street, Eye, Suffolk IP23 7AF
Admin 01379 871142  BO 01379 870519
Fax 01379 871142
Artistic Director: Tom Scott
Administrator: John Hickey

# Fareham, Hampshire

Pop. 92,6000. London 70 miles. Newspapers: Southern

Evening Echo (Southampton); The News (Portsmouth) - both ntly. STD code 01329

## FERNEHAM HALL

Osborn Road, Fareham, Hampshire PO16 7DB
Tel 01329 824864 BO 01329 231942
Fax 01329 281528
ADMINISTRATION:
A prestigious multi purpose venue conveniently situated mid-way between Portsmouth and Southampton.
Props: Fareham Borough Council
Ferneham Hall Manager: Russell Davies
Policy: Mixed programme of entertainment with use for international variety artistes, cinema, classical and popular music, cabaret, dances, exhibitions, theatre and wrestling.
Seats: Solent/Meon Suite combined 1,022 inc. 200 tiered.
Octagon Lounge 120; Cinema 462. Bar, Coffee Lounge/Restaurant.
TECHNICAL:
Stage: Proscenium arch. Performing area 16m x 6m - pros opening 14m x 5.5m - wing width 2m SR, 2m SL, 2m US. No rake - floor sprung wood with Harlequin lino, suitable for all dance. Forestage 14m x 2m, entrance SR and SL. No pit, but could be constructed. Backstage crossover, stage not heated. Height of grid 6.5m - 3 hemp sets, 25kg permitted on bars - maximum flying height 7.5m, 1m and 2m apart - tab track - 2 x Wipe track, - 3 sets of tabs - silver, blue and black - white back wall used as cyclorama - red house tabs drawn. 10 x 13A independent circuits. Get-in via backstage dock doors, 2.5m x 3.5m. Various scale plans available.
Lighting: Celco Series 2 60 way plus 30 way wing board, 82 circuits @ 8A, 12 @ 20A, operated from lighting control room - 3 phase, 1 x 100A 3 phase and 1 x 200A 3 phase supplies available for temporary board - 33 spots, 36 parcans, 6 floods, Strand and Thomas - 2 followspots, operated from projection room. Separate dance floor lighting rig.
Sound: Soundcraft Series 20 24:4:2 desk, operated from sound control room - Yamaha, Hill, H&H amps - 4 x Bose 802 and 6 x Bose foldback speakers - Shure mics - Yamaha cassette tape system - Rediffusion PA system. Facilities for recording and editing. Acoustics suitable for music and spoken word.
Stage Management: Prompt corner SL - ring intercom, 8 outstations, show relay to dressing rooms.
Backstage: 3 dressing rooms, access by stairs backstage - Green Room - 2 power points in dressing rooms, 8 in Green Room. Staff - 1 stage, 1 lighting, 1 sound - casuals available. Backstage facilities not accessible to disabled performers and staff.
Projection Equipment: 2 cinemaccanica Victoria 5 projectors with C x 16T lamphouses, for 35mm wide screen and cinemascope formats, Dolby surround sound system.

# Farnham, Surrey

Pop. 32,000. London 40 miles. Newspapers: Farnham Herald (fri). STD code 01252

## THE MALTINGS

Bridge Square, Farnham, Surrey GU9 7QR
Tel 01252 726234
Manager: John Heath
Marketing Manager: Sally Ann Lowe

# Felixtowe, Suffolk

Pop. 35,000. London 83 miles. STD code 01394

## SPA PAVILION THEATRE

Undercliff Road West, Felixtowe, Suffolk IP11 8AQ
Mgt 01394 283303 BO 01394 282126
ADMINISTRATION:
Props: Suffolk Coastal District Council
Managed by: Apollo Leisure. For all booking information and further details please contact Sam Shrouder or Nicky Monk at Apollo Leisure (UK) Ltd., Grehan House, Garsington Road, Cowley, Oxford OX4 5NQ. Tel: 01865 782900; Fax: Oxford 01865 782910.
General Manager: Miles Cowburn
Resident Stage Manager: Roger Miller
Policy: Professional Shows, Festivals, Concerts, Amateur Productions.
Perfs: 8.00 generally
Seats: 919. Licensed Bar and refreshments.
TECHNICAL:
Stage: Proscenium Arch, 32ft wide, 24ft deep, wings 9 x 9ft. No flying space above stage.
Lighting: Board: 72 ways M24 computer FX patch; F.O.H. spots 12 Patt.15/28, 6 Patt.T84, 4 Patt.263, 4 Patt.223, 2 Patt.818, 1 Batten; 7 Dips; 2 Spots Bars 10 Patt.814, 2 Harmony F spot bar 1; 4 Harmony F each spot bar 2 & 3; Extra LX; 6 minuette floods; 18 Parcans.
Sound Equip: RR Tape Deck & Record Deck O.P.; 8 Channel mixer & Stereo HH Amp + Pro 150 speakers + Bose 802 system also foldback + independant paging to dressing rooms. 200 watt amp O.P.
Dressing Rooms: 6; Accom. 40; Orchestra Pit.

# Filey, N.Yorks

Pop. 5,390. London 230 miles. Newspapers: Scarborough Evening News (dly); Scarborough Mercury (sats). STD code 01723 (Scarborough)

## SUN LOUNGE

The Crescent Gardens, Filey, North Yorkshire YO14 9HZ
Correspondence address: Londesborough Lodge
The Crescent, Scarborough YO11 2PW
Admin 01723 232323 Fax 01723 376941
ADMINISTRATION:
Props: Scarborough Borough Council
General Manger: Keith Norton (01723 376774)
Policy: Summer Variety
Seats: 250. Light Refreshments. Bar facilities.
TECHNICAL:
Stage: Proscenium Arch. Depth 12ft 10 inches; Width front 27ft; width rear 22ft.
Lighting: Tempus 2G 24 way Lighting Board. 1 lighting trough, 6 fresnels (3 each side); FOH spot bar, 6 fresnels, 7 spots, 2 mini spots; 2 floods.
Sound: 1 TOA 3 mike inputs plus auxiliary; 1 Techniel twin cassette tape deck; 3 shure Prologue Microphones, 3 microphone stands.
Dressing Rooms: 2, 4 to 6 people in each.
Limited amount of parking by stage door but doors cannot be obstructed.

# Fleetwood, Lancs

Pop. 29,530. London 234 miles. Newspapers: Evening Gazette (6 days per week); Fleetwood Weekly News (fri). STD code 01253

### MARINE HALL
The Esplanade, Fleetwood, Lancashire FY7 6HF
Mgt 01253 771141 BO 01253 770547
ADMINISTRATION:
Props: Wyre Borough Council
Hall Manager: Michael Brook
Events Manager: Mrs V Tindall
Policy: Corporation Multi-purpose Hall.
Seats: 636. Restaurant with Bar. Wyre Lounge and Beer
Garden.
TECHNICAL:
Stage: Proscenium, Raked; Pros. opening 8.53m; Ht. of
Pros. 4.27m; Depth of S/Line 7.01m; Ht. of Grid 4.88m;
W/Widths P.S. 2.59m, O.P. 2.59m.
Lighting: Switchboard: Eurolight-Ovation 240 CH. C105
output - standard back up computer 96 channels - 10V
output demux rigger control. F.O.H. No. 1 Spot Bar 12
circuits, No. 2 Spot Bar 6 circuits, Arena 8 circuits;
Stage: 5 x 10 x 2kw, Dips 4 x 2kw, 2 x 1kw Follow Spots
CSI, 6 Patt.743 1kw, 6 Patt.763 1kw, 10 16/30 Profiles,
12 Patt. 60 Flood, 8 Patt.749 1kw Flood, 75 x 500w
Fresnels/Profiles, 1 Batten Floats.
Sound: 1 Soundcraft Venue II 24:8:2 Feeding Audio low-
mid-high. Yamaha SPX 900. Graphic GQ mics various,
Shure AKG, 4 radio mics.

## Folkestone, Kent
Pop. 45,490. London 70 miles. Newspapers:
Folkestone, Hythe & District Herald (thurs); Folkestone &
Hythe Extra (wed). STD code 01303

### LEAS CLIFF HALL
The Leas, Folkestone, Kent CT20 2DZ
Mgt 01303 254695 BO 01303 253193
Fax 01303 221175
ADMINISTRATION:
Props: Shepway District Council
Managed by Apollo Leisure (UK) Ltd
For all booking information and further details please
contact Sam Shrouder or Nicky Monk at Apollo Leisure
(UK) Ltd., Grehan House, Garsington Road, Cowley,
Oxford OX4 5NQ. Tel: 01865 782900; Fax: Oxford
01865 782910.
General Manager: Jo Barnes
Policy: One Night Stands, Variety, Cabaret, Orchestral
Concerts, Snooker, Rock Concerts, etc.
Perfs: From 7.00p.m. and 8p.m.
Seats: 825 - standing concerts 1,500. Two Licensed
Bars, One Restaurant, Two Buffets.
TECHNICAL:
Stage: Proscenium, Flat; Pros. opening 6.10m; Ht. of
Pros. 6.10m; W/Widths P.S. 3.5m, O.P. 3.5m + 12 x
mobile extensions giving additional 48' x 12'.
Lighting: Zero 88 Eclipse 60 way with 48 memories 60
circuits at 2.5kw operated from F.O.H. Control box 40
Par 64 Lanterns with a selection of wide, medium and
narrow raylight reflectros. 10 T 84's, 10 Patt.123's. C.S.I.
follow spots operated from control box.
Sound: Soundcraft Series 200B 24 Channel Desk
Harrison AC 600 Crossover, Harrison GO 215 Graphic,
Harrison GP 230 Graphic, Digital delay, 7 Shure SM
58's, 3 Shure SM 57's, 1 AKG C451 E, 1 AKG CK1, 3 x
shure 845, 3 x Sennheiser 421, 1 AKG D 12 E, 1 C
Ducer Stereo Piano Pick up, 4 B55 AR 116 Active DI
Boxes, 20 Assorted microphone stands.
Backstage: 6 dressing rooms, access by side of stage -
green room - band room. 2 x 13 a power points.
Rehearsal rooms, rehearsal piano, good. Advice given on
accommodation. Staff - 1 stage, 1 lighting, sound as

required - casuals available - security personnel.

## Forfar

### REID HALL
Castle Street Forfar Angus DD8 3AE Scotland
Tel 01307 462958
Director of Cultural Servics.: Gavin N. Drummond
Tel 01307 461460  Fax 01307 462590
Arts Officer: Sandy Thomson
Contact: Catherine Wallace
Seating/Capacity: 829

## Frinton-on-Sea, Essex
Pop. (Frinton & Walton) 12,710. London 71 miles.
Newspapers: East Essex Gazette (fri); Essex County
Standard (fri); East Anglian Daily Times. STD code 01255

### SUMMER THEATRE
Frinton-on Sea Essex
Tel 01255 674443
ADMINISTRATION:
Theatre Lessee: Jack Watling
Producer: Seymour Matthews.
Write to: 21 Queens Road, Frinton, Essex CO13 9BL
Policy: One play per week, July- September
Seats: 230
Proscenium Stage.

## Frome, Somerset
Pop. 20,000. London 105 miles. STD 01373

### MERLIN THEATRE AND ARTS CENTRE
Bath Road, Frome, Somerset BA11 2HG
Admin 01373 461360 BO 01373 465949
Fax 01373 453900
ADMINISTRATION:
Merlin Theatre Trust Ltd.
Director: Rachael Collinge
Technical Manager: Ned Dahl
Administrator: Helen Franks
Marketing Officer: Chris Parker
Policy: The theatre promotes visits by touring companies
- drama, ballet, mime and music. It is available for hire. It
is a community theatre (drama workshop and college
facility during school hours).
Exhibition space in foyer.
Perfs: 7.45 (Mats. variable)
Seats: 240. Bar, Coffee Bar, Ice Cream.
TECHNICAL:
Stage: Adaptable. Open, Proscenium, Round; Flat; Pros.
Opening 9.00m; Ht. of Pros. 5.50m; Depth of S/Line
10.50m; Ht. of Grid 5.50m; W/Widths P.S. 4.00m, O.P.
4.00m; Prompt Cnr. P.S.
Lighting: 6 x T Spots (T84 1000w); 4 Patt.23; 6 SPR
Profile 500w, 8 MFR Fresnel 1,000w TH: 4 Cantata PC
1,200w, 4 MFL 500w Flood Lights, Cyc. Lighting: 3 6B
Lengths of Batten 3 x 6CY Trough Groundrows; 4 colour
circuits, 900w per circuit above, 900w per circuit below.
Total 1,800w per colour; Voltage 240; Max. Load of
control board 200 amps; 57 circuits; 24 Dimmers,
(Action 24 Computerised), wattage 2,000. Most sockets
can be paired.
Sound Equip: Please contact venue for details.

Dressing Rooms: 2; Accom. 20; 2 Showers.

# Glasgow

Pop. 861,898. London 394 miles. Newspapers: Daily Record (dly); Evening Times (ntly); Herald (dly); The Scotsman (dly). STD code 0141

## JAMES ARNOTT THEATRE

University of Glasgow, 9 University Avenue, Glasgow G12 8QQ
Mgmt: 0141 330 5522 Fax: 0141 330 3857
Email: e.rae@tfts.arts.gla.ac.uk
Centre Manager: Eileen Rae
Technical Resource Development Officer: Patrick Brennan
Technician: Ruth Alexander
Policy: Mixed programme of theatre,dance, music from the UK and abroad.
Student productions by University Departments including the Department of Theatre, Film and Television Studies. Available for conferences and space can be hired as a film studio facility.
Wheelchair spaces. Retractable seating bank. Licensed bar at performance times.
Dressing Rooms: 2 x Dressing rooms, total capacity 20 actors, one floor below theatre level. Green room, showers and laundry facilities also available on this floor.
Stage: Floor area = 10.7m wide x 20.2m long (with seating fully retracted) Height to trampoline grid = 6.1m. Height to scenery/tab bars = 5.8m. Several possible audience layouts - details available on request. Get in via stage lift to theatre level.
Lighting: Board - ETC Insight 2X with ETC Net Remote Interface Unit (mobile design station). Dimmers - 180 ETC Sensor. Lanterns - 18 x selection 1200W fresnels, 12 x 650W Selecon Acclaim variable profiles, ETC Source 4 fixed beam profiles: 14 x 19 degrees, 22 x 26 degrees, 24 x 36 degrees, 16 x 50 degrees, 18 x strand 500W Coda floods (10 x singles, 4 x 3's, 4 x 4's), 18 x Selecon 1200W PC's, 30 x ETC Source 4 500W Pars, 1 x Selecon Performer Quartz 2KW followspot (8-14 degree beam).
Sound: Desk - Yamaha 02R Digital Recording Console. Twin cassette deck - Tascam 302. CD player - Tascam CD401 MKII. Minidisc player - Tascam MD-801P. Minidisc recorder - Tascam MD-801R. DAT player - Tascam DA-30 MKII. Reel to reel tape recorder - Studer B77 MKII Stereo. Amplification - 7 x QSC USA900 amps, 2 X QSC USA1310 amps, 2 x Ashley MQX 2150 stereo 15 band graphic equalisers, 2 x Ashley MQX 2150 stereo 31 band graphic equalisers, Community DSC42 speaker system control. 48 x microphone positions at ground level. 8 x speaker outlets at grid level. 10 x speaker outlets at ground level. 4 x CSX38-2 monitors. 8 x SLS 920 loudspeakers. 4 x SBS 22 sub-bass speakers. Microphones - 4 x AKG SE300B vocal mics, 5 x Shure Beta 58A vocal mics, 1 x Sennheiser MKE300 directional mic. Communications system - four Canford Audio Techpro comms stations at ground level, two in LX control box, and one each in sound control box, FOH office and Green Room.

## BARROWLAND

244 Gallowgate, Glasgow, G4 0TT Scotland
Tel 0141 287 5024 Fax 0141 552 4997
ADMINISTRATION:
Props: Margaret McIver Ltd
Manager: Tom Joyes

Contact: A. S. Riddet. (Company Secretary)
Capacity: 1,900 standing.

## CITIZENS THEATRE

119, Gorbals Street, Glasgow G5 9DS Scotland
Mgt/SD 0141 429 5561 BO 0141 429 0022
Fax 0141 429 7374
ADMINISTRATION:
Props: Glasgow City Council
Lessees: Citizens' Theatre Ltd
Director: Giles Havergal
Company Manager: Lynn Pullen
Technical Manager: Dave Jensen
Policy: Repertory of Plays, Christmas Show and Seasons of Visiting Companies
Perfs: 7.30
Seats: Three Theatres (600, 120, 60). Three Bars
TECHNICAL:
Stage: Proscenium, Raked 25/500mm; Pros. Opening 7.75m; Ht. of Pros. 6.10m; Depth of S/Line 11.00m; Ht. of Grid 16.35m; Flying: 39 counterweight sets Ht. 6.10m; Flying Width 9.20m; W/Widths P.S. 4.27m; O.P. 4.27m; Prompt Cnr. P.S.; 39 counterweight sets; LX - Arri Imagine 250/210 way Lighting Board.
Lighting: On Stage - No.1 Spot Bar, 15 circuits, PS/OP Boom Poles, 10 circuits (linked), Fly Floor - 3 patch panels, each 10 circuits (7 x 2kw + 3 x 5kw), FOH - Gallery Front, 9 circuits, No. 1 Spot Bar, 12 circuits, No. 2 Spot Bar, 12 circuits, Box Booms PS/OP, 8 circuits (4 pairs), Circle Ends PS/OP, Each 12 circuits.
Dressing Rooms: 7; Accom. 21; 3 Showers.
Membership: TMA

## CITY HALL

Candleriggs Glasgow G1 1NQ Scotland
Tel 0141 287 5024 Bookings 0141 287 5005
BO 0141 287 5511 Fax 0141 287 5533
Seating/Capacity: 775-1,216

## GLASGOW PAVILION

121 Renfield Street, Glasgow G2 3AX Scotland
Mgt 0141 332 7579 BO 0141 332 1846
SD 0141 332 5568 Fax 0141 3312745
Party Bookings: 0141 333 1791
Fully computerised Box Office.
ADMINISTRATION:
Props: George Martin Associates
Manager & Licensee: Iain J Gordon
Policy: Plays, Variety & Pantomime, Rock and Pop, Conference
Perfs: Variable depending on show
Seats: 1,449 + 107 standing total 1556
TECHNICAL:
Stage: Proscenium, Raked; Pros. Opening 10.97m; Ht. of Pros. 7.62m centre arch; Depth of S/Line 5.49m; Ht. of Grid 15.24m; 28 lines, C/W; Scenery Flying Ht. 7.62m; Flying Bars 10.36m; W/Widths P.S. 2.74m, O.P. 4.88m; Prompt Cnr. O.P.; Stage extension available to cover Orchestra Pit.
Lighting: Switchboard: Lightboard M 96 ways, Stage: No.1 Bar 20 Par 64, 3 Sil 40; No. 2 Bar 1 Batten 4 colour; No. 3 Bar 1 Batten 4 colour; No. 4 Bar 20 Par 64, 4 Patt.23, 2 Sil; No. 5 Bar 8 Iris IS; No. 6 Bar 1 Batten 4 colour; Ladders 16 Par 64; FOH: 10 Par 64, 4 Sil 40; Follow Spots 2 1kw CSI; Special effects available.
Dressing Rooms: 11; Accom. 30; 2 Showers; Orchestra Pit 9 plus M.D.

## GLASGOW ROYAL CONCERT HALL

2 Sauchiehall Street Glasgow G2 3NY Scotland
Tel 0141 332 6633 BO 0141 287 5511
Fax 0141 333 9123
ADMINISTRATION:
Props: Glasgow Cultural Enterprises Ltd;
Director: Louise Mitchell
Concert Hall Bookings Contact: Karen Taylor
Capacity: 2,500 seated, including choir.

## HENRY WOOD HALL

(Royal Scottish National Orchestra Centre) 73 Claremont
Street Glasgow G3 7HA Scotland
Tel 0141 226 3868
ADMINISTRATION:
Chief Executive: Simon Crookall
Administrator: Ann Elliott
Seating/Capacity: 500, moveable.
Facilities for disabled.

## KING'S THEATRE

297 Bath Street, Glasgow G2 4JN Scotland
Mgt 0141 287 5429 SD 0141 248 5153
BO 0141 287 5511 Fax 0141 248 3361
ADMINISTRATION:
Department of Performing Arts, Glasgow City Council.
Director: Bridget McConnell
Head of Programming: Neil Levine
Theatre Operations Manager: Stephen Kelly
Event Marketing Manager: Julie Tait
Media and Public Relations: Lesley Booth
Stage Manager: Eddie O'Toole
Policy: All purpose
Perfs: Vary from week to week.
Seats: 1,785 with provision for five invalid wheelchairs.
There is a licensed Bar on each of the four floors - stalls,
grand circle, upper circle and balcony.
TECHNICAL:
Stage: Proscenium arch. Performing area 21m wide,
pros opening 9.14m x 8.38m, Stage raked, 1 in 24, floor
suitable for all dance, crossover, stage heated. Height of
grid 16.6m, 52 counterweight sets, 0.15m, 0.45m apart,
tab track, black box masking, 4 soft black legs, 4 soft
black borders, Gerriets 'Opera' cyclorama, neutral, red
house tabs, flown Slider trap SL, star trap SR.
Tallescope. Safety curtain. Scale stage, fly and lighting
plans available.
Lighting: Rank Strand Gemini 18 board, 170 circuits
2.5Kw, 3 phase, operated from FOH, grand circle, 330A
3 phase supply available for temporary board, 60 spots,
100 fresnels, Rank Strand, 2 x 2Kw solo followspots,
operated from upper circle, SL and SR. Sound DDA 32
into 8 into 8 matrix output desk, operated from FOH
centre upper circle. FOH speakers and amplifiers by
Tannoy. Various Shure, AKG, Sennheiser, Crown, Beyer
Phillips and Audio Technica microphones. 2 x Revox
B77 15/7.5 ips, 1 x Revox A77 7.5/3.25 ips, 1 x cassette
recorder 1 x CD player. Facilities for recording & editing.
Acoustics suitable for music and spoken word. Stage
management Cue lights to all technical areas. Show
relay/Tannoy to dressing rooms/FOH.
Backstage: 18 dressing rooms, some with own shower.
Kitchen area. Band room - wardrobe. Rehearsal piano.
Advice given on accommodation. Staff - 4 stage, 3
lighting 3 sound, 1 wardrobe - security personnel.
Membership: TMA

## MITCHELL THEATRE

6 Granville Street, Glasgow G3 7DR Scotland

Tickets available from computerised Box Office at the
Theatre Centre, Candleriggs, Tel 0141 287 5511 Theatre
Admin: Glasgow City Council, Department of
Department of Performing Arts & Venues,
Tel 0141 287 5429 Fax 0141 287 5533
ADMINISTRATION:
Props. Glasgow City Council, Dept. of Performing Arts &
Venues
Head of Programming: Neil Levine
Theatre Operations Manager: Stephen Kelly
Policy: Mixed programme, mainly drama and dance.
Amateur and professional use. Conferences, exhibitions
and social events.
Perfs: Variable, week to week
Seats: 418, with accommodation for up to five invalid
wheelchairs; Lecture/Exhibition Hall - 400. Coffee Bar,
Licensed Bar Services, Coffee/Snack Bar also open
10.30 - 4.30 and at perf. times.
TECHNICAL:
Stage: Proscenium, Flat; Pros. opening 10.10m; Pros.
Height 4.10m; Depth of S/Line 12.5m; 25 bars including
tab tracks and electric bars; Scenery flying height 3.65m,
flying bar area 10.2m; W/Widths P.S. and O.P. 2.8m av.;
Prompt Cnr. P.S.
Lighting: Switchboard: AMC 80 way with M24, 3 preset
FOH; FOH No.1 bridge 12 T64, No. 2 bridge 8 T64;
Alcoves 3 T54 aside; No. 1 Spot Bar 12 Patt.743, 3 T64;
No.2 Spot Bar 12 Patt.743, 3 T64; Floodbar 16 Patt.60;
Portable Equipment: 6 x 4'6" Tele stands, 4 Patt.123, 4
Patt.23, 2 Follow Spots.
Full 16mm Film Projection and A.V. facilities. Show relay,
paging.
Sound Equip: Soundcraft Delta 24 into 4 into 2; 4
Tannoy speakers - 3 MOS FET V800 amps; 2 Tannoy
speakers - 2 EV 9000 amps; 5 TOA Radio Mics. 4
Foldback H/H Pro 200; 2 Cassette Decks Various Shure,
AKG, Beyer Mics. 14 in total; 1 CD Player; Boss Reverb
effect unit
Dressing Rooms: 4; Accommodation 40 approx; 2
Showers; No Orchestra Pit but accommodation for small
orchestra in front of stage.

## ROBIN ANDERSON THEATRE

The Scottish Ballet, 261 West Princes Street,
Glasgow G4 9EE Scotland
Tel 0141 331 2931 Fax 0141 331 2629
ADMINISTRATION:
Props: The Scottish Ballet Ltd
Managing Director: Norman Quirk
Marketing Director: Keith Cooper
Bookings: Caroline Notman
Policy: Small scale performances by Scottish Ballet and
visiting companies; classes, demonstrations,
conferences and lectures.
Perfs: Wide variation according to requirements.
Seats: 182 - tiered.
TECHNICAL:
Contact: Caroline Notman
Dressing Rooms: 2-6 male/6 female. Restaurant: open
by arrangement. Licensed Bar: open by arrangement.
Membership: TMA

## SCOTTISH EXHIBITION & CONFERENCE CENTRE

Exhibition Way, Finnieston, Glasgow, G3 8YW Scotland
Tel 0141 248 3000 Fax 0141 226 3423
ADMINISTRATION:
Props: Scottish Exhibition Centre Ltd
Director - Marketing: Robert Eynon.
Seating/Capacity: Hall 1: 2,000; Hall 2/3: 3,600; Hall 4:

9,300; Hall 5: 5,500.

## THEATRE ROYAL
Hope Street, Glasgow G2 3QA Scotland
Mgt/SD 0141 332 3321 BO 0141 332 9000
Fax 0141 332 4477
ADMINISTRATION:
Props: Scottish Opera Theatre Royal Ltd
Theatre Manager: Diane Long
Technical Director: Julian Sleath
Director of Marketing and Press: Roberta Doyle
Box Office Manager: Gary Haldane
Policy: Scottish Opera Home Season. Visiting ballet and
drama companies, classical and light concerts.
Perfs: 7.15 and 2.15
Seats: 1,547. Four Bars. 3 Buffets.
TECHNICAL:
Stage: Proscenium, Flat. Pros. opening 10.362m; Ht. of
8.53m; Depth of S/Line 13.563m; Ht. of Grid 17.678m;
47 lines, c/weight; Flying Ht. 17.373m; Flying bars
15.849m; W/Widths P.S. 2.438m, O.P. 2, 133m;
Prompt. Cnr. P.S.
Lighting: Switchboard: Galaxy - 1st Circle 240 ways;
spots as required; dips as rig requires; spot bars as
required.
Sound Equip: 10 chan. Mixer; 2 x Revox.
Dressing Rooms: 10; max accom. 69; Showers to all
rooms.
Backstage: Orchestra pit for 110 (60 below stage).
Dock storage - inner dock. 100 sq.m., outer 50 sq.m.
Staff restaurant (green room) - Snacks 10.00a.m. to end
of interval.
Coaching room 24ft sq. (or extra wardrobe or dressing
room). (24).
Front of pit on lift to form apron.
Membership: TMA

## TRAMWAY
25 Albert Drive, Glasgow G41 2PE Scotland
Mgt 0141 422 2023 BO 0141 227 5511
Fax 0141 422 2021
ADMINISTRATION:
Revenue Funding: Glasgow City Council and Scottish
Arts Council
Project Funding: Trust Foundations Sponsorship, Foreign
Sources
Theatre Operations Manager: Stephen Kelly
Policy: Producing, coproducing; international
performance visual arts space with an emphasis on
innovative, challenging and radical work in three
disciplines. The programe is artist-centred and provides
appropriate public contexts for completed or developing
work by artists of all nationalities. Other emphases
include cross-border exchange and co-operation.
Touring productions occasionally hosted.
Perfs: Vary from week to week. Open 7 days
Seating: Capacities - Area 1: 719 raked seating
(moveable) 870 standing. Area 2: 1500 Standing. Area
4,122 (122 raked seating).
TECHNICAL:
Stage (Area One): Dimensions 40m x 26m. Performing
area 26m (10m between side pillars) x 16m. No rake -
floor concrete, suitable for dance only if stage provided,
backstage crossover, stage heated. Height of grid 7.7m
- fixing points as required - tab track - black tabs at rear
- red plaster back wall can be used a cyclorama. 13A
independent circuits. Get-in via rear of stage through
small scene dock, stage level - dock doors 2.7m x 3.2m.
Tallescope. Scale stage plans and full technical schedule
available.

Lighting: Strand Gemini board, 100 circuits, operated
from lighting box at rear of auditorium.
Sound: No equipment. Operating position in lighting box
or at rear of floor area. PA system. Acoustics suitable for
music and spoken word.
Stage Management: Prompt corner position variable -
cue lights and headsets. Show relay/Tannoy to dressing
rooms.
Backstage: 6 dressing rooms accommodating 60 plus
by side of stage - area can be made available for green
room - wardrobe at stage level, washing machine, drier,
drying room, several 13A sockets. Advice given on
accommodation by Greater Glasgow Tourist Board. No
permanent technical staff, but casuals available - security
personnel. Backstage facilities accessible to disabled
performers and staff.

Stage (Area Two): Dimensions 57m x 27m - height to
ceiling 7.7m. Concrete floor. No lighting or sound
equipment - supply available for temporary lighting -
equipment may be borrowed from Area One. Backstage
details as for Area One.

Stage (Area Three): Small performance gallery. Total
dimensions 8m x 32m, height 3.5m. No lighting or sound
equipment.

Stage (Area Four): Small performance gallery.
Dimensions  as Area Three. 36-way manual lighting
board available.

## TRON THEATRE
63 Trongate, Glasgow G1 5HB Scotland
Mgt 0141 552 3748 BO 0141 552 4267
Bar 0141 552 8587 Fax 0141 552 6657
Web Site: www.tron.co.uk
ADMINISTRATION:
Props: Tron Theatre Ltd
Artistic Director: Irina Brown
General Manager: Neil Murray
Press & Marketing Manager: Damon Scott
Production Manager: Jo Masson
Technical Manager: Malcolm Rogan
Bars Manager: Peter Hand
Policy: Theatre, Dance and Music from the UK and
Abroad, plus 2/3 productions a year by Tron Theatre Co.
Perfs: 7.30p.m.
Seats: Theatre 272 (109 stalls, 163 gallery). Raked fixed
seating. Bar - 100. Two cafe/bar spaces. Bar open all
day.
TECHNICAL:
Stage: Working dimensions - 9.45m wide x 6.3m.
Prompt corner SL or SR. Entrances - USL, USR, DSL,
DSR, USC. Get-in - various methods of access, please
phone for details if in doubt.
Lighting: Grid - 8.5m. Board - 48 channel Zero 88 Sirius.
Dimmers 48 Strand Tempus (2.4kw per channel).
Lanterns - 10 x harmony 22/40 1kw Variable Beam
Profiles, 4 x Harmony 15/28 1 kw Variable Beam
Profiles, 8 x Prelude 16/30 500w Variable Beam Profiles,
1 x Solo 2kw Follow Spot, 18 Harmony F 1kw Fresnels
with barn doors, 8 x ADB 1kw Fresnels, 8 x CCT 500w
Fresnels, 12 x Par 64/CP62. Supply - 100A 3 Phase.
Sound: Desk - A&H or Soundcraft 2000 16-4-2. Reel to
Reel Tape Recorders - 2 x Revox B77 (1 3.25/7.5 ips, 1
7.5/15 ips with Varispeed). Cassette Recorder -
Memorex Twin Deck. Amplification - Tannoy SR840,
480w/channel, Raunch DVT 400w per channel.
Speakers - 2 x Tannoy Leopards, 2 x Bose 101's, 2 x
100w Kudos.  Microphones - 1 x Bayer M300, 4 x
SM58.  Communication system - 4 way Strand Beltpack

and Headsets.
Dressing Rooms: 6. Capacity - flexible. Showers - 2
laundry - automatic washing machine, tumble drier, iron
and board.
Miscellaneous: assorted soft and hard blacks, weights,
braces and limited workshop and storage facilities.

### UNIVERSITY STUDENT'S UNION
32 University Avenue Glasgow G12 8LX Scotland
Tel 0141 339 8697 Fax 0141 334 2216
Seating/Capacity: 400, standing 600.
Contact: David O'Neill, Functions Manager

# Glenrothes

### ROTHES HALLS
Rothes Square, The Kingdom Centre, Glenrothes,
Fife KY7 5NX Scotland
Tel 01592 612121 BO 01592 611101
Fax 01592 612220
Email: rothes_halls@dial.pipex.com
Web Site: dspcce.dial.pipex.com/town/plaza/gx70/index
.html
ADMINISTRATION:
Theatre Manager: Frank Chinn
Technical Manager: Nick Weeks
A theatre, entertainment and conference venue with two
halls, adaptable stage and theatre seating, dance floors
and full catering.  Main hall capacity 720 seated (theatre),
1400 standing.  Located 30 minutes by car from
Edinburgh and St. Andrews.
TECHNICAL:
Stage (Hall A): A modular Sico staging system total 96 sq
metres at variable heights of 750, 900, 1050 and 1200
mm provides conference use staging. For heavier duty,
18 sections of steeldeck are available (heights as for
sico). Ramp available on request. Retractactable and
mobile tiered seating with further rows of linked stalls
seats available depending on stage layout. All seating
removable for flat floor space of 775 sq metres.
Full catwalk system 8.5m above floor, with numerous
500kg hanging points, from which fixed lighting bars at
8.75m above floor are accessible. For end stage use,
minibeam trussing on 6x chain hoists normally supports
2x full-width wipe tracks, and upstage black tabs.
Lighting: Control Board: Lightboard M. 144 channels
EC90 dimmers (120 @ 2k, 24 @ 5k), with outlets on 15A
(/32A Ceetorm for 5k's). DImmer outlets paralleled to
`Socapex` outlets. A variety of 16A SP, 32 TPNE, 63A
TPNE etc outlets are available on the catwalks, and tails
to 200A three-phase in the scenedock area. Full outlets
plan available on request.
Lanterns: 18 Cantata 1.2k 18/32, 8 Cantata 1.2k 11/26,
18 Cantata fresnel 1.2k, 18 Cantata PC 1.2k, 18 long-
nosed PAR cans, 12 short-nosed PAR cans, 9 Nocturne
1k.
Sound: TOA mixer 16:4:2 in control room at gallery level
FoH (opening window). 8x TOA bi-amped 380SE
speakers normally flown at catwalk level. 4 circuits stage
monitors (TOA wedges). Control room monitoring if
needed by pair TOA 280 reference monitors. Revox B
series (7.5/15ips), CD, cassette, etc. Assorted mics
including SM57s and SM58s. One diversity hand-held
and one diversity tieclip radiomic. 4x Dr boxes. Mic and
aux. lines to stage, also mic lines to catwalks.
Yamaha piano available on request. Also a Grotrian
Steinweg 6'6" concert grand piano available for
appropriate events. Music stands etc. stored on site.

Backstage: Fully fitted dressing rooms. Cars and vans
may be driven into the scenedock for unloading.

Stage (Hall B): Permanent alcove stage extendable by
sico or steeldeck units as required. Mobile tiered seating
used normally but can be removed leaving flat floorspace
of 225 sq metres.
Lighting: MX48 control system in control room at  gallery
level FoH. EC90 dimmers supply outlets on fixed lighting
bars. 5 Quartet fresnel 650w, 3 short-nosed PAR cans, 2
hi-lite 23 discharge profiles (suit gobos). Other lanterns
available from Hall A as required.
Sound: Adequate TOA sound system to 12:3:2 desk
located in gallery FoH. Multicore available to stage - suits
small bands. 2 circuit monitors (TOA wedges). Usual CD,
cassette etc. Mic`s shared with Hall A.
Other: Shared with Hall A

# Gloucester

### GLOUCESTER LEISURE CENTRE
Bruton Way Gloucester GL1 1DT
Tel: 01452 306498
Closed for refurbishment, expected to re-open in the
summer of 2001. For all enquiries and further information
contact Ken Meekings, Entertainment Manager on
01452 396936.

### THE NEW OLYMPUS THEATRE
Barton Street, Gloucester GL1 4EU
Admin 01452 525917 BO 01452 505089
SD 01452 507549 Fax 01452 387519
Manager: Mark Barsby-Finch
Technical Manager: Mark Payne
Props. Gloucester Operatic and Dramatic Society.
Policy: Touring, concert, Local amateur, conferences,
panotmime, studio, etc.
Seats: 427 inc. 6 wheelchair spaces (main), 70 (studio),
licensed bars, coffee bar.
Dressing Rooms: 3 accommodating 28, additional space
required.
Main Auditorium Technical:
Stage flat Pros. Opening 9m. Ht of Pros. 4.9m. Depth of
stage 6.5m. w/width P.S. 2m, OP 1.8m opens to 7.5m.
Scene dock area; Ht. of grid 9m.11 Hemp fly lines. 1 tab
track and 3 wipe tracks available. Orchestra pit 8.3m x
3.5m with optional raised area. SM desk on S.R.
Stage Lighting: Control rear of auditorium. Strand GSX
with Genius software, 75 way. Three stage light bars, 4
FOH perches. Luminaires : 14 x Patt 743, 8 x Harmony
F, 14 x Par 64, 6 x 1KW Sil, 6 x Thomas 650, 2 x
Prelude 16/30, 2 x Prelude 28/40, 2 x Solo KW
Followspots, 1 x Patt 294 Followspot, 4 x Coda 3
asymmetrical floods.
Sound: Allen and Heath 16/4/2 mixer, 1 x Denon 730R
cassette deck, 1 x Denon DCD-825C.D., 1 x Denon
DMD 10 CO Minidisk, 1 x Peavey Deltafex Digital F.X.
unit, 2 x Citromic PPX900 amps running 4 x Peavey
Impulse 200 speakers, 1 x Quad 405 amp running 2 x
Bose802 stage monitors. Selection of lead mics, 1 x
AT1100 diversity Radio Mic. 1 x Beyer S150 Radio Mic.
SM desk - Full cue light system, Canford TechPro
intercom to PS sound, lighting, F/Spots, Orch.pit Paging
and Relay system. Infr-red monitor of stage. Induction
loop amplifier.
Studio Technical:
Stage flat Pros. Arch. Opening to 3.9m, Ht of Pros.2.2m,
depth of stage 3.3m, 600mm removable at front to

create Thrust; w/widths PS 1.2m, OP 800mm.
Studio Lighting: Control rear of studio, Strand LX 12 way desk. 2 x Act 6 dimmers. 2FOH light bars with 22 circuits. Luminaires: $ x Quartet PC's, 4 x Minim F, 2 x Minim P, 6 x Patt 123, 2 x Quartet Profiles.
Studio Sound: Carlborough Eclipse 12 powered mixer, 2 x Warfedale Force 9 speakers, 8 way multicore from stage to box. 1 x Teac W - 780R Double Cassette deck.
F.X.: Dry ice and Smoke Machines, strobe light, UV, Gun, Helicopter light, Le Maitre Pyrotechnics System.

# Glyndebourne, East Sussex

London 52 miles. Newspapers: Sussex Express & County Herald (fri); Evening Argus (Brighton) mon-sat. STD code 01273

### GLYNDEBOURNE FESTIVAL OPERA HOUSE
Glyndebourne, Ringmer, Lewes, East Sussex BN8 5UU
Mgt 01273 812321 SD 01273 812321
Fax 01273 812783
ADMINISTRATION:
General Director: Nicholas Snowman
Director of Productions: Graham Vick
Music Director: Andrew Davis, CBE
Technical Director: Peter Horne
Finance Director: Mrs Sarah Hopwood
House Manager: Julie Crocker
Press & Public Relations: Nicky Webb
Policy: Festival Opera Season
New Opera House opened in May 1994.
Please contact venue for further details.

# Gravesend, Kent

Pop. 88,000. London 22 miles. Newspapers: Gravesend & Dartford Reporter (fri); Dartford Times (fri); (Kentish Times); Kent Today (mon-fri); Kent Messenger; New Shopper (wed). STD code 01474

### THE WOODVILLE HALLS THEATRE
Woodville Place, Gravesend, Kent DA12 1DD
Manager 01474 337456 Admin 01474 337611
BO 01474 337459/60 Fax 01474 337458
BO Manager (PL) 01474 337461
ADMINISTRATION:
Props: Gravesham Borough Council
Arts & Entertainments Manager: Brian N. Tourle
Theatre Manager: Robert Allen
Policy: Touring. One Night Stands, Music Hall, Pantomime, Repertory, Opera.
Perfs: 2.30, 5.30 or 7.30; Sun.8.00
Seats: 835. Two Bars fully licensed. Coffee Bar.
TECHNICAL:
Stage: Width 36' X 38@ (backstage to apron), 36' X 28' (backstage to main tabs), Proscenium with safety curtain 36' high X 27' wide. False proscenium opening min. 12' high X 24' wide, max. 18' high X 30' wide. 20 X counterweight flybars. Dock doors onto loading bay 10' wide X 16' high. Height to grid 65', Orchestra pit 26' X 8', Prompt corner stage left.
Lighting: 1 X Celco Venturerdesk 72 channels, 72 X 2kw dimmer circuit racks, 2 X CSI Coemar 1kw follow spots, 2 X Patt. 293 follow spots, 8 X Battens floods, 20 X Patt. 264 profile spots, 16 X Patt. 223 Fresnel spots, 6 X Patt.

243 Fresnel spots, 32 X Parcan Raylite, 6 X Martin Robo Scans PR0218, 2 X CCT profile spots, CCT minuets, 2 X Strobes, 4 X Helicopter lights, 9 X Patt. 23 profile spots, 1 X Elecrosonic 24 channel portable desk, 2 X Electrosonic power packs, 2 X T stands, 1 X Mirror Ball, 1 X Martin Junior smoke machine, ELF 16mm projectors, 1 X 32mm slide projector. Special Power Supply: 3 phase 100amp stage left, 32amp single phase supply (optional) Single phase 60amp stage left or right.
Sound: Soundcraft 24 channel sprit live sound console call over system to all dressing rooms with show relay. 2 TEC cassette players, 1 X Tascam tape deck, 1 CD Player. Speakers: 4 X RCF Event 1000 X 600w horns, 2 mounted permanently each side of proscenium arch, powered by RCF 1200MCF amplifier 1200w per channel. 4 X Fane, 1 X 15 200w floor wedge monitors/foldback driven by a Harrison 900w amplifier. 4 X TOA control 160w infills powered by TOA 1300 amplifier 1200w per channel. Microphones: 16 microphone inputs paired 16 SL & SR, 4 rifle mics, 7 vocal mics, 6 hand-held Sennheiser radio mics or 6 label Sennheiser radio mics. Headset intercom system to stage, flys, spots & control box.
General: 8 Dressing Rooms in basement for 50 all with shower & toilet facilities plus larger orchestra room for 70 Dressing room relay & cue call.

# Grays, Essex

Pop. (Borough) 127,000. Newspapers: Thurrock Gazette; Yellow Advertiser (both Friday). STD code 01375

### THAMESIDE THEATRE
Orsett Road, Grays, Essex RM17 5DX
Mgt 01375 382555 BO 01375 383961
Fax 01375 392666
ADMINISTRATION:
Props: Thurrock Borough Council
Arts Manager: Mark Allinson
Policy: Small scale tours, Pantomime, Amateurs, Films, Concerts, Conferences, Lectures, One Night Stands
Seats: 303. Licensed Bar, Coffee Lounge
THAMESIDE TWO
40 seat large screen video auditorium.
Umatic - VHS
TECHNICAL:
Stage: Proscenium, Flat; Pros. opening 9.07m; Ht. of Pros. 2.97m; Depth of S/Line 7.01m; W/Widths P.S. 1.83m, O.P. 0.61m; Prompt Cnr. O.P.
Lighting: Switchboard: Strand Lightboard M projection room; 46 ways; F.O.H. Spots. Good range of profile

flood and beam lanterns.
Fully equipped for 35mm and 16mm Projection and
Slide Projection. Curved Apron Stage. Comprehensive
video playback facilities on U-Matic VHS & SVHS.
Sound Equip: CD and Tape, full Dolby for cinema JBL
speakers, 16 way mixer.
Dressing Rooms 4; 4 Showers.
No Orchestra Pit but can accom. approx. 7 musicians.

## THURROCK CIVIC HALL
Blackshots Lane, Grays, Essex RM16 2JU
Mgt 01375 652397 BO 01375 383961 Fax 01375
652397
ADMINISTRATION:
Props: Thurrock Borough Council
Manager: Charles Curtis
Arts Manager: Mark Allinson
Policy: Dance hall, catering, hires, trade shows, stage
shows on any deal.
Seats: 747. 948 standing, 425 dance/dinner.
TECHNICAL:
Stage: Proscenium, flat with apron. Pros height: 4.8m,
width: 12.1m, depth 0.5m. Stage depth: 10.3m. Wing
width: 1.5m (max) OP & PS. Apron width: 13.8m, depth:
1.9m. Apron height from dancefloor: 0.9m. Stage height
from apron: 0.2m. BP Screen (centre stage) dimensions:
height: 5.5m, width 10.5m.
Dance Floor: 21.5m x 23.4m.
Electrics: 4x 13a sockets on stage. 4x CEE form 63a
mains sockets on stage: 1 portable sound mains (max
load = 63a). 3 portable LX mains (man load 100a).
Lighting: Desk: Strand Gemini II (360 channels). 84
Strand permus dimmers. 2 CCT silhouette follow spots
(Iris, Dimmer, Colour change).
Disco rig control. Light processor.
Sound: Desk: Soundcraft 200B (16:4:2). 2 PPX 900
amps, 1 H&H power amp. 4 Bose 802's, 2 Bose 301's,
2 tannoy lynx monitors. 2 Technics CD Players. 1
Double Kenwood cassette player. 5 AKG Mics (D321S)
Other: 1 Chapell Grand Piano. 1 Chapell Upright piano.
9 Sico stage extensions 2.45m x 1.22m.
Dressing room1 large splits into 3 with Marley doors.
Shower and toilets.

# Great Yarmouth, Norfolk
Pop. 49,830. London 126 miles. Newspapers: Yarmouth
Mercury (fri). STD code 01493

## BRITANNIA THEATRE
Britannia Pier, Marine Parade, Great Yarmouth,
Norfolk NR30 2EH
Mgt 01493 842914 BO 01493 842209
SD 01493 844171
ADMINISTRATION:
Props: Family Amusements Ltd
Theatre Co-ordinator: Irene Weir
Stage Manager: Alan Freeman
Policy: All year round hire available.
Perfs: To suit show.
Seats: 1,429. Long John Silvers Bar adjoining and
Restaurant on pier.
TECHNICAL:
Stage: Proscenium, Raked 1 in 26; Pros. opening
11.89m; Ht. of Pros. 4.72m at centre; Depth of S/Line
9.14m; Ht. of Grid 10.36m; 17 C/Ws 7 Hemp; Scenery
Flying Ht. 5.18m; Flying Bars 12.19m; W/Widths P.S.
1.52, O.P. 1.52; Prompt Cnr. P.S.  4 Futore Scans plus
smoke.

Lighting: Switchboard: Rank Strand M24 Memory
board. F.X. Effects board; 12 F.O.H. Spots; 4 Battens 4
circuits; 1 Float 4 circuits; 4 Dips 3 circuits; 1 Floodbar;
2 Spot Bars; 2 Follow Spots.
Sound Equip: Studio Master Series 5 16 way mixer, 2
banks speakers F.O.H. Foldback Monitors on stage, 1
Foldback Monitors pit, Mixing Unit; 2 Bans Speakers
40w.
Dressing Rooms 10; Accom 37.
Orchestra Pit.

## GORLESTON PAVILION
Pier Gardens, Gorleston, Great Yarmouth,
Norfolk NR31 6PP
Tel 01493 662832
ADMINISTRATION:
Props: Great Yarmouth Borough Council
Management controlled by K Lynch, Gypsy Productions,
0410 498641
Publicity and Entertainments Officer: S Malkovich
TECHNICAL:
Stage: Proscenium, Raked; Pros. Opening 7.26m; Ht. of
Pros. 4.52m; Depth of S/Line 4.80m; Ht. of Grid 3.96m
8 line sets, Hemp; W/Widths P.S. 3.66m, O.P. 2.28m;
Prompt Cnr. O.P.
Lighting: Switchboard: Strand Electric, Front R Wing; 24
ways, 3 phase; F.O.H. Spots 7 pre-focus; 2 Battens &
Foots.
Sound: 2 x 120w amps. 6 way mixer, 6 column
speakers Audit, 2 column speakers foyer. 5 mic. input
points, 1 music input point, cassette recorder, CD Deck.
General: 4 Dressing Rooms ; Accom 10.

## THE NEW WELLINGTON THEATRE
Marine Parade, Great Yarmouth, Norfolk NR30 3JF
Mgt 01493 843635 BO 01493 842244
Fax 01493 331304
ADMINISTRATION:
Lessee: Jim Davidson
Manager: Frank Woodruff
Built in 1903, auditorium reconstructed in 1960. Situated
in centre of pier, 500 feet from the centre of the seafront.
Funding: Venue is self-financing
Policy: Summer shows, pantomime, 1 night stands,
amateur productions. Willing to premiere show.
Perfs: Open 7 days - evening shows start at 7.45p.m.,
8.00p.m. on Sunday, matinees by arrangement.
Booking terms: hire, box office split, by negotiation.
Non-performance activities: Conferences, exhibitions.
Seating: 1,160, raked, fixed.
Catering: Buffet bar, coffee bar, 2 licensed bars.
Ticket outlets: Box Office, local travel agents. Shop/sales
area. Access: nearest public car park - 300 yards;
railway station - 1 mile; coach terminal - half mile; bus
routes - local routes.
Facilities for the disabled: 5 wheelchair spaces - parking
at pier entrance - level access - all house facilities except
toilets fully accessible.
TECHNICAL:
Stage: Proscenium arch. Performing area 8.69m +
9.3m, 5.64m + 9.14m. DS X 8.2m - pros opening
8m x 5.34m - wing widths 3.05m + recess SR, 3.05m
SL; Stage slighted raked, 1 in 16 - floor sprung wood,
suitable for all dance, backstage crossover, stage
heated. Height of grid 6.55m - 26 hemp sets - cloths
tumble only - blue legs - white cloth cyclorama - red
velvet house tabs, drawn. Several 13A independent
circuits. Forestage 8m x 0.91m, auditorium steps.
Orchestra pit 8m x 2.74m, accommodates 10. Get-in via

scene dock at rear of theatre, ground level + 5 steps, large double doors. Safety curtain.
Lighting: Strand SP40 board, 40 circuits, operated from SL gantry - no supply available for temporary board - 30 various lanterns, Strand - 2 followspots.
Sound: 40 channel mixing desk, operated in SL gantry - 4 FOH speakers, 1 monitor speaker - 1 amplifier - 3 mics, 1 radio mic. Shure-2 cassette decks - PA system. Acoustics suitable for music and spoken word.
Stage Management: Prompt corner SL - cue lights and headsets, 4 outstations - show relay/Tannoy to dressing rooms.
Backstage: 14 dressing rooms, accommodating 30, access by stairs or at stage level - wardrobe at rear of stage, iron and board, several 13A sockets. Advice on accommodation from Tourist Authority. Staff - 2 technicians - casuals available - caretaker. Backstage facilities not accessible to disabled performers and staff.

# Grimsby, North East Lincs.

### GRIMSBY AUDITORIUM
Cromwell Road, Grimsby,
North East Lincolnshire DN31 2BH
Tel 01472 311300 Fax 01472 311301
BO: 01472 311311
Auditorium Manager: Justine Wheelan
Technical Manager: Colin Ashman
Capacity: 1,441 seated, 1,700 standing.

# Grizedale

### THEATRE IN THE FOREST
Grizedale Hawkeshead Ambleside Cumbria LA22 0QJ
Mgt/BO 01229 860291 Fax 01229 860050
Theatre Assistant: Rachel Capovila
Seating/Capacity: 225
Multi-media venue.

# Guernsey, Channel Islands

Pop. 60,000. Newspapers: Evening Press & Star (ntly); Guernsey Weekly Press (sat); Guernsey Globe (thurs). STD code 01481

### BEAU SEJOUR CENTRE
Amherst Road, St. Peter Port, Guernsey GY1 2DL
Channel Islands
Mgt 01481 727211 BO 01481 728591
Fax 01481 714102
ADMINISTRATION:
Props: States of Guernsey Recreation Committee;
Centre Manager: David Ferguson
Policy: Theatre, Films, Conferences
Seats: 403 raked. Theatre Bar and other facilities of the Centre available.
TECHNICAL:
Stage: Area - 58'4" x 28'9"; Pros. opening 39'8"; Height of Pros. 12'1"; Orchestra Pit 30' x 4'.
Lighting: Switchboard: LBX 36 Way.
Sound Equip:16 mic lines to a Sound System; 16 x 4

TOA desk; various tape/CD.
Projection Equip: The Theatre has a projection room equipped with 2 - 35mm projectors, 1 - 16mm projector, 35mm slide, front projection screens - 10'6" x 24'.
Dressing Rooms: 6 plus showers.

# Guildford, Surrey

Pop. 124,700. London 290 miles. Newspapers: Surrey Advertiser (wkly); Surrey Times (wkly). STD code 01483

### CIVIC HALL
London Road, Guildford, Surrey GU1 2AA
Mgt 01483 444720/1 Fax 01483 301982
ADMINISTRATION:
Props: Guildford Borough Council
Ents & Civic Hall Manager: John Holmes
Policy: Touring, Concerts, Variety, Rock, Jazz, Opera, One Night Stands.
Seats: 1,150. Standing 1,500. Two Bars. Restaurant.
TECHNICAL:
Stage: Stage Width 16.8m. Stage Depth 8.41m. Stage Height 7.32m. Height above floor 1.2m. Stage Facilities: 3 flying bars, black borders, 4 black legs. Blacks across rear of stage. Orchestra Pit with space for 20 persons. Stage extension over pit. 4 rows of removable orchestra tiering across the stage.
Power: 3 phase 160A per phase (on Camlocks). 3 phase 60A per phase. 30A ring main.
Lighting: 72 way Sirius Desk, 72 x 10A Pulsar Rack, etc., etc., 2 x 1k CSI Rank Strand Solo Followspots; 3 bars over stage, 3 bars over auditorium. (3 flown, 2 access by catwalk. 2 vertical over side balconies. 36 Parcans. 42 1k Fresnel. 8 Sil 30. 2 Sil 15. 4 asymetric Flood. 10 Minuette Fresnel. 4 4Cell minutett flood, 30 par 16.
Sound Equip: 2.4k Martin Rig, 16:4:2 Soundcraft Delta Desk, Yamaha 31 Band Eq., SPX 90 Effects Cassette Deck, AKG/Shure Mics. 4 Wedge, 2 Celestion SRI Wedge/Fill. Mix from Control Room or rear of auditorium.
Communications: 5 station intercom. Telephones to all key areas. Paging to FOH and auditorium (from Box Office). Paging and show relay to backstage. Pianos: Steinway Model D Orchestral Concert Grand, Knight upright.
Dressing Rooms: 1 large male, 1 large female dressing room, all with toilets and showers. Capacity of 100 persons. 3 smaller dressing rooms all with individual facilities. Wardrobe area with washing machine, tumble dryer and iron. Production Office with phone (01483 303546). Backstage pay phone (01483 573572).

### YVONNE ARNAUD THEATRE
Millbrook, Guildford, Surrey GU1 3UX
Mgt/SD 01483 440077 BO 01483 440000
Fax 01483 564071
Email: yat@yvonne-arnaud.co.uk
Web Site: yvonne-arnaud.co.uk
ADMINISTRATION:
Props: Yvonne Arnaud Theatre Trust;
Lessees: Yvonne Arnaud Theatre Management Ltd;
Director: James Barber
Finance Officer: John Bostock
General Manager: David Lindsey
Commercial Operations: Paul Marshall
Box Office Manager: David Flockhart
Marketing Manager: Amanda Barry
Press Officer: Hannah Carter
Technical Stage Manager: Liza Cheal
Policy: Mainly 2-3 week runs of No. 1 tours and pre-

West End shows. Also mounts own in-house
productions with view to subsequent touring and
possible West End transfer.
Perfs: Mon-Thurs 7.45; Fri & Sat 8.00; Mats: Thurs  and
Sat. 2.30.
Seats: 590
All catering facilities open to theatregoers and non-
theatregoers alike. Harlequin Restaurant, a la carte and
table d'hote, open for lunch before, during and after
performances; Figaro's piano bar and restaurant;
Riverbank Cafe open from 10.00a.m. until the end of the
last interval, serving hot and cold snacks; foyer bar open
for normal theatre hours.
TECHNICAL:
Stage: Proscenium, Flat; Pros. opening 10.06m; Ht. of
Pros. variable 4.57m - 5.49m; Depth of S/Line 8.92m;
Ht. of Grid 11.78m; 31 C/W lines, Hemp rigged as
necessary; Scenery Flying Ht. 5.48m; Flying Bars 9.75m
with extn. 12.19m; W/Widths P.S. 7.92m, O.P. 7.92m;
Prompt Cnr. P.S.
Lighting: Switchboard: Arri Imagine 250 100 Ways.
Lanterns: 52 Patt. 264; 22 Silhouette 30; 38 Patt. 743; 8
Patt. 243 BP; 14 AC1001; 34 x 110v PAR 64 6 x T/64, 6
sections "S" type groundrow; 5 internally wired bars.
Sound: 1 Revox B77; 1 Revox B795 direct drive
turntable; 1 Soundcraft mixer (16-4-2); 1 Roland Graphic
Equaliser (Seq-331); 4 Martin CX2 speakers FOH; 4
Martin speaker wedges (FX or monitors); 1 Denon
DCM510 cassette machine; 1 Denon DCD520 CD
player; 1 Yamaha SPX900 effects processor; 4 Realistic
PRM's; 2 Rauch Power Block 44 (stereo driving FOH); 2
Rauch Power Block 22 (stereo driving ROH).
Dressing Rooms 10; Accom. 48; 4 Shower, 4
Bathrooms; Orchestra Pit up to 18.
Membership: TMA

# Halifax, West Yorkshire

Pop. 90,320. London 193 miles. Newspapers: Evening
Courier (ntly). STD code 014225

### BRIGHOUSE CIVIC HALL
Bradford Road, Brighouse, West Yorkshire HD6 1RS
Tel/Fax 01484 713262
ADMINISTRATION:
Props: Metropolitan Borough of Calderdale
Capacity: Main Hall 320

### CLAY HOUSE
Clay House Park, Greetland, Halifax,
West Yorkshire HX4 8AN
Tel 01422 378586
ADMINISTRATION:
Props: Metropolitan Borough of Calderdale
Capacity: Main Hall 100; Ante Room 50.

### SHELF VILLAGE HALL
Halifax Road, Shelf, Halifax, West Yorkshire HX3 7NT
Tel/Fax 01274 675774
ADMINISTRATION:
Props: Metropolitan Borough of Calderdale
Supervisor: Bill Turton
Capacity: Main Hall 225

### TODMORDEN TOWN HALL
Rise Lane, Todmorden, Lancashire OL14 7AB
Tel/Fax 01706 813597

ADMINISTRATION:
Props: Metropolitan Borough of Calderdale
Supervisor: Duncan Thomas
Capacity: Main Hall 400; Room 'A' 36; Room 'B' 20;
Room 'C' 40.

### THE VICTORIA THEATRE
Wards End, Halifax, West Yorkshire HX1 1BU
Mgt 01422 351156 BO 01422 351158
SD 01422 363299
ADMINISTRATION:
Props: Calderdale Metropolitan Borough Council
General Manager: George Candler
Policy: Concerts, Shows, Amateur Societies, Exhibitions,
Conferences, Rock, Pop, Opera, Dance.
Perfs: As required.
Seats/standing: 1,585. Two Bars, coffee lounge.
TECHNICAL:
Stage: Proscenium, Flat; Pros. opening 13.72m; Ht. of
Pros. 5.49m; Depth of S/Line 7.32m; Ht. of Grid 14.33m;
33 lines C/W. Flying Ht. 6.71m; Flying Bars 12.19m;
Prompt Cnr. P.S.
Lighting: Strand Gemini 2 plus Lighting Board. 2 C.S.I.
Follow spots. 4 on stage LX Bars. Combination of Par
Cans, Harmony P.C. SIL 15, SIL 30. Harmony 15 - 28,
743. Power Supply: 2 x 3 phase 200 amps, 1 x sphere
63 amp. Lighting Control back of Balcony,
Sound: Contact Venue for details.
Dressing Rooms: 12; to accommodate 100; 4 showers.
Orchestra Pit: Accommodate 20 musicians.

### WAINWRIGHT HALL
Jepson Lane, Elland, West Yorkshire HX5 0PY
Tel/Fax 01422 370198
ADMINISTRATION:
Props: Metropolitan Borough of Calderdale
Supervisor: Ian Dobson
Capacity: 120

# Harlech, Gwynedd

Pop. 2,000. STD code 01766

### THEATR ARDUDWY
Harlech, Gwynedd LL46 2PU Wales
Mgt/Fax 01766 780778 BO 01766 780667
ADMINISTRATION:
Theatre Director: Valerie Wynne-Williams
Marketing Officer: Rhian Jones
Status: National Touring House
Purpose-built theatre opened in 1972 - attached to
Coleg Harlech (Residential College).
Funding: Venue funded by Arts Council of Wales,
Gwynedd Council
Policy: Receiving theatre for professional companies
performing in Welsh and English. Willing to premiere
show.
Perfs: performances on approx.3-4 days a week -
evening shows regularly start at 7.30p.m. - matinees
held at 1.00p.m. on weekdays, 2.30p.m. on Saturdays.
Booking terms: Box Office split, guarantee and split.
Non-performance activities: Film, hire to community,
snooker, art exhibitions, craft exhibitions, conferences,
workshops.
Facilities: seating 266; raked. Catering: Bar and coffee
shop/sales area. Access: theatre car park, railway station
Harlech. Facilities for the disabled: assistance available
for disabled, ramped entrance, not all facilities

accessible. Other facilities: showers in dressing rooms.
TECHNICAL:
Stage: open stage with centre thrust, 'token'
proscenium. Performing area 13.10m (apron 3.5m) x
9.90m (inc. apron) - pros. opening 13.10m x 4.72m (min)
- 5.63 (max) - wing widths 1.52m. SR, 1.52m. SL No
rake - floor sapele timber on joists, suitable for all dance,
lino available, crossover, stage heated. 10 hemp sets
plus 5 winch sets, tab track. 2 borders, 1 set tabs,
surround, 4 tormentors, all black. 4 x 15A independent
circuits. Forestage (apron) 3.50m x 13.5m. Get-in via
dock door, 3.05m hjigh. Manual scenery hoist.
Tallescope. Technical information sheets available.
Lighting: Strand M24 memory board, 60 circuits, 58 @
2kw, 2 @ 5kw, 160A, 3 phase, operated from Control
Room at rear of auditorium - 60A single phase supply
stage right - 15 x Sil 30 1k Profiles, 19 x 1k Fresnels (9 x
Patt.743, 6 x Harmony F, 4 x ADB0), 6 x Patt.123, 3 x
Patt.23, 5 x 6ft battens, 1 x 2kw follow spot.
Sound: Operated from Control Room - Soundcraft Delta
200B 8-4-2 mixer, 2 x Carver 1.5 amps, 4 x Tannoy
Puma speakers, 1 x Revox A77, 1 x Phillips CD, 2 x
Casette Decks, 3 x Shure SM 58, mics, 3 x Shure 545F.

# Harlow, Essex

Pop. 84,000. London 25 miles. Newspapers: Harlow
Citizen (wed); Harlow Star (thurs); Herts and Essex
Observer (thurs). STD code 01279

### THE PLAYHOUSE
Playhouse Square Harlow, Essex CM20 1LS
Admin 01279 446760 BO 01279 431945
Fax 01279 424391
ADMINISTRATION:
General Manager: Lawrence Sach
Marketing Manager: Nicola Bowland
Development Manager: Philip Dale
Facilities Manager: Nicole Walton
Technical Manager: John Mann
Stage Manager: Anthony Osborne
Box Office Manager: Samantha Ballington
Recently re-opened. Available for all kinds of touring
productions.
Capacity 430
Please contact venue for technical information.

# Harrogate, N.Yorks

Pop. 64,000. London 204 miles. Newspapers: Harrogate
Advertiser (fri). STD code 01423

### HARROGATE INTERNATIONAL CENTRE
Kings Road, Harrogate, North Yorkshire HG1 5LA
Mgt 01423 500500 BO 01423 537230
SD 01423 537222 Fax 01423 537210
ADMINISTRATION:
Props: Harrogate District Council.
Director: Paul Lewis
Deputy Director: Stuart Quin
Technical Manager: David Wilmore
Policy: Conferences, Commercial and Trade
Presentations, Product Launches, Popular and Classical
Concerts, TV Shows, Sports Events
Perfs: Various. Interlinked to Exhibition Centre and Royal
Hall.
Seats: 2009 on single tier (578 removable from main
arena). Licensed Bar and Restaurant. Banqueting Hall

adjacent for up to 900. VIP/Press suites and
simultaneous interpretation booths overlooking
auditorium.
TECHNICAL:
Stage: Concert platform style, overall size to walls 15m
wide x 7.2m deep x 0.975m high, tapered at front.
Central section in three screw jack lifts each 10m wide x
2.4m deep, travels from arena floor to 1m above normal
stage level. Stage extendable to 0.975m height to
maximum 15m wide x 24m deep (with loss of seats).
Total floor area of lowered stage plus cleared arena 350
sq.m. approx. Access to stage and arena via 10 tonne
car lift 6.2m long x 3.00m wide x 3.7m high. Up to nine
electric hoist bars (250 kg - 750 kg) for drapes, lighting
etc. 10 fixed 300 kg electric point hoists over arena. 6 x
1000kg mobile electric chain hoists plus rigging
equipment.
Lighting: Galaxy 3 168 way with designer's remote plus
Galaxy pin patch/effects unit. Dimmers - 144 x 2.5kw, 18
x 5kw, 6 x 10kw, 16 x 2kw profile, 64 x 1kw profile, 12 x
2kw fresnel, 40 x 1kw fresnel, 50 x 1kw PAR 64, 2 Pani
1200 W HMI follow spots. Additional equipment available
on request.
Sound: 2 x Soundcraft 24:8:8 mixers, one mobile for
centre stalls, one in control room. 64 mic lines, 5.6KW
Electro Voice cluster system plus Nexos for concerts.
Flying facilities for touring P.A. 2 x Revox PR99, 1 Teac
A3440S, 2 x Tascam 112 cassette decks, CD player,
Tascam DAT Player, full concert Fx rack. AIRO Assisted
Resonance System, 2 x Micron radio mics.
AKG/Shure/Beyer microphones. Technical Projects
intercom, VHF radio comms. Tie lines to Royal Hall and
Exhibition Halls. Misc: 3 x Elmo Xenon 35mm slide
projectors, 1.6kw Xenon 16mm cine projector, AVL
Eagle presentation computer plus Dove X control
modules VHS, Betamax and 2 x U-matic video players
(all PAL/SECAM/NTSC). Cinema screen max 11m x
4.7m with variable masking. Colour CCTV system with
tie lines to Royal Hall and Exhibition Halls. Staff radio
pagers. Induction loop for hard of hearing.
Dressing Rooms: Principal - 2 x 2 person, 2 x 1 person.
Chorus - 2 x 24 person. Additional accommodation
available.

### HARROGATE THEATRE
Oxford Street, Harrogate, North Yorkshire HG1 1QF
Mgt 01423 502710 BO 01423 502116
SD 01423 569296 Fax 01423 563205
ADMINISTRATION:
Props: Harrogate District Council
Lessees: Harrogate (White Rose) Theatre Ltd
Artistic Director: Rob Swain
Marketing Manager: Rita Mulvey
Production Manager: Phil Day
Finance Manager: Brian Beetham
Policy: Resident Repertory Company through autumn &
spring touring season with full mix of the performing arts
- drama, dance, music, mime, children's shows etc., one
night to whole weeks.
Perfs: Evenings 7.45p.m.; Sat Mat.2.30p.m.
Seats: Main Theatre 500. Studio Theatre 50. Licensed
Bars and Restaurant.
TECHNICAL:
Stage: Proscenium, Raked; Pros. Opening 7.90m; Ht. of
Pros. 4.50m; Depth of S/Line 7.00m; SR to 10.16m Sl;
Ht. of Grid 13.72m; 34 line sets, Hemp; Scenery Flying
Ht. 6.86m; Flying Bars 10.97m; W/Widths P.S. 3.35m,
O.P. 3.35m; Prompt Cnr. P.S.
Lighting: Control - Arri impulse 2. 88 channels, 6 x 5k,
81 x 2k, 1 x 10k house light dimmer, 20 x 2k dimmers.
Lanterns Permanent F.O.H., Dress circle 6 x Cantata

18/32 profiles, Balcony 10 x Cantata 18/32 profiles, Gods 4 x Cantata 11/26 profiles, 2 x Selecon Performers f.spots, 2 x Sil 15 profiles 2k. Stage stock - 4 x Cantata Pebble Convex, 9 x Cantata 18/32 profiles, 2 x Cantata optique 8/17 profiles, 2 x Cantata optique 15/42 profiles, 10 x prelude fresnels, 10 x prelude 28/40 profiles, 20 x Cantata fresnels, 6 x Strand alto-fresnels 2K, 40 x par 64 cans CP60, 61, 62, 95 heads available please specify. 12 x Iris 1 manual one floods.
Miscellaneous - 2 x Flame F/X to fit pat 123 or 264.  2 x Cadenza E.P. effects projectors, 2 x CCT minuette profiles, 2 x CCT minuette fresnels, 4 x Coda 500/4 flood battens.
Old Stock - 11 x pat 223, 10 x ADB 1k fresnels, 6 x pat 243 2k fresnels, 9 x sil 30 profiles, 10 x pat 123, 10 x pat 23, 5 with shutters, 5 x pat 23n snouts, 1 x adb 2k fresnel, 12 x AC1000 floods, 30 x pat 264 and 263.  Old stock is for sale. Any serious offers considered.
Sound: Mixing desk - Soundcraft Spirit Studio 24 - 24-8-2, 2 feeds to auditorium speakers, 2 feeds to stage speakers, 4 spare feeds to pit, stage.
Cabling - 24 way multicore stage - control room, 16 tie lines, 8 speaker sends, 10 way multicore stage - O.P. stage / pit, 8 tie lines (1-8/9-16), 2 speaker sends (5-6/7-8).
Main PA - Nexos PS10, arranged in two stereo pairs on proscenium arch, Amcron 1200 power amp, Nexo PS10 controller.
Equipment - 2 1/4" reel to reels, Revox B77, 7.5/15ips, 1 1/4" reel to reel Revox B77 3.75/7.5 ips, 2 CD players Marantz CD-52, 2 Double cassette decks Onkyo TA-RW 313, 1 DAT recorder Sony DTC-690, 1 Multi Effects Processor Lexicon LXP-15, 1 Reverb Alesis Microverb, 1 Digital Display Roland SDE-3000.
Computer - IBM PC SLC2-50, Turtle Beach Tahiti 16 bit sampler card, SAW - Software Audio Workshop, Digital Recording and Editing package.
Other Items- Sound effects CD's, De Wolfe SFX, CD's 1-6, BBC Effects Library. Access to Discs 1.-40
Positions F.O.H.; 8 under balcony; 6 either side of control room, 2 booms in boxes.
Dressing Rooms 6;
Accom. 30; 2 Showers
Membership: TMA

### ROYAL HALL
Ripon Road, Harrogate, North Yorks
Mgt 01423 500500 (24 Hrs.) BO 01423 537230
SD 01423 537222 Fax 01423 537210
ADMINISTRATION:
Props: Harrogate District Council
Director: Paul Lewis
Deputy Director: Stuart Quin
Technical Manager: David Wilmore
Policy: Conferences, Trade and Commercial Presentations, Popular and Classical Concerts, Touring Shows, Pantomime etc.
Perfs: Variable
Seats: 1,275 on three levels plus boxes. Licensed Bar and Buffet. Stalls seats (527) removable to fully sprung maple dance floor.
Interlinked to Harrogate Conference and Exhibition Centres.
TECHNICAL:
Stage: Proscenium - Raked 1 in 40; Pros. opening 9.7m; Ht. of Pros 5.3; Depth - from S/Line 7.4m, from stage from 10.4m; Ht. of Grid 11m; Double purchase counterweight system - 18 bars at 200mm centres. House tabs centred on addition set controlled from SR prompt or fly floor. Main fly floor located SL. Maximum loading on any bar 300kg.  Bar length: 10m.  3 line hemp

sets are available US of bar 18; W/Widths P.S. 1.5m; O.P. 1.5m; Prompt corner SR. Stage side walls taper to rear.
Lighting: Vision 10 ADB control desk and 175 ways of dmx dimming. Lanterns - 36 Starlettes, 12 Sil 30, 8 Sil 15, 4-way cyc bar, 20 x 1kw PAR 64, 2 x Solo 1kw CSI Follow Spots; extra equipment on request.
Sound: Nexos 4kw system with delays, effects etc., and Soundcraft 24:8:2 mixer with 8 way matrix. Revox PR99 or A77 tape decks, Tascam 112 cassette decks, AKG/Beyer/Shure microphones. Technical Projects intercom. Induction loop for hard of hearing.
Other: AV facilities: 35mm slides. Conference set with 3.6m square rear projection screen.
Video and audio tielines to Conference Centre and Exhibition Halls.
Sound and Lighting controls located in control room at the rear of the Grand Circle.
Dressing Rooms: 8; Accom. 52; Orchestra Pit 10.

# Hartlepool, Cleveland
Pop. 90,000. Newspapers: The Hartlepool Mail (ntly). STD code 01429

### BOROUGH HALL
Middlegate, Headland, Hartlepool, Cleveland TS24 0JD
Mgt 01429 266269 Hall Direct Line 01429 266269
BO 01429 890000
ADMINISTRATION:
Props: Hartlepool Borough Council
Hall Manager: Garry Marshall
Capacity: 1,300.
Regularly hired for cabaret and pop one-nighters.
TECHNICAL:
Stage: Equipment entrance - W 6' H 6' 6". Stage - D 48' W 21'. Drop - 4'. Position - Middle of 105' wall. Dressing rooms - 2. Accoustics 0.5secs. Power Supply - 3 phase 100 amp. 13 Amp on stage. Off stage - 6/N.
Lighting: Fully computerised rig. Number of Banks - N/A 36 par cans, 6 profiles, 2 battens. Console - Sirius zero 88 24 channel. Position - N/A F.O.H. Other information
Sound: House P.A. - Peavey Mono. Wattage & Impedance - 1600 watts. Speakers - 4. Mics - 4/5 + radio mic shure 58, 2 x AKG C451. Connections - N/A XLB. Mic Stands - 4.5. Monitors - No. Position - F.O.H. Mixer - Yes TASCAM 1016. Channels - 8 x LR mic inputs 6 stereo inputs.

### TOWN HALL THEATRE
Lauder Street, Hartlepool, Cleveland TS24 8AY
Mgt 01429 860663  BO 01429 890000
Fax 01429 864370
ADMINISTRATION:
Props: Hartlepool Borough Council
Theatre & Halls Manager: Mr. E. Merrilees
Policy: Mixed Programme, mostly one nighters. 2 seasons per annum: Feb-May & Sep-Dec.
Capacity: 406 raked, 140 cabaret style, 200 standing.
Licensed Bar.
TECHNICAL:
Stage: Flat, pros. opening 8.3m, pros height 4.97m (from stage), stage height 1.23m. Apron depth 2.7m, stage depth 5.25m, SL wing/w 3m, SR wing/w 1.6m. House tabs and full black box masking, 3 sets of black tabs on travellers (DS, MS & US), 5 x US hemp sets (restricted height). Equipment access 2.25m(w) x 2.8m(h). Parking available, 4 station TechPro comms, 2 large dressing rooms with video/audio show relay, close to stage.

Auditorium on two levels.
Lighting: Control desk: Strand M24+FX wing at rear of audit. Dmmers: 30 x 5amp, 30 x 15amp. FOH. Semi-permanent ring; 8 x prelude F, 12 x Parcans, 8 x Prelude 28/40, 4 x Furse MPR/TH profiles, 4 x strand T/2 profiles, 8 x Cantata F, 1 x UV flood, 1 x strobe, 6 x ass. 1 kw profiles, 4 x coda/4(200w). No 3-phase.
Sound: Accoustics 0.5s, Mixer: Soundcraft Spirit Live 24:2 at rear of audit. Effects: Peavey Digital Effects Processor. Loudspeakers: Peavey International (Total Power 1.6kw). Mics 22 assorted with stands. Backline power on stage.
Grand Piano available.

# Hastings, East Sussex

Pop. 76,000. London 63 miles. Newspapers: Hastings & St. Leonards Observer (fri); Hastings News (wed). STD code 01424

### WHITE ROCK THEATRE
White Rock, Hastings, East Sussex TN34 1JX
Mgt 01424 781010 BO 01424 781000
SD 01424 434091 Fax 01424 781170
ADMINISTRATION:
Props: Hastings Borough Council
Theatre Manager: Andy Mould
Stage Manager: Peter Higson
Policy: All purpose Theatre
Seats: 1,165 (or 1,470 standing and seats) Two Bars, Buttery
SUSSEX HALL: 300 seats or 3090 sq.ft.
TECHNICAL:
Stage: Proscenium, Raked 1 in 48; Pros. opening 9.14m; Ht. of Pros. 5.49m; Depth of S/Line 5.79m; Ht. of Grid 9.75m; 15 lines C/W, 21 Hemp; Scenery Flying Ht. 4.88m; Flying Bars 12.19m; W/Widths PS 2.25m, US 4.57m, DS OP 8.97m, US 4.57m DS. Stage Extension 10m wide 2m deep. Prompt Cnr. PS.
Lighting: Switchboard: Strand Light Board 'M' 72 x 2.5kw circuits, F.O.H. Spots - 26 Patt. Harmony 15/28 12 PAR 64 (F.O.H. & side). No. 1 LX 12 PAR 64, No. 2 LX 10 Harmony F, and 12 Par 64, No. 3 LX 12 Par 64, Cyc 10 Coda 500/3 (plan available).
Sound Equipment: Soundcraft 400B 16/2/4 and 200B 8/2/4 -16/2/4 F.O.H. mixer position. 5 Altec and 2 Electrovoice pros. mounted speakers; Revox B77 reel to reel. Revox cassette deck, Denon CD and cassette decks. Echo and reverb. Units selection of AKG and Shure microphones Radio mics. Show relay and call system to all dressing rooms. Rank Strand intercom system, induction loop system.
Dressing Rooms 7; Accom. 40/50. 5 Showers.
Membership: TMA

# Hatfield, Herts

Pop. 29,000. London 27 miles. Newspapers: Welwyn TImes (thurs); The Review (thurs); Herald and Post (thurs). STD code 01707

### THE FORUM ENTERTAINMENT CENTRE
Lemsford Road, Hatfield, Hertfordshire AL10 0EB
Admin 01707 263117 BO 01707 271217
Fax 01707 272376
ADMINISTRATION:
Props: Welwyn Hatfield Council
General Manager: Graham Pinson

Administration: Shirley Nicholas
Assistant Manager: Nigel Bangs
Policy: Two seasons of light entertainment, variety, one night stands, concerts, dinner dances, panto, cabaret, dance, alternative comedy, regular weekly community events, exhibitions, conferences, day rehearsal facilities.
Seats: 746, seats can be cleared away to create flat floor with capacity of 1000. Cinema facilities in circle seating 233.
TECHNICAL:
Stage: Dimensions (no Proscenium Arch); Width 12.98m; Picture Frame Opening (with tabs) 9.42m x 5.19m; Max Depth 9.04m; Max Flying Ht. 10.64m. Stage Ht. from floor level 1.03m; Stage Extension available 10.34m x 3.80m; Flying System Barrels 10.34m x 25.4mm; 13 Barrels on 4 lines Hemp Set; Lighting Barrels on winch sets; 2 pairs Black Twill draw tabs; 3 sets Back Twill legs and borders. Motorised Red House tabs, 1 Cyc 12.16m x 6.69m.
Lighting: Lighting board, Jands ESP 48 channel lighting console; 2 CCT silhouette CSI follow spots (1kw), 2 x 650w 16/30 Prelude profile spots, 12A C1001 Floods; 24 x 1kw Fresnels, 8 x 500w Minim F Fresnels; 38 Par 64s; 6 x 1kw Silhouette Profiles.
Sound Equip: 16 into 4 Allen & Heath Brenell SR20 Mixer M/C Line X.L.R. F.O.H. 2 x H&H S500D Amps, 2 stereo graphic equalisers, 4 JBL 4682 speakers. 1 H&H Foldback, 1 H&H S500D Amp; 1 stereo graphic equalisers, 4 Shure 702 monitors plus 2 Martyin LE 200 Monitors; Mics AKG D12, 224E, D190E, 4 x SM58, 5 x SM57, 1 x SM58 (Switchable). 15 Mic. Stands, 9 Boom Arms, 2 desk stands, 3 music stands with lights. Get-in via back stage doors, Ht. 3 x 2.5m ground level.
Dressing Rooms: 3, accom. 30-40 each. Showers 2.
Auxiliary mains supply: 3 Phase 100 amp 13 amp socket outlets on ste. Piano: Baby Grand. 1 I.L.S. Loop.
Disabled access: ground floor only.

# Hayes, Middlesex

### BECK THEATRE
Grange Road Hayes Middlesex UB3 2UE
Mgt 0181 561 7506 BO 0181 561 8371 (3 lines)
Fax 0181 569 1072
ADMINISTRATION:
Props: Apollo Leisure (UK) Ltd.
For all booking enquiries contact Sam Shrouder (Joint Deputy Managing Director) or Nicky Monk (Theatre Bookings Manager) on tel: 01865 782900 or fax: 01865 782910, Grehan House, Garsington Road, Cowley, Oxford OX4 5NQ.
Theatre Manager: Graham Bradbury
MAIN AUDITORIUM: Policy: Major theatre tours and concerts, children's shows, pantomime, films, plus local amateur and daytime conference hirings.
Open 7 days per week.
Seats: Deluxe tiered, fixed auditorium seating: 600.
Seating with orchestra pit/thrust stage: 564.
Second Performance Area: Foyer area seating up to 250 around central performance floor of semi-sprung Canadian maple, dimensions up to 30' x 30'.
Policy: Cabaret performances, dance evenings, folk, jazz, dance workshop, fringe theatre, etc.
Licensed bar, kiosk, bistro restaurant .
Rooms available for private functions and meetings of up to 70; catering by arrangement.
Exhibition areas in foyer and function rooms.
Perfs: Variable, generally 8.00 p.m. for plays and single performance concerts.

TECHNICAL:
MAIN AUDITORIUM:
Stage: Polished Canadian Maple wood flat stage.
Proscenium arch - Height: 5.9m; Width: variable
opening, either11.6m, 12.8m or 14m; Depth: 9.5m to
cyclorama. Stage to Grid: max height 7.5m - NO FULL
FLYING FACILITY. Wing Widths: 3.5m to 1m. Walls taper
upstage.
Lighting: Arri Imagine 2 console - 100 channels. 5 Rank
Strand STM 20-way dimmer racks - includes 18 x 5kw
circuits. Tempus 2G - 12 manual lighting board (12-way,
2-preset) for use in the foyer. 2 x 6-way, 10 amp.
Tempus dimmer racks for use in the foyer.
Lanterns: 10 Cantata 11/26 - 1200w profile; 15 Cantata
18/32 - 1200w profile; 15 Cantata 26/44 - 1200w profile;
3 Leko 11 - 1000w profile; 2 Leko 18 - 1000w profile; 4
Leko 26 - 1000w profile; 2 Leko 40 - 1000w profile; 5
Prelude 28/40 - 650w profile; 5 Prelude 16/30 - 650w
profile; 25 Patt. T.64 - 1000w profile; 25 Cantata P.C. -
1200w prism convex; 5 Prelude P.C. - 650w prism
convex; 25 Cantata F. - 1200w fresnel; 5 Prelude F. -
650w fresnel; 35 Patt. 743 - 1000w fresnel; 30 Par
Cans - 1000w beamlights (Par 64); 12 Coda 500Mk2-
500w floods; 32 Iris 1 - 625w floods (20 rigged on cyc.
LX bar); 2 Patt. 293 Follow Spots - 2000w; 4 LX Stands.
Good stock of "Strand" Chromoid and Cinelux colour
filters.
Power Supplies: Stage left: 63 Amp 3 phase Cee-Form
Socket; 63 Amp 1 phase Cee-Form Socket; (only one
socket can be used at a time). 32 Amp 3 phase Cee-
Form Socket; 32 Amp 1 Phase Cee-Form Socket; 13
Amp Ring Main (RCD protected). Stage Right: 63 Amp 3
phase Cee-Form Socket; 13 Amp Ring Main (RCD
protected). We do not have the facility for 'tailing-in'. All
power supplied must be via cee-form or ring main.
Special effects: 1 Zero 88 sound-to-light unit. Mirror ball
and rotator. 2 Pan-can heads and controllers.
Projection and audio visual: 1 Westrex 35mm film
projector with cinemascope. 1 full size cinema screen. 1
Kodak Carousel S-AV2000 slide projector. 2 Kodak
Carousel S-AV2000 slide trays. 3 Kodak S-AV2000
lenses 1 x f=100mm: 2 x f=150mm. 1 portable screen 4'
x 4'. 1 overhead projector. 1 flipchart/wipeboard. 1 VHS
Video recorder and 24" Television (a small hire charge
will be incurred for the above items).
Sound: 1 Soundcraft 200SR 24-4-2 mixer desk; 1
Yamaha graphic equaliser - Q2031A, 31 band, 2
channel; 1 BSS frequency dividing system "Series 300";
2 H/H stereo power amplifiers - VX900 - Mosfet;
1 Pair Martin speaker stacks - 1.8kw total output (Bass -
BR125; Mid - MH112; High - HF2R); 1 Yamaha
SPX9011 digital effect processor; 1 Technics M222 twin
cassette player; 1 Studiomaster monitor mixer Model
Stagemaster 24-8 monitor mixer; 2 Yamaha graphic
equalisers, Q2031A, 31 band, 2 channel; 3 H/H stereo
power amplifiers VX300 - Mosfet; 4 JBL radial wedge
speakers, Model 4728P; 2 Martin wedge speakers,
Model LE200
Microphones: 5 Shure SM58. 1 Shure 565. 4 AKG 321.
1 AKG 202ES. 1 AKG D12E. 5 AKG D190E. 2 AKG
D900 rifle. 4 Sennheiser K30/ME80. 3 Calrec
CB20c/CC50/K10. 1 x SM58 radio Freq. 174.5 mHz
MPT 1345. Various microphone stands - boom,
telescopic, floor, etc.
For use in foyer: Bose sound system - 2 x Bose 302
Bass speakers, 4 x Bose 802 Series II speakers, 2 x
Bose speaker stands, Bose 802-C system controller,
PA300 Mosfet mixer amplifier (5 inputs), Tascam 225
cassette recorder.
A digital acoustic system is installed in the theatre:
S.I.A.P. (System for Improved Accoustic Performance).

Other: Equipment: Stage Manager's Desk - with full cue
lighting system, 2 intercom circuits and backstage
paging system. Desk movable and situated stage left.
Two sided (black/white) Harlequin full stage dance floor.
Soft plastic (Rosco) white/blue cyclorama. Full soft black
box. 12 black wood frame wing flats - 5.5m height, 1.5m
width; 15 wood frame rostra - 5 x 18" high; 5 x 36" high
5 x 56" high surface 6' x 4';. 12 metal frame rostra - 12"
high, surface 3' x 3'. 1 conductor's "RAT" music stand
with lights. 11 "RAT" music stands with lights. 30
lightweight music stands without lights.
Backstage Facilities: 8 Dressing Rooms - including 2
holding 20 each; 4 with private shower facilities. 2
additional shower units. 4 single unit W.C.s. 2 multiple
unit W.C.s (1 male/1 female). Laundry facilities , coin
operated washing machine and tumble dryer.
Direct access to scene dock through ramp and shutter
door. Difficult access for low ground clearance trucks.
Parking space for trucks.
Orchestra Pit lift (2.7m deep); 3 positions - as pit; as
auditorium floor; as stage apron.
11 bars (14.6m length) winch operated; 3 tab tracks; 7
wipe tracks. 5 lighting bars - including cyc lighting bar. 4
pianos - Steinway 'C' Concert Grand (on stage);
Daneman Baby Grand in foyer; Knight Upright; Yamaha
PF80 electric piano and stand.

# Helensburgh

## VICTORIA HALLS
Sinclair Street, Helensburgh, Dumbartonshire G84 8TU
Tel 01436 673275
Contact: John Niven
Seating/Capacity: 450 seated

# Hemel Hempstead

## THE DACORUM PAVILION
Marlowes, Hemel Hempstead, Hertfordshire HP1 1HA
Tel 01442 228727 Fax 01442 228735
BO: 01442 228700 Mkt 01442 228717
ADMINISTRATION:
Props: Dacorum Borough Council
General Manager: T Kealey.
Policy: Multi-purpose hall used for concerts, dances,
dinner dances, exhibitions, seminars, etc., available for
private hire or co-promotion.
Seating/Capacity: 1,055 seats (1,500 standing).
TECHNICAL:
Stage: Open stage, flat with adaptable rostra for
concerts. 58' x 28', height to grid 20'.
Lighting: Switchboard: Rank Strand Tempus M24 + FX
patch board 96 way working 152 lanterns.
Sound: Fixed Bose sound system, 16 way mixer.
Portable H+H sound system.

# Henley-On-Thames, Oxfordshire

Pop. 11,780. London 36 miles. Newspapers: Henley
Standard (fri). STD code 01491

## KENTON THEATRE
Newl Street, Henley-on-Thames, Oxfordshire RG9 2BG

BO 01491 575698
ADMINISTRATION:
Props: Kenton Theatre (Henley-on-Thames Management
Society) Ltd. For bookings contact
Mrs L. Chesterton Tel 01491 572031
Policy: For hire to Touring & Repertory, Concerts and
Amateur Productions. Cinema in between live stage
productions. 4th oldest working Theatre in the country.
Seats: 240.
TECHNICAL:
Technical Contact: Jim Birney Tel 01491 413150 or
Chris Colborne Tel 0118 940 3350

# Hereford

Pop. 47,500. London 138 miles. Newspapers: Evening
News (dly); Hereford Times (thurs). STD code 01432

## THE COURTYARD
Formerley Hereford Theatre & Arts Centre
Edgar Street, Hereford Hereford HR4 9JR
Tel 01432 268785 Fax 01432 274895
Marketing Manager: Kate Bull (01432 346500)

# High Wycombe,
# Buckinghamshire

STD code 01494

## WYCOMBE SWAN
St. Marys Street, High Wycombe, Buckinghamshire
HP11 2XE
Mgt 01494 514444 BO 01494 512000
Fax 01494 538080
ADMINISTRATION:
General Manager: Stuart Griffiths
Assistant General Manager: Roger Keele
Technical Manager: Carlos Queiroz
Proprietors: Wycombe Arts Management Limited
Status: National Touring House. Opened in November
1992. Red brick building, designed by county architects.
Central location. Venue is self financing.
Policy: Major theatre tours, concerts, children's shows,
pantomime, local amateur shows.
Performance Schedule:  Open 7 days - performances
generally start at 8.00pm. Booking terms by negotiation.
Non-performance activities: Conferences, trade shows,
functions, exhibitions.
Seating: Theatre 1,076, raked. Town Hall: 400, loose
chairs. Oak Room: 130, loose chairs. Catering: 2
licensed bars - hot food available. Ticket outlet: Shop
/Sales area. Access: Adjacent public car park. High
Wycombe railway station, 5 minutes walk. Local bus
routes. Facilities for the disabled: 12 wheelchair spaces -
infra-red hearing enhancement system - lift - assistance
available, contact duty managers -parking - level access
- all house facilities fully accessible.
TECHNICAL:
Stage: Proscenium arch and forestage. Performimg area
23.6m x 11m - pros opening 13.6m x 7.2m. No rake -
floor timber suspended on concrete frame, suitable for all
dance, lino and floorcloth available, backstage
crossover, stage heated. Height to grid 18m - 25
counterweight sets, single purchase, 400mm apart -1
tab track - 500kg permitted on bars - black legs and
borders, 1 black gauze, 3 sets tabs, 1 black, 1 gold, 1
red - white plastic cyclorama - red house tabs, flown.

Several 13A sockets. 4 traps CS - no machinery at
present. Forestage 13.6m x 3m. Orchestra pit on
screwjack lift (doubles as forestage), accommodates 48.
Get-in via ramp to scene dock SL, large shutter lift 8m
high. Tallescope. Safety curtain. Scale stage, fly and
lighting plans available.
Lighting: Compulight Applause board and rigger control,
200 circuits, 164 @ 2Kw, 36 @ 5Kw, operated from
control room at rear of stalls - 400A 3 phase supply
available for temporary board - 70 spots, 50 fresnels, 20
pars, 6 x 4-circuit groundrows, 6 x 4-circuit cyc battens,
Teatro - 2 Pani followspots, operated from upper circle.
Sound: Allen & Heath Saber 24:8:8 desk, operated from
control room at rear of stalls - 8 amps - graphic
equalisers - 8 x JBL speakers as infill, 10 x JBL speakers
as infill, 4 effects speakers, 4 foldback, 2 crossover units
- 14 Shure & AKG mics - 2 x Revox B77 reel-to-reel,
Tascam tape systems - Tascam CD player - record deck
- PA system - facilities for recording and editing.
Acoustics suitable for music and spoken word.
Stage Management: Prompt corner SR or SL - cue lights
and intercom, 8 outstations - show relay/Tannoy to
dressing rooms.
Backstage: 9 dressing rooms, access by lift and stairs,
accommodates 50 - band room - possible quick change
rooms - wardrobe SR, equipment washing machine and
dryer. Refreshments available from FOH. Rehearsal room
on 3rd floor, piano, upright, new. Advice given on
accommodation. Staff - 9 technicians - casuals available.
Backstage facilities accessible to disabled performers
and staff. Steinway D grand and 2 Boston upright pianos
plus one Boston Baby Grand available.

TOWN HALL
Adjacent to main Theatre.
Stage composed of Merricks Sico units, variable size,
maximum performing area 12.2m x 6.1m. Floor modules
on carpet, dance floor available. Height to ceiling 8m
from floor, 7.5m to trusses. Several 13A sockets. Get-in
via ramp at side of stage.
Lighting: Celco Pathfinder - 10 x profiles 1,000w - 10
fresenel 1,000w - 40 x parcans 1,000w. 6 x Martin Pro
218 Roboscans and 2208 controller.
Sound: Soundcraft Spirit SR 16:4:2 mixer. JBL speaker
system 4K (Including Foldback).
Backstage: 2 of theatre's dressing rooms can be used.

OAK ROOM
Above Town Hall - used for small events. Performing
area 4.57m x 6.1m - floor flat, carpeted. Height to ceiling
3.6m. Several 13A sockets. No lighting equipment -
sound equipment from Theatre stock.

# Hoddesdon

## BROXBOURNE CIVIC HALL
High Street Hoddesdon Hertfordshire EN11 8BE
Tel 01992 441931 BO 01992 441946
Fax 01992 451132
Manager: David Cooper
Technician: David Cowan
Seating/Capacity: 566

Projectors: 2 x 35mm slide projectors. 35mm projector
and screen. 16mm film projector. Overhead projector.
Sound: Full theatrical sound set up inc. 24 channel
mixing desk. 31 band graphic equipment. 2 lapel worn
microphones. Various cardoid and condenser
microphones. CD player, tape machine. Sound system

inside or out.

Lights: 80 channel programmable lighting board: 26 x 1kw focusable spots. 30 x 1kw fresnel lamps. 40 x 64 parcans. 4 movable 1kw flood lights. 12 x 1kw cyclorama asymetric floodlights. Various disco effects. Portable lighting desk and dimmer racks.

We are able to obtain (on your behalf) Rear screen projector, Data projection and Stage effects.

# Holyhead

## HOLYHEAD CONCERT HALL

Town Hall Newry Street Holyhead Gwynedd
LL65 1HN North Wales
Tel (office hrs) 01407 764608 Tel (outside office hrs)
01407 764335 Fax: 01407 765156
Seating/Capacity: 350 hall, 75 balcony.
Contact: L.G. Owen

# Hornchurch, Essex

Pop. 134,000. London 17 miles. Newspapers: Romford Recorder; Havering Post Extra; Yellow Advertisers; Brentwood Gazette. STD code 01708

## QUEEN'S THEATRE

Billet Lane, Hornchurch, Essex RM11 1QT
Mgt 01708 456118 BO 01708 443333
SD 01708 442078 Fax 01708 452348
ADMINISTRATION:
Props: Borough of Havering
Lessees: Havering Theatre Trust Ltd
Administrative Officer: Henrietta Duckworth
Artistic Director: Bob Carlton
Production Manager: Brod Mason
Publicity Manager: Emma Bagnall
Education Officer: Caroline Barth
Policy: Four weekly repertory, concerts, Sunday lunchtime jazz, children's events.
Seats: 506. Large Bar (Licensed);
Coffee Bar - Buffet (lunch and evening).
Access for the disabled, signed and audio described performances. Induction loop.
TECHNICAL:
Stage: Proscenium, Flat; Pros. opening 10.4m; Ht. of Pros. 6.2m; depth of S/Line 9.14m; Ht. of Grid 17.68m; Lines 30, 20 C/W, 2 Hemp, 2 Winch; Scenery Flying Ht. 5.49m; Flying Bars 12.4m; W/Widths P.S. 9.07m, O.P. 7.32m; Prompt Cnr. O.P.
Lighting: Switchboard: Rear Auditorium Eurolight Microlite Mk II. 98 dimmers; F.O.H. Spots approx. 30; Dips 10 each side; 3 Spot Bars; 1 Flood Box.
Sound Equip: 2 minidisks, 9 radio mics, 2 Turntables, Full stereo control rear of Auditorium; Speakers General P.A. and Music Auditorium plus misc. effects speakers.
Dressing Rooms 6; Accom. 30; 2 Showers; Orchestra Pit 20 musicians.
Membership: TMA

# Horsham, West Sussex

Pop.26,830. London 38 miles. Newspapers: West Sussex County Times (fri). STD code 01403

## HORSHAM ARTS CENTRE

North Street, Horsham, West Sussex RH12 1RL

Admin 01403 259708 BO 01403 268689
Fax 01403 211502
ADMINISTRATION:
Props: Horsham District Council
Manager: Kevin Parker
Assistant Manager: Michael Gattrell
Assistant Manager: Cliff Evans
Opened in 1984, the centre is a converted 1934-built ABC cinema and is uniquely embellished throughout with 1930s art deco styling.

CAPITOL THEATRE
Policy: Number one, middle and small-scale touring drama, opera, music, dance and film. Available for private functions including (in flat-floor format) banquets, trade shows.
Seats: 450, or 415 with orchestra pit/apron stage. Front stalls removable and rear stalls on bleacher units facilitating conversion of auditorium to flat-floor hall where necessary. Licensed bar and restaurant in Capitol Foyer.
TECHNICAL:
Stage: Proscenium with optional thrust apron/orchestra pit or flat floor. Pros. opening: 10.2m; Pros arch-back wall; 12m; Working stage depth: 8.89m; Stage floor sprung maple (covered with ply for protection), Ht. of grid 13.1m; fly floors: 6.5m; Flying width 14m; Wing width 2m SL, 2m SR; dock door 5m x 2m; full flying facilities: 29 c/w sets, 4 moveable hemp sets, 3 tab tracks (handline). Control room: rear auditorium.
Lighting: Control: Rank Strand Gemini 2 computer control, 80-way, plus 80-way 2 preset manual board.
Sound: control: Seck 18-8-2 mixer. Bose speaker system.
Projection: 1 Cinemaccanica 35mm platter system, Dolby SR sound system.
Stage: SM desk; CCTV stage monitor; 12 way cue light control; ring intercom system; phone ringer; clock and stop clock. Show relay and paging.
Dressing Rooms: 4, accom. 20; plus use of Studio for large companies.
Green Room: TV, automatic washing machine, tumble drier, iron, fridge, cooker.
Orchestra Pit: 30. Band room at rear.

RITZ CINEMA
Policy: First-run films seven days per week; available for daytime hire for lectures and seminars.
Technical: 1 35mm Cinemeccanica platter system. Dolby SR sound system. 2 Kodak Carousel projectors. 1 A.V. lecturn with remote controls. 8 into 2 mixer. 100 watt per channel PA system.

STUDIO
Policy: Classes and workshops, studio theatre, visual art exhibitions, lectures and meetings. Available for hire.
Format: large studio area with semi-sprung maple floor, seating up to 100 persons.
Technical: Lighting control 24 way 2 preset Zero 88 desk with effects panel. Sound 100 watt mono mixer/amp system. 1 twin deck disco console. Stage 12 2m x 1m variable height units.

RITZ/CAPITOL FOYERS
Visual arts exhibitions. Catering in both foyers. Licensed bar in Capitol foyer on first floor.
For full technical information and equipment list contact the Assistant Manager (Technical).

# Hounslow, Middx

## PAUL ROBESON THEATRE
Centrespace, 24 Treaty Centre, High Street, Hounslow,
Middlesex TW3 1ES
For admin. queries please contact: Arts, Events &
Venues Chiswick Town Hall, Heathfield Terrace,
Chiswick, London W4 4JN
Admin/Mgt 0181 862 6502  Admin Fax 0181 862 6570
BO 0181 577 6969  BO Fax 0181 572 3758
ADMINISTRATION:
Props: London Borough of Hounslow.
Business Manager: Mary Tennant
Operations Manager: Laurie Woollcott
Senior Technician: Rachel Francis
Press Officer: Nicole Flammer
Policy: Mixed programme of evening performances
including theatre, dance, multicultural events, music and
children's shows. Daytime activities include youth
workshops, children's events and senior citizen events.
The theatre is also available for commercial and
community hire.
Closed Sundays.
Seats: 280.
Fully licensed bar and Café/Restaurant. Community
Room - adjacent to the theatre, can be used as Green
Room or as a separate facility.
Dressing Room: 2 - shower facility.
TECHNICAL:
Stage:  No actual stage. Performance space same level
as row A; Performance Space: 39ft x 18ft (inc. cross
over and tab bunching); Performance Area: 25ft x 14ft;
Height to Grid: 30ft; Flying Lines: None, 3 x Wipe Tracks
D.S./C.S./U.S.; Tabs: Black tabs at  rear & mid stage,
plus legs and borders; House Tabs: Blue/Green
(Motorised); Cinema Screen: Picture Size 18ft x 9ft max
(C.S.); Cinema Projector: Elmo Lx 2200 16mm; Slide
Projector: Elmo Omnigraphic 552 Xenon; Power Supply:
One 32A Cee Form (P.S.) 16 x 13A sockets (S.R.).
Lighting: Lighting Desk: Zero 88, Sirius 48; Dimmers:
Electrosonic ES6000 series 2kw/chan also 4 x Non dim
circuits (1kw each); Stage Bars: 3, 1 x 12 way, 1 x 10
way, 1 x 6 way (all internally wired); Stage Dips: 4
(U.S.L.), (All stage bars and dips are patchable across
22 circuits); F.O.H. Bridges: 2 each 6 way (both paired
and internally wired); Follow Spot: 1 x Strand Solo 1kw
CSI; Lanterns: Various types of luminaries are available.
Sound: Sound Desk: Yamaha MC2404 II 24 Chn.  Main
Amps: Harrison Xi 600 (300w/chn) Mustang 200
(100w/chn); House Speakers: 4 x Tannoy Puma (Flown
above pros), 2 x Yamaha S2 15ES (floor level); Foldback
System: A basic 2 mix monitor system is available;
Yamaha CDX480 CD player. Tape Decks: Revox B77
(1/2 Track 1/4 inch) JVC TD-X502, Denon M12 XR
(Cassette Decks); Effect Units: Alesis Midiverb II;
EMP100; Yamaha Comp/LIM. Equalisation: Citronic
SPX 7-21 Graphic (Pre Set). Mics: Various types of vocal
and instrument mics are available along with 5 passive
D.I.s.

# Huddersfield

## LAWRENCE BATLEY THEATRE
Queen's Square, Queen Street, Huddersfield,
West Yorkshire HD1 2SP
Tel: 01484 425282 BO: 01484 430528
Fax: 01484 425336

General Manager: Vaughan Curtis
Artistic Director: Ron McAllister
S/Cap: 471. Cellar Theatre: S/Cap: 150

## HUDDERSFIELD TOWN HALL
Ramsden Street, Huddersfield, W Yorks HD1 2TA
Tel 01484 221900 BO: 01484 223200
ADMINISTRATION:
Seating/Capacity: 1,200.
For hall bookings contact Sue Wood
Tel 01484 221947, Fax 01484 221878

## ST PAUL'S HALL
Huddersfield University, Queensgate, Huddersfield, W
Yorks HD1 3DH
Tel 01484 472130 Fax 01484 451547
Contact: Joan Wragg
Seating/Capacity: 400

# Hull, East Yorkshire

## THE DONALD ROY THEATRE
(Gulbenkian Centre), University of Hull, Cottingham
Road, Hull East Yorks HU6 7RX
Admin 01482 466141 BO 01482 465236
ADMINISTRATION:
Props: University of Hull
Manager: A.J.Meech
House Manager: Joy Ward
Policy: Adaptable Teaching Theatre for Drama
Department Productions and Classes. Accepts Touring
Professional Companies, Experimental work, Films etc.
by arrangement.
Seats: 160 - 240. Coffee Bar.
Perfs: 7.45p.m.
TECHNICAL:
Stage: Adaptable, Flat; Pros. opening 8.31m; Ht. of
Pros. 4.88m; Depth of S/Line 10.51m; Ht. of Grid
12.80m; 30 lines C/W, 20 Hemp; Scenery Flying Ht.
6.10m; Flying Bars 10.36m; W/Widths P.S. 4.50m; O.P.
3.81m; Prompt Cnr. P.S.
Lighting: Switchboard: Lightpalette 90 - 4D 90 Dimmers,
96 ways.  Patt.264, Patt.233, Patt.243, Parcans, Codas,
Sil 30.
Sound Equip: 3 Tape Decks, 2 Gram Decks, Mic. Mixer,
rear Audit; Speakers 11, positions varied.
Dressing Rooms: 3; Accom. 26; Orchestra Pit small 4-6.
Get-in off road through 4.88m x 2.44m doors.
Cyclorama cloth tracked on 3 sides. Stage trapped over
basement.

## HULL CITY HALL
Victoria Square Paragon Street Hull HU1 3NA
Tel 01482 610610 Admin: 01482 613818/9
BO 01482 226655 Fax 01482 613961
ADMINISTRATION:
Operations Manager: Tony Ridley
Programme Manager Michael Lister
Capacity: 1,824 seating and standing (concerts).

## HULL NEW THEATRE
Kingston Square, Hull East Yorks HU1 3HQ
Admin 01482 613818/9 Admin Fax 01482 613961
BO 01482 226655 SD 01482 320244
SD Fax 01482 587233

ADMINISTRATION:
Props: Kingston Upon Hull City Council
Theatre Director: Russell E Hills
Programming & Development Manager: Alison
Duncan (Tel 01482 613811)
Administration Officer: Claire Elsdon
Marketing & Publicity Officer: Marie Burkitt (Tel 01482
613808)
Technical Manager: Allan Green
Chief Electrician: Allan Edwards
House Manager: Val Peacock
Policy: Major touring Plays, Ballet, Opera, Musicals,
Variety, Concerts and Pantomime season.
Seats: Flexible between 1104 - 1198.
Perfs: 7.30p.m. Stalls Bar/Restaurant and Circle Bar.
TECHNICAL:
Stage: Proscenium with apron if required; flat. Pros.
opening 10.98m; ht of pros. 7.01m; depth of S/Line
12m; Ht. of Grid 14.78m; 46 lines C/W, 7 of which are
double purchase, 2 hemp. Scenery flying Ht. 14.63m;
Flying Bars 12.19m. W/Widths PS 4.88m. OP 5.18m.
Prompt Cnr. PS.
Lighting/Sound: For specifications of new systems
please ring management number.
Dressing rooms: 17, accom. 80. 6 Showers. Flexible
Orchestra Pit 7 - 70.
Membership: TMA

### HULL TRUCK THEATRE
Spring Street, Hull East Yorks HU2 8RW
Mgt 01482 223800 BO 01482 323638
Publicity 01482 325012 Fax 01482 581182
Email: admin@hulltruck.co.uk
ADMINISTRATION:
Props: Hull Truck Theatre Co Ltd
Artistic Director: John Godber
Executive Director: Simon Stallworthy
Production Manager: Graham Hawkins
Policy: Resident productions; incoming tours, plays,
concerts.
Seats: 320 max.
TECHNICAL:
Stage: Thrust stage - Thurst 8.5m x 7.5m; Ht to Grid
3.64m. Electrics: operated from control room
overlooking stage on S.R. side of auditorium
Lighting: 60 way Lee Colotran computerised board; 30 x
1kw fresnels; 20 x 650w PC's; 6 x Sil 30's. Full list on
demand. 3 phase supply in SR wings.
Sound Equip: New system being installed. Contact
venue for information. Revox, cassette, quadreverb and
assorted mics.
Dressing Rooms: 2. Accom. 20.
Membership: ITC

### THE MIDDLETON HALL
The University, Cottingham Road, Hull
East Yorks HU6 7RX
Tel 01482 465056 Fax 01482 466511
Email: m.bucknell@admin.hull.ac.uk
ADMINISTRATION:
Props & Lessees: The University of Hull
Contact: Melanie Bucknall
Campus Services Offices Tel 01482 466540
Policy: Some Touring Bookings taken.
Seats: 514. Catering available by arrangement.
TECHNICAL:
Stage: Proscenium and Thrust, Flat; Pros. opening
11.28m; Ht. of Pros. 6.71m; Depth of S/Line 8.15m; Ht.
of Grid 8.99m; 8 Hanging Bars 13.11m, W/Widths P.S.
3.05m, O.P. 5.49m; Prompt Cnr. O.P.
Lighting: Desk light board M 78 channels., F.O.H. 32

circuits; stage 46 circuits. Lamps: 16 Cantata 26/44; 10
18/32; 4 CCT Minuettes; 25 Strand 743; 3 Strand Patt
23; 2 Strand Patt 123; 5 Patt S/64 Battens; 21 Patt
500w floods; 8 Par 64 Par Cans; 11 Strand Patt 264; 30
RAT music stands.
Sound Equip: C Audio RA 2000 amp, Crest VS 450
amp; Soundcraft Spirit Live 16-4-2 mixer; 2 650w
speakers, 4 Martin EM15s; Dressing relay system. CD
player, cassette player, Pro-Tech communication
system. Facilities for 16mm, slide and video projection.
Dressing Rooms 2; Accom 20; 2 Showers. additional
room(s) if required.

# Hunstanton, Norfolk
Pop. 4,500. London 124 miles. Newspapers: Eastern
Daily Press & Lynn News & Advertiser. STD code 01485

### PRINCESS THEATRE
The Green, Hunstanton, Norfolk PE36 5AH
Mgt 01485 535937 BO 01485 532252
Fax 01485 534463
ADMINISTRATION:
General Manager: Howard Barnes
FOH Manager: Margaret Allchorn
Stage Manager: Michael Mayes
Seating Capacity: 464
TECHNICAL:
Stage: Proscenium; Raked; Pros. opening 7.50m.
Extended apron of 1.67m over orchestra pit; 7 Section
removeable to form orchestra pit 8.0 x 1.67m. Ht. of
pros. 3.56m Depth of S/L 4.21m; Ht. of Grid 10.10m; 10
lines; Hemp. Scenery Flying Ht. 5.60m. Flying bars
10.10m. W/Widths; P.S. 3.21m; O.P. 4.11m; Prompt
Cnr. P.S.
Lighting: Switchboard Sirius Zero 88, 48 way; 6 F.O.H.
1kw. Spots: 16 F.O.H. 500w spots; 14 on stage 500w
spots; 1.2kw & 2kw follow spots, 9 X 1kw cyc lighting.
Sound Equipment: 1 set Bose 802 speakers, 1 set Bose
302 speakers, Soundcraft 200 SR 16/4/2 mixing desk.
Carver PM 1.5 Amp to power house system. Art stereo
Multiverb unit. 3 M400 Beyer Microphones. 1 SM58 Sure
Microphone. 2 PE 85L Sure Microphones. 1 DI200E
AKG Microphone. 2 Denon DRM 07 Cassette tape decks
with Dolby BC noise reduction. 3 Traynor Foldback
monitors on stage. Paging/relay system to 5 dressing
rooms. 2 X sm58 sure, 2 X Beta 58 sure, 2 X Denon
DRM 550 cassette decks, sony CDP-30 CD player, 2 X
Yamaha foldbacks.
Piano: Concert Grand Grotrian Steinweg 1989.
Dressing Rooms to accom. 12 plus 1 quick change
room for 2.
Intercom from S.M. desk to follow spot positions and
sound/lighting room.

# Huntly

### STEWART'S HALL
Gordon Street Huntly Aberdeenshire Scotland
Tel/Fax 01486 792779
Seating/Capacity: Stalls, 313 (portable, linked), balcony
38 (fixed)

# Ickenham, Middlesex

**COMPASS THEATRE AND ARTS CENTRE**
Glebe Avenue, Ickenham, Uxbridge,
Middlesex UB10 8PD
Admin 01895 632488 BO 01895 673200
Fax 01895 623724
Administration:
Manager: Bryony Flanagan
Administration: Jackie Forwood
Technical Manager: Jevan Sheperd
Purpose built theatre with retractable seating for 160,
refurbished in 1990.
Policy: Plays, musicals, concerts, pantomime and
children's performances. Willing to premiere a show.
TECHNICAL:
Stage: Proscenium arch, stage extensions available. No
rake.  Basic performing area: 6.1m x 6.1m. Pros
opening: 6.1m x 3.2m. Wing widths: 3.05m SR, SL.
Forestage: 6.1m x 1.37m, entrance from auditorium.
Height of grid: 7.01m
Lighting: Sirius 48 way lighting board, 100 amp three
phase power supply. Operated from control box at rear
of auditorium. Temporary three phase power supply to
grounds and cafe. 26 profiles, 32 fresnels, source fours
and codas available. Scaffolding tower available. 1 fixed
position lighting bar, 3 hemp flown lighting bars, cyc
flood bar plus 2 FOH bars.
Sound: Soundcraft Spirit Folio 10 operated from stage
left. Main amp switch PL500. Peavey Eurosys 350w
speakers. Second amp revox B251 for effects and
foldback. 2 cassette tape system, 1 reel to reel.
Stage Management: Prompt corner DSL. Show relay to
dressing rooms and green room. Tech relay with 6
outstations.
Backstage: 2 permanent dressing rooms, accom. for 30
performers. Large green room, catering available.
Washing, drying facilities. Workshop space for set
maintenance, fully equipped. Large studio available
backstage for rehearsal. 3 pianos available. 1 Yamaha
Grand Piano

# Ilfracombe, Devon

Pop. 9,140. London 203 miles. Newspapers: North
Devon Journal-Herald (thurs). STD code 01271

**THE LANDMARK**
The Promenade, Wilder Road, Ilfracombe,
Devon EX34 9BE
Tel 01271 865655
Contact: Karen Turner

# Inverness

Pop. 37,000. London 529 miles. Newspapers: Highland
News (thurs); Inverness Courier (tues/fri); Press and
Journal. STD code 01463

**EDEN COURT THEATRE**
Bishops Road, Inverness IV3 5SA Scotland
Mgt/SD 01463 239841 BO 01463 234234
Fax 01463 713810
Email: ecmail@cali.co.uk
Web Site: edencourt.uk.com
ADMINISTRATION:
Director: Colin Marr
Technical Manager: Jim Clark
Policy: Open all year housing all forms of touring
entertainment from drama, ballet and opera to films,

country music and pop shows. Full Conference facilities.
Seats: 800 on three levels. Three Foyer Bars, Restaurant
and Cocktail Bar, Exhibitions in the stalls foyer and in
additional adjacent rooms. 84 seat Cinema.
TECHNICAL:
Contact venue for required information.

# Ipswich, Suffolk

Pop. 123.070. London 72 miles. Newspapers: East
Anglian Daily Times; Evening Star (ntly); Suffolk Mercury
(thurs); Suffolk Extra (fri). STD code 01473

**CORN EXCHANGE**
King's Street Ipswich IP1 1DH
Tel 01473 255851 BO 01473 215544
Fax 01473 250951 Publicity Fax 01473 262688
Email: corn@ipswich-ents.co.uk
Web Site: www.ipswich-ents.co.uk
ADMINISTRATION:
General Manager: Billy Brennan
Marketing Manager: Hazel Clover
Capacity: 900 (including 176 in balcony).

**IPSWICH REGENT**
3 St. Helens Street, Ipswich Suffolk IP4 1HE
Mgt 01473 263555 Mgt Fax 01473 288236
Publicity 01473 255851 Pub. 01473 262688
BO 01473 281480 Technical 01473 721690
Email: regent@ipswich-ent.co.uk
Web Site: www.ipswich-ents.co.uk
ADMINISTRATION:
Policy: Live entertainment, single nights or week runs.
Manager: Roy Stephenson
Marketing Manager: Hazel Clover
Technical Manager: Alan Stimson
Seating capacity: 1,781
TECHNICAL:
Stage: Size: 19.5m x 8.4m + 2.4m extension over pit;
Slight Rake: Pros. opening 11.8m wide x 7m high;
Below stage crossover Grid Ht. 11.6m, 16 Hemp Lines,
4 winches; 6 x 1 ton chain hoists.
Stage Power: 300A x 3 Phase; 100A x.3 Phase; 100A x
Single Phase.
Lighting: Control 2 x 48 way Serius; Position - F.O.H.
Rear Stalls; Dimmers - 96 x 2kw Betapak; Lanterns: 30
x 1kw Fresnels, 18 x 2kw Fresnels, 24 x 1kw Profiles.
Circuit Distribution: 4 x 18 way - stage bars; 2 x 12 way
- dips; 2 x 12 way + 2x6 way F.O.H. bars; 2 x 12 way -
F.O.H. wich truss.
Sound: 200 watt speech only - full system hire arranged.
Dressing Rooms: 8 to accommodate 60.
Orchestra Pit: 20 can be extended by removing 50
seats.

**WOLSEY STUDIO**
St. George's Street, Ipswich Suffolk
Mgt 01473 218911 BO 01473 253725
SD 01473 255143 Fax 01483 212946
ADMINISTRATION:
Policy: 2-3 week runs of home-produced shows with
occasional visiting companies.
Perfs: 7.30p.m.; Sat. 4.p.m & 8p.m.; Wed. 2.30p.m.;
October to March.
Seats: Flexible (95-175). Bar open during performances
only.
TECHNICAL:
Stage: Stage area flexible. Minimum 6.20m x 5.10m;

maximum 10.70m x 7.80m.
Lighting: Board: ADB Cantor 36 way; 25 x 650w PCs + 10 x 650W zoom profiles; 6 x 1K Fresnels.
Sound: Allen Heath SC + 6 Mong 3 stereo input; 4 x 4 matrix output; 6 channel C audio amp outputs; 1 Revox B77, 1 cassette, 1 CD.
Dressing Rooms: 2, accommodation 10.

## WOLSEY THEATRE
Civic Drive, Ipswich Suffolk IP1 2AS
Mgt 01473 218911 BO 01473 253725
SD 01473 255143 Fax 01483 212946
ADMINISTRATION:
Lessees: Wolsey Theatre Co. Ltd
Artistic Director: Andrew Manley
Administrative Director: Lorna Anderson
Marketing & Business Development Manager: John Grice
Policy: Three and four weekly repertory
Perfs: 7.45; Sat. 4.30 & 8.00; Wed. 2.30
Seats: 400. Bar open during performances and normal licensing hours.
TECHNICAL:
Stage: Open (Thrust) Stage and Rear Stage. Flat; Thrust Stage Depth 12.25m; Max Width 14.20m; Width at Opening to Rear Stage 8.25m; Rear Stage Depth 6m; Width 8.25m; Wing Space P.S. 10.33m; O.P. 3.70m; Ht. over Thrust Stage 8.5m. Ht. over Rear Stage 7.5m; Prompt Cnr. O.P. (mobile to Control Room F.O.H.) No Fly Tower.
Lighting: Switchboard: Rank Strand Galaxy III 120 ways, 60 Profiles, 50 Fresnels, 7 x 5kw circuits.
Sound: DDA 24/8/2 mixer inc. theatre matrix. 3 Revox B77, 1 TEAC 4 track, 1 cassette, 1 CD, Bose 802/302 system.
Dressing Rooms 5; Accom. 25. Showers 3.
Membership: TMA

# Irvine, North Ayrshire
Pop. 58,000. Glasgow 26 miles. London 417 miles. STD code 01294

## MAGNUM THEATRE
Magnum Leisure Centre, Harbourside, Irvine, Ayrshire, KA12 8PP Scotland
Mgt/BO 01294 278381 Fax 01294 311228
Technicians 01294 275852
ADMINISTRATION:
Props: North Ayrshire Council
Manager: Andy Robinson
Entertainments Manager: Willie Freckleton
Policy: Magnum Theatre is a combined theatre/cinema and all types of entertainments are presented in the widest possible range.
Perfs: Variable
Seats: 323. Two Bars, a Cafeteria and Restaurant.
TECHNICAL:
Stage: Proscenium, opening 32ft; rear wall (drapes) 21ft, rear wall to sky cloth 20ft, depth of stage (without FOH) 20ft; depth of stage (using FOH) 27ft; Height of flats 16ft.
Lighting: Tempus M24 Lighting Board, Tempus M24 Effects Board, 60 channels & 185 memories.
Sound: TOA 12 channel mixing console, TOA front of House speakers, Talk Back system (wireless). Twin cassette deck, CD player, Alesis Midiverb Unit, Shure SM58 microphones, on stage monitors.
Other: 2 x 35mm projectors, 24ft x 12ft cinema screen, remote control slide carousel projector, overhead

projector, portable screens, lectern, VHS video & monitor, portable PA systems, flip charts and black board.

MAGNUM MAIN HALL:
Capacity 1,200 seated, 1,800 standing.
Size: 115ft x 102ft, height 40ft.
Stage: 40ft wide, 24ft deep, 4ft high (plus 16ft x 16ft PA wings.)

# Irvinestown, N.Ireland

## BAWNACRE CENTRE
Castle Street, Irvinestown, Enniskillen, County Fermanagh, BT94 1EE Northern Ireland
Tel 01365 621177 Fax 01365 628082
Centre Manager: George Beacom.
Seating: 900 in main hall. Purpose built stage with full lights and curtains. Minor hall: seating for 320. Excellent workshop, exhibition & cafe facilities available.

# Jersey, Channel Islands
Pop. 84,082. Newspapers: Jersey Evening Post (dly). STD code 01534

## GLOUCESTER HALL
Fort Regent Leisure Centre, St Helier, Jersey JE2 4UX Channel Islands
Mgt 01534 500200 Fax 01534 500225
ADMINSTRATION:
Props: States of Jersey
Commercial Manager: Moya Fenoughty
Sales & Marketing Manager: Victoria Carnegie
Policy: Multi-purpose
Seats: Variable from 800 to max 1,977
TECHNICAL:
Stage: Concert platform in accoustically correct bowl. 12.80m deep x 17.07m wide.
Lighting: Strand GSX 75 full theatre lighting system available.
Sound Equip: Combination of Bose loudspeakers with a Soundcraft 400B 32 channels.

## OPERA HOUSE
Gloucester Street, St Helier, Jersey, Channel Islands
Closed for refurbishment, expected to re-open July 2000. For enquiries contact: Sarah Clare Hugh, Executive Officer at the Jersey Arts Trust, St James Street St Helier JE2 3QZ
Tel 01534 617521 Fax 01534 610624

# Kelso

## TAIT HALL
Edenside Road, Kelso, Roxburghshire TD5 7BS
Tel 01573 224233
Manager: Tom Frizzell
Seating/Capacity: 700; balcony fixed, loose stacked in stalls.

# Kendal

### KENDAL LEISURE CENTRE
Burton Road Kendal Cumbria LA9 7HX
Tel 01539 729511 BO 01539 729702
Fax 01539 731135
Manager: Paul Stewart
Recreation Officer For Events: Dawn Garnett
Seating/Capacity: 893 max.

# Keswick, Cumbria

Pop. 5,169. London 283 miles. Newspapers: Keswick
Reminder (fri); Times & Star; News & Star; Lake District
Herald; Cumberland News. STD code 017687

### THEATRE BY THE LAKE
Lake Road, Keswick, Cumbria CA12 5DJ
Mgt 017687 72282 BO 017687 74411
Fax 017687 74698
ADMINISTRATION:
Props: Cumbria Theatre Trust Ltd
Executive Director: Patric Gilchrist
Policy: Professional repertoire of plays, July-October.
Also functions as a receiving venue for small-scale
drama, opera and ballet.
TECHNICAL:
Theatre opening during the summer of 1999.

# Kidderminster

### GLADES ARENA
Wyre Forest Glades Leisure Centre, Bromsgrove Street,
Kidderminster, Worcestershire DY10 1PP
Tel 01562 515151 Fax 01562 861458
General Manager: Nick Lewis
Centre & Events Manager: Stuart Booton
Capacity: 1,400 seated; 1,800 standing.

# Kilmarnock

Pop. 48,785. London 391 miles. Newspapers:
Kilmarnock Standard (thurs). STD code 01563

### PALACE THEATRE
9 Green Street, Kilmarnock, Ayrshire KA1 3BN Scotland
Mgt 01563 537710 BO 01563 523590
Fax 01563 573047
ADMINISTRATION:
East Ayrshire Council
Theatre Manager: Bruce Gilmour
Assistant Theatre Manager: Laura Brown
Stage Manager: James Miller
Policy: Professional & Amateur Drama, Opera, Ballet,
Concerts and Variety etc.
Perfs: 7.30p.m.
Seats: 503
Bars: 2
TECHNICAL:
Stage: Pros, slight rake; Pros. opening 7.47m; Ht. of
Pros. 4.88m; Depth of S/Line 7.32m; Ht. to Grid
10.06m; 20 Hemp sets.
Lighting: Switchboard: Tempus M24 120 circuits + FX
Desk. F.O.H. 20 T-Spots, 8 Profile Spots, Stage 20

Harmony F. 16 500w Floods. For details of further
lanterns please contact management.
Sound Equip: Fully professional sound system.
Upgraded + CC Pro Audio 1994. Please apply to
management for details.
Dressing Rooms 7.

# King's Lynn, Norfolk

Pop. 30,220. London 98 miles. Newspapers: Lynn News
& Advertiser (tues/fri); Eastern Daily (dly). STD code
01553

### KING'S LYNN ARTS CENTRE
29 King Street, King's Lynn Norfolk PE30 1HA
Mgt 01553 765565 BO 01553 764864
Fax 01553 762141
ADMINISTRATION:
General Manager: Howard Barnes
Technical Manager: John Holden
Policy: Plays, Dance, Music, Films throughout year.
Seats: 349. Theatre Bar.
TECHNICAL:
Stage: Proscenium, Flat; Pros. opening 6.71m; Ht. of
Pros. 3.50m; Depth of S/Line 5.64m; 15 lines, Hemp;
Flying Bars 7.32m; W/Widths P.S. 0.91m, O.P. 0.91m;
Prompt Cnr. P.S.
Lighting: Switchboard: 40 way, 2 pre-set, prompt side;
F.O.H. Spots 6 Patt.123, 10 Patt.23; 2 Battens 3 col;
Dips 4 each side; 1 Spot Bar 4 Patt.123, 1 strip.
Sound Equip: 1 Brennel Tape Deck, 1 4-speed Pan, 1
stereo Cassette Deck, prompt side; Speakers: 4 in Hall,
1 Stage; 2 H & H Power Amps (10 inputs).
Dressing Rooms: 4, Accom. 30, Orchestra Pit 16.
Max. height of Flats 3.66m; Max, width of Flats 1.91m.

### KING'S LYNN CORN EXCHANGE
Tuesday Market Place, King's Lynn, Norfolk PE30 1JW
Mgt 01553 765565 BO 01553 764864
Fax 01553 762141
ADMINISTRATION:
General Manager: Howard Barnes
Marketing Officer: Amanda McKee
Technical Manager: Paul Pomfret
Front Of House Manager: Ellen McPhillips
Capacity: 738 seated, 1,200 standing
TECHNICAL:
Stage: Open flat stage 12m x 8m (extends 10.6m). Wing
width 1.75m each side, grid height 8m. 6 x winched
double barrels.
Lighting: ETC Impression 2 Control Board (250 channels)
80 dimmers 66 @ 10A, 12 @ 25A. Hard wired to socket
outlets. 60 x par 64, 30 x 1.2k fresnels, 12 x 1.2k 22/40
profiles, 4 x 1.2k 15/28 profiles: 2 x 1200 MSR
followspots.
Sound: Crest century GT 24 channel mixer, 7 x crest
amplifiers, 8 community FOH speakers, 6 x peavey
wedges, Yamaha SPX 990, 2 channel compressor, 2
channel noise gate, 6 channels of graphic equalisers, 2 x
Tascam 112 mkII cassette decks, 1 x Tascam CD401
Mk II CD player, 6 shure SM58, 4 AKG SE 300B c/w
CK91, 2 x MD4 21, 2 AKG 112, 1 X SM57.
Dressing Rooms: 5, accomodating up to 70.
Other: 160A TPN Stage LX power supply, 160A SPN
stage sound. Intercom systems. Portable staging. Piano
available, and music stands.

# Kirkby In Ashfield

## FESTIVAL HALL

Festival Hall Leisure Centre, Hodgkinson Road, Kirkby-
in-Ashfield, Nottingham NG17 7DJ
Tel 01623 457100 Fax 01623 457099
Manager: Dennis Nichols
Seating/Capacity: 520

# Kirkcaldy

Pop. 150,000. London 398 miles. Newspapers: Fife Free
Press (fri). STD code 01592

## THE ADAM SMITH THEATRE

Bennochy Road, Kirkcaldy, Fife KY1 1ET Scotland
Mgt 01592 412567 SD 01592 266193
BO 01592 412929
ADMINISTRATION:
Props: Fife Council
General Manager: Alan Falconer
Theatre Manager: Sheila Thomson
Stage Manager: Roger Jackson
Film Theatre Manager: Mark Robson
Policy: All forms of touring entertainment including plays,
musicals, ballet, opera, concerts, jazz, rock, country, folk
etc.
Regional Film Theatre. Stereo Dolby Sound System.
Perfs: 7.30p.m.
Seating: 475 on one raked tier. Licensed Bar.
Restaurant. Three Functions Suites.
TECHNICAL:
Stage: Proscenium Arch; width 10.00m; height 6.00m.
Level Apron. Curved Apron extends over Orchestra Pit.
Depth - Prosc. to back wall 7.40m. Prosc. to Apron
edge, Centre 2.5m. Ends 1.5m. Curved orchestra pit
extension 2.0m. Stage width between dip traps 13.0m.
Grid height 8.60m. 30 sets 3 line polyester ropes on
48mm. O.D. alloy barrels, length 12.19m. One
counterweighted set and steel barrel. Eight motor
winches with 4 line sets and steel barrels. Stage plan
available. Fly floor S.L. only. Full black masking available.
Get-in by 3.00m. square lift (O.P. stage) from ground
level 5.00m below stage level. 6 dressing rooms on three
levels accom. 55. Wardrobe room, 2 washing machines,
ironing board, 2 tumble dryers. Deep sink. Car Park.
House tabs. Manual winch (drawn across) grand piano,
also upright. One large and one small Tallescope.
Orchestra pit seats 34 approx.
Lighting: Control Room rear auditorium projection suite.
138 dimmer channels. 2 lighting bridges: 2 vertical slot
booms (Apron sides), 14 ways No. 1 Spot Bar. Other
bars hung to order. 4 circuit CODA 4 Flood Bar. 2 HMI
Follow Spots or Patt.774 on dimmers. For list of lanterns
available apply to theatre. Auxillary mains supply (S.L.)
100 amps, 3 phase AC supply. 2 pole booms and 4
ladders available.
Sound: Control from rear of auditorium or stage.
Soundcraft 24 channel mixer or Studiomaster 8 into 4.
H.H. MOS-FET Amplifiers. Loudspeakers. Bass Reflex
cabinets or wedge monitors position as required.
Selection of Shure and AKG microphones. Headset
inter-comm. to all work stations. Paging and relay to
dressing rooms. Revox 2 track reel to reel tape deck.
Cassette tape deck. One 'Audio' Radio-Mic. For further
information apply to theatre.

# Kirkcudbright

## KIRKCUDBRIGHT, TOWN HALL

St Mary Street Kirkcudbright DG6 4JG
Tel 01557 330191 extn 66235 Fax 01557 330005
Seating Capacity: 250
Contact: Mrs May Monteith

# Lancaster, Lancs

Pop. 49,820. London 223 miles. Newspapers: Lancaster
Guardian (fri). STD code 01524

## ASHTON HALL

Dalton Square Lancaster Lancs LA1 1PJ
Tel 01524 582512 Admin: 01524 582000
Fax: 01524 582161
ADMINISTRATION:
Head of Arts and Events: Jon Harris
General Theatre Bookings: Graham Cox/Angela Kipling
Tel 01524 582504 Fax: 01524 582505
Capacity: 800

## THE DUKES

Moor Lane, Lancaster Lancs LA1 1QE
Mgt 01524 67461 BO 01524 66645 Fax 01524 846817
ADMINISTRATION:
Props: Lancaster City Council
Lessees: Duke's Playhouse Ltd
Administration Director: Mary Caws
Stage Manager: John Newman-Holden
Chief Electrician: Brent Lees
Policy: Repertory, outdoor site specific work, regional
film theatre, education, community and outreach work.
2 auditoria. End Stage (322 seats). In-the-round (198
seats) stage approx 5.3m x 6.1m.
TECHNICAL: End Stage
Proscenium Stage with apron, Flat; Pros. opening 10.67;
Ht. of Pros. 5.79m; Depth of Line 9.14m; Ht. of Grid
6.10m; Winch No. 1 Bar, other bars hemp as required;
Flying Bars 11.89m W/Widths P.S. 2.47m, O.P. 2.47m;
Prompt Cnr. Portable prompt desk.
Computerised Box Office.
Sound Equip: Revox Tapes Goldring Pan & Bose 80L;
Speakers as required. Dolby 35 + 16mm film sound
track. Soundcraft Mixing Desk.
Dressing Rooms 3 Accom. 12; 3 showers.
Membership: TMA

## GRAND THEATRE

St. Leonards Gate, Lancaster Lancs LA1 1NL
Mgt/BO 01524 64695 PCB (Foyer) 01524 381349
ADMINISTRATION:
Owners: Lancaster Footlights Club
Chairman of Theatre Mgt Committee: Mr Sim Lane-
Dixon
Policy: Available for hire.
Perfs: Variable according to production.
Seats: 465. Licensed Bar.
Toilets for the disabled installed.
TECHNICAL:
Stage: Proscenium Raked. Pros. opening 6.4m; Ht. of
Pros. 5.2m; Stage depth 6.4m; Ht. of grid 12.2m; 30
lines hemp; W/widths PS 2.4m; OP 1.8-4.8m
Lighting: Switchboard: Strand AMC 40 channels, OP
perch; circuit distribution F.O.H.  8, Flys 22, Stage 10.

Spots 10 Patt. T.84, 9 Patt.123, 17 patt 23, 3 minim, 1 minuette, 2 silouette 90, 4 starlette.
Dressing Rooms: 5; accom. 40. Orchestra Pit 12.
Costume hire.
Membership: Little Theatre Guild of Great Britain.

## NUFFIELD THEATRE
University of Lancaster, Bailrigg, Lancaster
Lancs LA1 4YW
Mgt 01524 594157 BO 01524 594151
Fax 01524 39021
Email: j.s.davies@lancaster.ac.uk
Web Site: www.lancs.ac.uk/users/nuffield
ADMINISTRATION:
Props: University of Lancaster
Director: Adrian Harris
Administrator: Jayne Davies
Chief Technician: Stephanie Sims
Stage Manger: Simon Attwood
Policy: Multi-Purpose Theatre accepts Touring
Professional Theatre, Experimental Theatre Lab. Work,
Dance, Mime, adapted classics.
Seats: 220 (max). Licensed Bar.
TECHNICAL:
Stage: Open Studio 22.86m.sq., Flat; Depth of S/Line
depends on Stage Form; Ht. of Grid 5.18m; Lines as
required, Hemp; Scenery Flying Ht. 3.05m; W/Widths
adaptable; Prompt Cnr. either.
Lighting: Switchboard: Gemini or Jands ESP II 24 way,
124 way board; 24 way sirius; 124 dimmers; F.O.H.
Spots as required; Dips as required; Full range of
lanterns.
Sound Equip: Professional Mixing Desk, 8 channel 3
group; Speakers 4 Tannoy York etc.
Dressing Room: 1, large (can be divided); Accom. 20;
Bathrooms; Orchestra Pit as required.
Very Flexible Studio 22.86m centre pit 1.52m deep,
15.24m.sq. Stage/s adaptable to any part of Studio.
Seating can be tiered or flat, 6.71m. Wheelchair access
and disabled toilets.

# Leamington Spa, Warwickshire

Pop. 42,300. London 90 miles. STD code 01926

## ROYAL SPA CENTRE
Newbold Street, Leamington Spa, Warwickshire CV32
4HN
Mgt/BO 01926 334418 Fax 01926 832054
ADMINISTRATION:
Props: Warwick District Council
Entertainments Manager: Peter B Nicholson
Assistant Entertainments Manager: David Phillips
Venue Technicians: Chris Whalley & Samantha Booth
TECHNICAL:
Avon Hall: Main season runs from September to May.
Programme consists of mainly one-nighters offering a full
spectrum of entertainment; comedy, ballet, rock, opera,
jazz, big bands, children's shows, variety, dance
competitions and a recognised talent competition. Ideal
for conferences and seminars, exhibitions and fairs.
Perf: Regularly 7.45 with 7.30 or 8.00 variances.
Seats: 800 (495 of which are removable on the ground
floor). 2 Licensed bars. Coffee bar.
Stage: Floor area: 54' x 54' flat maple floor (outer edges
limited to 7'8" height clearance). Entrance for cars etc.
8'w x 7'h. Plan available.

Stage: 3'9" high from hall floor. Main proscenium giving
stage working area 34'w x 26'd. Soft black masking -
fixed. Tabs and runners. Limited wing space.
Understage crossover. Blue painted back wall
cyclorama. Full motorised flying facilities, 18'h x 40'w
clothsize. 14' clearance height to lighting bars
(permanent).
100A 3 phase and 60A single phase power supply
available for temporary rigs.
Orchestra pit available. 4'deep apron available. Limited
rostrums available. Get-in via dock (to rear of stage) on
stage level. Plan available.
Lighting: Jands Hog desk to 168 dimmers. Rig consists
of various parcans, fresnels, pro 400s and limited spots
in fixed focus washes. 2 x Clay Paky Shadow HM1 1200
follow spots
Sound: Soundcraft Venue desk. Bose system with Hill
amps. Various FX, microphones and stands.
Stage Management: Techpro headset communication
system linked to sound, lights, followspots, flys and
additional capacity. Tannoy and show relay to dressing
rooms.
Backstage: 5 dressing rooms accomodate 25. 2
showers.
Staff: 3 full time Technicians. Casuals available.

Newbold Hall:
Policy: Conferences and meetings. Film shows.
Seats: 208, raked conference style.
Stage: No stage, flat floor area with curved cinema
screen behind, with associated masking and tabs. No
flying facility. 41" screen TV and video and slide
projection facilities available.

# Leeds, W. Yorks

## CITY VARIETIES MUSIC HALL
Swan Street, Leeds W Yorks LS1 6LW
Mgt 0113 242 5045 BO 0113 243 0808
SD 0113 245 3119 Fax 0113 234 1800
ADMINISTRATION:
Props: Leeds Grand Theatre & Opera House Ltd
General Manager: Peter Sandeman
Chief Technician: Tom Blackband
Policy: Music Hall, Pantomime, Variety, Tours, Celebrity
Concerts, Conferences
Perfs: 7.30 weekdays, Sat 5.00 & 8.00
Seats: 531, Stalls, Circles and Boxes.
TECHNICAL:
Stage: Proscenium, Raked; Pros. opening 6.10m; Ht. of
Pros. 5.18m; Depth of S/Line 4.88m; Ht. of Grid 9.75m;
16 lines, Hemp; Flying Bars 6.71m; Prompt Cnr. P.S.
Lighting: Switchboard: 48 way Sirius 12 Profiles, 10
Fresnels, 10 Pebble Convex, 3 x 4 compartment Cyc.
floods, 2 x 2kw Follow Spots.
Sound Equip: AHB 16 into 4 into 2 Sound Desk, 2 Nexo
PS15 speakers, 2 Nexo PS10 speakers, 1 Nexo 1000
Sub bass, 1 crown 2400 amplifier to PS15, 1 Crown
1200 Amplifier to PS10, 1 crown 1200 amplifier to sub
bass. 1 digital delay & 1 31 band graphic equaliser, both
preset to house characteristics. HH 450 watt and 200
watt foldback amps. 1 twin cassette deck. 1 DAT player.
1 mini disk player. 1 Grand and 1 Upright Piano.

## LEEDS CIVIC THEATRE
Cookridge Street, Leeds W Yorks LS2 8BH
Mgt 0113 245 6343 BO 0113 247 6962/245 5505
Bar/Catering 0113 243 4389

Web Site: www.leeds.gov.uk/civictheatre
ADMINISTRATION:
Props: Leeds City Council Leisure Services
General Manager: Steven Cartwright
Assistant Manager: Vivien Simpson
Chief Technician: Peter Waddicor
Policy: Mixed programme professional and amateur
productions of drama, dance concerts, opera,
pantomime, children's shows, light entertainment,
touring theatre companies.
Separate additional rehearsal rooms available at
Stansfeld Chambers 100 yards from theatre.
TECHNICAL:
Pros. Opening 8.69m; Ht. of Pros. 3.85m; Depth from
S/Line 5.54m; Ht. of Grid 9.1m.
Switchboard: Strand Gemini 28 circuits FOH 56 on
stage, 180 channel console Control room rear of stalls; 3
Spot Bars, 1 Batten, 2 F/Spots.
Dressing Rooms 7; Accom. 30. 1 Shower.

## LEEDS GRAND THEATRE AND OPERA HOUSE

46 New Briggate, Leeds W Yorks LS1 6NZ
Artists 0113 245 3930 Mgt 0113 245 6014
BO 0113 222 6222 Fax 0113 256 5906
Opera North (Switchboard) 0113 243 9999
ADMINISTRATION:
Props: Leeds Grand Theatre and Opera House Ltd
General Manager: Warren Smith
House and Catering Manager: Ann Baxendale
Stage Manager: Alan Dawson
Chief Electrician: David Yates
Policy: Touring plays, musicals, ballet, dance, concerts,
home of Opera North, licensed catering centre.
Facilities: Main theatre, 5 tier, seats 1550 + 84 stand.
Conference, exhibition, concert reception, rehearsal
rooms, 7 licensed Bars, 4 Coffee Lounges, 1 Sponsors
Bar - Linacre Room.
Studios: Seats 192 stands 250. Dimensions 10m x 14m
x 5m _ two side Studios each 4.9m. x 12m x 2.43m.
Grand Hall: Seats 100 stands 160. Dimensions 8.2m x
13.4m x 6.1m.
Assembly Rooms: Dimensions 13m x 22.75m x 2.95m
minimum for rehearsals only.
Advanced Booking Office with RITA computer ticket
issuing system plus 120 booking agents.
TECHNICAL:
Stage. Rake 1 in 24, Pros. opening 9.90m, Pros. Ht.
8.23m; Depth from setting line 13.61m; Grid Ht. 18.29m;
60 Double purchase Counterweight lines; P.S. Wings
3.76m; O.P. Wings 2.66m; Prompt Cnr. Control P.S.; 2
Stage and conductor TV cover cameras, 2 Portable TV
monitor; Rank Strand Gemini control box; Get-in: for
ordinary scenery etc via single deck hoist (.89m x 4.5m x
7m high) 1000kg; for baggage etc via passenger lift
(2.50m x .95m x 2m); for large bulk via steel roller shutter
doors 5.41m above street level using swing jib and push
travel trolley with electric chain hoist 500kg; cloth shute
from stage to street; stage 2 floors up (5.41m from
street).
Lighting: Switchboard: 160 operative ways + 36
unconnected; 200 rehearsal and plotting remote control
board. LX equip: 12 X Alto; 8 X Cantata 11/26; 6 X
Cantata 18/32; 6 X Cantata Fresnels; 6 X Cantata 26/44;
8 X Source 4's; 25 X 223's; 12 X IRS floods; 8 X 20' 11w
barrels; Stands 2 X 8'6"; 8 X 4'6", 2 x 1000 watt CSI
follow spots; 5 battens x 4 circuits, floats 4 circuits; dips
8 circuits per side; 2 tallescope ladders; 3 ph supply
240/415 Ex.sup 150 amp.
Sound Equip: MCM Series 12 input; 6 output channels,

plus metal cassette deck; P.S. control; 1 Revox tape
deck; 15 Ass.Mics.; Speakers - 6 Bose 802, Auditorium;
2 stage; + delay line to balcony and rear stalls show calls
and relay to all backstage areas.
Dressing Rooms 14; Accom. 80 persons; 12 shower
rooms; orchestra pit 25-70 musicians; music stands 20;
2 band rooms. Instrument store, music library, 3
rehearsal rooms. Wardrobe, backstage bar and canteen.
Digs, technical and press lists and stage plans available
on request.
Membership: TMA, Yorkshire Tourist Board, West
Yorkshire Arts Marketing Consortia.

## LEEDS PLAYHOUSE

Please refer to The West Yorkshire Playhouse.

## LEEDS UNIVERSITY UNION

Lifton Place, off Clarendon Road, Leeds, Yorks LS1 1UH
Tel 0113 243 9071 BO 0113 231 4208
Fax 0113 244 8786
ADMINISTRATION:
All correspondence to: PO Box 157, Leeds, LS1 1UH
Contact: Fran Owen, Entertainments Manager,
Tel: 0113 231 4236
Capacity: 1,800

## WEST YORKSHIRE PLAYHOUSE

Playhouse Square, Quarry Hill Leeds
West Yorkshire LS2 7UP
Admin 0113 213 7800 BO 0113 2137700
Press 0113 213 7272 Fax 0113 213 7250
Minicom 0113 213 7299
ADMINISTRATION:
Chief Executive & Artistic Director: Jude Kelly
Head of Casting and Scheduling: Kay Magson
Head of Operations: Dan Bates
Head of Marketing: Anne Torreggiani
Black Arts Co-Ordinator: Jackie Christie
Producing Theatre. Two auditoria seating 350 & 750.
Policy: Subsidised Repertory, year round programme;
touring welcome National and Regional Drama and
Dance. Young People's Theatre programme and black
arts events: concerts, foyer events, cabaret and late
night shows, Schools Company. It also includes
community work in its artistic policy. Restaurant, bar,
shop, rehearsal room, function & entertainment facilities,
full workshops. Facilities for the disabled.
QUARRY THEATRE
Seats: 750
Stage: Open Thrust stage; air conditioned. 16m wide x
7.4m deep. Flat modular stage surface with basement
under thrust stage area.
Opening to rear stage area: 18m wide x 8m high.
Movable panel reduces size to 15m wide x 6m high.
Rear stage area: 30m wide x 18m deep. Suspension grid
at 10m over front 5m section of stage. Full
counterweight grid at 20m over centre 11m section of
stage. 10 winches to underside of ceiling, at 7.5m, over
rear 9.5m section of stage. Thrust stage wagon: 16m
wide x 12.8m deep, with compensator lift.
Lighting, sound and SM controls: At rear of auditorium. 2
Auditorium lighting bridges. 'Juliet' balconies to either
side of stage opening.
Dressing Rooms: 9; total accom. 30. Crew dressing
rooms: 2; total accom. 30-40. Wardrobe maintenance
laundry.

COURTYARD THEATRE
Seats: 350. Courtyard Theatre. Air-conditioned. 2

Audience Galleries and end stage.
Stage: Flat modular stage surface with basement area below. 10.7m deep x 11.7m wide. SR & SL Wings 3.2m wide with 5m clearance under galleries. Grid at 10m with combination of winches, temporary counterweights & hemp line suspensions. Main seating block: 10.5m x 11.7m wide on bleachers. Technical galleries and winch/Hemp suspensions above auditorium.
Dressing Rooms: 5; total accom. 16.Backstage facilities accessible to disabled performers and staff.
Membership: TMA, Yorkshire and Humberside Tourist Board, NCA.

# Leicester, Leics

Pop.281,440. London 100 miles. STD code 0116

## DE MONTFORT HALL

Granville Road, Leicester Leics LE1 7RU
Mgt 0113 233 3113  BO 0113 233 3111
Fax 0113 233 3182
ADMINISTRATION:
Props: Leicester City Council
House Manager: Peter Cooper
Operations Manager: Alvin Hargreaves
Finance Manager: Sharon Brown
Box Office Manager: Jean Wolfe
Marketing Development Manager: Nick Hallam
Technical Manager: John Sippitt
Policy: One Night Concerts, Dances, Conferences, Weekly shows for children and Musicals
Seating/Capacity: 1,973 seated, 1,600 tiered, 2,200 standing.

## THE FLAMING COLOSSUS

57 Welford Road Leicester LE2 7AE
Admin 0116 233 4788 BO/Fax 0116 233 4777
ADMINISTRATION:
Manager: Richard Smith
A purpose built venue with a full on licence, and entertainments licence untill 2am.
The venue is by no means crowded at its full occupancy figure of 700 people. Superb views of the stage are available in the main area, this includes raised seating and a gantry running the entire length of the bar area at the front of the building. The bar is situated opposite the stage and space has been allotted for front of house and monitor mixing desks.  This makes an ideally proportioned showcase venue suited to the highest quality shows.
TECHNICAL:
Stage: 14' x 25' x 2'6" High 14' Head clearance.  Plain white backdrop.  Power: 60 amp independent supply with 12 sockets and RCD output.
Lighting: 12 x Martin Roboscan scanners projecting 17 colours and white by 290 watt mercury sodium lamps manually or computer controlled for fully programmable co-ordinated sequences.
Sound: P.A. To be arranged with Midland Sound and Light, subject to requirements.  The building is situated in a town centre location, close to both universities with parking for 50 or more cars.

## HAYMARKET THEATRE

Belgrave Gate, Garrick Walk, Leicester Leics LE1 3YQ
Mgt 0116 253 0021 BO 0116 253 9797
SD 0116 253 0021 Fax 0116 251 3310
ADMINISTRATION:

Props: Leicester City Council
Lessees: Leicester Theatre Trust Ltd
Executive Director: Kathleen Hamilton
Artistic Director: Paul Kerryson
Theatre Manager: Samantha Ireson
Production Manager: John Page
Technical Stage Manager: Mike Barry
Co.Manager: Harriet Roy
Policy: Subsidised repertory, and touring.
Seats: 752. Two Licensed Bars. One Coffee Bar.
TECHNICAL:
Stage: Proscenium with semi-thrust fly-tower over stage and thrust, Flat; Orchestra Pit (electric lift) in thrust; Pros. opening 14.63m; Ht. of Pros. 7.92m; Depth of S/Line to Back Wall 11.58m; S/Line to front of thrust 6.55m; Ht. of Grid 17.98m; 52 lines, C/W; Scenery Flying Ht. 17.68m; Flying Bars 14.02m; 17.07m; W/Widths P.S. 6.71m, O.P. 6.71m; Prompt Cnr. flexible.
Lighting: Switchboard: Rank Strand Galaxy II rear of balcony and also stalls control; 220 x 2kw and 20 x 5kw; F.O.H. Back bridge 10 x Patt.253 (2kw); 4 x Silhouette 15 (2kw); Front Bridge 28 x T84; Middle Bridge 8 x T84; Fly dips O.P., 35 x 2kw, 8 x 5kw. Flood Bar. 15 x Patt.49.
Sound Equip: 4 Sonifex u500 cartridge machines, 3 Revox A77 tape decks; 28 into 10 Fleximix rear of balcony. F.O.H. speakers systems, 4 Tannoy 10" dual concentric speakers, Vitavox horn units; Stage Speakers, 2 x Vitavox horn units; Stage Speakers, 2 x Vitavox bitone majors, 7 Quad 405 amps. Microphones AKG 'CMS' system. Also Recording Studio.
Dressing Rooms 8; Accom. 42; 4 Showers; Orchestra Pit 50; Fire curtain set D/Stage of thrust.
Membership: TMA

## HAYMARKET THEATRE - STUDIO THEATRE

Belgrave Gate, Garrick Walk, Leicester Leics LE1 3YQ
Mgt 0116 253 0021 BO 0116 253 9797
SD 0116 253 0021 Fax 0116 251 3310
ADMINISTRATION:
Props: Leicester City Council
Lessees: Leicester Theatre Trust Ltd
Executive Director: Kathleen Hamilton
Artistic Director: Paul Kerryson
Theatre Manager: Samantha Ireson
Production Manager: John Page
Technical Stage Manager: James Mulholland
Policy: Own productions in part year, co-productions and tours-in with small/medium scale companies.
Seats: 120. Two Bars, Coffee Bar (shared with main auditorium).
TECHNICAL:
Flat;  Roof Trusses 3.65m under, Prompt Cnr.
Switchboard: M24, Dimmers: 60 x 2kw; 32 Profiles; 58 Fresnels; 6 Floods. Spot bars fixed lighting grid at 3.66m. Shares building, facilities and management with large auditorium.

## LITTLE THEATRE

Dover Street, Leicester, Leicestershire LE1 6PW
Mgt 0116 254 2266 BO 0116 255 1302
Wardrobe Hire 0116 254 0472
ADMINSTRATION:
Manager: James O'Donoghue
Scenic Artist: Ann Jennimgs
Seats: 349
TECHNICAL: Please contact venue for details.

## PHOENIX ARTS CENTRE

21 Upper Brown Street, Leicester Leics LE1 5TE
Mgt 0116 224 7700 BO 0116 255 4854
Fax 0116 224 7701
ADMINISTRATION:
Partnership Initiative: De Montfort University & Leicester
City Council
Lessees: Leicester Arts Centre Ltd
Director: Richard Haswell
Head Of Live Programme: Judi Hughes
Technical Manager: Paul Noble
Policy: Broad based arts centre promoting the best
contemporary dance, drama, music, film, multi-cultural
arts exhibitions.
Perfs: Eves 6 days a week, Saturday Family Film
Matinees.
Seats: 270. Phoenix cafe open 12 - 8p.m. and during
interval. Licensed bar open normal licensing hours.
Building open 7 days a week. Jazz: Sunday lunchtimes;
Folk Saturday lunchtimes.
TECHNICAL:
Stage: Open, semi thrust, flat. Width of stage 14.40m,
depth of stage 8.25m, maximum height 5.20m for
scenery.  Height of fixed grid from 5.92m/6.40m.
Prompt desk in control room, rear of auditorium or S.L.
The stage surface is black. There are no flying facilities.
The back wall of the stage is a white plaster cyclorama.
Various soft black masking is available by pre-
arrangement, 13 x adjustable stage braces, 15 x stage
weights, 1 8'x4'x18' rostrum. Upright 8 octave piano.
Reversible black/grey dance floor covering main stage
area (11m wide and the full stage depth). Advance notice
is required to lay dance floor. A smoke machine and a
dry ice machine available by pre-arrangement.
Lighting Equipment: There are no follow-spots or followspots position in the Phoenix. All Phoenix equipment is
fitted with 15A plugs and sockets, including the stage
worker and independent sockets. However the Phoenix
can provide jumpers from 13A as required. Control: 84 x
2kw dimmers, Strand Lightboard M, 84 channels,
patchable to any dimmer. 36 channels under 2 preset
manual control. 200 Q memories, 2 timed/manual
playbacks, 1 timed only playback, 24 sub masters, 2
chase effect playbacks. Lanterns: 16 x Patt.23 500w
profiles (7 with shutters), 12 x Iris 1 750w floods, 18 x
Par can (various beam width Par 64s), 6 x Sil 30 1kw
profiles, 14 x Patt.743 1kw fresnels, 14 x prelude 16/30
500w profiles, 10 x Harmony 15/28 1kw profiles, 4 x
Berkey 6" 1 kw fresnels, 14 x Harmony PC 1kw pebble
convex, 4 x Patt.243 2kw fresnels, 2 x Cadenza F 2kw
fresnels, 12 x Patt.123 500w fresnels, 2 x Minuet F 500
fresnels, 1 x Patt.223. Other: 6 x 10A indepdent 15A
sockets in the stage area switched from control box, 6 x
unswitched 15A worker sockets in stage area for general
power requirements. The maximum possible load on the
independents and the workers combined is 60A,
protected by ELCB.
Sound Equip: microphones: 8 x Shure SM58, 4 x AKG
C451E 2 x AKG C100s, 2 x AKG CK1, 2 x Beyer 201, 2
x AKG CK5, 1 x Beyer M380, 2 x AKG CK8, 4 x AKG
310s, 1 x Sennheiser MD441, 2 x Sennheiser MD521,  1
x TAC Scorpion 26:8:2, 1 x Studiomaster Powerhouse
12-2 mixer, 2 x 1kw JBL  PA stacks, 2 x 250w Ramsa
speakers (fixed auditorium front), 4 x 200w BOSE
speakers (fixed auditorium sides and rear, but also
available for onstage monitors), 2 x 150w Carlsbro
speakers, 1 x Alesis Quadraverb, 1 x single channel
digital delay, 1 x single channel digital reverb/echo, 1 x
Denon cassette deck, 1 x Teac stereo cassette deck, 2 x
revox B77 reel-to-reel tape decks, 15 x boom mic
stands, 3 x D.I. boxes. 12 way microphone patch

(balanced XLR) between USL and control room. Ring -
intercom system with 5 belt packs and headsets
connecting control room, projection room, SL and SR.
Dressing Room show relay and paging system.
Projection: 2 x 35mm Westrex 2000 projectors; 1 16mm
Fumeo H2200 projector; 1 Dolby CP50 processor;
screen on roller over stage.
General: 4 13A skts. rear of stage; Cue LX as required;
show relay/FOH relay with paging; Comms. Technical
projects throughout theatre.
Touring: 13 Prelude PCs; 4 Goliath stands.
Dressing Rooms: 3; Accom. 18. 1 Shower. Iron, ironing
board, washing machine, tumble drier. Very limited
backstage space. No wing space.

# Leighton Buzzard

Pop.33,000. London 40 miles. Newspapers: Leighton
Buzzard Observer (thurs). STD code 01525

## LEIGHTON BUZZARD THEATRE

Lake Street, Leighton Buzzard, Bedfordshire LU7 8RX
Mgt 01525 850290 BO 01525 378310
Infoline 01525 381414 Fax 01525 851368
ADMINISTRATION:
Props: Bedfordshire County Council
Manager: Lois Wright
Technician: Edward Everest
Funded by Beds CC, EA.
Policy: Mixed programme of film, professional small scale
touring drama, music recitals, plus performance by local
amateurs. Childrens films, drama shows and workshops.
Exhibitions. Performing arts workshops.  Perfs: Mon-Sat
8.00, mats. 2.30p.m
Hire, box office split, guarantee & split, guarantee by
negotiation.
Seats: 170, raked.
Daytime coffee bar. Licensed bar on performance nights.
Foyer coffee servery on film nights.
Limited wheelchair space, lift-assistance available,
contact Manager, level access.
TECHNICAL:
Stage: Proscenium arch with 0.85m apron. Performing
area 8.25m x 5.65m - pros. opening 7.15m x 4.6m -
wing widths 1.38m SR, 1.38m SL. No rake - floor sprung
wood, suitable for dance, backstage crossover, stage
heated. Grid:4.9m. Tab track - black tabs - white cloth
cyclorama - turquoise house tabs, electrically drawn.
Get-in via public lift.
Lighting: Rank Strand MX48 board, operated from
projection room or wings - 51 lanterns.
Sound: Diamond Studiomaster Pro 12-3 mixerdesk.
RevoxB77mk2 reel-to-reel, TEAC W-750 R double
cassette system, TEAC CD-P3200, PA system.
Operated from projection room. Paging - 100w power
amplifier and 100v line transformer - speakers in various
locations. 6 inputs - foldback facility - 4 mics and stands.
Acoustics suitable for music and spoken word.
Stage Management: Prompt corner position SL -
phone/intercom cue system, 6 outstations - show
relay/Tannoy to dressing rooms. Backstage: 2 dressing
rooms, access by lift and stairs - band room - quick
change rooms - 4 power points in each room. Coffee bar
which is open limited hours daytime only and evening
licensed bar. Rehearsal rooms, piano, good. Staff - 1
part-time lighting/sound - casuals not available - security
personnel. Backstage facilities not accessible to disabled
performers and staff.

# Lerwick, Shetland Islands

### GARRISON THEATRE
Market Street Lerwick Shetland Scotland
Tel 01595 692114
ADMINISTRATION:
Props: Shetland Islands Council
Manager: John Bulter
Assistant Manager: Karen Clubb
Booking/Enquiries: Islesburgh Community Centre, King
Harald Street, Lerwick. Tel. 01595 692114. Fax 01595
696470.
Policy: Local & Touring Drama, concerts, recitals, films,
opera, ballet & pantomime.
Perfs: 7.30 / variable.
Seats: 287 max. (250 raked, up to 37 removable to
increase orchestra space).
Provision for disabled patrons: level access, toilet,
inductive loop, 4 wheelchair bays.
TECHNICAL:
Stage: Proscenium Stage: Pros. opening 6.7m; Ht. of
Pros. 2.9m; Stage Depth 5.5m plus apron 0.9m; Split
height grid from Pros. extending up stage 1.8m, height
6.45m, remaining US grid to stage rear 4.2m, height
3.65m.
Wing widths - SR 1.3m, SL 1.2m, rear crossover. Stage
floor - no rake, sprung wood, suitable for dance, lino
available. Stage heated. 7 hemp sets - tab track - black
or grey legs & borders - black or grey curtain as
cyclorama - wine house tabs, drawn. 16 x 13A
independent circuits, 6 x 15A independent circuits
controlled from control room. Scale stage plans
available. Get-in via rear double doors, off Market Street.
Show relay and paging to dressing rooms & Control
Room, 2 channel 12 station intercom system (six belt
packs and 4 fixed stations), 6 cue light stations. SM
Desk SL.
Lighting: 48 x 2.5kw channels controlled by Rank Strand
Action 48 desk normally situated in control room at rear
of auditorium but can be used from SL next to SM desk.
F.O.H. bar - 10 circuits & 2 x 15A independents, 4 x T84
c/w colour wheels, 2 x Harmony, 2 x Patt.263 and 2 x
Patt.23. Access from above auditorium. Followspots - 2
x Rank Strand Cantata operated from positions above
either side of auditorium, 1 x dimmer circuit & 1 x 15A
independent circuit in each position. Access from above
auditorium. No. 1 Stage LX bar - 10 circuits & 2 x 15A
independents, Manual winch. No. 2 Stage LX bar - 7
circuits & 2 x 15A independents. No. 3 Stage LX bar - 6
circuits & 2 x 15A independent. No. 4 Stage LX bar - 4
circuits. All attached to rear grid, height 3.65m. Boom -
SL & SR 1 circuit & 1 independent each. Dips - 7
circuits; Stage perimeter - 7 circuits. 60A Single Phase
Temporary Supply SL, 32A Three Phase Temporary
Supply SL. 6 x Coda Flood, 8 x Patt.60 Flood, 10 x
Patt.23 profile, 5 x Patt.123 Fresnel, 4 x minum F, 2 x 4
circ., 8 comp. Battens, UV fittings,
Le Maitre Pyroflash system & Rosco Fog machine.
Video Equip: 2 remotely controlled Panasonic F10
cameras wall mounted either side of the auditorium
linked to Panasonic MX10 Production Mixer & Pioneer
Titling computer located in control room at rear of
auditorium.
Sound Equip: An extremely versatile system with limited
control from side of stage or full control facilities from
control room at rear of auditorium. On-stage control; 6
channel Tascam mixer into 400w stereo audio system,

patch panel, line amps, 20 stage inputs, cassette deck.
Control room operation; 12 channel Tascam mixer,
inputs from stage at line level, 20 stage inputs. 400w
auditorium stereo audio system & 2 x 200w per channel
stage monitors. Tape playback cartridge cassette or reel
to reel. Recording facility 8 track 1/2" with 6 channel
premix, 2 track Tascam mastering & cassette. 20 stage
inputs. 7 headphone monitors on stage, 2 x 200w stage
monitors. Access for external P.A. system.
Dressing Rooms: Accommodating 20 each, two
showers, two toilets, refreshments from kitchen, access
by stairs. Prop room/quick change room at rear of
stage, Workshop off prop room. Staff - casual available
from community centre - security personnel. Backstage
facilities presently not accessible to disabled.

# Lichfield, Staffs
Pop. 30,000. London 112 miles. Newspapers: Lichfield
Mercury. STD code 01543

### LICHFIELD CIVIC HALL
Castle Dyke, Lichfield, Staffordshire WS13 6HR
Mgt 01543 256505 BO 01543 254021
Fax 01543 268263
ADMINISTRATION:
Props: Lichfield District Council
Manager: Richard Dabrowski
Policy: Touring concerts, Films, Pantomime, Drama,
Light Entertainment, Cabaret, Private Functions, Opera,
Ballet, Orchestral, Choral, Banquets arranged.
Conference facilities - meeting rooms available.
Perfs: 7.30pm or 8.00pm; Sat 2.30pm.
Seats: 394. Daytime restaurant/coffee shop, evening
coffee and light refreshments, licensed bar.
TECHNICAL:
Stage: Proscenium, flat; Pros. opening 11.582m; Ht. of
pros. 4.572m; Depth of S/Line 7.924m; Ht. of Grid
4.572m; 2 lines Hemp; W/Widths P.S. 2.438m; O.P.
2.133m; Prompt Cnr. P.S.
Lighting: 60 x 2kw Dimmers. Control: Microset 40s + 20
way ring. 4 spot bars, 2 FOH Bars. Lanterns: 16 X
Harmony F, 22 X Cantata F, 6 X Patt 743, 10 x
Patt.123,9 X Cantata 18/32, 6 X Cantata 26/88, 12 X
Patt 764, 3 x Patt 23, 9 x Nocturne Floods, 12 Patt 60,
30 Parcan, 1 Patt 793 follow spot.
Sound Equip: Allen & Heath 24:2 mixer, Tannoy/JBL
speakers; selection of Mics; Projection: 35mm projector,
35mm Carousel Slide Projector, Dolby Stereo.
Dressing Rooms 2; Max. accom. 20; showers. Band
room accom. 30. No Orchestra Pit but one can be
accommodated by removal of first two rows of seating.

# Lincoln, Lincs
Pop. 73,810. London 132 miles. Newspapers:
Lincolnshire Echo (ntly); Lincoln, Rutland & Stamford
Mercury (fri); Lincolnshire Chronicle (fri); Lincolnshire Free
Press (tue); Lincolnshire Standard (fri). STD code 01522

### THEATRE ROYAL
Clasketgate, Lincoln Lincs LN2 1JJ
Mgt 01522 523303 BO 01522 525555/534570
SD 01522 523303 Fax 01522 545490
CC Hotline 01522 519999
ADMINISTRATION:
Lessees: Chris Moreno Entertainments Ltd
Theatre Director: Chris Moreno

Theatre Manager: Keith Richards
Production Manager: Art Walker
Box Office Manager: Sylvia Coldron
Policy: Touring shows, drama films, concerts, amateur, productions.
Perfs: Nightly 7.30. Saturdays usually 6.15pm & 9pm.
Seats: 482. 2 Bars.
TECHNICAL:
Stage: Proscenium arch. Performing area 9.5m x 7m slight rake; Pros. opening 6.55m x 5.49m wing widths 3.66m SR, 3.66m SL. Stage raked, 1 to 72 - floor plywood with hardboard top, suitable for all dance, understage crossover, stage heated. Height of grid 12.8 - 36 hemp sets, 0.2m apart, 2 tab tracks, 350/400kg permitted on bars. Max flying height 12.6 black masking, white sharkstooth filled gauze cyclorama, maroon house tabs, flown. 10 x15A independent circuits. Forestage 7.5m x 2m entrances both sides. Orchestra pit 6.55m x 2m, accommodates 14. Get-in via dock doors 1m above street level, 2.5m x 4.7m. Tallescope, safety curtain. Scale stage, fly and lighting plans available.
Lighting: Switchboard: Rank Strand Gemini 2+ 100 circuits, 90 x 2kw, 10 x 5kw, operated from SL perch: 2 x 60A 3-phase supplies for temporary board. F.O.H. 16 x cantata 18/32 and pattern 23's. No.1 Spot bar 12 x Patt.743's. Flood bar 12 x 500w coda CYC floods. Extra equipment: 20 x 1kw profiles, 24 x 1kw Fresnels, 12 x 1000w Parcans, 8 x Patt 243's, 14 x patt.23's. 9 Lengths S. Type Batten. Follow Spots - 2 x 2kw Solos in Upper Circle.
Sound: Soundcraft 200 16 into 4 into 2 desk, operated from prompt corner, basic system outline suitable for all sound reinforcement, 5 x Sennheiser K3 U with ME40 and ME80 heads, 2 x SM58, 2 x Revox B77 tape decks, 1 x Sansui D100 cassette deck. P.A. system. Facilities for recording and editing. Acoustics suitable for music and the spoken word.
Stage Management: Prompt corner SL headphones, 6 outstations, CCTV system to P.C. and other outstations, show relay/Tannoy to dressing rooms. Backstage 9 dressing rooms, access by stairs from stage level. Rehearsal piano, advice given on accommodation. Facilities for the disabled: 2 wheelchair spaces. Contact House Manager.

# Liverpool, Merseyside

Pop. 588,600. London 167 miles. Newspapers: Liverpool Daily Post; Liverpool Echo (ntly); Liverpool Weekly News (thurs). STD code 0151

## CENTRAL HALL

Renshaw Street Liverpool Merseyside L1 2SF
Tel 0151 709 4435/6 Fax 0151 709 5832
Seating/Capacity: Concert Hall 1,000; Lonsdale Hall: 250
Theatre Manager: Harry Gardam

## EMPIRE THEATRE

Lime Street, Liverpool Merseyside L1 1JE
SD 0151 708 3200 BO 0151 708 3206 Admin 0151 708 3211 Fax 0151 709 6757 Party Bookings 0151 708 3231 CC 0151 709 1555
ADMINISTRATION:
Props: Apollo Leisure Ltd
Theatre Manager: Rachel Miller
Box Office Manager: Paul Black
Stage Manager: Tony Saunders
Technical Manager: Andrew Smith
Chief Electrician: Derek Pennington

For all booking information and further details please contact Sam Shrouder or Nicky Monk at Apollo Leisure (UK) Ltd., Grehan House, Garsington Road, Cowley, Oxford OX4 5NQ. Tel: 01865 782900; Fax: Oxford 01865 782910.
Policy: Touring - Opera, Ballet, Variety, Plays, Concerts and Pantomime
Perfs: Eve. 7.30. Mat. 2.30
Seats: 2,348. 2 Bars, 1 Coffee Bar.
TECHNICAL:
Stage: Proscenium. Pros. Opening 14.1m; Ht. of Pros. 7m; Depth of S/Line 11.58m; Ht. of Grid 22.2m; 57 c/w lines, 840lbs single purchase, C/W Scenery Flying ht. 7.62m; Flying Bars 18.29m; W/Widths P.S. 4.57m; O.P. 6m; Prompt Corner P.S.
Lighting: Gemini +2; (52 F.O.H.); Follow Spots Teatro MSR. 1 Ton Advance Truss (18 ways); 25 x T64s; 25 x 1k Fresnels (Berkey); No. 1 Bar 12 x 743s; 8 x Iris Is; 6 x Sil 15s (2k).
Sound Equip: Communication: 6 Outstation Strand Intercom.
Dressing Rooms 17; Accom. 105; Showers; Orchestra Pit 84.

## EVERYMAN THEATRE

Hope Street, Liverpool Merseyside L1 9BH
Admin 0151 709 0338 BO 0151 709 4776
Fax 0151 709 0398
ADMINISTRATION:
Props: New Everyman Ltd
Chief Executive: Rose Cuthbertson
General Manager: Sharon Duckworth
Production Manager: Paul Morgan
Policy: Innovative Repertory, some commissioned new plays and touring work.
Perfs: 8 p.m. Mon to Sat - usually.
Seats: 402, some variation available depending on stage arrangement. All day cafe/bar in exhibition foyer.
Restaurant lunch and evening to 11.30p.m.
Youth Theatre.
Education Department.
TECHNICAL:
Stage: Open, Flat. 10m wide x 15m deep. No flying. Ht. to grid 5.4m.
Lighting: Switchboard: Arri Image 96 x 2KW dimmers. 198 sockets on grid 9 dips. Fully patchable.
Sound Equipment: selection of mics, Revox, cassette, CD. 24-8-2 Soundcraft Venue (control room or auditorium), eq and FX units. 6 Community RSjr, 2 EV 15-2, foldback and effects speakers.
Dressing Rooms 3; accom. 20; 6 showers.
Membership: TMA

## NEPTUNE THEATRE

Hanover Street, Liverpool Merseyside L1 3DY
Tel 0151 709 7844 Fax 0151 225 6695
ADMINISTRATION:
Lessees: Liverpool City Council
Manager: Diane Jenks
House Manager: Linda Goulden
Stage Manager: David Saville
Policy: Visiting Amateur & Professional Companies. Home of Neptune Comedy Club.
Perfs: Various Times.
Seats: 445. Bar (evenings).
TECHNICAL:
Stage: Proscenium Stage with apron. Raked; Pros. Opening 8.33m; Ht. of Pros. 4.5m; Depth of Stage: a) including apron 10.3m, b) with orchestra pit open 7.80m, c) from setting line 7.10m, d) restricted sightlines max.

depth 3.3m centre stage; Ht. 4.27m; Flying Bars 8.99m;
W/Widths P.S. 2.74m; O.P. 2.59m; Prompt Cnr.O.P.
Lighting: Switchboard in circle: 66 ways; F.O.H. spots,
22 x 1k, Dips 5 each side, spot bars, patt 23 and 123,
pat 743 and par cans.
Sound Equipment: 12-2 Revox, B77, Cassette and C.D.
D.R. relay system.
Dressing Rooms 5; Accom. 40; 2 Showers; Orchestra
Pit 18-25.

## PHILHARMONIC HALL

Hope Street Liverpool Merseyside L1 9BP
Mgt 0151 210 2895 BO 0151 709 3789
Fax 0151 210 2902
ADMINISTRATION:
Chief Executive: Anthony Lewis-Crosby
Principal Conductor, RLPO: Petr Altrichter
Philharmonic Hall Director: Alex Medhurst
Events Co-ordinator (Bookings): Iona Horsburgh
Technical Services Manager: Miriam Stone
Marketing Director: Ian Archer
Built in 1939, original architect Herbert Rowse.
Refurbished 1991-95, architect Peter Carmichael.
Renowned art deco concert hall famous for its acoustics
and wall reliefs. Central location, between the two
cathedrals and both universities. Owned and managed
by RLPS. Underwent major refurbishment (open 1995)
giving it vastly expanded facilities and programme.
Winner of 1996 RICS Building Conservation Award.
Funding: venue funded by Arts Council of England, Local
Authorities in Merseyside, Lancashire and Cheshire.
Local Authority: Liverpool City Council.
RAA: NWAB
Catering: Lower Place Restaurant - award winning
restaurant, 70 covers. Open every event evening and all
lunchtimes. Substantial hospitality and event catering
facilities. Banqueting for up to 100 people.
Ticket Outets: on site box office. 25 agencies throughout
Merseyside. Shop and sales area.
Access: Car parks close by, very convenient for central
train and bus terminals, also airport and motorway links.
Facilities for the disabled. Level access and ramps,
assistance available. 10 wheelchair spaces. Grand foyer
bars, bistro, infra red and loop system.
Policy: Wide ranging international programme, including
resident and visiting orchestras, solo recitals, pop, jazz,
choral concerts, cinema, cabaret, comedy. Venue is
home to the Royal Liverpool Philharmonic Orchestra,
Principal Conductor Petr Altrichter. Promotions by the
Royal Liverpool Philharmonic Society, joint promotions,
hires. Willing to premiere show. Performance times vary,
normally 7.30pm.
Booking terms: Hire, box office split, by negotiation.
Seating: 1682 fixed, slightly raked, plus 102 platform
seats.
TECHNICAL:
Stage: Width - useable 18.5m, max 20m. Depth useable
11m, max 12m. High 0.86m. Both front and rear
platforms are curved. Get in with goods lift available
width min 1.03m height min 2.04m. 24 X 1 ton flying
points(eye bolt fixed to steel above concert ceiling). 15
positions over platform, 9 positions FoH allowing
Left/Right PA clusters to be flown separately from main
FoH truss. Temporary motor supply can be run to
platform on 3 phase 32amp 'C' form. 3 phase 16amp
'C' form motor connector @ 11 flying points. Flying can
only be done from official, designated points.
Lighting: In house concert and theatre lighting systems.
Control: Strand 430 - 250 ways active 134 ways
connected. Dimmers 4 x 24 way 2.5kw Strand LD90 - 2
x 24 way 2,5 kw ADB. Outlets all single 15 amp - one

outlet per dimmer. 32 ways of production lighting, 42
ways of concert lighting, 60 ways of house lighting, 6 x
16amp non dim - 2 used for follow spots. Lanterns 12 x
2kw Alto zoom 28/38 (second roof slot in front of
platform), 40 x 1kw 240v PAR64 (24 nearest roof slot to
stage - 12 inside slots), 2 x PANI HMI standard throw
follow spots in roof space, 60 x 1kw 110v PAR64 over
platform for concert lighting. Concert lighting cannot be
coloured, refocused or units moved elsewhere.
Sound: Mixing Desk Allen & Heath 24:4:2:1, six Aux
sends. Outboard, Alesis Reverb, Sabine Dual Channel
Feedback Suppressor, 2 Channels of Behhringer
Composer compressor/limiter/gate. Amplifiers deliver
approx 3.6kw distributed - mixture of Amcron and
Ramsa. Loudspeakers Nexo. Microphones, 3 x Beyer
M88, 1 Shure SM58, 4 x Calrec 1050, 2 x Calrec 1051,
4 x Trantec radio mics (2x handhed, 2x lav). BBC facility
in rack with feed to o/p panel with BBC compatible
connection system. Surround loudspeakers, suitable for
cinema sound. Multi microphone positions to stage.
Dolby cinema system.
Other: Stage Management: CCTV to auditorium with
monitor locations front and back of house. Public
address to all areas with microphone locations at front
and back of house. Show relay to all performers and to
public areas. Cue system with out-stations, loop
intercom system.
Backstage: Dressing/soloists/green rooms available.
Rehearsal piano in green room. Refreshments available.
Backstage fully accessible to wheelchair users. In-
house stage and lighting sound and casual technical and
get in staff available.
Additional Information: Organ - Rushworth and Dreaper
1939, refurbished 1983 by Rushworth and Dreaper, 3
chambers behind grilles at side and rear of concert
platforms; electro-pneumatic action with solid state
switching; 70 speaking stops, 15 couplers, 3 manuals
and pedal, 2930 pipes, very good condition; console on
electrically raised lifts CS - can swivel to face audience,
face the rear of the platform or sideways; the console
can be played under stage as well as at stage level.
Pianos: two stage pianos, to include at least one
Steinway D, excellent condition.

## ROYAL COURT THEATRE

Roe Street, Liverpool Merseyside L1 1HL
Admin 0151 709 1808 BO 0151 709 4321
Fax 0151 709 2678
ADMINISTRATION:
Chief Executive: Simon Geddes
Manager: Edward Grant
Policy: Pop concerts, standing or seated downstairs,
seating in circle and balcony. A rock venue as well as a
theatre. Seating: 1,796
TECHNICAL:
Stage: Proscenium; Flat, Pros. Opening 9.74m; Ht. Pros.
8.98m; Depth from S/Line 12.18m; Ht. grid 17.97m; 70
lines cwt. Flying Ht. 17.67m, length bars 12.18m.
Lighting: Switchboard:Strand Grand Master 94 ways,
FDH 12 x Patt.73, 8 x T64, 6 Battens 4 CCTS, each
floats 4 CCTS 8 ends centres. 6 Dips PS & OP, 2 Spot
bars 12 x Patt.743, Flood Bar 12 x Patt.49. Get-in Dock
Doors (Stage 3ft above street level) Metal roller 6.09m x
2.43m. Power on Stage: 3 x 300amp; 3 x 63amp; 3 x
32amp; 1 x 100amp.
Sound: Contact venue for required information.

## UNIVERSITY OF LIVERPOOL

Guild Of Students PO Box 187 160 Mount Pleasant
Liverpool Merseyside L69 7BR

Tel 0151 794 4131 Fax 0151 794 4174
Contact David Dennehy Tel 0151 794 4161
Contact: David Dennehy
Tel: 0151 794 4161
A £1.7 million redevelopment took place in 1994.
Mountford Hall - 891 seated - 1500 standing.
Lounge Hall, Courtyard Hall - T.B.C.
Stanley Theatre - 370 seated - standing n.a.

# Livingston

## THE FORUM

Almondvale Centre, Almondvale South, Livingston, West
Lothian EH54 6NB Scotland
Venue Closed at present.

# Llandrindod Wells, Powys

Pop. 3,470. London 170 miles. Newspaper: Radnor
Express (wed); Shropshire Journal (fri); County Times &
Gazette (sat). STD code 01597

## THE ALBERT HALL

Ithon Road, Llandrindod Wells, Powys LD1 6AS Wales
ADMINISTRATION:
Props: Committee of Management
Chairman: W Shewan, Belvedere Park Crescent,
Llandrindod Wells LD1 6AB. Tel 01597 822324
Stage Manager: Gerald Corfield
Booking, information, and key obtainable from D.A.C.
Hendriksen (Secretary), Chatsworth, Spa Road,
Llandrindod Wells. Tel 01597 822726
Policy: Stage Plays, Concerts, Repertory, Pantomime,
Meetings, etc. Hiring only. No promotion.
Perfs: as required.
Seats: 450 approx. Kitchen and Refreshment Room in
Lower Hall.
TECHNICAL:
Stage: Proscenium, Flat; Pros. opening 7.82m; Ht. of
Pros. 4.88m; Depth of S/Line 5.49m plus 3.05m Apron;
Ht. of Grid 7.32m; W/Widths P.S. 3.66m approx. O.P.
0.91m.
Lighting: Switchboard: 3 Strand Dimmer Packs each of
12 x 1000w capacity with provision for another pack.
Movable console 2 x 24; F.O.H. Spots 8 x 1000w profile
plus 2 x 500w Follow Spots; 2 Battens; Front 8 x 500w.
Back 6 x 300w.
Sound Equipment: Available if required. Speakers above
P.S.
Dressing Rooms 4; Orchestra Pit 6.

## THE PAVILION

Spa Road Llandrindod Wells Powys LD1 5EY Wales
Tel 01597 823532 Fax 01597 824413
Seating/Capacity: 565
Contact: Mrs Carolyn Flynn

# Llandudno

Pop. 17,620. London 226 miles. Newspapers:
Llandudno Advertiser (fri); North Wales Weekly Press
(thurs); North Wales Pioneer (wed). STD code 01492

## NORTH WALES CONFERENCE CENTRE

The Promenade, Penrhyn Crescent, Llandudno,
Conwy LL30 1BB Wales
Tel 01492 879771 Fax 01492 860790
ADMINISTRATION:
Props: Conwy County Borough Council
General Manager: Nick Reed
Policy: Orchestral Concerts, Touring Companies, One-
nighters, Conferences, Exhibitions, Fairs, Television
Studios etc.
Perfs: usually 8.00p.m.
Seats: Theatre style, 970. Two bars. Banqueting: 500;
Cabaret 700.
TECHNICAL:
Stage: Portable 28' x 16' (not proscenium). Flat floor.
7,500 square feet - Main Hall. 5000 square ft. lounge.
Lighting: Two spot bars, 12 x 1kw spots on each bar.
Sound: 12 way mixer, output to four speakers. 8
microphones/stands, etc. Tape recorder, 3.75 and 7.50
IPS. Multiple cassette recording.

## NORTH WALES THEATRE

The Promenade, Penrhyn Crescent, Llandudno,
Conwy LL30 1BB Wales
Mgt 01492 879771 BO 01492 872000
Fax 01492 860790
Email: info@nwtheatre.co.uk
Web Site: www.nwtheatre.co.uk
ADMINISTRATION:
General Manager: Nick Reed
Operations Manager: Bridget Jones
Technical Manager: John Owen
Seating: Total 1,500: stalls 698, (432 retractable, 266
demountable) creating 421 sq. metres for Exhibition
space; balcony 169 (148 fixed, 21 demountable); Circle:
638 (620 fixed high back, 18 removable).
TECHNICAL:
Superb new, technically state-of-the-art theatre.
Housing one of the largest stages in Britain. The perfect
venue for the best in classic arts and popular
entertainment.
Stage: Structural proscenium - width 14 metres, height
8 metres. Width - From centre line. S.R. 11.3 metres
(to counterweight frame) S.L. 14.45 metres. Depth -
from fire curtain to back wall 13.7 metres. Height - to
underside of grid 20m - to underside of fly galleries 7.5
metres. above stalls floor 1 metre. Surface: vinyl
covered on 25 mm ply flat stage. Stage designed for
load of 7.5kn per sq. metre.
Auditorium - Area 421 Sq. metres.
Machinery: 58 single purchase counterweight free sets
excluding house tabs and header, and side masking.
500kg. loading per bar. Counterweight bar length 15.6m
+ 2m extensions. 3 sets for proscenium header, house
tabs and side masking. 3 bar hoists over forestage,
500kg. (motorised) 1 up, 1 down counterweight set per
side of stage. 1 up, 1 down motorised hoist per side of
stage.
S.M. - Working corner S.L. mobile desk ( plugs into S.L.
S.R. stalls and control) Cue lights , show relay, C.C.T.V.
ring intercom.
Lighting: Control - Strand Mini Light Palette LP90 in
control room. Rear of level 1 (1st floor). Rehearsal desk
position at front of level 1. Riggers control.
On Stage power - 400 amp 3 phase. 200 amp, STP.
Dimmers LD90 - 204 x 10 amp. 36 x 20 amp. 19 non
dim outlets (remotely operated).
Sound: P. A. and Sound - Mixer - Allen and Heath Saber
2.24 into 8, 8 matrix into 2. Graphic equaliser, effects
unit, reel to reel, stereo cassette, compact disc player,

monitor speakers in control room, speakers above pros. arch, centre cluster and pros. left and right. 4 mobile effects speakers, 4 stage monitor speakers, 148 mic lines (including 24 in the orchestra pit), 24. S.L., 24 S.R. Other: Access - from car/truck park 3.5 metres high x 4.5 metres wide (tailgate high).
Cross over - Passage way open to stage. (Behind stage).
Understage - Trap area 7.2 metres wide x 3.6 metres front to back. 9 removable stage modules each measures 1.2 metres x 2.4 metres. Band store x 2. Band/crew room. General store. Female/Male W .C. (crew). Translation - 1st floor, 4 x translation booths at rear of seating.
Orchestra pit - Area 116 sq metres. Maximum front to back dimension 7.4 metres. Maximum width 18 metres, maximum front to back dimension of rostra infill section 2.1 metres. Maximum front to back dimension of life section 2.1 metres. Can be elevated to create more auditorium space for exhibitions, conferences etc.
Hard of Hearing - Infra red system (radiators, modulators, receivers, headsets etc).
Dressing rooms - Ground floor - 2 x Star dressing rooms with w.c. and showers. 1st floor - 1 x 16 person, 2 x 10 person, 1 x 8 person, w.c., wash and shower facilities. 2nd floor - 2 x 10 person, wig room costume and laundry, w.c., wash and shower facilities.

# Llanelli, Carmarthenshire

### LLANELLI ENTERTAINMENT CENTRE
Station Road, Llanelli, Carmarthenshire SA15 1AH Wales
Tel 01554 774057 Fax 01554 741632
ADMINISTRATION:
Props: Carmarthenshire County Council
Centre Manager: Carwyn Matera-Rogers
Policy: Mixed-use Entertainment Centre, with three auditoria.
Seats: 493 (Theatr Elli).
TECHNICAL:
Stage: Proscenium, Flat; Pros. Opening 10.44m; Ht. of Pros. 4.60m; Depth of S/Line 9.40m; Stage Apron 2.42m max. depth. Ht. to Grid 6.10m; Grid comprises 7 lines of 127mm x 64mm steel channels at approx. 2.35 centres over full stage depth; Rear wall cyc. plastered and painted soft black, limited height of 3.91m; No Machinery; Prompt Cnr. P.S.
Lighting: Switchboard: Tempus M24. 120 channel, 155 memory in projection room rear of auditorium. Good selection of lanterns, etc. Details available from management.
Sound Equip: Philips SQ 4 100w mixer amp plus extra 5 channel mixer with interchangeable P.C. boards to allow various input arrangements. Treble and bass controls and master fader. Output 100v, 70v, 50v and 4 ohms. 2.36w column speakers in auditorium.
Dressing Rooms 4; Accom. 32.
Rehearsal Room at ground floor level 10.50 x 9.20m.
Get-in: Theatre and workshops are at first floor level. Access via scenery lift 5.20m long x 1.10m wide x 2.20m high from street level directly at stage right. Workshop door 2.51m wide x 3.00m high.

# Llangollen

### ROYAL INTERNATIONAL PAVILION
Abbey Road Llangollen Denbighshire LL20 8SW Wales
Tel 01978 860111 Fax 01978 860046
Spectacular venue which can seat 1,500, 4,500 in a semi-outdoor arena or 400 in a heated indoor hall.
Manager: Jeremy Miles

# Lochgelly, Fife

### LOCHGELLY CENTRE THEATRE
Bank Street, Lochgelly, Fife KY5 9RD Scotland
Tel 01592 418141 Fax 01592 418080
ADMINISTRATION:
Head of Centre: Verdi Herriot
Seats: 454 in two tiers + 6 wheelchair bays.
Foyer, exhibition space, Coffee Bar, Licensed Bar.
TECHNICAL:
Stage: Proscenium arch, width: 9.1m, height 5.1m. Wing space: 3.4m per side. Grid height: 8.3m.
Apron depth: 2.43m, width: 10.8m.
Lighting: Arri Impuls manual/memory board with effects DMX 512, Rank Strand M24 memory board (in tandem with Arri Impuls), 60 dimmers (all circuits 2kw, 15 amp outputs.) FOH bridge 10 circuits, cantata 11/26, T spots, 2 2kw follow spots. Further equipment available.
Sound: DDA Q series 24:8:2 mixer. Auditorium equalised by 2 x 31 band graphic equalisers, preset with use of spectrum analyser. Flown speaker system 2kw RMS (4kw peak). Revox B77, Denon CD, Denon cassette. Microphones, induction loop.
Dressing Rooms: 3, accom. 30. Showers, basins and toilets. Workshops

# Loughborough, Leics

Pop. 146,800. London 114 miles. Newspapers: Loughborough Echo (wkly); Loughborough News (free wkly); Herald & Trader (free wkly); Echo Extra (free wkly); Leicester Mercury (wkly). STD code 01509

### CHARNWOOD THEATRE
Town Hall, Market Place, Loughborough, Leicestershire LE11 3EB
Admin 01509 634774 BO 01509 231914
Fax 01509 634914
ADMINISTRATION:
Charnwood Borough Council.
General Manager: Ian Stephens
Policy: Mixed programme of professional, Youth and Community Productions, Concerts, Conferences and Exhibitions
528 seat raked auditorium (150 fixed circle, 286 bleacher, 92 flat). Victoria Room - 250 seat studio.
Four Bars. Coffee Bar/Restaurant. Full Catering facilities. Various meeting rooms. Exhibition areas. Rehearsal spaces. Theatre. Exhibition Area. Banquet area etc.
TECHNICAL:
Stage: Proscenium, flat. Pros. opening 7.3m, Pros. Ht. 4.3m, Depth of S/Line 6.24m, Total depth 8.2m, Onstage width 14.9m, Hydraulic apron stage width 9m, Depth 2m, Scene Dock and access upstage centre. Lowered apron forms auditorium floor or orchestra pit with understage access. Flys 16 bar CW fly platform located SL clearance underneath 4.6m, Grid ht. 10.7m, Cloth ht. 6.1m, Bar width 9.1m
Prompt Cnr. Full head set system and show relay and paging to dressing rooms.

Lighting: 48 way, Sirius board Control Room rear of circle. Plus 48 way 2 preset slave board D.S.L. 5 pre-plugged barrels all winched. FOH 10 x 1kw cct profiles, 10 x 1kw cct fresnels, 16 x 1kw par cans. Stage 24 x 1kw furse profiles, 6 x cct minuettes, 6 x 23's, 4 x 1kw par cans, 12 x cct coda floodlights.
Sound: 16 Channel Inkel Mixer; 2 x Revox B77's; Record deck; Cassette deck; 8 on stage mike inputs. 2 x 50w monitor wedges; various shore and AKG mikes and 4 Sennheiser Mke 80R 5 Shore 5m 58, Telex hand held of tie clip radio mike FMR 25. Various stand leads. Baby Grand and Upright pianos.
Dressing Rooms: 4, Orchestra Room Pit accom. 25.

## LOUGHBOROUGH TOWN HALL
Market Place, Loughborough, Leicestershire LE11 3EB
Mgt 01509 634776  BO 01509 231914
Fax 01509 634914
Catering & Room Hire 01509 634775
Theatre Programming & Marketing 01509 634913
Email: townhall@charnwoodbc.gov.uk
ADMINISTRATION:
Manager: Ian Stephens  Tel 01509 634774
528 capacity venue which features a varied programme including comedy, drama, musicals, classical music, rock and children's shows. Also restaurant, cafe and bars. Bookings terms are varied but include box office splits, guarantees and co-promoting. All the facilities are available for hire.

## LOUGHBOROUGH UNIVERSITY SIR ROBERT MARTIN THEATRE/STUDIO
Department of English & Drama Loughborough University, Ashby Road, Loughborough, Leicestershire LE11 3TU
Admin 01509 222870
Director of Drama: Dr. Michael Mangan
No booking enquiries by telephone
Disabled: Ramp to foyer doors, special toilet, flat run into stalls of theatre. Side entrance, one small step into Studio. Wheelchairs placed in floor row - front of bleachers in both performance spaces.
TECHNICAL DETAILS
Common to both Venues
Dressing Rooms: 2 (1 x 10, 2 x 6) each with wash-hand basins and w.c's. Mirror lights and ample power sockets. Crowd room and warm-up space available by prior arrangement.
Laundry: Automatic washer, tumble dryer, steam iron & ironing board. Wardrobe store and making wardrobe in adjoining building.
F.O.H.: Box Office and Cloakroom in foyer. 6 station House phone to both venues.
Carpentry: Scenery workshop (availalble for hire) Prop. making space, scene dock, production office.
Sound: Recording studio and control cubicle in adjoining building - drapes on tab track, acoustic screens.
Cubicle: Graphic equaliser, Technics C.D. and disc Players, double cassette deck, echo unit, Alessis special effects, jackfield, Revox B77, Teac 8 into 4 mixer, Teac 4 track deck. Disc & CD special effects library. Monitoring & talk-back facilities.
Plan & Calls: Stage, Ground, socket outlet, and Campus site plans and digs list available from S.M. Colour and STAFF CALLS by prior arrangement.
Publicity: 100 posters, 250 throwaways; press release & foyer photos.
SIR ROBERT MARTIN THEATRE:
Seating: 92 tip-up seats in 4-row balcony; 162 seats on 9 tier bleacher. (254) floor rows over orchestra pit if

necessary. (Max cap. 300)
Staging: Pros. Stage with ramp forestage. Often shows play over covered orchestra kit at front of bleachers, backed by neutral safety curtain (bottle green to go with walls). Forestage can be counter-ramped. Ramp stops 2' above stalls floor. Rostrum forestage can be provided to 24' x 12'. For thrust or in the round, bleachers come out to 3 or 7 tiers.
Stage: Pros. width 27'. Ht. to RSJ's: 18'. Clear (i.e. flying ht..: 15' 6"). Ht. to pros. border 12' 9". Depth (@ sides) 21'; centre 25'. Forestage 8'.
Wall to wall: 45'. curved rendered rear wall as Cyclorama.
Cross-over passage.
13 hemp sets + house tabs operated from S.L. fly floor.
Drape set: blacks including runners working corner D.S.L. Two ring intercom with show relay and cue-call to dressing rooms and talk-back cans to technical areas. Cue lights, house phone and CCTV from camera out front.
Lighting: Board: Strand Lightboard M: Permus dimmers: 102 ways - 96 x 2.5k; 6 x 5k (cyc).F.O.H.: 2 bridges - each with 18 circuits in two internally wired barrels. 2 internally wired booms with 12 circuits wired across from top to bottom. 6 way plug boxes @ top of wing towers. Bridge laterns - Cantatas, T-spots 264's. MFR's. Booms - Berkelys and 23's.
Stage: 12 way No. 1; 12 way No. 2; way No. 3. Cyc. batten & pit - 3 circuits each. Extra positions: Pros. booms, up and down high level bars (non internally wired).
Lanterns: Berkey 1K., JFR's with bardoors, 123's, 23's. 4 way plug boxes mid stage left & right - head height: 2 way plug boxes fly floor wired across.
Limes: 2 x 23N Mk. II on cans,
Sound: 8 x JBL bins, 2 x Voice of the Theatre bins, 1 x Altec bin. 14 x mike inputs (12 stage, 2 house). Stage monitor facility. In control room: Soundcraft Delta 16/2 desk, HH Mosfect Amplification, EQ, & Alesis special effects to 10 x speaker outlets. 2 x Revox decks and Penon cassette deck. control room monitors; talkback.
Music: Small orch pit (2' deep). Piano available (grand by prior arrangement and removal fee). Mains feed and cue light in pit.
STUDIO THEATRE
Seating: 100 on moveable bleachers (two sections). Uncomfortable tip-up seats extra in single row gallery. Bleachers most commonly set end to end.
Dimensions: 45' square (no stage). Gallery 3' wide runs around all four walls 9' above floor. Ht to LX bars 15' 6".
Control Room: Over entrance doors and vestibule.
Lighting: Board: AVAB 211 with 72 x 2k dimmers. 10 x 6 way internally wired bars accessible from bridges. 8 x dip circuits. 4 spares on dimmer rack.
Lanterns: mainly Starlettes and Minuette Zoom Profiles.
Sound: 1 ea. REVOX A77 & B77 Decks, Penon cassette deck, A + H 16/4/2 mixer, H & H stereo amp. 150w. per channel, EQ and Alesis special effects to 4 x JBL column speakers - (one in each corner). Mike sockets @ floor level below control room.
Music: Upright Piano available WITH PRIOR NOTICE.
Other Facilities: 3 camera colour T.V. system. Low-band U-matic V.T.R. and editing.
Stage Management: Spectrum Q-Comm talk-back cans are plugged up as necessary.
Get-Ins: A get-in road runs behind the studio up to the workshop dock doors. Will take any size of wagon. Wagons can be parked there, and left overnight if necessary.
Standard get-in time: 2 pm on day of perf. Refreshment: Off the theatre foyer is the Senior Common Room

serving tea, coffee, hot meals and sandwiches at lunch. Open 9 - 2.15: 2.45 - 4.00. It is usually booked as the theatre bar for performance.

# Lowestoft, Suffolk

Pop. 58,000. London 116 miles. Newspapers: Lowestoft Journal (fri); Eastern Daily Press. Freesheets: Waveney Advertiser (fri). STD code 01502

### MARINA THEATRE
The Marina, Lowestoft, Suffolk NR32 1HH
Admin 01502 523443 BO 01502 573318
SD 01502 569431
ADMINISTRATION:
Props: Waveney District Council
Theatre Manager: David Shepheard
Technical Manager: Darryl Franklin
Perfs: Variable
Seats: 751. Fixed and raked. Bars and cafe/teashop in theatre.
TECHNICAL:
Lighting: Switchboard: Compulite Ovation, 40 controller 386, 1000 mem, 96 circs.
4 pars 56, 10 Prelude 16/30, 6 Cant 11.26, 5 Prelude 28/40, 5 Cant 18.32, 8 X ADB F, 10 X CCT F, 6 X CCT PC, Theatre Fresnels, 18 Prelude F, 3 Cant F, 12 Prelude PC, 12 Coda 500/1, 4 Parblazer, 8 Iris 1, Barndoors.
Followspots: 2 Strand Solo 2k C/W 6 colour magazines.
F/S operated from rear sides of stage.
Cinema 35mm x 16m. Projection Equip: 1 Prevost Westar P 93, flown screen projection surface 7.88mm (wide) x 4.5m (height), manual draw tabs. 2 x elf 16mm projectors, mobile screens. Fully Dolby sound.
Sound Equip: Venue theatre 24-8-2. Effects SP x 900. FOH tannoy and EV SPCIS, ROH, tannoy 20 ass mikes. 2 cassette deck, Revox B77Hs, CD.
Control room at rear stalls. Talkback: 6 headsets/ outstations, FOH & ROH calls and show relay.
Other: 1 Grotrain Steinway Grand Piano, 1 Upright overstrung Knight Piano. Theatre operating and security staff available as required.

# Luton, Beds

Pop. 162,930. London 32 miles. Newspapers: The Luton News (wed); The Herald (thurs). STD code 01582

### THE LIBRARY THEATRE
St. Georges Square, Luton Beds LU1 2NG
Mgt 01582 547475 BO 01582 547474
ADMINISTRATION:
Props: Luton Borough Council
Theatre Manager: Doc Watson
Policy: Small Touring Companies. One Night Stands, Film Theatre, Recitals, Amateur Lessees.
Perfs: times variable.
Seats: 238. Bar and Coffee Bar.
TECHNICAL:
Stage: Proscenium, Flat: Pros. opening 7.62m; Ht. of Pros. 3.66m; Depth of S/Line 5m; W/Widths P.S. 2.44m; O.P. 1.22m; Prompt Cnr. P.S.
Lighting: Switchboard: In projection box, Sirius 48 board memory and manual. 8 Spots; 2 Battens; 1 Float; Dips 2 each side; 4 Spot Bars. 8 Fresnel, 8 Stage Spots.
Sound Equip: Record Player, CD player, Cassette deck, Revox Tape eck, 30w amp P.S.: Speakers either side of stage.

Dressing Rooms: 4; Accom.25.

# Mabelthorpe, Lincs

Pop. 6,340. London 149 miles. Newspapers: see Lincoln. STD code 01507

### DUNES THEATRE
Central Promenade, Mabelthorpe Lincs LN12 1RG
BO (TIC) 01507 472496 Fax 01507 478765
ADMINISTRATION:
Props: East Lindsey District Council
Hall Bookings: R Suich, 01507 601111;
Foreshore Manager: G K Brader
Policy: Summer Show
Seats: 350. Licensed Bar and Children's Bar.
TECHNICAL:
Stage: Proscenium, Raked; Pros. Opening 7.32m; Ht. of Pros. 3.66m; Depth of S/Line 2.08m; Ht. of Grid 3.74m; W/Widths P.S. 1.11m, O.P. 1.11m; Prompt Cnr. P.S.
Lighting: Zero 88XLS board, 24 circuits, operated backstage/front of house; F.O.H. Spots 14; 2 Battens; 6 Dimmers; 2 Spot Bars. 1 followspot operated from the rear of the theatre.
Sound Equip: 1 Amplifier, 2 Speakers, 5 Microphones.
Dressing Rooms: 4.

# Macclesfield

### MACCLESFIELD LEISURE CENTRE
Priory Lane, Upton Priory, Macclesfield,
Cheshire SK10 4AF
Tel 01625 615602 Fax 01625 434694
Manager: David McHendry
Policy: Multi-purpose Hall with stage facilities.
Seating/Capacity: Main Hall: 1,200; Small Hall: 300

# Maesteg

### TOWN HALL
Talbot Street, Maesteg, Mid Glamorgan
CF34 9DA Wales
Tel 01656 733269 Fax 01656 739546
Email: dbos340547@aol.com
Seating/Capacity: 650
Manager: Dave Bostock
Stage Manager: Mario Williams

# Maidstone, Kent

Pop. 130,000. London 37 miles. Newspapers: Kent Messenger (fri), KM Extra (wed). STD code 01622

### CORN EXCHANGE COMPLEX
Earl Street, Maidstone, Kent ME14 1PL
Admin 01622 753922 BO 01622 758611
SD 01622 756777 Fax 01622 602194
ADMINISTRATION:
Props: Maidstone Borough Council
Commercial Manager: Mandy Hare
Policy: For hire; all types of stage shows, pantomimes, films, guaranteed split, 1st call & % deals.
THE EXCHANGE

Seats: Up to 389, Bar, Coffee Lounge.
TECHNICAL:
Seating and stage flexible within hall, 10m x 27m. Floor
Canadian maple, suitable for all dance, no crossover,
area heated. Various 13A/15A independent circuits. Get-
in via Rose Yard. Tallescope.
Lighting: Sirus 24 Programmable, 36 circuits, operated
from balcony or floor - various lanterns - 1 followspot,
operated from balcony.
Sound: Soundcraft 16:4:2 desk operated from balcony -
various mics - 1 cassette deck. Acoustics suitable for
music and spoken word. 1 CD.
Backstage: 3 dressing rooms, Piano, upright. Advice
given on accommodation. Staff - 1 stage, 1 lighting -
casuals available - security personnel.

HAZLITT THEATRE
Seats: 353-381 Bar, Coffee Lounge.
TECHNICAL:
Stage: Proscenium arch. Performing area 6.4m x 3.23m;
No rake - pros. opening 6.23m x 3.93m. floor PVC
dance lino on wood, suitable for all dance, backstage
crossover, stage heated. Height of grid 9.13m; 25 Hemp
sets tab track, basic masking available in black, blue and
pink, blue canvas cyclorama, gold/blue house tabs
flown. Various 15A independent circuits. Orchestra pit
accommodates 28. Get-in via 1st floor auditorium or
back doors 2m x 3.93m. Tallescope. Safety curtain.
Lighting: Rank Strand LBX, plus single preset manual
board and FX board, 60 circuits, operated from rear of
auditorium, supply available for temporary board, various
lanterns, 2 followspots, operated from rear of
auditorium.
Sound: Allen & Heath,16:4:2 operated at rear of
auditorium, several mics, 1 cassette deck. Acoustics
suitable for music and spoken word, 1 CD, 1 Yamaha
SPX.
Stage Management: Prompt corner SL headphones, 4
outstations show relay/Tannoy to dressing rooms.
Backstage 5 dressing rooms, access by stage door, 2
pianos, 1 grand, 1 upright, advice given on
accommodation. Staff - 1 stage, 1 lighting, casuals
available, stage doorkeeper. Backstage facilities
accessible to disabled performers and staff.

## MAIDSTONE LEISURE CENTRE-MOTE HALL

Mote Park, Willow Way, Maidstone, Kent ME15 7RN
Mgt 01622 672443 BO 01622 761111
Fax 01622 672462
ADMINISTRATION:
Events Officer: Barry Reynolds
Policy: Full range of performing arts, musicals and
variety productions.
Auditorium: The Mote Hall
Seats: 1,200. Licensed Bar and Cafe.
TECHNICAL:
Multi-function hall. Stage fully demountable to maximum
size of 14m x 8m. Pros. arch created using Drapes. Full
front tabs and mid stage tabs. Rear cyc. screen. Power
available 3 x 200 amp, 1 x 150 amp.
Lighting: In-house lighting controlled by Strand M24. 60
x 10 amp circuits. Limited range of lamps. Followspot
available.
Sound: In-house sound Ramsa speaker, AHB 12
channel mixer; Selection of mics and stands.
Dressing Rooms: 2 large Artistes dressing rooms, one
with private toilet and wash, large amount of sports
changing available

# Malvern, Worcester

Pop. 31,000. London 119 miles. Newspapers: Malvern
Gazette (fri). STD code 01684

## MALVERN THEATRES

Grange Road, Malvern, Worcestershire WR14 3HB
Mgt 01684 569256 BO 01684 892277
Fax 01684 893300
ADMINISTRATION:
Props: Malvern Theatre Trust Ltd
Chief Executive: E. Nicholas Lloyd
Technical Manager: Stuart Davis
Policy: Plays, Variety, Ballet, Opera, Music, One
Nighters, Films, Pantomime, etc.
Perfs: 8.00pm, Mat. 2.30pm.
Seats: 880. Bars. Buffet, Coffee etc.

FESTIVAL THEATRE
Policy: No 1 Tours, per west end shows. Co-
productions, Variety, Opera, Dance, One Night Stands.
Seats 860 Cafe, Bar, Circle Bar etc.
TECHNICAL:
Stage: Proscenium, raked 1.24, pros opening 9.20m, Ht
of pros, 5.98m. Depth of s/line 7.85m, Ht of Grid
15.70m. 33 counterweight sets plus 2 up and down
stage sets. Max. flying Ht. 15.30m. flying bars 9.20 ext.
to 11.00m.
Lighting: Control: Arri Imagine 2 120 ways (Control
Room rear of auditorium). Dimmers: LD90s, various
profile and fresnel luminaires.
Sound: Soundcraft 6000, Tascam tape machines, Teac
CD and cassette machines. Operate from control room
or rear of stalls. Comprehensive tie lines and speaker
outlets to stage and F.O.H.  Good selection of mics and
speakers.
General: Communications: Intercom and telephones to
all key areas. Paging to F.O.H., Auditorium and
backstage. Dressing Rooms: 9 plus wardrobe,
bathrooms and showers. Orchestra pit: accommodates
20.

THE NEW SPACE
Policy: Concerts, Variety, Opera, Dance, Jazz,
Conferences, Exhibitions, Film.
Seats: Balcony - 217 seats, flat floor - 500sqm, or raked
seating and flat floor seating 640 seats. Cafe bar, circle
etc.
TECHNICAL:
Stage: Thrust, flat, modular type, size from 7.32m X 17m
to 9,76m X 17m. Stage can also be used in the round. A
truss type grid suspends over the whole stage area.
Lighting: ETC expression from control room, at side of
auditorium or operated from rear of auditorium. Assorted
Profile and Fresnel Lanterns.
Sound: Tascam 312B, Sherman speaker clusters
surround sound speakers with Dolby processer for
35mm film projection. Operated from control room or
rear of auditorium or projection room. Comprehensive
TIE lines and speaker outlets.
General: Communications: Intercom and telephone to all
key areas. Paging to F.O.H., auditorium and backstage
areas. Dressing Rooms: 5 plus band room.

THE CINEMA
Policy: First run films, 7 days a wek, day time
conferences, lectures, seminars.
Seats: 400 with balcony.
TECHNICAL:
Stage: Flat, size 7.95m X 3.08m.

Lighting: Srius 24 way desk - rear of circle. Assorted Profile and Fresnel Lanterns.
Sound: 312B, Tannoy speakers, surround sound speakers with Dolby procceor. Audio TIE lines and speaker outlets.
General: 35mm & 16mm projection with full Dolby stereo sound. Screen - 7.42m X 3.8m. Full satalite facilities with video projection. Full 35mm slide projection facilities.

# Manchester, Gtr. Manchester

Pop. 531,270. London 184 miles. Newspapers: Manchester Evening News (fri). Other regional papers monthly. STD code 0161

## THE BOARDWALK

Little Peter Street, Manchester M15 4PS
Tel 0161 228 3555 Fax 0161 237 1037
Email: colindsinclair@msn.com
Web Site: www.boardwalk.co.uk
ADMINISTRATION:
Prop: Colin Sinclair
Club Manager: Athena Caramitsos
Events Assistant: Lee Donnelly
Policy: Venue for Indie bands, up and coming major bands, local band showcases, available for hire to other promoters. Rehearsal rooms available.
Technical details on request.
Seating/Capacity: 440 standing.

## BRIDGEWATER HALL

Lower Mosley Street, Manchester M2 3WS
Tel 0161 950 0000 Fax 0161 950 0001
ADMINISTRATION:
Operated and managed: Hallogen Ltd
Chief Executive: Howard Raynor
Director of Sales and Marketing: Sue Vanden
Acting Director of Operations: Mike Cowley
Technical Manager: Chris Wright
Concert Administrator: Anne Richardson
Seats: 2,330 over four levels (24 wheelchair seats).

TECHNICAL:
Stage: Open concert platform, 19m wide at the front, tapering 12.3m at rear. Built in stage lifts, the first at 5.5m from front of stage with a total depth of 12.8m allow for total flexibility on the platform. Platform is 1m high from stalls floor.
Lighting: ADB Vision 10. 200 production circuits, full production lighting rig in addition to concert platform lighting. 2 x 2500w follow spots. Power source: 400a 3 phase + neutral Bus Bars, or 4 X 125a sockets, 3 phase + neutral, located stage left.
Sound: Full 32 channel speech and music reinforcement system. Cable traps and runs to most parts of the auditorium on all levels. Sennheiser infra-red hard of hearing system. Power sources: 100 amp single phase located stage right. Independent: various 15a & 13a non-dim circuits.
General: Rigging: ample fixed points above stage and/or in roof with equipment available for hire. Clearance above stage approximately 13m. Pyrotechnics and smoke effects by prior arrangement only. Production office with telephone available. Dressing Rooms: Four ensuite changing rooms on platform level to accommodate 25-30 each. Guest Conductor and five solo ensuite dressing rooms on first floor level. Lift access to all levels..

## CONTACT THEATRE

(Manchester Young People's Theatre Ltd.)
Oxford Road, Manchester M15 6JA
Mgt 0161 274 3434 BO 0161 274 4400
Fax 0161 273 6286
ADMINISTRATION:
Props: Contact Theatre Company
The Theatre is closed for rebuilding and is due to reopen in Autumn 1999. For further details and information contact Helen Jones.

## DANCEHOUSE THEATRE

10 Oxford Road, Manchester M1 5QA
Mgt/SD/Makting 0161 237 1413 BO 0161 237 9753
Fax 0161 237 1408
ADMINISTRATION:
Theatre Manager: Crispin Radcliffe
Box Office Manager: Matthew White
Seats: 433, raked, retractable and moveable.
TECHNICAL:
Stage: Performing area 13.7m wide + 2 side aisles 2m wide each x 12.55m depth. Backstage area 16m x 6m, 2.47m to rear balcony. No rake, floor sprung wood, suitable for all dance. Height to ceiling 6.3m at apex, sloping sides.
Lighting: Arri Mirage DMX 512 board, 125 channels, 48@2.5kw, 6@5kw, operated from control box by auditorium rear - 200A 3 phase supply available 20IT Profile 10 500w profile, 24 fresnels, 12 pars, 12 floods, 8 x Dance Booms.
Sound: Yamaha 16:4:2 desk, operated from audio-visual room next to LX control room - 2 x H&H amps - 2 x Bosc 802, 2 x Tannoy Speakers. 1 mic, 1 x Revox B77 reel-to-reel, 1 x Denon, PA system. Acoustics suitable for music and spoken word.
Backstage: Changing facilties in Green Room, accomodates 30; other rooms available. Wardrobe adjacent to Green Room, iron and board, washing machine and dryer, sewing machine.
Technics electric piano. Backstage facilties accessible to disabled performers and staff with difficulty. Help needed.

## FORUM THEATRE

Civic Centre, Leningrad Square, Wythenshawe, Manchester M22 5RT
Mgt 0161 935 4073 BO 0161 236 7110
SD 0161 935 4071
ADMINISTRATION:
Props: Manchester City Council (Arts and Leisure Committee)
Artistic Director: Christopher Honer
Production Manager: Michael Williams
General Manager: Adrian J P Morgan
Policy: Tours and repertory.
Perfs: 7.30p.m. Tues-Thurs; 8.00p.m. Fri-Sat (Forum)
Seats: 485. Two Bars, Coffee Bar, Licensed Restaurant.
TECHNICAL:
Stage: Proscenium, Flat; Pros. Opening 10.97m; Ht. of Pros. 5.79m; Depth of S/line 9.14m; Ht. of Grid 13.41m; 37 lines, C/W; Scenery Flying Ht. 6.10m; Flying bars 13.41m; W/Widths P.S. 3.66m, O.P. 7.32m; Prompt Cnr. P.S.
Lighting: Switchboard: Viking, rear of Audit; 160 ways; F.O.H. Profiles: 40 264's 1kw, 24 Sill 11/26's 1kw. Fresnels: 33 243's 1kw, 10 243's 2kw. Floods: 18 Starlette 1kw Asymetrical. Beam Lights: 10 Long-nose Par64 Assorted bulbs (CP60 CP62 CP61), 11 Patt 750's 1kw. Follow-spots: 2 CCT CID Sill 10.
Sound Equip: 3 Tape, 1 Record, rear of Auditorium;

Speakers 4 circuits F.O.H., 8 circuits stage.
Dressing Room 4; Accom. 24; 6 Bathrooms; Orchestra
Pit 12. Part of Wythenshawe Forum Complex.
Membership: TMA

## G-MEX CENTRE
Windmill Street, Manchester M2 3GX
Tel 0161 834 2700 Fax 0161 833 3168
General Manager: David Mallard
Seating/Capacity: 9,376

## THE GREEN ROOM
54/56 Whitworth Street West, Manchester M1 5WW
Mgt 0161 950 5777 BO 0161 950 5900
Fax 0161 950 9776
ADMINISTRATION:
General Manager: Garfield Allen
Technical Manager: Steve Curtis
Seats: 166
TECHNICAL:
Stage: Width 12m, depth 8m. Semi-sprung ply surface
skinned floor with hardboard. Old black Rosco dance
floor used as general work surface. Stage accessible
from either upstage left or upstage right and whole
performing space is on the same level.
Lighting: Control: Celco Aviator T180 control desk with
180 output channels scrolled accross 30x soft channel
faders. 1000 cue memories. 220 LX circuits to 96 twin
dimmer outlets, 8 x Celco 12 channel `Fusion` dimmer
racks supplying the patchbay (normally rated at 10 amps
per channel). Can be altered to 16, 25 or 32 amp on
request.
Grid: Main lighting grid is installed at 4.3m with side bars
at heights of 4m and 3.53m. 176 circuits above floor
level and 44 dip circuits.
Lanterns: 3 selecon 2k Arena 8" fresnels + barndoors;
18 x selecon 1.2k High performance PCs and
barndoors; 6 x selecon 1.2k high performance fresnels +
barndoors; 24 x selecon 650w Acclaim PCs +
barndoors; 8 x selecon 650w acclaim fresnels +
barndoors; 2 x selecon 1.2k zoomspot - medium (18-
34); 12 x selecon 1.2k condensor zoom - wide (28-52);
10 x selecon 650w acclaim condensor zoom - wide (24-
44); 8 x drop-in iris and rotatable gobo holders for 1.2k
profiles; 10 x drop-in iris and rotatble gobo holders for
650w profiles; 12 x selecon acclaim asymmetric cyc
floods (800w); 12 x ETC source 4 pars (575w= 1k
equivalent) + lens set (comprising variety of lenses.); 3 x
compulite whisper 10" scrollers for 2k lanterns (16
colours); 6 x compulite whisper 8" scrollers for 1.2k
lanterns (16 colours); 8 x chameleon 6" scrollers for
650w lanterns (10 colours.)
Sound: 1 x Soundcraft spirit live-4 mixing desk
(12/16:4:2), 1 x Allen & Heat GL2 rack-mounted mixing
desk (10/14:4:2), 1 x stage-box and multicore from USL
to sound-control room paralleled with lighting control
room. 6 x Nexo PS10 speakers + 3 controllers; 2 x Nexo
LS500 sub-bass speakers, 4 x Nexo flying frames, 2 x
Nexo tripod speaker stands, 3 x Crest CA6 amplifiers (for
PS10s), 1 x Crest CA9 amplifier (for bass). Variety of
system effects available inc. graphic equaliser.CD,DAT,
cassette, Revox, 8 X mics & stands.

## LIBRARY THEATRE
St. Peters Square, Manchester M2 5PD
Mgt 0161 234 1913 BO 0161 236 7110
Fax 0161 228 6481
ADMINISTRATION:
Props: Manchester City Council (Leisure Services

Committee);
Artistic Director: Christopher Honer
Production Manager: Michael Williams
General Manager: Adrian J P Morgan
Policy: Repertory & occasional touring
Perfs: 7.30p.m. Mon-Thurs, 8p.m. Fri & Sat. Occasional
Mats 3p.m.
Seats: 308. Coffee Bar open all day. Licensed Bar.
TECHNICAL:
Stage: Proscenium, Raked. Pros. opening 9.14m; Ht. of
Pros. 3.66m; Depth of S/Line 4.64m; Ht. of Grid 4.27m;
Modular Grid System.
Lighting: Ctrl AVAB Viking, 96 circuits (380 socket outlets
on patch fields). Compr. CCT, STK lanterns including
follow spots.
Sound Equip: Comprehensive sound system available up
to 4kw.
Dressing Rooms 5; Accom. 19; 2 Shower rooms, 1
male, 1 female. Situated in basement of Central Library -
difficult get-in.
Membership: TMA

## MANCHESTER ACADEMY
Oxford Road, Manchester M13 9PR
Admin/BO 0161 275 2930 Fax 0161 275 2936/80
Contact: Sean Morgan

## MANCHESTER APOLLO
Ardwick Green, Stockport Road, Manchester M12 6AP
Mgt 0161 273 6921 BO 0161 242 2560
SD 0161 273 2958 Fax 0161 273 3033
ADMINISTRATION:
Props: Apollo Leisure (UK) Ltd
Theatre Manager: Ian Coburn
Chief Technician: P Gates
For all booking information and further details please
contact Sam Shrouder or Nicky Monk at Apollo Leisure
(UK) Ltd., Grehan House, Garsington Road, Cowley,
Oxford OX4 5NQ. Tel: 01865 782900; Fax: Oxford
01865 782910.
Policy: International Concerts, Live Shows, Pantomime &
Cinema.
Seats: 2,641. Standing capacity: 3,500.
Licensed Bar and Catering
TECHNICAL:
Stage: Thrust, Raked; Pros. opening 14.02m; Ht. of
Pros. 7.62m; Depth of S/Line 1.83m; Ht. of Grid 19.81m;
19 lines, 5 C/W, 14 Hemp; Scenery Flying Ht. 19.81m;
Flying Bars 13.72m; W/Widths P.S. 8.53m, O.P. 8.53m;
Prompt Cnr. O.P.
Dressing Rooms 16; Accom. 19. No Orchestra Pit.

## MANCHESTER METROPOLITAN
## UNIVERSITY STUDENTS' UNION
Oxford Road, Manchester M1 7EL
Tel 0161 273 1162 Fax 0161 273 7237
Entertainments Manager: Tanya Ager
Capacity: 400 seated, 900 standing

## OPERA HOUSE
Quay Street, Manchester M3 3HP
Mgt 0161 834 1787 BO 0161 242 2525
SD 0161 834 1787 Group Bookings 0161 242 2578
Fax 0161 834 5243
ADMINISTRATION:
Props: Apollo Leisure (UK) Ltd.
Chairman: Paul Gregg
General Manager James Howarth

Deputy General Manager: Joe Waldron
Stage Manager: Sean Curran
Chief Electrician: Paul Binks
For all booking information and further details please
contact Sam Shrouder or Nicky Monk at Apollo Leisure
(UK) Ltd., Grehan House, Garsington Road, Cowley,
Oxford OX4 5NQ. Tel: 01865 782900; Fax: Oxford
01865 782910.
Policy: No.1 Touring Theatre presenting extended runs
of major musicals.
Seats: 2,000. Four Licensed Bars. Two Coffee Bars.
TECHNICAL:
Stage: Proscenium, Pros. Opening 11.24m. Ht. of pros.
7.6m. Stage depth, working 12.8m. ht. of Grid: 17.6m.
bar length 12.19m. 60 lines.
Lighting: Control: Eurolite 200 Way. Dimmers: 176 at
2kw, 24 at 5kw. Patch panel to Front of House
proscenium booms, circle front and gallery front.
Sound: Control: 60amp single phase clean feed
provided. Permanent mixing position at rear of stalls,
powered by 8 x 13 amp outlets fed from the above.
Orchestra Pit: 10.6m wide x 2.64m deep in the centre
and 2.13m deep at the ends. 3 stage lifts - Nos. 1 & 2
travel to 0.8m above stage and 2.54m below stage. No.
3 to 1.83m above and 1.22m below.
Communications: Controlled from stage manager's
portable desk, stage left. Ring intercom and cue light
stations serving all key technical working areas. Paging
to all dressing rooms, band room, workshop and office
areas.
Dressing Rooms: 45 positions plus Co. Managers office,
Band Room, Wig Room, Wardrobe.

## PALACE THEATRE

Oxford Street, Manchester M1 6FT
Mgt 0161 228 6255 BO 0161 242 2503
SD 0161 228 6255 Group Bookings 0161 242 2578
Publicity 0161 236 7671 Fax 0161 237 5746
ADMINISTRATION:
Props: Apollo Leisure (UK) Ltd
Chairman: Paul Gregg
Marketing Manager: Sue Hibbert
General Manager: Peter Evans
Deputy General Manager: Jennie Rainsford
Stage Manager: Chris Mckee
Chief Electrician: Mark Spall
For all booking information and further details please
contact Sam Shrouder or Nicky Monk at Apollo Leisure
(UK) Ltd., Grehan House, Garsington Road, Cowley,
Oxford OX4 5NQ. Tel: 01865 782900; Fax: Oxford
01865 782910.
Policy: No. 1 Touring Theatre (Opera, Musicals etc.)
Seats: 2,000. Seven licensed bars. Theatre pub 'The
Stage Door'.
TECHNICAL:
Stage: Proscenium, Pros. opening 12.95m; Ht. of Pros.
7.95m; Stage Depth, working 17.07m; Ht. of Grid
21.95m; Bar Length (downstage) 18.29m, (upstage)
17.07m, centred at 0.17m; 73 lines.
Lighting: Rank Strand Galaxy 3; Dimmers 300 capacity,
240 fitted. Lighting Equip: floats 6 x 6; 20 x RS808 8kw
profiles, 32 x RST84 1kw profiles. 12 x RS743 1kw
fresnels, 10 x Iris 4 cyc units 1kw, 8 x Pallas 4
groundrows 650w, 2 Pani 1200w HMI follow spots.
Sound: Bose 1800 dual channel distribution amp with
gain control; 250 watts RMS into 8 ohms, 400 watts
RMS into 4 ohms; 4 x Bose 802 speakers with equaliser;
9 x AKG C451 mics, 6 with rifles; 7 table or footlight
stands, 3 telescopic floor stands; all mic and
loudspeaker lines distributed from two XLR patch panel
inside sound control room at rear of stalls.

Communications: controlled from Stage Manager's
portable desk, stage right. Comprising 9 way cue light
system, twin ring intercom system, paging to dressing
rooms, office, annexe and F.O.H. control rooms. The
stage door can also page selectively if the SM is not
doing so.
Facilities are installed for television cameras and other
visual systems.
Dressing Rooms for 150 artistes; orchestra pit for 100
musicians.

## ROYAL EXCHANGE THEATRE

Royal Exchange Theatre, Royal Exchange Studio,
St.Ann's Square, Manchester M2 7DH
Management: 0161 833 9333 Fax: 0161 832 0881
Marketing: 0161 833 9938 BO: 0161 833 9833
Web Site: www.royalexchange.co.uk
ADMINISTRATION:
Funded by NWAB; Association of Greater Manchester
Authorities;
Local Authority: Manchester City Council
Artistic Directors: Braham Murray, Gregory Hersov
Associate Directors: Marianne Elliott, Matthew Lloyd,
Sophie Marshall, Wyllie Longmore, Chris Monks
General Manager: Patricia Weller
Deputy General Manager: Richard Morgan
Financial Controller: Valerie Hawkin
Marketing Director: Andy Ryans
Press and PR Officer: Shelagh McGouran
Production Manager: Clive Richards
Seats: 740 raked on three levels.
Catering facilities: Self Service Cafe-bar (open 10am-
curtain up). Public bar, 2 interval bars. Group catering for
pre-show refreshments on request. Function rooms for
hire accomodating up to 200. Foyer area - catering
facilities for up to 700.
Facilities for the disabled: Up to 8 wheelchair spaces -
sound re-inforcement system lift - level access - ramp at
entrance - assistance available, contact Theatre
Manager - braille programme - all house facilities fully
accessible.
TECHNICAL:
Stage: 'In the round'. Performing area 8.5 diameter. No
rake - floor wood block parquet, suitable for dance, lino
available. Height to underside of trusses 7.6m - 6
counterweight sets, single purchase - no tab track. 1 x
13A ring, 2 x S/W 13A sockets. 7 entrances to stage.
Get-in via 27 steps, St Ann's Square - 2 sets dock doors
1.3m x 2.35m, 1.7m x 2.1m. Tallescope. Scale stage
and lighting plans available, 1:25.
Lighting: Strand Galaxy c/w Theatre Playback board,
120 circuits, 100 @ 10A, 20 @ 20A, 3 phase, operated
from 2nd gallery of auditorium - 60A 3 phase supply
available for temporary board - 100 profiles, 40 parcans
80 fresnels, Strand/CCT - followspots operated from 2nd
gallery or lighting bridge.
Sound: Desk custom made Cadac with 40 modules,
each module can be configured to be an input, group or
output for optimum flexibility. The sound system
comprises of the desk with associated jackfield, amps
JBL, EV, ProAc speakers, ASC Dart and CD replay
machines. There are speaker and microphone tie-lines
around the theatre. Operated from 2nd gallery with LX
and SM controls. Acoustics suitable for music, and
spoken word English. Facilities for recording and editing.
Stage Management: Prompt corner 2nd gallery with LX
and Sound - 18 way cue lights - show relay/Tannoy to
dressing rooms.
Backstage: 4 single, 2 for four, 1 for six, 1 for seven
dressing rooms, access by stage door - green room -
band room - quick change room - wardrobe on 1st floor

with coin operated washing and drying machines. Tea, coffee, soft drinks, sandwiches etc available. Rehearsal room, piano. Advice given on accommodation. Staff - 10 stage, 3 sound, 6 wardrobe casuals available - security personnel.
Main piano - Steinway Model D concert grand.

## ROYAL NORTHERN COLLEGE OF MUSIC OPERA THEATRE

124 Oxford Road, Manchester Gtr Manchester M13 9RD
Admin 0161 273 6283 BO 0161 273 4504
Fax 0161 273 7611
ADMINISTRATION:
Props: Royal Northern College of Music
Production Manager: Matt English
Resident Stage Manager: Nick McCoy
Administrator: Phillip Jones
Policy: Productions of Opera and Drama. Available for hire by Opera and Ballet and Theatre Companies.
Perfs: 7.15 or 7.45
Seats: 626. Coffee Bar and Licensed Bar.
TECHNICAL:
Stage: Proscenium, Flat; Pros. opening 13.72m; Ht. of Pros. 6.10m; Depth of S/Line (Main stage) 8.53m; Ht. of Grid 15.54m; 33 lines C/W; 4 lines Hemp; Scenery Flying Ht. 7.32m Flying bars 17.07m; W/Widths P.S. 4.88m, O.P. 10.36m; Prompt Cnr. O.P. Rear Stage 12.19m wide, 6.40m high, 9.14m deep, 7 Hemp sets.
Lighting: Switchboard: Galaxy 180 ways; F.O.H. 40 circuits. Equipment list available on request.
Sound Equip: Dressing Rooms Relay and Calls only.
Dressing Rooms 6; Accom. 26; 4 Showers. Additional rooms available if required. Orchestra Pit 70.
Pit lift at higher level gives forestage 4.88m deep.
Ground plan and section available; 2 Follow Spots, piano, black masking.

# Mansfield, Notts

Pop. 97,000. London 173 miles. Newspapers: The Chad (thurs). STD code 01623

## MANSFIELD LEISURE CENTRE

Chesterfield Road South, Mansfield, Nottinghamshire NG19 7BQ
Mgt 01623 646082 SD 01623 646081
Fax 01623 651729
ADMINISTRATION:
Manager: Mike Darnell
Duty Officers: David Norcliffe, Shaun Hird
Policy: Multi-purpose Hall used for concerts, exhibitions, trade shows, sporting and special events.
Seating/Capacity: 1,100 seated; 1,500 standing.

## THE PALACE THEATRE

Leeming Street, Mansfield, Nottinghamshire NG18 1NG
Mgt 01623 412951 Fax 01623 412922
BO 01623 633133
ADMINISTRATION:
Props: Mansfield District Council
Cultural Services Manager: Andrew Tucker
Technical Manager: Dai Evans
Policy: Midscale Touring, Pantomime, Amateur, Dance, Ballets, Operatic, Orchestral, Workshops.
Perfs: As required.
Seats: 553/605. Foyer Bar, Coffee Lounge
TECHNICAL:

Stage: Proscenium, 8.5m wide by 5.5m high, stage depth; max. 10m, flat stage; scenery flying height 7m; 27 counterweight sets @ 500kg each; flying bars 10.5m, upstage to 14m downstage; height of grid 14m, wing widths P.S. 65m O.P. 6m (approx); SM control P.S. Full orchestra pit with lift; loading bay at rear of stage - level access.
Lighting: ETC. Express 250 + wired remote; 120 ways ETC. Smartrack dimming; 9 X 15A independent circuits. DMX network. 20 X Cantata F, 20 X Harmony F, 4 X Alto F, 4 X Quartet F, 10 X P.123, 10 x T84, 20 x Cantata 18/32, 12 X Cantata 26/44; 12 X Prelude 16/30; 6 X 'S' type battens, 1 Coda; 21 Par 64; Pani HMI 1200 F/Spots.
Sound: DDA CS3 32:4:3, CD Player, Mini Disc recorder/player,2 X cassette player: 2 FX units, graphic eq; Assorted microphones inc. SM58, Beta 58, Crown PCC 160. 4 Bose 802 for monitor use. F.O.H. speakers d&b full range; delay system above and below balcony. 4 AudioTechinca and 2 Trantec diversity misc.
General: 10 Dressing Rooms; 3 Showers (1 of which has access for disabled). Access for disabled to all areas.
Other Facilities: Rehearsal room, dance studio, function/conference room, bar and restaurant, computerised box office.

# Margate, Kent

Pop. 52,000. London 74 miles. Newspapers: Isle of Thanet Gazette (fri); Thanet Times (tues); Freepapers: Adscene (tues); Thanet Extra (thurs). STD code 01843

## QUEEN'S HALL

Fort Crescent, Margate, Kent CT9 1HX
Mgt 01843 296111 BO 01843 292795
Fax 01843 292795
ADMINISTRATION:
Props: Thanet D.C.
General Manager: Chris Wolfe
Policy: Summer Shows, Concerts, Conferences, Dances, Exhibitions, Film Show, Banquets.
Perfs: Vary.
Seats: 442. Bars, Buffets.
TECHNICAL:
Stage: Proscenium, Flat; Pros. opening 8.53m; Ht. of Pros. 3.35m; Depth of S/Line 2.13m; Ht. of Grid 3.66m; Prompt Corner P.S.
Lighting: Switchboard: Strand MX 24, 18 - X650 prelude, 6 x 1200W cantanas with colour changers. 1 x 1K C.I.D. follow spot, stage 2 x battens - codas.
Sound Equipment: 1 x 16-4-2 Soundcraft 200B, 4 x Martin wall speakers 6 x JBL 1 speakers, amps - Mxf's & 200s, monitors - available, radio mics - available.
Dressing Rooms 6; Accom. 12; Orchestra Pit 5.
Stage extension 1.22m permanent Run out 2.44m.

## THEATRE ROYAL

Addington Street, Margate, Kent CT9 1PW
Admin 01843 293878 BO 01843 293877
ADMINISTRATION:
The Theatre Royal has been bought by two preservation trusts and is available for hire/percentage deals. All enquiries should be addressed to Mr. M.E. Wheatley-Ward at the theatre.
S/cap 510
TECHNICAL:
All technical details contact: Richard Thomas, Stage Director.

**WINTER GARDENS**
Fort Crescent, Margate, Kent CT9 1HX
Mgt 01843 296111 BO 01843 292795
Fax 01843 292795
ADMINISTRATION:
Props: Thanet D.C.
General Manager: Chris Wolfe
Policy: Summer Shows, Concerts, Conferences,
Dances, Exhibitions, Film Shows, Banquets.
Perfs: Variable according to attraction
Seats: 1,414. Bars, Buffets.
TECHNICAL:
Stage: Proscenium; Flat, Pros. Opening 10.26m; Height
of Pros. 5.59m; Depth of S/Line 7.14m; Height of Grid
8.07m; 30 lines, Hemp; Scenery Flying Height 2.44m;
Flying Bars 10.97m; W/Widths P.S. 3.28m, O.P. 3.28m;
Prompt Corner P.S.
Lighting: Switchboard: Strand lightboard M 60 faders
and 24 submasters controlling 4 permus dimmers
(96x2.5kw).
FOH 24,650W Quartets. 6, 1200w Cantatas. Pros. Bar 6
1000WT64 Fixed Spots - 4 Way Sem. Units. 6
1000WT64 Fixed Spots - 4 Way Sem. Units. Spot Bar
12 Patt.23, 6 Patt.B243 Fresnels. 3 Battens. Dips 12, 2
ind. F/Spots. 2 Sillhouettes 1kw C.I.D. 2kw F.O.H.
Sound Equip: 1 Soundcraft 200B 24/4/2 Mixer.8
Speakers. Sound total, 600w/monitor total 6 speakers.
Radio Mics available.
Dressing Rooms 9; Accom. 40; 3 Showers; Orchestra
Pit 14.
Stage Extension 1.22m. Permanent. Tab track 6 plus top
tab.

# Melton Mowbray, Leics

Pop. 157,200. London 247 miles. Newspapers: Northern
Echo (dly); Evening Gazette (ntly). STD code 01642

**MELTON THEATRE**
Asfordby Road, Melton Mowbray,
Leicestershire LE13 0HJ
Mgt 01664 567431 BO 01664 569280
Fax 01664 410556
ADMINISTRATION:
Contact: Richard Smith (ext.127)
Bookings: Linda Hallam (ext.137)
Technical Manager: Paul Duval (ext.126/140)
Policy: Touring, Pantomime, Concerts, Films, Amateur
shows.
Seats: 337 raked with room for 4 wheelchairs. Bars and
refectory.
TECHNICAL:
Proscenium stage, flat; pros. opening 10.21 max. 6.96m
min; Ht. of pros. 4.16m; Depth S/Line 10.67m with
2.74m apron; stage width 13.23m; Ht. of grid 8.32m; 18
lines C/W; max Scenery Flying Ht. 6.40m; length of flying
bars 10.67m; W/Widths 2.7m- 2.06m P.S. and O.P.
Prompt Cnr. P.S.
Lighting Equipment: Strand 100 Channel GSX memory
control with Genius and Kaleidoscope software. DMX to
remote position on stage. Tempus 2G 72 Channel
manual wing. Stock of assorted luminares totaling 75. 1
x 2k follow spot.
Sound Equipment: Yamaha MR16:4:2 mixing console
with phantom power. 1 MTR SPA 400 stereo Power
Amplifier (200WPC) to carlsrbo 18 inch and horn speaker
cab left and right of pros., 1 TOA P75D stereo power
amp to TOA 18 inch and horn auditorium left and right
rear fills. Alessis MEQ 230 graphic x 2; 1 Revox B77 MKII
Reel to Reel, 1 GX 4000/DB Akai Reel to Reel, 1

Technics Stereo Twin Cassette, 1 Hitachi HT 20S
Record Deck. For B/S monitoring 1 RPA60 TOA Stereo
Power Amplifier (60 WPC), 2 x Carlsbro 50 watt monitor
wedges. Mics: 3 x AKG D190E/60, 3 x Stennheisser K30
(M.E. 80 heads), 3 x AKG C451 EV (with CK1S heads)
Various boom and mic stands.
S.R.E, Show relay system to 14 stations, S.R.E. Stage
Managers desk (O.P.) to 8 stations. T.I.S. headphone
communication system to 6 stations. Internal theatre
communication system to 11 stations. Induction loop
system. Musical Equipment: Baby Grand, Upright Piano.
Dressing Rooms: 7 with max accom. for 120. Showers.
Orchestra pit for 15/20. Music Suite.
Opened June 22nd 1976.

# Middlesbrough, Cleveland

**MIDDLESBROUGH THEATRE**
The Avenue, Linthorpe, Middlesbrough,
Cleveland TS5 6SA
Admin 01642 824490 Admin Fax 01642 818947
BO 01642 815181 BO Fax 01642 824487
ADMINISTRATION:
Props: Middlesbrough Borough Council
Acting Theatre Manager: Judith Croft
Stage Manager: Peter Stockwell
Policy: All types of events especially drama, dance,
classical and folk music, jazz, poetry. Full/split weeks,
single nights. Will premiere Childrens, producing house.
Perfs: Usually 7.30
Seats: 486. Licensed Bar and Coffee Bar above Foyer.
TECHNICAL:
Stage: Proscenium with optional forestage, Flat; Pros.
opening 7.92m; Ht. of Pros. 4.27m; Depth of S/Line
12.19m; Ht. of Grid 7.92m; 17 lines, Hemp; Scenery
Flying Ht. 3.05m; Flying Bars 9.14m; W/Widths P.S.
6.10m, O.P. 6.10m; Prompt Cnr. P.S.
Lighting: Switchboard: Strand GSX, with effects
package, 60. Racks 60 ways at 2kw, located in
Projection Suite at rear back circle. Patching to 100
circuits. All Spots moveable to suit particular
productions; 10 Patt.264, 8 Patt.23N, 9 Patt.23, 12
Patt.123, 27 Patt.743, 4 Patt.223, 12 Patt.60, 2
Patt.764; 10 x Patt.123; 12 par cans, 12 codas, 1
Patt.252, 20 circuits F.O.H.; Bar 1 12 circuits; Bar 2 12
circuits; Bar 3 6 circuits; Bar 4 6 circuits; Bar 5 8 circuits;
Dips P.S. 8 circuits; Dips O.P. 12 circuits. Booms P.S. 3
circuits; Booms O.P. 3 circuits.
Sound Equip: Allen & Heath SC + series 16-4-2; mixing
desk; 2 x Mustang 100w into 100v line amps, Revox
B77 (7.5 + 3.75 IPS) JVC twin cassette deck, 3 Amcron
plate mics, various microphones; 1 x Technics D D
Turntable.
Dressing Rooms: 5; Accom.72; 2 Showers; Orchestra
Pit; Approx 20.

**TOWN HALL CRYPT, MIDDLESBROUGH**
Dances, Exhibitions, Concerts.
Capacity: 450 seated; 600 standing

**TOWN HALL, MIDDLESBROUGH**
PO Box 69 Middlesbrough, Cleveland TS1 1EL
Tel 01642 263848 Fax 01642 221866
ADMINISTRATION:
Theatre Manager: Jean Hewitt

Arts/Events Officer: Judith Croft
Capacity: 1,190 seated; 1,350 standing.
All types of events, especially classical and popular
music, rock, jazz, comedy, variety, craft fairs and
exhibitions, conferences.

# Milford Haven, Pembrokeshire

Pop. 13,960. London 250 miles. STD code 01646

## THE TORCH THEATRE

St. Peters Road, Milford Haven,
Pembrokeshire SA73 2BU Wales
Mgt 01646 694192 BO 01646 695267
Fax 01646 698919
ADMINISTRATION:
Artistic Director: Peter Doran
Finance Director: Roland Williams
Technical Manager: David Thomas
Publicity and Marketing Manager: Lesley Jones
Policy: Mixed programme theatre with in house repertory
company 3/4 times a year. Also visiting companies,
opera, dance, music, children's shows, choirs, variety,
films, exhibitions.
Perfs: Vary. Mon -Sun 7.30 pm.
Seats: 297. Bar
TECHNICAL:
Stage: Proscenium, Flat; Pros. Opening 11m; Ht. 5.6m;
Depth of S/Line 9m; Ht. of Grid 14m; 9 C/W lines: 10
hemp lines; Flying Ht. 13.5m; Length Flying Bars 13m; 2
L/X Winches; W/Widths 3-4m; apron Thrust/Pit 1.9m.
Lighting: Gemini 80 CCT; 30 T-Spot, 4 Sil 25's, 20
ADB's 1kw, 12 743's, 4 243's, 10 Par Cans. 1 35mm
Projectors with Tower System. 1 16mm projector.
Sound: Spirit live 4 mixer 24 - 4 - 2, Revox A77, Revox
B77, 6 Toa Radio Mics, 1 SPX990, 1 Denon Cassette
Player, 1 Denon CD Player. All stage boxes 3 pin XCR
Mic Line Speakers all Speakon plugs.
Dressing Rooms: 3 to accommodate 16; 3 Showers;
Orchestra Pit 12-15. Films: The theatre is fully equipped
for all types of 35mm presentations.
Membership: TMA

# Milton Keynes, Buckinghamshire

Pop. 185,000. London 55 miles. Newspapers: Milton
Keynes Herald; Milton Keynes Citizen; Chronicle and
Echo. STD code 01908

## BLETCHLEY LEISURE CENTRE

Princes Way, Bletchley, Milton Keynes,
Buckinghamshire MK2 2HQ
Tel 01908 377251 Fax: 01908 374094
Manager: Michael Robertson
Seating Capacity: 1,400

## JENNIE LEE THEATRE

Bletchley Leisure Centre, Princes Way, Bletchley,
Milton Keynes Buckinghamshire MK2 2HQ
Mgt 01908 377251  Fax 01908 374094
ADMINISTRATION:
Props: Borough of Milton Keynes
Manager: Michael Robertson
Policy: One Night Stands: childrens  films/sports films.

childrens theatre. Lectures.
Perfs: Variable.  No promotions, hirings only.
Seats: 120. Bars and cafeteria.
TECHNICAL:
Stage: Traditional, flat; Pros. opening 7.31m; depth of
S/Line 5.49m.
Lighting: Switchboard: 2 present, Electrosonic, 30 ways.
Spots: 12 Patt.23, 12 Patt.123k, 6 60's.
Sound Equip: Electrosonic tape and deck, movable
speaker system. 16mrn optical projector Fumeo.
Dressing Rooms 1; Accom. 12; Showers.

## THE NATIONAL BOWL

Watling Street Milton Keynes
Tel 01908 691691
ADMINISTRATION:
Contact: Helen Smith 01908 252443
Milton Keynes Council, Civic Offices, Saxon Gate East,
Milton Keynes MK9 3HG
Policy: Venue for major concerts.
Car parking for 12,000 cars.
1000 KVA power available.
Booking on a daily or weekly basis.
Capacity: 65,000.

## STANTONBURY CAMPUS THEATRE

Stantonbury Campus Purbeck, Stantonbury,
Milton Keynes Bucks MK14 6BN
Mgt 01908 224234
ADMINISTRATION:
Props: Stantonbury Campus
Theatre Director: Roy Nevitt
Technical Manager: Jason Greenaway
Professional theatre, dance, opera, classical and other
music, community theatre, pantomime, folk/popular
concerts, youth theatre, brass bands, children's theatre,
exhibitions/conferences.
Perfs.  To suit each performance.
Seats 200/450 Bar and buffet facilities.
NB.  Box Office facilities are not available at the Theatre.
Available however, from Stantonbury Campus Leisure
Centre on Milton Keynes 314466 and Milton Keynes Box
Office on Milton Keynes 234466.
TECHNICAL:
Stage: Round, Thrust or Proscenium, Flat (Audience
Raked); Pros.  opening 7.32m max; Ht of Pros Tab Track
24.38m.  Depth of S/Line 79.75m - 10.97m.  W/Widths
P.S. 2.44m; Prompt Cnr. Mobile.
Lighting: Arri mirage 125 with 72 ways of dimming, 10
spots, 34 fresnels, 1CCT follow spot (from rear), 6 x 3
way coda floods, 12 CP62 Parcans.
Sound: 16:4:2 Yamaha MX400 mixer operated from rear
CD/Tape/Revox/microphones. Switchboard control
room back of auditorium.
Dressing rooms 4, accom 20, orchestra pit 18 max.

# Mold, Flintshire

Pop. 8,180. London 191 miles. STD code 01352

## CLWYD THEATR CLMRU

Civic Centre, Mold, Clwyd CH7 1YA Wales
Mgt 01352 756331 BO 01352 755114
Fax 01352 758323
Email: drama@celtic.co.uk
Web Site: www.theatre-clwyd.co.uk
ADMINISTRATION:
Props: Flintshire County Council

Director: Terry Hands
Company Stage Manager: Andrew Gordon
Policy: A mixed programme theatre, built around a professional company performing at Theatr Clwyd and on tour around major Welsh theatres and through Britain - opera, concerts, dance, youth & schools drama and music, films.
Theatr Clwyd has four auditoria: Anthony Hopkins Theatre, Emlyn William Theatre, Film Theatre, Clwyd Room.
Perfs: Vary; Generally Drama 7.30; Films 7.45; Concerts 8.00.
Seating: Anthony Hopkins Theatre 580; Studio Theatre 300 max;
Clwyd Room 300 max; Film Theatre 129; Bars & Restaurant.
TECHNICAL:
Stage (Anthony Hopkins Theatre): Proscenium Stage with or without apron or endstage, Flat; Pros. opening 10.65m; Ht. of Pros. variable 5.20m - 6.50m; Depth of S/Line 11.00m; Stage to Grid 18.48m; 59 lines, single purchase C/W; Flying Bars 13m with 3m extensions; W/Widths P.S. 5m, O.P. 11m; Prompt Cnr. P.S. or Control Box rear auditorium.
Lighting: Switchboard: Rank Strand Galaxy (Control Room at rear of auditorium); 192 ways; Lighting Equip: 15 Patt.23, 6 Patt.123, 34 Patt.743, 10 Patt.243, 8 'T' Spot 64, 4 Patt.774, 2 Patt.793, 30 CCT Sil 30, 12 Patt.49, 6 Patt.60, 6 S/64 Batten, 2 S/34 Batten, 5 Iris 4, 16 Thomas P.A.R. Cans and others.
Sound Equip: Yamaha O2R mixer, Meyer speakers, 1 Samplers, hard disk recorders, Cassette Player, CD, DAT. Comprehensive microphone, tie line and speaker sockets throughout stage & F.O.H.; Good selection of mikes and speakers.
Stage (Emlyn Williams Theatre): An extremely variable space, with five main seating variations (End stage, L shape, Taverse, Thrust, Round). Stage area will be dependent on seating configuration, minimum stage area 5m x 7m, maximum stage area 7m x 16m. Good access for Lighting Rigs via gantry and catwalk system, max. height under catwalk 6.050m, tracking for cyclorama and black drapes (end stage only) Various hard masking.
Lighting: Switchboard: Rank Strand 530 (Control Room); 124 ways. Lighting Equip: 16 Patt.23, 10 Patt.123, 12 Patt.743, 12 'T' Spot 54, 6 Patt.264W, 4 Patt.264, 12 Patt.263W, 4 Patt.263, 6 Patt.263F, 12 Rochette. P.A.R Cans and others.
Sound Equip: Yamaha O2R mixer. Sampler and hard disk recorders. Cassette, CD, Microphone and speaker sockets throughout theatre. Mics and speakers shared with main house.
Dressing Rooms: Main Theatre 8 to accom. 40, Emlyn Williams Theatre (Studio) 4 to accom. 16. Showers in all dressing rooms plus bathroom.
Full Orchestra Pit with Band Rooms & Conductor's Room with Shower.
Films: The Film Theatre is fully equipped for widescreen presentations on 35mm and 16mm to BFI specifications.
There is a very large Exhibition Concourse.
Membership: TMA

# Motherwell

Pop. 149,000. London 379 miles. Newspapers: Motherwell Times; Wishaw Press. STD code 01698

## MOTHERWELL CONCERT HALL

Civic Centre, Motherwell, Lanarkshire
ML1 1TW Scotland
Admin/BO 01698 267515  Fax 01698 268806
ADMINISTRATION:
Director of Leisure Services: Norman Turner
Head of Cultural Services: Ann Malloy
Theatre Manager: Alastair Bayne
Technical Manager: Stewart Archibald
Seats: 1,008; Tiered: 883
Standing: 1,800
TECHNICAL:
Stage: Proscenium. Pros. opening 15.09m; Ht. of Pros. 4.95m; Depth of S/Line 7.92m; Ht. of Grid 5.99m; 20 lines; W/Widths P.S. 2.90m, O.P. 2.90m; Prompt Cnr. P.S.
Lighting: - Strand Gemini 2.71 2kw circuits - full range of lanterns, smoke, strobe and dry ice.
Sound Equip: 16 channel, mixing desk - full range of microphones including radio mics.
Dressing rooms - 8 Theatre/concert hall)

## MOTHERWELL THEATRE

Civic Centre, Motherwell, Lanarkshire ML1 1TW
Admin/BO 01698 267515  Fax 01698 268806
ADMINISTRATION:
Director of Leisure Services: Norman Turner
Head of Cultural Services: Ann Malloy
Theatre Manager: Alastair Bayne
Technical Manager: Stewart Archibald
Seats: 395
TECHNICAL:
Lighting:strand Gemini 96 2Kw circuits - fulll range of lanterns.  Smoke, strobe and dry ice.
Sound Equipment: Channel Soundcraft, Venue II - full range of microphones including radio mics.
Dressing rooms: Theatre/Concert Hall - 8.

# Mull, Isle of, Argyll

Pop. 3,500. Newspapers: An Muileach, Rounc & About, Oban Times, Oban Star. STD code 01688 400

## THE MULL THEATRE (TAIGH-CLUICHE MHUILE)

Dervaig, Tobermory, Isle of Mull Argyll
PA75 6QW Scotland
Admin/Fax 01688 400 267
Email: mulltheatr@aol.com
ADMINISTRATION:
Artistic Director: Alasdair McCrone
Chairman: Gillian King
Policy: Repertory and Touring
Perfs: April-Sept, 7 nights, 8.30pm, Occasional Matinees 4.15pm.
Seats: 43. Adjoining Buffet.
TECHNICAL:
Stage: Removeable Proscenium Stage, Flat; Pros. Opening 3.05m; Ht. of Pros. 2.74m; Depth of S/Line 1.83m; W/Widths P.S. 0.30m, Hearing Loop Installed.
Lighting: Switchboard: Junior Eight; F.O.H. Spots 5 Patt.45; 3 Battens; 3 Spot Bars Patt.45.
Sound Equip: Four Tape Recorders, 6 input, 4 output mixer, 10-way Speaker switch box and 13 speakers.
Dressing Rooms 2.
Membership: TMA

# Musselburgh

Pop. 17,249. London 369 miles. Newspapers: Musselburgh News, East Lothian News, East Lothian Courier (fri). STD code 0131

## BRUNTON THEATRE

Bridge Street, Musselburgh, Midlothian
EH21 6AA Scotland
Admin 0131 665 9900 BO 0131 665 2240
Fax 0131 665 7495
ADMINISTRATION:
Props: Brunton Theatre Trust
Chairman of Brunton Theatre Trust: Councillor T Ferguson
Director of Education & Community Services: Alan Blackie
Artistic Director: David Mark Thomson
General Manager: Lesley Smith
Policy: Seasonal Repertory. Also available for letting to Touring Companies for plays, opera, dance, concerts, variety, films, lectures etc.
Perfs: 7.30; matinees 10a.m., 2.30p.m.
Seats: 312. Exhibition area. Bar and Buffet facilities.
TECHNICAL:
Stage: Octagonal/Thrust, Flat; Pros. opening 10.2m; Ht. of Pros. 4.62m; Ht. of grid 5.63m; Depth of S/Line 6.40m; wrape around cyc.; induction loop.
Lighting: Switchboard: Rank Strand SP40/2 and R.S. Memory Board M24 + Duet; 40 ways; 12 harmony profiles, 10 263 (fresnel lens), 4 263 (P.C. lens), 4 23, 16 743, 8 Harmony fresnel, 4 min. fresnel, 2 min. profile, 2 coda 4 500w battens (4 comp. 2 circuit), 6 cada 1 500w flood, 5 stype battens (8 comp. 4 circuit), 4 500w floods.
Sound: Talkback: Bantam Headsets - various outlets. 16/4/2 Soundcraft Series 200B Mixing Console; 4 Tannoy Pumas F.O.H.; 2 Tannoy Pumas (moveable); 4 C Audio SR202 Amplifiers; 3 Yamaha Q2031 A Graphic Equalisers; 1 Revox B77 Tape Recorder, 1 Kenwood KX54 Cassette Recorder; 36 mic lines (12 Pit, 6 USC, 6 PSL, 6 DSR, 6 Catwalk). Technics SLP 777 CD Player; Revox B77 Mark II; Tape Deck Kenwood KX 54; BBC collection sound effects on compact disc; 3 AKG 451 microphones.

# Neath Port Talbot

## AFAN LIDO

Aberavon Seafront, Port Talbot SA12 6QN Wales
Tel 01639 871444 Fax 01639 893203
Seating/Capacity: 2,400 (700 raked, 1,800 retractable)
Manager: Paul Walker

## GWYN HALL

6 Orchard Street, Neath West Glamorgan SA11 1DU
For Hall Bookings contact: Angie Dickinson
on 01639 635013
Seating/Capacity: 731 (Main Hall)
Art Gallery/Museum

# New Brighton, Merseyside

Pop. 70,000. London 199 miles. Newspapers: Liverpool Echo (ntly); Daily Post (dly). STD code 0151

## FLORAL PAVILION THEATRE

Virginia Road, Wirral, Merseyside L45 2LH
Admin 0151 639 1794 BO 0151 639 4360
Fax 0151 692 2459
ADMINISTRATION:
Props: Wirral Borough Council
General Manager: Paul Holliday
Policy: Bands, One Night Concerts, Pantomime, Various Amateur Productions.
Perfs: Variable.
Seats: 972. Bar and Buffet.
TECHNICAL:
Stage: Proscenium stage flat; Pros. Opening 8.5m; Ht. of Pros. 3.66m; Depth of Stage 6.40m; Ht. of Grid 4.88m 14 lines; W/Widths P.S. 6.10m.
Lighting: Switchboard: Strand Sirrius 30 way. 10 T-spots, 4 Harmony, 8 Parcans, 2 Patt 123; 6 Harmony, 2 Iris, 4 Patt 137, 8 Fresnel, 8 Patt 123.
Sound: Allen & Heath 24 channel GL3 mixer, 2-4 monitor lines, Digital Effects unit, Tape Deck.
General: Dressing Rooms 7; Showers 3; Orchestra Pit (Capacity) 16.

# New Galloway

## TOWN HALL

High Street, New Galloway, Dumfries & Galloway, Scotland
Tel 01557 330291 Fax 01557 330005
For Hall Bookings contact: Mrs McQueen, Hallkeeper, on 01644 420204
Seating/Capacity: 153.

# Newark, Notts

Pop. 24,646. London 125 miles. Newspapers: Newark Advertiser and Herald; Nottingham Evening Post (ntly); Lincolnshire Echo. STD code 01636

## PALACE THEATRE

Appleton Gate, Newark, Nottinghamshire NG24 1JY
Mgt 01636 671636 BO 01636 671156
Fax 01636 701402
ADMINISTRATION:
Props: Jointly administered by Newark & Sherwood District Council/Newark Town Council.
Acting Theatre Director: David Piper
Acting Stage Manager: Mark Noutch
Policy: Mixed programme of Professional and Amateur Productions of Plays, Musicals, Concerts and Films.
Seats: 607. Licensed Bar, Coffee Bar, Room hire and rehearsal facilities.
TECHNICAL:
Stage: Proscenium. Flat; Pros. opening 8.47m; Ht. of Pros. 6.68m; Depth of S/Line 9.34m; HT. of Grid 13m; 18 lines, C/W Hemp; Scenery Flying Ht. 12m; Flying Bars 10m; W/Widths P.S. 4.98m, O.P. 3.70m; Prompt Cnr. O.P.
Lighting: Control: Strand Lightboard M 60 ways rear of Circle - Remote Riggers Control. Various Lanterns.
Sound: Control: Soundcraft 16-4-2 mixer, 2 Pair Bose 802's, 1 x 900w HH Amplifier, 1 x 600w HH Amplifier, 2 Pairs Bose 802 Speakers.
Dressing Rooms 6; Accom. 45; Showers 1 male, 1 female, Orchestra Pit 20. Provides apron stage, when not in use 3m x 8m.

# Newbury, Berkshire

London 56 miles. Newspapers: Newbury Weekly News
(thurs); Newbury & Thateham Chronicle (fri). STD code
01635

## THE CORN EXCHANGE
Market Place, Newbury, Berkshire RG14 5BD
Admin/Marketing 01635 582666 BO 01635 522733
Fax 01635 582223
ADMINISTRATION:
General Manager: Jane Morgan
Policy: Mixed programme of performing arts, visual art,
film and conferences.  Operates 7 days a week, all year.
Performances: Evenings, 19.45; Matinees, variable.
Seats: 424; retractable, raked seating, variable
stage/seating layouts.  Also a meeting room; 65 seats,
theatre-style; variable layouts.  Public Cafe/Bar in main
foyer, open all day.  Private catering available.
TECHNICAL:
Stage: variable size, beech veneered blocks to a
maximum of 80 sq.m.  If Pros. arch format used, stage
area 14m x 6m.  Pros opening 9.5m x 6.5m; wings SR
3.2m, SL 3m.  No rake.  Stage height variable up to 1m.
Dance lino and reversible lino, black/grey available.
Height to grid from floor, 9.2m, 7 winches, SWL 300 kg,
7 hemp lines, SWL 150 kg, 1 tab track, 3 pairs black
borders, 3 pairs black legs, 1 house tab and track,
manually drawn, white cyclorama, 15m x 7m;
Lighting: Strand LBX Board, 24 sub masters, 200
memories; 120 HDS dimming system, 108 x 3kw, 12 x 5
kw operated from FOH Control Room/Auditorium. 50
profile spots; 40 fresnels, 28 pars; 4 x 4 compartment
top lighting units; 8 x 1 compartment top lighting units.
Sound: Soundcraft Delta 200 Deluxe, 16 x 4 x 2 mixing
desk operated from Control room/Auditorium.  6 x JBL
speakers, Revox reel to reel; Tascam cassette tape
machines; Denon CD player.  Techpro 2 channel
intercom system.  Paging show relay system to FOH &
backstage. Paging from Box Office & SM desk.
Induction loop system. Additional Sound: Assortment of
AKG and Shure microphones
Dressing rooms: 4, accommodates 20 people; showers
in all rooms; Band room.
Other: 35mm film projection system.
Steinway D Concert Grand Piano.
Membership: TMA

## WATERMILL THEATRE
Bagnor, Newbury, Berkshire RG20 8AE
Mgt 01635 45834 BO 01635 46044 SD 01635 44532
Restaurant 01635 47025 Fax 01635 523726
ADMINISTRATION:
Artistic/Executive Director: Jill Fraser
Production Manager: Laurence T. Doyle
Policy: February to January
Perfs: 7.30 Mon-Sat,Thur & Sat 2.30 matinees.
Seats: 216
Bar and Restaurant open until 11.30
TECHNICAL:
Stage: Proscenium/Thrust, Flat; Pros. opening 4.88m;
Ht. of Pros. 4.88m; Depth of S/Line 3.96m; Ht. of Grid
8.53m; Scenery Flying Ht. 3.66m; Flying Bars 4.88m;
W/Widths P.S. 1.83m, O.P. 1.83m; Prompt Cnr. back of
auditorium.
Lighting: Switchboard: At the rear of Auditorium central;
Tempus M-24 Memory Lighting Board with optional FX
panel. Spot Bars 8; Various Lanterns.
Sound Equip: Variable as needed.
Dressing Rooms 3; Accom. 10 persons.

Actors live in theatre houses whilst rehearsing and
performing.
Membership: TMA

# Newcastle Upon Tyne, Tyne and Wear

Pop. 217,220. London 274 miles. Newspapers: Evening
Chronicle (ntly); The Journal (dly). STD code 0191

## CITY HALL
Northumberland Road, Newcastle upon Tyne NE1 8SF
Tel 0191 261 2606 SD 0191 232 3937
Manager: Peter Brennan  Private Line 0191 222 1778
Seating/Capacity: 2,133

## NEWCASTLE PLAYHOUSE AND GULBENKIAN STUDIO THEATRE
Barras Bridge, Newcastle upon Tyne
Tyne & Wear NE1 7RH
Admin 0191232 3366 BO 0191 230 5151
Fax 0191 261 8093
ADMINISTRATION:
Executive Director & Co Sec: Mandy Stewart
Artistic Director: Alan Lyddiard
Policy: Both auditorium and foyer are available for
concerts with six months each year being devoted to
festivals, touring theatre, dance and comedy. Both
spaces are also used for presentation events, exhibitions
and conferences.
Seats: Playhouse auditorium 512 seats. Foyer capacity
200 persons. Full bar and catering facilities. Gulbenkian
Studio 160 seats, 5 raked rows. Small coffee bar,
licensed bar.
TECHNICAL:
Stage: Flat sprung blockboard/matt black. Width
between edge walls 12.65m. Height to first lighting
bridge 6.7m. Height to grid 12.37m. Total depth 11.25m.
Dock door X 11.215 onto stage left 5.79m x 2.13m. 18
counterweight flying bars. Maximum flying height 11.6m.
Length of flying bars 18m.
Lighting: ETC Insight 2 at rear of auditorium (324
Channels with X, Y wheels) 150 dimmers (DMX 512 &
Strand D54 compatible) inc. 6 x 5kw dimmers 6 x
independent circuits around the stage. House lights are
dimmable on LX board.
Lanterns of various types which can be rigged anywhere
on the 4 FoH bridges or on stage.
Sound: Soundspirit 40:8:2, TAC Scorpion 24:8:2 Mixing
Desk. 5 x Yamaha GEQ 1031B, 1 x Klark tecknics
DN3602 x Yamaha SPX90II, 1 x Klark Teckniks DN716,
1 x Sabine FBX900, 1 x Yamaha Rev 7, Cassette deck,
revox. Speakers: 2 x Sherman CA3 1600w full-range bi-
amped speaker, 4 x TOA Bass Bins, 300w Bass
speaker, 6 x Martin CX2 300w full range speaker, 8 x
TOA 38SD 360w full range speaker, 14 Proac Tablet
80w full range speaker. Mics, comms.
Power: Located stage right 3 phase, 100A per phase,
busbar box 3 phase 32A cee-form outlet single phase
32A cee-form outlet.
Other: Dressing Rooms: 1 Large male dressing room for
16, 1 large female dressing room for 8, 2 small dressing
rooms for three.

Gulbenkian Studio Theatre:
Lighting: Arri Imagine2, 64 dimmable circuits (Strand
JTM, STM, ACT 6) 2kw, 132 x 15 amp sockets
distributed over the grid plus 8 on-stage dips, returning

to 15 amp patch panels. 14 x Strand Patt 223/743, 4 x Strand Patt 243, 10 x Strand Harmony F, 6 x Strand Patt 123, 2 x CCT Minuette, 12 x CCT Silhouette, 30 8 x Prelude, 16/30, 4 x Prelude 28/40, 4 x Patt 23's, 6 x Thomas Parcans, 5 x strand CODA 500/3.
Sound: Soundcraft 400B 12:4:2 Mixing desk.

## PEOPLE'S THEATRE
Stephenson Road, Newcastle upon Tyne,
Tyne & Wear NE6 5QF
BO 0191 265 5020 Greenroom 0191 265 5191
ADMINISTRATION:
Props. & Lessees: Peoples Theatre Arts Group Ltd.
Honorary Secretary: T Childs
Policy: Repertory, Arts Centre, Amateur.
Perfs: Evenings 7.30
Seats: Variable up to 550, Studio 90. Two Bars.
TECHNICAL:
Stage: Proscenium, Flat; Pros. Opening 10.36m; Ht. of Pros. 4.27m - 6.10m; Depth of S/Line 10.36m + 4.60m thrust forestage; Ht. of Grid 10.67m; 10 lines, Hemp; Scenery Flying Ht. 4.87m; Flying Bars 9.14m; W/Widths P.S. 5.49m, P.O. 1.83m; Prompt Cnr. P.S.
Lighting: Switchboard: Strand GSX, 96 ways; 22 F.O.H. Spots, all 1k various Flats 3 circuits; Cyc. 4 circuits; Dips 8 each side; 2 Perches; 3 Spot Bars, 30 Spots Patts.243,223,123; Bridge 12 circuits T-spots (12) + Patt.93's.
Sound Equip: Uher 5 channel stereo mixer; Stereo amplifier 200w (Pioneer 8500); Mono R.A. Amplifier; 2 Akai 4000 DS Stereo tape decks; Pioneer PC112D turntable; Shure cartridge M75D; 4 Moving coil mics (AKG - 2 hand, 2 shotgun); 4 mic stands; 2 stage speakers; 2 F.O.H. speakers (tannoy); 2 Overhead speakers; 4 channel microphone mixer Shure M68FCE; 4 point low impedance microphone system.
Dressing Rooms 3; Accom. 40; 2 Showers; 1 Bathroom; 3 lavatories; 5 hand basins; Orchestra Pit 20.

## RIVERSIDE
57-59 Melbourne Street, Newcastle upon Tyne NE1 2JQ
Tel 0191 261 4386 Fax 0191 261 4129
ADMINISTRATION:
Props: Riverside Operations Ltd
Bookings Manager: Andy Hockey.
Seating/Capacity: Venue 1 - 600, Venue 2 - 400.

## THEATRE ROYAL
100 Grey Street, Newcastle upon Tyne,
Tyne & Wear NE1 6BR
Mgt 0191 232 0997 BO 0191 232 2061
Fax 0191 261 1906
ADMINISTRATION:
General Manager: Peter Sarah
Marketing Manager: Jo Watkins
Stage Manager: J J McMullen
Chief Electrician: Andrew Kent
Policy: No.1 Touring, Children's Shows and Concerts and Pantomime.
Perfs: Variable. Computerised Box Office (Rita).
Seats: 1,294. 4 Bars, Coffee Shop, Restaurant.
TECHNICAL:
Stage: Proscenium, Raked 1 in 24; Pros. opening 9m; Ht. of Pros. 9.53m; Ht. of Grid 17.7m; 54 lines C/W; Scenery Flying Ht. 16.5m; Flying Bars 10.97m; W/Widths P.S. 4.88m, O.P. 1.83m; Ht. to Fly Floor 7.9m; Distance between fly rails: 11.89m; Prompt Cnr. P.S.; Footlights to back wall 18m.
Lighting: Switchboard: Galaxy Premier 2 325 Dim Cuirts,

48 Non Dim Located G.C. 33 Prelude F, 12 x 223, 26 x 743, 16 x Harmony F2 x 243, 12 x Cadenza P.C., 36 x T64, 14 x T84, 26 Harmony Prof, 36 x Cadenza Profile, 2 x 808, 8 x Patt.23, 20 x CCT 1k, 29 x Coda 4, 60 Punchlites.
Sound: DDA Series Mixer 28 Channel into 8 into 2. 2 Revox B77, 2 Luxman Cassette, Luxman CD, 2 x Yamaha SPX 90 FX, Trident Compressor located rear Grand Circle. Main PA 10 x Meyer series 500; Foldback JBL's: FX 2 x JBL Bins & Horns. Wide selection mics + Stands. Comms: Ring intercom etc.
Dressing Rooms: 16 to accommodate 86 (+), rooms 1-6 internal toilet and shower. Rooms 7-16 two or three internal showers, three bathrooms, two bandrooms, company office, green room, rehearsal room, wardrobe equipped laundry, wig room. Orchestra Pit 23, 50 or 75.
Membership: TMA

## TYNE THEATRE AND OPERA HOUSE
Westgate Road, Newcastle upon Tyne
Tyne & Wear NE1 4AG
Admin 0191 232 1551 BO 0191 232 0899
Fax 0191 230 1407
ADMINISTRATION:
Props: Tyne Theatre & Opera House Ltd
Manager: Ann Palmer
Front of House: Alison McGarrigal
Technical: Peter Millican
Policy: Touring Shows, One Night Concerts, Conferences.  Seats 1,100, Bars, Cafe, 200 seat cabaret venue.
TECHNICAL:
Victorian Theatre (1867).
Stage: Proscenium 8.63m.  Depth of stage: 11.7m 29 C/W Flying bars, Grid Height 17.5m, Rake 1 in 24.
Lighting: Gemini 1 control Berkey/Green Ginger Dimmers 16 x harmony PC 25 x Harmony F 8 x Prelude 16/30 10 Harmony 22/40 20 x Harmony 15/28 4 x Cantata 18/32 8 x Cadenza 9/15 12 x Pars, 2 x CSI follow spots.
Sound: No sound equipment.

# Newport, I.O.W.
Pop. 22,430. London 91 miles. (inc. ferry). Newspapers: Isle of Wight County Press (fri). STD code 01983

## MEDINA THEATRE
Mountbatten Centre, Fairlee Road, Newport,
Isle of Wight PO30 2DX
Tel 01983 527020  Fax 01983 822821
ADMINISTRATION:
Props: Isle of Wight Council (Wight Leisure)
Secretary: Irene Groves
Theatre Technician: Darren Smith
Policy: Professional and touring performances and events encouraging school and community involvements. Music concerts, recitals, variety, theatre, mime, meetings, lectures includes Local Amateur Societies etc.
Perfs: Flexible
Seats: 419 (Extended stage), 519 (small stage) plus facilities for disabled.
TECHNICAL:
Stage: Open Stage (fan-shaped); Black velour cyclorama curtains on looped track, flat working depth 7m(min) - 10m (max); Working width 10m(min) - 13m (max); Ht. 6m clear; No scenery flying; limited flying facilities.
Lighting: Switchboard: ETC Express 48 waym, 42 X 2.5kw dimmer, 6 X 4kw dimmer; F.O.H: 10 X 1.2kw

spots, 6 X 1kw spot, 2 X 500w ARC follow spots, 10 X
1w Fresnels/PC, 12 X 1kw PAR 64. Over Stage: 16 X
500w Fresnel, 6 X 1kw Fresnel/PC, 6 x 500w flood.
Sound Equip: Yamaha 24:4:2 mixer in control room, 2 X
250w Yamaha amplifier driving JBL 4670 speakers, 4 X
Peavey monitor wedges (100w each), 1 X record deck, 3
X cassette deck, 1 X CD player, 1 X Revox B77, 20
various mics, 4 radio mics (lapel or hand), various mic
stands, cables, DI boxes etc.
Dressing Rooms 4 small, 1 large, Green room, no
laundry facilities, showers in adjacent leisure centre.
Direct road access to green room and stage.

# Newport, South Wales

Pop. 135,000. London 130 miles. STD code 01633

### NEWPORT CENTRE

Kingsway, Newport, Gwent NP9 1UH South Wales
Tel 01633 662662 Fax 01633 662673
Gen Enq. & Sports Booking 01633 332332 Concerts
Tickets 01633 662666 Catering 01633 670737
ADMINISTRATION:
Director of Leisure Services: A G Ropke, Civic Centre,
Newport, Gwent NP9 4UR
Manager: Simon Jones
Policy: Mixed programme of entertainments, and sports
events.
Seats: Up to 2,024 in multi-purpose main hall. Easy
access for disabled. Fully licensed bar and full catering
service available. 7 function suites.
TECHNICAL:
Stage: Main Hall: Height adjustable 0 - 2m. Dimensions -
17m x 7m (extendable). Floor: Material - Granwood. Area
- 1,250m. Max loading 9kn/m. Lighting: 24 lighting
barrels (16 winched, 8 fixed). 60 channel, 3 pre-set
lighting control console with 3 independent groups per
pre-set. Full mastering with automatic dipless crossfade.
Power: 300 amp 3 phase supply and 60 amp single
phase clean supply backstage.
Sound: Show sound system with relay system to other
areas. Up to 36 microphone inputs. Ring intercom
system. Audio deaf-aid induction loop. Broadcasting
Facilities: Power - 300kw (3-phase) for specialist lighting.
50kw (single) for control vehicles. Communication lines.
Comprehensive high level catwalk. 24 lighting barrels.
Access and Parking: 2.65m x 3.71m elephant door
giving direct access for get-ins. On site parking for event
vehicles; adjacent car parks for 2,000.
Dressing Rooms: Function suite adjacent to stage has
been designed specifically to double as artistes' dressing
rooms.

# Northampton, Northants

Pop. 127,460. London 66 miles. Newspapers: Chronicle
& Echo (ntly); The Mercury (thurs). STD code 01604

### DERNGATE

19/21 Guildhall Road, Northampton Northants NN1 1DP
Mgt 01604 626222 BO 01604 624811
SD 01604 626289 Fax 01604 250901
Tech email: Hopwood@derngate.demon.co.uk
Email: postbox@derngate.demon.co.uk
Web Site: www.derngate.org
ADMINISTRATION:
Props: Northampton Borough Council/Derngate Trust
Operations Director: Roger Hopwood

Technical Manager: Kevin Roach
Programming Manager: Rosemary Jones
Box Office Manager: Hilary Atlas
Events Manager: Andrew M Wright
Policy: Multi-purpose entertainment centre. Wide
programme including ballet, opera and all forms of
touring theatre, big band concerts, orchestral concerts,
spectator sports and conferences. Large concourse area
for exhibitions and special events. Bars, meeting rooms
and restaurant.
Seats: Depending on layout. 1200 as Lyric theatre, 1450
as concert hall, 1600 arena style, or flat floor area of 600
sq.m. for exhibitions, banqueting and dinners with
cabaret.
TECHNICAL:
Stage: Width 28m, depth 12.6m, height to grid 22m;
Pros. arch height 11.4m, width 14m. 41 double
purchase C/W of 500kg capacity. Bar length 17m.
Orchestra elevator 17m x 3.4m, variable depth.
Lighting: Switchboard Arri Imagin 250. FOH 46 x
Silhouettes; Stage 43  Starlettes; 18 x Sil 30's, 8 x 2k
ADB fresnels, 90  x Parcans, 5 x AC1004; 6 x Minuette
Groundrows; 2 x Coemar Followspots.
Sound: Soundcraft 24:8:2. Comprehensive range of
equipment based on JBL speakers and C audio amps
with various Calrec/Sennheiser/AKG mics. No radio
mics. 2 x Revox PR99 and various Technics audio
equipment. SM desk left or right, ring intercom and cue
lights in all working areas.
Dressing Rooms: 13; Accom. 65; Showers, wardrobe
containing washing machine and tumble dryer. Direct
access for 'get in' under cover.

### ROYAL THEATRE

Guildhall Road, Northampton Northants NN1 1EA
Mgt 01604 638343 BO 01604 632533
SD 01604 634520 Marketing 01604 624485
TIE, Community Touring & Youth 01604 627566
Admin/Fax 01604 602408
ADMINISTRATION:
Props: Northampton Borough Council
Lessees: Northampton Repertory Players Ltd.
Artistic Director: Michael Napier Brown
Administrative Director: Nigel Lavender
Education and Community Associate Dir.: Sean Aita
Marketing Manager: Elizabeth Richards
House Manager: Colin Greening
Production Manager: Jack Tripp
Policy: 46 weeks per year of 3 or 4 week repertory,
including traditional pantomime, 3 weeks per year of
studio work, all professional, plus 1 week per year
schools/amateur work, in the main house; 12 weeks per
year touring in the community; 18 weeks per year touring
TIE in schools.
Perfs: Mon-Sat 7.30p.m. (some Sats 8.30p.m.), Thurs
matinees 2.30p.m., Sat matinees 5.00p.m.
Seats: 583, raked on three tiers. Two Bars, Royalties
Cafe-Bar, Costume Hire Dept.
TECHNICAL:
Stage: Proscenium, Slight Rake with 7.92m revolve
(electric); Pros. opening 6.30m; Ht. of Pros. 4.27m;
Depth of S/Line to 10.36m; Ht. of Grid 19.81m; 27 lines,
Hemp; Scenery Flying Ht. 5.49m; Flying Bars 9.14m;
W/Widths P.S. 2.13m (open through to side stage), O.P.
2.13m; Prompt Cnr. P.S.
Lighting: 22 x 500w fresnels, 32 x 1kw fresnels, 6 x 2kw
fresnels, 14 x 500w profiles, 14 x 1kw profiles, 26 x
1.2kw profiles, 6 x 500w floods, 10 x 1kw floods, 32 x
par cans, 5 x 4 x 1.2kw battens, 2 follows spots. Gemini
1 controlling 60 108 x 2kw dimmers plus 12 x 5kw
dimmers.

Sound: 16-4-2 DDA S Series PA Mixer, 2 B77 Revox
71/2 ips, 1 twin cassette deck, 1 x 31 twin band graphic,
4 Bose 802 speakers, 2 Shure 112 W speakers, 2
channel Mosfet H/H V800 amp, 2 channel Bose 1800
amp, various mics, Infra red hard of hearing system.
Membershp: TMA

# Norwich, Norfolk

Pop. 119,600. London 111 miles. Newspapers: Eastern
Daily Press (dly); Eastern Evening News (ntly); Norwich
Mercury; Norwich Advertiser (fri). STD code 01603

## MADDERMARKET THEATRE
St. Johns Alley, Norwich, Norfolk NR2 1DR
Mgt 01603 626560 BO 01603 620917
SD 01603 626560 Fax 01603 661357
ADMINISTRATION:
Props: Maddermarket Theatre Trust Ltd
General Manager: Michael Lyas
Artistic Director: Andrew Kitchen
Stage Manager: Paul Stimpson
Policy: Amateur - 12 productions per year, occasional
visiting companies.
Perfs: Nightly 7.30, Mat. 2.30.
Seats: 310 with Stewards. Exhibition Space. Licensed
Bar.
TECHNICAL:
Stage: Open neo Elizabethan, Flat with Thrust, Overall
Pros. Width 9.75m; Max. Ht. 4.88m; Total Depth 7.8m.
Lighting: Switchboard: 48 way Strand GSX; F.O.H. Front
and Rear.
Dressing Rooms: 2, accom. 40.

## NORWICH PLAYHOUSE
42-58 St. Georges Street, Norwich, Norfolk NR3 1AB
Mgt 01603 612580 Fax 01603 617728
ADMINISTRATION:
General Manager: Caroline Richardson

## NORWICH PUPPET THEATRE
St James, Whitefriars, Norwich, Norfolk NR3 1TN
Mgt 01603 615564 BO 01603 629921
Fax 01603 617578
Email: norpuppet@hotmail.com
Web Site: www.geocities.com/Broadway/Stage/2041
ADMINISTRATION:
General Manager: Ian Woods
Artistic Director: Luis Boy
Technician: Peter Butler
Administration: June Hutton
Status: Puppet Theatre
Policy: Norwich Puppet Theatre is a touring company
with almost unique benefit of own home theatre base
with raked auditorium, studio performance space and
workshops. Produces work for all ages from 3 years
upwards which tours throughout the UK and Europe.
Where possible live music is included in productions.
Willing to premiere show.
Facilities: Seating in main house 198 raked. Studio
theatre 50 informal, 4 wheelchair spaces, level access -
all house facilities fully accessible. Induction loop
system.
The Octagon exhibition gallery. Licensed bar. Food
brought in for specific functions.
TECHNICAL:
Stage: Proscenium arch. Performing area 5m x 6m -
pros opening 5.5m x 5.5m wing width 5.3m US. No rake

- floor sprung wood composition, suitable for dance (not
barefoot) backstage crossover, trench DS. Height of grid
3.05m - variable hemp sets - tab track - maximum flying
height 5.5m. Black masking - black house tabs, drawn.
10 x 13A, 16 x 15A sockets. Get-in via road to stage
area - dock doors 1m x 2m. Scale stage plan available.
Lighting: Green Ginger Microset + circuits @ 2.5K, can
be moved and operated from various positions - no
supply available for temporary board - 21 spots, 25
fresnels, CCT/Rank Strand followspots could be
operated from various positions.
Sound: Alesis equaliser - Amcron amp - 2 x JBL
speakers - 3 mics. Technics double cassette tape
systems. Acoustics suitable for music and spoken word.
Stage management Prompt Corner available.
Backstage: 1 green room, doubling as dressing room
with shower. Iron, 4 power points available. Advice given
on accomodation. No permanent staff - casuals
available - no security personnel. Backstage facilities
partially accessible to disabled performers and staff.
Rehearsal rooms, piano fairly good.

Technical Studio Theatre - Flat wooden floor with
informal seating 5m x 3m - no masking. In house lighting
facility 18 x 15a socket outlets, Lighting equipment
borrowed from main theatre - 8 x 13A socket outlets. No
sound equipment.

## ST ANDREW'S & BLACKFRIARS HALLS
St. Andrews Hall Plain, Norwich, Norfolk NR3 1AU
Tel 01603 628477 Fax 01603 762182
Contact: Tim Aldous
Seating/Capacity: St. Andrews Hall: 900; Blackfriars Hall:
370

## THEATRE ROYAL
Theatre Street, Norwich, Norfolk NR2 1RL
Mgt 01603 623562 Mgt Fax 01603 762904
BO 01603 630000 BO Fax 01603 622777
Marketing 01603 762240
ADMINISTRATION:
Chief Executive: Peter Wilson
Programming & Operations Director: Roger Richardson
Marketing & Publicity Director: Mark Hazell
Technical Co-Ordinator: Arthur Hoare
Stage Manager: Will Hill
Chief Electrician: Ian Greeves
Stores & Maintenance Manager: Jack Bowhill
Seats: 1,318. 3 Licensed Bars. 3 Licensed Corporate
Rooms. Coffee Bar. Full catering facilities. Full disabled
facilities.
TECHNICAL:
Stage: Proscenium stage 'flat'. Proscenium opening
9.68m x 6.63m high. Flys C/W 52 lines plus 2 lateral
bars. Modelbox ground plan.
Lighting: Strand 550, 180 way.
Sound: Reinforcement system.
Dressing Rooms: 9 (6 en suite), 3 Chorus (2 en suite).
Orchestra Dressing room facilities: Orchestra pit
particulars on application.

Studio Theatre:
Seats: 150: Rehearsal facilities.
Workshop facilities.
Specialists in scenery and costume hire, scenery design.
Scenic Artist. Building facilities.
Full technical specification available on application.

# Nottingham, Notts

Pop. 294,420. London 123 miles. Newspapers:
Nottingham Evening Post (ntly). STD code 0115

## BONINGTON THEATRE

Arnold Leisure Centre, Front Street, Arnold,
Nottingham Notts NG5 7EE
Mgt/BO 0115 967 0114 and 0115 956 0733
Fax 0115 956 0731
ADMINISTRATION:
Props: Gedling Borough Council
Manager: Lynda Jordan
Policy: Mixed amateur and professional programme of
drama, music, light opera, ballet.
Perfs: 7.30 or 8.00
Seats: 178. Theatre Bar.
TECHNICAL:
Stage: Proscenium, flat are 7.4m x 7.4m, 1.5m forming
apron. Little wing space.
Lighting: Switchboard: Eclipse Board 2 preset control
extends to 4 preset if required spread over 3 phases;
F.O.H. booms and dips and stage bars, 32 x MFR 1kw
fresnel spots, 9 x MPR 1kw profile spots, 3 x 6ft lighting
battens, as fixed. Top cyclorama on No. 3 bar 3ft x 6ft
portable lighting patterns 4 x MFL400w tungsten
floodlights.
Sound Equipment: 3 mics lines to 6 outlet points.
Cassettes and gram decks available.
Dressing Rooms: 2.

## NOTTINGHAM PLAYHOUSE

Wellington Circus, East Circus Street,
Nottingham Notts NG1 5AF
Mgt 0115 947 4361 BO 0115 941 9419
SD 0115 947 4361 Fax 0115 947 5759
Web Site: nottinghamplayhouse.co.uk/playhouse
ADMINISTRATION:
Props. & Lessees: Nottingham Theatre Trust Ltd
Executive Director: Venu Dhupa
Artistic Director: Martin Duncan
Theatre Manager: Katie Yapp
Production Manager: Simon Bourne
Policy: All year round Repertory with occasional visiting
companies, concerts and late-night events.
Perfs: 7.30 Mon - Sat
Seats: 685-766 (adaptable). Licensed bars, coffee bars
and adjoining Restaurant and Bars.
TECHNICAL:
Stage: Proscenium with two forestages (3.96m in all).
Flat; Pros. opening 9.75m; Ht. of Pros. 6.71m; Depth of
S/Line 9.75m; Ht. of Grid 18.58m; 32 lines, C/W;
Scenery Flying Ht. 7.18m; Flying Bars 12.19m; Widths
P.S. 3.66m, O.P. 7.32m; Prompt Cnr. O.P.
Lighting: Switchboard: Galaxy 3 rear of stalls; 192 ways
inc. 24 5kw. LX Equipment: 70 x Profiles. 50 x 1k
Fresnels & 20 x 2k Fresnels, 60 Parcan, 2 Follow Spots,
20 x Iris 1.
Sound Equipment: Soundcraft 32-8-2 Main Mixer; 4 x
B77 Revox; 2 x cassette decks; 1 x turntable; assorted
mics and stands. Main installed speaker system Meyer
UPA and USW system front of house, Bose 802's &
302's on stage. 3 X Denon 990R mini disks.
Dressing Rooms: 10, accom. 39, showers, Orchestra Pit
3.96m x 10.67m.
Membership: TMA

## ROCK CITY

8 Talbot Street, Nottingham NG1 5GG

Admin 0115 941 2544 Fax 0115 941 8438
BO: 0115 958 8484
ADMINISTRATION:
Managers & Promoters: Andy Copping, George Akins
Policy: Concert venue, club and disco, Mon-Tues-Wed
venue for live bands, Thur student night, Fri rock night,
Sat alternative night. Venue consists of a ground floor,
balcony and smaller disco room, four drinks bars and a
fast food bar. Sunday - available for bands.
Seating/Capacity: 1,700 standing.
TECHNICAL:
Stage: dimensions 31ft (10m) wide x 19ft (6m) deep x 3ft
(1m) high, fully carpeted. P.A. Risers: Stage Left 2 (4ft x
3ft); Stage Right 1 (4ft x 3ft) - due to Fire Exit on this
side. Stage to ceiling clearance - Stage Rear: 12ft (4m);
Front truss clearance - 22ft - with house flying chains.
Power: Lights 3 x 100 amp - 3 phase.  Sound: 3 x 60
amp - 3 phase.
Mixing Point: on raised area 40ft from stage centre - 4ft x
3ft. Rostra available on raised dais - 4ft x 8ft.
Backstage: catering facilities available.

## ROYAL CENTRE

See the Theatre Royal and the Royal Concert Hall

## ROYAL CONCERT HALL

Theatre Square, Nottingham Notts NG1 5ND
Mgt 0115 989 5500 Fax 0115 947 4218
BO 0115 989 5555 BO Fax 0115 950 3476
SD 0115 989 5500 SD Fax 0115 979 9145
Theatre Royal Co Office 0115 989 5612
Royal Concert Hall Office 0115 989 5606
ADMINISTRATION:
Props: Nottingham City Council
Managing Director, Royal Centre: J M Grayson
Operations Director: J D Ashworth
House Managers: Peter Ireson (Merchandise);
R Smedley (Conferences):P. Burgess (Finance)
Technical Manager: Dave Mason
Stage Manager: J. V. McCluskey
Chief Electrician: Martin Hunter
Catering Mgr: Mrs J Fletcher -
Lindley Catering Ltd Tel 0115 989 5569
Policy: Classical concerts. Popular music and variety
concerts, Conferences, Films, Ballet.
Seats: 2,500
Two large bars and buffet.
The Royal Concert Hall is on the main touring circuit for
the world's leading orchestras, major contemporary
bands and solo stars and as a major conference venue.
Clients include Shell and the Liberal Democrats.
TECHNICAL:
Stage: Platform - polished hardwood finish. With choir
stall seating retracted - width at front 19.10m. Width at
rear 14.30m, Depth 10.8m, Area 206 sq.m.; With four
levels of choir stall seating - width at front 19.10m, width
at rear 12.10m, depth 8.80m, area 137 sq.m.; Platform
equipment includes 3 levels of Orchestra Rostra and
Conductor's podium. Suspension point hoists. 25
positions with 25 motors in the are above the platform
and forward of the acoustic canopy with 350kg lifting
capacity per point.
Lighting: Switchboard: Rank Strand Galaxy 120 ways 75
2.5kw and 45 5kw positioned in rear stalls control room.
Houselighting: Full memory system. Auditorium lighting
can be programmed to suit individual events. Additional
power 400 amp TPN, platform left. 200 amp power
supplies and cable ducts for TV outside broadcast units.
Touring equipment location rear stalls seating removable
to allow touring sound and lighting control system

allocation. Cable ducts from platform left and right to position in stalls. Follow spots platforms provided at rear of gallery left and right. Follow spots 2 Neithammer 1200 HMI.
Projection Room: 2 x 35mm and 1 x 16mm projectors; 2 Kodak Carousels, Electronically operated rollsafe screen unit 47ft x 25ft.
Sound Equip: 24/4/2 Soundcraft Delta, tape and disc machines; Supplementary mobile speaker towers, positioned down-stage left and right: Main overhead array of bass bins, horns and high frequency units mounted on adjustable sound bridge through acoustic canopy. Variable acoustics: An adjustable acoustic reflector incorporating two lighting bridges and orchestra lighting units is suspended above platform, so that acoustic conditions can be changed to suit scale of on-stage activity, and size of audience. Height variable - 3.25m to 10.25m.
2 x Bosendorfer Grand Pianos. 1 x Yamaha Grand Piano.
Dressing Rooms: 6 Principal, 3 Orchestra; Orchestra Pit: 5 rows of stalls seating removed - 92 sq.m.

### THEATRE ROYAL
Theatre Square, Nottingham Notts NG1 5ND
Mgt 0115 989 5500 Mgt Fax 0115 947 4218
BO 0115 989 5555 BO Fax 0115 950 3476
SD 0115 989 5500 SD Fax 0115 979 9145
Theatre Royal Co Office 0115 989 5612
Royal Concert Hall Co Office 0115 989 5606
ADMINISTRATION:
Props: Nottingham City Council
Managing Director: J M Grayson
Operations Director: J D Ashworth
House Managers: Peter Ireson (Merchandise);
R Smedley (Conferences): P. Burgess (Finance)
Technical Manager: Ken Marshall
Stage Manager: Ian McCarthy
Chief Electrician: Austen Lee
Catering Mgr: Mrs J Fletcher -
Lindley Catering Ltd Tel 0115 989 5569
Policy: Touring Opera, Ballet, Drama, Variety, Pantomime and Concerts.
Seats: 1,186. Three Bars, Buffet and Restaurant
The modernised Victorian Theatre Royal is on the No 1 Touring Circuit and plays host to Companies such as the Royal Shakespeare Company, Royal National Theatre, Opera North, Northern Ballet and pre and post West End Tours.
TECHNICAL:
Stage: Proscenium, Raked 1/25. Pros. opening 9.10m; Ht. of Pros. 8.5m; Depth of S/Line 13.15m; Ht. of Grid 18.90m; D/S 18.3m; 55 lines C/W 1 up and downstage C/W set each side; Scenery Flying Ht. 18.00m, Flying Bars 12.55m, 50mm diam; W/Widths PS 3.10m, OP 3.95m. Scene Dock OP 9.8m x 13.00m; Rear stage area 17.3m x 6.3m; Prompt desk OP can be PS. Tabs swagged by motor. Forestage elevator forms pit size for 25 musicians. Larger Orchestra Pit with 5 rows of seats removed accommodates 65 musicians.
Lighting: Switchboard: Rank Strand Galaxy 3 174 ways, 154 2kw, 20 5kw dimmers positioned at rear of Upper Circle. 12 x 1200 Watt Cantata in ceiling slots; Gallery front 10 source 4; Circle sides 16 T spots; Pros Booms 12 Patt.23/123; Floodbar 6 Iris 4 units; Additional lantern stock available; 3 internally wired spotbars; 4 6way ladders on tracks; Limes 2 x PANI 1200.
Sound Equip: Hill Audio 16:8:2 desk; Revox A77 tape deck, Technics cassette player, Yamaha SPX 90, 10 AKG and shure mics, installed speaker system in proscenium boxes - Martin CT2 speakers with Amcron MA600 amplifiers.
Dressing Rooms: 16 accommodating 120, with showers and bathrooms, bandroom and wardrobe with automatic washing machine and tumble drier, 20 music stands, Yamaha 6'6" grand piano.

## Oban, Argyll
Pop. 8,134. London 506 miles. Newspapers: The Oban Times. STD code 01631

### CORRAN HALL
Corran Esplanade, Oban, Argyll PA34 5AB Scotland
Tel 01631 564046
Manager: Kevin Baker
Seating/Capacity: 758; stacking chairs.

### HIGHLAND THEATRE
George Street, Oban, Argyll PA34 5NX
Mgt/BO 01631562444 Fax 01631 566160
ADMINISTRATION:
Director: David Webster,
Highland Discover Centre Limited
Technical Manager: John Twort
Policy: Summer shows, Touring, One night stands, cinema.
Seats: 250
TECHNICAL:
For technical details please contact venue.

## Oldham, Lancashire
Pop. 227,000. London 185 miles. Newspapers: Oldham Evening Chronicle (ntly); Weekend (free wkly); Advertiser (free wkly). STD code 0161

### COLISEUM THEATRE
Fairbottom Street, Oldham Gtr. Manchester OL1 3SW
Mgt 0161 624 1731 BO 0161 624 2829
Mktg 0161 628 7748 Fax 0161 624 5318
ADMINISTRATION:
Props: Oldham Coliseum Theatre Ltd.
Chief Executive: Kenneth Alan Taylor
Technical Director: Richard Pattison
Policy: Four weekly Repertory + tours + one nighters.
Perfs: Mon-Sat 7.30p.m. except Friday 8.00p.m., One Sat Mat. per run 3.00p.m.
One nighters: Sun - 7.30pm
Seats: 580. 2 Bars. Coffee shop.
PASS Box office
TECHNICAL:
Stage: Proscenium, Flat; Pros. opening 8.90m; Ht. of Pros. 4.27m; Stage Depth 13.10m; Depth from S/Line 9.75m; Ht. of Grid 10.66m; 30 lines; Scenery Flying Ht. 5.25m; Flying Bars 9.8m; W/Widths P.S. 4.88m, O.P. 6.40m; Prompt Cnr. P.S.
Lighting and Sound: Control: F.O.H.: Switchboard: Compulite Applause; 96 Dimmers 27 x 1k Profiles, 16.5k Profiles. 22 1k Fresnels, 19 x .5k Fresnels 3 x 2k Fresnels, 38 Par64, 12 Floods, 1 x CSI F/S.
Sound Equip: 29-8-2 Soundcraft Ghost, 6 x Bose 802E, 4 x Pro 100's, 5 x Poweramps, 7 Rifles, 8 vocals, 10 Radio/mics. 2 x B77, 1 record desk. 1 x Cass.
Dressing Rooms 6; Accom. 20; 4 Showers.
Orchestra Pit.

## GRANGE ARTS CENTRE

Rochdale Road, Oldham Gtr Manchester OL9 6AA
Admin 0161 785 4238  BO 0161 785 4239
Technical 0161 785 4242
ADMINISTRATION:
Props: Oldham College Corp.
Director: Veronica Conlon
Manager: Andrea Bowler
Policy: Amateur and Professional programme of drama, music, and dance, often with special educational performances.
Perfs: Usually 7.30p.m. Mats. various.
Seats: 84 - 434. One Bar. Exhibition facilities in two foyer areas.
TECHNICAL:
Stage: The main performance area is cruciform in design with 4 bleachers of 84 seats and capable of accommodating any form of staging (round, arena, traverse, thrust, 2 pros. sets of varying dimensions and auditoria).
Lighting: A lighting bridge surrounds the performance area and a 48mm modular Grid is suspended 5.5m above the acting area and continued into the seating bays in the form of ornamental balustrading.
Control by Strand 430 memory board with integral sub-masters and Effects Generator controlling 140 fixed circuits through 120 dimmers, all terminated in 15 amp 3 pin sockets distributed at grid and floor level. In addition to the above there are 8 independent 5 amp circuits.
Lanterns available (all Rank Strand): 90 .5kw and 1kw Profile Lanterns, 6 with colour wheels. 65 .5kw, 1kw and 2kw Fresnels C/W barndoors. 48 .5kw and 1kw floods.
3 Follow spots C/W integral colour change and Iris. Specific requirements for incoming shows can be rigged by prior arrangement. The Centre is also equipped with a Mini 2/12 and 2-30 amp auxiliary power supplies and carries a large stock of colour medium in both Cinemoid and Lee.
Sound Equip: Main P.A.: 4 Bose 802 Speakers; 1 Citronics PPX 900 Stereo Amplifier 280w per channel into 8 ohms. Bay Reinforcement: 6 JBL Control 1, 1 Quad 405-5 Stereo into 4-16 ohms. Mixing/Effects: 1 Studiomaster Series 2 16/8/2, 1 Steven Digital Reverb. Amplifiers: 1 Quad 405-5 100w stereo into 4-16 ohms, 3 Quad 303 45w stereo into 4-16 ohms. Speakers available for Spot Sound and Foldback: 8 Toa F-300 8 ohm cabinets (150w), 4 KF 15 ohm cabinets (50w), 4 Kudos cabinets (50w). Microphones: 40 various inc. Diversity Radio Hand Held and lavalier. Tape Decks: 2 Revox B77 (7.5 & 15 ips) 1 Memorex Cassette Deck (Dolby B & C). Transcription Deck: 1 Technics Quartz. The Centre carries a full range of Microphone Stands and an Induction Loop System is installed for the benefit of the hard of hearing.
Backstage: Talkback and Cue Lights are available at any point within the Auditorium and Backstage, with Show Relay and Communication to all Dressing Rooms.
The Centre is equipped with monochrome C.C.T.V. equipment, which is used as a stage management aid.
Rostra: 34 Sico Stage units with elevators and 18 King Cole units.
Access: At tail-gate height via Scene Dock Door 5.5m high x 2.5m wide with similar aperture into Auditorium.
Full technical details are available on request.

## OLDHAM THEATRE WORKSHOP

Harrison Street, Oldham Gtr Manchester OL1 1PX
Mgt/BO 0161 911 3240 Fax 0161 911 3244
ADMINISTRATION:
Props: Oldham Metropolitan Borough Council

Director: Victoria Munnich
Policy: Touring productions; own Company productions; Summer Schools; Workshops.
Perfs: Usually 7.30p.m. Mats. various.
Seats: 120
TECHNICAL:
Stage: Flexible performance area.
Lighting and Sound Control: F.O.H.:Switchboard: Tempus M24 & FX 96 ways; 72 circuits used with a 99way patch terminated in 15 amp sockets. 19;650w prelude FR. 15;650w prelude PC. 10;650w prelude 28/40. 9;650w prelude 16/30. 6;1200w cantata 26/44. 8;1200w cantata PC. 16;1kw pars. 10;500w nocturn floods. 4;Coda 500w/3 cyc. batton. 4;500w Minuette FR. 4;500w Minuette PC. 2;500 Minuette TT PR. 2 x 2kw 2000w follow spots; Sirius 24 ways; Slicklite truss touring rig on Doughty stands; UV tubes; flash boxes; smoke machine. 1 x H & H 16 way system 8; 1 x Revox B77; 2 x Bose 802E; 2 x Bose 302; 2 x Pro. 200's; 1 x H&H v500 amp; 1 H & H vx45 amp; 8 x Lavalier Radio mics; 6 x ME40 & ME80 Rifle mics; 1 x Carlsbro-Cobra 3 channel keyboard combo; 1 x Korg T1 Synth.; Assorted Mic stands. The performance area is equipped with C.C.T.V. Full stage relay system. F.O.H. paging system. Full intercom and QLX system.

## QUEEN ELIZABETH HALL

West Street, Oldham OL1 1UT
Admin 0161 911 4071 BO 0161 911 4072
Fax 0161 620 9952
General Manager: Jasmin Hendry
Contact: Shelagh Malley
Seating/Capacity: 1,500

# Oundle, Northants

Pop.3,500. London 83 miles. Newspapers: See Peterborough. STD code 01832

## STAHL THEATRE

West Street, Oundle, Peterborough Northants PE8 4EJ
Mgt 01832 273930
ADMINISTRATION:
Props: Oundle School
Director: Robert Lowe
Policy: To provide a well-equipped stage for Oundle School and other local productions, and professional entertainment: the best of small drama groups, small opera and dance companies, mime, puppets, children's theatre, revue, readings. Occasionally whole week, mainly half-week or one-night bookings.
Seats: 264 on single raked tier.
TECHNICAL:
Stage: End stage  wing space and optional forestage/orchestra pit; Width 7.5m, Depth 8.1m (max) 3.3m (min); Typical flying bar ht. 5.7m. 2 winches and 4 hemp sets, Wing Widths P.S. 4m O.P. 1.5m.
Lighting: Switchboard: Eurolight Applause with 62 Dimmers. Two lighting bridges acros auditorium, and follow spot positions. Approx. 80 lanterns (various).
Sound Equip: Yamaha MC 1204 12/4/2 mixer. One gram deck, one Revox B77; one Revox A77 7.5/3.75 tape machine and Hitachi cassette deck, 6 speakers. Microphone and speaker sockets (100V) distributed through stage and auditorium.
Dressing Rooms 1-6, 2-4; Green room. 2 Showers, 2 WCs. Orchestra Pit 12 sq.m. approx. 12 players.
Get-in door 1.8m wide by 4.2m high into scene dock of 20 sq.m. by 4.3m high. Workshop/scene store 60 sq.m.

by 4.3m high.

# Oxford, Oxon

Pop. 111,680. London 57 miles. Newspapers: Oxford
Mail (ntly); Oxford Times (fri). STD code 01865

## APOLLO THEATRE

George Street, Oxford Oxon OX1 2AG
Mgt 01865 243041 BO 0870 606 3500
SD 01865 241631 Fax 01865 791986
Visiting Company Office 01865 248266
ADMINISTRATION:
Props: Apollo Leisure (UK) Ltd
Managing Director: Paul R Gregg
General Manager: Louise Clifford
Stage Manager: Lesley Griffiths
Chief Electrician: David Manion
For all booking information and further details please
contact Sam Shrouder or Nicky Monk at Apollo Leisure
(UK) Ltd., Grehan House, Garsington Road, Cowley,
Oxford OX4 5NQ. Tel: 01865 782900; Fax: Oxford
01865 782910.
Policy: Touring Plays, Ballet, Opera, Musical, Comedy,
Concerts, Pantomime.
Seats: 1,826. Four Bars. Adjacent wine bar and
Downtown Manhatten Nightclub.
TECHNICAL:
Stage: Proscenium Stage, Flat; Pros. opening 13.72m;
Ht. of Pros. 7.32m; Depth of S/Line 12.19m; Ht. of Grid
18.29m; 62 lines, C/W, Scenery Flying Ht. 17.68m;
Flying Bars 15.24m, 63mm dia., W/Widths P.S. 12.19m
x 4.27m plus Scene Dock 2.44m x 12.19m, O.P. 4.57m
x 5.49m plus 6.10m x 10.67m; Prompt Cnr. O.P.
Lighting: Switchboard: ETC Express 250, 132 ways (12 x
5kw), 12 Source 4, 12 1200w starlett fresnels + sils +
stock etc. Rear of Circle; F.O.H. House Boom 6 Sil 30
each side, Balcony 18 Sil 15.12 x source 4. Lantern
stocks available. Piano.
Projection: 2 Gaumont Kalee 35mm, rear of Circle.
Limes: 2 Teatros, rear of Balcony. Local supplier of
additional equipment exists also.
Dressing Rooms: One suite, 11 rooms accommodating
seventy +; Showers. Orchestra Pit 24; Accom. 2 rooms
plus washing facilities. Artiste's call box at the stage door
245691.

## THE OLD FIRE STATION THEATRE

40 George Street, Oxford Oxon OX1 2AQ
Mgt 01865 794494 BO 01865 794490
Fax 01865 790554
ADMINISTRATION:
Props: Apollo Leisure (UK) Ltd.
Theatre Manager: Ted Doan
Technical Manager: Adam Leigh
Seats: 183
Bookings are direct.
TECHNICAL:
Stage:Removeable. Width 7.32m; depth 3.66m (overall
depth 5.16m),
Lighting: 100 channel ARRI Image desk with DMX512
protocol to the racks, 92 ways Green Ginger/Eurolight
dimmers. Stands and cabling available.
Sound: Soundcraft Spirit Live 4 Mark II 16:4:2 mixing
desk, 1 x AB 1200 stereo amplifier, 2 x Bose 800 full-
range speakers (with hook clamps) and equaliser. Denon
cassette deck. Mics etc available.
For full technical details please contact venue.

## OXFORD PLAYHOUSE

Beaumont Street, Oxford Oxon OX1 2LW
Mgt 01865 247134 BO 01865 798600
SD 01865 792758 Marketing 01865 792055
Press 01865 721091 Fax 01865 793748
ADMINISTRATION:
Props: Oxford Playhouse Trust
Theatre Directors: Hedda Beeby & Tish Francis
Front of House Manager: Jonathan Nash
Technical Manager: Tim Boyd
Policy: Drama, Dance, Opera, Music, Concerts
Perfs: 7.30p.m. Matinee: Thurs & Sat 2.30p.m.
Seats: 600. Licensed cafe, bar.
TECHNICAL:
Stage: Proscenium with forestage, Flat; Pros. opening
8.38m; Ht. of Pros. 4.88m; Depth of S/Line 7.77m; Ht. of
Grid 12.04m; 25 lines C/W, Scenery Flying Ht. 5.33m;
Flying Bars 11.28m; W/Widths P.S. 1.52m, O.P. 2.44m;
Prompt Cnr. S.R.
Lighting: Lanterns: Profiles: 16 x Cantata 1200w, 15 x
Prelude 650w, 6 x Harmony 16, Fresnels 26 x 743, 10 x
Cantata 1k, 12 x Cadenza 2k, 20 x Pars 120V 12 x Pars
240v, (2's and 5's), 12 x Cyc Floods 1k; Control: Arri
Impuls; Racks Strand EC 90, 132 Circuits, 120 x 2k, 12
x 5k. Communications: Cue lights x 6; Headsets x 6 +
SM.
Sound: 24-8-2 DDA Q Series with mutes and matrix
mixer; 2 x Martin Audio PM3 full-range speakers; 2 x
Martin Audio sub-base speakers; 4 x Community CSX
35 speakers; 2 x Community 220 speakers; 1 x Revox
B77 high-speed (7.5 & 15 IPS) reel-to-reel; 1 x Denon
cassete deck. 1 x Denon 1000w CD Player, SPX 9.
Dressing Rooms: 7; Showers 4. Orchestra pit - 30
musicians when forestage lowered below auditorium
level.
Membership: TMA

## PEGASUS THEATRE

Magdalen Road, Oxford Oxon OX4 1RE
Admin 01865 792209 BO  01865 722851
Fax 01865 204876
ADMINISTRATION:
Policy: Small scale touring venue.  Home of the Oxford
Youth Theatre
Perfs: Approx. evenings 8.00.
Director: Euton Daley
Technician: Roy Paterman
Administrator: Alison Byard
Marketing Officer: Gill Jaggers
Community Development Officer: Simon Floodgate
Youth Theatre Worker: Taryn Storey
TECHNICAL:
Stage: Floor level.  Performing area 9.5m x 7.2m - wing
width 3m SR.  No rake - floor sprung wood with optional
double-sided Harlequin Dance Lino, suitable for dance,
backstage crossover possible, stage heated.  Height of
grid 5.2m. Get in direct to stage - back doors 1.3m x
3m. Tallescope + Ext Ladder.
Lighting: Sirius 48 board, 100 patch circuits.6 x
independents, suitable lantern stock.
Sound Equipment: Soundcraft Delta 16:4:2 Mixer, 16
way mic patch 1 x 100W per channel amp, 2 x cassette
deck, 1 x Revox B77 reel-to-reel , Alesis Quadroverb, 1
CD player, 1 Graphic Equaliser (31 band stereo).  2 x
Meyers and 2 x JBL control 10, cans comms.  Acoustics
suitable for music and spoken word.  Basic mic
stock.Details and plans available on request.
Backstage: 1 Dressing room, accom. up to 10 people;
access by stairs; iron and board; 6 power points.
Rehearsal rooms.  Advice given on accommodation.

Staff - casuals available. Backstage facilities are partially accessible to disabled performers and staff - dressing room can be arranged in adjacent building.

## SHELDONIAN THEATRE
Broad Street, Oxford OX1 3AZ
Tel 01865 277299
Manager: Sue Waldman
Seating/Capacity: 900

# Penzance, Cornwall
Pop.19,110. London 281 miles. Newspapers: The Cornishman (thurs). STD code 01736

## THE MINACK THEATRE
On the Open Cliff-side, Porthcurno, Churchtown, St. Levan, Penzance, Cornwall TR19 6JU
Mgt 01736 810694 BO 01736 810181
Fax 01736 810779
Email: info@minack.com
Web Site: www.minack.com/minack
ADMINISTRATION:
Prop: The Minack Theatre Trust
Theatre Manager: Philip Jackson
Policy: Weekly change of Company and production through season of sixteen weeks (late May - mid September).
Perfs: Five evenings at 8.00, usually two Mats. at 2.00.
Seats: 750. Coffee and Light Refreshments served in interval and before performance.
TECHNICAL:
Stage: Adverse Rake Stage
Lighting: Strand LBX lighting control board, 36 dimmers.
Sound: Allen and Heath GL2 16:4:2 control desk with graphic equaliser etc., connected to amplifiers. 16 channels. CD, DAT and cassette available.
Dressing Rooms: Accommodate up to 40.

# Perth
Pop. 42,583. London 417 miles. Newspapers: Perthshire Advertiser (tues/fri). Dundee Courier (dly). STD code 01738

## PERTH THEATRE
185 High Street, Perth PH1 5UW Scotland
Mgt 01738 472700 BO 01738 621031
SD 01738 621436 Fax 01738 624576
ADMINISTRATION:
Props: Perth Repertory Theatre Co Ltd
Artistic Director: Michael Winter
General Manager: Paul Hackett
Technical Manager: John Chapman
Policy: Repertory Season and Tours.
Perfs: 7.30. Mats Sat. 2.30
Seats: 490. Licensed Bar, Coffee Bar, Restaurant, Exhibition Area.
TECHNICAL:
Stage: Proscenium, Raked; Pros. opening 7.35m; Ht. of Pros. 6.10m; Depth of S/Line 8.23m; Ht. of Grid 13.41m; 36 C/W lines single, 2 Fixed Bars 8.9m; W/Widths P.S. 3.50m, O.P. 6.02m; Prompt Cnr. variable.
Lighting: GSX/Auto Board.  92 circuits.  Control room at rear of circle.  Lanterns: F.O.H. - 26 (1KW 650w) Profiles, Stage - 36 1KW Fresnels, CYC - 12 1KW

Floods, Follow Spots - 2 x 2KW Gallery Level.  Various other types of lanterns and equipment are available. Please contact Electrics Department for details.
Temporary supplies: 1 x 60A Single Phase, 1 x 63A Three phase.  Situated below Stage DSR.
Sound: 1 Soundcraft 500 24:8 mixer - 4 x C-Audio Amplifiers, 4 x Turbosound TMS 1 speakers (FOH), 4 BOSE 802 speakers (onstage) - 12 Yamaha Delay speakers (4 in circle, 4 in stalls, 4 in pit) 3 x Shure SM58 Mics, 4 x Sennheiser MKH 416 Mics, 6 Crown PCC 160 Mics, 3 x Neuman KM84i mics - 1 Otari MX5058 2 track machine, 2 RevoxB77 2 track tape machines, 1 Tascam 122 cassette machine - 1 CASIO DAT Machine - 1 Revox B226 CD player-1 LAD CA944 record deck.  1 Yamaha SPX 90II Effects processor.  Large sound effects library.  Tapes can be compiled to specification. Infra Red Enhanced Hearing/Audio Description/Simultaneous Translation facilities.  Induction loop system for the Hard of Hearing.  The acoustic is suitable for the spoken word.
Dressing rooms 6; Accom 43; 10 showers; Orchestra Pit 40; Large rehearsal room/Studio Theatre accom. 120.

Studio Theatre: 7m x 5m, seating: 120 max, lighting controlled by BBC micro 36 channels. Pulsar software 20 minuette profiles, 20 minuette fresnels. Fixed rig.

Membership: TMA; Federation of Scottish Theatres, Ltd. Salvo.

# Peterborough, Cambs
Pop. 124,000. London 81 miles. Newspapers: Peterborough Citizen (thurs); Peterborough Evening Telegraph (nlty); Peterborough Herald & Post (fri). STD code 01733

## THE CRESSET
Bretton Centre, Bretton, Peterborough Cambs PE3 8DX
Mgt 01733 332263 BO 01733 265705
Fax 01733 332544
ADMINISTRATION:
Props: The Cresset (Peterborough) Ltd. Registered Charity 308213
Director: John Roberts
Sales & Marketing: Gail Arnott
Policy: Mixed variety, one night stands, Celebrity Concerts, sports events, programme of all music, Conferences, banquets and social events.
Seats: 850, 200, 120 and 100 (four auditoria), 1,000 standing. Four bars, restaurant, pub and coffee bar.
TECHNICAL:
Full Technical specification on request.

## KEY THEATRE
Embankment Road, Peterborough Cambs PE1 1EF
Mgt 01733 552437 Bo 01733 552439
SD 01733 565040 Fax 01733 567025
ADMINISTRATION:
Props: Peterborough City Council
Director: Derek Killeen
Stage Manager: Phil Bracey
Policy: Touring in-house productions and concerts
Perfs: 7.30 Mon-Thurs. Fri and Sat 8.00; Mat Thurs 2.30 and Sat 5.00.
Seats: 399.
One Bar. One Coffee Bar (11.00a.m. Mon-Sat)
TECHNICAL:
Stage: Thrust stage with easy access between stage

and auditorium. No safety curtain. Auditorium and stage share a common roof; there is no ceiling and no physical proscenium arch, the upper limit of the audience's aspect being defined rather by the exposed lighting grid and black painted structural ironwork.
Stage Dimensions: Overall width including wings: 20.7m (68ft). Overall depth including 2.4m (8ft) thrust: 10.6m (35ft). Approx depth from setting line if tabs used: 7.2m (23ft 6ins). Pros opening: 13.1m (43ft) wide can be reduced to a minimum of 9.7m (32ft) by semi-permanent black tormentors). Minimum overhead clearance on stage is dictated by the roll-up cinema screen at 5.5m (18ft), structural ironwork at 5.9m (19ft 4ins) and fixed LX bars at 6.4m (21ft). Overall height stage floor to roof: 8.2m (27ft).
Hemp Lines - 2 sets, 0.48m o.d. barrels, max height of bar 8m (26ft 3ins) above stage floor (ie approx 1.4m (7ft) above grid height). One additional set, light duty only, against back wall (max flying height 5.4m (17ft 10ins).
Stage floor - Black hardboard. No rake.
Masking - Complete black masking (except top masking) as follows:- Midstage - black screen-masking tabs. These tabs can be fully closed if required, reducing depth of stage to 4.9m (16ft), including thrust. Upstage - 5.5m (18ft) black legs on wrap-around track to give full or partial rear masking.
Cyclorama - Canvas cyc 14.6m (48ft) wide x 5.5m (18ft) high on straight track immediately upstage of black masking track. Cyc track is approx. 9m (3ft) downstage from back wall.
House tabs - Cherry coloured draw-tabs operated by hand-drum OP. Not recommended for fast curtain calls.
Orchestra pit - 9.1m (30ft) wide x 3m (10ft) deep, accommodates up to 18 musicians. All or part of the front row of seating is lost (ie up to 26 seats), depending on size of pit required. Please advise as early as possible if the orchestra pit is required.
Get-in - Good access for lorries up to get-in doors 2m (6ft 6ins) wide x 3m (10ft) hight. Doors open directly on to stage (OP side), with a loading height of .8m (2ft 8ins) above outside ground level.
Scene dock - adjacent to stage, PS. Usable storage space approx 3m x 1.83m (10ft x 6ft) for props, wardrobe etc. Access from stage via doors 6.1m (20ft) high x 2m (6ft 6ins) wide.
Wardrobe area - in scene dock. Equipment comprising washing machine, tumble dryer, iron and ironing board.
Dressing rooms - No1. 4 seats, No 2. 4 seats, No 3. 8 seats (all on stage level), No 4. 4 seats (first floor), No 5. Portakabin 8 seats at rear. Special arrangements for large companies if necessary. All dressing rooms have wash basins, power points, mirror (with lights) and costume rails. (Portakabin does not have wash basin), Shower and WC at stage level (Gents) and 1st floor (Ladies).
Cueing system - SM desk on PS. Headset intercom system is provided. Paging facility to dressing rooms and foyers; show relay to dressing rooms.
Lighting: Positions - Two bridges FOH, with 0.48m o.d. hanging rail at 6.7m (22ft) above stage level. 6 LX bars on stage at a fixed height of 6.4m (21ft). 4 telescopic stands. For further details see stage plan.
Lighting control - ETC Insight 2X (8 x 5kw, 124 x 2kw, 18 non-dim).
Lanterns - 12 x Teatro 22/40, 12 x Teatro 15/28, 4 x Patt 243, 24 x Patt 743 with barndoors, 5 x 4 cell Cyc floods, 6 x starlette 1kw floods, 24 x par 64.
Colour - Lee.
Lime positions - with LX and sound control. 2 x solo C.I.D.
Sound: Control position rear of auditorium in same room

as LX control. Equipment - 6 x Shure SM58, 2 x Beyer 201, 2 x Revox B77 (71/2 x 15 ips), 1 x Soundcraft Venue 32-8-2 mixer, 1 x SPX-90 II, 5 x mic stands. For companies touring large sound rigs a FOH mixing position is available, centre back row, at the expense of 8 seats. Please advise as early as possible if this is required. Length of multicore needed to reach the stage is approx 100ft.
Ground Plans - 1:24 scale ground plans are available on request

# Pitlochry, Perthshire

Pop. 2,419. London 444 miles. STD code 01796

### PITLOCHRY FESTIVAL THEATRE
Pitlochry, Perthshire PH16 5DR Scotland
Admin 01796 484600  BO 01796 484626
Fax 01796 484616
ADMINISTRATION:
Administered by Pitlochry Festival Society Ltd.
Festival Director: Clive Perry
Administrator: Sheila Harborth
Theatre and Box Office Manager: Margaret Pirnie
Production Manager: Elaine Kyle
Marketing Officer Groups: Helen Stevenson
Marketing Officer: Charles Barron
Policy: Festival of plays in repertoire (April-October); Sunday Celebrity Concerts, Art Exhibitions
Perfs: Eves. 8.00. Mats. 2.00.
Seats: 540 + 4 wheelchair spaces. Restaurant & Bars open daily (exc. Sunday) during Season. Parking for 120 cars and disabled 10.
TECHNICAL:
Stage: Proscenium, Flat; Pros. opening 10.47m; Max Ht. to adjustable house border 6.80m; Depth: Setting line to back wall; 13.10m; Curved forestage 2.00m deep (max), Width: Centre line to P.S. wall 10.80m; Centre line to O.P. C/W frame 8.80m; Height: to underside Grid 9.15m; to underside fly floor O.P. 7.64m; Flying: 22 Hemp, 5 line sets; 15 sets single purchase C/W. Max Bar load 250 kg. All bar lengths 13.50m. Prompt Cnr. Variable Storage: Scene dock P.S. 140 sq.m. Scene dock O.P. 132 sq.m.; Get-in in P.S. scene dock. Door with 0.20 step, 3.37m x 6.95m high.
Lighting: Control: Rank Strand 139 way Gemini situated in Control Suite above rear stalls; Circuits: F.O.H. 44 (3 slots each side paired across, and 2 bridges), Grid. 54, Dips. 28 (including 3 ladders on track each side); Equipment: 34, Sil 30, 12. Starlett, 18. Minuette, 2 Patt.243, 40 Patt.743, 23 Patt.123, 26 Patt.264, 18 Patt 23II, 23 Patt. 23, 14 1001 Flood, 4 (3 circuit) PAR batten, 8 (4 circuit) Pallas groundrow 2 Sil 15.
Sound Equip: Soundcraft 24-16, 3 x Revox B77, 2 x Cassette Decks, 1 x CD player, all situated in Control Suite above rear stalls; 15 balanced microphone inputs, 3JBL speakers each side of pros.; 4 portable speakers.
Artistes' Accommodation: 5 Dressing Rooms capable of taking 5 artistes each. 4 Showers. With financial assistance from Scottish Arts Council and Perth & Kinross District Council.
Membership: TMA; Federation of Scottish Theatre.

# Plymouth, Devon

Pop. 257,900. London 211 miles. Newspapers: Western Evening Herald (ntly); The Western Morning News (dly); South Devon Times (fri); Sunday Independent. STD code 01752

# PLYMOUTH PAVILIONS

## The Premier Venue

# SOLD OUT!

**Seal    M People    Eternal    Shirley Bassey    Bottom
Reeves & Mortimer    Daniel O'Donnell    Prodigy
Wet Wet Wet    Gary Barlow    Boyzone
. . . and many more!**

2,512 full seated    3,060 full standing    3,500 standing/seated
1,236 recital format (seated)

Catchment area from Bristol to Penzance
Full technical support and catering facilities

Part of **The Royal Shakespeare Company** Plymouth residency

Chief Executive Adrian Vinken
All concert enquiries, please contact the Event Manager
**Tel: (01752) 222200  Fax: (01752) 262226**

## ATHENAEUM
Derrys Cross, Plymouth Devon PL1 2SW
Mgt 01752 266079 BO 01752 266104
ADMINISTRATION:
Props: The Plymouth Athenaeum
Hon. Theatre Manager: Mr. C. C. Rowe
Perfs: 7.30, 2.30 Sat.
Seats: 352. Coffe/Wine/Ice-cream/Confectionary
available.
TECHNICAL:
Stage: Proscenium, Flat with Stage Revolve 6.10m dia;
Pros. opening 7.87m; Ht. of Pros. 4.27m; Depth of
S/Line 7.62m; Ht. of Grid 8.15m; 22 lines. Orchestra
pit/forestage 7.45m x 2.3m. 35mm Cinemascope
Projector. Upright piano and Steinway Grand Model B.
Lighting: Strand Tempus 36 way board, 36 circuits, 3
phase, operated from lighting platform or projection box
(stalls). 60A 3 phase supply available for temporary
board - 56 Spots, 16 Fresnels, 8 Floods, battens.
Sound: Audio unit at prompt corner with 100w main
amp, twin tape deck, mixer unit with inputs for 3 mics +
phono + aux tape deck and audio mics etc.  Feeds
auditorium and backstage playback speakers output to
slave amp for balcony speakers.  Unit incorporates 50w
amp for stage relay to dressing rooms and directors mic.
Reel to reel tape deck and 4 mics available induction
loop for heard of hearing.
Dressing Rooms 6; Accom. 32; Orchestra Pit 12.

## THE BARBICAN THEATRE
Castle Street, Plymouth PL1 2NJ
Tel: 01752 267131 Fax: 01752 222209
ADMINISTRATION:
Props: The Barbican Theatre Plymouth Ltd
General Manager: Sarah Pym

Artistic Directors: Sheila Snellgrove, Mark Laville
Policy: Young People's Theatre Centre, home of Rent a
Role Drama service, small scale touring venue for Dance
and experimental/new work.
TECHNICAL:
Stage: Open end 9.14 x 9.14m - hinged flats create
wings. Sprung wood floor.
Lighting: MX board, 24 circuits, 2 preset, 96 memories
effects page, 3 tempus 10A/15 dimmers max load 10A
per dimmer, 14 spots, 6 pc's, 4 floods.
Sound: Teac audio cassette - 6 channel powered mixer
amp (Yamaha).
Dressing Rooms: 2. 1 Shower.
Membership: ITC

## PLYMOUTH PAVILIONS
Millbay Road, Plymouth Devon PL1 3LF
Tel 01752 222200 Fax 01752 263505
Admin Fax: 01752 262226
ADMINISTRATION:
Props: Plymouth Pavilions Ltd.
Chief Executive: Adrian Vinken
Head of Operations: Margaret Garcia
Policy:  Concert Venue opened summer 1991, also
available to host conferences, exhibitions and major
sporting events. Full light and sound system, large scale
in-house catering service, seven meeting/green rooms
plus dressing rooms. City Centre based.
Seating/Capacity: 2,512 seated, 3,060 standing; 1,236
recital.

## THEATRE ROYAL
Royal Parade South, Plymouth Devon PL1 2TR
Mgt/SD 01752 669292 BO 01752 267222
Mgt Fax 01752 671179 BO Fax 01752 252546

Mktg Fax 01752 601382
ADMINISTRATION:
Props: Theatre Royal (Plymouth) Ltd
Chief Executive: Adrian Vinken
General Manager Theatrical Services: Alan Finch
General Manger Operations Services: Margaret Garcia
Marketing Manager: Trina Jones
Artistic Director: Simon Stokes
Finance Manager: Brenda Buckingham
Education Co-ordinator: Claire Binden
Policy: Mainly in-house productions of large-scale
musicals and plays, often with partner theatres or
producers which either transfer to London or make
national tours. A number of touring in shows particularly
opera, ballet, musicals and children's shows. Home of
the annual RSC residency from 1997.
In the Drum Theatre (studio) an extensive range of new
drama work, children's shows and festivals.
Seats: Main House Auditorium 1,296 max - adjustable
ceiling reduces seating to 768. Drum Theatre - studio
theatre with variable seating and staging a max of 250
seats. Two Bars, Patisserie, Gallery dining area,
Sponsor's Bar, Function Room and Mezzanine Art
Gallery with work by local artists. Facilities for disabled
patrons include internal wheelchair lift, audio described
and signed performances.
TECHNICAL:
Stage: Proscenium with thrust fly tower over stage and
forestage. Flat stage, Modular, total of 40 (2.4m x 1.2m)
removable sections 2 double deck orchestra pit lifts;
Pros. opening 12.6m; Ht. of Pros. (Max) 8.6m; Stage
depth from front of stage to back wall 14m (from US of
orchestra); Depth of forestage 3.15m; Grid 25m; 78
single purchase counterweight sets at 200mm centres; 4
motor sets over forestage; Flying bars 14.5m (extendable
to 18.5m); 1 up and downstage counterweight set each
side; 2 up and downstage hemp seats each side; 2
motor up and downstage sets each side (Each half
depth of stage); Stage manager's desk P.S., O.P. or
control room.
Lighting: Control: Rank Strand 530. Control room at rear
of stalls; alternative positions in auditorium. 274
channels; 185 2.5kw circuits; 350 channels, 186 X
2.5kw circuits; 81 X 5.00kw circuits; 8 X 10kw circuits.
Sound: Sound control room rear of stalls. 62 microphone
and 52 loudspeaker sockets located around stage and
auditorium.
Dressing Rooms 20; accom. 113 (rooms shared with
Drum Theatre). Most rooms with Showers.
Orchestra Pit to accommodate 76 musicians. 4 Band
Rooms.
DRUM THEATRE
Stage: Clear height beneath lighting catwalks 5.75m.
Lighting: Control room at gallery level. Alternative position
for desk available; Control, Rank Strand 430, 144 X
2.5kw dimmers
Sound: Control room side gallery. 16 microphone and 20
loudspeaker sockets located at all levels.

# Poole, Dorset

Pop. 125,000. London 112 miles. Newspapers: Poole &
Dorset Advertiser; Bournemouth Evening Echo. STD
code 01202

## POOLE ARTS CENTRE

Kingland Road, Poole, Dorset BH15 1UG
Mgt 01202 665334 BO 01202 685222
Fax 01202 670016
ADMINISTRATION:

Props: Poole Borough Council
Lessees: Poole Arts Trust Ltd
Chief Executive: Ruth Eastwood
Programme Director: Alistair Wilkinson
Marketing and Publicity Manager: Sarah Chapman
Technical Manager: Robin Cave
Policy: Mixed programme with Concert Hall used for
classical and popular music and in its flat floor mode for
rock, cabaret, dances and exhibitions. Theatre used for
touring repertory company, opera and ballet. Full-time
cinema, dance studio, art gallery, craft studios and
function rooms.
Seats: Concert Hall - 1473; Rock; 2459; Theatre 670;
Cinema 109; Function Rooms (available for parties) 240;
Rehearsal Studio 120; Coffee Shop. Foyer Bars and
Cafe Bar.
TECHNICAL:
Wessex Hall: Orchestra seating for 120 and choir seating
for 140.
Platform Lighting: Rank Strand SPH0/2P, preset in rear
Auditorium Control Room. 38 x Patt.743; F.O.H. lighting
and 20 x Patt.T64; Effects Lighting: 24 x Par for wall
washing.
Sound Equip: Phillips SMH Amplifier with 8 Channel
Mixing Column, Music and foldback speakers. 7 Mics
and Stands. Steinway 'D' concert and 1 other grand
piano available.
Dressing Rooms: 4 Guest Artiste Rooms each with
shower. 1 Male Changing Room for approx 25; 1 Female
Changing Room for approx 25; Green Room for approx.
30.

Towngate Theatre:
Stage: Proscenium: Width 9900mm, Ht. 5400mm; Max.
Width 19880mm; between Flyrails 13899mm; Depth
9900mm. Orchestra Pit: Approx 25 persons, on lift.
Converts to forestage.
Lighting: Strand Light Pallette/in rear aud. control room.
80 x 2kw Dimmers. Equipment: 36 x T64, 36 x 743, 16
x Patt. 23, 8 x Minuette Fresnel, 10 x Patt. 60, 8 x Iris
One, 4 sections compartment Batten. 16 x par, 6 x patt
243 fresnel. Cinemechanica, Victoria 2, 35mm projector
and Fumeo 16mm projector.
Sound Equip: Phillips SM4 Amplifier with 8 Channel
Mixer F.O.H. and foldback speakers. 7 mics and stands.
Reel-to-reel Tape Decks, piano.
Machinery: 26 single purchase counterweight sets and
10 Hemp sets. Full cue light and talk-back system with
show relay and F.O.H. call system.
Dressing Rooms: Band Rooms: 9 Dressing Rooms each
with shower; capacity 30; Chorus Room; 12.60m x
4.20m.
Company Manager's Office with phone.

The Cinema:
35mm projection (1 x 7000 Westrex 35mm).

# Portsmouth, Hants

Pop. 187,000. London 71 miles. Newspapers: The News
(ntly); Streetlife (wkly); Journal (wkly). STD code 01705

## GUILDHALL

Guildhall Square, Portsmouth Hants PO1 2AB
Mgt 01705 834146 BO 01705 824355
Fax 01705 834177
ADMINISTRATION:
Managed by Amey Facilities Mgt Ltd in a joint venture
with DC Leisure Mgt Ltd on behalf of Portsmouth City
Council.

## PLYMOUTH THEATRE ROYAL

**"A regional powerhouse"**
The Independent

- major producing house

- producer of 1998's **West Side Story** and **Gross Indecency**

- home of the RSC's South West Residency

Theatre Royal seats 1,294
Drum Theatre seats up to 200 in flexible formats

Chief Executive Adrian Vinken
Artistic Director Simon Stokes
**Tel: (01752) 668282  Fax: (01752) 671179**
Registered Charity No. 284545

General Manager: Martin Dodd
Deputy General Manager: Danny Green
Front of House Manager: Roger Cripps
Box Office Manager: Stephanie Jendrys
Stage Manager: Nick Coles
Stage Productions Office: 01705 851451
Policy: Rock/Pop Concerts, live shows, major conferences, exhibitions, orchestral concerts, dinners, dances, product launches, sporting events.
Capacity: 2,228 Standing. 2,017 seated. Harlequin Restaurant. Full catering service and bars service available.
TECHNICAL:
Stage: Concert Hall (no proscenium arch), Flat; pros opening 21.78m x 8.9m high. Depth of stage 10.84m. stage width reduces to 10.64m at rear clearance 7.2m. 3 rows of 6 flying points (500 kg each).
Lighting: The lighting at the Guildhall consists of 120 way Arri dimming system of 5kw modules. The circuits are grouped in boxes of 3 situated above the stage. These can be linked to 3 trusses, (front, mid, rear stage). By multi-core cables F.O.H. consists of 25 circuits situated above the stalls. The lighting consists of par can, 2 kw pc, and 2 kw, 2.5kw sils. Behind the NO. 2 bar are three Follow Spot positions each with a PANI HMI 1200w follow spot.
Lighting control is possible from two positions a) Out Front in auditorium b) in control room at side of stage. For outfront control the Guildhall has a Arri Image and effects desk with 72 ways of manual back up mounted in a mobile console. The desk in the side of stage control room is a Arri Image.
Sound: The sound system for the Guildhall main auditoria consists of a Turbosound TSE central cluster system giving 180 degrees horizontal dispersion and 90 degree vertical dispersion over the frequency range 80

Hz to 20 Khz. The system is designed for central audio source perception and has a Maximum S.P.L. of 127 dBa at 1m with a maximum seat to seat variation of +/- 1.5dB and a maximum front to rear S.P.L. varience of 6dBa.
The Cluster is powered via 5 C-Audio 606 power amplifiers and feed in mono via a Yamaha Q 1027 Graphic equalizer. To increase the frequency response underneath the rear of the balcony 6 Bose 101's have been installed as at this point the cluster is not visible. The Bose 101's are fed only the same information as the TSE111 Mid High Packs all information above 250Hz. The 101's are installed in an arc with the cluster having the same centre point. A fixed delay time is applied to the signal to the 101's allowing for a difference in propagation plane.
The system can be controlled from two positions:
a) Stage right in a sound proof control room on the side of the stage at 20ft. above the stage level.
b) Out front in the Auditorium at stalls level below the front of the balcony.
The desk is a soundtracs "Solo live" 32/4/2. The 32 channels can be either line or mic level of which each channel has four band equalization and six auxillary sends. The inputs and outputs to the desk are accessed via a BT patch bay located in the FX rack. Connected via the patch bay. Yamaha SPX 90, Two denon cassette decks, A denon CD player. Revox B77. The patch bay also has connections for a BBC broadcast link input to the 100v line distributed system in the corridors around the main hall and links into the Technical Projects communications system which has loudspeaking outstations in all five dressing rooms and a technical circuit covering both lighting and sound control positions, follow spots, stage left and right. By termination of a coms line on the patch bay any microphone line can be

used to feed a communications outstation once patched in. Continuous monitoring of the auditorium is available by two AKG 568EB show relay microphones positioned in the roof which are fed into the Technical projects twin rings and governed by a gain control on the master unit placed in the Stage Managers Corner off stage. Single balanced line tie lines are positioned on the stage and at the rear of the auditorium with other links off stage and in the minor halls giving a total of 26 tie lines connected to the mixer patch bay an additional 8 tie lines are available on stage from a single mobile stage box which also terminates in the control room patch bay. Four foldback lines down to stage are installed feed from a Turner B302 power amplifier which has dedicated feeds from the patch bay. These sockets are marked foldback output and are down stage left and right. Two styles of foldback cabinet are available, 4 x turbo sound wedges or JBL Cabaret cabinets on stands as side fills. Systems in the sub halls can be set up separately using the tie lines and a portable Toa 3 channel mono mixer. Or relay the main system into the small halls is possible using the auxiliary feeds from either desk Microphones; 4 Micron hand held mics, 4 radio lapel mics.
Dressing Rooms 5; Accom. 150; 2 with showers. Open stage option or mobile staging units available to provide orchestra risers and/or Stage extensions.

### NEW THEATRE ROYAL
Guildhall Walk, Portsmouth Hants PO1 2DD
Mgt 01705 646477 BO 01705 649000
Fax 01705 646488
ADMINISTRATION:
Props: The New Theatre Royal Trustees
(Portsmouth) Ltd
Administrator: Gareth Vaughan
Technical Manager: Sue McClory
Theatre currently undergoing extensive restoration of auditorium and complete re-building of stage and backstage facilities.
Seats: Currently 250, anticipated capacity 850 approx.
Now in operation: The Conservatory Cafe (10.30a.m. - 5.00p.m. Mon-Sat) and the Dress Circle Bar (12 noon - 2.30p.m.).
A temporary small scale theatre within the auditorium allows occasional events or performances on a raised stage (28ft wide x 17ft deep) but with no technical facilities apart from lighting. Licensed for 160 in stalls and 90 in Dress Circle.

# Prestatyn

### NOVA CENTRE
Central Beach, Bastion Road, Prestatyn,
Denbighshire LL19 7EY Wales
Tel 01745 888021
Seating/Capacity: 300
Manager: Frank Gledhill

# Preston, Lancs
Pop. 95,450. London 212 miles. Newspapers: Lancashire Evening Post (dly). STD code 01772

### CHARTER THEATRE
Lancaster Road, Preston Lancs PR1 1HT
Tel 01772 203456 Fax 01772 881716
ADMINISTRATION:

Props: Preston Borough Council
General Manager: John Shedwick
Policy: Various
Seats: 780. Bars, Restaurant, Cafeteria
TECHNICAL:
Stage: Proscenium, Flat; Pros. opening 9.45m; Ht. of Pros. 5.15m; Depth of S/Line 11.12m; Ht. of Grid 14.63m; 37 lines, 33 C/W, 4 Hemp; Scenery Flying Ht. 6.8m; Flying Bars 10.06m; W/Widths P.S. 2.44m, O.P. 9.75m; Prompt Cnr. P.S.
Lighting: Ovation 3B/40 150 x ARRI dimmers (144x2.5k, 6 x 5k). Control room FOH. 36 x 1.2k profiles. 30 x 1.2k fresnels, 12 x 650W profiles. 12 x 650w fresnels 4 colour cyc floods plus various extras.
Sound: DDA 'Q' Series 24, 8, 2 mixer. Turbosound speakers (6 FOH, 4 Foldback). Tascam DA30 DAT, 1 Revox B77. 2 cassette decks. Cinema: 35mm projector and cakestand. JBL speakers (+ sub-bass + surround). Dolby processing.
Dressing Rooms 7; Accom. 34; 16 Showers, Orchestra Pit 24; Hydraulic Apron/Orchestra Pit.
Membership: I.L.A.M., A.E.A.M.

### GUILD HALL
Lancaster Road, Preston Lancs PR1 1HT
Tel 01772 203456 Fax 01772 881716
ADMINISTRATION:
Props: Preston Borough Council;
General Manager: John Shedwick
Policy: Concert Hall, mixed use.
Seats: 2,020. Bars, Restaurants, Cafeteria.
TECHNICAL:
Stage: Concert Stage - 6 piece hydraulic stage - 0.76m x 7.60m x 18.24m, plus choir area. Various positions for flying trusses available.
Lighting: Switchboard: Jands Event 40 x 2k fresnels, 12 x 2k profiles. Advance truss with 48 parcans. All round spot rail and sockets.
Sound Equip: 16:4:2 mixer, 1 Akai Reel, 2 Denon Cassette Decks, 1 Marantz CD Player. Speakers stage only. Turbosound P.A. + foot monitors. Dressing room relay.
Dressing Rooms: 6 + large Band Room. 2 showers and shared dressing room and shower facilities with Theatre, when available.

# Ramsgate, Kent
Pop. 40,070. London 74 miles. Newspapers: Thanet Times (tues); Isle of Thanet Gazette (fri). STD code 01843 (Thanet)

### GRANVILLE THEATRE
East Cliff, Victoria Parade, Ramsgate, Kent CT11 8DG
Tel 01843 591750
ADMINISTRATION:
Props: B.C. Stout
Policy: Summer Show, Repertory, Panto, Operatic, Arts, Films, Hiring, etc.
Perfs: 7.30
Seats: 587. Licensed Bar.
TECHNICAL:
Stage: Proscenium, Raked; Pros. opening 9.75m; Ht. of Pros. 5.49m; Depth of S/Line 7.32m; Ht. of Grid 10.97m; 21 lines, various; W/Widths P.S. 6.10m. O.P. 4.27m. 35mm Proj. Dolby sound.
Lighting: Switchboard: Strand Major; 48 ways; F.O.H. Spots 6 Fresnels Patt.243; 4 Battens; 3 circuits; Dips up to 4 each side; 4 Spot bars 10AA's 6A 23.

Sound: Speakers: Column 4 (sides of stage).
Dressing Rooms 6; Accom. 32; Orchestra Pit 20 max.
Membership: TMA

# Reading, Berks

Pop. 136,400. London 48 miles. Newspapers: Evening
Post (ntly); Reading Chronicle (fri); Reading Standard
(thurs); Midweek Chronicle (tues). STD code 0118

## THE HEXAGON

Queen's Walk, Reading Berks RG1 7UA
Mgt 0118 939 0390 BO 0118 960 6060
SD 0118 939 0018 Fax 0118 939 0028
Email: hexagon@beta.reading-bc.gov.uk
ADMINISTRATION:
Props: Reading Borough Council
Operations Manager: William Brooker
Business Manager: Shirley Britton
Technical Manager: Paul Kennedy
Marketing Manager: Andrew Jones
Head of Arts & Theatre: Andrew Ormston
Programme Co-ordinator: Ann Brown
Policy: Adaptable Concert Hall and Theatre. Touring and
in-house productions, concerts, etc.
Perfs: by arrangement.
Seats: 514 to 1686 depending upon format.
The auditorium is equipped with Sennheiser hard of
hearing infr-red system.
TECHNICAL:
Stage: Stage area 162m, Variable use including open
stage with or without choir stalls; and proscenium format
(opening 10.5m to 17m; ht up to 9.25m). Stage height
1m, Height of grid 10m. 19 hemp line sets and 5
motorised lighting bars; length of flying bars 10m - 18m
incl. W/Widths variable; stage manager's desk stage left.
Orchestra Pit lift available as pit, floor, or thrust to stage
(3.5m x 12m). Orchestra pit accommodation 48. Access
to stage: scene dock prompt side; good loading access.
Dimensions of stage entrance: height 2.5m; width
1.84m; diagonal 3.15m.
Lighting: Control: Strand Galaxy 2, 144 circuits (situated
rear of balcony in control room). Lanterns: 8 x Alto 8/16
(2.5KW), 8 x Sil 10 (2KW), 16 Cantata 11/26, 18 x T64,
12 x Sil 30, 16 x Prelude 16/30, 18 x Patt 243, 8 x
Cadenza F, 48 x Patt 743, 68 x Par 64 cans, 8 x 1KW
Floods, 8 x Iris 2, plus some miscellaneous stock, 2 x
Pani HMI 1200w follow spots.
Sound: Soundcraft Vienna 2 48 channel and Soundcraft
200B 16 channel mixing desks. Amplifiers: Crest 4001's
and 8001's. Speakers: Turbosound approx. 8k F.O.H.
plus Turbosound stage monitors. Microphones: Mainly
Shure and AKG, 1 x Revox A77, 2 x Revox B77's plus
various cassette and CD players. Projection: Twin 35mm
Cinemeccanica Victoria 5's. Dolby stereo with surround
sound, also Dolby S.R. Screen size 45' x 28'.
Dressing Rooms - 9 plus chorus and bandroom
accommodation. 10 backstage showers.
Membership: TMA

## THE MILL AT SONNING THEATRE

Sonning Eye, Reading Berks RG4 6TY
Mgt 0118 969 6039 BO 0118 969 8000
Fax 0118 944 2424
ADMINISTRATION:
Props: R D Richards
Artistic Director: Sally Hughes
Assistant Administrator: Ann Seymour
Policy: 6/5 weekly repertory

Perfs: Tues-Sat 8.15p.m. Mat Sat. 2.15p.m.
Restaurant opens 6.30p.m. Sats 12.30p.m.
Capacity: 212
TECHNICAL:
Stage: Thrust stage, semi-circular. Depth of stage 5.40m
width at centre 9.42m, width at US line 10.44m, width at
DS line 3.95m; max setting depth (for box sets) 1.37m,
max height 3.50m.
Lighting: Strand GSX lighting desk. 60 2kw circuits.
Sound Equipment: 2 x teac 2 track reel-to-reel tape
decks; 1 x 8 channel mixer; 4 x 100w Bose speakers.
Dressing Rooms: 5, Accom. 12.

## RIVERMEAD LEISURE COMPLEX

Richfield Avenue, Reading Berkshire RG1 8EQ
Tel 0118 901 5000 Fax 0118 901 5006
ADMINISTRATION:
Props: Reading Borough Council
Manager: Iain Davies
Policy: Leisure centre with concert facilities. Car parking
facilities for 650, 3 phase power supply.
Seating/Capacity, Main Hall: 2,400 seated, 3,000
standing.

# Redcar

## REDCAR BOWL

Majuba Road, Redcar, Cleveland TS10 5BJ
Tel 01642 479277 Fax 01642 479048
Seating/Capacity: Seats 900; cabaret 650; standing
1,400.
Entertainments Officer: Christina Bates

# Redditch, Worcs

Pop. 75,000. London 126 miles. Newspapers: Redditch
Advertiser; Birmingham Evening Mail; Redditch
Standard; Bromsgrove Messenger. STD code 01527

## PALACE THEATRE

Alcester Street, Redditch, Worcestershire B98 8AE
Mgt 01527 61544 Gen 01527 65203
BO Credit Cards 01527 68484 Fax 01527 60243
ADMINISTRATION:
Props: Redditch Borough Council; Lessees: Palace
Theatre Redditch Ltd.
General Manager and Artistic Director: Michael Dyer
Technical Manager: Andy Sheriff
Policy: Professional and amateur productions; brought-in
one/two night stand music, theatre, dance, exhibitions,
youth theatre and holiday youth activities. Policy of
community involvement and access to the arts.
Perfs: Normally 7.30.
Seats: 399.
Bar, Restaurant.
TECHNICAL:
Stage: Proscenium, raked, with removable flat apron
over orchestra pit; pros. opening 6.70m; Ht. to tabs
3.80m; Ht. to iron 4.70m; Depth of stage no apron
5.95m. Tip of apron 7.80m; Ht. of grid 11.60m; 16 lines
hemp; Scenery flying Ht. 5.49m; flying bars 8.00m;
W/Widths P.S. 3.66m O.P. 3.60m prompt cnr. P.S. Q
Light, Talkback wired & radio sets dressing room call
system.
Lighting: Switchboard: Strand Lightboard M; FOH Bar &
Booms; On stage 3 7.15m bars; 2 booms, dips 4 each
side; 4 Patt.263, 4 Patt.764; 2 T-Spot; 8 Patt.23; 2

Patt.23N; 2 Patt.823; 6 Prelude 16/30; 4 Patt.803; 3
Patt.123; 4 Furse 650 fren; 7 Patt.223 (743); 7 Furst 1k
fren; 4 Furst 500w fren; 4 code 500/3; 11 Patt.60 500w;
4 Patt.137 200w; 1 1kw par blazer; 1 Patt.252; f/spots 2
Patt.293 2k.
Sound Equip: Soundcraft 16 Channel Mixer, speakers 4
in auditorium.

# Redhill, Surrey

Pop. 55,000. London 18 miles. Newspapers: Surrey
Mirror (thurs); Independent (fri). STD code 01737

## THE HARLEQUIN
Warwick Quadrant, London Road,
Redhill Surrey RH1 1NN
Mgt 01737 773721 01737 765547 Fax 01737 765549
ADMINISTRATION:
Props: Reigate & Banstead Borough Council
Manager: Tom Kealey
Administration Officer: Bobby Weekes
Publicity and Marketing Manager: Audrey Ryan
Technical Manager: John Hewitt
Assistant Technical Manager: Ken Berreen
Seating: 17 800mm wide x 24 500mm long together
with a balcony at one end with four rows of permanently
installed seats. Proscenium panels are hinged and fold
flat against stage walls. Retractable bleachers store
beneath balcony; tiered seating on orchestra pit may be
rolled away beneath auditorium floor to provide large or
small pit giving:- full config. 494, small pit: 470, large pit:
422, in the round: 562.
Standing & Seated: 764
TECHNICAL:
Stage: Proscenium - 11 950 wide x 7600 high to fixed
pelmet. Height may be reduced with flown header. Width
- Centreline to St. Right 8900; Centreline to St. Left
8900. Distance between Fly Floors 14 000. Depth - Rear
of House Curtain to stage edge 400. Height - Clear
beneath Fly Floors 8335; beneath u/side of Grid 10 337.
Floor - Flat and level, covered in 'Harlequin' dance
flooring. Flying System - 30 installed hemp sets,
generally 200mm centres. Maximum bar capacity 150
kg. 9 electrically operated winch bars max. capacity 250
kg. Bar length 13000. Stage manager working corner on
Stg. left. Mobile control desk with extension cable. Get-
in: from servce loading bay 1 floor below stage with lift
access to stage level upstage R. Max. dimensions of lift
5740 x 2290 x 2450 high. Access to stage 2175 x 2075
high. Orchestra: Pit - 45 m.sq. on lift. Maximum depth
below stage/auditorium level 1050mm. Access to Pit via
auditorium.
Lighting: 120 way 550 by Strand in control room at rear
of Balcony. Dimmers - 24 x 5kw (to 32a CEE 17 s/o with
changeover to 4 x 15a 3-pin s/o). 96 x 2.5kw (to 15a 3-
pin s/o). Dimmer Room one floor above stage, upstage
left. Additional Power - 200a TPN designated 'Special
Effects' situated downstage Actors' left. Projection
Equipment: Single 16/35mm  projector by Kineton.
Rolled projection screen on electrically powered winch
bar. Full Dolby stereo. Sound and Communications.
Allen & Heath 32/8/2 Soundcraft 400B 20/4/2 mixer
desk, Patchfield with 38 microphone inputs, 20 tielines
from Prompt corner facilities panel to jackfield in control
room.
2 Revox B77 tape recorders, 2 Cassette Recorders, 1
record deck, 1 C.D. player, Yamaha SPX 90 2 Peavey
Autograph Eq, Drawmer Compresser/
Limiter, Alesis Quadraverb, Digital Sampler. 5 31 band
Yamaha graphic equalisers. Microphones: 3 Shure

SM58s, 3 AKG 321s, 3 224s, 9 AKG C451 bodies, 7
AKG CK8 heads, 4 AKG CK1 heads, 2 AKG CK22
heads. Various Microphone floor stands. Full P.A. with
Bose P.A. with separate monitor mix. Contact theatre for
full spec. Infra-red hearing aid system in auditorium.
Stage Management: SM desk by Showstrand
incorporates paging and show relay, twin-ring intercom,
cue lights and effects circuits. Induction loop. Yamaha
Grand and upright pianos and Roland D50.
Accommodation: 5 rooms for 39 artists at stage level.
Green Room at stage level St. left. 4 showers (2 each
sex). Detailed equipment list and drawings from the
technical manager.

# Rhyl, Denbighshire

Pop. 22,000. London 211 miles. Newspapers: Rhyl
Journal; Prestatyn Weekly (thurs); Rhyl & Prestatyn
Visitor. STD code 01745

## COLISEUM THEATRE
West Parade, Rhyl, Denbighshire LL18 1HB Wales
Tel/Fax 01745 351126
Props: Catlins Coliseum Ltd
Resident Administrator: A. Phillips
Technical Manager: D. Denver
Seats: 614
Reopened Spring 1997, new lighting and sound
installed, 16mm sound projection. All year round
operation.

## LITTLE THEATRE
Vale Road, Rhyl, Denbighshire LL18 2BS Wales
Mgt/BO 01745 342229
ADMINISTRATION:
Contact: Mrs L Roberts
Treasurer: Mrs E H Baker
Chairperson: Ms T Gwilliam
Policy: Repertory (Amateur and Professional),
Pantomime and Variety
Perfs: Usually 7.30 (occasional Saturday Matinees 2.30)
Seats: 190 + 3 wheelchair spaces. Access for disabled.
Coffee Bar.
TECHNICAL:
Stage: Proscenium stage with removable Apron, Flat;
Pros. Opening 6.71m; Ht. of Pros. 3.35m; Depth of
S/Line 7.45m; Ht. of Grid 6.71m; 16 sets, Hemp;
Scenery Flying Ht. 6.50m; W/Widths P.S. 2.83m, O.P.
3.76m; Prompt Cnr. P Side (R).
Lighting: Switchboard: Strand JSN24 (Control Room
Rear of House, Single Phase); 24 ways (patch panel);
F.O.H. Spots 12 Patts.243, 23, 263; 2 Battens plus
Cyc.; Dips 2 P, 3 O.P. (11 way); 3 Spot Bars Patts.23 &
123.
Sound Equip: 2 Turntables, Tape Recorder (Control
Room); Westrex Speakers Pros. and Stage.
Dressing Rooms 2; Accom. 12 - 15. Orchestra Pit 6.
Apron Stage 5.53m x 1.47m. Dock Doors 1.98m x
1.52m. Car Park at rear of Theatre - Railway Station 200
yards away.

## PAVILION THEATRE
Promenade, East Parade, Rhyl,
Denbighshire LL18 3AQ Wales
Mgt 01745 332414 BO 01745 330000
Fax 01745 339819  Tech 01745 360088
Props: Denbighshire County Council
Head of Tourism and Leisure: Lloyd Conaway

Theatre Manager: Gareth Owen
Marketing Officer: Jenny Brownlees
Technical Manager: Andy Hughes
Theatre Administrator: Val Simmons
Policy: Professional and amateur productions; brought-in one/two night stand music, theatre, dance, concerts etc. Also available for conferences.
Perfs: 7.30 or 8.00p.m.
Seats: 1,032. Coffee Bar, Licensed Bars and Restaurant.
TECHNICAL:
Stage: Proscenium, raked (1:35). Proscenium Width 12.9m; Pros. Ht. 6.2m; Max. Stage Width 25m; Max. Stage Depth (to front forestage) 10.9m (13.2m); Orchestra Pit: 50 sq.m. - to seat 30 maximum, can be covered. Stage Surface Grey Flecked hardboard; 44 single purchase counter-weight sets; 500 kg maximum loading per bar; Bar Length 16.25m; Distance between bar centres 200mm; Grid Height 16.5m.
Lighting: Gemini 2+ 156 Channels; Assortment of Strand Lanterns; 2 CSI Follow Spots; 5 Martin Roboscans; 2 Front of House Bridges; 2 Front of House Booms ; 4 Internally Wired Bars.
Sound: 24.4.2. Sound Tracs, Desk; SPX 900 and ART FX Units; Mini-disc Revox; CD; Cassette; Selection of Microphones & radio mics.
Dressing Rooms: 12; Accom. 70.
Membership: TMA

# Richmond, N.Yorks

Pop. 7,260. London 234 miles. Newspapers: Darlington & Stockton Times (sat); Northern Echo. STD code 01748

## GEORGIAN THEATRE ROYAL

Victoria Road, Richmond, North Yorkshire DL10 4DW
Mgt 01748 823710 BO 01748 823021
ADMINISTRATION:
Manager and Licensee: Bill Sellars
Stage Manager: Jim Russell
Policy: Professional Drama and Concerts, Local Amateur Societies.
Seats: 200
TECHNICAL:
Stage: Proscenium, Raked; Pros. opening 4.72m; Ht. of Pros. 3.50m; Depth of S/Line 6.40m; Ht. of Grid 5.18m; 15 lines, Hemp; Prompt Cnr. P.S.
Stage Plan available.
Lighting: Switchboard: Tempus 2G36 in Pros. box P.S.; Circuits: 10 FOH on barrels, 4 Pros. Box, 3 Dips, 1 Footlights, 4 battels - 43 circuits. Lamps: 34 Patt.23, 2 Patt.23N, 24 Patt.123 11 Patt.137.
Sound: Please contact venue.
Other: Dressing Rooms 4; Accom. 20.
Membership: TMA

# Richmond, Surrey

## RICHMOND THEATRE

The Little Green, Richmond, Surrey TW9 1QJ
Mgt/SD 0181 940 0220 BO 0181 940 0088
Fax 0181 948 3601
ADMINISTRATION:
Props: Richmond Theatre Trust.
Theatre Director: Karin Gartzke

Marketing Manager: Lucy Dale
Theatre Manager: Simon Pearce
Box Office Manager: Jane Caldwell
Technical Manager: John Young
Policy: Touring Drama, Opera and Ballet, Concerts and Pantomime.
Perfs: Evenings at 7.45 pm, Matinees Wed and Sat at 2.30 pm.
Seats: 840 on three levels. Three licensed bars and entertaining suite.
TECHNICAL:
Stage: Proscenium raked 1:24. Pros opening 8.16m. Ht. of Pros. 7.0m. Depth of Stage 9.1m. Ht. to Grid 14.0m. Wings 5.5m. P.S. 3.0m O.P. x over stage level. Flying system 35 sets single purchase counterweight 350kg S.W.C., bars 10m long. Get-in street level P.S. Removable rostra (row A) over orchestra pit 10m x 2m approx.
Lighting: Control: Eurolight Applause at rear of stalls. Dimmers 168 x 2.5kw and 12 x 5kw. Lanterns. Full permanent F.O.H. rig - details on application.
Sound & Communications: Full wiring infrastructure for sound control on stage or by prior arrangement at rear of stalls. Details of equipment on application. Full cuelight system, ring intercom and paging to all the usual areas.
Other: Dressing Rooms 9, accom. 26 on 3 floors; 8 Showers; Green Room; Bandroom; Wardrobe and Laundry.

# Rickmansworth, Herts

Pop. 78,000. London 20 miles. Newspapers: Watford Observer; Focus. STD code 01923

## WATERSMEET THEATRE

Salters Close, High Street, Rickmansworth, Hertfordshire WD3 1HJ
Mgt 01923 896484  BO 01923 771542
Fax 01923 710121
ADMINISTRATION:
Props: Three Rivers District Council
General Manager: Sandra Bruce-Gordon
Technical Manager: Peter Brown
Policy: Mixed Programme of entertainment - Theatre, Concerts, Cinema & Discotheque.
Seats: 481. Bars, Restaurant and full catering facilities for any function.
TECHNICAL:
Stage: Proscenium, Flat; Pros. opening 11.40m; Ht. of Pros. 4.97m; No. of Lines 22; C/W Hemp 16 Hands, 6 Winch; Flying Bars 12.00m; Prompt Cnr. P.S.
Lighting: Switchboard: Zero 88 Eclipse (48 way).
Sound Equip: Console in Projection Room; A.H.B. 12 Channel into 2 Mixer plus Foldback; 16 & 35mm Cinema Projection.
Dressing Rooms 4; Accom. 33; 1 Shower; Orchestra Pit 14 plus.
The Floor is raked by mechanical screw jacks which allows the seating to be raked or flat.
Colne Suite
Seats 70. Mixed programme of entertainments and functions.
Chess Restaurant
Seats 100. Mixed programme of Entertainments and Functions.

# Rochdale, Gtr Manchester

Pop. 91,454. London 221 miles. Newspapers: Rochdale Observer (wed/sat); and Manchester newspapers. STD code 01706

## GRACIE FIELDS THEATRE

Hudsons Walk, Greave Avenue, Oulder Hill, Rochdale, Lancashire OL11 5EF
Mgt 01706 645522 Fax 01706 648404
ADMINISTRATION:
Props: Rochdale M.B.C.
Manager: Phil Machin
Stage Manager: David Harrison
Policy: Available for hire and some promotions.
Seats: 688. Bar and Coffee Bar.
TECHNICAL:
Stage: Proscenium, flat; Pros. opening adjustable over 21.33m; Ht. of Pros. 7.34m; Depth of S.lne 7.15m; Ht. of Grid 15.24m; 24 lines, Hemp; Max. Scenery Flying Ht. 6.70m; Flying Bars 12.19m; W/Widths adjustable depending on proscenium opening, plus scene dock; Prompt Cnr. P.S.
There is 3.05m of stage in front of setting line, and to the rear a stepped choir area with 6 x 0.46m risers each 1.67m wide in half hexagonal shape.
Lightboard: Switchboard: Rank Strand SP60, in control room, rear auditorium, 60 ways; 20 T-Spots; No. 1 spot bar 12 Patt.743, No.2 spot bar 12 Patt.743, No.3 bar 14 Patt.60.
Sound Equip: 1 Ferrograph, 1 Garrard Gram Deck, 6 mic. inputs and mixer; 6 Carlsboro 100w speaker, side walls of auditorium.
Dressing Rooms 2; Accom. 24 plus. Showers. Orchestra Pit for 20 approx.

# Rotherham, S. Yorks

Pop. 250,000. London 161 miles. Newspapers: South Yorkshire & Rotherham Advertiser (fri). STD code 01709

## CIVIC THEATRE

Catherine Street, Rotherham, South Yorkshire S65 1EB
Mgt 01709 823640 BO 01709 823640
SD 01709 377196 Fax 01709 823638
ADMINISTRATION:
Props: Rotherham Borough Council
Theatre Manager: Terry Dobson
Stage Manager: Jayne Globe
Policy: Plays, Opera, Ballet, Musicals, Orchestral & Band Concerts, Celebrity Nights, Revue, etc.
Perfs: Nightly at 7.15. (Sunday 7.30).
Seats: 354. Coffee Lounge and Licensed Bar.
TECHNICAL:
Stage: Proscenium, Flat; Pros. Opening 8.07m; Ht. of Pros. 4.27m; Depth of S/Line 11.89m; Ht. of Grid 7.62m; 20 lines; Flying Bars 8.53m; W/Widths P.S. 9.14m, O.P. 2.44m; Prompt Cnr. P.S.
Lighting: Switchboard: Strand SP60 plus Tempus M24 and FX board, rear of auditorium; F.O.H. Spots 12; 2 Spot Bars, 12 Patt.743, 10 Patt.123, 9 Patt.23, 10 Patt.60; Dips 4 each side.
Sound Equip: Peavey XR 800 Mixer Amp, Revox B77 Tape Recorder plus cassette deck, 9 Mic inputs. 2 F.O.H. Speakers, 2 Backstage. Dressing Room Show Relay & Call System.
Dressing Rooms 4; Accom. 40; Orchestra Pit 12

## ROTHERHAM ARTS CENTRE

Walker Place, Rotherham, South Yorkshire S65 1JH
Admin: 01709 823623 BO: 01709 823621
Fax: 01709 823653
Manager: Martyn Green
Seating/Capacity: Main Hall 200; raked through 126 usual

# Salisbury, Wilts

Pop. 35,890. London 84 miles. Newspapers: Salisbury Journal (thurs). STD code 01722

## CITY HALL

Malthouse Lane, Salisbury Wilts SP2 7TU
Mgt 01722 334432 BO 01722 327676
Fax 01722 337059
ADMINISTRATION:
Salisbury District Council
Entertainment Manager: Phillip Smith
Technical Manager: Phillip Manning
Auditorium Seating: Variable up to 1,050
TECHNICAL:
Stage: Proscenium arch, max width 12m, max height 6m. Stage width 15.5m, depth 7m, height 11m. Extension 2.25m.
Lighting: Strand Action 48 Lighting board, 48 channels 2k per channel, 100 amp, 3PH supply for auxiliary use. 8 x 6 way dimmer packs on gantry stage left, 18 patt 60 floodlights, 10 500w Minuette fresnel spotlights, 12 1kw silhouette 30 profile spot lanterns, 12 1kw starlette fresnel spotlights, 2 chromatic mix wheels with remote controllers, 4 telescopic light stands, 2 2kw silhouette follow spots, 3 lighting bars onstage, 2 lighting bars over Auditorium, 6 dip boxes on stage, 9 front of house lighitng positions in Auditorium ceiling, 4 vertical lighting bars in Auditorium with 4 x 2kw outlets on each. Stage ring main with 8x13 amp sockets, 100 amp 3 phase supply for auxillary use.
Sound: 12 channel mixer in control room desk, third generation 400w amplifiers in control room desk. 2 column loudspeakers, one each side pros. 200w each. 14 mics, 1 radio mic, cassette player, 30 amp single for sound equipment. 6 mic sockets.

## THE MEDIEVAL HALL

Sarum St Michael, The Close, Salisbury Wilts SP1 2EY
Tel 01722 324731/412472 BO 01722 324731
Fax 01722 339983
ADMINISTRATION:
Props: John and Jane Waddington
Policy: Music, theatre, exhibitions etc.
Perfs: 7.30p.m. Sun. 7p.m.
Seats: 140 (comfortable stacking chairs & padded wall benches).
TECHNICAL:
Stage: Flat stage 14ft x 31ft, with wooden rostrum available. Flat york stone floor; 150ft. of linear hanging space.
Lighting: Purpose designed picture lighting; stage lighting with 18 channel dimmer circuit.
Sound: PA and sound equipment available.
Other: Limited catering facilities.
For further technical details apply to John or Jane Waddington at 10 Shady Bower, Salisbury SP1 2RG

## SALISBURY PLAYHOUSE

Malthouse Lane, Salisbury Wilts SP2 7RA

Mgt 01722 320117 BO 01722 320333
SD 01722 327670 Fax 01722 421991
ADMINISTRATION:
Props: Salisbury Arts Theatre Ltd
Artistic Director: Jonathan Church
Executive Director: Rebecca Morland
Production Manager: Chris Bagust
Stage Manager: Brum Gardner
Policy: Four-weekly Repertory, Studio, Touring and
education work.
Perfs: Mon, Tues, Wed 7.30; Thurs 2.30 & 8.00; Fri 8.00.
Sat 2.30 & 8.00.
Seats: 516 (open stage)
TECHNICAL:
Stage: Hexagon shape, max width 12.2m; Max Depth
12.2m (incl forestage); Ht. of Pros. 5.8m; Ht. to Grid
13.0m; Ht. to Fly Gallery 5.3m; Ht. understage 2.1m; Ht.
of stage riser 0.86m; Stage flat; side Stage left 6.7m x
6.4m.
Machinery: 19 Double Purchase CW sets (No. 0 used for
house tab, No. 1 used for LX Bar), Cradle. Modular
trapped forestage, full width 3m (forms small orchestra
pit); modular trapped floor in centre 3m section of stage.
Lighting: 2 Auditorium Bridges, 1 Pros Bridge.
Auditorium slot positions within tower walls. Internally
wired bars (1 x 12 way, 1 x 16 way).
Control: Strand Lighting 520: 116 ways (72 x 2kw, 36 x
2.5kw, 8 x 5kw). 12 independent circuits. All circuits fed
to 129 outlets via 2 patch-panels. Auditorium bridges
and towers; red phase; stage and fly tower, yellow
phase. 60 amp 3 phase supply on stage.
Luminaires: profile 40 x T64 (1kw) 2 x Patt 264 (1kw), 10
x CCT Silhouette 30 (1kw), 12 x Patt 23 (500w), 6 x
Model 823 (650w), 12 x Prelude 16/30 (650w), 24 x
Strand Cantata 18/32 (1.2kw). Fresnel: 4 x Minim
F(500w), 27 x Patt 743 (1kw), 10 x Patt 243 (2kw).
Floods: 12 x ADB AC1001 (1kw), 20 x Patt 60 (500w), 6
x Patt 137 (150w), 6 x S/63 Batten. Other: 18 x Cantata
PC (1.2kw), 24 x Par can (All CP61 lamps). Followspots:
2 x Patt 765 (1kw CSI).
Sound: Soundcraft K3. Also 2 mini disc players. 2 x
Yamaha Q2031A Graphic Equalisers. Dynacord DDL204
Delay Unit. Yamaha SPX 900 Effects Processor,
Technics RS-B655 Cassette Deck, Sony CDP-M50
Compact Disc Player, Technics SL-D202 Record Deck,
2 x Revox A77 Tape Decks (7.5ips). 2 x Carver PM900
Power Amplifiers, 1 x Carver PM300 Power Amplifier, 3 x
HH TPA 100D Power Amplifiers (Mono), 4 x EV S200
Loudspeakers (Permanently installed in Auditorium Roof),
4 x Altec 604-8G Speakers for onstage use. 2 x A & R
Column Speakers in Auditorium.
Microphone and Loudspeaker points in all areas of
auditorium. Communications: SM Desk situated DSR
corner on 10m multicore cable. 20 x Q lights to all parts
of stage and auditorium. Ring Intercom. FX-Bell and
telephone ringing circuits. Paging to dressing rooms,
foyers and stage. Show relay to dressing rooms and
backstage areas. Production desk in stalls with
complete comms. facilities.

Studio Theatre
Seating: Variable depending upon layout. Maximum 149.
Stage: Dimensions: 13.4m x 10.9m. Ht. to underside of
roof steels: 5m. Ht. to underside of gallery: 2.9m. No
stage rake. No stock masking.
Machinery: None.
Lighting: Control: LBX 150 - 2kw per channel. 6 x
independent outlets. All circuits fed to outlets around
studio via patch panel from 48 dimmers.
Luminaries: 17 x Patt 23 (500w), 12 x Prelude 16/30
(650w), 23 x Patt 123, (500w), 4 x Patt 743 (1kw), 2 x

Prelude PC (650w).
Sound: Soundcraft Spirit Folio Mixer (10/2), Revox A77
tape deck, 2 x HH TPA 100D power amplifiers, 2 x
Tannoy 15" speakers.
Communications: Show relay, paging to backstage and
foyers. Ring intercom.

# Scarborough, N Yorks

Pop. 43,080. London 231 miles. Newspapers:
Scarborough Evening News (dly); Scarborough Mercury
(sat); Trader & Weekly News (thurs). STD code 01723

## FUTURIST THEATRE
Foreshore Road, Scarborough,
North Yorkshire YO11 1NT
Mgt 01723 365789 BO 01723 374500
SD 01723 351712 Fax 01723 365456
Admin 01723 370742
ADMINISTRATION:
Props: Apollo Leisure (UK) Ltd.
General Manager: Ian Carpendale
Stage Manager: Richard Bielby
Assistant Manager: Alicia Fowler
For all booking information and further details please
contact Sam Shrouder or Nicky Monk at Apollo Leisure
(UK) Ltd., Grehan House, Garsington Road, Cowley,
Oxford OX4 5NQ. Tel: 01865 782900; Fax: Oxford
01865 782910.
Policy: Summer Season, One Night Stands, Films,
Conferences.
Perfs: 6.10 and 8.40 (Mats). variable depending on
show.
Seats: 2,155. Two Theatre Bars.
TECHNICAL:
Stage: Proscenium, Raked 1 in 24; Pros. opening
10.87m; Ht. of Pros. 5.55m; Depth of S/Line 11.28m;
Ht. of Grid 13.75m; 35 lines, C/W; Scenery Flying Ht.
6.71m; Flying Bars 10.97m; W/Widths P.S. 0.91m, O.P.
0.91m; Promt Cnr. O.P.
Lighting: Switchboard: Gemini 2+; 100 ways, 92 2kw
and 8 5kw circuits F.O.H. 16, Flies 29, Stage Dips 43; 20
Patt.764; 1 Flood Bar (12 x 1000w Floods); 4 x 4 circuit
Battens; Advance bar 12, 18 Patt.743; 2 Patt.765 Follow
Spots; No Footlights. 12 Harmony Fresnels, 14 Harmony
Profiles. Advance Bar with 12 Parcans. 14 Sil 30's, 28
Par 64 Cans, 12 Pat 49.
Sound Equip: 3 way system with graphic equaliser and
digital reverb. Hill B Series 3 24-4-2 desk Bose 800
monitor system.
Dressing Rooms 10; 4 Showers; Orchestra Pit 13.
Dressing Room Call System - Strand Cue Board Star
Suite.
Membership: TMA

## SPA GRAND HALL
The Spa, Scarborough, North Yorkshire YO11 2HD
Mgt 01723 376774 BO 01723365068
Fax 01723 355821
ADMINISTRATION:
Props: Scarborough Borough Council
Spa Manager: Keith Norton
Policy: Light orchestral concerts Summer Season,
Conferences; Occasional One-night stands.
Seats: Seating: Theatre style seats - Ground floor -
1225; balcony - 745; ground floor seats removable;
disabled access.
Bar and Restaurant.
TECHNICAL:

Stage: Width - 16.61m; Full Depth - 9.14m; Depth - Centre of curved frontage to steps 3.66m; 5 steps - 0.91m depth x 0.31m rising. Stage columns - from s/r 4.27m x 4.27m from stage front, from s/l 3.66m x 4.27m from stage front. Front tabs behind columns, drawn; 2 hemp sets, 2 winch LX bars, 2 fixed tab tracks; 2 pair gold tabs; get-in through auditorium - doors 2.43m x 1.52m; Stage entrance s/l, s/r.
Lighting: Strand 60 Channel 2 preset manual board; 16 1KW floods, 14 Parcans, 6 Cantatas; 8 Strand T84; 1 2KW follow spot.
Visual Aids: 1 overhead projector, 2 slide projectors.
Sound: 14 Audio Technica mics; 3 hand held radio mics; 1 tie mic radio; 16 channel FBT Sound Desk; 8 Bose 802 speakers, 2 Bose 402 speakers, 2 Twin cassette desks.
Backstage: 4 dressing rooms; 1 band room (with partition).
Piano: 1 Steinway Model D - full size concert grand.

## SPA THEATRE
The Spa, Scarborough, North Yorkshire YO11 2HD
Mgt 01723 376774  Fax 01723 355821
BO 01723 365068
ADMINISTRATION:
Props: Scarborough Borough Council
General Manager: Keith Norton
Policy: Resident Summer Show and occasional one-night stands and amateur shows out of season plus Christmas Panto.
Auditorium: Seating raked - total 567 Stalls 408 Circle 159 Disabled access and wheelchair spaces.
Buffet and Bar.
TECHNICAL:
Stage: Proscenium arch pros. opening 6.73m x 5.49m; Performing area 8,57m x 7.11m; Wing widths 1.6m s/l, 4.15, s/r; Backstage crossover 0.9m; Grid height 7.32m; Dock s/r wide 3m; 5 hemp sets; 4 winch bars (3 for lx); red house tabs, drawn - 4 tab tracks; 3 pair black curtain legs; 3 black borders; Black cyclorama; blue tabs; gold tabs; white gauze; stage raked, wooden floor covered with MDF boarding; get-in via rear doors, door 2.13m x 2.3m; scale drawing available.
Lighting: Strand MX48 channel memory board; 48 channels - 2KW per channel; s/r 10 dips s/l 42 dips FOH 18 dips (14 x 5A plug cap)(4 x 15A plug cap). 2 x 2 KW follow spots; 10 parcans, 8 fresnels, 10 x 1000w spots, 3 cyc battens, 2 footlight battens, 2 internally wired LX bars.
Sound: Carlsbro 12 into 2 desk - 2 speakers; 1 Technics tape deck; 6 mic stage boxes; Shure mics.
Backstage: Stage management s/l - 2.13A Sockets; 6 dressing rooms (3 with showers) - wardrobe; no show tannoy to dressing rooms; no disabled access to dressing rooms or stage.

## STEPHEN JOSEPH THEATRE
Westborough, Scarborough, North Yorkshire YO11 1JW
Mgt/SD 01723 370540 BO 01723 370541
Fax 01723 360506
ADMINISTRATION:
Props: Scarborough Theatre Trust Ltd
Artistic Director: Alan Ayckbourn
Financial Administrator: Keith McFarlane
Theatre Manager: Elizabeth Brown
Production Manager: Alison Fowler
Press & Marketing Officer: Andie Hawkes
Policy: Repertory. April to January. New plays every season.
Perfs: 7.30p.m.; (Sat. 3p.m. & 7.30p.m.)
Seats: The Round 406 max; McCarthy 165 max.

Restaurant, Bar.
Studio Theatre seats 75 for Lunch-time and Late Night plays and music.
TECHNICAL:
Stage (The Round): Performing area 6.7m x 6.1m. 3 Vom entrances. Fixed grid 4.26m.
Lighting: Strand Gemini 2+ with FX panel, floppy disc, 130 patches to 60 x 2.5 dimmers. Lanterns: 52 x 500w Fresnels, 22 x 1kw Fresnels, 33 x 100w Profiles, 12 x 1kw Profiles, 16 x 650 PC's, 3 x Par 64, 10 x 500w Nocturne Floods, 6 x CCT colour wheels.
Sound Equip: DDA D Series 16-8-2 via Matrix to 8 x H/H TPA 50w amps via speaker switching system to 16 outlets. 4 x Revox B77; 2 x Revox A77 reel to reel tape systems. 6 x Shure SM58. Speakers: 8 x Electrovoice 512-1 100w, 4 x Wharfedale 100w, 3 x Tannoy Puma.

Stage (McCarthy): End stage, performing area 5.95m x 3.66m, various levels. Fixed grid 3.67m.
Lighting: Board Pulsar 30 x 2 preset, 30 x patch to 30 x 1.2kw dimmers. Lanterns from stock.
Sound Equip: Seck 12:2 mixer. Cambridge Audio Amps. Tannoy Lynx speakers.

# Scunthorpe, North Lincolnshire
Pop. 70,330. London 160 miles. Newspapers: Scunthorpe Star (fri); Scunthorpe Evening Telegraph. STD code 01724

## THE BATHS HALL
59 Doncaster Road, Scunthorpe,
North Lincolnshire DN15 7RG
Admin 01724 297861 BO 01724 842332
Fax 01724 861341
ADMINISTRATION:
Props; North Lincolnshire Council
Manager: Terry Wincott.
Policy: Multi-purpose Hall hosting diverse events, cabaret, dance, concerts, opera, etc. Stage, conference and seminar facilities.
Seating/Capacity: Main Hall with upstairs, 1,000

## PLOWRIGHT THEATRE
Laneham Street, Scunthorpe,
North Lincolnshire DN15 6JP
Mgt 01724 859129 BO 01724 840883
Fax 01724 270423
ADMINISTRATION:
Props: North Lincolnshire Council
Licensee/Manager: Terry Wincott
Policy: Touring, Mixed programme.
Perfs: Normally 7.30.
Seats: 353. Licensed Bar, Tea and Coffee Bar.
Disabled access to most parts of building.
TECHNICAL:
Stage: Proscenium, Flat; Pros. opening 7.24m; Ht. of Pros. 3.60m; Depth of S/Line 6.71m plus apron 2.21m; Ht. of Grid 7.32m; 7 lines Hemp; W/Widths P.S. 7.62m; O.P. 6.40m; Prompt Cnr. O.P. 14 lines hemp.
Lighting: Strand LBX board - 60 dimmer channels, 3 bars on stage, 1 FOH and 2 side bars. Lanterns: 6 no T84, 6 no Prelude 16/30, 11 no starlette, 6 no minim PC, 6 no parcan, 10 no Patt 23, 6 no patt 123. Follow spot: Strand 818 2 kw. 20 lamp 4 channel cyc batton, 5 no ground row battens.
Sound: Inkel MX1600 Mixer 16:4:2, 16 No XLR Mic lines

+ 8 1/4 jack lines from the stage. Amps: Custom sound 150+150w. 4 no Mustang 50w. Speakers: 2 no 12" 150w cabs rear FoH. 2 no columns - pros arch, 2 no accoustech 12" 200w, 2 no W+T 12" 200w cabs 4 no 100v lime 2 dip skts on apron and 1 each side of stage. Revox B77, Garrard DD131, turntable, cassette deck, CD, various mics inc radio mic.
Dressing Rooms 4; Accom.40; Showers.

# Sevenoaks, Kent

Pop. 105,931. London 25 miles. Newspapers: Sevenoaks Chronicle (thur); Focus (tue); Kentish Times Leader (tues). STD code 01732

### STAG THEATRE

London Road, Sevenoaks, Kent TN13 1ZZ
Mgt 01723 451548 BO 01723 450175
Fax 01723 743306
ADMINISTRATION:
Props: Stag Theatre Ltd
General Manager: Terry Shaw
Production Manager: Tony Moore
Chief Technician: Jess Skoplos
Publicity ad Marketing Manager: Francis V Price
Administration Manager: Jane Grater
Policy: Professional and amateur productions, drama, musicals, dance, opera, concerts, touring shows, films, lectures.
Perfs: Usually 7.30/8.00pm
Seats: 139-700 variable.
Cinemas x 2: 141 and 109 seats.
General Facilities: Variable capacity refurbished auditorium from 139 seats studio style - 454 main auditorium - 700 seats in the round. 2 wheelchair spaces in main auditorium in the round and one in each cinema. Cinemas also available for hire comprising 141 seats and 109 seats (main house also has full 35mm projection facilities - 454 seats. Large conference/function/rehearsal suite available - part of the complex bookable separately. Heating and ventilation with adbiatic cooling system. In-house advertising and publicity department.
Public areas: large theatre bar/restaurant serving light lunches 10.00 am - 2.30 pm and pre-show suppers - cast and crew catering available. Carlton bar used for studio and in the round performances. Large light ground floor foyer with access to disabled lift. Upper foyer with coffee bar and cloakroom. Disabled and toddler facilities. Fully computerised box office.
TECHNICAL:
Stage: Size 60ft x 60ft performing area, 96 way dimmers, Arri Image lighting board. Manual lighting board, two lighting control boxes, Tech Pro headset system, full sound system/mixing desk, radio mic etc. Induction loop in each auditoria.
Lighting: Large in house lighting rig - inc 24 x Starlette fres. 36 x Cantata profile 14 x P743 Fres. Parcans, Codas, Minuettes and 2 x 1k csi followspots. 65 amp 3 phase supply on stage. 2 x 65 amp single phase supply on stage. Large scenery truck (horizontal flying system) 20ft x 20ft in 10ft x 5ft sections.
Dressing rooms: 2 principals with en-suite showers, wash basin etc. Large chorus room for up to 70 with shower block, WC's etc.
Orchestra pit for up to 50 musicians, removal lid on forestage. Prompt corner usually p.s. Baby grand and rehearsal pianos available. Large vehicle hoist to lift level with stage for get in (up to 7 ton short wheel base lorry). Large public car park at rear.

Full technical support by our 3 in house technicians, casuals available.

# Shanklin, I.O.W.

Pop. 16,000. Newspapers: Isle of Wight; Weekly post (thurs); Isle of Wight; County Press (fri). STD code 01983

### SHANKLIN THEATRE

Prospect Road, Shanklin, Isle of Wight PO37 6AJ
Mgt 01983 862739 BO 01983 868000
SD 01983 862916
ADMINISTRATION:
Props: I.W. Theatres Ltd.
Director: David Redston
Technical Manager: Chris Gardner
Policy: All year Repertory, Touring Repertory, Amateur Societies, One Night Stands, Musical Productions, Conferences, Exhibitions, Multi-Purpose Hall.
Perfs: Summer 8.15. Other times variable.
Seats: 670; cabaret style 420. Bar
TECHNICAL:
Stage: Proscenium, raked. Proscenium opening 8.99m. Height of proscenium 5.50m. Depth of S/Line 8.99m. Height of grid 9.90m. 20 lines hemp. W/widths P.S. 3.66m, O.P. 3.66m. Prompt corner P.S.
Lighting: Switchboard: Eurolight Micron Memory Board, 43 circuits 2kw. 3 phase. Normally operated FoH stalls. 100 amp 3 phase supply available for temp. board. Switched independents in flys, stage and F.O.H. Large lamp stock available.
Sound: A&H S.R. Series 12.2 Mixer.FoH P.S.L. VE500 250w P.C. Foldback MM 130w P.C. Revox B77 tape deck; Teac cassette deck; Mics AKG CMS system. Acoustics suitable for music or spoken word.
Stage management: Dressing room call and relay. Intercom and Q lights to all technical stations.
Backstage: 7 dressing rooms accommodating 40.
Orchestra pit: with grand piano.
Staff: 1 stage, casuals available.

# Sheffield, S Yorks

Pop. 513,310. London 160 miles. Newspapers: The Star (ntly); Telegraph (wkly). STD code 0114

### SHEFFIELD ARENA

Broughton Lane, Sheffield S9 2DF
Mgt 0114 256 2002 BO 0114 256 5656
Fax 0114 256 5520
ADMINISTRATION:
For all booking information and further details please contact Sam Shrouder or Nicky Monk at Apollo Leisure (UK) Ltd., Grehan House, Garsington Road, Cowley, Oxford OX4 5NQ. Tel: 01865 782900; Fax: Oxford 01865 782910.
General Manager: David Vickers
Staging major sporting events, exhibitions and conferences for the 12,000 seat capacity venue.

### SHEFFIELD CITY HALL

Barkers Pool, Balm Green, Sheffield S1 2JA
Mgt 0114 273 4242 Mkt/Press 0114 273 4595
BO 0114 278 9789 Fax 0114 276 9866
General Manager: Maire McCarthy
Seating/Capacity: Oval Hall 2,346; Memorial Hall 522; Central Suite 850.

**SHEFFIELD THEATRES**
Crucible Theatre & Lyceum Theatre Norfolk Street,
Sheffield S Yorks S1 1DA
Mgt 0114 276 0621 BO 0114 276 9922
ADMINISTRATION:
Props: Sheffield Theatres Trust
Chief Executive: Grahame Morris
Artistic Director: Deborah Paige
Finance Director: Andew Snelling
Marketing Director: Angela Galvin
Policy: Producing Theatre with full education team.
Perfs: Eves. 7.30 (Studio 7.45)
Seats: 1,000 approx.
Licensed Bar, Coffee Shop, Restaurant, 'Cues' Gift
Shop, and frequent foyer exhibitions.
Lyceum seats 1,100 on three levels.  No 1 touring
theatre, ballet, opera, musicals, drama, and pantomime.
4 bars.
TECHNICAL:
Please contact venue for full listings.

**SHEFFIELD'S OCTAGON**
Octagan Centre Western Bank, Sheffield S10 2TQ
Tel 0114 222 8888 Fax 0114 272 9097
Seating/Capacity: 1,250, retractable. 1,500 standing.
Entertainments Manager: Matthew Wooliscroft
Direct Line 0114 222 8556

# Sheringham, Norfolk

Pop. 4,770. London 130 miles. Newspapers: North
Norfolk News (fri); Eastern Daily Press (dly). STD code
01263

**LITTLE THEATRE**
2 Station Road, Sheringham, Norfolk NR26 8RE
Admin 01263 822117  Fax 01263 821963
BO 01263 822347
10am-4pm (Mon-Fri), 10am-5pm (Sat)
Policy: Summer repertory - rest of year on hire; also
35mm films.
Perfs: 8.00 normal
Seats: 181
ADMINISTRATION:
Props: Sheringham Little Theatre Society
Theatre Manager: Jonathan Emery
TECHNICAL:
Stage: Proscenium, Pros. Opening 5.26m; Ht. of Pros.
3.20m; Ht. of Grid 3.74m; Prompt Cnr. O.P.
Lighting: Switchboard: Sirius 24, Zero 88.
Sound: peakers: 2 - one each side of Pros.
Film: Twin 35mm.
Dressing Rooms 2; Accom. 9 Male, 10 Female.

# Shrewsbury, Shropshire

Pop. 57,300. London 148 miles. Newspapers:
Shropshire Star (btly); Shrewsbury Chronicle (thurs);
Shrewsbury Ad-Mag (thurs). STD code 01743

**MUSIC HALL**
The Square, Shrewsbury Shropshire SY1 1LH
Admin 01743 352019 BO 01743 244255
Fax 01743 358780
ADMINISTRATION:
Props: Shrewsbury and Atcham Borough Council
General Manager: Lezley Picton

House Manager: David Jack
Chief Technician: Grant Wilson
Policy: Week, Part-week and single performances of
Drama, Dance, Opera, Variety, Concerts etc.  Seats 398
on rectractable units (48 on arena floor). Promenade
450.
Licensed bars, coffee shops, function catering facilities.
Funding Authority: Shrewsbury and Atcham Borough
Council.
TECHNICAL:
Stage: Proscenium, width 9.41m depth 7.60m.  Upstage
crossover.  Flat floor wood on joists.  Three pair legs,
one set black tabs, four borders.  House tabs in red, 1
black, 1 white gauze, white cyc cloth, various other
cloths - information on request.  Stage management
from prompt side with TV monitor, or from control box at
rear of auditorium.
Lighting: Zero 88 Sirius control feeding 102 x 2.5kw
circuits.  Profile: 4 x Cadenza 18/32; 6 Cantata 18/32; 2
x Cantata 26/44; 4 x Prelude 16/30; 2 x Cantata 11/26;
4 x Sil; 2 x T-84; 2 x CSI follow spots.  Fresnels: 2 x
Cadenza PCs 2kw; 14 x Cantata PC 1.2kw; 8 x Cantata
F; 2 x Harmony F; 10 x Patt 743; 3 x Thomas 650w; 9 x
Prelude 650w; Beam lights: 8 x Tomcat par;  Floods: 8 x
Nocturne; 3 x Coda 500w; 1 x Monster Strobe; 1 x
Roscoe 1500; Fog machine; 1 x Mirror ball; 4 colour
wheels.
Sound: Studiomaster series two 16-8-2 Mixer; Alesis
Quadreverb; 2 x Boss GE131 Graphic Eq., 2 x Denon
twin cassette decks; 1 x Denon CD player, 1 x Tascam
32 and 1 A77 reel to reel; Six dressing rooms
accommodating up to 30 plus performers.  Backstage
relay/paging.  2 showers.

# Sidmouth, Devon

Pop. 12,500. London 163 miles. Newspapers: Sidmouth
Herald (sat). STD code 013958

**MANOR PAVILION**
Manor Road, Sidmouth, Devon EX10 8PR
Mgt 01395 516551 (Extn 401) for hiring enquiries
Fax 01395 577853
ADMINISTRATION:
Props: East Devon District Council
Lessees: Charles Vance Ltd
Artistic Director: Charles Vance
Policy: Summer Repertory July to September inclusive.
Also Amateurs and Concert Recitals throughout the year.
Seats: 282

# Skegness, Lincs

Pop. 15,000. London 139 miles. Newspapers: Skegness
Standard (fri); Skegness News (wed). STD code 01754

**EMBASSY CENTRE**
Grand Parade, Skegness, Lincolnshire PE25 2UG
Mgt 01754 768444 BO 01754 768333
Fax 01754 761737
ADMINISTRATION:
Props: East Lindsey District Council
For bookings contact Bob Suich, Head of Leisure and
Tourism
Tel: 01507 601111
Centre Manager: Steve Wattam
Policy: Concerts, Summer Shows, Conferences,
Exhbitions, Multi-purpose venue.

Seats: 1168 in fully seated configuration. Lower level 760 seats (332 loose, 428 retractable); balcony seats fixed. Catering facilities. Licensed Bar.
TECHNICAL:
Stage: Proscenium with fixed apron; Proscenium opening 7.00m; Ht. of Pros. 3.5m; Depth 4m curved. Vario's available for stage extensions. Soundcraft 200 sound desk.
Lighting: Switchboard: Celco 'Series 2' - 55 Spots - 2 Follow Spots.
Sound Equip: 4 Amplifiers, 10 Speakers, microphones 11, 4 foldback speakers.
Dressing Rooms 5.
Please apply to Centre for full technical specification.

### FESTIVAL PAVILION THEATRE
Tower Esplanade, Skegness, Lincs
Mgt 01754 767425  Fax 01754 765065
ADMINISTRATION:
Props: East Lindsey District Council
Management: Ian Wright & M. Dodson
Policy: Summer Shows/Conferences/Multi-Purpose/ Pop Concerts/Variety.
Seats: 1,000. Licensed Bars.
TECHNICAL:
Stage: Width 10.5m, Ht. 3m. Depth 5m.
Lighting: Furse, Backstage; F.O.H. Spots 8 2000w Lime Spot 1, 3 Battens, Footlights, Dimmers 6 Spot Bars.
Sound Equip: Amplifier, 4 Speaker twin mounted 4 microphone.
Dressing Rooms 4; Showers in 2.

# Solihull, West Midlands

Pop. 198,700. London 110 miles. Newspapers: Solihull News (thurs); Solihull Times (fri). Plus Birmingham Newspapers. STD code 0121

### SOLIHULL ARTS COMPLEX - LIBRARY THEATRE & EXHIBITION HALL
Homer Road, Solihull, West Midlands B91 3RG
Mgt 0121 704 6961 BO 0121 704 6962
Fax 0121 704 8195
ADMINISTRATION:
Props: Solihull MBC
Arts & Entertainments Manager: Lawrence Smith
Policy: Mixed use
Seats: 340 (theatre), 200 Exhibition Hall, Coffee Bar and Theatre Bar.
TECHNICAL:
Stage: Pros. opening 9.00m; Ht. of pros 4.00m (permanent with safety curtain); Stage 13m wide between galleries; 17.37m wall to wall; Ht. of Stage 11.75m to grid, 5.7m to underside of galleries; Stage surface soft wood boarding, Cyc permanent; 15 hemp fly lines.
Lighting: Strand 72 channel LBX LX board;  Stage Managers control desk (working corner SL) operating house tabs; intercom to FOH, Backstage show relay FOH; Backstage cue light system.
Sound Equip: Soundcraft K3 32-8-2-1; Denon Cassette deck; Bose 802-302 speaker; C Audio amps DN360 Graphics.
Projection facilities: Elmo 16mm Kodak SAV2010.
Dressing Rooms: 2 principal, shower/wash basin/wc; 2 chorus with 2 wash basins and wc; Wardrobe Green Room.
Get-in: 5.75m high x 3.00m wide dock door direct off carpark, drop to road .80m.

Also in complex , Exhibition Hall, Art Gallery, Bar and Coffee Lounge in addition to Library itself.

# South Shields, Tyne and Wear

### TEMPLE PARK CENTRE
Temple Memorial Park, John Reid Road, South Shields, Tyne and Wear NE34 8QN
Tel 0191 456 9119 Fax 0191 456 6621
ADMINISTRATION:
Props: South Tyneside Metropolitan Borough Council; Centre Manager: H. Blackett.
Policy: Multi-purpose Hall used for concerts, shows, sporting and special events, conferences and exhibitions.
Seating/Capacity: 2,000 seated; 3,500 standing.
TECHNICAL:
Main Hall: 155' x 119' (47.5m x 36.5m); Height 36' (11.0m); Total Area 18,445 sq. ft. (1,733 sq.m.).
Power: 100 amp 3 phase; 60 amp 3 phase; backstage external generator feed point.
Sound and Lighting: In-house P.A. and full sound system. Strand lighting system with control room.
Flying Facilities: 15 suspension points at 11.0 metres. Overall loading of 4 tons.
Other: Backstage: dressing rooms (private and communal); showers, w.c.; laundry and ironing.
Catering: Separate crew catering and dining fully equipped.
Changing: Large communal areas all with showers, hairdryers and w.c.
Production: Offices available with metered telephone, fax etc.
Access and Loading: Direct points adjacent to Main Hall.

# Southampton, Hants

Pop. 213,710. London 77 miles. Newspapers: Southern Evening Echo (ntly); Southampton Advertiser (thurs). STD code 01703

### MAYFLOWER THEATRE
Commercial Road, Southampton Hants SO15 1GE
Mgt 01703 711800 BO 01703 711811 Group Bookings 01703 711812 SD 01703 330071 Fax 01703 711801
ADMINISTRATION:
Props: Mayflower Theatre Trust Ltd.
Director: Dennis Hall
Financial Controller: Wycliffe Musuku
P.A the to Director: Mo Loader
Head of Marketing & Operations: Paul Lewis
Marketing Manager: Julia Lewis
Technical Manager: Richard Vidler
Stage Manager: Roy Osborne
Chief Electrician: Eric Butler
Customer Services Manager: Gill Wyatt
Box Office Managers: Melanie Newington & Carole Butt
House Manager: Bill Wiseman
Policy: No. 1 Touring Companies including National Ballet and Opera, Musicals (Pre/Post West End), Concerts, One Nighters, Conferences etc.
Seats: 2,289 plus 130 standing - total capacity 2,419.
TECHNICAL:
Stage: Pros. opening 13.5m; Ht. 7m, depth 12m P.S. 3m, O.P. 5.9m, stage width overall 22.6m.

Lighting: Control 300 channel Strand 530. Dimmers 5kw.
Dimmer 48 2kw Dimmer 252. Stage management
control desk has full dual queueing system of lights and
head-set communication video cameras can monitor
orchestral pit and stage.
Sound: 'Martin 10k' system controlled by a Soundcraft
800B Board.
Dressing Rooms: 18 (accommodating up to 120
persons) all on individual call system, plus show relay
facility. Band rooms; situated under the stage with direct
access to orchestra pit, 2 rooms with accommodation
for approx. 20 in each. Lifting front of Proscenium 6 x 1
tonne Points Stage Grid 16 x 1 tonne Scene height 6.4m
Dock, Width 4.3m; Depth 16.2m; new ramp unloading
height 1.3m.
Touring Managers Office.
Power: 3 x 3ph 200 amp.

## NUFFIELD THEATRE

University Road, Southampton Hants SO17 1TR
Mgt 01703 315500 BO 01703 617771
SD 01703 555414 Fax 01703 315511
ADMINISTRATION:
Props: The Nuffield Theatre Trust
Artistic Director Patrick Sandford
Licensee & Administrative Director: Mark Courtice
Production Manager: Julien Boast
Chief Technician: Greg Head
Policy: 3/4 weekly repertory (Sept-May) occasional tours
and amateur hire.
Perfs: Mon-Thurs Eve 7.30 pm; Fri & Sat eves 8 pm.
Mats: occasionally Mid-Week 2.30pm & Sat 2.30pm.
Seats: 481 (varies according to stage). Fully licensed
Theatre Bar, Restaurant.
Audio Description on last Wednesday of professional
run. Sighed performance on last Thursday of
professional run.
TECHNICAL:
Stage: Proscenium arch with thrust. Pros.opening 8.8m
x 4.5m - wing widths 4.11m SR, 4.11 SL. No rake - floor
hardboard covered, backstage crossover, stage heated.
Height of grid 9.57m - 20 hemp sets, 4 cw's, 0.2m apart
- tab track - maximum flying height 4.5m - black serge
legs and tabs - white filled cotton cloth cyclorama - blue
house tabs flown on c/w. Forestage (not rectangular) in 2
parts, 1st forestage: 2m 60 x 7m 50, 2nd forestage 2m
30 x 8m. Tensioned wired grid above the foredtage.
Orchestra pit accomodates 15 with single forestage or
25 if double. 15 lit music stands available. Get-in via
doors 2100 x 3000. Tallescope. Safety curtain. Scaled
1.25 plans available.
Lighting: Colortran Compact Elite board, 228 circuits,
200A, 3 phase, operated from rear of auditorium - no
supply for temporary board. Profiles: 30 CCT Sil 30 -1k,
20 CCT Sil 30 - 1.2k, 4 CCT Sil 40 - 1k, 10 Strand 263 -
1k, 4 Strand 764 - 1k, 4 Tulla Lito - 650w, 4 CCT
Minuette - 650 w, 3 Strand 23 - 500w Fresnels: 22
Strand 743 - 1k (c/w barndoors), 10 Tulla Lito - 1k (c/w
barndoors), 4 Strand 243 - 2k (c/w barndoors), 6
Coemar - 2k (c/w barndoors), 4 CCT Minuette - 650w
(c/w Barndoors), 2 Strand 123 - 500w (c/w barndoors),
3 Strand Beamlights, 40 Thomas Parcan (12 CP61/ 12
CP62/ 12 CP60), Floods: 5 Iris 4 -1k, 4 CCT Minuette -
500w, 6 Strand Patt 60, 6 Strand Coda 4's, Follow
Spots: 2 Strand 293 - 2k, 6 Rainbow 2-16 8" color
Scrollers.
Sound: 1 32 channel Soundcraft Ghost 32:8:8, 1
Yamaha 02R, 1 Soundcraft 200B 16 channel,1 Spirit
Folio 12.2 (restaurant), Speakers: 2 Bose 802 +
controller, 2 Ohm wedges 150w, 2 Bose 101, 2 Courts,
2 TOA full range speakers (restaurant), 2 Tannoy Mercury

(Controlroom monitors), 4 Ramsa A10 (front fills), Amps:
1 Quad 306 (controlroom monitors), 1 Quad 520, 1
Carver, 1 TOA (restaurant), 1 Amcron, 1 Crown CSL 460
(front fills), Main PA: 4 TOA Hi-Mid (spx), 2 TOA sub-bass
(spx), 1 TOA DPA-800amp (hi) + controller, 1 TOA DPA-
1200amp (Mid) + controller, 1 TOA DPA-2000amp
(Bass) + controller, Recorders & Players: 2 Tascam MD-
801R, 1 Akai S3000XL midi stereo digital sampler & Opti
driver 230mb, 1 Akai DR4VR hard disk recorder 2gb, 1
Denon twin cassette recorder, 1 Denon CD player, 1
Panasonic record player, 1 Teac portable DAT player, 3
Revox players/recorders, Effects Processors: Alesis
MidiVerb III, 1 Yamaha SPX50D, 1 TOA digital signal
processor DP0204, 1 Alesis M-EG 230, Microphones: 3
RS dynamic mics, 4 PZM, 1 AKG D955, 4 Audio
Technica rifle mics, 1 Sennheiser rifle mic, 1 Sennheiser
MD421 dynamic mic + strands (describing mics), 3
Shure SM58, Accessories: 3 Adjustable boom arm mic
stands (chrome), 2 adjustable boom arm mic stands
(black), 2 adjustable small mic stands, 2 DI boxes, 116
way XLR-XLR multi-core. Infra red system available.
Stage Management: Prompt corner SL - cue system, 10
outstations, show relay/tannoy to dressing rooms.
Backstage: 2 dressing rooms - green room - wardrobe
rear of stage with iron, washing machine, dryer and 3
power points. Rehearsal rooms by arrangement, piano
good. Advice given on accomodation. Staff - 1 stage, 2
lighting - casuals available - no security personnel.
Backstage facilities accessible to disabled performers
and staff.

## SOUTHAMPTON GUILDHALL

Northguild, Civic Centre, Southampton Hants SO14 7LP
Mgt 01703 832451 BO 01703 632601
Fax 01703 233359
ADMINISTRATION:
Props: Southampton City Council
Manager: Sue Cheriton
Southampton Guildhall comprises of three multi-purpose
auditorium.
Policy: Rock Concerts, Conferences, Dinners, Dances,
Exhibitions.
Capacities: Guildhall: 1,749 standing/balcony seating,
1,315 seated; Solent Suite: 300; Lecture Theatre 118.
Bar and Catering facilities.
TECHNICAL:
GUILDHALL
Stage: Proscenium with 1.24 rake; Pros. opening 14.8m;
Ht. of Pros. 8.4m; Stage depth 9.7m (11.7m with stage
extension); 8 winch bars.
Lightboard: Switchboard zero 88 sinus, boch Avolites,
Pearl (incl. grachics both dimming and control talk DMX
Full lighting rig Par 64's, CYC units, 8 X 1 ton winches in
auditorium, trussing available.
Sound: 32:8:2 Allen and Heath FOH/Monitor; 16:4:2
Soundcraft Delta FOH; 4 Base 802 and 10 Base (along
auditorium wall); full AV equipment; Compton double
consol pipe organ.
Choir stalls - seating 120.
Dressing Rooms: 6 - 2 with shower, toilet.
SOLENT SUITE
Performance/Auditorium space 31.5m X 8.78m.
Permanent dance floor.
LECTURE THEATRE
Opened 1993 tiered seat auditorium, full AV equipment
Stage: Proscenium opening 4.3m, height 2.57m, stage
depth 4.93m; full stage width 6.27m.
Lighting: 2 bars on stage, 1 bar FOH.
General: Indction loop.

### SOUTHAMPTON UNIVERSITY

University Road, Highfield, Southampton
Hants SO17 1BJ
Tel 01703 595200 Fax 01703 595252
ADMINISTRATION:
Events Officer: Dawn Perry
Main venue: seating/capacity: 800 (but only available for hire on weds. and sat.)
Other venues: Seating/Capacities: 500 and 400 (Both are available for hire throughout the week.)

### TURNER SIMS CONCERT HALL

University of Southampton, University Road, Southampton Hants SO17 1BJ
Mgt 01703 592223 BO 01703 595151
Fax 01703 592505
Seating/Capacity: 461 max, raked.
Concert Hall Manager: Peter Bolton

# Southend-On-Sea, Essex

Pop. 175,300. London 40 miles. Newspapers: Evening Echo (ntly); Standard Recorder (wkly); Yellow Advertiser (wkly). STD code 01702

### CLIFFS PAVILION

Station Road, Westcliff-on-Sea, Essex SS0 7RA
Mgt 01702 331852 BO 01702 351135
SD 01702 347394 Fax 01702 433015
Admin 01702 390657 Marketing 01702 390472
ADMINISTRATION:
Props: Southend-on-Sea B.C.
General Manager: Charles Mumford, AILAM(Dip)
Stage and Events Officer: Lester Sayer
Marketing: Paul Driscoll
Policy: Multi-Purpose
Perfs: Various
Seats: 1,630 Concerts, Shows; 1,000 Arena Events; Standing: 2,000.
Licenced Bars.
Full Conference Facilities.
TECHNICAL:
Stage: Get in: Loading bay with access to stage and auditorium via large lift 2.3m x 2.1m x 5.5m . Dressing Rooms: 8 medium sized rooms, large wardrobe with two twin tubs and 1 tumble dryer.
Power: Located u.s.r. Visiting lighting supply 200 amp three phase. Visting sound supply 63 amp three phase.
Stage Dimensions: Stage Raked: 1 in 25. Proscenium Width: Variable 9.75m to 14.33m. Proscenium Height: 5.33m. Stage Height: 1.1m. Stage Depth: 9.75m. Stage Width: 18.3m to 22.7m. Height of Grid 11.28m. Scenery flying height: 5.49m Height to fly floor 6.4m.
Control room to stage front: 25.45m. Stage Equipment: Flying lines: 27 Counterweight sets, Bars 16.45m at 23cm centres. Weight capacity: 396 kilo per craddle additional 3 Hemp sets. Rostra 20 Merricks Sico, wheeled rostra various heights. Curtains Full set blacks, full set blue, Set of Silvers with festoon, Cyclorama, assorted gauze and painted cloths. Pianos 1 Baldwin Grand, 1 Bluther Grand. Misc. Assorted Weights etc.
Lighting: Control: Arri Image 2 c/w riggers control & reflexion as back up. System is multiplexed at the desk and demultiplexed to drive the JTM dimmers situated sub-stage by the Arri Connexion. Follow Spots - 2 Patt 765 1KW CID (situated half way back in auditorium) Profile Spots - 16 Patt 264 1KW 4 T64 Spots 1 KW Fresnels - 19 Patt 743 1 KW 6 Patt 243 2KW.
Dimmer Outlets are situated as follows: NB All are

terminated in a 15a socket with the exception of the 5 KW circuits which terminate in a 32 amp. C-Form or 4 x 15 amp sockets. 1-20 - Bridge 2 FOH, 21-32 - Bridge 1 FOH, 33-50 - Patchable circuits FOH, 41-50 - PS flys DS onstage, 51-66 - PS flys DS onstage, 67-82 - PS flys CS onstage, 83-104 - PS flys US onstage, 105-107 - DSL Dips, 108-110 - CSL Dips, 111-112 - USL Dips, 113-116 - USR Dips, 117-118 - DSR Dips, 119-PS flys US 5KW, 120 - OP Back Wall 5KW
Sound: Mixer Soundcraft venue 32-8-4 positioned in either control room or centre stalls. Amplifiers: Main PA (2.5kw 5 Ashly FET 2000C), Monitors (1 kw), Monitors (1 kw) 2 Ashly FET 2000C. Processing: SPX 900, Drawmer compresser, Digital Delay. Loudspeakers: 6 Community RS220, 2 Community NFB, 2 Community VBS 212, 2 Community RS JR, 2 Community CSX 38M (wedges monitors), 4 JBL 4628B (on stage), 3 Shure 702 Wedges. Microphones: 4 SM58 LC, 3 Shure SM78, 4 Shure SM77, 1 Shure SM85, 2 Shure PE 75L, 1 Sennheiser 509, 2 AKG C451/CK8, 2 C-ducers, 1 Micron CNS non-diversity Lavalier, C/W MKE-2 mic. Mic Lines 24 lines from stage, 12 lines from pit, (Various lines around Building 96 in total). Coms: 6 Beltpacks and headsets.

### PALACE THEATRE CENTRE

London Road, Westcliff-on-Sea, Essex SS0 9LA
Mgt 01702 347816 BO 01702 342564
Fax 01702 435031
ADMINISTRATION:
Props: The Palace Theatre Trust (Southend-on-Sea) Ltd
Artistic Director: Christopher Dunham
Policy: Repertory. Infra-red audio/description system.
Perfs: Nightly 8.00; Wed. Mats 2.30 Sat Mats.4.00
Bar, Bistro, FOH Theatre completely refurbished 1987.
TECHNICAL:
Stage: Proscenium Arch: 8m wide, 5.5m high. 4.88m depth @ Centre Line (NB: Back wall does not run parallel). Alcove at rear, understage crossover. Rake 1:18. Grid 16.76m. 13 Lines hemp. 6 Lines CWT. Flying bars 9m long. Orchestra pit (coverd when not in use) accom. 12.
MAIN HOUSE
Sound: Soundcraft K3 24 channel, Court Proflex and Bose 802.C speakers, Yamaha amps,1 amp spare for on stage.
Lighting: Rand 430 with Genius+ Version 1.5, working dimmers. Harmony 15/28, Harmony 22/40, Cantata 26/44, Prelude 16/30, Harmony PC, Harmony F, ADB F, Prelude F, Minuette PC, Prelude PC, PAR 64, Nocturne flood, AC1001L floods, Coda battens.
STUDIO
Sound: The Studio has a basis sound system.
Lighting: Rand action 24 way board dimmers. SIL 30 (AXIAL), PAT 803 F, T64, PAT 743, PAT 813 PC.
Playback: Revox B77, CD players, cassette deck. Mics: AKG D330BT, Shure SM58, Sennhiser K6 (ME66 Capsules).
General: Dressing rooms: 4, accommodates 20.
Wardrobe with full laundry facilities. Workshop.
Paintshop. Complex also incorporates the Dixon Studio with its own LX and Sound systems, Cueing facilities and Show Relay.
Membership: TMA

# Southport, Merseyside

Pop. 89,400. London 210 miles. Newspapers: Southport Midweek Visitor (wed); Southampton Champion (wed); Southport Visitor (fri). STD code 01704

## FLORAL HALL

Promenade, Southport, Merseyside PR9 0DZ
Mgt 01704 540454 BO 01704 540404
SD 01704 540404 Fax 01704 536841
ADMINISTRATION:
Props: Sefton Metropolitan Borough Council
Managed by Apollo Leisure (UK) Ltd,
PO Box 960, Oxford OX4 5ND.
Tel: 01865 782900 or Fax 01865 782910.
General Manager: Lisa Chu
Resident Technical Managers: P Bateman, J. Hopper, P.
Bowes.
Seats: 1,000
TECHNICAL:
Stage: Proscenium. Pros. opening 36' x 16'. Falso pros.
28' x 12'. Stage depth 22'. Forestage 6'. 10 Hemp
Lighting: Switchboard: Rank Strand Memory System 46
way, lightboard M.
Sound: Soundcraft mixer, 16 channel, Rowland Spale
Echo. Speakers Proscenium Side Walls.
Dressing Rooms: 4 Showers 1.
Film equipment available 16mm.

## SOUTHPORT ARTS CENTRE

Lord Street, Southport, Merseyside PR8 1DB
Mgt 01704 540004 BO 01704 540011
ADMINISTRATION:
Props: Sefton Metropolitan B.C.
Arts Service Officer: John Taylor
Administration: Leslie Wilson
Arts Operations Manager: Mark Ratcliffe
Perfs: Small/mid scale touring productions, film, dance,
all kinds of music, exhibitions etc.
Seats: New Cambridge Theatre: 472; Studio 1: 260
seats; Studio 2: 85 seats. Bar/Buffet.
All venues available for hire at competitive rates.
TECHNICAL:
NEW CAMBRIDGE THEATRE:
Stage: Open end Proscenium, Flat; Pros. Opening
14.75m; Depth of S/Line 11.75m; Ht. of grid 7.80m; 24
lines, Hemp; W/Widths P.S. 10.50, O.P. 7.60; Prompt
Cnr P.S.
Lighting: Switchboard: Eclipse, rear of auditorium; 80
ways; Circuits: F.O.H. 28, Files 42, Dips 10, Ind. 6 at
Stage level, 6 at Grid level; Lamps: 31 1k TH Profiles, 30
1k TH Fresnels.
Sound Equip: 1 Turntable, 2 Tape Decks Revox A77 .50
track, rear auditorium; Speakers in dressing rooms, bars,
foyer area.
Dressing Rooms 6; Accom. 44; 2 Showers; Orchestra
Pit 19 sq.m
STUDIO 1:
Stage: Totally flexible working space, round, thrust, club
style, etc. Space 64' deep x 52' wide. Electronic
bleacher seating, giving 19 seats per row and up to ten
rows. 200 separate chairs, 24 Sico rostra 45 matching
tables.
Lighting: Board: Zero 88 Eclipse 72 channel. 12 1.2kw
Fresnels, Cantata; 8 1.2kw p.c. Canatata; 2 1.2kw
Profiles, Cantata; 18 1kw Parcans.
Sound: Desk AHB 16/4/2 mixing desk; 3 Ramsa amps;
1 Harrison graphic equaliser; 1 Yamaha SPX 900 effects
unit; 1 Revox B77 reel-to-reel 2 tack recorder; Technics
record deck; Tascam stereo cassette deck; 6 speakers
rig; 20 various microphones. Get-in via lift to rear of
stage.
Dressing Rooms: 6, accom. 44; 2 Showers.
STUDIO 2:
Small (30ft x 30ft), flexibile multi-purpose space ideal for
experimental or small scale drama, recitals, etc.Sound

and lighting installed to suit performances dictates but
facilities include 12 channel lighting system and 16
channel sound rig, video equip. and 35mm film projector.
Full access for performers to all backstage facilities.

## SOUTHPORT THEATRE

Promenade, Southport, Merseyside PR9 0DZ
Mgt 01704 540454 BO 01704 540404 Prod 0151 934
2444 Prod Fax 0151 934 2445 SD 0151 934 2407
Fax 01704 536841
ADMINISTRATION:
Props: Sefton Metropolitan Borough Council
Managed by Apollo Leisure (UK) Ltd.
For all booking information and further details please
contact Sam Shrouder or Nicky Monk at Apollo Leisure
(UK) Ltd., Grehan House, Garsington Road, Cowley,
Oxford OX4 5NQ. Tel: 01865 782900; Fax: Oxford
01865 782910.
General Manager: Lisa Chu
Resident Technical Managers: P. Bateman, J. Hopper,
P. Bowes.
Policy: Pantomime, Summer Season, Concerts, Touring,
Cinema.
Seats: 1,651. Four Bars, Restaurant.
TECHNICAL:
Stage: Proscenium with 3.35m deep thrust. Flat; Pros.
Opening 13.41m; Ht. of Pros. 5.18m; Depth of S/Line
7.32m; Ht. of Grid 9.14m; 20 lines, Hemp; Scenery
Flying Ht. 5.18m, O.P. 5.18m; Prompt Cnr. P.S.
Lighting: Switchboard: Lightboard M 96 channels,
Projection Room; 80 ways; F.O.H. Spots 20 Patt.764; 2
Patt.765; Battens 6 Patt.S/64; Dips 6 P.S. 6 O.P.; 3
Spot Bars, Patt.764, Patt.743, Patt.60.
Sound Equipment: 18 channel Soundcraft desk Mosfet &
Crown Power amps. Crown Power amps projection
room; Speakers Pros. side walls.
Dressing Rooms 13; Showers 4; Orchestra Pit 20.
Film Equipment fitted for 70mm, 35mm and 16mm with
optical or magnetic sound - Dolby Stereo Sound.

# Southsea, Hants

(see Portsmouth for information). STD code 01705

## KING'S THEATRE

Albert Road, Southsea, Hampshire PO5 2QJ
Mgt 01705 811294 BO 01705 812082
SD 01705 811396  Fax 01705 735242
ADMINISTRATION:
Co-Lessees: Joan N Cooper & I S Barnes
General Manager: Vanessa Dowling
Stage Manager: John Pike
Chief Electrician: Mandi Branch
Theatre Secretary: Anne Kennedy
Policy: Weekly Tours, Season, Pantomime, Plays, Ballet,
Opera, One-Night Stands
Perfs: Mon-Fri 7.30; Mats. Thurs 2.30; Sats 5.00 & 8.00
Seats: 1,500. Four Bars.
TECHNICAL:
Stage: Proscenium arch. Performing area 13.41m x
11.59m - pros opening 9.14m x 7.92m - wing widths
4.27m S.R. 4.27m S.L. plus scene dock. Stage raked, 1
in 24 - floor hardboard on sprung wood, suitable for
dance. No lino available, backstage crossover, stage
heated. Height of grid 16.76m - 50 hemp sets, 0.18m
apart - 2 tab tracks - maximum flying height 8.23m - 3
sets black twill legs and borders- 1 black twill, 1 white
cyclorama - red with gold trim house tabs, flown.
Orchestra pit 10.67m x 2.44m, accommodates 19. Get-

in via side of theatre, 1.22m above street - dock doors 3.66m x 3.05m. Tallescope. Safety curtain. Scale stage, fly and lighting plans available.

Lighting: Berkey Colortran board, 88 circuits, 82 @ 2.5kw, 6 @ 5kw, operated from box at left of auditorium - 100A 3 phase and 60A single phase & 200 A3 Phase supplies available for temporary board - 22 spots, 30 fresnels, 22 pars, 8 floods, 2 x Patt.23, various - 2 x CSI followspots, operated from rear of gallery.

Sound: Sound craft 24-3 desk, operated from box at left of auditorium or variable positions - Oval 250w stereo & 800w Power Amp, 4 x Bose FOH speakers - 1 x Revox B77 reel-to-reel, twin cassette tape systems. Acoustics suitable for music and spoken word.

Stage Management: Prompt corner SR - cue lights and headsets, various outstations - show relay/Tannoy to dressing rooms.

Backstage: 11 dressing rooms, accommodating 40, access by stairs - band room - temporary quick change rooms - wardrobe on ground floor, with coin-operated washing machine and tumble drier. 1 upright rehearsal piano, good. Advice given on accommodation. Staff - 2 technicians - casuals available - security personnel as required.

1 Yamaha upright piano.

# Southwold, Suffolk

Pop. 2,010. London 107 miles. STD code 01502

### SOUTHWOLD SUMMER THEATRE

Cumberland Road, Southwold, Suffolk IP18 6JP
Tel 01502 722389
ADMINISTRATION:
Props: Church Council
Contact: Mrs P Bumstead, Bookings Secretary
Tel: 01502 723591
Lesses: Jill Freud & Co
In season: Westons, Walberswick, Southwold, Suffolk IP18 6UH. Tel: 01502 723077
Out of season: 22 Wimpole Street, London W1m 7AD
Tel 0171 580 2222  Fax 0171 580 2334
Policy: Available for Repertory, Summer Season, Pantomime
Perfs: As required (ex. Sunday)
Seats: 240
TECHNICAL:
Proscenium Stage, Flat
Sound Equip: 2 F.O.H. Speakers
Dressing Rooms 2; Accom. up to 12.

# Spennymoor

### SPENNYMOOR LEISURE CENTRE

The High Street, Spennymoor,
County Durham DL16 6DB
Tel 01388 815827 Fax 01388 810098
Centre Manager: Jean Burton
Seating/Capacity: 1,100

# St Albans, Herts

Pop. 53,000. London 21 miles. Newspapers: Herts Advertiser (fri). STD code 01727

### ABBEY THEATRE & STUDIO

Westminster Lodge, Holywell Hill, St. Albans,
Hertfordshire AL1 2DL
Mgt 01727 847472 BO 01727 857861
Fax 01727 812742
ADMINISTRATION:
Props: Abbey Theatre Trust (St. Albans) Ltd
Manager: David Griffiths
Policy: Own amateur use; also occasional touring companies and other local society use.
Perfs: 8.00
Main Theatre: 244, Studio Theatre 70, Bar and Coffee.
TECHNICAL:
Stage: Proscenium Stage, Main Stage, Flat; Pros.
Opening 7.32m; Depth of S/Line 6.10m; Ht. of Grid 9.14m approx; Hemp lines 13, C/W sets 7 (inc. act drop); Flying Bars 7.92 approx.; W/Widths P.S. 3.35m, O.P. 3.55m; Prompt Cnr. P.S.
Lighting: Switchboard: Strand in LBX F.O.H. control room; 72 channels; F.O.H. Bar plus 4 perches - 20 circuits. No. 1 Bar 12 circuits., No. 2 Bar 12 circuits., Cyc Bar 4 Circuits., Dips 12 Circuits, 10 CCT Minuettte zooms, 10 Patt.264, 10 Patt.223, 8 Patt.123, 13 Patt.23, 16 Patt.60 floods, 4 3 circuit compartment Battens. 4 4-way coda cyc light.
Sound Equip: 24 into 8 mixer, 2 tape decks, 1 CD, 1 Cassette Deck; Speakers 2 F.O.H., 2 Stage. Infrared hearing aid system installed.
Dressing Rooms 4; Accom. 20.
Wardrobe: Very extensive.

Studio: 11m x 10m. Moveable raked seating for 70.
Switchboard: Strand Tempus, 2 pre-set 24 channels, in control room.
Sound: 8 input stereo mixer, 2 tape decks, CD, Cassette. Infra-red hearing aid system installed. Both venues take wheelchairs by prior arrangement.
Dressing Rooms: 2.

### THE ARENA

Civic Centre, St. Peters Street, St. Albans,
Hertfordshire AL1 3LD
Mgt 01727 861078 BO 01727 844488
SD 01727 850345 Fax 01727 865755
ADMINISTRATION:
Props: St. Albans Leisure Ltd.
Manager: Roger Cramer
Assistant Managers: Ray Daynes
Technical Manager: Tony Ayre
Policy: Mainly one night stands, professional concerts, touring productions, shows and amateur productions, conferences, films and dances. General purpose venue also used for exhibitions etc.
Seats: 856 Retractable stalls, fixed circle. 2 Licensed Bars and 1 Coffee Bar.
TECHNICAL:
Stage: Proscenium, Flat; Pros. Opening 12.01m; Grid height 10.08m. Prompt corner stage left. Apron width 50'. 15.2m x 2.43m deep. Orchestra pit 13.68m x 3.04m deep. One Weber Baby Grand Piano. Flying 23 c/w. 6 LX Winch.
Lighting: Control from projection room. Zero 88 eclipse, 72 channel, extended level memory, programmable chasers and cartridge fx. 2 x 1kw CSI followspots. FOH 12 1kw TH furse, 12 patt 263 (TH) 8 parcans. Stage No.1 bar 6 x 1kw TH furse. 4 Cantata, 6 x parcans (booms). Stage No.2 bar 6 x 1kw fresnel, 4 x parcans, 2 Cantata, Coda 3's. Stage No.3 bar 6 x Coda 3's (3CCT) 4 x patt 23's, 6 x patt 123's. Stage floor 3 CCT's D/S, 3 CCT's Mid Stage, 3 CCT's U/S. Stage Power - 2 x 13

amp rings (30 amp loading each). Prompt Cnr - 1 x 100 amp 3 phase supply and 60 amp single phase supply. (N.B. The above lamps may not always be in the position allocated).
Sound Equip: Mixers - Soundcraft K1; 8 mic + 2 st.(control room); Soundcraft K3; 28 theatre + 4st + matrix O/P stalls. Processors: BSS Varicurve + Omnidrive, on main; + KT Graphics on monitors. Amplifiers: C Audio on main; H/H mosfet on monitors. Speakers: Turbosound TCS system with sub/base - main JBL Tannoy - side fill + wedges + personal monitors. Effects: Yahama SPX 990, Roland 201. Mics: 14 assorted AKG C451s + accessories, 6 AKG D310, 6 AKG Tri Power, 4 Crown PCC's.
Sundry: Denon Mini Disc, Denon DAT, Denon CD, TEAC 122 cassette, Revox A77 H/S, Technics t/table; Sennheiser Infra Red System for hard of hearing; S.I.A.P. Acoustic system. Film Equip: 2 x Westrex 7000 35mm, Dolby surround, Opt/sound/silent speeds: 1 x fumero x 900 16mm Opt/mag/sound/silent. Harkness flown screen opening to 3.56mm high x 7.3m wide (5 ratios, inc scope).
Dressing Rooms: Rear stage 6; Accom. 32, 2 Showers.

## MALTINGS ARTS THEATRE

The Maltings, St. Albans, Hertfordshire AL1 3HL
Tel 01727 844222  Fax 01727 836616
ADMINISTRATION:
Manager: Jo Askham
Technical Manager: Jason Caswell
Policy: The centre aims to be a venue for professional touring companies. The programme includes Profesional theatre and childrens theatre, concerts, dance and many participatory classes and workshops.
TECHNICAL:
Stage: The Studio Theatre has end-on playing on the level, with black drapes and legs. Racked bleecher bench seating for 100, maximum audience 140/200. The flat floor playing area can be adjusted to any size (maximum 37 feet wide, 30 feet deep) the usual format being 25 by 25 feet square, providing 6 feet wing space at either side and access behind the black drape to both sides. Maximum height of the theatre is 11 feet 6 inches.
Lighting: 44 circuits into 24 way Sirius MKII Lighting desk (2 preset manual/memory) 12 x 650w Minuette Fresnels; 6 x 650w Pulsar Fresnels; 8 x 650w Minuette Zoom Profiles; 6 x 650w Pulsar P/C's; 6 x 500w Pulsar Floods. Sound: 8 Channel Soundcraft 'Spirit' desk, 6 Shure mic with stands, Revox, twin cassette. Yamaha Grand Piano (5).
Dressing room, toilet and shower available.

# St Andrews

Pop. 11,633. London 422 miles. Newspapers: The Courier (dly); East Fife Mail (wed); St. Andrew's Citizen (fri); Fife Herald (wed); Fife News ( fri); Fife Free Press (fri). STD code 01334

## BUCHANAN THEATRE

University of St Andrews 79 North Street, St. Andrews, Fife KY16 9AJ Scotland
Tel 01334 462521 Fax 01334 462500
Contact: Linda Richardson (01334 462521)
Seating/Capacity: 386

## BYRE THEATRE

Abbey Street, St. Andrews, Fife KY16 9LA Scotland

NB The theatre will be closed for rebuilding until the summer of 2000. For any enquiries, contact Tom Gardner on Tel 01334 476288 or Fax 01334 475370

## YOUNGER GRADUATION HALL

University of St Andrews 79 North Street, St. Andrews, Fife KY16 9AJ Scotland
Tel 01334 462226 Fax 01334 462500
Contact: Alison Malcolm for Hall bookings during term time.
Contact: Linda Richardson (01334 462521) for Hall bookings outside term time.
Seating/Capacity: 968

# St Austell, Cornwall

Pop. 80,000. London 260 miles. Newspapers: Cornish Guardian; The West Briton; Western Morning News. STD code 01726

## CORNWALL COLISEUM

Carlyon Bay, St. Austell, Cornwall PL25 3RG
Mgt 01726 814261 BO 01726 814004
Fax 01726 817231
ADMINISTRATION:
General Manager: David Hyslop
Props: Domaine Leisure Ltd., Carlyon Bay, St. Austell, Cornwall PL25 3RG. Tel 01726 814261
Policy: Multi-purpose venue used for Concerts, Summer Shows, Sporting & Special Events and Exhibitions.
Seating/Capacity: 3,326 standing, 2,306 seated.
TECHNICAL:
Full technical details available on request.

# St Helens, Merseyside

Pop. 104,430. London 191 miles. Newspapers: St.Helens Reporter (fri); Star. STD code 01744

## THEATRE ROYAL

Corporation Street, St. Helens, Merseyside WA10 1LQ
Mgt/BO 01744 451175 Fax 01744 613267
ADMINISTRATION:
Props: Theatre Royal St. Helens Trust
Theatre Administrator: Ken Irwin
Technical Manager: Mike Littlewood
Policy: Touring Companies, childrens prods, Ballet, Pantomimes, Concerts, Pop, Classic, Brass Bands, Small & Large scale musicals.
Perfs: By mutual agreement Morn/Mat/Eve.
Seats: 703. Licensed Bar & Coffee Bar.
TECHNICAL:
Stage: Proscenium, portable Apron 3.35m deep, Raked; Pros. opening 8.30m; Ht. of Pros. 7.01m; Depth of S/Line 10.36m; Ht. of Grid 14.63m; 42 lines Hemp; Scenery flying Bars 11.28m; W/Widths P.S. 3.35m, O.P. 3.66m; Prompt Cnr. P.S.
Lighting: Switchboard: Rank Strand 3 set 80 way board; 27 circuits to F.O.H.; 34 circuits in hanging positions over stage and 19 independent Dips. 75 of the ways are 2kw and 5 are 5kw.
Sound Equip: Phonic Stereo Audio mixed MX881 with 8 channels. National Panasonic cassette Deck; echo unit to all channels or single channels. Facilities for playing F.H.O. and 5 backstage outlets. Playback to dressing rooms, Talk back between Prompt Cnr. files, switchboard and limes.
Sound and Lighting: Control Rear Stalls. 16mm and

35mm Film Projection. Independent 100 amp 3 phase supply set of lines over the auditorium for extra lighting (pop groups, etc.).
Dressing Rooms 6; Accom. 109; Showers Back Stage. Orchestra Pit 19 plus M.D.

# Stafford, Staffs

Pop. 55,000. London 140 miles. Newspapers: Stafford Newsletter (fri); Express & Star (ntly); Evening Sentinel. STD code 01785

## STAFFORD GATEHOUSE

Eastgate Street, Stafford Staffs ST16 2LT
Mgt 01785 253595 BO 01785 254653
Fax 01785 225622
ADMINISTRATION:
Props: Stafford Borough Council
Manager: Daniel Shaw
Administration Manager: Lynn Elkin
House Manager: Alan Vernon
Technical Manager: Ken Moore
Marketing Officer: Johanna Alcock
Policy: The Gatehouse is a complete Arts and Entertainments complex, with theatre/concert hall, Studio Theatre, and pub performance space. Professional and amateur use.
Seats: 570 in one raked tier (reduces to 490 when orchestra pit fully extended); Malcolm Edwards Theatre:End Stage 96, In the Round 116; Cinema-style 120.
TECHNICAL:
Stage: Pros. opening 9.00m variable to 12.20m; Ht. of Pros. 6.00m, normal working ht. 4.60m; Flying Ht. 10.30m, bars 10.50; Depth of stage (house curtain to back wall) 7.10m, from front of stage 10.00m; orchestra Pit 27 sq.m. (reduces seating capacity to 490); Stage Machinery: 22 4 lines hemp sets 7 4 line winch sets. Dimensions: Pros. width 9000 (can open out to 12,200); Pros. height 6000 (normal working height 4,600); Flying height 10,400 (bar length 10,500); Depth (house curtain/back wall) 7,100; Depth (house curtain/front of stage) 1,000; Wings S.L. 3,100 (with 9m prox); Wings S.R. 3,100 (with 9m pros.).
Lighting: Rank Strand Gemini +2 desk in control room at rear of auditorium. (112 channels 108 x 2.5kw, 4 x 5kw). There are 2 auditorium lighting bridges, 2 booms and a gallery above the control room. 3 stage bars, 1 x 4 Iris 3 cyc bar. Equipment includes the following: 30 CCT Silhouette 30, Profiles 1kw; 4 CCT Silhouette 15, Profiles 2kw (2 fitted as follow spots); 40 CCT Starlette, 1 kw Fresnels; 4 R.S. Patt.123, 500w Fresnels; 6 R.S. Patt.23, 500w Profiles; 1 R.S.Patt.223, 1kw Fresnels; 6 R.S. Patt.264, 1kw Profiles; 2 R.S. Patt.2kw Fresnels; 2 R.S. CSI Followspot; 40 Par Cans; 10 Floor Cans.
Film projection equip: 35mm 1kw lamp, projector; perforated screen.
Sound Equip: Purpose designed installation with operating positions in control room and rear of auditorium. Mixing desk: Studiomaster Series III 24.4.2. Amplifiers: H/H VX600 H/H V80 0(3) H/H TPA 100D; Speakers: (4) Bose 802; (2) Bose 302; (5) Electrovoice; (2) Monitor Wedges. Tapes etc. (1) Revox B77; (1) Tascam 122 MkII cassette; (1) Sony TC K77R cassette; (1) Revox B226 Compact Disc; (1) Technic SL-DL1 Tuntable; (1) Yamaha SPX90; (1) Roland Chorus Echo RE-501; 1 EXR Exiter Spl; 1 MXR Dual fifteen band E.Q. Mics: 1 Micron Hand Held Radio Mic; 1 Sennheiser Radio Mic SK2012; (3) Sure SM58; (5) Sure 565; (5) AKG 202; (2) AKG D12; (2) AKG C414 EB; (3) Sennheiser

ME88, ME40 + K3; 2 AKG D321; (5) Calrec CB21C (5) DI Boxes; Infrared receiver headset facilities available for partially deaf patrons.
Dressing Rooms: 2 for 8, 2 for 4, Chorus Changing Green Room, shares use of studio dressing rooms. Get-in: Lift to first floor 2.70m x 2.00m, door 2.00m x 1.80m; Good sized staircase: Service yard difficult lorry access, inspection advised; also scenery hoist to pavement through OP dock door.
Orchestra pit: 27 square metres, 9 metres x 3 metres.

MALCOLM EDWARDS THEATRE
Stage: Dimensions dependent on form. Grid Ht. 4.00m. Lighting: Electrosonic Multiway 3 control, 36 way, 3 preset, 3 group mixing desk in control room, 36 x 2.5k dimmers. Electrosonic 36-way 3 group 3 preset board + RS Tempus M24 + FX Desk; 12 RS Prelude PC; 10 RS Prelude F; 30 CCT 500w Fresnel; 30 CCT 500w Profile. Film Projection: Furneo 9315 (500w Xenon), 16mm Projector, Optical and magnetic sound 24fps, 30 watt amp, zoom lens 35/65mm and amporphic lens. Reel capacity 5000 ft. Screen 4000 x 1900 matt white perforated roller screen.
Sound: Studiomaster Series II 24:16:24:2 Desk (in control room); Revox PR99HS & Revox B77 reel-to-reel machinery; AIWA Exceling XK009 Cassette Deck; Fostex A8 8-track recorder; AKAI:AM 24 track; Panasonic SL-H302 turntable; Midiverb; Midifix; Harrison Xi 600 MOSFET amp into 2 x Bose 802 2 off H/H TOA 100D amps for foldback. Show Relay. Mics from Gatehouse List.
Communications: Open ring intercom (Compac M) 6 stations; Cue lights 6 outstations; paging/show relay to dressing rooms.
Dressing Rooms: 2 each for 6 (each with shower) (can be increased by upper level dressing rooms). Get-In: Ground Floor - domestic size doors).

# Stamford, Lincs

Pop. 18,000. London 92 miles. Newspapers: Stamford (fri). STD code 01780

## STAMFORD ARTS CENTRE

27 St. Marys Street, Stamford, Lincolnshire PE9 2DL
Mgt 01780 480846 BO 01780 763203
Fax 01780 766690
ADMINISTRATION:
Props: South Kesteven District Council
Manager: David Popple
Policy: Integral part of Stamford Arts Centre. Theatre is used by touring professional companies/artistes and is available for hire by amateur groups. Drama, dance, mime and music presented. Induction loop and lift for disabled.
Seats: 166. Bar and catering facilities available.
TECHNICAL:
Stage: Proscenium flat; Pros. opening 8.27m. Ht. of Pros. 3.35m; W/Widths P.S. 0.91m, O.P. 0.91m
Lighting: Switchboard: Sirius 24. Control room rear of auditorium; F.O.H. spots. Lanterns: 10 CCT Minuette Profile 650w, 6 Strand Patt 813 Profile 500w, 2 Patt 23 Profile 500w, 17 Patt 803 Fresnels 650w, 8 CCT Minuette Fresnels 650w.
Sound Equip: Speakers either side of pros. arch. Hill LC 400 Amplifier, Technics Cassette Player, Denon CD player, 8 channel mixer desk.
Dressing Rooms 2; Accom. 24; Basins and toilets. No Orchestra Pit

# Stevenage, Herts

Pop. 77,000. London 31 miles. Newspapers: Stevenage Comet; Stevenage Gazette; Stevenage Herald. STD code 01438

## GORDON CRAIG THEATRE

Stevenage Arts & Leisure  Centre, Lytton Way, Stevenage, Hertfordshire SG1 1LZ
Mgt 01438 766642 BO 01438 766866
Fax 01438 766675
ADMINISTRATION:
Props: Stevenage Borough Council
Director of Leisure Services: M McCardle
Arts & Entertainments Manager: Bob Bustance
Marketing Manager: Maggi Turfrey
Technical Stage Manager: Nigel Hewlett
Policy: Mixed Programme
Perfs: 7.45
Seats: 506. Bar, Restaurant.
TECHNICAL:
Stage: Proscenium Stage, Flat; Pros. opening adjustable 9.15m - 12.2m; Black Harlequin Dance Floor. Ht. of Pros. 5.38m; Depth of S/Line 7.62m; Ht. of Grid 15.04m; Flying Bars 13.41m; 29 Double Purchase Counterweight Bars total. Prompt Cnr. P.S.
Lighting: Strand 430 control desk, storage to 3.5" disk. Strand LD90 Dimmers, 136 x 2.5kw + 36 x 5kw, 24 x non-dim. 400a Three phase power. Operated from control suite rear of auditorium. Temporary/Touring supply 2 x 63a Three Phase supply SL. 72 x 1kw Profile spots, 64 x 1kw fresnels. 2 x 1kw CSI followspots operated from control suite rear of auditorium.
Sound: Soundcraft Delta SR mixer, operated from control suite near rear of auditorium. D&B audiotechnik full range speaker system, 4 x foldback monitors. 5 x PCC160, 5 x SM58, 2 x SM57, DI Boxes, CD, Revox 7.5"/15ips, graphics and processing available. ACS Acoustic Control System. Variable acoustics for music and drama.
Steinway Concert and Kwai Baby Grand pianos; Christie ten-rank 3-manual theatre organ.
Stage Management: Prompt desk/corner SL, full cue light intercom with 12 outstations. Full headset intercom. Show/Conductors view monitor screens. Show relay and tannoy to all dressing rooms/backstage areas.
Dressing Rooms: 16, accom. 65. Showers. Orchestra pit 20. Wardrobe room with automatic washing machine and tumble dryer.
Rehearsal room with practice bar and piano. Hydraulic apron. 35mm projection facilities.

## STEVENAGE ARTS AND LEISURE CENTRE CONCERT HALL

Lytton Way, Stevenage, Hertfordshire SG1 1LZ
Mgt 01438 766642 BO 01438 766866
Fax 01438 766675
ADMINISTRATION:
Props: Stevenage Borough Council
Director of Leisure Services: M McCardle
Technical/Stage Manager: Nigel Hewlett
Arts & Entertainments Manager: Bob Bustance
Marketing Manager: Maggi Turfrey
TECHNICAL:
Stage: Floor space 35m x 35m, height 10m. Staging 25 x Merrick Sico units 8ft x 4ft x 4ft. Various configurations possible. Floor sprung maple. Flying points available. 13a Ring main available. Get In via car park to side at floor level through double width doors.
Lighting: 300a Three Phase Supply

(Camlock/Ceeform/Tails) available for toured lighting and sound equipment.
Sound: No equipment.
Backstage: Several Dressing Rooms/Band room available.

# Stirling

Pop. 30,047. London 410 miles. Newspapers: Stirling Observer (wed/fri). STD code 01786

## MACROBERT ARTS CENTRE

University of Stirling Stirling FK9 4LA Scotland
Mgt 01786 467155 BO 01786 461081
Fax 01786 451369
ADMINISTRATION:
Director: Elizabeth Moran
Technical Manager: Colin Proudfoot
Policy: Mixed touring - Opera, Ballet, Drama, Concerts, Recitals, etc. Stirling Film Theatre.
Perfs: Usually 7.30 or 8.00p.m.
Seats: 497 in one raked tier. Bar, Coffee Bars, Studio Theatre (av. seats 140 on three sides), Art Gallery.
TECHNICAL:
Stage: Proscenium with Forestage/Pit and lifts; Pros. opening 9.75m; Ht. of Pros. 5.49m; Depth of S/Line 9.14m; Ht. of Grid 14.33m; 38 lines, 31 C/W, Hemp lines plotted to requirements.
Lighting: Switchboard: Rank Lightpallett 90 Rank Strand 120 way M24 Backup, rear of Audit; 25 F.O.H. Spots; 20 Dips; 55 Flys (20 still to be installed); Stage Manager's Desk P.S., D.S. Wander mic. operation.
Sound Equip: 2 x 500 amps dedicated F.O.H., 5 x 100w Turner amps (Foldback Facilities) 16 into 8 mixer, 2 Revox B77. Sony Cassette Desk; mics; Philips FP20 Projectors; 1 x 15mm Philips FP16 Projection.
Dressing Room 6; Accom. 35; 6 Showers; Orchestra Pit 45 max.

STUDIO
Tech. Info: Seating 120 on 3 sides. 30 Circs., controlled by MX48 board.
Sound: Stereo Amp 8-2 mixer.

# Stockport, Cheshire

Pop. 138,750. London 177 miles. Newspapers: The Messenger (thurs); Manchester Evening News; Stockport Express (thurs). STD code 0161

## ROMILEY FORUM

The Precinct, Compstall Road, Romiley, Stockport, Cheshire SK6 4EA
BO 0161 430 6570 Fax 0161 406 6782
ADMINISTRATION:
Props & Lessees: Met.Borough Stockport. Community Services Division.
Manager: June Gibbons
Policy: Touring, Repertory, Dance, Music, Comedy.
Perfs: 7.30pm, Mats. 2.30pm
Seats: 410. 1 Bar, Theatre Cafe.
TECHNICAL:
Stage: Proscenium arch, flat. Pros opening 11.58m, Ht. of Pros. 4.27m, Depth of S/Line 3.96m; Ht. of Grid 5.49m; apron depth 2.44m, 10 lines, hemp. W/Widths 3.05m S.R., 3.05m S.L.; Prompt Cnr S.L.; backstage crossover; Tab track - black masking - blue house tabs, safety curtain.

Lighting: Zero 88 Sirius 48 way board. 84 circuits. 64
amp socket available for touring systems - 24 1.2k
profiles, 8 1.2k PC's, 14 650w fresnels, 12 650w PC's,
17 1k parcans CP62 beam angle, 5 x 4 circuit battens, 2
followspots.
Projection facilities 16mm.
Sound: Yamaha 16:4:2 and Yamaha 12:4:2 linkable
mixers, 4 Bose 802, 2 bass driver speakers, foldback
system, 1 Yamaha SPX90 effects unit, 1 Bose RE 1000
reverb unit, 1 Alesis Noisegate, 1 Harrison 600, 1 H&H
600 amps, 19 mics, cassette tape system, CD player,
PA system.
Other: Backstage: 2 dressing rooms, accom 5, 2
Showers/toilets. Band/chorus accom 20+, Scenery hoist
and lift, tallescope, rehearsal piano, show relay/tannoy to
dressing rooms.

# Stoke-On-Trent, Staffs

Pop. 262,120. London 147 miles. Newspapers:
Staffordshire Sentinel (daily); Staffordshire Advertiser
(thurs). STD code 01782

## THE NEW VIC

Etruria Road, Newcastle Under Lyme ST9 0JG
Mgt 01782 717954 BO 01782 717962
Fax 01782 712885
ADMINISTRATION:
Props: Stoke on Trent and North Staffordshire Theatre
Trust Limited
Artistic Director: Gwenda Hughes
General Manager: Ludo Keston
Production Manager: David Martin
Policy: Repertoire with permanent company. Concerts.
Perfs: Normally Mon-Sat 7.30, many mats in summer,
Xmas.
Seats: 635. Standing 60. Self service Restaurant, Coffee
Bar, Two Bars, Bookshop, Exhibition space, Rehearsal
Room with small performance capability (seats 150).
TECHNICAL:
Theatre in the Round (Perm).
Lighting: Switchboard: Rank Strand Gemini; 120
channels, Lanterns: 12 Harmony 15/28, 15 Harmony F,
20 Patt.23, 25 Patt.123, 2 Patt.223, 12 Patt.264, 4 ADB
1000 TNH, 17 Patt.23N, 2 Patt.774, 48 Prelude 16/30, 6
Cadenza, 2 Fresnel + 55 Parcans.
Sound Equipment: DDA (D Series) Mixing Console, 12,
channels. 4 x Martin CX2 speakers. 5 Revox Tape
Decks, 4 Quad Amps. Induction Loop Rehearsal Room
(flex open space). Projection facility.
Dressing Rooms: 4; 20m, 6m, 10f, 4f.
Membership: TMA

## QUEEN'S THEATRE

Wedgwood Street, Burslem,
Stoke-on-Trent Staffs ST6 4EA
For all enquiries contact Carole Salmon Tel 01782
232732  or Fax 01782 236691
ADMINISTRATION:
Props: Stoke-on-Trent City Council, Property & Facilities
Management Division.
General Manager: Alan Bolton
Policy: Private Hire only but suitable for Ballet, Opera,
Musicals, Pantomimes, Concerts (Orchestral Choral,
Pop) and Film Shows.
Rents negotiable.
Seats: Arena Tiered Seats 362; Balcony 654. Licensed
Bars and Refreshment after Show. Additional catering by
arrangement as required.

TECHNICAL:
Stage: Proscenium Stage with Apron 3.05m x 14.02m
Flat Pros. opening 12.19m. Ht. of Pros. 4.88m; Depth of
S/Line 6.71m to footlights, 9.75m Ht. of Grid 10.82m; 20
lines; Scenery Flying Ht. 5.49m; Flying Bars 13.72m;
W/Widths P.S. 3.05m Prompt Cnr. P.S. Safety Curtain &
Drencher system installed.
Lighting: 96 channel Event Board control desk complete
with 14" colour monitor F.O.H. Spots 28 Patt.264, 3
Battens, Dips 12 plus, 2 each side, 2 Spot Bars, 1 Front
Patts.264, 223, 123, 23 1 Pro Spot Patt.293; 2 Follow
Spots (Pani HMVI200).
Sound Equip: 16 Channel Soundcraft; 200 Delta Mixer -
16 microphone points (4 radio); Stage Effects System;
Twin Tape deck. Dressing Room and other areas paging
system. Intercom system - backstage - lighting (2)
Sound - Gentry.
Dressing Rooms 8 (3 Sep. 1 room divided into 5
cubicles) Accom. 100. 4 Showers. Orchestra Pit 18.

## THE ROYAL

Pall Mall, Hanley, Stoke-on-Trent Staffs ST1 1EE
Mgt 01782 206000 BO 01782 207777
Fax 01782 213432
ADMINISTRATION:
Props: Mike Lloyd Theatres Ltd. Managing Director -
Mike Lloyd, 14/20  Brunswick Street, Hanley,
Stoke-on-Trent ST1 1DR.
Assistant: Nigel Bamford
Manager: Ian Price
Marketing Manager: Mary Worsdale
Technical Manager: Brian Beech
Policy: Mixed programme
Seats: 1,450
TECHNICAL:
Stage: Proscenium width - 40'; height - 22'. Stage depth
back wall to back of safety curtain - 31' 8"; back wall to
front edge - 34' 9". Full stage width (including wings) -
58' 6". Wing width stage left - 7' 6"; stage right - 11' US,
15' 8" DS. Height to underside of grid - 50'. Scene dock
area-situated stage right: with height of 22' - 29' 8" X 16'
8", with height of 15' - 13' 6" X 14' 6".
Flying: 56 single purchase counterweight lines at 6"
centres, average length of flying bars 42'. All lines
controlled from fly gallery on SL. Line 1 is fitted with a
stage level brake to enable house tabs to be flown from
both levels. Grid structure is steel, and has a safe loading
of up to 10 tons. A front of house box truss is situated
above the front gangway, fitted with motorised hoists to
bring it to auditorium level, controlled from the SM
position. The truss is 40' wide, and has a safe loading of
up to 2 tons, and is equipped with access ladder and a
green border.
Lighting: Control: ADB Vision 10/ST computerised
control system capable of controlling up to 1024 DMX
channels, storage for over 500cues, 99 special effects,
10 dimmer laws, 99 chasers. It is equipped with both
hard disk storage and 3.5" floppy disk, has twin
playback pannels, 48 submasters, motion control panel
and is equipped with 2 SVGA monitors, infra red riggers
control and full tracking backup. Dimmers: 180 X 3kw
circuits, 12 X 5kw circuits, 6 dedicated non dim circuits.
A DMX network and 16A ring provided for the powering
and control of moving lights/scrollers. Follow spot
positions are in the rear upper circle boxes. A further 2 X
16A sockets are provided at the rear of the upper circle
should more than 2 spots be required. Luminaires: 60 X
1kw Par 64 cans; 10 X 1kw Par 64 floor cans; 50 X
1.2kw Fresnels; 22 X DS105 1.2kw 15/31 medium angle
Profiles; 12 X DSN105 1.2kw 11/23 narrow angle
Profiles; 4 X DS205 2kw 13/36 medium angle Profiles; 5

X 4way 1kw Cyc units; 5 X 4way 1kw Groundrows; 10 X 500w single floods; 8 X 650w Fresnels; 2 X 1.2kw HMI follow spots with stands and accessories.
General: SM desk situated on SR with 12 way cue light system, paging and show relay system to dressing rooms and FOH. Additional paging points are provided at SD and in FOH at the BO. It also contains control for ring intercom system with 8 headsets and belt packs.

## VICTORIA HALL
Bagnall Street, Hanley. Stoke-on-Trent
Staffordshire ST1 3AD
Tel 01782 213808 Fax 01782 214738
ADMINISTRATION:
Launch Director: David Blyth
Office Administrator: Sue Wilkinson
Marketing Manager: David Brownlee
Assistant Marketing Manager: Sam Calvert
Operations Manager: Andrew Macduff
Box Office Manager: Helen Bottomley
Stage Door Supervisor: Nicola Ratcliffe
Press Officer: Faye Corlett
Stage Manager: Martin Lund
Education Officer: Kirsty Simons
Seating/Capacity: Stalls: 576 loose chairs or 492 loose chairs with stage extension. Circle: 294. Balcony 391. Choir: 100-120. Wheelchair spaces ( 4 at each level): 12. 1393 max, 900 max with no stage extension.
TECHNICAL:
Stage: Rectangular concert platform. Flat, hardwood floor, lower side balconies impinge on stage at front corners. Platform depth: Additional 1.2m or 2.4m. Platform ht. 1.2m above stalls floor. Permanent choir seating on padded benches for 100-120 dependent on details being finalised.
Access: Flat access to platform from undercover loading area via double door USL and USR. Space for two trucks to unload and park. Power and cable ducts in loading area. Backstage storage and circulation area.
Backstage Accommodation: 6-7 unfitted dressing rooms, 7 principal dressing rooms. Green room, circulation/assembly area. Stage door keeper's office, passenger lift.
Suspensions: 10m clearance below chandeliers. Each lighting bridge has 5 x 500kg strong points, of which any 3 may be used at any one time. 8 x 500kg chain hoists and controller. Seven line winch carries curved truss with acoustic masking curtain in front of choir seating.
Orchestral Concert Lighting: Dedicated permanent lighting designed to achieve 1000lux over the whole platform. Two dimmers for lit music stands.
Production Lighting: Installed dimmers: 96 x 2.5kw; 12 x 5kw; RCD protection. Installed control ETC express 125 with riggers' control. Programmable concert lighting control. Principal lighting positions on lighting bridges and upper balcony front. Remote control (DMX 512) and non-dim circuits at all lighting positions. DMX links for touring dimmers and controls. Socket outlets. Follow spots located on lighting bridge. 2no. Pani 1200/35 long throw with manual colour changers.
Communications: Control position PM's corner; cue lights at choir and orchestra doors; ring intercom (techpro single channel); show relay and paging to backstage and foyers, also video show relay.
Sound: Permanently installed sound system with delay and image shift loudspeakers suitable for speech and music but not designed to cope with rock and roll. 44 microphone lines/sockets. Backstage patchbay links to audio bus and allow access to mic lines for broadcasting and recording. House mixers 16-4-21. Outboard gear includes DAT, CD player, Minidisc, compact cassette,

digital reverb, compressor and de esser. Infra red show relay system for hard of hearing and 2 channels allow for audio described performances.
Control Positions: PM's corner - SR. Technical control room - Rear of circle (SR). Temporary sound and lighting desks can be erected at the back of the stalls and balcony stage right.
Power supplies: SL: 200a TPN supply available on busbars; 32a Ceeform TPN, 63a Ceeform TPN and 125a Ceeform SPN. SR: 125a Ceeform SPN. Rigging: 63a TPN. Parking area: 200a TPN. Technical earth. RCD protection on all low current supplies.
Other Equipment: Chairs, pianos, conductor's rostrum, powered access tower, zarges ladders, safety harnesses.
NB: The information in this issue of technical information is given in good faith but changes may occur and potential users of the facilities should check for accuracy when the theatre is open.

# Stranraer, Wigtownshire

## THE RYAN CENTRE
Fairhurst Road, Stranraer, Wigtownshire
DG9 7AP Scotland
Mgt 01776 703535 Fax 01776 706880
ADMINISTRATION:
Head of Leisure and Sport for Dumfries and Galloway Council: Stewart S Atkinson
Centre Manager: David S Hislop
Technician: Eric McCune
Status: Leisure Centre and Theatre
Architects Dumfries and Galloway Regional Council.
Venue financed by Wigtown District Council, Dumfries and Galloway Regional Council.
Local authority: Dumfries and Galloway Council
Policy: To provide the widest range of performing arts, both professional and community based, side by side with sports and leisure provision. Willing to premiere show. Performance schedule open 7 days; performance times by arrangement. Booking terms by negotiation.
Facilities: Seats: Theatre 263, Games Hall 600, catering cafeteria, bar, entertainment licence. Access car park, at centre, station Stranraer, 1km; coach terminal: Stagecoach, Lewis Street, 40m; bus routes, none for the disabled 4 wheelchair spaces - lift chair/stair lift - assistance available, contact David Hislop - level access, all house facilities fully accessible. Other facilities: rehearsal dance studio, sprung wood floor, ballet barre and mirrors.
TECHNICAL:
Stage: Proscenium arch. Performing area 18.5m x 7.7m - pros opening 10m x 6m - wing widths 4.2m SR, 4m SL. No rake - floor soft wood, suitable for all dance, backstage crossover, stage heated. Height to grid 10.37m, 13 counterweight double purchase sets - maximum flying height 4.27m - tab track - 3 set black legs and borders - white cyclorama - claret house tabs, flown. 3 phase power supply. Orchestra pit 9m wide, 2m deep, accommodates 12. Get-in via dock doors on Fairhurst Road, 3.5m x 3.5m. Tallescope. Scale stage, fly and lighting plans available.
Lighting: Strand MX manual/memory board, 48 circuits at 2kw at present, 3 phase, operated from projection room at rear of auditorium - a 2 x 32A supplies available for temporary board - 10 spots, 10 fresnels, 10 650 watt preludes, 10 300 watt, parcans, 4 side stands. Follow spot (Strand 2kw).
Cinema Facilities: Cinemactor Projector CX20H Dolby

surround (digital).
Sound: Allen & Heath: 16:2 desk - 2 x Yamaha P2150 amps - 2 x Yamaha Q2031A graphic equalisers - 4 x Shure SM58, 8 x AKG D190E mics, 3 radio mics - tape deck and CD player. Acoustics suitable for music and spoken word. Stage management Prompt corner SR - Canford Audio cue system, beltpacks and headsets, 4 outstations. Backstage - 2 dressing rooms, accommodate 25, access via passage from Leisure Centre foyer. Rehearsal room and pianos, Collard & Collard, upright new and Yamaha baby grand. Advice given on accommodation.
Staff: 2 technicians - casuals not available. No security personnel. Backstage facilities accessible to disabled performers and staff.
Games Hall - Open space 36m x 18m. Floor sprung wood. Height to ceiling 9.14m. 20 x 16A 3 phase supplies available for lighting, 32A supply for sound - equipment from theatre.

# Stratford-Upon-Avon, Warwicks

Pop. 19,760. London 92 miles. Newspapers: Stratford-upon-Avon Herald (fri). STD code 01789

## THE OTHER PLACE

Southern Lane, Stratford-upon-Avon,
Warwickshire CV37 6BH
Mgt 01789 296655 Fax 01789 415192
ADMINISTRATION:
Props: Royal Shakespeare Theatre
Administrator: Bronwyn Robertson
Policy: Small budget productions. Classical and Modern Plays.
Perfs: Usually 7.30. Seats: 280 max. Refreshments.
TECHNICAL:
Stage: Open stage theatre with balcony. Performance area approx. 9.40m x 9m.
Lighting: Gemini 2+, 175 dimmers; 120 lanterns, various.
Sound Equip: 10 into 4 mixer. various speakers. 2 Revox tapes.
Dressing Rooms: 3/4, accom. 21; 3 Showers.
Membership: TMA

## ROYAL SHAKESPEARE THEATRE, SWAN THEATRE

Waterside, Stratford-upon-Avon,
Warwickshire CV37 6BB
Mgt 01789 296655 Mgt Fax 01789 294810
BO 01789 295623 BO Fax 01789 261974
ADMINISTRATION:
Artistic Director: Adrian Noble
Licensee & Manager: Graham Sawyer
Technical Manager: Simon Bowler
Policy: Royal Shakespeare Company's own season from March to January. Winter season of visiting companies. Occasional Sunday concerts.
Perfs: Evening 7.30, Mats. Thurs & Sat 1.30
Seats: RST 1508, Swan 464, The Other Place 220. Box Tree and River Terrace Restaurants. Dress Circle Coffee Bar, Balcony Buffet Bar, 3 other bars.
TECHNICAL:
ROYAL SHAKESPEARE THEATRE
Stage: Proscenium, Flat; Pros. Opening 8.94m; Ht. of Pros. 9.20m; Depth from S/Line 13.60m; Ht. of Grid 19.81m; 60 lines, C/W; Flying Bars 12.19m; W/Widths P.S. 12.19m, O.P. 12.19m; Prompt Cnr. P.S.

Lighting: Switchboard: Rank Strand Galaxy 240 way, rear of Dress Circle, F.O.H. Spots as required; Spot Bars as required.
Sound Equipment: Tape built to specification; Speakers as required.
Dressing Rooms 14; Accom. 60; 9 Bathrooms.
NB: Technical information above relates to Winter Season conditions. During RSC's Shakespeare Seasons there is an apron stage, steeply raked, no orchestra pit, and many other changes from the information given.
Membership: SWET, TMA

SWAN THEATRE
FACILITIES:
Seating: 400; on 2 galleries and ground level.
Catering: Wide range available in adjacent Royal Shakespeare Theatre. 1 bar sells all range of drinks and has theatre licence.
Ticket outlets: Own box office and usual agents.
Computerised box office system: RITA.
Shop/sales area.
Access: Nearest public car park: in front of RST; railway station: Stratford upon Avon; coach terminal: Stratford upon Avon.
Facilities for the disabled: 4 wheelchair spaces available, but have prior warning - deaf loop system - assistance available, contact Attendant - parking - ramp at entrance - all house facilities fully accessible.
TECHNICAL:
Stage: Thrust, gallery, 3 sides. Performing area 5.81m x 13.09m - pros opening 7.04m x 5.24m. No rake - floor plywood, suitable for dance, no lino available. Backstage crossover, stage heated. No tab track - back wall used as cyclorama. 4 x 15A independent circuits. Lift, centre stage, entrances DS. Scenery lift. Scale stage and lighting plans available, 1 to 25.
Lighting: Strand Galaxy board, 288 circuits, 300A, 3 phase, operated from 2nd gallery DS - no supply for temporary board - 100 profiles, 35 fresnels, 60 pars, 40 pc's, Strand - 2 followspots operated from centre technical gallery DS.
Sound: DDA 16 into 10 into 10 desk, operated from 2nd gallery DS - Harrison amps driving Tannoy Lynx and Puma speakers - AKG, Beyer mics - ASC dart replay machines - dubbing room available. Acoustics suitable for music and spoken word.
Stage management: Prompt corner SR - show relay/Tannoy to dressing rooms.
Backstage: Various dressing rooms, access by backstage - green room - wardrobe backstage with irons, washing machines, dryers. Refreshments from green room serving snacks and main meals. Rehearsal rooms, piano, good. Advice given on accommodation.
Staff - 1 stage, 2 lighting, 1 sound, 1 wardrobe - casuals available - security personnel.

# Street, Somerset

Pop. 11,000. London 130 miles. Newspapers: Central Somerset Gazette (thurs); Shepton Mallet Journal (fri); Bridgewater Mercury (tues); Wells Journal (fri); Western Gazette (thurs). STD code 01458

## STRODE THEATRE

Strode College, Church Road, Street,
Somerset BA16 0AB
Admin 01458 446529 BO 01458 442846
Fax 01458 446529
ADMINISTRATION:
Props: Strode College

Manager: Liz Leyshon
Technician: Rob Russell
Policy: Mixed programme, professional tours, mostly one nighters but some split weeks. Also amateur and educational users and Regional Film Theatre.
Seats: 393. Bar and refreshments.
Disabled facilities: 4 wheelchair spaces - deaf loop system - parking - level access - adjacent disabled toilet on ground floor.
TECHNICAL:
Stage: Proscenium arch. Performing area 13.41m x 6.4m - pros opening 9.75m x 5.5m. No rake - floor wood covered in black vinyl, suitable for dance, vinyl floor available, backstage and sub-stage crossovers, stage heated. Height to grid 9.14m - 14 hemp sets - tab track - black legs - white painted wall used as cyclorama - red drawn house tabs. Several 13 amp sockets. De-mountable Apron stage - 12m x 1.2m., Orchestra pit - accommodates 30, Get-in S.R. 1.7m x 2.4m - tailboard height - stage and lighting plans available.
Lighting: Avab expert 256 way control desk situated in control room - rear stalls. DMX512 - 60 channels Permus dimmers - 30 Profile spots - 8 x Cantata 16/30, 6 x T84, 6 x Sil 30, 8 x Prelude 16/30, 21 fresnels, 9 x Harmony F, 5 x 743, 7 x Starlets PC, 12 par 64, 5 x floods, 4 x 3 cyc floods, 2 x MSR follow spots. Supply available for temporary racks by arrangement.
Projection:35mm and 16mm projection, Dolby S.R., Flown screen on stage.
Sound: Allen and Heath SC Series 24-4-2 desk rear side stalls - reverb and effects - Revox, Dat, cassette, CD and sampler available, QSR Amps, EV speakers - L&R and stage, surround loudspeakers throughout auditorium. 2 channels on-stage foldback system, various microphones.
Stage Management: Prompt corner S.L. talkback - show relay tannoy to dressing rooms and FOH. Casual staff available by arrangement.
Backstage: 4 dressing rooms, accommodates 25, band room - below stage.
Piano: Steinway B7 grand.

# Sudbury, Suffolk

Pop. 17,911. London 50 miles. Newspapers: Suffolk Free Press (wkly); Mercury (wkly). East Anglian Daily Times. STD code 01787

### THE QUAY THEATRE
Quay Lane, Sudbury, Suffolk CO10 2AN
Admin 01787 883443 BO 01787 374745
Fax 01787 312602
ADMINISTRATION:
Props: The Quay at Sudbury Trustees
Director: Richard Way
Technical Manager: Steve Betteridge
House Manager: Lisa Croft
Policy: Touring plays; childrens' theatre, music (jazz, folk, classical and popular); amateur dramatic, light operatic, jazz, T.I.E. and youth groups.
Perfs: Mon-Sun evenings and occasional days. Box Office open 11am - 3pm & 6pm - 9.30pm Mon-Sat, 11am - 2.30pm Sun.
Seats: 125. Licenced Bar, restaurant.
TECHNICAL:
Stage: Open stage, end on. Raked auditorium. Stage width 6.1m. Depth 8 m. Wing space and get-in SR only.
Lighting: Zero 88 Eclipse 36 way 250 memory, 36 x 2Kw dimmers.

Sound: Peavey MD-II 12-2 mixer desk. Technics cassette deck. 6 independent speakers, mono or stereo. Teac X-7 spool tape deck + remote.
Dressing Rooms: 2; accommodating 12 and 6.

# Sunderland, Tyne & Wear

Pop. 215,280. London 269 miles. Newspapers: Echo (ntly); Sunderland Star (wkly). STD code 0191

### EMPIRE THEATRE
High Street West, Sunderland Tyne & Wear SR1 3EX
Mgt 0191 510 0545 BO 0191 514 2517
SD 0191 565 6750 Fax 0191 553 7427
ADMINISTRATION:
Props: Sunderland Empire Theatre Trust
Managing Director: Symon Easton
Deputy Managing Director: Stuart Anderson
Operations Manager: Christabel Brett
Technical Manager: Melvyn P James
Box Office Manager: Rachel Thompson
Policy: Touring, Opera, Ballet, Pantomime, etc.
Perfs: 2.30 & 7.30
Seats: 1,900. Green Room Bar, Stalls Bar, Coffee Bar, Dress Circle Bar, Studio Coffee Bar.
TECHNICAL:
Stage: Proscenium arch. Performing area 13.72m x 12.8m, pros. opening 10.5m x 5.9m. Stage raked, 1 in 19.5", floor sprung wood covered with ply, suitable for all dance, backstage crossover, stage heated. Height of grid 18.34m - 2 hemp sets, 35 counterweight, double purchase sets 0.15m - 0.22m apart tab track, max flying height 19.8m, black masking. White cyclorama, brown house tabs, flown. Forestage 9.75 x 2.13m entrances from stage. Orchestra pit 12.5 x 2.13m x 1.3m deep, accommodates up to 100. Get-in via street level. Tallescope, safety curtain. Scale stage and fly plans available.
Lighting: Rank Strand Gemini board, 120 circuits, operated from box at back of circle - 200A 3 phase supply available for temporary board, OP side - 34 Profiles, 36 Fresnels, Rank Strand 2 follow spots operated from front of Gallery; single phase 60 amps for sound P.S. . Stage management Prompt corner can be OP or PS. Cue lights, 10 permanent show relay/Tannoy to dressing rooms. Backstage Green room, band room, wardrobe on 2nd floor with industrial washing machine & drier, coin-op, iron and 5 double 13A sockets. Piano. Advice given on accommodation. Staff, 2 stage, 2 lighting, casuals available, security personnel. Backstage facilities not accessible to disabled performers and staff.
Sound: Soundcraft 500 40 channel desk, operated from rear of circle - 10k FOH Apogee speakers - 11 x SM58, 6 x Beyer 86, 10 x radio mics - 2 x Revox Reel-to-reel, 1 x Denon cassette tape systems - 1 x Denon CD player. Acoustics suitable for music and spoken word.
Studio (Films): 35mm optical sound; Projector Victoria 5 Cinemaccanica.

# Sunninghill, Berkshire

### NOVELLO THEATRE
High Street, Sunninghill, Ascot, Berks SL5 9NE
Tel 01344 620881
ADMINISTRATION:
Contact: June Rose
Stage Manager: Julie Fox

Box Office Manager: Diana Stein
Independently owned, specialises in work for children
and young people - resident company and some visiting
touring companies doing similar work. mainly morning
and afternoon performances also weekends. Open
throughout the year except August.
Available for occasional lettings evenings only.
Licensed bar. Coffee bar.
Seats 158 raked Auditorium.
Wheelchair access. No stairs.
TECHNICAL:
Proscenium stage. Opening 28ft depth. No flying, 3
traps, lighting box at back of auditorium. Full PA sound
system/2 tape decks. Board - Zero 88 Sirius 24 Twenty
four channel 2 pre-set, 99 programmable memories.
Cue lights, strobe, UV lights, smoke and dry ice
machine, 24 lanterns. Orchestra pit. 1 piano, 1
keyboard. Get-in at street level. 2 dressing rooms seat
5/6 in each. Scene dock/workshop. Washing machine
etc.

# Sutton Coldfield, West Midlands

Pop. 84,160. London 112 miles. Newspapers: Sutton
Observer (fri); Sutton Coldfield News (fri); Metro News
(thurs). STD code 0121

## HIGHBURY LITTLE THEATRE
Sheffield Road, Sutton Coldfield,
West Midlands B73 5HD
Chairman 0121 373 1961 Admin 0121 373 2761
ADMINISTRATION:
Props: Highbury Theatre Centre Ltd
Chairman: Mollie Randle
For Technical Information Contact: Steve Bowyer
Policy: Amateur Little theatre presenting 7 plays per
season for 10 performances each and Studio
productions 4 (3 nights each) and touring professional
companies (one-night stands).
Perfs: 7.30
Seats: 140. Coffee Bar and Licensed Club Bar.
Disabled access, toilets and lifts.
TECHNICAL:
Stage: Proscenium, Flat; Pros. opening 4.72m; Ht. of
Pros. 3.50m; Depth of S/Line 6.55m; Ht. of Grid 7.62m;
42 lines, Hemp; Scenery Flying Ht. 3.66m; Flying Bars
5.49m; W/Widths P.S. 1.83m, O.P. 0.61m; Prompt Cnr.
O.P.
Lighting: Please contact venue.
Sound Equip: 3 Tape Decks; Speakers Auditorium
ceiling and Stage. Induction loop.
Dressing Rooms 3; Accom. 24.
Private Membership Theatre.
Membership: L.T.G.B.

# Sutton, Surrey

## SECOMBE THEATRE
Cheam Road Sutton Surrey SM1 2ST
Mgt/Admin 0181 770 6998 BO 0181 770 6990
ADMINISTRATION:
Props: London Borough of Sutton
Theatre Manager: Shirley Carpenter
(Tel 0181 770 6986)
Press & Publicity: Michael Coventry

Policy: Mixed programme, professional one nighters,
drama, tours, variety, dance, cinema, children's shows,
pantomime, annual talent show, amateur theatre,
lettings.
Seats: 347 (Max. 400). Foyer Bar, Foyer Buffet. Second
performance space/letting room available.
TECHNICAL:
Stage: Proscenium stage, flat: Pros. opening 8.50m; Ht.
of Pros. 4.57m; Depth of Stage 9.00m; Wing Space
3.00m S.L., 5.00m S.R.; Ht. of Grid 9.00m; 18 hemp
sets; House tabs on C/W ; Prompt desk S.L.
Lighting: Control, strand MX 48 plus MX12,
2.5kw/channel; circuits: 42 on stage, 18 F.O.H. and 15
independents; 1 F.O.H. spotbar, 4 F.O.H. vertical
booms, 4 overstage spotbars on winches. Lanterns: 16
Silhouette 30, 10 Starlette Fresnel, 3 Starlette PC, 18
Minuette Fresnel, 8 Minuette PC, 24 x 1k Par, 15
Minuette Flood, Le Maitre pyroflash system (2 pods),
2x2K FOH follow spots.
Sound Equipment: Soundcraft series 400B 16/4/2, 400
watts per channel stereo amp into 6 fixed position
F.O.H. speakers (Bose system). 100 watts per channel
stereo amp into 2 mobile effects speakers. Revox B77,
tape-to-tape Teac cassette 4 radio mics (Trantec),
Various Shure and AKG mics and stands.
Other: Communications: Promps desk PS; 9 cue lights;
ring intercom, show relay. Dressing Rooms 3, accom.
10 each; 2 Showers; Orchestra Pit 15. Second
performance: 11m wide x 11.8m length, small stage at
one end; seats 120 max; no stage lighting installation.
Can be used for performance or functions, own bar.

# Swanage, Dorset

Pop. 7,660. London 123 miles. Newspapers: Purbeck
Advertiser. STD code 01929

## THE MOWLEM THEATRE
The Mowlem, Shore Road, Swanage, Dorset BH19 1DD
Mgt 01929 422229 BO 01929 422239
ADMINISTRATION:
Props: Mowlem Theatre
Policy: Touring, Repertory and Film Shows
Administrator: Carol Sharpe
Seats: 400
TECHNICAL:
Stage: Proscenium, Flat; Pros. opening 9.14m; Ht. of
Pros. 4.88m; Depth of S/Line 6.55m; W/Widths P.S.
1.52m, O.P. 2.89m.
Lighting: Switchboard: 24 way Zero 88 'Sirius', 30 way
Electrosonic "Linkit".
Sound: "Custom Sound" speakers; "Any-Tronics"
amplifiers; "Seck" mixer; 35mm projectors.
Dressing Rooms: 2.
Lift to all floors.

# Swansea, W Glam.

Pop. 171,520. London 192 miles. Newspapers: South
Wales Evening Post 9ntly); Western Mail (dly); Herald of
Wales (thurs for sat). STD code 01792

## BRANGWYN HALL
Swansea Market, The Guildhall, Swansea
SA1 3PE South Wales
Tel/Fax 01792 635489
Brangwyn Hall Manager: Sean Keir
Capacity 1,198

Available for hire or split, concerts, recordings, conferences, functions, dinner.

## DYLAN THOMAS THEATRE
7 Gloucester Place, Maritime Quarter, Swansea
W Glamorgan SA1 1TY S Wales
Tel 01792 473238
ADMINISTRATION:
Administration and Technical Manager: Steve Williams
Seats: 200
TECHNICAL:
Open Ground Stage, ballet floor. Width 13.7m; Depth 10.2m; White cyc. Raked auditorium.

## PATTI PAVILION
Victoria Park, Cradock Street, Oystermouth, Swansea
West Glamorgan SA1 3EP S Wales
Tel/Fax 01792 635489
Manager: Sean Keir
Seats: 490

## PENYRHEOL THEATRE
Penyrheol Leisure Centre, Pontardulais Road,
Gorseinon, Swansea W Glamorgan SA4 4FG S Wales
Mgt/BO 01792 897039 Fax 01792 894931
ADMINISTRATION:
Owner: City & County of Swansea
Manager: David Osborne
Policy: Arts. Mixed and balanced Arts and Entertainments programmes of professional productions and available for hire.
Seats: Max. 600; Balcony 160; (seating is retractable). Main auditorium - 480 seats maximum. Partition available to split seating, if required (300 front, 200 rear and 200 balcony). The seating in the main auditorium is not a fixed arrangement and can be arranged according to the function/production within the maximum seating.
TECHNICAL:
Stage: Width: (Wall to wall) - 14.2m. Proscenium: 10.6m wide, 4.7m high. Stage Depth: 7.0m to front tabs; Stage Apron: 1.0m; Stage Rake: None; Stage Height: To hangers - 7.1m; To lighting Grid - 6.0m. Cyclorama: The stage is equipped with full cyclorama measuring 10.9m wide x 6.0m high. Curtains: One pair front tabs (red in colour); 2 pairs black traverse tabs; 3 pairs black legs; 3 black borders.
Machinery: None.
Green Rooms: Two (1 male, 1 female) situated behind the stage on stage left. Dance Studio: Situated at the rear of the stage with access onto stage from both sides.
Lighting: Control: Furse EDRC 36 way electric switchboard. Each dimmer is rated at 2kw; 48 way patch panel. Control Desk: 36 way 2 preset control desk with master sliders and blackout switches. Location: In control room front of house. A remote control point is switched in the wing stage right. Intercom: 7 stations provided - 4 front of house. 4 on stage.
Sound Equip: One TOA 12 channel mixer & TOA Power Amp (300 watt) fitted Bose speakers & Equaliser, 3 Shure microphones + 2 audio technica. Prompt Corner.
Get-in: Stage left or stage right; Main access through foyer at ground floor level and door No. 7 for very long equipment.
Other: Access Equipment: Tallescope.
Piano. 1 Danemann Baby Grand.
Stage Manager's Desk: Located stage wings.
Power: The theatre also has a three phase electrical supply at 100 amps per phase. Each supply is at

220/240 volts per phase. Fifty cycles are fused/switch junction box and the power is supplied by a 5 wire system (3 positive), 1 neutral return and 1 earth and one additional isolated phase of sixty amps to be available for sound.

## SWANSEA GRAND THEATRE
Singleton Street, Swansea
West Glamorgan SA1 3QJ South Wales
Mgt 01792 475242 BO 01792 475715
SD 01792 478535 Fax 01792 475379
ADMINISTRATION:
Owners: The City and County of Swansea
Manager and Licensee: Gary Iles
Assistant General Manager: Gerald Morris
Marketing Officer: Paul Hopkins
Front of House Manager: Ray Foulton
Box Office Manager: Nigel Waters
Stage Manager: Brian Martin
Policy: Touring, Opera, Ballet, Drama, Children's Shows, Pantomime, Sunday Concerts. Various in-house productions plus Co. Productions with commercial producers.
Perfs: Variable depending upon attraction.
Seats: 1,021
Bars and Coffee Bars at all levels. Exhibition Areas.
TECHNICAL:
Stage: Proscenium, flat; Pros. opening 8.80m; Ht. of Pros. 8.00m; Depth of S/Line 14.00m; Working widths PS 7.80m, OP 12.00m; Ht. of Grid 21.50m; Flying Lines: 70 single purchase 500k sets at 200m centres, 8 motorised sets; all 13m long, with 2m extensions each side. On each side of stage 1 up and down C/W set, 1 up and down hemp set, 1 full length and half length up (2 nr.) and down motorised sets; motorised cloth hoist; Prompt Cnr. normally PS, alternative OP. Approx. 2/3 of acting area trapped in separate 2.4m x 1.2m modules.
Lighting: Switchboard: Rank Strand Galaxy 3 184 channel rear of gallery; 4 x 10kx 36 x 5k, 144 x 2.5k dimmers.
Sound Equipment: 24 channel into 8 group mixer; 36 mic lines; permanent auditorium PA + 47 other loudspeaker lines; cassette tape deck, gram deck 2 x Revox B77 tape decks.
Dressing Rooms: 16, accom. 100, most with showers. 1 Dance Studio, 1 Rehearsal Studio.
Orchestra Pit to accommodate 90 in two independent lifts adjusted to stage floor or pit level.
4 Band Rooms and Music Store.
Membership: TMA

## TALIESIN ARTS CENTRE
University of Wales, Swansea Singleton Park, Swansea
W Glamorgan SA2 8PZ S Wales
Admin 01792 295491 Tech 01792 295492
BO 01792 296883 Fax 01792 295899
ADMINISTRATION:
Props: University College of Swansea
Manager: Sybil Crouch
Senior Technicians: Andrew Knight/David Palmer
Policy: Drama, dance, opera, concerts, films. Mixed programme touring and in-house productions.
Perfs: 7.30 nightly plus occasional late-nights, and Sundays.
Seats: 328/365 (Theatre), Space for 2 wheelchairs. Bar, Foyer, Ceri Richards Art Gallery, Bookshop, Music, Art and Pottery Studios.
TECHNICAL:
Stage: Flat floored stage with adjustable proscenium

walls; forestage lift to pit; wood floor covered hardboard. Stage opening 11.9m to 15.9m. Max width 20m. Depth 9.3m, with thrust 11.6m. Floor to roof beams 10.5m. Floor to fly galleries 6.2m.  18 x No 4 line hemp sets. 3 x 250kg winch bars. 2 x 250 kg motorised lighting bars. Stage managers desk (prompt), rehearsal desk auditorium/control room, intercom and cue lights to all areas, 4 x dressing rooms for 28 artists at stage level. green room, laundry, showers, access to workshop and scene dock at stage level from roadway.
Lighting: Rank Strand Gemini 2. 120 Channels. 108 x 2.5Kw and 12 x 5Kw. Control to rear of auditorium. 4 x F.O.H. Bridges + booms on adjustable side walls. 4 x lighting stands.
Lanterns: 8 x Harmony 15/28, 20 x Harmony 22/40. 10 x harmony PC's . 20  x Harmony Fresnels. 10 Prelude 16/30. 10 Prelude fresnels. 10 x Coda Floods. 10 x Nocturn Floods. 24 Par Cans.
Film: 2 x Westrex 7000 35mm film projectors, 1 x fumeo 16mm film projector, 2 x Kodak 2010 slide projectors, 2 x Simda 3040 slide projectors with dissolve.
Sound: 24/8/2 Soundcraft Venue 2 mixer.  F.O.H. speakers: 2 x bose 302, 4 x bose 802. Rear of auditorium: 2 x Bose 802. portable monitors 4 x JBL (M330) MK2. 2 x Monitor wedges   Microphones 2 x shure beta 58 radio mics, 6 x shure beta 58, 2 x SM58, 4 x shure beta 57, 2 x beyer 201, 2 x AKG D3600 Cardiod Instrument mics, 4 x AKG 1200, 4 x AKG 1903 x crown p.c.c. 2 x revox B77 tape machines, 1 x denon twin cassette deck, 1 x denon cd player, 1 denon DN-1100 minidisc machine, 1 tascam DA20 DAT machineR 1 Yamaha SPX 990, 3 x Yamaha 2301 equalisers, 1 x Alesis midiverb.

# Swindon, Wilts

Pop. 175,000. London 79 miles. Newspapers: Evening Advertiser (ntly); Wiltshire Gazette & Herald (thurs); Wiltshire Star (thurs); Swindon Messenger (thurs). STD code 01793

## OASIS LEISURE CENTRE

North Star Avenue, Swindon Wiltshire SN2 1EP
Tel 01793 445401 Fax 01793 465132
ADMINISTRATION:
Props: Swindon Borough Council
Manager: Alan Greer
Product Development Manager: Steve Skull
Policy: Leisure centre with multi-purpose used for concerts, sporting  and social events, conferences and exhibitions.
Seating/Capacity: 1,600 seated: 2,200 standing
TECHNICAL:
Dimensions of concert hall 126' x 108'; height 29'; no flying facilities.
Power: Lighting - 100 Amp 3 phase; Sound - 60 Amp 3 phase. Lighting basic white or colour spots only. Stage: standard layout 40' x 24', multi-height 2'6'-4,20 units 8' x 6' available. Access ground floor direct from car park.

## WYVERN THEATRE & ARTS CENTRE

Theatre Square, Swindon Wilts SN1 1QN
Mgt 01793 535534 Bo 01793 524481
Fax 01793 480278
ADMINISTRATION:
Props: Swindon Borough Council
Licensees: Wyvern Arts Trust Ltd
Management: Apollo Leisure (UK) Ltd
Theatre Manager: Lizzie Jones

Deputy Managers: David Hollingworth & Jeff Jones
Publicity & Marketing Manager: Mags Rowles
Stage Manager: David Wicks
For all booking information and further details please
contact Sam Shrouder or Nicky Monk at Apollo Leisure
(UK) Ltd., Grehan House, Garsington Road, Cowley,
Oxford OX4 5NQ. Tel: 01865 782900; Fax: Oxford
01865 782910.
Policy: Touring Drama, Opera and Dance, Concerts,
Children's Theatre, Mixed Programme, Exhibitions.
Perfs: Variable.
Seats: 617. Harlequin Bar and Restaurant, Stalls
Licensed Bar, Refreshments Bar.
TECHNICAL:
Stage: Proscenium Fully Trapped Stage, Flat; Apron
1.22m plus Orch. Lift 1.83m; Pros. opening 10.67m -
13.41m; Ht. of Pros. 6.10m; Depth of S/Line 9.14m; Ht.
of Grid 18.29m; 40 lines 35 C/W, Scenery Flying Ht.
14.33m, 18.29m Hemp; Flying Bars 13.72m; W/Widths
P.S. 6.40m, O.P. 6.40m; Prompt Cnr. O.P.
Lighting: Switchboard: Strand lighting lightboard M two
pre-set 48 submaster control with 200 split time
playback memories and built-in effects. 76 2k dimmers;
4 5k dimmers. Lanterns: Profiles - 20 Harmony 15/28
1000 watts; 16 Patt.264 1000 watts; 10 Patt.23 500
watts; Fresnels - 10 Patt.243 2000 watts; 31 Patt.743
1000 watts; 10 Patt.123 500 watts; Beamlights: 20
Parcans with CP62 lamps; Floodlights: 15 Iris 1
Floodlight 1000 watts; 6 Patt.60 Floodlights 500 watts; 5
Coda 3 Groundrows/Cyc Flood; 5 S63 Groundrows
Floods. Follow Spots 2 Altman MT1 400.
Sound Equip: TAC Scorpion 32-8-2 Revox B77; Otari
MX 5050; Yamaha Cassette Deck; Bose speakers, 3
pairs flown; 6 Foldback monitors; 5 SM58 microphones;
3 SM57 microphones; 10 microphone stands with
booms; 1 SPX 90 effects; 1 Yamaha graphic equaliser.
Dressing Rooms 7; Accom.2 5; 4 Showers; Orchestra
Pit 40.

Arts Centre:
Studio and Meeting Room.
Band Room and Store; Scenic Workshops. Wardrobe.
Membership: TMA

# Swinton & Pendlebury, Gtr Manchester

Pop. 40,124. Newspapers: Swinton & Pendelbury
Journal (thurs). STD code 0161

## LANCASTRIAN HALL THEATRE

177 Chorley Road, Swinton, Manchester Gtr
Manchester M27 4AE
Admin/BO 0161 790 4548 (out of hours) 0161 794 7466
Fax 0161 702 6920
ADMINISTRATION:
Props: City of Salford
Policy: Multi-Purpose: Pantomime, Touring Companies.
Manager: David Heyes
Perfs: Various.
Seats: 478. Bars, Buffet.
TECHNICAL:
Stage: Proscenium Stage, Flat; Pros. Opening 9.75m;
Ht. of Pros. 4.57m; Depth of S/Line 7.62m; Ht. of Grid
10.97m; 16 lines, Hemp; Scenery Flying Ht. 4.88m;
Flying Bars 11.58m; W/Widths P.S. 3.05m, O.P. 3.05m;
Prompt Cnr. P.S.
3rd Floor Theatre, Stage lift 7.32m x 3.05m to back wall
of stage.

Lighting: Switchboard: Strand 40, 3 way, rear of theatre;
F.O.H. Spots 78 Fresnel, 6 Patt.223, 6 Patt.23, 6
Halogen 1000w; 3 Battens; 1 Float; Dips 4 each side; 8
Spots Patt.23N Fresnels.
Sound Equipment: Tape, Disc. 100w Selmer, Stage P.S.
Sonifex, Reverb.
Dressing Rooms 8; Accom. 60; 2 Bathrooms; Orchestra
Pit 12.

# Taunton, Somerset

Pop. 65,000. London 142 miles. STD code 01823

## THE BREWHOUSE THEATRE & ARTS CENTRE

Coal Orchard, Suffolk Crescent, Taunton,
Somerset TA1 1JL
Mgt/SD 01823 274608 BO 01823 283244
Fax 01823 323166
ADMINISTRATION:
Props: The Brewhouse Theatre and Arts Centre
Chief Executive: Jim Robertson
Marketing Manager: Gordon Webber
Programme Co-ordinator: Glenys Gill
Technical Manager: Sebastian Petit
Policy: Mid scale professional touring drama, dance,
opera, one person shows, poetry, conference, amateur
drama, operatic & pantomime companies, jazz and folk
and classical music.
Perfs: 7.45. Mats. usually Thurs & Sat 2.30.
Seats: 352. Bar and Buffet/Restaurant.
TECHNICAL:
Stage: Pros. width 10.10m; Height 6.30m, with header
4.93m; Pros. header 1.37m (h); Depth of pros. to cyc.
7.00m; Max flying height 6.40m; Hemp bar width
13.00m; Prompt side wing width 3.50m; Opp. prompt
side wing width 7.50m; Dock doors opening 4.00m (w) x
6.00m (h); Depth of apron 3.00m; Height of stage above
1st row auditorium.
Lightboard: Rank Strand Gemini 2 memory board with
integral effects panel operated from control room at rear
of auditorium. Riggers control and plotting position in
auditorium. 96 X 2.5kw circuits (LD 90 Racks): Phase 1
(c.no.1-16+49-64) = bridge + juliets, Phase 2 (c.no. 17-
32+65-80) = adv. bar +LX1, Phase 3 (c.no. 33-48+81-
96) = LX2 +12 dip sockets. Patch panel located in SL
juliet balcony. Equipment: 10 X Vision 1200ZN; 10 X
Altman Shakespeare 15/35; 11 X Prelude 16/30; 8 X
Freedom 28/58; 8 X Vision 650ZW 23/40; 2 X Clay Paky
Shadow follow spots; 8 X Patt 23c/w shutters; 12 X Par
64 (CP62); 9 X Harmony F +b/d; 10 X Vision 1200F +
b/d; 10 X Cantata F + b/d; 12 X Vision 650F + b/d; 10 X
Prelude F + b/d; 8 X Vision 2.5k PC + b/d; 12 X
Spotlight Domino 1k floods; 6 X booms; 4 X shin stands.
Sound Equip: 1 x Revox B77 (HS); 1 x Pioneer cassette
deck, 1 X Allen & Heath mixer (24-4-2); 24 way hardwire
multicore to stage (inclusive of speaker routes); 6 X
Tannoy Lynx speakers; 2 x Citronic PPX amplifiers;1 X
Carver PM950 amp; 9 X mic stands; 3 X SM58 mics; 5
X assorted AKG mics; 1 X Yamaha graph. equaliser.
General: Dressing Rooms 2 large, 2 small; Total
accommodation 40 3 showers, 4 Toilets. Green
Room/Crew Room with fridge, small cooker &
microwave, 1 disabled toilet & shower.

# Telford, Shropshire

Pop. 140,000. London 148 miles. Newspapers:
Shropshire Star (ntly); Telford Journal (fri). STD code

01952

## OAKENGATES THEATRE
Limes Walk, Oakengates, Telford, Shropshire TF2 6EP
Admin 01952 610163 BO 01952 619020
Fax 01952 610164
ADMINISTRATION:
Props: Telford & Wrekin Council
Manager: Chris Maddocks
Technical Managers: Brian Eades & Ray Newall
Policy: One Night Stands, Concerts, Exhibitions,
Pantomime, Amateur Musicals; Lettings for Banquets,
Concerts, Variety, Discos, Dances etc.
Seats: 651 Concert. 315 on retractable rake. Bars and
Servery.
Box Office: 14 agents.
TECHNICAL:
Stage: Proscenium arch. Performing area 16.5m by
12.5m, pros opening 12.2m by 4.2m. Wing widths 2m
SR, 2m SL no rake. Floor sprung wood, suitable for
dance (not barefoot). Backstage and understage
crossovers, stage not heated. Height of grid 6m - black,
beige, burgundy masking - white canvas cyclorama -
red house tabs, drawn. 4 by 2 13A sockets, 4 by 15A
independent circuits. 100 A3 phase visitors supply. 1
lift in front of stage. Get in via stage lift - dock doors 2m
by 2m. Tallescope. Scale stage and lighting plans
available.
Lighting: Rank Strand GSX. 72 circuits, 15 amp 2kw per
channel. Operated rear of auditorium. Visitors supply 3
phase stage left. 33 profile spots, 19 fresnels, 8 floods,
16 pars and 1 cyc batten, 6 Scans.
Sound: Yamaha 24 channel desk EV Delta boxes,
Crown amps.
Stage Management: Prompt corner SL. Tecpro cue
system with 5 outstations. Show relay to dressing
rooms.

## Tewksbury, Glos
Pop. 9,104. London 104 miles. STD code 01684

## ROSES THEATRE
Sun Street, Tewkesbury, Gloucestershire GL20 5NX
Admin 01684 290734 BO 01684 295074
Fax 01684 290732
ADMINISTRATION:
Director: Robert Hamlin
Technical Manager: Louise Pounder
Marketing Manager: Judy Gibson
Finance: Sheila Smith
Policy: Pantomime, One Night Stands, Concerts,
Drama, Cabaret, Films, Conferences, Touring Shows.
Perfs: Daily.
Seats: 370. Licensed Bar, Kiosk.
TECHNICAL:
Stage: Proscenium stage, Flat; Pros. opening 12.19m;
Ht. of Pros. 5.79m; Depth of S/Line 8.92m; Ht. of Grid
14.17m; 18 lines, 6 C/W, 9 hemp, 2 Motor Tabs, power
O.P. screen; Scenery Flying Ht. 6.71m; Flying Bars
12.19m; W/Widths P.S. 3.05m av., O.P. 3.05m av.
Prompt Cnr. P.S.
Lighting: Switchboard: Rank Tempus 48 channel.
Spots 1 Follow, 2 Perches (8 circ. paired) Gallery (10
circ. paired); Dips 6 P.S., 6 O.P.; 3 Spot Bars, No. 1 15
circuits, No. 2 10 circuits, No. 3 6 circuits.
Sound Equip: Spirit Folio 12 way, tape deck, 4 AKG
190, Quad 303 amps, all in projection box. Speakers:
Tannoy Mansfield 2 stage, 2 auditorium.

Dressing Rooms 3 plus; Accom. 40; 1 Shower;
Orchestra Pit 14. Disabled persons provision (own toilet,
demountable auditorium seating to accommodate
wheelchairs, all disabled facilities on common level with
street).
Separate Conference Room.

## Tonbridge

### ANGEL LEISURE CENTRE
Angel Lane, Tonbridge, Kent TN9 1SF
Tel 01732 359966 Fax 01732 363677
Manager: Gary Littlejohn
Policy: Multi-purpose Hall used for theatre, cinema,
concerts, meetings, sports and social events,
conferences, fairs and markets.
Seating/Capacity: 307 seated; 400 standing.

## Torbay, Devon
Pop. 112,000. London 193 miles. Newspapers: Herald
Express (ntly); Western Morning News (dly); Torbay
Weekender (thurs). STD code 01803

### BABBACOMBE THEATRE
Babbacombe Downs Road, Torquay, Devon TQ1 3LU
Mgt 01803 328385 Admin 01803 322233
Fax 01803 322244
ADMINISTRATION:
Props: Matthews Productions Ltd
Cary Point, Babbacombe, Downs Road, Torquay,
Devon TQ1 3LU Tel 01803 322233 Fax 01803 322244
Contact: Colin Matthews
Seats: 600
TECHNICAL:
Stage: Proscenium Stage, Flat; Pros. opening 8.46m;
Ht. of Pros. 4.19m; Depth of S/Line 5.03m; Ht. of grid
5.79m; 17 lines, 11 Hemp-to-wire, 6 Hemp; Scenery
Flying Ht. 2.89m; Flying Bars 9.75m; W/Widths P.S.
0.91m, O.P. 1.22m; Prompt Cnr. P.S.
Lighting: Switchboard: Sirius 48 way memory board.
Full lighting rig-details on request.
Sound Equip: Stereo slave PSL 12-16, 1200W 4 Hz Full
range cabinets. Soundcraft spirit stereo desk 12
channel - 5 monitors for foldback.
Dressing Rooms 5; Accom. 20.

### BRIXHAM THEATRE
New Road, Brixham, Devon
Mgt/BO 01803 852829
ADMINISTRATION:
Props: Torbay Borough Council
For bookings and further information contact
Peter Carpenter Tel 01803 201201
Policy: Summer play season, private hirings remainder of
year.
Perfs: Variable.
Seats: 342
TECHNICAL:
Stage: Proscenium, Flat; Pros. opening 7.77m; Ht. of
Pros. 3.05m (very high raised stage); Prompt Cnr.
1.83m.
Lighting: Switchboard: Strand 3 preset 18 way; F.O.H. 4
Patt.264; 2 light battens; 1 front spot bar 3 Patt.137, 2
Patt.123, 1 Back Spot for 8 Patt.113, 1 Patt.223, Stage
Dips run from Dimmer Pack 4 Patt.223.

Sound Equip: 4 track tape recorder.
Dressing Rooms 4; Accom. 20. When Orchestra rail installed. Accom. 10 musicians.

## PALACE AVENUE THEATRE

Palace Avenue, Paignton, Devon TQ3 3HF
Mgt 01803 558367 BO 01803 665800
Fax 01803 665800
ADMINISTRATION:
Props: Torbay Council
Theatre Manager: Alan Davies
Policy: Private hirings throughout the year.
Perfs: Variable.
Seats: 391
TECHNICAL:
Stage: Proscenium, Raked; Pros. opening 7.32m; Ht. of Pros. 6.10m; Depth of S/Line 9.75m; 15 lines; W/Widths P.S. 1.83m, O.P. 1.83m; Prompt Cnr. P.S.
Lighting: Arri 75 channel memory desk; 48 channel dimmer (10 amp/channel); Extra 100amp 3 Phase supply; controlable FOH or Side Stage. Lanterns - 8 Source 4 Profiles; 2 Profiles 500w; 4 Pat 23; 16 Quartet PC with barn doors; 4 PAT 264 with barn doors; 12 Pat 123; 8 PAT 64 floods; 3 X 3 channel batterns; followspot. FOH grid - 16 channels.
Sound Equip: 12 channel stereo mixer, 500w per channel; two FOH speakers.
General: Dressing Rooms 5; Accom. 24. Grand Piano - Concert Pitch. When Orchestra Rail installed accom. 5 or 6 musicians. Accommodation for 6 wheelchairs at front of stalls. Access to auditorium can be obtained by chair lift accommodating one person without chair. Hearing loop installed for the partially deaf.

## PRINCESS THEATRE

Torbay Road, Torquay Devon TQ2 5EZ
Mgt 01803 290288 BO 01803 290290
SD 01803 297072 SM 01803 290068
Production Office 01803 290075 Fax 01803 290170
ADMINISTRATION:
Props: Torbay Borough Council
Management: Apollo Leisure (UK) Ltd
For all booking information and further details please contact Sam Shrouder or Nicky Monk at Apollo Leisure (UK) Ltd., Grehan House, Garsington Road, Cowley, Oxford OX4 5NQ. Tel: 01865 782900; Fax: Oxford 01865 782910.
Theatre Manager: Wendy Bennett
Stage Manager: Martyn Jenkins
Chief Electrician: Martin Roberts
ASM: Eric Payne
Policy: Summer Shows, Pantomime, Tours (plays, opera, ballet), conference facilities, Repertory, Concerts.
Perfs: Variable according to function.
Seats: 1,495. bar within Theatre, Restaurant adjacent.
TECHNICAL:
Stage: Proscenium, Flat; Pros. Opening 10.58m, Ht of Pros. 4.87m, Fire curtain to back wall 7.5m, Forestage to back wall 9.41m. Stage width: W to W 18.34m. P.S. 3.90m. O.P. 2.80m. Ht of grid 12.60m, 30 lines, C/W: Scenery flying Ht. 5.49m. Flying Bars 12.50m. Power supply; 200 amp P.S. 100 amp O.P. both 3 phase. Forestage 1.02m x 11.96m. Prompt cnr. P.S. Orchestra pit 11 plus M.D. Street level get in dock doors 2.45m wide by 3.36m high.
Lighting: Switchboard: Strand Gemini 112 way. F.O.H. 8 Patt. 53 (Auto) 8 Patt. 53, 8 Prelude 16/30. 6 Patt. 743, 4 Silhouettes. Stage. Foots 3 circuit. Bar 1. 8 x Cantata F, 5 Patt 60, 4 743, 2 Cantata 26/44. Bar 2. 8

ADB 1000, 4 Patt 60, 2 patt 743, Cyc Bar 6 Coda 4 circuits: Circuits F.O.H. 18, Foots 3, Dips 8 a side, Flys 50. Additional lighting. 20 Parcans, 6 243, 12 Patt 60, 5 Patt 123, 8 23N's, Lycian 1290XLT Follow Spots at rear of Balcony, 1 x 9 station intercom, Show relay.
Sound Equip: Soundcraft K1 24-4-2 desk, 2 JBL Tri lamps, 1 JBL 6290, 2 x 60w, 1 JBL 6260, 2 x 300w. 2 Yamaha P2201, 2 x 200w, 1 Yamaha P2050, 2 x 90w. 2 x Cabinets loaded with 15" + Horn 250w. 1 Revox B77, 1 Denon CD + Rev 100 effects unit, 2 Denon cassettes, 2 Yamaha 2031 Graphic , 1 MXR 172 Graphic. Stands 4 Pump type, 2 Boom type, 5 short type. Mics: 7 SM58, SAKG 451, 5 Sennheiser ME80/K30, 1 PZM, 2 Shure Unisphere, 2 DI boxes, 1 Shure SM57, 1 AKG D12, 3 Crown PCC.
Dressing Rooms 9: Wardrobe with W/M & T/D. Accom 40; 4 showers.

## TORBAY LEISURE CENTRE

Clennon Valley, Penwill Way, Paignton, Devon TQ4 5JR
Tel/Fax 01803 522240
ADMINISTRATION:
General Manager: A. D. Westwood.
Policy: Multi-purpose leisure & sports centre with facilities for exhibitions, conferences, sports displays and concerts. Also has an outdoor showground and sports pitches.
Seating/Capacity: 2,400 seated; or 3,000 standing & 400 seated.
TECHNICAL:
Full power and stage available, please apply to venue for further details.

## TORQUAY RIVIERA CENTRE

Chestnut Avenue Torquay Devon TQ2 5LZ
Mgt 01803 299992 BO 01803 206333
Fax 01803 206320
General Manager: Barry Cole
Seating/Capacity: 1,850 (standing); 1,500 (theatre); 1,100 (cabaret).
Major concert, conference and exhibition venue, one night, summer season, rock and pop, boxing, etc.

# Tredegar

## TREDEGAR LEISURE CENTRE

Stable Lane, Tredegar, Gwent NP2 4BH Wales
Tel 01495 723554 Fax 01495 724146
Manager: David Allan
Seating/Capacity: Hall: 600

# Troon

## TROON CONCERT HALL

South Beach, Ayr Street, Troon, Ayrshire KA10 6EF
Scotland
Tel 01292 313555 Fax 01292 318009
Contacts: Carol Murray, Debbie Gavin, Lynn Wright
Seating/Capacity: 850

# Trowbridge

## ARC THEATRE
College Road, Trowbridge, Wiltshire BA14 0ES
BO: 01225 756376/01225 766241 Fax: 01225 756211
Theatre Director: Deryck Newland
Chief Technician: Louise Birchall
Marketing and Administration Assistant: James Clifford
Policy: Small scale touring, theatre, dance, children's
performance. Folk and jazz. Emphasis on young people
and participatory activity.
Two dressing rooms and access to two further changing
facilities for larger casts or choruses.
Rehearsal Studio: 11.5m x 6.5m with fully sprung floor.
Fully mirrored down one length. Piano. Simple lighting rig
available for use by negotiation.
Theatre: Full floor space with all seating retracted = 14m
x 11.5m. End on performance space (capacity 150) =
10m x 8m.
Entire floor space is fully sprung. Black dance floor is
available 10m x 8m. Rostra to create a raised stage is
available if required but remember all the seating is
tiered. Front tabs and back cyclorama for end on
performance. Piano.
Technical: 96 circuit rig extending throughout the space
for fully flexible use of floor space. Dimmable House
Lighting. 40 lanterns inc. follow spot and cyc. Battens.
LBX Strand desk with Genius software.
Sound: Soundcraft Spirit live 16-4-2 mixer. Sound
system includes cassette, CD, DAT and minidisc. 4 x
200W speakers + 2 x foldback/FX speakers.
S.M: 8 way cuing desk with show relay and 5 beltpacks.
Facility panels allow for flexible siting of control desks.

# Tunbridge Wells, Kent

Pop. 96,500. London 37 miles. Newspapers: Kent &
Sussex Courier (fri). STD code 01892

## ASSEMBLY HALL THEATRE
Crescent Road, Tunbridge Wells, Kent TN1 2LU
Mgt 01892 526121 BO 01892 530613
SD 01892 527702 Fax 01892 525203
ADMINISTRATION:
Tunbridge Wells Borough Council
Theatre Manager: Pat Casey
Operations Manager: John Sumner
Business Manager: Brian McAteer
Technical Assistant: Terry Hill
Box Office Supervisor: Monica Brennan
Policy: Multi-purpose hall. Repertory, pantomime,
concerts, plays, exhibitions, dances, dinners, meetings,
musicals, drama festivals, etc.
Perfs: Vary
Capacity: 934 Seated; 700 standing.
Bar and Buffet.
TECHNICAL:
Stage: Proscenium. Width: 39', Height: 22', Depth: 33',
Stage Depth to setting line 29', Stage Width: 56'. flying
Equipment: 24 double purchase counterweight (lines 2-
25), 1 single purchase counterweight (line 1), 1 electric
winch bar (line 26). All flying bars rated at 500 kg. 14
hemp sets, 4 verlinde 1000 kg chain hoists. Stage
equipment: Rostra 8 6'3"x3'6"x1'0", 4 6'6"x3'9"x1'0", 4
8'0"x4'0"x1'0". Masking and Tabs. 3 sets black legs
12'x22', 3 black borders 6'x50', 4 pairs of tabs, 22'
drop with tab tracks; red, gold, blue, black. 1 pair
house tabs, with motorised track, 1 rosco cyclorama on

frame 40' x 20', 1 show cloth, 1 projection screen on
frame 20'x15'.
Lighting: Dimming and Control - control room - rear of
circle. Strand Gemini II, Thorn 120 x 10 way matrix with
effects. 120 2.5kw dimmers distributed 34 FOH, 52 PS
fly floor, 18 stage perches, 16 stage dips. Stage power:
1 60A TP&N Prompt side, 1 200A TP&N Prompt side, 1
315A TP&N T.V. supply. Lanterns: FOH Lighting bar 20
x T84 (12 with colour wheels), FOH Booms PS and OP 5
x Cantata 11/26 each side, FOH follow spots (rear of
circle) 2 x 765 CID.
Patt 743 26, Patt 828 6, Cantata F 6, Minim F 4, Sil 30
4, Prelude 16/30 2, Par Can 38, Par 36 8 way bars 4,
Coda 4 10, AC 1001 12. 4'6" stands 6, 40' 18 way
lighting bars 3 (with working lights). Kodak Carousel
35mm projector 1.
Sound: Control (circle mixing position), 1 Yamaha MC
2404, 24 channel, 4 group, 4 aux, 1 Klark Teknik DN
332 Graphic, 2 Yamaha Q2031 Graphic, 2 Yamaha SPX
90 Effects, 1 Yamaha GC2020 Compressor/Limiter, 1
Tascam 112R cassette Deck, 1 Pioneer LT-W700R Twin
Cassette Deck. Also available: 1 TEAC 1/2 Track Tape
Recorder, 1 AKAI 1/4 track tape recorder, 1 Goldring
Lenco record deck. Speakers and amps: FOH 8 Martin
Audio CX 2, 4 Martin Audio BX 2, 2 Martin Audio CX 2
(circle fill). Foldback: 5 Yamaha S 2112-H, 12" Wedge
Monitors, 1 Yamaha S 10 x Mini Monitors, 4 Fostex SP
11, Mini Monitors. Amplifiers: 4 HHM 900, 1 Yamaha P
2250, 2 Spectrum 100 W, 1 Yamaha P2350, Tie lines:
Prompt corner 25 Mic Ties, 6 return ties. Microphones:
12 AKG C 451 E Bodies, 5 AKG CK 1 Capsules, 5 AKG
CK 3 Capsules, 2 AKG CK 8 Capsules, 1 AKG CK 9
Capsules, 3 AKG CK 22 Capsules, 4 AKG C 535, 4
AKG D 190, 1 AKG D 320, 3 AKG D 707, 3 Shure
SM58, 1 Audio Pocket Radio with Sony ECM 50 1
Sennheiser SKM 4031 Hand Held Radio, 2 DI Boxes,
selection of straight, boom and table microphone
stands. Prompt corner (PS): Stage relay and SM call to
dressing rooms. Ring Intercom (Tec-Pro) Prompt
corner, PS Stage, OP Stage, Fly Floors, Orch. Pit, Under
Stage, Control Room, Follow Spots, Sound Desk.
Closed Circuit Television, Prompt Corner, OP Stage,
Stage, Orch. Pit, Foyers and Bars. Cue lights to
Orchestra Pit. Maxon Portable Radios - interfaced with
ring intercom.
Orchestra pit: 3 section pit lift (approx total size 44'x6'9")
access to pit from understage. 19 RAT Lit music
stands.
Piano: Steinway Concert Grand, Steinway Boudoir
Grand.
Dressing rooms: Ground floor (stage level) 3 rooms
15'x9', 1 Prop Store/dressing room. First floor, 2 rooms
15'x17', 1 room 15'x9'. Understage: 1 room 15'x15' 1
band room.

# Ulverston, Cumbria

Pop. 13,500. London 270 miles. Newspapers:
Advertiser (thurs); Evening Mail (dly). STD code 01229

## CORONATION HALL THEATRE
County Square, Ulverston Cumbria LA12 7LZ
Mgt 01229 582610 BO 01229 587140
ADMINISTRATION:
Props: South Lakeland D.C.
Policy: All types of Stage Performance including Tours,
Repertory, Drama, Dance, Opera, Light Entertainment,
Comedy, Concerts, etc; also Dances, Conferences etc.
Manager: Janet Ridal
Seats: 636.

We are interested in joint promotions.
TECHNICAL:
Stage: Proscenium, Raked (overall width 16.46m; Pros. opening 8.53m; depth 8.53m)
Lighting: Switchboard: Spots, Limes, etc.
Sound Equip: Microphones and Amplifications systems.
Dressing Rooms 5; Orchestra Front.

# Uppingham, Rutland

Pop. 3,067. London 89 miles. STD code 01572

## UPPINGHAM THEATRE

Stockerston Road, Uppingham, Rutland LE15 9UD
Mgt 01572 823318  Fax 01572 821872
Uppingham School Tel 01572 822216
ADMINISTRATION:
Props: The Trustees of Uppingham School
Director of Drama: Julian Freeman
Theatre Manager: Andrew Swift
Policy: Tours, local school and amateur prods.
Perfs: 7.30 (no matinees usually), variable.
Seats: 296, Bar and Buffet for most shows.
TECHNICAL:
Stage: Proscenium arch/performing area 12.2m x 9.75m. Proscenium opening 12.2m x 4.75m. Lift and trap DSC. Forestage 1.22m deep. Orchestra pit 3.05m deep, 9.14m wide, 2.28m height, accommodates 30. Get-in via SR exit - dock doors 3.05m x 6.0m. Tallescope.
Lighting: Eclipse memory board, 60 circuits 300 amps, operated from LX box at back of auditorium.
24 spots, 24 fresnels. Follow spots operated from LX box or back gantry.
Sound: Teac mixer 8 into 2, 2 quad amp 100 watts, 2 x FOH speakers, 2 x movable ROH speakers. Cassette and CD, operated from LX box . Acoustics suitable for music and spoken word.
Dressing rooms: 3. Rehearsal piano fair.

# Ventnor, I.O.W.

Pop. 7,000. Newspapers: Isle of Wight County Press (fri); South Wight Chronicle (thurs). STD code 01983

## THE WINTER GARDENS

Pier Street, Ventnor, Isle of Wight PO38 1SZ
Tel 01983 855215 Fax 01983 853314
ADMINISTRATION:
Props: Ventnor Town Council
Manager: John Farrant
Technical Manager: Tim Warry
Policy: Multi-Purpose Hall
Seats: 400 (Removable)
Bar and Restaurant.
TECHNICAL:
Stage: Proscenium, Raked. Pros. opening 10.30m, ht of Pros. 4.00m; Depth of Stage 5.80m; W/Widths P.S. 3.00m, O.P. 0.60m; Prompt Cnr. P.S.; Ht. to Grid 6.40m.
Lighting: Switchboard - Strand JP40/3 located prompt cnr. 40 circuits 2kw. FOH: 6 x Prelude 16/30.2 x 5IL30, 6 x Harmony P.C., 4 x Harmony F, 4 x Cantata F, 6 x Parcan.  Stage: 10 x Prelude F, 1 x 4 circuit batten, 18 x Parcan, 10 x CODA 500w Floods. Follow Spots available on request.
Sound Equip: 8 into 2 mixer x 200w, foldback x 50w; Shure mics, tape deck and cassette deck.

Dressing Rooms 2. Accom. 8. Additional space available to accommodate 50.

# Wakefield, West Yorkshire

Pop. 300,000. London 200 miles. Newspapers: Yorkshire Post (dly); Evening Post (dly); Wakefield Express (fri). STD code 01924

## THEATRE ROYAL & OPERA HOUSE

Drury Lane, Wakefield, West Yorkshire WF1 2TE
Admin 01924 215531 BO 01924 211311
Fax 01924 215525
ADMINISTRATION:
Props: Wakefield Theatre Trust
General Manager: Murray Edwards
Marketing Manager: Sandra Wood
Theatre Operations Manager: Marie Dalton
Seats: 504
Policy: Professional touring, in-house professional pantomime, amateur work, community and outreach projects.  Guarantees, fees and Box Office splits.
TECHNICAL:
Stage: Pros opening 7.26m, Height to tabs 4.88m, Stage depth 9.15m (raked 1:30), Flying 20 c/w lines, bar width 8.3m.
Lighting: Strand Gemini 108 circuits.
Sound: Tascam 16/4/2 desk, EV speakers, 5 dressing rooms c/w showers.
Orchestra Pit 16 people.

# Warrington

## PARR HALL

Palmyra Square South, Warrington Cheshire WA1 1BL
Tel 01925 651178 BO 01925 634958
Fax 01925 234144
Email: parrhall@warrington.gov.uk
Web Site: www.info-quest.com/parrhall
Manager: John Perry
Technician: Richard Fleming
Capacity: 1,100

## SPECTRUM ARENA

PO Box 12, Bonson Road, Birchwood, Warrington, Cheshire WA3 7FB
Tel: 01925 810002 Fax: 01925 838043
Capacity: 1, 500 seated; 2,400 partially seated/standing

# Watford, Herts

Pop.77,690. London 17 miles. Newspapers: Watford Observer (fri). STD code 01923

## THE COLOSSEUM

Rickmansworth Road, Watford Herts WD1 7JN
Mgt 01923 445300 BO 01923 445000
Fax 01923 445225
ADMINISTRATION:
Managers: Paul Scarbrow and John Wallace
Manager (Marketing & Publicity): James Delanoy
Capacity: Standing 1,794 (1,500 stalls/294 balcony); Seated 1,440 (1146 Stalls/294 balcony).Catering

facilities.
TECHNICAL:
Stage: Width 50ft, Depth 31.5ft; Height 4.5ft; Clearance
from stage 40ft approx. Dressing rooms: 1 master, 2
standard, 1 Touring production office.
No fire curtain.Power supplies: 200A 3 Phase (Lighting),
100A Single Phase (Audio);
Lighting: 16 x 1k Fresnels, 8 per side, mounted on
brackets over the stage area. All lamps have barn doors
and are coloured on request. Plus full concert rig.
Follow spots: 2 x Coemar Pilots. Intercom lines situated
at the spot positions and on stage left . Rigging points
are rated at 1 ton per point. Mixer positions will be
situated centrally at the rear of the hall below the
balcony. Risers will be available (1ft + 2ft).
Sound: Systems can be designed to suit your
requirements - please contact for further details.

## PALACE THEATRE

Clarendon Road, Watford Herts WD1 1JZ
Mgt/SD 01923 235455 BO 01923 225671
Fax 01923 819664
ADMINISTRATION:
Lessees: Palace Theatre Watford Ltd
Artistic Director: Giles Croft
Administrative Director: Alastair Moir
Production Manager: Fergus Gillies
Policy: 4 weekly Repertory.
Perfs: 7.45, Fri. & Sat. 8.00.
Seats: 663. Bar and Bistro.
TECHNICAL:
Stage: Proscenium, Rake 1:48. Pros. opening 8.26m;
Ht. of Pros. 4.8m; Depth of S/Line 6.10m plus 2.12
Forestage; Ht. of Grid 11m; 23 lines Hemp, House Tabs
C/W; Scenery Flying Ht. 5.3m; Flying Bars 9m;
W/Widths P.S. 1.9m, O.P. 2.7m; Prompt Cnr. O.P.
Lighting: Switchboard: Gemini II + board - 96 ways.
Sound Equip: 16-4-2 DDA mixer + House PA. Theatre
Projects Head Set System.
Prompt Call System.
Dressing Rooms 5; Accom. 30; Orchestra Pit 15.
Membership: TMA

# Wellingborough, Northamptonshire

Pop, 68,500 London 70 Miles. Newpapers: Evening
Telegraph (Daily), Citizen (Thur), Northampton Chronicle
& Echo (Daily), herald and Post (Thur), TV Advertiser
(Wed) STD Code: 01933

## THE CASTLE

Castle Way, Wellingborough, Northamptonshire NN8
1XA
Mgt 01933 229022  BO 01933 270007
Fax 01933 229888
Email: pat@thecastle.org.uk
ADMINISTRATION:
The Castle (Wellingborough) Ltd
Executive Director: Graham Brown
Artistic Director: Daniel Austin
Marketing Manager: Gordon Glass
Customer Services Manager: Michaela Lewis
Technical Manager: Lesley Gash
Food & Beverage Manager: Eric Fernando
Administrator: Pat Souster
POLICY: The Castle provides a vibrant mixture of 70%
professional touring music, dance, drama, film and

comedy and an in-house Christmas production. The
remaining 30% are hires by local societies and
community groups.
Seats: Main Auditorium 501, Studio Theatre 84 (raked
seating) - 120 (cabaret seating/standing)
Fully licensed bar & brasserie, exhibition space, art
gallery, function rooms including conference facilities,
craft workshop.
TECHNICAL:
Main Auditorium: Proscenium stage, flat, country maple
flooring (Harlequin dance floor available): Pros. opening
9.72m - 11.88m; Pros. height 5.49m - 6.45m; Depth of
S/Line 10.5m - 13.5m with thrust, stage width 20m,
Height of Grid 15m; to fly floor 7.5m; 28 C/W Bars & 6
Hemp, 2 tab tracks; Prompt Desk DSL; Backstage or
Understage Crossover; Auditorium capable of flat floor
format for exhibitions, conferences and dances, full
catering and bar facilities on site. Orchestra Pit (12m x
3m) accommodates 25.
Lighting: Control: Galaxy Nova 120 Channel in Control
Room at Rear of Stalls + Riggers Control; 3 on stage LX
Bars + 3 ladders P.S. & O.P.; 3 x FOH Bridges & 2 x
FOH Booms each side. Lanterns available: 22 x 2.5kW
14/32 Alto Profiles; 24 x 1.2kW Cantata PC's; 8 x 1.2kW
Cantata Fresnels; 36 x 1.2kW Cantata 11/26 Profiles; 5
x 1.5kW Iris 4 cyc battens; 8 x 2kW Cadenza PC PALS
lanterns; 2 x 1kW Solo CSI Followspots. Dimmers: 112 x
2.5kW & 8 x 5kW; 18 non-dimming independent
channels (16A).
Sound: Soundcraft Spiritlive 16 channel mixer; PA's: 2C-
Audio RA1001 & 1 C-Audio SR 707; Speakers flown in
central cluster in front of prosc. arch - 2 Community
PC264, 1 Community LF212 & 1 JBL2445 & stereo pair
(Community) auditorium left & right; 4 full range monitor
wedges, 6 stage LS outputs, 24 stage mic inputs, 1
Revox B77 MkII 7.5 & 15 i.p.s. + remote; 2 Denon
cassette desks, 1 Marantz CD player, Yamaha SPX 990
multi effects processor, 1 Denon Mini-disc player.
Facilities: 2 x 63A single phase and 1 x 32A single phase
located in workshop 15m from SL.
Dressing Rooms: Accommodate 64 total, 2 Ground
Level with Toilets & Showers; 5 Basement with shared
Toilets & Showers; 2 Green Rooms (smoking & non-
smoking); Full washing & drying facilities.
Cinema: Flown screen with Integral Dolby Sound System
JBL; 16mm & 35mm projectors located in projection
room at rear of balcony.
Car Parking: 120 space car park + overspill multi-storey.

STUDIO THEATRE
Multi purpose space available in theatre format 84 seats
(chairs on retractable seating unit in raked format);
Performance area 8m x 7.5m; cabaret format 112-120
seats or clear space. Beech floor (no rake). No floor
coverings available.
Masking: Full set of soft blacks at each end of room, 2
side masking flats.
Lighting: Strand LX 24 Channel 2-way preset desk; 4 x
Act 6 dimmers; selection of Lee Colortran lanterns -
500W club profiles, fresnels etc. Fixed grid covering
whole area (approx. 5m from floor).
Sound: Soundcraft Spirit Power Station: 10 mic
channels, 2 L&R; QSC Audio USA 850 Amplifier (2
monitor mix) 2 EV SX 200 full range speakers and
stands. Mics, playback equipment, monitors available on
request.
Facilities: 2 x Dressing Rooms accommodating 12
people; Male & Female toilets.

# Welwyn Garden City, Herts

Pop. 47,000. London 23 miles. Newspapers: Welwyn Times (wed); Review (thurs). STD code 01707

## CAMPUS WEST THEATRE

The Campus, Welwyn Garden City Herts AL8 6BX
Mgt 01707 357165 BO 01707 332880
Fax 01707 357185
ADMINISTRATION:
Props: Welwyn Hatfield Council
General Manager Leisure Services: Richard Masters
Theatre Manager: Mark Woolman
Policy: Concerts, Ballet, Orchestral, Variety, Film, etc.
Seats: 364
TECHNICAL:
Stage: Proscenium. Flat; Pros. Opening 10.34m; Ht. of Pros. 4.96m; Depth of S/Line 7.72m; Ht. of Grid 12.19m; 21 lines, 5 C/W, 10 Hemp; Scenery Flying Ht. 7.24m; W/Widths P.S. 5.43m, O.P. 0.91m; Prompt Cnr. P.S.
Lighting: Switchboard: Zero 88 Eclipse 60 channel memory board. 57 double outlets (2k) + 3 x 5k channels, 15 amp 3 pin BESA circuits F.O.H. Lighting Lamps: 36 x 1kw Profiles; 5 x Prelude Profiles; 2 x Minuette Profiles; 16 x Furse 650w Profiles; 28 x 1kw Fresnels. Follow Spots: 30 x P123; 6 x CCT 2 circ; 2 x 1kw Solo CSI's battens; 4 x Par.64; 16 x Patt.60's.
Sound Equip: Allen & Heath SR plus 416 sound mixer. F.O.H. speakers: 2 prs Bose 802 speakers, 2 Bose 302 speakers; monitor speakers - 1 pr. JBL speakers; Revox B77 Tape Recorder; Denon DCD 620 CD player; Denon DRM 700 cassette player; 12 mix inputs either side of stage. 4 Shure SM58 mics, 4 Shure SM57 mics.
Dressing Rooms: Paging and Show Relay; Intercom to lighting control; Limes, Fly P.S. Stage, Orchestra.
Dressing Rooms: 4; accom. 30/40. Orchestra Pit: 20 - 30 RAT music stands + 1 RAT conductors stand.
Full Box Office facilities. Film theatre - 35mm & 16mm. Projection facilities. Most A/V aids for conferences.

# Weston-Super-Mare, North Somerset

Pop. 80,000. London 136 miles. Newspapers: Weston Mercury (fri); Weston & Worle News (thur). STD code 01934

## PLAYHOUSE

High Street Weston Super Mare
North Somerset BS23 1HP
Mgt 01934 627457 BO 01934 645544
SD 01934 623974 Fax 01934 622888
ADMINISTRATION:
Props: North Somerset District Council
Director of Leisure Services: Mr R F C Acland
General Manager: Murray MacDonald
Policy: Touring, Plays, Pantomime, Ballet, Musical Productions, Drama, Opera, One Night Stands, Summer Season, Films
Perfs: 7.30 (once nightly). 6.00 & 8.45 (twice nightly).
Seats: 658. Licensed Bars, Light Refreshments.
TECHNICAL:
Stage: Proscenium, Flat; Pros. Opening 9.14m; Ht. of Pros. 5.49m, Depth of S/Line 6.55m; Ht. of Grid 13.72m; 36 lines, 30 C/W, 6 Hemp; Scenery Flying Ht.

7.32m; Flying Bars 11.28m; W/Widths P.S. 2.59m, O.P. 5.18m; Prompt Cnr. P.S.
Lighting: Switchboard: Strand 430 162 way, 57 x 743 - 12 x Cantarter 11/26, 26 x Patt.23's - 4 x 243's 30 Parcans - 6 x 808's, 8 x 15 Silloetts - 6 x 30 silloetts, 20 x 264's - 10 minuetts fresnel, 15 x minuett profiles, 20 x 500w minuett floods, 4 x 1000w ADB floods.
Sound Equip: Allen and Heath 24/4/2 Film Equip: 2 35mm Projectors, 2 16mm Projectors.
Screen - all formats.
Dressing Rooms 9; Accom. 50 plus; 2 Showers; Orchestra Pit 15.
Other: Large Rehearsal Room. Orchestra Pit connects to forestage. Committee or Meeting Room available for private hire (accommodation up to 40).

## WINTER GARDENS PAVILION

Royal Parade, Weston Super Mare
North Somerset BS23 1AQ
Mgt 01934 417117 BO 01934 645544
ADMINISTRATION:
Props: North Somerset District Council
Director of Leisure Services: Mr R F C Acland
General Manager: Mrs Vivienne Thompson
Seating/Capacity: 400
Refurbishment now completed.
For technical details please contact venue.

# Wexford, Eire

Pop. 15,000. Newspapers: New Ross Standard (fri for sat); The People (fri for sat). STD code 00 353 53

## THEATRE ROYAL WEXFORD

High Street, Wexford Eire
Mgt 00 353 53 22400 Fax 00 353 53 24289
BO 00 353 53 22144 BO Fax 00 353 53 47438
ADMINISTRATION:
Props: Loch Garmen Enterprises
Lessee: Wexford Festival Opera
Artistic Director: Luigi Ferrari (for Festival)
Chief Executive: Jerome Hynes
Policy: Mainly H.Q. for Wexford Festival Opera
Perfs: 8.00
Seats: 550. Canteen and Wine Bar.
TECHNICAL:
Stage: Proscenium Stage, Raked; Pros. opening 6.79m; Ht. of Pros. 5.43m; Depth of S/Line 5.33m; Ht. of Grid 13.72m; 20 lines; Scenery Flying Ht. 6.10m; Flying Bars 10.36m; W/Widths P.S. 1.83m; O.P. 1.83m;
Lighting: Switchboard: Location F.O.H. System; Berkey Colortrack, memory system, 96 ways. Lanterns include, Silhouette 30's, Patt.764's, Patt.264's, Patt.223's, 123's, 23's and 23N's.
Sound: Speakers backstage and F.O.H. and all Dressing Rooms.
Dressing Rooms 10; Accom. 100. Orchestra Pit 45.

# Weymouth, Dorset

Pop. 70,000. London 132 miles. Newspapers: Dorset Evening Echo (ntly). STD code 01305

## WEYMOUTH, THE PAVILION COMPLEX

The Esplanade, Weymouth, Dorset DT4 8ED
Admin/BO 01305 783225 Fax 01305 761654
ADMINISTRATION:

Props: Leisure Entertainments & Tourism
Complex Manager: Stephen Young (01305 765218)
Deputy Manager: Ken Ramsey (01305 765214)
Stage Manager: Mark Thorne (01305 765241)
Bar 01305 765227
Policy: Touring house, policy of star name summer show
and panto, one night shows, Concerts (Classical &
Modern) - facilties for Conferences and Exhibitions.
Open all year.
Performances: By arrangement.
Facilities, Seating: Theatre 1012 (raked), Ocean Room:
Up to 720 (flat floor), 9,000 sq.ft. exhibition.
TECHNICAL:
Stage: Proscenium, Flat; Pros. opening 13.11m; Ht. of
Pros. 5.33m; Depth of S/Line 8.23m; Ht. of Grid
15.85m; 30 lines, C/W; Scenery Flying Ht. 7.32m;
Prompt Cnr. P.S.
Lighting: Control: Rank Strand 'Gemini'. Rear centre
stalls 104 circuits. Equipment: F.O.H. 8 Sil. 15 4 Sil. 30:
Boxes (P.S. + O.P.) 4 each harmony 22/40 Pros. Arch
each side: 4 Par Cans. On Stage: 12 Starlettes. 16
Harmony F. 14 P60. 6 Iris 1. 30 Par Cans. Follow Spots:
2 Cid Strand Solos.
Sound: 1 HMI Pani Sound Desk - Soundcraft 24 into 4
into 2 situated rear centre stalls. Speakers - Turbo
Sound.
Amplifiers: Yamaha system completed with Graphic
Equalisers and SPX90 effects.
Dressing Rooms: 12; Band Room

Ocean Room: 18 Comma Fennes 650's; 4 Teatro
Fennes 1000 watts; 12 Comma Profile Spots; 8
Microlight Mini Profile Spots; plus Sirius 48 Zero 88
lighting console. Shure sound vocal master, J.V.C.
stereo cassette deck KD 720.
Ocean Room Dressing Rooms: 2.

# Whitby, Yorks

Pop. 12,850. London 243 miles. Newspapers: Whitby
Gazette (fri). STD code 01947

### WHITBY PAVILION THEATRE
West Cliff, The Spa, Whitby, North Yorkshire YO21 3EN
Mgt 01947 820625 BO 01947 604855
Fax 01947 604487
ADMINISTRATION:
Props: Scarborough Borough Council
Director of Tourism & Amenities: Peter Dahl
Manager: Ann Stevenson
Policy: Variety (Summer Season). Available Winter
Touring. Also used by amateur groups during the winter
providing plays, musicals, ballet, pantomime, song
tournaments, and arts festivals.
Seats: 507. Theatre Bar, Cafe and full Catering facilities.
TECHNICAL:
Stage: Proscenium, Raked; Pros. Opening 7.92m; Ht. of
Pros. 4.42m; Depth of S/Line 6.40m; Ht. of Grid 5.79m;
10 line sets, Hemp; W/Widths P.S. 1.83m - 2.44m, O.P.
1.83m - 2.44m; Prompt Cnr. O.P.
Lighting: Switchboard: Strand LBX C/W Genius 75
software situated F.O.H. 6 x 763s, 8x 264s, 2 x Cantata
18/32, 2 x Cantata 11/26 12 parcan, 1 x Harmony
22/40, 12 x 743s, 6 x Harmony F, 5 x 23s, 5 x 123, 2 x
Coda 3 Batten, 2 x Coda, 2 x Nocturne, 2 x
Colourwheels, 1 x CSI follow spot.
Sound: Studiomaster 12-2 mixer, 4 x JBL speakers
FOH, 2 x A.T. Radio mics available. Digital FX processor,
foldback system, 2 F.O.H. 1 Cassette Player.
Dressing Rooms 4; Accom. 12.

Cyclorama fitted - Prop. Room & Green Room.

# Whitchurch, Shropshire

Pop, 7,768. London 146 miles. Newspapers: Shropshire
Star (dly); Whitchurch Herald (wkly). STD code 01948

### CIVIC CENTRE
High Street, Whitchurch, Shropshire SY13 1AX
Mgt/BO/SD 01948 663403 Fax 01948 666011
ADMINISTRATION:
Props: Whitchurch Town Council
Administrator: Anthony Rains
Policy: One night stands, Touring Theatre, Children's
Shows, Live Music, also available for hire.
Seats: 450
TECHNICAL:
Stage: Proscenium, opening 8.7m, Ht. 3.4m, Depth
13.8m, Bars 10.2 long.
Lighting: Control 20 way. Zero 88 Eclipse with 48
programme matrix and 8 pattern programmable chase.
F.O.H. 4 x Patt.23 500w, 6 x Minuette 500w, 4 x
Patt.123 500w, 4 x Patt.164 (remote control colour
wheel). 2 x 3 Batt., 8 baby floods, 1 x 3 Batt. cyc floods.
1 follow spot.
Sound: P.A. Speakers F.O.H.
Easy get-in on stage level.
Dressing Rooms: 3, 1 Shower.

# Whitehaven, Cumbria

Pop. 27,000. London 309 miles. Newspapers: Evening
News & Star (ntly); Cumberland News; Whitehaven
News; Times & star (all wkly). STD code 01946

### ROSEHILL THEATRE
Moresby, Whitehaven, Cumbria CA28 6SE
Mgt 01946 694039 BO 01946 692422
ADMINISTRATION:
Props: Rosehill Arts Trust Ltd.
Director: Christopher Lloyd
Policy: Small scale touring venue - drama, classical &
popular music, dance & mime, comedy, films, children's
shows, youth theatre. Theatre available for private hire.
Perfs: generally 8.00. Season: September to July.
Seats: 208. Bar. Bistro. Car Park.
TECHNICAL:
Stage: Proscenium, Flat; Pros. opening 5.38m; Ht. of
Pros. 3.38m; Depth of S/Line 5.18m; Ht. of Grid 5.33m;
16 lines, Hemp; Scenery Flying Ht. 5.33m; Flying Bars
6.71m; W/Widths P.S. 3.38m, O.P. 3.38m; Prompt Cnr.
O.P.
Dressing Rooms 2; Accom. 10.
Other: Steinway Concert Grand Piano. Rosehill Theatre
was founded in 1959 by the late Sir Nicholas Sekers,
and designed by Oliver Messel. Set designer for
Glyndebourne.

### SOLWAY CIVIC THEATRE
Whitehaven Civic Hall, Lowther Street, Whitehaven,
Cumbria CA28 7SH
Tel 01946 852821  Fax 01946 592250
ADMINISTRATION:
Props: Copeland Borough Council
Civic Hall Manager: Mrs Dorothy Graham
Policy: Plays, One Night Stands of all kinds, Cabaret,
Pantomime, Celebrity Lectures, etc.

Perfs: Generally 7.30. Sunday Concerts 8.00; Mat. Variable.
Seats: 400. Daily Luncheon Restaurant, Bars & Refreshments available at every production.
TECHNICAL:
Stage: Proscenium 9.00m wide, 4.27m high (permanent, with safety curtain and drencher; Stage Width from centre line 4.42m S.L. and S.R.; Stage depth Pros. to back wall 7.62m; Forestage nil extending to 2.74m; 28 lines, 8 bars, 1 wipe track, 3 winched tab tracks.
Lighting: Switchboard: Rank Strand Tempus 4 Pre Set 45 circuits patching into 30 ways; operated from FOH, Sl or SL gantry; FOH 10 CCT 1000w fresnels, 2 Patt.23, 2 Majors 500w, 2 1000w Strand spots, 4 Patt.123; Stage: 4 bars 9 Patt.137, 8 Patt.23, 4 Patt.60, 2 Patt.123, 1 3 circ Cyc Bar, 3 x 3 circ Ground Row (available).
Sound Equip: H&H into 2 speakers, 4 auxillary speakers; operated from SR; 3 mix stands, 2 boom stands, 4 mics. Hospital relay service.
Prompt desk operated from SR including cue lights to pit, stage and switchboard. Bar bells, Tannoy to dressing rooms and intercom to switchboard FOH.
Other: Storage Space in scenery dock. Get-in via dock doors with chain hoist 3.66m above street.
Dressing Rooms 5; Accom. 30; Wash & Toilet facilities; Green Room; Tannoy; Orchestra Pit approx. 20. 1 illuminated conductor stand.
Crossover passage under stage. One upright Piano. One Clavinova.
Multi-purpose entertainment and catering complex built 1969 in the centre of Whitehaven.

# Widnes

### QUEEN'S HALL
Victoria Road, Widnes, Cheshire WA8 7RF
Tel/BO 0151 424 2339 Fax 0151 420 5762
ADMINISTRATION:
Manager: Brian Pridmore
QH: Capacity 150 balcony raked; 500 stacking; 800 standing.
The Studio: (same address) 200 stacking; 300 standing; 150 cabaret style.

# Wimborne, Dorset

### TIVOLI THEATRE
West Borough, Wimborne Minster, Dorset BH21 1LT
Mgt: 01202 849103  BO: 01202 848014
Fax: 01202 849483
ADMINISTRATION:
General Manager: Malcolm V Angel
Technical Manager: Andy Day
Policy: Concerts, Musicals, Plays, Touring, Opera, Ballet, Comedy, Cinema
Seats: 467-494 (depending on format), permanently raked stadium design balcony and stalls. Accoustically designed auditorium.
Licensed Bar.
TECHNICAL:
Stage: Proscenium opening with apron. Proscenium opening 9.40. Ht of Pros. 6.40. Depth of apron 2.50. Depth of stage (inc. apron) to back wall 8.40. Width of stage inc. wings 12.94. Wings 1.20.

4 Bars length 9.15m for backcloths. Maximum Ht.7.3m.
Lighting: 3 lighting bars over stage. 1 lighting bar F.O.H. Control - Sirius 24 MK.1 (24 channels).
Sound: Soundcraft Spirit 8. 24 channel mixing desk Behringer Crossovers. In house speaker units powered by B.K.amps or hire in.

# Winchester, Hants

Pop. 88,800. London 65 miles. Newspapers: Southern Evening Echo (ntly); Hampshire Chronicle (fri); Winchester Extra (thurs). STD code 01962

### THEATRE ROYAL
Jewry Street, Winchester, Hampshire SO23 8SB
Theatre closed for major refurbishment. For further details contact Keith Powers on 01962 842226 or Fax 01962 841015

# Windsor, Berks

Pop. 30,360. London 23 miles. Newspapers: Windsor, SLough & Eton Express (fri). STD code 01753

### FARRER THEATRE
Eton College, Windsor, Berkshire SL4 6DW
Tel 01753 671164  Fax 01753 671059
ADMINISTRATION:
Props: Eton College
The Controller: Mr Peter Broad
Manager: Bryan Samuel
Policy: Private productions, with occasional amateur and professional performances.
Seats: 401
TECHNICAL:
Stage: Proscenium or Thrust Stage, Flat; opening 11.43m; Ht of Pros. 4.57m or 5.18m; Depth of S/Line 9.14m; Ht of Grid 12.80m; 14 lines C/W 8 hemp; Scenery Flying Ht. 5.03; Flying Bars 11.58m; W/Widths P.S. 3.05m, O.P. 3.05m; Prompt Cnr. P.S. Orchestra Pit: 20.
Lighting: Switchboard: Strand Tempus M24/M24FX; 60 ways; 10 Sil 80; 10 Harmony 15/28; 12 Iris 1kw; 20 Prelude F; 10 Prelude 16/30; 6 Harmony PC; 16 Harmony F; 6 Prelude PC; 5 Coda 4 Batten; 4 Strand T84.
Sound Equip: Soundcraft Delta Mixer, Millbank and C Audio amplifiers; Tanoy and JBL speakers, Revox B77 HS, Sony cassette, AKG D190 and C1000S microphones. TecPro Intercom System. Contact Bryan Samuel or Peter Broad for further details.
Dressing room complex - large capacity with show relay.

### THEATRE ROYAL
Thames Street, Windsor, Berkshire SL4 1PS
Mgt 01753 863444 BO 01753 853888
SD 01753 863444 Fax 01753 831673
ADMINISTRATION:
Props: Windsor & Maidenhead Borough Council
Lessee: Windsor Theatre Ltd
Executive Producer: Bill Kenwright
Executive Director: Mark Piper
Theatre Manager: Amanda Parker
Production Manager: Rob Gale
Policy: Three-weekly (six weeks Pantomime). Own productions without resident company and co-productions.

Perfs: Mon-Sat 8.00; Matinees Thurs 2.30, Sat 4.45,
Day-time business conference facilities available.
Seats: 633. Two Bars, Buffet.
TECHNICAL:
Stage: Proscenium, Raked; Pros. opening 8.53m; Ht. of
Pros. up to 5.49m; Depth of S/Line 9.14m; Ht. of Grid
16.46m; 40 lines, Hemp; Scenery Flying Ht. 7.62m;
Flying Bars 9.75m; W/Widths P.S. 1.83m, O.P. 1.83m;
Prompt Cnr. O.P.
Lighting: Strand lighting Gemini 2+ upgrade. 129
circuits (122x2.5kw, 7x5w).
Dressing Rooms 8; Accom. 40; 2 Showers; Orchestra
Pit 12.

# Winsford, Cheshire

London 172 miles. Newspapers: Chester Chronicle,
Warrington Guardian; Manchester Evening News;
Liverpool Echo. STD code 01606

## CIVIC HALL

Dene Drive, Winsford, Cheshire CW7 1AX
Mgt 01606 592944 BO 01606 867593
Fax 01606 867539
ADMINISTRATION:
Props: Vale Royal Borough Council, Leisure Services,
Wyvern House, The Drumber, Winsford, Cheshire. Tel
01606 862862.
General Manager: Linda Brocklehurst
Stage Technician: Andries Dewitt
Policy: Variety, One-Night Stands, Pop Concerts,
Pantomime, Childrens Shows, Exhibitions, Private and
Commercial Hire, Wrestling.
Perfs: Negotiable.
Seats: 997. 2 Bars, Snack Bar & Lounge.
TECHNICAL:
Stage: Proscenium Stage, Flat; Pros. opening 9.14m;
Ht. of Pros. 5.49m; Depth of S/Line 7.32m; Ht. of Grid
6.10m; W/Widths P.S. 1.83m, O.P. 1.83m; Prompt Cnr.
O.P.
Lighting: Switchboard: Statelight 100 Memory, 65
Channel Desk, and 8 Channel Colour Wheel Memory
Unit; F.O.H. Spots 5 x 100w TI Spots 4 with colour
wheels, 11 Patt.23 500w 8 with colour wheels, 2 follow
spots.
Sound Equip: 1 Toa 12 Channel Mixing Desk with stage
foldback circuit; 1 Toa P 300 D300 watt + 300 watt
power amplifier; 1 Electro Voice TL 606 DX Low
Frequency Drive unit; 1 Electro Voice HR 90 Horn
loudspeaker; 1 Electro Voice HR 40 Horn loudspeaker; 2
Electro Voice DH 1506 high frequency driver; 1 Electro
Voice EVT 2210 1/3 octave graphic equalizer; 1 Electro
Voice XEQ 2 2 way Active cross over.
Dressing Rooms 2; Accom. 24; additional
accommodation under stage.
Orchestra Pit removable.

# Wisbech, Cambs

Pop. 18,000. London 106 miles. Newspapers: Wisbech
Standard (fri); Fenland Citizen (wed); Eastern Daily Press;
Evening Telegraph (ntly). STD code 01945

## ANGLES THEATRE & ARTS CENTRE

Alexandra Road, Wisbech, Cambridgeshire PE13 1HQ
Mgt 01945 585587 BO 01945 474447
ADMINISTRATION:
Props: Wisbech Christian Spiritualist Church & Wisbech

Town Council
Lessees: Angles Centre Trust
Centre Director: Michael Burrell
Administrator: Adrian Bell
Policy: Small scale touring, amateur productions by
resident company, other amateur productions, childrens
theatre, workshops. The Angles is an original Georgian
Theatre built in 1793. It closed during the 1840's and
was turned to several different uses before being re-
discovered by a group of enthusiasts in 1978. It has now
been returned to its original use and is to be restored to
recapture its original character.
Seats: 112. Bar, Terrace, 2 studios.
TECHNICAL:
Stage: Open, Flat; width wall to wall 7.90m; Ht. to Grid
4.50m; Depth of stage 4.80m; rear of stage extends an
extra 1.80m but with only 2.40m height; no wing space -
small area at rear of stage.
Lighting: Control is via a Rank Strand MX 24 way board
situated at the rear of the auditorium. Grid consists of
I.W.B.'s wired 15 amp patched at racks. Lanterns: 6 x
Patt.743, 12 x Minuette, 1 x Patt.123, 3 x Patt.23, 1 x Sil
30. Other lanterns are available.
Sound Equip: Anytronics A12 250W Power Amp. 3G 8-
2 Mixing Desk. Bose 402 Speakers. Cassette Deck.
Daewoo Baby Grand Piano. Other equipment is
available.
Dressing Rooms 1; Accom. 20 (1 extra dressing room
occasionally available).

# Woking, Surrey

Pop. 90,000. London 28 miles. Newspapers: Woking
News and Mail (wkly); Surrey Advertiser (wkly). STD
code 01483

## THE NEW VICTORIA THEATRE THE RHODA MCGAW THEATRE

The Ambassadors, The Peacocks Centre, Woking,
Surrey GU21 1GQ
Tel 01483 747422 Fax 01483 770477
Mkt 01483 748300 Mkt Fax 01483 740477
BO 01483 761144 Bookings Robert Cogo-Fawcett
Tel/Fax 01225 311248
Web Site: ww.theambassadors.com/woking
ADMINISTRATION:
Chief Executive: David Blyth
General Manager: Richard Wingate
Marketing Manager: Pat Westwell
Stage Manager: Kevin Shelfer
Chief Electrician: Mark Allington
Policy: Touring, Drama, Opera, Ballet, Musicals, Panto
and Concerts.
Seats: New Victoria Theatre: 1,338 without orchestra.
1,308 with orchestra.
Rhoda McGaw Theatre: 230.
Also: 3 fully licensed bars. Sponsors Rooms. 2 Coffee
Bars. 6 screen multiplex. Cinemas.
TECHNICAL (NEW VICTORIA):
Stage: Proscenium Arch: Grid Height 19840mm; Prosc
Width 7480mm; Width of stage: CL to SL 11460mm:
Width of stage CL to SR 11460mm: Distance between
fly galleries 18270mm: Back of Prosc wall to rear wall
12000mm: Rear of Dock Door area Width 15000mm:
Depth 5000mm. Counterweight bars length 14.00m
(with 2m extensions either end); 2 up and down stage
motorised bars plus 2 hemp, and 2 counterweight bars.
Trapped area centre stage: Width 6.10m, Depth 4.88m;
Rear Stage: Width 15.00m, Depth 5.00m. Get-in direct

onto rear stage understage crossover.
Lighting: Switchboard: Strand 550 400 channels &
moving light software. 202-2.5kw, 36-5kw, 2-10kw, 20
switched non dims. 45-1k Fresnells, 10-2k Fresnells,
60-1k Profiles, 10-2k Profiles, 6-1k cyc Floods, 6-1k
Ground rows, 16 x IWBs, 16-Multicore, 2-colour arc
follow spots.
Sound and Communication: Soundtrack Mega 32-8-2
with matrix. Desk has two positions, either Control
Room or Stalls. Electrovoice P.A. Full range music and
speech. 180 x 16 Tie lines, 40 video lines 6-F.X.
Speakers (Fold back). Stage Managers Desk: Positions
Stage Left, Stage Right, Stalls. Twin ring intercom: Infra
red hard of hearing, Video and Audio lines to all areas.
Other: Accommodation: 10 Dressing Rooms on 3 levels,
all with showers, accommodation for 53, 2 large Band
Rooms, Visiting Company Managers Office, Wardrobe
with Laundry Rooms.
Lift to all floors.
Orchestra Pit: Max dimensions - width 12.60m, depth
3.40m, max travel from stage level 2.80m. Forestage
suspension; 3 motorised flying bars.
TECHNICAL (RHODA MCGAW): Please contact
venue.

# Wolverhampton, West Midlands

Pop. 252,462. London 123 miles. Newspapers: Express
& Star. STD code 01902

## ARENA THEATRE

University of Wolverhampton, Wulfruna Street,
Wolverhampton West Midlands WV1 1SB
Mgt/Bo 01902 322380 Fax 01902 322680
Email: arena@wlv.ac.uk
ADMINISTRATION:
Administrator: Kevin O'Sullivan
Technician: Peter Webb
Policy: Arena Arts present a programme of its cultural
events provided by the University for its students and the
wider community. Offering a multi-media venue for the
performing arts, the adaptable and professionally
equipped Arena is used as a resource with specialist
teaching facilities for Theatre Studies students at the
University of Wolverhampton. The Arena is also a venue
for West Midlands Arts small-scale touring theatre, and
presents traditional, alternative and ethnic theatre by
professional, community and student groups.
TECHNICAL:
Stage: Main acting area 7.5m x 9.35m. Height (to
lighting grid) 4.55m. Semi-permanent seating in one tier
for 95. Additional seating may be added (with
consequent loss of acting area) to fire limit of 120.
Lighting: Avolite Rolacue Sapphire/manual lighting desk.
72 x 10 amp dimmer racks patched to 72 X 15amp
outlet sockets. 4 x Harmony 15/28. 6 X Harmony Fs. 2 X
Harmony 12s. 6 X Prelude Fs. 7 x Prelude 16/30. 4 X
Minuettes. 7 X Cantata Profile's. 6 X Cantata Fs. 8 X
Cantata P.C. 6 X Quartet P.C. 6 x Parkans. 2 X Coda
Floodlights. 1 X Effects Projector. 8 X Robocolour Pro
400. 2 X Trakspots.
Sound: 32 Channel Yamaha PM 1200 Sound Mixer.
Revox B77 Tape Deck.. 2 Cassette Decks. CD player.
Dual 504 Record Turntable. Various microphones.
Other facilities: 2 x Kodak Carousel S-AV2000 Slide
Projectors. 6.1m X 2.4m film projection screen. 7mts X
3mts white cyc. Bluther Leipzig Grand piano. Dressing
room with shower, washing facilities and WC.

## CIVIC HALL

North Street, Wolverhampton WV1 1RQ
Mgt 01902 552122 BO: 01902 552121
Fax 01902 552123
Outdoor Events Dept: 01902 552099
ADMINISTRATION:
Manager: Mark Blackstock
Policy: Concert Hall/Theatre used for comedy, pop,
classical.
Terms by negotiation.
Capacity: 2,039 seated 2,126 standing.
TECHNICAL:
Full light and sound facilities suitable for all product,
turbosound, mobile lights and theatre lights.

## GRAND THEATRE

Lichfield Street, Wolverhampton
West Midlands WV1 1DE
Tel 01902 573300 BO 01902 429212
Fax 01902 573301
ADMINISTRATION:
Props: Wolverhampton Metropolitan Borough Council
Lessees: Wolverhampton Grand Theatre (1982) Ltd.
Chief Executive: Brian Goddard
General Manager: Tony Pugh
Financial Controller: Gary Postins
Technical Manager: Ian Griffiths
Marketing Manager: Joseph Hocking
BO Manager: Steve Collins
Policy: No 1 Touring: Musicals, Plays, Opera, Ballet,
Variety, Concerts & Pantomime.
Seats: 1,200. 3 Bars. Facilities for disabled patrons.
Traditional 3 tier theatre, built 1894, Major refurbishment
during 1998. Computerised box office (RITA). Perfs:
Variable.
TECHNICAL:
Stage: Proscenium stage, raked 1 in 26; wooden floor;
pros. opening 10.41m; Ht. of Pros. 6.50m; Depth of
Stage (safety curtain to back wall); P.S. 11.90m, O.P.
12.70m; Depth to last C/W set 10.20m (bridge over rear
of stage); Ht. to Grid 16.00m; 45 double purchase c/w
sets, length of C/W barrels 12.20m, max load 318kg per
barrel; clearance between fly rails 13.00m; clearance
under fly galleries and up-stage bridge (min) 6.50m;
Wing Widths P.S. 3.60m, O.P. 3.00m; additional storage
dock OP side (restricted); Prompt Cnr. PS. (Stage plans
available on request).
Lighting: Rank Strand 430 board, 124 circuits, operated
from rear of upper circle. 200A 3-phase supply for
incoming equipment. 24 spots, 6 parcans, and 2
fresnels permanently rigged FOH. 12 spots, 26 fresnels,
26 parcans, 10 PCs, 14 floods, 1-4 way coda batten,
and 8 aeros for use on-stage. 2-CSI follow spots
operated from rear of upper circle.
Sound Equip: 1-Soundcraft 32 channel Venue 11
console, & 1-Soundcraft 8 channel Spirit console.
Comprehensive JBL system (725s, 728s & 726s). For
FOH and EV SX200s and Martin CX1s for monitoring. 2-
Revox B77s & cassette deck. 60A single phase supply
for incoming equipment.
Stage Management: Prompt corner SL Metro Audio (TP
compatible) with outstations as required. CCTV to green
room, dress circle bar, and prompt corner. Show relay
to dressing rooms. Tannoy to Backstage, FOH and
auditorium. Infra Red system for impaired hearing fitted.
Dressing Rooms: 14 (all with showers); accom. 70.
Band Room, Green Room, Wardrobe/Laundry Room.
Other: Get-In Doors: Centre back wall, street level, 4.4m
high x 2.5m wide.
Orchestra Pit: Approx 22 sq.m. (extends to 50 sq.m. by

# It's Grand to be back!

**On 17 December 1998 the Grand re-opened after its spectacular £8 million refurbishment.**

Now appearing at our bigger, better, brighter theatre:

★ Magnificently redecorated Victorian auditorium with air conditioning, 1200 brand new seats and a new higher revenue seating plan

★ Strengthened and raised fly tower with enlarged grid, external crossover, enlarged wing storage space, full size hydraulic orchestra pit, backstage lift, two band rooms and 14 new-look dressing rooms

★ Three brand new bars, Front of House lift, cloakroom, two reception rooms, sweet kiosk, spacious foyer and improved toilet facilities

An exciting new chapter in the Grand Theatre's success story is just beginning. To play your part, call Chief Executive Brian Goddard on 01902 57 33 00.

WOLVERHAMPTON

**GRAND** THEATRE

LICHFIELD STREET WOLVERHAMPTON WV1 1DE
www.grandtheatre.co.uk

removing up to 3 rows stalls and rostra). Basic pit accommodation 15-20; fully extended can accommodate up to 55.
Stock Equipment: Full set black serge masking; Izora cyclorama; various rostra, masking flats and drapes.

## WULFRUN HALL

Mitre Fold, North Street, Wolverhampton WV1 1RQ
Mgt 01902 552122    BO 01902 552121
Fax: 01902 552123
Outdoor Events Dept: 01902 552099
ADMINISTRATION:
Manager: Mark Blackstock
Policy: Concert Hall/Theatre used for concerts, comedy, pantomime.
Terms by negotiation.
Capacity: 672 seated - 756 standing.
TECHNICAL:
Full light and sound facilities suitable for all product, turbosound, mobile lights and theatre lights.

# Woodbridge, Suffolk

Pop. 7,640. Menton 3,700. London 74 miles.
Newspapers: Mercury; Advertiser; East Anglian Daily Times (wkly); Evening Star (ntly). STD code 01394

## RIVERSIDE THEATRE

Quay Street, Woodbridge, Suffolk IP12 1BX
Mgt/BO 01394 382174 Rest 01394 382587
ADMINISTRATION:
Theatre Manager: David Marsh
Policy: Amateur and charity productions, country and western, conferences, seminars etc.
TECHNICAL:
Cinema and Theatre 288 seats. Dolby Stereo Spectral Recording Sound. Stage acting area 30' wide x 21' deep. 120 circuits lighting. Tannoy P.A.
Dressing Rooms: 60 persons.

# Worcester

Pop. 75,000. London 113 miles. Newspapers: Evening News (ntly); Berrow's Worcester Journal (thurs). STD code 01905

## SWAN THEATRE

Worcester Theatre Company The Moors, Worcester WR1 3EF
Mgt 01905 726969 BO 01905 27322
Fax 01905 723738
ADMINISTRATION:
Props: Worcester Arts Association (SAMA) Ltd
Artistic Director: Jenny Stephens
General Manager: Alison Catlin
Policy: Professional repertory season September-April; also resident amateur company (Swan Theatre Company). Sunday Concerts, Saturday Children's Theatre, Professional tours.
Perfs: 7.30. Mats. Thur 2.30
Seats: 353. Restaurant, Bar (full licensed).
TECHNICAL:
Stage: Proscenium with Thrust Apron. Flat; Pros. opening 10.30m; Ht. of Pros. 4.27m; Depth of S/Line 7.32m; Ht. of Grid 5.49m; 21 lines, Hemp; W/Widths P.S. 4.57m, O.P. 4.57m; Prompt Cnr. P.S.
Lighting: Switchboard: Arri Image + FX at rear of

auditorium 72 dimmers; Lantern Stock 12 CCT Sil. 30, 18 ADB 1k Fresnel, 8 Patt. 743, 8 Patt. 264, 6 x Cantata P.C.,10 x Prelude Profile, 8 x Par 64, 12 x 1kw Flood, 5 X Patt 243, 2 X 265 follow spots.
Sound Equip: 3 Quad 405's, 2 Revox flat Bed A77 with Varyspeed, 1 x Revox B77, 1 CD Player, 1 Record Deck, Various mics, 2 Cassette Deck, 1 16/4/2 mixer, 2 Tannoy Golds in Auditorium, 4 speakers on stage, sound controlled from F.O.H. control room.
Dressing Rooms: 6; Accom. 20; 1 Shower. Orchestra Pit 8.
Membership: TMA

# Workington, Cumbria

Pop. 28,000. London 310 miles. Newspapers: West Cumberland Times & Star (wkly); Evening News & Star. STD code 01900

## CARNEGIE THEATRE AND ARTS CENTRE

Finkle Street, Workington, Cumbria CA14 2BD
Tel 01900 602122 Fax 01900 67143
ADMINISTRATION:
Manager: Paul Sherwin
Adminstrator: Alex Fitzgerald
Status: Theatre & Arts Centre
Funding: Venue funded by Allerdale B.C.
Regional Arts Association: Northern Arts
Policy: Promote folk, rock, jazz, ballet, M.O.R., variety, country, children's drama. Hire to amateur drama etc. Also promote festivals, rhythm n' blues. Michael Monroe's bar promotes national and local rock, rhythm and blues, and Indie bands.
Perfs: Available for use 7 days.
Booking Terms: Hire split, guarantee and split, 1/2 calls co-production, negotiation.
Non-performance activities: meeting rooms, rehearsal spaces, photography exhibition space, socials, craft activities, etc.
Facilities: Seats 361, Monroe's bar 200.
Theatre raked. Catering - coffee shop.
Bar - special hours certificate to 1.00 a.m. Shop sales area available.
Access: nearest public car park: Brow Top, Railway - Workington Main, Coach terminal - Workington.
Facilities for disabled - 8 wheelchair spaces (level access). Assistance available (contact manager). All house facilities available.
Other facilities: Dance studio 12m x 10m also used for meetings and rehearsal.
TECHNICAL:
Theatre Stage: Proscenium arch. Performing area 9m x 8m - pros opening 7m x 6m - wing widths 2m SR, 2m SL, 6m US. Stage raked, floor sprung wood, suitable for all dance, backstage crossover, stage heated. Height of grid 6m; 2 tab tracks; black Bolton twill legs and borders; gold silk and white canvas cyclorama; gold house tabs, drawn. 4 x 60A and 2 x 30A independent circuits. Forestage 3m x 1m. Orchestra pit 7m x 2m, accommodates 15. Get-in via understage; dock doors 1.5m x 3m. Scale stage and lighting plans available.
Lighting: Strand MX48, operated from lighting control room; 22 spots + 48 parcans, 36 fresnels, Rank Strand - 2 followspots, operated from lighting control room.
Sound Shure and AKG mics - 1 x cassette - HH PA and Bose theatre speakers. Acoustics suitable for music and the spoken word. Stage Management: 4k Peavey Rig available locally. Intercom to lighting control.
Piano: Kawai Baby Grand
Backstage: 5 dressing rooms, access by stage and

theatre balcony; green room; adequate supply of power points. Beverages, liquor and sandwiches available. Rehearsal rooms, piano, good. Advice given on accommodation. Staff - stage and lighting; casuals available; security personel. Backstage facilities not accessible to disabled performers and staff.

Michael Monroe's Bar
Stage: performing area 5m x 2.5m; floor carpeted; height to grid ceiling 3.5m; 8 x 13A sockets.
Lighting: 5 Spots, Strand.
Sound: Shure & AKG mics, cassette tape, H + H PA, Bose speakers. Acoustics suitable for music and spoken word. 4k Peavey Rig available locally.

# Worksop, Notts

Pop. 37,760. London 160 miles. Newspapers: Worksop Guardian (fri); Worksop Trader (wed); Worksop Star (ntly). STD code 01909

### REGAL CENTRE
Carlton Road, Worksop, Nottinghamshire S80 1PD
Admin 01909 474458 BO 01909 482896
Fax 01909 472918
ADMINISTRATION:
Props: Bassetlaw District Council
Manager: Julie Lawrence
Assistant Manager: Karry Batty
Technical Officer: Steve Crisp
Policy: Touring, International & Cultural Shows, Pantomime, Plays, Variety, Amateur, Operatic, Orchestral, Pop, Folk, Jazz, Children's Shows, Concerts, Films, Dance, One Nighters
Perfs: As required
Seats: 326
TECHNICAL:
Stage: Proscenium Stage, Raked 1 in 24, Pros. opening 8.35m; Ht. of Pros. 4.84m; Depth of S/Line 3.7m; 12 lines, Hemp; Scenery Flying Ht. 8.90m; Flying Bars 8m; W/Widths P.S. 2.15m O.P. 2.71m.
Lighting: Control desk - 48 way Sirus memory board which is operated from the control room at the rear of theatre - centre stage.
Stage area - there are three on stage lighting bars.  Bar 1 - 12 sockets, 12 CCT 650 watt minuette floods, Bar 2-10 sockets 8 CCT 650 watt minuette floods, 2 par 64s, bar 3 - 3 x 4 bank syke lights.  Dip sockets - 8 and they are paired.  The first four sockets on bars 1 and 2 are paired going inwards to centre stage. Leaving four individual sockets on bar 1 and two on bar 2.
FOH - FOH Stage bar - 20 sockets with 14 minuette floods and barn doors.  6 CCT 650 watt zoom profiles. Once again the first 8 sockets are paired to centre stage leaving 4 individual sockets.  FOH stage left - side bars - 8 individual circuits with 2 CCT 650 watt profiles.  1 par 64 1kw, 2 sill 30s, 1 sill 15.  FOH stage right side bars - as stage left.  There are also 2 par 64s 1kw and 2 x 500 watt Powerblazers for use if required.  There is no objection to lights being moved around to suit the production being staged.
Follow spot - one 2kw spot and stand.
Film Equip: 1 x 35mm Projector, 4 track Quadrophonic Sound. Dolby Stereo SR. Dressing Rooms: 4 Accom. 25.
Sound: 12 channel Soundcraft Spirit desk, 12 channels from stage to control room, 2 Bose 802 speakers, 4 fold back monitors, 1 600 watt power amp, 1 250watt power amp for fold back, 3 SM 58 vocal mics, 5 AKG mics, 3 Sure wide range mics, various types of mic

stands, 1 twin cassette deck, the Centre does not have a Revox machine.
Communication system - Master station prompt side to LX box, front of house, with head sets or monitors, cue speakers in dressing rooms, two belt packs with sockets on stage, fly floor and numerous places throughout the building.  If any further information is required please contact our Technical Officer, Steve Crisp who will be only be too pleased to help.

# Worthing, Sussex

Pop. 98,210. London 58 miles. STD code 01903

### ASSEMBLY HALL
Stoke Abbott Road, Worthing, West Sussex BN11 1HQ
Tel 01903 239999 extn 2502/3/4/2530
BO 01903 820500 Fax 01903 821124
SD (PCB) 01903 211654
Mgt offices at: Pavilion Theatre, Marine Parade, Worthing, Sussex BN11 3PX.
ADMINISTRATION:
Props: Worthing Borough Council.
Borough Community Services Officer: Hywel Griffiths B.A., D.L.P., M.I.L.A.M.
Theatre Manager: Peter Bailey F.I.E.A.M.
Business Development Manager: Trevor Gray A.I.E.A.M.
Marketing Manager: Louise Sommerstein
House Manager: Paul Gordon
Policy: Mixed entertainments, programme of shows, concerts, classical concerts, rock concerts, dance, exhibition, conferences etc.
Concert Hall - seating 930 or 1,100 standing.
Buffets, refreshments and bar.  Computerised box office system Prompt Data.
TECHNICAL:
Stage: Concert stage (stepped).  Performing area 13.1m x 10.67m.  Floor oak strip, suitable for dance, backstage crossover, stage heated.  Height to ceiling 9m.  Brown tabs at rear.  7 x twin 13A sockets.  Forestage 13.1m x 3.66m.
Lighting: Sirius 48 board, 68 circuits, 200A, 3 phase, operated from projection room, 100A 3 phase supply available for temporary board - 48 x 1kw parcans - 2 x Pani 1202 followspots operated from rear of balcony.
Sound: Soundcraft 200B 16:4:2 desk, operated from control room - 6 x TOA 305D full range in stereo through 3 x Harrison x 600 amps - 4 x SM58 and 5 x 545 SD mics, radio mic available on written request - 1 x Denon cassette. Acoustics suitable for music and spoken word.
Other: Stage management: prompt corner SL.  No show relay/Tannoy to dressing rooms.
Backstage: 4 dressing rooms, access by rear of stage.
Staff - 1 stage, 1 lighting, 1 sound - casuals available - security personnel upon request.  Backstage facilities not accessible to disabled performers and staff.
Additional Information: Steinway concert grand piano available for performers on written request. Organs: Wurlitzer, composite, built 1922 and 1928, installed in present location in 1981.

### CONNAUGHT THEATRE
Union Place, Worthing, West Sussex BN11 1LG
Mgt 01903 231799 BO 01903 235333
SD 01903 238856 Publicity 01903 239770
Co Mgr 01903 820593 Fax 01903 215337
ADMINISTRATION:
Theatre Administrator: David Smith

Technical Manager: Derek Oakley
Deputy Administrator: Glenda Harkess
Policy: Mixed programme, including films and amateur.
Perfs: Evening Mon-Fri 7.30p.m.; Sat 8p.m.; Mat. Wed
2.00p.m.; Sat. 2.30p.m.
Seats: 514. Two bars and one Restaurant.
TECHNICAL:
Stage: Proscenium with apron raked; (apron flat) DS
apron from iron 1.75m; width of apron and pros opening
10.97m; Ht of pros 5.49m; Iron to back wall 7.93m; Ht
of grid 12.26m; 32 lines. 7 C/W 27 Hemp; Flying Ht
11.33m; Bars 11.9m. W/Widths PS 1.93m; OP3.90m.
Prompt corner movable.
Lighting: Switchboard: Control room in rear audit;
Eurolight ovation 96 ways, FOH 21 x 264, 12 CCT 30's,
7 x 764's. Follow Spots 2 x Coemar Pilota 2000. 30 x
1K Fresnels, 3 x 3kw Fresnels. 10 x CCT colour wheels,
fully patchable outlet system. 18 Par cans.
Full 35mm projection facilities
Sound Equip: Control Room, Speakers, 2 FOH, 2 rear
auditorium, 2 stage, 2 Revox, B77, 1 x Ferrograph, 1 x
cassette deck, 1 x CD deck, 1 x soundcraft 16-4-2,
various Mics, 1 x MGL09. Dressing rooms 6; Accom.
32; 4 Showers.
Membership TMA

RITZ THEATRE
TECHNICAL:
225 seats Thrust, Round, Pros.Arch. Cabaret. Clear
height beneath lighting rig 7.31 Studio acting area 10 x
10m. Pros acting area 10.97 x 4.25m.
Lighting control in gallery 24 channels. 24 x 2.5kw
dimmers, 40 outlets, full 35mm projection facilities
dressing room, accomodation 10.

### NORTHBROOK THEATRE
Littlehampton Road, Goring-by-Sea, Worthing, West
Sussex BN12 6NU
Admin 01903 606162 BO 01903 606162
SD 01903 263067 Fax 01903 821124
ADMINISTRATION:
Theatre Manager: Marilyn Floyde
Technical Manager: Michael Finch
Seating: 192

### WORTHING PAVILION THEATRE
Marine Parade, Worthing, West Sussex BN11 3PX
Mgt 01903 23999 ext 2502/3/4/2530
BO 01903 820500 Fax 01903 821124
SD (PCB) 01903 211353
ADMINISTRATION:
Props: Worthing Borough Council;
Borough Community Services Officer: Hywel Griffiths
B.Sc., D.L.P. M.I.L.A.M.
Theatre Manager: Peter Bailey F.I.E.A.M.
Business Development Manager: Trevor Gray A.I.E.A.M.
House Manager: Paul Gordon
Marketing Manager: Louise Sommerstein
Technical Manager: Dave Lamb
Policy: Varied attractions; Summer entertainment June
to September. Star concerts, exhibitions, conferences,
dinners, dances, wrestling, local society productions.
Perfs: Varied times. Mats. Usually Wed & Sat.
Seats: 850. Cafe Denton, Buffets, Refreshments & Bar.
Computerised Box Office System (Prompt Data).
TECHNICAL:
Stage: Proscenium Stage, Raked; Pros. opening 32ft;
Ht. of Pros. 20ft; Stage width 32ft, height 20ft, depth
22ft;

Raisable forestage; Prompt Cnr. S.M.'s desk with
Dressing Room paging & PAC system, 8 station
intercom. Control room.
Lighting: Control Boards: Celco Gold 90 linked to
Eurolight Applause with designers remote 120 ways
Eurolight/Green Ginger Dimming.
Lanterns: F.O.H. 4 Harmony F, 4 Harmony 12, 10
Harmony 22/40 with colour changes, 4 T Spots.
Cyc. Bar. 5. 4 section codas.
Stage: 40 par cans, 2 Harmony F, 10 Patt.223, plus
Patt.60's, 4 Cadenza 12/32, Patt.123's, Patt.243's, 5
Patt.823. 6 Prelude F, 2 Solo CSI Follow Spots.
Sound: Sound Desk: DDA Q Series 32:8:2. Speaker
System - 6 JBL 1750 Mid/Top enclosures, 2 JBL 1746
Bass enclosures, 2 JBL control 8 SR (delay system).
FPOH Drive system: 2 crest audio CA12 1225w PC. 3
crest audio CA8 900w PC, 2 crest audio CA4 450w PC.
Monitor drive: 2 H&H VX900's, 1 H&H VX600, 1 H&H
VX600 (Delay system drive unit). Monitor wedges
available: 4 MA700 JBL loaded wedges. 1 2x15" + Horn
Drum fill. 5 JBL control mone personal monitors. FOH
Control: DDA Q series 32-8-2 console. 4 aux returns
(max). 6 monitor returns (max). Urei platform total FOH
control system. Digital processing system controlling
FOH crossovers, delays, parametric EQ. Outboard: 2
Yahama SPX900 Stereo digital effects processors. 2
Yahama GC2020B comp/limiters, 1 drawmer DS201
noise gate, 3 E/V 2x10 Graphic EQ's, 1 EMO 2x31
graphic (dedicated to monitor returns), 1 EMO 2x15
Graphic EQ (dedicated to monitor returns). Denon dual
cassette deck, denon CD player, Revox B77 reel to reel.
Microphones: 7 SM58's, 4 SM57's, 2 SM545's, 2EV
PL80's, 4 Sennheiser 509's. 3 AKG C451 EB's, 3 CK1
Heads, 2 CK5 heads, 2 C300B's, 2 CK91's, 2 CK98's,
2 PZM's, 1 crown tie mic. Radio microphones: 2
Sennheiser hand held diversity radio mics, frequencies
175 & 176.4MHZ, 1 Sennheiser lapel mic frequency.
32 way stage box on stage with accompabnying stage
tails. Stage box also acts as monitor splitters with 32
ways split at stage level.
Other: Dressing Rooms: 7; 4 Showers.
Steinway piano available.
Membership: TMA

# Wrexham

### WILLIAM ASTON HALL
Mold Road, Wrexham, LL11 2AW Wales
Tel 01978 293221  Fax 01978 290008
ADMINISTRATION:
Props: North East Wales Institute
Licensee: Nicola Dwyer
Policy: Music, Dance, Opera, Orchestral and Choral
Concerts.
Perfs: 7.30pm
Seats: 890
TECHNICAL:
Stage: Proscenium opening with apron. Flat. Pros
opening 8.50; Ht of Pros 4.25. Depth of apron 3m,
Depth of stage to cyc 7.50m. Ht of grid 6.50m. 11
hemp lines, no c/w. Width of stage 12m. P/S wings
2.40. O/P wings 2m. Flying bars 10m.
Lighting: Switchboard: Movable, 60 ways.
Sound Equipment according to presentation.
Dressing Rooms: 8 Accom 40 + Orchestra Pit 20.

### WREXHAM STUDIO THEATRE
Yale College, Grove Park Road, Wrexham,

LL12 7AA Wales
Tel 01978 311794 ext 2217 & 2252 Fax 01978 291569
ADMINISTRATION:
Props: Yale College
Licensee: Emlyn Jones
Manager: Paul Hernon
Policy: Drama, Dance, Music, Touring small scale.
Perfs: 7.30pm
Seats: 137 Theatre style. Max 200

TECHNICAL:
Stage: Studio Theatre 12m square/acting area. End on flexible seating.
Lighting: Switchboard: Colourmaster 60, 116 dimmers.
Sound as needed.
Dressing Rooms: flexible spaces, showers. Accom. 15-20.

# Yeovil, Somerset

Pop. 42,000. London 126 miles. Newspapers: Express & Star (thurs); Western Gazette (fri); Weekly News (sat); Western Daily Press; Evening Post. STD code 01935

## OCTAGON THEATRE

Hendford, Yeovil, Somerset BA20 1UX
Mgt 01935 422836 BO 01935 422884
SD 01935 431075 Mktg 01935 422720
Fax 01935 475281
ADMINISTRATION:
Props: South Somerset District Council
General Manager: John G White, MILAM (DipME)
Chief Technician: Robert Sinnick
Marketing: Dianne Wynn
Theatre Manager: Nick Mountjoy
Administration Officer: Margaret Milner
Policy: Touring, Pantomime, Musicals, Plays, Opera, Ballet, Conferences, Concerts.
Seats: 625 permanently raked.
3 Bars and Cafe Bar.
TECHNICAL:
Stage: Proscenium. Flat; Pros. opening 12.95m; Ht. of Pros. 5m (Var. False Pros & Portals) Depth 10.82m; Ht. of Grid 9.2m; 25 lines; Hemp; Flying Bars 15.24m; W/Widths 4.88m each side; Prompt Corner P.S.
Lighting: Control: Rank Strand 430 150 channel Memory (92 channels Connected); FX Desk; F.O.H. bridge; 4 stage spot bars; Lanterns: 18 Patt.264; 35 Patt.743; 4 Patt. T84; 48 x 1000w Pars; 12 Patt.60; 4 Starlettes; 3 UV Floods; 3 UV Tubes; 12 Cantatas 18/32, 16 Dips PS, 4 Dips OP. Additional and 100 amp 3 phase power 60 amp 3 phase power PS: Follow spots; 2 CCT 1000w CSI,
Sound: 16 Channel Mixer plus fold back; Tape Deck; Cassette Deck. Additional or alternative sound equipment as required. Ring intercom with headsets to all technical Depts plus Cue Lights. Dressing Room Call Back; Induction Loop.
Dressing Rooms: 6; all with Showers; Quick Change Room, Green Room, Props Room, Wardrobe. Staff - 3 Technicians, Stagedoor Keeper, Orchestra Pit accommodates 20.

# York, N Yorks

Pop. 104,780. London 196 miles. Newspaper: Yorkshire Evening Press (ntly). STD code 01904

## DE GREY ROOMS

Exhibition Square, York YO1 2HB
For all enquiries and further information contact Steve Owen Tel: 01904 613161 ext.3418
or Fax: 01904 553424.
Seating/Capacity: 200

## GRAND OPERA HOUSE

Cumberland Street, York YO1 9SW
Admin 01904 655441 BO 01904 671818
Backstage Corridor 01904 671857 Fax 01904 671858
ADMINISTRATION:
For all booking information and further details please contact Sam Shrouder or Nicky Monk at Apollo Leisure (UK) Ltd., Grehan House, Garsington Road, Cowley, Oxford OX4 5NQ. Tel: 01865 782900; Fax: Oxford 01865 782910.
General Manager: Ian Sime

Deputy Manager: David Turner
Assistant Manager: Vanessa Kendal
Box Office Manager: John McWilliam
P.A. to General Manager: Charlotte Rose
Technical Manager: Dave Jackson
Stage Manager: Paul Veysey
Catering & Bars Manager: Corrina Cotterill
Group Bookings Manager: Nikki Levey
Catering available: Main bar/coffee/food area + 3 bars.
Capacity: 1,030
TECHNICAL:
Stage: Iroko, tongue and groove, semi-sprung. Brown in colour. Get-in straight from street to USR; Get in doors: 2x4m (no parking available for waiting).
Pros. width 8.093m. Depth of stage: From iron: 9.064m to crossover; from front: 9.803m to crossover. Grid height: 13.25m; barrel length: 10m; wing space: stage left 3.6m; DS 4.8m; stage right 4.8m. Upstage walkover: 1.3m.Proscenium height 6.1m; Bars: 29 3-line hemp sets (OP fly floor; 12 4-line motorised 350kg line with speed control; 5 4-line hand winches 500kg. Power and winch bars operated PS fly floor. Front tabs: On counterweight controlled from prompt corner. Iron and drencher: controlled from prompt corner and stage door. Other tab tracks: 2; drapes: 1 black box.
Cyclorama: White, normally on hemp set 29. Rake: none. House tab: Admiral red with gold braid, flown; 1 pair black tabs 5.5m by 7m drop; 8 black legs 2.5m x 7m drop; 4 black borders 10.2m by 4m drop.
Independent sockets: 240v power 6 x 13A twin sockets located around stage . 30A ring.
Prompt desk: either PS or OP. Paging to FOH and backstage. 9 Q-lites (DSL, USL, DSR, USR, sound, lighting, OP flies, PS flies). Stop watch. Low voltage effects output.
Comms: 2 channel, 8 (+prompt desk) outstations, locations as above. Flying: 29 hemp sets, 12 speed control 350 kg motorised bar, 5 x 500kg hand winched bars. Front tabs on counterweight (DSL).
Safety Curtain: Eurotraks, metal, motorised. Dry ice available by prior consultation.
Lighting: Board located stage left back of stalls or prompt corner. Power supply: 200A. 3 phase up stage left. House light control: Prompt corner, LX control room. Lanterns: Follow spots: 2 Rank Strand "Solo" CID 1kw, rear of upper circle. FOH lighting: 21 circuits Grand Circle Ceiling (20 Cantat 11/26) Box booms 2 x 11/26 (6 x cirs either side). Circle front: 3 x cirs (1 x tab warmer). 36 x cirs FOH o.a. Lighting control: 360 way Rank Strand Gemini 2+. 96 ways of 2.5kw dimmers. 24 (FOH) Cantata 11/26 1.2kw Profile; 6 Cantata 18/32 1.2kw Profile; 1 (Tab warmers) Cantata PC 1.2kw Pebble Convex; 40 Cantata F 1.2kw Fresnels (all with barndoors); 24 Punchlites 1kw (220v) Par 64; 10 Coda 4 500w 4-section batten; 1 (no1 bar Fixed IWB 24w ladder section; 3 Moyable DNB 18w ladder section. Accessories: 6 Gobo holders; 4 Tall stands; 2 Medium stands; 2 bench bases; 8 lit music stands; 1 conductor's lit stand. Follow spot: Rank Strand "Solo". CSI 1kw lamp. 5 colour magazine . 1 Black out card. Positioned at rear of Upper Circle. NB Loses 3 x seat per side (K6-8 and K21-23). Controls and dimmers: There are 96 ways of Rans Strand Permus dimmers, controlled by a 360 way Rank Strand Gemini 2+. 48 x P/S fly floor, 4 x DSR, 3 x USL, 2 x understage, 3 x OP fly floor, 21 x FOH Grand circle ceiling, 12 x FOH Grand Circle boxes (6 x either side), 3 x Circle front.
Sound: Board located centre back row of stalls, or prompt corner. Power supply: 100 amps. 1 phase, down stage left + 16A clean supply DSL. Mixer: Allen & Heath SRC 24-4-2. Amplifiers: 4 x HH VX 900. Digital

delays: 2 x TOA 310D. Graphic EQ's: 2 x Yahama Q2031A 31 band stereo. Speakers: Upper circle-2 x TOA 380 SD, Dress circle-2 x TOA FOH, Stalls 2 x TOA F 600, On stage 2 TOA 380 SD, 2 x TOA 30, SDM monitors. Microphones: 2 x AKG D112, 3 x AKG D222, 2 x AKG D321. Accessories: 6 x microphone stands. Induction loop: Broadcasts to stalls only.
Other: Dressing rooms: 3 + company office at stage level. 3 + production/wardrobe next level up.
Orchestra pit 9.5m x 4.6m accomodating 40. Access for prompt corner. Seats and lit music stands as available. Piano: Boudoir grand.

## THEATRE ROYAL

St. Leonards Place, York YO1 7HD
Admin 01904 658162 BO 01904 623568
Restaurant 01904 632596 Fax 01904 611534
24hr Info Line 01904 610041
ADMINISTRATION:
Props: York City Council
Lessees: York Citizens' Theatre Trust
Executive Director: Elizabeth Jones
Artistic Director: Damian Cruden
Production Manager: Matt Nodings
Theatre Manager: Jim Melvin
Policy: Resident Repertory Company, occasional Tours, Pantomime
Perfs: 7.30, Sat. 4.00 & 8.00. Wed. Mat. 2.30.
Seats: 863. Restaurant, Coffee Bar, Licensed Bar.
TECHNICAL:
Stage: Proscenium, Raked; Pros. opening 9.14m; Ht. of Pros. 6.40m; Depth of S/Line P.S. 9.75m O.P. 8.53m; Ht. of Grid 14.02m; 30 lines C/W (plus 3 Hemp);
Scenery Flying Ht. 6.71m (to mask); W/Widths P.S. 3.66m, O.P. 3.66m. Between Fly Rails 14.02m. Prompt Cnr. P.S. Scene Dock 4.9m x 7.3m extends from P.S. of stage.
Lighting: Switchboard: ADB Vision 10, 160 circuits, 24 X Cantata 18-32, 20 X Sil 30, 2 X Sil 15, 2 X Source 4, 2 X Solo 1k, 30 X 743, 24 X Vision F, 11 X 243, 6 X Starlette 2k Fresnel, 4 X Starlette 2kw PC, 70 X PAR64, 5 X 4 Cell Thomas Batterns, 16 X ADB AC1001 floods.
Sound Equip: Mixer 24-8-2 Soundtracs MX, 16-3 and 8-3 Soundcraft Spirits.2 X Tascam MD801-R MiniDisc, 2 x Revox B77, 2 x Cassette decks, 2 x CD, FOH
Wharfedale Force 9 powered by HH amps. Microphones 4 x SM58, 3 X PCC160, 5 X Rifles, 1 X D112.
Dressing Rooms 8; Accom. 62 (all rooms have showers) plus Wardrobe and Laundry.
Orchestra Pit variable by removing stalls seats.
Membership: TMA

## YORK ARTS CENTRE

Micklegate, York N Yorks YO1 1JG
Admin Tel/Fax 01904 642582
Information & Membership 01904 627129
Converted Medieval Church used for theatre, music and dance. Retractable seating for 160 or standing cap 200 on 3 sides with raked, fliexible arrangement.
Theatre facilities. Dressing room. Bar.
Seating: 160 raked or 200 standing.

## YORK BARBICAN CENTRE

Paragon Street, York YO10 4NT
Mgt 01904 628991 BO 01904 656688
Fax 01904 628227
ADMINISTRATION:
Props: City of York Council
Entertainments Manager: Craig Smart
Technical Manager: Daniel Brookes
Policy: Flexible auditorium can stage classical, pop, comedy, opera, childrens shows, product launches, exhibitions, sport and televised events.
Perfs: by arrangement.
Seats: 1500 - 1880 depending on format. Facilities for the disabled. Three licensed bars. Brasserie.
The auditorium acoustic has been designed primarily for music, infra-red system for hard of hearing.
TECHNICAL:
Stage: Variable size demountable Steeldeck units (mainly 8x4) max size 17.1m x 10m x 1m (other shapes and sizes by arrangement) Ht to grid 12.1m (from the floor). 5 Power bars 750kg loading; 4 x 20.2m; 1 x 23.2m. Full grid also available for rigging. SM desk SR, SL Control Room. Full comms links. Get-in access to auditorium via ground floor doors (various routes available). Parking for 3-4 artics.
Lighting: Control: ETC Insight 2X; Dimmers ETC Smartrack 108 2.5kw, 34 5kw; Lanterns: Juliate 1.2kw profiles X 10, Juliate 1.2k PC X 10, CYC floods 1kw X 20, Par cans 1kw X 86, Teatro profiles 2kw X 19, Coamar fresnels X 20, other fresnels X 8 Music stands: lit X 20, unlit X 44..
Sound: Alan and Heath Sabre 24-8 Matrix into JBL central cluster 4 JBL Power Monitors; various mics.
Other equipment available on request.
Other: Dressing rooms - 3 plus chorus and bandroom accommodation, en suite showers and toilets.
Car parking for 110; additional multi-storey for 400.

# AMATEUR THEATRES

**ANGLESEY**
**THEATR FACH**
**Pencraig Llangefni, Anglesey, Gwynedd LL77 7LA**
**Tel 01248 722412**
Chairman: Mr Gareth Jones  (01407 741594)
Seats: 100

**BATH**
**THE RONDO**
**St. Saviour's Road, Larkhall, Bath BA1 6RT**
**Tel 01225 444003**
**ADMINSTRATION:**
Props: Rondo Trust for the Performing Arts
Contact: Mrs Leonard
Fully equipped, comfortable studio theatre for small
scale tours and amateur companies
Seats: 105
Performing area: 7.9m x 4m

**BINGLEY**
**BINGLEY LITTLE THEATRE**
**Bingley, Yorkshire BD16 2JZ**
**Tel 01274 564049**
Artistic Director: Patricia Clough  01535 630022
House Manager: Jeff Peacock
Seats: 150

**BIRMINGHAM**
**HALL GREEN LITTLE THEATRE LIMITED**
**Pemberley Road, Acocks Green,**
**Birmingham B27 7RY**
**Tel 0121 706 1541  BO 0121 707 1874**
Seats: 200
**TECHNICAL:**
Stage Pros. Opening 7.6m; ht. of Pros. 3.7m; Depth of
Stage 7.6m; W/Widths P.S. 3.7m, O.P. 3.35m.
Also Studio Theatre seating up to 100 (variable seating).

**BLACKWOOD**
**BLACKWOOD LITTLE THEATRE**
**Woodbine Road, Blackwood, Gwent NP2 1QJ**
**Tel 01495 223485**
Technical Director: Alwyn Price
Seats: 146

**BOLTON**
**BOLTON LITTLE THEATRE**
**Hanover Street, Bolton, Lancs BL1 4TG**
**BO 01204 524469**
**ADMINISTRATION:**
Secretary: Mr. Michael English
22 The Glen, Bolton BL1 5DB
Tel 01204 491540
**TECHNICAL:**
**MAIN THEATRE:**
Seats: 157
Stage: Pros. Opening 6.70m; Ht. of Pros. 3.66m; Depth
of Stage 9.15m; W/Widths P.S. 2.44m, O.P. 2.44m.
FORGE THEATRE: (Studio)
Seats: 60. Thrust Stage.

**BRADFORD**
**THE PRIESTLEY CENTRE FOR THE ARTS**
**Chapel Street, Bradford, West Yorkshire BD1 5DL**
**Admin/BO 01274 820666  Fax 01274 822701**
Chairman: David Rosendale

Manager: Graham Colon
Seats: 272
**TECHNICAL:**
Stage Proscenium. Opening 7.01m; Height of Pros.
3.66m; Depth of Stage 6.10m; W/Widths P.S. 2.74m,
O.P. 2.74m.

**BROMLEY**
**BROMLEY LITTLE THEATRE LTD**
**North St., Bromley, Kent BR1  1SD**
**Tel 0181 460 3047**
**ADMINISTRATION:**
Administrative Director: Sue Court
Policy: Membership Theatre, presenting plays, one
each month except August.
Seats: 112

**CHEADLE**
**HEALD GREEN THEATRE COMPANY**
**Heald Green Theatre, Cheadle Royal Hospital, 100**
**Wilmslow Rd., Heald Green, Cheadle, Cheshire**
**Tel 0161 428 9704**
**ADMINISTRATION:**
Secretary: Mrs Barbara Ritchie, 94 Brown Lane,
Hill Green, Cheshire. Tel: 0161 437 4635

**CHEADLE HULME**
**CHADS THEATRE COMPANY**
**Mellor Road, Cheadle Hulme, Cheshire SK8 5AU**
**Tel 0161 486 1788**
**ADMINISTRATION:**
Secretary: Mrs E. C. J. Stock, 7 Ridge Park, Bramhall,
Stockport, SK7 2BJ
Tel 0161 439 2924
Seats: 141.
**TECHNICAL:**
Stage: Pros. Opening 6.10m; Depth of Stage 6.70m;
Pros. Ht. 2.70m.

**COVENTRY**
**CRITERION THEATRE**
**Berkeley Road South, Earlsdon, Coventry**
**Tel 01203 675175**
Seats: 120

**GATESHEAD**
**LITTLE THEATRE**
**Saltwell View, Gateshead, Tyne & Wear NE8 4JS**
**Tel 0191 478 2563  BO 0191 478 1499**
**ADMINISTRATION:**
Progressive Players Secretary: Janet Wind
Tel: 0191 417 2956
Secretary: Mrs. D. E. McGinn, 3 Grange Court,
Heworth, Gateshead. Tel 0191 469 4221
Seats: 188
**TECHNICAL:**
Stage: Pros. Opening 7.32m; Ht. of Pros. 3.66m; Depth
of Stage, 3.96m (5.18 with apron); W/Widths irregular,
min 1.22m.

**GLOUCESTER**
**THE NEW OLYMPUS THEATRE**
**Barton Street, Gloucester GL1 4EU**
**Admin 01452 525917  BO 01452 505089**
**SD 01452 507549  Fax 01452 387518**
Main Theatre seats: 427

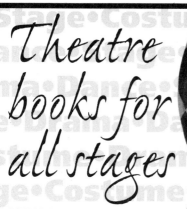

Studio Theatre seats: 80
**TECHNICAL:**
Stage Pros. Opening 9.0m; Ht. of Pros. 4.9m; Depth of
Stage 6.25m; W/Widths P.S. 2.0m, O.P. 1.8m opens to
scene dock; Ht. of grid 8.75m.
Membership: NODA.

**GRIMSBY**
**THE CAXTON THEATRE AND ARTS CENTRE**
**(The Caxton Players)**
**128 Cleethorpe Road, Grimsby,**
**North East Lincolnshire DN32 3HW**
**Tel 01472 345167**
Secretary: Cathy Bennett-Ryan  01472 231753
Seats: 184
**TECHNICAL:**
Stage: Ht. of Pros. 3.65m; W/Widths P.S. 0.91m. O.P.
2.74m. Depth of Stage 5.2m; Opening 7.3m; No
scenery above 12ft high.

**HALIFAX**
**THE PLAYHOUSE (The Halifax Thespians)**
**Kings Cross Lane, Halifax, West Yorks, HX1 2SH**
**Tel 01422 365998**
**ADMINISTRATION:**
Secretary: Mrs. Judith Priestley, Quaker Cottage, 10
Quaker Lane, Hightown, Liversedge WF15 6NF
Tel: 01274 878967
Seats: 288
**TECHNICAL:**
Stage: Pros. Opening 8.54m; Ht. of Pros. 4.27m;
Depth of Stage 7.62; W/Widths P.S. 1.83m, O.P. 1.83.

**ILKLEY**
**THE PLAYHOUSE (The Ilkley Players)**
**Weston Road, Ilkley, West Yorkshire LS29 8DW**
**Tel 01943 609539**
**Website www.theplanet.net/ilkley/arts/iphs.hts**

**KENILWORTH**
**THE PRIORY THEATRE**
**Rosemary Hill, Kenilworth, Warwickshire CV8 1BN**
**Tel 01926 855301**
Secretary: Mrs.S Hunt
Seats: 120
**TECHNICAL:**
Stage Pros. Opening 5.49m; Ht. of Pros. 3.66m; Depth
of Stage 14.65m; W/Widths P.S. nil, O.P. 2.75m; Fly
Tower 9.25m.

**TALISMAN THEATRE COMPANY**
**Talisman Theatre and Arts Centre, Barrow Road,**
**Kenilworth, Warwickshire, CV8 1EG.**
**Tel 01926 856548**
**ADMINISTRATION:**
Chairman: Wendy Anderson, 215 Duggins Lane,
Coventry CV4 9GP   Tel 01203 465179
Seats: 156
**TECHNICAL:**
Stage: Pros. Opening 7.32m; Depth of Stage 9.10m.

**LANCASTER**
**GRAND THEATRE**
**St. Leonardgate, Lancaster LA1 1NL**
**Mgt/BO 01524 64695**
Seats: 465
For further details please see entry in Provincial
Theatre Section.

**LEAMINGTON SPA**
**THE LOFT THEATRE**
**Victoria Colonnade, Leamington Spa,**
**Warwickshire CV31 3AA**

**Tel 01926 422566  BO 01926 426341**
Chairman: David Fletcher
Seats: 200
**TECHNICAL:**
Stage: Pros. Opening 9.20m; Ht. of Pros. 4.57m;
Depth of Stage 8.38m; W/Widths P.S., O.P. 3.81m.

**LEICESTER**
**LEICESTER DRAMA SOCIETY LITTLE THEATRE**
**Dover Street, Leicester LE1 6PW**
**Admin 0116 254 2266  BO 0116 255 1302**
Theatre Manager: James O'Donoghue
Seats: 349
**TECHNICAL:**
Stage: Pros. Opening 7.62m; Ht. of Pros. 3.81m;
Depth of Stage 9.8m; Widths P.S. 4.57m, O.P. 2.13m.

**LONDON**
**JACKSONS LANE COMMUNITY CENTRE**
**Archway Road, London N6 5AA**
**Tel 0181 340 5226**
**Fax 0181 348 2424**
For full details please see entry in Fringe Theatre
Section.

**THE QUESTORS THEATRE**
**Mattock Lane, Ealing, London W5 5BQ**
**Mgt 0181 567 0011  BO 0181 567 5184**
For details see entry in London Theatres Section.

**SOUTH LONDON THEATRE**
**2a Norwood High Street, London SE27 9NS**
**Tel 0181 670 3474**
Member's Club 0181 670 4661
Seats: 96
**TECHNICAL:**
Stage: Pros. Opening 6.40m; Ht. of Pros. 3.05m,
Depth of Stage 6.10m; W/Widths P.S. 3.05m, O.P.
1.52m. Studio Theatre - Prompt corner. Seats 50.

**THE TOWER THEATRE**
**Canonbury Place, Islington, London N1 2NQ**
**Mgt 0171 226 5111**
For details see entry in London Theatre Section.

**NEWCASTLE UPON TYNE**
**PEOPLE'S THEATRE**
**Stephenson Road, Newcastle upon Tyne NE6 5QF**
**Tel 0191 265 5020**
For details see entry in Provincial Theatre Section.

**NEWPORT, GWENT**
**DOLMAN THEATRE**
**Kingsway, Newport, Gwent NP9 1EX**
**Tel 01633 263670  BO 01633 251338**
President: Mrs Ruth Ferguson
Seats: 400
**TECHNICAL:**
Stage: Pros. Opening 7.93m to 11.98m; Ht. of Pros.
4.88m; Depth of Stage 9.76m; W/Widths P.S. 7.62m,
O.P. 5.79m.

**NEWPORT, I.O.W.**
**APOLLO THEATRE (Little Theatre Guild member)**
**Pyle Street, Newport, Isle of Wight PO30 4JZ**
**Tel 01983 527267**
**ADMINISTRATION:**
Director: Michael Whitehead 01983 298839
Secretary: Pam Underwood 01983 522309
Publicity Officer: Tony Rolle 01983 760798
Seats: 132
**TECHNICAL:**
Stage: Pros. Opening 4.88m to 9.15m; Ht. of Pros.

4.42m; Depth of Stage 7.62m; W/Widths variable 0.61m to 2.44m.
The theatre is available for hire. We do not pay companies to perform.

**OLDBURY**
**BARLOW THEATRE**
**Spring Walk, Oldbury, Warley, West Midlands**
**B69 4SP**
**Tel 0121 552 2761**

**READING**
**PROGRESS THEATRE**
**The Mount, Christchurch Road, Reading, Berks**
**RG1 5HL**
**Admin 0118 987 4230**
ADMINISTRATION:
Secretary: Dorothy Grugeon
Tel: 0118 957 3561 (day)
Tel: 0118 926 4053 (evenings)
Seats: 99 (inc. disabled)
TECHNICAL:
Stage Pros. Opening 5.49m; Ht. of Pros. 2.70m; Depth of Stage 6.0m; moderate wing space. Car park - free.

**ST ALBANS**
**ABBEY THEATRE**
**The Company of Ten, Westminster Lodge,**
**Holywell Hill, St. Albans, Herts AL1 2DL**
**Admin 01727 847472 BO 01727 857861**
ADMINISTRATION:
Manager: David Griffiths
Seats: 244
Studio Theatre seats 70

**STOCKPORT**
**STOCKPORT GARRICK THEATRE**
**Exchange Street, Wellington Road South,**
**Stockport SK3 0EJ**
**BO 0161 480 5866 SD 0161 480 3287**
ADMINISTRATION:
Secretary: John & Pat Baker, 4 Corbar Road, Davenport, Stockport SK2 6EP. Tel 0161 483 4574
Seats: 155
TECHNICAL:
Stage: Pros. Opening 6.10m; Ht. of Pros. 5.49m; Depth of Stage 11.98m; W/Widths P.S. 2.13m, O.P. 2.44m.

**STOKE-ON-TRENT**
**STOKE-ON-TRENT REPERTORY THEATRE**
**Leek Road, Stoke-on-Trent ST4 2TR**
**Admin 01782 209897 BO 01782 209784**

**SUNDERLAND**
**ROYALTY THEATRE**
**The Royalty, Sunderland, Tyne and Wear SR2 7PP**
**Tel 0191 567 2669**

**SUTTON COLDFIELD**
**HIGHBURY LITTLE THEATRE**
**Sheffield Road, Sutton Coldfield,**
**West Midlands B73 5HD**
**Admin 0121 373 2761**
For details see entry in Provincial Theatre Section.

**SUTTON ARTS THEATRE**
**South Parade, Sutton Coldfield,**
**West Midlands B72 1QU**
**Admin/BO 0121 355 5355**
ADMINISTRATION:
Secretary: Miss Joanne Ellis Tel 0121 355 5954
Seats: 124

**TEIGNMOUTH**
**CARLTON THEATRE**
**The Den, Teignmouth, Devon TQ14 8BD**
**Tel 01626 778991**
ADMINISTRATION:
Props: Teinbridge D.C.
Lessees: Teignmouth Players
Theatre Manager: A A P Butler, 25 Salisbury Terrace, Teignmouth TQ14 8JG.
Seats: 217. Lounge Bar.
For Hire Only.
TECHNICAL:
Prosceium Stage, slight rake; Pros. opening 7.32m; Ht. of Pros. 3.05m; Depth of S/Line 5.79m; W/Widths P.S. 1.52m, O.P. 1.52m; Prompt Cnr. P.S.
Switchboard: Rank Strand Tempus 2G 36 ways; Permus Dimmers above OP side of stage: 4 battens on stage; 2 battens F.O.H. 4 dips. 2 Patt.23; 4 Prelude 19/30; 4 Patt.223; 12 floods; 5 Flood-battens; 2 Patt.123.
Sound Equipment: Realistic P.A. 2 speakers controlled from lighting box rear of auditorium.
Dressing Rooms 5; Accom. 6; Orchestra Pit 4.

**TONBRIDGE**
**THE ANGEL LEISURE CENTRE**
**Angel Lane, Tonbridge, Kent TN9 1SF**
**Tel 01732 359966**
Manager: Gary Littlejohn
Leisure Centre with two halls and rehearsal rooms. Jim May Hall with seating for 1,100. Medway Hall, seating for 317.

**WIGAN**
**WIGAN LITTLE THEATRE**
**Crompton Street, Wigan, Lancs WN1 3SL**
**Admin 01942 491000 BO 01942 242561**
ADMINISTRATION:
Secretary: Mr. J. Dean, Ince Hall, Ince Hall Avenue, Ince, Wigan, WN2 2HY. Tel 01942 821904
Seats: 230
TECHNICAL:
Stage Pros. Opening 9.15m; Ht. of Pros. 3.66m; Depth of Stage 6.70m; very restricted Wing Space.

**WINCHESTER**
**CHESIL THEATRE**
**Chesil Street, Winchester, Hants SO23 8HU**
**Tel 01962 889356**
ADMINISTRATION:
Contact: Tom Williams
Policy: Amateur dramatic company, puts on six shows a year. New members always welcome. member of the Little Theatre Guild of Great Britain.
Seats: 70

**WREXHAM**
**GROVE PARK THEATRE**
**Hill Street, Wrexham,**
**Mgt 01978 351981 BO 01978 351091**
Secretary: Mrs Mary Braid
Seats: 212
TECHNICAL:
Stage: Pros. Opening 6.40m; Ht. of Pros. 3.81m; Depth of Stage 7.62m plus 1.22m apron; W/Widths P.S. 2.13m, O.P. 0.91m.

# COMEDY & CABARET VENUES

**ACTON COMEDY CLUB**
Kings Head, Acton High Street, London W3
Tel 0181 992 0282
Capacity: 150

**APPLES AND SNAKES**
BAC, Lavender Hill, London SW11
Office: Unit 7. Theatre Place, 489A New Cross Road,
London SE14 6TQ
Tel 0181 692 0393
Capacity: 80
Contact: Programmer

**AZTEC COMEDY CLUB**
Borderland Restaurant, 47-49 Westow Street,
London SE19 3RW
Tel 0181 771 0885
Capacity: 120
Contact: Patrick or Kevin

**ASTRO BAR & COSMIC COMEDY CLUB**
175/177 Fulham Palace Road, London W6
Tel 0171 381 2006

**AZTEC CLUB**
Westow Street, London SE19
Tel 0181 771 0885

**BAC**
Lavender Hill, Battersea, London SW11 5TF
Admin 0171 223 6557  BO 0171 223 2223
Fax 0171 978 5207
Director: Tom Morris
General Manager: Steve Mannix

**BANANA CABARET**
The Bedford, 77 Bedford Hill, London SW12 9HD
Tel 0181 673 1756
Capacity: Ground floor 200. First floor 130.
Contact: Andy Waring

**BEARCAT CLUB**
The Turks Head, Winchester Road,
St. Margaret's, Twickenham, Middlesex
Tel 0181 892 1972
Capacity: 150
Contact: James Punnett
Season: Sept-May, performances on Mon + Sat

**THE BEDFORD**
Bedford Hill, London, SW12
Tel 0181 673 1756

**BEYOND A JOKE**
Contact tel 0171 277 8604

**THE BLACKFRIARS**
36 Bell Street, Glasgow
Tel 0141 552 5924
Capacity: 100

**BOUND AND GAGGED**
**(Palmers Green)**
The Fox, 413 Green Lanes, Palmers Green,
London N13
Tel 0171 483 3456.
Capacity: 180

**BOUND AND GAGGED**
**(Tufnell Park)**
Tufnell Park Tavern, 162 Tufnell Park Road,
London N7
Tel 0171 483 3456
Capacity: 130

**BULL & BUSH**
No 1Kew Road, Richmond
Tel 0181 940 5768

**BUNJIES COFFEE HOUSE**
(Formerly Out To Lunch)
27 Lichfield Street, London WC2H 9NI
Tel: 0171 240 1796
Capacity: 50

**THE BUZZ**
Venue: The Southern Hotel, Nell Lane,
Chorlton, Manchester M21
Tel 0161 881 7048
Programmed by John B. Marshall.
PO Box 13, Bramhall SK7 1DZ
Tel 0161 440 8662
Every Thursday at 8pm.
Capacity: 200

**CANAL CAFÉ THEATRE**
The Bridge House, Delamere Terrace,
Little Venice, London W2 6ND
Tel 0171 289 6054  Fax 0171 266 1717
Capacity: 60

**CHATS PLACE ARTS CENTRE & VENUE**
42-44 Brooksby's Walk, Chatsworth Road,
Hackney, London E9 6DF.
Tel 0181 986 6714 /533 0227
Fax 0181 985 6878
Contact: Michelle Gregory, Programmer

**THE CITADEL ARTS CENTRE**
Waterloo Street, St. Helen's WA10 1PX.
Tel 01744 735436
Capacity: 200 standing or 185 seated.

**CLUB JAMMIN**
WKD, 18 Kentish Town Road, Camden Town,
London NW1
Tel 0171 482 5042  Tel/Fax 0171 482 5042
Contact: Lee H. Simba
Cap: 400

**COLCHESTER COMEDY CLUB**
Colchester Arts Centre, Church Street,
Colchester CO1 1NF
Tel 01206 577301
Contact: Anthony Roberts
Cap. 250

**COMEDY AT THE OLD TROUT**
River Street, Windsor, Berks
Contact Tel: 01753 831751
Capacity: 200.

**COMEDY AT THE TOWNGATE**
St. Martins Square, Basildon, Essex SS14 1DW
Tel 01268 531343 (box office)  Fax 01268 525415

**COMEDY CAFÉ**
66 Rivington Street, London EC2A 3AY

Tel 0171 739 5706
Capacity: 170
Contact: Noel Faulkner and Mario Baotic

**COMEDY CAFÉ**
Tyne Theatre and Opera House, Westgate Road,
Newcastle upon Tyne
SD 0191 232 1551  BO 0191 232 0899
Capacity:150

**COMEDY CUPBOARD**
170 East Road, Cambridge CB1 1DB
Contact Tel 01223 508533
Capacity: 250

**THE COMEDY SPOT**
29/30 Maiden Lane, London WC2
Contact Tel 0171 379 5900
Capacity: 70

**COMEDY STORE**
In 1A Oxendon Street, (corner of Coventry Street),
London SW1Y 4EE
Tel 01426 914433 (voice bank information service)
or 0171 839 6642 (admin)
Credit Card Bookings: 0171 344 4444 (Ticketmaster)
Capacity: 400

**COMEDY SUPERSTORE**
Student Union, Warwick University, Gibbet Hill Road,
Coventry CV4 7AL
Tel 01203 417220
Capacity: 300

**COMICS ON SATURDAY NIGHT**
Fulmar and Firkin, 51 Parker Street,
London WC2B 5PS
Tel 0171 405 0590
Contact: Andy Fox on 0181 801 4689
Capacity: about 100

**THE CRACK COMEDY CLUB**
Queens Arms, High Street, Wealdstone, Harrow
Tel: 0181 427 3332
Capacity: 120, performances 8pm to midnight.
For information and enquiries contact 0181 907 9659

**THE CRACK'S 90 COMEDY CLUB**
The Dealcroix Inn, Buncrana Road, Derry
Tel: 01232 776680

**CROCODILE CABARET**
Venue: Concorde Bar, Madeira Drive, Brighton
Performances: Thursdays
Capacity: 200
Office: 24a Bute Street, Brighton, Sussex BN2 2EH
Tel 01273 677836
Contact: Lucy Barry

**DOWNSTAIRS AT THE KING'S HEAD**
2 Crouch End Hill, London N8
Tel 0181 340 1028
Contact: Peter Graham on 01920 823265
Capacity: 120

**THE DRILL HALL**
16 Chenies Street, London WC1
Tel 0171 637 8270

**THE DRUM**
The Fenton, 161 Woodhouse Lane, Leeds LS2 3ED
Tel 0113 245 0624/245 3908
Capacity: 110

**THE EMPIRE LAUGHS BACK**
Botanic Avenue, Belfast
Tel 01232 776680
Capacity: 200

**FINNEGAN`S WAKE**
2 Essex Road, London N1
Tel 0171 813 4478

**THE FOX**
413 Green Lanes, London N13
Tel 0171 483 3456

**FRIDAY ALTERNATIVE**
South Hill Park, Bracknell, Berks RG12 4PA.
Tel 01344 484123 (box office)
Capacity: 120
Contact: Simon Hullahan
Show starts 8:30pm

**THE FULMAR AND FIRKIN**
51 Parker Street, London WC2
Tel 0171 405 0590

**GUILTY PEA**
The Wheatsheaf, 25 Rathbone Place, London W1
Tel 0171 580 1585
Capacity: 80

**HA BLOODY HA**
The Viaduct Inn, Uxbridge Road, Hanwell, London W7
Tel 0181 566 4067
Contact: Simon Randle
Capacity: 120. Performances Fri + Sat night at 9pm

**THE HAMPSTEAD COMEDY CLUB**
(Downstairs at The Washington)
Englands Lane, Belsize Park, London NW3
Tel 0171 207 7256

**HECKLERS**
The Goose & Granite, 204 Hoe St, Walthamstow,
London E17 3AX
Tel 0181 520 0465
Capacity: 140

**HELLFIRE COMEDY CLUB**
Wycombe Town Hall, Queen Victoria Road,
High Wycombe Bucks
Tel 01494 512000
Capacity: 250

**HOT SPOTS!**
The Academy, Union of Brunel Students, Cleveland
Road, Uxbridge, Middx. UB8 3PH
Tel 01895 813504
Fax 01895 810477
Capacity: 300

**THE ISOBAR**
South Bank University Students' Union,
Keyworth Street, London SE1 6NG.
Tel 0171 815 6060
Entertainments Manager: Tom Dinnis
Performances: Alternate Thursdays (in association with
Comedy Network on Channel 5; with an open mike
sponsored by The Daily Telegraph)
Capacity: 200-300

**JACKSONS LANE**
269a Archway Road, London N6 5AA.
Tel 0181 340 5226  Fax 0181 348 2424
Programmer: John Walmsley

Capacity: 150 approx/or 80 seat studio

**THE JOKER COMEDY CLUB**
Cliffs Pavillion Maritime Bar, Station Road,
Southend on Sea, Essex.
Tel 01702 393339 (booking office)
Capacity: 250.

**JONGLEURS BATTERSEA**
49 Lavender Gardens, London SW11.
Admin 0171 924 2766  BO 0171 924 2766
Fax 0171 924 5175  Promotions 0171 924 3080
Contacts: Promotions: Richard Sirot
Bookings: Clare Britton
Capacity: 300

**JONGLEURS CAMDEN LOCK**
**(AKA DINGWALLS)**
Camden Lock, Chalk Farm Road, London N1
Admin 0171 924 2248  BO 0171 924 2766
Tel(10am-4pm) 0171 267 1577
Fax 0171 924 5175  Promotions 0171 924 3080
Contacts: Promotions: Richard Sirot
Bookings: Clare Britton
Capacity: 450 seated, 70 standing

**MECCANO CLUB**
Market Tavern, 2 Essex Road, London N1
Tel 0181 800 2236
Capacity: 60

**MELTDOWN**
Club Ilfor Bach, Womanby Street, Cardiff
Tel 01222 485554
Capacity: 150

**ORANJE BOOM BOOM**
De Hems Dutch Café Bar, 11 Macclesfield Street,
London W1
Tel 0171 437 2494
Capacity: 100

**PAISLEY ARTS CENTRE**
New Street, Paisley
Tel 0141 887 1010
Capacity: 160

**PILLAR TALK**
Pillar Room, Town Hall, Imperial Square,
Cheltenham, Glos. GL50 IQA
Tel 01242 561621
Capacity: 320

**RAILWAY INN**
3 St Paul's Hill, Winchester, Hants SL22 5AE
Tel 01962 867795

**RED ROSE CLUB**
129 Seven Sisters Road, London N7 7QG
Tel 0171 263 7265
Capacity: 200

**ROSEMARY BRANCH THEATRE**
Shepperton Road, London N1
Tel 0171 704 6665

**THE ROYAL OAK**
Coombe Road, Surrey
Tel 0181 940 6882

**SCREAMING BLUE MURDER**
The Ferryboat Tavern, 6 Bridge Road,
Hampton Court, Surrey

For Bookings Contact Pete Harris on 0181 339 0506
Capacity: 120.

**SCREAMING BLUE MURDER**
The Mitre Tavern, Hampton Court Road,
Hampton Court, London
Tel 0181 979 9988
For Bookings Contact Pete Harris on 0181 339 0506
Capacity: 150

**SCREAMING BLUE MURDER**
The Old Town Hall Arts Centre, High Street,
Hemel Hempstead HP1 3AE
Tel 01442 242827
For Bookings Contact Pete Harris on 0181 339 0506
Shows: Every other monday.
Capacity: 85

**SCREAMING BLUE MURDER**
Wimbledon Top of the Hill, Dog and Fox, High Street,
WImbledon Village, SW19
For Bookings Contact Pete Harris on 0181 339 0506
Capacity: 250

**SOHOHO**
Crown and Two Chairmen, 31 Dean Street, London W1
Tel 0181 340 3627
Capacity: 80

**THREE LEGGED DOG CLUB**
Hull Truck Theatre, Spring Street, Hull
BO 01482 323638
Contact: Steve Shaw or Matt Stephenson
Tel 01482 345438
Capacity: 300

**TUFNELL PARK TAVERN**
Tufnell Park Road, London N7
Tel 0171 483 3456

**TUT AND SHIVE**
Upper Street, Islington, London N1
Tel 0171 359 7719

**UP THE CREEK**
302 Creek Road, London SE10
Tel 0181 858 4581
Contact: Malcolm Hardee
Performances: Fri, Sat, Sun
Capacity: 300

**UPFRONT COMEDY CLUB**
1 Chippenham Mews, London W9
Tel 0171 286 1656
Performances: First Friday of every month.

**THE VIADUCT**
Uxbridge Road, London W7
Tel 0181 566 4067

**WORLD OYSTER CLUB**
(Formerly Nuff Said)
27 Lichfield Street, London WC2
Tel 0171 240 1796
Contact: Will Smith on 0171 278 1929
Capacity: 50 ish

# ARTS CENTRES

**ALDERSHOT**
**WEST END CENTRE**
**Queens Road, Aldershot, Hampshire GU11 3JD**
**Tel 01252 408040 BO 01252 330040**
**Fax 01252 408041**
Capacity: 100 (theatre), 250 (promenade), 200 (gigs)
Fully equipped and refurbished Victorian listed building.
Regional reputation for theatre, world music, rock,
roots, film plus related workshops. Bar and diner.
Promotors welcome.

**ALFRETON**
**ALFRETON HALL**
**Church Street, Alfreton, Derbyshire DE55 7AH**
**Tel 01773 832201**
Centre Manager: Glenda Cresswell-Cast
Seats: 180.
Stage: 5.49 x 3.66m extending to 10.97m x 4.88m; Ht.
4.57m.
Lighting: 16 lamp console. 24 lanterns.
No dressing rooms, but multi-purpose space available.

**ALSAGER**
**ALSAGER ARTS CENTRE**
**Crewe & Alsager Faculty**
**Manchester Metropolitan University, Hassall Road,**
**Alsager, Stoke on Trent ST7 2HL**
**Tel 0161 247 5302 Fax 0161 247 6377**
Arts Centre Co-ordinator: Neil Mackenzie

**BARNSTAPLE**
**NORTH DEVON COLLEGE NEW THEATRE**
**Old Sticklepath Hill, Barnstaple, Devon EX31 2BQ**
**Tel 01271 388120**
Seats: 120
Open stage theatre, licensed bar and art gallery, full
lighting.

**BASINGSTOKE**
**CENTRAL STUDIO**
**Queen Mary's College, Cliddesden Road,**
**Basingstoke RG21 3HF**
**Tel 01256 479221 Fax 01256 326097**
Centre Manager: Mervyn Heard
Technical Manager: Steve Robson
A purpose built studio theatre with extended thrust
stage (7.60m x 9.12m).
Lighting: 36 way bar. Full stage management, Green
Room, 2 Dressing Rooms, Workshops.
Seats: 126.
We present a large mixed programme of professional
music, drama, mime, dance and childrens events. We
have a particular interest in workshops, educational
projects and innovative work. Part of Queen Mary's
Centre.

**BEAFORD**
**BEAFORD CENTRE**
**Beaford Winkleigh, Devon EX19 8LU**
**Tel 01805 603201 Fax 01805 603202**
**e-mail beaford@globalnet.co.uk**
**Website www.castlelink.co.uk/beaford/**
Director: Bob Butler
Wide range of activities in N. Devon, including
extensive professional events programme. Rural
Resources Unit, hiring theatrical lighting and sound
systems and rostra units to community groups.
Residential Courses, Children's Activities, Participatory

Projects, Photographic Archive.
Incorporating The Plough Arts Centre.

**BILLERICAY**
**THE FOLD ARTS CENTRE**
**72 Laindon Road, Billericay, Essex CM12 9LD**
**Tel 01277 659286**
Chairman: Margaret White
Events Co-ordinator: Sharron Mahony
Secretary: Edmond Philpott
The Billericay Arts Association is a voluntry
organisation promoting the arts in Billericay. It operates
at the Fold Arts Centre, which has a performance area
accomodating up to 80 people on flexible seating
layouts. The Association welcomes enquiries from
professional and amateur groups wishing to stage an
event and will give full marketing support. The building
also houses two exhibition galleries and three class
rooms.

**BINGLEY**
**BINGLEY ARTS CENTRE**
**Main Street, Bingley, West Yorkshire BD16 2LZ**
**Tel 01274 751576 Fax 01274 751523**
Full theatre facilities, with stage, apron, curtains and
orch. pit when necessary.
Manager: Mark Davies
Seats: 373 retractable seating.
Rank Strand lighting systems.
Dressing Rooms: 2 , approx. 25 in each.
Also used for dinner dances, exhibitions, antique sales etc.

**BIRKENHEAD**
**WIRRAL YOUTH THEATRE**
**St Benedilt's School, New Hey Road,**
**Upton, Wirral L49 9BZ**
**Tel 0151 677 0753 Fax 0151 677 5781**
Drama Worker: Shiralea Drewett
Technical Worker: Mo White
Admin Assistant: Liz Jones

**MAC - THE CENTRE FOR BIRMINGHAM**
**(Midlands Arts Centre), Cannon Hill Park,**
**Birmingham B12 9QH**
**Admin 0121 440 4221 BO 0121 440 3838**
**Fax 0121 446 4372**
Director: Geoff Sims
Programme Director: Dorothy Wilson
Open from 9am to 11pm 362 days a year.
Programme includes new productions and touring
theatre, wide range of music and dance performances,
cinema, literary events. Year round courses for adults
and children in Arts and Crafts, Music and Dance.
MAC houses: The Theatre (202 seats), The Hexagon
(88 seats), Cinema (144 seats), the Arena (450 seats),
Dance, Music and Fine Art Studios, Foyle, Cotton and
Foyer Galleries plus other exhibition areas, Restaurant,
Cafe, Bar, Bookshop, Parkside Function and Meeting
Rooms.
Dressing Rooms: The Theatre - 2; The Hexagon - 2;
Showers.
Membership: TMA

**BOSTON**
**BLACKFRIARS ARTS CENTRE**
**Spain Lane, Boston, Lincolnshire PE21 6HP**
**Tel 01205 363108**
Director: Ian Whiteside

For technical details see entry in Provincial Theatres Section

**BRACKNELL**
**SOUTH HILL PARK ARTS CENTRE**
**Bracknell, Berkshire RG12 7PA**
**Tel 01344 427272  Fax 01344 411427**
Director: Tim Brinkman
For Technical details of Wilde Theatre see entry in Provincial Theatre Section

**BRADFORD**
**BRADFORD THEATRE IN THE MILL**
**Bradford University, Richmond Rd., Bradford BD7 1DP**
**Tel 01274 383185  BO 01274 383200**
**Fax 01274 383187**
Contact: Jemima Thomas
For technical details see entry in Provincial Theatres Section.

**BRAINTREE**
**THE TOWN HALL CENTRE**
**Market Square, Braintree, Essex CM7 3YG**
**Tel 01376 557776**
Manager: Mrs J A Grice
Administrator: Tony Edmunds

**BRENTWOOD THEATRE**
**Shenfield Road, Brentwood, Essex CM15 8AG.**
**Admin 01277 230833  BO 01277 200300**
Props: Brentwood Theatre Trust
Theatre Administrator: Karen Fisher
Capacity: 100-198 seated. 270 standing.

**BRIDGNORTH**
**BRIDGNORTH LEISURE CENTRE**
**Northgate, Bridgnorth, Shropshire WV16 4ER**
**Tel 01746 761541  Fax 01746 768118**
Manager: Mike Burnell
Main Hall: Seats 650. Raked auditorium 286, 364 on floor area. Full lighting system. H/Way unit. Modular stage unit additional seating or stage in the round. Dressing Rooms.
Small Hall: Seats 250. Suitable for many events, e.g. Mime and Dances. Full lighting system. Exhibition areas. Licensed Bar, Coffee Bar, 4 Squash Courts, Swimming Pool, outside public areas, Tennis Courts, Badminton Courts, etc.

**BRIDGWATER**
**BRIDGWATER ARTS CENTRE**
**11-13 Castle Street, Bridgwater, Somerset TA6 3DD**
**Tel 01278 422700  Fax 01278 447402**
Director: Richard Crowe
Seats 196. Ground Floor 160 (Variable), Balcony 36. Pros. Arch Theatre with apron stage. 7.92m wide, 6.10m deep with 2.44m wing space on each side. Lighting and Sound Facilities.Dressing Rooms. F.O.H. Gallery, 4 Conference Rooms, Licensed Bar and Kitchen. Garden for outdoor sculpture.
Policy: to promote a well balanced programme of events that reaches a wide section of the local community within the Bridgwater area. The Centre promotes professional and amateur theatre, literature events, rock, blues, jazz and classical music, films and schools workshops. It is keen to promote work of social relevance and also contemporary work.

**BRIDPORT**
**BRIDPORT ARTS CENTRE**
**South Street, Bridport DT6 3NR**
**Tel 01308 427183  BO/Fax 01308 424204**
Administrator: Frances Everitt

Marketing Officer: Lorna Richards
Director: Chris Huxley
Seats: 200
Width of stage across prosc. arch opening 6.12m. The wings up to wall each side 3m. Archway opening 5.88m. Depth back of Archway 2.61m. Tabline to front of stage 61cm. Prosc. Arch height 4m, adjustable with border. Grand Piano. Used by local art and drama societies, plus a full programme of national touring companies, contemporary and traditional. Over 40 professional performances per year. Excellent, large exhibition Room and Club Room for meetings available.

**BRIGHTON**
**GARDNER ARTS CENTRE**
**University of Sussex, Falmer, Brighton BN1 9RA**
**Tel 01273 685447  BO 01273 685861**
**SD 01273 696975  Fax 01273 678551**
General Manager: Norma Binnie
For technical details see entry in Provincial Theatre Section.

**THE ZAP**
**187-193 King's Road Arches, Brighton BN1 1NB**
**Tel 01273 821588  Fax 01273 206960**
**e-mail office@zapuk.com**
For further details please see entry in Provincial Concert Venue Section.

**BRISTOL**
**ALBANY CENTRE**
**Shaftesbury Avenue, Montpelier, Bristol BS6 5LL**
**Tel 0117 954 2154**
Seats Max. 110. Can be arranged to seat end-on, traverse or 3-sides. Small scale theatre. Mime, Music & Dance. Dressing rooms. Part-time Technician. Limited disabled access.

**HOPE CENTRE**
**Hope Chapel Hill, Bristol BS8 4ND**
**Tel 0117 921 5271  Fax 0117 929 1883**
Manager: Gill Loats
Technician/Caretaker: Joe Sutton
Publicity: Hellie Mulvaney
Community Worker: Jason Hull
Administrative Assistant: Sue Bennett
The Hope Centre is a lively community arts centre. Originally a congregational chapel, it is now leased by the Community Association to be both a local cultural resource and promoter of fringe theatre, dance and music events at weekends, and a community resource, working with others in the community - Hotwells School, Dowry Square Resource & Activity Centre, H.A.N.D.S., Trinity Day Care etc.; the Community Worker promotes and supports play provision, community education, information sharing, advice sessions etc.

**WATERSHED MEDIA CENTRE**
**1 Canons Road, Bristol, BS1 5TX**
**Tel 0117 927 6444  Fax 0117 921 3958**
Director: Luke Sapsed
An arts venue with a photographic exhibition gallery and two cinemas. Also available for private hire: Gallery Two - 6,000 square feet on one level. Will take a maximum of 250 people seated or 400 standing. Cinemas One & Two - fully equipped tiered conference auditoria (with excellent audio visual and technical support provided free of charge). 200 and 50 person capacity, available between 9-5pm.

**BROMLEY ARTS COUNCIL**
**RIPLEY ARTS CENTRE**
**24 Sundridge Avenue, Bromley, Kent BR1 2PX**

Tel 0181 464 5816
Contact: Mrs Jean Dyne
Policy: Promoting the Arts.

**BROXBOURNE**
**BROXBOURNE ARTS CENTRE**
**Lowewood, High Street, Hoddesdon, Herts.**
**Tel 01992 465032**
Hon. Secretary: Mavis Winter

**BURY**
**THE MET ARTS CENTRE**
**Market Street, Bury, Lancs. BL9 0BW**
**Mgt 0161 761 7107  BO 0161 761 2216**
**Fax 0161 763 5056**
Director: Alan Oatey
Technical Manager: Jonathan Clark
Marketing Manager: Chantelle Brandon
Catering Manager: Mike Atkinson
Disabled access throughout, except technical boxes.
Seats: Theatre 130-250; Studio Theatre: 80; Cafe Bar:
100.

**CHESTERFIELD**
**THE ARTS CENTRE**
**Chesterfield College, Infirmary Road, Chesterfield,**
**Derbys. S41 7NG**
**Tel 01246 500578**
Administrator: Siân Davies
Recital Room, raked seating for 175.

**ZONE**
**Church Street, Brimington, Chesterfield,**
**Derbyshire S43 1JG**
**Tel 01246 271548**
Centre Manager: Sue Carrott
Seats: About 75.
Variable flat performance area. Lighting and Sound
facilities available. Dressing Rooms. Disabled access
and toilet facilities.

**CHICHESTER**
**CHICHESTER CENTRE OF ARTS**
**St. Andrews Court, East Street, Chichester,**
**West Sussex PO19 1YH**
**Tel 01243 779103**
Contact: Mr L.B. Bluestone
Main Hall 19.8m x 6.6m with 150 stacking chairs. No
stage. Seating Capacity: 150
Studio: 14 ft x 16 ft. Seating Capacity: 25-40.

**CHIPPING NORTON**
**THE THEATRE**
**Spring Street, Chipping Norton, Oxon. OX7 5NL**
**Admin 01608 642349  BO 01608 642350**
**Fax 01608 642324**
Director: Tamara Malcolm
General Manager: Mathew Russell
Policy: Touring theatre, concerts, cinema, schools &
childrens theatre & workshops, produces own
pantomimes & touring productions.
Seats: 235. Bar. Art Gallery.
For technical details see Provincial Theatre Section.

**CHRISTCHURCH**
**THE REGENT CENTRE**
**51 High Street, Christchurch, Dorset BH23 1AS**
**Tel 01202 479819  BO 01202 499148**
**Fax 01202 479952**
General Manager: David Hopkins
Seats: 483 Stage 24' x 24' (Live & Cinema)
Studio-seats: 80 Foyer Gallery, Coffee & Licensed bar.

**CIRENCESTER**
**BREWERY ARTS**
**Brewery Court, Cirencester, Gloucestershire**
**GL7 1JH**
**Tel 01285 657181  Fax 01285 644060**
**e-mail breweryarts@enterprise.net**
Artisitic Director: Danny Scrivener
120 seat theatre showing small to medium scale
touring shows. The past twelve months has seen
companies and individuals of international status
performing theatre, folk, jazz and classical music,
opera, literature events and cultural dance.
Performances are also given by our resident theatre
company, Kaos Theatre who tour nationally. The Arts
and Craft Centre also houses a gallery of national
importance, a Crafts Council selected Craft Shop, an
Egon Ronay recommended Coffee House and 17
resident craftworkers, including a jeweller, willow
basket weaver, ceramicist, textile artist and stainded
glass artist.
**Kaos Theatre:**
Resident theatre group at Theatre - ongoing policy of
performance research.
Kaos Theatre Director: Xavier Leret

**COLCHESTER**
**COLCHESTER ARTS CENTRE**
**St. Mary-at-the-Walls, Church Street, Colchester,**
**Essex CO1 1NF**
**Tel 01206 577301  Fax 01206 764334**
Seating: 250
Licensed Bar

**COVENTRY**
**WARWICK ARTS CENTRE,**
**University of Warwick, Coventry CV4 7AL**
**Admin 01203 523734  BO 01203 524524**
**Fax 01203 523883**
For technical details see entry in Provincial Theatres
Section.

**DARLINGTON**
**THE ARTS CENTRE**
**Vane Terrace, Darlington DL3 7AX**
**Admin 01325 483271  BO 01325 483168**
**Fax 01325 365794**
Centre Manager: Peter Cutchie
Theatre seating between 140 and 350 in flexible
layouts. Ballroom for cabaret and functions, Film
Theatre with 35mm projector and screen seating 200.
Garden Bar seating 80 to 100 for cabaret, folk, jazz etc.
Dance studio, galleries, foyer, self-service restaurant
and bar. Wide range of meeting rooms and practical
workshop facilities, artists' and craftspersons' studios,
sound and video recording facilities, residential
accommodation available for visiting performers,
course participants and conference visitors, resident
theatre companies; also base for Cleveland Theatre
Company. Darlington Borough Council provides this
service.

**DORCHESTER**
**DORCHESTER ARTS CENTRE**
**School Lane, The Grove, Dorchester,**
**Dorset DT1 1XR**
**Tel 01305 266926**
Director: Ruth Harris
2 Halls, maximum theatre capacity: 60

**DURHAM**
**DURHAM LIGHT INFANTRY MUSEUM**
**and**
**DURHAM ART GALLERY**
**Aykley Heads, Durham DH1 5TU**
**Tel 0191 384 2214 Fax 0191 386 1770**
Arts Manager: Zoë Channing
Capacity: 120
Performances held in exhibitions area. Ceiling height
8 ft. Disabled access to all buildings; disabled toilet.

**ULEY, NR. DURSLEY**
**PREMA ARTS CENTRE**
**South Street, Uley, Gloucestershire GL11 5SS**
**Admin/BO 01453 860703 Fax 01453 860123**
**e-mail admin@prema.demon.co.uk**
Contact: Gordon Scott, Director
Theatre size: 30 sq ft, 120 seats.
Programme: Live Art, Dance, Cross Art performance,
video.

**EVESHAM**
**EVESHAM ARTS CENTRE**
**Victoria Avenue, Evesham, Worcs., WR11 4QH**
**Tel 01386 48883 only when an event is on,**
**otherwise - 01386 446067**
Contact: Lauri Griffith Jones
Fully equipped theatre, 312 seats, flat stage, raked
auditorium. Cinema screen. Licensed and Coffee Bars.
(Joint use with Prince's Henry's School, Evesham).

**EXETER**
**EXETER & DEVON ARTS CENTRE**
**Bradninch Place, Gandy Street, Exeter,**
**Devon EX4 3LS**
**Admin 01392 219741 BO 01392 421111**
Programme Manager: Andy Morley
Marketing Manager: Alison Fordham
Venue closed for renovations and will reopen spring
1999, meanwhile arts centre activities continue
elsewhere.

**FALMOUTH**
**FALMOUTH ARTS CENTRE**
**Church Street, Falmouth, Cornwall TR11 3EG**
**Admin 01326 314566 BO 01326 212300**
Administrator: Michael Carver
Programme Director: Dominic Power
Tel 01326 317090
Arts Theatre with Pros. Arch Stage, seating 200 on
fixed seats. Gallery, seating 150 moveable seats.
Theatre Facilities and Dressing Rooms.

**FAREHAM**
**THE ASHCROFT ARTS CENTRE**
**Osborn Road, Fareham, Hants. PO16 7DX**
**Tel 01329 235161 BO 01329 310600**
**Fax 01329 825661**
Director: Steve Rowley

**FOLKESTONE**
**THE METROPOLE ARTS CENTRE**
**The Metropole, The Leas, Folkestone, Kent CT20 2LS**
**Tel 01303 255070/244706**
Acting Director: Ann Fearey
Drama, Dance, Workshops, Exhibitions, Jazz,
Literature, Classical Music etc. Seating 200: General
cover lighting, PA, stage blocks and wooden floor. Ideal
venue for one person/two person shows.

**FROME**
**MERLIN THEATRE AND ARTS CENTRE**
**Bath Road, Frome, Somerset BA11 2HG**

**Admin 01373 461360 BO 01373 465949**
**Fax 01373 453900**
For full details see entry in Provincial Theatre Section.
**GAINSBOROUGH**
**TRINITY ARTS CENTRE**
**Trinity Street, Gainsborough, Lincs. DN21 2AL**
**Admin 01427 810298 BO 01427 810710**
**Fax 01427 811198**
Seats: 208

**GOOLE**
**THE GATE**
**c/o Goole Town Council, Alfred Taylor House,**
**17/23 Gladstone Terrace, Goole, East Yorkshire**
**DN14 5AQ**
**Tel 01405 763652**
Arts and Leisure Development Officer: Charlie Studdy
New, flexible space with moveable staging and seating
for a maximum of 100. Full technical specification
available on request. Small and middle scale
companies booked. Two dressing rooms with shower
and toilet.

**GREAT TORRINGTON**
**THE PLOUGH THEATRE/ARTS CENTRE**
**Fore Street, Great Torrington, Devon EX38 8HQ**
**Tel 01805 622552 Fax 01805 624624**
Director: Bob Butler

**GREAT YARMOUTH**
**ST. GEORGES THEATRE AND CENTRE FOR THE**
**ARTS**
**King Street, Great Yarmouth, Norfolk NR30 2PG**
**Tel 01493 858387**
Administrator: Betty Taylor
Seats: 225. Stage 15' x 20' widening to 34'.

**GRIMSBY**
**CAXTON THEATRE & ARTS CENTRE**
**128 Cleethorpe Road, Grimsby, North East**
**Lincolnshire DN32 3HW**
**Tel 01472 345167 (not daytime)**
Secretary: Cathy Bennett-Ryan Tel 01472 231753
Opened in 1982 to house the Caxton Players and offer
venue for touring professionals, facilities for workshops,
exhibitions and foyer events.
Seating Capacity: 184
2 Dressing rooms plus Green Room. Coffee bar,
control room, store and Licensed Bar.

**GWENT**
**BLACKWOOD MINERS INSTITUTE**
**High Street, Blackwood, Gwent NP2 1BB**
**Admin 01495 224425  BO 01495 227206**
**Fax 01495 226457**
Manager: Lyn Evans
400 seat theatre/cinema, dance hall, live music and
cabaret bar, bistro and arts gallery. Presents nationally
acclaimed professional and high class community
product and a full timetable of community workshops,
projects and productions. Available for private hire and
functions/seminars.

**HARROW**
**HARROW ARTS CENTRE/TRAVELLERS**
**STUDIO THEATRE**
**Uxbridge Road, Hatch End, Harrow,**
**Middlesex HA5 4EA**
**Tel 0181 428 0123  BO 0181 428 0124**
**Fax 0181 428 0121**
**e-mail harrowarts@getsurfed.co.uk**
**Website harrowarts.org.uk/**
Programme Manager: Chris Mellor
**Studio Theatre:** Moveable staging and seating — 130
maximum. Standard lighting and sound facilities.
Performing area flexible. 2 Dressing Rooms with
Shower and Toilet. Fully accessible to disabled
performers.
**Elliot Concert Hall:** 600 seats. Used for Dance and
Music events. Sirius lighting system. 3 dressing rooms,
disabled access. Licensed bar.

**HASTINGS**
**STABLES THEATRE & ART GALLERY**
**The Bourne, Hastings, East Sussex TN34 3EY**
**Tel 01424 423221**
Secretary: Mabel E. Stringfellow
Chairman: C J Lacey
Pros. Arch Stage, 160 seats. Full theatre facilities.
Dressing Rooms.

**HAVANT**
**HAVANT ARTS CENTRE & BEDHAMPTON ARTS**
**CENTRES)**
**Managed by Havant Arts Active**
**Havant, Hants. PO9 1BS**
**Admin 01705 480113  BO 01705 472700**
**Fax 01705 498577**
Arts Active Director: Paul Sadler
Twin venues 1 mile apart.
**BAC: Participatory Centre**, studio stage area 8m x
3.5m x 4m to grid. Raked seating 65. Technical list on
request.
**O.T.H.: Performance based centre**. Studio theatre,
stage area 6.9m x 6.55m x 4m to grid. Raked seating
135. Technical list on request.

**HEBDEN BRIDGE**
**ARVON FOUNDATION**
**Lumb Bank, Hebden Bridge, West Yorkshire**

**Tel/Fax 01422 843714**
Centre Director: Amanda Dalton
Performance Area in converted barn (12.77m x 6.38m).
Not suitable for public performance.

**HEMEL HEMPSTEAD**
**Boxmoor Arts Centre for Young People**
**Boxmoor Hall, St John`s Road, Hemel Hempstead,**
**Herts. HP1 1JR**
**Tel 01442 233456**
Borough Arts Manager: Sarah Railson
Centre Manager: Paula Leonard
Seating capacity 100. Raked audit, or Flat Performance
area 25' x 25'. Full stage lighting available. Rostra
available. Versatile & flexible space.

**OLD TOWN HALL ARTS CENTRE**
**High Street, Hemel Hempstead, Herts. HP1 3AE**
**Tel 01442 228095  BO 01442 228091**
**Fax 01442 234072**
General Manager: Sarah Railson
Seating Capacity 120. Raked audit. Flat Performance
area 25' x 25'.
Full stage lighting available.

**HEREFORD**
**THE COURTYARD - HEREFORD'S CENTRE FOR**
**THE ARTS**
**Edgar Street, Hereford HR4 9JR**
**Mgt 01432 268785  BO 01432 359252**
**Fax 01432 274895**
Opening Autumn 1998.
Artistic Director: Jonathan Stone
Administrator: Vicky Stackhouse
Policy: Presenting and producing house.
Seats: Main House - 400. Studio - 140.

**HEXHAM**
**QUEEN'S HALL ARTS CENTRE,**
**Beaumont Street, Hexham, NE46 3LS**
**Mgt 01434 606787  BO 01434 607272**
**Fax 01434 606043**
**ADMINISTRATION:**
Arts Manager: Geof Keys
Administrator: Joyce Stonehouse
Senior Technician: Andrew Biscoe
Assistant Technician: Alex Perry
Marketing Officer: Mylee Hall
Front of House Supervisor: Caroline Reay
Arts Outreach Worker: Pauline Moger
Policy: to promote a full range of middle and small
scale touring of Performing Arts complemented by
Outreach Work throughout the year. The Visual Arts is
an important part of our programming with The Gallery
and Studio in constant use.  A suite of Darkrooms is
available for assisted or unassisted hire.  Queen's Hall
Arts Centre houses a restaurant, library plus features, a
stained glass foyer and the Tynedale Tapestry.
**TECHNICAL**
400 seats, first three rows (51) seats demountable.
Dimensions: pros width 9.04m, pros line to rear wall
7.56m, fore stage to rear wall 8.66m.  Grid height
12.00m, stage width (acting area) 8m. Limited wings
space. Flying - 11 sets double purchase counter
weight, 15 3 line hemp sets, all operated from fly floor,
bar length 9.10m. Lighting Arri Image + 24 subs
(manual backup), 96 dimmers (88 x 2kw 8 x 5kw), 36 x
fresnels, 12 x sil 30, 6 x p.c., 16 x par cans, 4 x cyc
floods, 2 x CSI follow spots, minimal colour (lee), 100
amp 3 phase supply.  Sound: 1 x revox B77 (7 1/2 x
15), 2 x cassette decks), soundcraft 16/4/2 mixer, 2 V x
800 amps, 4 x Bose 802 speakers.  F.O.H. 3 x SM57, 3
SM x 58, 3 x AKG D 310 (mics), 6 x boom stands.

Disabled facilities, wheelchair access, lift, disabled toilets.

**HORSHAM**
**HORSHAM ARTS CENTRE**
**North Street, Horsham, West Sussex RH12 1RL**
**Admin 01403 259708 BO 01403 268689**
**Fax 01403 211502**
Manager: Kevin Parker
450 seat theatre, 100 seat studio, 126 seat cinema.
Drama, Plays, Dance, Children's Shows, Orchestras etc.

**HULL**
**HULL TRUCK THEATRE**
**Spring Street, Hull HU2 8RW**
**Mgt 01482 224800 BO 01482 323638**
**Fax 01482 581182**
General Manager: Simon Stallworthy
Seats: 320 max
For technical details see entry in Provincial Theatre Section.

**ILMINSTER**
**DILLINGTON HOUSE**
**Ilminster, Somerset TA19 9DT**
**Tel 01460 52427  Fax 01460 52433**
General Manager: Wayne Bennett
Recital room seating 170. Lighting, sound and audio-visual facilities available. Residential accommodation on site.

**IPSWICH**
**CORN EXCHANGE**
**King Street, Ipswich, Suffolk, IP1 1DH**
**Mgt 01473 255851 BO 01473 215544**
**Fax 01473 250951**
General Manager: Billy Brennan
Publicity Officer: Hazel Clover

**JERSEY**
**JERSEY ARTS CENTRE**
**Phillips Street, St. Helier, Jersey JE2 4SW**
**Tel 01534 68080**
Contact: Rod McLoughlin, Director
Seats: 250, fixed and steeply raked

**KENDAL**
**BREWERY ARTS CENTRE**
**Highgate, Kendal, Cumbria LA9 4HE**
**Tel 01539 725133  Fax 01539 730257**
Director: Anne Pierson
**Theatre:** New building 30' x 30' stage, 253 seats.
Malt Room: Movable stage. Seats 250-300. Ceiling height approx 8'. Level access.
**Studio Theatre:** Flexible seating for 60-80 in 18' x 50' space (performance area usually 18' x 18' end on). Basic grid. 60 circuits.

**KING'S LYNN**
**ARTS CENTRE**
**29 King Street, King's Lynn, Norfolk PE30 1HA**
**Tel 01553 774725  BO 01553 773578**
**Fax 01553 770591**
General Manager: Howard Barnes
Theatre with small pros. stage. Seats 349 on raked seating. Theatre facilities, 4 Dressing Rooms.

**KINGSBRIDGE**
**SOUTH HAMS THEATRE & ARTS TRUST**
**Town Hall Theatre, Fore Street, Kingsbridge, South Devon**
**Tel 01548 856636**

Chairman: W Stanton

**LEICESTER**
**LEICESTERSHIRE ARTS**
**Knighton Fields Centre, Herrick Road, Leicester LE2 6DH**
**Tel 0116 270 0850**
Head of Service: Peter Baker

**PHOENIX ARTS CENTRE**
**21 Upper Brown Street, Leicester LE1 5TE**
**Tel 0116 224 7700  BO 0116 255 4854**
Centre Director: Richard Haswell
Head of Live Programme: Judi Hughes
Head of Film & Media: Laraine Porter
Head of Marketing & Customer Services: Jennie Jordan
For technical details see entry in Provincial Theatre Section.

**LETCHWORTH GARDEN CITY**
**PLINSTON HALL**
**Letchworth, Herts SG6 3NX**
**General 01462 480245  Hall Bookings 01462 672003**
General Manager: Denis Hill
Seats: 300.
Stage 46' x 20' x 13' clearance. Lighting and sound equipment. Dressing Rooms, Green Rooms etc.

**LEWES**
**ALL SAINTS CENTRE (Arts & Youth)**
**Friars Walk, Lewes, East Sussex BN7 2LE**
**Tel 01273 477583**
Community Arts Development Officer: Sally F Staples.

**LEYLAND**
**WORDEN ARTS AND CRAFTS CENTRE**
**Worden Park, Leyland, Lancs, PR5 2DJ**
**Tel 01772 455908**
Contact: Richard Blackburn
**LIVERPOOL**
**BLUECOAT ARTS CENTRE**
**Bluecoat Chambers, School Lane, Liverpool L1 3BX**
**Tel 0151 709 5297  Fax 0151 707 0048**
**e-mail bluecoat@netmatters.co.uk**
Director: Brian Biggs
**Concert Hall:** Seats 200, retractable seating unit, semi-sprung wooden floor, performance space maximum 30' x 30'. Fixed lighting bars, Rank Strand 18-way Mimi 2, single phase supply, 10 x 50 w lanterns, six microphones, small p.a., six into one mixer. Bechstein concert grand. Suitable for small scale dance and mime, music, jazz, music theatre, etc. Licensed restaurant, bar.

**GREAT GEORGES COMMUNITY CULTURAL PROJECT (THE BLACKIE)**
**Great George Street, Liverpool L1 5EW**
**Tel 0151 709 5109**
**Minicom/Fax 0151 709 4822**
Co-directors: Bill Harpe & Sally Morris
Cultural programme plus play, games, youth work, recreation & education. Borrowing facilities. Resources available - rehearsal/performance/exhibition spaces; lights, sound equipment, video, darkroom.

**LONDON**
**AFRICA CENTRE**
**38 King Street, Covent Garden, London WC2E 8JT**
**Tel 0171 836 1973  Fax 0171 836 1975**
**e-mail africacentre@gn.apc.org**
Programme Co-ordinator: Shukura Nduhukire

Main Hall seats 150. Size 15.24m x 6.09m x 4.57m.

**THE ALBANY**
**Douglas Way, London SE8 4AG**
**Admin 0181 692 0231 BO 0181 692 4446**
**Fax 0181 469 2253**
Administrator: Howard Francis
Programmer: Sandra Doran
Director: Andrew Broadley
Production Manager: Andrew Siddall
Policy: 1 or 2 in-house productions a year, plus full programme of music, cabaret, touring theatre and dance reflecting social and cultural mix of South East London.
The building possesses probably the best house PA and sound system in a comparable venue, it is able to cope with incoming rock bands and with any rival theatre event. The lighting system is on the way to rivalling the sound system in proficiency. Seats 300, 425 standing.

**ALL SAINTS ARTS CENTRE**
**122 Oakleigh Road North, London N20 9EZ**
**Tel 0181 445 8388/445 4654**
**Fax 0181 445 6831**
Director: A V Benjamin

**BAC**
**Lavender Hill, Battersea, London SW11 5TF**
**Tel 0171 223 6557 BO 0171 223 2223**
**Fax 0171 978 5207**
Director: Tom Morris
General Manager: Steve Mannix
For technical details see entry in London Theatre Section.
**BANGLADESH ARTS CENTRE**
**24 Pembridge Gardens, London W2 4DX**
**Tel 0171 229 9404**

**BARBICAN CENTRE**
**Silk Street, London EC2Y 8DS**
**Admin 0171 638 4141 Fax 0171 920 9648**
Managing Director: John Tusa
For full details see entry in London Theatre Section.

**BHAVAN INSTITUTE OF INDIAN ART & CULTURE**
**4a Castletown Road, London W14 9HQ**
**Tel 0171 381 3086/4608 Fax 0171 381 8758**
**Website www.sakti.com/bhavan**
Executive Director: Dr. M. N. Nandakumara

**CHAT'S PLACE**
**Arts Centre & Venue**
**42-44 Brooksby's Walk, London E9 6DF**
**Tel 0181 986 6714/533 0227 Fax 0181 985 6878**
Contact: Michelle Gregory — Programmer
Various Arts Workshops. 1 Bar. Open Tue-Sat events include Music, Theatre and Cabaret.

**THE DRILL HALL**
**16 Chenies Street, London WC1E 7EX**
**Admin 0171 631 1353 BO 0171 637 8270**
**Fax 0171 631 4468**
**e-mail admin@drillhall.co.uk**
Artistic Director: Julie Parker
Administrator: Conrad Lynch
Marketing Manager: Simone Lennox-Grodon
Box Office Manager: Sarah Chamber
Technical Manager: Kim Holt
Main auditorium seating 200. Recently upgraded lighting system and in-house PA system. Licensed Bar and Cafe. Small exhibition space. Companies invited to perform. No hires.

Rehearsal Rooms and Dark Rooms to hire, extensive workshop programme. Disabled access, bar etc & ground floor.

**FAIRFIELD HALLS, CROYDON**
**Park Lane, Croydon CR9 1DG**
**Tel 0181 681 0821 Fax 0181 686 7944**
Chief Executive: Derek Barr
For technical details see entry in London Concert Venue Section.

**FAIRKYTES ARTS CENTRE**
**51 Billet Lane, Hornchurch, Essex RM11 1AX**
**Tel 01708 456308 Fax 01708 475286**
**Arts Office contact at the Broxhill Centre,**
**Broxhill Road, Romford**
**Tel 01708 773950 Fax 01708 773853**
Converted Georgian house used for many kinds of arts and craft activities. Small Hall: 100 seats.
Main room (seating capacity 40) is occasionally used for small-scale music and poetry events, etc. and tickets need to be sold in advance to overcome licensing difficulties. Spacious garden is suitable for drama performances if a company tours all its own equipment. Run adult & children's workshops.

**GLOBE EDUCATION CENTRE**
**Bear Gardens, Bankside, London SE1 9ED**
**Tel 0171 928 6342 Fax 0171 928 7968**
**(incorporating the SHAKESPEARE GLOBE**
**EXHIBITION, New Globe Walk, London**
Open 7 days a week, 10am - 5pm.**)**
Mon-Fri, opening at 10am. Evening classes and play readings at week ends, advertised seasonally.

**HARINGEY ARTS COUNCIL**
**Selby Centre, Selby Road, Tottenham N17 8JN**
**Tel 0181 801 9520 Fax 0181 885 2767**
Contact: Bhavini Chavda
**HOXTON HALL**
**130 Hoxton Street, London N1 6SH**
**Tel 0171 739 5431 Fax 0181 729 3815**
An original Victorian saloon, Music Hall. Two galleries and an open stage. Theatre facilities, two dressing rooms and rehearsal space. Resident Company, Hoxton Hall Theatre Project, run the theatre as a Community Arts Centre & Theatre Venue. Theatre programme of professional and community companies. Theatre training centre (performance skills and theatre technicals)
Available for hire — for performances and for film or TV work.

**INSTITUTE OF CONTEMPORARY ARTS (ICA)**
**The Mall, London SW1Y 5AH**
**Postal Address: 12 Carlton House Terrace,**
**London SW1Y 5AH**
**Offices 0171 930 0493 BO 0171 930 3647**
**Fax 0171 873 0051**
ICA Theatre.
For details see entry in Fringe Theatres Section.

**INTERCHANGE STUDIOS**
**Dalby Street, Kentish Town, London NW5 3NQ**
**Tel 0171 267 9421 Fax 0171 482 5292**
Director: Alan Tomkins
2 halls with 100 fixed & 80 unfixed seats. 3 rehearsal/small dance studios. Showers etc.

**ISLINGTON ARTS FACTORY**
**2 Parkhurst Road, London N7 0SF**
**Tel 0171 607 0561 Fax 0171 700 7229**

**JACKSONS LANE COMMUNITY CENTRE**
**Archway Road, Highgate, London N6 5AA**
**Tel 0181 340 5226 Fax 0181 348 2424**
Please contact Theatre co-ordinator.
Seats:129
For full details please see entry in Fringe Theatres
Section.

**MILLFIELD HOUSE ARTS CENTRE**
**Silver Street, Edmonton, London N18 1PJ**
**Tel 0181 803 5283 Fax 0181 807 3892**
Two large studios seating up to 80 max. people
suitable for recitals, master-classes, dance or drama
plus several smaller rooms, including an attractive
committee/conference room.
Pottery, painting studio, studio cinema and licensed
bar. Regular monthly art exhibitions. Landscaped
gardens.

**THE BULL**
**68 High Street, Barnet, Herts EN5 5SJ**
**Admin 0181 449 5189  BO 0181 449 0048**
**Fax 0181 364 9037**
Director: Alison Duthie
176 Seat Main Theatre (Stage 42' x 20'). Studio
Theatre (Stage 15' x 30'); Art Gallery, Craft Gallery and
Shop. Bar. Full performance programme of
professional Drama, Dance, Music, Visual Arts and
weekly courses and classes. Childrens Shows,.
Programme of community and education work. Eight
resident craftspeople.
Disabled access: ramped access to studio. Lift to first
floor theatre. Hearing aid induction loops fitted.
**OVAL HOUSE**
**52-54 Kennington Oval, London SE11 5SW**
**Tel 0171 582 0080  Fax 0171 820 0990**
**e-mail ovalhouse@dial.pipex.com**
**Website dspace@dial.pipex.com**
Two Studio Theatres with moveable seating. Seats:
100 and 50.
Theatre Facilities. Dressing Room. Rehearsal spaces,
classes and workshops, Arts Education Centre, cafe.
Available for hire, May-July. BO split Oct-March. Bar,
very good wheelchair access.

**POLISH SOCIAL & CULTURAL ASSOCIATION**
**238-246 King Street, Hammersmith,**
**London W6 0RF**
**Tel 0181 741 1940**
Arts co-ordinator: Stefan Lubomirski De Vaux

**RIPLEY ARTS CENTRE**
**24 Sundridge Avenue, Bromley BR1 2PX**
**Tel 0181 464 5816**
Administrator/Secretary: Mrs. J. M. Dyne
Bromley Arts Council, 24 Sundridge Avenue, Bromley,
Kent BR1 2PX
Seats: 120 max

**RIVERSIDE STUDIOS**
**Crisp Road, Hammersmith, London W6 9RL**
**Mgt 0181 741 2251  BO 0181 741 2255**
**Fax 0181 563 0336**
Contact for Hires: Jon Fawcett
Studio 1 - 500 seats, Studio 2 - 400 seats, Studio 3 -
100 seats, Studio 4 - rehearsal space.
Cinema, 200 seats.
For more information, see entry in London Theatre
Section.

**THE TABERNACLE**
**Powis Square, London W11 2AY**

Closed for refurbishment. Re-opening spring 1998.
Contact for enquiries: Mike Owen on 0181 964 5297

**WATERMANS ARTS CENTRE**
**40 High Street, Brentford**
**Admin 0181 847 5651  BO 0181 568 1176**
**Fax 0181 569 8592**
Contact: Performance Officer/Live Arts Team
Policy: Full programme of artistic activity in the Theatre,
Cinema, Gallery, Foyer and Studio, reflecting the social
and cultural mix in West London. Origins: purpose built
by Hounslow Arts Trust, opened in October 1984.
Subsidy: London Borough of Hounslow, LAB and
LBGU funded.
The Arts Centre has a permanent full-time staff
including two technicians. Audiences: Theatre seats
228-239 with removable forestage. Mostly a West
London audience. Cinema seats 126 with small stage
for talks, lectures, etc. (12' x 5').
**TECHNICAL:**
**Stage:** Width at pros 8.73m; Depth 6.35m; Depth with
demountable foerstage (1) 7.70m; Depth with
demountable foerstage (2) 9.38m; Height to pros
4.14m; Height to grid 4.72m.
**Sound:** Soundcraft K1 16-4-2 desk, 2 pairs tannoy
Lynx, 1 pair tannoy Puma, 1 Revox PR99 7.5/15 ips, 1
Tascam 112 cassette deck,1 Tascam 122b cassette
deck, 1 Denon DCD 825 CD player.
**Lighting:** Control: ARRI Impulse 2 with colour monitor,
handheld remote and Reflexion backup console 72
Dimmers @ 2.5k, 8 @ 5k. Lanterns: 10 X Strand
Prelude 28/40 profile spot 650w; 8 X Strand Prelude
16/30 profile spot 650w; 10 X Strand Prelude Fresnel
650w; 8 X Strand Harmony Fresnel 1000w; 6 X Strand
Coda 500/1; 6 X CCT Starlette PC 1000w; 4 X CCT
Minuette PC 650w; 16 X Thomas PAR 64 lantern; 1 X
CCT Silhouette 2000/15 follow spot. All lantrens have
colour frame and safety chain. All Fresnel and PC's
have barn doors.
**General:** 1 Baby Grand Piano (Kawai). Dressing
Rooms: 2 capacity 10. Green Room, Induction loop for
hard of hearing.

**YAA ASANTEWAA ARTS AND COMMUNITY**
**CENTRE**
**1 Chippenham Mews, London W9 2AN**
**Tel/BO 0171 286 1656  Fax 0171 266 0377**
Seats: Theatre 120 max; Main Space 250
Limited hiring. Meeting room also available for hires.
Lighting and sound facilities.

**LOUGHBOROUGH**
**CHARNWOOD ARTS COUNCIL**
**Fearon Hall, Rectory Road, Loughborough,**
**Leics. LE11 1PL**
**Tel 01509 269416**
Contact: Kevin Ryan
Chairman of Charnwood Arts: Keith Stubbs
Tel: 01509 268996
Available venues range from 80 to 500 seats.

**LOWESTOFT**
**SEAGULL THEATRE**
**Morton Road, Lowestoft**
**Tel 01502 562863  Fax 01502 515338**
Contact: Rory Kelsey
Studio Theatre, end Stage. Seats: 108.
Theatre Facilities, Bar, Dressing Room.

**LUTON**
**LUTON COMMUNITY ARTS CENTRE ('33')**
**33 Guildford Street, Luton, Bedfordshire LU1 2NQ**
**Tel 01582 419584  Fax 01582 459401**

Contact: Linda Farrell or Paul Jolly.
**TECHNICAL:**
Cabaret space. 2 spaces both approx 35' long and 14' wide including seating. Equipped with light and sound facilities from a separate technical/projection box with foldback system. Seating is flexible up to a maximum of 70 in ground floor cabaret space which has wheelchair access, and an excellent upright acoustic Yamaha piano. U-Matic & VHS Recording & Edit facilities. Photographic Gallery and Darkroom. '33' has a policy of running workshops in conjunction with exhibitions and performances.
Other Equipment: Upright piano, cinema screen, Sony 50' video projector, U-Matic, V.H.S. Player/Recorders.
Other facilities: Photographic Darkroom, and video Editing. 16 track recording studio with fully comprehensive midi programming suite. Vegetarian Cafe.

**LYMINGTON**
**LYMINGTON COMMUNITY CENTRE**
**New Street, Lymington, Hants SO41 9BQ**
**Tel 01590 672337  Fax 01590 678147**
Director: Mr K. Cromar
Pros. Arch Theatre with 110 fixed tiered seats.
Lighting and sound facilities. 1 Dressing Room.

**MANCHESTER**
**THE FORUM**
**Civic Centre , Leningrad Square, Wythenshawe, Manchester M22 5RT**
**Mgt 0161 935 4073 Fax 0161 935 4092**
Artistic Director: Christopher Honer
For technical details see entry in Provincial Theatre Section.

**THE GREEN ROOM**
**54/56 Whitworth Street West, Manchester M1 5WW**
**Mgt 0161 950 5777  BO 0161 950 5900**
**Fax 0161 950 9776**
General Manager: TBA
Technical Manager: Steve Curtis
Artistic Manager: Bush Hartshorn
Seats: 166
Please see entry in the Provincial Theatres section for a full technical readout.

**ROYAL NORTHERN COLLEGE OF MUSIC**
**124 Oxford Road, Manchester M13 9RD**
**Admin 0161 273 6283  BO 0161 273 4504**
**Fax 0161 273 7611**
Production Manager: Matt English
Resident Stage Manager: Nick McCoy
Administrator: Phillip Jones
For technical details see entry in Provincial Theatre Section.

**MANSFIELD**
**THE OLD LIBRARY**
**Leeming Street, Mansfield, Notts NG18 1NG**
**Tel 01623 635225  Fax 01623 635240**
**e-mail art@nperspex.demon.co.uk**
Artistic Director: Gavin Stride
Buildings Manager: Bryan Angus
Managed by New Persectives Theatre Company.
Fully equipped theatre space with retractable seating (100), large rehearsal room, foyer and exhibition area. Mainly participation based, with some small scale productions..

**MELKSHAM**
**RACHEL FOWLER CENTRE**
**Chapel Court, Melksham, Wiltshire SN12 6EX**
**Tel 01225 702234**

Chairman: Mr A Jackson

**MELTON MOWBRAY**
**MELTON LEISURE CENTRE & THEATRE**
**Asfordby Road, Melton Mowbray, Leics. LG13 OHJ**
**Mgt 01664 67431  BO 01664 69280**
**Fax 01664 410556**
Contact: Richard Smith (ext.127)
Bookings: Linda Hallam (ext.137)
Technical Manager: Paul Duval (ext.126/140)
For technical details see entry in Provincial Theatre Section.

**NEWARK**
**THE PALACE THEATRE**
**Appletongate Newark, Notts, NG24 1JY**
**Admin 01636 71636  BO 01636 71156**
**Fax 01636 701402**
For technical details see entry in Provincial Theatre Section.

**NEWBURY**
**THE ARTS WORKSHOP**
**Northcroft Lane, Newbury, Berks RG13 1BU**
**Tel 01635 47851**
Director: Trish Lee
Full range of activities and art and craft courses plus professional theatre, music and visual arts events. Seating: Main Hall (40' x 27') 60-120; additional upper rooms for studio use and meetings.
Lighting Equipment: Please contact venue for details.
No Sound Equipment . Portable raised seating, no flats, tabs etc. Kodak 2010 Carousel.

**NEWCASTLE UPON TYNE**
**PEOPLE'S THEATRE ARTS GROUP**
**Stephenson Road, Newcastle upon Tyne NE6 5QF**
**BO 0191 265 5020  Greenroom 0191 265 5191**
Honorary Secretary:T Childs
For technical details see entry in Provincial Theatre Section.
**NEWENT**
**NEWENT ARTS CENTRE**
**Ross Road, Newent, Glos. GL18 1BD**
**Tel 01531 820629**
Youth & Community Worker: Nigel Burgess

**NEWPORT Isle of Wight**
**THE QUAY ARTS CENTRE**
**Sea Street, Newport, Isle of Wight PO30 5BD**
**Admin 01983 822490  BO 01983 528825**

**NORTHAMPTON**
**NORTHAMPTON COLLEGE ARTS CENTRE**
**Northampton College, Booth Lane, Northampton NN3 3RF**
**Admin/BO 01604 734218**
Mixed programme of small/middle scale theatre, dance, music, literature and cabaret. Adaptable theatre seats 80, bar and rehearsal facilities.

**NORWICH**
**NORWICH ARTS CENTRE**
**Reeves Yard, St. Benedicts Street, Norwich, Norfolk NR2 4PG**
**Admin 01603 660387  BO 01603 660352**
Centre Manager: Pam Reekie
100-120 seats, variable, raked or raised stage. Converted church with no fixed stage, max. 19' wide x 18' deep. LX Stock Sirrus 48, 9 Fresnels, 5 Profiles, FX Stock RSD 16-8 mixer 9 stage lines. 300 watt max.

**OLDHAM**
**GRANGE ARTS CENTRE**
Rochdale Road, Oldham,
Greater Manchester OL9 6EA
Mgt 0161 624 8012 BO 0161 624 8013
Director: Veronica Conlon
Seats: 84 - 434
For further details see entry in Provincial Theare
Section.

**OXFORD**
**OLD FIRE STATION**
40 George Street, Oxford OX1 2AQ
Mgt 01865 794494 BO 01865 794490
Fax 01865 794491
Managed by Apollo Leisure (UK) Ltd.
Theatre Manager: Ted Doan
Technical Manager: James Wooldridge
183 seat theatre. Open end or traverse. Student Drama
during term time. Premieres of new work during rest of
year.

**PEGASUS THEATRE**
Magdalen Road, Oxford, OX4 1RE
Admin 01865 792209 BO 01865 722851
Fax 01865 204976
For full details see entry in Provincial Theatre Section.

**PAISLEY ARTS CENTRE**
New Street, Paisley, Renfrewshire PA1 1EZ
Tel 0141 887 1010 Fax 0141 887 6300
Contact: John Harding
Receiving venue for professional theatre, comedy,
music (rock & pop, jazz, folk, classical), mime & dance.

**PENZANCE**
**ACORN THEATRE**
Parade Street, Penzance, Cornwall TR18 4BU
Tel/Fax 01736 365520
Project Director: Julia Twomlow
Fenton-Wood Hall: open stage 28' x 14' + 2.6' wings,
capacity 130; Little Theatre: stage 14' x 12' + 6' wings,
capacity 80
Closed for refurbishment. Re-opens summer 1998

**PETERBOROUGH**
**PETERBOROUGH ARTS CENTRE**
Orton Goldhay, Peterborough PE2 5JQ
Tel 01733 237073 Fax 01733 235462
e-mail postmaster@p-arts.demon.co.uk
Arts Development Director: Lynda Wilson
Studio: 120 capacity
Also housing a Gallery

**PONTYPRIDD**
**THE MUNI ARTS CENTRE**
Gelliwastad Road, Pontypridd, Mid Glam CF37 2DP
Admin/BO 01443 485934 Fax 01443 401832
Director: Judith Jones
Multipurpose Arts Centre housing a theatre, cinema, art
gallery, restaurant and two bars. Seating cap. Main
auditorium 355 (tiered seating). Cabaret setting 200.
6.7m x 7.6m stage. Comprehensive lighting and sound
facilities.

**POOLE**
**POOLE ARTS CENTRE**
Poole, Dorset BH15 1UG
Mgt 01202 665334 BO 01202 685222
Fax 01202 670016
Chief Executive: Ruth Eastwood
Programme Director: Alistair Wilkinson
Marketing and Publicity Manager: Brent Ellis
Technical Manager: Robin Cave

Concert Hall, Theatre, Cinema, Art Gallery, Craft
Workshop, Studio, Meeting Rooms, Headquarters
Accommodation for Bournemouth Symphony Orchestra
and Bournemouth Sinfonietta.
Technical details see entry Provincial Theatre Section.

**PORTSMOUTH ARTS CENTRE**
Reginald Road, Southsea, Hants. PO4 9HN
Tel 01705 732236 Fax 01705 734424
Director: Currently vacant.

**POTTERS BAR**
**WYLLYOTTS CENTRE**
Darkes Lane, Potters Bar, Herts. EN6 2HN
Tel 01707 645005 Fax 01707 649849
Centre Manager: Ursula Corcoran
Marketing Manager: Chris Jordan
420 seat, proscenium stage, bar, catering. Cinema,
Conference Rooms availble for hire.

**PRESTON**
**GUILD HALL & CHARTER THEATRE**
Lancaster Road, Preston, Lancs. PR1 1HT
Tel 01772 203456 Fax 01772 881716
General Manager: John Shedwick
For technical details see entry in Provincial Theatre
Section.

**WORDEN ARTS AND CRAFTS CENTRE**
Worden Park, Leyland, Preston, Lancs. PR5 2DJ
Tel/Fax 01772 455908
Contact: Richard Blackburn, Technical Support Officer
Main Hall: Capacity: 90-94, raked.

**THE ARTS CENTRE**
University of Central Lancashire
St. Peter's Square, Fylde Road, Preston PR1 2HE
Tel 01772 893001 Fax 01772 892979
Co-ordinator: Trevor Lloyd
Administrative Assistant: Sondra McEwan
Capacity: 120

**READING**
**THE HEXAGON**
Queens Walk, Reading RG1 7UA
Mgt 0118 939 0390 BO 0118 960 6060
SD 0118 939 0018 Fax 0118 939 0028
e-mail hexagon@beta.reading-bc.gov.uk
Operations Manager: William Brooker
Business Manager: Shirley Britton
Technical Manager: Paul Kennedy
Marketing Manager: Ruth Spicer
Programme Co-ordinator: Ann Brown
For full details see entry in Provincial Theatre Section.

**21 SOUTH STREET**
21 South Street, Reading, Berkshire RG1 4UA
Tel/Fax 0118 950 4911 BO 0118 960 6060
A leisure facility run by Reading Borough Council's
Theatres & Museums Division.
South Street Co-ordinator:Tim Bennett-Goodman
Policy: Professional arts performances and workshop
programme; community use including local arts
performance, functions, meetings etc.
**TECHNICAL:**
Auditorium with open stage (variable size, up to 24ft x
12ft) or floor area 25ft x 25ft, 24 way Strand Action
lighting control and lanterns, PA system. Variable, flat
or tiered seating layout, capacity 125 (220 standing).
Bar in auditorium. Separate bar (MacDevitt's) with area
for music and cabaret performances. Photographic
dark room. Video edit suite opened September 1993.
One large and one small dressing room for

approximately 20.

**ROTHERHAM**
**ROTHERHAM ARTS CENTRE**
**Walker Place, Rotherham, South Yorkshire S65 1JH**
**Tel 01709 823621**
Head of Museums & Arts: Jane Glaister
Arts Centre Manager: Martyn Green

**RUNCORN**
**RUNCORN LIBRARY (ARTS)**
**Shopping City, Runcorn, Cheshire WA7 2PF**
**Tel 01928 715351  Fax 01928 790221**

**ST. ALBANS**
**MALTINGS ARTS THEATRE**
**The Maltings, St. Albans, Herts. AL1 3HL**
**Tel 01727 844222**
Manager: Tony Peters
The centre aims to be a venue for professional touring companies. The programme includes professional theatre and childrens theatre, folk chamber concerts, and many participatory classes and workshops. For technical information see Provincial Theatre Section.

**ST. AUSTELL**
**THE ARTS CENTRE**
**87 Truro Road, St. Austell, Cornwall PL25 5HJ**
Professional programme bookings contact: Phil Webb, Director, Restormel Arts, 14 High Cross Street, St Austell, Cornwall PL25 4AN. Tel: 01726 68532
Theatre has permanent stage, 150 in fixed seats. Lighting Facilities. Basic Sound Equipment. 2 Dressing Rooms. Full Cinema equipment. Additional concert space, seats 50/60, available. Box office splits welcome. Disabled access to theatre.

**SAFFRON WALDEN**
**CORN EXCHANGE ARTS CENTRE**
**2 King Street, Saffron Walden, Essex CB10 1ES**
**Tel 01799 523178  Fax 01799 513642**
Manager: Mrs. J. Crofts
Facilities for theatre, concerts and recitals, film and an art gallery. Audience capacity: 150-200.

**SALISBURY**
**SALISBURY ARTS CENTRE**
**Bedwin Street, Salisbury, Wilts SP1 3UT**
**Tel 01722 321744**
Director: Jill Low
Converted church now used for theatre, music, dance, workshops and exhibitions. Restaurant and licensed bar. Max. s/cap: main area 250, standing 400, other smaller spaces available.

**SCARBOROUGH**
**UNIVERSITY COLLEGE OF SCARBOROUGH**
**The North Riding College, Filey Road,**
**Scarborough, North Yorkshire YO11 3AZ**
**Tel 01723 362392  Fax 01723 370815**
Senior Lecturer, Theatre Studies: Eric Prince
Annual programme of small-scale touring theatre and dance.
Capacity: 150

**SHREWSBURY**
**SHREWSBURY AND DISTRICT ARTS**
**ASSOCIATION**
**The Gateway, Chester Street, Shrewsbury SY1 1NB**
**Tel 01743 361120  Fax 01743 358951**
Flexible, purpose-built studio for small-scale theatre, equipped with collapsible blocks for staging/raked seating. Multi-purpose lighting grid and curtain tracks.

Seating capacity approximately 120.

**SOUTHPORT**
**SOUTHPORT ARTS CENTRE**
**Lord Street, Southport, PR8 1DB**
**Tel 01704 540004  BO 01704 540011**
**Fax 0151 934 2126**
Administration: Lesley Wilson
Two performance spaces, 472 & 260 seat, conventional and variable layouts. Visual Art Gallery, Two Meeting/Rehearsal Rooms, Exhibition space available.
For technical details see entry in Provincial Theatre Section.

**SPALDING**
**SOUTH HOLLAND CENTRE**
**Market Place, Spalding, Lincs. PE11 1SS**
**Tel 01775 725031**
Arts Officer: Nigel Hawkins
Recently refurbished venue. Auditorium with facilities for theatre and cinema. Maximum seats 372. Large function hall, meeting rooms, cafe and bar areas with in-house catering

**STAFFORD**
**THE GATEHOUSE**
**Stafford Gatehouse, Eastgate Street,**
**Stafford ST16 2LT**
**Tel 01785 253595  BO 01785 254653**
**Fax 01785 225622**
Manager: Daniel Shaw
Seats: 570 in one raked tier (reduces to 490 when orchestra pit fully extended); Malcolm Edwards Theatre:End Stage 96, In the Round 116; Cinema-style 120.

**STAMFORD**
**STAMFORD ARTS CENTRE**
**27 St. Mary's Street, Stamford, Lincs. PE9 2DL**
**Mgt 01780 480846  BO 01780 763203**
**Fax 01780 766690**
Manager: David Popple
Seats: Theatre 166; Ballroom 250.
Music, Theatre and Dance. Details from the above. Stamford Arts Centre offers extensive facilities in spacious and historic Georgian premises, set in the finest stone town in England.

**STEVENAGE**
**GORDON CRAIG THEATRE**
**Lytton Way, Stevenage, Herts. SG1 1LZ**
**Mgt 01438 766642  BO 01438 766866**
**Fax 01438 766675**
Director of Leisure Services: M McCardle
Arts & Entertainments Managers: Bob Bustance
Marketing Manager: Maggi Turfrey
Technical Stage Manager: Richard Crumpton
Capacity: 506

**STOCKTON**
**ARC**
**Dovecot Street, Stockton-on-Tees TS18 1LL**
**Tel 01642 611625/611659**
**Fax 01642 613425**
Director: Frank Wilson
Capacity: 150.
Opening November 1998. Theatre facilities: 3 auditoria. Production facilities: Digital studies with facilities & record and screen work in all auditoria.
Policy: We are interested in commissioning work and receiving touring work of a high standard. Guarantees, box office splits and hire all considered.

**SWINDON**
**THE ARTS CENTRE**
**Devizes Road, Swindon, Wilts SN1 4BJ.**
**Tel 01793 466565**
Arts Centre Manager: Clarry Bean
**TECHNICAL:**
Pros. Arch stage with small apron. 228 fixed seats.
Stage area: 6.5m x 7m. Pros opening 6.5m x 3.12m
Access to theatre by stairs only.
Theatre Facilities: Lighting and Sound Equipment: 2 x
Sirius 48 Lighting desks; PEP 1200 sound desk.
Dressing Rooms 2. Green room.

**TAMWORTH**
**TAMWORTH ARTS CENTRE**
**Church Street, Tamworth, Staffordshire B79 7BX**
**Tel 01827 53092  Fax 01827 313044**
Manager: David Kreps

**TAUNTON**
**BREWHOUSE THEATRE & ARTS CENTRE**
**Coal Orchard, Taunton, Somerset TA1 1JL**
**Admin 01823 274608  BO 01823 283244**
**Fax 01823 323116**
Chief Executive: Jim Robertson
Marketing/Press: Deborah Hull Brown
Technical Manager: Sebastian Petit
Full theatre facilities: see entry in Provincial Theatres
Section.

**TORRINGTON**
**THE PLOUGH THEATRE**
**Fore Street, Torrington, Devon EX38 8HQ**
**Tel 01805 622552  BO 01805 624624**
**Fax 01805 623238**
Manager: Paulene Warren
Performance Evening shows regularly start at 8pm
matinees at 2.30pm.
Seats: 132
**TECHNICAL:**
Lighting: 20 assorted lanterns; mains supply 60 amp from
lighting box, or F.O.H.
2 Dressing Rooms accom, total 12 people. Full 35mm
Cinema Projects/Screen and 16mm facility. Two exhibition
spaces/ small meeting rooms. Bar and Kitchen facilities.
PA. Equipment can be supplied by the theatre.

**TOTNES**
**DARTINGTON ARTS & DARTINGTON**
**INTERNATIONAL SUMMER SCHOOL**
**Dartington Hall, Totnes, Devon TQ9 6DE**
**Admin 01803 865864  BO 01803 863073**
**Fax 01803 868108**
Arts Manager: Paul Goddard
Great hall seats 400. Barn Theatre, 180 fixed well-
raked seats (open from April 1997). Two Studios,
seating 100-150. Theatre and film facilities. 3 Dressing
Rooms.

**TUNBRIDGE WELLS**
**TRINITY THEATRE & ARTS CENTRE**
**Church Road, Tunbridge Wells, Kent**
**Admin 01892 525111  BO 01892 544699/544690**
Manager: Les Miller

**WAKEFIELD**
**WAKEFIELD ARTS CENTRE**
**Wakefield College, Thorns Park Centre, Thorns**
**Park, Wakefield WF2 8Q2**
**Tel 01924 789815  Fax 01924 789340**
Administrator: Jayne Oxley
Seats: 222

**WALLINGFORD**
**CORN EXCHANGE**
**Market Place, Wallingford, Oxon OX10 0EG**
**Tel 01491 825000**
Bookings Manager: Patrick Williams (01491 838193)
**TECHNICAL:**
Performance area 8.2m x 6.1m; proscenium; good
flying facilities; wood surface.
Lighting: extensively equipped ESP II two-preset
manual/memory system; 100 amps single phase supply.
Sound Equipment: Allen & Heath 16:8:2 mixer plus full
outboard equipment. 2 Dressing rooms, 8/20.
Auditorium seats 187.

**WALLSEND**
**BUDDLE ARTS CENTRE**
**258b Station Road, Wallsend,**
**Tyne and Wear NE28 8RH**
**Tel 0191 200 7132  Fax 0191 200 7142**
**Minicom 0191 200 7140**
**e-mail buddle@ntynearts.demon.co.uk**
Managed by North Tyneside Arts.
Arts Resources Officer: Geoffrey A. Perkins
Administrator: Pauline Douglas
Theatre (capacity 160 cabaret-style seating),
workshops/rehearsal spaces, gallery, office units.

**WASHINGTON**
**THE ARTS CENTRE, WASHINGTON**
**Biddick Lane, Fatfield, District 7, Washington,**
**Tyne & Wear**
**Mgt/BO 0191 219 3455  Fax 0191 219 3466**
Props: City of Sunderland.
Assistant Director of Community Services: Jeffrey P
Devine
Manager: Marie Kirbyshaw
High Barn used for performances. End stage with
seating for 130, or cleared for informal presentations.
Theatre facilities. 1 Dressing Room. Also Low Barn
ideal for conference and small-scale theatre.

**WATFORD**
**PUMP HOUSE THEATRE AND ARTS CENTRE**
**Local Board Road, Lower High Street, Watford,**
**Herts. WD1 2PJ**
**Tel 01923 241362**
Administrator: April Read
Theatre with open-end stage and nominal proscenium.
Seats 129 on tiered seats. Theatre facilities. 2 Dressing
Rooms. Second auditorium, flat floor seats 100
(movable).

**WATFORD YOUTH ARTS CENTRE**
**Theatreyard, Grosvenor Road, Watford WD1 2QT**
**Tel 01923 233439**
Director: Ian Milton
Regular workshops and productions for 13-25s in
theatre, dance, drama, music, video and visual arts.

**WESTRIDGE**
**WESTRIDGE (Open Centre and Studio)**
**Andover Road, Highclere, Nr. Newbury, Berks**
**RG20 9PJ**
**Tel 01635 253322**
Hon. Director: Dorothy Rose J. Gribble
Showcase for visiting drawing room recitals and
solo/duo drama. Attractive garden setting for outdoor
events. Seats: 24. Comfortable accommodation for
holidays and small study groups.

**WINDSOR COMMUNITY ARTS CENTRE**
**The Old Court, St. Leonards Road, Windsor,**
**Berks SL4 3BL**

**Tel 01753 859421**
Community arts centre. Mixture of professional and
amateur activities, creating a regular all-year round
programme. Premises opened February 1981 suitable
for music of all kinds, poetry, dance, theatre, classes
and courses, children's activities, films.
**TECHNICAL:**
Auditorium: Fixed raked balcony (96 seats) and
retractable seating unit (63 seats). Flat floor stage area
7m x 7m 750, wood block. Studio: 7m750 x 14m,
accommodate up to 100 people. Coffee/Bar area.
Lighting Equipment: AX10M 24/48 2 Preset Board with
DMX 512 output..
Sound Equipment: Mixer MM/MP 180 into 2 channel.
Amp: MM/AP 360 dual channel. Speakers: 2 x 100w,
Projector: Fumeo HD 2000.

**WORCESTER**
**WORCESTER ARTS WORKSHOP**
**21 Sansome Street, Worcester WR1 1UH**
**Tel 01905 21095 Fax 01905 21088**
General Manager: John Denton
Seats: up to 80

**WORKSOP**
**REGAL CENTRE**
**Carlton Road, Worksop, Notts. S8 1PD**
**Tel 01909 474458 BO 01909 482896**
**Fax 01909 472918**
**ADMINISTRATION:**
Props. Bassetlaw District Council
Manager: Julie Lawrence
Assistant Manager: Lorraine Neep
Technical Officer: Steve Crisp.
Policy: Touring, Pantomime, Plays, Variety, Amateur,
Operatic, Orchestral, Pop, Folk, Jazz, Childrens
Shows, Concerts, Films, Dance, One Nighters.
Perfs: As required. Seats: 326
**TECHNICAL:**
**Stage:** Proscenium, Raked 1-24, Pros. opening 8.35m;
height of Pros 4.84m; Depth of S/Line 3.7m, 12 lines,
Hemp; Scenery Flying Ht. 8.90m; flying Bars 8m;
W/Widths P.S. 2.15m O.P. 2.71m.
**Lighting:** Switchboard: Stage Area: There are three on
stage lighting bars. Bar 1 12 Sockets: 12 CCT 650 watt
minuette floods. Bar 2 10 Sockets: 8 CCT 650 watt
minuette floods, 2 par 64s. Bar 3: 3, 4 Bank syke lights.
Dip Sockets: 8 and they are paired. The first four
sockets on bars 1 and 2 are paired going inwards to
centre stage. Leaving four individual sockets on bar 1
and 2 on bar 2. F.O.H.: F.O.H. Stage Bar: 20 sockets,
with 14 minuette floods and barn doors. 6 CCT 650
watt zoom profies. Once again the first 8 sockets are
paired to centre stage leaving 4 individual socekts.
F.O.H. Stage Left, Side bars: 8 individual circuits with 2
CCT 650 watt profiles, 1 par 64 1kw, 2 Sill 30s, 1 Sill
15. F.O.H. Stage Right, Side bars: As stage left. There
are also 2 par 64s 1kw, 2 500 watt Powerblazers, for
use as required. No objection to lights being moved
around to suite the production being staged. Control
Desk: 48 way Sirus Memory Board which is operated
from Control Room at the rear of Theatre Centre Stage.
Follow Spot: One 2kw follow spot and stand.
**Sound Equipment:** H/H 600w amp. 12 Channel
Soundcraft Spirit Mixer with foldback, Tape Deck,
Speakers, F.O.H., Intercom/Dressing Rooms Relay.
Film Equip: 1 x 35mm Projector, 4 track Quadrophonic
Sound. Dressing Rooms: 4 accom. 25.

**YORK**
**YORK ARTS CENTRE**
**Micklegate, York YO1 1JG**
**Admin 01904 642582**

**BO 01904 627129**
Converted Medieval Church used for theatre, music
and dance. Retractable seating for 160 or standing
cap 200 on 3 sides with raked, flexible arrangement.
Theatre Facilities. Dressing Room. Bar.

# SCOTLAND
**ABERDEEN**
**ABERDEEN ARTS CENTRE**
**King Street, Aberdeen AB24 5AA**
**Tel 01224 635208**
Programmes/Venues Manager: Martin L Milne
Administrator: Verna Ward
Asst. Administrator: (evening) Arthur Deans
Full equipped proscenium arch theatre with 350 fixed
raked seats.

**HADDO**
**Haddo House Choral and Operatic Society,**
**Haddo House, Aberdeen AB41 0ER**
**Tel 01651 851770 BO 01651 851111**
Performance auditorium adaptable to proscenium
thrust or platform.
Seats: 400 chairs available.

**AIRDRIE**
**AIRDRIE ARTS CENTRE**
**Anderson Street, Airdrie, Lanarkshire ML6 0AA**
**Tel 01236 755436**
Honorary Secretary: Mrs. D. Patterson
Small Theatre: 169 seats

**BELLSHILL**
**BELLSHILL CULTURAL CENTRE**
**John Street, Bellshill, Lanarkshire ML4 1RJ**
**Admin/BO 01698 267515 Fax 01698 268806**
Manager: Alasdair Bayne
Seats: Main Hall 146; Standing 220.
**TECHNICAL:**
Floor space 160 square metres; Staging: Mirror and
Barre; Picture Rail.
Sound Equipment: Tape, Cassette, Gram. Mics; 4
channels.
Lighting Control: One Act 12.
Green Room. Disabled access.

**CUMBERNAULD**
**CUMBERNAULD THEATRE**
**Kildrum, Cumbernauld G67 2BN**
**Admin 01236 737235 BO 01236 732887**
**Fax 01236 738408**
Artistic Director: Simon Sharkey
Administration: Debbie Murdoch
Drama, Community Drama, Dance, Exhibitions, Films,
Workshops.
Seats 258 (main auditorium), 60 (studio)
Disabled access, disabled toilet, loop system.

**DALKEITH ARTS CENTRE**
**White Hart Street, Dalkeith, Midlothian**
**Tel 0131 663 6986**
Director of Community Services: 1 White Hart Street,
Dalkeith.
Dalkeith Arts Guild Secretary: Mrs. W. Sleater
Performance area with 150 seats in rows. 120 seats for
in-the-round. Limited facilities. No lighting. No Dressing
Room. Piano. Stage made up of 8 blocks.

**DUMFRIES**
**DUMFRIES GUILD OF PLAYERS**
**Theatre Royal, Shakespeare Street, Dumfries**
**DG1 2JH**

Tel 01387 254209

**GRACEFIELD ARTS CENTRE**
**28 Edinburgh Road, Dumfries DG1 1JQ**
**Tel 01387 260445/6 (Arts Association)**
**Fax 01387 253383  e-mail dgaa.demon.co.uk**

**DUNDEE**
**BONAR HALL**
**University of Dundee, Park Place, Dundee DD1 4HN**
**Tel 01382 345466  Fax 01382 345467**
Administrator: Sheena Jack
Capacity 494

**DUDHOPE ARTS CENTRE**
**St. Mary Place, Dundee DD1 5RB**
**Tel 01382 201035  Fax 01382 206574**
Emphasis on community drama, dance, radio, visual
arts and crafts, with a programme of incoming small-
scale touring drama and dance. A well-equipped 112
seat studio theatre, plus arts, crafts, rehearsal rooms
and licensed cafe.

**EDINBURGH**
**CRAIGMILLAR FESTIVAL SOCIETY ARTS CENTRE**
**58 Newcraighall Road, Edinburgh**
**Tel 0131 669 8432**
Organising Secretary: Jack O'Donnell

**THE NETHERBOW**
**43 High Street, Edinburgh EH1 1SR**
**Tel 0131 556 9579  Fax 0131 556 7478**
Director: Donald Smith
Seating 75. Fully equipped. Access for disabled
performers. 1 Dressing Room.

**THEATRE WORKSHOP**
**34 Hamilton Place, Edinburgh EH3 5AX**
**Tel 0131 225 7942  Fax 0131 220 0112**
Director: Robert Rae
Administration Manager: Helen Green
Technical Manager: Allan Woolfe
**TECHNICAL:**
Adaptable hall with flexible seating for 100-200. Studio
Seating for 60. Full lighting and sound equipment.
Dressing room, other arts facilities, cafe, licensed bar.
All areas accessible to disabled.

**ERSKINE**
**PARK MAINS THEATRE**
**Park Mains, Erskine, Renfrewshire PA8 6EY**
**Tel 0141 812 2801  Fax 0141 812 0119**
For Bookings contact the Management Committee
370 seats plus accommodation for three wheelchairs.
Open stage with apron. Apron removable to reveal
small orchestra pit. Rank Strand SP440 2Kw dimmer
board. Facility to patch-in Rank Strand M24 Memory
Desk.
2 Dressing Rooms. Estonia Concert Grand Piano.
Upright Piano.

**GLASGOW**
**CCA**
**Centre for Contemporary Arts**
**350 Sauchiehall Street, Glasgow G2 3JD**
**Admin 0141 332 7521  BO 0141 332 0522**
**Fax 0141 332 3226**
**e-mail gen@cca-glasgow.com**
**Website www.cca-glasgow.com**
Director: Graham McKenzie
Head of Programme: Francis McKee
Technical Manager: Bob Pringle
Press & Marketing: Chris Lord

CCA is one of the UK's premier venues for new art,
offering an innovative and varied programme of
exhibitions, performance, talks and events, by artists
from Britain and abroad. CCA supports artists in
making possible the creation of original work and aims
to increase the accessibility and strengthen the
understanding of contemporary arts through a broad
range of activities including talks, tours, writers' events,
classes and workshops. The centre houses two gallery
spaces, two performance spaces, a cafe-bar and
bookshop.
Spaces within the Centre are available for private hire,
please contact Kevin Meek (House Manager) 0141 332
7521.

**KILMARDINNY HOUSE ARTS CENTRE**
**East Dunbartonshire Council,**
**Arts & Events Service**
**50 Kilmardinny Avenue, Bearsden,**
**Glasgow G61 3NN**
**Tel 0141 931 5084**
Arts & Events Manager: Joan Riddell
Monday - Friday (10-12noon/2-4pm)
Performance area with conventional stage. 140 seats.
Limited theatre facilities.
2 Dressing Rooms, Grand Piano.

**INVERNESS**
**EDEN COURT THEATRE**
**Bishops Road, Inverness IV3 5SA**
**Mgt 01463 239841  BO 01463 234234**
**Fax 01463 713810**
**e-mail ecmail@cali.co.uk**
**Website edencourt.uk.com**
Director: Colin Marr
For technical details see Provincial Theatre Section.

**IRVINE**
**HARBOUR ARTS CENTRE**
**114 - 116 Harbour Street, Irvine, Ayrshire KA12 8PZ**
**Admin 01294 271419  BO 01294 274059**
Chairman: Ian J Dickson
Centre Development Manager: Marie Blackwood
Arts Outreach Worker: Janet Wallace
Small theatre equipped for thrust stage presentations.
Seats 96. Theatre facilities. Dressing Room. Technical
Gallery. T loop.

**LIVINGSTON**
**HOWDEN PARK CENTRE**
**Howden, Livingston, West Lothian  EH54 6AE**
**Tel 01506 433634  Fax 01506 434525**
Contact: Val Bickford
Modern purpose-built Arts Centre designed and
equipped for flexibility of productions and to meet the
highest needs of the theatrical profession. The seating
capacities for the theatre and other accommodations in
the centre are as follows: Theatre — Fixed raked
seating for 276 plus capacity to seat on the level 75
persons when thrust stage not used. Conference Room
— 200 seats; Dining Room — 152 seats. In addition to
the above accommodation there are: 2 Dressing
Rooms, Workshop, Foyer/Box Office, Art Gallery and
Studio, Exhibition Area.

**LOCHGELLY**
**LOCHGELLY CENTRE THEATRE**
**Bank Street, Lochgelly, Fife KY5 9RD**
**Tel 01592 418141  Fax 01592 418080**
Head of Centre: Norman Lockhart
Fully equipped theatre. Seating Capacity in two tiers -
454 seats with 6 additional wheelchair bays.
Please see entry in the Provincial Theatres Section.

**PAISLEY**
**PAISLEY ARTS CENTRE**
**New Street, Paisley PA1 1EZ**
**Tel 0141 887 1010  Fax 0141 887 6300**
Administrators: John Harding, Mike Jones and Gayl
Paterson
Capacity: Theatre 158

**PETERHEAD**
**PETERHEAD COMMUNITY EDUCATION CENTRE**
**Balmoor Terrace, Peterhead, Aberdeenshire**
**AB42 1EP**
**Tel 01779 477277  Fax 01779 471041**
Full theatre facilities. Tiered auditorium with 300 seats.
Proscenium arch stage area 10m x 6.80m. 2 Dressing
Rooms. Wing space either side. Control room rear of
auditorium. Lighting and sound equipment.

**ST. ANDREWS**
**CRAWFORD ARTS CENTRE**
**93 North Street, St. Andrews, Fife KY16 9AL**
**Tel 01334 474610  Fax 01334 479880**
Director: Diana Sykes
Studio Theatre: 5.48 sq.m floor space.
Seats 66. Zero 88 lighting board, 30 channel 3 preset.
Sound equipment.

**STIRLING**
**MACROBERT ARTS CENTRE**
**University of Stirling FK9 4LA Scotland**
**Mgt 01786 467155  BO 01786 461081**
**Fax 01786 451369**
For further details see Provincial Theatre Section.

**WICK**
**LYTH ARTS CENTRE**
**Near Wick KW1 4UD**
**Tel 01955 641270  Fax 01955 641414**
Director: William Wilson
Operates as a venue for touring theatre, music and
dance companies. Open April - September each year,
closed in Winter. Studio theatre 39' x 21' x 15' with
wooden floor, adaptable raked seating for 70, blackout,
some lighting, P.A., excellent Welmar upright piano.
Option for special bar licence and equipped to produce
buffet suppers etc. Some accommodation available at
the centre. Maintains local mailing facilities. Scottish
Arts Council subsidy.

# WALES

**ABERYSTWYTH ARTS CENTRE**
**Penglais Road, Aberystwyth SY23 3DE**
**Admin 01970 622882  BO 01970 623232**
**Fax 01970 622883  Stage Manager: 01970 622892**
For technical details see Provincial Theatre Section.

**BANGOR**
**THEATR GWYNEDD**
**Ffordd Deiniol, Bangor, Gwynedd LL57 2TL**
**Admin 01248 351707  BO 01248 351708**
**Fax 01248 351915**
Director: Dafydd Thomas
Theatre has end stage. 346 fixed seats in one tier. Full
theatre facilities. 4 Dressing Rooms.
See Provincial Theatre Section for full technicnical details.

**BUILTH WELLS**
**WYESIDE ARTS CENTRE**
**Castle Street, Builth Wells, Powys LD2 3BN.**
**Tel 01982 553668 BO 01982 552555**

**Fax 01982 552515**
Multi-use Arts Centre - 2 Auditoria, Gallery.
Director: Jonathan Morgan
Technical Manager: Chris Sennett
**Castle Theatre/Cinema**
End stage 9m x 7m. Fixed seating max. 216.
Two level projection/control room auditorium rear. 2 x
Westrex 35mm projectors. No wing space, limited
height, limited lighting facilities. Bechstein Grand.
**Market Theatre**
Unique performance area 19m x 10m, flat floor, stone
finished interior with alcoves on 3 sides. Max. seating
approx. 250. Usual use: end stage 7m x 10m, raked
seating. Disabled symbols for wheelchair and hard of
hearing.
Rank Strand M24 into 7 ways hard wired. Bechstein
Grand.
For full details please see entry in Provincial Theatre
Section.

**CARDIFF**
**CHAPTER ARTS CENTRE**
**Market Road, Canton, Cardiff,**
**South Glamorgan.CF5 1QE**
**Tel 01222 396061  Fax 01222 225901**
Theatre Director: Gordana Vnuk
**TECHNICAL:**
Studio theatre with retractable seating rake, 96 seats on
rake and 2 removable rows on floor - capacity 120.
Theatre facilities: 2 Dressing Rooms. AHB 16 into 8 into 2
mixer, 4 Tannoy Puma, 2 Tannoy Jaguar, 2 Bose 8022E
speakers. 1 Harrison X1000. 1 x 600, 2 Quad 520F amps.
36 way 3 group, 3 preset DTI multiset with auto preset
(200 memories). 120 outlets on Grid. 16 Dip circuits, 3
Eurolight patch panels (s x 60 amp phases). Good stock of
lanterns. Four rehearsal rooms.
Second equipped studio: capacity 60.

**LLANOVER HALL ARTS CENTRE**
**Romilly Road, Canton, Cardiff CF5 1FH**
**Tel 01222 342022  Fax 01222 384937**
Director: John Lightwood
Performances in converted gymnasium. Seats for
about 150 max., flexible. Operational Theatre Venue,
Educational Arts Centre; Gallery well equipped studio
facilities, Coffee Bar.

**ST DONATS ARTS CENTRE**
**St. Donats Castle, Nr. Llantwit Major,**
**South Glamorgan, CF61 1WF**
**Tel 01446 792151  BO 01446 794848**
**Fax 01446 794711**
Director: David Ambrose
Performance area with flexible staging. Maximum (with
smallest stage size) 225 seats. Seats can be arranged
in "cabaret" style (150 approx.)
Other facilities: very small Gallery — (6m x 5.5m  approx.)

**HARLECH**
**THEATR ARDUDWY**
**Arts Centre, Harlech, Gwynedd**
**Tel 01766 780667  Fax 01766 780778**
Fully equipped Theatre with Licensed bar.
Open stage, seats 266, in curved steeply raked single tiers.

**MILFORD HAVEN**
**TORCH THEATRE**
**St. Peters Road, Milford Haven,**
**Pembrokeshire SA73 2BU**
**Mgt 01646 694192  BO 01646 695267**
**Fax 01646 698919**
Artistic Director: Mike James
For technical details see Provincial Theatre Section.

**MOLD**
**THEATR CLYWD**
**Mold, Flintshire CH7 1YA**
**Mgt 01352 756331  BO 01352 755114**
**Fax 01352 758323**
**email: drama@celtie.co.uk**
For technical details see Provincial Theatre Section.

**NANTYMOEL**
**BERWYN CENTRE**
**Ogwy Street, Nantymoel, Nr. Bridgend,**
**Mid-Glamorgan CF32 7SA**
**Tel 01656 840439  Fax 01656 841393**
Deputy Administrator: Ruth Bees
Theatre capacity: 296

**NEWTOWN**
**THEATR HAFREN**
**Llanidloes Road, Newtown, Powys SY16 4HU**
**Admin 01686 625447 BO 01686 625007**
**Fax 01686 625446**
Administrator: Sara Clutton
Deputy Administrator: Laurence Hanna
Box Office Managers: Liz Healy & Anne Grieve
Technical Manager: Peter Whitehead
Deputy Technical Manager: Nick Johnson Walker

**RHYL**
**RHYL LIBRARY MUSEUM & ARTS CENTRE**
**Church Street, Rhyl, Flintshire LL18 3AA**
**Tel 01745 353814  Fax 01745 331438**
**e-mail rhyllib@dircon.co.uk**
Administrator: Denbighshire County Council. Library
and Information Service.

**SWANSEA**
**TALIESIN ARTS CENTRE**
**Singleton Park, Swansea SA2 8PZ**
**Tel 01792 295438**
Manager: Ms. Sybil Crouch

Technical: David Palmer/Andrew Knight
For full technical details see entry in Provincial Theatre
Section.

**THEATR FELINFACH**
**Felinfach, Llanbr-Pont-Steffan,**
**Ceredigion SA48 8AF**
**Tel 01570 470697  Fax 01570 471030**
Administrator: D Euros Lewis
Capacity: 260

**WREXHAM**
**WREXHAM ARTS CENTRE**
**Rhosddu Road, Wrexham, North Wales  LL11 1AU**
**Tel 01978 261932  Fax 01978 361876**
**e-mail gallery@wrexhamlib.u-net.com**
Visual Arts Officer: Stephen West
Education Officer: Dawn Parry

# NORTHERN IRELAND

**COLERAINE**
**THE UNIVERSITY OF ULSTER**
**Cromore Road, Coleraine**
**Northern Ireland BT52 1SA**
Arts Development Officer: Terence Zeeman
Tel 01265 324449, Fax 01265 324924
Theatre Manager: Janet Mackle Tel 01265 324683
Technical Supervisor: David Coyle
Concert Hall: The Diamond Concert Hall - 1,500 seat
hall with central sprung wooden floor surrounded by
raised concrete plinth - organ.  The Octagon - 500 seat
recital room.  Theatre - The Riverside Theatre (see
entry in Provincial Theatre Section).  Art Galleries  The
Octagon Gallery, the Riverside Theatre Foyer Gallery.

ENGLAND & WALES

LONDON BOROUGHS

SCOTLAND

COUNTY LEISURE DEPARTMENTS

NORTHERN IRELAND

Local Authorities

# LOCAL AUTHORITIES

## ENGLAND & WALES

**Please note: Theatres marked * are not necessarily controlled by the local authority under which they are listed, and are included for location purposes only. See full entries in the Provincial Theatres Section.**

## ALLERDALE Cumbria

Allderdale Borough Council, Allderdale House, Workington, Cumbria CA14 3YJ
Tel 01900 326333 Fax 01900 326346

The following venues all have Sunday Licences and Stage facilities.

**CARNEGIE THEATRE***
Finkle Street, Workington, Cumbria CA14 2BD
Tel/BO 01900 602122 Fax 01900 67143
S/Cap. 360
Manager: Mr. P. Sherwin

**MICHAEL MONROE'S BAR**
Address as Carnegie Theatre (see above)
Tel 01900 602122 Fax 01900 67143
Manager: Mr. P. Sherwin
Standing 200

**MARYPORT CIVIC HALL**
Lower Church Street, Maryport, Cumbria CA15 6LE
Tel 01900 812652
Manager: Paul Sherwin
Contact: Margaret Craig
S/Cap: 400, standing 600.

## ARNOLD Nottinghamshire

Gedling Borough Council, Civic Centre, Arnet Hill Park, Arnold, Nottingham NG5 6LU
Tel 0115 901 3901 Fax 0115 901 3921
Arts Development Officer: Alison Clark
Tel 0115 901 3713 Fax 0115 901 3928

**BONINGTON THEATRE***
Arnold Leisure Centre, High St. Arnold,
Nottingham NG5 7EE
Manager: Mrs Lynda Jordan,
Tel 0115 967 0114 Fax 0115 956 0731

## ARUN West Sussex

**THE WINDMILL ENTERTAINMENT COMPLEX**
The Green, Windmill Road, Littlehampton,
West Sussex BN17 5LM
Tel 01903 724929 Fax 01903 725606
**Administration:**
Complex Manager: Sue Dunn
Deputy Complex Manager: Bob Price
S/Cap: 252.
Amateur shows, community events, one-night stands, Theatres Own Craft Fayres, First Run Feature Films, Conferences and Seminars.

## ASHFIELD Nottinghamshire

Ashfield District Council, Council Offices, Urban Road, Kirkby-in-Ashfield, Nottinghamshire NG17 8DA
Tel 01623 450000 Fax 01623 457587
Community Services, Leisure Division
Tel 01623 457284 Fax 01623 457530
Director of Community Services: Stephen Brown
Assistant Director, Leisure Dept: John Colgan

**FESTIVAL HALL LEISURE CENTRE**
Hodgkinson Road, Kirkby-in-Ashfield NG17 7DJ
Tel 01623 457100 Fax 01623 457099
**Administration:**
Manager: D. Nicholls
S/Cap. Sports Hall 550, Gallery Room 200
Sunday Licence and Stage Facilities.

**SUTTON CENTRE**
High Pavement, Sutton-in-Ashfield, NG17 1EE
Tel 01623 457600 Fax 01623 457606
Sports Hall Bookings: 01623 457666
**Administration:**
Manager: Mr David. Royal
S/Cap. 236
Sunday Licence and Stage Facilities.

**HUCKNALL LEISURE CENTRE**
Linby Road, Hucknall, NG15 7TX
Tel 0115 956 8750 Fax 0115 956 8760
**Administration:**
Acting Manager: Sandra McRobert
S/Cap. 400.
Sunday licence.

**HUTHWAITE LEISURE CENTRE**
New Street, Huthwaite, Sutton-in-Ashfield NG17 2LR
Tel 01623 550076 Fax: 01623 552025
**Administration:**
Manager: Sandra McRobert
S/Cap. 100.
Sunday Licence.

## ASHFORD Kent
Borough Health & Leisure Services Officer:
Ian Kirkland
Ashford Borough Council, Civic Centre, Ashford,
Kent, TN23 1PL
Tel 01233 637311  Fax 01233 645654

**STOUR CENTRE**
Tannery Lane, Ashford, Kent TN23 1PL
Tel 01233 639966  Fax 01233 665791
Manager: John Argent
Multi-purpose Hall (seats 1,300) Thomas Hall (seats 350).

## AYLESBURY VALE, Bucks
Aylesbury Vale District Council, Bearbrook House,
Oxford Road, Aylesbury, Buckinghamshire HP19 3RJ
Tel 01296 585210  Fax 01296 488887

**CIVIC CENTRE, AYLESBURY**
Market Square, Aylesbury, Bucks HP20 1UF
Tel 01296 585527  Fax 01296 392091
Manager: Phil Barker
S/Cap, Reg. Maxwell Hall: 700 seated, 800 dancing and 1,150 standing.  Aston Hall 150 seated or 200 dancing.  Several Meeting Rooms.

## BARNSLEY South Yorkshire
Barnsley Metropolitan Borough Council, Education & Leisure Department, Berneslai Close, Barnsley, South Yorkshire S70 2HS
Tel 01226 773500  Fax 01226 773599

**CIVIC HALL**
See Provincial Venues for details

## BARROW-IN-FURNESS, Cumbria
**FORUM 28**
See Provincial Venues for details

## BASINGSTOKE, Hampshire
Basingstoke and Deane Borough Council
Arts & Heritage Manager.
Civic Offices, London Road, Basingstoke,
Hampshire RG21 4AH
Tel 01256 845736  Fax 01256 845642

**THE ANVIL**
See Provincial Venues for details

**HAYMARKET THEATRE**
See Provincial Venues for details.

## BASSETLAW Nottinghamshire
Bassetlaw District Council
West House, Hundred Acre Lane, Carlton Forest,
Worksop, Notts S81 0TS
Head of Leisure & Amenity Services Manager:
Neil Jackson
Tel 01909 534437  Fax 01909 733769
Principal Leisure Services & Amenities: Richard Mervill
Tel 01909 533486  Fax 01909 733769

**REGAL ARTS CENTRE**
Carlton Road, Worksop, Notts. S80 1PD
Mgt 01909 474458  BO 01909 482896
Fax 01909 472918
Manager: Julie Lawrence
Capacity 326 (Theatre), 153 (Cinema), Music, theatre, dance events, and films.

**BASSETLAW LEISURE CENTRE**
Eastgate, Worksop, Notts S81 OQH
Tel 01909 480164  Fax 01909 530951
**Administration:**
Manager: Tony Lewis
Arena S/Cap: 400 - 700
Orchestral Concerts, Pop Concerts, Exhibitions, Sporting Events.

**BIRCOTES LEISURE CENTRE**
Off Whitehouse Road, Bircotes, Doncaster DN11 8EF
Tel 01302 743979  Fax 01302 751271
Manager: Theresa Hodgkinson
S/Cap: Approx 700 max

**WORKSOP TOWN HALL**
Potter Street, Worksop, Notts S81 2AH
Tel 01909 533533  Fax 01909 501758
Manager: Keith Circuit
S/Cap: Ceres Suite, 200; Assembly Room, 200; Venetian Room, 16.

**RETFORD TOWN HALL**
17b The Square, Retford, Notts DN22 6DB
Tel 01777 706741  Fax 01777 713810
Superintendent: Carl Gibson(0177 713748)
S/Cap: Ballroom, 300; Council Chamber, 80;
Butter Market, 230 (for exhibitions).

**RETFORD LEISURE CENTRE**
West Carr Road, Retford, Notts DN22 7NN
Tel 01777 706500  Fax 01777 705205
Manager: Glynn Davies

**WORKSOP LEISURE CENTRE**
Valley Road, Worksop, Notts S81 7EN
Tel 01909 473937  Fax 01909 530957
Manager: David Rose

## BATH, North Somerset
Bath & North East Somerset Council
Pump Room, Stall Street,
Bath BA1 1LZ
Tel 01225 477000  Fax 01225 477709

**ASSEMBLY ROOMS**
See Provincial Venues for details

**GUILDHALL\***
See Provincial Venues for details

**PAVILION\***
See Provincial Venues for details.

**PUMP ROOMS\***
See Provincial Venues for details

## BEDFORD Bedfordshire
Bedford Borough Council
Borough Arts & Leisure Officer: Mr. J Moore
Town Hall, St. Paul's Square, Bedford MK40 1SJ
Tel 01234 267422  Fax 01234 221606

**BEDFORD CORN EXCHANGE**
St. Paul's Square, Bedford MK40 1SL
Admin 01234 344813  BO 01234 269519
Fax 01234 325358  MKtg 01234 364464
General Manager: Ian Morrison
Operations Manager: Carl Amos
**Main Auditorium**
Multi-purpose venue with staging accommodating up
to 1,000. Offers complete sound and flexible stage
lighting systems. Includes 50 seat Miller and Bunyan
Rooms. Full bar and catering services.

**Howard Room**
S/Cap. 150. No permanent stage. Multi-purpose venue
with bar and catering services available.

**Harpur Suite**
S/Cap. 210. Stage. Stand alone multi-purpose venue
with separate bar. Catering service available.

**CIVIC THEATRE**
S/Cap. 289. Classic Victorian stage. Portable PA and
lighting systems. Bar service.

# BERWICK-UPON-TWEED, Northumberland
Chief Executive: E. O. Cawthorn
Borough Treasurer: Clive Batson
Environmental and Community Services Officer:
Rob Marriner
Council Offices, Wallace Green,
Berwick-upon-Tweed, TD15 1ED
Tel 01289 330044  Fax 01289 330540

# BEVERLEY, East Riding of Yorkshire
Head of Recreational & Contract Services: John Moran
County Hall, Beverley HU17 9BA
Tel 01482 887700  Fax 01482 884940

**HALTEMPRICE LEISURE CENTRE**
Springfield Way, Anlaby, Hull, HU10 6QJ
Tel (Enquiries) 01482 652501  Fax 01482 650577
Centre Manager: S. Stevens.

**HORNSEA FLORAL HALL**
The Esplanade, Hornsea, East Yorkshire, HU18 1NQ
Tel 01964 532919
Manager: Len Cheer
S/Cap: 450. General Purposes Hall, Dance, Theatre,
Trade Fairs, Cafe and Licensed Bar.

# BIRMINGHAM
Director of Leisure and Community Services
P.O. Box 2122, Baskerville House, Broad Street,
Birmingham B1 2NE
Arts Facilities Manager: Neil Johnston
Tel 0121 605 5111  Fax 0121 303 1394

**OLD REP THEATRE**
See Provincial Venues for details

**TOWN HALL, BIRMINGHAM**
Closed for a 3 year refurbishment programme.

**TOWN HALL, SUTTON COLDFIELD**
Upper Clifton Road, Sutton Coldfield, Birmingham
B73 6AB
Tel 0121 355 8990  Fax 0121 355 8255
**Administration:**

Manager: John Finlayson
S/Cap: 404
Concerts, Musicals, Plays, Exhibitions, Dinners,
Dances, Conferences.

For other Birmingham theatres see Provincial Venues.

# BLABY Leicestershire
Countryside & Leisure Officer: Mr M Harris
Council Offices, Narborough, Leicester LE9 5EP
Tel 0116 275 0555  Fax 0116 275 0368

**ENDERBY COMMUNAL HALL**
Queens Drive, Enderby, Leicestershire
Tel 0116 286 3818
Contact: Mrs D Barrow
Stage. S/Cap. 126.

**LITTLETHORPE COMMUNAL HALL**
Biddle Road, Littlethorpe, Leics.
Tel 0116 275 0555 ext.2328
Contact: Martin Wells
No Stage. S/Cap. 140

**ELMESTHORPE SOCIAL CENTRE**
Station Road, Elmesthorpe, Leics.
Tel 01455 842197
Contact: Mrs Joan Rampton
Stage. S/Cap. 126

**HUNCOTE LEISURE CENTRE**
Sportsfield Lane, Huncote LE9 3BN
Tel 0116 275 0246  Fax 0116 286 1851
Manager: Justine Davies
S/Cap. 300. No Stage.

**ENDERBY LEISURE CENTRE**
Mill Lane, Enderby LE9 5NW
Tel 0116 275 0234  Fax 0116 286 1256
Manager: Joanne Smith
S/Cap. 400 max. No Stage.
(Swimming Pool available for Galas)

# BLACKBURN, Lancashire
Director of Community and Leisure Services:
Mr. E. Runswick
General Manager: Mr Geoff Peake
Tel 01254 582579
Entertainments Bookings: Steve Burch
Tel 01254 582579  Fax 01254 667277

**KING GEORGE'S HALL***
Northgate, Blackburn BB2 1AA
S/Cap: 1,853. Standing/Cap: 2,000.
**Technical:**
**Stage:** Open stage. Performing area 16m x 6.5m (to
rise) 3.6m u/s. Floor wood, suitable for all dance.
Demountable pros. arch opening to 44'(W) x 24'(H)
with house tabs. Backstage cross over. Stage heated.
Height of grid 8.25m - 3 Tab Tracks, 8 Hemplines, 3
Tonnes permitted (even) or 1.5 tonnes (point). Black
legs, runner, white cyclorama. Get in via goods lift,
2.5m sq. 3.7 tonne load, tallescope. Scale stage plan
available.
**Lighting:** Jands event plus 96 way board, 100 2KW
circuits, operated from rear of balcony 1 x 200A 3
Phase, 1 x 100A single phase supplies for temporary
board, 31 +32A motor feed 29 spots, 71 fresnels, 188
parcans and 2 Solo 1k follow spots.
**Sound:** Hill Soundmix 24:4:2 desk, operated from rear
of balcony, 10 community CSX 35 PA cabinet

speakers (house), upto 4KW speaker stacks, 8 x ATM, 4 x Beyer, 4 x sennheiser ME80 x 3KU, 5 x TOA and 1 x Samson radio mics. Revox B77 Reel-to-Reel, Teac Cassette Tape systems, H & H Hill PA. Acoustics suitable for music and spoken word.
Stage management prompt corner as required — technical projects cue system, 8 outstations.
**Backstage** 5 en suite dressing rooms, production office, utility room, show-relay, access by stairs/rear of stage — ample power sockets. Refreshments as required. Rehearsal piano, Steinway Model D concert grand. Advice given on accommodation. Staff — casuals available — security personnel available. Backstage facilities not accessible to disabled performers and staff.
**WINDSOR SUITE**
Concert venue/banquet room offering excellent facilities for shows, discos, lectures, dinner functions, etc. Capacity: 584 seated; 750 standing.
**Technical:**
**Stage:** Proscenium Arch. Performing area 12m x 5m — floor sprung wood, suitable for all dance, backstage crossover, stage heated. Height of grid 3.2m (clear) — 3 tab tracks — black runners, legs — back wall used as cyclorama — red drawn house tabs. Get in via goods lift 2.5m sq. 3.7 tonne load.
**Lighting:** Zero 88 eclipse 48 channel board. 36 onstage 2kw circuits, operated from F.O.H. (rear). 100A 3 Phase 60A single phase for temporary board. Lanterns as for King George's Hall.
**Sound:** Hill Soundmix 24-4-2 (portable) desk, operated from rear F.O.H., 1KW EV house PA mics and additional PA as for King George's Hall. Acoustics suitable for music and spoken word.
Stage management: prompt corner as required. Technical projects cue system, 6 outstations.
**Backstage:** 2 dressing rooms, access by stairs, SL and SR power points.
Refreshments as required. Rehearsal piano, Neindorf Grand. Backstage facilities not accessible to disabled performers and staff.

**STUDIO**
Currently undergoing a refit.

## BLACKPOOL Lancashire
Director of Community & Tourism Services:
Terry Gregson
125 Albert Road, Blackpool, Lancashire FY1 4PW
Tel 01253 478002  Fax 01253 478010
Head of Tourism: Mrs J Seddon
Conference and Promotions Manager:
Mrs Caroline Gallagher
1 Clifton Street, Blackpool, Lancashire FY1 1LY
Tel 01253 477477  Fax 01253 478210

## BLAENAU Gwent
Director of Community Services:Robin Morrison
Central Depot, Barleyfield Industrial Estate,
Brynmawr NP3 4YF
Tel 01495 355601  Fax 01495 312357

**THE BEAUFORT THEATRE & BALLROOM**
Beaufort Hill, Ebbw Vale, Blaenau Gwent  NP3 5QQ
Admin/Fax 01495 308996  BO 01495 302112
Arts Development Officer: Geoff Cripps
S/Cap: 381, Beaufort Room; 150, Ballroom.

**METROPOLE THEATRE**
Market Street, Abertillery, Blaenau Gwent NP3

Tel 01495 321724  BO 01495 216563
S/Cap: 420

## BLYTH VALLEY Northumberland
Arts Development Officer: David Garrett
Blyth Valley Leisure Services.Council Offices,
Seaton Delaval, Tyne & Wear NE25 0DX
Tel 01670 542348  Fax 01670 542344

**BLYTH SPORTS CENTRE**
Bolam Avenue, Blyth NE24 5BT
Tel 01670 352943  Fax 01670 368384
Manager: Bill Sharp
S/Cap for concerts: 800

**CONCORDIA LEISURE CENTRE**
Town Centre, Cramlington NE23 6YB
Tel 01670 717423  Fax 01670 590648
Manager: Richard Calvert
S/Cap for Concerts: 700

## BOLTON Greater Manchester
**ALBERT HALLS**
**Albert Hall**
See Provincial Venues for details.
**Festival Hall**
See Provincial Venues for details.

## BOURNEMOUTH Dorset
Director: Kevin Sheehan
Entertainments and Events Manager: Rob Zuradzki
Exeter Road, Bournemouth BH2 5BH
Tel 01202 456400  Fax 01202 456500

**BOURNEMOUTH INTERNATIONAL CENTRE***
See Provincial Venues for details

**PAVILION THEATRE***
See Provincial Venues for details

## BRACKNELL Berkshire
Director of Leisure Services: Vincent Paliczka
Bracknell Forest Borough Council,
Easthampstead House, Town Square, Bracknell,
Berkshire RG12 1AQ
Tel 01344 424642  Fax 01344 352187

**BRACKNELL SPORT & LEISURE CENTRE**
Bagshot Road, Bracknell, RG12 9SE
Tel 01344 454203  Fax 01344 868511
Sport Centre Manager: P. Dodds  Tel 01344 861717
Main Hall S/Cap: 1,000; Function Suite S/Cap: 450.
Sporting Events, Tours, Conference Hall, Exhibitions.
(For information on South Hill Park Arts Centre see entries in Provincial Theatre and Arts Centres section).

## BRADFORD West Yorkshire
Head of Recreation: Jim Mackay
Jacobs Well, Bradford BD1 5RW
Tel 01274 752646  Fax 01274 757646
Theatres General Manager: John Botteley
Tel 01274 752375  Fax 01274 752185

**ALHAMBRA THEATRE***
See Provincial Venues for details

**ST. GEORGE'S HALL**
See Provincial Venues for details.

**BINGLEY ARTS CENTRE**
Main Street, Bingley, West Yorkshire BD16 2LZ
Tel 01274 751576  Fax 01274 751523
**Administration:**
Contact: Mark Davies
S/Cap: 379. Stage Facilities.
One Night Stands, Jazz Concerts & Speciality.

**KINGS HALL/WINTER GARDENS**
22 Station Road, Ilkley, West Yorkshire LS29 8HE
Tel 01274 751576  Fax 01274 751523
**Administration:**
Contact: Mark Davies
S/Cap: 540.
Stage Facilities.
Shows, Conferences, Classical Concerts.

**VICTORIA HALL**
Victoria Park, Hard Ings Road, Keighley,
West Yorks. BD21 3JN
**Administration:**
Booking Contact: Louise Newton, 01535 681763
S/Cap: 550-600
Limited Stage Facilities.
Boxing, Wrestling, Ballroom Dancing, Sporting Events,
Conferences.

**VICTORIA HALL**
Victoria Road, Saltaire, West Yorkshire BD18 3JS
Tel 01274 752375  Fax 01274 751523
Contact: Mark Davies
S/Cap: 500

**KIRKLANDS**
Kirklands Community Centre, 119 Main Street,
Menston, Ilkley, West Yorks
Tel 01943 874335
Booking Contact: Louise Newton on 01535 681763
S/Cap: 200

**QUEENS HALL**
Main Street, Burley-in-Wharfedale, Ilkley, West Yorks.
Tel: 01943 864062
Booking Contact: Louise Newton on 01535 681763
S/Cap: 300

**HOLDEN HALL**
Colne Road, Oakworth, Keighley, West Yorks LS29 7BT
Tel: 01535 644197
Booking Contact: Louise Newton on 01535 681763
S/Cap: 130

**SILSDEN TOWN HALL**
Kirkgate, Silsden, Keighley, West Yorks.BD20 0PB
Tel: 01535 652466
Booking Contact: Louise Newton on 01535 681763
S/Cap: 200

**VICTORIA HALL**
Station Road, Queensbury, Bradford,
West Yorkshire BD13 1AD
Contact: Alison Keddie
Tel 01274 883978
S/Cap: 250

**IAN CLOUGH HALL**
Hall Cliffe, Baildon, Shipley, West Yorkshire BD17 6ND
Tel 01274 752375  Fax 01274 751523
Contact :Mark Davies
S/Cap: 220

**MECHANICS INSTITUTE**
Main Road, Denholme, Bradford,
West Yorkshire BD13 4LN
Tel 01274 833613
Booking Contact: Louise Newton on 01535 681763
S/Cap: 200

# BRAINTREE Essex
Causeway House, Bocking End, Braintree,
Essex CM7 9HB
Tel 01376 552525  Fax 01376 552626
Head of Leisure Services: Denis Housden

**BRAINTREE LEISURE CENTRE**
Pamfield Lane, Braintree, Essex CM7 1FF
Tel: 01376 552585  Fax: 01376 344195
Manager: Andrew Killin

# BRECKLAND Norfolk
The Guildhall, Dereham, Norflok NR19 1EE
Tel 01362 695333  Fax 01362 692582
Chief Executive: Mr. R.N. Garnett
Client Manager for Leisure: Julian Sims

**BRECKLAND SPORTS AND LEISURE CENTRE**
Croxton Road, Thetford, Norfolk IP24 1JD
Tel 01842 753110  Fax 01842 761056
Manager: John Walker

# BRECKNOCK Powys
County Hall, Llandrindod Wells, Powys LD1 5LG
Tel 01597 826469  Fax 01597 826243
Director of Community Leisure & Recreation:
Mr Ian Hill

**STRAND HALL, BUILTH WELLS**
Strand Streeet, Builth Wells, Powys LD2 3AA
Tel 01982 552461
For Bookings Contact: Lil Jarman-Harries  Tel 01982
553535

# BRENTWOOD Essex
All recreational facilities are under the control of the
Director of Community Services: Robert McLintock,
Brentwood Borough Council
Ingrave Road, Brentwood, Essex  CM15 8AY
Tel 01277 261111  Fax 01277 200152

**THE BRENTWOOD CENTRE, THE INTERNATIONAL
HALL\***
See Provincial Venues for details

**OLD HOUSE ARTS AND COMMUNITY CENTRE**
5 Shenfield Road, Brentwood, Essex CM15 8AG
Tel 01277 211827  Fax 01277 217831
Please see entry in Arts Centres Section.

# BRIDGEND Mid-Glamorgan
Sunnyside, Bridgend, CF31 4AR
Tel 01656 642610  Fax 01656 642675
Director of Education, Leisure and Community
Services: David Matthews
**BERWYN CENTRE, NANTYMOEL**
Ogwy Street, Nantymoel, Bridgend CF32 7SD
Tel 01656 840439  Fax 01656 841393
Manager: Mari Major
Theatre Seating Capacity: 296
Art Gallery, Library and purpose built disco.

**GRAND PAVILION, PORTHCAWL**
The Esplanade, Porthcawl, CF36 3YW
Tel 01656 783860  Fax 01656 772111
Manager: Jason Crook
Theatre: Variety, Concerts, Plays, Dances, Opera,
Pantomime.
Seating Capacity for Theatre: 635 / Standing, 1,000
Jubilee Room: Discos, Private Parties, Wedding
Receptions.
Seating Capacity for Jubilee: 100
New Cafe Bar.

**MAESTEG TOWN HALL**
Talbot Street, Maesteg CF34 9DA
Tel 01656 733269  Fax 01656 739546
Dance Hall/Theatre.
Seating Capacity: 650
Contact: David Bostock

**PYLE LEISURE CENTRE**
Helig Fan, Pyle, Bridgend CF33 6BS
Tel 01656 743712  Fax 01656 745875
Site Manager: Ceri Randall
Dance Hall Seating Capacity: 300
Theatre Seating Capacity: 250
Portable staging and movable curtains. Suitable for
Plays, Exhibitions, Meetings, etc.

**BRIDGEND RECREATION CENTRE**
Angel Street, Bridgend CF31 4AH
Tel 01656 657491  Fax 01656 647886
Operations Manager: Mike Payne
Concert Hall and Sports Hall.
Concert Hall Seating Capacity: 500
Stage lighting and dressing rooms.
Sports Hall Seating Capacity: 900

**BLAENGARW WORKMEN'S HALL**
Blaengarw Road, Blaengarw, Bridgend CF32 8AW
Tel 01656 871142  Fax 01656 870507
Manager: Steve Clarke
Variety, Concerts, Plays - Dance Studio and stage
lighting
Seating Capacity: 268

# BRIDGNORTH Shropshire
Westgate, Bridgnorth WV16 5AA
Tel 01746 713100  Fax 01746 764414
Chief Executive & Clerk: Mrs Trudi Elliott, BSc(Econ)

**BRIDGNORTH LEISURE CENTRE**
Northgate, Bridgnorth, Shropshire WV16 4ER
Tel 01746 761541  Fax 01746 768118
Manager: Mike Burnell
Seating Capacity: 500

# BRIDLINGTON, Yorkshire
Entertainments Officer: P.M. Naylor
The Spa Offices, Bridlington YO15 3JH
Tel 01262 678257
Fax 01262 401769

**SPA ROYAL HALL, BRIDLINGTON***
See Provincial Venues for detailsVenue.

**SPA THEATRE, BRIDLINGTON***
See Provincial Venues for details
**LEISURE WORLD**
See Provincial Venues for details

# BRIGHTON & HOVE
## East Sussex
Arts, Recreation and Tourism Services
Kings House, Grand Avenue, Hove BN3 2LS
Director of Arts, Recreation & Tourism: Deborah Grubb
Tel 01273 292530  Fax 01273 292532
Head of Leisure Services: David Fleming
Tel 01273 292700  Fax 01273 292555

**BRIGHTON CENTRE***
See Provincial Venues for details

**DOME COMPLEX**
See Provincial Venues for details
**Dome Theatre***
See Provincial Venues for details
**Corn Exchange**
See Provincial Venues for details
**Pavilion Theatre***
See Provincial Venues for details

**HOVE TOWN HALL**
Norton Road, Hove, East Sussex BN3 4AH
Tel 01273 292910  Fax 01273  292936
Contact: Chris Jones
Seats: Great Hall: 1,300; Banqueting Room: 250.
Reception Room also available.

# BRISTOL
Bristol City Council, Colston House, Colston Street,
Bristol BS1 5AQ
Director of Leisure Services: Stephen Wray
Tel: 0117 922 2632  Fax: 0117 922 3991

**COLSTON HALL***
See Provincial Venues for details

# BROADLAND Norfolk
Thorpe Lodge, Yarmouth Road, Norwich NR7 0DU
Tel 01603 703265  Fax 01603 701859

# BROMSGROVE
## Worcestershire
The Recreation and Tourism Section
The Council House, Burcot Lane,
Bromsgrove, Worcestershire B60 1AA
Head of Recreation & Tourism: Adrian Lowther
Tel 01527 873232  Fax 01527 875660
e-mail daleh@bromsgrove.gov.uk
DX 17279Bromsgrove

# BROXBOURNE Hertfordshire

**BROXBOURNE CIVIC HALL**
High Street, Hoddesdon, Herts EN11 8BE
See Provincial Venues for details (Hoddesdon)

# BROXTOWE Nottinghamshire
Director of Technical & Leisure Services: Mr. P. Davison
Community Development Officer: Mrs Mary Bentley
Directorate of Technical and Leisure Services,
Broxtowe Borough Council, Council Offices, Foster
Avenue, Beeston, Nottingham NG9 1AB
Tel 0115 917 7777  Fax 0115 917 3600

# BURNLEY Lancashire

**BURNLEY MECHANICS**
Manchester Road, Burnley BB11 1JA
Mgt 01282 430005  BO 01282 430055
Fax 01282 457428
General Manager: David Peirce
Seats: 427; Standing: 500

# BURY Lancashire
Metropolitan Borough of Bury
Dept. of Competitive Services, Central Bookings,
3rd Floor, Craig House, Bank Street, Bury,
Lancashire BL9 0DN
Tel 0161 253 5903  Fax 0161 253 5902

**RAMSBOTTOM CIVIC HALL**
Market Place, Ramsbottom BL0 9HT
Tel 01706 822988  Fax 01706 829455
Manager: Muriel Morris
Seating/Capacity: 200

**RADCLIFFE CIVIC HALL**
Thomas Street, Radcliffe, Manchester M26 2UH
Tel 0161 253 7812  Fax 0161 253 7813
**Administration:**
Venue Manager: James Adnams
S/Cap: 400. Bookings for private functions, local
operatics, exhibitions and conferences.  Full
entertainments programme September to June.
Catering facilities and licensed bar.

**LONGFIELD SUITE**
Longfield Centre, Prestwich M25 5AY
Tel 0161 253 7227  Fax 0161 253 7229
**Administration:**
Venue Manager: David Curtis
S/Cap: 400. Bookings for private functions, local
operatic and theatre group productions. Full catering
and bars service.

**ELIZABETHAN SUITE TOWN HALL**
Knowsley Street, Bury, Lancashire BL9 0SW
Tel 0161 253 5196  Fax 0161 253 5198
**Administration:**
Venue Manager: Peter Heath
S/Cap: 350. Bookings for private functions and Civic
Entertainment promotions. Full catering and bars
service.

# CAERPHILLY
Leisure Services Department, Caerphilly Road, Ystrad
Mynach, Hengoed CF82 7EP
Tel 01443 815588  Fax 01443 862153
Principal Leisure Officer: Bill Thompson
Leisure Officer: Alwyn Evans

**BLACKWOOD MINERS INSTITUTE**
High Street, Blackwood, NP2 1BB
Tel 01495 224425  BO 01495 227206
Fax 01495 226457
Manager: Lyn Evans
S/Cap: 404, Main Auditorium.

# CALDERDALE West Yorkshire
Metropolitan Borough of Calderdale, Leisure Services
Department, Wellesley Park, Halifax,
West Yorkshire HX2 0AY
Tel 01422 359454  Fax 01422 342499

Director: Ms Carolyn Downs

**PIECE HALL**
Halifax HX1 1RE
Tel 01422 358087  Fax 01422 349310
Commercial Manager: Mark Humphreys
S/Cap: unlimited. Exhibitions, Outdoor Entertainments
- theatre, bands, etc. Licensed Restaurant, Cafeteria,
Meeting Room, Industrial Museum, Art Gallery &
Tourist Information Centre.

**VICTORIA THEATRE, HALIFAX**
See Provincial Venues for details

**HEBDEN BRIDGE CINEMA**
Tel 01422 351156
Halls Manager: Fi Godfrey Faussett
Available for small theatre productions/concerts.
Saturday morning junior show (Film).

**HEBDEN BRIDGE PUBLIC HALLS**
Tel 01422 358087
Commercial Manager: Mark Humphreys

# CAMBRIDGE Cambridgeshire
The Guildhall, Cambridge CB2 3QJ
Tel 01223 457000
Cambridge City Council Director of Leisure Services:
Ian Cooper  Tel 01223 457502  Fax 01223 457519
Marketing and Promotions Manager: Pauline Haughey
Tel 01223 457510  Fax 01223 457529

**CAMBRIDGE CORN EXCHANGE***
See Provincial Venues for details

**THE GUILDHALL***
To book contact Martin Beaumont
Tel 01223 457000 ext. 7441  Fax 01223 457039
Concert and Dance Hall Seating Capacity: 619
Small Hall Seating Capacity: 200
Lecture and Recital Hall.

**KELSEY KERRIDGE SPORTS HALL**
Queen Anne Terrace, Gonville Place,
Cambridge CB1 1NA
Tel 01223 462226  Fax 01223 462228
Manager: Keith Allison
S/Cap: 1,500
Bookable for concerts, dances and exhibitions.

# CANNOCK CHASE Staffordshire
Head of Leisure Services: Duncan Lowndes
Entertainments and Promotions Officer: Andrea Pugh
Cannock Chase Council, Civic Centre, Beecroft Road,
Cannock, Staffs WS11 1BG
Tel 01543 462621  Fax 01543 462317

**AQUARIUS BALLROOM**
Victoria Street, Hednesford, Staffs WS12 5BT
Tel 01543 422417  Fax 01543 428005
**Administration:**
Manager: Jo Bird
S/Cap: 300 max

**CIVIC SUITE**
Civic Centre, Beecroft Road, Cannock WS11 1BG
Tel 01543 462621  Fax 01543 462317
Halls Manager: Arthur Rails
Bookings: Sue Logan
S/Cap: 375

**CHASE LEISURE CENTRE**
Stafford Road, Cannock WS11 2AL
Manager: Steve Dodd
Tel 01543 504065  Fax 01543 502655
S/Cap: 1,250

**CONISTON HALL**
Cannock Road, Chadsmoor, Cannock
Tel 01543 462621  Fax 01543 462317
**Administration:**
Halls Manager: Arthur Ralls
Bookings: Sue Logan
S/Cap: 140

**PRINCE OF WALES CENTRE\***
Church Street, Cannock.
Tel 01543 578762
Manager: Richard Kay
S/Cap: 439

**PYE GREEN COMMUNITY CENTRE**
Bradbury Lane, Hednesford.
Tel 01543 462621  Fax 01543 462317
**Administration:**
Halls Manager: Arthur Ralls
Bookings: Sue Logan
S/Cap: 100

**ST. MICHAEL'S COMMUNITY CENTRE**
Main Road, Brereton, Rugeley.
Tel 01543 462621  Fax 01543 462317
**Administration:**
Halls Manager: Arthur Ralls
Bookings: Sue Logan
S/Cap: 120

**RUGELEY ROAD PAVILION**
Rugeley Road, Hednesford, Cannock
Tel 01543 462621  Fax 01543 462317
**Administration:**
Halls Manager: Arthur Ralls
Bookings: Sue Logan
S/Cap: 50

**THE RED ROSE THEATRE & COMMUNITY HALL**
Taylors Lane, Rugeley, Staffs WS15 2AA
Tel 01889 576281
Contact: Paul Smith
S/Cap: 210

**HAYES GREEN COMMUNITY CENTRE**
Heath Hayes, Cannock.
Tel 01543 462621  Fax 01543 462317
**Administration:**
Halls Manager: Arthur Ralls
Bookings: Sue Logan
S/Cap: 150

# CANTERBURY Kent
City Estates & Leisure Officer: M. D. Burgess
Council Offices, Military Road, Canterbury, CT1 1YW
Tel 01227 763763  Fax 01227 763727

**THE MARLOWE THEATRE\***
See Provincial Venues for details

**KINGS HALL**
Kings Hall, Herne Bay, East Cliff, Herne Bay
Kent CT6 5JP
Tel 01227 781381  Fax 01227 371514
**Administration:**

Manager: Lawrence Fenlon
S/Cap: 625.
Banqueting, Dances, Exhibitions, Plays, Musicals,
Shows and Revues.

**PIER PAVILION LEISURE CENTRE**
Central Parade, Herne Bay, Kent CT6 5JN
Tel 01227 366921  Fax 01227 742260
S/Cap: 500.
Multi-Purpose Leisure Centre

# CARADON Cornwall
Chief Executive: Jack Neal
Luxstowe House, Liskeard, Cornwall PL14 3DZ
Tel 01579 341000  Fax 01579 341001

**LUX PARK LEISURE CENTRE**
Cold Style Road, Liskeard, Cornwall, PL14 3HZ
Tel 01579 342544  Fax 01579 344435
Manager: Richard Tuxford
S/Cap: Main Hall: approx 600 max.

# CARDIFF
Head of Arts and Cultural Services: Judi Richards
Cardiff County Council, St.David's Hall, The Hayes,
Cardiff CF1 2SH:
Tel 01222 878514  Fax 01222 878517

# CARLISLE Cumbria
Carlisle City Council, Civic Centre, Carlisle CA3 8QG
Clerk & Chief Executive: Rod Brackley
01228 817000  Fax 01228 817048
Director of Leisure: Evan Cartwright
Tel 01228 817351  Fax 01228 817369

**THE SANDS CENTRE**
See Provincial Venues for details

**STANWIX ARTS THEATRE**
Cumbria College of Art, Brampton Road, Carlisle,
Cumbria CA3 9AY
Professional Programme Managed by Carlisle City
Council, The Arts Unit, Tullie House Museum, Castle
St., Carlisle CA3 8TP
Tel 01228 534781  Fax 01228 810249
Contact: Mick North
**Technical:**
Performance space 9.94m x 8.23m; seating 275 raked.
Contact venue for lighting and sound details. 2
dressing rooms; bar and refreshment facilities.
Rehearsal rooms - 2 pianos.

# CARMARTHEN Carmarthenshire
Town Clerk: Mrs C.F Thomas
St. Peter's Civic Hall, Nott Square,
Carmarthen SA31 1PG
Tel 01267 235199  Fax 01267 221607

**AMAN CENTRE\***
See Provincial Venues for details (Ammanford)

**ST. PETER'S CIVIC HALL**
See Provincial Venues for details

# CARRICK Cornwall
Carrick House, Pydar Street, Truro, Cornwall TR1 1EB
Tel 01872 224400  Fax 01872 242104

Head of Tourism, Leisure & Economic Development:
Terry Beckett  Tel 01872 224400  Fax 01872 272239

**THE HALL FOR CORNWALL**
Back Quay, Truro TR1 2LL
Tel 01872 262465  BO 01872 262466
Fax 01872 260246
Artistic & Operations Director: Chris Warner
A multi purpose hall for theatre, concerts, exhibitions,
conferences, sales and private functions. Full technical
facilities and up to 1,000 seats. Four performance
modes, shutting down from 1,000 to 800 to 600 to 400.
Restaurant, cafe and full catering facilities available.

**PRINCESS PAVILION**
Melvill Road, Falmouth TR11 4AR
Tel 01326 311277  Fax 01326 315382
BO 01236 211222
**Administration:**
Manager: R.D. Phipps
S/Cap: 400.
Multi-purpose Hall/Theatre.
Policy: Concerts, Exhibitions, Conferences, etc. Bar
and catering facilities. Full stage and sound facilities.

**TRURO LEISURE CENTRE**
College Road, Truro, Cornwall TR1 3XX
Tel 01872 261628  Fax 01872 261978
Manager: Mrs Sue Popham

# CASTLE MORPETH
# Northumberland
Chief Executive: P. Wilson
Council Offices, The Kylins, Loansdean, Morpeth,
Northumberland NE61 2EQ
Tel 01670 514351  Fax 01670 510348

**STOREY PARK COMMUNITY CENTRE**
St. Mary's Field, Morpeth, Northumberland NE61 2QE
S/Cap: 200. Stage

**TOWN HALL**
Market Place, Morpeth, Northumberland NE61 1LZ
Caretaker: Jim Buchanan  Tel 01670 513438
S/Cap: 380. (Ground floor 200, first floor 180). Stage.

**ST. JAMES COMMUNITY CENTRE**
Wellway, Morpeth, Northumberland NE61 1BN
Caretaker: Sylvia Scott  Tel 01670 518848
Stage. S/Cap: 200.

**HADSTON COMMUNITY CENTRE**
The Precinct, Hadston, Northumberland NE65 9YF
Tel 01670 761034
Caretakers: Gail Shannon  Tel 01670 761241,
Jen Fairburn  Tel 01670 761230
S/Cap: 250.

**RIVERSIDE LEISURE CENTRE**
Newmarket, Morpeth, Northumberland NE61 1PR
Tel 01670 514665  Fax 01670 510169
Manager: Mrs J Binks
S/Cap: 1000

# CASTLE POINT Essex
Civic Halls Manager: T. Clifford
Council Offices, Kiln Road, Thundersley, Benfleet,
Essex SS7 1TF
Tel 01268 882200  Fax 01268 882464

**THE PADDOCKS**
Long Road, Canvey Island, Essex SS8 0JA
Tel 01268 695271  Mgt 01298 882200
Fax 01268 882464
S/Cap: 450 max

**RUNNYMEDE HALL**
Council Offices, Kiln Road, Thundersley, South
Benfleet, Essex SS7 1TF
Management Tel 01268 882200  Fax 01268 882464
S/Cap: 300 approx.

# CEREDIGION
Cultural Services, Education & Community
Services Dept, County Offices, Aberystwyth,
Ceredigion SY23 2DE
Assistant Director: Mr D Geraint Lewis
Tel 01970 633700  Fax 01970 615348

# CHARNWOOD Leicestershire
Admin & Contract Services, Town Hall, Market Place,
Loughborough, Leics. LE11 3EB
Tel 01509 634774

**LOUGHBOROUGH TOWN HALL**
Market Place, Loughborough LE11 3EB
BO 01509 231914  Mgt 01509 634776
Fax 01509 634914
e-mail: townhall@charnwoodbc.gov.uk
528 capacity venue which features a varied
programme including comedy, drama, musicals,
classical music, rock and children's shows. Also
restaurant, cafe and bars. Booking terms are varied
but include box office splits, guarantees and co-
promoting. All the facilities are available for hire.

# CHELMSFORD Essex
Chelmsford Borough Council, Civic Centre,
Duke Street, Chelmsford, Essex CM1 1JE
Tel 01245 606606
Director of Leisure Services: Bernard Mella
Civic Centre, Duke Street, Chelmsford
Tel 01245 490490
Administration Tel: 01245 606635  Fax 01245 606977
Arts/Entertainments Manager: Jim Gillies M.I.L.A.M.
Tel 01245 495248

**CHANCELLOR HALL***
See Provincial Venues for details

**CIVIC THEATRE***
See Provincial Venues for details.

**CRAMPHORN THEATRE***
See Provincial Venues for details

# CHELTENHAM
# Gloucestershire
Head of Festivals and Entertainments: J. P. Tyndall
Town Hall, Imperial Square, Cheltenham,
Glos. GL50 1QA
Tel 01242 521621  Fax 01242 573902

**EVERYMAN THEATRE***
See Provincial Venues for details

**PITTVILLE PUMP ROOM**
See Provincial Venues for details
**PLAYHOUSE THEATRE**

49 Bath Road, Cheltenham, Glos GL53 7HG
Tel 01242 522852
S/Cap: 232. Amateur Theatre

**TOWN HALL\***
See Provincial Venues for details

# CHERWELL Oxfordshire
Chief Executive: G. J. Handley, B.A., M.Sc., M.R.T.P.I.
Head of Leisure Services: Ian Davies
Arts & Tourism Manager: Vicky Hope-Walker, B.A.,
P.G.Dip., D.M.S.
Bodicote House, Bodicote, Banbury, Oxon OX15 4AA
Tel 01295 252535  Fax 01295 270028

# CHESTER Cheshire
Chief Executive: P. Durham, I.P.F.A., F.C.A.A.,
F.B.I.M.
The Forum, Chester CH1 2HS
Tel 01244 324324  Fax 01244 324338

**GATEWAY THEATRE\***
Hamilton Place, Chester CH1 2BH
Tel 01244 344238  BO 01244 340392
Fax 01224 317277
Seats: 440
See entry in Provincial Theatre Section

# CHESTERFIELD Derbyshire
Borough Recreation & Leisure Officer: G. Cass
Recreation & Leisure Department, Queen's Park,
Chesterfield S40 2LD
Tel 01246 345111  Fax 01246 345110

**THE WINDING WHEEL**
13 Holywell Street, Chesterfield S41 7FA
Tel 01246 345333  BO 01246 345334
Fax 01246 345330
S/Cap: 850 Main Auditorium, 550 stalls, 300 circle.;
Ballroom/Recital Room, 300; Function Room, 150.

# CHESTER LE STREET County Durham
Leisure Development Manager: Bill Lightburn
Chester Le Street District Council,
Civic Centre, Newcastle Road, Chester Le Street,
Co Durham DH3 3UT
Tel 0191 387 1919  Fax 0191 387 1583

# CHICHESTER West Sussex
Chichester District Council, East Pallant House,
East Pallant, Chichester, West Sussex PO19 1TY
Arts & Heritage Development Manager: Ann Bone
Tel 01243 785166  Fax 01243 776766
Chichester City Council, The Council House, North
Street, Chichester, West Sussex PO19 1LQ
Tel 01243 788502  Fax 01243 773022

**WESTGATE LEISURE CENTRE**
Cathedral Way, Chichester, West Sussex PO19 1RJ
Tel 01243 785651  Fax 01243 533849
Manager: Kevin McCoy

**ASSEMBLY ROOM & OLD COURTROOM**
The Council House, North Street,
Chichester PO19 1LQ
Tel 01243 788502  Fax 01243 773022

S/Cap: Assembly Room, 185; Old Courtroom, 60.
Available for hire. Contact the Custodians for booking
details.

# CHILTERN Buckinghamshire
Chief Executive & Secretary to Chiltern D.C.:
A Goodrum
Chief Community and Leisure Officer: T. D. Clitherow,
Council Offices, King George V Road, Amersham,
Bucks HP6 5AW
Tel 01494 732019  Fax 01494 586503

# CHORLEY Lancashire
Chorley Borough Council, Astley Hall, Astley Park,
Chorley PR7 1NP
Director of Community Services: R. B. Stagles
Curator: Dr Nigel Wright
Tel 01257 515555  Fax 01257 515556

**LANCASTRIAN SUITE**
Town Hall, Market Street, Chorley, PR7 1DP
Tel 01257 515151  Fax 01257 515150
Management: Roger Handscombe, Head of
Commercial Development for Chorley Borough Council
Bookings Contact: Alison Brandwood
Tel: 01257 515312  Fax 01257 515319
S/Cap: 450 max. Concert Facilities.

**TATTON COMMUNITY CENTRES**
Silverdale Road, Chorley
Tel: 01257 270854
Manager: Liz Morey Tel: 01257 515650
S/Cap: 100. Stage Facilities.

# CHRISTCHURCH, Dorset
Chief Executive & Town Clerk: MA Turvey BA, MBA,
DMS, FMS, MIMgt
Civic Offices, Bridge Street, Christchurch BH23 1AZ
Tel 01202 495000  Fax 01202 482200

# COLCHESTER, Essex
Event Co-Ordinator: Claire Jackson
Community Services, PO Box 331, Town Hall,
Colchester, Essex CO1 1GL
Tel 01206 282946  Fax 01206 282916

**CHARTER HALL**
Colchester Leisure World, Cowdray Avenue,
Colchester, CO1 1YH
Mgt 01206 282946  BO 01206 282020
Fax 01206 282916
S/Cap: 1,200

# COLWYN, Conwy
Director of Tourism and Leisure: Peter Gibson
Conwy County Borough Council Civic Offices,
Colwyn Bay LL29 8AR
Tel 01492 575374  Fax 01492 513664

**THEATRE COLWYN**
Abergele Road, Colwyn Bay, Conwy LL29 7RU
BO 01492 532668  SD 01492 530892
Fax 01492 533971
Events Manager: Philip Batty
S/Cap: 434

# CONNAH'S QUAY, Flintshire

**CIVIC HALL, CONNAH'S QUAY**
Wepre Drive, Connah`s Quay, Deeside,
Flintshire CH5 4HB
Correspondence Address: Connah`s Quay Town
Council Offices, Greenacre, Wepre Drive, Connah`s
Quay, Deeside, Flintshire CH5 4HB
Civic Hall 01244 811102
Council Offiices 01244 819420
**Administration:**
Controlled by Connah's Quay Town Council; full
catering/bars facilities by arrangement with on-site
Lessees.
Contact: D.A.Cooper, Clerk + Financial Officer
Tours, Variety, Dances all Catering Functions,
Conferences.
**Technical:**
S/Cap 500. Stage Width 7.32m, Ht. 5.49m, Stage Left
3.66m, Stage Right 5.49m. Electrics: Voltage 230-250
with additional range of supply. 28 Circuits; Wattage
10,000; F.O.H. Spot Bars 4; Batten Floods on Batten
Bar 9; Batten Floods on back stage reserve 3; Wing
Floods 2. Licensed Bar and Cafe facilities available.
Dressing Rooms 3. Separate Lounge available. S/Cap 50.

# CONGLETON Cheshire

Amenities Services Manager: Bob Hardiker
Arts Development Officer: Carole MacGregor
Amenities Dept, Community Services, Council Offices,
Westfields, Middlewich Road, Sandbach CW11 1HZ
Tel 01270 763231  Fax 01270 768460

**TOWN HALL, CONGLETON**
High Street, Congleton, Cheshire CW12 1BN
Tel 01270 290771
Town Hall Manager: Jack Wimpenny
Contact: Frank Macintosh
Catering Manager: David Hughes
Community Development Manager: Jo Money
S/Cap with stage extension 430, without 472 (disabled
access).
Main Hall with stage, bar facilities, etc.

**TOWN HALL, SANDBACH**
High Street, Sandbach, Cheshire
Tel 01270 762885
For bookings contact Barry Johnson.
Tel 01270 763231  Fax 01270 768460
S/Cap with stage extension 200, without 240 (disabled
access).
Main Hall with stage, bar facilities, etc.

**CIVIC CENTRE, ALSAGER**
Newcastle Road, Alsager, Cheshire ST7 2AE
Tel 01270 873116/875354
For Bookings Contact Barry Johnson
Tel 01270 763231  Fax 01270 768460
S/Cap 350 (disabled access).
Main Hall with stage, bar facilities, etc.

**CIVIC HALL, MIDDLEWICH**
Civic Way, Middlewich, Cheshire CW10 9AT
Tel 01606 837175
For Bookings contact Barry Johnson
Tel 01270 763231  Fax 01270 768460
Contact: Neil Brooker
S/Cap 300 (disabled access).
Main Hall with stage, bar facilities, etc.

# COPELAND Cumbria

Council Offices, Catherine Street, Whitehaven,
Cumbria CA28 7NY
Tel 01946 852585  Fax 01946 852791
Leisure Manager: M. Beveridge
(Tel/Fax 01946 590089)

**WHITEHAVEN CIVIC HALL***
See Provincial Venues for details (Solway Civic Theatre)

**CLEATOR MOOR CIVIC HALL**
The Square, Cleator Moor, Cumbria CA25 5AR
Tel/Fax 01946 810176
S/Cap: 250
Stage and Lighting Facilities. Dressing Rooms, Bar
and Refreshments.

**EGREMONT MARKET HALL**
Market Street, Egremont CA22 2DF
Tel 01946 820254
**Administration:**
Contact: Margaret Woodburn
S/Cap: 200 - 300
Stage and Lighting Facilities. Dressing Rooms. Bar
and Refreshments.

# CORBY Northamptonshire

Corby Borough Council, Grosvenor House, George
Street, Corby, Northamptonshire
Director of Leisure Services: Chris Stephenson
Tel 01543 402551  Fax 01543 206757

**FESTIVAL HALL**
**THEATRE/CINEMA**
**WILLOW ROOM**
George Street, Corby, Northamptonshire  NN17 1QB
Tel 01536 402551  BO 01536 402233
Fax 01536 400200
**Administration:**
Props: Corby Borough Council
Gemeral Manager: Charles L Sanders
Operations Manager: Ted Blair
Technical Manager: Duncan Mitchell
Catering Manager: Mike Green
Policy: Multi-Purpose Arts and Entertainment Centre
able to stage arts, entertainment, cinema, conferences,
exhibitions, catering events and functions.
Capacities: Festival Hall: 690 stalls, 274 balcony in
theatre style.  Theatre/Cinema: 490 seats. Willow
Room: 300 standing, 150 cabaret style.
**Technical:**
**Festival Hall**: 48ft wide x 18ft deep stage, front 9ft
made up of 6ft x 3ft x 1.5ft blocks able to be configured
to suit requirements. Basic theatre lighting and sound
system upgraded 1997.
**Theatre/Cinema**: 30ft x 30ft proscenium arch stage
with street level access. Full lighting rig and sound
system. Orchestra pit for up to 20 and baby grand
piano located on stage or in pit as required. Video
cinema with 14ft screen.

# COTSWOLD Gloucestershire

Director of Community Services: Andrew Grant
Trinity Road, Cirencester, Glos GL7 1PX
Tel 01285 643643  Fax 01285 657334

**COTSWOLD LEISURE CENTRE**
Tetbury Road, Cirencester, Glos. GL7 1US
Tel 01285 654057  Fax 01285 655763
Contact: Ian Green

**ADMINISTRATION:**
Props: Cotswold Leisure Services Ltd
Abberley House, Park Street, Cirencester,
Glos GL7 2BX
Tel 01285 640349  Fax 01285 653713
Leisure Centre Hall Capacity: approx 600

**THE CORN HALL**
Market Place, Cirencester, Glos
Contact: Margaret Mernagh
ADMINISTRATION:
Props: Cotsworld Leisure Services Ltd
Abberley House, Park Street, Cirencester,
Glos GL7 2BX
Cornhall Capacity: 300 (Theatre style)

# COVENTRY West Midlands
Council House, Coventry CV1 5RR
Tel 01203 833333
Chief Executive & Town Clerk: Iain Roxburgh
Tel 01203 831100  Fax 01203 833680

**BELGRADE THEATRE***
See Provincial Venues for details

# CRAVEN North Yorkshire
Craven District Council, 9 High Street, Skipton,
North Yorkshire BD23 1AB
Tel 01756 700600  Fax 01756 700658
Arts Development Officer: Liz Humphry-Williams
Tel 01756 706408

**SKIPTON TOWN HALL**
High Street, Skipton, North Yorkshire
Caretaker: Tony Beck  Tel 01756 706322
Bookings contact Rachel Hall, Craven District Council,
Granville Street, Skipton, North Yorks.BD23 1PS
Tel 01756 706313  Fax 01756 700658
S/Cap: approx 350. Stage.

# CRAWLEY West Sussex
Theatre & Arts Manager: Kevin Eason
Hawth Avenue, Crawley RH10 6YZ
Tel 01293 552941  Fax 01293 533362

**CRAWLEY LEISURE CENTRE**
Haslett Avenue, Crawley RH10 1TS
Tel 01293 537431  Fax 01293 523750
Bookings: Dave Watmore
Tel 01293 552941  Fax 01293 533362
Fully Equipped. Large Capacity Venue. Max. capacity
1,700 seated concert, 2,400 standing concert -
available for one-night stand concerts, rock concerts,
light entertainments, major sporting events, fairs,
exhibitions, etc.

**BEWBUSH LEISURE CENTRE**
Breezehurst Drive, Bewbush, Crawley RH11 6AB
Tel 01293 546477  Fax 01293 545225
Bookings: Dave Watmore
Tel 01293 552941  Fax 01293 533362
Large capacity Sports Hall. Max. capacity 1,200 seated
concert. Available for one night stands, concerts, rock
concerts, exhibitions, etc.

**THE HAWTH***
See Provincial Venues for details

# CREWE & NANTWICH Cheshire
Head of Leisure: Byron J. Davies
Delamere House, Delamere Street, Crewe,
Cheshire .CW1 2JZ
Tel 01270 537249  Fax 01270 537757

**LYCEUM THEATRE, CREWE***
See Provincial Venues for details

**CIVIC HALL, NANTWICH***
Market Street, Nantwich, Cheshire CW5 5DG
Tel 01270 628633  Fax 01270 537369
Contact: Kaye Hollinshead

**VICTORIA COMMUNITY CENTRE, CREWE***
West Street, Crewe ,Cheshire CW1 2PZ
Tel 01270 211422  Fax 01270 537960
Contact: Elly McFahn

**CROWSFOOT COMMUNITY CENTRE**
Crowsfoot Lane, off Beam Street, Nantwich,
Cheshire CW5 5DR
Tel 01270 629665  Fax 01270 537369
Contact: Kaye Hollinshead

**COPPENHALL LEISURE CENTRE**
Coronation Street, Crewe, Cheshire CW1 4DJ
Tel 01270 585698  Fax 01270 250681
Contact: Edward Braney

**SHAVINGTON LEISURE CENTRE**
Rope Lane, Shavington, Cheshire CW2 5DJ
Tel 01270 663221  Fax 01270 650773
Contact:Gerald Baldwin

# DACORUM, Hertfordshire
Chief Executive: Keith Hunt
Director of Community & Leisure: Mrs. C. M. Pedlow,
Civic Centre, Hemel Hempstead, Herts HP1 1HH
Tel 01442 228500  Fax 01442 228618

**PAVILION, HEMEL HEMPSTEAD***
See Provincial Venues for details

**HEMEL HEMPSTEAD OLD TOWNHALL
ARTS CENTRE**
High Street, Hemel Hempstead, Herts.HP1 3AE
Tel 01442 228095  BO 01442 228091
Fax 01442 234072
General Manager: Sarah Railson
Seating Capacity 120. Raked audit. Flat Performance
area 25' x 25'.
Full stage lighting available.

**CIVIC CENTRE, BERKHAMSTED**
High Street, Berkhampstead, Hertfordshire HP4 3HB
Tel 01442 228917
Contact: Sue Geraghty
Pros. arch stage. S/Cap: 250 for Shows, Dances,
Rehearsal Room. Private hiring - dances, meetings,
exhibitions, etc.

**VICTORIA HALL, TRING**
Akeman Street, Tring, Hertfordshire HP23 6AA
Tel 01442 228951  Fax 01442 823001
Manager: Edward Dean
S/Cap: 350 Local Amateur Productions, Meetings. Two
Halls and Meeting Room. Private Hire, Weddings,
Banquets, Community use.

## DARLINGTON Co. Durham
Vicarge Road, Darlington, County Durham DL1 1JW
Tel 01325 380880  Fax 01325 486987
Director of Contract Services: C. J. Brown
Head of Theatre & Arts: Peter Cutchie

**DARLINGTON CIVIC THEATRE***
See Provincial Venues for details

**DARLINGTON ARTS CENTRE**
Vane Terrace, Darlington DL3 7AX
Admin 01325 483271  BO 01325 486555
Fax 01325 365794
Theatre seating between 140 and 350 in flexible
layouts.

**DOLPHIN CENTRE***
Horsemarket, Darlington, County Durham DL1 5RP
Tel: 01325 388406  Fax 01325 369400
Sports and Recreational facilities. Banqueting hall and
smaller rooms suitable for meetings and lectures. In-
house catering and bar service. For full details apply to
Leisure Contract Manager: Terry Collins.

## DAVENTRY Northants
Arts Officer: Sonia Hawes
Leisure and Community Services,
Daventry District Council, Lodge Road,
Daventry, Northants NN11 5AF
Tel 01327 302482  Fax 01327 703823

**DAVENTRY LEISURE CENTRE**
Lodge Road, Daventry, Northants NN11 5AF
Tel 01327 871144  Fax 01327 301686
Manager: Phil Steele
Saxon Suite: 320

## DENBIGHSHIRE
Chief Executive: H.V. Thomas
Council Offices, Wynnstay Road, Ruthin,
Denbighshire  LL15 1YN
Tel 01824 706000  Fax 01824 706137
Head of Tourism & Leisure: Lloyd Conaway
Russell House, Churton Road, Rhyl,
Denbighshire LL18 3DP
Tel 01824 706410  Fax 01745 344516

**CORWEN PAVILION**
London Road, Corwen, Denbighshire LL21 9RW
Tel 01490 412600
Manager: Adrian Roberts
S/Cap: 1,250
Stage and Lighting Facilities.

**PAVILION THEATRE***
See Provincial Venues for details

**NOVA, Prestatyn***
See Provincial Venues for details

**THE SCALA CINEMA/ARTS CENTRE**
High Street, Prestatyn, Denbighshire
Tel 01745 854365  Fax 01745 886850
Contact: Gary Jones

**LITTLE THEATRE***
See Provincial Venues for details

## DERBYSHIRE DALES
## Derbyshire
Chief Executive: Mr. D. Wheatcroft
Town Hall, Bank Road, Matlock, Derbyshire DE4 3NN
Tel 01629 580580  Fax 01629 580482

## DERBY Derbyshire
The following halls all have Sunday licence and Stage
Facilities.

**ASSEMBLY ROOMS***
See Provincial Venues for details

**DARWIN SUITE**
See Provincial Venues for details

**GUILDHALL THEATRE**
See Provincial Venues for details

## DERWENTSIDE, Co Durham
Civic Centre, Consett, Co. Durham DH8 5JA
Director of Community Services: Mike Clark
Tel 01207 218000  Fax 218302

**CONSETT CIVIC HALL**
Medomsley Road, Consett, County Durham DH8 5JA
Tel 01207 218191  Fax 01207 218200
Manager: Mr. D. Barrett
Dances, receptions, concerts, Meetings.

**STANLEY CIVIC HALL**
Front Street, Stanley, County Durham DH9 0NA
Tel 01207 218899  Fax 01207 284035
Manager: Sandra Lathbury
S/Cap: (inc. balcony) 430. Multi-purpose hall for
Concerts, Theatre, Cinema, Dances and Receptions.

**EMPIRE THEATRE, CONSETT**
Front Street, Consett, County Durham DH8 5AB
Tel 01207 218171
Manager: Mrs. A. D. Northwood
S/Cap: 535. Theatre, Cinema, Concerts.

## DONCASTER South Yorkshire
Council House, Doncaster, South Yorkshire DN1 3AF
Tel 01302 737320  Fax 01302 737309

**DONCASTER CIVIC THEATRE**
Waterdale, Doncaster DN1 3ET
Tel 01302 342349  Fax 01302 367223
Manager: Jeremy Hartill
S/Cap: 511
8 Dressing Rooms, 2 Showers, Daily Luncheon
Restaurant, Orchestra Pit, Professional Ent., Amateur
Productions, One Night Stands, Conferences.
Available for private hire.

## DOVER Kent
Director of Economic Development: Mr. R. Madge
Event Co-ordinator: Donna Sowerby
Dover District Council, White Cliffs Business Park,
Dover, Kent CT16 3PD
Tel 01304 821199  Fax 01304 872062

**DOVER TOWN HALL**
Biggin Street, Dover CT16 1DL
Tel/Fax 01304 201200
Manager: Trevor S. Jones

S/Cap: 600. Public Meetings, Conferences, Local Amateurs, Dances, Banquets, etc.

# DUDLEY West Midlands
Dudley Planning & Leisure Department,
Claughton House, Blowers Green Road,
Dudley, West Midlands, DY2 8UZ
Tel 01384 815521 Fax 01384 815599

**BRIERLEY HILL CIVIC HALL**
Bank Street, Brierley Hill, West Midlands DY5 3DA
Tel 01384 812900  Fax 01384 812370
S/Cap: 741
Contact: John WIlliams

**DUDLEY TOWN HALL**
See Provincial Venues for details

**NETHERTON ARTS CENTRE**
See Provincial Venues for details

**STOURBRIDGE TOWN HALL**
Crown Centre, Stourbridge DY8 1YE
Tel 01384 812948  Fax 01384 812946
Contact: Laurence Hanna
S/Cap: 650

**CORNBOW HALL**
Hagley Street, Halesowen
Tel: 01384 812800
Contact: Paul Dodge
S/Cap: 384

# DURHAM, Co. Durham
87 Claypath, Durham DH1 1RG
Tel 0191 386 6111  Fax 0191 384 8543
Deputy Director of Technical & Leisure Services: Keith Walton

# EASINGTON, Co. Durham
Community Development Officer: David Moore
Council Offices, Seaside Lane, Easington Village,
Peterlee, Co. Durham, SR8 3TN
Tel 0191 527 0501  Fax 0191 527 3868
Economic & Tourism Development Office: Adam Sutherland

**PETERLEE LEISURE CENTRE**
St Cuthbert`s Road, Peterlee, Co. Durham SR8 1AF
Tel 0191 586 2400  Fax 0191 586 5479
**Administration:**
Manager: Paul Irwin
S/Cap: 1,500.
Multi-use Leisure Centre. Conferences, Exhibitions, Dances, Sporting Events.

**SEAHAM LEISURE CENTRE**
Daneside Recreation Ground, Daneside, Seaham, Co Durham SR7 8AD
Tel 0191 581 6366  Admin 0191 581 6788
Fax 0191 581 6852
Manager: Julia Berrystone
S/Cap: 300. Multi-use Leisure Centre. Conferences, Exhibitions, Dances, Sporting Events.

# EASTBOURNE East Sussex
Department of Tourism & Community Services,
College Road, Eastbourne, East Sussex BN21 4JJ

Tel 01323 415401  Fax 01323 638686
Director: Ronald G. Cussons

**THE CONGRESS THEATRE\***
See Provincial Venues for details

**DEVONSHIRE PARK THEATRE\***
See Provincial Venues for details

**WINTER GARDEN\***
See Provincial Venues for details

# EAST CAMBRIDGESHIRE
## Cambridgeshire
The Grange, Nutholt Road, Ely,
Cambridgeshire CB7 4PL
Tel 01353 665555  Fax 01353 668819
Economic & Community Development Officer: Ray Harding

**THE MALTINGS PUBLIC HALL, CONFERENCE & BANQUETING CENTRE**
Ship Lane, Ely, Cambs CB7 4BB
Tel 01353 662633  Fax 01353 669379
Manager: Mrs T. Ingram
S/Cap: 330

# EAST DEVON Devon
Chief Executive: F. J. Vallender, LL.B., Solicitor.
Council Offices, Knowle, Sidmouth, Devon EX10 9RX
Tel 01395 516551 ext 401  Fax 01395 577853

**EXMOUTH PAVILION**
S/Cap: 400. Dancing, Summer Shows, Operatic Society and Exmouth Players Productions, Conferences and Exhibitions.

**SIDMOUTH MANOR PAVILION\***
See Provincial Venues for details

**SEATON TOWN HALL**
S/Cap: 276
Stage productions, concerts, exhibitions, dances, excellent stage and auditorium facilities.

# EAST HAMPSHIRE
East Hampshire District Council
Community and Leisure Services Division
Penns Place, Petersfield, Hants. GU31 4EX
Tel 01730 266551  Fax 01730 234385

# EAST HERTFORDSHIRE
## Hertfordshire
Leisure Services Officer: Mr. T. Osborne
East Hertfordshire District Council Leisure Division,
PO Box 103, Wallfields, Pegs Lane, Hertford,
Herts SG13 8EQ
Tel 01279 655261  Fax 01992 554877

**CASTLE HALL**
The Wash, Hertford, Herts SG14 1PS
Tel 01992 589024  Fax 01992 589025
BO 01992 589026
Manager: Eoin Baird
Seats: 500; standing: 600.
**Technical:**
Full Stage Facilities. Pros. Width 10.23m. Ht. 4.86m.

Depth of Stage 9m. Ht. to Grid 11.96m, 3-level lift - Stage level (apron), Floor level or as Orchestra Pit, Own Scenery Dock. 72 way Strand M.24 Memory control desk. 4 Dressing Rooms.

## EASTLEIGH Hampshire
Arts Officer: Cheryl Butler
Civic Offices, Leigh Road, Eastleigh, Hants SO50 9YN
Tel 01703 614646  Fax 01703 629466

### THE POINT DANCE & ARTS CENTRE
The Point, Town Hall Centre, Leigh Road,
Eastleigh SO50 9DE
Mgt 01703 629226  BO 01703 652333
Fax 01703 641261
Manager: Mary Dawson
S/Cap: 318. Stage Facilities.

### FLEMING PARK LEISURE CENTRE
Passfield Avenue, Eastleigh SO50 9NL
Tel 01703 641555  Fax 01703 629248
Manager: Richard Millard
S/Cap: 980

## EAST LINDSEY Lincolnshire
Tedder Hall, Manby Park, Louth, Lincolnshire LN11 8UP
Tel 01507 601111/329411  Fax 01507 327149
Head of Leisure & Tourism: Bob Suich

### DUNES FAMILY ENTERTAINMENT CENTRE, MABELTHORPE*
Central Promenade, Mablethorpe, Lincs LN12 1RG
Tel 01507 472496  Fax 01507 478765
Hall Bookings: Bob Suich, 01507 601111 ext.471

### EMBASSY CENTRE, SKEGNESS*
Grand Parade, Skegness, Lincs PE25 2UG
Mgt 01754 768444  BO 01754 768333
Fax 01754 761737
Hall Bookings: Bob Suich, 01507 601111 ext.471

### FESTIVAL PAVILION, SKEGNESS*
Tower Esplanade, Skegness, Lincs
BO 01754 768333  Fax 01754 761737
Hall Bookings: Bob Suich, 01507 601111

## EAST STAFFORDSHIRE Staffordshire
Town Hall, Burton-upon-Trent, Staffordshire
Tel 01283 508000  Fax 01283 508388
Head of Leisure: J. White
Arts Officer: Alison Betteridge
Midland Grain Warehouse, Derby Street,
Burton-upon-Trent,Staffordshire DE14 2JJ
Tel 01283 508656  Fax 01283 508388

### BURTON TOWN HALL
King Edward Place, Burton-upon-Trent,
Staffordshire DE14 2EB
Tel 01283 508458
For bookings contact Caroline Berwick
Tel 01283 508548  Fax 01283 508733
Seating/Capacity 557 (concerts)
Also available for weddings, dinner dances, exhibitions and conferences. Separate facilities are available in The Lingen Room and The Rochefort Room.

## EDEN Cumbria
Chief Executive: I. W. Bruce

Town Hall, Penrith, Cumbria CA11 7QF
Tel 01768 864671  Fax 01768 890470
e-mail chief.exec@eden.gov.uk

## ELLESMERE PORT Cheshire
Chief Executive & Town Clerk: S. Ewbank, L.L.B., F.B.I.M.
Borough Leisure, Tourism & Amenities Officer:
P. A. Hearfield, B.Sc., (Econ.), D.M.A., M.I.L.A.M.
Council Offices, 4 Civic Way, Ellesmere Port, South Wirral L65 0BE
Tel 0151 356 6789  Fax 0151 355 0508

### ELLESMERE PORT, CIVIC HALL
Civic Way, Ellesmere Port, South Wirral L65 0BE
Tel 0151 356 6780  Fax 0151 355 0508
Contact: Miles Veitch
S/Cap: 636. Multi-purpose Hall.

### E.P.I.C. LEISURE CENTRE
McGarva Way, Ellesmere Port, South Wirral L65 9HH
Tel 0151 355 6432  Fax 0151 356 5886
Manager: Anji Jackson
Multi-purpose Sports Hall and Cinema

### NESTON CIVIC HALL
Hinderton Road, Neston, South Wirral L64 9PE
Tel 0151 336 1077  Fax 0515 353 8223
Manager: Trudi Harris
S/Cap: 250. Multi-purpose Hall

## ELMBRIDGE Surrey
Head of Leisure and Community Services: Ivy Harris
Civic Centre, High Street, Esher, Surrey  KT10 9SD
Tel 01372 474568/474474
Fax 01372 474939

### THE PLAYHOUSE
Hurst Grove, Walton-on-Thames
Contact: Mrs P Ling on 01372 474569
S/Cap: 180
Pros stage, large hall 60ft x 26ft.

### VINE HALL
Vine Road, East Molesey
Contact: Mrs P Ling on 01372 474569
S/Cap: 195

### THE MOLE HALL
Bishop Fox Way, West Molesey
Contact: Mrs P Ling on 01372 474569

### THE BARN THEATRE
High Street, West Molesey KT7 2LY
Contact: Maggs Latter on 0181 941 1090
seats: 70
Semi-professional supper theatre.

### VERA FLETCHER HALL
4 Ember Court Road, Thames Ditton, Surrey
Contact: Val Walker Tel 0181 398 4289

## EPPING FOREST Essex
Arts Officer: Carien Meijer
Epping Forest Arts, The House, rear of Loughton Pool,
Traps Hill, Loughton Essex IG10 1SZ
Tel 0181 532 1103  Fax 0181 532 1106

## EPSOM & EWELL Surrey

Borough Recreation Department, Town Hall, The Parade, Epsom, Surrey KT18 5BY
Community Services Officer: Dick Harris
Tel 01372 732000  Fax 01372 732488
Entertainments Officer: Trevor Mitchell
Tel 01372 742226  Fax 01372 726228

**EPSOM PLAYHOUSE***
See Provincial Venues for details

**BOURNE HALL**
Spring Street, Ewell, Surrey KT17 1UF
Tel 0181 393 9571  Fax 0181 786 7265
Manager: Sandra Dessent
S/Cap: 360 approx. variable according to nature of function. Stage facilities, concerts, lectures, dances, catering and conferences.

**EWELL COURT HOUSE**
Lakehurst Road, Ewell, Surrey
Tel 0181 393 9571  Fax 0181 786 7265
Manager: Sandra Dessent
Rooms for lectures, receptions, adult education and smaller functions.

## EREWASH Derbyshire

Chief Leisure Services Officer: Tony Harris
Town Hall, Long Eaton, NG10 1HU
Tel 0115 946 1321  Fax 0115 946 1900

## EXETER Devon

Civic Centre, Paris Street, Exeter EX1 1JN
Tel 01392 277888  Fax 01392 265265
Director of Community & Environment: James Kelly
Halls Promotions Manager: David Lewis

**ST. GEORGE'S HALL, EXETER***
St. George's Hall, Market St, Exeter EX1 1BW
Tel 01392 265866  Fax 01392 422137
S/Cap: 500, standing 500
**Technical:**
Main stage or portable available. Full stage facilities, 3 Phase Electric, 3 Dressing Rooms with show relay. Suitable for one-night stands, stage shows, pantomimes, wrestling, films, fashion shows and community events. Bar and catering facilities.

## FAREHAM, Hampshire

Civic Offices, Civic Way, Fareham,
Hampshire PO16 7PP
Tel 01329 236100  Fax 01329 822732
Chief Leisure Officer: Peter Grimwood
Tel 01329 824541

**FERNEHAM HALL***
See Provincial Venues for details

**SOLENT SUITE**
See Provincial Venues for details

**OCTAGON LOUNGE**
See Provincial Venues for details

## FENLAND Cambridgeshire

Head of Leisure: Dennis Bell
Arts Development Officer: Andy O'Hanlon
Fenland Hall, County Road, March, Cambs PE15 8NQ

Tel 01354 654321  Fax 01354 622358

## FLINTSHIRE

County Offices, St Davids Park, Ewloe, Deeside, Flintshire CH5 3ZQ
Director of Culture, Leisure and Tourism: Howard Fowler  Tel 01352 702450  Fax 01352 702458
Assistant Director - Leisure: Mike Hornby
Tel 01352 702452  Fax 01352 702458
Assistant Director - Development & Support: Ray Large  Tel 01352 702470  Fax 01352 702458

**DEESIDE LEISURE CENTRE**
Chester Road West, Queensferry, Deeside, Flintshire CH5 1SA.
Tel 01244 810540  Fax 01244 836287
Contact: Alan Reed
Staging up to 50' x 40' with P.A. wings available.  Full electrics and T.V. connections.
S/Cap. Large Sports Hall 2,300.

**HOLYWELL LEISURE CENTRE**
Fron Park Road, Holywell, Flintshire CH8 7UZ
Tel 01352 715056  Fax 01352 714478
Bookings 01352 712027
Contact: Chris Travers

## FOREST OF DEAN Gloucestershire

Assistant Leisure Services Officer: M G Derbyshire
Council Offices: High Street, Coleford,
Glos. GL16 8HG
Tel 01594 812381  Fax 01594 812314

## FYLDE Lancashire

Tourism Officer: Paul Norris
290 Clifton Drive South, Lytham St. Annes,
Lancs FY8 1LH
Tel 01253 724141  Fax 01253 713754

**LOWTHER PAVILION**
Lytham.
S/Cap: 450. Multi-Purpose Hall/Theatre

## GATESHEAD Tyne and Wear

Director of Arts & Libraries: William J. Macnaught, M.A., A.L.A.
Assistant Director of Arts: Mike White
Central Library, Prince Consort Road,
Gateshead NE8 4LN
Tel 0191 477 3478  Fax 0191 477 7454

**CAEDMON HALL**
at Central Library (as above)
S/Cap: 240.
Portable Stage 2.44m x 4.88m.

## GILLINGHAM Kent

See Medway District Council

## GLOUCESTER Gloucestershire

Leisure Management, Gloucester City Council, Herbert Warehouse, The Docks, Gloucester GL1 2EQ

Tel 01452 396620  Fax 01452 396622
Head of Leisure Services: Steve Elway

**GLOUCESTER LEISURE CENTRE***
See Provincial Venues for details

**GUILDHALL ARTS CENTRE**
23 Eastgate Street, Gloucester GL1 1NS
Mgt 01452 505086  BO 01452 505089
Fax 01452 384734
Arts Officer: Andy Woods
Bookings: Angela Hetheridge
**Technical:**
Performance Space: 200 - 260 seated; Flat floor
performing area 30'/40', 400 dancing; fixed platform
40'/15'. Cinema: 125
Recital Suite: 60.
also bar, workshops and gallery.

## GOSPORT, Hampshire
Town Hall, Gosport PO12 1EB
Tel 01705 584242  Fax 01705 545238
Economic Development Manager: R. Wilson

## GRAVESHAM Kent
Entertainments Manager: Brian N. Tourle
Woodville Halls, Woodville Place,
Gravesend DA12 1DD
Tel 01474 337456  Fax 01474 337458

**WOODVILLE HALLS***
See Provincial Venues for details:

**KENT ROOM**
S/Cap: 100.

**WOODVILLE BALLROOM**
S/Cap: 450 (Dances)
S/Cap: 835
Cap: 1,000 Discos/Rock Concerts

## GREAT GRIMSBY, North East Lincolnshire
Head of Leisure: Keith Davis
Principal Arts Development Officer: Mr Chris Jones
Arts Development Officer: Lynne Conlan
Leisure Services Department, Civic Offices, The Knoll,
Cleethorpes, North East Lincolnshire DN35 8LN
Tel 01472 323000  Fax 01472 323005

**GRIMSBY AUDITORIUM**
See Provincial Venues for details

**TOWN HALL**
Town Hall Square, Grimsby,
North East Lincolnshire DN31 1HX
Tel 01472 324101  Fax 01472 324108
Town Hall Manager: J. Callison
Assembly Room: Seating up to 450.

## GREAT YARMOUTH Norfolk
Engineering & Leisure Services, Town Hall, Great
Yarmouth, Norfolk NR30 2QF
Tel 01493 856100  Fax 01493 846365
Borough Engineer: R Dornan
Head of Community Services: T Whitmill
Leisure Services Officer: Miss Marie Tacon

**GORLESTON PAVILION***
See Provincial Venues for details

**WELLINGTON PIER THEATRE***
See Provincial Venues for details

**WELLINGTON PIER WINTER GARDEN**
See Provincial Venues for details

## GUILDFORD Surrey
Director of Leisure Services: Jim Miles, BA, DipAA,
MILAM
Millmead House, Millmead, Guildford, Surrey GU2 5BB
Tel 01483 444700  Fax 01483 444717

**GUILDFORD SPECTRUM**
Guildford Spectrum, Parkway, Guildford GU1 1UP.
Tel 01483 443322
Fax 01483 443311
General Manager of Spectrum: Peter Gunn
Policy: Concerts, Variety, Ice Shows, Corporate Events
Seated: 1,800 - 3,000, standing 2,000 - 3,000.
Bars, restaurant, cafeterias, free parking.

**CIVIC HALL***
See Provincial Venues for details

**ELECTRIC THEATRE**
Onslow Street, Guildford, Surrey GU1 4SZ
Mgt 01483 444788  BO 01483 444789
Fax 01483 563913
**Administration:**
Props: Guildford Borough Council
Manager: James Powell
Policy: Small Scale amateur theatre, jazz, opera,
comedy, music.
Seats: 210; Standing: 250. Cafe/bar.

## GWYNEDD
Shirehall Street, Caernarfon, Gwynedd LL55 ISH
Tel 01268 672255  Fax 01268 676998
Director of Technical Services: Ievan Lewis

**NEUADD DWYFOR**
Stryd Penlan, Pwllheli, Gwynedd LL53 5DN
Box Office/Management: 01758 704088
Fax 01758 701228
Manager: Ann Rowena
Box Office open 10-1/2-4 plus 1 hour before
performance.
Cinema & Theatre
Re-opened 1995 after extensive refurbishment.
Receiving Theatre for all types of entertainment, plays,
concerts, dance etc. Access for disabled via lift to first
floor. Open throughout the year.

**NEUADD BUDDUG**
Bala, Gwynedd LL23 7SR
Tel 01678 520800
Contact: Mrs Linda Newell
Seating/Capacity: 280

**FFESTINIOG PUBLIC HALL**
Penybryn, Ffestiniog, Gwynedd
Secretary: Mrs. E. Ayres

## HALTON Cheshire
Halton Borough Council, Town Hall, Heath Road,
Runcorn WA7 5TD
Tel 0151 424 2061  Fax 0151 471 7303

Asst. Director of Cultural and Leisure Services:
Howard Cockcroft BA(Hons); Dip. Lib; ALA.

**QUEEN'S HALL, WIDNES**
Victoria Road, Widnes, Cheshire WA8 7RF
Tel 0151 424 2339/2061  Fax 0151 420 5762
Manager: Brian Pridmore
Concerts, Plays, Exhibitions, Dinners.
S/Cap: 650

# HAMBLETON North Yorkshire
Chief Executive: P. Simpson
Civic Centre, Stone Cross, Northallerton DL6 2UU
Tel 01609 779977  Fax 01609 780017

**HAMBLETON COMMUNITY CENTRE**
**NORTHALLERTON**
Bullamoor Road, Northallerton, North Yorks DL6 1PE
Tel 01609 776230
Manager: Richard Dowson
S/Cap: 400.
Full Stage, Dressing Rooms, Bar and Catering
facilities.

# HARBOROUGH Leicestershire
Chief Executive: M C  Wilson
Council Offices, Adam and Eve Street,
Market Harborough LE16 7AG
Tel 01858 410000  Fax 01858 821000

# HARROGATE North Yorkshire
Department of Leisure and Amenities Services,
Brandreth House, St.Lukes Avenue, Harrogate,
North Yorkshire HG1 2AA

Tel 01423 500600  Fax 01423 556710
Director of Leisure & Amenities Services: Kevin Douglas

**HARROGATE INTERNATIONAL CENTRE***
**ROYAL HALL***

# HART Hampshire
Hart District Council, Harlington Way, Fleet,
Hampshire, GU13 8AE
Tel 01252 622122  Fax 01252 626886

**THE HARLINGTON CENTRE**
Fleet Road, Fleet, Hampshire GU13 8BY
Tel 01252 811009  Fax 01252 812191
Manager: Lindsay Hopkins (Tel 01252 774468)
Seating/Capacity: 400

# HARTLEPOOL Cleveland
Municipal Buildings, Church Square,
Hartlepool TS24 7EQ
Tel 01429 266522  Fax 01429 523450
Director of Community Services: Janet Barker

**TOWN HALL THEATRE**
See Provincial Venues for details

**BOROUGH HALL**
See Provincial Venues for details

# HASTINGS East Sussex
Head of Leisure Services: Mike Marsh
Hastings Borough Council 5 Robertson Terrace,
Hastings, TN34 1JE
Tel 01424 781122  Fax 01424 781133

**WHITE ROCK THEATRE***
See Provincial Venues for details

**MARINA PAVILION**
Lower Promenade, Marina, St.Leonard's on Sea,
East Sussex, TN38 0BU
Tel 01424 781850  Fax 01424 781899
Props: Hasting Borough Council
Leasees: D.C. Leisure Ltd
Manager: Chris Lawrence

**SUMMERFIELD LEISURE CENTRE**
Bohemia Road, Hastings, East Sussex TN34 1ET
Tel 01424 781777  Fax 01424 781810
Props: Hastings Borough Council
Leasees: D.C. Leisure Ltd
Manager: Steve Tytherleigh

# HAVANT Hampshire
Leisure & Community Services, Civic Offices,
Civic Centre Road, Havant PO9 2AX.
Tel 01705 474174 ext. 406
Fax 01705 446418
Leisure & Tourism Manager: Maria Wilkinson

# HEREFORD
## Hereford City Council
Grange House, off Etnam Street, Leominster,
Herefordshire HR6 8ZD
Head of Culture Services & Education for Life: Geoff
Cole (Tel 01432 260721)
Head of Cultural Services: Natalia Silver
(Tel 01432 260732)
Leisure Services Manager: Tony Featherstone
(Tel 01432 260728)
Heritage Services Manager: Isabel Churcher
(Tel: 01432 260623)
Correspondence Address: PO Box 44 Leominster,
Herefordshire HR6 8ZD Fax: 01568 611046
Director of Policy & Community Services:
Mrs Jane Jones "Brockington" 35 Hafod Road,
Hereford HR1 1SH
Tel 01432 260037 Fax 01432 340189

**HEREFORD LEISURE CENTRE**
Holmer Road, Hereford HR4 9UD
Tel 01432 278178  Fax 01432 266281
Manager: Pete Williams
S/cap: 2,216

**HEREFORD  THEATRE AND ARTS CENTRE**
Edgar Street, Hereford HR4 9JR
See Provincial Venues for details (The Courtyard)

# HERTSMERE Hertfordshire

**HERTSMERE LEISURE**
Rudolph Road, Bushey, Hertfordshire WD2 3DV
Head of Operations: Chris Rushton
Tel 0181 386 4044  Fax 0181 386 4621

**THE WYLLYOTTS CENTRE, POTTERS BAR**
Darkes Lane, Potters Bar, Herts EN6 2HN
Venue Direct Line 01707 645005
S/Cap: 421 for stage shows, 120 for dinners,
exhibitions, art gallery, museum, 3 conference rooms,
cafe and bar.

**THE HARTSPRING SUITE, BUSHEY**
Park Avenue, Bushey, Hertfordshire WD2 3BJ
Tel 01923 233039  Fax 01923 213318
Manager: Stuart Leggett
S/Cap: 110 for sit down meals.
Direct line to suite: 01923 243963

# HIGH PEAK Derbyshire
Director of Leisure Services: Richard Tomlinson,
Environmental Health & Leisure Dept., Town Hall,
Buxton, SK17 6EL
Tel 01298 28404  Fax 01298 28425

**PAVILION GARDENS, BUXTON**
St Johns Road, Buxton, SK17 6XN
Tel: 01298 23114
Manager: M. R. Roberts
S/Cap: 1,100. Used for Exhibitions, Conferences,
Concerts (Orch), Dances, Wrestling, etc.

**BUXTON OPERA HOUSE***
See Provincial Venues for details

# HORSHAM West Sussex
North Street, Horsham, West Sussex RH12 1RL
Tel 01403 215100  Fax 01403 215268
Director of Leisure Services: Chris Dier

**HORSHAM ARTS CENTRE THEATRE**
See Provincial Venues for details

# HUNTINGDONSHIRE
## Cambridgeshire
Head of Leisure Services: Tony Davies
Pathfinder House, St. Mary's Street,
Huntingdon PE18 6TN
Tel 01480 388046  Fax 01480 388273

**ST. IVO RECREATION CENTRE**
Westwood Road, St. Ives, Huntingdon,
Cambs. PE17 4WV
Tel 01480 388500  Fax 01480 388513
Manager of Centre: Ian Cousins
Civic Hall with S/Cap of 700. Stage facilities.

**PRIORY CENTRE, ST. NEOTS**
St. Neots Town Council, Priory Lane, St. Neots,
Huntingdon, Cambs.
Tel 01480 388922
**Administration:**
Manager of Centre: Adam Clarke
Great Hall, with full stage and changing facilities
including showers.
S/Cap: 400.

# HYNDBURN Lancashire
Chief Executive: Mike Chambers
Hyndburn Leisure, Town Hall, Blackburn Road,
Accrington, Lancs. 1LA
Tel 01254 380296  Fax 01254 380291
Chief Executive: Mike Chambers

**OSWALDTWISTLE CIVIC THEATRE**
Oswaldtwistle, Accrington, Lancs.BB5 3DF
Tel 01254 232172  Fax 01254 388038
Manager: Peter Baron
S/Cap: 470.

**ACCRINGTON TOWN HALL**
Blackburn Road, Accrington, Lancashire BB5 1LA
Tel 01254 380296 Fax 01254 380291
Manager: Peter Baron
S/Cap: 400

**HYNDBURN SPORTS CENTRE**
Henry Street, Church, Accrington, Lancs.BB5 4EZ
Tel 01254 385945 Fax 01254 301949
Manager: Geoff Pickles
S/Cap: 1,200. Stage Facilities.

# ISLE OF WIGHT
Wight Leisure, I.O.W. Council, 17 Quay Street,
Newport, Isle of Wight PO30 5BA
Managing Director: Annie Horne
Tel 01983 823828 Fax 01983 823369

**MEDINA THEATRE**
See Provincial Venues for details

**MEDINA LEISURE CENTRE**
Fairlee Road, Newport, Isle of Wight PO30 2DX
Tel 01983 523767 Fax 01983 822821
Manager: Paul Broome

**RYDE THEATRE**
Lind Street, Ryde, Isle of Wight PO33 2NL
Tel/Fax 01983 568099
Manager: Malcolm Bennett
S/Cap: 500. Drapes, Licenced Bar, Full Kitchen.

**SANDOWN LEISURE CENTRE**
The Broadway, Sandown, Isle of Wight PO36 9ET
Tel 01983 405594 Fax 01983 405037
Operations Manager: Mrs Lynn Burford

**PIER PAVILION, SANDOWN***
See Provincial Venues for details

**SHANKLIN THEATRE***
See Provincial Venues for details

**WINTER GARDENS, VENTNOR***
See Provincial Venues for details

# IPSWICH Suffolk
Ipswich Borough Council
Civic Centre, Ipswich IP1 2EE
Tel 01473 263501 Fax 01473 263636
Corporate Director: J.A. Orr

**IPSWICH REGENT**
See Provincial Venues for details

**CORN EXCHANGE/TOWN HALL COMPLEX**
See Provincial Venues for details

**GRAND HALL**
(A part of the Corn Exchange Complex)
Multi-purpose Hall.
S/Cap: 896.
Comp. lighting and sound system.
Dressing Rooms.

**ROBERT CROSS HALL**
(A part of the Corn Exchange Complex)
Multi-purpose Hall
S/Cap: 200.
Sound system.

**COUNCIL CHAMBER**
(A part of the Corn Exchange Complex)
S/Cap: 200. Some stage lighting and amplification.
Plus miscellaneous meeting rooms and exhibition
spaces.

# KENNET Wiltshire
Leisure Services Manager: A. P. Smith
Browfort, Bath Road, Devizes, Wiltshire SN10 2AT
Tel 01380 724911 Ext. 690
Fax 01380 729146

# KETTERING
# Northamptonshire
Municipal Offices, Bowling Green Road,
Kettering NN15 6QX
Tel 01536 410333 Fax 01536 410795
Community Development Manager: Lynn Chapman

# KING'S LYNN AND WEST
# NORFOLK Norfolk
Head of Leisure and Tourism: John Barrett
Valentine Road, Hunstanton, Norfolk PE36 5EZ
Tel 01485 532516 Fax 01485 533090

**CORN EXCHANGE***
See Provincial Venues for details

For the Regis Rooms and The Town Hall contact:
General Manager - Community Services, Mr S Beales,
Kings Court, Chapel Street, Kings Lynn,
Norfolk PE30 1EX
Tel 01553 692722

**REGIS ROOMS**
Wellesley Street, King's Lynn, Norfolk PE30 1QD
Enquiries and Bookings, Tel 01553 692722
S/Cap: 250. Portable stage available.

**TOWN HALL & ASSEMBLY ROOMS**
Saturday Market Place, King's Lynn, Norfolk PE30 5DQ
Enquiries and Bookings, Tel 01553 692722
S/Cap: 200. Portable stage available.

**DOWNHAM MARKET TOWN HALL**
Priory Road, Downham Market, Norfolk PE38 9JT
Tel 01366 383287 Fax 01366 385042
For bookings & further details contact Wendy Allen.
S/Cap: 350. Permanent Stage.

**PRINCESS THEATRE**
See Provincial Venues for details

# KINGSTON UPON HULL
# East Yorkshire
Director of Leisure Services: C. Brown
79 Ferensway, Kingston upon Hull HU2 8LE
Tel 01482 610610 Fax 01482 615656

**HULL NEW THEATRE***
See Provincial Venues for details

**CITY HALL**
See Provincial Venues for details

## KIRKLEES West Yorkshire
Cultural Services Department, Huddersfield Town Hall,
Ramsden Street, Huddersfield, West Yorkshire HD1 2TA
Tel 01484 226300  Fax 01484 226342
Head of Cultural Services: Jonathan Drake

### BATLEY TOWN HALL
Market Place, Batley WF17 5DA
Tel 014924 326002
Manager: Julia Robinson (01484 221902)
Superintendent: Barry Phillips
For bookings contact Gary Ellis or Sue Wood
Tel 01484 221913/221947  Fax 01484 221876
S/Cap: 300. Stage facilities.

### CLECKHEATON TOWN HALL
Bradford Road, Cleckheaton BD19 3RH
Tel 01274 335029
Manager: Julia Robinson (01484 221902)
Superintendent: Dave Johnson
For bookings contact Gary Ellis or Sue Wood
Tel 01484 221913/221947  Fax 01484 221876
S/Cap: 500. Stage facilities.

### DEWSBURY ARTS CENTRE
Upper Road, Batley Carr, Dewsbury WF17 7LT
Manager: Julia Robinson Tel 01484 221902
For bookings contact Gary Ellis or Sue Wood
Tel 01484 221913 or 01484 221947
Fax 01484 221876
S/Cap: 176. Stage facilities.

### DEWSBURY TOWN HALL
Wakefield Road, Dewsbury WF12 8DQ
Tel: 01924 324502
Manager: Julia Robinson (01484 221902)
Superintendent: Sue Lenton
For bookings contact Gary Ellis or Sue Wood
Tel 01484 221913 or 01484 221947
Fax 01484 221876
S/Cap: 685. Stage Facilities.

### HOLMFIRTH CIVIC HALL
Huddersfield Road, Holmfirth HD7 1AS
Tel 01484 222452
Caretaker: Sharon Baxter
For bookings contact Gary Ellis or Sue Wood
Tel 01484 221913 or 01484 221947
Fax 01484 221876
Seats: 320 (large hall), 120 (small hall). Stage facilities.

### HONLEY COMMUNITY CENTRE
Stoney Lane, Honley HD7 2DY
Tel 01484 222388
Caretaker: Christine Holroyd
For bookings contact Gary Ellis or Sue Wood
Tel 01484 221947
Fax 01484 221876
S/Cap: 170.
Stage facilities.

### HUDDERSFIELD TOWN HALL*
Ramsden Street, Huddersfield HD1 2TA
Tel 01484 221900
Manager: Julia Robinson (01484 221902)
For bookings contact Gary Ellis or Sue Wood
Tel 01484 221913 or 01484 221947
Fax 01484 221873
S/Cap: 1,200. Stage facilities. Willis Concert Organ.

### MELTHAM CIVIC HALL
Huddersfield Road, Meltham HD7 3AG
Tel 01484 854534
Caretaker: Mrs Jackie Levitt

For bookings contact Gary Ellis or Sue Wood
Tel 01484 221947
Fax 01484 221876

### SLAITHWAITE CIVIC HALL
New Street, Slaithwaite HD7 5AB
Tel 01484 842419
Caretaker: Joan Brooke
For bookings contact Gary Ellis or Sue Wood
Tel 01484 221947
Fax 01484 221876
S/Cap: 260. Stage facilities.

### THE LAWRENCE BATLEY THEATRE
See Provincial Venues for details

## KNOWSLEY Merseyside
Director of Leisure Services: John Bell
Leisure Services Department, Council Offices,
Archway Road, Huyton L36 9UX
Tel 0151 443 3459  Fax 0151 443 0349
Head of Arts: Paul Bewick
Tel 0151 443 5619  Fax 0151 443 5618

### KIRKBY SUITE
Cherryfield Drive, Kirkby L32 1TX
Venue Tel 0151 443 4063  Fax 0151 443 4064
S/Cap: 500 (Theatre style).
Sunday Licence. Stage Facilities.

### HUYTON GALLERY
Poplar Bank, Huyton L36 9UX
Tel 0151 443 3761  Fax 0151 443 3573

### HUYTON SUITE
Poplar Bank, Huyton L36 9UX
Tel 0151 443 3761  Fax 0151 443 3573
S/Cap: 450. Sunday Licence. Stage Facilities.

### PRESCOT LEISURE CENTRE
Warrington Road, Prescot, Merseyside L35 5AD
Tel 0151 430 7202  Fax 0151 289 4425
Manager: Geoff Pollitt
Facilities for sport, catering and entertainment.
Capacity 150 to 500 depending on function.

### KNOWSLEY VILLAGE HALL
School Lane, Knowsley Village, L34 9EN
Tel 0151 548 4545
Bookings: Charlie Price, Clerk to the Council
S/Cap: 174
Stage Facilities.

## LANCASTER Lancashire
Festival & Events Officer: Keith Lamb
Palatine Hall, Lancaster LA1 1PW
Tel 01524 582828  Fax 01524 582323

### ASHTON HALL, LANCASTER
Dalton Square, Lancaster LA1 1PJ
Multi-purpose civic hall with buffet/bar area plus
banqueting suite. Max. capacity 800; 600 stalls, 200
balcony. Open stage backed by large organ. Dance
floor. Used for dancing, exhibitions, conferences,
banquets, concerts, fashion shows, boxing,
private/commercial hire.
Building Superintendent: Mrs Sheila Hall
Tel 01524 582515
For bookings telephone 01524 582000 or fax 582161

### THE PLATFORM, MORECAMBE
Station Buildings, Central Promenade, Morecambe,

Lancashire LA4 4DB
Contact Kirk Worley
Tel 01524 582814 Fax01524 832745
Unique multi purpose venue, newly restored former
Edwardian Railway Station, Exhibitions, Conferences,
Community Arts, Jazz and live music. Capacity
400+theatre, 1000 standing. Private & commercial
hire.

## LEEDS West Yorkshire
Acting Director of Leisure Services: Denise Preston
Leeds Town Hall, The Headrow, Leeds LS1 3AD.
Tel 0113 247 8337  Fax 0113 247 7747
Website www.leeds.gov.uk

**LEEDS CIVIC THEATRE***
See Provincial Venues for details

## LEICESTER Leicestershire
New Walk Centre, Welford Place, Leicester LE1 6ZG
Tel 0116 254 9922  Fax 0116 255 4894
Director of Arts & Leisure: Michael Gallagher

**DE MONTFORT HALL***
See Provincial Venues for details

## LEOMINSTER Herefordshire

**COMMUNITY CENTRE**
School Road, Leominster HR6 8NS
Tel 01568 616411
Manager: Jennifer Gough

**LEISURE CENTRE**
Coningsby Road, Leominster HR6 8LL
Tel 01568 612540  Fax 01568 610031
Manager: Mick Ligema
Seating/Capacity: 900

## LEWES, East Sussex
Leisure Services Department,Lewes District Council,
Southover House, Southover Road, Lewes,
East Sussex BN7 1DY
Tel 01273 471600  Fax 01273 479011
Director of Leisure Services Fax 01273 484462

**TOWN HALL LEWES**
High Street, Lewes, East Sussex BN7 2DQ
Tel 01273 484009
Caretaker: G. Ticehurst
**Assembly Hall:**
Stage. S/Cap: 400. max.
Portable.
**Corn Exchange:**
No fixed stage, but portable stage available.
S/Cap: 400 max.
**Lecture Room:**
No stage. S/Cap: 80.

**SOUTHOVER GRANGE, LEWES**
Grange Road, Lewes, East Sussex
Tel: 01273 471600
**Evelyn Room:**
S/Cap: 35
**Ainsworth Room:**
S/Cap: 65
**Newton Room:**
S/Cap: 60

**DOWNS LEISURE CENTRE, SEAFORD**
Sutton Road, Seaford, East Sussex BN25 4QW
Tel 01323 490011  Fax 01323 491531
General Manager: Peter Crowley
Centre Manager: Stuart Adcock
**Blatchington Hall:**
Stage. S/Cap: 200
**Sutton Hall:**
No Stage. S/Cap: 100
**Committee Room:**
No Stage. S/Cap: 60.
**Sports Hall:**
No fixed stage but portable stage available.
S/Cap: 500. max.

**SALTS HALL, Seaford**
Tel 01323 490011
No Stage. S/Cap: 80.

## LICHFIELD Staffordshire
Head of Leisure Services: Mrs S. Smith
Lichfield District Council, Frog Lane,
Lichfield WS13 6YX
Tel 01543 414000  Fax 01543 250673

**CIVIC HALL***
See Provincial Venues for details

## LINCOLN Lincolnshire
City Hall, Beaumont Fee, Lincoln LN1 1DD
Tel 01522 881188  Fax 01522 560049

**THEATRE ROYAL***
See Provincial Venues for details

**BROADGATE DRILL HALL**
Broadgate, Lincoln LN2 5AE
Tel/Fax 01522 524393
S/Cap: 800.
Stage facilities.

**YARBOROUGH LEISURE CENTRE**
Riseholme Road, Lincoln LN1 3SP
Tel 01522 524228.  Fax 01522 683946
Manager: Peter Wray
Sports Hall. Seating: 900. Stage can be erected.

**THE LAWN**
Union Road, Lincoln.LN1 3BL
Tel 01522 560330  Fax 01522 524400
Manager: Terry Smith
Main Hall seats 468, Stage portable.
Small Theatre seats 100. Stage permanent.

## LIVERPOOL Merseyside
Director of Leisure Services: J. Davies, B.A., D.M.S., Dip.Lib,
MILAM
Head of Tourism, Arts and Heritage: Keith Davies
3rd Floor, Millennium House, Victoria Street,
Liverpool L1 6JH
Tel 0151 233 6340  Fax 0151 233 6399

## LLANDUDNO Conwy

**CANOLFAN/ABERCONWY CENTRE***
Canolfan Aberconwy Centre, Promenade, Llandudno
Tel 01492 879771
Fax 01492 860790
S/Cap: 950 theatre style; 500 cabaret.

**NORTH WALES THEATRE**
Tel 01492 879771 BO 01492 872000
Fax 01492 860790
S/Cap: 1,500

# LLANELLI Carmarthenshire
Centre Manager: Carwyn Rogers
Llanelli Entertainment Centre, Station Road, Llanelli,
Carmarthenshire, SA15 1AH
Tel 01554 774057  Fax 01554 741632

**LLANELLI ENTERTAINMENT CENTRE***
3 Auditoriums.
**Theatr Elli:**
S/Cap: 493. Repertory, Variety, Concerts, Recitals,
etc., also Cinema.
**Theatre 2:**
S/Cap: 330. Suitable for Concerts and limited Drama
Productions, also Cinema.
**Theatre 3:**
S/Cap: 122. Cinema. No stage. Rehearsal Room and
Theatre Workshop available.
See Provincial Venues for further details

# LUTON Bedfordshire
Director of Leisure and Cultural Services: David Sutton
Luton Borough Council Leisure & Cultural Services
Dept, Wardown Park Offices, Old Bedford Road, Luton
LU2 7HA
Tel 01582 746700  Fax 01582 546762
**THE LIBRARY THEATRE***
St. George's Theatre, St. George's Square,
Luton LU1 2NG
Mgt 01582 730637  BO 01582 547474
Manager: Doc Watson

# MACCLESFIELD Cheshire
Chief Leisure Services Officer: H.M. Hartley
Macclesfield Borough Council, Town Hall,
Macclesfield, Cheshire SK10 2EA
Tel 01625 500500  Fax 01625 504515

**MACCLESFIELD LEISURE CENTRE**
Priory Lane, Macclesfield SK10 1EA
Tel 01625 615602  Fax 01625 434694
Manager: David McHendry
S/Cap: 1,200 Main Hall. 275 Small Hall.
Stage Facilities. Multi-purpose venue.

**WILMSLOW LEISURE CENTRE**
Rectory Field, Wilmslow SK9 1BU
Tel 01625 533789  Fax 01625 532481
Manager: Miss Kim Walker
S/Cap: 528. Main Hall. Stage Facilities. Multi-purpose
venue, with specialist sound and lighting.

Various other venues used for year-round Arts
programme. For further details contact Mark Wheelton
Tel 01625 504506  Fax 01625 504515

# MAIDSTONE Kent
Leisure Policy Officer: Brian Latimer
Directorate of Borough Services, 13 Tonbridge Road,
Maidstone, ME16 8HG
Tel 01622 602000  Fax 01622 602764

**CORN EXCHANGE COMPLEX***
See Provincial Venues for details

**THE HAZLITT THEATRE***
See Provincial Venues for details

**THE EXCHANGE***
(Part of the Corn Exchange complex)
See Provincial Venues for details

**MAIDSTONE LEISURE CENTRE**
Motes Park, Maidstone, ME15 7RN
Tel 01622 761111  Fax 01622 672462
Manager: Mike Packham
For Bookings contact: Barry Reynolds
Main Hall S/Cap: 1,080 ground floor, 360 balcony.

# MALDON Essex
Chief Executive: E. A. P. Plumridge
Council Offices, Princes Road, Maldon, Essex CM9 5DL
Tel 01621 854477
Fax 01621 852575

# MALVERN HILLS
# Hereford and Worcester

**WINTER GARDENS COMPLEX FESTIVAL
THEATRE***
See Provincial Venues for details

# MANCHESTER
Manchester City Council Leisure Division, Crown
Square, Manchester M60 3BB
Tel 0161 234 7064  Fax 0161 234 7241
Head of Leisure: Jim Byrne

**LIBRARY THEATRE COMPANY**
See Provincial Venues for details

**FORUM THEATRE**
See Provincial Venues for details

# MANSFIELD
# Nottinghamshire
Civic Centre, Chesterfield Road, South Mansfield,
Notts NG19 7BH
Tel 01623 656656  Fax 01623 420197
Head of Leisure Services: Iain Hook

**PALACE THEATRE**
Leeming Street, Mansfield Notts NG18 1NG
Mgt 01623 412951  Fax 01623 412922
BO 01623 663133
Policy: Midscale Touring, Pantomime, Amateur,
Dance, Ballets, Operatic, Orchestral, Workshops.
Perfs: As required.
Seats: 553/605. Foyer Bar, Coffee Lounge

**MANSFIELD LEISURE CENTRE***
Chesterfield Road, South Mansfield, Notts NG19
Tel 01623 646081  Fax 01623 651729
Manager: Mike Darnell
Seats up to 1,000.

**OAK TREE LANE CENTRE**
Jubilee Way, South Mansfield, Notts NG18 3RT
Tel/Fax 01623 420492
Manager: Ian Waller
Seats up to 400.

## MEDWAY Kent
Medway District Council Civic Centre, Strood, Rochester, Kent ME2 4AV
Director of Leisure Arts & Libraries: Dennis Holmes
Tel 01634 306000  Fax 01634 732848

## MENDIP Somerset
Mendip District Counci, Cannards Grave Road, Shepton Mallet BA4 5BT
Tel 01749 343399  Fax 01749 344050
Arts Development Officer: Nicola Epps

## MERTHYR TYDFIL Mid-Glamorgan
Leisure Services Department, Civic Centre, Castle Street, Merthyr Tydfil CF47 8AN
Tel 01685 725000  Fax 01685 722146
Leisure Services Manager: John Davies
Tel 01685 725277  Fax 01685 722146

## MID BEDFORDSHIRE Bedfordshire
Dir. of Environmental Services: David Stewart
23 London Road, Biggleswade SG18 8ER
Tel 01767 313137  Fax 01767 316717

## MID DEVON DISTRICT COUNCIL
Leisure Services Officer: Rob Kelley
Ailsa House, Tidcombe Lane, Tiverton, Devon  EX16 4DZ
Tel 01884 255255  Fax 01884 255584

**CULM VALLEY SPORTS CENTRE**
Meadow Lane, Cullumpton EX15 1LL
Tel 01884 32853
Bookings Contact: Corinne Parnell
S/Cap: 500 approx

**LORDS MEADOW LEISURE CENTRE**
Commercial Road, Crediton EX17 1ER
Tel 01363 776190
Main Hall and Ancillary Room available for hire.
Bookings Contact: Samantha Bennion

## MIDDLESBROUGH Cleveland
Head of Arts, Entertainments and Events: Judith Croft
Tel 01642 300202  Fax 01642 300276
P.O. Box 69, Vancouver House, Central Mews, Gurney Street, Middlesbrough, Cleveland TS1 1EL

**MIDDLESBROUGH THEATRE***
See Provincial Venues for details

**TOWN HALL, MIDDLESBROUGH**
See Provincial Venues for details

**TOWN HALL CRYPT, MIDDLESBROUGH**
Dances, Exhibitions, Concerts.
S/Cap: 450, standing: 600

## MID SUSSEX West Sussex
Department of Leisure Services, Administration Office, Mid Sussex District Council "Oaklands", Oaklands Road, Haywards Heath, West Sussex RH16 1SS

Tel 01444 458166  Fax 01444 450027
Leisure Planning & Development Manager: Katherine Nicolas
Arts Development Manager: Sarah Elderkin
(Fax 01444 414669)

**CLAIR HALL, HAYWARDS HEATH**
Perrymount Road, Haywards Heath, West Sussex RH16 3DN
Tel 01444 455440  Fax 01444 440041
Manager: Martin Thomson
Capacity: Seats: 360; Dances: 400.
Multi-purpose hall.

**MARTLETS HALL**
Civic Way, Burgess Hill, West Sussex RH15 9NN
Tel 01444 242888  Fax 01444 870550
Manager: Sally Willcock
Multi-purpose Hall.

## MILTON KEYNES Buckinghamshire
Arts Development Manager: Pauline Scott-Garrett
502 Avesbury Boulevard, Milton Keynes, Buckinghamshire MK9 3HS
Tel 01908 691691  Fax 01908 253304

**WILTON HALL**
Wilton Avenue, Bletchley Bucks MK3 6BN
Tel 01908 372852
For bookings contact the Duty Officer at Bletchley Leisure Centre: Tel 01908 377251  Fax 01908 374094
**Administration:**
Halls Officer: Fiona McRae
Contact also for Bookings: Helen Palmer
S/Cap: 330
Stage Facilities.

**STANTONBURY CAMPUS LEISURE CENTRE**
Purbeck, Stantonbury, Milton Keynes MK14 6BN
Tel 01908 314466  Fax 01908 318754
Manager: Matthew Partridge
Bookings: Bob Fletcher
Main Hall 800-1,000.
See Provincial Venues for further details

**BLETCHLEY LEISURE CENTRE**
See Provincial Venues for details

**JENNIE LEE THEATRE***
See Provincial Venues for details

## MOLE VALLEY Surrey
Head of Leisure Services: John Cawdell
Pippbrook, Reigate Road, Dorking, Surrey RH4 1SJ
Tel 01306 885001  Fax 01306 740866

**DORKING HALLS**
Reigate Road, Dorking RH4 1SG
Contact: Vanessa Hart, Manager, on 01306 879200
Fax 01306 877277
3 Halls; Capacities: 801, 252 & 99.
Open from March 1997

**LEATHERHEAD LEISURE CENTRE**
Guildford Road, Leatherhead
2 Halls, Capacities: 1,200 & 350.
Enquiries to: Elena Glynn, Leatherhead Leisure Centre, Guildford Road, Leatherhead.
Tel 01372 377674  Fax 01372 386749

## MONMOUTHSHIRE
Manager, Leisure Libraries and Culture: Peter Ellis
Monmouthshire County Council, County Hall,
Cwmbran NP44 2XH
Tel 01633 644644  Fax 01633 644666

**BOROUGH THEATRE, ABERGAVENNY**
See Provincial Venues for details

## NEATH PORT TALBOT
## West Glamorgan
Chief Executive: Ken Sawyer
Director of Leisure Services: John Powell
Assistant Director of Leisure Services: Russell Ward
Civic Centre, Port Talbot, West Glamorgan SA13 1PJ
Tel 01639 763333  Fax 01639 763444

**AFAN LIDO***
See Provincial Venues for details

**THE PRINCESS ROYAL THEATRE**
Civic Centre, Port Talbot, West Glamorgan SA13 1PJ
Tel 01639 763214  Fax 01639 763444
Manager: Terry Doyle
Multi-Purpose Hall, fully air conditioned, with maximum
832 seat capacity, 11.5 x 6.5 metre stage, orchestra pit
and comprehensive lighting and sound facilities.

## NEWARK & SHERWOOD
## DISTRICT Nottinghamshire
Director of Recreation and Tourism: Gerry Croad
Deputy Director of Recreation & Tourism: Jim Todd
Arts & Marketing Manager: Mark Stephens
District Council Offices, Kelham Hall, Newark, Notts
NG23 5QX
Tel 01636 605111  Fax 01636 708267

**PALACE THEATRE***
See Provincial Venues for details

## NEWCASTLE-UNDER-LYME
## Staffordshire
Head of Leisure Services: J. W. Martin, M.I.L.A.M.,
M.Inst.B.R.M. (Dip.)
Principal Leisure Officer Culture, Development and
Leisure Management: C Ayres
Civic Offices, Merrial Street, Newcastle, Staffordshire
ST5 2AG
Tel 01782 717717  Fax 01782 711032

## NEWPORT South Wales
Leisure & Catering Division, Civic Centre, Newport,
South Wales NP9 4UR
Tel 01633 232824  Fax 01633 232808
Arts Development Officer: Adrian Ross
Arts Development Assistant: David Power
Direct Line: 01633 232849
Arts Officer: Chris Smith Direct Line: 01633 232158

**NEWPORT CENTRE***
See Provincial Venues for details

## NORTH CORNWALL Cornwall
North Cornwall District Council
Director of Housing & Environmental Services:
T. W. Magee responsible for Leisure & Sports Facilities

Council Offices, Trevanion Road, Wadebridge,
Cornwall PL27 7NU
Tel 01208 893333  Fax 01208 893455

## NORTH DORSET Dorset
Arts Development Officer: Kate Montefiore
Nordon, Salisbury Road, Blandford DT11 7LL
Tel 01258 484034  Fax 01258 484007

## NORTH EAST DERBYSHIRE
## Derbyshire
Director of Development & Leisure: Mr I.D. Boothroyd
Council Offices, Saltergate, Chesterfield S40 1LF
Tel 01246 231111  Fax 01246 221260

**DRONFIELD SPORTS CENTRE**
Civic Centre, Dronfield, Sheffield S18 1PD
Tel 01246 416166  Fax 01246 410466
Area Manager: Mike Blythe

**SHARLEY PARK LEISURE CENTRE**
Market Street, Clay Cross, Derbyshire S45 9LX
Tel 01246 862461  Fax 01246 864629
S/Cap: 800

## NORTH HERTFORDSHIRE
Head of Leisure Services:  Steve Welsh
Gernon Road, Letchworth SG6 3JF
Tel 01462 474000  Fax 01462 474500

**HITCHIN TOWN HALL**
Brand Street, Hitchin SG5 1HX
Tel 01462 434650
For Bookings contact: Scott McMurray or John Cox
Tel/Fax 01462 456202
S/Cap: 457. Stage Facilities.

## NORTH LINCOLNSHIRE
Pitwood House, Ashby Road, Scunthorpe,
North Lincolnshire, DN16 1AB
Tel 01724 296296
PO Box 35, Hewson House, Station Road, Brigg,
Lincolnshire DN20 8XJ
Fax 01724 297258
Senior Leisure Officer: Paul Clark: Tel 01724 297094
Leisure Development Officer: Simon Seal
Tel 01724 297265

**THE PLOWRIGHT THEATRE**
See Provincial Venues for details

**THE BATHS HALL**
59 Doncaster Road, Scunthorpe,
North Lincolnshire DN15 7RG
Tel 01724 842332  Fax 01724 861341
Entertainments Manager: Terry Wincott
Multi-purpose Hall, hosting diverse events - Cabaret,
Discos, Concerts, Opera, etc. Stage Facilities.

## NORTH NORFOLK Norfolk
North Norfolk District Council, Tourism & Leisure
Officer: Mr. S. W. Baker
Arts Officer: Jan Legge
Council Offices, Holt Road, Cromer NR27 9EL
Tel 01263 513811  Fax 01263 515042

**PIER PAVILION, CROMER***
**LITTLE THEATRE, SHERINGHAM***
2 Station Road, Sheringham, Norfolk NR26 8RE
Tel 01263 822347  Fax 01263 821963
Capacity: 186

**FAKENHAM COMMUNITY CENTRE**
Oak Street, Fakenham, Norfolk
Tel 01328 862791
S/Cap: 300.
Sunday Licence. Stage Facilities.
Note: Little Theatre and Fakenham Community Centre
are not under local authority control.

# NORTH SHROPSHIRE
Edinburgh House, New Street, Wem,
Shropshire SY4 5DB
Tel 01939 232771  Fax 01939 238444

**ELLESMERE TOWN HALL**
1-3 Willow Street, Ellesmere, Shropshire SY12 0AL
Tel 01691 622188
S/Cap: 240
Light Tours, Concerts, Amateur Events, Dances, etc.
(Ellesmere Town Council).

**WEM TOWN HALL**
Venue closed for redevelopment and expected to
reopen in December 1999. For further details contact:
Jane Drummond, Town Clerk Tel 01939 232733.

**WHITCHURCH CIVIC CENTRE**
High St., Whitchurch, Shropshire, SY13 1AX
Tel 01948 663403  Fax 01948 666011
Administrator: Anthony Rains
One Night Stands, Touring Theatre, Live Music, etc.
Main Hall Capacity: 400.

# NORTH SOMERSET
Town Hall, Weston Super Mare BS23 1UJ
Tel 01934 888888  Fax (Gen Enqs.) 01934 418194
Fax (Leisure Services Dept) 01934 612006
Director of Economic Development & Community
Leisure: Mr R.F.C. Acland

**THE PLAYHOUSE**
See Provincial Venues for details

**WINTER GARDENS**
See Provincial Venues for details.

# NORTH TYNESIDE
## Tyne and Wear
Principal Arts Officer: Mike Campbell
258b Station Road, Wallsend NE28 8RH
Tel 0191 200 7133
Head of Community Services: Brian Topping
7 Northumberland Square, North Shields NE30 1QQ
Tel:0191 200 5161

**WHITLEY BAY PLAYHOUSE**
Marine Avenue, Whitley Bay, Tyne & Wear NE26 1LZ
Tel 0191 252 6857  BO 0191 252 3505
Fax 0191 251 4949
Manager: Tim Flood
S/Cap: 746
Fully equipped theatre.

**BUDDLE ARTS CENTRE**
258b Station Road, Wallsend, NE28 8RH

Tel 0191 200 7132
Director: Mike Campbell
S/Cap: 150.
Stage Facilities.

# NORTH WARWICKSHIRE
## Warwickshire
Leisure Services Officer: Alan Freeman
South Street, Atherstone, Warwickshire CV9 1BD
Tel 01827 719207  Fax 01827 719225

**ATHERSTONE LEISURE COMPLEX**
Long Street, Atherstone, Warwickshire CV9 1AX
Manager: Claire Lodge
Tel 01827 719201  Fax 01827 719225

# NORTH WILTSHIRE
## Wiltshire
Arts Development Officer: Ms Kerry N. Wilkins
The Citadel, Bath Road, Chippenham, Wiltshire
SN15 2AA
Tel 01249 706111  Fax 01249 462283

# NORWICH, Norfolk
Chief Leisure & Community Services Officer:
David Albutt
Arts Officer: Ruth Churchill  Tel 01603 212147
Community Arts and Events Officer: Helen Selleck
Gladstone House, 28 St. Giles Street, Norwich  NR2 1TQ
Tel 01603 212137  Fax 01603 213003
Website www.norwich.gov.uk

**ST. ANDREW'S AND BLACKFRIARS HALLS***
See Provincial Venues for details

**THEATRE ROYAL**
See Provincial Venues for details

# NOTTINGHAM
## Nottinghamshire
Profile Nottingham c/o The Galleries of Justice, Shire
Hall, High Pavement, The Lace Market,
Nottingham NG1 1HN
Tel 0115 915 9231/5  Fax 0115 915 9230
e-mail: tourism@nottinghamcity.gov.uk

**ROYAL CENTRE***
See Provincial Venues for details
# NUNEATON Warwickshire
Nuneaton & Bedworth Borough Council, The Town Hall,
Coton Road, Nuneaton CV11 5AA
Tel 01203 376376
Fax (Leisure Services Dept) 01203 376551

**BEDWORTH CIVIC HALL**
High Street, Bedworth, Warwicks CV12 8NF
Mgt 01203 376705  BO 01203 376707
Fax 01203 376730
Entertainments & Civic Hall Manager: David Matthews
Seats: 813 approx. Bar, Coffee Bar, Small Hall and
Meeting Rooms.

# OLDHAM Lancashire
Civic Centre, West Street, Oldham,
Lancashire OL1 1XJ
Tel 0161 911 4260  Fax 0161 911 3221
Director of Education and Leisure Services: Mike Willis

Assistant Director (Culture & Entertainments): Nick
Ford Tel 0161 911 4052
Arts in the Community Manager: Paul Barnett
Tel 0161 911 4080 Fax 0161 911 4220

**QUEEN ELIZABETH HALL***
See Provincial Venues for details

**ROYTON ASSEMBLY HALL**
Market Square, Royton OL2 5QD
Tel 0161 911 4071 Fax 0161 620 9952
For Bookings: Sheila Malley at the Queen Elizabeth Hall
S/Cap: 400.
Sunday Licence. Stage Facilities. Bar Facilities.

# OXFORD Oxfordshire
Leisure Services Deptartment, 109-113 St. Aldates,
Oxford OX1 1DS
Tel 01865 249811 Fax 01865 252254
Head of Leisure: Tricia Ormiston Kilsby Tel 01865 252740
Arts Officer: Al Williams Tel 01865 252829

**TOWN HALL**
Oxford OX1 1BX
Tel 01865 252351
Fax 01865 252388
S/Cap: Oxford Town Hall - Assembly Room 200; Main
Hall 812; Old Library 150.

# PEMBROKESHIRE
Cultural Services Manager: Mrs Mary John
County Library, Dew Street, Haverfordwest SA61 1SU
Tel 01437 775240 Fax 01437 769218

**THEATR GWAUN**
West Street, Fishguard, Pembrokeshire SA65 9AD
Tel 01348 873421
S/Cap: 188
Limited Stage Facilities.

# PENDLE Lancashire
Pendle Borough Council
Leisure Services Manager: Phil Storey
Bank House, Albert Road, Colne, Lancs BB8 OBP
Tel 01282 661661 ax 01282 661221

**SILVERMAN HALL**
Pendle Street, Nelson BB9 7NH
Tel 01282 661911
For Bookings Contact Gary A. Hood, 01282 661220
S/Cap: 300. Sunday Licence; Stage Facilities.

**MUNICIPAL HALL**
Albert Road, Colne BB8 OBP
Tel 01282 661216
For Bookings Contact Gary A. Hood, 01282 861026
S/Cap: 611. Sunday Licence, Stage Facilities.

**CIVIC THEATRE**
Stanley Street, Nelson
Tel 01282 661913
For Bookings Contact Gary A. Hood, 01282 861026
S/Cap: 338. Sunday Licence, Stage Facilities.

**BARNOLDSWICK CIVIC HALL**
Station Road, Barnoldswick
Tel 01282 666717
For Bookings Contact Gary A. Hood, 01282 861026
S/Cap: 180. Sunday Licence.

**BARROWFORD CIVIC HALL**
Maud Street, Barrowford, Nelson
Tel 01282 661796
For Bookings Contact Gary A. Hood, 01282 661220
S/Cap: 150. Sunday Licence.

# PENWITH Cornwall
Director of Central Services: Mrs J.R Cross I. P.F.A.
Council Offices, St. Clare, Penzance TR18 3QW
Tel 01736 362341 Fax 01736 364292

**ST. JOHN'S HALL**
Alverton Street, Penzance, TR18 2QR
Foyer Tel 01736 363244
Bookings: Mrs Clare James
Tel 01736 362341 ext 2178
S/Cap: 399

**ST. IVES CONCERT HALL**
Street Anpol, St Ives, TR26 2DT
Foyer Tel 01736 795749
Bookings: Mrs Clare James
Tel 01736 362341 ext. 2178
S/Cap: 399

**ST. JUST TOWN HALL**
Foyer Tel 01736 788375
Bookings: Mrs Clare James
Tel 01736 362341 ext. 2178
S/Cap: 110

# PETERBOROUGH
# Cambridgeshire
Director of Leisure Services: Paul Martin
Bayard Place, Broadway, Peterborough PE1 1HZ
Tel 01733 742658 Fax 01733 742600

**KEY THEATRE***
See Provincial Venues for details

**BUSHFIELD SPORTS CENTRE**
Bushfield, Peterborough PE2 5RQ
Tel 01733 234018 Fax 01733 394043
Manager: Richard Thompson

**WERRINGTON SPORTS CENTRE**
Stanilard Way, Werrington, Peterborough PE4 6JT
Tel 01733 570064 Fax 01733 320053
Manager: Z Abdulla

# PLYMOUTH Devon
Principal Arts Development Officer: Paul Kelly
Department of Heritage and Leisure, 3rd Floor,
Windsor House, Tavistock Road, Plymouth,
Devon PL1 2AA
Tel 01752 307000 Fax 01752 307003

# POOLE Dorset
Civic Centre, Poole, Dorset BH15 2RU
Head of Leisure Services: David Neudegg
Tel 01202 633500 Fax 01202 633706

# PORTSMOUTH Hampshire
Civic Offices, Guildhall Square,
Portsmouth PO1 2AD
Tel 01705 834171 Fax 01705 834159
City Leisure Officer: David Knight

**PORTMOUTH GUILDHALL\***
See Provincial Venues for details

## POWYS
Cultural Services Manager: John Greatorex
Powys County Council, County Hall, Llandrindod
Wells, Powys LD1 5LG
Tel 01597 826464  Fax 01597 826243
Head of Leisure Services: Paul Griffiths

**PAVILION**
See Provincial Venues for details

**RHAYADER LEISURE CENTRE**
North Street, Rhayader LD6 5BU
Tel 01597 810355  Fax 01597 811022
S/Cap: 460 approx
Stage & Lighting Facilities available.

**COMMUNITY CENTRE, Knighton**
Community Centre Management Committee, 5 Swan
Court, Knighton LD7 1BT
Tel 01547 528011
Secretary: K.J. Kell
S/Cap: 500 approx.
Stage Facilities available.

**THE ALBERT HALL THEATRE, Llandrindod Wells**
See Provincial Venues for details

## PRESTON Lancashire

**GUILD HALL\***
Lancaster Road, Preston PR1 1HT
Tel 01772 203456

General Manager: John Shedwick
Policy: Concert Hall, mixed use.
Seats: 2,020. Bars, Restaurants, Cafeteria.

## READING Berkshire
Head of Theatres and Museums: Michael Eakin
Tel 0118 939 0123
Arts Development Officer: Tammy Bedford
Tel 0118 939 0394
Based at the Hexagon Theatre, Queen`s Walk,
Reading RG1 7UA

**THE HEXAGON\***
See Provincial Venues for details
**21 SOUTH STREET\***
21 South Street, Reading, Berkshire, RG1 4QR
Tel 0118 901 5234  Fax 0118 901 5235
e-mail: 21southstreet@reading.gov.uk
S/Cap: 125, 220 standing.

**RIVERMEAD CENTRE**
See Provincial Venues for details

**TOWN HALL**
Blagrave Street, Reading, Berkshire RG1 1QH
Tel 0118 939 9809  Fax 0118 956 6719
Manager: Christine Johnson
Conference, function and arts venue, comprising:
**Victoria Hall**
Comfortable elegant room, 220 sq.m., seating up to 200
for concerts, performances, conferences, exhibitions,
dinners, etc. High level audio-visual equipment, including
video, full sound equipment, film projection, etc. Rostra
stage; piano; basic theatre lighting.
**Meeting Rooms**
Four ancillary rooms for meetings, conferences and

functions.
Capacities:
**Waterhouse Room** - 70 sq.m. Seating for up to 60 theatre style with bar facilities.
**Silverthorne Room** - 40 sq.m. Seating for up to 40.
**Oscar Wilde Room** - 20 sq.m. Seating for up to 25.
**Jane Austen Room** - 20 sq.m. Seating for up to 25.

## REDCAR & CLEVELAND
Redcar & Cleveland Borough Council
Leisure and Library Dept., Redcar and Cleveland House, P.O. Box 86, Kirkleatham Street, Redcar, Cleveland TS10 1XX
Tel 01642 444000  Fax 01642 444341

**REDCAR BOWL***
See Provincial Venues for details

**COATHAM MEMORIAL HALL, REDCAR**
Concerts, Dances, Exhibitions

**JAMES FINEGAN MUNICIPAL HALL, ESTON**
Tel 01642 453974
Concerts, Dances, Exhibitions

**SOUTHBANK ACTIVITIES CENTRE**
Branch Street, Southbank
Tel 01642 454427
Community Hall.

## REDDITCH Worcestershire
Head of Leisure Services: Paul Patten
Town Hall, Redditch, Worcs. B98 8AH
Tel 01527 64252  Fax 01527 65216

**PALACE THEATRE***
See Provincial Venues for details

## REIGATE & BANSTEAD Surrey
Chief Executive: Martin Bacon
Town Hall, Castlefield Road, Reigate, RH2 0SH
Tel 01737 276000  Fax 01737 276013

**HARLEQUIN THEATRE AND CINEMA***
See Provincial Venues for details

## RESTORMEL Cornwall
Director of Tourism and Leisure: B. E. Arthur
Borough Offices, 39 Penwinnick Road,
St. Austell PL25 5DR
Tel 01726 74466  Fax 01726 68339

## RHONDDA CYNON TAFF Mid Glamorgan
Director of Leisure & Tourism: E. Hitchings
Rhondda Cynon Taff County Borough Council,
The Town Hall, Mountain Ash, CF45 4EU
Tel 01443 472461  Fax 01443 476012

**ABERCYNON SPORTS CENTRE**
Parc Abercynon, Abercynon, Mid Glamorgan CF45 4UY
Tel 01443 740141  Fax 01443 742337
Manager: Mrs Mair Taylor
750-1,000 seats.

**COLISEUM THEATRE**
See Provincial Venues for details

**HAWTHORN LEISURE &  RECREATION CENTRE**
Fairfield Lane, Pontypridd CF37 5LN
Tel 01443 843406  Fax 01443 841880
**Administration:**
Senior Assistant Manager: Keith Nicholls
For Bookings Contact: Duty Managers
S/Cap: Multi-purpose Sports Hall 750; Modern Concert Hall 450.
Stage facilities.

**LLANTRISANT LEISURE CENTRE**
Southgate Park, Llantrisant CF72 8DJ
Tel 01443 228538  Fax 01443 229727
Manager: Dave Matthews
S/Cap: Multi-purpose Sports Hall 900; Concert Hall 400.

**MICHAEL SOBELL SPORTS CENTRE**
Ynys, Aberdare, CF44 7RP
Tel 01685 874323  Fax 01685 870876
Manager: B Williamson
Capacity: 1,250 - 1,500 seats (Stage Available)

**MUNI ARTS CENTRE**
The Muni, Gelliwastad Road, Pontypridd CF37 2DP
Tel 01443 485934  Fax 01443 401832
**Administration:**
For Bookings Contact: Judith Jones, Manager, or Leon Kruger and Tyrone Pope, Assistant Managers.
S/Cap: 350
Multi-purpose Arts Centre (Theatre, Art Gallery, Cinema).
S/Cap: Main auditorium 355 (tiered seating); Cabaret setting 200.  6.7m x 7.6m stage.
Comprehensive lighting and sound facilities.

**PARK AND DARE, Treorchy**
Station Road, Treorchy, Rhondda, Mid-Glamorgan CF42 6NL
BO 01443 773112  Fax 01443 776922
**Administration:**
For Bookings Contact: Entertainment Officer: Derek Ward, M.I.L.A.M,
Tel 01443 472461  Fax 01443 476012
Manager: Enid Bowen
S/Cap: 770. Fully Equipped theatre, used also as cinema.

## RIBBLE VALLEY Lancashire
Director of Commercial Services: John Heap
Council Offices, Church Walk, Clitheroe BB7 2RA
Tel 01200 425111  Fax 01200 426339

## RICHMOND North Yorkshire
Leisure and Economic Development Unit Manager: Tony Clark
Friars Wynd, Richmond, North Yorkshire DL10 4RT
Tel 01748 829100  Fax 01748 850897

## ROCHDALE Lancashire
Municipal Offices, Smith Street, Rochdale OL16 1XG
Tel 01706 647474  Fax 01706 864104

**CIVIC HALL, HEYWOOD**
Wood Street, Heywood OL10 1LW
Tel 01706 368130  Fax 01706 867389
Manager: Brian Johnston
S/Cap: 400. Dancing 400.
General Purpose Hall

**CIVIC HALL, MIDDLETON**
Fountain Street, Middleton M24 1AF
Tel 0161 643 2470  Fax 0161 654 0211
Manager: Graham Duckworth
S/Cap: 600. Dancing 600. General Purpose Hall

**GRACIE FIELDS THEATRE***
Hudsons Walk, Oulder Hill, Rochdale,
Greater Manchester OL11 5EF
Mgt 01706 645522  Fax 01706 648404
Contacts: Phil Machin and Brian Robertson
S/Cap: 688

# ROCHESTER UPON MEDWAY Kent
Now Medway District Council.

**CENTRAL THEATRE***
See Provincial Venues for details

# ROCHFORD Essex
Council Offices, South Street, Rochford,
Essex SS4 1BW
Tel 01702 546366  Fax 01702 545737

**CLEMENTS HALL LEISURE CENTRE**
Clements Hall Way, Hawkwell, Hockley,
Essex SS5 4LN
Tel 01702 207777  Fax 01702 205307
Manager: Mrs Wendy Edwards
Managed by Circa Leisure Plc, Cottis House,
Locks Hill, Rochford, Essex SS4 1BB
Tel 01702 544331  Fax 01702 544766
Chief Executive: Peter Johnson
Marketing Manager: Mike Fitch

**THE MILL HALL**
Bellingham Lane, Rayleigh, Essex SS6 7ED
Tel 01268 778171  Fax 01268 778737
Manager: Jane Pepper
Managed by Circa Leisure Plc, Cottis House,
Locks Hill, Rochford, Essex SS4 1BB
Tel 01702 544331  Fax 01702 544766
Chief Executive: Peter Johnson
Marketing Manager: Mike Fitch

# ROSSENDALE Lancashire
Town Hall, Rawtenstall, Rossendale, Lancs BB4 7LZ
Tel 01706 217777  Fax 01706 224958
Venues Manager: Chris J Reed
Tel/Fax 01706 217797

**HASLINGDEN PUBLIC HALL**
Regent Street, Haslingden, Rossendale,
Lancs BB4 5HQ
Tel 01706 214477
S/Cap: 400

**BACUP LEISURE CENTRE**
Burnley Road, Bacup, Lancs OL13 8AE
Tel 01706 875550
Manager: Fred Thomas
S/Cap: 350

**ASTORIA BALLROOM**
The Valley Centre, Rawtenstall, Rossendale,
Lancs BB4 7QQ
Tel 01706 216965

Manager: Bill Wood
S/Cap: 700

**WHITWORTH CIVIC HALL**
Main Street, Whitworth, Lancs OL12 8JJ
Tel 01706 852866
Manager: Keith Brierley
S/Cap: 400

# ROTHER East Sussex
Tel 01424 787577  Fax 01424 787520
Director of Recreation & Tourism: Anthony Leonard
14 Beeching Road, Bexhill on Sea,
East Sussex TN39 3LG

**DE LA WARR PAVILION***
See Provincial Venues for details

# ROTHERHAM South Yorkshire
Head of Museums and Arts: Jane Glaister
Arts Centre Manager: Martyn Green
Senior Arts Development Officer: Rushiraj Munshi
Arts Officers: C McManus & J.McCoy
Museums and Arts Services Department, Rotherham
Arts Centre, Walker Place, Rotherham S65 1JH
Tel 01709 382121  Fax 01709 823653

**CIVIC THEATRE***
See Provincial Venues for details

# RUGBY Warwickshire
Head of Leisure Services: R. Honeybunn
Technical Services Dept., Town Hall, Evreux Way,
Rugby CV21 2LB
Tel 01788 533533  Fax 01788 533778

**THE BENN HALL**
Newbold Road, Rugby CV21 2LB
Tel 01788 541516  Fax 01788 533719
Manager: Mrs Kay O'Neill
Stage and dressing rooms (with showers) available.
S/Cap: 650 (Main Hall); 200 (Rokeby Room).
Bar, full catering facilities, easy access from
motorways, ample parking. Brochures and details
available from the Manager

# RUNNYMEDE Surrey
Venue Bookings Co-ordinator: B Lupton
Civic Offices, Station Road, Addlestone,
Surrey KT15 2AH
Tel 01932 838383  Fax 01932 855135

**CHERTSEY HALL**
Hariot Road, Chertsey KT16 9DR
Tel 01932 566645
Bookings Contact: Barbara Lupton on 01932 705437
Stage. Max. S/Cap. Large Hall: 290 (inc. raked 184)
Small Hall 90.

**HYTHE SOCIAL CENTRE**
Thorpe Lea Road, Staines TW18 3HD
Tel 01784 452102
Bookings Contact: Barbara Lupton on 01932 705437
Stage. Max. Seating Large Hall 300, Small Hall 75.

**LITERARY INSTITUTE**
51 High Street, Egham TW20 9EA
Tel 01784 431514

Bookings Contact: Barbara Lupton on 01932 705437
Stage.
S/Cap: 168 max.
Newly refurbished.

**THORPE VILLAGE HALL**
Coldharbour Lane, Thorpe, TW20 8TE
Tel 01932 562587
Bookings Contact: Barbara Lupton on 01932 705437
S/Cap: 113
Newly Refurbished

# RUSHCLIFFE Nottinghamshire
Chief Recreation & Community Services Officer:
P Chalmers
Recreation Department, Civic Centre, Pavilion Road,
West Bridgford, Nottingham NG2 5FE
Tel 0115 981 9911  Fax 0115 945 5882

# RUSHMOOR Hampshire
Council Offices, Farnborough Road, Farnborough
Hampshire GU14 7JU
Tel 01252 398398  Fax 01252 524017
Arts Officer: Richard Mann

**PRINCES HALL***
Princes Way, Aldershot, Hampshire GU11 1NX.
Mgt 01252 327671  BO 01252 329155
Fax 01252 320269
General Manager: Steven C Pugh
Chief Technician: David Goddard
S/Cap: 680

# RUTLAND
Chief Executive: Dr Janice Morphet
Community Development Officer: Mrs Pam Ellis
Catmose, Oakham, Rutland LE15 6HP
Tel 01572 722577  Fax 01572 758307

# RYEDALE North Yorkshire
Arts, Grants and Lottery Officer: Clare Slater
Ryedale District Council, Ryedale House, Malton,
North Yorkshire YO17 7HH
Tel 01653 600666  Fax 01653 696801

**THE MILTON ROOMS**
Malton, North Yorkshire YO17 7LX
Tel 01653 697195
**Administration:**
Chairman: Mr BR Mawtus, Lora House, Wykeham,
Scarborough YO13 9QB
Tel 01723 862845
Secretary/Treasurer:Roger Willis Tel 01653 694289

# ST. ALBANS Hertfordshire
Civic Centre, St. Peter's Street, St. Albans,
Hertfordshire AL1 3JE
Tel 01727 866100  Fax 01727 861561
Leisure Services Manager: Julie Simpson

**HARPENDEN PUBLIC HALLS**
South Down Road, Harpenden, Hertfordshire AL5 1PL
Tel 01582 762880  Fax 01582 762324
Manager: Joan Keast
Props: St. Albans Leisure Services
Mainly private functions, local operatic society ,craft fairs,
weddings, conferences, seminars and exhibitions.

S/Cap: 363 to 440

# ST. EDMUNDSBURY Suffolk
Director of  Leisure Services: S. Palframan
Borough Offices, Angel Hill, Bury St. Edmunds,
Suffolk IP33 1XB
Tel 01284 763233
Full details of all facilities contact: Tom Deller on:
Tel 01284 763233  Fax 01284 757091

**THEATRE ROYAL***
See Provincial Venues for details

**CORN EXCHANGE**
Abbeygate Street, Bury St Edmunds, Suffolk
Tel 01284 761315  Fax 01284 705025
Halls Administrator: Justin Morse
S/Cap: 400
Stage Facilities.

**TOWN HALL ARTS CENTRE**
High Street, Haverhill, Suffolk CB9 8AR
Tel 01440 714140
Manager: Julian Hartshorn
S/Cap: 235

# ST. HELENS Merseyside
Recreation Dept:
Principal Recreations Officer: Hugh Evans,
4th Floor, Century House, Hardshaw Street, St Helens,
Merseyside WA10 1RN
Tel 01744 455453  Fax 01744 455330
Youth and Community Services Dept:
Senior Officer: Melyn Riding,
Rivington Centre, Rivington Road, St Helens,
Merseyside WA10 4ND
Tel 01744 455461  Fax 01744 455350

**HAYDOCK LEISURE CENTRE**
Clipsley Lane, St Helens, Merseyside WA11 0JG
Manager: Vicky McDowell
For Bookings call 01744 24006
S/Cap: 400

**BROADWAY COMMUNITY LEISURE CENTRE**
Broadway, Grange Park, St Helens,
Merseyside WA10 3RY
Tel/Fax 01744 612822
Centre Manager: Gary Forde
For Bookings Contact: Mike Cooper on 01744 24349
S/Cap: 400 (at Broadway Community High School)

**PETERSTREET COMMUNITY CENTRE**
Peter Street, St. Helens WA10 2EQ
Tel 01744 24293
For Bookings Contact: Kathryn Northover, Manager
S/Cap: 200. Hall and Stage.

**QUEENS PARK COMMUNITY LEISURE CENTRE**
Boundary Road, St. Helens WA10 2LT
Tel 01744 22339
For Bookings Contact: Terry Bates, Manager
Large Hall 32m x 17m. Stage available.
S/Cap: 600

**SUTTON COMMUNITY LEISURE CENTRE**
Eltonhead Road, St. Helens WA9 5AU
Tel 01744 810910  Fax 01744 810695
For Bookings Contact: Jerry Caughey, Duty Manager.
Large Hall 33m x 36m. Stage available.
S/Cap: 1,000

## SALFORD
## Greater Manchester
Head of Arts, Leisure & Community Services:
Ted Tootill
Vulcan House, Albion Place, The Cresent, Salford
M5 4NL
Tel 0161 736 9448  Fax 0161 745 7806

**LANCASTRIAN HALL**
See Provincial Venues for details

**PEMBROKE HALLS**
High St., Walkden, Worsley, Manchester M28 3BR
Tel 0161 790 4584  Fax 0161 702 6920
Contact for Bookings: David Heyes
Multi-purpose venue for cabaret and banqueting.
S/capacity: 550 approx.

**PHOENIX THEATRE**
Westerham Avenue, off Liverpool Street
Salford M5 4PS
Tel 0161 736 1556
Community Theatre and Arts Centre

## SALISBURY Wiltshire
Chief Executive: R. K. Sheard
Principal Arts & Community Officer: Rachel Efemey
Salisbury District Council, The Council House,
Bourne Hill, Salisbury SP1 3UZ
Tel 01722 434307  Fax 01722 434632

**CITY HALL**
See Provincial Venues for details

**GUILDHALL**
Guildhall Square, Market Place, Salisbury SP1 1JH.
Tel 01722 412144
Fax 01722 434369
Contact for Bookings: Anita Waddington, Manager
S/Cap: 200. Flexible  Stage/Seating Facilities.

## SANDWELL West Midlands
Arts in Sandwell, Department of Education and
Community Services, Sandwell Metropolitan Borough
Council, PO Box 41, Shaftesbury House, 402 High
Street, West Bromwich, West Midlands B70 9LT
Tel 0121 569 4927  Fax 0121 544 3854

## SCARBOROUGH
## North Yorkshire
Director of Tourism & Leisure: Peter Dahl
Department of Tourism & Amenities, Londesborough
Lodge, The Crescent, Scarborough, N. Yorks
YO11 2PW
Tel 01723 232323  Fax 01723 376941

**SPA GRAND HALL***
See Provincial Venues for details

**SPA THEATRE***
See Provincial Venues for details.

**WHITBY PAVILION THEATRE**
See Provincial Venues for details

**SUN LOUNGE, FILEY***
See Provincial Venues for details

## SEDGEFIELD Co. Durham
Leisure Services Officer: P. K. Ball
Green Lane, Spennymoor, Co. Durham DL16 6JQ
Tel 01388 816166  Fax 01388 815374

**NEWTON AYCLIFFE LEISURE CENTRE**
Beveridge Arcade, Newton Aycliffe DL5 4EH
Tel 01325 300500  Fax 01325 301726
Manager: Jean Burton
S/Cap: 3 Halls: 30, 180 and 700.
Fully Licensed. Portable Stage. Lighting & PA
Available

**SPENNYMOOR LEISURE CENTRE**
High Street, Spennymoor, Co. Durham DL16 6DB
Tel 01388 815827  Fax 01388 810098
Manager: Jean Burton
S/Cap: Entertainment Hall 300. Stage Facilities.
Lighting & PA Available, Fully Licensed.
Sports Hall 1,198.

**SHILDON SUNNYDALE LEISURE CENTRE**
Midridge Lane, Shilden, Co. Durham DL4 2EP
Tel 01388 777340  Fax 01388 778659
Manager: Cathy Hartnell.
S/Cap: 300 max. Portable Stages.

**FERRYHILL LEISURE CENTRE**
Lambton Road, Ferry Hill, Co. Durham DL17 8BQ
Tel 01740 654121  Fax 01740 651158
Bookings Contact: Peter Kirtley on 01740 654123
S/Cap: 1 Hall - 450. Portable Stage. Licensed.

## SEDGEMOOR Somerset
Chief Executive: Mr A.G. Lovell, C. Eng
Bridgwater House, King Square,
Bridgwater TA6 3AR
Tel 01278 435435  Fax 01278 444076

**THE PRINCESS, Burnham on Sea**
Burnham on Sea, Somerset TA8 1EH
Tel 01278 784464  Fax 01278 455260
Manager: Jan Wilson
S/Cap: 210. Full Stage Facilities.
**BRIDGWATER TOWN HALL**
Hogh Street, Bridgwater, Somerset TA6 3AS
Tel 01278 435453
S/Cap: 400. Full Stage Facilities.

**BRIDGWATER ARTS CENTRE LTD**
Arts Centre Director: Mrs Charlie Dearden
Tel 01278 422700
S/Cap: 200. Full Stage and Licensed Facilities
For full details see Arts Centres

## SEFTON Merseyside
P.O. Box 25, Promenade, Southport PR9 0DZ
Tel 01704 533133 or 0151 934 2416
Fax 0151 934 2418
Chief Economic Development & Tourism Officer:
Ken Wainman, Economic Development & Tourism
Division, PO Box 25, Promenade, Southport, PR9 0DZ
Tel 0151 934 2418  Fax 0151 934 2438

**SOUTHPORT THEATRE & FLORAL HALL
COMPLEX***
(NB: Owned by Local Authority but managed by Apollo
Leisure)
See Provincial Venues for details

**SOUTHPORT ARTS CENTRE***
See Provincial Venues for details

**CIVIC HALL, CROSBY**
Crosby Road North, Liverpool L22 OLQ
Tel 0151 928 1919  Fax 0151 257 6419
Arts Operation Manager: Mark Ratcliffe
Multi-purpose Hall. Capacity 401. Concerts,
Promotions, Civic and Private Functions, Bar Facilities.

# SELBY North Yorkshire
Chief Executive & Clerk of the Council: Martin Connor
Civic Centre, Portholme Road, Selby YO8 4SB
Tel 01757 705101  Fax 01757 292020

**ABBEY LESIURE CENTRE**
Scott Road, Selby, North Yorkshire YO8 OBL
Tel 01757 213758  Fax 01757 210313
Manager: Bob Lancaster
Capacity Main Hall: Seats: 300; Standing: 480.

# SHEFFIELD
# South Yorkshire

**CITY HALL**
See Provincial Venues for details
**Oval Hall**
S/Cap: 2,346.
Rock, Pop, Comedy, Orchestral Concerts, Ballet,
Theatre, Meetings & Conferences, etc.
**Central Hall**
Ballroom Capacity: Club nights and Dances, 850. .
Dinner Dances 500, Exhibitions, Central Suite
comprising: North Hall (Bar), South Hall (Bar), Central
Hall (Ballroom), The Arches (Refreshments).
**Memorial Hall**
S/Cap: 522.
Concerts, Comedy, Meetings, Lectures, Conferences,
etc.

**LIBRARY THEATRE, CENTRAL LIBRARY**
Surrey Street, Sheffield, S1 1XZ
Tel 0114 273 4102  Fax 0114 273 5009
For Bookings Contact: Ann Bradley on 0114 273 4102
S/Cap: 260. Used mainly by local pop groups, amateur
dramatic societies and for meetings.

# SHEPWAY Kent
Civic Centre, Castle Hill Avenue, Folkestone,
Kent CT20 2QY
Tel 01303 850388  Fax 01303 258854
Executive Director of Tourism Services: Stephen
Hagues

**LEAS CLIFF HALL, FOLKESTONE***
**The Leas, Folkestone, Kent CT20 2DZ**
**Mgt 01303 254695  BO 01303 253193**
**Fax 01303 221175**
**ADMINISTRATION:**
Props: Shepway District Council
Managed by Apollo Leisure (UK) Ltd
For all booking information and further details please
contact: Sam Shrouder or Nicky Monk at Apollo
Leisure (UK) Ltd, PO Box 960 Oxford OX4 5NO, Tel:
01865 782900 Fax: 01865 782910
General Manager: Louise Guedalla

# SHREWSBURY Shropshire
Shrewsbury & Atcham Borough Council, The Guildhall,
Dogpole, Shrewsbury, Shropshire SY1 1ER

Tel 01743 232255  Fax 01743 271594
Director of Environmental Health, Tourism & Leisure:
Geraint Morgan, Oakleigh Manor, Belle Vue Road,
Shrewsbury, Shropshire SY3 7NW
Tel 01743 231456  Fax 01743 271593

**MUSIC HALL***
The Square, Shrewsbury, Shropshire SY1 1LH
Admin 01743 352019  BO 01743 244255
Fax 01743 358780
General Manager: TBA
House Manager: David Jack
Chief Technician: Grant Wilson
Seats 398 on rectractable units (48 on arena floor).
Promenade 450.

# SOLIHULL West Midlands
P.O. Box 20, Council House, Solihull B91 2QU
Tel: 0121 704 6000  Fax 0121 704 6669
Director of Education, Libraries & Arts: David Nixen

**SOLIHULL ARTS COMPLEX**
See Provincial Venues for details

# SOUTHAMPTON Hampshire
West Marland Road, Civic Centre,
Southampton SA14 7LP
Tel 01703 832453  Fax 01703 233359

**SOUTHAMPTON GUILDHALL***
See Provincial Venues for details
**SOLENT SUITE**
Civic Centre, Southampton SA14 7LP
Tel 01703 832200
Manager: Martin Orman
S/Cap: 300. Concerts, Banqueting, Meetings, Dances,
Exhibitions.

# SOUTH BEDFORDSHIRE
Leisure Services Manager: Catherine Doherty
The District Offices, High Street North, Dunstable,
Beds LU6 1LF
Tel 01582 472222  Fax 01582 474009

**QUEENSWAY HALL, DUNSTABLE**
Vernon Place, Dunstable, LU5 4EU
Tel 01582 603326/609620
Fax 01582 471190
NB: Facility now managed by Sports and Leisure
Foods Ltd.
Director: Tony Jupp
Hall Manager: Yvonne Mullens
S/Cap: 900. Full Stage Facilities.

# SOUTH BUCKS
# Buckinghamshire
Chief Executive: Chris Furness
Head of Leisure: Hamish Pringle (ext: 215)
Arts & Play Officer: Debbie Stubbs (ext: 347)
Council Offices, Windsor Road, Slough SL1 2HN
Tel 01753 533333  Fax 01753 676214
DX 42266 Slough West

**BEACON THEATRE AND LEISURE CENTRE**
Holtspur Way, Beaconsfield, Bucks HP9 1RJ
Direct Tel/Fax 01494 677764
NB: Managed by Glendale Leisure on behalf of South
Bucks District Council.

## SOUTH CAMBRIDGESHIRE
### Cambridgeshire
Chief Executive: J.S. Ballantyne
Arts Development Officer: Celia Bell
South Cambridgeshire Hall, 9-11 Hills Road,
Cambridge CB2 1PB
Tel 01223 443000  Fax 01223 443149
e-mail celia.bell@scambs.gov.uk

## SOUTH DERBYSHIRE
### Derbyshire
Leisure Facilities Manager: Chris Mason
Civic Offices, Swadlincote, Derbyshire DE11 0AH
Tel 01283 228094  Fax 01283 228158

**GREEN BANK LEISURE CENTRE**
Civic Way, Swandlincote, Derbyshire DE11 OAH
Tel 01283 216269  Fax 01283 210979
Manager: Paul Dowling
S/Cap: 1,100. Stage Facilities.

## SOUTHEND-ON-SEA Essex
Civic Centre, Victoria Avenue, Southend on Sea
Essex SS2 6ER
Tel 01702 215000  Fax 01702 215631
Director of Leisure Services: John Dallaway

**CLIFFS PAVILION***
**Station Road, Westcliff-on-Sea, Essex SSO 7RA**
**Mgt 01702 331852  BO 01702 351135**
**SD 01702 347394  Fax 01702 433015**
**Admin 01702 390657  Marketing 01702 390472**
See Provincial Venues for details

## SOUTH GLOUCESTERSHIRE
Council Offices, Broad Lane, Engine Common,
Yate, BS17 5PN
Tel 01454 868686  Fax 01454 865819
Arts & Events: Diana Hatton

**THORNBURY LEISURE CENTRE**
Alveston Hill, Thornbury, Bristol, BS12 2JB
Tel 01454 865777  Fax 01454 865775
Manager: R.Sims
Portable Stage.
S/Cap: 1,000.
Concerts, Dances, Exhibitions, etc.

**YATE LEISURE CENTRE**
Kennedy Way, Yate, Bristol, BS17 4XE
Tel 01454 865800  Fax 01454 865805
Manager: Kath Lerebourg
Portable Stage.
S/Cap: 1,500.
Concerts, Dances, Exhibitions etc.

## SOUTH HAMS Devon
South Hams District Council
Leisure Services Manager: M. Thomas
Follaton House, Plymouth Road, Totnes TQ9 5NE
Tel 01803 861234  Fax 01803 866151

**CIVIC HALL, TOTNES**
Tel 01803 862003
Caretaker: Mr Tom Joyce
For Bookings Contact Town Clerk: Mr. D Edwards
Esq., The Guildhall, 5 Ramparts Walk, Totnes,
Devon TQ9 5QH

Tel 01803 862147  Fax 01803 864275
S/Cap: 324.
General Purpose Hall (Managed by Totnes
Town Council)

**QUAYSIDE LEISURE CENTRE**
Rope Walk, Kingsbridge TQ7 1HH
Tel 01548 857100  Fax 01548 856903
Manager: D. Day
Contact for Bookings: Reception, Kingsbridge
Sports Centre.
Large adaptable hall. Disabled access.
(Owned by South Hams District Council)

**SOUTH DARTMOOR LEISURE CENTRE**
Leonards Road, Ivybridge PL21 OSL
Tel 01752 896999  Fax 01752 895476
Contact for Bookings: Gill Knox, Manager.
Multi-purpose performance room, s/cap 2 - 300. Large
adaptable hall, s/cap: 800. Disabled access. (Owned
by South Hams District Council).

**TOTNES PAVILION**
Borough Park Road, Totnes TQ9 5JG
Tel 01803 862992  Fax 01803 867381
Contact for Bookings: Sarah Kellow, Manager.
Adaptable function suite, s/cap 200. Disabled access.
(Owned by South Hams District Council)

## SOUTH HOLLAND
### Lincolnshire
Arts Officer: Nigel Hawkins
South Holland District Council, Priory Road, Spalding,
Lincolnshire PE11 2XE
Tel 01775 761161  Fax 01775 711054

## SOUTH KESTEVEN
### Lincolnshire
Head of Amenity Services: J Slater
Arts Development Officer: K. P. Ross
Council Offices, St. Peter's Hill, Grantham, Lincs
NG31 6PZ
Tel 01476 406080  Fax 01476 406000

**BOURNE LEISURE CENTRE**
Queens Road, Bourne, PE10 9DT
Tel 01778 421435  Fax 01778 394528
Manager: John Foster
S/Cap: 600. Stage Facilities.

**CORN EXCHANGE, BOURNE**
Abbey Road, Bourne PE10 9EF
Tel 01778 423771
S/Cap: 300. Stage Facilities.

**DEEPINGS LEISURE CENTRE**
Park Road, Deeping St. James,
Peterborough PE6 8NF
Tel 01778 344072
Manager: Bob Pinder
S/Cap: 600. Stage Facilities.

**GRANTHAM MERES LEISURE CENTRE**
Trent Road, Grantham NG31 7XG
Tel 01476 581930  Fax 01476 581931
Manager: Lisa Harrison
S/Cap: 600. Stage Facilities

**GRANTHAM GUILDHALL ARTS CENTRE**
Correspondance Address: Council Offices, St Peters
Hill, Grantham, NG31 6PZ

Tel 01476 406159  Fax 01476 406001
Manager: Carol Drury
Theatre: 210 seat raked auditorium, full stage facilities.
S/Cap: 200, Function Hall, Studio Space & Gallery.

**STAMFORD ARTS CENTRE**
27 St.Mary's Street, Stamford, Lincolnshire PE9 2DL
Tel 01780 763203  Fax 01780 766690
Manager: David Popple
Theatre: 170 seat, full stage facilities.
S/Cap: 200 seat Function Hall, Studio Space & Gallery

## SOUTH LAKELAND Cumbria
Head of Tourism and Amenities: R. Read
Arts & Events Officer: Imelda Winters-Lewis
South Lakeland District Council, Leisure Services
Department, South Lakeland House, Kendal, Cumbria
LA9 4DL
Tel 01539 733333  Fax 01539 740300

**CORONATION HALL, ULVERSTON\***
See Provincial Venues for details

**KENDAL LEISURE CENTRE**
See Provincial Venues for details

**TOWN HALL, KENDAL**
Highgate, Kendal, Cumbria LA9 4DL
Tel 01539 725758  Fax 01539 734457
Assembly Room.
For Bookings Contact: Debbie McKee
S/Cap: 400. Dressing Rooms, Catering, Bar, Concerts,
Shows.

**VICTORIA HALL, GRANGE-OVER-SANDS**
Tel 01539 532375
S/Cap: Small Hall 300.
For bookings contact: Derek Whittington

## SOUTH NORTHAMPTONSHIRE Northamptonshire
Leisure Policy Officer: Richard Griffiths
Arts Manager: Anna Hayward
Council Offices, Springfield, Towcester, Northants
NN12 6AE
Tel 01327 350211  Fax 01327 359219

## SOUTH OXFORDSHIRE Oxon
Leisure Services Officer: Christine Gore
P.O. Box 140, Council Offices, Crowmarsh,
Wallingford OX10 8QX
Tel 01491 835351  Fax 01491 833390

**THAME SPORTS AND ARTS CENTRE**
Oxford Road, Thame, Oxon OX9 2BB.
Tel 01844 215607  Fax 01844 216927
Manager: Ray Boulton
Arts Officer: Alan Hamilton
S/cap: Large Hall: 600; Small Hall: 150.

**DIDCOT LEISURE CENTRE**
Mereland Road, Didcot, Oxon OX12 8AY
Tel 01235 811250  Fax 01235 816356
Manager: David Spring
S/Cap: Main Hall, 300.

## SOUTH PEMBROKESHIRE Dyfed

**PATER HALL, PEMBROKE DOCK**
Council Offices, Pater Hall, Lewis Street, Pembroke
Dock
Tel 01646 684410  Fax 01646 622788
Director: Mrs W.A. Vincent
S/Cap: 300.
Dance Hall, Conference Hall, Limited Theatre Licence.
Plays, Social Functions, Concerts, etc. Catering
facilities. Adjoining rooms for smaller functions.

## SOUTH RIBBLE Lancashire
Civic Centre, West Paddock, Leyland,
Lancashire PR5 1DH
Tel 01772 421491  Fax 01772 622287
Chief Executive: P Halsall, C.I.P.F.A.
Leisure Services Manager: Paul Callander, M.B.A.,
D.M.S., M.I.L.A.M.

**WORDEN ARTS AND CRAFTS CENTRE, LEYLAND**
Worden Park, Worden Lane, Leyland,
Lancashire PR5 2DJ
Tel/Fax 01772 455908
Arts Development Officer: Richard Blackburn  D.M.S.
Stage Facilties.
S/Cap: 130.

## SOUTH SHROPSHIRE Shropshire
Director of Environment & Development: W.N. Jones
Council Offices, Stone House, Corve Street, Ludlow,
Shropshire SY8 1DG
Tel 01584 874941  Fax 01584 875245

## SOUTH SOMERSET DISTRICT COUNCIL Somerset
Community & Leisure Manager: Paul C Greatorex,
MILAM
Holyrood Lace Mill, Holyrood Street, Chard,
Somerset TA20 2YA
Tel 01460 260359  Fax: 01460 265553

**OCTAGON THEATRE**
See Provincial Venues for details

## SOUTH STAFFORDSHIRE Staffordshire
Chief Executive: Mr. Les Barnfield
Council Offices, Wolverhampton Road, Codsall, South
Staffordshire WV8 1PX
Tel 01902 696000  Fax 01902 696800

## SOUTH TYNESIDE Tyne and Wear
Head of Leisure Services: David Marsden,
Leisure Services, Central Library, Prince George Square,
South Shields NE33 2PE
Tel 0191 427 1717  Fax 0191 427 0469
Arts Development Officer: Pauline Moger
Arts department, Custom House, Mill Dam, South
Shields, Tyne and Wear. NE33 1ES
Tel 0191 454 1234  Fax 0191 456 5979

**BOLINGBROKE HALL, South Shields**
Bolingbroke Street, South Shields NE33 2SS
Tel 0191 454 0914 Fax 0191 454 4684
S/Cap: 225 with small stage erected. Suitable for
Exhibitions, Conferences, etc.
Also for single performance tours.

**TEMPLE PARK CENTRE, South Shields***
John Reid Road, South Shields, NE34 8QN
Tel 0191 456 9119 Fax 0191 456 6621
Capacity: Seats: 2,200; Standing: 3,500
Suitable for all performance tours, exhibitions, concerts
and cabaret type entertainment with catering

# SPELTHORNE Surrey
Chief Executive: M. B. Taylor, LL.B.Solicitor
Director of Leisure Services: Kim Tighe
Council Offices, Knowle Green, Staines TW18 1XB
Tel 01784 451499 Fax 01784 463356

**SPELTHORNE LEISURE CENTRE**
Knowle Green, Staines, Middlesex TW18 1AJ
General Manager: Jay Jenkins
Tel 01784 417100 Fax 01784 417105
Main Hall S/Cap: 750
For Bookings Contact: Peter Davis

**SUNBURY LEISURE CENTRE**
Nursery Road, Sunbury-on-Thames, Middlesex
TW16 6LG
Tel 01932 772287 Fax 01932 772093
Manager: Dale Wild
Contact for Bookings: Lynne Phillips
S/Cap: 400+
**THE OLD TOWN HALL ARTS CENTRE**
Staines Theatre, Markets Square, Staines, Middlesex
TW18 4RH
Tel 01784 881885 BO 881880 Fax 01784 880965
General Manager: Sandra Bruce-Gordon
For General Enquiries contact: Sean Woodhead
**RIVERSIDE ARTS CENTRE**
59 Thames Street, Sunbury, Middlesex TW16 5QF
Tel 01932 789249
Manager: Eric Champion
For Bookings call: 01932 782850
S/Cap: 120 max

# STAFFORD Staffordshire
Civic Offices, Riverside, Stafford ST16 3AQ
Tel 01785 223181 Fax 01785 249371
Director of Development: D.J. Pinnock
Assistant Director (Leisure & Tourism): John Gilbert

**THE GATEHOUSE THEATRE***
Eastgate Street, Stafford ST16 2LT
Mgt 01785 253595 BO 01785 254653
Fax 01785 225622
Manager: Daniel Shaw
Administration Manager: Lynn Elkin
House Manager: Alan Vernon
Senior Technician: Ken Moore
Marketing Officer: Nathan Archer
Capacity: 570 in one raked tier (reduces to 490 when
orchestra pit fully extended)

**THE MALCOLM EDWARDS THEATRE***
Eastgate Street, Stafford ST16 2LT
Mgt 01785 253595 BO 01785 254653
Fax 01785 225622
Capacity: End Stage 96, In the Round 116; Cinema-

style 120.

# STAFFORDSHIRE MOORLANDS Staffordshire
Chief Executive: Mr B J Preedy
Moorlands House, Stockwell Street, Leek, Staffs
ST13 6HQ
Tel 01538 483483 Fax 01538 483474

# STEVENAGE Hertfordshire
Director of Community Services: Stephen Halsey
Department of Community Services, Daneshill House,
Danstrete, Stevenage, Hertfordshire SG1 1HN
Tel 01438 356177 Fax 01438 740296

**STEVENAGE ARTS AND LEISURE CENTRE**
Lytton Way, Stevenage, Herts SG1 1LZ
Mgt 01438 766642 BO 01438 766866
Fax 01438 766675
Director of Leisure Services: M McCardle
Arts & Entertainments Manager: Bob Bustance
Marketing Manager: Maggi Turfrey
S/Cap: 1,400, Concert Hall.

**GORDON CRAIG THEATRE***
**Stevenage Arts & Leisure Centre, Lytton Way,**
**Stevenage, Herts SG1 1LZ**
**Mgt 01438 766642 BO 01438 766866**
**Fax 01438 766675**
Director of Leisure Services: M McCardle
Arts & Entertainments Manager: Bob Bustance
Marketing Manager: Maggi Turfrey
Technical Stage Manager: Richard Crumpton
Seats: 506. Bar, Restaurant.

# STOCKPORT Greater Manchester
Stockport Metropolitan Borough Council, Town Hall
Complex, Piccadilly, Stockport SK1 3XE
Tel 0161 474 4444 Fax 0161 429 0335
Principal Arts Officer: Ms Jo McGrath
Leisure Services Division, Arts Officer, Compstall
Road, Romiley, Stockport SK6 4EA
Tel 0161 430 6570 Fax 0161 406 6782

**ROMILEY FORUM***
See Provincial Venues for details

**STOCKPORT TOWN HALL**
Wellington Street South, Stockport SK1 3XE
Tel 0161 474 3260 Fax 0161 477 9530
Contact: Ann Cullen
S/Cap: 720. Sunday Licence. Stage Shows, Banquets,
Dances, Conferences, etc.

# STOCKTON-ON-TEES Cleveland
Gloucester House, 72 Church Road, Stockton-on-
Tees, TS18 1YB
Tel 01642 393900
Fax 01642 393963

**BILLINGHAM FORUM**
See Provincial Venues for details

**GEORGIAN THEATRE**
Green Dragon Yard, Stockton on Tees,

Cleveland TS18 1AT
Tel/Fax 01642 674115
Concert hall for minority arts.
S/Cap: 140.

**THORNABY PAVILION**
New Town Centre, Thornaby, Stockton on Tees,
Cleveland TS17 9EW
Tel 01642 760971 Fax 01642 750235
Manager: David Seller
Concerts, Dances, Exhibitions & Conferences

**STOCKWELL HALL**
S/Cap: 1,500 including 384 fixed seats in balcony and
approx. 1,100 on floor according to size of staging.

**WATSON HALL**
Tel 01642 750235
S/Cap: 200

# STOKE-ON-TRENT
## Staffordshire
Civic Centre, Glebe Street, Stoke-On-Trent,
Staffordshire ST4 1RT
Tel 01782 232732 Fax 01782 236691
Director of Property Services: Stephen Costello

**ASSEMBLY HALL, TUNSTALL**
High Street Tunstall,
Staffordshire
Tel 01782 834656
Closed for refurbishment. For further details contact
Carole Salmon
Tel 01782 232732 Fax 01782 236691
**STOKE TOWN HALL**
Civic Centre, Glebe Street, Stoke on Trent, ST4 1RT
Tel 01782 232631

**JUBILEE HALL, STOKE**
Stoke Town Hall, Civic Centre, Glebe Street,
Stoke on Trent Staffordshire ST4 1RT
Tel 01782 232631
For bookings contact Pat Brayford on 01782 232832 or
Carole Salmon on 01782 232732
S/Cap: 300

**KING'S HALL, STOKE**
Stoke Town Hall, Civic Centre, Glebe Street,
Stoke on Trent Staffordshire ST4 1RT
Tel 01782 404732
For bookings contact Carole Salmon on 01782 232732
Fax 01782 236691
S/Cap: 1,372

**QUEENS THEATRE, BURSLEM**
See Provincial Venues for details

**VICTORIA HALL, HANLEY***
See Provincial Venues for details

**ALBERT HALL, LONGTON**
Times Square, Longton Staffordshire ST3 1BZ
Tel 01782 314364
For bookings contact Carole Salmon on 01782 232732
Fax 01782 236691
S/Cap 240

# STROUD Gloucestershire
Head of Leisure Services: Alan Caig, M.A., D.M.S.,
M.I.L.A.M.

Stroud District Council, Ebley Mill, Westward Road,
Stroud, GL5 4UB
Tel 01453 766321 Fax 01453 750932

**SUBSCRIPTION ROOMS**
George Street, Stroud, Glos., GL5 1AE
Booking Clerk: Kay Tanner on 01453 764999 (9am-
5pm)
Fax 01453 755930
S/Cap: 350 max. Stage Facilities.

# STOWMARKET, Suffolk
Town Clerk: M. Cansdale
Milton House, Milton Road South,
Stowmarket, IP14 1EZ
Tel 01449 612060 Fax 01449 775103

**REGAL THEATRE**
Ipswich Street, Showmarket, Suffolk IP14 1AY
Tel 01449 612825
Large open stage, no drapes, with dressing
accommodation. Theatre available for daytime
conferences.
S/Cap: 234.
Bar and refreshment facilities.

# SUFFOLK COASTAL Suffolk
Assistant Director of Leisure and Tourism:
Mr A Osmanski
Melton Hill, Woodbridge IP12 1AU
Tel 01394 383789 Fax 01394 385100

**SPA PAVILION, FELIXSTOWE***

**LEISURE & CONFERENCE CENTRE, FELIXSTOWE**
Undercliff Road West, Felixstowe, Suffolk IP11 8AB
Tel 01394 670411 Fax 01394 277456
For Bookings Contact: Paul Johnson, Manager
S/Cap: 250

# SUNDERLAND Tyne & Wear
Director of Education and Community Services:
Dr J Williams
Mautland Square, Houghton-Le-Spring, Tyne & Wear
DH4 4BL
Tel 0191 512 0444 Fax 0191 584 5059

**CROWTREE LEISURE CENTRE**
Crowtree Road, Sunderland SR1 3EL
Tel 0191 553 2600
Manager: Miss A O'Neill

**WASHINGTON LEISURE CENTRE**
Town Centre District 1, Washington NE38 7JF
Tel 0191 219 3400 Fax 0191 219 3424
Manager: Mike Poulter
Main Hall available for booking.

**NORTHUMBRIA CENTRE**
Stephenson Road, Stephenson, District 12,
Washington
Tel 0191 416 3380 Fax 0191 219 3424
Manager: Mike Poulter
Seating: 3,460

**WASHINGTON ARTS CENTRE**
Biddick Lane, Fatfield, Washington 7, NE38 8AB
Tel 0191 416 6440 Fax 0191 219 3466
Manager: Helen Hogg
Capacities: 150, 85. Theatre: 130

**SEABURN CENTRE**
Whitburn Road, Seaburn, Sunderland SR6 8AA
Tel 0191 529 4091  Fax 0191 529 3958
Manager: Steve Crewe

# SURREY HEATH Surrey
Arts Business Manager: Karen Turner BA (Hons)
Surrey Heath House, Knoll Road, Camberley, Surrey
GU15 3HD
Tel 01276 686252

**ARTS LINK, CAMBERLEY***
Knoll Road, Camberley, Surrey
Tel 01276 26978  BO 01276 23738

# SWANLEY Kent
Town Clerk: C. A. Roddan
Council Offices, St. Mary's Road, Swanley, Kent BR8 7BU
Tel 01322 665855  Fax 01322 613000

**WOODLANDS THEATRE**
Hilda May Avenue, Swanley, BR8 7BU
Tel 01322 613900  Fax 01322 664739
For Bookings Contact: Paula Smith and Angela
Warren
S/Cap: 220.
Policy: Local Shows including Ballet. Available also for
Conferences and Banquets. Large car park.

# SWANSEA
Director of Leisure: David Evans
The Guildhall, Swansea SA1 4PE
Tel 01792 635401  Fax 01792 635408

**BRANGWYN HALL**
Tel 01792 635489
Contact: Mr. S. Keir
S/Cap: 1,198
Choral & Orchestral Concerts, Dances, Dinners,
Exhibitions and Conferences

**GRAND THEATRE***
Tel 01792 475242
Contact: Mr. G. Iles
S/Cap: 1,021
Touring Ballet, Opera, Drama, One Night Concerts and
Comedians, Musicals. Pantomime plus own repertory
productions.

**PATTI PAVILION***
Victoria Park, Oystermouth Road, Swansea SA1 3EP
Tel 01792 477710
Contact: Mr T Lloyd
S/Cap: 490
Variety, etc. Conferences, Tours, Rep. and General
Purpose Building - Boxing, Wrestling, Exhibitions,
Meetings, Dances, etc.

**PENYRHEOL THEATRE***
Tel 01792 897039

**SWANSEA LEISURE CENTRE**
Oystermouth Road, Swansea SA1 3ST
Tel 01792 649126  Fax 01792 457231
For Bookings Contact: Alan Woodman, Manager
S/Cap: 900
Variety, Concerts, Conferences, Exhibition & General
Purpose rooms.

**THEATR CWMTAWE***
Tel 01792 830111

# SWINDON Wiltshire
Civic Offices, Euclid Street, Swindon,
Wiltshire SN1 2JH
Tel 01793 493000  Fax 01793 490420
Head of Arts and Museums: Julia Holberry
Fax 01793 466484

**OASIS LEISURE CENTRE**
North Star Avenue, Swindon SN2 1EP
Tel 01793 445400  Fax 01793 465132
Manager: Alan Greer
S/Cap: 1,680; Standing: 2,250. Main S./Cap: 2,250.
Portable stage, three phase electrics. Restaurant for
80 persons. Ample free car parking adjacent to
complex.

**ARTS CENTRE**
Devizes Road, Swindon, Wilts SN1 4BJ
Tel 01793 614837  Fax 01793 422827
**Administration:**
Manager: Clarry Bean
Marketing: David Kingsbury
Technician: Matthew Herring
**Technical:**
Pros. Arch stage with small apron. Lighting and sound
equipment. Dressing room facilities. Bar facilities.
S/Cap: 220

**TOWN HALL STUDIOS**
Regent Circus, Swindon SN1 1QF
Tel 01793 493697  Fax 01793 611181
Manager: Jane Hyde-Walsh
Bookings Contact: Marie McClusky
Studio theatre for small scale productions, S/Cap: 98,
raked. Multi-purpose lighting and sound equipment.
Limited disabled access. Dressing room facilities. Bar
facilities.

**LINK CENTRE**
Whitehill Way, Westlea, Swindon, Wiltshire SN5 7DL
Tel 01793 445566  Fax 01793 886115
**Technical:**
Main Hall: 1,500 seated, 1,900 standing. 3 phase
supply, variable height staging, dressing rooms and
catering facilities. Extensive free parking.
Arb Studio: Flexible stage and raked seating area with
upper balcony. Sound and lighting equipment.
Dressing room and bar facilities.

# TAMWORTH Staffordshire
Municipal Offices, Marmion House,
Lichfield Street, Tamworth B79 7BZ
Tel 01827 311222  Fax 01827 52769
Arts Development Officer: Angela Watson, on tel
01827 311222 ext.325.

**TAMWORTH ARTS CENTRE & ASSEMBLY ROOMS**
Church Street, Tamworth, Staffs B79 7BX
Tel 01827 53092
**Administration:**
Manager: Joanne Sands
S/Cap: Arts Centre: 96, Assembly Rooms: 360
Sunday licence 7:30 - 10:30pm.

**PALACE MEDIA CENTRE**
Lower Gungate, Tamworth, Staffs, B79 7AW

Tel 01827 57100  Fax 01827 57707
Bookings Contact: Joanne Sands (Tel 01827 53092)
S/Cap: 200 approx.

## TANDRIDGE, Surrey
Leisure & Business Development Manager: Paul Clark
Council Offices, Station Road East, Oxted,
Surrey RH8 0BT
Tel 01883 722000  Fax 01883 722015

## TAUNTON DEANE Somerset
General Manager: Mrs S. Douglas
Leisure & Recreation Officer: A. R. Itter
Technical Services Division, The Deane House,
Belvedere Road, Taunton TA1 1HE
Tel 01823 356356  Fax 01823 356326

### MUNICIPAL HALL
Contact: Peter Cottell on 01823 356356
Medieval Hall. S/Cap: 100.
Refreshment Facilities. P.A. System available.

### WELLINGTON SPORTS CENTRE
Tel 01823 663010
Manager: G. Fletcher
S/Cap: 800
Portable stage facilities.

### BLACKBROOK PAVILION
Tel 01823 333435
Manager: Miss J. Dickinson
S/Cap: 800

## TEESDALE Durham
Chief Executive: C. M. Anderson
43 Galgate, Barnard Castle, Co. Durham DL12 8EL
Tel 01833 690000  Fax 01833 637269
e-mail tourism@teesdale.co.uk

### TEESDALE SPORTS CENTRE
Strathmore Road, Barnard Castle, Co Durham
CL12 8DS
Tel 01833 690400  Fax 01833 695034
For Bookings Contact: Gordon Hall, Manager
Main Hall: 33m x 18m
S/Cap: approx 500

## TEIGNBRIDGE, DEVON
Leisure & Tourism Officer: Karen Christie
Forde House, Newton Abbot, TQ12 4XX
Tel 01626 61101  Fax 01626 330162

The Dyrons and Dawlish Leisure Centres are under
the management of the Leisure and Tourism Officer;
other venues are used for promotions.

## TELFORD Shropshire
Derby House, Lawn Central, Telford,
Shropshire TF3 4LA
Tel 01952 202100  Fax 01952 201053
Director of Leisure and Community Services: N Rollo
Tel 01952 202552  Fax 01952 290628
Arts & Entertainments Officer: Mrs. J. Escott
Tel 01952 202579  Fax 01952 290628

### OAKENGATES THEATRE*
Limes Walk, Telford, Shropshire TF2 6EP
Admin 01952 610163  BO 01952 619020

Fax 01952 610164
**Administration:**
Theatre Manager: Chris Maddocks
S/Cap: 650
**Technical:**
Full stage facilities. 72-way Duet 2 with Pin Patch.
Hymo Stage Lift. 24 input Sound System. 4 Main
Dressing Rooms. Suitable for one-night stands,
pantomime, wrestling, films, banquets and community
events, conferences and seminars. Bar and catering
facilities.

### DAWLEY TOWN HALL
New Street, Dawley, Telford, Shropshire, TF4 3JR
Tel 01952 630414
S/Cap: 200
Other halls for hire . For information contact Leisure &
Community Services on tel 01952 202552

## TENDRING Essex
Entertainments Officer: Bob Foster
Leisure Section, Town Hall, Station Road,
Clacton-on-Sea, Essex CO15 1SE
Tel 01255 253208  Fax 01255 253139

### PRINCES THEATRE*
Station Road, Clacton-on-Sea, Essex
Tel 01255 253208
Contact: Bob Foster
S/Cap: 820

## TEST VALLEY Hampshire
Arts Officer: Michael Johnson
Leisure Services, Beech Hurst, Weyhill Road,
Andover, Hampshire SP10 3AJ.
Tel 01264 343204  Fax 01264 332214

### CRICKLADE THEATRE*
Charlton Road, Andover, Hampshire SP10 1EJ
Tel 01264 363311
Administrator: Stuart Morris, on 01264 365698

### PLAZA THEATRE, ROMSEY
Tel 01794 523054

### WINTON STUDIO THEATRE
Winton School, London Road, Andover,
Hampshire SP10 2PS
Administrator: Derek Ware, on tel 01264 351822

## THANET Kent
Cecil Street, Margate, Kent CT9 1XZ
Tel 01843 225511  Fax 01843 290906
Head of Tourism & Leisure Services: Peter Miller
Fax 01843 852744

### PAVILION GARDEN ON THE SANDS, BROADSTAIRS
Harbour Street, Broadstairs, Kent CT10 1EU
Tel 01843 865726  Fax 01843 604004
Entertainment & Theatre Manager: Brian Stout
S/Cap: 275
Open concert stage. Light orchestral concerts, variety
concerts, drama, conferences, exhibitions. Full stage
lighting and sound systems.

## THREE RIVERS Hertfordshire
Three Rivers House, Northway, Rickmansworth, Herts

TENDRING DISTRICT COUNCIL

# CLACTON-ON-SEA

## Princes Theatre 820 Capacity
### With New Tiered Retractable Seating

Available for shows, concerts, conferences, exhibitions etc.
Details from **Bob Foster**, Entertainments Officer, Town Hall,
Station Road, Clacton-on-Sea, Essex. Tel: 01255 253208 Fax: 01255 253200

WD3 1RL
Tel 01923 776611  Fax 01923 896119

**WATERSMEET THEATRE**
High Street, Rickmansworth
Tel 01923 771542/896484  Fax 01923 710121
S/Cap: 481  Full Stage & Cinema Facilities
COLNE SUITE: S/Cap: 70
CHESS SUITE: S/Cap: 100

**THE CENTRE, SOUTH OXHEY**
Gosforth Lane, Oxhey, Herts WD1 6AX
Tel 0181 428 4954  Fax 0181 421 4254
S/Cap: 100

## THURROCK Essex
Thameside Theatre, Orsett Road, Grays, Essex
Tel 01375 382555
Thurrock Civic Hall, Blackshots Lane, Grays,
Essex RM17 5DX
Tel 01375 652397  e-mail mallinson@thurrock.gov.uk

**THAMESIDE THEATRE***
Orsett Road, Grays, Essex
Tel 01375 382555
S/Cap: 303.

**THURROCK CIVIC HALL***
Thurrock Civic Hall, Blackshots Lane, Grays,
Essex RM16 2JU
Tel 01375 652397
S/Cap: 747
Multi-Purpose Hall.

## TONBRIDGE & MALLING Kent
Chief Executive: R. G. T. Thompson
Tonbridge & Malling Borough Council
Gibson Drive, Kings Hill, West Malling, Kent ME19 4LZ
Tel 01732 844522  Fax 01732 842170

**ANGEL LEISURE CENTRE, Tonbridge**
Angel Lane, Tonbridge, Kent TN9 1SF
Tel 01732 359966  Fax 01732 363677
General Manager: G. Littlejohn
Stage Facility, Project Room.
S/Cap: 300/350 depending on seating layout.

## TORFAEN  Gwent
Civic Centre, Pontypool, Gwent NP4 6YB.
Tel 01495 762200  Fax 01495 755513

## TORRIDGE Devon
Chief Executive: R K Brasington
Head of Leisure Services: Dave Fursman
Riverbank House, Bideford, Devon EX39 2QG.
Tel 01237 476711  Fax 01237 478849

**BEAFORD CENTRE**
Beaford Arts Centre, Winkleigh, Devon EX19 8LU
Director: Jennie Hayes
Tel 01805 603201  Fax 01805 603202
Rural arts centre, with licensed area which seats up to
132, works throughout North Devon. See also Plough
Arts Centre, Torrington EX38 8HQ

**BIDEFORD COLLEGE THEATRE**
Abbotsham Road, Bideford, Devon EX3 9AR
Tel/Fax 01237 428110
Manager: Neil Bennion
S/Cap: 181. Floor Stage.

**GRENVILLE COLLEGE ASSEMBLY HALL**
Belvoir Road, Bideford, Devon EX39 3JR
Tel 01237 472214
S/Cap: 410  Full Stage.
Contact: The Bursar

**THE PLOUGH ARTS CENTRE**
9-11 Fore Street, Torrington, Devon EX38 8HQ
Tel: 01805 622552  Fax 01805 624624
Managed by The Beaford Centre, Wimkleigh,
Devon EX19 8LU
Tel 01805 603201  Fax 01805603202
Arts Director: Catriona Rose
S/Cap: 320. Floor Stage.

## TRAFFORD Greater Manchester
Director of Housing & Environmental Services: Ken
Ivatt  Fax 0161 912 4613
Assistant Director of Education, Arts & Leisure:
Graham Luccock
Trafford Town Hall, Talbot Road, Stretford,
Manchester M32 0ZR
Tel 0161 912 1212  Fax 0161 912 4184

## TUNBRIDGE WELLS Kent
Town Hall, Tunbridge Wells, Kent TN1 1RS
Tel 01892 526121  Fax 01892 534227

**ASSEMBLY HALL THEATRE***
Crescent Road, Tunbridge Wells, Kent TN1 2LU
Tel 01892 518645  Fax 01892 525203
Manager: Pat Casey

S/Cap: 934

## TYNEDALE Northumberland
Director of Leisure and Tourism and Economic Developmemt: Richard. A. D. Mercer, B.A., D.M.S.
Prospect House, Hexham, Northumberland NE46 3NH
Tel 01434 652200  Fax 01434 652425

## UTTLESFORD Essex
Head of Leisure & Amenities: Sarah McLagan
Council Offices, London Road, Saffron Walden, Essex CB11 4ER
Tel 01799 510560  Fax 01799 510550

## VALE OF GLAMORGAN
## South Glamorgan

**MEMORIAL HALL, BARRY**
(Barry Town Council)
Tel 01446 738663
**Administration:**
Contact: Sue Baddeley
S/Cap: 1,111
Full Stage Facilities. Activities: One Night Stands, Pop Concerts, Symphony Concerts, Exhibitions, Conferences, Private Functions etc.,
Dances and Dinners.
Small Halls available for hire.

**PAGET ROOMS, PENARTH**
Correspondance Address: Penarth Town Council, West House, Stanwell Road, Penarth CF64 2YG
Tel 01222 700721  Fax 01222 712574
For Bookings Contact: The Town Clerk
S/Cap: 398
Stage Facilities, Sunday Licence.

## VALE OF WHITE HORSE
## Oxon

**CIVIC HALL**
Portway, Wantage OX12 9BX
Tel 01235 763456  Fax 01235 764696
Contact: Christina Denton-Powell
S/Cap: 350. Stage.

## VALE ROYAL Cheshire
Leisure Services Officer:C Bottomly
Community Services Directorate, Wyvern House, The Drumber, Winsford, Cheshire CW7 1AH
Tel 01606 867533
Entertainments & Events Officer: Sue Gillett

**CIVIC HALL, WINSFORD***
For information and Bookings contact: 01606 867533
Seating: 997.

**MEMORIAL HALL, NORTHWICH**
For information and Bookings contact: 01606 867533
Seating: 500

## WAKEFIELD
## West Yorkshire
Senior Development Officer: Adele Poppleton
Public Services Dept, Museums and Arts,
The Elizabethan Gallery, Brook Street,
Wakefield WF1 2QW

Tel 01924 305799  Fax 01924 305793

**CASTLEFORD CIVIC CENTRE**
Ferrybridge Road, Castleford, West Yorks WF10 4JH
Tel 01977 727015
Manager: Les Pickins
S/Cap: 600

**OSSETT TOWN HALL**
The Marketplace, Ossett, Wakefield, West Yorks
Tel 01924 302999  Fax 01924 305793
Contact for Bookings: Ray Cox, Manager
S/Cap: 400

**PONTEFRACT TOWN HALL**
S/Cap: 420

## WALSALL West Midlands
Promotions and Events Manager: Antonia Pompa
Civic Centre, Darwall Street, Walsall WS1 1TZ
Tel 01922 653170  Fax 01922 721682

**BLOXWICH LIBRARY THEATRE**
Elmore Row, Bloxwich, Walsall WS3 2HR,
West Midlands
Tel: Shirley Stone 01922 653183
Fully equipped theatre, raised auditorium seating 130, kitchen facilities.

## WANSBECK Northumberland
Leisure Services Manager: Tony Goodwin
Bomarsund Depot, East View, Stake Ford, NE62 5TR
Tel 01670 819802  Fax 01670 520457

**ASHINGTON LEISURE CENTRE**
Institute Road, Ashington, Northumberland NE63 8HP
Tel 01670 813254  Fax 01670 857189
Bookings Contact: Colin Ray, Manager, 01670 813254
S/Cap: 180. Sunday Licence.
Minimal Stage Facilities. Sport Hall S/Cap: 900

**BEDLINGTON COMMUNITY CENTRE**
Fund Street West, Bedlington, Northumberland
NE22 5TT
Tel 01670 824141
Contact for Bookings: Simon Baxter, Manager
S/Cap: 200.

**NEWBIGGIN SPORTS & COMMUNITY CENTRE**
Woodhorn Road, Newbiggin by the Sea,
Northumberland
Tel 01670 817713  Fax 01670 857189
Bookings Contact: Colin Ray, Manager, 01670 813254
Sunday Licence.
S/Cap: 250, Sports Hall S/Cap: 525.

## WARRINGTON Cheshire
New Town House, Buttermarket Street, Warrington,
Cheshire WA1 2NH
Tel 01925 444400
Director of Community Services: Alan Stephenson on fax 01295 442888
Entertainments Manager: John Perry
Arts Officer: Gail Thorne

**WARRINGTON PARR HALL**
Palmyra Square, Warrington, WA1 1BL
Tel 01925 651178
Manager: John Perry
Marketing Manager: Nick Shaw
Variable S/Cap: 200 to 1,100. Concerts, Dances,

Pantomimes, etc. Disabled access.

# WARWICK Warwickshire

Amenities Officer: Dale G. Best, B.Ed., D.M.S. (Rec. Man.) M. Inst.B.R.M., M.R.M.A.
Regent Square House, Regent Street,
Leamington Spa CV32 4UJ
Tel 01926 450000 Ext. 2050 Fax 01926 887260
Entertainments Manager: Peter Nicholson
Royal Spa Centre, Newbold Terrace, Leamington Spa
CV32 4HN
Tel 01926 334418 Fax 01926 832054

### ROYAL PUMP ROOMS, LEAMINGTON SPA

The Parade, Leamington Spa, CV32 4AB
Tel 01926 884668 Fax 01926 832054
For Bookings Contact: Peter Nicholson, 01926 334418
Entertainment Suite
S/Cap: Concerts 250, Dinners 200
An elegant Assembly Room suitable for a wide range of events.

### ROYAL SPA CENTRE, LEAMINGTON SPA
### AVON HALL

Newbold Terrace, Leamington Spa CV32 4HN
Tel 01926 334418 Fax 01926 832054
For Bookings Contact: Peter Nicholson
Multi-Purpose venue.
S/Cap: Theatre 799; Dances 500; Dinners 350 Max.
Full Stage Facilities including fly tower. Suitable for Stage Productions, Opera, Ballet, Pantomime, Celebrity Concerts, Orchestral Concerts, Film Shows, D/Dances. Ideal for Conferences, Seminars, Exhibitions, Wrestling, Boxing. Fully Licensed Bar and Coffee Lounge.

# WATFORD Hertfordshire

Town Hall, Watford, Herts WD1 3EX
Tel 01923 226400 Fax 01923 226133
Director of Leisure: Michael Bond
Executive Assistant to the Director of Leisure: Gaynor Bradley on fax 01923 249729

### PALACE THEATRE*

Clarendon Road, Watford, Herts WD1 1J2
Mgt/SD 01923 235455 BO 01923 225671
Fax 01923 819664
Artistic Director: Giles Croft
Administrative Director: Alastair Moir
Production Manager: Fergus Gillies
S/Cap: 663

# WAVENEY Suffolk

Chief Leisure Officer: Peter Waring
Principal Arts & Heritage Officer: Sue Webster
Community Services, Waveney District Council,
Mariner's Street, Lowestoft NR32 1JT
Tel 01502 523302 Fax 01502 514617

### MARINA THEATRE

Marina, Lowestoft, NR32 1HH
Mgt 01502 523443 BO 01502 573318
Fax 01502 538179
Bookings Contact: Sue Webster or David Shepheard.
S/Cap: 751

# WEAR VALLEY DISTRICT COUNCIL County Durham

Leisure and Marketing Director: Paul Dobson
Arts Development Officer: Mary O'Malley
Civic Centre, Crook, Co. Durham, DL15 9ES
Tel 01388 765555
Fax 01388 766660

### CIVIC HALL, CROOK

Military Row, Crook, Co. Durham DL15 9DL
Tel 01388 763665
S/Cap: 250 . Stage Facilities.

### TOWN HALL, STANHOPE

Front Street, Bishop Auckland, Co. Durham
Tel 01388 528516
S/Cap: 200. Stage Facilities.

### SPECTRUM LEISURE COMPLEX

Hunwick Lane, Willington Crook,
Co. Durham DL15 OJA
Tel 01388 747000 Fax 01388 747098
Contact for Bookings: Neil Phillipson
2 Halls: S/Cap: 600 and 200.
Stage Facilities.

### WEARDALE LEISURE COMPLEX

Eastgate, Bishops Auckland, Co. Durham, DL13 2AA
Tel 01388 517567
Contact for Bookings: Neil Phillipson
S/Cap: 250. Stage Facilities.

### BISHOP AUCKLAND TOWN HALL

Marketplace, Bishop Auckland DL14 7NP
Tel 01388 602610
Centre Manager: Gillian Wales
A joint project between Wear Valley District Council and Durham County.
S/Cap: 220. Bar. Stage sound and lighting facilities.

# WELLINGBOROUGH Northamptonshire

Recreation and Amenities Officer: P. Morrall
Council Offices, Swanspool, Wellingborough NN8 1BP
Tel 01933 229777 Fax 01933 229318

### GLAMIS HALL

Goldsmith Road, Wellingborough NN8 3RU
Tel 01933 677326
Manager: Maureen McDonald
For Bookings call: 01933 229777 ext.4426
S/Cap: 220. Stage.

### TITHE BARN

Tithe Barn Road, Wellingborough
Tel 01933 229777 ext.4420
For Bookings call: 01933 229777 ext.4426
S/Cap: 200. Stage.

# WELWYN-HATFIELD Hertfordshire

The Campus, Welwyn Garden City,
Hertfordshire AL8 6AE
Tel 01707 357000 Fax 01707 357257
General Manager of Leisure Services: Pauline Lawrence
Tel 01707 357183 Fax 01707 357185

**HATFIELD LEISURE CENTRE**
Travellers Lane, Hatfield, Hertfordshire AL10 8TJ.
Tel 01707 268769 Fax 01707 267500
Manager: Stuart West

**CAVENDISH HALL**
Maryland, Hatfield, Hertfordshire
For bookings contact Mia Hall
Tel 01707 357192 Fax 01707 357185
Contact: Susan Ford
S/Cap: 120.

**VINEYARD BARN**
The Vineyard, Welwyn Garden City, Herts
For bookings contact Mia Hall
Tel 01707 357192 Fax 01707 357185
Bookings: Pam Bates
S/Cap: 2 Halls, 60 and 40.

**WOODHALL COMMUNITY CENTRE**
Mill Green Road, Welwyn Garden City, Herts
For bookings contact Mia Hall
Tel 01707 357192 Fax 01707 357185
For Bookings Contact: Pam Bates
S/Cap: 300

# WEST BERKSHIRE Berkshire
Chief Executive: Stella Manzie
Head of Culture and Tourism: Alison Coates
Council Offices, Market Street, Newbury, Berkshire
Tel 01635 42400 Fax 01635 519431

# WEST DEVON Devon
Chief Executive: David Incoll
Economic and Leisure Development Mgr: Tim Bevan
West Devon Borough Council, Kilworthy Park,
Drake Road, Tavistock, Devon PL19 0BZ
Tel 01822 615911 Fax 01822 614840

# WEST DORSET Dorset
Contact: Patrica Jackson, Leisure and Tourism
Division, 58/60 High West Street, Dorchester,
Dorset DT1 1UZ
Tel 01305 252261 Fax 01305 251481

**MARINE THEATRE, LYME REGIS**
Church Street, Lyme Regis, Dorset DT7 3BS
Mgt 01297 442394 BO 01297 442138
Fax 01297 443773
**Administration:**
Manager: Peter Hammond
Under control of Town Clerk,
The Guildhall, Bridge Street, Lyme Regis
Tel 01297 445175
S/Cap: 200
**Technical:**
**Stage:** Proscenium arch, performing area 9.45m x
4.6m, pros opening 6.7m x 2.95m. Stage slightly
raked. Height 3.66m.
**Lighting:** Lighting rig just installed. Lighting technician
available.
**Sound:** Operated from SR or balcony. No equipment.
**Other:** Backstage: 2 dressing rooms. Piano. No
permanent staff but casuals available.

**BRIDPORT ARTS CENTRE***
South Street, Bridport, Dorset DT6 3NR
Tel 01308 427183
Administrator: Frances Everitt
S/Cap: 200

**DORCHESTER ARTS CENTRE**
School Lane, The Grove, Dorchester,
Dorset DT1 1XR
Tel 01305 266926

**SHERBORNE ARTS CENTRE**
Sherborne House, Newland, Sherborne DT9 3JG
Tel 01935 813433
Director: Sally Wallace

# WEST LANCASHIRE
## Lancashire
Director of Development & Amenities: Les Abernethy
52 Derby Street, Ormskirk, Lancs L39 2DF
Tel 01695 577177 Fax 01695 585113

**CIVIC HALL**
Southport Road, Ormskirk
Tel 01695 720837
Bookings: Sue McIntyre
S/Cap: 320
Sunday Licence. Stage Facilities.

# WEST SOMERSET
## Somerset
Chief Executive Officer & Clerk: Colin W. Rockall
Council Offices, 20 Fore Street, Williton, Taunton,
Somerset TA4 4QA
Tel 01984 632291 Fax 01984 633022

# WEST WILTSHIRE
## Wiltshire
Contact: Nicola Clench, Arts & Entertainments
Manager, Direct Leisure, West Wiltshire District
Council, Bradley Road, Trowbridge BA14 0RD
Tel 01225 776655 Fax 01225 774085

**THE CIVIC HALL**
St. Stephen's Place, Trowbridge, Wiltshire BA14 8AH
S/Cap: 360
For Bookings Contact: Pat Bowler
Tel 01225 775335 Fax 01225 774085

**THE ASSEMBLY HALL**
Market Place, Melksham, Wiltshire SN12 6ES
For Bookings Contact: Pat Bowler
Tel 01225 775335 Fax 01225 774085
S/Cap: 450/500 Standing 650 max;

**ST. MARGARET'S HALL**
St Margaret's Street Bradford on Avon,
Wiltshire BA15 1DE
For Bookings Contact: Pat Bowler
Tel 01225 775335 Fax 01225 774085
S/Cap: 200 Standing 400

**THE LAVERTON HALL**
Bratton Road, Westbury, Wiltshire BA13 3EN
For Bookings Contact: Pat Bowler
Tel 01225 775335 Fax 01225 774085
S/Cap: 160

**THE ASSEMBLY HALL**
Warminster, Wiltshire BA12 8LB
For Bookings Contact: Pat Bowler
Tel 01225 775335 Fax 01225 774085
S/Cap: 400

# WEYMOUTH & PORTLAND

Leisure, Entertainments & Tourism General Manager:
Harvey G. Bailey
The Pavilion Complex, The Esplanade, Weymouth,
Dorset DT4 8ED
Tel 01305 786732  Fax 01305 761654

**THE PAVILION COMPLEX***
The Pavilion Complex, The Esplanade, Weymouth,
Dorset DT4 8ED
Tel 01305 786732  Fax 01305 761654
Pavilion Complex Manager: Stephen Young

# WIGAN
## Greater Manchester

Director of Leisure: R. F. Hill
Trencherfield Mill, Wallgate, Wigan, WN3 4EF
Tel 01942 828508  Fax 01942 828540

**DERBY ROOM**
Turnpike Centre, Leigh Library, Civic Square, Leigh
WN7 1EB
Tel 01942 404404  Fax 01942 404567
For Bookings Contact: Wendy Heaton, Library
Manager, or Cathy Grundy, Secretary.
S/Cap: 180

**FORMBY HALL**
Alder Street, Atherton, Manchester M46 9DS
Tel 01942 876496
Manager: Mrs M. Davies
Concerts, Dancing.
S/Cap: 350

**HAIGH HALL**
Haigh, Wigan, WN2 1PE
Tel 01942 832895  Fax 01942 831081
Events Manager: Colin Hurst
Conference, Dances, Dining
S/Cap: 150

**HOWE BRIDGE SPORTS CENTRE**
Leigh Road, Atherton, Manchester M46 OPJ
Tel 01942 870403  Fax 01942 886802
Manager: Jean Hodges
S/Cap: 1,000 or 1,500. (Concerts only).

**LOWTON CIVIC HALL**
Hesketh Meadow Lane, Lowton, Warrington WA3 2AJ
Tel 01942 672971
Dances, Concerts
S/Cap: 400

**THE MILL AT THE PIER**
Wigan Pier, Wallgate, Wigan WN3 4EU
Tel 01942 323666
Concerts, dancing, exhibitions.
S/Cap: 500

**MONACO BALLROOM**
Atherton Road, Hindley WN2 3EW
Tel 01942 255138
Contact Mrs Winders
Concerts, Dancing
S/Cap: 400

**THE PALACE OF VARIETIES**
Victorian themed music hall venue of Wigan Pier.
Tel 01942 323666
S/Cap: 65

**ROBIN PARK SPORTS COMPLEX***
Robin Park Road, Wigan WN5 0UY
NB: Under redevelopment for 2 years. For information
or enquiries contact Mr Mick Hannan, Manager.
Tel 01942 245212

# WIMBORNE Dorset

Chief Executive: Mr. A. Breakwell
Head of Leisure: Neil Farmer
East Dorset District Council, Council Offices, Furzehill,
Wimborne, Dorset BH21 4HN
Tel 01202 886201  Fax 01202 841390

# WINCHESTER Hampshire

Tourism Services Manager: Joanna Child
Tourist Information Centre, Guildhall, The Broadway,
Winchester SO23 9LJ
Tel 01962 840500/848180  Fax 01962 850348

**THEATRE ROYAL***
Jewry Street, Winchester, Hants S023 8SB
Theatre closed for major refurbishment and is
expected to re-open in spring 1999.
For further details contact: Keith Powers on 01962
842226 or Fax 01962 841015.

**CHESIL LITTLE THEATRE**
Chesil Street, Winchester, Hants SO23 8HU
Tel 01962 889356
Contact: Tom Williams
Seats: 70

**WINCHESTER GUILDHALL**
The Broadway, Winchester, Hampshire S023 9LJ
Manager: Pamela Sanderson
Tel 01962 840820  Fax 01962 878458
S/Cap: 615 max

**JOHN STRIPE THEATRE**
King Alfred's College, Winchester, Hampshire
Theatre Co-ordinator: Mr. P. Chamberlain
King Alfred's College
Tel 01962 868725  BO 01962 827492
S/Cap: 291 + 2 Wheelchair spaces.

**TOWER ARTS CENTRE**
Romsey Road, Winchester, Hampshire SO22 5PW
Tel 01962 867986  Fax 01962 849337
Director: John Tellett
S/Cap: 118

# WINDSOR & MAIDENHEAD
## Berkshire

Arts Development Officer: Patricia Cowe
4th Floor, Berkshire House, Queens Street,
Maidenhead, Berks SL6 1NF
Tel 01628 796100  Fax 01628 796121

**DESBOROUGH SUITE**
Maidenhead Town Hall, Park Street, Maidenhead,
Berkshire SL6 1RF
Tel 01628 796033
S/Cap: 350
Stage Facilities

**ASTOR SUITE**
Maidenhead Town Hall, Park Street, Maidenhead,
Berkshire SL6 1RF
Tel 01628 796033

S/Cap: 70
No stage Facilities, Bar.

**MAGNET LEISURE CENRE**
Holmanleaze, Maidenhead, Berkshire SL6 8AW
tel 01628 796103  Fax 01628 777010

**WINDSOR GUILDHALL**
High Street, Windsor, Berkshire SL4 1LR
Tel 01753 743920  Fax 01753 743917
Manager: Emmanuelle Veille
Guildhall Chamber: S/Cap: 120
No stage facilities.  Also 3 Conference Rooms.

# WIRRAL Merseyside
Director of Leisure Services and Tourism:
Andrew Worthington
Westminster House, Hamilton Street, Birkenhead
Wirral L41 5FN
Tel 0151 647 2366  Fax 0151 666 1343

**BEBINGTON CIVIC CENTRE**
Civic Way, Bebington, Wirral L63 7PN
Tel 0151 643 7237
Manager: Dennis Tobin
S/Cap: Civic Suite: 120; Phoenix Suite: 120
For Booking contact Ian Scarratt
Tel 0151 643 7239  Fax 0151 643 7231

**BROMBOROUGH CIVIC HALL**
Allport Lane, Bromborough, Wirral L67 7HR
Tel 0151 334 6849
Manager: Dennis Tobin
S/Cap: Large Hall: 250; Small Hall: 80
For Booking contact Ian Scarratt
Tel 0151 643 7239  Fax 0151 643 7231
Plus small hall. Entertainments, Meetings, Socials, etc.
plus rooms at Civic Centre, Bebington

**FLORAL PAVILION THEATRE, NEW BRIGHTON***
Virginia Road, New Brighton, Wirral, L45 2LH
Admin 0151 639 1794  BO 0151 639 4360
Fax 0151 691 2459
General Manager: Paul. Holliday
Seats: 972

**GROSVENOR BALLROOM, WALLASEY**
Grosvenor Street, Wallasey, Wirral L44 1AQ
Tel 0151 638 4431
For Bookings contact Chris Lewis on 0151 639 1386
S/Cap: 250
Dancing, Bingo, Meetings

**HESWALL HALL**
Telegraph Road, Heswall, Wirral L60 0AF
Tel 0151 342 2614
Manager: Paul Irons
Bookings: Sally Anderson
S/Cap: 290
Entertainments, Clubs, Drama, Opera

**THE TOWN HALL, BIRKENHEAD**
Town Hall, Hamilton Square, Birkenhead L41 5BR
Tel: 0151 666 3963
For Bookings Contact: Pat Ramsden
0151 652 4177  Fax 0151 670 0253
S/Cap: 284 raked, balcony 60. Max: 392
Dances, Conferences and Civic Functions, etc.

**VICTORIA HALL, HIGHER BEBINGTON**
Village Road, Higher Bebington, Wirral L63 8PT
Tel 0151 608 1527

Manager: Dennis Tobin
S/Cap: Large Hall 180; Small Hall: 80
For Booking contact Ian Scarratt
Tel 0151 643 7239  Fax 0151 643 7231

# WOKINGHAM Berkshire
Chief Executive: Mrs Gillian Norton
Council Offices, Shute End, Wokingham,
Berks RG40 1WQ
Tel 0118 974 6000  Fax 0118 978 9078

**LECTURE THEATRE**
Palmer Building, Reading University, Whiteknights,
Reading, Berks RG6 6AH
Tel 0118 987 5123
S/Cap: 400
Cinema Licence.

**THE THEATRE**
Faculty of Letters, Reading University.
Tel 0118 987 5123

**WOKINGHAM THEATRE**
Cantley, Twyford Road, Wokingham,
Berks, RG40 5TU
Tel 0118 989 0395
S/Cap: 125
Audio Loop.

**SHINFIELD PLAYERS THEATRE AND
ARTS CENTRE**
Whitley Wood Lane, Shinfield, Berkshire RG2 9DF
Tel 0118 987 3057
**Administration:**
Licensee: Mrs E. Denny  Tel 0118 988 3946
For Bookings contact: Jim Taylor, Secretary, 18
Keswick Road, Tile Hurst, Reading RG30 4SD
Tel 0118 942 4606
S/Cap: 142. Wheelchair facilities.

**WOODCLYFFE HALL**
High Street, Wargrave, Berks.
Licensee: Wargrave Parish Council

**THE WOODLEY PLAYHOUSE**
Headley Road, Woodley, Reading, Berks
Licensee: Mr S.J. Atkins

# WOLVERHAMPTON
# West Midlands
Civic Hall, North Street,
Wolverhampton WV1 1RQ
Tel 01902 312029  Fax 01902 713047

**CIVIC HALL**
Manager: Mark Blackstock
S/Cap: 2,039 (seated), 2,126 (standing).
Concerts, Conferences, Meetings, Banqueting, etc.
General purpose.

**WULFRUN HALL**
Contact Manager: Mark Blackstock for Conferences,
Exhibitions, Small Scale Theatre, Concerts.
S/Cap: 672, standing 756, Flexible multi-purpose
performance space.

# WORCESTER
# Hereford and Worcester
Director of Leisure Services: Mr. A. Audas

Orchard House, Farrier Street, Worcester WR1 3BW
Tel 01905 723471  Fax 01905 722350

# WORTHING West Sussex
Director of Community Services: Hywel Griffiths, B.Sc.,
D.L.P., M.I.L.A.M.
Portland House, Richmond Road, Worthing, West
Sussex BN11 1HQ
Tel 01903 239999 exts 2502/3/4/2530
Fax 01903 207035

**ASSEMBLY HALL**
Stoke Abbott Road, Worthing, West Sussex
Tel 01903 239999
Box Office at Pavilion 01903 820500
See Provincial Venues

# WREXHAM
Guildhall, Wrexham LL11 1WF
Tel 01978 292000
Director of Education & Leisure: Terry Garner
Roxburgh House, Hill Street, Wrexham LL11 1SN
Tel 01978 297420  Fax 01978 297422
Entertainments Officer: G.A. Lacy
Tel 01978 292683  Fax 01978 297422

**PLAS MADOC LEISURE CENTRE**
Acrefair, Wrexham LL14 3HL
Tel 01978 821600  Fax 01978 824633
Manager: Neil Devlin
S/Cap: 800 approx.

# WYCHAVON
## Hereford & Worcester
Chief Executive: Stephen Nott
Civic Centre, Queen Elizabeth Drive, Pershore,
Worcs WR10 1PT
Tel 01386 565000  Fax 01386 561089

# WYCOMBE Buckinghamshire
Chief Leisure Officer: Neil Roberts
Wycombe District Council, Queen Victoria Road, High
Wycombe, Bucks HP11 1BB
Tel 01494 421801

**SHELLEY THEATRE**
Court Garden Leisure Complex, Pound Lane,
Marlow FL7 2AE
Tel 01628 898080  Fax 01628 473277
**Administration:**
Contact: Tracy Smith
250 seat flat floor hall, flat stage.
Stage lighting and sound facilities. Dressing rooms,
projection room, bar, restaurant and sporting facilities
adjoining. Suitable for Dancing, Theatre, Exhibitions,
Conferences and social events.

**WYCOMBE SWAN**
St. Mary Street, High Wycombe HP11 2XE
Leased to Wycombe Arts Management
Tel 01494 514444
1,076 seat auditorium, full professional support
systems; incorporates Town Hall. Oak room suite
suitable for all conference and social events.

# WYRE, Lancashire
Events Manager: Vicky Tindall

Leisure & Sports Manager: Grant Sellars
Wyre Civic Centre, Breck Road,
Poulton, FY6 7TU
Tel: 01253 891000

**MARINE HALL***
Events Manager: Vicky Tindall
The Esplanade, Fleetwood, Lancs FY7 64F
Tel 01253 771141/770547
Leisure & Sports Manager: Grant Sellars
Full stage facilities.
S/Cap: 636

**LECTURE HALL, THORNTON CLEVELEYS**
Leisure & Sports Manager: Grant Sellars
Four Lane Ends, Thornton Cleveleys, Lancs
Tel 01253 858529
200 seats.

**POULTON YOUTH & COMMUNITY CENTRE**
Leisure & Sports Manager: Grant Sellars
Parrys Way, Poulton-Le-Fylde Lancs, Lancs FY6 7PU
Tel 01253 895115
S/Cap: 150.

**FRANK TOWNEND COMMUNITY CENTRE**
Leisure & Sports Manager: Grant Sellars
Kensington Road, Cleveleys, Lancs FY5 1ER
Tel 01253 863369
S/Cap: 100

# WYRE FOREST
## Hereford and Worcester
Head of Leisure Services: Andrew Dickens, MBA
M.Inst SRM (Dip) M.I.L.A.M.
Wyre Forest District Council, 99 Coventry Street,
Kidderminster, Worcs. DY10 2BL
Tel 01562 820505  Fax 01562 825141
e-mail leisure@wfdc@online.rednet.co.uk

# YNYS MÔN-Isle of Anglesey
## Borough Council
Llangefni, Anglesey LL77 7TW
Tel 01248 752000  Fax 01248 750365
Director of Leisure & Heritage: Elspeth Mitcheson

**PLAS ARTHUR SPORTS CENTRE**
Llangefni, Isle of Anglesey LL77 7NF
Tel 01248 724701

**BEAUMARIS LEISURE CENTRE**
Canolfan Beaumaris, Rating Row, Beaumaris,
LL58 8AL.
Tel/Fax 01248 811200
Manager: Sian Mai Jones
375 Seat Multipurpose Venue available for Exhibitions,
Concerts, TV Shows, Sporting Competitions, Dances,
Professional lighting/Sound available. Tiered
retractable seating.

# LONDON

## BARKING & DAGENHAM

London Borough of Barking and Dagenham
Civic Centre, Rainham Road North, Dagenham,
Essex RM10 7BN
Tel 0181 592 4500  Fax 0181 252 8053

### BROADWAY THEATRE
Broadway, Barking IG11 7LU
Tel 0181 592 4500 ext.3466  BO 0181 591 9662
Fax 0181 591 9662
Manager: Ms C Oatham
S/Cap: 800

### GORESBROOK LEISURE CENTRE
Ripple Road, Dagenham, Essex
Tel 0181 593 3270
Manager: T Stephens

## BARNET

Head of Recreation: Mr. Lockwood
Leisure Department, London Borough of Barnet, Great
North Way, Hendon, London NW4 1PS
Tel 0181 457 9900
Fax 0181 203 7512

## BEXLEY

Lesiure Development Manager: Janet Stone
Leisure Department, London Borough of Bexley,
Leisure Link, Howbury Centre, Slade Green Road,
Erith DA8 2HX
Tel 0181 303 7777 Ext. 3919
Fax 0181 308 4972

### CRAYFORD TOWN HALL
Crayford Road, Crayford
Tel 0181 303 7777 ext.2203
Contact for Bookings: April Leask
S/Cap: 300. Stage Facilities

### CIVIC SUITE
Bexley Civic Offices, Broadway, Bexley Heath
DA6 7LB
Contact for Bookings: April Leafk, 0181 303 7777
ext.2203
S/Cap: 300. Portable Staging.

### CROOK LOG SPORTS CENTRE
Brampton Road, Bexleyheath, Kent DA7 4HH
Tel 0181 304 5386
Fax 0181 304 5597
For Bookings Contact: Terry Murphy
S/Cap: 1,000 (Portable staging and seating).
Concerts, Displays, Exhibitions, Conferences, etc.

## BRENT

London Borough of Brent
Brent House Annex, 356-368 High Road, Marriott
Services. Brent Town Hall, Forty Lane, Wembley,
Middlesex HA9 9HT
Tel 0181 937 6207

### ASSEMBLY HALL
Brent Town Hall, Wembley HA9 9HT

Tel 0181 937 6204
**Administration:**
S/Cap: 946. Tours, Opera, Ballet, Plays, Conferences,
Weddings, Films, Shows, Recordings.
Catering: Licensed Bars, main foyer, Refreshment Bar,
Servery same level.
**Technical:**
**Stage:** Pros. Stage (raked); Pros. Opening 12.19m x
7.62m; Depth of Setting Line 9.14m.
**Lighting:** Switchboard: 230/240 volt AC 60 way
Thyristor dimmer board (operation F.O.H.) (pre-set).
**Other:** Dressing Rooms: 2 large, 2 small, Orchestra
Pit, Scenery - Side Dock Door access.

## CAMDEN

London Borough of Camden.
Director of Leisure and Community Services: John
Mothersole
Assistant Director of Leisure & Comminuty Services:
Frances Mangan
Leisure Service Department, The Crowndale Centre,
218 Eversholt Street, London NW1 1BD
Tel 0171 911 1606
Fax 0171 911 1587
e-mail leis.director@camden.gov.uk
Website www.camden.gov.uk

## CITY OF LONDON

Corporation of London.
Guildhall, London EC2P 2EJ
Tel 0171 606 3030

### THE BARBICAN
Silk Street, Barbican, London EC2Y 8DS
Administration:
Mgt 0171 638 4141  Fax 0171 920 9648
SD 0171 628 3351  BO 0171 638 8891
ADMINISTRATION:
Managing Director: John Tusa
Arts Director: Graham Sheffield
Director of Public Affairs: Ruth Hasnip
Engineering Director: Mark Chapman
Technical Services Manager: Kim Little
Senior House Manager: Sue Patterson
Press & PR Manager: Valerie Gillard
Head of Box Office Services: Eileen Tench
Head of Marketing: Chris Travers
Facilities for the disabled: Barbican Hall, 16 wheelchair
spaces plus escorts; Barbican Theatre, 8 wheelchair
spaces plus escorts; The Pit, 1 wheelchair space plus
escort. Lifts, chairlifts and assistance available, ring
box office on 0171 638 8891. Level access and free
parking on presentation of disabled car registration
certificate.

## CROYDON

Head of Recreation Services Dept: Rob Hardy
Croydon Council, Crosfield House, Mint Walk,
Croydon, Surrey CR9 1BS
Tel 0181 760 5402

### FAIRFIELD CONCERT HALL*
Park Lane, Croydon CR9 1DG
Tel 0181 681 0821
S/Cap: 1,800

**ASHCROFT THEATRE***
Park Lane, Croydon CR9 1DG
Tel 0181 681 0821
S/Cap: 763

# EALING

London Borough of Ealing.
Halls & Events Team, Ground Floor, Perceval House,
Uxbridge Road, Ealing W5 2HL
All enquiries to 0181 758 5624/0181 758 8079
Fax 0181 566 5088

**TOWN HALL, EALING**
New Broadway, W5
Tel 0181 758 5219  Fax 0181 280 1099
S/Cap: 518

**TOWN HALL, ACTON**
High Street, W3
Tel 0181 758 5219  Fax 0181 280 1099
S/Cap: 830

**GREENFORD HALL**
Greenford Broadway
Tel 0181 578 1076
S/Cap: 580

# ENFIELD

London Borough of Enfield
Community Arts Development Officer: Penny Wilkinson
Arts Development Unit, Millfield House Arts Centre,
Silver Street, Edmonton, London N18 1PJ
Tel 0181 803 5283
Fax 0181 807 3892

**MILLFIELD HOUSE ARTS CENTRE**
Silver Street, Edmonton, London N18 1PJ
Tel 0181 803 5283

**ANGEL COMMUNITY CENTRE**
Raynham Rd., Edmonton, London N18 2JG
Tel 0181 807 4511
For bookings contact Alison Durston on 0181 982 7032

**FORTY HALL BANQUETING SUITE AND MUSEUM**
Forty Hill, Enfield, Middlesex EN2 9HA
Tel 0181 363 4046
For bookings contact Alison Durston on 0181 982 7032

# GREENWICH

London Borough of Greenwich
147 Powis Street, Woolwich, London SE18 6JL
Tel 0181 854 8888
Arts & Entertainments Department
Tel 0181 317 5417  Fax 0181 317 2822

**WOOLWICH PUBLIC HALL**
Market Street, London SE18
Tel 0181 854 8888
Hall Superintendent: Steve Williams
For bookings contact Sales Unit on 0181 317 8687
S/Cap: 600
Daily Lettings

# HACKNEY

Head of Arts & Cultural Services: Lesli Good (on 0171
762 6825)
Events & Projects Officer: Fahim Qureshi, (on 0171
762 6828)

Arts Development Officers:
Donna Pieters (on 0171 762 6827)
Caroline Jenkinson (0171 762 6829)
Administrator: Joyce Anthony (0171 762 6823)
Edith Cavell Building, Enfield Road, London N1 5BA
Tel 0171 214 8400
Fax 0171 214 8531

**ASSEMBLY HALL, HACKNEY TOWN HALL**
Mare Street, Hackney, London E8
Tel 0181 986 3123
Contact for bookings: Sonia Joseph (0181 525 3299)
S/Cap: 500

**ASSEMBLY HALL, STOKE NEWINGTON**
Church Street, London N16 OJR
Tel 0181 442 5000
Contact For Bookings: Sonia Joseph, 0181 525 3299
S/Cap: 500

**BRICK LANE MUSIC HALL**
134-146 Curtain Road, London EC2A 3AR
Tel 0171 739 9996/7
Contact: Vincent Hayes/Zara Kattan

**HACKNEY EMPIRE**
291 Mare Street, Hackney, London E8 1EJ
Tel 0181 985 0171
Director: Roland Muldoon
S/Cap: 1,600

# HAMMERSMITH & FULHAM

London Borough of Hammersmith and Fulham
Public Information & Civic Facilities Manager: Dee Little
Bookings: Dee Little, Alan Wall & Helen Pinnington
Town Hall, King Street, London W6 9JU.
General 0181 748 3020
Lettings 0181 576 5008

**HAMMERSMITH TOWN HALL**
Hammersmith, London W6 9JU
For Bookings Contact: Dee Little, Alan Wall or Helen
Pinnington on 0181 576 5008
Assembly Hall· S/Cap: 950. All purpose Small Hall:
S/Cap: 150. All purpose

**FULHAM TOWN HALL**
Fulham Broadway, London SW6
Tel 0181 748 3020
For Bookings Contact: Dee Little, Alan Wall or Helen
Pinnington on 0181 576 5008
Grand Hall: S/Cap: 456, all purpose hall. Concert Hall:
S/Cap: 200, all purpose.

**RIVERSIDE STUDIOS***
Crisp Road, Hammersmith, London W6 9RL
Tel 0181 741 2251
S/Cap: 500 max.

**LYRIC THEATRE***
King Street, Hammersmith, London W6 0QL
Tel 0181 741 0824
Administrative Producer: Simon Mellor
S/Cap: 537

# HARROW

London Borough of Harrow, Civic Centre, Station
Road, Harrow, Middlesex HA1 2US
Tel 0181 863 5611
Fax 0181 424 1209

**CEDARS YOUTH CENTRE**
Chichley Gardens, Harrow Weald

Centre Manager: Tony Skeel
For Bookings Contact: Education Lettings Dept on
0181 863 5611 Ext. 2525
S/Cap: 150-200

**GRANT ROAD YOUTH COMMUNITY CENTRE**
Grant Road, Harrow HA1
Tel 0181 427 6559
Centre Manager: Colin Edgly
For Hall Bookings Contact: Education Lettings on
0181 863 5611

**HARROW ARTS CENTRE**
Uxbridge Road, Hatch End, Middx. HA5 4EA
Enquiries 0181 428 0123   BO 0181 428 0124
Fax 0181 428 0121

**PINNER YOUTH & COMMUNITY CENTRE**
Chapel Lane, Pinner HA5 1AA
Tel 0181 868 8865
For Bookings Contact: Harrow Civic Centre on 0181
863 5611
S/Cap: 120

# HAVERING
London Borough of Havering
Halls Manager: Brian Ford
Hall Bookings: Pat Long
Broxhill Centre, Broxhill Road, Harold Hill, Romford
RM4 1XN
Tel 01708 773861
Fax 01708 773859
Management of 5 Public halls and their letting to
members of the public.
The following halls are licensed for Music and Dancing.

**DUKES HALL**
May Green Crescent, Off Park Lane, Hornchurch,
Essex RM11 1EJ
Tel 01708 773861
For Bookings Contact: Pat Long on 01708 773892
Stage, lighting system.

**NEW WINDMILL HALL**
St Mary`s Lane, Upminster RM14 2QH
Tel 01708 773861
For Bookings Contact: Pat Long on 01708 773892
S/Cap: 250. Dancing, Concerts, Variety Shows, Stage
Plays etc. Multi-use stage facilities F.O.H. spots,
Dressing Room accommodation.

**TWEED WAY HALL**
Tweed Way, Rise Park, Romford  RM1 4A2
Tel 01708 773861
S/Cap: 200, stage.
For Bookings Contact: Pat Long, 01708 773892

# HILLINGDON
London Borough of Hillingdon
Arts Co-ordinator: Joan Gallacher
Central Library, High Street, Uxbridge, Middx UB8 1HD
Tel 01895 250711
Fax 01895 811164

**WINSTON CHURCHILL HALL**
Pinn Way, Ruislip, Middx HA4 7QL
Tel 01895 678800
Fax 01895 677555
Manager: Gill McCallum, Anne Tiernan
S/Cap: 438 Multi-purpose hall.

**COMPASS ARTS THEATRE**
Glebe Avenue, Ickenham, Middx UB10 8PD
Tel 01895 632488  BO 01895 673200
Fax 01895 623724
Theatre Manager: Bryony Flanagan
Community Arts Theatre
S/Cap: Aud. 160 (raked seating).
Other rooms and facilities.

# HOUNSLOW
London Borough of Hounslow
Civic Centre, Lampton Road, Hounslow,
Middlesex TW3 4DN
Tel 0181 570 7728  Fax 0181 572 4819
Director of Leisure Services: Howard Simmons
Tel 0181 862 5793  Fax 0181 862 5847

**PAUL ROBESON THEATRE**
CentreSpace, 24 Treaty Centre, High Street,
Hounslow, Middlesex TW3 1ES
Admin/Mgt 0181 814 0364  BO 0181 577 6969
Fax 0181 569 4330
Business Manager: Mary Tennant
Operations Manager: Laurie Woollcott
Marketing Manager: Hilary Coleman
Senior Technician: Miriam Stone
Press Officer: Audrey Ryan
Seats: 280
See London Theatres section for further details.

# KENSINGTON & CHELSEA
Royal Borough of Kensington & Chelsea
Director of Libraries and Arts: C. J. Koster
Central Library, Phillimore Walk, London W8 7RX
Tel 0171 937 2542
Fax 0171 937 0515

**CENTRAL LIBRARY THEATRE**
Central Library, Phillimore Walk, London W8 7RX
Tel 0171 937 2542
Contact: A. Carrion
S/Cap: 162
Suitable for Meetings, Recitals, Concerts and Film
Shows.  Music and entertainment licence.
**Central Library Meeting Room**
S/Cap: 50
Suitable for Meetings and Rehearsals.
Contact: A. Carrion

**BROMPTON LIBRARY - MEETING ROOM**
210 Old Brompton Road, London SW5 0BS
Tel 0171 373 3111
Fax 0171 244 6469
Contact: Chris Moore
S/Cap: 45
**Technical:**
Room 24' x 23' with rostra. Small kitchen available.
Suitable for meetings, quiet private functions. Not
licensed.

**LEIGHTON HOUSE MUSEUM**
12 Holland Park Road, London W14 8LZ
Tel 0171 602 3316
**Administration:**
The Main Studio S./Cap: 152.
Opening times: Monday to Saturday 11.00am - 5.30pm
Closed Sundays and Bank Holidays.
Atmospheric period building licensed for use as a
Concert Hall. Available from 6.30pm - 10.00pm. Limited
dressing room facility. Theatrical entertainment not
permitted.

Exhibition gallery available for the visual arts. (11am - 6pm Mon-Fri and to 5pm Sat.) No facilities available Sunday.

### HOLLAND PARK THEATRE
Holland Park, Kensington, London W8 6LU
Mgt 0171 603 1123  BO 0171 602 7856
Fax 0171 371 2467
**Administration:**
For Bookings Contact: Gabriel West on 0171 603 1123.
726 seater Summer Theatre set amid the ruins of the Jacobean Holland House and completely covered by an innovative tensile canopy. Full lighting rig; sound enhancement; F.O.H. catering facilities. No flying. Season runs from June to mid-August, featuring Opera, Music, Theatre and Dance staged by independent and touring companies.

## KINGSTON
Royal Borough of Kingston upon Thames
Director of Education and Leisure Services: John Braithwaite
Guildhall 2, Kingston upon Thames KT1 1EU
Tel 0181 547 5220  Fax 0181 547 5297
Arts Development Officer: Colin Bloxham
Kingston Library, Fairfield Road, Kingston upon Thames KT1 2PS
Tel 0181 547 6416  Fax 0181 547 6426
e-mail webmaster@councillors.kingston.gov.uk
Website www.kingston.gov.uk

### THE DOUGLAS CENTRE
(community arts centre for the Borough of Kingston)
Douglas Road, Tolworth, Surbiton, Surrey KT6 7SB
Tel 0181 296 9012

### LJ'S THEATRE BAR
140 London Road, Kingston upon Thames,
Surrey KT2 6QL
Tel 0181 288 1448

## LAMBETH
London Borough of Lambeth
Arts Officer: Menika Van Der Poorten
Halls Officer: Paul Griffiths
Directorate of Environmental Services, Arts and Halls,
5th Floor, Courtenay House, 9 - 15 New Park Road,
SW2 4DY
Tel 0171 926 0168
Fax 0171 926 0179

### LAMBETH TOWN HALL
(Assembly Hall), Brixton Hill, London SW2 1RW
Direct Town Hall Line 0171 926 1000
For Bookings Contact: Karen Vince on: 0171 926 2116
S/Cap: 300
General purpose hall used for small scale shows, dances, etc.

### NETTLEFOLD HALL*
West Norwood Library, Norwood High Street, London
SE27 9JX
Tel 0171 926 8070
Fax 0171 926 8071
Halls Officer: Paul Griffiths
S/Cap: 213. General Purpose Hall. Raised retractable seating for theatre shows. Full sound, lighting and projection facilities/induction loop.

### NORWOOD HALL
38 Knights Hill, London SE27 0JD
Tel 0171 926 8072  Fax 0171 926 8072
Halls Officer: Paul Griffiths
S/Cap: 280. General Purpose Hall. Sound, lighting facilities, induction loop.

## LEWISHAM
London Borough of Lewisham
Programming Manager: Chris Hare
Promotions Manager: Martin Costello
Rushey Green, Catford, SE6 4TU
Tel 0181 690 2317
Fax 0181 314 1716

### LEWISHAM THEATRE*
### LEWISHAM THEATRE STUDIO
Mgt 0181 690 2317  BO 0181 690 0002
Fax 0181 314 1716
Joint General Managers: Martin Costello and Chris Hare.
Technical Manager: Kath O`Sullivan
Policy: Touring, Pantomime, Concerts, Variety, Musical, Opera, etc.
Perfs: variable.
Seats 851. Two Bars.

## MERTON
London Borough of Merton
Assistant Director for Education, Leisure and Library Services: R. G. Hobbs
Tel 0181 545 3651  Fax 0181 545 3443
Merton Civic Centre, London Road, Morden,
Surrey SM4 5DX
Tel 0181 543 2222

## NEWHAM
London Borough of Newham
Acting Director: Simon Parkinson
Leisure Services Dept., 292 Barking Road, East Ham,
London E6 3BA
Tel 0181 472 1430
Fax 0181 557 8845

## REDBRIDGE
London Borough of Redbridge
Central Library, Clements Road, Ilford, Essex IG1 1EA
Tel 0181 478 7145
Fax 0181 553 3299
Borough Arts Officer: Ms H. Colborne
Lynton House, High Road, Ilford, Essex 1GI 1NY
Tel 0181 514 5110

## RICHMOND UPON THAMES
London Borough of Richmond upon Thames
Principal Arts Officer: Nigel Cutting
Leisure Services Dept., Langholm Lodge,
146 Petersham Road, Richmond TW10 6UX
Tel 0181 831 6138
Fax 0181 940 7568

## SOUTHWARK
London Borough of Southwark
Principal Arts Officer: Mr. Vaughan Aston
Southwark Arts Service, The Civic, 600 - 608 Old Kent Road, Peckham, London SE15 1JB
Tel 0171 635 6841

**THE CIVIC**
600 - 608 Old Kent Road, Peckham,
London SE15 1JB
Tel 0171 732 3232
Fax 0171 732 5868
**Administration:**
Bookings Contact: Debbie Spencer
S/Cap: 326
General purpose hall used for Concerts, Theatrical
Productions, Banquets, Variety Shows, Wedding
Receptions, Conference and Seminar facilities.

# SUTTON
London Borough of Sutton
Head of Community Lifestyles: Colin Beech
Central Library, St Nicholas Way, Sutton SM1 1EA
Tel 0181 770 4642

**CENTRAL LIBRARY (Europa Gallery)**
St Nicholas Way, Sutton SM1 1EA
For Bookings Contact: Lesley Vye on 0181 770 4749
S/Cap: 325
Recitals, Lectures, Poetry Readings, Exhibitions.

**SECOMBE THEATRE***
Cheam Road, Sutton, Surrey SM1 2ST
Tel 0181 642 2218/9
Manager: Shirley Carpenter on 0181 770 6986
S/Cap: 400 max
Musicals, Plays, One Night Attractions, Recitals,
Professional and Amateur Productions.

**CHARLES CRYER STUDIO THEATRE***
Tel 0181 770 4960
Director: Keith Lancing
S/Cap: 100-180 (Flexible)
Alternative Arts, Cabaret, Jazz, Rock, Minority Arts,
Disability Arts and professional producing venue.

# TOWER HAMLETS

**WHITECHAPEL THEATRE**
189 Whitechapel Road, London E1 1DN
Tel 0171 377 8735

# WALTHAM FOREST
London Borough of Waltham Forest.
Mr. P. Wilkinson, Entertainments Manager, PO Box
416, Sycamore House, Forest Road,
Walthamstow E17 4SY
Tel 0181 527 5544 ext. 4642.
Also Andrew Lemarke ext.4568

**WALTHAMSTOW ASSEMBLY HALL***
Forest Road, London E17 4JD
Mgt 0181 527 5544 Ext. 4420  BO 0181 521 7111
SD 0181 527 5394  Fax 0181 531 8642
Entertainments Manager: Eamonn O'Machaill
S/Cap: 1,150

**CHINGFORD ASSEMBLY HALL**
Station Road, Chingford E4 7EN
Tel 0181 529 0555
**Administration:**
S/Cap: 480.
Policy: Touring, Pantomime, Concerts, Variety, Music
Hall, Drama, Dances, Dinners, Conferences,
Weddings, etc.
**Technical:**
**Stage:** Width 10m; Depth 9m; Height 4m, no flying

Facilities; Wings 3.5m. Electrics: 100amp x 3 phase x
240 volt in wings.
**Lighting:** Rank Strand A.M.C. 30 way x 3 pre-sets;
F.O.H.; One Dozen Profile/Fresnel Spots + 2 x 2Kw
Follow Spots. Stage: 3 Battens (Floods and Spots) +
Portable Wing Floods. Effects: Mirrorball.
**Sound:** 8 Channel Mixer with monitor facility and
cassette deck - Output 100 watts. Sound/Lighting
Control Room located above foyer at rear of theatre.

**WALTHAM FOREST THEATRE**
Winns Terrace, Walthamstow E17 6EJ
Tel 0181 527 5544
**Administration:**
S/Cap: 430
Policy: Touring, Pantomime, Concerts, Variety, Music
Hall, Drama, Dances, Dinners, Conferences,
Weddings, etc.
**Technical:**
**Stage:** Width 9m; Depth 7.5m; Height 3.7m, no Flying
Facilities; Wings: Stage Right 2m, Stage Left 8m (inc.
scene dock). Electrics: 100 amp x 3 phase x 240 volt in
wings.
**Lighting:** Rank Strand A.M.C. 300 way x 3 pre-sets;
F.O.H.; 2 Dozen Profile/Fresnel Spots + 2 x 2Kw
Follow spots. Stage: 3 Battens (Floods and Spots) +
Portable Wing Floods. Effects: Mirrorball, Colour
Change Wheels and Effects. Projector.
**Sound:** 16 Channel Mixer with monitor facility and
cassette deck. Output 200 watts. Intercom.
Sound/Lighting Control Room located above foyer at
rear of theatre. Artistes Portable Sound/ Lighting
Desks to be located at centre rear of hall - 35m
multicore required.

# WANDSWORTH

**GRAND HALL, BATTERSEA TOWN HALL***
170 Lavender Hill, Battersea SW11 5TF
Tel 0181 738 0908
Fax 0171 978 5207
**Administration:**
Manager: Catherine Thornborrow
Bookings Contact: Maria Lunnis
S/Cap: 400
Flat floor. Multi-Purpose.

**CIVIC SUITE, WANDSWORTH TOWN HALL**
High Street, Wandsworth SW18 2PU
Tel 0181 871 6394/5
Bookings Contact: Terry Sammons, Manager
S/Cap: 475. Multi-Purpose.

**LOLA JONES HALL**
Greaves Place, Garratt Lane, SW17 0NE
Hall Superintendent: 0181 871 7176
S/Cap: 300. Multi-Purpose

# WESTMINSTER
Westminster City Council
Arts Manager: Joanne Gray
Westminster City Hall, 64 Victoria Street,
London SW1E 6QP
Tel 0171 641 6000
Fax 0171 641 8083

# Scotland

**ABERDEEN CITY COUNCIL**
St Nicholas House, Aberdeen AB10 1XJ
Tel 01224 522472
Fax 01224 648256
Chief Executive: Douglas Paterson
Director of Arts & Recreation: Brian Woodcock
Principal Officer Arts and Recreation Dept: Ciaran Monaghan
General Manager (Performing Arts Venues): Robert Robson

**ABERDEENSHIRE**
Woodhill House, Westburn Road, Aberdeen AB16 5GB
Tel 01224 620981
Chief Executive: Alan Campbell
Tel 01224 665400 Fax 01224 665444
Director of Leisure and Recreation: Gil Carling
Tel 01224 665515 Fax 01224 665444
Arts Development Officer (North): Hazel Weeks
Tel 01261 813384 Fax 01261 833646
Arts Development Officer (Central): Sheila Waterhouse
Tel 01467 628379 Fax 01467 624285
Arts Development Officer (South): Mindy Grewer
Tel 01569 768358 Fax 01569 765455
**Aberdeen Arts Centre** (374)
**Aberdeen International Youth Festival and Aberdeen Alternative Festival** is funded by the City Council but is managed independently.
**Banchory Town Hall** (290)
**Banff Town Hall** (200)
**Cowdray Hall** (370/476)
**Dalrymple Hall**, Fraserburgh (400)
**Deeside Community Education Centre**, Aboyne (270)
**Fordyce Street**, Rosehearty (200)
**His Majesty's Theatre, Aberdeen** (1,456)
**Inverurie Town Hall** seats 534
**Learney Hall**, Torphins (300).
**Lumphanan Village Hall** (100)
**Macduff Town Hall** (350)
**Madcuff Arts Centre** (200)
**Music Hall, Aberdeen** (1,274)
**Peterhead Community Education Centre** (321 seats but 306 if orchestra used).
**Portsoy Town Hall** (350)
**Rescue Hall**, Peterhead (250)
**St. Laurence Hall**, Laurencekirk (300)
**Stewarts Hall**, Huntly (400)
**Stonehaven Town Hall** (474)

**ANGUS**
County Buildings, Market Street, Forfar DD8 3WF
Tel 01307 461460
Fax 01307 461968
Chief Executive: Sandy Watson
Director of Cultural Services: Gavin Drummond
Arts Officer: Sandy Thomson
**Webster Theatre**, Arbroath (606)
**City Hall**, Brechin (430)
**Inglis Memorial Hall**, Edzell (180)
**Reid Hall**, Forfar (829)
**Town Hall**, Kirriemuir (372)
**Town Hall**, Montrose (674)
**Wharncliffe Hall**, Newtyle (120)

**ARGYLL & BUTE**
Kilmory, Lochgilphead PA31 8RT
Tel 01546 602127
Fax 01546 604444

Director of Environmental Services: Tom McKay
Head of Leisure: Paul Weatherall
Principal Leisure Resources Officer: Willie Young
The Leisure Development unit within the Department of Environmental Services is responsible for Arts, Library, Museum and Sports Services. Arts Development is co-ordinated by the unit's Principal Leisure Resources Officer, Willie Young and is presently concerned with organising a range of events in the Council's Halls and advising on grant assistance to local and national arts organisations.
Argyll and Bute is a large mixed urban, rural and island area with a scattered population of 90,500.

**CLACKMANNANSHIRE**
Greenfield, Alloa FK10 2AD
Tel 01259 452487
Fax 01259 452240
Chief Executive: Robert Allan
Team Leader -Arts: Rosa McPherson
Executive Director Education & Community Services: Keir Bloomer

**DUMFRIES AND GALLOWAY**
Council Offices, English Street, Dumfries DG1 2DD
Tel 01387 260000
Fax 01387 260034
Chief Executive: Ian Smith
Director for Community Resources: Leslie Jardine
Director for Education: Kenneth McLeod
Head of Economic & Community Development: Graeme Trickey
Head of Leisure & Sport: Stewart Atkinson
Arts Development Officer: Rebecca Coggins
Museums Manager: David Lockwood
Tel 01387 253374
The Council operate a wide range of facilities across the region including:
**Loreburn Hall - Dumfries; Sanquhar Town Hall, Hillview Leisure Centre - Kirkconnel; Robert Burns Centre Film Theatre; Dumfries Museum; Dumfries Ice Bowl; Burns House; Sanquhar Tolbooth Museum; Old Bridge House Museum; Dumfries Archive Centre and Robert Burns Centre.
Birchvale Theatre; Dalbeattie (privately owned).
Town Halls in Kirkcudbright, Castle Douglas, Dalbeattie and New Galloway.
Langholm Buccleuch Hall (400); Annan, Lockerbie, Lochmaben and Moffat.**
In addition, suitable school halls are available to outside organisations for entertainment and recreation.
Population 148,000
Area 2,459 sq miles
Employment is mostly in agriculture, forestory, hotels catering, food processing, textiles, clothing, rubber goods, mechanical engineering and distributive trades.

**DUNDEE CITY**
McManus Galleries, Albert Square, Dundee DD1 1DA
Tel 01382 434000
Fax 01382 434666
Chief Executive: Alex Stephen
21 City Square, Dundee DD1 3BY
Tel 01382 434000 Fax 01382 434666
Chief Arts Officer: Andrea Stark
Art Development Officer: Norrie Coulson
McManus Galleries, Albert Square, Dundee DD1 1DA
Tel 01382 432020 Fax 01382 432052

The **Caird Hall** (capacity 2,400) consists of a full set of platform retiring rooms, cloak rooms, lounge foyer, spacious corridors and a grand organ. The Hall is let for concerts, conferences, exhibitions, graduation ceremonies etc. Within the Caird Hall complex is: The **Marryat Hall** - capacity varies from 225 to 344 depending on use.

The **Steps Theatre** has a seating capacity of 250 showing quality cultural films as arranged by the Dundee Film Theatre. Additional purposes include informal musical concerts, lectures, etc. Incorporated in the complex is a conference room having audio visual equipment available. These facilities are located within the Central Library, Wellgate.

The **Repertory Theatre** opened in May 1982. Current entertainments under Council aegis include pop concerts, orchestral concerts, variety, opera and amateur productions.

Dundee, the industrial heart of holiday country has a population of 187,371.

## EAST AYRSHIRE
London Road, Kilmarnock KA3 7DU
Tel 01563 576000
Fax 01563 574062
Chief Executive: David Montgomery
Director of Community Services: William Stafford
Arts & Cultural Development Officer: David Bett
**The Palace Theatre, Kilmarnock** (503)
**Cumnock Town Hall** (500)
**Cumnock Academy Assembly Hall** (250)
**The Grand Hall, Kilmarnock** (900)
**Town Hall Darvel** (400)
**Morton Hall Newmilns** (400)
**Institute Stewarton** (300)
**Public Hall Dunlop**
**John Fulton Memorial Hall Fenwick.**

## EAST DUNBARTONSHIRE
Director of Education & Leisure: Ian Mills
Boclair House, 100 Milngavie Road,
Bearsden G61 2TQ
Tel 0141 942 9000  Fax 0141 942 6814
Head of Leisure & Cultural Services: Sue Selwyn
The Triangle, Kirkintilloch Road, Bishopbriggs G64 2TR
Tel 0141 772 9000  Fax 0141 772 0934
Arts and Events Manager: Joan Riddell
Kilmardinny House, Kilmardinny Avenue,
Bearsden G61 3NN
Tel 0141 931 5084
Libraries Manager: Elizabeth Brown
Library Headquarters, 2 West High Street,
Kirkintilloch G66 1AD
Tel 0141 776 5666  Fax 0141 776 0408
The Council aims "to provide a balanced programme to cater for the leisure and cultural requirements of residents within the district", which has a population of some 110,220 in seventy-seven square miles.
Financial aid is given to the Fort Theatre, Bishopbriggs. The Leisuredrome, The Allander, Twechar and Campsie Recreation Centres have a wide range of sporting and recreational facilities. There are 14 public halls, **Kirkintilloch Town Hall, Lenzie Hall, War Memorial Hall Bishopbriggs, Brackenbrae House, Milton of Campsie Hall, Memorial Hall Lennoxtown, Caldwell Hall, Torrance Community Centre , Westerton Hall, Kessington Hall, Bearsden Hall, Milngavie Town Hall, Kilmardinny House, Maxholme.**
There is no stated entertainment programme, however many halls are used for performances of various types throughtout the year.

## EAST LOTHIAN
Council Buildings, Haddington, East Lothian EH41 3HA
Tel 01620 827827
Fax 01620 827888
Chief Executive: John Lindsay
Director of Education & Community Services: Alan Blackie
Manager of Cultural Services: Margaret O'Connor
Principal Arts Officer: Lesley Smith
Tel 0131 665 3711
Present policy is to provide a balanced programme of entertainment. Population is roughly 80,000 and the district is rural with farming, fishing and tourism the main industries.
The **Brunton Theatre** at Musselburgh seats up to 305and is home to the Brunton Theatre Company.
Props: East Lothian Council; Principal Arts Officer: Lesley Smith; Artistic Director: Robin Peoples; Marketing Officer: Sally Wilson. **The Brunton Hall** in that town accommodates 900.

## EAST RENFREWSHIRE
Council Offices, Eastwood Park, Rouken Glen Road,
Giffnock, Glasgow G46 6UG
Tel: 0141 577 3000
Fax: 0141 620 0884
Chief Executive: Peter Daniels
Tel 0141 577 3009
Fax 0141 638 8969
Director of Community & Leisure: Ann Saunders
Tel 0141 577 3096
Fax 0141 577 3100
Head of Cultural Services: Ken McKinlay
Tel 0141 577 3103
Fax 0141 577 3100
Principal Leisure Officer: Mrs Chris Wyse
Tel 0141 577 3912
Fax 0141 577 3919
The **Eastwood Theatre** has S/Cap of 300. Main halls are **Fairweather Hall, Crookfur Pavilion, Capelrig House,** at Newton Mearns; **Thorntree Hall** at Thornliebank; **Rhuallan House, Carmichael Hall, Eastwood House, Woodfarm Mini-Sports Centre** and **Woodfarm Pavilion** all at Giffnock; **Duff Memorial Hall** at Busby; **Montgomery Hall** at Eaglesham; **Muirend Pavilion** at Muirend; **Netherlee Pavilion** at Netherlee and **Clarkston Hall and Overlee Pavilion** both at Clarkston.
This suburban residential district on the south side of Glasgow has a population of 60,000 in 45.3 square miles.

## EDINBURGH (CITY OF)
PO Box 3232, Edinburgh EH1 1YX
Tel 0131 469 3086
Fax 0131 469 3010
Chief Executive: Tom Aitchison
Director of Recreation: Roger Jones
Assistant Director: Leslie Evans
17 Waterloo Place, Edinburgh EH1 3BG

## FALKIRK
Town Hall, Municipal Buildings, Falkirk FK1 5RS
Tel 01324 506176
Fax 01324 506171
Director of Community & Leisure Services: Loudon Craig
Principal Officer Entertainments: A Craig Murray
Entertainments Officer: Jane Clark
Assistant Entertainments Officers:
Morag Cochrane
**Falkirk Town Hall** Theatre 250 -650, Concert Hall 900; **Grangemouth Town Hall** (600); **Bo'ness Town Hall** (500).

# CARNEGIE HALL DUNFERMLINE

Fully equipped theatre seating 596 with orchestra pit, large stage and excellent acoustics. Available for hires and joint promotions.

For full details and technical specification contact:

Phone **01383 314110**
Fax **01383 314131**

## FIFE
The Tower Block, Auchterderran Centre, Woodend
Road, Cardenden, Fife KY5 0NE
Tel 01592 414714
Fax 01592 414727
Community Services, Fife Council aims to encourage
and support the development of the arts through
participation and enjoyment for the widest possible
diversity of interests throughout Fife communities. The
programme includes involvement in community
festivals, performance and exhibitions from the local to
the International Youth Performance groups, residential
and short courses and an information service.
Professional arts events are programmed in theatres,
halls, schools and colleges often linking with
community events. Lending services include staging,
lighting, arts works and music. A focus on arts
development results in the formation of many new
companies and societies which become dynamic
independent organisations.
Fife is situated in the East of Scotland, just North of
Edinburgh. The region covers an area of 505 square
miles with a coastline of 115 miles. The main centres of
population are Dunfermline, Kirkaldy, Glenrothes and
St.Andrews.

Community Services West
Music Institute, Eastport,
Dunfermline, KY12 7JA
Tel 01383 314110
Fax 01383 314131
Service Manager Sports & Parks: Grant Ward
Arts Co-ordinator: Lesley O'Hare
Theatre Manager: Vacant
Lochgelly Centre Manager: Verdi Harriot
Community Centres Manager: Alice Callaghan
Theatres: **Carnegie Hall, Dunfermline** (590 seats),
**Lochgelly Centre** (463 seats)
Halls: **Iverkeithing Civic Centre** (400); **Lochgelly
Town Hall** (300); **Baldridgeburn** (390); **Dell
Farquaarson** (390).

Community Services Central
Town House, Kirkcaldy KY1 1XW
Tel 01592 412900
Fax 01592 417847
Service Manager (Arts, Libraries, Museums):
Iain Whitelaw
Arts Co-ordinator: Vacant
Theatre Manager: Adam Smith Theatre: Sheila Thomson
Manager, Rothes Halls: Frank Chinn (01592 612220)
Events & Promotions Manager: Margaret Anderson
Hall Development Officers: Isobel Ramage,
Frances Geddes
Theatres: **Adam Smith Theatre**, Kirkcaldy, including
Auditorium (475 seats); **Beveridge Studio** (200);
**Function Suite** (200), **Rothes Halls**, Glenrothes

(700/300).
Halls: numerous and varied in 18 communities with
capacities up to 460.

Community Services East
County Buildings, Cupar, Fife KT15 4TA
Tel 01334 412200
Fax 01334 412110
Service Manager (Community Education): Tom Bain
Arts Co-ordinator: Andrew Neil
Halls Administrator/Events & Promotions: Paul Marshall
Main Halls are **St. Andrews Town Hall** (350); **Corn
Exchange Cupar** (450); **Blyth Hall** Newport (400);
**Easter Town Hall** Anstruther (250); **Gregory Hall**
Tayport (250 seated). Stage & Lighting available in
halls.

## GLASGOW (CITY OF)
Department of Performing Arts & Venues, Exchange
House, 229 George Street, Glasgow G1 1QU
Tel 0141 287 5429
Fax 0141 287 5533
Director of Performing Arts: Christine Hamilton
Head of Programming: Neil Levine
Principal Operations Manager: Billy Garrett
Technical Manager: Peter Green
Event Marketing Manager: Julie Tait
Media & PR: Lesley Booth
**King's Theatre**
297 Bath Street, Glasgow G2 4JN
Tel 0141 332 2661
Tickets 0141 227 5511
S/Cap: 1,785. Jan - Dec. One of the UK's premiere
touring venues: theatre, pantomime, drama, opera,
dance, variety.
**Tramway**
25 Albert Drive, Glasgow G41 2PE
Tel 0141 422 2023  BO 0141 287 5511
Fax 0141 422 2021
Tickets 0141 227 5511
Seating: Capacities - Area 1: 719 raked seating
(moveable) 870 standing. Area 2: 1500 Standing. Area
4,122 (122 raked seating).
**Mitchell Theatre & James Moir Hall Complex**
Granville Street, Glasgow G3 7DR
Tel 0141 221 3198  BO 0141 287 5511
Fax 0141 221 0695
Tickets: 0141 227 5511
S/Cap: 418 Mitchell Theatre; 400 James Moir Hall. Jan
- Dec. Multi-use theatre & conference complex: theatre,
drama, music, dance, exhibitions, conferences.
**City Hall**
Candleriggs, Glasgow G1 1NQ
Tel 0141 287 5005  BO 0141 287 5511
Fax 0141 287 5533
Tickets: 0141 227 5511
Capacity: 1216 Grand Hall. Jan - Dec. One of

Glasgow's most popular venues for concerts, conferences and exhibitions.
Old Fruitmarket
Albion Street, Glasgow G1
Capacity: 850. Jan-Dec. A fully flexible "found space" presenting jazz, live music, theatre, exhibitions.

## HIGHLAND

Headquarters, Glenurquhart Road, Inverness IV3 5NX
Tel 01463 702000
Fax 01463 711177
Director of Cultural & Leisure Services: Alan J Jones
The Highland Council covers the geographic area previously administered by the regional council and eight district councils. An audit of all facilities is currently being conducted. the council has access to a variety of venues, including 100 seat drama studio and several well-eqiupped school halls, and helps subsidise The Eden Court Theatre, Inverness.
The council is interested in improving arts and entertainments provision and welcomes approaches from groups and individuals interested in appearing in the Highlands. The Cultural & Leisure Services Department is happy to promote incoming tours and acts as co-ordinators for all incoming tours within the area. Population of this rural region is 200,000 on a density of 20 per square mile area.

BADENOCH & STRATHSPEY
Council Offices, Ruthven Road, Kingussie PH21 1EJ
Tel 01540 664500
Fax 01540 661004
Area Cultural & Leisure Services Manager: Graham Watson

CAITHNESS
Offices: District Council Offices, Wick,
Caithness KW1 4AB
Tel 01955 603761
Fax 01955 604524
Area Cultural & Leisure Services Manager: Ian Robertson
**Assembly Rooms** Wick (636)
**Town Hall** Thurso (250)

INVERNESS
Offices: The Town House, Inverness IV1 1JG
Tel 01463 724224
Fax 01463 712850
Arts Officer: Adrian Clarke
Area Cultural & Leisure Services Manager: Gunars Libeks
**Eden Court Theatre** (800)

LOCHABER
Offices: Highland Council, Mamore House, Fort William PH33 6EL
Tel 01397 702102
Fax 01397 702107
Area Cultural & Leisure Services Manager: Hugh Allison

NAIRN
Offices: The Court House, High Street, Nairn IV12 4AU
Tel 01667 458521
Fax 01667 452056
Area Cultural & Leisure Services Manager: Graham Watson
Recreation & Entertainment Assistant: Miss Anne Sudder
The Council will provide a programme of municipal entertainment summer seasons in addition to allowing

the usual Fair and visiting Circus.

ROSS & CROMARTY
Offices: County Buildings, Dingwall IV15 9QN
Tel 01349 868477
Fax 01349 863107
Arts Development Officer: Nick Fearne
Area Cultural & Leisure Services Officer: Peter Hoffman
There is a great deal of local voluntary effort in promotion of entertainment in this area which has increased over the years. Professional shows are making use of the large halls. The Duthac Centre (formerly the Tain Town Hall) has been leased by the Highland Council to a Management Committee and there is a part-time Management on the premises. (Telephone Tain 894422). Local drama groups continue to develop and there are three Art Societies and one Film Society and a very active Camera Club in the area. Other main halls are **Dingwall** (400); **Fearn** (100); **Evanton** (120); **Portmahomack** (120); **Averon Centre,** Alness (200); **Invergordon Arts Centre** (100); **Fortrose** (80-100); **Muir of Ord** (150); **Cromarty** (150); **Milnafua** (60); Population is now 44,000 in 1,236,000 acres, mostly settled on eastern coastal plain where industry has arrived; sparsely populated in central and Wester Ross. Tourism is strong on western seaboard. Industry in the east includes farming, distilling, oil rig platform construction, oil support, related industries. Two Arts Development Officers have been appointed for the Area and a Burgeoning Community Arts Movement involving a number of artists in residence and general arts residencies is under way. Artists in residence include Dance, Community Drama, Writer, Traditional Music, Visual Arts and Music.

SKYE & LOCHALSH
Offices: Tigh na Sgire Park Lane, Portree,
Isle of Skye IV51 9GP
Tel 01478 612341
Fax 01478 613828
Area Cultural & Leisure Services Manager: Roger Miket

SUTHERLAND
Offices: Main Street, Golspie, Sutherland, KW10 6RB
Tel 01408 633033
Fax 01408 633120
Area Cultural & Leisure Services Officer: Graham Nichols

## INVERCLYDE

Municipal Buildings, Greenock PA15 1LY
Tel 01475 724400
Fax 01475 882010
Chief Executive: Graeme Bettison
Head of Services (Libraries, Arts & Community Education): Joy Monteith
Arts Development Officer: Catriona Henderson

## MIDLOTHIAN

Midlothian House, Buccleuch Street,
Dalkeith EH22 1DJ
Tel 0131 663 2881
Fax 0131 660 7565
Chief Executive: Trevor Muir
Director of Community Services: Graeme Marwick
No theatres but halls include **Cowan Institute,** Penicuik (300); **Danderhall Leisure Centre** (400); **Mayfield Leisure Centre** (400); **Gorebridge Leisure Centre** (400); **Newtongrange Leisure Centre** (350); **Ladywood Leisure Centre,** Penicuik (450); **Dalkeith Arts Centre** (150); **Bonnyrigg Leisure Centre.**

## MORAY

Council Office, High Street, Elgin IV30 1BX
Tel 01343 543451
Fax 01343 540183
Chief Executive: Anthony Connell
Director of Tech & Leisure Services: John Summers
Chief Leisure Officer: Rod Stone
Seven halls of which **Elgin** is best equipped for theatre (accommodates 743)

## NORTH AYRSHIRE

Cunninghame House, Friars Croft, Irvine KA12 8EE
Tel 01294 324112
Fax 01294 324114
Performing Arts Officer: William Freckleton
Assistant Performing Arts Officer: Craig Smart
**Magnum Main Hall**: Capacity 1278 seated and 2000 standing.
**Magnum Theatre, Irvine**: 323 capacity.
Lighting: Tempus M24; Tempus M24 F/X; 60 Channel; 189 Memories; 18 T Spots; 17 Fresnel; 12 Floods; 6 Profiles, Total 53 lamps.
Sound: T.O.A. c/x 124 Mixing Desk; 12 Channel; 2 F.O.N. Speakers; Tape Deck; CD Player.
Theatres are: **The Magnum Leisure Centres Main Hall and Theatre Complex** in Irvine (as above); **Barrfields Pavilion**, Largs (470); **Civic Theatre**, Ardrossan (250); The Council also gives financial assistance to the Harbour Arts Centre at Irvine Main Halls are: **Blacklands Hall**, Kilwinning (300); **Saltcoats Town Hall** (200); **Dunlop Memorial Hall**, Dreghorn (350); **Walker Memorial Hall**, Kilbirnie (500 main hall, 150 lesser hall); **Hayocks Hall** (150); **Dalry Public Hall** (200 main hall, 50 lesser hall); **Beith Townhouse** (200); **William Knox Institute**, Kilbirnie (120); **West Kilbride Public Hall** (200); **Millport Town Hall** (300 main hall, 200 lesser hall); **Garrison Ballroom, Millport** (800); **Development Association Hall**, Millport (220); **Volunteer Rooms**, Irvine (400). The Council has a policy of assisting the arts by providing live entertainment and currently this ranges from regular performances of plays and variety shows through to cabaret and cultural items. The Council also aids arts organisations, professional theatre, arts guilds, civic weeks and festivals.

## NORTH LANARKSHIRE

PO Box 14, Civic Centre, Motherwell ML1 1TW
Tel 01698 302222
Chief Executive: Andrew Cowe
Director of Leisure Services: Norman Turner
Head of Cultural Services: Ann Malloy
The **Motherwell Theatre** (395); **Concert Hall** (S/Cap: 1,008, Standing/Cap: 1,800 and **Bellshill Cultural Centre** are main venues. The Council promotes all forms of entertainment with special emphasis on the pantomime season.

Offices: Buchanan Tower, Buchanan Business Park, Stepps, Glasgow
Tel 0141 304 1800
Arts & Venues Manager: Lizanne McMurrich
Artistic Director of Cumbernauld Theatre: Simon Sharkey
Tel: 01236 737235
**Airdrie Arts Centre Theatre** (170). **Sir John Wilson Town Hall**, Airdrie has a Large Hall (900) and a Lesser Hall (110).
Population of about 200,000.

## RENFREWSHIRE

High Street, Paisley PA1 2BA
Tel 0141 889 3151
Fax 0141 889 9240
Director of Leisure Services: Howard Hann
Policy is to provide a community-based Arts Service to all people resident in Renfrew District. There are approximately 40 halls and community centres, the largest being **Paisley Town Hall; Johnstone Community Hall;** and **Tweedle Hall**, Linwood. There is an Arts Centre containing a 165 seat fully equipped theatre, workshop area, bar and bistro.
The District has urban, rural and industrial areas, and the total population is 196,000

## ORKNEY ISLANDS COUNCIL

Offices: Council Offices, Kirkwall, Orkney KW15 1NY
Tel 0185687 3535
Fax 0185687 6327
Recreation and Leisure are responsibilities of the Education Department and the official responsible is Alan G Clouston, Assistant Director of Education and Recreation Services.
There are three Community Education Officers. The main theatre provision is based on **Orkney Arts Theatre**, which has a capacity of 324. The Council also owns and runs the **Phoenix Cinema** which is also used for concerts. The seating capacity is 520. Outside these theatres activities are centred on community centres. There is a strong tradition of dramatic and musical activity within the islands. The region is an island community with farming the main economic activity. Services, industries, etc. centre around the two towns Kirkwall and Stromness. Due mainly to oil development, the population has increased over recent years to 19,500.

## PERTH & KINROSS

3 High Street, Perth PH1 5JU
Tel 01738 475211
Fax 01738 441690
Director of Leisure and Cultural Services: Jim Blair
The Council do not actively promote but encourage entertainments. The Leisure and Cultural Services Department provide and maintain facilities. Organisers of charities and professional promoters initiate concerts and events. A Community Arts Officer occasionally hires productions. **Perth City Hall** (1,500) is available for conferences, concerts, etc. Other public halls for hire at Pitlochry, Aberfeldy, Crieff, Auchterarder, Kinross, Coupar Angus and Blairgowrie **Perth Lesser City Hall** (350) for smaller productions. **Perth Theatre** (600) stage repertory drama with a resident company - Tel: 01738 621031. **Pitlochry Festival Theatre** (500) has summer rep.
Tel 01796 3054

## SCOTTISH BORDERS

Regional Headquarters: Newtown St. Boswells, Melrose, TD6 0SA
Tel: 01835 824000
Fax: 01835 825031
Director of Leisure & Recreation: Ian Yates
Head of Cultural Services: Brian J Croft

Offices: District Council Offices
8 Newtown Street, Duns. TD11 3DT
Tel 01361 882600
Fax 01361 883711
Chief Executive: Alistair Croall
Sports & Recreational Services: Tom Leighton
Tel 01835 824000 ex 265
Cultural & Interpretive Dept: Brian Croft
Tel 01835 824000 ex 266

Offices: Albert Place, Galashiels TD1 3DL
Tel 01896 754751
Fax 01896 757003
Venues: **Volunteer Hall, Galashiels** (capacity 553 seats); **Victoria Hall, Selkirk** (capacity 664 seats); **Corn Exchange, Melrose** (capacity 304 seats).

Offices, High Street, Hawick TD9 9EF
Tel 01450 375991
Fax 01450 378526
Tourist/Leisure Manager: Max Arthur
The Council encourage concerts, band displays, holiday entertainment, sheep dog trials, play groups, dances, piping contests, shows and all forms of public entertainment.
Facilities include **Hawick Town Hall** (634), **Kelso Talt Hall** (700), **Jedburgh Town Hall** (450).
Population is 35,000 in rural district area of 587 square miles with farming, tweeds and knitwear the main industries.

## SHETLAND ISLANDS COUNCIL
Offices: Leisure and Recreation Department, Town Hall, Lerwick ZE1 0HB, Shetland
Tel 01595 693535
Fax 01595 744509
Director of Community & Education: Jim Halcrow
Deputy Director: Rob Anderson
Shetland Arts Trust is a charitable organisation formed by the Shetland Islands Council to promote, support and develop the arts in Shetland.
Offices: Pitt Lane, Lerwick ZE1 0DW
Tel 01595 694001
Fax 01595 692941
Arts Officer: Mr A. Watt.
The Shetland Islands Council, in consultation with Shetland Arts Trust, Local Groups and Scottish Arts Council, continues to assess how best the various art forms can be promoted with a view to these interests being adequately supported and accommodated.
Shetland's 552 square miles consists of over 100 islands, 17 of which are inhabited. The population is almost 23,000 with the main town Lerwick (7,500) situated on the largest "Mainland" Isle. Main industries are fishing, agriculture, tourism, knitwear and oil. The **Garrison Theatre** in Market Street, Lerwick re-opened in 1990 following major refurbishment. It is Britain's most northerly theatre with a capacity of 287, and is managed as part of Islesburgh Community Centre, King Harald Street, Lerwick. The **Islesburgh Community Centre** is used regularly for a variety of events including the Shetland Folk Festival, Accordion and Fiddle Festival, exhibitions, drama, dance and music productions and workshops. In addition there are 56 community halls, many of which have been renovated and refurbished over the past 10 years. These community halls are managed by local committees and most include stage/performance facilities.

## SOUTH AYRSHIRE
PO Box 1996, Wellington Square, Ayr KA7 1DS
Tel 01292 612000
Fax 01292 612419
Chief Executive: George Thorley
Director of Education Services: Michael McCabe
Theatres Manager: Gordon Taylor
Alan Davies, M.I.L.A.M.
The **Gaiety Theatre** Ayr seats 570 and is open all the year round: Revue, Panto, Drama, Opera, Dance, etc.
**The Civic Theatre**, Ayr seats 345 and offers a professional season of small scale touring productions throughout the year apart from **Town Hall** which seats 700 persons, the area also has the following medium

and municipal halls. **Beach Pavilion** Girvan, total seating 610-summer shows, dances, sporting and general purpose use as well as private hire. **The Citadel,** Ayr, total audience capacity 1,200, dependent on layout for rock concerts, conferences, etc. Available for private hire. **Troon Concert Hall** - 886 for theatrical shows. Available for dances, conferences, private hire. **Walker Hall,** Troon - 294 for concerts, film shows, small functions. (Part of the concert hall complex and is adjacent to Troon Concert Hall). **Maybole Town Hall** - for concerts, films, private hire. Seating 260.

## SOUTH LANARKSHIRE
Council Building, Almada Street, Hamilton ML3 OAA
Tel 01698 454444
Fax 01698 454275
Chief Executive: Alastair McNish
Executive Director of Community Resources: Douglas Henry
**East Kilbride Arts Centre**
Arts Centre: A. McBain
Tel 01355 261000
Fax 01355 261280

Offices: South Vennel, Lanark ML11 7JT
Tel 01555 661331
Arts Officer: Colin McAllister
**Carluke Recreation Centre** (350)
**Municipal Hall,** Biggar (520)
**Memorial Hall,** Lanark (550)
**New District Hall,** Carluke (500).

## STIRLING
Viewforth, Stirling FK8 2ET
Tel 01786 443322
Fax 01786 442538
Chief Executive: Keith Yates
Director of Community Services: Helen Munro
Head of Libraries, Heritage & Culture: Allan Gillies
**Albert Hall** (850); **Mayfield Centre** (200); **Cowane Theatre** (140).

## WEST DUMBARTONSHIRE
Castle Street, Dumbarton, G82 1JY
Tel 01389 738280
Fax 01389 733244
Director of Environmental Protection & Leisure Services: Norman Rae
Policy: Halls in the area are available for booking by outside agencies. Some promotions also negotiated, box office split, guarantee, negtiable.
Population: 98,000, mixed urban, rural and industrial district.
**Denny Civic Theatre**, Dumbarton: (345)
used by both professional and amateur companies for hire will promote.
**Burgh Hall**, Dumbarton: varied use, concert dance etc.
**Clydebank Town Hall**, Clydebank: (550)
musicals, pantomime, concerts etc. Both amateur and professional bookings, terms negotiable.
Booking information Tel: 01389 738280

## WESTERN ISLES
## COMHAIRLE NAN EILEAN SIAR
## (WESTERN ISLES COUNCIL)
Town Hall, Stornoway, Isle of Lewis HS1 2BE
Tel 01851 703773
Fax 01851 704209
Responsible Officer: Norman MacLean, Principal Officer, Cultural & Community Education Services.
Policy is to support local initiatives in the voluntary sector and to encourage professional companies, groups, ensembles or orchestras wishing to visit the Western Isles. The Council does not book performers as a promoter.
The Council prefers visiting performers to try to visit each of the four major population centes of the Isles viz. Barra, the Uists, Harris and Lewis during their tours. It has a very strong Gaelic tradition, which is reflected throughout the area.
The Council operates one theatre at Sgoil Lionacleit in Benbecula and the Town Hall in Stornoway. In addition, it has performance spaces in a number of local schools, and village halls and community centres are also available. Details of the facilities throughout the Western Isles obtainable from the Responsible Officer.

## WEST LOTHIAN
Arts Unit, Almondbank Campus, The Mall, Craigshill, Livingston, West Lothian EH54 5EJ
Tel 01506 777585
Arts Manager: Brian Duguid
Arts Development Officer: Susan Thores
Arts Development Programme.
**Howden Park Centre, Howden, Livingston EH54 6AE, Tel  01506 433634.**
Howden Park Centre is an Arts Centre comprising 270 seat theatre with conference hall and workshop space. Many community halls throughout the district.
Situated in East Central Scotland the District forms the western part of the Lothian Region.

# COUNTY LEISURE DEPARTMENTS

## BEDFORDSHIRE
Director of Education Arts & Libraries: Paul Brett
Director of Environmental & Economic Development:
Mike Kenworthy
Bedfordshire County Council, County Hall, Bedford
MK42 9AP
Tel 01234 228309
Fax 01234 228921

## CHESHIRE
Principal Arts Officer: Sue Davies
Cheshire County Council Arts Services, Goldsmith
House, Hamilton Place, Chester CH1 1SE
Tel 01244 602834
Fax 01244 602620
e-mail daviessh@cheshire-cc.btx400.co.uk

## CLEVELAND
County Librarian and Leisure Officer: Neil Bennett
Central Library, Victoria Square, Middlesbrough,
Cleveland TS1 2AY
Tel 01642 263397
Fax 01642 230690

## HAMPSHIRE
County Arts Office
Mottisfont Court, High Street, Winchester SO23 8ZD
Senior Arts Officer: Michael Fuller
Arts Development Officer: Dawn Langley
Arts Marketing Officer: Julie Eaglen
Tel 01962 846965
Fax 01962 841644
e-mail artsmf@hants.gov.uk

## ISLE OF WIGHT
Arts Development Officer: Lorna Brown
The Guildhall, High Street, Newport PO30 1TY
Tel 01983 823825
Fax 01983 823841

## KINGSTON-UPON-HULL
Director of Leisure Services: Colin Brown
79 Ferensway, Kingston-upon-Hull,
East Yorks, HU2 8LE
Tel 01482 615609
Fax 01482 61556
Also at Brunswick House, Strand Close, East Yorkshire
Tel 01482 885758
Fax 01482 883162

## LEICESTERSHIRE
Director of Museums: Mrs Sarah Levitt
"The Rowans", College Street, Leicester LE2 OJJ.
Tel 0116 255 4100
Fax 0116 247 3011
Arts Development Officer: Brigitte Cattell
Tel 0116 247 3240
Fortnightly lunch time Concert Season: Oct-March
(Thursdays).
Leicestershire County Council Arts Development
Officer: Stephanie Edmonds: Tel 0116 247 3003.

## LINCOLNSHIRE
Education and Cultural Services
County Arts Development Officer: David Lambert
County Offices, Newland, Lincoln LN1 1YL
Tel 01522 552831
Fax 01522 552811

## NORFOLK
Director Norfolk Museums Service: Catherine M.
Wilson, F.S.A., F.M.A.
Castle Museum, Norwich NR1 3JU
Tel 01603 223624
Fax 01603 765651
Occasional theatrical productions Norwich Castle.
Whiffler Theatre Castle Gardens in Norwich. Details
from the Museum.

## NORTHAMPTONSHIRE
Principal Arts Officer: Lesley Hagger
Leisure Services, Northamptonshire County Council,
PO Box 149, County Hall, Guildhall Road,
Northampton NN1 1AU
Tel 01604 2323
Fax 010 23188

## NOTTINGHAMSHIRE
Assistant Director of Community Services (Leisure
Services): Tim Challans
Head of Arts: Tim Harris
Trent Bridge House, Fox Road, West Bridgford,
Nottingham NG2 6BJ
Tel 0115 977 4206
Fax 0115 977 2428

## OXFORDSHIRE
Director of Leisure and Arts: Thomas Forrest
Central Library, Westgate, Oxford OX1 1DJ
Tel 01865 815549
Fax 01865 810187
e-mail ref.occdja@dial.pipex.com

## SOMERSET
County Museums Officer: D. P. Dawson
The Castle, Taunton TA1 4AA
Tel 01823 355510
Fax 01823 320229
The County Museums Service collects, conserves and
exhibits material evidence of peoples activities and the
natural environment of Somerset for the education and
enjoyment of residents and visitors to the area.

## WILTSHIRE
Head of Service: Pauline Dyer, ALA DMS MIMgt
Department of Libraries & Heritage
Bythesea Road, Trowbridge, Wilts BA14 8BS
Tel 01225 713709
Fax 01225 713993

## CHANNEL ISLANDS
## GUERNSEY
Director of Recreation: David Chilton
Events Manager: Penny Weaver
Amherst, St. Peter Port, Guernsey,
Channel Islands GY1 2DL
Tel 01481 727211
Fax 01481 714102

# NORTHERN IRELAND

## ANTRIM
Chief Leisure and Tourism Officer: Philip A. Lucas
Antrim Borough Council, The Steeple,
Antrim BT41 1BJ
Tel 01849 463113
Arts & Heritage Development Officer:
Mrs Maureen Armstrong
Clotworthy Arts Centre, Antrim Castle Gardens,
Randalstown Road, Antrim BT41 4LH
Tel 01849 428000

## ARDS BOROUGH COUNCIL
**ARDS ARTS CENTRE**
Town Hall, Conway Square, Newtownards,
Co. Down BT23 4DB
Tel 01247 810803
Fax 01247 823131

**THE QUEENS HALL**
West Street, Newtownards
Tel 01247 824000
Contact: Maryl Graham

## ARMAGH
Director of Leisure and Tourism: J. Sanderson
The Palace Demesne, Armagh BT60 4EL
Tel 01861 529600
Fax 01861 529601

## BALLYMENA
Arts Officer: Rosalind Lowry
Ballymena Borough Council, "Ardeevin", 80 Galgorm
Road, Ballymena BT42 1AB
Tel 01266 44111
Fax 01266 46296

**TOWN HALL**
Bridge Street, Ballymena BT42 1AD
Tel 01266 656262
For Bookings Contact: Chief Executives Dept
Tel 01266 44111
Superintendant: Kenneth McGookin
S/Cap: Main Hall, 539; Balcony, 130; Minor Hall 120
max. Stage Facilities.

**SEVEN TOWERS LEISURE CENTRE**
Trostan Avenue, Ballymena BT43 7BL
Tel 01266 41427
S/Cap: Main Hall 1,760. Minor Hall 120.
Stage and Catering Facilities.

## BALLYMONEY
Chief Recreation and Amenities Officer: W. J. Paul
Cultural Services Officer: Margaret Higgins
Riada House, Charles Street, Ballymoney BT53 6DZ
Tel 01265 662280
Fax 01265 667659

## BANBRIDGE
Director of Leisure & Tourism: Mike Reith
Council Offices, Downshire Road, Banbridge,
Co. Down BT32 2JY
Tel 018206 662991
Fax 018206 662595

## BELFAST CITY
Head of Community and Leisure Services: Brian
Morrison
Client Services Department, Leisure Services Section,
The Cecil Ward Building, 4-10 Linenhall Street, Belfast
BT2 8BP.
Tel 01232 320202
Fax 01232 244301

**ARTS THEATRE**
23/41 Botanic Ave, Belfast BT7 1JG
Admin 01232 316901  BO 01232 316900
Fax 01232 316906
Administrator: Anthony Stott
S/Cap: 550, 26' Pros. with 14' Apron.

**GRAND OPERA HOUSE\***
Great Victoria Street, Belfast BT2 7HR
Admin/SD 01232 240411  BO 01232 241919
Fax 01232 236842
Theatre Director: Derek Nicholls
S/Cap: 1,001 on three levels.

**GROUP THEATRE\***
Bedford Street, Belfast BT2 7FF
Mgt 01232 323900  BO 01232 329685
Fax 01232 247199
Manager: R. E. Flaherty
S/Cap: 240

**LYRIC PLAYERS THEATRE\***
55 Ridgeway Street, Belfast BT9 5FB
Mgt 01232 669660
BO 01232 381081
Theatre Manager: P. McBride
S/Cap: 304

**ULSTER HALL**
Bedford Street, Belfast BT2 7FF
Mgt 01232 323900
Fax 01232 247199
Manager: R. E. Flaherty
**Technical:**
S/Cap: 1,270. F.O.H. (Balcony 446), plus 174 choir
(behind stage). Stage open (only). Half moon 11.5 x
5.8m. Auditorium 500 sq. m. Mulholland Grand Organ.
Pop and classical concerts. Conferences, Exhibitions,
Boxing, Snooker, Darts.

## CARRICKFERGUS
**JOYMOUNT TOWN HALL**
Joymount, Carrickfergus,
Co. Antrim BT38 7DL
Tel 01960 351604
Fax 0196 366676

**CARRICKFERGUS LEISURE CENTRE**
Prince William Way, Carrickfergus,
Co. Antrim BT38 7HP
Tel 01960 351711
Fax 01960 360504

Manager: Norman Houston
S/Cap: 1,200

## CASTLEREAGH
Director of Leisure Services:
James D. Rose, B.Ed., D.R.L.P., M.Sc.
Dundonald International Ice Bowl, 111 Old Dundonald
Road, Dundonald BT16 0XT
Tel 01232 482611
Fax 01232 489604

## COLERAINE
Cloonavin, 41 Port Stewart Road, Coleraine,
Co. Londonderry BT52 1EY
Tel 01265 52181
Fax 01265 53489

### RIVERSIDE THEATRE*
The University of Ulster, Coleraine,
Co. Londonderry, Northern Ireland BT52 1SA
Mgt 01265 44141 exts 4683, 4456, or 4459
BO 01265 51388  Fax 01265 324924
**ADMINISTRATION:**
Arts Development Officer: Terence Zeeman
Tel 01265 324449  Fax 01265 324924
Theatre Manager: Janet Mackle
Technical Supervisor: David Coyle
Theatre Assistant: Mary Acheson
Policy: Touring, Ballet, Opera, Own Summer Show,
Christmas Show
Perfs: Mon-Sat 8.00p.m.; Occasional Schools Mat.
10.30a.m. or 1.30 p.m.
Seats: Thrust 358, Pros. 274, bar, Foyer, Art Gallery.

## COOKSTOWN
Development Manager: A McCreesh
Council Offices, Burn Road, Cookstown, BT80 8DT
Tel 01648 762205
Fax 01648 764360

## CRAIGAVON
Arts Development Officer: Rosaleen McMullan
Pinebank House Arts & Community Centre, Tullygally
Road, Craigavon BT65 5BY, Co. Armagh, N. Ireland
Tel 01762 341618
Fax 01762 342402

## DERRY CITY COUNCIL
Director of Recreation and Leisure: C. S. Logue
Venues Manager: David McLaughlin
Administrative Assistant: Paula Bradley
Rialto Entertainment Centre, Market Street, Derry
BT48 6EF
Tel 01504 260516
Fax 01504 374757

## DOWN
Director of Museum Services: Dr Brian Turner
Arts Officer: Jill Holmes
Down County Museum, The Mall, Downpatrick, Co.
Down BT30 6AH
Tel 01396 615218
Fax 01396 615590

### DOWN LEISURE CENTRE
Market Street, Downpatrick, Co. Down

Tel 01396 613426
Fax 01396 616905
General Manager: Mr. Macartan Bryce
S/Cap: 600. Stage and audio-visual facilities.
S/Cap: 600. Meeting rooms, Conference facilities.

### BALLYNAHINCH CENTRE
Windmill Street, Ballynahinch, Co. Down BT24 8HB
Tel 01238 561950
Fax 01238 565606
Contact: Tom Breen
S/Cap: 400. Stage and audio-visual facilities.
S/Cap: 50. Meeting room.

### DOWN ARTS CENTRE
Irish Street, Downpatrick, Co. Down
Tel: 01396 615283
S/Cap: 200. Stage and Audio Visual facilities.
S/Cap: 200 Meeting rooms, Conference facilities,
Exhibition area.

### NEWCASTLE CENTRE
Central Promenade, Newcastle
Tel 013967 25034
S/Cap: 30
Stage and audio visual facilities; meeting rooms
available.

## DUNGANNON
Arts and Administrative Officer: Theresa McNicholl
Dungannon District Arts/Entertainment Committee,
Council Offices, Circular Road, Dungannon BT71 6DT
Tel 01868 720300
Fax 01868 720368

## FERMANAGH
Town Hall, Enniskillen, Co. Fermanagh BT74 7BA
Tel 01365 325050
Fax 01365 322024
Director of Recreation: Rodney Connor, B.Sc.(Econ),
D.M.S.

### ARDHOWEN THEATRE & ARTS CENTRE*
Dublin Road, Enniskillen, Co. Fermanagh.
Manager & Artistic Director: Eamonn Bradley
Admin 01365 323233  BO 01365 325440
Fax 01365 327102
S/Cap: in Main Theatre 295.
S/Cap: in Studio 60.

### TOWN HALL
Town Hall, Enniskillen, Co. Fermanagh BT74 7BA
Tel 01365 325050
Superintendent: Frankie Roofe
S/Cap: 182. Stage Facilities.

### LAKELAND FORUM
Broadmeadow, Enniskillen BT74 7EF
Tel 01365 324121
Fax 01365 328622
Manager: Iain Kennedy
S/Cap: Main Hall 1,000

### CASTLE PARK CENTRE
11 Water Street, Lissnaskea BT92 OL2
Tel 01365 721299
Manager: Elizabeth Wilson
S/Cap: Main Hall, 395. Stage Facilities.

### BAWNACRE CENTRE
Irvinestown, Co. Fermanagh, BT94 1EE
Tel 01365 621177

Fax 01365 628082
Manager: George Beacom
S/Cap: Main Hall 800
Purpose built stage facilities with full lights and curtains.
Minor Hall - Suitable for workshops and exhibitions and concerts. S/Cap: 320

### COMMUNITY CENTRES

**Belcoo Community Centre,** Garrison Road, Belcoo
For Bookings and Enquiries Contact: Jim Ledwirth, at the Fermanagh Community Services Department on 01365 325050.
S/Cap: 360
Stage Facilities.
**Belleek Community Centre,** Station Road, Belleek
For Bookings and Enquiries Contact: Jim Ledwirth, at the Fermanagh Community Services Department on 01365 325050.
S/Cap: 50.
Stage Facilities.
**Ederney Community Centre,** High Street, Ederney.
For Bookings and Enquiries Contact: Jim Ledwirth, at the Fermanagh Community Services Department on 01365 325050.
S/Cap: 360
Stage Facilities.
**Kesh Community Centre,** Mantlin Road, Kesh, Co. Fermanagh BT93 1TT
Contact: The Kesh Development Association
S/Cap: 360
Stage Facilities.
**Newtownbutler Community Centre,** Bridge Street, Newtownbutler
For Bookings and Enquiries Contact: Jim Ledwirth, at the Fermanagh Community Services Department on 01365 325050.
S/Cap: 150.
Stage Facilities.
**Rosslea Community Centre,** Monaghan Road, Rosslea
For Bookings and Enquiries Contact: Jim Ledwirth, at the Fermanagh Community Services Department on 01365 325050.
S/Cap: 360.
Stage Facilities.

## LARNE BOROUGH COUNCIL

Promotions & Community Services Officer:
Mr. H. G. Francis
Smiley Buildings, Victoria Road, Larne BT40 1RU.
Tel 01574 272313
Fax 01574 260660

## LIMAVADY

Chief Recreation/Tourist Officer: S. T. McGregor
Limavady Borough Council, 7 Connell Street, Limavady, Co. Londonderry BT49 OHA
Tel 015047 22226

### TOWN HALL

Main Street, Limavady
S/Cap: 360.
Stage Facilities.

### ROE VALLEY RECREATION CENTRE

Greystone Road, Limavady.
S/Cap: 800
Stage Facilities.

## LISBURN BOROUGH COUNCIL

Director of Leisure Services: Mr N. G. Ferris
The Borough Offices, The Square, Hillsborough,
Co. Down BT26 6AH
Tel 01846 682477
Fax 01846 689984

### HARMONY HILL ARTS CENTRE

54 Harmony Hill, Lisburn BT27 4ES
Tel 01846 682477
Fax 01846 662679
Arts Development Officer: Ms. S.S. Stewart

## MAGHERAFELT

Chief Recreation Officer: Michael Browne
Council Offices: 50 Ballyrowan Road, Magherafelt, Co Londonderry BT45 6AN
Tel 01648 32151
Fax 01648 31240

## MOYLE

Leisure Services Manager: K McGarry
Moyle District Council, Sheskburn House, 7 Mary Street, Ballycastle, Co. Antrim BT54 6QH
Tel 012657 62225
Fax 012657 62515

## NEWRY AND MOURNE

Leisure & Sports Facility Officer: Dermot Russell
District Council Offices, Greenbank, Newry BT34 ZQU
Tel 01693 767226
Fax 01693 766177

### TOWN HALL, NEWRY

Bank Parade, Newry BT35 6HR
Tel 01693 764780
**Administration:**
District Council Offices, Greenbank, Newry.
Tel 01693 767226
For bookings contact the Administrative Director, Mark Hughes, Newry Arts Centre, 1A Bank Parade, Newry, Co. Down BT35 6HP
Tel 01693 766232
Fax 01693 766839
Policy - Musicals, Theatre, Pantomime
Seating: 150 Balcony, 300 Main Hall
**Technical:**
**Stage:** Stage Area - depth 5 metres, width 7 metres. Wing space 35 metres each side. Total Stage Depth 8.5 metres (to Cyc Cloth). Pros Arch Height 4.25 metres.
**Lighting:** Rank Strand AMC St Lighting system with 60 Circuits (58 wired).
**Other:** Dressing Rooms 5,(1 quick change). Passenger lift to Main Hall, Dressing Rooms and Back Stage. Intercom to all areas.

### ST. COLMAN'S PAROCHIAL HALL

Trevor Hill, Newry
Tel 01693 66276
S/Cap: 610.
Good stage facilities and lighting.

### ARTS CENTRE NEWRY

1a Bank Parade, Newry, Co. Down BT35 6HP
Tel 01693 766232
Fax 01693 766839
**Administration:**

For Bookings Contact the Administrative Director:
Mark Hughes
Policy: To promote good Theatre and Arts in the Newry
and Mourne area.
Seating: Auditorium - 162 seats.
**Technical:**
**Stage:** Area: Flat stage with Proscenium Arch. Width
6.28m, Depth 6.28m, Height 6.5m.
Passenger lift to all floors. House intercom system.
**Lighting:** Rank Strand AMC System with 60 No.
circuits.
**Other:** Rooms: Auditorum. 2 Dressing Rooms. Green
Room. Exhibition Areas. Coffee Bar. Photographic
Studio etc. Rehearsal room.

**WARRENPOINT**
Town Hall - Warrenpoint, Church Street, Warrenpoint,
BT34 3HN
Tel 01693 752256
**Administration:**
District Council Offices, Greenbank, Newry.
Tel 01693 767226
For bookings contact the Administrative Director, Mark
Hughes, Newry Arts Centre, 1A Bank Parade, Newry,
Co. Down BT35 6HP
Tel 01693 766232
Fax 01693 766839
Policy: Theatre, Musicals, FEIS events, Drama.
Seating: 500 Main Hall
**Technical:**
**Stage:** Depth 6.1m. Width 7m. Height to Pros. Arch.
4.25m. House PA system with microphone outlets.
Intercom to backstage area and dressing rooms.
**Lighting:** Rank Strand Mini-2 with twelve circuits and
2 presets.

**KILKEEL**
Town Hall - Kilkeel, Newry Street, Kilkeel.
Tel 01693 763092
**Administration:**
District Council Offices, Greenbank, Newry.
Tel 01693 767226
Bookings: Kilkeel Community Complex, Mourne
Esplanade, Kilkeel.
Tel: 01693 764666
Fax 01693 763495
(Newry, Warrenpoint and Kilkeel are part of Newry
local authority).Policy: Theatre used as Cinema 4
nights per week. Available for concerts and plays,
drama etc.
Seating: Main Hall - 325 Balcony 88 Total 413.
**Technical:**
**Stage:** Depth 6.4m. Width 8.3m. Wing space St Rt
3.65m St Lt 1.83m. 2 Dressing Rooms off stage right.
Kitchen area and House PA system with microphone
outlets.
**Lighting:** Rank Strand Mini 2 with 30 circuits and 2
presets.

# NEWTOWNABBEY
Department of Leisure & Technical Services: TBA
Glenmount House, 49 Church Road, Newtownabbey,
Co. Antrim BT36 7LG
Tel 01232 868751
Fax 01232 365407

**THE COURTYARD THEATRE AT BALLYEARL**
585 Doad Raod, Newtownabbey,
Co. Antrim BT36 5RZ
Tel 01232 848287
Fax 01232 844896

# NORTH DOWN BOROUGH COUNCIL
Arts Officer: Ms P. Clamp
Town Hall, The Castle, Bangor BT20 4BT
Tel 01247 270371
Fax 01247 271370

# OMAGH, Co. Tyrone
Head of Arts and Tourism: F. Sweeney
Arts Development Officer: Jean Brennon
Council Offices, The Grange, Mountjoy Road, Omagh,
Co. Tyrone BT79 7BL
Tel 01662 245321
Fax 01662 243888

**OMAGH LEISURE CENTRE**
Old Mountfield Road, Omagh
S/Cap: 550
Portable stage facilities.

# PRODUCING MANAGEMENTS

# BALLET, OPERA AND DANCE COMPANIES

# ORCHESTRAS

# PRINCIPAL FESTIVALS

# SMALL SCALE TOURING COMPANIES

# MIDDLE SCALE TOURING COMPANIES

# COMMUNITY THEATRE

# MIME & PHYSICAL THEATRE

# CHILDREN'S, YOUNG PEOPLES THEATRE & TIE

# CIRCUS PROPRIETORS

# PUPPET COMPANIES

# Production

# PRODUCING MANAGEMENTS

## ABA DABA PRODUCTIONS
30 Upper Park Road, London NW3 2UT
Tel/Fax: 0171 722 5395

## ABSTRACT IMAGES
117 Willoughby House, Barbican, London EC2Y 8BL
Tel/Fax: 0171 638 5123
Email: productions@abstract-images.co.uk
Contact: Howard Ross
London, fringe and middle-scale tours of UK and
Europe. 1999 productions include a critically-acclaimed
production of Martin Sherman's ground-breaking play
"Bent".

## ACORN ENTERTAINMENTS
Winterfold House, 46 Woodfield Road, Kings Heath,
Birmingham B13 9UJ
Tel/Fax 0121 444 7258
Email: jim@acornent.demon.co.uk
Web Site: http:\www.acornent.demon.co.uk

## ACT THEATRE PRODUCTIONS LTD
110 St.Martin's Lane, London WC2N 4AD
Tel: 0171 304 7922 Fax: 0171 867 1131

## ACTORS TOURING COMPANY
Alford House, Aveline Street, London SE11 5DQ
Tel: 0171 735 8311 Fax: 0171 735 1031
Email: atc@cwcom.net
Artistic Director: Nick Philippou
Executive Producer: Gavin Barlow
Administrator: David Kelleher

## A.I.R LTD
AIR House, Spennymoor, County Durham DL16 7SE
Tel: 01388 814632 Fax: 01388 812445
Email: air@agents-uk.com
Senior Personnel: Colin Pearson - Director,
John Wray - Director

## ALBEMARLE OF LONDON
74 Mortimer Street, London W1N 7DF
Tel: 0171 631 0135 Fax: 0171 323 3074
Email: sales@albemalelondon.demon.co.uk
Managing Director: Basil Critchley
Assistant: Sulie Branscombe
Producing pantomime & summer seasons. Scenic &
costume departments, construction & hire.

## ALTERNATIVE THEATRE COMPANY LTD
Bush Theatre, Shepherds Bush Green,
London W12 8QD
Tel: 0171 602 3703 Fax: 0171 602 7614
Email: thebush@dircon.co.uk
General Manager: Deborah Aydon
Artistic Director: Mike Bradwell
Administrator: David Wright

## AMBASSADOR THEATRE GROUP/ TURNSTYLE GROUP LTD
25 Shaftesbury Avenue, London W1V 7HA
Tel: 0171 240 9891 Fax: 0171 379 5748
Managing Director: Howard Panter
General Manager: Meryl Faiers

## APOLLO LEISURE UK LTD
Grehan House, Garsington Road, Cowley,
Oxford OX4 5NQ
Tel: 01865 782900 Fax: 01865 782910
Managing Director: Sam Shrouder
General Manager: Nicky Monk

## ARCADEIA MUSIC MANAGEMENT
Unit 8a, Western Road Complex, Western Road,
Hockley, Birmingham B18 7QD
Tel: 0121 507 0933
Managing Director, Promotions: George de Rosa

## ARTS MANAGEMENT
"Redroofs" Littlewick Green, Maidenhead,
Berkshire SL6 3QY
Tel: 01628 822982 Fax: 01628 822461
Specialising in: Young People

## ASSOCIATED CAPITAL THEATRES LIMITED
110 St.Martin's Lane, London WC2N 4AD
Tel: 0171 304 7922 Fax: 0171 867 1131
Email: Firstname.Surname@act-arts.co.uk

## BARKING DOG THEATRE COMPANY
Room 49 Millmead Business Centre, Mill Mead Road,
Tottenham Hale, London N17 9QU
Tel: 0181 880 9977 Fax: 0181 880 9978
Email: bdog@bdog.globalnet.co.uk
Director: Patrick Jacobs
Administrator: Mike Brooks
Children's Theatre Company.

## MARTIN BARRY PRODUCTIONS
39 Godre'r Coed, Gwernymynydd, Mold,
Clwyd CH7 4DS
Tel: 01352 758266 Fax: 01352 759511
Managing Director: Martin Barry

## B.A.S.A. PRODUCTIONS
Suite 5, 37a The Centre, Walton-on-Thames,
Surrey KT12 1QY
Tel: 01932 269393 Fax: 01932 240038
Directors: Jon Barker, Kenny Martyn & Jackie Brown
Entertainment for on-board ships

## B.E. EVENT HIRE
Ashtrees, Kirby Bellars, Melton Mowbray,
Leicestershire LE14 2DU
Tel: 01664 812627 Fax: 01664 813727

Partners: Caroline Evans and Simon Evans

## BEVERLEY ARTISTES

Beverley House, 22-34 Dean Road, South Shields,
Tyne and Wear NE33 3PT
Tel: 0191 456 2428 Fax: 0192 456 0978
Senior Personnel: Bill Reeve, Bob Gladwin,
Ralph Phillips.
Bill Reeve's Office (2nd Office)
Corby House, East Rainton DH5 9QN
Tel: 0700 900 0282
Fax: 0191 512 0165
E-mail: billbevs@aol.com

## BIG BEAR MUSIC

PO Box 944, Birmingham B16 8UT
Tel: 0121 454 7020 Fax: 0121 454 9996
Email: bigbearmusic@compuserve.com
Senior Personnel: Tim Jennings
Big Bear Music specialise in Jazz, Blues and Swing.

## THE BIRMINGHAM STAGE COMPANY

The Old Rep Theatre, Station Street,
Birmingham B5 4DY
Tel: 0121 643 9050 Fax: 0121 643 8099 London
Office: Tel: 0171 437 3391 Fax: 0171 437 3395
Actor/Manager: Neal Foster
Administrator: Caroline Dunn

## BLAKE/RAWSON PRODUCTIONS LTD - THE SHOW PEOPLE

The Show People Academy, 1 Kirkby Avenue,
Doncaster, South Yorkshire DN5 9TF
Office Tel/Fax: 01302 787567 Studio: 01302 320447

## BOB SONS PRODUCTIONS LTD

The Penthouse, 10 Abbey Orchard Street,
London SW1P 2JP
Tel: 0171 222 1154 Fax: 0171 222 1147
Contact: Robert Willis

## BRIGHT TRACKS PRODUCTIONS

PO Box 27, Stroud, Gloucestershire GL6 0YQ
Tel/Fax: 01453 836877

## GARRY BROWN ASSOCIATES (INT) LTD

27 Downs Side, Cheam, Sutton, Surrey SM2 7EH
Tel: 0181 643 3991/8375 Fax: 0181 770 7241
Email: gbaltd@compuserve.com
Senior Personnel: Garry Brown, John Cheney, Helen
Machell, Brenda Capper, Denise Webb
Specialising in: Entertainment for Major Shipping Lines
and Hilton Hotels Worldwide.

## RICHARD BUCKNALL MANAGEMENT (RBM)

3rd Floor, 18 Betterton Street, London WC2H 9BP
Tel: 0171 287 5010 Fax: 0171 287 5020

## NICA BURNS PRODUCTIONS

Duchess Theatre, Catherine Street,
London WC2B 5LA
Tel: 0171 836 7333 Fax: 0171 836 7444

# Abstract Images

THEATRE PRODUCTIONS

117 Willougby House, Barbican,
London EC2Y 8BL

0171-638 5123

e-mail: productions@abstract-images.co.uk

Contact: Howard Ross

## CALM FEELINGS

101 Valiant House, Vicarage Crescent,
London SW11 3LX
Tel: 0171 223 3218 Tel/Fax: 0171 924 7037
Partners: Cass Allen & Libby Morris
Production Company, Cabaret Bookers and Outdoor
Entertainment Agents.

## KENNY CANTOR PRODUCTIONS

"Uppham Hall" Green Lane, Kessingland, Lowestoft,
Suffolk NR83 7RP
Tel/Fax: 01502 742045 Tel/Fax: 07000 KCANTOR
Tel/fFax: 07000 522 6867
Email: kenny.c@virgin.net
Senior Personnel: Kenny Cantor, Caron Heggie

## CAVALCADE THEATRE COMPANY LTD

57 Pelham Road, Wimbledon, London SW19 1NW
Tel: 0181 540 3513 Fax: 0181 540 2243
Administrator: Carol Crowther
Artistic Director: Graham Ashe
Clowning & Comedy, Musical Theatre, Pantomimes,
Plays, Cabaret & Themed Evenings.
Theatre in Education.

## CHALMERS WOOD LTD

74 Ormonde Crescent, Netherlee, Glasgow G44 3SW
Tel/Fax: 0141 633 3894
Senior Personnel: Peter de Rance, Scott de Rance

## CHANCE PROMOTIONS

Blowell House, Fulham Lane, Whitley, Nr. Selby,
Yorkshire DN14 0JL
Tel: 01977 662222 (3 Lines) Fax: 01977 662233
Specialising in: Look/Sound Alike Shows & Tributes.

## CHANNEL THEATRE COMPANY

Central Studios, 130 Grosvenor Place, Margate,
Kent CT9 1UY
Tel: 01843 280077 Fax: 01843 280088
Artistic Director: Philip Dart
Associate Director: Claudia Leaf
Policy: Channel Theatre is a middle and small scale
touring company based in South East England and
operating nationally. It has also an attached
Community and T.I.E. Company, dealing with new and
innovative work.

## CHAPLINS PANTOS (CHAPLINS LTD)
Chaplins House, 16a Barclay Road, London E17 9JJ
Tel: 0181 521 6300 Fax: 0181 521 4900
Managing Directors: J. Wenborn & J Holmes
Touring Christmas Pantomimes.
Full Package provided.

## DUGGIE CHAPMAN ASSOCIATES
The Old Coach House, 202 Common Edge Road,
Blackpool FY4 5DG
Tel/Fax: 01253 691823 Mobile: 0976 925504
Director: Duggie Chapman
PA: Beryl Johnson
Duggie Chapman Associates is Britain's longest
running promoter of touring music hall presenting Star
Variety Summer Shows and Pantomimes. Specialists
in late bookings for managements. Package shows
always available at short notice.

## GUY CHAPMAN ASSOCIATES
1-2 Henrietta Street, Covent Garden,
London WC2E 8PS
Tel: 0171 379 7474 Fax: 0171 379 8484
Email: chapman@dircom.co.uk
Managing Directors: Guy Chapman
Associates: Matthew Bartlett, Michael Parke, Steven
Drew, Jenny Eldridge, Jonathan Russell &
Ryan Peterson
Press/Marketing/Tour Booking/General Management

## CHICKEN SHED THEATRE COMPANY
Chase Side, Southgate, London N14 4PE
Tel: 0181 351 6161 Fax: 0181 292 0202
Managing DIrector: John Bull
Registered Charity.

## CHILDRENS SHOWTIME PRODUCTIONS
PO Box 127, Heathfield, East Sussex TN21 0ZR
Tel: 01435 864008 Fax: 01435 868919
Specialising in: Theatre for Children.

## CHURCHILL THEATRE BROMLEY
High Street, Bromley Kent BR1 1HA
Admin/SD 0181 464 7131 BO 0181 460 6677
Marketing and Publicity 0181 460 1401
Goldcard Hotline 0181 460 5838 Fax 0181 290 6968
See Theatre of Comedy Company Ltd in Producing
Managements.

## CLASSIC PRESENTATIONS LTD
85 Ladbroke Road, London W11 3PJ
Tel/Fax: 0171 229 0635
Director: Martin Starkie
Manager: Christopher Dean

## RON COBURN INTERNATIONAL
## PRODUCTIONS
"A Breath of Scotland" Vaudevilla, Elliot Road,
Dundee DD2 1SY
Tel/Fax: 01382 669025

## MICHAEL CODRON PLAY LTD
Aldwych Theatre Offices, Aldwych, London WC2B 4DF
Tel: 0171 240 8291 Fax: 0171 240 8467

Director: Michael Codron
General Manager/Productions: Paul O'Leary

## COLE KITCHENN
20-21 Store Street, London WC1E 7DH
Tel: 0171 580 2772 Fax: 0171 580 2992
Contact: The General Manager

## MAX COLLIE RHYTHM ACES
26 Wendover Road, Bromley, Kent BR2 9JX
Tel: 0181 460 1139 Fax: 0181 466 7005
Email: bouquetc52@aol.com
Senior Personnel: Max Collie
Specialising in: Traditional and New Orleans Jazz

## COMMUNICATIONS HUB LTD
257 Summer Lane, Birmingham B19 2PX
Tel: 0121 333 3543 Fax: 0121 333 3442
Managing Director: Andrew Patterson
Director: Dawn Evans

## COURT THEATRE COMPANY
The Courtyard Theatre, 10 York Way, King's Cross,
London N1 9AA
Tel/Fax: 0171 833 0870
Senior Personnel: June Abbott
Based in a former stables/carriage block, the company
produce old and new work either solely or in
association with another company.

## DANCE FOR EVERYONE LTD
30 Sevington Road, London NW4 3RX
Tel/Fax: 0181 202 7863
Artistic Director: Naomi Benari

## DELFONT MACKINTOSH THEATRES LTD
Prince of Wales Theatre, Coventry Street,
London W1V 8AS
Tel: 0171 930 9901 Fax: 0171 930 8970
Managing Director: George Biggs
Technical Director: Peter Roberts

## DELPHINE Y DOMINGO
4 Cormorant Rise, Worcester WR2 4BA
Tel: 01905 424083/0181 697 5960
Contact: James Peterson
Specialising in quality Flamenco Music and Dance for
Television, Theatre, Promotion and Education.

## WALLY DENT ENTERTAINMENTS
121a Woodlands Avenue, West Byfleet,
Surrey KT14 6AS
Tel: 01932 347885/351444/347826
Fax: 01932 336229 Car Phone: 0831 270976
Senior Personnel: Wally Dent, Jose Harknett
30 years experience in most aspects of the
entertainment industry: package shows, representing
after dinner sports personalities, comedians, groups,
speciality acts. Supply entertainment to the holiday
industry, corporate marketing and HM Forces.

## TERRY DENTON - DE GRAY'S WORLD OF FANTASY
Swans Nest, 2 Windmill Road, Hampton Hill,
Middlesex TW12 1RH
Tel: 0181 941 1595 Fax: 0181 783 1366
Web Site: www.world-of-fantasy.co.uk
Managing Directors: Sheila & Terry Denton-De Gray

## DGM PRODUCTIONS LTD
3-5 Latimer Road, Teddington, Middlesex TW11 8QA
Tel: 0181 977 8707 Fax: 0181 977 6909
Producer: David Graham
Administration: Elizabeth Wallace
Finance: Christine Watson
Bookings: Vanessa Gee
Press & Publicity: Yee-Lin Barr (0171 580 2919)

## THE DRAMA HOUSE
1 Hertford Place, London W1P 5RS
Tel: 0171 388 9140 Fax: 0171 388 3511
Managing Director: Jack Emery

## DRAMATIS PERSONAE LTD
19 Regency Street, London SW1P 4BY
Tel: 0171 834 9300
Directors: Nathan Silver & Nicolas Kent

## DYFEL MANAGEMENT
19 Fontwell Drive, Bickley, Bromley, Kent BR2 8AB
Tel: 0181 467 9605/07000 367687 (For Music)
Fax: 0181 249 1972
Senior Personnel: Jean Dyne

## E&B PRODUCTIONS (THEATRE) LTD.
Sutie 3, Waldorf Chambers, 11 Aldwych,
London WC2B 4DA
Tel: 0171 836 2795 Fax: 0171 379 4892
Managing Director: Paul Elliot

## VIVYAN ELLACOTT PRODUCTIONS
Kenneth More Theatre, Oakfield Road, Ilford,
Essex IG1 1BT
Tel: 0181 553 4464 Fax: 0181 553 5476
Email: vivyane@aol.com

## ENGLISH NATIONAL OPERA
London Coliseum, St.Martin's Lane,
London WC2N 4ES
Tel: 0171 836 0111 Fax: 0171 836 8379/0171 497
9052 (PR) Theatre Management: Fax: 0171 836 5769
Email: marketing@eno.org
Web Site: www.eno.org
Directors of the English National Opera:
Music Director: Paul Daniel
General Director: Nicholas Payne
Executive Director: Russell Willis Taylor
Technical Director: Laurence Holderness
Director of Public Relations: Maggie Sedwards
Financial Controller: Graeme Wallace

## ENGLISH STAGE COMPANY LTD
Royal Court Theatre, St.Martin's Lane,
London WC2N 4BG
Tel: 0171 565 5050 Fax: 0171 565 5001

Artistic Director: Stephen Daldry
Executive Director: Vicki Heywood

## FAME FACTORY PRESENTATIONS
Wits End, 300 Bishops Drive, Oakwood,
Derby DE21 2DR
Tel: 01332 833933 Fax: 01332 834279
Company Director: Maxine D Harrison
Music Director: Gerry Harrison
Pantomime, touring shows, show production,
educational theatre and workshops.

## FIRST LEISURE CORPORATION PLC
7 Soho Street, London W1V 5FA
Tel: 0171 437 9727 Fax: 0171 439 0088
Chairman: Michael Grade
Finance Director: Graham Coles

## FLAMENCO PRODUCTIONS
36 Rosenthal House, 45 Rushey Green,
London SE6 4AR
Tel: 0181 697 5960
Administrator: James Peterson

## FLAMENCO PRODUCTIONS - MIDLANDS SECTION
4 Cormorant Rise, Lower Wick, Worcester WR2 4BA
Tel: 01905 424083
Senior Personnel: D Auchterlonie
Specialising in: Quality Flamenco for all Media

## THE FOG & GAS CO LTD
The Pixie Hut, 238 High Road, Byfleet,
Surrey KT14 7DD
Tel: 01932 349762 Fax: 01932 353581
Directors: J. Karagianis and R Karagianis

## VANESSA FORD PRODUCTIONS
Upper House Farm, Upper House Lane,
Shamley Green, Nr. Guildford, Surrey GU5 0SX
Tel: 01483 278203 01483 268530 (messages)
Fax: 01483 278203
Email: VFPLTD@msn.com
Directors: Vanessa Ford & Glyn Robbins

## CLARE FOX ASSOCIATES LTD
9 Plympton Road, London NW6 7EH
Postal contact only please.

## JILL FREUD & COMPANY
18 York House, Montagu Street, London
Tel: 0171 724 5432 Fax: 0171 724 3210
Also at: 278a Earls Court Road, London SW5 9AS
Tel/Fax: 0171 373 1805
Web Site: www.users.globalnet.co.uk/~jneill
Artistic Director: Jill Freud
Administrator: Antony Falkingham

## GAIETIES MUSIC HALL AND VARIETY COMPANY
9 Beechwood Avenue, Earlsdon, Coventry CV5 6DF
Tel: 01203 778377/677173 Fax: 01203 778686
Mobile: 0585 430579

Manager: Sheila Payne

## GARRICKS
7 Garrick Street, London WC2E 9AR
Tel: 0171 240 0660 Fax: 0171 497 9242
Email: garricks@mcmail.com
Senior Personnel: Megan Willis

## TREVOR GEORGE ENTERTAINMENTS (UK)
PO Box 135 Torquay Devon TQ1 3YT
Tel: 01803 311932/313300 Fax: 01803 312004
Senior Personnel: Anne George, Lesley Burnett

## GLOBE PLAYERS THEATRE COMPANY
36 St.James' Avenue, Hampton Hill,
Middlesex TW12 1HH
Tel: 0181 979 5497 Fax: 0181 941 6776
Contact: Tony McAvoy

## GO ENTERTAINMENTS
The Arts Exchange, Mill Green, Congleton,
Cheshire CW12 1JG
Tel: 01260 276627 Fax: 01260 270777
Tel: 07000 CIRCUS / 07000 BIG TOP
Email: phillipgandey@netcentral.co.uk
Contact: Phillip or Carol Gandey
Mercury Court, Isle of Dogs, London
Tel 0171 730 0304
Specialising in: Circus, Ice Skaters, Mime, Street
Entertainers, Equestrian shows, Club DJ's, Celebrities,
Stunt Shows, and International Cabaret Revue Shows.

## HARVEY GOLDSMITH ENTERTAINMENTS LTD
The Glassworks, 3-4 Ashland Place, London W1M 3JH
Tel: 0171 224 1992 Fax: 0171 224 0111
Managing Director: Harvey Goldsmith
Promoters: Pete Wilson & Dennis Arnold

## FRANCIS GOLIGHTLY PRODUCTIONS
7 Riverside Walk, Colchester, Essex CO1 1RD
Tel/Fax: 01206 765057
Partners: Francis Golightly & Roy Cloughton

## GOOD COMPANY THEATRE PRODUCTIONS
48 Quebec Street, Brighton BN2 2UZ
Tel: 01273 606652 Fax: 01273 606926
Administrator: Emma Rees
Artistic Director: Sue Pomeroy

## CHARLES HALEY PRODUCTIONS
Toad Hall, 67 Poppleton Road, Whipps Cross,
London E11 1LP
Tel: 0181 989 8364/989 0060
Contact: Jennifer Haley

## HAYMARKET THEATRE COMPANY
Haymarket Theatre Wote Street,
Basingstoke, RG21 7NW
Production: 01256 323073 BO: 01256 465566
Fax: 01256 57130
Email: info@haymarket.org.uk
Web Site: www.haymarket.org.uk

Theatre Director: Alasdair Ramsay
Producing theatre - up to 8 in house shows +3 or 4
visiting shows. Season: September to June. Shows run
between 1 and 4 weeks. Developing community and
education programme.

## AL HEATH INTERNATIONAL
The New House, The Green, Semley, Shaftesbury,
Dorset SP7 9AU
Tel: 01747 830723/01747 830719 Fax: 01747 830723
Senior Personnel: Al Heath, Pippa Heath

## GLYNIS HENDERSON MANAGEMENT & PRODUCTION
52 Tottenham Street, London W1P 9PG
Tel: 0171 580 9644 Fax: 0171 436 1489
Senior Personnel: Glynis Henderson, Claudia Courtis,
Michael Brazier, Roy Luxford
Specialising in: Visual Musical, Comedy, Dance

## HILTON INTERNATIONAL ENTERTAINMENTS
27 Downs Side, Cheam, Sutton, Surrey SM2 7EH
Tel: 0181 643 3991/8375 Fax: 0181 770 7241
Email: GBALTD@compuserve.com
Senior Personnel; Garry Brown, John Cheney
Specialising in: Supplying artistes and Bands to
Hilton Hotels.

## PHILIP HINDIN LTD
66 Melbourne Way, Bush Hill Park, Enfield,
Middlesex EN1 1XQ
Tel/Fax: 0181 366 2978
Senior Personnel: P Hindin
Specialising in TV Game Shows & Pantomime Artistes.
Creator of "Call My Bluff" etc.

## THE HISS & BOO COMPANY
1 Nyes Hill, Wineham Lane, Bolney,
West Sussex RH17 5SD
Tel: 01444 881707 Fax: 01444 882057
Email: hissboo@msn.com
Web Site: www.hissboo.co.uk
Managing Director: Ian Liston

## PAUL HOLMAN ASSOCIATES LTD
20a Deane Avenue, South Ruislip,
Middlesex HA4 6SR
Tel: 0181 845 9408 Fax: 0181 582 2557
Managing Director: Paul Holman

## HUTT RUSSELL PRODUCTIONS LTD
PO Box 64, Cirencester, Gloucestershire GL7 5YD
Tel: 01285 644622 Fax: 01285 642291
Email: hutt_russell_productions@cemi.co.uk
Senior Personnel: Steven Hutt, Dudley Russell

## HWB PRODUCTIONS
17 Bargate Close New Malden Surrey KT3 6BG
Tel: 0181 942 5859 Fax: 0181 949 4107
Senior Personnel: Paul Barnard

**BRUCE HYMAN ASSOCIATES LTD**
47 Downshire Hill, London NW3 1NX
Tel: 0171 916 1984 Fax: 0171 435 5589
Managing Director: Bruce Hyman
Casting Director: Karen Sanders Young

**IMAGINATION ENTERTAINMENTS**
25 Store Street, London WC1E 7BL
Tel: 0171 323 3300 Fax: 0171 323 5801
Senior Personnel: Bob Eady

**BRIAN JACKSON FILMS LTD**
39/41 Hanover Steps, St Georges Fields,
Albion Street, London W2 2YG
Tel: 0171 402 7543 Fax: 0171 262 5736
Managing Director: Brian Jackson

**THE JAYWALKERS LTD**
The Manor House, Burgh Castle,
Great Yarmouth NR31 8JU
Tel: 01493 780223 Fax: 01493 781291
Managing Directors: Peter & Christine Jay

**JERICHO PRODUCTIONS**
Toynbee Studios, 28 Commercial Street,
London E1 6LS
Tel: 0171 377 2529 Fax: 0171 377 6010
Director: Geraldine Collinge

**JESTER PRODUCTIONS**
(Jack Seaton)
Flat 6, Shaftesbury House, Grange Road, Ealing,
London W5 5UA
Tel/Fax: 0181 840 5316

**KENNEDY STREET ENTERPRISES**
Kennedy House, 31 Stamford Street, Altrincham,
Cheshire WA14 1ES
Tel: 0161 941 5151 Fax: 0161 928 9491
Managing Director: Danny Betesh

**BILL KENWRIGHT LTD**
55/59 Shaftesbury Avenue, London W1V 8JA
Tel: 0171 439 4466 Fax: 0171 437 8370
Managing Director: Bill Kenwright
Executive Producer: Rod Coton
Chief Executive: Brett Finnegan
Producers: Julius Green & Mark Rubinstein
Marketing: Paul Savingden

**KERROY THEATRE PRODUCTIONS
(DIVISION OF KERROY GROUP LTD)**
2 Queensmead, St.John's Wood Park,
London NW8 6RE
Tel: 0171 722 9828 Fax: 0171 722 9886
CEO: Iain Kerr

**DAVID KIRK PRODUCTIONS**
12 Panmuir Road, West Wimbledon,
London SW20 0PZ
Tel: 0181 947 0130
Managing Director: David Kirk

**KNIGHTSBRIDGE THEATRICAL
PRODUCTIONS LTD**
21 New Fetter Lane, London EC4A 1JJ
Tel: 0171 583 8687 Fax: 0171 583 1040
Telex: 8811736 RANDK
G Cables: DIOSKUROI LONDON EC4

**ROLF KRUGER MANAGEMENT**
21 Eastcastle Street, London W1N 7PA
Tel: 0171 323 3733 Fax: 0171 323 3744
Email: rkruger@mail.com
Senior Personnel: Rachel Kruger

**STEPHEN LEATHERLAND PRODUCTIONS**
44 Highclere Street, London SE26 4EU
Tel/Fax: 0181 778 6038
Managing Director: Stephen Leatherland
Consultant: Donald Auty
Administrator: Barbara Barringer

**LEISURE AT SEA LTD**
27 Downs Side, Cheam, Surrey SM2 7EH
Tel: 0181 643 8375 Fax: 0181 770 7241
Email: GBALTD@compuserve.com
Contact: Garry Brown

**JOHNNY & BARBARA LEY TRAMPOLINE &
CLOWN PROMOTIONS**
14 Stanshaw Close, Frenchay, Bristol, BS16 1JY
Tel: 0117 956 5599
Contact: John & Barbara Ley

**LINE-UP PMC**
9a Tankerville Place, Newcastle Upon Tyne NE2 3AT
Tel: 0191 281 6449 Fax: 0191 212 0913
Email: line-up.co.uk
Senior Personnel: Chris Murtagh

**JIMMY LOGAN O.B.E.**
"Springvale", 73 East Princes Street, Helensburgh,
Dumbartonshire, G84 7DG
Tel: 01436 671503 Fax: 01436 672124
Managing Director: Jimmy Logan O.B.E.

**LONDON BUBBLE (BUBBLE THEATRE CO.
LTD)**
5 Elephant Lane, London SE16 4JD
Tel: 0171 237 4434 Fax: 0171 231 2366
Artistic Director: Jonathan Petherbridge
Admin Director: Helen Chamberlain

**THE LONDON COMPANY
(INTERNATIONAL PLAYS) LTD**
Registered Office: 37 Marylebone Lane,
London W1M 5FN
Tel: 0171 486 3166 Fax: 0171 486 2164
In association with Derek Glynne (London) Pty Ltd. of
Melbourne, Australia.

**MAC - THE CENTRE FOR BIRMINGHAM**
(Midlands Arts Centre), Cannon Hill Park,
Birmingham B12 9QH

Admin 0121 440 4221 BO 0121 440 3838 Fax 0121 446 4372

## CAMERON MACKINTOSH LTD
1 Bedford Square, London WC1B 3RA
Proprietor: Cameron Mackintosh
Director: Martin McCallum

## MARIANNE MACNAGHTON
Dundarave, Bushmills, Co.Antrim BT57 8ST
Tel: 01265 731215 Fax: 01265 732575
Director: Marianne MacNaghton

## MAD MONK PRODUCTIONS
22 Convent Close, Kenilworth, Warwickshire CV8 2FQ
Tel: 01926 854047
Directors: Stephen Boden, Adam Schumacher &
Hannah Plaistow

## MANCHESTER YOUNG PEOPLE'S THEATRE LTD
See Contact Theatre Company

## JOHNNY MANS CASTAWAY CRUISING PRODUCTIONS LTD
The Maltings, Brewery Road, Hoddesdon,
Hertfordshire EN11 8HF
Tel: 01992 470907 Fax: 01992 470516
Tel, Castaway Cruising Productions: 01992 470907
Managing Director: Johnny Mans
Administration: Julia Mumford, Philip Crowe, Hayley
Noble, & Lynn Aldridge

## MANTAPLAN LTD
Douglas Drive, Godalming, Surrey GU7 1HJ
Tel: 01483 420088 Fax: 01483 424566
Managing Director: Andy Ayres
Associate Director: Lisa Taylor

## MARCELLUS PRODUCTIONS LTD
11 Chelverton Road, Putney, London SW15 1RN
Tel: 0181 788 5663
Directors: Nina & Jimmy Thompson

## JOHN MARTIN PROMOTIONS LTD
The Homestead, Eastwick Road, Great Bookham,
Surrey KT23 4BA
Tel: 0181 786 3620 Fax: 0181 786 3621
Senior Personnel: John Martin

## MATTHEWS PRODUCTIONS
Matpro Ltd, Cary Point, Babbacombe Downs,
Torquay TQ1 3LU
Tel: 01803 322233 Fax: 01803 322244
Email: matpro@btinternet.com

## MAVERICK THEATRE COMPANY
32 Highbury Road, Kings Heath, Birmingham B14 7QN
Tel: 0121 444 0933 Fax: 0121 443 1426
Email: maverick.theatre@virgin.net
Web Site: freespace.virgin.net/maverick.theatre/mav.htm
Artistic Director/Producer: Nick Hennegan

Production Manager: John Slater
Sales Manager: Linda Jagger

## MCLEOD-HOLDEN ENTERPRISES LTD
Priory House, 1133 Hessle High Road, Hull HU4 6SB
Tel: 01482 565444 Fax: 01482 353635
Email: info@mcleod-holden.com
Web Site: www.mcleod-holden.com
Senior Personnel: Peter McLeod, Ian Gray, Robin
Carew, Dick Allix, Liz Hugill, Duncan Wood

## THE MEDIEVAL HALL
Sarum St Michael, The Close, Salisbury
Wilts SP1 2EY
Tel 01722 324731/412472 BO 01722 324731
Fax 01722 339983
ADMINISTRATION:
Props: John and Jane Waddington
Policy: Music, theatre, exhibitions etc.

## MEMORIAL FILMS LTD
6e Ladbroke Square, London W11
Tel: 0171 727 7107

## METHOD & MADNESS
25 Short Street, London SE1 8LJ
Tel: 0171 450 1990 Fax: 0171 450 1991
Minicom: 0171 450 1997
Email: methodandmadness@mcmail.com
Artistic Director: Mike Alfreds
Executive Director: James Williams
Marketing Manager: Margred Pryce
Policy: Repertoire touring throughout the year.

## MILLER LODGE
2 Lord Hills Road, London W2 6PD
Tel: 0171 286 7277 Fax: 0171 286 7377
Email: millerlodge@the-sound-company.co.uk
Directors: John Miller & Bubble Lodge

## AL MITCHELL ASSOCIATES
5 Anglers Lane, Kentish Town, London NW5 3DG
Tel: 0171 482 5113 Fax: 0171 485 4254
Senior Personnel: Al Mitchell, Tony Humphreys

## MONTROSE ENTERTAINMENTS LTD
Glassenbury Hill Farm, Glassenbury Road, Cranbrook,
Kent TN17 2QF
Tel: 01580 715755 Fax: 01580 713285
Email: montroseent@enterprise.net
Producer: Christopher Yates
Accounts: Naomi Russell
Casting: Anne Molyneux

## THE NATIONAL SYMPHONY ORCHESTRA
Jumps Road, Churt, Farnham, Surrey GU10 2JY
Tel: 01252 252315 Fax: 01252 255120
President: Perry Montague-Mason
Managing Director: E. Anne Collis
Principal Conductor: Martin Yates

## NEVADA PRODUCTIONS/BARRIE STACEY U.K. PRODUCTIONS LTD
Third Floor, 9 Denmark Street, London WC2H 8LP
Tel: 0171 836 6220/4128 Fax: 0171 836 2949
Director: Barrie Stacey

## NEW SHAKESPEARE COMPANY - OPEN AIR THEATRE
Regents Park, London NW1 4NP
Tel: 0171 935 5756 & 5884 Fax: 0171 487 4562
Artistic/Managing Director: Ian Talbot
General Manager: Sheila Benjamin

## NEWPALM PRODUCTIONS
26 Cavendish Avenue, Finchley, London N3 3QN
Tel: 0181 349 0802/0181 346 8011
Fax: 0181 346 8257
Managing Director: John Newman
also: Civic Theatre, Chelmsford, Essex
Tel: 01245 268998

## PAUL NICHOLAS & DAVID IAN ASSOCIATES LTD
7 Great Russell Street, London WC1B 3NH
Tel: 0171 637 8182 Fax: 0171 323 1601
Managing Director: David Ian

## NOEL GAY
22-25 Dean Street, London W1V 5AL
Tel: 0171 836 3941 Fax: 0171 287 1816
Senior Personnel: A J Armitage, G X Constantinidi,
N Ranceford-Hadley

## NORMAN MEADMORE LTD
23 Westfield Road, Bishop's Stortford,
Herfordshire CM23 2RE
Tel/Fax: 01279 652371
Managing Director: Andrew Meadmore

## NORTHERN STAGE
Newcastle Playhouse, Barras Bridge,
Newcastle-upon-Tyne NE1 7RH
Tel: 0191 232 3366 Fax: 0191 261 8093
Email: Northern.Stage@ncl.ac.uk
Artistic Director: Alan Lyddiard
Executive Director: Mandy Stewart

## THE OKAI COLLIER COMPANY LTD
103 Lexington Building, The Bow Quarter, Fairfield
Road, Bow, London E3 2UH
Tel/Fax: 0181 983 0858
Manager: Simon Collier

## OPERA NORTH
Grand Theatre, 46 New Briggate, Leeds LS1 6NU
Tel: 0113 243 9999 Fax: 0113 244 0418 (admin)
0113 243 5745 (Tech) Telex: 265871
Email: 74:MUS252
Company Director: Richard Mantle
Controller of Planning: Christine Chibnall
Technical Director: Rick Green
Music Adviser: Elgar Howarth
Head of Marketing: Richard Whitehouse
Head of Community Education: Dominic Gray

Production Manager: Ray Hain
Company Manager: Jane Bonner

## OPERETTA FOR ALL
185 Syon Lane, Isleworth, Middlesex TW7 5PU
Tel/Fax: 0181 560 5988
Performing Management: Angela Jenkins & John
Noble

## ORBIT
6 Fortnam Road, London N19 3NR
Tel: 0171 263 9934
Director: Kenneth Parrott

## ORCHARD THEATRE COMPANY
108 Newport Road, Barnstaple, Devon EX32 9BA
Tel: 01271 371475/373356 Fax: 01271 371825
Email: orchardtheatre@compuserve.com
Artistic Director: Bill Buffery
Administrator: Frederica Notley
Community & Education Officer: Gill Nathanson

## OSPREY GROUP
Osprey House, 10 Little Portland Street,
London W1N 6LX
Tel: 0171 637 8575 Fax: 0171 208 1001
Creative Director: Mike Reynolds

## OVATION PRODUCTIONS
1 Prince of Wales Passage, 117 Hampstead Road,
London NW1 3EF
Tel: 0171 387 2342 Fax: 0171 380 0404
Email: OvationGB@aol.com
Partners: Katie & John Plews

## OXFORD STAGE COMPANY
131 High Street, Oxford OX1 4DH
Tel: 01865 723238 Fax: 01865 790625
Email: info@oxfordstage.co.uk
Web Site: www.oxfordstage.co.uk
Artistic Director: John Retallack
General Manager: Patrick Martin

## PAINES PLOUGH
4th Floor, 43 Aldwych, London WC2B 4DA
Tel: 0171 240 4533 Fax: 0171240 4534
Email: paines.plough@dial.pipex.com
Artistic Director: Vicki Featherstone
Administrative Director: Belinda Hamilton
Literary Director: Mark Ravenhill
Literary Manager: Jessica Dromgool
A national touring company specialising in accessible
new plays.

## PERFORMING ARTS MANAGEMENT
Canal 7, Clarence Mill, Clarence Road, Bollington,
Macclesfield, Cheshire SK10 5JZ
Tel: 01625 575681 Fax: 01625 572839
Email: clare.scott@performingarts.co.uk
Web Site: www.performingarts.co.uk
Senior Personnel: Nicholas Smith, Sally Smith,
Clare Scott
Promoter of outdoor classical concerts with fireworks.

## PHYSICALITY LTD
265-267 Ilford Lane, Ilford, Essex IG1 2SD
Tel: 0181 491 2800 Fax: 0181 491 2801
Email: physicality@pavilion.co.uk
Senior Personnel: Wayne Pritchett
Specialising in: Physical Arts.

## PLANTAGENET PRODUCTIONS
Westridge Open Centre, Andover Road, Highclere,
Newbury, Berkshire RG20 9PJ
Tel: 01635 253322
Director: Dorothy Rose J.Gribble

## THE PLAYBOARD PUPPET THEATRE
94 Ockendon Road, London N1 3NW
Tel: 0171 226 5911 Fax: 0171 704 1081
Director: Ian Allen

## PLAYERS THEATRE
The Arches Villiers Street London WC2N 6NG
Tel 0171 976 1307 BO 0171 839 1134
Fax 0171 839 8067
Email: info@theplayerstheatre.co.uk
Web Site: www.theplayerstheatre.co.uk
ADMINISTRATION:
Props: Players Theatre Club
Trustees: Geoffrey Brawn; Dominic Le Foe
Manager: Stephen Grey
Policy: Victorian Music Hall, Melodrama & Pantomime.
Perfs: Tues-Sun 8.15. Seats: 256

## PLAYTIME PRODUCTIONS
Beech House, Great Sturton, Horncastle,
Lincolnshire LN9 5NX
Tel/Fax: 01507 578435
Directors: Dan Dobson & Hiroko Yoshikawa

## P&O CRUISES (UK) LTD
Richmond House, Terminus Terrace, Southampton,
Hampshire SO14 3PN
Tel: 01703 534245 Fax: 01703 534280
Head of Entertainment: David Llewhellin

## POLA JONES ASSOCIATES LTD
14 Dean Street, London W1V 5AH
Tel: 0171 439 1165 Fax: 0171 437 3994
Managing Director: Andre Ptaszynski

## PRELUDE
The Old Stables, 10 Timber Lane, Caterham,
Surrey CR3 6LZ
Tel: 01883 344300 Fax: 01883 347712
Email: prelud@globalnet.co.uk
Senior Personnel: Phillippa Lunn
Specialising in: Entertainment for Business, including
After Dinner Speakers, Cabaret and Background
Music.

## PREMIER PRODUCTIONS
4 Haywood, Bracknell, Berkshire RG12 7WG
Tel: 01344 453888 Fax: 01344 305151
Senior Personnel: Connie Hayes
Specialising in Children's Theatre Shows and Personal
Appearances.

## Q20 BRADFORD'S THEATRE COMPANY
"Ivy Lea", Fyfe Lane, Baildon,
West Yorkshire BD17 6DP
Tel/Fax: 01274 591417 (9am - 12pm Mon-Fri)
Artistic Director: John Lambert

## PAUL RAYMOND ORGANISATION (PRO)
2 Archer Street, Piccadilly, London W1Y 1FG
Tel: 0171 734 9191 Fax: 0171 734 5030

## THE REALLY USEFUL GROUP LTD
22 Tower Street, London WC2H 9NS
Tel: 0171 240 0880 Fax: 0171 240 1204
Proprieter: Andrew Lloyd Webber

## MICHAEL REDINGTON LTD
10 Maunsel Street, London SW1P 2QL
Tel: 0171 834 5119 Fax: 0171 828 6947

## THE REP COLLEGE
17 St. Mary's Avenue, Purley-on-Thames, Berkshire
RG8 8BJ
Tel/Fax: 0118 942 1144
Contact: David Tudor, Elizabeth Lane

## THE RIPLEY-DUGGAN PARTNERSHIP
Theatre Production Brokerage
52 Tottenham Street, London W1P 9PG
Tel: 0171 436 1392 Fax: 0171 436 1395
Email: ripleyduggan@sompuserve.com

## BRIAN RIX ENTERPRISES
68 South Lambeth Road, London SW8 1RL
Tel: 0171 820 0082 Fax: 0171 820 0806
Directors: Lord Brian Rix, CBE, DL & Elspet Gray

## RODGERS & PAYNE PRODUCTIONS
9 Beechwood Avenue, Earlsdon, Coventry, West
Midlands CV5 6DF
Tel: 01203 778377/677173 Fax: 01203 778686 Mobile:
0585 430579
Senior Personnel: Sheila Payne, John Rodgers
Specialises in Music Hall and Variety Package Shows
for theatre, corporate functions, theme evenings, etc.

## MICHAEL ROSE LTD
The Old Dairy, Throop Road, Holdenhurst,
Bournemouth, Dorset BH8 0DL
Tel: 01202 522711 Fax: 01202 522311
Directors: Michael Rose & David Morgan

## ROYAL EXCHANGE THEATRE COMPANY LTD
Royal Exchange Theatre, Royal Exchange Studio,
St.Ann's Square, Manchester M2 7DH
Management: 0161 833 9333 Fax: 0161 832 0881
Marketing: 0161 833 9938 BO: 0161 833 9833
Web Site: www.royalexchange.co.uk
ADMINISTRATION:
Funded by NWAB; Association of Greater Manchester
Authorities;
Local Authority: Manchester City Council
Artistic Directors: Braham Murray, Gregory Hersov

Associate Directors: Marianne Elliott, Matthew Lloyd, Sophie Marshall, Wyllie Longmore, Chris Monks

## ROYAL NATIONAL THEATRE
Upper Ground South Bank London SE1 9PX
Mgt/Admin 0171 452 3333 SD 0171 452 3333 BO
0171 452 3000 Information 0171 452 3400
Fax 0171 452 3344
ADMINISTRATION:
Director of the National: Trevor Nunn
Company Secretary & Head of Finance:
Lew Hodges
General Manager: Maggie Whitlum
Head of Touring: Roger Chapman
Associate Directors: Michael Bryant, Howard Davies,
Declan Donnellan, Peter Gill, David Hare, Nicholas
Hytner, Sir Ian McKellen, Deborah Warner, Nicholas
Wright.

## ROYAL SHAKESPEARE COMPANY
Royal Shakespeare Theatre,
 Stratford-upon-Avon CV37 6BB
Tel: 01789 296655 Fax: 01789 294810 Barbican
Theatre, Silk Street, London EC2Y 8DS Tel: 0171 628
3351 Fax: 0171 374 0818
Artistic Director: Adrian Noble
General Manager: Will Weston

## ROYSTON PRODUCTIONS
2 Coaching Walk, Westone, Northampton NN3 3EX
Tel: 01604 411413
Contact: Roy Gilbert

## SANDOW CLOWNS
59 Thoresby Close, Bridlington,
East Yorkshire YO16 7EN
Tel: 01262 671492
Contact: Tom Bratby
Children's and Variety Shows on stage, on the floor, in
schools and in the round.

## SANDPIPER PRODUCTIONS LTD
Flat B, Abingdon Court, Allen Street, London W8 6BP
Tel: 0171 937 9593 Fax: 0171 937 3536
Producer: Harold Sanderton

## SCENIC HAPPENINGS LTD
PO Box 178, Elvington, York YO4 5YY
Tel: 01904 607607 Fax: 01904 607608
Director: Martin Witts
Office Manager: David Forster
Production Manager: Phil Lawson
Specialists in all aspects of production management,
stage management and orchestral management.

## THE SCOTTISH CHAMBER ORCHESTRA
4 Royal Terrace, Edinburgh EH7 5AB
Tel: 0131 557 6800 Fax: 0131 557 6933
Managing Director: Roy McEwan

## SERIO ENSEMBLE
The Pigeon Loft, 443-445 Holloway Road,
London N7 6LJ
Tel: 0171 281 7683 Theatre: 0171 281 7745

Artistic Director: Charles Serio
Venue available for rehearsal space hire.

## VINCENT SHAW ASSOCIATES LTD
20 Jay Mews, London SW7 2EP
Tel: 0171 581 8215 Fax: 0171 225 1079
Email: vincentshaw@clara.net
Web Site: http://home.clara.net/vincentshaw
Director: Vincent Shaw

## SHOW OF STRENGTH
Hebron House, Sion Road, Bedminster,
Bristol BS3 3BD
Tel: 0117 987 9444 Fax: 0117 963 1770
Artistic Directors: Sheila Hannon & Alan Coveney

## SMALLHYTHE PRODUCTIONS LTD
1 Hogarth Hill, London NW11 6AY
Contact by post only.

## SNAP THEATRE COMPANY
Snap People's Theatre Trust, Unit A, Causeway
Business Centre, Bishop's Stortford,
Hertfordshire CM23 2UB
Tel: 01279 504095/503066 Fax: 01279 501472
Artistic Director: Andy Graham
Administrative Director: Mike Wood

## EDWARD SNAPE ASSOCIATES LTD
22/24 Torrington Place, London WC1E 7HF
Tel: 0171 580 6792 Fax: 0171 580 6652
Director: Edward Snape

## SOHO THEATRE COMPANY
21 Dean Street, London W1V 7RD
Tel: 0171 287 5060 Fax: 0171 287 5061
Email: mail@sohotheatre.com
Artistic Director: Abigail Morris
Admin Producer: Mark Godfrey
Literary Manager: Paul Sirett
Soho Theatre Company is dedicated to the discovery
and development of new writers. The company reads
and reports on over 1500 scripts a year and runs an
extensive development programme, which gives
writers advice, support, workshops, rehearsed
readings and commissions. In 1996 the company
bought a building with money from the National Lottery
through the Arts Council of England. The building, on
Dean Street W1, is due to open in November 1999.
The new building will include a 200 seat theatre and a
Writers' Centre as well as a bar, restaurant, offices,
rehearsal rooms and, uniquely, space for writers -
everything the company needs to house its bold,
artistic policy under one roof. For further information on
the project or the company's work with writers contact
Soho Theatre Company.

## SOOTY INTERNATIONAL
Heath End, The Flats, Reading Road, Blackwater,
Camberley, Surrey GU17 0AR
Tel: 01252 872060 Fax: 01252 860190
Cheif Executive: James Corsan

## SOUTHWESTERN MANAGEMENT
13 Portland Road, Street, Somerset BA16 9PX
Tel: 01458 445186 Fax: 01458 841186
Email: chris@sw-management.co.uk
Web Site: www.sw-management.co.uk
Senior Personnel: Chris Hannam
Production tour & stage management services.

## SPARE TYRE THEATRE COMPANY
Interchange Studios, Dalby Street, London NW5 3NQ
Tel/Fax: 0171 267 5252
Email: sttc@dircon.co.uk
Director: Claire Chapman
Administrative Director: Angela Kelly
Theatre training company running projects with
disadvantaged groups such as the young unemployed
and the elderly. Productions are toured locally.

## SPYWAY ARTS LTD
15c Commercial Road, Swanage, Dorset BH19 1DF
Tel: 01929 424007
Email: spyway@avnet.co.uk
Partners: Peter Cooper & Annette Sumption

## STAGE DOOR PRODUCTIONS & THEATRICAL AGENCY
20 Dewar Drive, Millhouses, Sheffield S7 2GQ
Tel: 0114 236 3083 Fax: 0114 262 1281
Mobile: 0370 865953
Sole Proprieter: Peter Wright

## STAGE FURTHER PRODUCTIONS LTD
2 Archangel Way, Dunston Park, Thatcham,
Berkshire RG18 4EB
Tel: 01635 523363 Fax: 01635 872845
Director: Garth Harrison

## STAGE ONE THEATRE COMPANY
34 Jasmine Grove, London SE20 8JW
Tel: 0181 778 5213 Fax: 0181 778 1756
Email: admin@stageone.demon.co.uk
Web Site: www.stageone.demon.co.uk
Admin Director: Desmond Maurer

## STAGESTRUCK PRODUCTIONS
Stowe March, Barnet Lane, Elstree,
Herfordshire WD6 3RQ
Tel: 07000 227526 Fax: 0181 905 1511
Director: Simon Caplan

## STAGEWORKS WORLDWIDE PRODUCTIONS
525 Ocean Boulevard, Blackpool FY4 1EZ
Tel: 01253 342426 Fax: 01253 342702
President: Amanda Thompson
Vice-President: Lorraine Trangmar
Entertainment Secretary: Marie Cavney

## THE STENNETT COMPANY
Craig-y-Nos, Rhiwbina Hill, Cardiff CF4 6UP
Tel: 01222 625276 Fax: 01222 611009
Partners: Stan Stennett, Ceri Stennett,
Elizabeth Stennett & Roger Stennett

## STOLL MOSS THEATRES LTD
21 Soho Square, London W1V 5FD
Tel: 0171 494 5200 Fax: 0171 434 1217
Chief Executive: Richard Johnston
Production Directors: Nica Burns & Gareth Johnston
Concerts and Hirings Manager: David Kinsey

## SWALLOW PRODUCTIONS (UK) LTD
32 Blenheim Gardens, Wembley Park,
Middlesex HA9 7NP
Tel/Fax: 0181 904 7024
Producer: John B Hobbs

## SWANSEA LITTLE THEATRE COMPANY LTD
Dylan Thomas Theatre, Maritime Quarter,
7 Gloucester Place, Swansea SA1 1TY
Tel: 01792 473238 Fax: 01792 416899
Artistic Chairman: Anneilie Williams
Assistant: Ned Williams

## SWANSFLIGHT PRODUCTIONS
Swans Nest, 2 Windmill Road, Hampton Hill,
Middlesex TW12 1RH
Tel: 0181 941 1595 Fax: 0181 783 1366
Managing Directors: Sheila and Terry Denton-De Gray

## TALKBACK MANAGEMENT
36 Percy Street, London W1P 0LN
Tel: 0171 631 3940 Fax: 0171 637 5105
Senior Personnel: Melanie Coupland, Anna Wilkes
Directors: Mel Smith, Griff Rhys Jones &
Peter Fincham

## T.B.A. MUSIC LTD
1st Floor, 361 Edgware Road, London W2 1DY
Tel: 0171 723 1307 Fax: 0171 724 7287
Email: tbamusic@globalnet.co.uk
Director: Peter Benda
TMA Members

## THEATRE OF COMEDY COMPANY LTD
Shaftesbury Theatre, 210 Shaftesbury Avenue,
London WC2H 8DP
Tel: 0171 379 3345 Fax: 0171 836 8181
Chief Executive: Andrew Leigh
Company founded in 1983 by Ray Cooney and leading
comedy actors and writers. Manages the Churchill
Theatre, Bromley and owns the Shaftesbury Theatre.
Not reading unsolicited scripts in 1999.

## THE THEATRE OF MARIONETTES
Barntimpin House, St.Anns, Lockerbie,
Dumfriesshire DG11 1HL
Tel: 01576 470222
Directors: Peter & Frances Grant

## THEATRE ROUNDABOUT LTD
859 Finchley Road, London NW11 8LX
Tel: 0181 455 4752
Key Personnel: Sylvia Read & William Fry

## THEATRE ROYAL, STRATFORD EAST
Gerry Raffles Square London E15 1BN

Mgt 0181 534 7374 BO 0181 534 0310
Press Office 0181 534 2178 Fax 0181 534 8381
ADMINISTRATION:
General Manager: Nick Jones
Artistic Director: Philip Hedley
Associate Director: Kerry Michael
Production Manager: Bob Irwin
Policy: The bulk of the year is taken up with own
productions of new plays with the occasional classic.
No permanent company and a minimum technical and
administrative staff. Play choice ranges from family
shows like pantomimes, musicals, melodramas and
farces through to controversial modern work,
particularly with appeal to young audiences.
On Sundays, once a month, run our own Variety
Shows or have in guest bands, dance companies or
fringe groups.
Seats: 464

### TKO MUSIC GROUP
PO Box 130, Hove, East Sussex BN3 6QU
Tel: 01273 550088 Fax: 01273 540968
Email: management@tkomusicgroup.co.uk
Senior Personnel: Jeffrey Kruger, Howard Kruger,
Adam Clavering
Specialising in: Concert & Event Promotions and
Management

### TOPAZ PRODUCTIONS LTD
46 Wormholt Road, London W12 0LS
Tel: 0181 749 2619 Fax: 0181 749 0358
Director: Malcolm Taylor

### TRENDS PRODUCTIONS (LONDON) LTD
54 Lisson Street, London NW1 5DF
Tel: 0171 723 8001 Fax: 0171 258 3591
Senior Personnel: Jamie Phillips, Linda Smith

### TRIANGLE PRODUCTIONS
"Twynings", Church Road, Fordham, Colchester,
Essex CO6 3NJ
Tel: 01206 240467 Fax: 01206 240467
Administrator: Graham B. Hewes
To present entertaining "middle of the road" drama to
as wide a range of audiences as possible.
Productions range from adaptations of well-known
stories to new commission work.
A greater emphasis has recently been placed on
Children's shows, and the Company have nine young
people's shows currently in repertoire.
The Company carries all its own equipment, and is
entirely self-contained. All types of venue are
acceptable.

### TRIUMPH PROSCENIUM PRODUCTIONS LTD
(See also Duncan C Weldon Productions Ltd)
Suite 4, Waldorf Chambers, 11 Aldwych,
London WC2B 4DA
Tel: 0171 343 8800 Fax: 0171 343 8801

### THE TURNSTYLE GROUP
25 Shaftesbury Avenue, London W1V 7HA
Tel: 0171 494 0333 Fax: 0171 494 0034
Managing Director: Howard Panter
Head of Production: Meryl Faiers

### TURTLE KEY ARTS
Ladbroke Hall, 79 Barlby Road, London W10 6AZ
Tel: 0181 964 5060 Fax: 0181 964 4080
Email: turtlek@globalnet.co.uk
Contact: Charlotte Cunningham, Alison King
Turtle Key Arts is launching itself as a dynamic and
versatile arts management company that combines
production, technical services, education and training
to serve theatre and dance companies and venues,
special schools, disability arts organisations and the
rest of the education sector.

### UK ARTS INTERNATIONAL/
### FIFTH AMENDMENT LTD
2nd Floor, 6 Shaw Street, Worcester WR1 3QQ
Tel: 01905 26424 Fax: 01905 22868
Email: jan.ryan@amendmnt.demon.co.uk
Web Site: www.ukarts.com
Director: Jan Ryan
Administration: Lucy Bowen
Presents work from the US, UK and elsewhere.

### UK PRODUCTIONS LTD
Lime House, 78 Meadrow, Godalming,
Surrey GU7 3HT
Tel: 01483 423600 Fax: 01483 418486
Directors: Peter Frosdick & Martin Dodd

### UNCLE BRIAN LTD
The Wood Cottage, Brompton-by-Sawdon,
Scarborough YO13 9DD
Tel/Fax: 01723 859497 Mobile: 0850 615554
Director: David Reid-Frow
General Manager: Brian Frow

## UPSTAGE ENTERTAINMENT GROUP
Abingdon Chambers, 23 Abingdon Street,
Blackpool FY1 1DG
Tel: 01253 292 676 Fax: 01253 292165
Email: upstage@btinternet.com
Senior Personnel: Margaret Todd, Neville Skelly,
Graeme Todd

## CHARLES VANCE PRODUCTIONS
Hampden House, 2 Weymouth Street,
London W1N 3FD
Tel: 0171 636 4343 Fax: 0171 636 2323
Email: cvtheatre@aol.com
Chairman: Charles Vance
Administrative Director: Jill Streatfeild
Production Manager: Mark Alexander
Production Executive: Erika Vincent
Marketing Manager: Dawn Kellogg

## ANTHONY VANDER ELST PRODUCTIONS
The Studio, 14 College Road, Bromley, Kent BR1 3NS
Tel: 0181 466 5580

## DENIS VAUGHAN MANAGEMENT
Bond Street House, 14 Clifford Street,
London W1X 2JD
Tel: 0171 486 5353 Fax: 01372 742448
Senior Personnel: Denis Vaughan

## W & J THEATRICAL ENTERPRISES LTD
15 Brookland Hill, London NW11 6DU
Tel/Fax: 0181 458 1608
Senior Personnel: Bill Roberton

## WARRICK PRODUCING CONSULTANTS
40-42 Parker Street, London WC2B 5PQ
Tel: 0171 404 0546 Fax: 0171 404 1555
Producing Director: C.J. Warrick
Production Assistant: Tarryn Davis

## DUNCAN C WELDON PRODUCTIONS LTD
(See also Triumph Proscenium Productions Ltd)
Suite 4, Waldorf Chambers, 11 Aldwych,
London WC2B 4DA
Tel: 0171 343 8800 Fax: 0171 343 8801
Managing Director: Duncan Weldon
Deputy MD: Peter Williams

## WESTMINSTER PRODUCTIONS LTD
Westminster Theatre, 12 Palace Street,
London SW1E 5JF
Tel: 0171 834 7882 Fax: 0171 828 7609
Contact: Jeffrey Craig and David Channen

## WHIRLIGIG THEATRE
14 Belvedere Drive, Wimbledon, London SW19 7BY
Tel: 0181 947 1732 Fax: 0181 879 7648
Directors: David Wood & John Gould
Administrator: Barry Sheppard

## MICHAEL WHITE ENTERTAINMENTS LTD
48 Dean Street, London W1V 5HL
Tel: 0171 734 7707 Fax: 0171 734 7727

Managing Director: Michael White
Contact: Mac Mackenzie

## JOHN WILLIAMS
PO Box 423, Chislehurst, Kent BR7 5TU
Tel: 0181 295 3639 Fax: 0181 295 3641
Senior Personnel: John Williams

## ROBBIE WILSON EVENT MANAGEMENT LTD
54-56 Station Approach, South Ruislip,
Middlesex HA4 6SA
Tel: 0181 841 9588 Fax: 0181 841 2113
Managing Director: Robbie Wilson

## MAURICE WINNICK (ASSOCIATES) LTD
66 Melbourne Way, Enfield, Middlesex EN1 1XQ
Tel/Fax: 0181 366 2978

## WIZZARD PRODUCTIONS
60 Cromford Way, Combeside, Surrey KT3 3BA
Affiliated to Millet Productions,
Touring - West End Productions.

## WSG PRODUCTIONS LTD
14 Belvedere Drive, Wimbledon, London SW19 7BY
Tel: 0181 947 1732 Fax: 0181 879 7648
Contact: David Wood, John Gould

## THE YOUNG VIC THEATRE COMPANY
66 The Cut London SE1 8LZ
Tel 0171 633 0133 BO 0171 928 6363
Fax 0171 928 1585
ADMINISTRATION:
Artistic Director: Tim Supple
Admin Producer: Caroline Maude
Policy: Theatre
Seats: Main Theatre 500 max, Studio Space 80-90.

## ZAP PRODUCTIONS
Third Floor, 7a Middle Street, Brighton BN1 1AL
Tel: 01273 821588 Fax: 01273 206960
Directors: Robin Morley, Dave Reeves & Pat Butler

# BALLET, OPERA & DANCE COMPANIES

## ADONAIS BALLET COMPANY

183 Aston Clinton Road, Weston Turville, Aylesbury,
Buckinghamshire HP22 5AD
Tel/Fax: 01252 543838 or 01296 630390
Email: adonais@pebbles.eurobell.co.uk
Web Site: www.zynet.co.uk/pebbles/adonais
Artistic Director: Jan Kitteridge
Administrative Director: Graham Mitchell
Company policy to take high quality new work to
audiences nationwide.

## RICHARD ALSTON DANCE COMPANY

(controlled by Contemporary Dance Trust)
The Place, 17 Duke's Road, London WC1H 9AB
Tel: 0171 387 6332 Fax: 0171 383 4851

## BALLET CENTRAL

10 Herbal Hill, Clerkenwell Road, London EC1R 5EJ
Tel: 0171 837 6332 Fax: 0171 833 5571
Directors: Ann Stannard, Greg Horsman
Ballet Central Company Manager: Ruth Tisdall
A company of 15 young dancers sponsored by British
Gas and undertaking British regional tours from March
to July each year. Mixed programme of classical, jazz
and contemporary works.

## BALLET CREATIONS

3 Blackbird Way, Bransgore, Hampshire BH23 8LG
Contacts: Ursula Hageli, Richard Slaughter
Small to middle scale classical ballet company with
resident musicians. Lecture demonstrations,
educational work and workshops.

## BANK OF IRELAND ARTS CENTRE

Foster Place, Dublin 2
Tel 00 353 1 671 1488 Fax 00 353 1 670 7556
Contact: Barry O'Kelly
The Bank of Ireland's Arts Centre stages live
performances as well as exhibitions. It has provided the
first major public platform for many young Irish artistes.

## BIRMINGHAM ROYAL BALLET

Birmingham Hippodrome, Thorp Street,
Birmingham B5 4AU
Tel: 0121 622 2555 Fax: 0121 622 5038
Artistic Director: David Bintley
Administrative Director: Derek Purnell
The sister company to the Royal Ballet, based in
Birmingham and touring to London, other cities
throughout Great Britain and overseas.

## BUXTON FESTIVAL

1 Crescent View, Hall Bank, Buxton,
Derbyshire SK17 6EN
Admin: 01298 70395 BO: 01298 72190
Fax: 01298 72289
Chairman: Sir Philip Haworth
General Manager: Glyn Foley
Buxton Opera House S/Cap: 930

## CARL CAMPBELL DANCE COMPANY 7

Thomas Carlton Centre, Alpha Street, Peckham,
London SE15 4NX
Tel/Fax: 0171 639 4875 (daytime)
Minicom/Answermachine/Fax
Email: ccdc7@easynet.co.uk

## THE CEDAR DANCE THEATRE

42 Gunton Road, London E5 9JS
Tel: 0181 806 4609

## THE CHOLMONDELEYS

(See also the Featherstonehaughs)
Unit 1, Lafone House, The Leather Market,
11-13 Leather Market Street, London SE1 3HN
Tel: 0171 378 8800 Fax: 0171 378 8810
Artistic Director: Lea Anderson
Administrative Director: Sue Wyatt

## CHOU CHOU BALLET COMPANY

27 Iona Close, Ravensbourne Park, Catford,
London SE6 4YN
Tel: 0181 690 6329 Fax: 0181 690 6329
A company of young performers (age 8-17) who
perform both classical repertoire and authentic
character dance from many cultures. Available for
concerts, open-air and indoor. Videos, workshops,
demonstrations undertaken.

## CITY BALLET OF LONDON

International Buildings, 71 Kingsway,
London WC2B 6SX
Tel: 0171 405 0044 Fax: 0171 405 2050
Web Site: freespace.virgin.net/david.browne/cbl.htm
Artistic Director: Harold King
The London based neo-classical ballet company with
22 dancers tours Great Britain and abroad with full
length productions and mixed programmes.

## CLONTER OPERA THEATRE

Swettenham Heath, Congleton, Cheshire, CW12 2LR
Admin: 01260 224638 BO: 01260 224514
Fax: 01260 224742
Artistic Director: Jeffery Lockett
Musical Director: Leonard Hancock
Assistant Musical Director: Wyn Davies
Box Office: Jane Edwards

## COMMON GROUND SIGN DANCE THEATRE

4th Floor, Crane Building, Hanover Street,
Liverpool, L1 3DY
Tel/Fax: 0151 707 8033 Minicom: 0151 707 8380
(Typetalk 0800 515152)
Administrator: Barry Avison

## CRYSTAL CLEAR OPERA

The Old Refectory, Grafham, Cambridgshire PE18 0BB
Tel: 01480 810261 Fax: 01480 812835
Artistic Director: Martin McEvoy

Mid-scale touring company; opera sung in English and 14 piece orchestra. Accessible, understandable, affordable & available to all. Touring throughout the UK.

## CWMNI BALLET GWENT
30 Glasllwch Crescent, Newport,
South Wales NP9 3SE
Tel: 01633 253985 Fax: 01633 221690
Email: cwmniballet@dial.pipex.com
Artistic Director: Darius James
Administrative Director: Yvonne Williams
Wales' own independent ballet company specialising in National and International touring.

## DANCE UMBRELLA
October - November annually
20 Chancellors Street, London W6 9RN
Tel: 0181 741 4040 Fax: 0181 741 7902
Email: mail@danceumbrella.co.uk
Web Site: www.danceumbrella.co.uk
Artistic Director: Val Bourne
Administrator: Toby Beazley
Programme Manager: Betsy Gregory
Marketing Manager: David Pratt
Dance Umbrella support and encourages the best of the new in contemporary dance work both in Britain and overseas.

## DELPHINE Y DOMINGO
4 Cormorant Rise, Worcester WR2 4BA
Tel: 01905 424083/0181 697 5960
Contact: James Peterson
Specialising in quality Flamenco Music and Dance for Television, Theatre, Promotion and Education.

## DIVERSIONS DANCE COMPANY
Ebenezer Studio, Charles Street, Cardiff CF1 4EA
Tel: 01222 228855 Fax: 01222 227176
Director: Roy Campbell-Moore
A company of 8 dancers touring a mixed programme of contemporary dance by international choreographers throughout the UK and overseas.

## THE D'OYLY CARTE OPERA COMPANY
Valley Park, Cromer Gardens, Wolverhampton,
West Midlands WV6 0VA
Tel: 01902 744555 Fax: 01902 744333
Chairman: Sir Michael Bishop CBE
General Manager: Ray Brown
Music Director: John Owen Edwards
Administration Manager: Ian Martin

## DV8 PHYSICAL THEATRE
c/o Artsadmin, Toynbee Studios,
28 Commercial Street, London E1 6LS
Tel: 0171 247 5102 Fax: 0171 247 5103
General Manager: Leonie Gombrich

## ENGLISH NATIONAL BALLET LTD
Markova House, 39 Jay Mews, London SW7 2ES
Tel: 0171 581 1245 Fax: 0171 225 0827
Email: info@ballet.org.uk
Stores, wardrobe, electrics, and scenic studio:
Units 9 and 10, Fairway Estate,

Fairway Drive,
Greenford, Middlesex
UB6 8PW
Tel: 0181 575 6204
Artistic Director: Derek Deane
Executive Director: Carole McPhee
Deputy Executive Director: Richard Shaw
Finance Director: Jack Haslam
Music Director: Patrick Flynn
Technical Director: Alan Riches
Education Manager: Iryna Pyzniuk

## ENGLISH NATIONAL OPERA
London Coliseum, St.Martin's Lane,
London WC2N 4ES
Tel: 0171 836 0111
Fax: 0171 836 8379/0171 497 9052 (PR)
Theatre Management: Fax: 0171 836 5769
Email: marketing@eno.org
Web Site: www.eno.org
Directors of the English National Opera:
Music Director: Paul Daniel
General Director: Nicholas Payne
Executive Director: Russell Willis Taylor
Technical Director: Laurence Holderness
Director of Public Relations: Maggie Sedwards
Financial Controller: Graeme Wallace

## ENGLISH TOURING OPERA
W121, Westminster Business Square, Durham Street,
London SE11 5JH
Admin: 0171 820 1131 Press: 0171 820 1141
Fax: 0171 735 7008
Chairman: Nick MacAndrew
Chief Executive: Katharine Herbert
Music Director: Andrew Greenwood
Director of Productions: Robert Chevara
Development Director: Lucy Anderson Jones
Press Officer: John Haywood
Orchestra Manager: Peter Thompson
Education Manager: Paul Reeve

## ENGLISH YOUTH BALLET
## JANET LEWIS ENTERPRISES
85 Brockley Grove, Brockley, London SE4 1DZ
Tel: 0181 691 2806
Email: juliet@ndtc.org
Artistic Director: Janet Lewis
Administration: Bridget Hearne & Juliet Hayes
Choreographers: Ursula Hageli, Richard Slaughter

## THE FEATHERSTONEHAUGHS
(See also the Cholmondeleys)
Unit LF 1.1, Lafone House, The Leathermarket,
11-13 Leathermarket Street, London SE1 3HN
Tel: 0171 378 8800 Fax: 0171 378 8810
Artistic Director: Lea Anderson
General Manager: Sue Wyatt

## FIRST ACT OPERA INTERNATIONAL
The Thatched House, West Farleigh, Maidstone,
Kent ME15 0NJ
Tel: 01622 747762 Fax: 01622 745276
Email: figaro@globalnet.co.uk
Web Site: http://www.users.globalnet.co.uk/~figaro/news
Managing Director: Elaine Holden
Musical Director: Kenneth Roberts

Producer: John von Nuding

## GLYNDEBOURNE FESTIVAL OPERA HOUSE
Glyndebourne, Ringmer, Lewes,
East Sussex BN8 5UU
Mgt 01273 812321 SD 01273 812321
Fax 01273 812783
ADMINISTRATION:
General Director: Nicholas Snowman
Director of Productions: Graham Vick
Music Director: Andrew Davis, CBE
Technical Director: Peter Horne
Finance Director: Mrs Sarah Hopwood
House Manager: Julie Crocker
Press & Public Relations: Nicky Webb
Policy: Festival Opera Season
New Opera House opened in May 1994.
Please contact venue for further details.

## THE GUIZERS DANCE AND MIME THEATRE
Johnny Haynes 24 Howard Street, Loughborough,
Leicestershire LE11 1PD
Tel: 01509 236522
Keith Barlow 6 Victoria Road, Woodhouse Evans,
Leicesterhsire LE12 8RF
Tel: 01509 891 010

## HEARTSTONE
Office 2, Mayfield, High Street, Dingwall, Invernesshire
Tel: 01349 865400 Fax: 01349 866066
Director: Sita Kumari

## IRIE! DANCE THEATE
The Albany Centre, Douglas Way, Deptford,
London SE8 4AG
Tel: 0181 691 6099 Fax: 0181 694 8464
Web Site: http://www.deptfordnet/arts/irie/irie.html
IRIE!'s dance style is a unique fusion of African,
Caribbean and Western Contemporary Dance.
Artistic Director: Beverley Glean

## JIVING LINDY HOPPERS
35 Newton Avenue, London W3 8AR
Tel: 0181 992 8128 Fax: 0181 752 0683
Email: 100630.1655@compuserve.com
Contacts: Caroline Hinds, Terry Monaghan, Warren
Heyes, Russell Sargeant
Authentic Jazz Dance Company.

## KALAMANDALAM VIJAYAKUMAR (KATHAKALI ACTOR)
1 Holland Road, Woolston, Southampton SO19 9FW
Tel: 01703 420114 Fax: 01703 444468
Email: kathakal@interalpha.co.uk
Web Site: http://www.intent.co.uk/kathakali/index.html
Offers solo Kathakali performances, workshops,
courses, full company performances to include top
international artists from India. We tour nationally and
internationally to make quality Kathakali available to
all. 1999 tour will include Theyam, a ritual dance from
Kerala, South India.

## KENT OPERA
Pembles Cross, Egerton, Ashford, Kent TN27 9BN

Tel/Fax: 01233 756237 Fax: 01233 756704

## KOKUMA DANCE THEATRE COMPANY
418-419 The Custard Factory, Gibb Street, Digbeth,
Birmingham B9 4AA
Tel: 0121 608 7744 Fax: 0121 608 7755
Artistic Director: Patrick Acogny

## THE KOSH
6 Brewery Road, London N7 9NH
Tel: 0171 607 4185 Fax: 0171 607 2491
Artistic Director: Michael Merwitzer
Choreographer: Sian Williams

## LONDON OPERA PLAYERS LTD
Broadmeade Copse, Westwood Lane, Wanborough,
Surrey GU3 2JN
Tel: 01483 811004 Fax: 01483 811 721
Managing Director: Elisabeth Parry

## LONDON SAVOYARDS
23 Westfield Road, Bishop's Stortford,
Hertfordshire CM23 2RE
Tel: 01279 652371
Managing Director: Andrew Meadmore

## LUDUS DANCE COMPANY
Ludus Dance Centre, Assembly Rooms, King Street,
Lancaster LA1 1RE
Tel: 01524 389901 Fax: 01524 847744
Email: ludus@easynet.co.uk
Web Site: www.dancenorthwest.org.uk
Director: Deborah Barnard
Head of Touring: Jacqueline Greaves
Britain's leading dance company for young people.
Award winning shows, workshops, teaching packs,
inset, videos, the works! High impact in Theatres,
Festivals, Schools and the Community. Still unique
after 23 years.

## MOVING VISIONS DANCE THEATRE
St.Margaret's Lodge, 300 St.Margaret's Road,
Twickenham TW1 1PT
Tel: 0181 891 0121 (24 hours) Fax: 0181 891 0487
Contact: Ross McKim

## NORTHERN BALLET THEATRE
West Park Centre, Spen Lane, Leeds LS16 5BE
Tel: 0113 274 5355 Fax: 0113 274 5381/220 8007
Email: @nbtdance.demon.co.uk
Web Site: www.nbt.co.uk
Artistic Director: TBC
Executive Director: Mark Skipper
Music Director: John Pryce-Jones
Head of Finance: Julia Grime
Head of Marketing: Katherine Scott
Head of Press & PR: Anna M. D. Izza
Britain's leading classical dance drama company
produces new full length versions of the classics as
well as new classical and modern works. Touring the
UK for up to 26 weeks a year with availability for
overseas tours. Current repertoire includes: Cinderella,
A Christmas Carol, Carmen, Dracula, Giselle, A Simple
Man, Jardi Tancat, Jazz Concerto.

## NORTHERN OPERA
24 Bankside, Morpeth, Northumberland NE61 1XD
Tel: 01670 514149 or 0191 236 3118
Fax: 0191 514149
Contact: Roy Beasley, Administration.
Semi-professional stages productions in Newcastle
upon Tyne, regional tours of small scale productions
and operatic concerts.

## OPERA DELLA LUNA
7 Cotmore House, Fringford, Bicester OX6 9RQ
Tel: 01869 278145 Fax: 01869 277594
Email: operadellaluna@lineone.com
Web Site: http://ourworld.compuserve.com/homepages
/davidcookson/luna.htm
Artistic Director: Jeff Clarke
Administrator: Graham Watson

## OPERA NORTH
Grand Theatre, 46 New Briggate, Leeds LS1 6NU
Tel: 0113 243 9999 Fax: 0113 244 0418 (admin)
0113 243 5745 (Tech) Telex: 265871
Email: 74:MUS252
Company Director: Richard Mantle
Controller of Planning: Christine Chibnall
Technical Director: Rick Green
Music Adviser: Elgar Howarth
Head of Marketing: Richard Whitehouse
Head of Community Education: Dominic Gray
Production Manager: Ray Hain
Company Manager: Jane Bonner

## OPERA RARA
134-146 Curtain Road, London EC2A 3AR
Tel: 0171 613 2858 Fax: 0171 613 2261
Musical Director: Patric Schmid

## PAVILION OPERA
Thorpe Tilney Hall, Thorpe Tilney,
Near Lincoln LN4 3SL
Tel: 01526 378 231 Fax: 01526 378315

## PHOENIX DANCE COMPANY
3, St.Peters Buildings, St.Peters Square,
Leeds LS9 8AH
Tel: 0113 242 3486 Fax: 0113 244 4736
Email: phoenix@dircon.co.uk
Web Site: www.phoenix.dircon.co.uk
Contact: Dawn Fuller
A contemporary repertory company of 11 dancers,
touring on the middle scale nationally and
internationally.

## PICCOLA OPERA
Park Hills, 6 Clevelands Park, Northam, Bideford,
Devon EX39 3QH
Tel: 01237 425217
Director: Kenneth Campbell
Mainly student productions of Italian and French Opera
in the original language.

## PLAN B
Dundee Arts Centre, St.Mary Place, Dundee DD1 5RB
Tel: 01334 654866
Contact: Amanda Chinn

## POWYS DANCE
The Dance Centre, Arlais Road, Llandrindod Wells,
Powys LD1 5HE
Tel/Fax: 01597 824370
Manager: Louise Ingham

## RAMBERT DANCE COMPANY
94 Chiswick High Road, London W4 1SH
Tel: 0181 995 4246 Fax: 0181 747 8323
Directors: Christopher Bruce (Artistic),
Christopher Nourse (Executive)
Director of Finance & Administration: Geoff Hunt
Director of Marketing: Jackie Friend
Development Manager: Ellen Plant
Education Manager: Sarah Dekker

## ROMANSKA
Flat 6 1 Little Russell Street, London WC1A 2HR
Tel/Fax: 0171 436 8497
Email: mimische@compuserve.com
Contacts: Stephen Rouse, Natasha Crawford
Specialising in Ukranian, Spanish and Gypsy Dance.
Romanska dancers are available for theatre, film,
cabaret, festival and school performances.

## ALEXANDER ROY
## LONDON BALLET THEATRE
North House, 69 Eton Avenue, London NW3 3EU
Tel: 0171 586 2498 Fax: 0171 722 9942
Artistic Director: Alexander Roy
Associate Director: Christina Gallea
London based company which undertakes both British
and regional tours and international tours on a world-
wide basis. Company of 10-16 performs both classical
and contemporary ballet-theatre productions.

## ROYAL OPERA HOUSE
Floral Street Covent Garden London WC2E 9DD
Tel 0171 212 9123
Props: Royal Opera House, Covent Garden, Ltd
Closed for redevelopment until late 1999, meanwhile
The Royal Opera & The Royal Ballet will perform in
other venues in London, regionally and abroad. For
information please phone the above number.

## SCOTTISH BALLET
261 West Princes Street, Glasgow G4 9EE
Tel: 0141 331 2931 Fax: 0141 331 2629
Email: scotballet@msn.com
Web Site: www.scottishballet.uk.com
Chairman: Peg Beveridge
Acting Artistic Director: Kenneth Burke
Managing Director: Norman L. Quirk
Director of Marketing & Press: Roberta Doyle
Head of Finance: Renton Thomson, C.A.
Music Director: Alan Barker

## SCOTTISH OPERA
39 Elmbank Crescent, Glasgow G2 4PT
Tel: 0141 248 4567 Fax: 0141 221 8812
Chairman: Sandy Orr
General Director: Ruth MacKenzie
Music Director: Richard Armstrong

## TANI MORENA
Info: 0181 452 0407
Studio in the West End of London.

## TEMUJIN DANCE COMPANY
The Downshall Centre, Aldborough Road South,
Seven Kings, Ilford, Essex IG3 8HZ
Tel: 0181 599 7726 Fax: 0181 599 1288
Contact: Jo Walker, Temujin Gill
Specialising in Traditional Jazz Dance which includes
Tap, Charleston, Blues and the acrobatic Lindy Hop.

## TRIPSICHORE PERFORMING COMPANY
143 Sandringham Road, London NW2 5EJ
Tel: 0181 459 2416 Fax: 0181 621 4082
Email: Tripsichore@msn.com
Artistic Director: Edward Clark
Performers: Martin McDougall, Diana Harland, Desiree
Kingerod, Claire Best, Elizabeth Tullock,
Gideon Reeve.
Perform as Tripsichore Yoga Theatre.

## UNION DANCE COMPANY
Culturally Diverse Contemporary Dance
Marylebone Dance Studio, 12 Lisson Grove,
London NW1 6TS
Tel: 0171 724 5765 Fax: 0171 324 8911
Artistic Director: Corrine Bougaard
Administrative Director: Pippa Bound
Education Officer: Rachel Attfield

## WELSH NATIONAL OPERA
John Street, Cardiff CF1 4SP
Tel: 01222 464666 Fax: 01222 483050
Chairman: The Lord Davies of Llandinam
General Director: Anthony Freud
Musical Director: Carlo Rizzi
Director of Opera Planning: Isobel Murphy
Director of Administration: Geoffrey Rowe
Technical Director: Alan Parr
Company Manager: Barbara Stuart

## WEXFORD FESTIVAL OPERA
Theatre Royal, High Street, Wexford,
Tel: 00 353 53 22144 Fax: 00 353 53 24289
Chief Executive: Jerome Hynes

## YORKSHIRE DANCE CENTRE
3, St.Peters Building, St.Peters Square,
Leeds LS9 8AH
Tel: 0113 243 9867 Fax: 0113 259 5700
Email: admin@yorkshiredance.org.uk
Web Site: http://www.yorkshiredance.org.uk
General Manager: Catherine Woodall
Marketing Officer: Cathy O'Neill
Classes and workshops from beginners to
professionals. Also studio hire for auditions,
rehearsals, etc. Phone for details and free programme.
Also hot desks for short or long term letting. Flexible
way of hiring individual office spaces. Fully accessible.
Meeting room hire and reception & administration
services.

# ORCHESTRAS

### THE ACADEMY OF ANCIENT MUSIC
10 Brookside, Cambridge CB2 1JE
Tel: 01223 301509 Fax: 01223 327377
Email: administrator@aam.co.uk
Director: Christopher Hogwood
Assistant Director & Concert Master: Andrew Manze
Associate Conductor: Paul Goodwin
General Manager: Christopher Lawrence
Concerts & Tours Manager: Fiona Seers
Administrator: Madeleine Holmes

### ACADEMY OF LONDON
Studio 26, Building 56, GEC Estate, East Lane,
Wembley, Middlesex HA9 7PX
Tel: 0181 908 4348 Fax: 0181 908 4713
Conductor: Richard Stamp

### ACADEMY OF ST MARTIN IN THE FIELDS
Raine House, Raine Street, London E1 9RG
Tel: 0171 702 1377 Fax: 0171 481 0228
Music/Artistic Director: Sir Neville Marriner
Artistic Directors: Iona Brown, Kenneth Sillito

### ACADEMY OF THE LONDON MOZARTEUM
7 Woodland Glade, Farnham Common,
Buckinghamshire SL2 3RG
Tel: 01753 648113 Fax: 01753 648114

### AEOLIAN SINFONIA (23-70)
25 Roy Road, Northwood, Middlesex HA6 1EQ
Tel: 01923 828055
Music Director: Philip Gibson

### ALL SOULS ORCHESTRA
All Souls Music Office, St Pauls Church, Robert Adam
Street, London W1M 5AH
Tel: 0171 487 3508 Fax: 0171 224 6087
Music Director/Principal Conductor: Noel H Tredinnick

### AMBACHE CHAMBER ORCHESTRA
9 Beversbrook Road, London N19 4QG
Tel: 0171 263 4027
Music Director: Diana Ambacke
General Manager: Heather Baxtor

### AMICI CHAMBER ORCHESTRA
20 Oakhill Drive, Welwyn, Hertfordshire AL6 9NW
Tel: 01438 715740
Music Director/Principal Conductor: Nigel Springthorpe

### BBC CONCERT ORCHESTRA
The Hippodrome, North End Road, London NW11 7RP
Tel: 0171 765 4010 Fax: 0171 765 4929
General Manager: Ian Maclay
Orchestra Manager: Adrian Evett
Promotions and Marketing Manager: Sarah Biggs

### BBC NATIONAL ORCHESTRA OF WALES
Broadcasting House, Landaff, Cardiff CF5 2YQ
Tel: 01222 322442 Fax: 01222 322575
Music Director: Mark Wigglesworth

Manager: Byron Jenkins

### BBC PHILARMONIC
New Broadcasting House, Oxford Road,
Manchester M60 1SJ
Tel: 0161 244 4005 Fax: 0161 244 4010

### BBC SCOTTISH SYMPHONY ORCHESTRA
Broadcasting House, Queen Margaret Drive,
Glasgow G12 8DG
Tel: 0141 338 2606 Fax: 0141 307 4312
Chief Conductor: Osmo Vanska
Prinicpal Guest Conductor: Martyn Brabbins
Manager: Alan Davis

### BBC SYMPHONY ORCHESTRA
Maida Vale Studios, Delaware Road, London W9 2LG
Tel: 0171 765 5751 Fax: 0171 286 3251
General Manager: Louise Badger

### BELMONT ENSEMBLE OF LONDON
30b Belmont Road, London N15 3TL
Tel: 0181 881 2995
Music Director: Peter Gilbert-Dyson
Administrator: Rebekah Gilbert-Dyson

### BIRMINGHAM ENSEMBLE
16 Yew Tree Road, Birmingham B15 2LX
Tel: 0121 440 5164
Artistic Director: Peter Thomas
Administrator: Constanza Lezama

### BIRMINGHAM SINFONIETTA
41 St Agnes Road, Birmingham B3 3RP
Tel: 0121 449 0225
Music Director: Jeremy Ballard
Orchestral Manager: Susan Savage

### BOURNEMOUTH SYMPHONY ORCHESTRA/BOURNEMOUTH SINFONIETTA
2 Seldown Lane, Poole, Dorset BH15 1UF
Tel: 01202 670611 Fax: 01202 687235
Web Site: www.orchestras.co.uk
Managing Director: Vacant

### BRANDENBURG CONSORT
97 Mill Lane, Lower Earley, Reading,
Berkshire RG6 3UH
Tel: 0118 935 2595 Fax: 0118 935 2627
Email: roy.goodman@virgin.net
Web Site: http://freespace.virgin.net/roy.goodman
Music Director: Roy Goodman
Administrator: Steven Jones

### BRANDENURG SINFONIA
57 Kingswood Road, London SW19 3ND
Tel: 0181 542 1661 Fax: 0181 540 1103
Artistic Director: Robert Porter

## THE BRITISH CONCERT ORCHESTRA

The British Concert Orchestra (Founded 1945) Ltd
147 Haling Park Road, South Croydon,
Surrey CR2 6NN
Tel: 0181 688 4605 Fax: 0181 667 0607
Orchestra Manager: Peter Craen

## BRITTEN SINFONIA

12d Kings Parade, Cambridge CB2 1SJ
Tel: 01223 300795 Fax: 01223 302092
Email: info@brittensinfonia.demon.co.uk
Artistic Director: Nicholas Cleobury
General Manager: David Butcher
Concerts Manager: Helen Thompson

## CERDDORION (THE MUSICIANS TOURING COMPANY)

Ty-wrth-y-Coed, Cwmystwyth, Aberystwyth,
Dyfed SY23 4AF
Tel/Fax: 01974 282631
Director: Robert Spearing
Administrator: Joanna Medcalf

## CHAMBER ORCHESTRA OF EUROPE

8 Southampton Place, London WC1A 2EA
Tel: 0171 831 2326 Fax: 0171 831 8248
Artistic Adviser: Claudio Abbado
General Manager: June Megennis
Personnel/Planning Manager: Simon Fletcher
Tours Manager: Christopher Smith-Gillard

## CHELTENHAM INTERNATIONAL FESTIVAL OF MUSIC

3 - 18 July 1999
Cheltenham Arts Festivals Ltd, Town Hall, Imperial
Square, Cheltenham, Gloucestershire GL50 1QA
Admin: 01242 521621 BO: 01242 227979
Fax: 01242 573902
Artistic Director: Michael Berkeley
Festival Organiser: Kim Berkeley
Principal Venues: Town Hall (cap: 1,000), Pittville
Pump Room (cap: 400) &
Everyman Theatre (cap: 650)

## CITY OF PETERBOROUGH SYMPHONY ORCHESTRA

55 Sapperton, Werrington, Peterborough PE4 5BS
Tel: 01733 576797 Fax: 01733 755939
Contact: Mrs Jackie Over
Conductor: Norman Beedie

## COLLEGIUM MUSICUM 90

71 Priory Road, Kew, Surrey TW9 3DH
Tel: 0181 940 7086 Fax: 0181 332 0879
Music Directors: Richard Hickox, Simon Standage
General Manager: Francesca McManus

## CONSORT OF LONDON

36 Minsterley Avenue, Shepperton,
Middlesex TW17 8QT
Tel: 01932 784925 Fax: 01932 782589
General Manager/Music
Director: Robert Haydon Clarke

## CORELLI CHAMBER ORCHESTRA

155 Hewlett Road, Cheltenham,
Gloucestershire GL52 6UD
Tel: 01242 570383
Director: Warwick Cole
General Manager: Rachel Abbess

## ARTHUR DAKIN ORCHESTRAS

The Old Posthouse, Hammond Street, Mappowder,
Sturminster Newton, Dorset DT10 2EH
Tel: 01258 817802 Fax: 01258 817844

## DANTE ALIGHIERI ORCHESTRA

East West Arts Ltd, 93b Cambridge Gardens,
London W10 6JE
Tel: 0181 960 5889 Fax: 0181 968 5541
Music Director: Anup Kumar Biswas

## EAST OF ENGLAND ORCHESTRA

Beaufort St. Business Centre, Beaufort Street,
Derby DE21 6AX
Tel: 01332 207570 Fax: 01332 207569
Email: orchestra@eoeo.freeserve.co.uk
Principal Conductor: Nicholas Kok
General Manager: Peter Helps

## ENGLISH BACH FESTIVAL ORCHESTRA

15 South Eaton Place, London SW1W 9ER
Tel: 0171 730 5925 Fax: 0171 730 1456
Artistic Director: Lina Lalandi

## ENGLISH BAROQUE ORCHESTRA

57 Kingswood Road, London SW19 3ND
Tel: 0181 542 1661 Fax: 0181 540 1103
Contact: Robert Porter

## ENGLISH BAROQUE SOLOISTS

Monteverdi Choir and Orchestra Ltd
61-63 Wandsworth High Street, London SW18 2PT
Tel: 0181 871 4750 Fax: 0181 871 4751
Email: montev@compuserve.com
Acting General Manager: Howard Gough

## ENGLISH CHAMBER ORCHESTRA

2 Coningsby, London W5 4HR
Tel: 0181 840 6565 Fax: 0181 567 7198
Principal Conductor: Jeffrey Tate

## ENGLISH CLASSICAL PLAYERS

25b Epsom Lane South, Tadworth, Surrey KT20 5TA
Tel/Fax: 01737 813273 Fax: 01737 215676
Muisc Director: Jonathan Brett
Administrator: Lyn Mumford

## ENGLISH CONCERT

8 St.George's Terrace, London NW1 8XJ
Tel: 0171 911 0905 Fax: 0171 911 0904
Artistic Director: Trevor Pinnock

## ENGLISH FESTIVAL ORCHESTRA

151 Mount View Road, London N4 4JT
Tel: 0181 341 6408 Fax: 0181 340 0021
General Manager: Trevor Ford

Concert Manager: Marianne Barton

## ENGLISH HAYDN ORCHESTRA
14 Upper Bar, Newport, Shropshire TF10 7EJ
Tel: 01952 825235 Fax: 01952 814734
Director: John Reid
Period Instruments

## THE ENGLISH HERITAGE ORCHESTRA
Hollybank, 5 The Orchard, Kislingbury NN7 4BG
Tel: 01604 830679/832461 Fax: 01604 830679
Music Director: Graham Mayo
Administrator: Jackie Mayo

## ENGLISH MOZART PLAYERS
28 Salutary Mount, Exeter EX1 2QE
Tel/Fax: 01392 275476
Conductor/Music Director: Antony Le Fleming

## ENGLISH NATIONAL OPERA ORCHESTRA
London Coliseum, St.Martin's Lane,
London WC2N 4ES
Tel: 0171 836 0111 Fax: 0171 836 8379
Orchestra Manager: Ian Killick
Assistant Orchestra Manager: Deborah West

## ENGLISH NORTHERN PHILARMONIA
The Orchestra of Opera North, Grand Theatre,
46 New Briggate, Leeds LS1 6NU
Tel: 0113 243 9999 Fax: 0113 244 0418

## ENGLISH PHILHARMONIA ORCHESTRA
57 Kingswood Road, London SW19 3ND
Tel: 0181 542 1661 Fax: 0181 540 1103
Music Director: Leon Lovett
Manager: Robert Porter

## ENGLISH SINFONIA
1 Wedgwood Court, Stevenage SG1 4QR
Tel: 01438 350990 Fax: 01438 350930
Web Site: www.Stevenage.gov.uk/EnglishSinfonia
Principal Conductor: Nicolae Moldoveanu
Leader: Janice Graham
Cheif Executive: Graham Pfaff

## ENGLISH SINFONIETTA
The Barn, Layston Park, Royston,
Hertfordshire SG8 9DS
Tel: 01763 242847 Fax: 01763 248048
General Manager: Graham Pfaff

## ENGLISH STRING & SYMPHONY ORCHESTRA
Rockliffe House, 40 Church Street, Malvern WR14 2AZ
Tel: 01684 560696/560045 Fax: 01684 560656
General Manager: Elizabeth Wilde

## EUROPEAN UNION BAROQUE ORCHESTRA
Hordley, Wootton, Woodstock OX20 1EP
Tel: 01993 812111 Fax: 01993 812911
Email: info@eubo.org.uk
Web Site: www.eubo.org.uk
Musical Director: Roy Goodman
General Administrator: Paul James

## EUROPEAN UNION CHAMBER ORCHESTRA
Fermain House, Dolphin Street, Colyton,
Devon EX13 6LU
Tel: 01297 552272 Fax: 01297 553744
Director General: Ambrose Miller

## EUROPEAN WOMEN'S ORCHESTRA
Toynbee Studios, 28 Commercial Street,
London E1 6LS
Tel: 0181 800 4131 Fax: 0181 802 6614
Conductor/Music Director: Odaline de la Martinez
Administrator: Jayne Rollason

## EX CATHEDRA BAROQUE ORCHESTRA
Suite 303, Jewellery Business Centre,
95 Spencer Street, Birmingham B18 6DA
Tel: 0121 523 1025 Fax: 0121 523 1026
Conductor: Jeffrey Skidmore
General Manager: Justin Lee

## GABRIELI CONSORT AND PLAYERS
Foresters Hall, 25-27 Westow Street,
London SE19 3RY
Tel: 0181 771 7974 Fax: 0181 771 7973
Email: gabrieliconsort@compuserve.com
Web Site: www.gabrieli.com
Director: Paul McCreesh
General Manager: Anita Crowe

## GUILDFORD PHILHARMONIC ORCHESTRA
Millmead House, Millmead, Guildford, Surrey GU2 5BB
Tel: 01483 444666
Email: guildfordphil@guildford.gov.uk
Web Site: www.guildfordphilharmonic.co.uk
Principal Conductor: En Shao
General Manager: Nicola Goold

## HALLE CONCERTS SOCIETY
The Bridgewater Hall, Manchester M2 3WS
Tel: 0161 237 7000 Fax: 0161 237 7029

## THE HANOVER BAND
45 Portland Road, Hove, East Sussex BN3 5DQ
Tel: 01273 206978 Fax: 01273 329636
Artistic Director: Caroline Brown

## HAVANT CHAMBER ORCHESTRA
152 West Street, Havant PO9 1LP
Tel: 01705 483228
Music Director: Peter Craddock

## HAVANT SYMPHONY ORCHESTRA
152 West Street, Havant PO9 1LP
Tel: 01705 483228
Music Director: Peter Craddock

## ISLE OF WIGHT SYMPHONY ORCHESTRA
5 Melcombe House, Queens Road, Cowes,

Isle of Wight PO31 8BW
Tel: 01983 290495
Administration: Jean Kirkpatrick

## THE BERT KAEMPFERT ORCHESTRA
PO Box 389, Banstead, Surrey SM7 1RT
Tel: 0181 393 4580 Fax: 0181 786 7884
Email: tony-fisher@pavilion.co.uk
Director: Tony Fisher

## THE KING'S CONSORT
34 St.Mary's Grove. London W4 3LN
Tel: 0181 995 9994 Fax: 0181 995 2115
Email: info@the-kings-consort.org.uk
Web Site: www.the-kings-consort.org.uk
Artistic Director: Robert King
Development Director: Nicky Oppenheimer
Artistic Manager: Edward Hossack
Administrator: Elizabeth Baines

## KREISLER STRING ORCHESTRA
57 Sunnyside Road, Chesham,
Buckinghamshire HP5 2AR
Tel: 01494 792572
Contact: Robert Wollard

## LANGHAM CHAMBER ORCHESTRA
9 Weylea Avenue, Burpham, Guildford,
Surrey GU4 7YN
Tel: 01483 573705

## LITTLE SYMPHONY ORCHESTRA
14 Beaumont Road, Purley, Surrey CR8 2EG
Tel: 0181 668 5883
Music Director: Darrell Davison

## LONDON CAMERATA
38 Vicarage Lane, Kingsthorpe,
Northampton NN2 6QS
Tel: 01604 712209
Music Director: Paul Hilliam

## LONDON CHAMBER PLAYERS
PO Box 84, London NW11 8AL
Tel/Fax: 0181 455 6799
Music Director: Adrian Sunshine

## LONDON CHAMBER SYMPHONY
Room 12, Second Floor, Toynbee Studios, 28
Commercial Street, London E1 6IS
Tel: 0171 247 2950 Fax: 0171 247 2956

## LONDON CHANTICLEER ORCHESTRA
Tickerage Castle, Pound Lane, Framfield, Uckfield,
East Sussex TN22 5RT
Tel: 01825 890348
Musical Director: Dr Ruth Gipps

## LONDON CITY CHAMBER ORCHESTRA
The Old School, 3-5 Bridge Street, Hadleigh,
Suffolk IP7 6BY
Tel: 01473 822596 Fax: 01473 824175
Administrator: M H V Reckitt

Publicity: Kathleen Grant
Music Director: Thomas McIntosh

## LONDON CONCERT ORCHESTRA
Raymond Gubbay Limited. 176a High Street, Barnet,
Hertfordshire EN5 5SZ
Tel: 0181 441 8940 Fax: 0181 441 0887

## LONDON FESTIVAL ORCHESTRA
The Warehouse, 13 Theed Street, South Bank,
London SE1 8ST
Tel: 0171 928 9251 Fax: 0171 928 9252
Email: lforchestra@compuserve.com
Web Site: www.lforch.org
Artistic Director: Ross Pople
General Manager: Ian Pressland
Education and Outreach: Beccy Jones

## LONDON HANDEL ORCHESTRA
The Coach House, Drury Lane, Redmarley d'Abitot,
Gloucestershire GL19 3JX
Tel/Fax: 01531 650616

## LONDON JUPITER ORCHESTRA
57 White Horse Road, London E1 0ND
Tel: 0171 790 5883 Fax: 0171 265 9170
Conductor: Gregory Rose

## LONDON LYRIC ORCHESTRA
4a Harewood Road, South Croydon, Surrey CR2 7AL
Tel/Fax: 0181 688 2430
Orchestral Manager: Judith Wordsworth

## LONDON MOZART PLAYERS
92 Chatsworth Road, Croydon CR0 1HB
Tel: 0181 686 1996 Fax: 0181 686 2187
Managing Director: Ian Lush
Music Director: Matthias Barnert

## LONDON ORPHEUS ORCHESTRA
2 Tenby Mansions, Nottingham Street,
London W1M 3RD
Tel: 0171 486 1929

## LONDON PHILANOVA ORCHESTRA
43 Briton Hill Road, Sanderstead, Surrey CR2 0JJ
Tel: 0181 657 1662
Music Director: Philip Winter

## THE LONDON PHILHARMONIC
35 Doughty Street, London WC1N 2AA
Tel: 0171 546 1600 Fax: 0171 546 1601

## LONDON PRO ARTE ORCHESTRA
121 Addiscombe Court Road, Croydon,
Surrey CR0 6TX
Tel: 0181 655 3950 Fax: 0181 654 9137

## LONDON SCHUBERT ORCHESTRA
27 Kendal Steps, St.Georges Fields, London W2 2YE
Tel: 0171 4052 7860 Fax: 0171 402 7172
Mobile: 0836 294833

Email: status.cymbal@argonet.co.uk

## LONDON SCHUBERT PLAYERS
72 Warwick Gardens, London W14 8PP
Tel/Fax: 0171 603 1396
Musical Director: Anda Anastasescu

## LONDON SINFONIA
Sinfonia, 1 The Bridle Path, Conventry CV5 9QF
Tel: 01203 404696
Musical Director: Gordon Heard

## LONDON SINFONIETTA
2nd Floor, Clove Building, 4 Maguire Street,
London SE1 2NQ
Tel: 0171 378 8123 Fax: 0171 378 0937
Principal Conductor: Markus Stenz
Managing Director: Cathy Graham

## LONDON VIENNESE CONCERT ORCHESTRA
52 Helen Avenue, Feltham, Middlesex TW14 9LB
Tel/Fax: 0181 751 0417

## MANCHESTER CAMERATA
Zion Arts Centre, Stretford Road, Manchester M15 5ZA
Tel: 0161 226 8696 Fax: 0161 226 8600
Email: mancam@compuserve.com
Web Site: www.manchestercamerata.org.uk
General Manager: Lucy Potter

## MANCHESTER MOZART ORCHESTRA
Zion Arts Centre, Stretford Road, Manchester M15 5ZA
Tel: 0161 226 8696 Fax: 0161 226 8600
General Manager: Lucy Potter

## MIDLAND PHILHARMONIC ORCHESTRA
Ridgeway House, Great Brighton,
Northampton NN7 4JA
Tel: 01604 770511 Fax: 01604 770022

## MIDLANDS SYMPHONY ORCHESTRA
14 Upper Bar, Newport, Shropshire TF10 7EJ
Tel: 01952 825235 Fax: 01952 814734

## MILTON KEYNES CITY ORCHESTRA
Acorn House, 369 Midsummer Boulevard,
Central Milton Keynes, MK9 3HP
Tel: 01908 692777 Fax: 01908 230099

## MORAY CHAMBER ORCHESTRA
Kildonan, Young Street, Elgin, Moray IV30 1TH
Tel: 01343 543531
Director: Peter Zanre

## MOZART ORCHESTRA
Sinfonia, 1 The Bridle Path, Coventry CV5 9QF
Tel: 01203 404696
Music Director: Gordon Heard

## MUSIC PROJECTS/LONDON
11 Elmwood Road, Chiswick, London W4 3DY
Tel: 0181 994 9528 Fax: 0181 994 9595

## NEW CHAMBER ORCHESTRA
130 High Street, Oxford OX1 4DH
Tel: 01865 724448 Fax: 01865 722953
Music Director: Andrew Zreczycki
Chair: Philip Vincent

## NEW ENGLISH CONCERT ORCHESTRA
23 Hitchin Street, Biggleswade,
Bedfordshire SG18 8AX
Tel: 01767 316521 Fax: 01767 317221
Email: neco@lindsaymusic.co.uk

## NEW ENGLISH ORCHESTRA
14 Woodbine Road, Barbourne, Worcester WR1 3JB
Tel/Fax: 01905 613771
Contact: Mrs A Hawcutt

## NEW LONDON ORCHESTRA
4 Lower Belgrave Street, London SW1W 0LJ
Tel: 0171 823 5523 Fax: 0171 823 6373
Musical Director: Ronald Corp

## NEW QUEEN'S HALL ORCHESTRA
c/o Manygate Management, 13 Cotswold Mews,
30 Battersea Square, London SW11 3RA
Tel: 0171 233 7265 Fax: 0171 585 2830

## THE NEW WIND ORCHESTRA
119 Woolstone Road, Forest Hill, London SE23 2TQ
Tel: 0181 699 1101 Fax: 0181 207 4554

## NORTHERN CHAMBER ORCHESTRA
1 Crescent View, Hall Bank, Buxton,
Derbyshire SK17 6EN
Tel: 01298 70395 Fax: 01298 72289 BO: 01298 73700

## THE ORCHESTRA AT BLACKHEATH
16 Shooters Hill Road, Blackheath, London SE3 7BD
Tel: 0181 858 9311 Fax: 0181 853 5936
Conductor: Rupert Bond
General Manager: Prue Corp

## ORCHESTRA DA CAMERA
41 Fishponds Road, Kenilworth,
Warwickshire CV8 1EY
Tel: 01926 858187
Music Director: Kenneth Page

## ORCHESTRA OF THE AGE OF ENLIGHTENMENT
5th Floor, Westcombe House, 56-58 Whitcomb Street,
London WC2H 7DN
Tel: 0171 930 0646 Fax: 0171 930 0626

## ORCHESTRA OF WELSH NATIONAL OPERA
John Street, Cardiff CF1 4SP
Tel: Main Line: 01222 464666
Orchestral Office: 01222 451574 Fax: 01222 483050

Manager: Peter Harrap

## ORCHESTRE REVOLUTIONNAIRE ET ROMANTIQUE
(See also English Baroque Soloists)
Monteverdi Choir & Orchestra Ltd
61-63 Wandsworth High Street, London SW18 2PT
Tel: 0181 871 4750 Fax: 0181 871 4751
Email: montev@compuserve.com
Acting General Manager: Howard Gough

## THE PALM COURT THEATRE ORCHESTRA & COMPANY
Winkton Lodge Cottage, Winkton, Christchurch,
Dorset BH23 7AR
Tel: 01202 484185 Fax: 01202 471920
Management: Palm Court Theatre Productions

## PHILHARMONIA ORCHESTRA
Philharmonia Ltd. 76 Great Portland Street,
London W1N 6HA
Tel: 0171 580 9961 Fax: 0171 436 5517
Email: philharmonia@philharmonia.co.uk
Web Site: www.philharmonia.co.uk
Managing Director: David Whelton

## THE PICCADILLY DANCE ORCHESTRA
50 Albert Street, Windsor, Berkshire SL4 5BU
Tel: 01753 855828 Fax: 01753 855801
Mobile: 0802 702232
Stylish and swinging stage and dance orchestra,
specialising in the 20's, 30's and 40's.

## THE ROSEBERY ORCHESTRA
51 Stradella Road, London SE24 9HL
Tel: 0171 274 8214 Fax: 0171 771 0957
Email: clarissa@mcmail.com
General Manager: Clarissa Melville

## ROYAL LIVERPOOL PHILHARMONIC ORCHESTRA
Philharmonic Hall, Hope Street, Liverpool L1 9BP
Tel: 0151 709 2895 Fax: 0151 709 0918

## ROYAL PHILHARMONIC ORCHESTRA
16 Clerkenwell Green, London EC1R 0DP
Tel: 0171 608 2381 Fax: 0171 608 1226
Managing Director: John Manger
Head of Development & Sponsorship: Sara Lorn
Head of Concert & Recordings: Simon Foster

## ROYAL SCOTTISH NATIONAL ORCHESTRA
Henry Wood Hall, 73 Claremont Street,
Glasgow G3 7HA
Tel: 0144 226 3868 Fax: 0141 221 4317
Email: rsno@glasgow.almac.co.uk
Web Site: www.scot-art.org/rsno

## SCOTTISH EARLY MUSIC CONSORT
11 Sandyford Place, Glasgow G3 7NB
Tel: 0141 221 4740 Fax: 0141 221 4786

## VICTOR SILVESTER JUNIOR AND THE VICTOR SILVESTER ORCHESTRA
Fir Tree Cottage, Tibberton,
Gloucestershire GL19 3AQ
Tel: 01452 790514

## SINFONIA OF LONDON
Pigeon House Meadow, 27 Grove Road, Beaconsfield,
Buckinghamshire HP9 1UR
Tel: 01494 677934 Fax: 01494 670443
General Manager: Peter Willison
Secretary: Sally Birkett

## SINFONIA VERDI
60 Cowper Road, Harpenden, Hertfordshire AL5 5NG
Tel/Fax: 01582 462137
Musical Director: David Murphy

## SOUTH YORKSHIRE SYMPHONY ORCHESTRA
1 Springfield Close, Eckington, Sheffield S21 4GS
Tel: 01246 431562
Email: paulsyso88aol.com

## ST. JAMES'S BAROQUE PLAYERS
200 Broomwood Road, London SW11 6JY
Tel: 0171 228 6388 Fax: 0171 738 1706

## STEINITZ BACH PLAYERS
London Bach Society
73 High Street, Old Oxted, Surrey RH8 9LN
Tel: 01883 717372 Fax: 01883 715851
Administrator: Mrs Margaret Steinitz
Orchestral Manager: Shauni McGregor

## PETER STUART ORCHESTRA
6 Coxwold Hill, Wetherby, West Yorkshire LS22 7PX
Tel/Fax: 01937 582573
Email: psmusic@globalnet.co.uk
Web Site: www.users.globalnet.co.uk~psmusic

## SURREY CHAMBER ORCHESTRA
25b Epsom Lane South, Tadworth, Surrey KT20 5TA
Tel: 01737 813273 Fax: 01737 215676
Music Director: Jonathan Brett
Administration: Lyn Mumford

## TAUNTON SINFONIETTA
29 French Weir Avenue, Taunton TA1 1XQ
Tel: 01823 275020
Chairman: Robin Carpenter

## TAVERNER PLAYERS
Ibex House, 42-46 Minories, London EC3N 1DY
Tel: 0171 481 2103 Fax: 0171 481 2865

## THAMES CHAMBER ORCHESTRA
41 Shirley Drive, Hounslow, Middlesex TW3 2HD
Tel: 0181 894 2068

## ULSTER ORCHESTRA
Elmwood Hall at Queen's, 89 University Road,

Belfast BT7 1NF
Tel: 01232 664535 Fax: 01232 662761
Chief Executive: Michael Henson
Principal Conductor/Artistic Adviser: Dmitry Sitkovetsky

## VIENNESE GALA ORCHESTRA

Five Bells Cottage, 132 St.Leonard's Street,
West Malling, Kent ME19 6PD
Tel: 01732 874285 Fax: 01732 874288
Artistic Director: John Bradbury
General Manager: Robert McIntosh
Directed from the violin in a traditional manner, John
Bradbury presents classics from the Viennese period.

## VIRTUOSI OF ENGLAND

14 Beaumont Road, Purley, Surrey CR8 2EG
Tel/Fax: 0181 668 5883
Musical Director: Darrell Davison

## VIVALDI CONCERTANTE

35 Laurel Avenue, Potters Bar, Hertfordshire EN6 2AB
Tel: 01707 650735/643355
Director/Conductor: Joseph Pilbery

## WELSH CHAMBER ORCHESTRA

100 Ystrad Fawr, Bridgend,
Mid Glamorgan CF31 3HW
Tel: 01656 658891 Fax: 01656 876675
Administration: Barbara Parish

## WORTHING SYMPHONY

New Connaught Theatre Ltd, Connaught Theatre,
Union Place, Worthing, West Sussex BN11 1LG
Tel: 01903 231799 Fax: 01903 215337
Orchestra Administrator: David Smith
Principal Conductor: John Gibbons

## YORKSHIRE CONCERT ORCHESTRA

Torridon House, 104 Bradford Road, Wrenthorpe,
Wakefield WF1 2AH
Tel: 01924 371496
General Manager: Brian Greensmith

# PRINCIPAL FESTIVALS

### Aldeburgh Festival of Music & the Arts
11 - 27 June 1999
Aldeburgh Foundation, High Street, Aldeburgh, Suffolk
IP15 5AX
Tel: 01728 452935 Fax: 01728 452715
Email: enquiries@aldeburghfestivals.org
Chief Executive: Jonathan Reekie

### Bath Fringe Festival
28 May - 13 June 1999
Fringe Committee, c/o The Bell, Walcot Street, Bath
Tel: 01225 480079
Email: Pcondo@compuserve.com
Web Site: www.bathfringe.co.uk
Chairperson: David Stevenson

### Bath International Music Festival
21 May - 6 June 1998
5 Broad Street, Bath BA1 5LJ
Box Office: 01225 463362 Fax: 01225 310377
Director: Tim Joss
Bath International Music Festival was founded in 1948.
It presents a diverse programme of music featuring
some of the finest performers in the world. Classical,
Early, Opera, Jazz, Flamenco, World, Contemporary,
Folk, etc.
The festival takes place over 17days in the beautiful
georgian city of Bath. Please contact the festival for full
details.

### The BBC Henry Wood Promenade Concerts
July - Sept 1999
Press & Publicity Office: Room 4114, Broadcasting
House, London W1A 1AA
Tel: 0171 765 4296 Fax: 0171 765 0619
Email: proms@bbc.co.uk
Web Site: www.bbc.co.uk/proms/

### Bracknell Festival
2/3/4 July 1999
South Hill Park, Bracknell, Berkshire RG12 7PA
Tel: 01344 427272 BO: 01344 484123 Fax: 01344
411427
Contact: Simon Chatterton

### Bridlington Festival
East Riding of Yorkshire Council
County Hall, Beverley, East Yorkshire HU17 9BA
Tel: 01482 884938 Fax: 01482 884940
Contact: June Mitchell

### Brighton Festival
1 - 23 May 1999
Brighton Festival Office, 21-22 Old Steine, Brighton
BN1 1EL
Tel: 01273 292950/1/2 Fax: 01273 622453
Email: info@brighton-festival.org.uk
Web Site: www.brighton-festival.org.uk
Largest Arts Festival in England. Covers theatre,
music, opera, dance, literature, street theatre, film &
media, exhibitions.

### Buxton Opera Festival
July 1999
1 Crescent View, Hall Bank, Buxton, Derby SK17 6EN
Tel: 01298 70395 BO: 01298 72190 Fax: 01298 72289
General Manager: Glyn Foley

### Cambridge Folk Festival
30 July - 1 August 1999
Organisation: The Guildhall, Cambridge CB2 3QJ
Tel: 01223 457515 Fax: 01223 457529
Venue: Cherryhinton, Cambridge

### Chaucer Festival
13 April 1998 (Southwark) TBA (Canterbury)
Chaucer Heritage Centre, 22 St.Peter's Street,
Canterbury CT1 2BQ
Tel: 01227 470379 Fax: 01227 761416
Founder/Director: Martin Starkie
Festival Manager/Organiser: Philippe Wibrotte
The Festival was founded in 1985 by Martin Starkie to
further the enjoyment of the work and life of England's
first great writer, Geoffrey Chaucer. There are concerts,
art exhibitions, productions of the musical 'Canterbury
Tales', costumed cavalcades, fairs, illustrated talks,
walks and visits to Chaucer sites.

### Cheltenham Festival of Literature
8 - 24 October 1999
Cheltenham Arts Festivals Ltd, Town Hall, Imperial
Square, Cheltenham, Gloucestershire GL50 1QA
Admin: 01242 521621 BO: 01242 227979 Fax: 01242
573902
Artistic Director: John Walsh
Festival Organiser: Sarah Smyth
Principal Venues: Town Hall (cap: 1,000), Everyman
Theatre (cap: 650) & Playhouse (cap: 220)

### Chichester Festival Theatre and Minerva Theatre
Summer Festival Season of Plays May - September
1999
Festival Theatre, Oaklands Park, Chichester, West
Sussex PO19 4AP
Tel: 01243 784437 Fax: 01243 787288 BO: 01243
781312
Email: admin@cft.org.uk
Web Site: www.cft.org.uk
Festival Director: Andrew Welch
General Manager: Paul Rogerson
Production Manager: Christopher Bush-Bailey

### Chichester Festivities
2 -18 July 1999
Canon Gate House, South Street, Chichester, Sussex
PO19 1PU
Tel: 01243 785718 Fax: 01243 528356
Festival Administrator: Chichester Festivities
Contact: Amanda Sharp

### Chippenham Folk Festival
Festival Office, The Bridge Centre, Chippenham,
Wiltshire SN15 2AA

Tel: 01249 657190 (24 hours)
Email: chippfolk@aol.com
Web Site: http://members.aol.com/chippfolk/index.html
A traditional based folk festival set in the heart of
Chippenham beside the River Avon. Up to sixteen
venues used daily plus fringe events. 2-3,000 people
attend the festival which is in its 28th year. Concerts,
ceilidhs, dances, morris and ritual displays. Workshops
and sessions abound in a family based festival to suit
all ages.

### City of London Festival
22 June - 15 July 1999
Festival Office, Bishopsgate Hall, 230 Bishopsgate,
London EC2M 4QD
Tel: 0171 377 0540 Fax: 0171 377 1972
Email: cityfest@dircon.co.uk
Web Site: www.city-of-london-festival.org.uk
Festival Director: Michael Macleod

### Glyndebourne Festival Opera
May - August 1999
Glyndebourne, Lewes, East Sussex BN8 5UU
Tel: 01273 812321 Fax: 01273 812783
ADMINISTRATION:
General Director: Nicholas Snowman
Director of Productions: Graham Vick
Music Director: Andrew Davis, CBE
Technical Director: Peter Horne
Finance Director: Mrs Sarah Hopwood
House Manager: Julie Crocker
Press & Public Relations: Nicky Webb
Policy: Festival Opera Season
New Opera House opened in May 1994.
Please contact venue for further details.

### Greenwich & Docklands International Festival
2 - 18 July 1999
6 College Approach, Greenwich, London SE10 9HY
Tel: 0181 305 1818 Fax: 0181 305 1188
Email: greendock@globalnet.co.uk
Artistic Director: Bradley Hemmings
Executive Director: Christine Mathews-Sheen
Production Administrator: Jenny Lambert

### Harrogate International Festival
First two weeks of July/August
Festival Office, Royal Baths, Harrogate HG1 2RR
Tel: 01423 562303 Fax: 01423 521264
Email: info@harrogate-festival.org.uk
Festival Director: William Culver Dodds
General Administrator: Fiona Goh

### International Jazz Day
29 May 1999
Registered Office: 55b Medfield Street, London SW15
4JY
Tel/Fax: 0181 785 4741
Email: IJD2000@hotmail.com
Company Secretary: Simon Liebesny
Patrons: Cedar Walton and Michael Denny
Jazz Concerts, workshops and masterclasses.
Registered charity.

### King's Lynn Festival
22 - 31 July 1999
Festival Office: 27 King Street, King's Lynn, Norfolk
PE30 1ET
Tel: 01553 767557 Fax: 01553 767688
Contact: Joanne Rutterford

### The Leeds International Pianoforte Competition
7 - 23 September 2000
Pianoforte Competition Office, The University of Leeds,
Leeds LS2 9JT
Tel/Fax: 0113 244 6586 Telex: 556473 UNILDS G
Hon.Administrator: Francoise Logan

### London International Festival of Theatre
June/July 1999
19-20 Great Sutton Street, London EC1V 0DN
Tel: 0171 490 3965/4 Fax: 0171 490 3976

### London International Mime Festival
9 - 24 January 1999
35 Little Russell Street, London WC1A 2HH
Tel: 0171 637 5661 Fax: 0171 323 1151
Directors: Joseph Seelig & Helen Lannaghan

### London Jazz Festival
12 - 21 November 1999
4th Floor, Windsor House, 83 Kingsway, London
WC2B 6SD
Tel: 0171 405 9900 Fax: 0171 405 9911
Email: info@seriousltd.demon.co.uk
Contact: John Cumming

### Ludlow Festival
26 June - 11 July 1999
Festival Office, Castle Square, Ludlow, Shropshire SY8
1AY
Tel: 01584 875070 Fax: 01584
Festival Administrator: A.C.Baynon

### Manchester Festival
Late September - Early October 1999
Offices: Central Library, St.Peters Square, Manchester
M2 5PD
Tel: 0161 234 1944/1964 Fax: 0161 236 7952
Email: mcrfest@libraries.manchester.gov.uk
Web Site: www.manchester-festivals.org.uk
Pop/Jazz music, comedy, club culture, special events
and digital art.

### Minack Theatre Festival
24 May - 18 September 1999
Minack Theatre, Porthcurno, Penzance, Cornwall TR19
6JU
Tel: 01736 810694 Fax: 01736 810779
Email: info@minack.com
Web Site: www.minack.com/minack
Manager: Philip Jackson
A different play/musical/opera each week. Open-air
theatre on the cliffs between Penzance and Lands End.

### National Arts Day
Arts Day Trust, 3 Earl Road, London SW14 7JH

Tel: 0181 876 2161 Fax: 0181 878 4403
Administrator: Al Weil
The nation's day for the arts. This special day is set aside once each year on Min-Summer day, June 24th, with the aim of praising the level of participation in the awareness of the arts generally.

## National Dance Week
19 - 27 June 1998
15 Rosslyn Road, Billericay, Essex CM12 9JN
Tel/Fax: 01277 630760
National Co-ordinator: Vin Harrop
To celebrate the richness and diversity of dance of the differing cultures and traditions of the community of these Islands, by co-ordinating an annual week of dance for all to enjoy. To promote a greater understanding of dance as a means of self-expression and enjoyment, and to enhance professional training for young people in particular, through an annual County and Regional Councils' Dance Prize to be awarded to promising students from each county or region. These are to be known as the "Footsies" - and the winners, the "Footsie Laureates".

## National Student Drama Festival
7 - 14 April 1999 in Scarborough
20 Lansdowne Road, Muswell Hill, London N10 2AU
Tel: 0181 883 4586 Fax: 0181 883 7142
Email: clive@nsdf.skynet.co.uk
Web Site: http://www.nsdf.uk.internet
Festival Director: Clive Wolfe
Seven concentrated days of performances of outstanding student productions selected from the whole of UK and Ireland, plus a huge number and range of professionally led workshops, talks and discussions, plus daily magazine produced by festival participants. All open to non-students. Venues include the Stephen Joseph Theatre and the Spa. Sponsored by The Sunday Times, Scarborough Borough Council & the BBC Broadcast. Arts Council-funded.

## Open Air Theatre Shakespeare Season
May - September 1999
New Shakespeare Company, Open Air Theatre, Regent's Park, London NW1 4NP
Mgmt: 0171 935 5756/5884 BO: 0171 466 2431/1933
Fax: 0171 487 4562
Artistic & Managing Director: Ian Talbot
Capacity: 1,187 (plus seats on grass bank when performances sold out).

## Polesden Lacey Open Air Theatre Festival
12 June - 4 July 1999
Polesden Lacey Open Air Th., National Trust, Polesden Lacey, Dorking, Surrey RH5 6BD
Admin: 01342 716433 BO: 01372 457223

## Richmond Festival
c/o Langholm Lodge, 146 Petersham Road, Richmond, Surrey TW10 6UX
Tel: 0181 831 6138 Fax: 0181 940 7568
Details: c/o Nigel Cutting, Borough Arts Officer

## Round Festival
The International Festival of Theatre in the Round

Email: round@wamda.demon.co.uk
Web Site: www.actual.co.uk/round
Annual - Summer

## Salisbury Festival
75 New Street, Salisbury SP1 2PH
Tel: 01722 323883 Fax: 01722 410552
A multi arts festival with an em[phasis on music of all kinds (theatre, dance,circus) and outdoor events.

## St. Albans International Organ Festival
8 - 17 July 1999
PO Box 80, St.Albans Hertfordshire AL3 4HR
Tel/Fax: 01727 844765

## Wansbeck Festival
October 1999
Leisure Department, Wansbeck District Council, East View, Stakeford, Choppington, Northumberland NE62 5TR
Tel: 01670 819802 Fax: 01670 520457

## York Early Music Festival
2 - 11 July 1999
The Administrative Director, PO Box 226, York YO30 5ZU
Tel: 01904 658338 Fax: 01904 612631
Email: yemf@netcomuk.co.uk
Web Site: www.netcomuk.co.uk/~yemf/festival.html
Britain's largest festival of early music. Concerts in historic houses, churches throughout York. Plus illustrated lectures, walks & talks.

## Northern Ireland

## Belfast Festival at Queen's
13 - 29 November 1998
Festival House, 25 College Gardens, Belfast BT9 6BS
Northern Ireland
Tel: 01232 667687 Fax: 01232 663733
Email: festival@qxb.ac.uk
Executive Director: Robert Agnew
Assistant Executive Director: Rosie Turner

## Scotland

## Edinburgh Festival Fringe
8 - 30 August 1999
Festival Fringe Society Ltd. 180 High Street, Edinburgh EH1 1QS
Tel: 0131 226 5257 Fax: 0131 220 4205
Email: admin@edfringe.com
Web Site: www.edfringe.com

## Edinburgh International Festival
August 1999
Edinburgh Int'l Festival, 21 Market Street, Edinburgh EH1 1BW
Tel: 0131 473 2001

## Perth Festival of the Arts
May - June each year
3-5 High Street, Perth PH1 5JS Scotland
Tel: 01738 475295 Fax: 01738 475295
Email: artsfestival@perth.org.uk

Web Site: www.perth.org.uk/perth/festival/htm
Festival Administrator: Mrs Sandra Ralston

## Pitlochry Festival Theatre Season
14 May - 16 October 1999
Pitlochry Festival Theatre, Pitlochry, Perthshire PH16 5DR
Mgmt: 01796 473054 BO: 01796 472680
Festival Director: Clive Perry
Administrator: Sheila Harborth
Theatre and Box Office Manager: Margaret Pimie
Production Manager: Elaine Kyle
Marketing Officer Groups: Helen Stevenson
Marketing Officer: Charles Barron
Seats: 540 + 4 wheelchair spaces. Restaurant and bars open daily (not Sundays) during season. Parking for 120 cars and disabled 10.

*Wales*

## Fishguard Music Festival
23 July - 31 July 1999
Festival Office, Fishguard, Dyfed SA65 9BJ
Tel/Fax: 01348 873612

## Llangollen International Musical Eisteddfod
6 - 11 July 1999
Eisteddfod Office, Victoria Square, Llangollen, Clwyd LL20 8NG
Tel: 01978 860236 Fax: 01978 861300
Email: lime@celtic.co.uk
Web Site: www.llangollen.org.uk
Director of Marketing: Mrs M A Jones

# SMALL SCALE TOURING COMPANIES

**ABA DABA**
30 Upper Park Road, London NW3 2UT
Tel/Fax: 0171 722 5395

**ACTION SPACE MOBILE**
PO Box 73, Barnsley, South Yorkshire S75 1NE
Tel: 01226 384944
Artistic Director: Mary Turner

**ACTORS INCORPORATED**
19 Rectory Gardens, London SW4 0EE
Tel: 0171 978 1142
Contact: Richard Leighton

**ACTORS TOURING COMPANY**
Alford House, Aveline Street, London SE11 5DQ
Tel: 0171 735 8311 Fax: 0171 735 1031
Email: atc@cwcom.net
Artistic Director: Nick Philippou
Executive Producer: Gavin Barlow
Administrator: David Kelleher

**ALARMIST THEATRE**
Top Offices, 13a Western Road, Hove,
East Sussex BN3 1AE
Tel: 01273 208739 Fax: 01273 720894
Artistic Directors: Helena Uren and Stephen Plaice
Touring theatre producing new writing.

**ANIMUS PRODUCTIONS
(AKA "THE SECRET THEATRE")**
13 Corsham Street, London N1 6DP
Tel: 0171 253 3999
Artistic Director: Adam Henderson
Associate Director: Sean Aita
Producer: Brad Lavelle
Musical Director: Ben Cole

**ANNEXE THEATRE COMPANY**
Unit 6, The Quadrangle, Ruchill Street,
Glasgow G20 9PX
Tel: 0141 945 4444 Fax: 0141 945 4358

**ARC THEATRE COMPANY**
The Malt House, Newbold Road, Desford,
Leicester LE9 9GS
Tel/Fax: 01455 828400

**BEAVERS ARTS**
16 Barracks Square, Barracks Road, Newcastle,
Staffordshire ST5 1LG
Tel: 01782 717326 Fax: 01782 717190
Email: BeaversArts@compuserve.com
Touring community projects. Youth Arts International
Exchanges. The company now has a project office in
Mostar, Bosnia Herzegovina.

**BENCHTOURS PRODUCTIONS**
Bonnington Mill, 72 Newhaven Road,
Edinburgh EH6 5QG Scotland
Tel/Fax: 0131 55 3585
Email: benchtours@hotmail.com
Morag Neil: Administrator
Peter Clerke: Director
Scotland's leading international theatre ensemble.
Specialising in education/outread programme,
including special needs work.

**BLACK THEATRE CO-OPERATIVE**
Unit 3p, Leroy House, 436 Essex Road,
London N1 3QP
Tel: 0171 226 1225 Fax: 0171 226 0233
Email: Felix.btc@virgin.net
Artistic Director: Felix Cross

**BONE IDOL THEATRE**
The Hazels, Belmont, Wantage,
Oxfordshire OX12 9AS
Tel: 01235 762000

**BORDERLINE THEATRE**
North Harbour Street, Ayr KA8 8AA
Tel: 01292 281010 Fax: 01292 263825
Chief Executive: Edward Jackson
Artistic Director: Leslie Finlay

**BRICKBATS VOLUNTEERS - COMEDY
IMPROVISATION**
33 Findon Road, London W12 9PP
Tel/Fax: 0181 743 6989
Contact: Peter Wear

**BRIGHT TRACKS PRODUCTIONS**
PO Box 27, Stroud, Gloucestershire GL6 0YQ
Tel/Fax: 01453 836877

**BILL BROOKMAN PRODUCTIONS**
101 Ashby Road, Loughborough,
Leicestershire LE11 3AB
Tel: 01509 236175 Fax: 01509 219873
Email: bill_brookman@compuserve.com
A large developed experienced street theatre company
combining street music, street gypsy dancing, fire,
stiltwalking, puppetry. Large sets. Celebratory theatre.
Our millennium project is a huge Exploding Cosmos
Tower.

**CAKES AND ALE THEATRE COMPANY**
40 Lucerne Road, London N5 1TZ
Tel/Fax: 0171 226 6483

**THE CENTRE FOR PERFORMANCE
RESEARCH**
8 Science Park, Aberystwyth, SY23 3AH
Tel: 01970 622133 Fax: 01970 622132
Email: cprwww@aber.ac.uk
Web Site: www.aber.ac.uk/~cprwww
Producer: Judie Christie
Artistic Director: Richard Gough

Administrator: Claire Swatheridge

## CENTRE OCEAN STREAM
1 Holland Road, Southampton SO19 9FW
Tel: 01703 420114 Fax: 01703 444678
Email: kathakali@interalpha.co.uk
Contact: Barbara Vijayakumar
To explore the Language of Living Colour and the creative connections between the visual and performing arts through the abstract work of Centre Ocean Stream and the classical work of Kathakali.

## CERTAIN CURTAIN THEATRE
Unit 112, Oyston Mill, Strand Road, Preston PR1 8UR
Tel: 01772 731024
Email: cctheatre@yahoo.com
Web Site: www.callnetuk.com/home/cctheatre
Directors: Claire Moore, John Woudberg
Original work tailored to all ages includes T.I.E., issue-based, public performances, musicals and workshops.

## CLEAN BREAK THEATRE COMPANY
2 Patshull Road, London NW5 2LB
Tel: 0171 482 8600 Fax: 0171 380 0308

## COMMON GROUND SIGN DANCE THEATRE
4th Floor, Crane Building, Hanover Street, Liverpool, L1 3DY
Tel/Fax: 0151 707 8033 Minicom: 0151 707 8380
(Typetalk 0800 515152)
Administrator: Barry Avison

## COMMUNICADO THEATRE COMPANY
2 Hill Street, Edinburgh EH2 3JZ
Tel: 0131 624 4040 Fax: 0131 624 4041
Email: comcado@dircon.co.uk
Artistic Director: Helena Kaut
Producer: Linda Borthwick
Tour Administrator: Debbie Forbes

## COMPASS THEATRE COMPANY
Carver Street Institute, 24 Rockingham Lane, Sheffield S1 4FW
Tel: 0114 275 5328 Fax: 0114 278 6931

## CORNELIUS & JONES PRODUCTIONS
49 Carters Close, Sherington, Newport Pagnell, Buckinghamshire MK16 9NW
Tel: 01908 612593 Fax: 01908 216400
Co-Directors: Sue Leech & Neil Canham

## CUT-CLOTH THEATRE
41 Beresford Road, London N5 2HR
Tel: 0171 503 4393

## DALIER SYLW
Chapter, Heol Y Farchnad, Treganna, Caerdydd CF5 1QE
Tel: 01222 236650 Fax: 01222 236651
Email: dalsylw@globalnet.co.uk
Artistic Director: Bethan Jones
Administrator: Mai Jones

## DEAD EARNEST THEATRE
84 Walkley Road, Sheffield S6 2XP
Tel/Fax: 0114 231 0687
Email: dead-earnest@pop3.poptel.org.uk
Artistic Director: Ashley Barnes
Production Manager: Neil Adleman

## EASTERN ANGLES THEATRE COMPANY
Sir John Mills Theatre, Gatacre Road, Ipswich, Suffolk IP1 2LQ
Tel: 01473 218202 Fax: 01473 250954
Box Office: 01473 211498
Artistic Director: Ivan Cutting
Administrator: Rebecca Farrar
Marketing Officer: Andrew Burton
Stage Manager: Penny Griffin
Assistant Administrator: Maggie Jones

## ECONOMICAL TRUTH CHARITABLE THEATRE COMPANY
98a Park Avenue South, London N8 8LS
Tel: 0181 341 4599 Fax: 0181 347 5881
Email: truth@economicaltruth.scl.co.uk
Web Site: www.economicaltruth.scl.co.uk
Economical Truth creates exciting performance, generated from the histories and experiences of company members, producing authentic insights into our everyday emotional lives.
Artistic Directors: David Jubb and Phil Seddon

## EMPTY SPACE THEATRE COMPANY
37 Nasmyth Street, London W6 0HA
Tel/Fax: 0181 563 1949
Artistic Director: Andrew Holmes

## ESCAPE ARTISTS
35 Halifax Road, Cambridge CB4 3QB
Tel: 01223 775731 Fax: 01223 775732
Email: EscapeArtists@compuserve.com
Director: Matthew Taylor
Administrator: Christopher Corner
Education Director: Vivien Ewington

## FECUND THEATRE
6 Cleland Road, Chalfont St Peter, Buckinghamshire SL9 9BG
Tel: 01753 882692
Contact: Beverley Reid - Administrator
Fecund theatre annually research and create an exciting, original and provocative theatrical experience; fusing current social issues with the physical potential of the actor. We are pioneering and pushing the bounds of the dramatic construct and the expectations of our audience.
Fecund tours nationally and provides educational and commercial residences and workshops; encouraging creative and experiential understanding of theatre and video technology.

## FORCED ENTERTAINMENT
Unit 102, The Workstation, 46 Shoreham Street, Sheffield S1 4SP
Tel: 0114 279 8977 Fax: 0114 221 2170
Email: fe@forced.co.uk
Web Site: www.forced.co.uk
General Manager: Deborah Chadbourn

Director: Tim Etchells
Administrator: Verity Leigh

## FOREST FORGE THEATRE COMPANY
The Theatre Centre, Crow Arch Lane, Ringwood,
Hampshire BH24 1SF
Tel: 01425 470188 Fax: 01425 471158
Email: theatre@forestforge.demon.co.uk
Web Site: http://www.forestforge.demon.co.uk
Artistic Director: Kevin Shaw
Company Administrator: Karen Jeffries
Outreach Director: Amanda Simpson
Funding Officer: Karen Shaw
Marketing and Projects Officer: Jessica Marklew

## FOURSIGHT THEATRE COMPANY LTD
Newhampton Centre for Arts, Dunkley Street,
Wolverhampton, WV1 4AN
Tel: 01902 714257 Fax: 01902 428413
Email: foursight.theatre@mcmail.com
Web Site: www.foursight.theatre.mcmail.com
Artistic Director: Naomi Cooke
Administrator: Sally Haines
Foursight Theatre creates unusual, uncompromising
and multi-disciplinary works which review history
through the eyes of women: unknown, famous and
infamous. Foursight is committed to creating total
theatre - an holistic style of performance rooted in
physical theatre. Work is experimented in both process
& form.
Foursight tours nationally & internationally and
provides educational workshops and residencies.
Funding: Arts Council of England, West Midlands Arts,
Wolverhampton Council.

## FRANTIC ASSEMBLY
BAC, Old Town Hall, Lavender Hill, Battersea,
London SW11 5TF
Tel/Fax: 0171 228 8885 Mobile: 0976 813064
Web Site: http://www.franticassembly.co.uk
Administrative Director: Vicki Coles
Artistic Director: Scott Graham
Artistic Director: Steve Hoggett
Frantic is one of the UK's most exciting, dynamic
physical theatre companies to rise in recent years.
Renowned for producing new, innovative work, rooted
in 1990's youth culture, Frantic tour nationally and
internationally, and provides educational workshops
and residencies. Our current show Sell Out, received a
1998 Time Out Live Award. (Best in off West End).
See our new web site for further details on the
company.

## FREAKSHOW
5 Ewhurst Road, London SE4 1AG
Tel: 0181 690 2798 Fax: 0181 690 4744

## ROSY GIBB
2 Aycliffe Road, London W12
Tel: 0181 749 7779 Fax: 0181 740 5504

## GOG THEATRE COMPANY
Ostia, Overleigh Street, Somerset BA16 0TJ
Tel: 01458 445494 Fax: 01458 840063
Directors: Tom Clark, Caryne Clark

Two shows currently touring abroad: "Lovebites"
Premiere Berlin September 1997; "Suitcase" Tbilisi,
Georgia, Pakistan Theatre Festival November 1997.
We are always interested to hear from adventurous
theatre people. Proposed project in Turkish Amphi
Theatre 1998-1999.

## GRAEAE THEATRE COMPANY
Interchange Studios, Dalby Street, London NW5 3NQ
Tel: 0171 267 1959/3164 (minicom)
Fax: 0171 267 2703
Email: graeae@dercon.co.uk
Web Site: www.users.dercom.co.uk/~graeae
Artistic Director: Jenny Sealey
Administrator Director: Kevin Dunn

## THE GRAND THEATRE OF LEMMINGS
Cliffhanger Lodge, 38 High Street, Manningtree,
Essex CO11 1AJ
Tel: 01206 391632 Fax: 01206 392402

## DEREK GRANT'S WORLD OF PUPPETS
93 Cutlers Place, Wimborne, Dorset BH21 2HX
Tel: 01202 887439 Fax: 01202 849493
Current production "The Puppet Factory" - available
with a new production each year. This polished
presentation features four different kinds of puppets in
fast-moving musical and dramatic cameos. Superb
family entertainment.

## GREEN GINGER
32 The Norton, Tenby,
Pembrokeshire SA70 8AB Wales
Tel/Fax: 0117 942 3212 Tel: 01834 842746
Email: gg.amyrose@netgates.co.uk
Touring theatre company using
actors/masks/puppets/projection. Last show "slaphead"
toured 10 countries. In preparation " Bambi...the
Wilderness Years". Available from March 2000. "Frank
Einstein" show available throughout 1999.

## GREEN PAVEMENT THEATRE COMPANY
35 Armadale Road, Chichester,
West Sussex PO19 4NR
Tel: 01243 771597

## HEADS TOGETHER PRODUCTIONS
32 Methley Terrace, Leeds LS7 3PB
Tel: 0973 172433 Fax: 0113 262 9223
Email: admin@heads.demon.co.uk
Artistic Director: Adrian Sinclair
Policy: To create unusual performances in unlikely
places. Founded in 1986 the company has developed
a style of theatre inspired by movement and image
working alongside the spoken word - physical theatre.
Heads Together has always strived to offer a range of
training opportunities of the highest quality and has
recently been cited as an example of good practice for
its vocational training under the European Union's
Horizon programme.
Funding: Arts Council of England; Yorks & Humberside
Arts; European Union's Employment Initiative; Leeds,
Bradford and other City Councils.

## HULLABALLOO CHILDREN'S THEATRE
21 St.Leonard's Lane, Edinburgh EH8 9SH

Tel: 0131 662 1645 Fax: 0131 662 1638
Artistic Director: Chris Craig
Musical Director: Angie Rew

## INNER STATE THEATRE COMPANY
15 Denmark Street, Lancaster LA1 5LY
Tel: 01524 37838
Contact: Andy Andrews/Christine Bissell
Highly adaptable theatre, suitable for a range of
venues both outdoor and indoor; from street to arts
centre. The company uses a distinctive style of
apparent chaos which owes more to stand up comedy
than recognised conventional theatre.

## INTIMATE STRANGERS
Melanie Thompson 46 The Archers Way, Glastonbury,
Somerset BA6 9JB
Tel/Fax: 01458 833846
Working on the hybridity principle. Collaborations
across the art forms. Focusing on commissions for
site-specific pieces.

## I.O.U. THEATRE
Dean Clough, Halifax, West Yorkshire HX3 5AX
Tel: 01422 369217 Fax: 01422 330203
Email: iou@globalnet.co.uk
Creating exciting, entertaining visual theatre with
music. Shows are devised for specific and unusual
locations as well as for purpose built theatre venues.
Features of work - new, visual/non-scripted, company
devised, live music, taped music.

## KALA CHETHENA KATHAKALI TROUPE LTD
1 Holland Road, Woolston, Southampton SO19 9FW
Tel: 01703 420114/0402 083214 (mobile)
Fax: 01703 444468
Email: kathakali@interalpha.co.uk
Web Site: http://www.intent.co.uk/kathakali/index.html
Policy: To present International Kathakali (Classical
dance drama from Kerala S. India) throughout G.B.
with full troupe performances, solo performances,
workshops, residences and courses. Plus an exhibition
of costumes with related performances and workshops.
In 1999 we will tour Kathakali and Theyam both highly
visual performed by top international artists and from
Kerala, South India.

## KNEEHIGH TOURING THEATRE COMPANY
14 Walsingham Place, Truro, Cornwall TR1 2RP
Tel: 01872 223159/271766 Fax: 01872 260487
Administrator: Julie Seyler
Local Work Co-ordinator: Amanda Harris
Artistic Directors: Bill Mitchell, Mike Shepherd

## LIP SERVICE
The Comedy Suite, 63 Nicholas Road, Chorlton,
Manchester M21 9LG
Tel/Fax: 0161 881 0061
Artistic Directors: Maggie Fox, Sue Ryding
Tour Organisation: UK Arts International
Tel: 01905 26424
Fax: 01905 22868
Marketing: Nick Sweeting

## LITTLE SQUIRT PRODUCTIONS
39 Elm Street, Cardiff CF2 3QS

Tel/Fax: 01222 486550
Contact: Paddy Faulkner
Touring theatres nationwide. Also available for private
functions, outdoor events and promotions. International
Award Winning Show 1997.

## LIVE THEATRE CO.
7/8 Trinity Chare, Quayside,
Newcastle-upon-Tyne NE1 3DF
Tel: 0191 261 2694 (4 Lines) BO: 0191 232 1232
Fax: 0191 232 2224
Venue: 27 Broadchare, Quayside,
Newcastle-upon-Tyne, NE1 3DQ

## LUDUS DANCE COMPANY
Ludus Dance Centre, Assembly Rooms, King Street,
Lancaster LA1 1RE
Tel: 01524 389901 Fax: 01524 847744
Email: ludus@easynet.co.uk
Web Site: www.dancenorthwest.org.uk
Director: Deborah Barnard
Head of Touring: Jacqueline Greaves
Britain's leading dance company for young people.
Award winning shows, workshops, teaching packs,
inset, videos, the works! High impact in Theatres,
Festivals, Schools and the Community. Still unique
after 23 years.

## LYNX THEATRE AND POETRY
1 Queen's Gate Villas, Victoria Park Road,
London E9 7BU
Tel: 0181 986 5477

## MASKARRAY
213 Rotherhithe New Road, London SE16 2BA
Tel: 0171 231 3827
Director: Brige Bidell

## MEETING GROUND THEATRE COMPANY
4 Shirley Road, Nottingham NG3 5DA
Tel: 0115 962 3009
Artistic Directors: Tanya Myers, Stephen Lowe,
Jonathan Chadwick
International and experimental collaborations. One
production per annum. Average audience 300.

## MERSEYSIDE YOUNG PEOPLE'S THEATRE
13 Hope Street, Liverpool L1 9BH
Tel: 0151 708 0877 Fax: 0151 707 9950
Administrator: Karen O'Donnell
Artistic Director: Wendy Harris

## THE MIGHTY PEN PRODUCTION CO.
18 Chiswick Green Studios, London W4 5BW
Tel: 0181 995 0445 Fax: 0181 995 0443

## MIKRON THEATRE CO. LTD
Marsden Mechanics, Peel Street, Marsden,
Huddersfield HD7 6BW
Tel/Fax: 01484 843701
Email: mikron-theatre@pop3.poptel.org.uk
Web Site: http://www.alden.u-net.com/mikron/moc.html
Artistic Director: Mike Lucas
Associate Administrators: Andrea Walker, Shelly Frape

## MIND THE...GAP

Queens House, Queens Road, Bradford, West
Yorkshire BD8 7BS
Tel: 01274 544683 Fax: 01274 544501
Artistic Director: Tim Wheeler
The company aims: to broaden public perception of
the arts, to ensure that people with a learning disability
are able to speak for themselves; to challenge
attitudes and physical inaccessibility.

## MOCKBEGGAR THEATRE COMPANY

Cotton Exchange Building, Old Hall Street,
Liverpool L3 9LQ
Tel/Fax: 0151 236 1292
Email: mockbeggar@cix.compulink.co.uk
Artistic Director: Di Christian
Administrative Director: Sue O'Brien
The company primarily works with disabled people of
all ages and employs disabled performers and where
possible disabled stage managers, directors, writers
and other practitioners on both performance and
workshop projects. The company also offers
workshops and disability equality training with non-
disabled people of all ages.

## MOONSHINE PRODUCTIONS

Alpine House, 4 Northfields, Kilburn, Belper,
Derbyshire DE56 0LW
Tel: 01332 780462
Contact: Sue Reaney
Moonshine formed in 1993 and is based in the Amber
Valley area of Derbyshire. The Company presents
original work of local writers focusing on the heritage of
the community. We also provide a mobile audio-
description service for all visual, artistic and musical
events.

## NATIONAL STUDENT THEATRE COMPANY

20 Lansdowne Road, Muswell Hill, London N10 2AU
Tel: 0181 883 4586 Fax: 0181 883 7142
Email: clive@nsdf.skynet.co.uk
Web Site: www.nsdf.uk.internet
Contact: Clive Wolfe
Reconstituted for each summer vacation. Over 110
productions (new and old work). 19 Edinburgh Fringe
awards. Auditions advertised in The Stage and on
Website.

## NATURAL THEATRE COMPANY

Widcombe Institute, Widcombe Hill, Bath,
North Somerset BA2 6AA
Tel: 01225 469131 Fax: 01225 442555
Email: naturals@compuserve.com
Web Site:
www.ourworld.compuserve.com/homepages/naturals
Contact: Dot Peryer

## NETI-NETI THEATRE COMPANY

George Orwell School, Turle Road, London N4 3LS
Tel/Fax: 0171 272 7302

## NOFIT STATE CIRCUS

PO Box 238, Cardiff CF2 1XS
Tel: 01222 788734 Fax: 01222 331367
Aims to produce large scale multi-media projects. Tour
with 350 seat big top, fully equipped with light/sound.

## NOT THE NATIONAL THEATRE

149 Eglington Hill, London SE18 3DU
Tel/Fax: 0181 855 3258

## NTC TOURING THEATRE COMPANY LTD

The Playhouse, Bondgate Without, Alnwick NE66 1PQ
Tel: 01665 602586 Fax: 01665 605837
Administrator: Anna Flood

## OPEN HAND THEATRE CO.

Dean Clough, Halifax, West Yorkshire HX3 5AX
Email: openhand@pop3.poptel.org.uk
Administrator: Angela Saville
Artistic Directors: Maureen Lunt, John Barber
Publicity and Marketing: Emma Davies

## OXFORDSHIRE TOURING THEATRE COMPANY

Unit 1, St John Fisher School, Sandy Lane West,
Oxford OX4 5LD
Tel: 01865 778119 Fax: 01865 714822
Artistic Director: Jeremy James

## PASCAL THEATRE COMPANY

35 Flaxman Court, Flaxman Terrace, Bloomsbury,
London WC1H 9AR
Tel: 0171 383 0920 Fax: 0171 419 9798
Email: JuliaPascal@aol.com
Artistic Director: Julia Pascal
Administrator: Graeme Braidwood

## THE PHANTOM CAPTAIN

618b Finchley Road, London NW11 7RR
Tel/Fax: 0181 455 4564
Email: zip@phancap.demon.co.uk
Artistic Director: Neil Hornick
Stage and Environmental shows, festival and
conference events, workshop residences, creative
event consultation. This year's speciality: Literary
themed events.

## PILOT THEATRE

Glasshoughton Cultural Centre, Redhill Avenue,
Castleford, West Yorkshire WF10 4QH
Tel: 01977 604852 Fax: 01977 512819
Email: pilot.theatre@geo.2.poptel.org.uk
Web Site: http://homepages.poptel.org.uk/pilot.theatre
Artistic Director: Marcus Romer
Administrator: Veronica Bailey
Produce new touring work for new audiences. National
brief funded by Arts Council of England & Yorkshire &
Humberside Arts.

## PRAXIS THEATRE COMPANY LTD

24 Wykeham Road, London NW4 2SU
Tel/Fax: 0181 203 1916
Email: praxisco@globalnet.co.uk
Web Site: www.users.globalnet.co.uk/~praxisco

Praxis is a theatre company dedicated to new writing for the stage and screen, crossing the great divide between text based theatre, visual theatre and cinematic imagery. Since its conception Praxis has grown from strength to strength, expanding its work force, delivering more and more ambitious and sometimes controversial productions and workshop programmes in conventional theatre and site specific venues.

Our corporate work draws on the expertise of partners from a variety of business and arts disciplines.

## PROTEUS THEATRE COMPANY

Fairfields Arts Centre, Council Road, Basingstoke, Hampshire RG21 3DH
Tel: 01256 354541 Fax: 01256 356186
Artistic Director: Mark Helyar

## PUBLIC PARTS THEATRE COMPANY

Epstein Building, Mivart Street, Easton, Bristol B55 6JL
Tel: 0117 939 3904
Artistic Director: Karen Hayes
Company Manager: Jo Weeks

## Q20 BRADFORD'S THEATRE COMPANY

"Ivy Lea", Fyfe Lane, Baildon,
West Yorkshire BD17 6DP
Tel/Fax: 01274 591417 (9am - 12pm Mon-Fri)
Artistic Director: John Lambert

## RAMBERT DANCE COMPANY

94 Chiswick High Road, London W4 1SH
Tel: 0181 995 4246 Fax: 0181 747 8323
Directors: Christopher Bruce (Artistic),
Christopher Nourse (Executive)
Director of Finance & Administration: Geoff Hunt
Director of Marketing: Jackie Friend
Development Manager: Ellen Plant
Education Manager: Sarah Dekker

## RED LADDER THEATRE COMPANY

3 St Peters Buildings, York Street, Leeds LS9 8AJ
Tel: 0113 245 5311 Fax: 0113 524 5351
Email: red-ladder@geo2.poptel.org.uk
Red Ladder is a national touring theatre company producing high quality theatre for young people, 13-25. Commissions new writing and performs in small scale theatre venues and youth and community venues.

Other activities include workshops, projects and training events for young people and youth workers.
Touring times: April - July & September - December.
Equipment carried - touring lighting rig and full sound.

## RED SHIFT THEATRE COMPANY

TRG2 Trowbray House, 108 Weston Street,
London SE1 3QB
Tel: 0171 978 9787 Fax: 0171 378 9789
Email: rshift@dircon.co.uk
Web Site: http://www.rshift.dircon.co.uk
General Manager: Sophie Elliott
Artistic Director: Jonathan Holloway
Administrator: Jess Lammin

## REMOULD THEATRE COMPANY

Humberside Cultural Enterprise Centre
Middleton Street, Hull HU3 1NB
Tel: 01482 226 157 Fax: 01482 326190
Artistic Director: Rupert Creed
Administrative Director: Averil Coult
Administrator: Sara Hawkins
Educator and Outreach Office: Carolyn Mendelsohn

## THE ROYAL BALLET BENEVOLENT FUND

45 Floral Street, London WC2E 9DD
Tel/Fax: 0181 643 4470
Secretary: Peter Wilson

## ROYSTON PRODUCTIONS

2 Coaching Walk, Westone, Northampton NN3 3EX
Tel: 01604 411413
Contact: Roy Gilbert

## IAN SAVILLE: MAGIC FOR SOCIALISM

8 Aylesbury Street, London NW10 0AS
Tel: 0181 621 0157
Email: ian@redmagic.dircon.co.uk
Web Site: http://www.redmagic.dircon.co.uk

## SCARLET THEATRE COMPANY

Studio 4, The Bull, 68 High Street, Barnet,
Hertfordshire EN5 5SJ
Tel: 0181 441 9779 Fax: 0181 447 0075
Email: admin@scarlettheatre.co.uk
Artistic Director: Grainne Byrne
Creates highly artistic theatre using a variety of starting points. The work is either: devised, made through radical adaptations of classics or little known European plays & new writing.

## SNAP THEATRE TRUST

Unit A, Causeway Business Centre, 2, The Causeway,
Bishop's Stortford, Hertfordshire CM23 2EJ
Tel: 01279 836200 Fax: 01279 501472
Contacts: Andy Graham and Mike Wood

## SNAPSHOT

76 Buxton Road, Disley, Stockport,
Cheshire SK12 2HE
Tel/Fax: 01663 765860 Mobile: 0589 745594
Email: a6-acts@mighty-micro.co.uk
Web Site:
www.mighty-micro.co.uk/users/personal/a6acts/default.htm
Artistic Director: Chris Bright
Administration: Michael Hobson

## SNARLING BEASTIES

27 Grosvenor Road, Harborne, Birmingham B17 9AL
Tel: 01203 365650

## SOLA ENERGY THEATRE COMPANY

31 Stirling Road, London SW9 9EF
Tel/Fax: 0171 326 0221

## SOUTH SOMERSET PERFORMANCE GROUP

Churchwalk, Aller, Near Langport, Somerset

Tel: 01458 250852
Contact: Di Dean

## THE SPHINX THEATRE COMPANY
25 Short Street, London SE1 8LJ
Tel: 0171 401 9993/4 Fax: 0171 401 9995

## STAGE ONE THEATRE COMPANY
34 Jasmine Grove, London SE20 8JW
Tel: 0181 778 5213 Fax: 0181 778 1756
Email: admin@stageone.demon.co.uk
Web Site: www.stageone.demon.co.uk
Admin Director: Desmond Maurer

## STRATHCONA THEATRE COMPANY
Unit 13, The Leathermarket, Weston Street,
London SE1 3ER
Tel: 0171 403 9316 Fax: 0171 403 9587
Email: STC@strathco.demon.co.uk
Artistic Directors: Ann Cleary, Ian McCurrach
Administrator: Barbara van Heel

## TAMASHA THEATRE COMPANY
Unit D, 11 Ronalds Road, London N5 1XJ
Tel: 0171 609 2411 Fax: 0171 609 2722
Joint Artistic Directors: Kristine Landon Smith and
Sudha Bhuchar

## TELLING TALES THEATRE COMPANY
19 Bradford Road, St.Johns, Wakefield,
West Yorkshire WF1 2RF
Tel: 01924 379654
Email: Bromtell@aol.com
The company presents original plays concerned with
significant social and political issues of our time, with
projected imagery and live music often complementing
the drama. Blue Murder: The Killing of Derek Bentley
received widespread acclaim (The Stage, The Times,
The Late Night Show on BBC2) as did Jacknife, set at
the time of the Yorkshire Ripper Murders. Latest
production is "Blistered", a one man show concerned
with a convicted arsonist.

## THEATRE OF FIRE
"Pyrotechnic Performance & Wizardry"
PO Box 315, Bamford, Sheffield S30 2BX
Tel: 01433 651215 Fax: 01433 651161

## THEATRE OF INCURABLE PLAYERS
c/o The Buddle Arts Centre, 258b Station Road,
Wallsend, Tyne and Wear NE28 8RH
Tel: 0191 200 7352 Fax: 0191 200 7142
Contact: Gary Cordingley
From festivals to schools, theatres to the street. We
utilise a wide variety of performance styles, including
physical and visual theatre, to enthralling effect.
Incurable Players has a strong community agenda
offering skills and issue based workshops and projects
created specifically for individual client groups.

## THEATRE ROTTO
Nanscawen Barn, Newmill, Penzance,
Cornwall TR20 8XN
Tel: 01736 365158

## THEATRE ROUNDABOUT LTD
859 Finchley Road, London NW11 8LX
Tel: 0181 455 4752
Key Personnel: Sylvia Read & William Fry

## THEATRE SET UP
12 Fairlawn Close, Southgate, London N14 4JX
Tel: 0181 886 9572

## THE THEATRE UNDERGROUND
The Theatre Underground, Department of Literature,
University of Essex, Wivenhoe Park,
Colchester CO4 3SQ
Tel: 01206 872635

## THEATRE WORKSHOP
34 Hamilton Place, Edinburgh EH3 5AX Scotland
Tel 0131 225 7942 Fax 0131 220 0112

## TRESTLE THEATRE COMPANY
Birch Centre, Hill End Lane, St.Albans,
Hertfordshire AL4 0RA
Tel 01727 850950 Fax 01727 855558
Email: trestle@dircon.co.uk
Contact: Penny Mayes

## TRIANGLE
5 Parrotts Grove, Coventry CV2 1NQ
Tel/Fax: 01203 362210
Email: triangletheatre@triangletheatre.demon.co.uk
Artistic Director: Carran Waterfield
Touring nationally and internationally. Current
repertoire: 'Looking for the Tallyman', 'My Sister My
Angel' and 'Nina and Frederick'.

## VOLCANO THEATRE
176 Hanover Street, Swansea SA1 6BP
Tel: 01792 472772 Fax: 01792 648230
Administrator: Irena Halder
Artistic Directors: Fern Smith & Paul Davies
Designer/Technician: Andrew Jones
Volcano theatre is a new generation of performers
committed to movement and meaning on stage. We
have chosen to reject both the use of "the script" and
the work of "the dramatist".

## WOMEN AND THEATRE
The Friend's Institute, 220 Moseley Road, Highgate,
Birmingham B12 0DG
Tel: 0121 440 4203 Fax: 0121 446 4280

# MIDDLE SCALE TOURING COMPANIES

### 7:84 THEATRE COMPANY (SCOTLAND)
2nd Floor, 333 Woodlands Road, Glasgow G3 6NG
Tel: 0141 334 6686 Fax: 0141 334 3369
Email: 7.84-theatre@btinternet.com

### BIG WHEEL THEATRE COMPANY (TIE)
54 William Street, Oxford OX3 0ER
Tel: 01865 241527 Fax: 01865 248041
Email: bigwheeltie@compuserve.com

### BIRTH GOF
Chapter, Market Road, Canton, Caerdydd,
Cardiff CF5 1QE
Tel: 01222 222682 Fax: 01222 238741
Contact: Alison Woods

### BRISTOL EXPRESS THEATRE COMPANY
Flat 2, 28 Saville Road, Chiswick, London W4 5HG
Tel/Fax: 0181 742 3952

### CHANNEL THEATRE COMPANY
Central Studios, 130 Grosvenor Place, Margate,
Kent CT9 1UY
Tel: 01843 280077 Fax: 01843 280088
Artistic Director: Philip Dart
Associate Director: Claudia Leaf
Policy: Channel Theatre is a middle and small scale
touring company based in South East England and
operating nationally. It has also an attached
Community and T.I.E. Company, dealing with new and
innovative work.

### THE CHELSEA CENTRE THEATRE
World's End Place King's Road London SW10 0DR
Tel: 0171 352 1967 Fax: 0171 352 2024
Email: chelseacentre@btinternet.com
Web Site: www.btinternet.com/~chelseacentre/
Artistic Director: Francis Alexander
General Manager: David Micklem
Administrator: Colman Stephenson
Policy: In-house producing and middle scale touring.
Committed to the presentation of new writing of high
literary value dealing with the issues of today. Also
workshops & full youth arts programme..
Seats: 84 - 122

### THE CHERUB COMPANY LONDON
Arches, 5/6 Midland Road, London NW1 2AD
Tel/Fax: 0171 383 0947
Director: Andrew Visnevski
Administrator: Vi Marriott

### COMMUNICADO THEATRE COMPANY
2 Hill Street, Edinburgh EH2 3JZ
Tel: 0131 624 4040 Fax: 0131 624 4041
Email: comcado@dircon.co.uk
Artistic Director: Helena Kaut
Producer: Linda Borthwick
Tour Administrator: Debbie Forbes

### EMERGENCY EXIT ARTS
PO Box 570 London SE10 0EE
Tel: 0181 853 4809 Fax: 0181 858 2025
Email: eea@easynet.co.uk
Web Site: www.eea.org.uk
Senior Personnel: Mark Allan, Les Sharpe, Deb Mullins
Marketing Officer: Paul Lowe

### FORKBEARD FANTASY
34 Balmoral Road, St.Andrews, Bristol BS7 9AZ
Tel: 0117 924 8141 Fax: 0117 949 1178
Co-directors: Tim Britton, Chris Britton,
Penny Saunders.
Administrator: Janice May

### GAY SWEATSHOP THEATRE COMPANY
The Holborn Centre, Three Cups Yard, Sandland
Street, London WC1R 4PZ
Tel: 0171 242 1168 Fax: 0171 242 3143

### DAVID GLASS ENSEMBLE
6 Aberdeen Studios, 22 Highbury Grove,
London N5 2EA
Tel: 0171 354 9200 Fax: 0171 354 0625

### THE GRAND UNION
14 Clerkenwell Green, London EC1R 0DP
Tel: 0171 251 2100 Fax: 0171 250 3009

### HORSE AND BAMBOO THEATRE
Horse & Bamboo Centre, Waterfoot, Rossendale,
Lancashire BB4 7HB
Tel: 01706 220241 Fax: 01706 831166
Email: horse.bamboo@zen.co.uk
Web Site: www.compnet.co.uk/bushome/~hobo/horse.htm

### HULL TRUCK THEATRE COMPANY
Hull Truck Theatre, Spring Street, Hull HU2 8RW
Tel: 01482 224800 Fax: 01482 581182
Email: admin@hulltruck.co.uk
Executive Director: Simon Stallworthy
Artistic Director: John Gobder
Marketing Officer: Tracy Milnes
Marketing Officer, Tours: Angela Marshall
Finance Manager: Grenda Halton
Admin Assistant: Christine Wild

### IMAGE THEATRE COMPANY
23 Sedgeford Road, Shepherds Bush,
London W12 0NA
Tel/Fax: 0181 743 9380

### I.O.U. THEATRE
Dean Clough, Halifax, West Yorkshire HX3 5AX
Tel: 01422 369217 Fax: 01422 330203
Email: iou@globalnet.co.uk

Creating exciting, entertaining visual theatre with music. Shows are devised for specific and unusual locations as well as for purpose built theatre venues. Features of work - new, visual/non-scripted, company devised, live music, taped music.

## KABOODLE PRODUCTIONS LTD
15 Hope Street, Liverpool L1 9BQ
Tel: 0151 709 2818 Fax: 0151 709 2440
Executive Producer: Suzie Boyd
Artistic Director: Lee Beagley

## LIVESPACE THEATRE COMPANY
River Studios, River Road, Westacre,
Norfolk PE32 1UD
Tel/Fax: 01760 755007 Fax: 01760 755800

## THE LONDON BUBBLE
3/5 Elephant Lane London SE16 4JD
Tel 0171 237 4434 Fax 0171 231 2366
Email: admin@londonbubble.org.uk
ADMINISTRATION:
Bubble Theatre Company Ltd.
Artistic Director: Jonathan Petherbridge
Administrator: Helen Chamberlain
Policy: Productions: to tour a variety of productions to adults and children throughout the Greater London area in community and traditional venues, and, during the summer, to London's parks and open spaces. The aim is to develop a popular theatre style which is bold and bright, fast and physical, open and accessible.
Seating on average: 250

## LUMIERE & SON THEATRE LTD
36 Leander Road, London SW2 2LH
Tel: 0181 674 7177 Fax: 0181 674 4309

## MADE IN WALES STAGE COMPANY
1st Floor, Mount Stuart House, Mount Stuart Square,
Cardiff CF1 6DJ
Tel: 01222 344737 Fax: 01222 484016

## NATURAL THEATRE COMPANY
Widcombe Institute, Widcombe Hill, Bath,
North Somerset BA2 6AA
Tel: 01225 469131 Fax: 01225 442555
Email: naturals@compuserve.com
Web Site:
www.ourworld.compuserve.com/homepages/naturals
Contact: Dot Peryer

## NOLA RAE/LONDON MIME THEATRE
49 Springcroft Avenue, London N2 9JH
Tel: 0181 444 6248 Fax: 0181 883 9751
Contact: Valerie West

## ORCHARD THEATRE COMPANY
108 Newport Road, Barnstaple, Devon EX32 9BA
Tel: 01271 371475/373356 Fax: 01271 371825
Email: orchardtheatre@compuserve.com
Artistic Director: Bill Buffery
Administrator: Frederica Notley
Community & Education Officer: Gill Nathanson

## PAINES PLOUGH
4th Floor, 43 Aldwych, London WC2B 4DA
Tel: 0171 240 4533 Fax: 0171240 4534
Email: paines.plough@dial.pipex.com
Artistic Director: Vicki Featherstone
Administrative Director: Belinda Hamilton
Literary Director: Mark Ravenhill
Literary Manager: Jessica Dromgool
A national touring company specialising in accessible new plays.

## PARASOL THEATRE COMPANY
Garden House, 4 Sunnyside, Wimbledon,
London SW19 4SL
Tel: 0181 946 9478 Fax: 0181 946 0228
Artistic Director: Richard Gill
Family entertainment and children's theatre.

## PASCAL THEATRE COMPANY
35 Flaxman Court, Flaxman Terrace, Bloomsbury,
London WC1H 9AR
Tel: 0171 383 0920 Fax: 0171 419 9798
Email: JuliaPascal@aol.com
Artistic Director: Julia Pascal
Administrator: Graeme Braidwood

## THE PEOPLE SHOW
St.James the Great Institute, Pollard Row,
London E2 6NB
Tel: 0171 729 1841 Fax: 0171 739 0203
Administrator: Jane Martin

## PILOT THEATRE
Glasshoughton Cultural Centre, Redhill Avenue,
Castleford, West Yorkshire WF10 4QH
Tel: 01977 604852 Fax: 01977 512819
Email: pilot.theatre@geo.2.poptel.org.uk
Web Site: http://homepages.poptel.org.uk/pilot.theatre
Artistic Director: Marcus Romer
Administrator: Veronica Bailey
Produce new touring work for new audiences. National brief funded by Arts Council of England & Yorkshire & Humberside Arts.

## QUEST THEATRE COMPANY
3c Mecklenburgh Street, Bloomsbury,
London WC1N 2AH
Tel/Fax: 0171 713 0342
Artistic Director: David Craik
Policy: To provide opportunities of seeing unusual and thought provoking plays from around the world, preferably in non-naturalistic and visually stimulating formats. Emphasis is on cross-cultural structure and interest.

## SHARED EXPERIENCE THEATRE COMPANY
The Soho Laundry, 9 Dufour's Place,
London W1V 1FE
Tel: 0171 434 9248 Fax: 0171 287 8763
Email: 106250.1562@compuserve.com
Policy: To explore a physical way of working through a diverse range of theatrical forms.

Recent successes: adaptions of "Anna Karenina",
"Jane Eyre" and "War and Peace". Touring nationally
and internationally in 1999 with "The House of
Bernarda Alba" and "Jane Eyre".

### TALAWA THEATRE COMPANY
3rd Floor, 23/25 Great Sutton Street,
London EC1V 0DN
Tel: 0171 251 6644 Fax: 0171 251 5969
Email: anthony@talawa.com
Personnel: Anthony Corriette, General Manager
Yvonne Brewster, Artistic Director

### TARA ARTS
356 Garratt Lane, London SW18 4ES
Tel: 0181 333 4457 Fax: 0181 870 9540

### THEATR POWYS
The Drama Centre, Tremont Road, Llandrindod Wells,
Powys LD1 5EB
Tel: 01597 824444 Fax: 01597 824381
Email: theatr.powys@powys.gov.uk
Powys County Council Cultural Development Officer:
John Greatovex
Artistic Director: Ian Yeoman
General Manager: Colin Anderson

### THEATRE DE COMPLICITE
20-24 Eden Grove, London N7 8ED
Tel: 0171 700 0233 Fax: 0171 700 0234
Email: email@complicite.co.uk
Artistic Director: Simon McBurney
Administrative Producer: Judith Dimant
Administrator: Chris Chibnall
Education & Marketing: Kate Sparshatt
Admin Assistant: Doug Rintoul

### TRESTLE THEATRE COMPANY
Birch Centre, Hill End Lane, St.Albans,
Hertfordshire AL4 0RA
Tel 01727 850950 Fax 01727 855558
Email: trestle@dircon.co.uk
Contact: Penny Mayes

### WEST GLAMORGAN THEATR GORLLEWIN MORGANNWG
Unit 3, Milland Road Industrial Estate, Neath, Neath
Port Talbot SA11 1NJ
Tel: 01639 641771 Fax: 01639 644213

### WORD AND ACTION (DORSET) LTD
61 West Borough, Wimborne, Dorset BH21 1LX
Tel: 01202 883197/889669 Fax: 01202 881061
Community theatre with twenty-five years language
arts experience. Practitioners of Instant Theatre,
Annual, International and National Tours. Offers
performances, workshops, publishing, business
courses. Co-founders of "The Round Festival".

### YORICK - INTERNATIONALIST THEATRE ENSEMBLE
5e Peabody Buildings, Rodney Road,
London SE17 1BT
Tel/Fax: 0171 701 6385

International and multi-cultural theatre - epic, richly
visual, and physical - with a strong ethical slant.
Patrons include Dario Fo, Isabel Allende,
George Tabori.
Contact: Michael Batz, Artistic Director

### ZIP THEATRE
Dunkley Street, Wolverhampton WV1 4AN
Tel: 01902 712251 Fax: 01902 713494
Email: jon.zip@dial.pipex.com
Web Site: http://dspace.dial.pipex.com/jon.zip
Company Secretary: Cathy Pemberton

# COMMUNITY THEATRE

## AGE EXCHANGE THEATRE TRUST
The Reminiscence Centre, 11 Blackheath Village,
London SE3 9LA
Tel: 0181 318 9105/318 3504 Fax: 0181 318 0060
Email: age-exhange@lewisham.gov.uk
Web Site: www.age-exchange.org.uk

## THE BARBICAN THEATRE
(Rent-a-Role Drama; YPT/TIE)
Castle Street, Plymouth PL1 2NJ
Tel: 01752 267131 Fax: 01752 222209
ADMINISTRATION:
Props: The Barbican Theatre Plymouth Ltd
General Manager: Sarah Pym
Artistic Directors: Sheila Snellgrove, Mark Laville
Policy: Young People's Theatre Centre, home of Rent
a Role Drama service, small scale touring venue for
Dance and experimental/new work.

## BREAKTHROUGH THEATRE GROUP
23 Newtown Road, Hove, East Sussex
Tel: 01273 736625
Administration: Nick Faulkner
Existing work, new work, company written/devised. 3
to 6 night runs. 6 productions a year. Brighton area.

## BRUVVERS THEATRE COMPANY
Ouseburn Warehouse, Workshops, 36 Lime Street,
Ouseburn, Newcastle-upon-Tyne NE1 2PQ
Tel/Fax: 0191 261 9230
Artistic Director: Michael Mould
One of the surviving sixties groups. Providing year
round theatre for all age ranges.
Focus of operation: Greater Newcastle
25 years touring experience at home and abroad, self
contained show for any venue. Award winning
company, ensemble musical theatre of the highest
order.

## CHANNEL THEATRE COMPANY
Central Studios, 130 Grosvenor Place, Margate,
Kent CT9 1UY
Tel: 01843 280077 Fax: 01843 280088
Artistic Director: Philip Dart
Associate Director: Claudia Leaf
Policy: Channel Theatre is a middle and small scale
touring company based in South East England and
operating nationally. It has also an attached
Community and T.I.E. Company, dealing with new and
innovative work.

## THE CHELSEA CENTRE THEATRE
World's End Place King's Road London SW10 0DR
Tel: 0171 352 1967 Fax: 0171 352 2024
Email: chelseacentre@btinternet.com
Web Site: www.btinternet.com/~chelseacentre/
Artistic Director: Francis Alexander
General Manager: David Micklem
Administrator: Colman Stephenson
Policy: In-house producing and middle scale touring.

Committed to the presentation of new writing of high
literary value dealing with the issues of today. Also
workshops & full youth arts programme..
Seats: 84 - 122

## DR.FOSTERS TRAVELLING THEATRE
Dr.Fosters, Bridge House, Paganhill Lane, Stroud,
Gloucestershire GL5 4JU
Tel: 01453 751903

## EMERGENCY EXIT ARTS
PO Box 570 London SE10 0EE
Tel: 0181 853 4809 Fax: 0181 858 2025
Email: eea@easynet.co.uk
Web Site: www.eea.org.uk
Senior Personnel: Mark Allan, Les Sharpe,
Deb Mullins
Marketing Officer: Paul Lowe

## HIJINX THEATRE
Suite One, Bay Chambers, West Bute Street, Cardiff
Bay CF1 6HG Wales
Tel: 01222 300331 Fax: 01222 300332
Artistic Director: Gaynor Lougher
Administrator: Val Hill
Publicity and Promotions: Lowri Jones

## HOXTON HALL THEATRE & ARTS CENTRE
130 Hoxton Street, London N1 6SH
Tel 0171 739 5431 Fax 0171 729 3815
Original victorian music hall theatre build in 1863 and
designed by Sir James Mortimer. Venue, theatre &
Arts training organisation. Weekend performances.
80 seat theatre venue available for hire.

## NEW PERSPECTIVES THEATRE COMPANY
The Old Library, Leeming Street, Mansfield,
Nottingham NG18 1NG
Tel: 01623 635225 Fax: 01623 635240
Email: art@nperspex.demon.co.uk

## OXFORDSHIRE TOURING THEATRE COMPANY
Unit 1, St John Fisher School, Sandy Lane West,
Oxford OX4 5LD
Tel: 01865 778119 Fax: 01865 714822
Artistic Director: Jeremy James

## PENTABUS ARTS LTD
The Old School, Bromfield, Near Ludlow,
Shropshire SY8 2JU
Tel: 01584 856564 Fax: 01584 856254
Email: admin@pentabus.prestel.co.uk
Contact: John Moreton, Development

## SPARE TYRE THEATRE COMPANY
Interchange Studios, Dalby Street, London NW5 3NQ
Tel/Fax: 0171 267 5252
Email: sttc@dircon.co.uk

Director: Claire Chapman
Administrative Director: Angela Kelly
Theatre training company running projects with disadvantaged groups such as the young unemployed and the elderly. Productions are toured locally.

## SPECTACLE THEATRE LIMITED
Rhondda Campus, Pontypridd College, Llwynpia,
Tonypandy, South Wales CF40 2TQ
Tel: 01443 430700/430704 Fax: 01443 423080
Artistic Director: Steve Davis
Administrator Director: Sandra Jones
Administrative Assistant: Michelle Collins
Tour Co-ordinator: Rachael Taylor
Company Stage Manager: George Davis-Stewart

## THEATR POWYS
The Drama Centre, Tremont Road, Llandrindod Wells,
Powys LD1 5EB
Tel: 01597 824444 Fax: 01597 824381
Email: theatr.powys@powys.gov.uk
Powys County Council Cultural Development Officer:
John Greatovex
Artistic Director: Ian Yeoman
General Manager: Colin Anderson

## THEATRE OF FIRE
"Pyrotechnic Performance & Wizardry"
PO Box 315, Bamford, Sheffield S30 2BX
Tel: 01433 651215 Fax: 01433 651161

## THEATRE OF INCURABLE PLAYERS
c/o The Buddle Arts Centre, 258b Station Road,
Wallsend, Tyne and Wear NE28 8RH
Tel: 0191 200 7352 Fax: 0191 200 7142
Contact: Gary Cordingley
From festivals to schools, theatres to the street. We utilise a wide variety of performance styles, including physical and visual theatre, to enthralling effect. Incurable Players has a strong community agenda offering skills and issue based workshops and projects created specifically for individual client groups.

## THEATRE VENTURE
The Resources Centre, Leywick Street,
London E15 3DD
Tel: 0181 519 6678 Fax: 0181 519 8769 Minicom:
0181 536 1353
Email: info@theatre-venture.org
Web Site: www.theatre-venture.org
Artistic Director: John Edward McGrath
Administrator/Marketing: Rosemary Evans
Production Manager: Helen Pringle
Associate Director (Youth Arts and Media):
John Riches
Visual Arts Development Worker: Kevin McKeon
Media Worker: Simone Pennant
Video Worker: Eelyn Lee
Music Worker: Tony Reid
Development Manager: Suzanne Rider

## THEATRO TECHNIS
26 Crowndale Road London NW1 1TT
Tel 0171 387 6617
Director: George Evgeniou

## TURTLE KEY ARTS
Ladbroke Hall, 79 Barlby Road, London W10 6AZ
Tel: 0181 964 5060 Fax: 0181 964 4080
Email: turtlek@globalnet.co.uk
Contact: Charlotte Cunningham, Alison King
Turtle Key Arts is launching itself as a dynamic and versatile arts management company that combines production, technical services, education and training to serve theatre and dance companies and venues, special schools, disability arts organisations and the rest of the education sector.

## WEST GLAMORGAN THEATR GORLLEWIN MORGANNWG
Unit 3, Milland Road Industrial Estate, Neath,
Neath Port Talbot SA11 1NJ
Tel: 01639 641771 Fax: 01639 644213

## WORD AND ACTION (DORSET) LTD
61 West Borough, Wimborne, Dorset BH21 1LX
Tel: 01202 883197/889669 Fax: 01202 881061
Community theatre with twenty-five years language arts experience. Practitioners of Instant Theatre, Annual, International and National Tours. Offers performances, workshops, publishing, business courses. Co-founders of "The Round Festival".

# MIME & PHYSICAL THEATRE

**PERI ASTON**
8 Wilton Crescent, London SW19 3QZ
Tel: 0181 540 4900
Creates and performs her one-woman shows on
spiritual and mythical themes using mime, masks,
storytelling, poetry and music. Innovative and exciting
use of scenery, costume and props.

**RICHARD CUMING**
7 East Street, Titchfield, Fareham,
Hampshire PO14 4AD
Tel: 01329 516422 Mobile: 0378 148814
Mime and Physical theatre performer using the clown
as a basis. Also with John Lee and company State of
Play. Available for bookings from Spring 1999.

**FRANTIC ASSEMBLY**
BAC, Old Town Hall, Lavender Hill, Battersea,
London SW11 5TF
Tel/Fax: 0171 228 8885 Mobile: 0976 813064
Web Site: http://www.franticassembly.co.uk
Administrative Director: Vicki Coles
Artistic Director: Scott Graham
Artistic Director: Steve Hoggett
Frantic is one of the UK's most exciting, dynamic
physical theatre companies to rise in recent years.
Renowned for producing new, innovative work, rooted
in 1990's youth culture, Frantic tour nationally and
internationally, and provides educational workshops
and residencies. Our current show Sell Out, received a
1998 Time Out Live Award. (Best in off West End).
See our new web site for further details on the
company.

**THE GUIZERS DANCE AND MIME THEATRE**
Johnny Haynes 24 Howard Street, Loughborough,
Leicestershire LE11 1PD
Tel: 01509 236522
Keith Barlow 6 Victoria Road, Woodhouse Evans,
Leicesterhsire LE12 8RF
Tel: 01509 891 010

**ADRIAN HEDLEY & CO.**
74 Park Hall Road, East Finchley, London N2 9PX
Tel: 0181 882 6414

**JOHN LEE & STATE OF PLAY**
12a Market Square, Oundle, Peterborough PE8 4BQ
Tel/Fax: 01458 251805 Tel: 01832 272 846
State of Play develops productions in theatre, cabaret
and festivals - the first being "Titanic" - a parallel story
of two musicians who are employed in the largest boat
ever built. Using innovative theatrical and film
conventions in a comedy full length theatre show.
Suitable for audiences of all types and especially for
middle scale touring.

**MIMIKA**
26 Highbury Terrace, Leeds LS6 4ET
Tel/Fax: 0113 274 0053

Email: mimika@btinternet.com

**JOHN MOWAT**
197 Croxted Road, London SE24 9DB
Tel: 0181 671 6495

**TRESTLE THEATRE COMPANY**
Birch Centre, Hill End Lane, St.Albans,
Hertfordshire AL4 0RA
Tel 01727 850950 Fax 01727 855558
Email: trestle@dircon.co.uk
Contact: Penny Mayes

# CHILDREN'S THEATRE, TIE COMPANIES AND YOUNG PEOPLES THEATRE

## THE BARBICAN THEATRE
(Rent-a-Role Drama; YPT/TIE)
Castle Street, Plymouth PL1 2NJ
Tel: 01752 267131 Fax: 01752 222209
ADMINISTRATION:
Props: The Barbican Theatre Plymouth Ltd
General Manager: Sarah Pym
Artistic Directors: Sheila Snellgrove, Mark Laville
Policy: Young People's Theatre Centre, home of Rent
a Role Drama service, small scale touring venue for
Dance and experimental/new work.

## BIG WHEEL THEATRE COMPANY (TIE)
54 William Street, Oxford OX3 0ER
Tel: 01865 241527 Fax: 01865 248041
Email: bigwheeltie@compuserve.com

## BLAH BLAH BLAH! (TIE)
East Leeds Community Base, Brooklands View,
Seacroft, Leeds LS14 6SA
Tel: 0113 224 3171 Fax: 0113 224 3685
Email: blahblahblah@pop3.poptel.org.uk
Artistic Director: Anthony Haddon
Administrator: Maureen McGough

## BRIGHTON DRAMA CENTRE
Office: 79 Sherwood Road, Seaford,
East Sussex BN25 3ED
Tel: 01323 897949 (24 hours) Fax: 01323 897972
Courses:
Acting workshops and tuition for the wide Brighton &
Hove area - teenagers and young adults.  Evening and
holiday courses.  Private lessons at anytime.

## BRUVVERS THEATRE COMPANY
Ouseburn Warehouse, Workshops, 36 Lime Street,
Ouseburn, Newcastle-upon-Tyne NE1 2PQ
Tel/Fax: 0191 261 9230
Artistic Director: Michael Mould
One of the surviving sixties groups. Providing year
round theatre for all age ranges.
Focus of operation: Greater Newcastle
25 years staging experience at home and abroad, self
contained show for any venue. Award winning
company, ensemble musical theatre of the highest
order.

## CHILDRENS SHOWTIME PRODUCTIONS
PO Box 127, Heathfield, East Sussex TN21 0ZR
Tel: 01435 864008 Fax: 01435 868919
Specialising in: Theatre for Children.

## COMMON LORE STORY TELLING AND MUSIC COMPANY
Brixton Small Business Centre, Unit 301, 444 Brixton
Road, London SW9 8EJ
Tel: 0171 738 7051

## CROYDON YOUTH THEATRE ORGANISATION (YPT)
New Shoestring Theatre, Oakley Road,
London SE25
Tel: 0181 655 1098
Director: S.Reynolds (0171 739 2973)

## DAYLIGHT THEATRE (TIE)
66 Middle Street, Stroud, Gloucestershire GL5 1EA
Tel: 01453 763808

## FIRST BITE (TIE) COMPANY
St Columbia's by the Castle, Victoria Terrace,
Edinburgh EH1 2PW
Tel: 0131 225 7993
Administrative Manager: Rebecca Kilbey
Also at: Pope John Paul RC High School, Alderwood
Avenue, Speke, Liverpool L24 2UB
Tel: 0151 448 1818
Administrator: Kris Needham

## FREEHAND THEATRE (CT)
1 Reynard Villas, Mayfield Grove, Baildon, Shipley
West Yorkshire BD17 6DY
Tel: 01274 585277
Co-Directors: Lizzie Allen and Simon Hatfield.
Freehand theatre was formed in 1982 when it has been
delighting audiences with its inventive style of puppetry.
Productions are aimed primarily at children (5 to 11
year olds) and family audiences. The company
regularly performs in schools, arts centres, small
theatres, etc. Technically sufficient. Maximum
audience: 140.

## GAZEBO THEATRE-IN-EDUCATION COMPANY
The Multi-Purpose Centre, Victoria Road, Darlaston,
West Midlands WS10 8AP
Tel/Fax: 0121 526 6877

## HADDO YOUTH THEATRE (YPT)
Haddo House, Aberdeen AB41 0ER
Tel: 01651 851770 Fax: 01651 851609 Ticket Hotline:
01651 851111

## HALF MOON YOUNG PEOPLE'S THEATRE (YPT)
43 Whitehorse Road, London E1 0ND
Tel: 0171 265 8138 Fax: 0171 702 7220
Email: halfmoon@dircon.co.uk
Leading provider of professional theatre training, youth
theatre and arts projects for young people across
London. Regular programme of shows for young
people.

## INTERPLAY THEATRE TRUST
Armley Ridge Road, Leeds LS12 3LE
Tel: 0113 263 8556 Fax: 0113 231 9285

Email: interplay@pop3.poptel.org.uk
Tour & Promotions Manager: Alexis Hutson
Artistic Director: Steve Byrne
Administrator: Gemma Kelmanson

## LAMBETH CHILDREN'S THEATRE CO LTD (CT)

27 Wingmore Road, London SE24 0AS
Tel: 0171 733 5270 Fax: 0171 326 0146
Email: lambch@globalnet.co.uk
Contact: Raymond Cook

## LEARNING THROUGH ACTION (TIE)

Founded 1983
Learning Through Action Centre Fair Cross, Stratfield
Saye, Reading RG7 2BT
Tel: 01256 883500 Fax: 01256 883700
Email: 100045.3465@compuserve.com

## THE LITTLE ANGEL MARIONETTE THEATRE (CT)

"Home of British Puppetry", 14 Dagmar Passage,
Cross Street, London N1 2DN
Tel: 0171 226 1787 Fax: 0171 359 7565

## LITTLE HANDS THEATRE COMPANY

Flat 10, 76 Gloucester Road, London SW1V 4EF
Tel/Fax: 0171 828 4068
Trustees: Judy Alexandria (Theatre Company
Director); Elizabeth Quinn; Morag Rosie MBE.
We are a non-profit theatre company currently seeking
charity status, dedicated to deaf/hard of hearing
children ages 4-11 within multi-cultural communities all
over the UK. The aim of the theatre is to break the
barrier between the deaf and hearing world through
entertainment and workshops communicating through
British sign language, speaking and mime, this is also
open to special needs communities where everyone
can communicate in their own way.

## LITTLE SQUIRT PRODUCTIONS

39 Elm Street, Cardiff CF2 3QS
Tel/Fax: 01222 486550
Contact: Paddy Faulkner
Touring theatres nationwide. Also available for private
functions, outdoor events and promotions. International
Award Winning Show 1997.

## M6 THEATRE COMPANY

Hamer C.P. School, Albert Royds Street,
Rochdale OL16 2SU
Tel: 01706 355898 Fax: 01706 711700
Email: info@m6theatre.freeserve.co.uk
Artistic/Education Controller: Dorothy Wood
Administrator: Jane Milne
Marketing: Beate Mielemeier

## MAGIC CARPET THEATRE COMPANY

18 Church Street, Sutton-on-Hull HU7 4TS
Tel: 01482 709939 Fax: 01482 787362
Mobile: 0385 260038
Email: jon@magiccarpet.demon.co.uk
Web Site: www.magiccarpet.demon.co.uk
Magic Carpet tour exciting new works to venues,
schools and festivals in the UK and abroad.

Formed in 1982 Magic Carpet are a professional
touring children's theatre company. During 1999 they
will tour Professor Funsling's Tricks by Anthony Peters
and present workshops.

## MERSEYSIDE YOUNG PEOPLE'S THEATRE

13 Hope Street, Liverpool L1 9BH
Tel: 0151 708 0877 Fax: 0151 707 9950
Administrator: Karen O'Donnell
Artistic Director: Wendy Harris

## MICK'S ENTERTAINMENTS

Oldwell House, Broad End Road, Walsoken, Wisbech,
Cambridgeshire PE14 7BQ
Tel/Fax: 01945 461383
Uncle Mick Children's Entertainer, Punch and Judy,
Magic Ventriloquism, Funfair, Rides and Stalls.

## OFF THE SHELF THEATRE

(Formerly known as Cambridge Syllabus Players TIE)
Gordon House, 12 Guilford Street, London WC1N 1DT
Tel: 0171 242 1046
Artistic Director: Tim Seward
Designer and Business Manager: Kim Hart

## OLDHAM THEATRE WORKSHOP

Harrison Street, Oldham Gtr Manchester OL1 1PX
Mgt/BO 0161 911 3240 Fax 0161 911 3244
ADMINISTRATION:
Props: Oldham Metropolitan Borough Council
Director: Victoria Munnich
Policy: Touring productions; own Company
productions; Summer Schools; Workshops.
Perfs: Usually 7.30p.m. Mats. various.
Seats: 120

## OPEN HAND THEATRE CO.

Dean Clough, Halifax, West Yorkshire HX3 5AX
Email: openhand@pop3.poptel.org.uk
Administrator: Angela Saville
Artistic Directors: Maureen Lunt, John Barber
Publicity and Marketing: Emma Davies

## OXFORD YOUTH THEATRE (OYT)

Pegasus Theatre, Magdalen Road, Oxford OX4 1RE
Tel: 01865 722851 (Box Office)
Administration: 01865 792209
Email: pegasust@dircon.co.uk
See Provincial Theatres (Pegasus Theatre) for further
details.

## PARASOL THEATRE COMPANY

Garden House, 4 Sunnyside, Wimbledon,
London SW19 4SL
Tel: 0181 946 9478 Fax: 0181 946 0228
Artistic Director: Richard Gill
Family entertainment and children's theatre.

## PIED PIPER THEATRE COMPANY

In Association with Yvonne Arnaud Theatre
1 Lillian Place, Coxcombe Lane, Chiddingfold,
Surrey GU8 4QA
Tel: 01428 684022 Fax: 01483 564071

## PLAYBOX THEATRE
1st Floor Suite, 74 Priory Road, Kenilworth,
Warwickshire CV8 1LQ
Tel: 01926 512388 Mobile: 0860 196405
In April 1999 Playbox Theatre moves into a custom
designed building The Dream Factory in Warwick. A
conception of Playbox with Glenn Howells Architects
(UK) and Sceno Plus (Montreal) this will be a national
focus for the performing arts and young people,
housing productions, workshops, special projects,
visiting companies, from UK and overseas. A theatre
exclusively for young people.

## POLKA THEATRE FOR CHILDREN
240 The Broadway Wimbledon London SW19 1SB
Mgt 0181 542 4258 BO 0181 543 4888
Fax 0181 542 7723
Email: polkatheatre@dial.pipex.com
Web Site: www.polkatheatre.com
ADMINISTRATION:
Prop: Polka Children's Theatre Ltd.
Artistic Director: Vicky Ireland
Admin: Stephen Midlane
Policy: Children's Theatre Repertoire and visiting
Children's Theatre Companies.
Seats: 300. Children's Restaurant, Exhibitions,
Playground.

## POP-UP THEATRE LTD (CT)
404 St. John Street, London EC1V 4NJ
Tel: 0171 837 7588 Fax: 0171 837 7599
Email: popup@dircon.co.uk
Web Site: http://www.popup.dircon.co.uk
National touring to theatres, arts centres and schools.

## PROFESSOR CRUMP
8 St. Marks Road, London W7 2PW
Tel/Fax: 0181 566 1575
Clown and Stilt Entertainer specialising in Children's
Entertainment.

## QUICKSILVER NATIONAL TOURING
## THEATRE (CT)
The Glasshouse, 4 Enfield Road, London N1 5AZ
Tel: 0171 241 2942 Fax: 0171 254 3119
Email: qsilver@easynet.co.uk
Web Site: www.quicksilvertheatre.org
Joint Artistic Director & Chief Executive: Guy Holland
Joint Artistic Director: Carey English
General Manager: Paula Van Hagen

## RAINBOW ENTERTAINMENTS
11 Waterside, Peartree Bridge,
Milton Keynes MK6 3DE
Tel: 01908 661017
Senior Personnel: Dawn Rainbow
Specialises in Childrens Entertainment.

## THE REGENERATOR THEATRE COMPANY
PO Box 31094, Chelmsley Wood,
Birmingham B37 6PY
Tel: 0121 772 8667
A fringe touring theatre in Health Theatre Company
targeting Community and Education issues, from drugs
to Shakespeare.

## ROYAL COURT YOUNG PEOPLE'S
## THEATRE (YPT)
309 Portobello Road, London W10 5TD
Tel: 0181 960 4641 Fax: 0181 960 1434
Email: yp69@dial.pipex.com
Artistic Director: Carl Miller

## ROYSTON PRODUCTIONS
2 Coaching Walk, Westone, Northampton NN3 3EX
Tel: 01604 411413
Contact: Roy Gilbert

## SANDOW CLOWNS
59 Thoresby Close, Bridlington,
East Yorkshire YO16 7EN
Tel: 01262 671492
Contact: Tom Bratby
Children's and Variety Shows on stage, on the floor, in
schools and in the round.

## IAN SAVILLE: MAGIC FOR SOCIALISM
8 Aylesbury Street, London NW10 0AS
Tel: 0181 621 0157
Email: ian@redmagic.dircon.co.uk
Web Site: http://www.redmagic.dircon.co.uk

## SCHOOLPLAY PRODUCTIONS LTD
15 Inglis Road, Colchester, Essex CO3 3HU
Tel: 01206 540111 Fax: 01206 766944
Drama workshops available for schools or youth
groups anywhere in the UK. Full, half-day or evening
sessions as required, covering almost any aspect of
theatre performance for any age up to 19 and involving
almost any number. Full publishing service of plays
and musicals.

## SHEFFIELD THEATRES EDUCATION
## DEPARTMENT (TIE, YPT & YT)
55 Norfolk Street, Sheffield S1 1DA
Tel: 0114 249 5999 Fax: 0114 270 1532

## SNAP THEATRE COMPANY
Snap People's Theatre Trust, Unit A, Causeway
Business Centre, Bishop's Stortford,
Hertfordshire CM23 2UB
Tel: 01279 504095/503066 Fax: 01279 501472
Artistic Director: Andy Graham
Administrative Director: Mike Wood

## SNAPSHOT
76 Buxton Road, Disley, Stockport,
Cheshire SK12 2HE
Tel/Fax: 01663 765860 Mobile: 0589 745594
Email: a6-acts@mighty-micro.co.uk
Web Site: http://www.mighty-micro.co.uk/users/person
al/a6acts/default.htm
Artistic Director: Chris Bright
Administration: Michael Hobson

## SPECTACLE THEATRE LIMITED
Rhondda Campus, Pontypridd College, Llwynpia,
Tonypandy, South Wales CF40 2TQ
Tel: 01443 430700/430704 Fax: 01443 423080

Artistic Director: Steve Davis
Administrator Director: Sandra Jones
Administrative Assistant: Michelle Collins
Tour Co-ordinator: Rachael Taylor
Company Stage Manager: George Davis-Stewart

## TAG THEATRE COMPANY
18 Albion Street, Glasgow G1 1LH
Tel: 0141 552 4949 Fax: 0141 552 0666
Artistic Director: James Brinng
General Manager: Jon Morgan
TAG is Scotland's leading theatre company for young
people.

## THEATRE CENTRE YOUNG PEOPLE'S THEATRE CO.
7-8 Toynbee Workshops, 3 Gunthorpe Street,
London E1 7RQ
Tel: 0171 377 0379 Fax: 0171 377 1376
Email: theacen@aol.com
Web Site: www.theatre-centre.co.uk

## THEATRE EXCHANGE
The Leisure Centre, Guildford Road,
Leatherhead KT22 9BL
Tel/Fax: 01372 362700
Email: theatre_exchange@tecres.co.uk
Web Site: www.bcity.com/theatre_exchange
Artistic Directors: Beth Wood and Andrew Pullen
Through a creative exchange between practitioners
and young people we seek to promote access to
training and production work to high numbers of young
people. We seek to explore and expand creative
techniques and to produce high standard theatre and
educational work with an emphasis on new writing.

## THEATRE WORKSHOP
34 Hamilton Place, Edinburgh EH3 5AX Scotland
Tel 0131 225 7942 Fax 0131 220 0112

## TICKLISH ALLSORTS
31 Highfield Road, Salisbury, Wiltshire SP2 7LZ
Tel: 01722 335654
Senior Personnel: Gary A Nunn
Specialising in: Medieval Banquets, Children's
Entertainers, Barn Dances.

## TIEBREAK TOURING THEATRE (TIE)
Heartsease High School, Marryat Road,
Norwich NR7 9DF
Tel: 01603 435209 Fax: 01603 435184
Email: tie.break@virgin.net
Artistic Director: David Farmer
Administrator: Anne Giles
Marketing & Development: Alison Smith

## WEST GLAMORGAN THEATR GORLLEWIN MORGANNWG
Unit 3, Milland Road Industrial Estate, Neath,
Neath Port Talbot SA11 1NJ
Tel: 01639 641771 Fax: 01639 644213

## WHIRLIGIG THEATRE
14 Belvedere Drive, Wimbledon, London SW19 7BY
Tel: 0181 947 1732 Fax: 0181 879 7648
Directors: David Wood & John Gould
Administrator: Barry Sheppard

## YOUNG PLEASANCE (YPT)
Pleasance Theatre Trust Ltd, Carpenter Mews, North
Road, Islington, London N7 9EF
Tel: 0171 700 6877 Fax: 0171 700 7366
BO: 0171 609 1800
Contact: Tim Norton and Kathryn Norton

## YOUTH THEATRE YORKSHIRE (YPT)
54a Nunthorpe Road, York YO23 1BP
Tel: 01904 639707
Artistic Director: Jill Adamson
Administrator: Van Wilson

## YVONNE ARNAUD THEATRE
Millbrook, Guildford, Surrey GU1 3UX
Mgt/SD 01483 440077 BO 01483 440000
Fax 01483 564071
Email: yat@yvonne-arnaud.co.uk
Web Site: yvonne-arnaud.co.uk

## ZIPPO'S CIRCUS (CT)
174 Stockbridge Road, Winchester,
Hampshire SO22 6RW
Admin: 01962 868092 BO: 07050 121416
Fax: 01962 868097 Mobile: 0836 641277
Email: zipposcircus@yahoo.com

# CIRCUS PROPRIETORS

## BERT BANGER'S CIRCUS
11 Waterside, Peartree Bridge,
Milton Keynes MK6 3DE
Tel: 01908 661017
Proprieter: Dawn Rainbow
Non-animal circus playing under 5's and family circus
shows, circus workshops and physical theatre cabaret.

## BLACKPOOL TOWER CIRCUS
Blackpool Tower, Promenade, Blackpool FY1 4BJ
Tel/Fax: 01253 27776
Contact: Laci Endresz
Tip Top Entertainments

## THE CHINESE STATE CIRCUS
(Go Entertainment Ltd)
Arts Exchange, Mill Green, Congleton,
Cheshire CW12 4AB
Tel: 01260 276627 Fax: 01260 270777
Tel: 07000 CIRCUS Tel: 0171 730 0304
Promoters of Gandey's Circus, Cirque Surreal, Circus
USA, Circus Starr, The Chinese State Circus and Ice
Fantasia.
Lady Boys of Bangkok.

## MARY CHIPPERFIELD'S TAME WILD ANIMALS
Croft Farm, Over Wallop, Stockbridge,
Hampshire SO20 8HX
Tel: 01264 781233 Fax: 01264 782411
Senior Personnel: Roger Cawley
Supplies a wide variety of animals for films, TV and
advertisments, including Camels, Elephants and
Chimpanzees.

## SALLY CHIPPERFIELD'S CIRCUS
(Clubb Chipperfield Ltd)
Church Hill, Wilmington, Dartford, Kent DA2 7DZ
Tel: 01322 225431 (HO) Fax: 01322 289932 Training
Quarters: 01608 683389

## COSMOS JUGGLERS
24 Grange Street, York YO10 4BH
Tel: 01904 654355 Fax: 01904 608972
Email: jjs3@york.ac.uk
Web Site: www.semlyen.demon.co.uk
Juggling shows either for all ages or for children and
their families. Specialists in fire and UV juggling.
Cosmos can also provide workshop and residential
teaching.

## GERRY COTTLE'S CIRCUS LTD
Addlestone Moor, Surrey KT15 2QF
Tel: 01932 828888 Fax: 01932 859902
Email: GerryCottle@btinternet.com
Operating the following shows:- Gerry Cottle's Circus;
Circus Ethiopia; Circus of Horrors; Moscow State
Circus

## SIR ROBERT FOSSET'S CIRCUS
Manor Farm, Towcester Road, Milton Malsor,
Northants N7 3AZ
Tel: 01604 858369

## NOFIT STATE CIRCUS
PO Box 238, Cardiff CF2 1XS
Tel: 01222 788734 Fax: 01222 331367
Aims to produce large scale multi-media projects. Tour
with 350 seat big top, fully equipped with light/sound.

## BILLY SMART'S CIRCUS
Seafront, Littlehampton, West Sussex BN17 5LL
Tel: 01903 721000 Fax: 01903 716663

## ZIPPO'S CIRCUS (CT)
174 Stockbridge Road, Winchester,
Hampshire SO22 6RW
Admin: 01962 868092 BO: 07050 121416 Fax: 01962
868097 Mobile: 0836 641277
Email: zipposcircus@yahoo.com

# PUPPET COMPANIES

## THE ALL ELECTRIC PUPPET THEATRE
8 Wyndham Road, Andover, Hampshire SP10 2JR
Tel: 01264 361924 Fax: 01264 337014
Email: all.electric@cwcom.net
Policy is to provide theatre of the highest professional
level for children, creative puppets, visual effects and
to entertain.

## JOE BARTON'S DUNCAN DRAGON PUPPET THEATRE OF MUSIC AND MAGIC
7 Brands Hill Avenue, High Wycombe,
Buckinghamshire HP13 5PZ
Tel: 01494 439056

## BOB THINGUMMYBOB'S ORIGINAL PUPPETS AND GUITAR ENTERTAINMENT
48 Tenby Avenue, Kenton, Harrow,
Middlesex HA3 8RX
Tel/Fax: 0181 907 4606
Director: Robert Leven

## THE BUCKMASTER PUPPETS
18 Cranmore, Netley Abbey, Southampton SO3 5GG
Tel: 01703 456586
Director: Michael Buckmaster

## CORNELIUS & JONES PRODUCTIONS
49 Carters Close, Sherington, Newport Pagnell,
Buckinghamshire MK16 9NW
Tel: 01908 612593 Fax: 01908 216400
Co-Directors: Sue Leech & Neil Canham

## PIP CRITTEN'S STRING CIRCUS
12 Trelawney Avenue, St.Budeaux,
Plymouth PL5 1RH
Tel: 01752 361210 Mobile: 0467 795576

## DUDLEY TELEPUPPETS
Lower Guscott, Huntshaw, Near Torrington,
North Devon EX38 7HE
Tel: 01271 858490
Director: John Dudley

## EMERGENCY EXIT ARTS
PO Box 570 London SE10 0EE
Tel: 0181 853 4809 Fax: 0181 858 2025
Email: eea@easynet.co.uk
Web Site: www.eea.org.uk
Senior Personnel: Mark Allan, Les Sharpe,
Deb Mullins
Marketing Officer: Paul Lowe

## FAR AND WIDE PUPPETS
Unit 16, Brook House, Darlington, Devon TQ9 6DJ
Tel: 01803 864890 Fax: 01803 864649
Storytelling, puppetry and theatre for a wide range of
venues. Specialised in workshops.

## FAULTY OPTIC - THEATRE OF ANIMATION
12 Savile Road, Huddersfield,
West Yorkshire HD3 3DH
Tel: 01484 536027 Fax: 01484 450239
Surreal puppetry for an adult rather than a kid's
audience - Tours UK and Europe.

## FREEHAND THEATRE (CT)
1 Reynard Villas, Mayfield Grove, Baildon, Shipley
West Yorkshire BD17 6DY
Tel: 01274 585277
Co-Directors: Lizzie Allen and Simon Hatfield.
Freehand theatre was formed in 1982 when it has
been delighting audiences with its inventive style of
puppetry. Productions are aimed primarily at children
(5 to 11 year olds) and family audiences. The
company regularly performs in schools, arts centres,
small theatres, etc. Technically sufficient. Maximum
audience: 140.

## DEREK GRANT'S WORLD OF PUPPETS
93 Cutlers Place, Wimborne, Dorset BH21 2HX
Tel: 01202 887439 Fax: 01202 849493
Current production "The Puppet Factory" - available
with a new production each year. This polished
presentation features four different kinds of puppets in
fast-moving musical and dramatic cameos. Superb
family entertainment.

## GREEN GINGER
32 The Norton, Tenby,
Pembrokeshire SA70 8AB Wales
Tel/Fax: 0117 942 3212 Tel: 01834 842746
Email: gg.amyrose@netgates.co.uk
Touring theatre company using
actors/masks/puppets/projection. Last show
"slaphead" toured 10 countries. In preparation "
Bambi...the Wilderness Years". Available from March
2000. "Frank Einstein" show available throughout
1999.

## HARLEQUIN MARIONETTE THEATRE
Cayley Promenade, Rhos-on-Sea, Colwyn Bay,
North Wales LL28 4EP
Tel: 01492 582062/548166

## IAN AND FRIENDS
35 Hibernia Point, Wolvercote Road, London SE2 9TL
Tel/Fax: 0181 310 4376
Email: ianth@mailbox.co.uk
Web Site: www.mailbox.co.uk/lycuk/ianandfriends.html
Contact: Ian Thom
Speciality Act/Puppets.

## IN THE BOAT THEATRE COMPANY
c/o Action Space Mobile, PO Box 73,
Barnsley S75 1NE
Tel: 01226 384944
Email: actimspacemob@pop3.poptel.org.uk
Co-ordinator: Rosy Cartwright, Special Needs Theatre
Company. Production "Snakes and Ladders".

## THE INTERNATIONAL PURVES PUPPETS
Biggar Puppet Theatre, Broughton Road, Biggar,
Lanarkshire ML12 6HA Scotland
Tel: 01899 220521 BO: 01899 220631
Fax: 01899 220750
Contact: Jill Purves, Laura Shirley (admin)
Touring shows also workshops, in-service courses,
guided tours in our own theatre. Puppet museum.

## JACOLLY PUPPET THEATRE
Kirkella Road, Yelverton, Devon PL20 6BB
Tel/Fax: 01822 852346
Directors: Jacqueline Ilett and Holly Griffin
Administrator: Sarah Berry

## DEREK LAWRENCE THE PUPPET MAN
36 Brynhyfryd Avenue, Rhyl, Denbighshire,
North Wales LL18 2DB
Tel/Fax: 01745 350586

## CHIRSTOPHER LEITH
25a Randolph Crescent, London W9 1DP
Tel: 0171 289 9653

## LITTLE ANGEL THEATRE "HOME OF BRITISH PUPPETRY"
14 Dagmar Passage Cross Street London N1 2DN
Admin 0171 359 8581 BO 0171 226 1787
Fax 0171 359 7565
ADMINISTRATION:
Co founder/Dept. Director: Lindy Wright
Director: Christopher Leith
Policy: Resident & Touring Puppet Theatre.
Perfs: Weekends: Sat. 11.00 and 3.00. Sun. 11.00 and
3.00. Daily School Holidays; some Evenings.
Disabled Access.
Seats: 100

## MAGIC PUPPETRY COMPANY
36 Brynhyfryd Avenue, Rhyl, Denbighshire,
North Wales LL18 2DB
Tel: 01745 350586
Director: Derek Lawrence

## MAJOR MUSTARD'S TRAVELLING SHOW
1 Carless Avenue, Harborne, Birmingham B17 9EG
Tel: 0121 426 4329
Director: Mike Frost

## MICK'S ENTERTAINMENTS
Oldwell House, Broad End Road, Walsoken, Wisbech,
Cambridgeshire PE14 7BQ
Tel/Fax: 01945 461383
Uncle Mick Children's Entertainer, Punch and Judy,
Magic Ventriloquism, Funfair, Rides and Stalls.

## MOVINGSTAGE MARIONETTE COMPANY
78 Middleton Road, London E8 4BP
Tel: 0171 249 6876
Email: puppet@mcmail.com
Directors: Juliet and Gren Middleton

Operators of the Puppet Theatre Barge. A fully
equipped puppet theatre with seating for 60 persons.
Able to tour most venues. Maximum audience 200.
Carry fully equipped puppet booth with lighting and
sound.

## NO STRINGS PUPPET THEATRE
Archway House, Mansfield Road, Edwinstowe,
Nottinghamshire NG21 9HF
Tel: 01623 824210
Director: Alan Kirkpatrick; Sue Murray
Indoor and outdoor performances for all ages,
workshops for schools and community projects. Street
specialist - queues, crowds, parks, town centres - will
venture anywhere. Can tailor to 'era' - medieval,
Victorian etc.

## NORTHERN BLACK LIGHT THEATRE
Black Light Base, 1 Neville Terrace, York YO3 7NF
Tel: 01904 651138

## NORWICH PUPPET THEATRE
St James, Whitefriars, Norwich Norfolk NR3 1TN
Mgt 01603 615564 BO 01603 629921
Fax 01603 617578
Email: norpuppet@hotmail.com
Web Site: www.geocities.com/Broadway/Stage/2041
ADMINISTRATION:
General Manager: Ian Woods
Artistic Director: Luis Boy
Technician: Peter Butler
Administration: June Hutton
Status: Puppet Theatre
Policy: Norwich Puppet Theatre is a touring company
with almost unique benefit of own home theatre base
with raked auditorium, studio performance space and
workshops. Produces work for all ages from 3 years
upwards which tours throughout the UK and Europe.
Where possible live music is included in productions.
Willing to premiere show.
Facilities: Seating in main house 198 raked.  Studio
theatre 50 informal, 4 wheelchair spaces, level access
- all house facilities fully accessible.  Induction loop
system.
The Octagon exhibition gallery.  Licensed bar.  Food
brought in for specific functions.

## PAPER MAGIC - SILHOUETTES ORIGAMI PAPER CUTTING
PO Box 32, Hastings, East Sussex TN34 1BD
Tel: 01424 439855 Fax: 01424 439855

## THE PARKER MARIONETTES
10 Hurley Road, Little Corby, Carlisle,
Cumbria CA4 8QF
Tel: 01228 560980
Director: Stan Parker

## PAVLOV'S PUPPETS
Vesper Cottage, Smarden, Ashford, Kent TN27 8NA
Tel: 01223 770513
Puppets for all occasions including pantomime, variety
and cabaret. Specialists in UV puppetry. Acts and
effect created for advertising, etc.

## JOHN PEEL MOBILE PUPPET THEATRES
52 High Street, Hampton Wick, Kingston,
Surrey KT1 4DB
Tel: 0181 977 2976 (24 hours) Fax: 0181 286 9894
Email: n.claire@cablenet.co.uk
Traditional Fairy Stories performed by traditional hand-made glove puppets in mobile theatre. No gimics, old fashioned values.
8 foot height clearance. Suitable for rooms, halls and studio theatres.

## PICCOLO PUPPET COMPANY
11a Walpole Gardens, Strawberry Hill, Twickenham,
Middlesex TW2 5SL
Tel: 0181 898 9247

## PLAYBOARD PUPPET THEATRE
94 Ockendon Road, London N1 3NW
Tel: 0171 226 5911 Fax: 0171 704 1081
Director: Ian Allen

## POLLY'S PUPPETS
24 Maple Road, Ashtead, Surrey KT21 2LX
Tel: 01372 270190 Fax: 01372 271002
Director: Morag Thorpe
Administrator: Heidi Brazil

## PRESTO PUPPET THEATRE
Greenwood, 13 College Road, Buxton,
Derbyshire SK17 9DZ
Tel: 01298 77845 (24 Hour Answer Service)
Fax: 01298 23946
Directors: Nigel Lawton and Robin Lawrence

## PROFESSOR ALEXANDER'S PUNCH & JUDY
59 Wilton Way, London E8 1BG
Tel: 0171 254 0416

## PUNCHINELLO'S PUPPETS
Punch's Oak, Cleobury Road, Far Forest,
Worcester DY14 9EB
Tel: 01299 266634 Fax: 01299 266561
Director: Mary Edwards
Small scale touring and schools, street theatre walkabouts. Traditional Punch & Judy and Fantoccini. A Puppetlink company supported by West Midlands Arts.

## THE PUPPET CENTRE TRUST
at Battersea Arts Centre, Lavendar Hill,
London SW11 5TN
Tel: 0171 228 5335
Email: pct@puppetcentre.demon.co.uk
Director: Loretta Howells
Administrator: Allyson Kirk

## PUPPETCRAFT
1 Venton Oak Cottages, Dartington, Totnes,
Devon TQ9 6DW
Tel/Fax: 01803 867778
Email: puppetcraft@hotmail.co
Web Site: www.angelfine.com/or/puppetcraft/index.html
Artistic Director: John Roberts

## THE PUPPETEERS' COMPANY
PO Box 350, Brighton BN2 1TZ
Tel/Fax: 01273 687183
Email: admin@puppco.demon.co.uk
Web Site: www.puppco.demon.co.uk

## SHADOWSTRING THEATRE
'Tropiquaria', Washford Cross, Watchet, West
Somerset TA23 0JX
Tel: 01984 640688
Director: Paul Doran

## SMALL WORLD THEATRE
Fern Villa, Llandygwydd, Cardigan, Dyfed SA43 2QX
Tel/Fax: 01239 682785
Email: smallworld@ent.com

## CHRIS SOMERVILLE PUPPETS
13 Walton Crescent, Llandudno Junction,
Gwynedd LL31 9ER
Tel: 01492 582062
Director: Chris Somerville

## STAR PUPPETS
Kerry Farm, Yardley Gobion, Towcester,
Northants NN12 7UF
Tel: 01908 542110
Director: Christopher Covington

## THE STOCKWELL PUPPETS
Vesper Cottage, Smarden, Ashford, Kent TN27 8NA
Tel: 01233 770513
Directors: Alan and Brenda Stockwell

## THE THEATRE OF MARIONETTES
Barntimpin House, St.Anns, Lockerbie,
Dumfriesshire DG11 1HL Scotland
Tel: 01576 470222
Directors: Peter & Frances Grant

## TICKLISH ALLSORTS
31 Highfield Road, Salisbury, Wiltshire SP2 7LZ
Tel: 01722 335654
Senior Personnel: Gary A Nunn
Specialising in: Medieval Banquets, Children's Entertainers, Barn Dances.

## TREASURE TROVE PUPPET COMPANY
The Old Chapel, Glyndwr Road, Gwernymynydd,
Near Mold, Flintshire CH7 5LW Wales
Tel: 01352 750 838
Director: Stephen Sharples
Operation includes: Puppets for all occasions, small/middle scale touring, workshops and demonstrations. Makers of puppets. Extensive touring nationally and internationally.

## WHISPER AND SHOUT COMPANY
"Thornhill", Ridgeway Lane, Lymington,
Hampshire SO41 8AA
Tel: 01590 672325
Directors: Di and Arthur Humphrey

Representing Agents in all Branches
of the Entertainment Industry

The Agents' Association (Great Britain)
54 Keyes House, Dolphin Square
LONDON SW1V 3NA
Tel: 0171 834 0515   Fax: 0171 821 0261
Email: association@agents-uk.com
www.agents-uk.com

# AGENTS and PERSONAL MANAGERS

**19 MANAGEMENT**
Unit 32, Ransomes Dock, 35-37 Parkgate Road,
London SW11 4NP
Tel: 0171 738 1919
Fax: 0171 738 1819

**1984 PERSONAL MANAGEMENT**
54 Peartree Street, London EC1V 3SB
Tel: 0171 251 8046
Fax: 0171 250 0933

**1ST CLASS ENTERTAINMENT AGENCY**
2 Scotts Way, Riverhead, Sevenoaks, Kent TN13 2DG
Tel/Fax: 01732 456446
Mobile: 0850 603500

**1ST FRAMEWORK**
44 Nelson Square, London SE1 0QA
Tel: 0171 803 0530
Fax: 0171 803 0531

**4.A.D**
15 Alma Road, London SW18 1AA
Tel: 0181 870 9724
Fax: 0181 874 6600

**A & B ENTERTAINMENTS**
PO Box 87, Southport, Merseyside PR8 2AP
Tel: 01704 550033
Fax: 01704 551333

**A & B PERSONAL MANAGEMENT LIMITED**
5th Floor, Plaza Suite, 114 Jermyn Street,
London SW1Y 6HJ
Tel: 0171 839 4433
Fax: 0171 930 5738

**A & J MANAGEMENT**
551 Green Lanes, Palmers Green, London N13 4DR
Tel: 0181 882 7716
Fax: 0181 882 5983
Email: ajmanagement@bigfoot.com

**A BETTER CLASS OF ACT**
Star House, 338 Abingdon Road, Oxford OX1 4TQ
Tel/Fax: 01865 794782

**A CROSSE THE WORLD**
11A Kensington Park Road, London W11 3BY
Tel/Fax: 0171 263 0034

**A-Z ANIMALS LTD/A-Z DOGS LTD**
Endeavor House, 6 Station Road, Stoke D'Abernon,
Cobham Surrey KT11 3BN
Tel: 0171 248 6222
Fax: 01932 866369

**THE A6 AGENCY**
76 Buxton Road, Disley, Stockport, Cheshire
SK12 2HE
Tel/Fax: 01663 765860
Mobile: 0589 745594
Email: a6-acts@mighty-micro.co.uk

**AAA ARMSTRONG ACADEMY AGENCY**
GMC Studio, Hollingbourne, Maidstone
Kent ME17 1UQ
Tel: 01622 880599
Fax: 01622 880020

**AB ENTERTAINMENTS**
48 Queens Drive, Cashes Green, Stroud
Gloucestershire GL5 4LZ
Tel: 01453 755155
Fax: 01453 755255

**ABACUS PROMOTIONS**
92 Ashridge Way, Sunbury-On-Thames
Middlesex TW16 7RR
Tel: 01932 783395
Fax: 01932 713822

**JUNE ABBOTT ASSOCIATES**
10 York Way, London N1 9AA
Tel: 0171 837 7826
Fax: 0171 833 0870

**ABDC ENTERTAINMENTS**
18 Halls Farm Close, Winchester,
Hampshire SO22 6RE
Tel/Fax: 01962 885628

**MARJORIE ABEL LTD**
50 Maddox Street, London W1R 9PA
Tel: 0171 499 1343/ 0171 493 6921
Fax: 0171 499 8131

**ABLE ARTISTES & ASSOCIATES**
32 Manor Road, Wallington, Surrey SM6 0AA
Tel: 0181 647 4783

**ABOVE ALL ENTERTAINMENT**
(In Association With Mick Urry Orchestras)
15 Eastport Lane, Lewes, East Sussex BN7 1TL
Tel: 01273 486622/472931 (3 Lines)
Fax: 01273 486633

**ABS AGENCY**
2 Elgin Avenue, London W9 3QP
Tel: 0171 289 1160
Fax: 0171 289 1162

**ABSOLUTELY PRODUCTIONS LTD**
27-31 Charing Cross Road, London WC2H 0AU
Tel: 0171 930 3113
Fax: 0171 930 4114
Email: info@absolutely-uk.com

## ACA MODELS & PROMOTIONS
10A Cregagh Road, Belfast BT6 9EP
Tel: 01232 739613
Fax: 01232 739614

## ACCESS V.I.P.
Media Suite, Sicklinghall, Wetherby, Leeds, LS22 4BD
Tel: 01937 588066

## ACCOLADE PRODUCTIONS LTD
PO Box 422, Accolade House Southampton SO18 2ZB
Tel: 01703 327000
Fax: 01703 327777

## ACE MUSIC ENTERTAINMENTS
103 Roman Road, Salisbury, Wiltshire SP2 9BZ
Tel: 01722 328755
Fax: 01722 414513

## ACJ ENTERTAINMENTS
29 Chapel Lane, Codsall, Wolverhampton WV8 2EJ
Tel: 01902 845566
Fax: 01902 842532

## ACKER'S INTERNATIONAL AGENCY
53 Cambridge Mansions, Cambridge Road,
London SW11 4RX
Tel: 0171 978 5885/5886
Fax: 0171 978 5882

## ACORN ENTERTAINMENTS
Winterfold House, 46 Woodfield Road, Kings Heath,
Birmingham B13 9UJ
Tel/Fax 0121 444 7258
Email: jim@acornent.demon.co.uk
Web Site: http:\www.acornent.demon.co.uk

## ACROBATS UNLIMITED
The Circus Space, Coronet Street, London N1 6HD
Tel/Fax: 0171 613 5259
Email: acrobats@btinternet.com
Web Site: http:/www.btinternet.com/~acrobats

## THE ACT SHOP
PO Box 23, Spennymoor, County Durham DL16 7YZ
Tel: 01388 818888
Fax: 01388 811222
Email: actshop@agents-uk.com

## ACTING ASSOCIATES
71 Hartham Road, London N7 9JJ
Tel/Fax: 0171 607 3562 (2 lines)

## ACTION ENTERTAINMENT
27 Fairholme Road, Croydon, Surrey CR0 3PG
Tel: 0181 689 7615
Fax: 0181 239 7987

## ACTION FORCE ENTERTAINMENTS
Regis House, 98 High Street, Billericay,
Essex CM12 9XU
Tel: 01277 633314

Fax: 01277 633315

## ACTIVE ARTS MANAGEMENT
347 Archway Road, Highgate, London N6 5AA
Tel: 0181 342 8555
Fax: 0181 342 8010

## ACTORS AGENCY
1 Glen Street, Tollcross, Edinburgh EH3 9JD
Tel: 0131 228 4040 (2 Lines)
Fax: 0131 228 4645
Mobile: 0831 403030

## ACTORS ALLIANCE
Bon Marche Building, 444 Brixton Road,
London SW9 8EJ
Tel/Fax: 0171 326 0070

## ACTORS EXCHANGE LTD
Unit 3/1, 11 Marshalsea Road, London SE1 1EP
Tel: 0171 378 8441
Fax: 0171 378 8152

## ACTORS FILE
61-71 Collier Street, London N1 9BE
Tel: 0171 278 0087
Fax: 0171 278 0364

## THE ACTORS GROUP
(TAG)
4 Newton Street, Piccadilly, Manchester M1 2AW
Tel: 0161 228 0771
Fax: 0161 236 6935

## ACTORS INC.
14 Dean Street, London W1V 5AH
Tel: 0171 437 4417
Fax: 0171 437 4221

## THE ACTORS LIST
Half Moon Chambers Chapel Walks,
Manchester M2 1HN
Tel: 0161 833 1605
Fax: 0161 832 5219
Web Site: www.bossagencies.co.uk

## ACTORS NETWORK AGENCY (SEE LISTING ANA)

## ACTORUM
3rd Floor, 21 Foley Street, London W1P 7LH
Tel: 0171 636 6978
Fax: 0171 636 6975

## ADA ENTERPRISES
78 St. Margarets Road, Twickenham,
Middlesex TW1 2LP
Tel: 0181 892 1716
Fax: 0181 892 5069

**ADASTRA**
2 Star Row, North Dalton, Driffield,
East Yorkshire YO25 9UR
Tel: 01377 217662
Fax: 01377 217754
Email: adastra@adastey.demon.co.uk
Web Site: http://www.wizardweb.co.uk/adastra

**AFTER DINNER SPEAKERS**
Saga Court, 3 Sibleys Rise, South Heath,
Great Missenden, Buckinghamshire HP16 9QQ
Tel: 01494 866289
Fax: 01494 890558

**AFTER DINNER WORLD**
"Lime Trees" Blackwood Hall Booth House Terrace,
Luddendenfoot, Halifax, West Yorkshire HX2 6HH
Tel: 01422 886006
Fax: 01422 884494
Email: roger.davis@comedians.co.uk

**THE AGENCY ( LONDON) LTD**
24 Pottery Lane, Holland Park, London W11 4LZ
Tel: 0171 727 1346
Fax: 0171 727 9037

**THE AGENCY**
370 City Road, Islington, London EC1V 2QA
Tel: 0171 278 3331
Fax: 720171 83746

**A.I.B. ENTERTAINMENTS**
41 The Quarryknowes, Bo'ness,
West Lothian EH51 0QJ
Tel/Fax: 01506 828976

**AIM (ASSOCIATED INTERNATIONAL MANAGEMENT)**
5 Denmark Street, London WC2H 8LP
Tel: 0171 836 2001
Fax: 0171 379 0848

**A.I.R LTD**
AIR House, Spennymoor, County Durham DL16 7SE
Tel: 01388 814632
Fax: 01388 812445
Email: air@agents-uk.com

**ALANDER AGENCY**
135 Merrion Avenue, Stanmore, Middlesex HA7 4RZ
Tel: 0181 954 7685

**ALBERT ALCHEMY ENTERTAINMENT**
5 Beech Avenue, Rawmarsh, Rotherham,
South Yorkshire S62 5HH
Tel: 01709 710780
Fax: 01709 399688
Email: albert@albertalchemy.com
Web Site: www@albertalchemy.com

**ALEXANDER PERSONAL MANAGEMENT**
16 Roughdown Avenue, Hemel Hempstead,
Hertfordshire HP3 9BH
Tel: 01442 252907
Fax: 01442 241099

**ALEXANDER'S**
31 Kirk Road, Mapperley, Nottingham NG3 6GX
Tel/Fax: 0115 962 3827

**ALL ELECTRIC THEATRE PRODUCTIONS**
8 Wyndham Road, Andover, Hampshire SP10 2JR
Tel: 01264 361924
Fax: 01264 337014

**ALL STAR SPEAKERS**
100 Farm Lane, London SW6 1QH
Tel: 0171 381 4693
Fax: 0171 385 6647
Email: speakers@globalnet.co.uk

**ALL STAR WRESTLING PROMOTIONS**
81 Fountain Street, Birkenhead, Merseyside L42 7JD
Tel: 0151 652 6507 (5 lines)
Fax: 0151 652 3090

**DEREK ALLEN ENTERTAINMENTS**
22 Auburn Grove, Blackpool FY1 5NJ
Tel: 01253 693195
Tel: 01253 791830

**JIM ALLEN MANAGEMENT**
Woodyers House, Thorpe in Balne, Doncaster,
South Yorkshire DN6 0DY
Tel/Fax: 01302 883545

**NICK ALLEN MANAGMENT**
4-7 Forewoods Common, Holt, Trowbridge,
Wiltshire BA14 6PJ
Tel/Fax: 01225 782281

**STEVE ALLEN ENTERTAINMENTS**
60 Broadway, Peterborough PE1 1SU
Tel: 01733 569589
Fax: 01733 564109

**ALLIED TALENT**
Mansfield House, 9 Great Chapel Street,
London W1V 3AL
Tel: 0171 437 2551
Fax: 0171 437 2295

**MICHAEL ALLISON ASSOCIATES**
Unit 3, The Apollo Building, 18 All Saints Road,
London W11 1HH
Tel: 0171 221 1062
Fax: 0171 2212390

**THE ALLOTT AGENCY**
8 Melbourne Avenue, Dronfield Woodhouse,
Derbyshire S18 5YW
Tel: 01246 412365

Fax: 01246 290338
Mobile: 0836 231859

## ALLSORTS CASTING
1 Cathedral Street, London SE1 9DE
Tel: 0171 403 4834
Fax: 0171 403 1656

## ALLSORTS DRAMA FOR CHILDREN
2 Pember Road, London NW10 5LP
Tel: 0181 969 3249/07071 225090
Fax: 0181 969 3249

## ALMA MANAGEMENT LTD
8 Swift Street, Fulham, London SW6 5AG
Tel: 0171 736 1772
Fax: 0171 731 3480

## ALPHA CONNECTION AGENCY
Suite 49, Charter House, Lord Montgomery Way,
Portsmouth PO1 2SH
Tel: 01705 732744
Fax: 01705 618817
Mobile: 0850 305631/2
Email: alpac@mcmail.com
Web Site: www.alphac.mcmail.com

## ALPHA PERSONAL MANAGEMENT
Berkeley House, 73 Upper Richmond Road,
London SW15 2SZ
Tel: 0181 870 7066/0181 870 7013
Fax: 0181 870 7077

## JONATHAN ALTARAS ASSOCIATES (JAA)
13 Shorts Gardens, London WC2H 9AT
Tel: 0171 836 8722
Fax: 0171 836 6066

## ALTERNATIVE ARTS
47a Brushfield Street, London E1 6AA
Tel: 0171 375 0441
Fax: 0171 375 0484

## ALVAREZ MANAGEMENT
86 Muswell Road, Muswell Hill, London N10 2BE
Tel: 0181 883 2206
Fax: 0181 444 2646

## ALW ASSOCIATES
5 Spring Street, London W2 3RA
Tel: 0171 262 5506/7
Fax: 0171 2402 4834

## AM ARTISTS
68c Randolph Avenue, London W9 1BG
Tel: 0171 286 4852

## AM MODEL & PROMOTION AGENCY
11 St. Marys Place, Newcastle upon Tyne NE1 7PG
Tel: 0191 233 1420/233 2331
Fax: 0191 233 1421

## BRIAN AMBER ENTERTAINMENTS
The White House, 9 Well Street, Tyldesley,
Manchester M29 8HN
Tel/Fax: 01941 891527

## AMBER PERSONAL MANAGEMENT LTD
28 St Margarets Chambers, 5 Newton Street,
Manchester M1 1HN
Tel: 0161 228 0236
Fax: 0161 228 0235

## AMG LTD
11-13 Broad Court, Covent Garden,
London WC2B 5QN
Tel: 0171 240 5052
Fax: 0171 240 4956

## AMI ARTISTE MANAGEMENT INTERNATIONAL
8 Buckfast Court, Runcorn, Cheshire WA7 1QJ
Tel 01928 579992

## AMOR REEVES MANAGEMENT
Bouverie House, Effra Road, London SW19 8PS
Tel: 0181 543 1999
Fax: 0181 543 1973

## AMP RECORDS
PO Box 387, London N22 6SF
Tel: 0181 889 0616

## ANA (ACTORS NETWORK AGENCY)
55 Lambeth Walk, London SE11 6DX
Tel: 0171 735 0999
Fax: 0171 735 8177

## NITA ANDERSON ENTERTAINMENT
165 Wolverhampton Road, Sedgley, Dudley,
West Midlands DY3 1QR
Tel: 01902 882211/681224
Fax: 01902 883356

## ANDERSSONS
PO Box 672, Chelmsford, Essex CM2 9TH
Tel: 01245 476187
Fax: 01245 471544

## AMANDA ANDREWS AGENCY
30 Caverswall Road, Blythe Bridge,
Stoke-on-Trent ST11 9BG
Tel/Fax: 01782 393889

## ANFIELD AGENCY
1 The Stiles, Ormskirk, Lancashire L39 3QG
Tel: 01695 576026
Fax: 01695 578757

## SUSAN ANGEL ASSOCIATES
1st Floor, 12 D'Arblay Street, London W1V 3FP
Tel: 0171 439 3086
Fax: 0171 437 1712

**ANGLE ENTERTAINMENTS**
P.O. Box 253, Maltby, Rotherham S66 7YL
Tel: 01709 812079
Fax: 01709 813182
Freephone: 0800 074 0312
Email: angle@globalnet.co.uk
Web Site: http://users.globalnet.co.uk/-angle

**ANGLIA ARTISTES**
19 Granville Road, Felixstowe, Suffolk IP11 8AT
Tel: 01394 283159
Fax: 01394 276162
Email: info@anglia-artistes.co.uk
Web Site: http://www.anglia-artistes.co.uk

**ANIMAL AMBASSADORS**
20 Croft Way, Woodcote, Reading,
Berkshire RG8 0RS
Tel/Fax: 01491 681202

**ANIMAL ARK**
29 Somerset Road, Brentford, Middlesex TW8 8BT
Tel: 0181 560 3029
Fax: 0181 560 5762

**ANIMAL FREE ADVISORY SERVICE**
270 Hithercroft Road, High Wycombe,
Buckinghamshire HP13 5RF
Tel: 01426 611569
Fax: 01494 441385

**ANIMAL WORLD**
28 Greaves Road, High Wycombe,
Buckinghamshire HP13 7JU
Tel: 01494 442750
Fax: 01494 441385

**API PERSONALITY MANAGEMENT**
141-143 Drury Lane, London WC2B 5TB
Tel: 0171 379 4625
Fax: 0171 836 1735

**APM (SEE ALEXANDER PERSONAL MANAGEMENT)**

**APOLLO PROMOTIONS**
3 Grove Farm House, Grove Hill, Osmington,
Weymouth, Dorset DT3 6EZ
Tel: 01305 834097

**APSLEY ENTERTAINMENTS LTD**
116 Belswains Lane, Hemel Hempstead,
Hertfordshire HP3 9PP
Tel: 01442 256856
Fax: 01442 256856

**ARAENA ENTERPRISES**
Oriel Lodge, 26 Linksway, Northwood,
Middlesex HA6 2XB
Tel: 01923 827047/01923 775480
Fax: 01923 827047

**BILLY F ARATA**
1 Vernon Avenue, Birmingham B20 1DB
Tel: 0121 554 4708
Fax: 0121 523 4603

**ARENA ENTERTAINMENT ORGANISATION**
Regents Court, 39 Harrogate Road, Leeds LS7 3PD
Tel: 0113 239 2222
Fax: 0113 239 2016
Email: stars@arenaentertainments.co.uk

**ARENA PERSONAL MANAGEMENT**
Room 11, Ground Floor, East Block, Panther House,
38, Mount Pleasant, London WC1X 0AP
Tel/Fax: 0171 278 1661

**ARLINGTON ENTERPRISES**
1-3 Charlotte Street, London W1P 1HB
Tel: 0171 580 0702
Fax: 0171 580 4994

**ARM (SEE ALAN ROBINSON MANAGEMENT)**

**ARMSTRONG ARTS PERSONAL MANAGEMENT**
9 Greville Hall Greville Place, London NW6 5JS
Tel: 0171 372 7110
Fax: 07070 746230
Email: armstrongartsltd@armstrongartsltd.demon.co.uk

**ALAN ARNISON ENTERTAINMENT CONSULTANTS**
PO Box 194, Stockport, Cheshire SK2 5FL
Tel: 0161 419 9930

**ARTFIELD LTD**
5 Grosvenor Square, London W1X 9LA
Tel: 0171 499 9941
Email: artfield@dial.pipex.com

**ARTISTE MANAGEMENT GROUP (SEE AMG)**

**ARTS MANAGEMENT**
"Redroofs" Littlewick Green, Maidenhead,
Berkshire SL6 3QY
Tel: 01628 822982
Fax: 01628 822461

**ARTS, SOUND AND LEISURE**
4 Keats Avenue, Grantham, Lincolnshire NG31 9NN
Tel/Fax: 01476 571096

**ARTSWORLD INTERNATIONAL MANAGEMENT LTD**
P.O. Box 13759, London W2 6FG
Tel: 0171 262 1500
Fax: 0171 262 1459
Web Site: www.agents-uk.com/59

## ASGARD
125 Parkway, London NW1 7PS
Tel: 0171 387 5090
Fax: 0171 387 8740

## ASHDOWN ASSOCIATES
Crescent Arts Centre, 2-4 University Road, Belfast,
Northern Ireland BT7 1NH
Tel/Fax: 01232 248861

## ASKONAS HOLT LTD
Lonsdale Chambers, 27 Chancery Lane,
London WC2A 1PF
Tel: 0171 400 1700
Fax: 0171 400 1799
Email: info@askonasholt.co.uk
Web Site: www.askonashold.co.uk

## DAVID ASPDEN
Tel: 01306 712120
Fax: 01306 713241

## ASQUITH & HORNER PERSONAL MANAGEMENT
The Studio, 14 College Road, Bromley, Kent BR1 3NS
Tel: 0181 466 5580
Fax: 0181 313 0443

## ASSOCIATED ARTS
8 Shrewsbury Lane, London SE18 3JF
Tel: 0181 856 4958
Fax: 0181 856 8189

## ASSOCIATED SPEAKERS
24a Park Road, Hayes, Middlesex UB4 8JN
Tel: 0181 848 9048

## ATA (SEE ALLIED TALENT AGENCY)

## ATHOLE STILL INTERNATIONAL MANAGEMENT LTD
Foresters Hall, 25-27 Westow Street,
London SE19 3TY
Tel: 0181 771 5271
Fax: 0181 771 8172
Email: athole@dial.pipex.com

## ATLANTIC VISION ENTERTAINMENTS
Unit 1, 29 Broadway Avenue, St Margarets,
Twickenham TW1 1RH
Tel: 0181 891 1446
Fax: 0181 892 0406

## ATS CASTING LTD
26 St. Michaels Road, Headingley, Leeds LS6 3AW
Tel: 0113 230 4300/0113 230 4334
Fax: 0113 275 6422

## ATTICUS TELEVISION LTD
5 Clarelawn Avenue, London SW14 8BH
Tel/Fax: 0181 876 0406

## AUTONOMOUS TALENT BOOKING
PO Box 7, Ware, Hertfordshire SG12 9UD
Tel: 01920 467780
Fax: 01920 466077

## AVALON PROMOTIONS LTD
4a Exmoor Street, London W10 6BD
Tel: 0171 598 7333
Fax: 0171 598 7334
Email: chrisw@avalonuk.com

## AVENUE ARTISTES LTD
47 The Polygon, Southampton SO15 2BP
Tel: 01703 227077
Fax: 01703 334625

## ELAINE AVON ARTISTES MANAGEMENT/CRUISE CONSULTANT
Montage, 127 Westhall Road, Warlingham,
Surrey CR6 9HJ
Tel: 01883 622317/0836 766608
Fax: 01883 627478

## AVVIC PERSONAL MANAGEMENT
6 Edgware Mount, Leeds LS8 5NG
Tel/Fax: 0113 248 4915

## BAD HABITS ENTERTAINMENT GROUP
PO Box 111 London W13 0ZH
Tel: 0181 357 2337
Fax: 0181 566 7215
Regional Office, PO Box 69, Daventry NN11 4ZY
Tel: 01327 312505
Fax: 01327 312545
Email: info@badhabitsent-group.com
Web Site: www.badhabitsent-group.com

## BAGENAL HARVEY ORGANISATION LTD
141-143 Drury Lane, London WC2B 5TB
Tel: 0171 279 4625
Fax: 0171 836 1735

## PAUL BAILEY AGENCY
22 Wolsey Road, East Molesey, Surrey KT8 9EL
Tel: 0181 941 2034
Fax: 0181 941 6304

## YVONNE BAKER ASSOCIATES
8 Temple Fortune Lane, London NW11 7UD
Tel: 0181 455 8687
Fax: 0181 458 3143
Email: yvonne@yvbaker.demon.co.uk

## DAVID G BALL
Fir Tree Cottage, Tibberton,
Gloucestershire GL19 3AQ
Tel: 01452 790514

## B.A.M. ASSOCIATES
The Old Fire Station, 82-84 York Road,
Bristol BS3 4AL
Tel: 0117 963 2855

Fax: 0117 953 5508

## BAMFORD MANAGEMENT
81 Russell Court, Ross Road, Wallington,
Surrey SM6 8QT
Tel/Fax: 0181 669 3074

## ANDREW BANCROFT ASSOCIATES
48 Mortimer Street London W1N 7DG
Tel: 0171 700 0432
Fax: 0171 436 0747

## JOE BANGAY ENTERPRISES
River House, Riverwood Drive, Marlow,
Buckinghamshire SL7 1QY
Tel: 01628 486193
Fax: 01628 890239
Mobile: 0860 812529

## AUSTIN BAPTISTE ENTERTAINMENT AGENCY
29 Court House Gardens, Finchley, London N3 1PU
Tel: 0181 922 3770
Tel/Fax: 0181 346 3984

## GAVIN BARKER ASSOCIATES
45 South Molton Street, Mayfair London W1Y 1HD
Tel: 0171 434 3801
Fax: 0171 494 1547

## BARN DANCE AGENCY
62 Beechwood Road, South Croydon,
Surrey CR2 0AA
Tel: 0181 657 2813
Fax: 0181 651 6080

## HARRY BARNES ENTERTAINMENTS
Braemar House, 5 Braemar Lane, Worsley,
Manchester M28 1HD
Tel: 0161 799 2684
Fax: 0161 799 5678

## PAUL BARRETT ROCK 'N' ROLL ENTERPRISES
16 Grove Place, Penarth, South Glamorgan CF64 2ND
Tel: 01222 704279
Fax: 01222 709989

## BEN BARRETTO ENTERTAINMENTS AGENCY
2 Oakham Road, Somerby, Melton Mowbray,
Leicestershire LE14 2QF
Tel: 01664 454888
Email: 106063.316@ compuserve.com
Web Site: http://ourworld.compuserve.com.homepages
/benbarretto

## TONY BARRIE ASSOCIATES
149 Kingfisher Drive, Merrow Park, Guildford,
Surrey GU4 7EY
Tel: 01483 502687

## BARRON KNIGHTS
Touchwood, Plantation Road, Leighton Buzzard,
Bedfordshire LU7 7JE
Tel/Fax: 01525 854443
Email: Templar@Powernet.co.uk

## BARROW GORDON ASSOCIATES LTD
53 Grosvenor Street, London W1X 9FH
Tel: 0181 876 4433
Fax: 0181 878 3942

## THE MARTIN BARRY AGENCY
39 Godre'r Coed, Gwernymynydd, Mold,
Flintshire CH7 4DS
Tel: 01352 758266
Fax: 01352 759511

## GEORGE BARTRAM
1 Sherborne Street, Birmingham B16 8DE
Tel: 0121 608 6000
Fax: 0121 608 2223

## BASEMENT MANAGEMENT
Park House, 37-51 Greenhill Crescent,
Watford WD1 8QU
Tel: 01923 220169

## B.A.S.I. C..D. AGENCYPEOPLE
3 Rushden House, Tatlow Road, Glenfield,
Leicester LE3 8ND
Tel: 0116 287 9594

## PETER FATS BAXTER
1A4 Third Avenue, Hove, East Sussex BN3 2PD
Tel/Fax: 01273 770818

## B.C.D ENTERTAINMENTS AGENCY
Lawnhaven, Coldharbour Farm, Castle Canyke Road,
Bodmin, Cornwall PL31 1DX
Tel: 01208 72614
Fax: 01208 72144

## B.D.A. (BRIAN DURKIN ASSOCIATES)
Bryson House, Chiltern Road, Culcheth, Warrington,
Cheshire WA3 4LL
Tel: 01925 766655
Fax: 01925 763073
Email: ybd349@aol.com

## BE-ALL & END-ALL MANAGEMENT
15 Essex Road Chesham, Buckinghamshire HP5 3HT
Tel/Fax: 01494 580753

## BEAT STREET ENTERTAINMENTS LTD
50/52 West Main Street, Darvel, Ayrshire KA17 0AQ
Tel: 01560 320383
Fax: 01560 320843
Email: promotions@beatstreet.co.uk
Web Site: http:\www.beatstreet.co.uk

## JOHN BEDFORD ASSOCIATES
40 Stubbington Avenue, Portsmouth,

Hampshire PO2 0HY
Tel: 01705 661339
Fax: 01705 643993

### BEE BOP PROMOTIONS
2 Council Houses, Bromley Wood, Rugeley,
Staffordshire WS15 3AQ
Tel/Fax: 01283 840382

### BEEJAYS PROMOTIONS
136 Pottinger Street, Ashton-under-Lyne,
Lancashire OL7 0HQ
Tel/Fax: 0161 344 1610
Mobile: 0850 450 609

### BEHIND THE SCENES UK
Tel/Fax: 01908 630256
Mobile: 0378 045813
Email: btsuk@aol.com

### JULIAN BELFRAGE ASSOCIATES
46 Albemarle Street, London W1X 4PP
Tel: 0171 491 4400
Fax: 0171 493 5460

### BELLTOWER ENTERPRISES
(See also Droagonsfire)
9 Hillside Road, Ashstead, Surrey KT21 1RZ
Tel: 01372 277703
Fax: 01372 278406

### AUDREY BENJAMIN AGENCY
278A Elgin Avenue, Maida Vale, London W9 1JR
Tel: 0171 289 7180
Fax: 0171 266 5480

### TONY BENNELL ENTERTAINMENTS
10 Manor Way, Kidlington, Oxfordshire OX5 2BD
Tel/Fax: 01865 372645
Mobile: 0585 204274

### THE JULES BENNETT AGENCY
PO Box 25, Moreton-In-Marsh,
Gloucestershire GL56 9YJ
Tel/Fax: 07000 458537
Tel/Fax: 01386 701571
Mobile: 0468 017293

### BENTLEY'S ENTERTAINMENTS
26a Winders Road, London SW11 3HB
Tel: 0171 223 7900
Fax: 0171 978 4062

### BEVERLEY ARTISTES
Beverley House, 22-34 Dean Road, South Shields,
Tyne and Wear NE33 3PT
Tel: 0191 456 2428
Fax: 0192 456 0978

### BGS PRODUCTIONS
Newtown Street, Kilsyth, Glasgow G65 0JX
Tel: 01236 821081

Fax: 01236 826900
Email: nscott@scotdisc.co.uk
Web Site: http//www.scotdisc.co.uk

### BIG BEAR MUSIC
PO Box 944, Birmingham B16 8UT
Tel: 0121 454 7020
Fax: 0121 454 9996
Email: bigbearmusic@compuserve.com

### BIG LIFE RECORDS (1994) LTD
15 Little Portland Street, London W1N 5DE
Tel: 0171 323 3888
Fax: 0171 636 3551

### BIG M PRODUCTIONS LTD
Big M House, 1 Stevenage Road, Knebworth,
Hertfordshire SG3 6AN
Tel: 01438 814433
Fax: 01438 815252

### BILLBOARD PERSONAL MANAGEMENT
The Co-op Centre, 11 Mowll Street, London SW9 6BG
Tel: 0171 735 9956
Fax: 0171 793 0426

### TONY BILLINGHAM MUSIC
Lapal House, Lapal Lane South, Halesowen,
West Midlands B62 0EF
Tel: 0121 550 1272/503 0326
Fax: 0121 550 1562

### BIRCHALL ENTERTAINMENT AGENCY
16 Granville Road, Jesmond,
Newcastle Upon Tyne NE2 1TP
Tel: 0191 386 7461

### MICHAEL BLACK PERSONAL MANAGEMENT
5 The Ridgeway, Radlett, Hertfordshire WD7 8PZ
Tel: 01923 856555
Fax: 01923 859871

### ALLAN BLACKBURN ARTISTES
7 Bd des Moulins, Monte Carlo, MC 98000 Monaco
Tel: +377 93 30 67 98
Fax: +377 92 16 01 94

### BLACKBURN SACHS ASOCIATES
Eastgate House, 16-19 Eastcastle Street,
London W1N 7PA
Tel: 0171 636 7744
Fax: 0171 636 5757

### BLACKMAIL MANAGEMENT & PRODUCTION
60 Cleveland Road, New Malden, Surrey KT3 3QJ
Tel/Fax: 0181 942 9511

**DEREK BLOCK ARTISTES AGENCY LIMITED**
Douglas House, 3 Richmond Buildings,
London W1V 5AE
Tel: 0171 434 2100
Fax: 0171 434 0200
Email: dbaa@derekblock.demon.co.uk

**REBECCA BLOND ASSOCIATES**
69A Kings Road, London SW3 4NX
Tel: 0171 351 4100
Fax: 0171 351 4600

**BLONDIE ENTERTAINMENTS**
39 The Chase, Off Penns Lane, Sutton Coldfield,
West Midlands
Tel: 0121 384 6460

**BLUE WAND PRODUCTIONS LTD**
2nd Floor 12 Weltje Road, London W6 9TG
Tel/Fax: 0181 741 2038

**BLUE WATER PRODUCTIONS**
Blue Water, Vinegar Hill, Undy,
Monmouthshire NP6 3EJ
Tel: 01633 882211
Fax: 01633 880045

**BLUEPRINT MANAGEMENT**
134 Lots Road, London SW10 0RJ
Tel: 0171 351 4333
Fax: 0171 352 4652

**BLUESTONE PROMOTIONS**
Fermoy, Farnham Road, Odiham,
Hampshire RG29 1HS
Tel/Fax: 01256 702535
Mobile: 0966 371747/371748

**B.M.A. (BODYLINE MODEL AGENCY)**
32 Akeman Street, Tring, Hertfordshire HP23 6AN
Tel: 01442 890490
FAX: 01442 890690

**BO PROMOTIONS**
PO Box 201, Macclesfield, Cheshire SK11 7BS
Tel/Fax: 01189 403516
Email: www.mrmethane.com

**BOBSONS PRODUCTIONS**
The Penthouse, 10 Abbey Orchard Street,
London SW1P 2JP
Tel: 0171 222 1154
Fax: 0171 222 1147

**JOHN BODDY AGENCY**
10 Southfield Gardens, Twickenham TW1 4SZ
Tel: 0181 892 0133/0181 891 3809
Fax: 0181 892 4283

**BODEN AGENCY**
6 Windmill Hill, Enfield, Middlesex EN2

Tel/Fax: 0181 367 1836

**BODO AGENCY**
186 Ashley Road, Hale, Altrincham,
Cheshire WA15 9SF
Tel/Fax: 0161 928 8136

**RICK BONNER ENTERTAINMENTS**
9 Mill Brooks, South Chailey, Lewes,
East Sussex BN8 4AW
Tel: 0273 401573

**BOO-BOO THE CLOWNS FAMILY ENTERTAINMENTS AGENCY**
90 Market Street, Ashby-De-La-Zouch,
Leicestershire LE65 1AP
Freephone: 0800 371266
Free Fax: 0800 371643 (24 Hrs)
Email: 101746.2275@ compuserve.com

**BOOK OF DREAMS**
73 Couchmore Avenue, Esher, Surrey KT10 9AX
Tel: 0181 398 0255
Fax: 0181 398 9022
Email: bookofdreams@compuserve.com

**BOOM CLOUD MANAGEMENT**
8 Botteville Road, Birmingham,
West Midlands B27 7YD
Tel: 0121 708 1349/0836 339142
Fax: 0121 707 6428

**BOOT MUSIC LTD**
PO Box 1745, London W9 3QL
Tel/Fax: 0181 968 0753

**BORDER LEISURE**
Top Floor, Richmond Place, 69/71 Edgar Street,
Hereford HR4 9JR
Tel: 01432 270470
Fax: 01432 353867

**JOE BORROW ENTERPRISES**
New House, Blue House Point Road,
Stockton-On-Tees, Cleveland TS18 2PJ
Tel: 01642 616710
Fax: 01642 615737

**JOHN BOSCO ENTERTAINMENTS**
The Talbot, High Street, Cuckfield, Haywards Heath,
West Sussex RH17 5JX
Tel: 01444 451043

**ADRIAN BOSS PROMOTIONS**
2 Elgin Avenue, London W9 2QP
Tel: 0171 286 1665
Fax: 0171 286 1573

**DEREK BOULTON MANAGEMENT**
76 Carlisle Mansions, Carlisle Place,
London SW1P 1HZ
Tel: 0171 828 6533

Fax: 0171 828 1271

**SHEILA BOURNE MANAGEMENT**
Bridge House, Three Mill Lane, London E3 3DU
Tel: 0181 215 2150
Fax: 0181 215 2159

**SANDRA BOYCE MANAGEMENT**
1 Kingsway Parade, Albion Road, London N16 0TA
Tel: 0171 923 0606
Fax: 0171 241 2313

**RALPH BOYD ENTERTAINMENTS**
17 Dundee Court, Ellesmere Port,
South Wirral L65 5EQ
Tel: 0151 355 7642/0151 356 4640
Fax: 0151 356 7796

**MICHELLE BRAIDMAN ASSOCIATES**
3rd Floor Suite, 10 Lower John Street,
London W1R 3PE
Tel: 0171 437 0817
Fax: 0171 439 3600
Email: michelle@braidman.com

**BRAITHWAITE'S THEATRICAL AGENCY**
8 Brookshill Avenue, Harrow, Middlesex HA3 6RZ
Tel: 0181 954 5638

**BREAK THE ICE**
200 Pennygate, Spalding, Lincolnshire PE11 1LT
Tel: 01775 766230
Fax: 01775 714107

**BRENT ENTERTAINMENT AGENCY**
87 Herbert Gardens, London NW10 3BH
Tel: 0181 965 2826
Fax: 0181 965 2991
Mobile: 0802 885557

**BRIAN DURKIN ASSOCIATES**
(See BDA),

**PAUL BRIDSON PRODUCTIONS**
Motte House, Marford Hill, Marford, Wrexham,
LL12 8SW
Tel: 01244 571708/01244 571709
Fax: 01244 571722

**BRIGHT MUSIC AGENCY LTD**
55 Fulham High Street, London SW6 3JJ
Tel: 0171 384 1599
Fax: 0171 384 2236

**BRIGHT TRACKS PRODUCTIONS**
PO Box 27, Stroud, Gloucestershire GL6 0YQ
Tel/Fax: 01453 836877

**BRISTOCK ENTERTAINMENTS**
5 Bartonia Grove, Brislington, Bristol BS4 5AG
Tel: 0117 977 3202

Fax: 0117 983 3800

**BRITISH STAGE PRODUCTIONS**
Unit 8, 132 Charing Cross Road, London WC2H 0LA
Tel: 0171 836 4128
Fax: 0171 836 2949
126 Victoria Road, Scarborough YO11 2FL
Tel: 01753 507186

**BRITT MANGEMENT**
59 Plains of Waterloo, Ramsgate, Kent CT11 8JE
Tel: 01843 850586/851656
Fax: 01843 850586

**BROADLAND ENTERTAINMENTS**
12 Broadland Drive, Thorpe End, Norwich NR13 5BT
Tel: 01603 432766/01603 439968

**BROADLEY MUSIC GROUP**
48 Broadley Terrace, London NW1 6LG
Tel: 0171 258 0324
Fax: 0171 724 2361

**DOLLY BROOK CASTING**
52 Sandford Road, East Ham, London E6 3QS
Tel: 0181 472 2561
Fax: 0181 552 0733

**BILL BROOKMAN**
101 Ashby Road, Loughborough,
Leicestershire LE11 3AB
Tel: 01509 236175
Fax: 01509 219873
Email: Bill_Brookman@compuserve.com

**CLAUDE BROOKS ENTERTAINMENTS**
1 High Street, Slough, Berkshire SL1 1DY
Tel: 01753 520717
Fax: 01753 520424

**BROTHERHOOD OF MAN MANAGEMENT**
Westfield, 75 Burkes Road, Beaconsfield,
Buckinghamshire HP9 1PP
Tel: 01494 673073
Fax: 01494 680920

**BARRY BROWN & PARTNER**
47 West Square, Southwark, London SE11 4SP
Tel: 0171 928 1229
Fax: 0171 928 1909

**GARRY BROWN ASSOCIATES (INT) LTD**
27 Downs Side, Cheam, Sutton, Surrey SM2 7EH
Tel: 0181 643 3991/8375
Fax: 0181 770 7241
Email: gbaltd@compuserve.com

**PETER BROWNE MANAGEMENT**
13 St. Martins Road, London SW9 0SP
Tel: 0171 737 3444
Fax: 0171 737 3446

## J & S BROWNHUT ENTERTAINMENT PROMOTIONS
(With S G Brownhut Promotions)
22 Kings Road, Bramhope, Leeds LS16 9JN
Tel: 0113 267 5127
Fax: 0113 261 2813
Mobile: 0374 816942

## DEREK BRUCE LTD
107 High Street, Evesham, Worcestershire WR11 4EB
Tel: 01386 442819/443456
Fax: 01386 443456

## BRUNSKILL MANAGEMENT LTD
Suite 8a, 169 Queens Gate, London SW7 5HE
Tel: 0171 581 2288/9; 0171 584 8060
Fax: 0171 589 9460
Email: 101234.2025@compuserve.com

## BTM
P.O. Box 6003, Birmingham B45 0AR
Tel: 0121 477 9553
Fax: 0121 693 2954
Email: barry@btm-gotham.demon.co.uk

## BTM LEISURE
Sunnyville House, Park Crescent, Wellingborough,
Northamptonshire NN8 4PJ
Tel: 01933 223575
Fax: 01933 225725

## BTWS (ENTERTAINMENTS) LTD
60 Granshaw Close, Kings Norton,
Birmingham B38 8RA
Tel: 0121 458 2462
Fax: 0121 628 2622

## BUBBLEGUM
Ealing Studios Ealing Green, London W5 5EP
Tel: 0181 758 8678
Fax: 0181 758 8664
Email: bubgm@aol.com

## RICHARD BUCKNALL MANAGEMENT (RBM)
3rd Floor, 18 Betterton Street, London WC2H 9BP
Tel: 0171 287 5010
Fax: 0171 287 5020

## STEPHEN BUDD MANAGEMENT
109B Regents Park Road, London NW1 8UR
Tel: 0171 916 3303
Fax: 0171 916 3302
Email: sb.stephenbudd.demon.co.uk

## BULLRUSH MANAGEMENT
Unit 5, Mart Road Industrial Estate, Minehead,
Somerset
Tel: 01643 708090
Fax: 01643 707009

## BURDETT-COUTTS ASSOCIATES
Riverside Studios, Crisp Road, London W6 9RL
Tel: 0181 563 1040
Fax: 0181 748 0430

## BARRY BURNETT ORGANISATION LTD
Prince of Wales Theatre, 31 Coventry Street,
London W1V 8AS
Tel: 0171 839 0202
Fax: 0171 839 0438

## MIKE BURTON MANAGEMENT LIMITED (MBM)
Bastion House, Brunswick Road, Gloucester GL1 1JJ
Tel: 01452 419666
Fax: 01452 387664
Email: management@mikeburtongroup.co.uk

## MEL BUSH ORGANISATION
5 Stratfield Saye, 20-22 Wellington Road,
Bournemouth BH8 8JN
Tel: 01202 293093
Fax: 01202 293080

## BUSINESS EVENT MANAGEMENT
The Old Manse, Horton Road, Hackleton,
Northampton NN7 2AW
Tel/Fax: 01604 870942

## THE BUSINESS THEATRICAL AGENCY
80 Larden Road, London W3 7SX
Tel: 0181 248 6574
Fax: 0181 749 7748

## CABAL MANAGEMENT
9/10 Regent Square, London WC1H 8HZ
Tel/Fax: 0171 837 9648

## CADS MANAGEMENT
48 Lightwoods Hill, Bearwood, Warley,
West Midlands B67 5EB
Tel: 0121 420 1996
Fax: 0121 434 4909
Email: cads_management@lineone.net
Web Site: website.lineone.net/~cads_management

## CALEDONIAN MUSIC AGENCY
1 Bridge Place, Shotts, Lanarkshire ML7 5JE
Tel: 01501 820999
Fax: 01501 820751

## CALYPSO VOICES
25-26 Poland Street, London W1V 3DB
Tel: 0171 734 6415
Fax: 0171 437 0410

## CAM
19 Denmark Street, London WC2H 8NA
Tel: 0171 497 0448
Fax: 0171 240 7384

**CAMBRIAN ENTERTAINMENTS INTERNATIONAL LTD**
Trefeglwys, Caersws, Powys SY17 5PU
Tel: 01686 430311
Fax: 01686 430331

**SARA CAMERON MANAGEMENT**
40 Redbourne Avenue, London N3 2BS
Tel: 0181 343 0433
Fax: 0181 343 0221

**ALISON CAMPBELL MODEL AGENCY**
10 Cregagh Road, Belfast, Northern Ireland BT6 9EP
Tel: 01232 739613
Fax: 01232 739614

**CAMPBELL ASSOCIATES**
4 McKiernan Court, Shuttleworth Road,
London SW11 3DY
Tel: 0171 228 3694
Hants. Office
Campbell Park, Fernhurst Road, Milland GU30 7LU
Tel: 01428 741646
Fax: 01428 741648

**CAMPBELL HINTON MANAGEMENT**
155 Park Road, Teddington, Middlesex TW11 0BP
Tel: 0181 977 3253
Fax: 0181 943 1024

**JOCK CAMPBELL PRODUCTIONS & VARIETY AGENCY**
1 Mountbatten Court, Belmont Street, Bognor Regis,
West Sussex PO21 1JN
Tel: 01243 866811

**CAMSCOTT LEISURE**
PO Box 101, Blackpool FY2 0QF
Tel: 01253 590007
Fax: 01253 595757

**CANA VARIETY AGENCY**
129 Bourne Hill, Palmers Green, London N13 4BE
Tel: 0181 886 5598
Fax: 0181 886 6482

**THE CANDLE MUSIC COMPANY**
44 Southern Row, London W10 5AN
Tel: 0181 960 0111
Fax: 0181 968 7008
Email: email@candlemusic.com
Web Site: www.candlemusic.demon.co.uk

**ALEXANDRA CANN REPRESENTATION**
12 Abingdon Road, London W8 6AF
Tel: 0171 938 4002
Fax: 0171 938 4228

**KENNY CANTOR PRODUCTIONS**
"Uppham Hall" Green Lane, Kessingland, Lowestoft,
Suffolk NR33 7RP
Tel/Fax: 01502 742045

Tel/Fax: 07000 KCANTOR
Tel/fFax: 07000 522 6867
Email: kenny.c@virgin.net

**CANTOR WISE REPRESENTATION**
Osborne House 111 Bartholomew Road,
London NW5 2BJ
Tel: 0171 284 2804
Fax: 0171 284 2805

**CAPITAL ARTS THEATRICAL AGENCY**
Wyllyotts Centre, Wyllyotts Place, Darkes Lane,
Potters Bar, Hertfordshire EN6 2HN
Tel/Fax: 01707 653800/654878
Tel/Fax: 0181 449 2342
Mobile: 0585 232414

**CARDIFF CASTING**
Chapter Arts Centre, Market Road, Canton,
Cardiff, CF5 1QE
Tel: 01222 233321
Fax: 01222 233380

**ROGER CAREY ASSOCIATES**
7 St. Georges Square, London SW1V 2HX
Tel: 0171 630 6301
Tel: 0171 630 0029

**IAN CARLILE MANAGEMENT**
70 Cross Oak Road, Berkhamsted,
Hertfordshire HP4 3HZ
Tel: 01442 877511
Fax: 01442 873019
Email: icmanagement@ compuserve.com

**CARNIVAL BAND SECRETARIES LEAGUE**
14 Launceston Road, Alvaston, Derby DE24 0NN
Tel: 01332 573266
Fax: 01332 573266
Mobile: 0378 141430

**CAROUSEL**
18 Westbury Lodge Close, Pinner, Middlesex
HA5 3FG
Tel: 0181 866 8816
Fax: 0181 933 1614

**CAROUSEL ENTERTAINMENT OF WINDSOR**
7 Lawn Close, Datchet, Berkshire SL3 9JZ
Tel/Fax: 01753 546374

**DAVE CARR MANAGEMENT**
42 Cockton Hill Road, Bishop Auckland,
County Durham DL14 6AH
Tel: 01388 608540
Fax: 01388 601905

**NORRIE CARR AGENCY FOR KIDS**
Holborn Studios, 49 Eagle Wharf Road,
London, N1 7ED
Tel: 0171 253 1771
Fax: 0171 253 1772

**FRANK CARSON**
175a Hampton Cove, Balbriggan, Co Dublin Eire
Tel: 00 353 1 841 1719
Fax: 00 353 1 841 1937

**HAL CARTER ORGANISATION**
101 Hazelwood Lane, Palmers Green,
London N13 5HQ
Tel: 0181 886 2801
Fax: 0181 882 7380

**CASAROTTO COMPANY LTD**
National House, 60-66 Wardour Street,
London W1V 4ND
Tel: 0171 287 4450
Fax: 0171 287 9128
Email: agents@casarotto.uk.com

**CASSELL ENTERTAINMENTS & LEISURE
CONSULTANTS**
Lavington, Margery Lane, Kingswood, Tadworth,
Surrey KT20 7BG
Tel/Fax: 01737 242966

**CASTCALL CASTING SERVICES**
106 Wilsden Avenue, Luton LU1 5HR
Tel: 01582 456213
Fax: 01582 826370
Email: admin@castcall.demon.co.uk

**CASTING UNLIMITED**
Mobile: 0956 254246
Web Site: casting.vossnet.co.uk

**CASTLE ENTERTAINMENT AGENCY**
19 Burton Street, Tutbury, Burton-On-Trent,
Staffordshire DE13 9NR
Tel: 01283 812069

**C C A**
4 Court Lodge, 48 Sloane Square, London SW1W 8AT
Tel: 0171 730 8857
Fax: 0171 730 6971

**CCM (CHANCERY CO-OPERATIVE
MANAGEMENT)**
Panther House, 38 Mount Pleasant,
London WC1X 0AP
Tel: 0171 278 0507
Fax: 0171 404 5406

**CDA (CAROLINE DAWSON ASSOCIATES)**
19 Sydney Mews, London SW3 6HL
Tel: 0171 581 8111
Fax: 0171 589 4800

**C.D.E.C**
11 Lammas Mead, Hitchin, Hertfordshire SG5 1YD
Tel: 01462 455699

**CEE BEE VARIETY AGENCY**
4a Queens Road, Sheffield S2 4DG
Tel: 0114 275 3909/275 4507
Fax: 0114 272 8091

**CELEBRATION ENTERTAINMENTS
MANAGEMENT & AGENCY**
PO Box 238, Lord Street, Southport,
Merseyside PR8 6GQ
Tel: 01704 514444
Fax: 01704 514433

**CELEBRATION MANAGEMENT**
32a Market Street, Hoylake, Wirral,
Merseyside L47 2AF
Tel: 0151 632 6626
Fax: 0151 632 5355
Mobile: 0374 737231

**CELEBRITY SPEAKERS**
Eton Place Burnham Bucks SL1 7PT
Tel: 01753 747015
Fax: 01753 747001

**THE CENTRAL AGENCY**
112 Gunnersbury Avenue, London W5 4HB
Tel: 0181 993 7441
Fax: 0181 992 9993

**CENTRAL CASTING INC**
14 Dean Street, London W1V 5AH
Tel: 0171 437 4211
Fax: 0171 437 4221

**CENTRAL ENTERTAINMENTS**
105 Blake Road, Corby, Northamptonshire NN18 9LW
Tel: 01536 398275
Fax: 01536 398468
Email: 106463.565@compuserve.com

**CENTRAL LINE CO-OPERATIVE
PERSONAL MANAGEMENT**
11 East Circus Street, Nottingham NG1 5AF
Tel: 0115 941 2937
Fax: 0115 950 8087

**CENTRAL MUSIC AGENCY**
Hartfield House 202 Wells Road, Malvern,
Worcestershire WR14 4HD
Tel: 01684 566102
Fax: 01684 566100

**CHALMERS WOOD LTD**
74 Ormonde Crescent, Netherlee, Glasgow G44 3SW
Tel/Fax: 0141 633 3894

**CHAMPION MANAGEMENT & MUSIC**
181 High Street, London NW10 4TE
Tel: 0181 455 2469
Fax: 0181 965 3948

**CHAMPION STAGE PROMOTIONS**
9 Bridge Street, Musselburgh,
Midlothian EH21 6AA Scotland
Tel: 0131 665 5477
Fax: 0131 653 6879

**CHANCE PROMOTIONS**
Blowell House, Fulham Lane, Whitley, Nr. Selby,
Yorkshire DN14 0JL
Tel: 01977 662222 (3 Lines)
Fax: 01977 662233

**CHARACTER ARTISTES**
153 Battersea Rise, London SW11 1HP
Tel: 0171 223 7827
Fax: 0171 924 2334
Email: lailadebs@msn.com

**DAVID CHARLES AGENCY**
2 Betjeman Way, Hemel Hempstead,
Hertfordshire HP1 3HH
TelFax: 01442 264402

**PETER CHARLESWORTH LTD**
2nd Floor, 68 Old Brompton Road, London SW7 3LQ
Tel: 0171 581 2478
Fax: 0171 589 2922

**CHARMENKO**
46 Spenser Road, London SE24 0NR
Tel: 0171 274 6618
Fax: 0171 737 4712

**CHATTO & LINNIT LTD**
123a Kings Road London SW3 4PL
Tel: 0171 352 7722
Fax: 0171 352 3450

**CHERRYSTAGE**
8 Botteville Road, Birmingham,
West Midlands B27 7YD
Tel: 0121 708 1349

**CHILDRENS SHOWTIME PRODUCTIONS**
PO Box 127, Heathfield, East Sussex TN21 0ZR
Tel: 01435 864008
Fax: 01435 868919

**CHILDS PLAY**
PO Box 234, Penn, High Wycombe,
Buckinghamshire HP10 8NQ
Tel: 01494 815758
Fax: 01494 815788

**CHILDSPLAY EVENT SERVICES**
Briar House, Caldbec Hill, Battle,
East Sussex TN33 0JR
Tel/Fax: 01424 775450
Mobile: 0850 311202
Email: kids_crew@compuserve.com

**CHIMES INTERNATIONAL
ENTERTAINMENTS LTD**
131 Mount Annan Drive, Kings Park, Glasgow
G44 4RX Scotland
Tel: 0141 569 7798
Fax: 0141 569 9990
Email: roychimes@aol.com

**MARY CHIPPERFIELD'S TAME WILD
ANIMALS**
Croft Farm, Over Wallop, Stockbridge,
Hampshire SO20 8HX
Tel: 01264 781233
Fax: 01264 782411

**CHORALE MUSIC PRODUCTIONS LTD**
54 High Street, Eton, Berkshire SL4 6BL
Tel: 01753 620801
Fax: 01753 620802

**CHRISTIAN'S TEAM**
11 Old Burlington Street, London W1X 1LA
Tel: 0171 494 2692
Fax: 0171 439 7234

**C.I.A. (CALAVEROCK INTERNATIONAL
AGENCY)**
4 Cambridge Road, Langford, Biggleswade,
Bedfordshire SG18 9SE
Tel: 01462 700456
Fax: 01462 701001
Email: ciaents@aol.com
Web Site: http://members.aol.com/cianents

**CINEL GABRAN MANAGEMENT**
254 Uxbridge Road, Mill End, Rickmansworth,
Hertfordshire WD3 2EA
Tel/Fax: 01923 896120

**CIRCUIT PERSONAL MANAGEMENT LTD**
Suite 71, S.O.T.E.C, Bedford Street, Shelton,
Stoke-On-Trent, Staffordshire ST1 4PZ
Tel: 01782 285388
Fax: 01782 264200

**CIRCUS PRODUCTIONS**
Black Horse Lodge, Wolverton Road, Great Linford,
Milton Keynes MK14 5AL
Tel: 01908 605938

**CITY ACTORS MANAGEMENT**
24 Rivington Street, London EC2A 3DU
Tel/Fax: 0171 613 2636

**CLARION/SEVEN MUSES**
47 Whitehall Park, London N19 3TW
Tel: 0171 272 4413/5125/8448
Fax: 0171 281 9687

**JEAN CLARKE MANAGEMENT**
6th Floor International House 223 Regent Street,
London W1R 7DB

Tel: 0171 495 2424
Fax: 0171 495 7742

## CLASS ACTS ENTERTAINMENT
139 Stranmillis Road, Belfast BT9 5AJ
Tel: 01232 681041
Fax: 01232 687747
Mobile: 0850 818859
9 Herbert Place, Dublin 2
Tel: 00 353 1 662 5484
Fax: 00 353 1 676 9298
Email: classacts@unite.co.uk

## CLASSIQUE PROMOTIONS
8 Skelcher Road, Shirley, Solihull,
West Midlands B90 2EZ
Tel: 0121 745 1920
Fax: 0121 244 0410

## TONY CLAYMAN PROMOTIONS
134 Wigmore Street, London W1H 0LD
Tel: 0171 486 1222
Fax: 0171 935 6276

## STEPHANIE CLIPSHAM
9 Pembridge Place, London W2 4XB
Tel: 0171 243 1325
Fax: 0171 792 9200

## CLUB SCENE
PO Box 11, Bathgate,
West Lothian EH48 1RX Scotland
Tel: 01506 636038
Fax: 01506 633900

## CLUBLINE PROMOTIONS
56 Rowner Lane, Gosport, Hampshire PO13 0DT
Tel/Fax: 01329 317285
Email: clubline1@aol.com

## CLW ENTERPRISES
1 Bridge Court, Stone Road, Stoke-on-Trent ST4 6SJ
Tel: 01782 747724/258369
Fax: 01782 412323
Mobile: 0378 349323
Email: hitcorp@dircon.co.uk

## CMO MANAGEMENT
Unit 32, Ransomes Dock, 35-37 Parkgate Road,
London SW11 4NP
Tel: 0171 228 4000
Fax: 0171 924 1608

## COACH HOUSE ENTERTAINMENT
The Coach House Kings Lane, Yelvertoft, Northampton
NN6 6LX
Tel: 01788 822336
Fax: 01788 823333
Email: Susan.Keyes@btinternet.com

## COAST TO COAST ENTERTAINMENTS
18 Afghan Road, Broadstairs, Kent CT10 3DT
Tel/Fax: 01843 603917

## RON COBURN INTERNATIONAL PRODUCTIONS
"A Breath of Scotland" Vaudevilla, Elliot Road, Dundee
DD2 1SY Scotland
Tel/Fax: 01382 669025

## ELSPETH COCHRANE AGENCY
11-13 Orlando Road, London SW4 0LE
Tel: 0171 220 3146
Fax: 0171 622 5815

## CODY'S WILD WEST
Black Horse Lodge, Wolverton Road, Great Linford,
Milton Keynes MK14 5AL
Tel: 01908 605938

## RAYMOND COFFER MANAGEMENT
Suite 1, Hadleigh House, 96 High Street, Bushey,
Watford WD2 3DE
Tel: 0181 420 4430
Fax: 0181 950 7617

## ERNEST COLCLOUGH ENTERPRISES
Newton House, 1 Newton Drive, Blackpool,
Lancs FY3 8BT
Tel: 01253 302262
Fax: 01253 300072
Email: colclough@cyberscape.net

## GRAHAM COLE MANAGEMENT
51 Grove Avenue, Weymouth, Dorset DT4 7RJ
Tel: 01305 777253

## MAX COLLIE RHYTHM ACES
26 Wendover Road, Bromley, Kent BR2 9JX
Tel: 0181 460 1139
Fax: 0181 466 7005
Email: bouquetc52@aol.com

## BARRY COLLINGS ENTERTAINMENTS
21a Clifftown Road, Southend-On-Sea SS1 1AB
Tel: 01702 330005
Fax: 01702 333309

## COLLINGWOOD PERSONAL MANAGEMENT
9 Blacksmiths Lane, Thorpe-on-the-Hill,
Lincoln LN6 9BQ
Tel: 01522 686931
FaX: 01522 684552

## SHANE COLLINS ASSOCIATES
39-41 New Oxford Street, London WC1A 1BH
Tel: 0171 836 9377
Fax: 0171 836 9388
Email: shane_collins@lineone.net

## COLLIS MANAGEMENT
182 Trevelyan Road, London SW17 9LW
Tel: 0181 767 0196
Fax: 0181 682 0973

**COMEDY CLUB**
165 Peckham Rye, London SE15 3HZ
Tel: 0171 732 3434
Fax: 0171 732 9292

**COMMERCIAL CASTING**
12 Colas Mews, London NW6 4LH
Tel: 0171 372 0009
Fax: 0171 372 2141

**COMPACT ENTERTAINMENT AGENCY**
98 Shellards Road, Longwell Green, Bristol BS30 9DT
Tel: 0117 932 4344
Fax: 0117 932 6006

**COMPLETE ENTERTAINMENT SERVICES**
PO Box 112, Seaford, East Sussex BN25 2DQ
Tel: 01323 492266
Fax: 01323 492234

**COMPLETE TALENT AGENCY**
1346 London Road, Leigh-On-Sea, Essex SS9 2UH
Tel: 01702 478787
Fax: 01702 478770
Mobile: 0850 111616
The Old Forge, Kingfield Road, Woking,
Surrey GU22 9EG
Tel: 01483 766655
Fax: 01483 722250
Email: bookings@entertainers.co.uk
Web Site: www.entertainers.co.uk

**CONCORDE INTERNATIONAL ARTISTES LTD**
101 Shepherds Bush Road, London W6 7LP
Tel: 0171 602 8822
Fax: 0181 603 2352

**CONNECTIONS**
70 Rowlands Avenue, Pinner, Middlesex HA5 4BP
Tel: 0181 420 1444
Fax: 0181 428 5836
Email: mail@connections.uk.com
Web Site: www.connections.uk.com

**CONNEXTIONS ENTERTAINMENT LTD**
399 Tildesley Road, Putney London SW15 3BD
Tel: 0181 789 6645
Fax: 0181 785 3533

**MIKE CONSTANTIA ENTERTAINMENTS**
41 Manchester Road, Woolston, Warrington,
Cheshire WA1 4AE
Tel:  01925 810979
Fax: 01925 850777

**CONWAY VAN GELDER LTD**
3rd Floor 18-21 Jermyn Street, London SW1Y 6HP
Tel: 0171 287 0077
Fax: 0171 287 1940

**COPPENDALE FOR COUNTRY**
23 Church Green, Shoreham-By-Sea,
West Sussex BN43 6JQ

Tel: 01273 596363
Fax: 01273 597272
Email: coppendale@hotmail.com

**PETE CORBY ENTERTAINMENTS**
4 Newnham Avenue, Ripley, Derbyshire DE5 3GX
Tel: 01773 747442
Fax: 01773 744072

**RAY CORNELL ARTISTES &
PRODUCTIONS LTD**
Applause House, 56 St. Annes Road, South Shore,
Blackpool, Lancs FY4 2AS
Tel: 01253 402463
Fax: 01253 404006

**CLIVE CORNER ASSOCIATES**
73 Gloucester Road, Hampton, Middlesex TW12 2UQ
Tel: 0181 941 8653
Fax: 0181 941 2866

**COSMIC COMEDY**
177 Fulham Palace Road, London W6 8QT
Tel: 0171 381 1288
Fax: 0171 385 3325
Email: cosmiccomedy.demon.co.uk

**COSMOS AGENCY**
26a Bellevue Crescent, Edinburgh EH3 6NF Scotland
Tel: 0131 558 3146

**LOU COULSON**
1st Floor, 37 Berwick Street, London W1V 3RF
Tel: 0171 734 9633
Fax: 0171 439 7569

**COUNTERFEIT COMPANY**
10 Barley Mow Passage, Chiswick, London W4 4PH
Tel: 0181 994 8397
Fax: 0181 742 7684

**CRACKTEAM MANAGEMENT**
Norden, 2 Hillhead Road, Newtonhill, Stonehaven,
Kincardineshire, Scotland
Tel: 01569 730962

**CRAWFORD**
2 Conduit Street, London W1R 9TG
Tel: 0171 629 6464
Fax: 0171 355 1084

**CREAM ENTERTAINMENTS**
248 Daws Heath Road, Thundersley, Benfleet,
Essex SS7 2TD
Tel: 01702 551448
Fax: 01702 551708

**THE CREAM THEATRICAL AGENCY**
58 Beale Close, Tottenhall Road, London N13 6DF
Tel: 0181 888 7593
Fax: 0181 888 5636
Mobile: 0956 316029

**CREEME ENTERTAINMENTS**
East Lynne, Harper Green Road, Doe Hey, Farnworth,
Bolton BL4 7HT
Tel: 01204 793441/793018
Fax: 01204 792655
Mobile: 0831 278963

**CRESCENT MANAGEMENT**
10 Barley Mow Passage, Chiswick, London W4 4PH
Tel: 0181 994 6477
Fax: 0181 994 0207

**CROMWELL MANAGEMENT**
4/5 High Street, Huntingdon,
Cambridgeshire PE18 6TE
Tel: 01480 435600
Fax: 01480 356250

**ROBERT CROSSLAND ENTERTAINMENTS**
Woodcroft, 60 Ashton Lane, Sale, Cheshire M33 6NS
Tel: 0161 962 7820
Fax: 0161 969 2172

**CROUCH ASSOCIATES**
9-15 Neal Street, London WC2H
Tel: 0171 379 1684
Fax: 0171 379 1991

**SARA CROUCH MANAGEMENT**
Suite 1, Ground Floor, 1 Duchess Street,
London W1N 3DE
Tel: 0171 436 4626
Fax: 0171 436 4627

**CROWD PULLERS (STREET PERFORMERS
AND BANDS)**
158 Old Woolwich Road, London SE10 9PR
Tel: 0181 305 0074
Fax: 0181 858 9045

**CROWN ENTERTAINMENTS**
103 Bromley Common, Bromley, Kent BR2 9RN
Tel: 0181 464 0454
Fax: 0181 290 4038

**CRUICKSHANK CAZENOVE LIMITED**
97 Old South Lambeth Road, London SW8 1XU
Tel: 0171 735 2933
Fax: 0171 820 1081

**C.S. ENTERTAINMENTS**
31 Sherwood Road, Winnersh, Berkshire RG41 5NH
Tel/Fax: 0118 978 5989

**C S M ARTISTES**
St Dunstans Hall, East Acton Lane, London W3 7EG
Tel: 0181 743 9982
Fax: 0181 740 6542

**CT ENTERTAINMENTS**
PO Box 52, Newtownards, County Down BT23 7FX
Northern Ireland

Tel: 01232 428800
Fax: 01232 428444

**CURTIS BROWN GROUP**
4th Floor, Haymarket House, 28-29 Haymarket,
London SW1Y 4SP
Tel: 0171 396 6600
Fax: 0171 396 0110

**CUSTOM THEATRICS UK LTD**
55-61 Great Queen Street, London WC2B 5DA
Tel: 0171 404 4232
Fax: 0171 436 8522

**CW ENTERTAINMENTS**
3, First Floor, The City Business Centre,
Llanthony Road, Gloucester GL2 5JH
Tel/Fax: 01542 331441

**D & S ARTISTES**
3 Wilton Crescent, North Wooton, King's Lynn,
Norfolk PE30 3RB
Tel: 01553 631498

**DABBER DAVIS PRODUCTIONS**
24a Park Road, Hayes, Middlesex UB4 8JN
Tel: 0181 848 9048

**JUDY DAISH ASSOCIATES**
2 St. Charles Place, London W10 6EG
Tel: 0181 964 8811
Fax: 0181 964 8966

**ARTHUR DAKIN ORCHESTRAS**
The Old Posthouse, Hammond Street, Mappowder,
Sturminster Newton, Dorset DT10 2EH
Tel: 01258 817802
Fax: 01258 817844

**DAVID DALY ASSOCIATES**
586A Kings Road, London SW6 2DX
Tel: 0171 610 9560
Fax: 0171 610 9512

**LARRY DALZELL ASSOCIATES LTD**
91 Regent Street, London W1R 7TB
Tel: 0171 287 5131
Fax: 0171 287 5161

**DANCERS AGENCY**
1 Charlotte Street, London W1P 1DH
Tel: 0171 636 1473
Fax: 0171 636 1657

**PAUL DANIELS**
PO Box 250, 140 Beckett Road, Doncaster,
South Yorkshire DN2 4BA
Tel: 01302 321233
Fax: 01302 321978
Email: Newton_Edwardsn.com
Web Site: http://user.itl.net/~encore/pd.html

**DANSATAK**
Worth House, Worth Street, Carlton,
Nottingham NG4 1RX
Tel: 0115 987 9000
Fax: 0115 987 1216

**DARK BLUES MANAGEMENT**
30 Stamford Brook Road, London W6 0XH
Tel: 0181 734 3292
Fax: 0181 740 5520

**DAUBNEY AGENCY**
53 Scarsdale Cross, Dronfield, Derbyshire S18 1SL
Tel: 01246 414400
Fax: 01246 413279
Email: derekd@daubneyagency.telme.com

**THE DAVID AGENCY**
153 Battersea Rise, London SW11 1HP
Tel: 0171 223 7720
Fax: 0171 924 2334
Email: laila@msn.com
Web Site: http://www.davidagency.euro-index.co.uk

**DAVID ANTHONY PROMOTIONS**
P.O. Box 286, Warrington WA2 8GA
Tel: 01925 632496
Fax: 01925 416589

**LENA DAVIS/JOHN BISHOP ASSOCIATES**
Cottons Farmhouse, Whiston Road, Cogenhoe,
Northampton NN7 1NL
Tel: 01604 891487
Fax: 01604 890405

**ROGER DAVIS ASSOCIATES**
Lime Trees Blackwood Hall Lane, Luddendenfoot,
Halifax, West Yorkshire HX2 6HD
Tel: 01422 884800
Fax: 01422 884494
Email: roger.davis@comedians.co.uk
Web Site: http://www.comedians.co.uk

**D.B. PRODUCTIONS**
1 Mallard Way, Yateley, Camberley, Surrey GU46 6PG
Tel: 01252 878922
Fax: 01252 878784

**YVONNE DE VALL ENTERTAINMENTS**
86 Upper Fant Road, Maidstone, Kent ME16 8BU
Tel: 01622 687154/688473
Fax: 01622 687154

**DAVID DEAN PROMOTIONS LTD**
Capilano, Clos de la Mare, La Rue de Maupertuis,
St. Clement, Jersey JE2 6NH Channel Islands
Tel/Fax:01534 872973

**RICKY DEAN ENTERTAINMENTS**
52 Bentley Street, Bolton, Lancs BL2 1NE
Tel: 01204 525929

**DEBIL MANAGEMENT**
114 Linkfield Road, Isleworth, Middlesex TW7 6QJ
Tel: 0181 847 1430
Fax: 0181 758 2017

**ALAN DENI ENTERTAINMENTS**
2 Queens Road, Crosby, Liverpool L23 5TR
Tel: 0151 924 8589

**THE DENMAN VARIETY & CASTING
AGENCY**
Commerce Chambers, Elite Buildings,
Upper Parliament Street, Nottingham NG1 2BP
Tel: 0115 941 8421/0115 947 3257
Fax: 0115 947 3257

**DENMARK STREET MANAGEMENT**
11 Packington Bridge Workspace Packington Square,
London N1 7UA
Tel: 0171 354 8555
Fax: 0171 354 8558

**WALLY DENT ENTERTAINMENTS**
121a Woodlands Avenue, West Byfleet,
Surrey KT14 6AS
Tel: 01932 347885/351444/347826
Fax: 01932 336229
Car Phone: 0831 270976

**TONY DENTON PROMOTIONS LTD**
19 South Molton Lane, London W1Y 1AQ
Tel: 0171 629 4666
Fax: 0171 629 4777

**DERI PROMOTIONS**
8 Wick Lane, Felpham, Bognor Regis,
West Sussex PO22 8QG
Tel: 01243 585545
Fax: 01243 586886
Mobile: 0860 509898

**DERRICK'S DOUBLES**
224 Commonwealth Way, Abbey Wood,
London SE2 0LF
Tel: 0181 311 2129
0181 488 3583
0181 312 4550
Fax: 0181 311 2129
Web Site: www.posers.co.uk/ent/ddub.htm

**DERWENT ENTERTAINMENTS**
42 St. Annes Gardens, Llanrhos, Llandudno,
Gwynedd LL30 1SD
Tel/Fax: 01492 573838

**DES REES SUNRISE GROUP**
Elm Croft, Thorn Wood Common, High Road,
Thornwood, Epping, Essex CM16 6LX
Tel: 07000 303130
Fax: 01992 570192
Mobile  0850 023522

**KEN DESMOND AGENCY & MANAGEMENT**
16 Clarence Road North, South Benfleet,
Essex SS7 1HW
Tel: 01268 793401

**DINGS ENTERTAINMENT**
44/46 Bunyan Road, Kempston, Bedford MK42 8HL
Tel: 01234 851166 (5lines)
Fax: 01234 840383

**DINOSAUR PROMOTIONS/PULSE (THE AGENCY)**
5 Heyburn Crescent, Westport Gardens,
Stoke-on-Trent ST6 4DL
Tel: 01782 824051
Fax: 01782 839513
Email: dinoprom@btinternet.com
Web Site: www.ukacts.com/agency/dinosaur

**DIRECT-LINE PERSONAL MANAGEMENT**
35 The CHEL Centre, 26 Roundhay Road,
Leeds LS7 1AB
Tel/Fax: 0113 244 4991

**DISCOVERY ENTERTAINMENT**
East Nook, Elsdon, Northumberland, Tyne & Wear
Tel/Fax: 01388 775439
Mobile: 0973 161616

**THE DIXON AGENCY**
58 Hedley Street, Gosforth,
Newcastle Upon Tyne NE3 1DL
Tel: 0191 213 1333
Fax:0191 213 1313

**DOWNES PRESENTERS AGENCY**
96 Broadway, Bexleyheath, Kent DA6 7DE
Tel: 0181 304 0541
Fax: 0181 301 5591

**DOWNSIDE MUSIC**
7 Layton Court, Weybridge, Surrey KT13 9AD
Tel: 01932 840314

**DRAGONSFIRE/BELLTOWER ENTERPRISES**
9 Hillside Road, Ashtead, Surrey KT21 1RZ
Tel: 01372 277703
Fax: 01372 278406

**STEVE DRAPER ENTERTAINMENTS**
2 The Coppice, Beardwood Manor Blackburn
Lancashire BB2 7BQ
Tel/Fax: 01254 679005

**DREAMS INTERNATIONAL MODEL & CASTING AGENCY**
Stanbrook House, 2-5 Old Bond Street,
London W1X 3TB
Tel: 0171 359 4786

**BRYAN DREW LTD**
Quadrant House, 80/82 Regent Street,
London W1R 6AU
Tel: 0171 437 2293
Fax: 0171 437 0561

**NEIL DROVER - THE AGENCY**
Event House, 437 Crow Road, Glasgow G11 7DZ
Scotland
Tel: 0141 257 3377

**DSA THEATRICAL AGENCY**
31 Carnaby Street, London W1V 1PQ
Tel: 0171 734 3121
Fax: 0171 734 4328

**DUKERIES ENTERTAINMENTS**
151 Mansfield Road, Clipstone Village, Mansfield,
Nottinghamshire NG21 9AA
Tel: 01623 635327
Fax: 01623 621133

**DUNBAR AGENCY**
2 Manse Street, Old Corstorphine Village, Edinburgh
EH12 7TR Scotland
Tel: 0131 334 4389

**EVAN DUNSTAN ASSOCIATES**
296 Whitchurch Lane, Kenons Park, Edgware,
Middlesex HA8 6QX
Tel: 0181 952 6563

**BARRY DYE ENTERTAINMENTS**
PO Box 888, Ipswich, Suffolk IP1 6BU
Tel: 01473 744287
Fax: 01473 745442
Mobile: 0831 700799
Email: BARRY DYE@AOL.COM

**DYFEL MANAGEMENT**
19 Fontwell Drive, Bickley, Bromley, Kent BR2 8AB
Tel: 0181 467 9605
07000 367687 (For Music)
Fax: 0181 249 1972

**KENNETH EARLE PERSONAL MANAGEMENT**
214 Brixton Road, London SW9 6AP
Tel: 0171 274 1219
Fax: 0171 274 9529

**SUSI EARNSHAW MANAGEMENT**
5 Brook Place, Barnet, Hertfordshire EN5 2DL
Tel: 0181 441 5010
Fax: 0181 364 9618

**EAST ANGLIAN ENTERTAINMENTS**
16 Rembrandt Way, Bury St. Edmunds,
Suffolk IP33 2LP
Tel: 01284 762775

**EAST LANCASHIRE ENTERTAINMENTS**
Old Earth, 33 Ighten Road, Burnley,
Lancashire BB12 0JF
Tel: 01282 422455

**THE EASTMAN MARLEY ORGANISATION**
7th Floor, 54-62 Regent Street, London W1R 5PJ
Tel: 0171 439 4052
Fax: 0171 287 2844

**E C 1**
1 Cowcross Street, London EC1M 6DR
Tel: 0171 490 8990
Fax: 0171 490 8987

**ECCENTRIC MANAGEMENT**
18 West Hill Park, London N6 6ND
Tel: 0181 348 8638
Fax: 0181 347 7099

**THE EDGE ENTERTAINMENT CONSULTANTS**
The Edge, Queens Street, March,
Cambridgeshire PE15 8SN
Tel: 01354 661122/661133
Fax: 01354 661144
Web Site: www.users.globalnet.co.uk/~edge/

**EFFECTIVE MANAGEMENT**
4 Hermitage Heights, Bridgnorth,
Shropshire WV15 5EN
Tel: 01746 761583
Fax: 01746 768302

**JAKE ELCOCK ENTERTAINMENTS**
67 Wolverhampton Road, Sedgley, Dudley,
West Midlands DY3 1RG
Tel: 01902 672972/884301
Fax: 01902 881060

**ELITE PROMOTIONS**
4 St. Michaels Walk, Newtonhill, Stonehaven,
Kincardineshire AB39 3GZ
Tel: 01569 731113
Fax: 01569 730006
Email: info@elite-promo.co.uk
Web Site: www.elite-promo.co.uk

**RON ELLIS**
5 Mayfield Court, Victoria Road, Formby,
Liverpool L37 7JL
Tel/Fax: 01704 834105

**EMERGENCY EXIT ARTS**
PO Box 570 London SE10 0EE
Tel: 0181 853 4809
Fax: 0181 858 2025
Email: eea@easynet.co.uk
Web Site: www.eea.org.uk

**EMKAY ENTERTAINMENTS**
Nobel House Regent Centre, Blackness Road,
Linlithgow, West Lothian EH49 7HU Scotland
Tel: 01506 845555
Fax: 01506 845566
Email: emkay.ents@virgin.net

**EMPIRE MANAGEMENT LTD**
Newton House, 147 St. Neots Road, Hardwick,
Cambridge, Cambs CB3 7QJ
Tel: 01954 212800
Fax: 01954 212801

**EMPTAGE HALLETT LTD**
24 Poland Street, London W1V 3DD
Tel: 0171 287 5511
Fax: 0171 287 4411

**DOREEN ENGLISH 95**
4 Selsey Avenue, Bognor Regis,
West Sussex PO21 2QZ
Tel/Fax: 01243 825968

**ENTERTAINMENT & MUSIC SUPPORT**
3 Littlecote Place, Pinner, Middlesex HA5 4RE
Tel: 0181 428 6456
Fax: 0181 428 6456
Email: raymond.e@virgin.net

**THE ENTERTAINMENT CO.**
John Cotton Buisiness Centre, 10 Sunnyside,
Edinburgh EH7 5RA
Tel: 0131 659 6549
Fax: 0131 661 4790

**ENTERTAINMENTS NETWORK UK
(HEAD OFFICE)**
The Landings, Burton End, West Wickham, Cambridge
CB1 6SD
Tel: 01223 290640
Fax: 01223 290643
Email: barriehawkins@compuserve.com
Web Site: www.entsnetuk.com.uk

**ENTERTAINMENTS NETWORK (UK)
ANGLIA**
The Chestnuts Queens Close, Balsham,
Cambridge CB1 6HL
Tel: 01223 890134
Fax: 01223 890134
Mobile: 0378 931310
Web Site: www.entsnetuk.com.uk

**ENTERTAINMENTS NETWORK (UK) KENT**
14 Varne Road, Folkestone, Kent CT19 6BG
Tel/Fax: 01303 226855
Mobile: 0498 647030
Web Site: www.entsnetuk.co.uk

**ENTERTAINMENTS NETWORK (UK)
LONDON CITY EAST**
Wickham House 10 Cleveland Way, London E1 4TR
Tel: 0171 791 1990

Fax: 0171 423 9411
Web Site: www.entsnetuk.com.uk

**ENTERTAINMENTS UK-EUROPE LTD.**
Tel: 01373 865546

**ENTERTAINMENTS UNLIMITED**
4 Greenford Road, Southport
Tel/Fax: 01704 574732
Email: info@ents-unltd.com
Web Site: http://www.ents-unltd.com

**JUNE EPSTEIN ASSOCIATES**
62 Compayne Gardens, London NW6 3RY
Tel: 0171 328 0864/0171 372 1928
Fax: 0171 328 0684

**EQUATOR MUSIC**
17 Hereford Mansions, Hereford Road,
London W2 5BA
Tel: 0171 727 5858
Fax: 0171 229 5934

**ESSANAY**
2 Conduit Street, London W1R 9TG
Tel: 0171 4093526
Fax: 0171 355 1084

**THE ESSENTIAL AGENCY**
Dance Attic Studios, 368 North End Road,
London SW6 1LY
Tel: 0171 385 2460
Fax: 0171 610 0995
Email: esslitd@aol.com

**ESSEX ENTERTAINMENT AGENCY**
78 High Road, Layer-de-la-Haye, Colchester,
Essex CO2 0DT
Tel: 01206 734163/734174
Fax: 01206 734165

**ETERNAL FLAME**
38 Houlton Road, Poole, Dorset BH15 2LN
Tel: 01202 686500
Fax: 01202 773915
Email: eternal.flame@virgin.net
Web Site: http://freespace.virgin.net/eternal.flame

**ETERNAL MANAGEMENT**
PO Box 45, Liverpool L69 2LE
Tel: 0151 734 1500
Fax: 0151 734 1611

**ETM LTD**
Mosley House, 122 Mosley Common Road, Worsley,
Manchester M28 1AN
Tel: 0161 790 4640/0161 799 7605
Fax: 0161 703 8521

**ETS ENTERTAINMENTS AGENCY**
11 Green Lane, Northgate, Crawley, West Sussex
RH10 2JX

Tel: 01293 519394
Fax: 01293 402342

**ETTINGER BROS**
3 Church Road, Wavertree, Liverpool L15 9EA
Tel: 0151 734 2240
Fax: 0151 733 2468

**EUROPEAN MUSIC PROMOTIONS**
19 Captains Close, Sutton Valence, Kent ME17 3BA
Tel/Fax: 01622 844088

**EVANS & REISS**
100 Fawe Park Road, London SW15 2EA
Tel: 0181 877 3755
Fax: 0181 877 0307

**JACQUE EVANS MANAGEMENT LIMITED**
4 Gorleston Street, London W14 8XS
Tel: 0171 610 5225
Fax: 0171 610 5335

**EWE-NIQUE PROMOTIONS**
PO Box 107, Grimston, King's Lynn, Norfolk PE32 1BB
Tel: 01485 600812
Fax: 01485 600233

**EXCASTING AGENCY**
Bank Chambers 375a Regents Park Road,
London N3 1DE
Tel: 0181 343 3838
Fax: 0181 343 4905

**EXTRA UNLIMITED**
209 Hatton Road, Feltham, Middlesex TW14 9QY
Tel: 0181 893 2573
Fax: 0181 384 2539
Mobile: 0956 254246

**F.A.B. (FORWARD AGENCY BOOKING)**
35 Britannia Row, London N1 8QH
Tel: 0171 704 8080
Fax: 0171 704 8999
Email: rob_challice@msn.com

**FAIRPLAY ENTERTAINMENTS**
8 Grig Place, Alsager, Stoke-On-Trent,
Staffordshire ST7 2SU
Tel: 01270 873848/01270 876054
Fax: 01270 873848

**FANFARE 3000 (INCORPORATING JOHNNY
HOWARD ASSOCIATES)**
Incorporating Johnny Howard Associates
The Folly, Pinner Hill Road, Pinner,
Middlesex HA5 3YQ
Tel: 07000 FANFARE
Tel: 0181 429 3000
Fax: 0181 868 6497
Email: entertainment@fanfare.co.uk
Web Site: http://www.fanfare.co.uk

## KATE FEAST MANAGEMENT
10 Primrose Hill Studios, Fitzroy Road, London
NW1 8TR
Tel: 0171 586 5502
Fax: 0171 586 9817

## FRANK FEENEY ENTERTAINMENT AGENCY
9a High Street, Normanby, Middlesbrough,
Cleveland TS6 0NQ
Tel: 01642 455366/455072
Fax: 01642 455532

## MALCOLM FELD AGENCY LTD
Malina House, Sandforth Road, Sandfield Park,
Liverpool L12 1JY
Tel: 0151 259 6565
ax: 0151 259 5006

## COLETTE FENLON PERSONAL MANAGEMENT
(Incorporating Chiltern Youn Set)
2a Eaton Road, West Derby, Liverpool L12 7JJ
Tel: 0151 252 1177
Fax: 0151 280 7998

## FI STEPS AGENCY
6 Cook Road, Horsham, West Sussex RH12 5GG
Tel/Fax: 01403 248626

## FICTION RECORDS
4 Tottenham Mews, London W1P 9PJ
Tel: 0171 323 5555
Fax: 0171 323 5323

## ALAN FIELD ENTERTAINMENT LIMITED
3 The Spinney, Bakers Hill, Barnet,
Hertfordshire EN5 5QJ
Tel: 0181 441 1137
Fax: 0181 447 0657
Email: Alan-Field@msn.com

## RICHARD FILLINGHAM AGENCY
22 Williamwood Park West, Netherlee,
Glasgow G44 3TE
Tel: 0141 633 2298
Fax: 0141 633 1100

## FILM RIGHTS LTD
101 Southbank House, Black Prince Road,
Albert Embankment London SE1 7SJ
Tel: 0171 735 8171

## FIRST EUROPEAN ARTISTS
100a Chalk Farm Road, London NW1 8EH
Tel: 0171 482 2825
Fax: 0171 482 2826

## FIRST MANAGEMENT
PO Box 24, London SW15 3NL

## FIRST TIME MANAGEMENT & PUBLISHING
Sovereign House, 12 Trewartha Road, Praa Sands,
Penzance, Cornwall TR20 9ST
Tel: 01736 762826
Fax: 01736 763328
Email: panamus@aol.com

## FIRSTARS LTD
1 Water Lane, Camden Town, London NW1 8NZ
Tel: 0171 267 1101
Fax: 0171 267 7071

## FISHER PROMOTIONS & MARKETING NATIONWIDE (AGENCY)
Clyn Pattel House Narberth, Pembrokeshire
SA67 8UD Wales
Tel: 01834 860568
Fax: 01834 860623

## ROGER FISHER MUSIC SERVICES
64 Whitley Court Road, Quinton, Birmingham B32 1EY
Tel: 0121 422 8590
Web Site: http://www.yell.co.uk/sites/rogerfishermusics
erv

## SHERIDAN FITZGERALD MANAGEMENT
87 Western Road, Upton Park, London E13 9JE
Tel: 0181 471 9814
Fax: 0181 470 2587

## FLAIR THEATRICAL AGENCY
Flair House, 28 Cornmill Lane, Liversedge,
West Yorkshire WF15 7DZ
Tel: 01924 408181
Emergency Let-Down 01421 496431
Fax: 01924 402651

## FLAMENCO PRODUCTIONS - MIDLANDS SECTION
4 Cormorant Rise, Lower Wick, Worcester WR2 4BA
Tel: 01905 424083

## THE FLYING MUSIC COMPANY LTD
110 Clarendon Road, London W11 2HR
Tel: 0171 221 7799
Fax: 0171 221 5016

## FOCUS MANAGEMENT LTD
Claremont House 22-24 Claremont Road, Surbiton,
Surrey KT6 4QU
Tel: 0181 241 2446
Fax: 0181 241 2447

## FOLK ENTERTAINMENTS
62 Beechwood Road, South Croydon,
Surrey CR2 0AA
Tel: 0181 657 2813
Fax: 0181 651 6080
Mobile: 0836 546225

## FOOL'S PARADISE
Sentrys Farm, Exminster, Exeter, Devon EX6 8DY

Tel: 01392 832268
Fax: 01392 833122

## JOHN FORD PRODUCTIONS
Bradford Court, Bradford Street, Birmingham B12 0NS
Tel: 0121 693 9911
Fax: 0121 693 7799
Email: info@jfp.co.uk

## MAL FORD ARTISTE AND LEISURE MANAGEMENT LTD
Suite 2, 8 Burlington Road West, Blackpool,
Lancs FY4 1JR
Tel/Fax: 01253 298035
Mobile: 0860 479092

## FOREIGN ARTISTES AGENCY
PO Box 10576, London SW1
Tel: 0171 828 6826
Fax: 0171 828 0922

## ROGER FORRESTER MANAGEMENT
18 Harley House, Regents Park, London NW1 5HE
Tel: 0171 486 8056
Fax: 0171 487 5663

## DAVID FORSHAW ENTERPRISES
68 Kirkstone Road South, Litherland,
Liverpool L21 5HW
Tel: 0151 928 7660
Fax: 0151 920 5688

## FORWARD AGENCY
35 Britannia Row, London N1 8QH
Tel: 0171 704 8080
Fax: 0171 704 8999
Email: robfab@dial.pipex.com / doobwan@dial.pipex.com

## JILL FOSTER LTD
9 Barb Mews, London W6 7PA
Tel: 0171 602 1263
Fax: 0171 602 9336

## FOSTER LOMAX PROMOTIONS
5 Keld Close, Tottington, Bury, Lancashire BL8 1UJ
Tel: 0161 763 6166
Fax: 0161 763 6167

## FOUR STAR WRESTLING PROMOTIONS
68 Bartram Avenue, Braintree, Essex CM7 3RB
Tel: 01376 327963

## FOX ARTIST MANAGEMENT LTD
Concorde House, 101 Shepherds Bush Road,
London W6 7LP
Tel: 0171 602 8822
Fax: 0171 603 2352

## KAYE FRANKLAND ENTERTAINMENT AGENCY
155/157 Cinderhill Road, Bulwell, Nottingham
NG6 8RQ

Tel/Fax: 0115 927 1319

## DEREK FRANKS ORGANISATION
Kexby Lodge, Kexby, York YO4 5LA
Tel: 01759 388900
Fax: 01759 380674

## FREE TRADE AGENCY
Free Trade Wharf, 350 The Highway, London E1 9HU
Tel: 0171 702 8111
Fax: 0171 702 8116

## FREWIN ASSOCIATES
65 Rectory Lane, London SW17 9PY
Tel: 0181 672 2859
Fax: 0181 672 1341

## FRONTLINE MANAGEMENT LTD
Colombo Centre, 34-36 Colombo Street,
London SE1 8DP
Tel/Fax: 0171 261 9466

## FUNHOUSE PRODUCTIONS
91 Regent Court, Promenade, Blackpool FY1 1RT
Tel: 01274 619832
Fax: 01274 610569

## FUNTIME PRODUCTIONS
4 Haywood, Bracknell, Berkshire RG12 7WG
Tel: 01344 453888
Fax: 01344 872369

## G.A.A. (GOLD ARTIST AGENCY)
16 Princedale Road, London W11 4NJ
Tel: 0171 221 1864
Fax: 0171 221 1606

## GABLES AND TTH MANAGEMENT
321 Leigham Court Road, London SW16 2RX
Tel: 0181 769 7411

## HILARY GAGAN ASSOCIATES
20-21 Store Street, London WC1E 7DH
Tel: 0171 916 4056/4059
Fax: 0171 916 4067

## GAILFORCE MANAGEMENT LTD
30 Ives Street, London SW3 2ND
Tel: 0171 581 0261
Fax: 0171 584 5774
Email: gailforc@dircon.co.uk

## GALAXY EVENTS
Dorn Heath Farmhouse, Stratford Road,
Moreton-in-Marsh, Gloucestershire GL56 9NQ
Tel/Fax: 01608 652548
Mobile: 0860 485578

## GALLOWAYS ONE
15 Lexham Mews, Kensington, London W8 6JW
Tel: 0171 376 2288

## G.A.M.E.
Game House, 11 Corncrake Close, Luton LU2 8EL
Tel: 01582 425474

## BRIAN GANNON MANAGEMENT
PO Box 106, Milnrow, Rochdale,
Lancashire OL16 4HW
Tel: 01706 860400
Fax: 01706 860406
Email: b.gannon@entertainment-net.com
Web Site: http://www.entertainment-net.com

## KERRY GARDNER MANAGEMENT
7 St. Georges Square, London SW1V 2HX
Tel: 0171 828 7748
Fax: 0171 828 7758

## GARRICKS
7 Garrick Street, London WC2E 9AR
Tel: 0171 240 0660
Fax: 0171 497 9242
Email: garricks@mcmail.com

## PATRICK GARVEY MANAGEMENT
Top Floor 59 Lansdowne Place, Hove,
East Sussex BN3 1FL
Tel: 01273 206623
Fax: 01273 208484
Email: patrick@patrickgarvey.demon.co.uk

## GB PROMOTIONS AND ENTERTAINMENT AGENCY
Point West, 27 Countess Wear Road, Exeter EX2 6LR
Tel: 01392 411194
Fax: 01392 278860

## RAY GELATO MANAGEMENT
143 Cannon Lane, Pinner, Middlesex HA5 1HU
Tel: 0181 868 0453
Fax: 0181 429 1880
Email: info@raygelato.com
Web Site: http://www.raygelato.com

## GEM PRODUCTIONS
35 Finsbury Terrace, Brynmill, Swansea,
South Wales SA2 0AH
Tel: 01792 646278
Fax: 01792 475109

## TREVOR GEORGE ENTERTAINMENTS (UK)
PO Box 135 Torquay Devon TQ1 3YT
Tel: 01803 311932/313300
Fax: 01803 312004

## ROBERTO GERMAINS AGENCY
20 Lower Hill Road, Epsom, Surrey KT19 8LT
Tel: 01372 747314
Fax: 01372 813735
Email: roberto.germains@which.net

## G.F. MANAGEMENT LTD
No 3, Pont Park, Berwick Hill, Ponteland,
Newcastle Upon Tyne NE20 0JX
Tel: 01661 821077
Fax: 01661 820589
Email: michael@gfmanagement.com

## TONY GIBBER PRODUCTIONS
116 Seven Sisters Road, London N7 6AE
Tel/Fax: 0171 794 5160

## ERIC GLASS LTD
28 Berkeley Square, London W1X 6HD
Tel: 0171 629 7162
Fax: 0171 499 6780

## GLASSHOUSE PRODUCTIONS LIMITED
Upper York Street, (Private Road East), Earlsdon,
Coventry, W Midlands CV1 3GQ
Tel/Fax: 01203 223892
Email: glasshouse@dial.pipex.com
Web Site: www.dspace.dial.pipex.com/glasshouse

## GLOBAL ARENA
Northside House 69 Tweedy Road, Bromley,
Kent BR1 3WA
Tel: 0181 466 8452
Fax: 0181 466 9292
Email: cbayliss1@aol.com

## GLOUCESTER ENTERTAINMENT AGENCY
Little Haven, Elmore Lane, Quedgeley,
Gloucester GL2 6NW
Tel: 01452 721966 (Two Lines)
Fax: 01452 722489

## GMM
(Also Greg Millard Management)
3rd Floor 91-93 Buckingham Palace Road,
London SW1W 0RP
Tel: 0171 630 7300
Fax: 0171 630 6464

## GO ENTERTAINMENTS
The Arts Exchange, Mill Green, Congleton,
Cheshire CW12 1JG
Tel: 01260 276627
Fax: 01260 270777
Tel: 07000 CIRCUS / 07000 BIG TOP
Email: phillipgandey@netcentral.co.uk

## CHRIS GORDON THEATRICAL AGENCY
29 Well Garth, Well Head, Halifax,
West Yorkshire HX1 2BJ
Tel: 01422 369995
Fax: 01422 252327

## JIMMY GRAFTON MANAGEMENT
26 Tavistock Court, Tavistock Square,
London WC1H 9HE
Tel/Fax: 0171 387 1773
Mobile: 0831 456425

## GOWN & GAUNTLET PROMOTIONS
1 Court Lawns, Tylers Green, High Wycombe,
Buckinghamshire HP10 8DH
Tel/Fax: 01494 814587

## GP ASSOCIATES
4 Gallus Close, Winchmore Hill, London N21 1JR
Tel: 0181 886 2263
Fax: 0181 882 9189

## LEA GRAHAM ENTERTAINMENT
Shelley House 1 Newport Road, Burgess Hill,
West Sussex RH15 8QG
Tel: 01444 235475
Fax: 01444 871577

## RICKY GRAHAM LEISURE
Suite 10, Brittannia House, Skinner Lane, Pontefract,
West Yorkshire WF8 1HG
Tel: 01977 600640
Fax: 01977 600974

## IAN GRANT MANAGEMENT
PO Box 107, Godstone, Surrey RH9 8YS
Tel: 01342 892074/01342 892178
Fax: 01342 893411
Email: ig@igma.demon.uk
Web Site: www.igma.demon.co.uk

## JAMES GRANT MANAGEMENT LIMITED
Syon Lodge, London Road, Isleworth,
Middlesex TW7 5BH
Tel: 0181 232 4100
Fax: 0181 232 4101
Email: jgrant.ftech.co.uk
Web Site: www.ftech.co.uk/~jgrant/

## GRANTHAM-HAZELDINE
5 Blenheim Street, New Bond Street,
London W1Y 9LB
Tel: 0171 499 4011
Fax: 0171 495 3370

## DARREN GRAY MANAGEMENT
2 Marston Lane, Portsmouth PO3 5TW
Tel: 01705 699973
Fax: 01705 677227

## JOAN GRAY PERSONAL MANAGEMENT
29 Sunbury Court Island, Sunbury-On-Thames,
Middlesex TW16 5PP
Tel: 01932 783544

## GRAYS MANAGEMENT
Panther House, 38 Mount Pleasant,
London WC1X 0AP
Tel/Fax: 0171 278 1054

## GREASEPAINT MAKE-UP AGENCY
143 Northfield Avenue, Ealing, London W13 9QT
Tel/Fax: 0181 840 3983
Tel: 0181 840 6000
Email: info@greasepaint.co.uk

Web Site: http://www.greasepaint.co.uk

## GREAT WESTERN ENTERTAINMENT AGENCY
46 Critchill Road, Frome, Somerset BA11 4HF
Tel: 01373 461666

## GREEN & UNDERWOOD
2 Conduit Street, London W1R 9TG
Tel: 0171 493 0308
Fax: 0171 355 1084

## GREEN MAN RECORDS
Tel: 01424 716576

## STAN GREEN MANAGEMENT
PO Box 4, Stoke Fleming, Dartmouth, Devon TQ6 0YD
Tel: 01803 770046
Fax: 01803 770075

## GREENS
Iona, North Orbital Road, Garston, Watford, Herts
WD2 6NB
Tel: 0973 642642/01923 677776
Fax: 01923 661527

## CARL GRESHAM PRESENTATIONS
PO Box 3, Bradford, West Yorkshire BD1 4QN
Tel:01274 735880
Fax: 01274 370313
Mobile: 0378 297787

## SANDRA GRIFFIN MANAGEMENT
6 Ryde Place, Richmond Road, Twickenham,
Middlesex TW1 2EH
Tel: 0181 891 5676
Fax: 0181 744 1812
Email: SGMgmt@aol.com

## EMLYN 'GRIFF' GRIFFITHS
59 Westmead, Windsor, Berkshire SL4 3NN
Tel: 01753 831860

## GROSVENOR PRODUCTIONS
14 Tavistock Street, London WC2E 7PY
Tel: 0171 379 9111
Fax: 0171 379 3478

## GROUP 3 ASSOCIATES
79 Hornsey Road, London N7 6DJ
Tel: 0171 609 9862

## GTA MUSIC CONSULTANTS AND AGENCY
14 Glamorgan Road, Hampton Wick,
Kingston Upon Thames, Surrey KT1 4HP
Tel: 0181 943 9113
Fax: 0181 943 9112

## J GURNETT PERSONAL MANAGEMENT LTD
2 New Kings Road, London SW6 4SA
Tel: 0171 736 7828

Fax: 0171 736 5455
Email: mail@jgpm.demon.co.uk
Web Site: www.jgpm.demon.co.uk

## H & MARCEL ENTERPRISES
282 Staniforth Road, Sheffield S9 3FT
Tel/Fax: 0114 244 4052

## H.A.T.S. (UK) LTD
Suite 1, Excelsior House, 3-5 Balfour Road, Ilford,
Essex IG1 4HP
Tel: 0181 478 1848/8382
Fax: 0181 553 1880
Mobile: 0402 031519

## CINDY HACKER ASSOCIATES
24 Cavendish Buildings, Gilbert Street,
London W1Y 1FD
Tel: 0171 629 2998
Fax: 0171 355 3510
Email: parrot@cerbernet.co.uk

## YVETTE HALES AGENCY
203 The Chart House, Burrells Wharf,
London E14 3TN
Tel: 0171 538 4736
Fax: 0171 538 4778

## TONY HALL GROUP OF COMPANIES
3rd Floor, 9 Carnaby Street, London W1V 1PG
Tel: 0171 437 1958
Fax: 0171 437 3852

## HAMILTON ASPER LTD
24 Hanway Street, London W1P 9DD
Tel: 0171 636 1221
Fax: 0171 636 1226

## HAMILTON'S ENTERTAINMENT CONSULTANTS
4 Heathfield Terrace, London W4 4JE
Tel: 0181 987 8889
Fax: 0181 987 8886

## SUE HAMMER PERSONAL MANAGEMENT
Otterbourne House, Chobham Road, Ottershaw,
Chertsey, Surrey KT16 0QF
Tel: 01932 874111/2
Fax: 01932 872922

## HAMPSONS THEATRICAL AGENCY
136 Hamstead Road, Handsworth,
Birmingham B20 2QR
Tel: 0121 554 2191
Fax: 0121 686 9220

## ROGER HANCOCK LTD
4 Water Lane, London NW1 8NZ
Tel: 0171 267 4418
Fax: 0171 267 0705

## HANDLE ARTISTS MANAGEMENT
Handle Group of Companies, Handle House,
1 Albion Place, Galena Road, London W6 0QT
Tel: 0181 846 9111
Fax: 0181 846 8011/2

## JEF HANLON PROMOTIONS LTD
1 York Street, London W1H 1PZ
Tel: 0171 487 2558
Fax: 0171 487 2584
Email: jhanlon@agents-uk.com

## HARBOUR & COFFEY
3rd Floor 5 Sedley Place, London W1R 1HH
Tel: 0171 499 5548
Fax: 0171 499 0884

## MIKE HARDING
Dean Clough Mill Dean Clough Office Park, Halifax,
West Yorkshire HX3 5AX
Tel: 01422 343949
Mobile: 0802 515737

## HARRIS PERSONAL MANAGEMENT
171 Junction Road, London N19 5PZ
Tel: 0171 281 0445
Fax: 0171 561 0105

## LES HART (SOUTHAMPTON) ENTERTAINMENTS
1st Floor, 225 High Street, Eastleigh, Hampshire
Tel: 01703 614889/01703 618311
Fax: 01703 611090

## HARTBEAT ENTERTAINMENTS
PO Box 3, Plympton, Plymouth, Devon PL7 5YL
Tel: 01752 335000
Fax: 01752 335060
Email: hartbeat@lineone.net

## RICHARD HATTON LTD
29 Roehampton Gate, London SW15 5JR
Tel: 0181 876 6699
Fax: 0181 876 8278

## JACK HAWKINS ORCHESTRA
Ferndale, 157 Portsmouth Road, Horndean,
Waterlooville, Hampshire PO8 9LG
Tel/Fax: 01705 596721

## HAWTHORN ENTERTAINMENT
1st Floor, York House, Tremains Road, Bridgend,
Mid Glamorgan CF31 1TZ
Tel: 01656 662835
Fax: 01656 661872
Email: hawthorn@link-connect.uk

## HAZARD CHASE LTD
Richmond House, 16-20 Regent Street, Cambridge,
Cambs CB2 1DB
Tel: 01223 312400
Fax: 01223 460827

Email: info@hazardchase.co.uk
Web Site: www.hazardchase.co.uk

## HAZEMEAD LTD
3rd Floor, 18 Hanover Street, London W1R 9HG
Tel: 0171 629 4817
Fax: 0171 629 5668

## HCA
(Also Howard Cooke Associates)
Apartment 1, 20 Courtfield Gardens, London SW5 0PD
Tel: 0171 835 0136
Fax: 0171 835 1391

## HEAD ON MANAGEMENT
88 Lewisham Way, New Cross, London SE14 6NY
Tel/Fax: 0181 469 2576

## DENNIS HEANEY PROMOTIONS
Whitehall, Ashgrove Road, Newry,
County Down BT34 1QN
Tel: 01693 68658
Fax: 01693 6673

## HEART OF ENGLAND PROMOTIONS LTD
Unit 1, White Cottage, Birmingham Road, Meriden,
Coventry CV7 7HY
Tel: 01676 522700
Fax: 01676 523876
Email: sales@heartofengland.co.uk
Web Site: www.heartofengland.demon.co

## AL HEATH INTERNATIONAL
The New House, The Green, Semley, Shaftesbury,
Dorset SP7 9AU
Tel: 01747 830723/01747 830719
Fax: 01747 830723

## GEORGE HEATHCOTE MANAGEMENT
58 Northdown Street, London N1 9BS
Tel: 0171 713 6959
Fax: 0171 713 6968

## HEAVY PENCIL MANAGEMENT
BAC, Lavender Hill, London SW11 5TF
Tel: 0171 738 9574
Fax: 0171 924 4636

## HELTER SKELTER
The Plaza, 535 Kings Road, London SW10 0SZ
Tel: 0171 376 8501
Fax: 0171 376 8336

## HEMMINGS LEISURE
Oakland, 16 Foxland Close, Shirley, Solihull,
West Midlands B90 4HL
Tel: 01564 702770
Fax: 01564 703931
Email: leisure@design-one.co.uk

## GLYNIS HENDERSON MANAGEMENT & PRODUCTION
52 Tottenham Street, London W1P 9PG
Tel: 0171 580 9644
Fax: 0171 436 1489

## HENDERSON MANAGEMENT
51 Promenade North, Thornton-Cleveleys,
Lancashire FY5 1LN
Tel: 01253 863386
Fax: 01253 867799
Email: agents@henderson-management.co.uk
Web Site: www.henderson-management.co.uk

## JOHN HESSENTHALER ENTERTAINMENTS
20 Green Willows, Lavenham, Sudbury,
Suffolk CO10 9SP
Tel: 01787 247838
Fax: 01787 247898

## JEREMY HICKS ASSOCIATES
12 Ogle Street, London W1P 7LG
Tel: 0171 636 8008
Fax: 0171 636 8880

## JACK L HIGGINS
Pear Tree Cottage, Weymarks, Bradwell-on-Sea,
Southminster, Essex CM0 7JB
Tel: 01621 776463
Fax: 01621 776671

## HIGHFIELD MANAGEMENT & PROMOTIONS
38 Cambridge Road Impington Cambridge CB4 4NU
Tel: 01223 233000
Fax: 01223 235252

## HIGHFIELD PRODUCTIONS
10 Imperial Square, Cheltenham,
Gloucestershire GL50 1QB
Tel: 01242 264902
Fax: 01242 264909
Email: highfield_productions@cemi.co.uk

## LOUISE HILLMAN & KATE THRELFALL
33 Brookfield, Highgate West Hill, London N6 6AT
Tel: 0181 341 2207
Fax: 0181 340 9309

## HILTON INTERNATIONAL ENTERTAINMENTS
27 Downs Side, Cheam, Sutton, Surrey SM2 7EH
Tel: 0181 643 3991/8375
Fax: 0181 770 7241
Email: GBALTD@compuserve.com

## BERNARD HINCHCLIFFE AGENCY
Arnold House, 73a Birkby Hall Road, Huddersfield,
West Yorks HD2 2TN
Tel: 01484 534622
Fax: 01484 535650

**DEE HINDIN ASSOCIATES**
Malvern House 15-16 Nassau Street,
London W1N 7RE
Tel: 0171 637 0616
Fax: 0171 637 0818

**PHILIP HINDIN LTD**
66 Melbourne Way, Bush Hill Park, Enfield,
Middlesex EN1 1XQ
Tel/Fax: 0181 366 2978

**HIRE-A-BAND ENTERTAINMENT AGENCY**
35 Trent Road, Ipswich, Suffolk IP3 0QL
Tel/Fax: 01473 712624

**HIRED HANDS**
12 Cressy Road, London NW3 2LY
Tel: 0171 267 9212
Fax: 0171 267 1030

**HIT & RUN MUSIC LTD**
30 Ives Street, London SW3 2ND
Tel: 0171 581 0261
Fax: 0171 584 5774

**HOBSON'S ARTISTES**
62 Chiswick High Road, London W4 1SY
Tel: 0181 747 8326
Fax: 0181 742 1511

**HOLLAND-FORD'S**
103 Lydyett Lane, Barnton, Northwich,
Cheshire CW8 4JT
Tel: 01606 76960

**DAVE HOLLY ARTS MEDIA SERVICES**
The Annexe 23 Eastwood Gardens, Felling,
Gateshead, Tyne and Wear NE10 0AH
Tel: 0191 438 2711
Fax: 0191 438 2722

**SALLY HOPE ASSOCIATES**
108 Leonard Street, London EC2A 4RH
Tel: 0171 613 5353
Fax: 0171 613 4848
Email: s-hope@dircon.co.uk

**ADRIAN HOPKINS PROMOTIONS**
24 Fulham Palace Road, Hammersmith,
London W6 9PH
Tel: 0181 741 9910
Fax: 0181 741 9914

**THE HORNE CONCERT AGENCY**
44 Linton Road, Castle Gresley, Swadlincote,
Derbyshire DE11 9HS
Tel: 01283 218335

**HOUGHTON WEAVERS (MANAGEMENT) LTD**
13 Hall Gate, Westhoughton, Bolton BL5 2SF
Tel: 01942 813033
Fax: 01942 818989

**HOUNDOG MUSIC & ENTERTAINMENT AGENCY**
49 Arthurton Road, Spixworth, Norwich NR10 3QU
Tel/Fax: 01603 897789

**HOUSE OF LORDS**
London SW1A 0PW
Tel: 0171 235 6600

**AMANDA HOWARD ASSOCIATES LTD**
7/8 Little Turnstile, London WC1V 7DX
Tel: 0171 404 2332
Fax: 0171 404 7456

**JOHN HOWE PRESENTATIONS**
2 Meadow Way, Ferring, Worthing,
West Sussex BN12 5LD
Tel: 01903 249912
Fax: 01903 507698

**HOWES & PRIOR LTD**
66 Berkeley House, Hay Hill, London W1X 7LH
Tel: 0171 493 7570/7655
Fax: 0171 408 0058

**HUGHES ENTERTAINMENT**
PO Box 502, Warrington, Cheshire WA4 2ER
Tel/Fax: 01925 602900

**JANE HUGHES MANAGEMENT**
The Coach House, PO Box 123, Knutsford,
Cheshire WA16 9HX
Tel: 01565 723000
Fax: 01565 722211

**MIKE HUGHES ENTERTAINMENTS**
C/O Gerald Goss Ltd, 6 Windmill Street,
London W1P 1HF
Tel: 0171 636 5547
Fax: 0171 636 0079

**OWEN HUGHES ENTERTAINMENTS**
12 Observer Buildings, Rowbottom Square, Wigan,
Lancashire WN1 1LN
Tel: 01942 322949/01942 510757
Fax: 01942 510758

**D HULL PROMOTIONS LTD**
46 University Street, Belfast,
Northern Ireland BT7 1HB
Tel: 01232 240360
Fax: 01232 247919

**BERNARD HUNTER ASSOCIATES**
13 Spencer Gardens, London SW14 7AH
Tel: 0181 878 6308
Fax: 0181 392 9334

**HURRICANE PRODUCTIONS LTD**
2 Spirit Quay, Vaughan Way, St Catherine's Dock,
London E1 9UT
Tel: 0171 480 6100

Fax: 0171 481 0668

## HUTT RUSSELL PRODUCTIONS LTD
PO Box 64, Cirencester, Gloucestershire GL7 5YD
Tel: 01285 644622
Fax: 01285 642291
Email: hutt_russell_productions@cemi.co.uk

## HWB PRODUCTIONS
17 Bargate Close New Malden Surrey KT3 6BG
Tel: 0181 942 5859
Fax: 0181 949 4107

## HYPER KINETICS
54 Harmood Street, London NW1 8DP
Tel: 0171 485 1563
Fax: 0171 485 5334

## I E MUSIC
59a Chesson Road, London W14 9QS
Tel: 0171 386 9995
Fax: 0171 610 0762
Email: info.ie.demon.co.uk

## ICM LTD
Oxford House, 76 Oxford Street, London W1M 0AX
Tel: 0171 636 6565
Fax: 0171 323 0101

## IDLE HANDS
PO Box 129 Stevenage, Hertfordshire SG1 2DN
Tel: 01438 311633
Fax: 01438 724777

## IMAGES ENTERTAINMENTS
78 Eversley Road, Thundersley, Benfleet,
Essex SS7 4JH
Tel/Fax: 01268 757975
Email: images@images.com

## IMAGINATION ENTERTAINMENTS
25 Store Street, London WC1E 7BL
Tel: 0171 323 3300
Fax: 0171 323 5801

## IMG ARTISTES
Media House, Hogarth Business Park,
3 Burlington Lane, Chiswick, London W4 2TH
Tel: 0181 233 5800
Fax: 0181 233 5801

## INDEPENDENT MANAGEMENT LIMITED
Finsbury Business Centre, 40 Bowling Green Lane,
London EC1R 0NE
Tel/Fax: 0171 833 4680

## INGPEN & WILLIAMS LTD
26 Wadham Road, London SW15 2LR
Tel: 0181 874 3222
Fax: 0181 877 3113

## INITIATIVE UNLIMITED
12a Station Road, Mill Hill, London NW7 2JU
Tel: 0181 959 6579
Fax: 0181 201 0659
Email: sales@mayhem.org.uk
Web Site: www.mayhem.org.uk

## INSPIRATION MANAGEMENT
Southbank House, Black Prince Road,
London SE1 7SJ
Tel/Fax: 0171 587 0947

## INSPIRATIONAL ARTISTE BOOKING
PO Box 1AS, London W1A 1AS
Tel/Fax: 0171 287 0060

## INTERNATIONAL ARTISTES LTD
Mezzanine Floor, 235 Regent Street,
London W1R 8AX
Tel: 0171 439 8401
Fax: 0171 409 2070
4th Floor, Television House, 10-12 Mount Street
Manchester M2 5FA
Tel: 0161 833 9838
Fax: 0161 832 7480
Email: (user)@intartistes.demon.co.uk

## INTERNATIONAL MANAGEMENT & AGENCY LTD
2 Bond Terrace, Rishworth Street Wakefield,
West Yorkshire WF1 2HW
Tel: 01924 299993
Fax: 01924 200750
Email: norman.thewlis@blinternet.com

## INTERNATIONAL THEATRE & MUSIC LTD
Claridge House, 29 Barnes High Street,
London SW13 9LW
Tel: 0181 876 8666
Fax: 0181 876 7594

## IRREPRESSABLE ARTISTES
39 Icen Way, Dorchester, Dorset DT1 1ET
Tel/Fax: 01305 261057/268977

## ISLAND RECORDS LTD
22 St. Peters Square, London W6 9NW
Tel: 0181 910 3333
Fax: 0181 910 3397

## ITALIA CONTI AGENCY LTD
Italia Conti House, 23 Goswell Road,
London EC1M 7AJ
Tel: 0171 608 0044
Fax: 0171 253 1430

## ITB (INTERNATIONAL TALENT BOOKING)
3rd Floor, 27a Floral Street, Covent Garden,
London WC2E 9DQ
Tel: 0171 379 1313
Fax: 0171 379 1744

**J B AGENCY LTD**
7 Stonehill Mansions, 8 Streatham High Road,
London SW16 1DD
Tel: 0181 677 5151
Fax: 0181 769 9567
Email: tonyjb@globalnet.co.uk
Web Site: http://www.jbagency.euro-index.co.uk

**J.S.E./KIDLEEWYNKS LEISURE HIRE**
PO Box 509, Bodiam Crescent, Eastbourne,
Herefordshire BN22 9HQ
Tel/Fax: 01323 540154
Mobile: 0378 642687

**JAA (SEE JONATHAN ALTARAS
ASSOCIATES LTD)**

**STEVE JACKSON SERVICES PROMOTIONS**
159 Rotherham Road, Monk Bretton, Barnsley,
South Yorkshire S71 2LL
Tel: 01226 205932/285453
Fax: 01226 205932

**JACLYN AGENCY**
Thackeray House, Mill Road, Hempnall, Norwich,
Norfolk NR15 2LP
Tel: 01508 499241
Fax: 01508 499077

**JOHNNY JALLAND ENTERPRISES**
8 Manners Road, Balderton, Newark,
Nottinghamshire NG24 3HW
Tel: 01636 701710
Fax: 01636 700841

**SUSAN JAMES PERSONAL MANAGEMENT**
15 Maiden Lane London WC2 7NA
Tel: 0171 740 1684
Fax: 0171 740 1685

**JOY JAMESON LTD**
2.19 The Plaza, 535 Kings Road, London SW10 0SZ
Tel: 0171 351 3971
Fax: 0171 352 1744

**J.A.V.A.MANAGEMENT**
24 Aviemore Road, Warmsworth Doncaster,
South Yorkshire DN4 9NE
Tel: 01302 310690
Fax: 01302 855997

**ALEX JAY PERSONAL MANAGEMENT**
137a Kensington High Street, London W8 6SU
Tel: 0171 376 2769
Fax: 0171 376 2769

**ELLIE JAY ENTERTAINMENT
CONSULTANTS LTD**
Elstree Film Studios, Shenley Road, Borehamwood,
Hertfordshire WD6 1JG
Tel: 0181 324 2277
Fax: 0181 324 2766

Email: entertainment@elliejay.co.uk

**JAYCO ENTERTAINEMENT**
53A Comber Road, Dundonald, Belfast,
Northern Ireland BT16 0AA
Tel: 01232 481783
Fax: 01232 487459
Mobile: 0831 677912

**JAZZ AND ARTS DIRECTIONS**
PO Box 118 Newport, Gwent NP9 2YN
Tel: 01633 211368
Fax: 01633 220422

**JAZZ MUSIC AGENCY**
16 Lancaster Road, London W11 1QP
Tel/Fax: 0171 221 7688

**JB AGENCY LTD**
7 Stonehill Mansions, 8 Streatham High Road,
London SW16 1DD
Tel: 0181 677 5151
Fax: 0181 769 9567

**JB ASSOCIATES**
3 Stevenson Square, Manchester M1 1DN
Tel: 0161 237 1808
Fax: 0161 237 1809
Email: united_cities@compuserve.com

**JBA LTD**
1st Floor, Chichester House, Kennington Park,
1-3 Brixton Road, London SW9 6DE
Tel: 0171 582 3048
Fax: 0171 793 8658
Email: jbaltd@globalnet.co.uk

**JEFFREY & WHITE**
9-15 Neal Street, London WC2H 9PU
Tel: 0171 240 7000
Fax: 0171 240 0007

**JGM**
15 Lexham Mews, London W8 6JW
Tel: 0171 376 2414
Fax: 0171 376 2416

**JIVE ENTERTAINMENT SERVICES**
4 Pasteur Courtyard, Whittle Road,
Phoenix Parkway Industrial Est Corby,
Northamptonshire NN17 5DX
Tel: 01536 406406
Fax: 01536 400082

**JK ROYALE PROMOTIONS**
20 Moorhead Mews, Cowgate Centre,
Newcastle Upon Tyne NE5 3AR
Tel: 0191 242 1009
Fax: 0191 242 1008

**JLA (JEREMY LEE ASSOCIATES LTD)**
13 Short's Gardens, Covent Garden,

London WC2H 9AT
Tel: 0171 240 0413
Fax: 0171 240 0371

## JLM PERSONAL MANAGEMENT
242 Acton Lane, London W4 5DL
Tel: 0181 747 8223
Fax: 0181 747 8286

## JM ASSOCIATES
77 Beak Street, London W1R 3LF
Tel: 0171 434 0602
Fax: 0171 434 0640

## JMS MANAGEMENT LTD
Membury Business Park, Ermin Street,
Lambourn Woodlands, Hungerford,
Berkshire RG17 7TP
Tel: 01488 72010
Fax: 01488 72075

## PETER JOHNSON ENTERTAINMENTS
Hastings Road, Hawkhurst, Cranbrook,
Kent TN18 4RT
Tel: 01580 754822
Fax: 01580 754808
Email: pjents@agents-uk.com
Web Site: www.business.u-net.com/~agents13/

## JOHNSON'S
17 Crofton Road, Woodside, Grays, Essex RM16 2GY
Tel: 01375 394845
Fax: 01375 394843
Email: philjohnson@cableinet.co.uk
Web Site: http://wkweb4.cableinet.co.uk

## JOKER ENTERTAINMENTS
Dwyfach Farm, Glanwyfach, Garndolbenmaen,
Gwynedd LL51 9LJ Wales
Tel: 01766 530726

## JOLLY ROGER ENTERTAINMENTS
19 Ashness Gardens, Greenford, Middlesex UB6 0RL
Tel: 0181 902 3373/0181 903 5533
Fax: 0181 902 9538

## JRS ENTERTAINMENTS
16 Carlton Square, Carlton Colville, Lowestoft,
Suffolk NR33 8JL
Tel/Fax: 01502 572578

## JS ENTERTAINMENTS
April Rise, Llanover Road, Blaenavon, Gwent NP4 9JQ
Tel: 01495 790619

## JUKES ENTERTAINMENTS
81 Terence Messenger Towers, Oliver Close,
London E10 5LH
Tel: 0181 518 7033
Fax: 0181 558 8288
Email: jukes@netcomuk.co.uk

## JUKES PRODUCTIONS LTD
PO Box 13995 London W9 2FL
Tel: 0171 286 9532
Fax: 0171 286 4739
Email: jukes@easynet.co.uk

## CHUCK JULIAN ASSOCIATES
Suite 51, 26 Charing Cross Road, London WC2H 0DH
Tel: 0171 437 4248
Fax: 0171 240 1296

## KAL MANAGEMENT
95 Gloucester Road, Hampton, Middlesex TW12 2UW
Tel: 0181 783 0039
Fax: 0181 979 6487

## KALEIDESCOPE CELEBRITY APPEARANCES
162 Roe Lane, Southport, Merseyside PR9 7PN
Tel/Fax: 01704 27805

## KALEIDESCOPE ENTERTAINMENTS & LEISURE INTERNATIONAL
Whyte House, 162 Roe Lane, Southport,
Merseyside PR9 7PN
Tel/Fax: 01704 27805

## KAMA ENTERTAINMENT SERVICES
2 Thornton Park Avenue, Thornton Park Estate,
Muxton, Telford, Shropshire TF2 8RF
Tel: 01952 603916

## ROBERTA KANAL AGENCY
82 Constance Road, Twickenham,
Middlesex TW2 7JA
Tel: 0181 894 2277
Fax: 0181 894 7952

## KCPM (KENNETH CLEVELAND PERSONAL MANAGEMENT LTD)
6 Ganton Street, London W1V 1LJ
Tel: 0171 734 7304
Fax: 0171 734 7318

## PAT KEELING MODEL AGENCY
99-101 Highcross Street, Leicester LE1 4PH
Tel: 0116 262 2540
Fax: 0116 253 7712

## GORDON KELLETT ENTERTAINMENTS
4 Moor Flatts Road, Middleton, Leeds LS10 3SW
Tel: 0113 270 8562/0113 270 2301
Fax: 0113 277 3267

## ROBERT C KELLY LTD
3 Athole Gardens, Glasgow G12 9AY Scotland
Tel: 0141 337 2244
Fax: 0141 337 1955

## KERNOW ENTERTAINMENTS
Commercial Road, Penryn, Cornwall TR10 8AE

Tel: 01326 377500
Fax: 01326 376600

## IVOR KIMMEL CASTING
PO Box 5601, London W9 1WH
Tel: 0171 289 7726
Fax: 0171 289 3098

## ADRIAN KING ASSOCIATES
33, Marlborough Mansions, Cannon Hill,
London NW6 1JS
Tel: 0171 435 4600/435 4700
Fax: 0171 435 4100

## GEORGE KING
44 Winchester Drive, Poulton-Le-Fylde,
Lancashire FY6 7PS
Tel: 01253 886432
Tel/Fax: 01253 896271

## KEVIN KING MANAGEMENT
16 Lime Trees Avenue, Llangattock, Crickhowell,
Powys NP8 1LB Wales
Tel: 01873 810142
Fax: 01873 811557

## KNIGHT AYTON MANAGEMENT
10 Argyll Street, London W1V 1AB
Tel: 0171 287 4405
Fax: 0171 434 3075

## RAY KNIGHT CASTING
21a Lambolle Place, Belsize Park, London NW3 4PG
Tel: 0171 722 1551
Fax: 0171 722 2322

## KRISTANNAR MUSIC
33 Park Chase, Wembley, Middlesex HA9 8EQ
Tel/Fax: 0181 902 5523

## ROLF KRUGER MANAGEMENT
21 Eastcastle Street, London W1N 7PA
Tel: 0171 323 3733
Fax: 0171 323 3744
Email: rkruger@mail.com

## KRYSTINA VARIETY AGENCY
251 Shinfield Road, Shinfield, Reading,
Berkshire RG2 8HF
Tel: 0118 986 4135/0831 635662
Fax: 0118 931 1219

## KUDOS MANAGEMENT
Crown Studios, 16-18 Crown Road, Twickenham,
Middlesex TW1 3EE
Tel: 0181 891 4233
Fax: 0181 891 2339

## L'EPINE SMITH & CARNEY ASSOCIATES
Suite 61/63, Kent House, 87 Regent Street,
London W1R 7HF
Tel: 0171 434 4143

Fax: 0171 434 4173

## L.O.E.ENTERTAINMENT LTD
159 Broadhurst Gardens, London NW6 3AU
Tel: 0171 328 6100
Fax: 0171 624 6384

## MICHAEL LA ROCHE MANAGEMENT
Anchor House 127-129 Mile End Road,
London E1 4UL
Tel: 0171 790 8828
Fax: 0171 790 8829

## LABEL SPINNERS
Box 1, 404 Footscray Road, London SE9 3TU
Tel: 0181 857 8775/0181 355 9700
Fax: 0181 857 8775
Email: spinners@dircon.co.uk
Web Site: www.labelspinners.co.uk

## MICHAEL LADKIN PERSONAL MANAGEMENT
Suite One, Ground Floor, 1 Duchess Street,
London W1N 3DE
Tel: 0171 436 4626
Fax: 0171 436 4627

## BETTY LAINE MANAGEMENT
The Studios, East Street, Epsom, Surrey KT17 1HH
Tel/Fax: 01372 721815

## LAINE MANAGEMENT
Matrix House, 301-303 Chapel Street, Salford M3 5JG
Tel: 0161 835 2122
Fax: 0161 839 3061

## LAMPLIGHT MUSIC LTD
109 Eastbourne Mews, London W2 6LQ
Tel: 0171 402 4169
Fax: 0171 723 2768

## DAVID LAND (AGENCY) LTD
46 Crawford Street, London W1
Tel: 0171 723 2456
Fax: 0171 723 7567

## LANGFORD ASSOCIATES
17 Westfields Avenue, London SW13 0AT
Tel: 0181 878 7148
Fax: 0181 878 7078

## LATIN ARTS SERVICES (LAS)
24 Blakes Terrace, New Malden, Surrey KT3 6ET
Tel/Fax: 07000 472572
Mobile: 0956 446342
Email: latin_arts_services@compuserve.com

## LATIN-TOUCH ENTERTAINMENTS
Fatima Community Centre, Commonwealth Avenue,
London W12 7QR
Tel: 0181 740 9020
Fax: 0181 749 8903

Email: latin_touch@compuserve.com
Web Site: http://www.latin touch.com

## TESSA LE BARS MANAGEMENT
54 Birchwood Road, Petts Wood, Orpington,
Kent BR5 1NZ
Tel/Fax: 01689 837084
Mobile: 0860 287255

## BERNARD LEE MANAGEMENT
Moorcroft Lodge, Farleigh Common, Warlingham,
Surrey CR6 9PE
Tel/Fax: 01883 625667

## LEE'S PEOPLE
238 Nelson Road, Whitton, Twickenham,
Middlesex TW2 7BW
Tel: 0181 898 9000
Fax: 0181 893 3600
Mobile: 07970 527252 / 527152 / 527052
Email: lee@lees-people.co.uk
Web Site: www.lees-people.co.uk

## JANE LEHRER ASSOCIATES
100A Chalk Farm Road, London NW1 8EH
Tel: 0171 482 4898
Fax: 0171 482 4899

## LEIGH MANAGEMENT
14 St. Davids Drive, Edgware, Middlesex HA8 6JH
Tel/Fax: 0181 951 4449

## THE LEIGHTON-POPE ORGANISATION
8 Glenthorne Mews, 115a Glenthorne Road,
Hammersmith, London W6 0LJ
Tel: 0181 741 4453
Fax: 0181 741 4289

## LEISURE MANAGEMENT
63 Clyde Terrace, Spennymoor,
County Durham DL16 7SQ
Tel: 01388 420050
Fax: 01388 420037
Email: leisure@agents-uk.com

## LEISURE SERVICES AGENCY LIMITED
1 Park Lane, Hemel Hempstead,
Hertfordshire HP2 4YL
Tel: 01442 230300
Fax: 01442 251678

## LEO MANAGEMENT & AGENCY
Nelson House, Castle Hill Road, Hindley, Wigan,
Lancashire WN2 4BH
Tel: 01942 701942
Fax: 01942 517151
Email: leo@agents-uk.com

## LEVO MANAGEMENT
2nd Floor, 12 Weltje Road, Hammersmith,
London W6 9TG
Tel/Fax: 0181 7412038

## LEWIS & VAUGHAN PROMOTIONS
76a Waterloo Road, Blyth, Northumberland NE24 1DG
Tel: 01670 360036/355082
Fax: 01670 355203
Mobile: 0403 128449

## LEY ENTERTAINMENT PRODUCTIONS
14 Stanshaw Close, Frenchay, Bristol BS16 1JY
Tel: 0117 956 5599

## WILLIAM LEYLAND
The Cricketer, Keats Avenue, Poolstock, Wigan,
Lancashire WN3 5UB
Tel: 01942 824555
Fax: 01942 824567

## BRIAN LIDSTONE REPRESENTATION
138 Westbourne Grove, London W11 2RR
Tel: 0171 727 2342
Fax: 0171 221 7210

## LIFEFORCE MANAGEMENT
"Avonside" 63 High Street, Tewkesbury,
Gloucestershire GL20 5BJ
Tel: 01684 850750
Fax: 01684 297717
Mobile: 0831 675489

## LIMELIGHT MANAGEMENT
33 Newman Street, London W1P 3PD
Tel: 0171 637 2529
Fax: 0171 637 2538

## LINCOLN MANAGEMENT ENTERTAINMENT
& LEISURE AGENCY
12 Grantham Road, Bracebridge Heath,
Lincoln LN4 2LD
Tel: 01522 540761 (4lines)
Fax: 01522 514020

## LINE-UP PMC
9a Tankerville Place, Newcastle Upon Tyne NE2 3AT
Tel: 0191 281 6449
Fax: 0191 212 0913
Email: line-up.co.uk

## LINKS MANAGEMENT
34-68 Colombo Street, London SE1 8DP
Tel/Fax: 0171 928 0806/3134

## LINKSIDE AGENCY
21 Poplar Road, Leatherhead, Surrey KT22 8SF
Tel: 01372 802374
Fax: 01372 801972

## LINTERN REES ORGANISATION
Unit 2, The Quarry, Kewstoke Road, Worle,
Weston-super-Mare, North Somerset BS22 9LS

## LIONHEART MUSIC
20 Grasmere Avenue, Kingston Vale,
London SW15 3RB

Tel: 0181 546 4047
Fax: 0181 546 0468

## LIP SERVICE CASTING LIMITED
4 Kingly Street, London W1R 5LF
Tel: 0171 724 3393
Fax: 0171 734 3373
Email: bookings@lipservice.co.uk

## LIPTON PARKER ENTERTAINMENTS LTD
6 Broadstrood, Loughton, Essex IG10 2SE
Tel: 0181 508 7744
Fax: 0181 508 7735
Mobile: 0374 483404
Email: laurie@link-connect.co.uk
Web Site: www.link-connect.co.uk/~link101575

## LIVE PROMOTIONS
The Millstone, 9 St. Thomas Road, Spalding,
Lincolnshire PE11 2XY
Tel: 01775 768661
Fax: 01775 768665

## LOESJE SANDERS
Pound Square, 1 North Hill, Woodbridge,
Suffolk IP12 1HH
Tel: 01394 385260
Fax: 01394 388734

## LONDON MANAGEMENT
Noel House, 2-4 Noel Street, London W1V 3RB
Tel: 0171 287 9000
Fax: 0171 287 3236

## LONDON MUSIC AGENCY
Wayside, Epping Green, Epping, Essex CM16 6PU
Tel: 01992 578617/8
Fax: 01992 578618

## LONDON MUSICIANS LTD
Cedar House, Vine Lane, Hillingdon, Uxbridge,
Middlesex UB10 0BX
Tel: 01895 252555
Fax: 01895 252556
Email: mail@lonmus.demon.co.uk

## LONDON PERFORMERS
The Young Vic, 66 The Cut, London SE1 8LZ
Tel: 0171 928 8353
Fax: 0171 928 8505

## THE LONDON SPEAKER BUREAU
The London House, 271 King Street, London W6 9LZ
Tel: 0181 748 9595
Fax: 0181 741 8273
Email: speakers@londonspeakerbureau.co.uk

## LONGTIME MANAGEMENT
668 High Road, London N17 0AB
Tel/Fax: 0181 801 4152

## LOOK ALIKES AGENCY
17-23 Lorn Road, London SW9 0AB
Tel: 0171 274 0666
Fax: 0171 274 4466
Email: looklikeuk@aol.com
Web Site: www.lookalikesuk.com

## LOOKALIKES - SUSAN SCOTT
26 College Crescent, London NW3 5LH
Tel: 0171 387 9245
Fax: 0171 722 8261

## DON LORD ENTERTAINMENTS
31 Fern Road, Rushden, Northamptonshire NN10 6AU
Tel/Fax: 01933 353221

## JOE LOSS LTD
PO Box 1901, Prince Albert Road, London NW8 7EJ
Tel/Fax: 0171 580 1212

## MARK LUNDQUIST MANAGEMENT
2 Woodlands, Woking, Surrey GU22 7RU
Tel: 01483 773373
Fax: 01483 767929
Mobile: 07971 401510
Email: marklundquist@dial.pipex.com

## RONNIE LUNDY AGENCY
208 Chester Road, Sunderland SR4 7HE
Tel: 0191 567 6633
Fax: 0191 567 4559

## LWA
18 Elliott Square, London NW3 3SU
Tel: 0171 586 5867
Fax: 0171 586 1583

## DENNIS LYNE AGENCY
108 Leonard Street, London EC2A 4RH
Tel: 0171 739 6200
Fax: 0171 739 4101

## CHRIS LYNN AGENCY
17 Kimber Close, Lancing, West Sussex BN15 8QD
Tel: 01903 755511/765377

## M.A.G.I.C.
19 South Audley Street, London W1Y 5DN
Tel: 0171 499 3377
Fax: 0171 499 3310
Email: info@magic-ltd.com

## M.A.P. AGENCY
Manor Grange, Piper Hill, Fairburn, Knottingley,
West Yorkshire WF11 9LF
Tel: 01977 675052
Fax: 01977 675053

## M.M & M
Pinewood Studios, Pinewood Road, Iver,
Buckinghamshire SL0 0NH
Tel: 01753 650808

Fax: 01753 650705

## M.S. ENTERTAINMENT GROUP
2A Bockhanger Court, Kennington, Ashford,
Kent TN24 9JJ
Tel/Fax: 01233 610023

## MACFARLANE CHARD ASSOCIATES
7/8 Little Turnstile, London WC1V 7DX
Tel: 0171 404 2332
Fax: 0171 404 7456

## HEATHER MACKENZIE
Upper Cultullich, Aberfeldy, Perthshire PH15 2EN
Scotland

## SCOTT MACKENZIE ASSOCIATES
6 Gardner Way, Kenilworth, Warwickshire CV8 1QW
Tel: 01926 859102/3
Fax: 01926 858966

## PAUL MADELEY
17 Valley Road, Arden Park, Bredbury, Stockport,
Cheshire SK6 2EA
Tel/Fax: 0161 430 5380/0161 430 7255

## MAGIC EYE RECORDS
PO Box 3037, Wokingham, Berkshire RG40 4RG
Tel: 0118 932 8320
Fax: 0118 932 8237

## MICHAEL MAGILL ENTERTAINMENTS
"Chez Nous", Burren Road, Warrenpoint, Newry,
County Down BT34 3SA Northern Ireland
Tel: 016937 73618/016937 52229
Fax: 016937 52020

## MAGNET PERSONAL MANAGEMENT
Unit 743 The Big Peg, 120 Vyse Street, Hockley,
Birmingham B18 6NF
Tel/Fax: 0121 628 7788

## MAGNOLIA MANAGEMENT
136 Hicks Avenue, Greenford, Middlesex UB6 8HB
Tel: 0181 578 2899
Fax: 0181 575 0369

## MAHONEY GRETTON ASSOCIATES (MGA)
Concorde House, 18 Margaret Street,
Brighton BN2 1TS
Tel: 01273 685970
Fax: 01273 685971

## MAINLINE ENTERTAINMENT
29 Manor Farm Road, Aston-on-Trent,
Derby DE72 2BW
Tel/Fax: 01332 792533

## MAINSTREAM EVENTS
The Signal Box 119-123 Sandycombe Road,
Richmond, Surrey TW9 2ER

Tel: 0181 940 3311
Fax: 0181 940 7404

## MAITLAND MUSIC (INC. CAPITAL VOICES)
Brook House 8 Rythe Road, Claygate, Esher,
Surrey KT10 9DF
Tel: 01372 466228
Fax: 01372 466229
Email: maitmus@aol.com / capvox@aol.com

## MAJOR ENTERTAINMENT AGENCY
6c Standbridge Lane, Sandal, Wakefield,
West Yorkshire WF2 7DY
Tel: 01924 254350
Fax: 01924 259414

## MIKE MALLEY ENTERTAINMENTS
10 Holly Park Gardens, Finchley, London N3 3NJ
Tel: 0181 346 4109
Fax: 0181 346 1104
Mobile: 0385 375661/2
Email: mikemall@globalnet.co.uk
Web Site: www.ukstars.co.uk

## MALONE & KNIGHT ASSOCIATES
26 Wellesley Road, London W4 4BN
Tel: 0181 994 1619
Fax: 0181 994 2992
Mobile: 07771 784895
Email: mka.agency@virgin.net

## MANHATTAN MANAGEMENT
(Representing theTEMBO Group of Companies)
Suite GO4, 6-8 Underwood Street, London N1 7JQ
Tel: 0171 477 6001
Fax: 0171 477 6002

## JOHNNY MANS PRODUCTIONS LIMITED
The Maltings, Brewery Road, Hoddesdon,
Hertfordshire EN11 8HF
Tel: 01992 470907
Fax: 01992 470516

## ANDREW MANSON
288 Munster Road, London SW6 6BQ
Tel: 0171 386 9158
Fax: 0171 381 8874

## MARCO POLO
23 Station Road, Hayling Island, Hampshire PO11 0EA
Tel: 01705 461934
Fax: 01705 461935
Mobile: 0802 500050
Email: MarkoPolo@compuserve.com

## HARRY MARGOLIS ENTERTAINMENT
## ORGANISATION
Entertainment Direct
14 Heathside Road, Giffnock,
Glasgow G46 6HL Scotland
Tel: 0141 638 0724
Fax: 0141 620 0799

## MARKHAM & FROGGATT LTD
Julian House 4 Windmill Street, London W1P 1HF
Tel: 0171 636 4412
Fax: 0171 637 5233

## MARLAN AGENCY
484 Bearwood Road, Warley, Smethwick,
West Midlands B66 4HB
Tel: 0121 429 5603
Fax: 0121 420 1957

## MARMONT MANAGEMENT
Langham House, 308 Regent Street,
London W1R 5AL
Tel: 0171 637 3183
Fax: 0171 323 4798
Email: (In Association with Penny Wesson)

## BILLY MARSH ASSOCIATES
174-178 North Gower Street, London NW1 2NB
Tel: 0171 388 6858
Fax: 0171 388 6848
Email: bmarsh@dircon.co.uk

## BRIAN MARSHALL MANAGEMENT
Fathom End, Unicorn Street, Bloxham, Banbury,
Oxfordshire OX15 4QA
Tel: 01295 720811
Fax: 01295 720595
Email: dates@msn.com

## SCOTT MARSHALL
44 Perryn Road, London W3 7NA
Tel: 0181 749 7692
Fax: 0181 740 7342

## JOHN MARTIN PROMOTIONS LTD
The Homestead, Eastwick Road, Great Bookham,
Surrey KT23 4BA
Tel: 0181 786 3620
Fax: 0181 786 3621

## MARINA MARTIN ASSOCIATES
12-13 Poland Street, London W1V 3DE
Tel: 0171 734 4818
Fax: 0171 734 4832

## RICHARD MARTIN MANAGEMENT
18 Ambrose Place, Worthing, West Sussex BN11 1PZ
Tel: 01903 823456 (3 Lines)
Fax: 01903 823847

## RON MARTIN MANAGEMENT
Willow Cottage, Oakley Hill, Wimborne,
Dorset BH21 1RJ
Tel/Fax: 01202 881247 (4 Lines)

## NIGEL MARTIN-SMITH MANAGEMENT LTD
41 South King Street, Manchester M2 6DE
Tel: 0161 832 8080
Fax: 0161 832 1613

## MASTERS ENTERTAINMENT CORPORATION
PO Box 10, Ilkeston, Derbyshire DE7 8XJ
Tel: 0115 944 1770
Fax: 0115 944 4644
Mobile: 0850 532000
Email: dd@dd.uk.com
Web Site: www.dd.uk.com

## MASTERS PERFORMING ARTS COLLEGE & AGENCY
Arterial Road, Rayleigh, Essex SS6 7UQ
Tel/Fax: 01268 770549
Tel: 01702 331616

## MATCHROOM LTD
10 Western Road, Romford, Essex RM1 3JT
Tel: 01708 782200
Fax: 01708 723425

## CLIFF MATHEWS MANAGEMENT & ENTERTAINMENT AGENCY
PO Box 95 Rotherham, South Yorkshire S60 5YH
Tel: 01709 363908/368889
Fax: 01709 360831

## MATTERS MUSICAL
The Loft, Rear of 8 West Street, Dorking,
Surrey RH4 1BL
Tel: 01306 741007
Fax: 01306 741008

## MAX MANAGEMENT PRODUCTIONS
7 Maxey Close, Market Deeping, Peterborough,
Cambs PE6 8DP
Tel: 01778 380451
Fax: 01778 348570

## MAX PROMOTIONS
26 Hill Rise, Kilgetty, Pembrokeshire SA68 0QS Wales
Tel/Fax: 01834 812443

## MAYER & EDEN LTD
(In Association with James Sharkey Associates Ltd)
34 Kingly Court, Kingly Street, London W1R 5LE
Tel: 0171 434 1242
Fax: 0171 287 5834

## MBM (SEE MIKE BURTON MANAGEMENT)

## NORMAN MCCANN CONCERT AGENCY LIMITED
The Coach House, 56 Lawrie Park Gardens,
London SE26 6JX
Tel: 0181 659 5955
Fax: 0181 659 4582

## JAMES MCDERMONT AGENCY
47 Roxborough Avenue, Isleworth,
Middlesex TW7 5HQ
Tel: 0181 560 5451

**MCINTOSH RAE MANAGEMENT**
Thornton House, Thornton Road, London SW19 4NG
Tel: 0181 944 6688
Fax: 0181 944 6624

**MCINTYRE MANAGEMENT**
2nd Floor, 35 Soho Square, London W1V 5DG
Tel: 0171 439 2270
Fax: 0171 439 2280

**BILL MCLEAN PERSONAL MANAGEMENT**
23B Deodar Road, Putney, London SW15 2NP
Tel: 0181 789 8191
Fax: 0181 789 8192

**MCLEOD-HOLDEN ENTERPRISES LTD**
Priory House, 1133 Hessle High Road, Hull HU4 6SB
Tel: 01482 565444
Fax: 01482 353635
Email: info@mcleod-holden.com
Web Site: www.mcleod-holden.com

**KEN MCREDDIE LTD**
91 Regent Street, London W1R 7TB
Tel: 0171 439 1456
Fax: 0171 734 6530

**RAY MCVAY ORCHESTRAS**
Courtyard Cottage, High Canons, Shenley
Hertfordshire WD6 5PL
Tel: 0181 207 2474
Fax: 0181 207 4473

**MEMORY LANE PROMOTIONS LIMITED**
110 Nelson Road Central, Great Yarmouth,
Norfolk NR30 2NJ
Tel: 01493 843383/332045
Fax: 01493 844150
Mobile: 0973 780361
Pager: 0839 985369
Email: rockstar@globalnet.co.uk

**MERLIN CHILDRENS ENTERTAINMENTS**
29 Norwood Drive, North Harrow, Middlesex
Tel: 0181 866 6327

**MG ENTERTAINMENTS**
11 Kirkless Villas, Cale Lane, New Springs, Wigan,
Lancashire WN2 1HQ
Tel: 01942 484757
Fax: 01942 231055
Mobile: 0831 861328

**MIDAS ENTERTAINMENTS**
23 Ledbury Road, Blackpool, Lancashire FY3 7SR
Tel: 01253 395062

**MIDLAND ENTERTAINMENT**
PO Box 259, Coventry CV5 8YU
Tel/Fax: 01203 715544

**JOHN MILES ORGANISATION**
Cadbury Camp Lane, Clapton in Gordano,
Bristol BS20 7SB
Tel: 01275 854675/856770
Fax: 01275 810186

**MILLENNIUM ARTISTES MANAGEMENT
LTD**
3 Dorin Court, Landscape Road, Warlingham,
Surrey CR6 9JT
Tel: 01883 626000
Fax: 01883 624579
Mobile: 0958 329912
Email: mam.ltd@mcmail.com
Web Site: www.mam.ltd.mcmail.com

**MIRACLE PRESTIGE INTERNATIONAL LTD**
1 Water Lane, Camden Town, London NW1 8NZ
Tel: 0171 267 5599
Fax: 0171 267 5155
Email: agents@mpi-agency.co.uk

**MISSION CONTROL ARTIST AGENCY**
50 City Business Centre, Lower Road,
London SE16 2XB
Tel: 0171 252 3001
Fax: 0171 252 2225
Email: agents@mission-control.co.uk
Web Site: www.mission-control.co.uk

**AL MITCHELL ASSOCIATES**
5 Anglers Lane, Kentish Town, London NW5 3DG
Tel: 0171 482 5113
Fax: 0171 485 4254

**MJM ENTERTAINMENT**
PO Box 453 Richmond Surrey TW10 6GW
Tel: 0181 332 7474
Fax: 0181 255 4279

**MJR GOSPEL MUSIC AGENCY**
29a Hythe Road, Thornton Heath, Surrey CR7 8QX
Tel: 0181 240 9848
Fax: 0181 251 2588

**MLR (ALSO MACNAUGHTON LORD
REPRESENTATION LTD)**
200 Fulham Road, London SW10 9PN
Tel: 0171 351 5442/376 5575
Fax: 0171 351 4560

**MM (MUIREAST MANAGEMENT)**
28 Chapter Chambers, Esterbrooke Street,
London SW1P 4NN
Tel: 0171 828 1407
Fax: 0171 834 3016
Email: muireast@dircon.co.uk

**MMA**
100 Malmesbury Road, Shirley,
Southampton SO15 5FQ
Tel: 01703 786373
Fax: 01703 345645

## MOCKINGBIRD MANAGEMENT (LEON FISK)
Meadow Cottage, Ferry Lane, Medmenham, Marlow,
Buckinghamshire SL7 2EZ
Tel: 01491 571235
Fax: 01491 579214

## MORGAN & GOODMAN
Mezzanine, Quadrant House, 80-82 Regent Street,
London W1R 5PA
Tel: 0171 437 1383/5293
Fax: 0171 437 5293/494 3446

## CHRIS MORGAN ASSOCIATES
79 Maindy Road, Cardiff CF2 4HL
Tel/Fax: 01222 345765
Mobile: 0589 887437

## WILLIAM MORRIS AGENCY (UK) LTD
1 Stratton Street London W1X 6HB
Tel: 0171 355 8500
Fax: 0171 355 8600

## JAE MOSS ENTERPRISES
16 Cambridge Road, Walton-On-Thames,
Surrey KT12 2DP
Tel/Fax: 01932 223233
Mobile: 0860 326406
Email: jmossent@aol.com

## MOTLEY MUSIC LTD
79 Parkway, London NW1 7PP
Tel: 0171 482 7166
Fax: 0171 482 7286

## MP THEATRICAL AGENCY
10 Princess Avenue, Haydock, St. Helens,
Merseyside WA11 0RG
Tel: 01942 725087/728108
Fax: 01942 726619

## MPC ENTERTAINMENT
MPC House 15/16 Maple Mews, Maida Vale,
London NW6 5UZ
Tel: 0171 624 1184
Fax: 0171 624 4220
Email: mpc@mpce.com
Web Site: www.mpce.com

## MPL
3 Soho Square, London W1

## MR "E" ENTERTAINMENTS
Little Greenfields Farm, Jack Haye Lane, Light Oaks,
Stoke-on-Trent ST2 7NG
Tel: 01782 304909
Mobile: 0831 311318
Web Site: http://www.yell.co.uk/sites/magic-show-mr-e/

## MRS CASEY MUSIC
PO Box 296, Aylesbury, Buckinghamshire HP19 3TL
Tel: 01296 394411

Fax: 01296 392300
Email: mcm@mrscasey.nildran.co.uk
Web Site: www.mrscasey.co.uk

## MTM PRESENTATIONS
Avron House, 37 Highmeadow, Ringley Wood,
Radcliffe, Manchester M26 1YN
Tel: 0161 725 9991
Fax: 0161 725 9199

## MUCH LOVED PRODUCTIONS LTD
6 Darton Lane, Darton, Barnsley,
South Yorkshire S75 5AH
Tel: 01226 380175
Fax: 01226 380566
Email: muchlovedproduct.demon.uk

## MULTI-MEDIA ENTERTAINMENTS
14 Canterbury Road, Penn, Wolverhampton WV4 4EH
Tel/Fax: 01902 344148

## ELAINE MURPHY ASSOCIATES
310 Aberdeen House, 22 Highbury Grove,
London N5 2EA
Tel: 0171 704 9913
Fax: 0171 704 8039

## MALCOLM MURRAY ENTERTAINMENTS
Incorporating the Cruising and Corporate Company
Suite 11, 3 Quay Walls, Berwick-Upon-Tweed,
Northumberland TD15 1HB
Tel: 01289 330148/9
Fax: 01289 308408
Email: malcolmmurrayents@link-connect.co.uk
Web Site: htth://www.link-connect.co.uk/~link0130

## MUSIC INTERNATIONAL
13 Ardilaun Road, London N5 2QR
Tel: 0171 359 5183
Fax: 0171 226 9792
Email: music@musicint.demon.co.uk

## MUSIC SCOTLAND
24 Ochil Road, Alva, Clackmannanshire
FK12 5JT Scotland
Tel/Fax: 01259 760126
Email: johndouglas@musicscotland.demon.co.uk
Web Site: http://www.musicscotland@demon.co.uk

## MUSICAL AGENCY AND MANAGEMENT LTD
The Seedbed Centre, Langston Road, Loughton,
Essex IG10 3TQ
Tel: 0181 501 2469
Fax: 0181 502 6863

## MUSICAL ASSOCIATES
60 Blacketts Wood Drive, Chorleywood,
Rickmansworth, Hertfordshire WD3 5QH
Tel: 01923 285415
Fax: 01923 286097
Email: musass@aol.com

**MUSICIAN MANAGEMENT**
132 Main Road, Quadring, Spalding,
Lincolnshire PE11 4PW
Tel: 01775 821215

**NARROW ROAD COMPANY**
22 Poland Street, London W1V 3DD
Tel: 0171 434 0406
Fax: 0171 439 1237

**NATIONWIDE CASTING AGENCY**
Gainsborough House, 109 Portland Street,
Manchester M1 6DN
Tel: 0161 236 4041
Fax: 0161 236 9993

**NATURAL SOUND**
17 St. Annes Court, London W1V 3AW
Tel: 0171 437 4860
Fax: 0171 437 4859

**N.B. MANAGEMENT**
Ashlea, Oakwood Drive, East Horsley, Leatherhead,
Surrey KT24 6QF
Tel: 01483 282666
Fax: 01483 284777
Email: nick.bomford@btinternet.com

**NDS MANAGEMENT SERVICES**
4 Newlands Road, Horsham, West Sussex RH12 2BY
Tel: 07000 637637/01403 276800
Fax: 01403 276801

**TONI NELSON ASSOCIATES**
42 Berrymead Gardens, London W3 8AB
Tel/Fax: 0181 993 2078

**NEM PRODUCTIONS(UK)**
Priory House, 55 Lawe Road, South Shields,
Tyne and Wear NE33 2AL
Tel: 0191 427 6207
Fax: 0191 427 6323
Email: 100604.2015@compuserve.com

**NEMESIS AGENCY LTD**
41 South King Street, Manchester M2 6DE
Tel: 0161 832 1133
Fax: 0161 832 1613

**NEMESIS CASTING LTD**
41 South King Street, Manchester M2 6DE
Tel; 0161 832 8737
Fax: 0161 832 1616

**NEVS AGENCY**
2nd Floor, Regal House, 198 Kings Road,
London SW3 5XX
Tel: 0171 352 4886 (Men)
Tel: 0171 352 9496 (Girls)
Fax: 0171 352 6068
Email: NEVS@nildram.co.uk

**NEW AGENCY/PROMOTIONS**
140 Kiln Place, London NW5 4AP
Tel/Fax: 0171 419 1996

**NEW CENTURY ASSOCIATES**
4 Terminus Road Chichester, West Sussex PO20 2NE
Tel: 01243 771992
Fax: 01243 528729

**NIGHT OWLS ENTERTAINMENT AGENCY**
21 The Pastures, Aylesbury,
Buckinghamshire HP20 1XL
Tel: 07000 202820
Fax: 01296 483828

**NINTH DIRECTION**
29 The Lynch, High Street, Hoddesdon,
Hertfordshire EN11 8EN
Tel: 01992 446921
Fax: 01992 450941

**NJ MEDIA ENTERPRISES**
10 Clorane Gardens, London NW3 7PR
Tel: 0171 794 0414
Fax: 0171 431 0786

**NOEL GAY**
22-25 Dean Street, London W1V 5AL
Tel: 0171 836 3941
Fax: 0171 287 1816

**JOHN NOEL MANAGEMENT**
5 Primrose Mews, 1a Sharpleshall Street,
London NW1 8YW
Tel: 0171 483 4468
Fax: 0171 586 0632

**NON STOP ENTERTAINMENTS**
PO Box 10, Garston, Liverpool L19 2RD
Tel: 0151 427 1910
Fax: 0151 494 9707

**NORTH OF WATFORD ACTORS AGENCY**
Bridge Mill, Bridge Gate, Hebden Bridge,
West Yorkshire HX7 8EX
Tel: 01422 845361
Fax: 01422 846503

**NORTH ONE MANAGEMENT**
18 Ashwin Street, London E8 3DL
Tel: 0171 254 9093
Fax: 0171 249 9989

**NORTH WALES ENTERTAINMENTS**
'Beric', Breeze Hill Estate, Bangor,
Gwynedd LL57 4LT Wales
Tel: 01248 351504
Email: iss041@bangor.ac.uk

## NORTHERN LIGHTS ACTORS MANAGEMENT
Dean Clough Office Park, Halifax,
West Yorkshire HX3 5AX
Tel: 01422 382203
Fax: 01422 360355
Email: northern.lights@btinternet.co

## NORTHERN MUSIC COMPANY
Cheapside Chambers, 43 Cheapside, Bradford,
West Yorkshire BV1 4HP
Tel: 01274 306361
Fax: 01274 730097
Email: Mailman@ntnmusic.demon.co.uk

## NORWELL LAPLEY ASSOCIATES LTD
Lapley Hall, Lapley, Staffordshire ST19 9JR
Tel: 01785 841991
Fax: 01785 841992
Email: chris@majmar.demon.co.uk

## NORWICH ARTISTES
'Bryden', 115 Holt Road, Hellesdon, Norwich,
Norfolk NR6 6UA
Tel: 01603 407101
Fax: 01603 405314

## NOW YOU'RE TALKING SPEAKERS AGENCY
Stone Cottage, Ireby, Carnforth, Lancashire LA6 2JQ
Tel: 01524 242221
Email: speakers@nyt.co.uk
Web Site: http://www.nyt.co.uk

## NSE ENTERTAINMENTS
Minster Cottage, Broomers Corner, Shipley, Horsham,
West Sussex RH13 8PS
Tel: 01403 741321

## NVB ENTERTAINMENTS
80 Holywell Road, Studham, Dunstable,
Bedfordshire LU6 2PD
Tel: 01582 873623
Fax: 01582 873618

## NVS ARTISTES MANAGEMENT
23 Napier Avenue, Blackpool FY4 1PA
Tel: 01253 298511
NVS Artistes Management
Crosswinds, Cimla Common, Neath SA11 3SU
Tel: 01639 633 198
Email: lukasuk@compuserve.com

## NYLAND MANAGEMENT
20 School Lane, Heaton Chapel, Stockport,
Cheshire SK4 5DG
Tel: 0161 442 2224
Fax: 0161 432 5407

## DEE O'REILLY MANAGEMENT
112 Gunnersbury Avenue, London W5 4HB
Tel: 0181 993 7441
Fax: 0181 992 9993

## OCTOBER AGENCY & MANAGEMENT
Third Floor, 27 Henniker Mews, Chelsea,
London SW3 6BL
Tel: 0171 351 9871
Fax: 0171 351 9872

## OFF THE KERB PRODUCTIONS
22 Thornhill Crescent, London N1 1BJ
Tel: 0171 700 4477
Fax: 0171 700 4646

## MERVYN O'HORAN AGENCY
140 Beckett Road, Doncaster,
South Yorkshire DN2 4BA
Tel: 01302 321233
Fax: 01302 321978

## ON LINE PROMOTIONS
West Lodge, Manchester Road, Warrington,
Cheshire WA1 3BF
Tel: 01925 576606
Fax: 01925 411133

## ONE MANAGEMENT
43 St. Albans Avenue, London W4 5JS
Tel: 0181 994 4422
Fax: 0181 994 1930

## OPAL MOON ENTERTAINMENTS AND PROMOTIONS
Opal House, 155 Castle Road, Bedford MK40 3RT
Tel/Fax: 01234 403593
Mobile: 07970 932944

## OPERA & CONCERT ARTISTS
75 Aberdare Gardens, London NW6 3AN
Tel: 0171 328 3097
Fax: 0171 372 3537

## ORBIT ENTERTAINMENTS AGENCY AND MANAGEMENT
77 Leyland Road, Penwortham, Preston,
Lancs PR1 9QH
Tel: 01772 744584

## ORDINARY PEOPLE LTD
8 Camden Road, London NW1 9DP
Tel: (For Booking Models) 0171 267 7007
Tel: (Enquiries/Membership) 0171 267 4141
Fax: 0171 267 5677

## ORGANISATION UNLIMITED
Central Building, Worcester Road,
Stourport-On-Severn, Worcestershire DY13 9AS
Tel: 01299 827197
Fax: 01299 827191

## ORIENTAL ARTS (BRADFORD) LIMITED
Glyde House, Glydegate, 18 Little Horton Lane,
Bradford, West Yorkshire BD5 0BQ
Tel: 01274 370190
Fax: 01274 370104

**OTB PRODUCTIONS**
5 Oldridge View, Tedburn St. Mary, Exeter EX6 6AB
Tel/Fax: 01647 61237

**OTTO PERSONAL MANAGEMENT LTD**
Workstation 15 Paternoster Row, Sheffield S1 2BX
Tel: 0114 275 2592
Fax: 0114 275 0550
Email: otto@mail.globalnet.co.uk

**OUT & OUT ENTERTAINMENT**
17 Hillside Close, Cheltenham,
Gloucestershire GL51 5AS
Tel: 01242 529957
Fax: 01242 234686

**OUTLET PROMOTIONS**
Suite 501 International House 223 Regent Street
London W1R 8QD
Tel/Fax: 01768 483748

**PATRICIA OWEN**
111 Tattersall Gardens, Leigh-On-Sea,
Essex SS9 2QZ
Tel: 01702 551265
Fax: 01702 553202

**SIAN OWEN MANAGEMENT & CASTING**
5 Elton Avenue, London NW3
Tel: 0171 435 2205

**P&R ENTERTAINMENTS LTD**
PO Box 99, Hockley, Essex SS5
Tel: 01702 202036
Fax: 01702 200886

**PAGE THREE MANAGEMENT**
PO Box 1AS London W1A 1AS
Tel: 0171 287 0060
Fax: 0171 287 0060

**PALM COURT THEATRE PRODUCTIONS**
Winkton Lodge Cottage, Salisbury Road, Winkton,
Christchurch, Dorset BH23 7AR
Tel: 01202 484185
Fax: 01202 471920
Email: godwin@palm-court.demon.co.uk

**JACKIE PALMER**
30 Daws Hill Lane, High Wycombe,
Buckinghamshire HP11 1PW
Tel: 01494 520978/01494 510479
Fax: 01494 510479

**PAN ARTISTS AGENCY**
1 Hollins Grove, Sale, Cheshire M33 6RE
tel: 0161 969 7419
Fax: 0161 973 9724

**PANTOWORLD LTD**
28 Birchfields Road, Manchester M13 0XR
TelFax: 0161 225 9339

**PARAMOUNT ENTERTAINMENTS**
44 Gordon Road, Gosport, Hampshire PO12 3QF
Tel/Fax: 01705 511995

**PARAMOUNT INTERNATIONAL MANAGEMENT**
204-226 Imperial Drive, Harrow, Middlesex HA2 7HH
Tel: 0181 429 3179
Fax: 0181 868 6475
Email: mail@paracody.demon.co.uk

**PARAPHERNALIA PUPPETS**
Church Studios, Common Road, Stafford ST16 3EQ
Tel: 01785 226326
Fax: 01785 220460

**PARK ASSOCIATES**
6 George Street, Nottingham NG1 3BE
Tel: 0115 948 3206
Fax: 0115 952 7203

**PARK MANAGEMENT LTD**
Unit 21, 11 Marshalsea Road, London SE1 1EP
Tel: 0171 357 0024
Fax: 0171 357 0047

**PARK PROMOTIONS**
PO Box 651, High Street, Cumnor, Oxford OX2 9QD
Tel: 01865 241717
Fax: 01865 204556

**PARLIAMENT COMMUNICATIONS**
(Head Office) Roddis House Old Christchurch Road,
Bournemouth BH1 1LG
Tel: 01202 242425/6/7
Fax: 01202 242428
(Manchester Office)
Resource House, 144 Castle Street,
Stockport SK3 9JH
Tel: 0161 429 5337
Fax: 0161 429 5338

**PARR'S THEATRICAL & TV AGENCY**
The Tom Thumb Theatre, Eastern Esplanade,
Cliftonville, Margate, Kent CT9 2LB
Tel: 01843 221791

**PARROT PRODUCTIONS LTD**
24 Cavendish Buildings, Gilbert Street,
London W1Y 1FD
Tel: 0171 629 2998
Fax: 0171 355 3510
Email: parrot@cybernet.co.uk

**PBJ MANAGEMENT LTD**
5 Soho Square, London W1V 5DE
Tel: 0171 287 1112
Fax: 0171 287 1448

**PBR MANAGEMENT**
138 Putney Bridge Road, London SW15 2NQ
Tel: 0181 871 4139

Fax: 0181 874 4847

## P.C. THEATRICAL MODEL AGENCY
101 Strathmore Gardens, Edgware,
Middlesex HA8 5HJ
Tel: 0181 381 2229
Fax: 0181 933 3418
Email: pag1646670@aol.com

## PELHAM ASSOCIATES
9-12 Middle Street, Brighton BN1 1AL
Tel: 01273 323010
Fax: 01273 202492
Email: pelhamassociates@btinternet.com
Web Site: http://www.btinternet.com/~pelhamassociate
s

## PELLER ARTISTES LTD
14 West Street, Beighton, Sheffield S20 1EP
Tel: 0114 247 2365
Fax: 0114 247 2156
Also: Pepys Court, 84-86 The Chase,
London SW4 0NF
Tel: 0171 978 3002
Fax: 0171 978 3003

## BARBARA PEMBERTON ASSOCIATES
53-54 Haymarket, London SW1Y 4RP
Tel: 0171 976 1577
Fax: 0171 976 2533

## PENGUINS ENTERTAINMENT
143 Arthur Road, Windsor, Berkshire SL4 1RU
Tel: 01753 833811
Fax: 01753 833754

## PERFORMANCE ACTORS AGENCY
137 Goswell Road, London EC1V 7ET
Tel: 0171 251 5716
Fax: 0171 251 3974

## PERFORMERS AGENCY
2-4 Chase Road, Corringham, Stanford-Le-Hope,
Essex SS17 7QH
Tel: 01375 672053
Fax: 01375 672353

## PERFORMING ARTISTES (PART OF THE F4 GROUP)
2 Thayer Street, London W1M 5LG
Tel: 0171 224 0107
Fax: 0171 224 0126
Email: enquiries@f4group.co.uk
Web Site: www.f4group.co.uk

## PERFORMING ARTS
6 Windmill Street, London W1P 1HF
Tel: 0171 255 1362
Fax: 0171 631 4631

## PERFORMING ARTS MANAGEMENT
Canal 7, Clarence Mill, Clarence Road, Bollington,
Macclesfield, Cheshire SK10 5JZ

Tel: 01625 575681
Fax: 01625 572839
Email: clare.scott@performingarts.co.uk
Web Site: www.performingarts.co.uk

## PERROTTS FOLLY AGENCY
Treverryl, Trenance, Mawgan Porth, Newquay,
Cornwall TR8 4DA
Tel: 01637 860866

## GEORGE PERRY PROFILE MANAGEMENT
6 Aberdeen Studios, 22 Highbury Grove,
London N5 2EA
Tel: 0171 354 9600
Fax: 0171 354 0625

## PERSONAL ANGLIAN LEISURE SERVICES
1 Blake Court, Sandringham Way, Swaffham,
Norfolk PE37 8BS
Tel/Fax: 01760 725161
Email: http://www.yell.co.uk/sites/pals-productions/

## PERSONAL APPEARANCES
20 North Mount, 1147-1161 High Road, Whetstone,
London N20 0PH
Tel: 0181 343 7748

## PERSONALLY SPEAKING
2 Hartopp Road, Four Oaks, Sutton Coldfield,
West Midlands B74 2RH
Tel: 0121 308 1267/0171 222 3434
Fax: 0121 308 5191

## PETERS FRASER & DUNLOP ARTISTES
503/4 The Chambers, Chelsea Harbour, Lots Road,
London SW10 0XF
Tel: 0171 344 1010 Actors Agency
Tel: 0171 344 1020 Account Department
Fax: 0171 352 8135
Web Site: http://www.pfd.co.uk

## GEORGE PETERS ENTERTAINMENTS
16 Uranus Road, Hemel Hempstead,
Hertfordshire HP2 5QF
Tel/Fax: 01442 267825

## JO PETERS MANAGEMENT LTD
56 Macready House, 75 Crawford Street,
London W1H 1HS
Tel: 0171 724 6555
Fax: 0171 724 5296

## PHA MODEL & CASTING MANAGEMENT
Tanzaro House, Ardwick Green North,
Manchester M12 6FZ
Tel: 0161 273 4444
Fax: 0161 273 4567

## PHAB
High Notes, Sheerwater Avenue, Woodham,
Addlestone, Surrey KT15 3DS
Tel: 01932 348174
Fax: 01932 340921

**PHILLIPS ENTERTAINMENT AGENCY**
6 Queen Victoria Road, Llanelli, Carmarthenshire
SA15 2TL Wales
Tel: 01554 750525
Fax: 01554 758336

**THE KEN PHILLIPS AGENCY**
PO Box 31, Warrington, Cheshire WA5 2BN
Tel: 01925 791000
Fax: 01925 791777

**NORMAN PHILLIPS AGENCY LIMITED**
2 Hartopp Road, Sutton Coldfield,
West Midlands B74 2RH
Tel: 0121 308 1267/0121 222 3434
Fax: 0121 308 5191

**VAL PHILLIPS ENTERTAINMENTS**
10 St. Davids Close, Heolgerrig, Merthyr Tydfil,
Mid Glamorgan CF48 1SH Wales
Tel: 01685 384848

**PHOENIX PROMOTIONS**
22 Athersley Gardens, Owlthorpe, Sheffield S20 6RW
TelFax: 0114 247 7314
Mobile: 0378 754419

**PHYSICALITY LTD**
265-267 Ilford Lane, Ilford, Essex IG1 2SD
Tel: 0181 491 2800
Fax: 0181 491 2801
Email: physicality@pavilion.co.uk

**HILDA PHYSICK**
78 Temple Sheen Road, London SW14 7RR
Tel: 0181 876 0073
Fax: 0181 876 5561

**PICCADILLY MANAGEMENT**
Unit 123, 23 New Mount Street, Manchester M4 4DE
Tel: 0161 953 4057
Fax: 0161 953 4001

**NIC PICOT AGENCY**
6 Thrush Green, Harrow, Middlesex HA2 6EZ
Tel: 0181 866 5585
Fax: 0181 868 3374
Email: nic@nicpicot.co.uk
Web Site: www.nicpicot.co.uk

**PINEAPPLE AGENCY**
159-161 Balls Pond Road, Islington London N1 4BG
Tel: 0171 241 6601
Fax: 0171 241 3006

**P.J. ENTERTAINMENTS**
15 Honeysuckle Avenue, Kingswinford,
West Midlands DY6 7ED
Tel/Fax: 01384 278982

**P.L.A. SCOTLAND (PAT LOVETT AGENCY)**
Picardy House, 4 Picardy Place, Edinburgh

EH1 3JT Scotland
Tel: 0131 478 7878
Fax: 0131 557 5565

**PLANET CLAIRE PRODUCTIONS**
6 Warminster Road, St Werburghs, Bristol BS2 9UH
Tel: 0117 955 1283

**PLANET EARTH ENTERTAINMENT LTD**
Broad Acres, 33 Cattle End, Silverstone, Towcester,
Northamptonshire NN12 8UX
Tel/Fax: 01327 857170

**PLASTIC SURGERY**
Coachhouse, Mansion Farm, Liverton Hill, Sandway,
Maidstone, Kent ME17 2NJ
Tel/Fax: 01622 858300

**PLAYTIME (AGENCY) LTD**
The Leisure Factory, Oldfields, Corngreaves Road,
Cradley Heath, West Midlands B64 6BS
Tel: 01384 637776
Fax: 01384 637227

**PLUNKET GREENE LTD**
(In Conjunction with James Sharkey Associates Ltd)
21 Golden Square, London W1R 3PA
Tel: 0171 484 8801
Fax: 0171 494 1547

## PM ORGANISATION
98 North Street, Scarborough,
North Yorkshire YO11 1DE
Tel/Fax: 01723 371255

## POOL PRODUCTIONS LTD
3rd Floor, 9 Carnaby Street, London W1V 1PG
Tel: 0171 437 1958
Fax: 0171 437 3852

## GORDON POOLE AGENCY LTD
The Limes, Main Road, Brockley, Backwell,
Bristol BS48 3BB
Tel: 01275 463222
Fax: 01275 462252

## MARTIN POOLE
30a Jackson Road, London N7 6EJ
Tel: 0171 607 9851

## POP VOX LTD
17 Berkeley Road, Tunbridge Wells, Kent TN1 1YR
Tel: 01892 531011

## PORTASS & CARTER ENTERTAINMENTS
The Music Shop, 26 Bridge Road, Sutton Bridge,
Spalding, Lincolnshire PE12 9UA
Tel: 01406 350407

## POSITIVE MANAGEMENT
1 The Stiles, Ormskirk, Lancashire L39 3QG
Tel: 01695 570258
Fax: 01695 578757

## POSITIVE PLUS LTD
Berkeley House, Berkeley Street, Ashton-under-Lyne,
Lancashire OL6 7DT
Tel: 0161 339 6667
Fax: 0161 339 4242

## BOB POTTER ENTERTAINMENT AGENCY
Entertainments House, Lakeside Wharf, Wharf Road,
Frimley Green, Camberley, Surrey GU16 6PT
Tel: 01252 836464
Fax: 01252 836777

## POWER PROMOTIONS
PO Box 61, Liverpool L13 0EF
Tel/Fax: 0151 230 0070

## PP PROMOTIONS
27 Leighton Avenue, Park South Estate, Swindon,
Wilts SN3 2HW
Tel/Fax: 01793 643280
Mobile: 07771 552974

## PRELUDE
The Old Stables, 10 Timber Lane, Caterham,
Surrey CR3 6LZ
Tel: 01883 344300
Fax: 01883 347712
Email: prelud@globalnet.co.uk

## PREMIER PRODUCTIONS
4 Haywood, Bracknell, Berkshire RG12 7WG
Tel: 01344 453888
Fax: 01344 305151

## PREMIERE PROMOTIONS
24 Briarwood Close, Fareham, Hampshire PO16 0PS
Tel: 01329 238449 (4 Lines)
Fax: 01329 233088
Email: premiere@agents-uk.com

## PRESENTER PROMOTIONS
123 Corporation Road, Gillingham, Kent ME7 1RG
Tel: 01634 851077/07000 Presenters
Fax: 01634 316771
Email: presenter-promotions@lineone.net

## PRESTIGE ARTISTES
Foxhollow, West End, Nailsea, Bristol BS48 4DB
Tel: 01275 853170
Fax: 01275 810279

## PRIMARY TALENT INTERNATIONAL
2-12 Pentonville Road, London N1 9PL
Tel: 0171 833 8998
Fax: 0171 833 5992
Email: mail@primary.uk.com
Web Site: http://www.ilmc.com

## PRIME PERFORMERS LTD
Camden House 156 Camden High Street,
London NW1 0NE
Tel: 0171 482 2730
Fax: 0171 482 2691

## PRINCIPAL ARTISTES
4 Paddington Street, London W1M 3LA
Tel: 0171 224 3414
Fax: 0171 486 4668

## PRO ACRO
100 Malmesbury Road, Shirley, Southampton,
Hants SO15 5FQ
Tel: 01703 786373
Fax: 01703 345645
Email: info@2ma.co.uk

## PROFESSIONAL SPORTS PARTNERSHIPS LTD
8 Chertsey Road, Chobham, Surrey GU24 8NB
Tel: 01276 858930
Fax: 01276 856974

## PROFESSOR NUTTY
74 Goldsmith Road, London N11 3JN
Tel: 0181 361 9110 (or 2070)

## PROFILE ARTISTES AGENCY
Unit 101 J, Tower Bridge Business Complex,
100 Clements Road, London SE16 4DG
Tel: 0171 394 0012/0700 PROFILE
Fax: 0171 394 0094

Liverpool Office
Tel: 0151 709 1111

**P.S.R ENTERTAINMENTS**
47 Abington Street, Northampton, Northants NN1 2AW
Tel: 01604 631831
Fax: 01604 231579

**PURE MANAGEMENT**
39 Bolton Gardens, London SW5 0AQ
Tel: 0171 373 6388
Fax: 0171 373 4499

**PURPLE PALACE**
34 Flower Lane, Mill Hill, London NW7 2JE
Tel/Fax: 0181 959 2825

**THE PURPLE PUPPETS**
3 Fir Avenue, New Milton, Hampshire BH25 6EX
Tel: 01425 621682

**TONY PUXLEY**
4 Vine Gate, Parsonage Lane, Farnham Common,
Slough, Buckinghamshire SL2 3NX
Tel: 01753 643696
Fax: 01753 642259

**PVA LTD**
2 High Street, Westbury-on-Trym, Bristol BS9 3DU
Tel: 0117 950 4504
Fax: 0117 959 1786

**QUALITY DOUBLES**
56 Kenerne Drive, Chipping Barnet, Barnet,
Hertfordshire EN5 2NN
Tel: 0181 440 3703
Fax: 0181 440 8045

**QUALITY ENTERTAINMENTS**
PO Box 97, Bridgnorth Grove, Willenhall,
West Midlands WV12 4RX
Tel: 01902 606316
Fax: 01902 607026
Email: qual_ents@compuserve.com

**QUICK FIRE MANAGEMEN/QFM
PUBLISHING/NATION RECORDS LIMITED**
19 All Saints Road, London W11 1HE
Tel: 0171 792 8167
Fax: 0171 792 2854

**R&B PRODUCTIONS**
1A, Raynham Terrace, Edmonton, London N18 2JN
Tel: 0181 884 3499

**R.B.M. (SEE RICHARD BUCKNALL
MANAGEMENT)**

**RAGE**
256 Edgware Road, London W2 1DS
Tel: 0171 262 0515

Fax: 0171 402 0507

**RAINBOW ENTERTAINMENTS**
11 Waterside, Peartree Bridge,
Milton Keynes MK6 3DE
Tel: 01908 661017

**RAINBOW INTERNATIONAL LTD**
87 Herbert Gardens, London NW10 3BH
Tel: 0181 965 2826
Fax: 0181 965 2991
Mobile: 0802 885557

**RATTLEBAG ACTORS AGENCY LIMITED**
Everyman Theatre Annexe, 13-15 Hope Street,
Liverpool, Merseyside L1 9BH
Tel: 0151 708 7273
Fax: 0151 709 0773

**RAVENSCOURT THEATRE SCHOOL
AGENCY**
Tandy House, 30/40 Dalling Road, London W6 0JB
Tel: 0181 741 0707
Fax: 0181 741 1786

**RAY'S NORTHERN CASTING AGENCY**
7 Wince Close, Middleton, Manchester M24 1UJ
Tel/Fax: 0161 643 6745

**RAZZAMATAZZ MANAGEMENT**
Crofters, East Park Lane, Newchapel, Lingfield,
Surrey RH7 6HS
Tel: 01342 835359
Fax: 01342 835433

**RDL**
132 Chase Way, London N14 5DH
Tel: 01992 629970
Fax: 0181 361 3757

**TANO REA - PERSONAL MANAGEMENT**
58 Alexandra Road, London NW4 2RY
Tel: 0181 203 1747
Fax: 0181 203 1064
Email: tandt@lineone.net

**REAL CREATIVES WORLDWIDE INC.**
13-14 Dean Street, London W1V 5AH
Tel: 0171 437 4211
Fax: 0171 437 4221
Email: RealCreate@aol.com

**REAL PEOPLE WORLDWIDE INC.**
14 Dean Street, London W1V 5AH
Tel: 0171 437 4211
Fax: 0171 437 4221

**RED GOLD MUSIC LTD**
87a Queens Road, East Grinstead,
West Sussex RH19 1BG
Tel: 01342 300949
Fax: 01342 410846

Web Site: www.egnet.co.uk/clients/music.rgm.html

**JOAN REDDIIN**
Hazel Cottage, Wheeler End Common, Wheeler End,
High Wycombe, Buckinghamshire HP14 3NL
Tel: 01494 882729
Fax: 01494 521 727

**REDROOFS ASSOCIATES**
School Lane, Littlewick Green, Maidenhead,
Berkshire SL6 3QY
Tel: 01628 822982
Fax: 01628 822461

**REDSKY MUSIC**
47 Northbrook Street, Leeds, Yorks LS7 4QH
Tel: 0113 237 1771
Fax: 0113 237 4141

**REGENCY AGENCY**
25 Carr Road, Calverley, Pudsey,
West Yorkshire LS28 5NE
Tel: 0113 255 8980

**JOHN REID ENTERPRISES**
32 Galena Road, London W6 0LT
Tel: 0181 741 9933
Fax: 0181 741 3938

**RENT-A-BAND**
Burnside House, 10 Burns Court, Birstall, Batley,
West Yorkshire WF17 9JB
Tel/Fax: 01924 441441

**REPRESENTATION JOYCE EDWARDS**
275 Kennington Road, London SE11 6BY
Tel: 0171 735 5735
Fax: 0171 820 1845

**JIMMY RETFORD'S AGENCY**
25 Offley Road, London SW9 0LR
Tel: 0171 735 1030
Fax: 0171 735 0814

**RETURN ENTERTAINMENTS LTD**
66/68 St. Loyes Street, Bedford MK40 1EZ
Tel: 01234 327123
Fax: 01234 353658
Email: phil@ceroc.powernet.co.uk

**SANDRA REYNOLDS AGENCY**
20-22 Maddox Street, London W1R 9PG
Tel: 0171 493 6161
Fax: 0171 493 5223
35 St Georges Street
Norwich NR3 1DA
Tel: 01603 623842/623921
Fax: 01603 219825

**RHIANNON MANAGEMENT**
20 Montague Road, London E8 2HN
Tel: 0171 275 8292

Fax: 0171 503 8034
Email: rhiannon@enterprise.net
Web Site: http://homepages.enterprise.net/rhiannon

**PENNY RICH**
35-42 Charlotte Road, London EC2A 3PD
Tel: 0171 613 3886
Fax: 0171 729 8500

**THE CLIFF RICHARD ORGANISATION**
PO Box 46c, Hare Lane, Claygate, Esher,
Surrey KT10 0RB
Tel: 01372 467752
Fax: 01372 462352

**THE LISA RICHARDS AGENCY**
28/9 Haymarket, London SW1Y 4SP
Tel: 0171 390 7370
Fax: 0171 396 6618
Email: LR@curtisbrown.co.uk

**STELLA RICHARDS MANAGEMENT**
42 Hazlebury Road, London SW6 2ND
Tel: 0171 736 7786
Fax: 0171 731 5082

**RICHMOND MANAGEMENT**
Coach House, Swinhope Hall, Swinhope,
Market Rasen, Lincolnshire LN8 6HT
Tel: 01472 399011
Fax: 01472 399025

**RIGAL MANAGEMENT**
109 Albert Bridge Road, London SW11 4PF
Tel: 0171 228 8689
Fax: 0171 738 1742
Email: rigal@mcmail.com

**RIPPLE MANAGEMENT**
344 Kings Road, London SW3 5UR
Tel: 0171 352 5628
Fax: 0171 351 7700

**RIVERSIDE PROMOTIONS**
38 Hickling Close, Bedford, Cambs MK40 4NA
Tel: 01234 266563
Fax: 01234 343488

**RIVIERA ARTISTES**
33 Warren Road, Torquay, S Devon TQ2 5TQ
Tel: 01803 200039
Fax: 01803 200821

**R.L.M. (RICHARD LAW MANAGEMENT)**
58 Marylands Road, London W9 2DR
Tel: 0171 286 1706
Fax: 0171 266 1293

**ALAN ROBINSON MANAGEMENT (ALSO A.R.M.)**
PO Box 177, New Malden, Surrey KT3 3YT
Tel: 0181 949 8885

Fax: 0181 949 3558

## GORDON ROBINSON ASSOCIATES
8 Lilac Avenue, Knutsford, Cheshire WA16 0AZ
Tel/Fax: 01565 652188
Mobile: 0403 185642

## RODGERS & PAYNE PRODUCTIONS
9 Beechwood Avenue, Earlsdon, Coventry,
West Midlands CV5 6DF
Tel: 01203 778377/677173
Fax: 01203 778686
Mobile: 0585 430579

## ROGUES & VAGABONDS MANAGEMENT
321 Essex Road, Islington, London N1 3PS
Tel: 0171 226 5885
Fax: 0171 226 0440

## ROLAND MILLER LTD
Encore House, 64 Singer Way,
Woburn Road Industrial Estate, Kempston,
Bedford MK42 7AF
Tel: 01234 855111 (7 lines)
Fax: 01234 85899
Email: roland.miller@dial.pipex.com

## ROLE MODELS
12 Cressy Road, London NW3 2LY
Tel: 0171 284 4337
Fax: 0171 267 1030

## DON ROSAY MANAGEMENT
3rd Floor, 21-25 Goldhawk Road, London W12 8QQ
Tel: 0181 743 0640

## KATHY ROSE MANAGEMENT
159 Earlsfield Road, London SW18 3DD
Tel: 0181 874 0744
Fax: 0181 874 9136

## ROSEBERY MANAGEMENT
123 Aberdeen House, 22 Highbury Grove,
London N5 2EA
Tel: 0171 354 5566
Fax: 0171 354 2154

## THE ROSEMAN ORGANISATION
Suite 9, The Power House 70 Chiswick High Road,
London W4 1SY
Tel: 0181 742 0552
Fax: 0181 742 0554

## ROSSMORE PERSONAL MANAGEMENT
Rossmore Road, Marylebone, London NW1 6NJ
Tel: 0171 258 1953
Fax: 0171 723 1040

## ROSTRUM PROMOTIONS
4 Ferniebank Brae, Bridge of Allan,
Stirling FK9 4PJ Scotland
Tel: 01786 834449

Fax: 01786 833949

## NIGEL ROUND MANAGEMENT AND ENTERTAINMENT AGENCY
119 Railway Road, Adlington, Chorley,
Lancashire PR6 9QX
Tel: 01257 480103
Fax: 01257 474879
Mobile: 0468 157666
Email: 106212.2745compuserve

## KEITH ROWLEY
5 Scotts Walk, Chelmsford CM1 2HB
Tel: 01245 603135
Fax: 01245 603925
Email: krowley@star-performers.com

## ROYCE MANAGEMENT
34a Sinclair Road, London W14 0NH
Tel: 0171 602 4992
Fax: 0171 371 4985

## ROYLE MANAGEMENT
Royle House, 77 Prospect Road, Woodford Green,
Essex IG8 7NA
Tel: 0181 559 2526

## RS ENTERPRISES
2 The Meadows, Milford, Salisbury SP1 2SS
Tel: 01722 322479

## RUNNING DOG MANAGEMENT LIMITED
PO Box 225 Sunbury-on-Thames,
Middlesex TW16 5RT
Tel: 0181 941 8180
Fax: 0181 941 8146
Email: Runningdog@compuserve.com

## DUDLEY RUSSELL CONCERT & THEATRE PRODUCTIONS
PO Box 64, Cirencester, Gloucestershire GL7 5YD
Tel: 01285 644622
Fax: 01285 642291

## SAFEHAVEN ENTERTAINEMENTS
59 Thoresby Close, Bridlington,
East Yorkshire YO16 5EN
Tel: 01262 671492

## KEITH SALBERG AGENCY & PRODUCTIONS
34 Telford Avenue, Streatham Hill, London SW2 4XF
Tel: 0181 671 1166/7

## SALVO THE CLOWN
(Founder of the International Clowns Directory)
13 Second Avenue, Kingsleigh Park Hart Road,
Thundersley, Essex SS7 3QD
Tel: 01268 745791

**NAT SANDERSON ENTERTAINMENTS**
263 Ayr Road, Newton Mearns,
Glasgow G77 6AW Scotland
Tel/Fax: 0141 639 3539

**SARABAND ASSOCIATES**
265 Liverpool Road, Islington, London N1 1LX
Tel: 0171 609 5313
Fax: 0171 609 2370

**SARDI'S ENTERPRISES**
6 Redbridge Lane East, Redbridge, Ilford,
Essex IG4 5ES
Tel: 0181 551 6720
Fax: 0181 551 1200
Email: SARDIS@axident.clara.net
Web Site: http://www.axident.clara.net/sardis.htm

**SARM PRODUCTIONS**
The Blue Building, 42/46 St. Lukes Mews,
London W11 1DG
Tel: 0171 221 5101
Fax: 0171 221 3374

**SAVANNA ENTERTAINMENTS AGENCY**
29 Court House Gardens, Finchley, London N3 1PU
Tel/Fax: 0181 346 3984

**SCA MANAGEMENT**
23 Goswell Road, London EC1M 7AJ
Tel: 0171 336 6122
Fax: 0171 253 1430

**ANNA SCHER THEATRE MANAGEMENT**
70-72 Barnsbury Road, London N1 0ES
Tel: 0171 278 2101
Fax: 0171 833 9467

**PETER SCHNABL**
72 Vincent Square, London SW1P 2PA
Tel: 0171 630 6955
Fax: 0171 233 5674

**SCOT-BAKER AGENCY**
35 Caithness Road, Brook Green, London W14 0JA
Tel: 0171 603 9988
Fax: 0171 603 7698

**TIM SCOTT PERSONAL MANAGEMENT**
Unit 5, The Cloisters Business Centre,
8 Battersea Park Road, London SW8 4BG
Tel: 0171 978 1352
Fax: 0171 498 2942

**SCREENLITE AGENCY**
Shepperton Studios, Studios Road, Shepperton,
Middlesex TW17 0QD
Tel: 01932 572271
Fax: 01932 566977

**DONALD SCRIMGEOUR ARTISTS AGENCY**
49 Springcroft Avenue, London N2 9JH

Tel: 0181 444 6248
Tel: 0181 883 9751

**VICTOR SEAFORTH AGENCY**
33 Norbury Crescent, Norbury, London SW16 4JS
Tel: 0181 764 8891

**DAVE SEAMER ENTERTAINMENTS**
46 Magdalen Road, Oxford OX4 1RB
Tel/Fax: 01865 240054

**SEAVIEW MUSIC**
28 Mawson Road, Cambridge CB1 2EA
Tel: 01223 508431
Fax: 01223 508449

**SEBA LTD**
Brackendale Forest Road, Hayley Green, Warfield,
Bracknell, Berkshire RG42 6DB
Tel/Fax: 01344 421688
Tel: 01344 883198

**DAWN SEDGWICK MANAGEMENT**
3 Goodwins Court, London WC2N 4LL
Tel: 0171 240 0404
Fax: 0171 240 0415
Email: dawnsedgwick@compuserve.com

**THE SESSION CONNECTION**
110-112 Disraeli Road, London SW15 2DX
Tel: 0181 871 1212
Fax: 0181 877 1214
Email: sconnection@msn.com

**SHADIVARIUS LTD**
Northmere House 12 Northmere Drive, Poole,
Dorset BH12 4DU
Tel: 01202 747417
Fax: 01202 381203
Email: nivram@globalnet.co.uk

**SHAKER'S DISCOTHEQUES**
Tel/Fax: 0181 398 3707

**SHALIT ENTERTAINMENT**
Cambridge Theatre, Seven Dials, Covent Garden,
London WC2H 9HU
Tel: 0171 379 3282
Fax: 0171 379 3238

**SHAMROCK MUSIC LTD**
9 Thornton Place, London W1H 1FG
Tel: 0171 935 9719
Fax: 0171 935 0241
Email: lindy@celtus.demon.co.uk

**JACK SHARPE ENTERTAINMENTS**
Tel: 01702 524169

**VINCENT SHAW ASSOCIATES LTD**
20 Jay Mews, London SW7 2EP

Tel: 0171 581 8215
Fax: 0171 225 1079
Email: vincentshaw@clara.net
Web Site: http://home.clara.net/vincentshaw

**MALCOLM SHEDDEN**
1 Charlotte Street, London W1P 1DH
Tel: 0171 636 1876
Fax: 0171 636 1657

**SHEPHERD & FORD**
13 Radnor Walk, London SW3 4BP
Tel: 0171 352 2200
Fax: 0171 352 2277

**ELIZABETH SHEPHERD AGENCY**
29 Eversley Crescent, Winchmore Hill,
London N21 1EL
Tel: 0181 364 0598
Fax: 0181 364 1624

**TONY SHERWOOD LTD**
5 Castleton Avenue, Carlton, Nottingham NG4 3NZ
Tel: 0115 961 7384
Fax: 0115 940 0092

**SHOWBIZ UK (HERTS)**
58 Broadlands Avenue, Chesham,
Buckinghamshire HP5 1AL
Tel/Fax: 01494 776666

**SHOWBIZ UK (KENT)**
3 Marwell, Westerham, Kent TN16 1SB
Tel/Fax: 01959 564439
Email: mikewheal@csi.com

**SHOWBIZ UK (THAMES VALLEY)**
St Ives, Coopers Lane, Bramley, Tadley,
Hampshire RG26 5DA
Tel/Fax: 01256 881411

**SHOWBUSINESS ENTERTAINMENT
AGENCY**
The Bungalow, Chatsworth Avenue, Long Eaton,
Nottingham NG10 2FL
Tel: 0115 973 5445
Fax: 0115 946 1831

**SHOWSTOPPERS!**
42 Foxglove Close, Witham, Essex CM8 2XW
Tel: 01376 518486
Fax: 01376 510340
Mobile: 0402 663618/0850 687720

**SHOWTIME ENTERTAINMENTS**
Highways House, 89-91 Highways Avenue, Euxton,
Chorley, Lancashire PR7 6QD
Tel: 01257 275489 (4lines)
Fax: 01257 265608

**SHURWOOD MANAGEMENT**
Tote Hill Cottage, Stedham, Midhurst,

West Sussex GU29 0PY
Tel: 01730 817400
Fax: 01730 815846

**SILVESTER MANAGEMENT**
122 Wardour Street, London W1V 3LA
Tel: 0171 734 7232
Fax: 0171 437 3450

**SIMONES INTERNATIONALE**
PO Box 15154 London W5 3FW
Tel: 0181 861 3900
Fax: 0181 381 1571
Mobile: 0860 400071

**SIMPSON FOX ASSOCIATES LTD**
52 Shaftesbury Avenue, London W1V 7DE
Tel: 0171 434 9167
Fax: 0171 494 2887

**SINCERE MANAGEMENT**
Flat B, 6 Bravington Road, London W9 3AH
Tel: 0181 960 4438
Fax: 0181 968 8458
Email: 106276.2056@compuserve.com

**SANDRA SINGER P.R.**
21 Cotswold Road, Westcliff-on-Sea, Essex SS0 8AA
Tel: 01702 331616
Fax: 01702 339393

**SINGERS AGENCY**
Caversham, 16 Harris Lane, Shenley, Radlett,
Hertfordshire WD7 9EB
Tel: 01923 852175
Fax: 01923 859636

**SJS PROMOTIONS**
159 Rotherham Road, Monk Bretton, Barnsley,
South Yorkshire S71 2LL
Tel: 01226 205932/01226 285453/01226 770730
Fax: 01226 605932

**SMAC ENTERTAINMENTS**
218 Westburn Road, Aberdeen AB25 2LT Scotland
Tel/Fax: 01224 632668

**BILL SMITH ENTERTAINMENTS**
74 Greenhill Avenue, Greenhill, Sheffield S8 7DT
Tel: 0114 274 9457
Fax: 0114 274 8345

**DOUG SMITH ASSOCIATES**
PO Box 1151, Heathfield Road, London W3 8EJ
Tel: 0181 993 8436
Fax: 0181 896 1778
Email: actonium@dial.pipex.com

**JIMMY SMITH**
Hill Farm, Main Road, New Hackleton, Hackleton,
Northampton NN7 2DH
Tel: 01604 870421

Fax: 01604 870153

**ROBERT SMITH AGENCY**
5 Vyvyan Road, Clifton, Bristol BS8 3AD
Tel: 0117 973 8265/0117 973 9535
Fax: 0117 970 6956

**SO WHAT ARTS LTD**
Lock-Keepers Cottage, Century Street,
Manchester M3 4QL
Tel: 0161 832 2111
Fax: 0161 832 2333

**SOLO AGENCY LTD**
55 Fulham High Street, London SW6 3JJ
Tel: 0171 736 5925
Fax: 0171 731 6921
Email: solo@solo.uk.com

**SOLOMON ARTISTES MANAGEMENT INTERNATIONAL**
30 Clarence Street, Southend-on-Sea SS1 1BD
Tel: 01702 392370
Fax: 01702 392385

**PAUL SOLOMONS ENTERTAINMENTS**
"Sunnyside" 15 Chantry Road, Harrow,
Middlesex HA3 6NT
Tel: 0181 421 4814
Email: haylard@msn.com

**SOME BIZARRE**
124 New Bond Street, London W1Y 9AE
Tel: 0171 495 2260
Fax: 0171 495 2344

**SOUL KITCHENS/PRIMARY TALENT INTERNATIONAL**
St Thomes Street Stables, St. Thomas Street,
Newcastle Upon Tyne NE1 4LE
Tel: 0191 230 1970
Fax: 0191 232 0262
Email: k&p@kware.demon.co.uk

**SOUND ADVICE**
30 Artesian Road, London W2 5DD
Tel: 0171 229 2219
Fax: 0171 229 9870
Email: mail@soundadvice.uk.com

**SOUND ENTERTAINMENTS**
16 Crofters Meadow, Lychpit, Basingstoke,
Hampshire RG24 8RX
Tel: 01256 354573

**SOUNDTRACK MUSIC MANAGEMENT LTD**
22 Ives Street, Chelsea, London SW3 2ND
Tel: 0171 581 0330
Fax: 0171 823 7086

**SOUTHWESTERN MANAGEMENT**
13 Portland Road, Street, Somerset BA16 9PX

Tel: 01458 445186
Fax: 01458 841186
Email: chris@sw-management.co.uk
Web Site: www.sw-management.co.uk

**SPEAK LTD**
46 Old Compton Street, London W1V 5PB
Tel: 0171 287 4646
Fax: 0171 287 5283

**SPEAK-EASY LTD**
37 Soho Square, London W1V 5DG
Tel: 01858 461961
Fax: 01858 461994

**SPEAKER'S CORNER**
94 Albury Drive, Pinner, Middlesex HA5 3RF
Tel: 0181 866 8967
Fax: 0181 868 4409
Email: speakers@agents-uk.com

**SPEAKERS FOR BUSINESS**
1-2 Pudding Lane, London EC3R 8AB
Tel: 0171 929 5559
Fax: 0171 929 5558
Email: info@afb.co.uk
Web Site: www.sfb.co.uk

**SPEAKING VOLUMES**
Huntindon Hall, Crowngate, Worcester WR1 3LD
Tel: 01905 611323
Fax: 01905 619958

**SPECIAL INTERESTS MANAGEMENT**
Douglas House, 3 Richmond Buildings, London
W1V 5AE

**SPECIALIST PROMOTIONS**
8 Oliver Street, Atherton, Manchester M46 9FN
Tel/fax: 01942 894159

**SPECTRUM INTERNATIONAL AGENCY**
20a Bedford Square, Brighton BN1 2PN
Tel: 01273 206569
Fax: 01273 723791

**IVOR SPENCER ENTERPRISES**
12 Little Bornes, Dulwich, London SE21 8SE
Tel: 0181 670 5585/0181 670 8424
Fax: 0181 670 0055
Car: 0860 313835
Email: ivor@ivorspencer.com
Web Site: http://www.ivorspencer.com

**KEN SPENCER PERSONAL MANAGEMENT**
P.A.G. Promotions, 138 Sandy Hill Road,
London SE18 7BA
Tel/Fax: 0181 854 2558

**SPINX MANAGEMENT & ENTERTAINMENT AGENCY**

Unity House, 2 Unity Place, Westgate Rotherham,
South Yorkshire S60 1AR
Tel: 01709 820379/820370/830999
Fax: 01709 369990

## SPLITTING IMAGES LOOKALIKE AGENCY
29 Mortimer Court, Abbey Road, St Johns Wood,
London NW8 9AB
Tel/Fax: 0171 286 8300

## SPORTS WORKSHOP PROMOTIONS
PO Box 878, Crystal Palace National, Sports Centre,
London SE19 2BH
Tel: 0181 659 4561
Fax: 0181 776 7772
Web Site: www.btinternet.com/~sports.promotions

## SPOTLIGHT ENTERTAINMENTS
9 Rostherne Avenue, Lowton, Warrington WA3 2QD
Tel: 01942 724405

## SPROULE ENTERTAINMENTS
29 Craven Road, London W2 3BX
Tel: 0171 706 1550
Fax: 0171 706 1546

## PAUL SPYKER MANAGEMENTS
1-2 Henrietta Street, London WC2E 8PS
Tel: 0171 379 8181
Fax: 0171 379 8282
Email: info@pspy.com
Web Site: www.pspy.com

## ST JAMES'S MANAGEMENT
19 Lodge Close, Stoke D'Abernon, Cobham,
Surrey KT11 2SG
Tel: 01932 860666
Fax: 01932 860444

## BARRIE STACEY PROMOTIONS & PRODUCTIONS
9 Denmark Street, Third Floor, London WC2H 0LA
Tel: 0171 836 6220
Fax: 0171 836 2949

## STACEY-GARRARD ASSOCIATES ENTERTAINMENT AGENCY
77 Central Avenue, Telscombe Cliffs, Peacehaven,
East Sussex BN10 7NB
Tel/Fax: 01273 587947

## HELEN STAFFORD MANAGEMENT
14 Park Avenue, Bush Hill Park, Enfield,
Middlesex EN1 2HP
Tel: 0181 360 6329
Fax: 0181 482 0371
Email: castnet@avnet.co.uk

## STAFFORD LAW
6 Barham Close, Weybridge, Surrey KT13 9PR
Tel: 01932 854489
Fax: 01932 858521

## STAG ENTERTAINMENTS
1 Moor Road, Findon, Portlethen,
Aberdeen AB12 4RY Scotland
Tel/Fax: 01224 780000

## STAGE CENTRE MANAGEMENT
41 North Road, London N7 9DP
Tel: 0171 607 0872
Fax: 0171 609 0213

## STAGE MEDIA EVENTS
54 Calderview Avenue, Coatbridge,
Lanarkshire ML5 4TQ
Tel: 01236 433040

## STAGE PALM ENTERTAINMENTS
140 Beckett Road, Doncaster,
South Yorkshire DN2 4BA
Tel: 01302 326117
Fax: 01302 361871

## STAGECOACH MANAGEMENT
The Courthouse, Elm Grove, Walton-On-Thames,
Surrey KT12 1LH
Tel: 01932 254333
Fax: 01932 222894
Email: stagecoach@dial.pipex.com

## STAGESTRUCK MANAGEMENT
Stowe March, Barnet Lane, Elstree, Borehamwood,
Hertfordshire WD6 3RQ
Tel: 0181 953 8300
Fax: 0181 905 1511

## STAR TURN INTERNATIONAL LTD
16 Campbell Drive, Cardiff CF1 7QE
Tel/Fax: 01222 387672
Email: CPSJPower@aol.com

## STARDREAM LTD
'Party House', Mowbray Drive, Blackpool,
Lancs FY3 7JR
Tel: 01253 302602
Fax: 01253 301000

## STARDUST ENTERTAINMENTS AGENCY
1 West Well Close, Tingewick, Buckingham,
Bucks MK18 4QD
Tel/Fax: 01280 848387
Mobile: 0421 613670

## STARFINDERS INTERNATIONAL MANAGEMENT
113 Walton Road, East Molesey, Surrey KT8 0DR
Tel: 0181 941 1765/6
Fax: 0181 941 1767

## STARLINGS THEATRICAL AGENCY
45 Viola Close, South Ockendon, Essex RM15 6JF
Tel/Fax: 01708 859109

**STARMAKER ENTERTAINMENTS**
574 Hertford Road, Enfield, Middlesex EN3 5SU
Tel/Fax: 0181 443 3900

**RICHARD STARNOWSKI MANAGEMENT**
1 Penylan Place, Edgware, Middlesex HA8 6EN
Tel: 0181 952 2941
Fax: 0181 952 1892

**STARS IN YOUR EYES ENTERTAINMENT
AGENCY**
59 Windsor Road, Prestwich, Manchester M25 0DB
Tel: 0161 720 8912
Fax: 0161 740 0474

**STELLAMAX ENTERPRISES LTD**
Nova House, 53 Nova Croft, Off Broad Lane,
Eastern Green, Coventry CV5 7FJ
Tel: 01203 469585

**STEPHEN HATTON MANAGEMENT**
Shepperton House, 83-93 Shepperton Road,
London N1 3DF
Tel: 0171 359 3593
Fax: 0171 354 2189

**ROBERT STIGWOOD ORGANISATION LTD**
Barton Manor, Barton Estate, East Cowes,
Isle of Wight PO32 6LB
Tel: 01983 280676
Fax: 01983 293923

**STIVEN CHRISTIE MANAGEMENT**
80a Dean Street, London W1V 5AD
Tel: 0171 434 4430/07000 ACTORS
Fax: 0171 434 4430
Mobile: 0831 403030

**ANNETTE STONE ASSOCIATES**
2nd Floor, 22 Great Marlborough Street,
London W1V 1AF
Tel: 0171 734 0626
Fax: 0171 434 2346/0171 439 2522

**THE RICHARD STONE ASSOCIATES**
2 Henrietta Street, London WC2E 8PS
Tel: 0171 497 0849
Fax: 0171 497 0869

**STONEYPORT AGENCY**
39 Shandon Crescent, Edinburgh EH11 1QF
Tel: 0131 346 8237/339 4279
Fax: 0131 313 2083/339 4279
Email:
jb@folkmus.demon.co.uk / bboo3@post.almac.co.uk
Web Site: http://www.stoneyport.demon.co.uk

**MIKE & MARGARET STOREY
ENTERTAINMENTS**
Cliffe End Business Park, Dale Street, Longwood,
Huddersfield HD3 4TG
Tel: 01484 657054

Fax: 01484 657055

**PETER STUART MUSIC**
6 Coxwold Hill, Wetherby, West Yorkshire LS22 7PX
Tel/Fax: 01937 582573

**STUDIO ONE ASSOCIATES**
19 St. Patricks Road, Coventry CV1 2LP
Tel: 01203 552903
Fax: 01203 229003

**STYLE PROMOTIONS**
18 Mill Road, Rye, East Sussex TN31 7NN
Tel: 01797 224601
Fax: 01797222617

**SUCCESS**
Suite 73-74, Kent House, 87 Regent Street,
London W1R 7HF
Tel: 0171 734 3356
Fax: 0171 494 3787

**SUCCESSFUL CHOICE**
13 Cambridge Drive, Lee Green, London SE12 8AG
Tel: 0181 852 4955
Mobile: 0966 536186

**BOBBY SUMMERS ENTERTAINMENT UK**
69a Bure Lane, Christchurch, Dorset BH23 4DL
Tel: 01425 278500/277226
Fax: 01425 279320
Mobile: 0411 445208

**MARK SUMMERS MANAGEMENT**
209 Hatton Road, Feltham, Middlesex TW14 9QY
Tel: 0181 893 2573
Fax: 0181 384 2539
Mobile: 0956 254246

**MICHAEL SUMMERTON MANAGEMENT LTD**
336 Fulham Road, Chelsea, London SW10 9UG
Tel: 0171 351 7777
Fax: 0171 352 0411

**SWAMP MUSIC**
PO Box 94, Derby DE22 1XA
Tel/Fax: 01332 332336
Mobile: 0402 564804
Email: Chrishall@swampmusic.demon.co.uk

**SWAN ENTERTAINMENTS**
73 Highgate Road, Sileby, Loughborough,
Leicestershire LE12 7PN
Tel: 01509 814889

**SWIFT ENTERTAINMENTS**
4 Woodcocks, Tollgate Road, London E16 3LE
Tel: 0171 473 0292
Fax: 0171 511 5115
Email: PBBUS@aol.com

**SYLVANTONE PROMOTIONS**
17 Allerton Grange Way, Leeds LS17 6LP
Tel: 0113 268 7788

**SYNWAVE PRODUCTIONS**
78 Mount Road, Hastings, East Sussex TN35 5LA
Tel: 01424 439465

**T D PROMOTIONS**
Torignie, Rue de Candie, St. Andrew, Guernsey
GY6 8UP Channel Islands
Tel: 01481 38907

**TALENT ARTISTS LTD**
4 Mews House, Princes Lane, London N10 3LU
Tel: 0181 444 4088
Fax: 0181 444 3353

**TALENT ENTERTAINMENTS AGENCY**
'Eastholme', Main Road, East Lyng, Taunton,
Somerset TA3 5AU
Tel: 01823 698609
Fax: 01823 698697

**TALENT INTERNATIONAL**
61 Howland Way, London SE16 1HW
Tel/Fax: 0171 231 2553
Email: TalentInt@aol.com

**TALENT INTRODUCTION CENTRE**
6a Mowbray Road, Upper Norwood,
London SE19 2RN
Tel: 0181 653 8111
Fax: 0181 653 3615

**TALKBACK MANAGEMENT**
36 Percy Street, London W1P 0LN
Tel: 0171 631 3940
Fax: 0171 637 5105

**TALKIES**
3 Charlotte Mews, London W1P 1LN
Tel: 0171 323 6883/6993

**TALKING CONCEPTS**
19 Bird Street, Lichfield, Staffordshire WS13 6PW
Tel: 01543 414666
Fax: 01543 416644

**TALKING HEADS**
Eastgate House, 16-19 Eastcastle Street,
London W1N 7PA
Tel: 0171 636 7755
Fax: 0171 636 5757
Email: 106700.3414@compuserve.com

**TAM MANAGEMENT**
192 Derby Lane, Stoneycroft, Liverpool L13 6QQ
Tel/Fax: 0151 259 6017

**TANWOOD THEATRICAL AGENCY**
46-48 Bath Road, Swindon, Wiltshire SN1 4AY
Tel: 01793 523895
Fax: 01793 643219

**TARGET CASTING LTD**
Rhodes House, St. Leonards Gate,
Lancaster LA1 1NN
Tel: 01524 67354
Fax: 01524 848812
Email: target@actorsuk.demon.co.uk

**RUTH TARKO AGENCY**
52 Cecil Street, Glasgow G12 8RJ Scotland
Tel: 0141 334 0555
Fax: 0141 334 0896

**BRIAN TAYLOR - NINA QUICK
ASSOCIATES**
50 Pembroke Road, Kensington, London W8 6NX
Tel: 0171 602 6141
Fax: 0171 602 6301

**TEACHER STERN SELBY**
37-41 Bedford Row, London WC1R 4JH
Tel: 0171 242 3191
Fax: 0171 242 1156 or 0171 405 2964
Email: gs@tsslaw.co.uk

**NORMAN TEAL (BLACKPOOL ARTISTES
MANAGEMENT)**
12 Queensway, Blackpool FY4 2DG
Tel: 01253 344061
Fax: 01253 407525

**PAUL TELFORD MANAGEMENT**
23 Noel Street, London W1V 3RD
Tel: 0171 434 1100
Fax: 0171 434 1200
Email: ptperform@aol.com

**TEMPLAR ENTERTAINMENT AGENCY**
'Touchwood, Plantation Road, Leighton Buzzard,
Bedfordshire LU7 7JE
Tel: 01525 854443
Fax: 01525 854403
Email: templar@powernet.co.uk

**TEMPLAR POLWYN ENTERTAINMENTS &
PROMOTIONS**
70 Wheble Drive, Woodley, Reading RG5 3DU
Tel: 0118 926 0399
Mobile: 0421 464611

**TEMPLE'S ENTERTAINMENT AGENCY
(EST. 1897)**
2 Knowle Close, Abington Vale,
Northampton NN3 3LW
Tel: 01604 639198
Fax: 01604 628204

**TH PROMOTIONS**
204 Fairview Avenue, Wigmore, Gillingham,
Kent ME8 0PX
Tel: 01634 371381

**THAT'S ENTERTAINMENT ASSOCIATES**
Upham Hall Green Lane, Kessingland, Lowestoft,
Suffolk NR33 7RP
Tel/Fax: 01502 742045
Tel/Fax: 07000 KCANTOR
Tel/Fax: 07000 522 6867
Email: kenny.c@virgin.net

**THEOBALD DICKSON PRODUCTIONS**
The Coach House, Swinhope Hall, Swinhope,
Market Rasen, Lincolnshire LN8 6HT
Tel: 01472 399011
Fax: 01472 399025
Web Site: www.barbaradickson.com

**THOMAS AND BENDA ASSOCIATION LTD**
310 Edgware Road, London W2 1DY
Tel: 0171 723 5509
Fax: 0171 724 7287

**DAVID THOMPSON ASSOCIATES**
50b Neal Street, London WC2H 9PA
Tel: 0171 836 3988

**JIM THOMPSON**
1 Northdown Road, Belmont, Sutton, Surrey SM2 6DY
Tel: 0181 770 3511/2
Fax: 0181 643 6687

**SYLVIA THORLEY ENTERTAINMENT**
1 Breakwaters, Shore Road, Bonchurch, Ventnor
Isle of Wight
Tel: 01983 854129
Fax: 01983 853796

**THORNTON AGENCY**
(For Dwarves, Midgets and Little People 5' and Under)
72 Purley Downs Road, South Croydon, Surrey
CR2 0RB
Tel: 0181 660 5588
Fax: 0171 385 6647

**TICKETY BOO**
The Boathouse Crabtree Lane, London SW6 6TY
Tel: 0171 610 0122
Fax: 0171 610 0133
Email: tickety-boo@tickety-boo.com
Web Site: www.tickety-boo.com

**TICKLISH ALLSORTS**
31 Highfield Road, Salisbury, Wiltshire SP2 7LZ
Tel: 01722 335654

**TIME ARTISTES**
13 Southwell Gardens, Ashton-Under-Lyne,
Lancashire OL6 8XS
Tel: 0161 343 7400
Fax: 0161 343 7294

**VICTORIA TINKER MANAGEMENT**
Birchen Bridge House Brighton Road,
Mannings Heath, Horsham, West Sussex RH13 6HY
Tel/Fax: 01403 210653

**ROY TIPPER**
'Karagola', The Drive, Skegness, Lincs
Tel: 01754 762805
Fax: 01754 761173

**TKO MUSIC GROUP**
PO Box 130, Hove, East Sussex BN3 6QU
Tel: 01273 550088
Fax: 01273 540968
Email: management@tkomusicgroup.co.uk

**WARREN TOLLEY PRODUCTIONS**
'Cherokee', 23 Napier Avenue, Blackpool,
Lancs FY4 1PA
Tel: 01253 403781
Fax: 01253 403785
Mobile: 0850 502001

**TOP HAT ENTERTAINMENTS**
Cecil Court, 75B Cecil Street, Newton,
Birmingham B19 3SU
Tel/Fax: 0121 359 6165

**TOP MODEL AGENCY**
3rd Floor, 21-25 Goldhawk Road, London W12 8QQ
Tel: 0181 743 0640
Fax: 0181 743 1413

**TOP TALENT AGENCY**
Yester Road, Chislehurst, Kent BR7 5HN
Tel/Fax: 0181 467 0808

**REG TRACEY**
'Scholars', Clayhill Road, Leigh, Reigate,
Surrey RH2 8PD
Tel: 01306 611339
Fax: 01306 611240

**TRANSART (UK) LTD**
8 Bristol Gardens, London W9 2JG
Tel: 0171 286 7526
Fax: 0171 266 2687

**TRENDS PRODUCTIONS (LONDON) LTD**
54 Lisson Street, London NW1 5DF
Tel: 0171 723 8001
Fax: 0171 258 3591

**TRIBE AGENCY**
PO Box 19, Kings Langley, Hertfordshire WD4 8BF
Tel: 01923 261985

**TRIPLE CREAM ENTERTAINMENT**
248 Daws Heath Road, Thundersley, Benfleet,
Essex SS7 2TP
Tel: 01702 551448

**GARY TROLAN MANAGEMENT**
30 Burrard Road, London NW6 1DB
Tel/Fax: 0171 794 4429
Tel: 0171 431 4367

**TROPICAL ENTERTAINMENTS
MANAGEMENT AGENCY**
34 Crest Road, London NW2 7LY
Tel: 0181 450 2084
Fax: 0181 830 6457
Email: tema@tropical.force9.co.uk

**TUBE (MANAGEMENT) PRODUCTIONS**
42 Park View Road, Neasdon, London NW10 1AL
Tel: 0181 450 5987

**TOMMY TUCKER AGENCY**
43 Drury Lane, London WC2B 5RT
Tel: 0171 497 2113
Fax: 0171 379 0451

**TUFF TUFF MANAGEMENT**
4 Durweston Mews, Crawford Street,
London W1H 1PB
Tel: 0171 935 3664
Fax: 0171 487 5385

**BILL TURNER MANAGEMENT**
140 Beckett Road, Doncaster,
South Yorkshire DN2 4BA
Tel: 01302 367495
Fax: 01302 321978

**GRAHAM TURNER**
56 Towncroft, Chelmsford CM1 4JX
Tel: 01245 491252
Fax: 01245 603925
Email: gt@star-performers.com

**THE TWO CITIES PROMOTIONS AGENCY**
(A Division of Class Acts Entertainments)
9 Herbert Place Dublin 2 Eire
Tel: 00 353 1 662 5484
Fax: 00 353 1 676 9298
139 Stranmillis Road, Belfast BT9 5AJ Northern Ireland
Tel: 01232 681041
Fax: 01232 687747
Email: classacts@unite.co.uk

**UGLY MODELS**
Tigris House, 256 Edgware Road, London W2 1DS
Tel: 0171 402 5564
Fax: 0171 402 0507

**UK BOOKING AGENCY**
Box 1, 404 Footscray Road, London SE9 3TU
Email: spinners@dircon.co.uk
Web Site: www.ukbookingagency.co.uk

**ULTIMATE ENTERTAINMENT
INTERNATIONAL**
Atlas House, London Road, Hindhead,

Surrey GU26 6AB
Tel: 01428 606566
Fax: 01428 606141

**UNCLE BRIAN LTD**
The Wood Cottage, Main Road, Brompton-by-Sawdon,
Scarborough, North Yorkshire YO13 9DD
Tel: 01723 859497
Fax: 01723 859497
Mobile: 0850 615554
Email: unclebrianltd@btinternet.com
Web Site: http://www.btwebworld.com/unclebrianltd

**UNIQUE ARTISTES LTD**
Avon House, Kensington Village, Avonmore Road,
London W14 8TS
Tel: 0171 371 5353
Fax: 0171 371 5352
Email: jcarlton@uniquegroup.co.uk

**UNIVERSAL BOOKING AGENCY**
Tel: 0181 355 0675

**MEL UNSWORTH**
52 Bede Burn Road, Jarrow,
Tyne and Wear NE32 5AJ
Tel: 0191 489 3114
Fax: 0191 428 6547

**UPBEAT MANAGEMENT**
Sutton Business Centre, Restmor Way, Wallington,
Surrey SM6 7AH
Tel: 0181 773 1223
Fax: 0181 669 6752
Email: info@upbeat.co.uk
Web Site: www.upbeat.co.uk

**UPSTAGE ENTERTAINMENT GROUP**
Abingdon Chambers, 23 Abingdon Street,
Blackpool FY1 1DG
Tel: 01253 292 676
Fax: 01253 292165
Email: upstage@btinternet.com

**ROXANE VACCA MANAGEMENT**
73 Beak Street, London W1R 3LF
Tel: 0171 734 8085
Fax: 0171 734 8086

**VALUE ADDED TALENT**
1-2 Purley Place, London N1 1QA
Tel: 0171 704 9720
Fax: 0171 226 6135

**VAN WALSUM MANAGEMENT LTD**
4 Addison Bridge Place, London W14 8XP
Tel: 0171 371 4343
Fax: 0171 371 4344
Email: vwm@vanwalsum.demon.co.uk

**DENIS VAUGHAN MANAGEMENT**
Bond Street House, 14 Clifford Street,
London W1X 2JD

Tel: 0171 486 5353
Fax: 01372 742448

**VEGAS ENTERTAINMENTS**
'Craigmore', 9 Riverside, Preston, Lancs PR1 8ET
Tel/Fax: 01772 822521

**VERN ALLEN**
'Marvern', 4 Newhayes Close, Exeter, Devon EX2 9JJ
Tel: 01392 273305
Fax: 01392 2426421

**CLARE VIDAL-HALL**
28 Perrers Road, London W6 0EZ
Tel: 0181 741 7647
Fax: 0181 741 9459

**MICHAEL VINE ASSOCIATES**
29 Mount View Road, London N4 4SS
Tel: 0181 348 5899
Fax: 0181 348 3277
Email: mpvine@aol.com

**VISIONS INTERNATIONAL MODEL
MANAGEMENT & AGENCY**
Gainsborough House, 109 Portland Street,
Manchester M1 6DN
Tel: 0161 236 4041
Fax: 0161 237 9993

**THE VOICE BOX**
PO Box 82, Altrincham, Cheshire WA15 0QD
Tel: 0161 928 3222
Fax: 0161 928 7849

**THE VOICE SHOP**
Bakerloo Chambers, 304 Edgware Road,
London W2 1DY
Tel: 0171 402 3966
Fax: 0171 706 1002
Email: voiceshop@compuserve.com

**W & J THEATRICAL ENTERPRISES LTD**
15 Brookland Hill, London NW11 6DU
Tel/Fax: 0181 458 1608

**THELMA WADE**
54 Harley Street, London W1N 1AD
Tel: 0171 580 9860/0171 637 8022
Fax: 0171 580 2337

**WALKER ENTERTAINMENTS**
53 Ravensworth Road, Dunston, Gateshead,
Tyne and Wear NE11 9AB
Tel: 01228 20609
Fax: 0191 460 0721

**GINGER WALKER AGENCY**
14 Gooding Rise, Tiverton, Devon EX16 5BX
Tel: 01884 256389/01803 322622

**NICKY WALKER ENTERTAINMENT
AGENCY**
The Office, 35 Gordon Avenue, Thorpe St Andrew,
Norwich, Norfolk NR7 0DP
Tel: 01603 300777
Fax: 01603 300888

**WALMSLEY ASSOCIATES**
37A Crimsworth Road, London SW8 4RJ
Tel: 0171 627 4393
Fax: 0171 720 2433

**ALAN WALTERS MANAGEMENT**
15 Waverley Road, Southsea, Hampshire PO5 2PH
Tel: 01705 874072
Fax: 01705 430403

**WANSBECK THEATRICAL AGENCY**
9 Station Street, Bedlington,
Northumberland NE22 7JN
Tel: 01670 823698
Fax: 01670 823718

**WAR ZONES**
33 Kersley Road, London N16 0NT
Tel: 0171 249 2894
Fax: 0171 254 3729
Email: wz33@aol.com

**WARING & MCKENNA**
Lauderdale House 11 Gower Street
London WC1E 2HB
Tel: 0171 691 1333
Fax: 0171 691 1335
Email: dj@waringandmckenna.demon.co.uk

**BARRY WEINBERG ASSOCIATES**
28 Blenheim Gardens, Wembley, Middlesex HA9 7NP
Tel: 0181 904 7025
Fax: 0181 933 5751
Mobile: 0956 372323

**JANET WELCH PERSONAL MANAGEMENT**
46 The Vineyard, Richmond, Surrey TW10 6AN
Tel: 0181 332 6544
Fax: 0181 948 6787

**WELL BRED PRODUCTIONS**
189 Bermondsey Street, London SE1 3UW
Tel: 0171 407 5301
Fax: 0171 234 0336

**WESSEX ENTERTAINMENTS**
The Old Barn, Owl Street, Stocklinch, Ilminster,
Somerset TA19 9JN
Tel/Fax: 01460 52109

**WEST CENTRAL MANAGEMENT**
4 East Block, Panther House, 38 Mount Pleasant,
London WC1X 0AP
Tel/Fax: 0171 833 8134

**WEST END THEATRICAL**
Windgrove House, Ponteland Road, Cowgate,
Newcastle upon Tyne NE5 3AJ
Tel: 0191 214 6883
Fax: 0191 286 7267

**JASON WEST AGENCY**
Saddlebow, King's Lynn, Norfolk PE34 3AR
Tel: 01553 617586 (3 Lines)
Fax: 01553 617734
Email: jwagency@aol.com

**TONY WEST ENTERTAINMENTS**
PO Box 25, Formby, Liverpool, Merseyside L38 0DA
Tel: 0151 929 2727
Fax: 0151 929 3030
Email: tonywestent@btinternet.com

**WESTLAND STUDIOS**
5-6 lonbard Street East, Dublin 2 Eire
Tel: 00 353 1 677 9762/6774229/6793364
Fax: 00 353 1 671 0421

**WHAT MANAGEMENT**
Tel: 01895 824674

**WHATEVER ARTISTES MANAGEMENT LTD**
1 York Street, London W1H 1PZ
Tel: 0171 487 3111
Fax: 0171 487 3311
Email: wam@agents-uk.com

**LAWRENCE WHEELER**
41 Ashby Road, Daventry,
Northamptonshire NN11 5QD
Tel: 01327 705243
Fax: 01327 877273

**MICHAEL WHITEHALL**
125 Gloucester Road, London SW7 4TE
Tel: 0171 244 8466
Fax: 0171 244 9060

**ALAN WHITEHEAD MANAGEMENT LTD**
10 Deacons Close, Elstree, Borehamwood,
Hertfordshire WD6 3HX
Tel: 0181 953 8877
Fax: 0181 207 0614

**WIENERWALD ENTERTAINMENTS**
Wienerwald, 52 Helen Avenue, Feltham,
Middlesex TW14 9LB
Tel/Fax: 0181 751 0417

**WIGAN PIER PROMOTIONS**
6 Essex Road, Standish, Wigan, Lancashire WN1 2TH
Tel: 01257 425707

**JOHN WILCOCKS MEDIA AGENCY LTD**
34 Carisbrooke Close, Enfield, Middlesex EN1 3NB
Tel: 0181 364 4556
Fax: 0181 292 5060

**TONY WILD PROMOTIONS**
5 Fisher Close, Wadebridge, Cornwall PL27 6DX
Tel/Fax: 01208 814930

**DAVID WILKINSON ASSOCIATES**
115 Hazlebury Road, London SW6 2LX
Tel: 0171 371 5188
Fax: 0171 371 5161

**JOHN WILLIAMS**
PO Box 423, Chislehurst, Kent BR7 5TU
Tel: 0181 295 3639
Fax: 0181 295 3641

**WILLOW PERSONAL MANAGEMENT**
63 St. Martins Road, Deal, Kent CT14 9NY
Tel: 0700 900 WILLOW (945569)
Fax: 01733 240392
Email: info@willowmanagement.co.uk

**NEWTON WILLS MANAGEMENT &
PRODUCTIONS**
Utopia Studios, 17 Church Street, Belton in Rutland,
Oakham, Rutland LE15 9JU
Tel/Fax: 01572 717314

**ALLAN WILSON ENTERPRISES**
Queens House, Chapel Green Road, Hindley, Wigan,
Lancashire WN2 3LL
Tel: 01942 258565
Tel/Fax: 01942 255158

**WINDSOR PROMOTIONS**
50 Albert Street, Windsor, Berkshire SL4 5BU
Tel: 01753 855828
Fax: 01753 855801
Mobile: 0802 702232
Email: windprom@agents-uk.com

**WINK LEISURE ENTERPRISES**
39 Blake Avenue, Wath-upon-Dearne, Rotherham,
South Yorkshire S63 6NT
Tel: 01709 872864
Fax: 01709 873916

**MAURICE WINNICK (ASSOCIATES) LTD**
66 Melbourne Way, Enfield, Middlesex EN1 1XQ
Tel/Fax: 0181 366 2978

**DAVE WINSLETT ASSOCIATES**
6 Kenwood Ridge, Kenley, Surrey CR8 5JW
Tel: 0181 668 0531
Fax: 0181 668 9216
Email: winslett@agents-uk.com

**WENDY WISBEY AGENCY**
2 Rupert Road, London W4 1LX
Tel: 0181 994 1210
Tel/Fax: 0181 994 5378

**WISE BUDDAH MUSIC RADIO LTD**
7a Great Titchfield Street, London W1P 7AF

Tel: 0171 307 1600
Fax: 0171 307 1601
Email: firstname.surname@wisebuddah.com

## WIZARD MANAGEMENT
5 Clarelawn Avenue, London SW14 8BH
Tel: 0181 876 0406
Fax: 0181 878 3821
Email: attwiz@aol.com

## ALAN WOOD AGENCY
346 Gleadless Road, Sheffield S2 3AJ
Tel: 0114 258 0338
Fax: 0114 258 0638
Email: alan wood@agents-uk.com

## WORLD OF MOVEMENT ENTERTAINMENT AGENCY
Southbank House, Black Prince Road,
Albert Embankment, London SE1 7SJ
Tel: 0171 587 1440
Fax: 0171 735 1555

## WORLD PREMIERE
6 Chantry Heath Crescent, Knowle, Solihull,
West Midlands B93 9NH
Tel/Fax: 01564 774783

## WORLD WIDE ENTERTAINMENTS
64 Main Street, Swithland, Loughborough,
Leicestershire LE12 8TH
Tel: 01509 890096
Fax: 01509 890965 & 2nd Line
Email: wwe@agents-uk.com

## EDWARD WYMAN AGENCY
Ty'r Sais Stables, Argoed, Blackwood,
Gwent NP2 0JA Wales
Tel: 01495 224297
Fax: 01495 220212
Voice Bank Service (24 Hours)
01495 959021

## CAROLYNNE WYPER MANAGEMENT
22 Ives Street, London SW3 2ND
Tel: 0171 581 0330
Fax: 0171 823 7086
Email: info@soundtrackcwm.co.uk

## BRIAN YEATES ASSOCIATES
Home Farm House, London Road, Canwell,
Sutton Coldfield, West Midlands B75 5SH
Tel: 0121 323 2200
Fax: 0121 323 2313
Email: ash@cyberphile.co.uk

## YELLOW BALLOON PRODUCTIONS LTD
Freshwater House, Outdowns, Effingham,
Leatherhead, Surrey KT24 5QR
Tel: 01483 281500/1
Fax: 01483 281502

## EDDIE YEOH MANAGEMENT
(Inc. London Oriental Artistes Agency)
37 Falmouth Gardens, Redbridge, Ilford,
Essex IG4 5JU
Tel: 0181 550 9994/0181 550 1916
Fax: 0181 550 0348
Mobile: 0385 924298

## YES!! BRAZIL
275 Acton Lane, London W11 5DH
Tel/Fax: 0181 742 8988

## PHILIP YOUD ENTERTAINMENTS & MANAGEMENT
40 Armstrong Close, Locking Stumps, Birchwood,
Warrington, Cheshire WA3 6DH
Tel: 01925 828278
Fax: 01925 824757

## APRIL YOUNG LIMITED
11 Woodlands Road, Barnes, London SW13 0JZ
Tel: 0181 876 7030
Fax: 0181 878 7017

## ANN ZAHL PERSONAL MANAGEMENT
57 Great Cumberland Place, London W1H 7LJ
Tel: 0171 724 3684
Fax: 0171 262 4143
Mobile: 0802 735103

## MARLENE ZWICKER & ASSOCIATES
No.3 101 Malvern Road, London NW6 5PU
Tel/Fax: 0171 328 6838

# CONCERT PROMOTERS

## ADASTRA
2 Star Row, North Dalton, Driffield,
East Yorkshire YO25 9UR
Tel: 01377 217662 Fax: 01377 217754
Email: adastra@adastey.demon.co.uk
Web Site: http://www.wizardweb.co.uk/adastra
Senior Personnel: Chris Wade

## AIKEN PROMOTIONS
348 Lisburn Road, Belfast BT9 6GH
Tel: 01232 381047 Fax: 01232 682091
Managing Director: Jim Aiken
Administrator: Cathy Wilson
Promoter: Peter Aiken

## A.I.R LTD
AIR House, Spennymoor, County Durham DL16 7SE
Tel: 01388 814632 Fax: 01388 812445
Email: air@agents-uk.com
Senior Personnel: Colin Pearson - Director,
John Wray - Director

## ALLIED TALENT
Mansfield House, 9 Great Chapel Street,
London W1V 3AL
Tel: 0171 437 2551 Fax: 0171 437 2295
Senior Personnel: Bill Crabbe, Liv Stainer, Jan Cotten

## ANGLO-EUROPEAN ARTS
25 Fournier Street, London E1 6QE
Tel: 0171 247 7219 Fax: 0171 247 6094
Director: Carolyn Humphreys
Classical concert management, arrangement of
projects, festivals and classical concert series,
orchestral fixing.

## APOLLO LEISURE UK LTD
Grehan House, Garsington Road, Cowley,
Oxford OX4 5NQ
Tel: 01865 782900 Fax: 01865 782910
Managing Director: Sam Shrouder
General Manager: Nicky Monk

## ASGARD
125 Parkway, London NW1 7PS
Tel: 0171 387 5090 Fax: 0171 387 8740
Senior Personnel: Paul Fenn, Paul Charles,
Mick Griffiths, Paul Taylor

## ASKONAS HOLT LTD
Lonsdale Chambers, 27 Chancery Lane,
London WC2A 1PF
Tel: 0171 400 1700 Fax: 0171 400 1799
Email: info@askonasholt.co.uk
Web Site: www.askonashold.co.uk
Senior Personnel: Martin Campbell-White,
Robert Rattray
Specialising in: Classical Music.

## AVALON PROMOTIONS LTD
4a Exmoor Street, London W10 6BD
Tel: 0171 598 7333 Fax: 0171 598 7334
Email: chrisw@avalonuk.com
Senior Personnel: Richard Allen-Turner, Jon Thoday,
Colin Jones, Rob Aslett, Fiona Pride, James Herring

## BANKHOUSE LEISURE LTD
Riverside House, Aspley Marina, Wakefield Road,
Huddersfield HD1 3AF
Tel: 01484 435353 Fax: 01484 423351
Contact: Janet Macintosh

## MARTIN BARRY PRODUCTIONS
39 Godre'r Coed, Gwernymynydd, Mold,
Clwyd CH7 4DS
Tel: 01352 758266 Fax: 01352 759511
Managing Director: Martin Barry

## BIG BEAR MUSIC
PO Box 944, Birmingham B16 8UT
Tel: 0121 454 7020 Fax: 0121 454 9996
Email: bigbearmusic@compuserve.com
Senior Personnel: Tim Jennings
Big Bear Music specialise in Jazz, Blues and Swing.

## DEREK BLOCK ARTISTES AGENCY LIMITED
Douglas House, 3 Richmond Buildings,
London W1V 5AE
Tel: 0171 434 2100 Fax: 0171 434 0200
Email: dbaa@derekblock.demon.co.uk
Senior Personnel: Derek Block, Simon Shaw,
Scott Miller

## MEL BUSH ORGANISATION
5 Stratfield Saye, 20-22 Wellington Road,
Bournemouth BH8 8JN
Tel: 01202 293093 Fax: 01202 293080
Senior Personnel: Mel Bush

## CAPITAL RADIO ENTERPRISES
30 Leicester Square, London WC2H 7LA
Tel: 0171 766 6000 Fax: 0171 766 6100
Managing Director: David Mansfield
Station Director: Martin King
Head of Personnel: Tracy Reed
Group Programming Director: Richard Park
Commercial Director: Fru Hazitt

## DUGGIE CHAPMAN ASSOCIATES
The Old Coach House, 202 Common Edge Road,
Blackpool FY4 5DG
Tel/Fax: 01253 691823 Mobile: 0976 925504
Director: Duggie Chapman
PA: Beryl Johnson

Duggie Chapman Associates is Britain's longest running promoter of touring music hall presenting Star Variety Summer Shows and Pantomimes. Specialists in late bookings for managements. Package shows always available at short notice.

## CHESTER HOPKINS INTERNATIONAL
24 Fulham Palace Road, London W6 9PH
Tel: 0181 741 9910 (5 Lines) Fax: 0181 741 9914
Managing Directors: Adrian Hopkins and Jo Chester

## BARRY CLAYMAN CONCERTS LTD
134 Wigmore Street, London W1H 0LD
Tel: 0171 486 1222 Fax: 0171 935 6276
Managing Director: Barry Clayman
General Manager: Elizabeth Kaye
Production Manager: Phil Bowdery
Theatrical Director: Adrian Leggett

## CONSOLIDATED BOOKING AGENTS
117 King Street, Knutsford, Cheshire WA16 6EH
Tel: 01565 654024 Fax: 01565 654671
Managing Director: Alec Leslie
Production: Pat King
PA: Clare Stuart

## THE PAUL DAINTY CORPORATION (UK) LTD
No.4 Yeomans Row, London SW3 2AH
Tel: 0171 589 1111 Fax: 0171 589 2211
Managing Director: Peter Lister-Todd

## DERI PROMOTIONS
8 Wick Lane, Felpham, Bognor Regis,
West Sussex PO22 8QG
Tel: 01243 585545 Fax: 01243 586886
Mobile: 0860 509898
Senior Personnel: Roy Cooper
Specialising in: Country & Western.

## DF CONCERTS
PO Box 1540 Blanefield, Glasgow Scotland
Tel: 01360 771177 Fax: 01360 771171
Director: Stuart Clumpus
Head Booker: Geoff Ellis

## MALCOLM FELD AGENCY LTD
Malina House, Sandforth Road, Sandfield Park,
Liverpool L12 1JY
Tel: 0151 259 6565 ax: 0151 259 5006
Senior Personnel: Malcolm Feld

## THE FLYING MUSIC COMPANY LTD
110 Clarendon Road, London W11 2HR
Tel: 0171 221 7799 Fax: 0171 221 5016
Senior Personnel: Derek Nicol, Paul Walden

## FUNNYFRIEND LTD
Queens House, 1 Leicester Place, London WC2H 7BP
Tel: 0171 432 3258 Fax: 0171 432 3268

## GLASTONBURY FESTIVALS
Worthy Farm, Worthy Lane, Pilton, Shepton Mallet,
Somerset BA4 4BY
Tel: 01749 890254 Fax: 01759 890285
Promoter: Michael Eavis
Booker: Martin Elborn

## HARVEY GOLDSMITH ENTERTAINMENTS LTD
The Glassworks, 3-4 Ashland Place, London W1M 3JH
Tel: 0171 224 1992 Fax: 0171 224 0111
Managing Director: Harvey Goldsmith
Promoters: Pete Wilson & Dennis Arnold

## RAYMOND GUBBAY LTD
Olivier House, 27/31 East Barnet Road, Barnet,
Hertfordshire EN4 8RN
Tel: 0181 216 3000 Fax: 0181 216 3001
Managing Director: Raymond Gubbay
Deputy MD: Robert Jolley
Events Director: Anthony Findlay

## JEF HANLON PROMOTIONS LTD
1 York Street, London W1H 1PZ
Tel: 0171 487 2558 Fax: 0171 487 2584
Email: jhanlon@agents-uk.com

## HERITAGE MUSIC - MUSIC CONSULTANTS & PRODUCTION COMPANY
50 Main Street, Peckleton, Leicester LE9 7RE
Tel: 01455 822604 Fax: 01455 828911
Mobile: 0374 785059
Email: heritagemu@aol.com
Artistic Director: Celia Davies

## JOHN HESSENTHALER ENTERTAINMENTS
20 Green Willows, Lavenham, Sudbury,
Suffolk CO10 9SP
Tel: 01787 247838 Fax: 01787 247898
Senior Personnel: John Hessenthaler
Stage PA & Lighting Systems, Stages, Disco Show.
Act representation and Concert tours.

## JACK L HIGGINS
Pear Tree Cottage, Weymarks, Bradwell-on-Sea,
Southminster, Essex CM0 7JB
Tel: 01621 776463 Fax: 01621 776671
Senior Personnel: Jack L Higgins

## BOB HOLLAND-FORD
103 Lydyett Lane, Barnton, Northwich,
Cheshire CW8 4JT
Tel: 01606 76960
Proprietor: Bob Holland-Ford

## DAVID HULL PROMOTIONS
46 University Street, Belfast BT7 1HB
Tel: 01232 240360 Fax: 01232 247919
Managing Director: David Hull
General Manager: Frankie Caldbeck

## INTERNATIONAL ARTISTES LTD
Mezzanine Floor, 235 Regent Street,

London W1R 8AX
Tel: 0171 439 8401 Fax: 0171 409 2070
4th Floor, Television House, 10-12 Mount Street
Manchester M2 5FA Tel: 0161 833 9838
Fax: 0161 832 7480
Email: (user)@intartistes.demon.co.uk
Senior Personnel: Laurie Mansfield, Stuart Littlewood,
Robert Voice, Graham Gunn, Craig Ramadhin,
Mandy Ward

## ITB (INTERNATIONAL TALENT BOOKING)
3rd Floor, 27a Floral Street, Covent Garden,
London WC2E 9DQ
Tel: 0171 379 1313 Fax: 0171 379 1744
Agents: Rod MacSween, Barry Dickins, David Levy,
Martin Horne, Mike Dewdney, Charlie Myatt,
Scott Thomas & Maria Hutt

## K-BELL PRODUCTIONS
16 Melrose Avenue, London SW19 8BY
Tel: 0181 947 0788 Fax: 0181 241 3572
Email: kmcdonald5@compuserve.com
Managing Director: Keith McDonald

## KENNEDY STREET ENTERPRISES
Kennedy House, 31 Stamford Street, Altrincham,
Cheshire WA14 1ES
Tel: 0161 941 5151 Fax: 0161 928 9491
Managing Director: Danny Betesh

## STEPHEN LEATHERLAND PRODUCTIONS
44 Highclere Street, London SE26 4EU
Tel/Fax: 0181 778 6038
Managing Director: Stephen Leatherland
Consultant: Donald Auty
Administrator: Barbara Barringer

## LINE-UP PMC
9a Tankerville Place, Newcastle Upon Tyne NE2 3AT
Tel: 0191 281 6449 Fax: 0191 212 0913
Email: line-up.co.uk
Senior Personnel: Chris Murtagh

## MIKE LLOYD ARTISTES LTD
Brunswick House, 14-20 Brunswick Street,
Stoke-on-Trent ST1 1DR
Tel: 01782 206000 Fax: 01782 213432
Managing Director: Mike Lloyd
Assistant: Nigel Bamford

## MARK LUNDQUIST MANAGEMENT
2 Woodlands, Woking, Surrey GU22 7RU
Tel: 01483 773373 Fax: 01483 767929
Mobile: 07971 401510
Email: marklundquist@dial.pipex.com

## JOHNNY MANS PRODUCTIONS LIMITED
The Maltings, Brewery Road, Hoddesdon,
Hertfordshire EN11 8HF
Tel: 01992 470907 Fax: 01992 470516
Managing Director: Johnny Mans
Administration: Julia Mumford, Philip Crowe, Elliot
Mans & Lynn Aldridge.

## MARSHALL ARTS LTD
Leeder House, 6 Erskine Road, London NW3 3AJ
Tel: 0171 586 3831 Fax: 0171 586 1422
Managing Director: Barry Marshall
Director: Doris Dixon
Agent: Rob Hallett

## JOHN MARTIN PROMOTIONS LTD
The Homestead, Eastwick Road, Great Bookham,
Surrey KT23 4BA
Tel: 0181 786 3620 Fax: 0181 786 3621
Senior Personnel: John Martin

## MATPRO LTD
Cary Point, Babbacombe Downs Road,
Torquay TQ1 3LU
Tel: 01803 322233 Fax: 01803 322244
Email: matpro@btinternet.com

## NORMAN MCCANN CONCERT AGENCY LIMITED
The Coach House, 56 Lawrie Park Gardens,
London SE26 6JX
Tel: 0181 659 5955 Fax: 0181 659 4582

## PHIL MCINTYRE PROMOTIONS
15 Riversway, Navigation Way, Ashton-on-Ribble,
Preston PR2 2YP
Tel: 01772 720205 Fax: 01772 720238
Director: Philip McIntyre
Managing Director: Paul Roberts

## MCP PROMOTIONS LTD
16 Birmingham Road, Walsall WS1 2NA
Tel: 01922 620123 Fax: 01922 725654
Promoters: Tim Parsons, Stuart Galbraith

## METROPOLIS MUSIC
491a Holloway Road, London N19 4DD
Tel: 0171 272 2442 Fax: 0171 263 2434
Managing Director: Bob Angus
Director: Paul Hutton

## JOHN MILES ORGANISATION
Cadbury Camp Lane, Clapton in Gordano,
Bristol BS20 7SB
Tel: 01275 854675/856770 Fax: 01275 810186

## MILLENNIUM ARTISTES MANAGEMENT LTD
3 Dorin Court, Landscape Road, Warlingham,
Surrey CR6 9JT
Tel: 01883 626000 Fax: 01883 624579
Mobile: 0958 329912
Email: mam.ltd@mcmail.com
Web Site: www.mam.ltd.mcmail.com

## ANDREW MILLER PROMOTIONS (INTERNATIONAL) LTD
55 Fulham High Street, London SW6 3JJ
Tel: 0171 736 5500 Fax: 0171 371 7728

**MRS CASEY MUSIC**
PO Box 296, Aylesbury, Buckinghamshire HP19 3TL
Tel: 01296 394411 Fax: 01296 392300
Email: mcm@mrscasey.nildran.co.uk
Web Site: www.mrscasey.co.uk
Senior Personnel: Steve Heap
Deals mainly with Festival Organisation.

**MUSIC FOR ALL OCCASIONS**
Torridon House, 104 Bradford Road, Wakefield,
West Yorkshire WF1 2AH
Tel: 01924 371496
Managing Director: Brian Greensmith
Bands, Orchestras, Palm Court and Discos

**MUSICSCOPE**
95 White Lion Street, London N1 9PF
Tel: 0171278 1133 Fax: 0171 278 4442
Email: licensing@psluk.com
Partners: John Sinfield, Chris Patrick & David Jensen
Contact: Patricia Millett
Copyright Holders.

**PERFORMING ARTS MANAGEMENT**
Canal 7, Clarence Mill, Clarence Road, Bollington,
Macclesfield, Cheshire SK10 5JZ
Tel: 01625 575681 Fax: 01625 572839
Email: clare.scott@performingarts.co.uk
Web Site: www.performingarts.co.uk
Senior Personnel: Nicholas Smith, Sally Smith,
Clare Scott
Promoter of outdoor classical concerts with fireworks.

**PREMIERE PROMOTIONS**
24 Briarwood Close, Fareham, Hampshire PO16 0PS
Tel: 01329 238449 (4 Lines) Fax: 01329 233088
Email: premiere@agents-uk.com
Senior Personnel: Mrs Del Mitchell

**RCL LEISURE LTD**
131 Mount Annan Drive, Glasgow G44 4RX
Tel: 0141 649 7798 Fax: 0141 632 6533
Email: roychimes@aol.com
Senior Personnel: Robert Pratt

**REGULAR MUSIC**
The Palladium, Broughton Place,
Edinburgh EH1 3RR Scotland
Tel: 0131 557 6578 Fax: 0131 557 6579

**RIGOLETTO LTD**
4 Wigton Court, Wigton Lane, Leeds LS17 8SB
Tel: 0113 269 3720
Directors: June & Stanley Sher

**THE ROCK GARDEN**
6-7 The Piazza, London WC2E 8HA
Tel: 0171 836 4052 Fax: 0171 379 4793
Email: art@rockgarden.co.uk
Chairman: Arthur Wicksom
Managing Director: Philip Matthews

**ROYSTON PRODUCTIONS**
2 Coaching Walk, Westone, Northampton NN3 3EX
Tel: 01604 411413
Contact: Roy Gilbert

**DUDLEY RUSSELL CONCERT & THEATRE PRODUCTIONS**
PO Box 64, Cirencester, Gloucestershire GL7 5YD
Tel: 01285 644622 Fax: 01285 642291
Senior Personnel: Dudley Russell

**HENRY SELLERS ENTERTAINMENTS**
PO Box 262, London NW8 0NJ
Tel: 0171 586 7963 Fax: 0171 586 6798

**JACK SHARPE ENTERTAINMENTS**
Tel: 01702 524169

**SOLO PROMOTIONS**
2nd Floor, 55 Fulham High Street, London SW6 3JJ
Tel: 0171 736 5925 Fax: 0171 731 6921
Managing Director: John Giddings
Promoter: Graham Pullin

**STONE RANGER PRODUCTIONS**
25 Whitehall, London SW1A 2BS
Tel: 0171 930 0661 Fax: 0171 839 5002
Company Managers: Ed Smith & Iain McCallum
Specialising in touring comedians.

**THEOBALD DICKSON PRODUCTIONS**
The Coach House, Swinhope Hall, Swinhope, Market
Rasen, Lincolnshire LN8 6HT
Tel: 01472 399011 Fax: 01472 399025
Web Site: www.barbaradickson.com
Senior Personnel: Bernard Theobald

**TKO PROMOTIONS LTD**
PO Box 130, Hove, East Sussex BN3 6QU
Tel: 01273 550088 Fax: 01273 540969
Email: tkoadam@tkogroup.com
Concerts: Adam Clavering

**UK PRODUCTIONS LTD**
Lime House, 78 Meadrow, Godalming,
Surrey GU7 3HT
Tel: 01483 423600 Fax: 01483 418486
Directors: Peter Frosdick & Martin Dodd

**VAN WALSUM MANAGEMENT LTD**
4 Addison Bridge Place, London W14 8XP
Tel: 0171 371 4343 Fax: 0171 371 4344
Email: vwm@vanwalsum.demon.co.uk
Senior Personnel: Joeske Van Walsum, Victoria
Rowsell, Roderick Thomson, Geoffrey Owen,
Rachel Bostock

**WELSH NATIONAL CONCERT AGENCY LTD**
The Coach House, 56 Lawrie Park Gardens,
London SE26 6XJ
Tel: 0181 659 5955 Fax: 0181 659 4582

**JOHN WILLIAMS**
PO Box 423, Chislehurst, Kent BR7 5TU
Tel: 0181 295 3639 Fax: 0181 295 3641
Senior Personnel: John Williams

**WORLD IN THE PARK LTD**
Millside, Mill Lane, Box, Corsham, Wiltshire SN13 8PN
Tel: 01225 743188 Fax: 01225 743481
Artistic Director: Thomas Brooman

# LITERARY AGENTS

### THE AGENCY ( LONDON) LTD
24 Pottery Lane, Holland Park, London W11 4LZ
Tel: 0171 727 1346 Fax: 0171 727 9037
Senior Personnel: Stephen Durbridge

### AITKEN AND STONE LTD
29 Fernshaw Road, London SW10 0TG
Tel: 0171 351 7561 Fax: 0171 376 3594
Agency Personnel: Gillen Aitken & Bryan Stone

### AQUARIUS LITERARY AGENCY & PICTURE LIBRARY
PO Box 5, Hastings, East Sussex TN34 1HR
Tel: 01424 721196 Fax: 01424 717704
Email: aquarius.lib@clara.net
Managing Director: Gilbert Gibson
Head of Picture Library: David Corkill

### YVONNE BAKER ASSOCIATES
8 Temple Fortune Lane, London NW11 7UD
Tel: 0181 455 8687 Fax: 0181 458 3143
Email: yvonne@yvbaker.demon.co.uk
Senior Personnel: Yvonne Baker
Specialising in: Writers for TV (drama, series, sitcoms) and stage.  Representing small scale full length stage shows, drama and children's shows.

### ALAN BRODIE REPRESENTATION LTD
(incorporating Michael Imison Playwrights)
211 Piccadilly, London W1V 9LD
Tel: 0171 917 2871 Fax: 0171 917 2872
Email: alanbrodie@aol.com
Managing Director: Alan Brodie
Director: S.McNair & Caroline Brodie
Consultant: Michael Imison

### CAMPBELL THOMSON & MCLAUGHLIN LTD
1 Kings Mews, London WC1N 2JA
Tel: 0171 242 0958 Fax: 0171 242 2408

### CASAROTTO COMPANY LTD
National House, 60-66 Wardour Street,
London W1V 4ND
Tel: 0171 287 4450 Fax: 0171 287 9128
Email: agents@casarotto.uk.com
Senior Personnel: Jenne Casarotto, Tracy Smith,
Rachel Swann, Charlotte Kelly, (Theatre Division):
Mel Kenyon, Tom Erhardt; (Technicians):
Catherine O'Shea, Sarah Prithard

### CASAROTTO RAMSAY LTD
60-66 Wardour Street, London W1V 4ND
Tel: 0171 287 4450 Fax: 0171 287 9128
Managing Director: Giorgio Casarotto
Agents: Tom Erhardt, Mel Kenyon

### C&B (THEATRE) LIMITED
126 Cornwall Road, London SE1 8TQ
Tel/Fax: 0171 633 0599
Managing Director: John Gordo

### JONATHAN CLOWES LTD
10 Iron Bridge House, Bridge Approach,
London NW1 8BD
Tel: 0171 722 7674 Fax: 0171 722 7677
Directors: Brie Burkeman, Jonathan Clowes &
Ann Evans

### ELSPETH COCHRANE AGENCY
11-13 Orlando Road, London SW4 0LE
Tel: 0171 220 3146 Fax: 0171 622 5815
Senior Personnel: Elspeth Cochrane, Roger Charteris

### ROSICA COLIN LTD
1 Clareville Grove Mews, London SW7 5AH
Tel: 0171 370 1080 Fax: 0171 244 6441
Managing Director: Joanna Marston

### RUPERT CREW LTD
1a King's Mews, London WC1N 2JA
Tel: 0171 242 8586 Fax: 0171 831 7914

### CRUICKSHANK CAZENOVE LIMITED
97 Old South Lambeth Road, London SW8 1XU
Tel: 0171 735 2933 Fax: 0171 820 1081
Senior Personnel: Harriet Cruickshank
Specialising in Directors, Designers &
Choreographers. Does NOT deal with actors.

### CURTIS BROWN GROUP
4th Floor, Haymarket House, 28-29 Haymarket,
London SW1Y 4SP
Tel: 0171 396 6600 Fax: 0171 396 0110
Senior Personnel: Jonathan Lloyd
Specialising in: writers, directors, some presenters.

### JUDY DAISH ASSOCIATES
2 St. Charles Place, London W10 6EG
Tel: 0181 964 8811 Fax: 0181 964 8966
Senior Personnel: J Daish, S Stroud, D Harwood,
L Newman

### NORMA FARNES MANAGEMENT
9 Orme Court, London W2 4RL
Tel: 0171 727 1544 Fax: 0171 792 2110
Contact: Norma Farnes

### LAURENCE FINCH LTD
101 Southbank House, Black Prince Road, Albert
Embankment, London SE1 7SJ
Tel: 0171 735 8171

### JILL FOSTER LTD
9 Barb Mews, London W6 7PA
Tel: 0171 602 1263 Fax: 0171 602 9336
Senior Personnel: Jill Foster, Ann Foster, Alison Finch,
Kim Dockrey

### SAMUEL FRENCH LTD
52 Fitzroy Street, Fitzrovia, London W1P 6JR

Tel: 0171 387 9373 Fax: 0171 387 2161
Email: theatre@samuelfrench-london.co.uk
Web Site: samuelfrench-london.co.uk
Managing Director: J Bedding
Editorial Director: A Smith

## BLAKE FRIEDMANN LITERARY, TV AND FILM AGENCY
37-41 Gower Street, London WC1E 6HH
Tel: 0171 631 4331 Fax: 0171 323 1274
Contact: Carole Blake, Fiction and
Non-Fiction manuscripts.
Julian Friedmann & Conrad Williams,
Film and TV scripts.

## PAMELA GILLIS MANAGEMENT
46 Sheldon Avenue, London N6 4JR
Tel: 0181 340 7868 Fax: 0181 341 5564
Proprieter: Pamela Gillis
No unsolicited manuscripts.

## ERIC GLASS LTD
28 Berkeley Square, London W1X 6HD
Tel: 0171 629 7162 Fax: 0171 499 6780
Senior Personnel: Janet Glass
Agency Personnel: David Capon

## DAVID GROSSMAN LITERARY AGENCY
118b Holland Park Avenue, London W11 4UA
Tel: 0171 221 2770 Fax: 0171 221 1445
Managing Director: David Grossman

## THE ROD HALL AGENCY LTD
7 Goodge Place, London W1P 1FL
Tel: 0171 637 0706 Fax: 0171 637 0807
Email: rod.hall@dial.pipex.com
Directors: Rod Hall and Clare Barker
Playwrights, screenwriters and directors.

## ROGER HANCOCK LTD
4 Water Lane, London NW1 8NZ
Tel: 0171 267 4418 Fax: 0171 267 0705

## A.M.HEATH & COMPANY LTD
79 St.Martin's, London WC2N 4AA
Tel: 0171 836 4271 Fax: 0171 497 2561

## MICHAEL HENSHAW
3 Stucley Place, London NW1 8NS
Tel: 0171 267 1311 Fax: 0171 267 7960
Contact: Michael Henshaw

## DAVID HIGHAM ASSOCIATES
5-8 Lower John Street, Golden Square,
London W1R 4HA
Tel: 0171 437 7888 Fax: 0171 437 1072
Directors: Bruce Hunter, Jacqueline Korn, Antony Goff,
Elizabeth Cree and Ania Corless.
Write to: Elizabeth Cree

## ICM LTD
Oxford House, 76 Oxford Street, London W1M 0AX
Tel: 0171 636 6565 Fax: 0171 323 0101

## INTERNATIONAL COPYRIGHT BUREAU LTD
22a Aubrey House, Maida Avenue, London W2 1TQ
Tel: 0171 724 8034 Fax: 0171 724 7662
Managing Director: Joy Westendarp

## JOHN JOHNSON LTD
Clerkenwell House, 45-47 Clerkenwell Green,
London EC1R 0HT
Tel: 0171 251 0125 Fax: 0171 251 2172
Agency Personnel: Andrew Hewson, Margaret Hewson
& Elizabeth Fairbairn.

## ROLF KRUGER MANAGEMENT
21 Eastcastle Street, London W1N 7PA
Tel: 0171 323 3733 Fax: 0171 323 3744
Email: rkruger@mail.com
Senior Personnel: Rachel Kruger

## TESSA LE BARS MANAGEMENT
54 Birchwood Road, Petts Wood, Orpington,
Kent BR5 1NZ
Tel/Fax: 01689 837084 Mobile: 0860 287255
Specialising in Mainly Comedy Writers. Member of
Personal Managers Association. Existing Clients Only.

## LEMON UNNA AND DURBRIDGE LTD
See The Agency (London) Ltd.

## CHRISTOPHER LITTLE LITERARY AGENCY
10 Eelbrook Studios, 125 Moore Park Road,
London SW6 4PS
Tel: 0171 736 4455 Fax: 0171 736 4490
Email: 100555.3137@compuserve.com
Partners: Christopher Little & Patrick Walsh

## ANDREW MANN LTD
1 Old Compton Street, London W1V 5PH
Tel: 0171 734 4751/2 Fax: 0171 287 9264
Managing Director: Anne Dewe
Director: Tina Betts

## JOHNNY MANS PRODUCTIONS LIMITED
The Maltings, Brewery Road, Hoddesdon,
Hertfordshire EN11 8HF
Tel: 01992 470907 Fax: 01992 470516
Managing Director: Johnny Mans
Administration: Julia Mumford, Philip Crowe, Elliot
Mans & Lynn Aldridge.

## MARJACQ SCRIPTS LTD
34 Devonshire Place, London W1N 1PE
Tel: 0171 935 9499 Fax: 0171 935 9115

## BLANCHE MARVIN (PMA)
21a St John's Wood High Street, London NW8 7NG
Tel: 0171 722 2313 Fax: 0171 722 2313
Director: Blanche Marvin
Plays for theatre, film and TV.

## M.B.A. LITERARY AGENTS LTD
62 Grafton Way, London W1

Tel: 0171 387 2076 Fax: 0171 387 2042
Email: agent@mbalit.co.uk

## BILL MCLEAN PERSONAL MANAGEMENT
23B Deodar Road, Putney, London SW15 2NP
Tel: 0181 789 8191 Fax: 0181 789 8192

## MLR (ALSO MACNAUGHTON LORD REPRESENTATION LTD)
200 Fulham Road, London SW10 9PN
Tel: 0171 351 5442/376 5575 Fax: 0171 351 4560
Senior Personnel: Patricia MacNaughton,
Annabel Lord

## WILLIAM MORRIS AGENCY (UK) LTD
1 Stratton Street London W1X 6HB
Tel: 0171 355 8500 Fax: 0171 355 8600
Managing Director: Steven Kennis
Literary Agent: Stephanie Cabbott

## MUSICSCOPE
95 White Lion Street, London N1 9PF
Tel: 0171278 1133 Fax: 0171 278 4442
Email: licensing@psluk.com
Partners: John Sinfield, Chris Patrick & David Jensen
Contact: Patricia Millett
Copyright Holders.

## NOEL GAY
22-25 Dean Street, London W1V 5AL
Tel: 0171 836 3941 Fax: 0171 287 1816
Senior Personnel: A J Armitage, G X Constantinidi,
N Ranceford-Hadley

## PETERS FRASER & DUNLOP ARTISTES
503/4 The Chambers, Chelsea Harbour, Lots Road,
London SW10 0XF
Tel: 0171 344 1010 Actors Agency Tel: 0171 344 1020
Account Department Fax: 0171 352 8135
Web Site: http://www.pfd.co.uk

## LAURENCE POLLINGER LTD
18 Maddox Street, Mayfair, London W1R 0EU
Tel: 0171 629 9761 Fax: 0171 629 9765
Email: laurencepollinger@compuserve.com
Agency Personnel: Gerald Pollinger, Juliet Burton,
Lesley Hadcroft & Heather Chalcroft

## RADALA & ASSOCIATES
17 Avenue Mansions, Finchley Road,
London NW3 7AX
Tel: 0171 794 4495 Fax: 0171 431 7636
Contact: Richard Gollner
We do not usually represent dramatists but do offer a
consultancy service by way of paid script evaluation
and advice.

## TESSA SAYLE AGENCY
11 Jubilee Place, London SW3 3TE
Tel: 0171 823 3883 Fax: 0171 823 3363
Literary Contact: Rachel Calder

## VINCENT SHAW ASSOCIATES LTD
20 Jay Mews, London SW7 2EP
Tel: 0171 581 8215 Fax: 0171 225 1079
Email: vincentshaw@clara.net
Web Site: http://home.clara.net/vincentshaw
Director: Vincent Shaw

## SHEIL LAND ASSOCIATES LTD
43 Doughty Street, London WC1N 2LF
Tel: 0171 405 9351 Fax: 0171 831 2127
Agency Personnel: Anthony Sheil, Sonia Land, Vivien
Green, Simon Trewin, Luigi Bonomi & John Rush

## SIEFERT DENCH ASSOCIATES
24 D'Arblay Street, London W1V 3FH
Tel: 0171 437 4551 Fax: 0171 439 1355
Agency Personnel: Linda Siefert & Elizabeth Dench

## JON THURLEY MANAGEMENT
213 Linen Hall, 162/168 Regent Street,
London W1R 5TA
Tel: 0171 437 9545 Fax: 0171 287 9208
Agency Associates: Jon Thurley & Patricia Preece

## WARNER/CHAPPELL PLAYS LTD
(formerly English Theatre Guild)
Griffin House, 161 Hammersmith Road,
London W6 8BS
Tel: 0181 563 5800 Fax: 0181 563 5801
Email: warner.chappell@dial.pipex.com
Manager: Michael Callahan
Play publishers and Play Agents.

## A.P WATT LTD
20 John Street, London WC1N 2DR
Tel: 0171 405 6774 Fax: 0171 430 1952
Plays Agent: Sam North

# VOICE-OVER AGENCIES

## CALYPSO VOICES
25-26 Poland Street, London W1V 3DB
Tel: 0171 734 6415
Fax: 0171 437 0410
Senior personnel: Jane Savage, Kim Wheeler
Voice Over Agency, call for details.

## CASTAWAY
3 Kingly Street, London W1R 5LF
Tel: 0171 439 7414
Fax: 0171 287 2202
Senior Personnel: Sheila Britten

## CELEBRITY SPEAKERS
Eton Place Burnham Bucks SL1 7PT
Tel: 01753 747015
Fax: 01753 747001
Senior Personnel: Alex Krywald
Enquiries: Aveline Hughes

## BRYAN DREW LTD
Quadrant House, 80/82 Regent Street,
London W1R 6AU
Tel: 0171 437 2293
Fax: 0171 437 0561
Senior Personnel: Bryan Drew, Susy Wootton,
Mina Parmar
Specialising in: Actors, Actresses, Writers, Directors,
Voice Overs

## FOREIGN VERSIONS LTD
5 Rostrevor Mews, London SW6 5AZ
Tel: 0171 610 6188
Fax: 0171 610 6189
Email: info@foreignversions.co.uk
Senior Personnel: Jenny Vincent
Provider of professional foreign language services to
the media and communication industries.

## HOBSON'S ARTISTES
62 Chiswick High Road, London W4 1SY
Tel: 0181 747 8326
Fax: 0181 742 1511
Senior Personnel: Gaynor Shaw, Linda Sacks

## LIP SERVICE CASTING LIMITED
4 Kingly Street, London W1R 5LF
Tel: 0171 724 3393
Fax: 0171 734 3373
Email: bookings@lipservice.co.uk
Also a roster of Foreign Artistes. Call for further details.

## ANDREW MANSON
288 Munster Road, London SW6 6BQ
Tel: 0171 386 9158
Fax: 0171 381 8874

Specialising in Actors, Presenters and Voice Over
Artistes.

## MBA
3rd Floor Suite 10-11 Lower John Street,
London W1R 3PE
Tel: 0171 734 3393
Fax: 0171 439 3600
Senior Personnel: Michelle Braidman

## EVANS O'BRIEN
Houstow Garage 115 Humber Road, London SE3 7LW
Tel: 0171 293 7077
Fax: 0171 293 7066
Senior Personnel: Kate Evans, Jo Davidson

## PRESENTER PROMOTIONS
123 Corporation Road, Gillingham, Kent ME7 1RG
Tel: 01634 851077/07000 Presenters
Fax: 01634 316771
Email: presenter-promotions@lineone.net
Senior Personnel: Colin Cobb
Specialising in: Presenters, Speakers,Voice Artistes.
Offering a casting service free to production
companies. Offering help to newcomers and artistes
without an agent.

## RABBIT VOCAL MANAGEMENT
23 Golden Square, London W1R 3PA
Tel: 0171 287 6466
Fax: 0171 281 6566
Senior Personnel: Melanie Bourne

## RHUBARB
Room 41 6 Langley Street, London WC2H 9JA
Tel: 0171 836 1336
Fax: 0171 836 0444
Email: www.rhubarb.mcmail.com
Web Site: www.rhubarb.co.uk
Senior Personnel: Stephen de Montaignac,
Ben Romer Lee

## TALKIES
3 Charlotte Mews, London W1P 1LN
Tel: 0171 323 6883/6993
Specialising in: Voice Overs.

## TALKING HEADS
Eastgate House, 16-19 Eastcastle Street,
London W1N 7PA
Tel: 0171 636 7755
Fax: 0171 636 5757
Email: 106700.3414@compuserve.com
Senior Personnel: Jennifer Taylor, John Sachs
Specialising in: Voice Overs, Atlantic, Character,
Impressionists, Broadcasters, DJ's, Personalities,
Actors, Foreign, Presenters.

## VOICE & SCRIPT INTERNATIONAL
132 Cleveland Street, London W1P 6AB
Tel: 0171 692 7700
Fax: 0171 692 7711
Web Site: www.v-s-i.com
Senior Personnel: Norman Darwood

## VOICE BOX
PO Box 82 Altrincham, Cheshire WA15 0QD
Tel: 0161 928 3222
Fax: 0161 928 7849
Senior Personnel: Vicki Robinson

## VOICE SHOP
Bakerloo Chambers 304 Edgware Road,
London W2 1DY
Tel: 0171 402 3966
Fax: 0171 706 1002
Email: voiceshop@compuserve.com
Senior Personnel: Maxine Wiltshire

## VOICES LTD
Suite 201 29 Great Pulteney Street, London W1R 3DD
Tel: 0171 734 3934
Fax: 0171 287 0064

**PRESS AND PUBLICITY AGENTS**

**PRESS CUTTING AGENCIES**

**THEATRE CRITICS**

**MAJOR NEWSPAPERS**

**LOCAL DAILY PRESS**

**LOCAL WEEKLY PRESS**

**INDEPENDENT TELEVISION**

**BBC TV**

**SATELLITE & CABLE TV**

**BBC RADIO**

**INDEPENDENT LOCAL RADIO**

# Media & Public Relatons

# PRESS CUTTING AGENCIES

## ASSOCIATED PRESS CUTTING SERVICES LTD
26 Aylmer Road, London N2 0BX
Tel: 0181 341 0091 Fax: 0181 348 3927

## THE BROADCAST MONITORING COMPANY UK INTERNATIONAL PRESS
89fi Worship Street, London EC2A 2BE
Tel: 0171 377 1742 Fax: 0171 377 6103

## CXT LTD
The Studio, CXT House, One Tanner Street,
London SE1 3UB
Tel: 0171 378 8139 Fax: 0171 378 8634

## DURRANTS PRESS CUTTINGS LTD
103 Whitecross Street, London EC1Y 8QT
Tel: 0171 588 3671 Fax: 0171 374 8171

## EDS PRESS CUTTINGS
19-23 Ironmonger Row, London EC1V 3QN
Tel: 0171 336 8899 Fax: 0171 336 8877

## INTERNATIONAL PRESS CUTTING BUREAU
224/236 Walworth Road, London SE17 1JE
Tel: 0171 708 2113 Fax: 0171 701 4489

## MCCALLUM MEDIA MONITER
Tower House, 10 Fossil Way, Glasgow G4 9SY
Tel: 0141 333 1822 Fax: 0141 333 1811

## NEWSCUP (UK) LTD
26 Aylmer Road, London N2 0BX
Tel: 0181 341 0091 Fax: 0181 348 3927

## PIMS UK LTD
PIMS House, Mildmay Avenue, London N1 4RS
Tel: 0171 226 1000 Fax: 0171 704 1360

## ROMEIKE & CURTICE LTD
Hale House, 290/296 Green Lane, London N13 5TP
Tel: 0181 882 0155/0800 289543 Fax: 0181 882 6716

# PRESS AND PUBLICITY AGENTS

## ASSASSINATION MUSIC PROMOTIONS
Tudor House, Pinstone Way, Gerrards Cross,
Buckinghamshire SL9 7BJ
Tel/Fax: 01753 8935 Mobile: 0966 256144
Promotions Manager: Rupert Withers

## AVALON PUBLICITY
Queens House, 1 Leicester Place, Leicester Square,
London WC2H 7BP
Tel: 0171 734 6677 Fax: 0171 437 3366

## GEORGE BARTRAM ASSOCIATES
1 Sherbourne Gate, Birmingham B16 8DE
Tel: 0121 608 6000 Fax: 0121 608 2223
Contact: Robert Holmes

## MARK BORKOWSKI PRESS AND PUBLICITY RELATIONS
12 Oval Road, London NW1 7DH
Tel: 0171 482 4000 Fax: 0171 482 5400

## TONY BRAINSBY PUBLICITY LTD
16b Edith Grove, London SW10 0NL
Tel: 0171 834 8341 Fax: 0171 352 9451

## PETER BROOKS ASSOCIATES
162-168 Regent Street, London W1R 5TB
Tel: 0171 734 2955 Fax: 0171 287 5744

## LYNNE BURTON
The Marketing Office: 9 Chiswick High Road,
London W4 2ND
Tel: 0181 994 0066 Fax: 0181 994 4499
Email: tmo@vossnet.co.uk

## CAUSE AND EFFECT MARKETING, PUBLICITY AND DISTRIBUTION
Paddock House, Muddles Green, Chiddingly,
Nr.Lewes, East Sussex BN8 6HS
Tel/Fax: 01825 873188 Mobile: 0850 978482
Flexible distribution company specialising in high
profile poster and leaflet/brochure campaigns dealing
with a large number of prominent theatre and
marketing offices. Operates nationwide.

## GUY CHAPMAN ASSOCIATES
1-2 Henrietta Street, Covent Garden,
London WC2E 8PS
Tel: 0171 379 7474 Fax: 0171 379 8484
Email: chapman@dircon.co.uk
Managing Directors: Guy Chapman
Associates: Matthew Bartlett, Michael Parke, Steven
Drew, Jenny Eldridge, Jonathan Russell &
Ryan Peterson
Press/Marketing/Tour Booking/General Management

## MAX CLIFFORD ASSOCIATES LTD
109 New Bond Street, London W1Y 9AA
Tel: 0171 408 2350 Fax: 0171 409 2294

## CORPORATE PUBLIC RELATIONS LTD
PO Box 12, Haselmere, Surrey GU27 3AH
Tel: 01428 654011 Fax: 01428 651401

## MARTIN J CORRIE
Wembley Stadium Ltd., Wembley HA9 0DW
Tel: 0181 902 8833 Fax: 0181 900 1045

**DENNIS DAVIDSON ASSOCIATES LTD**
Royalty House, 72-74 Dean Street, London W1V 5HB
Tel: 0171 439 6391 Fax: 0171 437 6358
Also in Los Angeles, New York and Sydney

**THE CLIVE DAVIS PARTNERSHIP**
Unit 9 Clyde Works, Clyde Road, Wallington,
Surrey SM6 8PZ
Tel: 0181 669 8268 Fax: 0181 773 4945

**JACKIE ELLIMAN**
5 Dryden Street, London WC2E 9NW
Tel: 0171 829 8465 Fax: 0171 240 5600
Press, marketing and publicity for drama, dance,
music, etc.

**CLIFFORD ELSON (PUBLICITY) LTD**
223 Regent Street, London W1R 7DB
Tel: 0171 495 4012 Fax: 0171 495 4175

**ENGLISH NATIONAL OPERA**
London Coliseum, St Martins Lane,
London WC2N 4ES
Tel: 0171 836 0111 Fax: 0171 497 9052

**IAN GRANT CUMMING PUBLIC RELATIONS**
8 St.Bernards Crescent, Edinburgh EH4 1NP
Tel: 0131 315 2424 Fax: 0131 332 9957

**HARDSELL LIMITED**
52 Thrale Street, London SE1 9HW
Tel: 0171 403 4037 Fax: 0171 403 5381
A specialist arts and entertainments full service agency
providing media planning & buying, marketing, PR,
sales promotion and in-house design and printing.

**HARRISON COWLEY**
154 Great Charles Street, Birmingham B3 3HU
Tel: 0121 236 7532 Fax: 0121 236 7220

**YVONNE I'ANSON PUBLICITY**
4 Penzance House, 2 Seaton Close,
London SE11 4EX
Tel: 0171 582 3172 Fax: 0171 793 1941

**JANET JUDD**
19 De Beauvoir Square, London WC2N 6EF
Tel: 0171 249 0412

**LYNNE KIRWIN ASSOCIATES**
21 Buckingham Street, London WC2N 6EF
Tel: 0171 930 7003 Fax: 0171 930 4226

**LAKE-SMITH GRIFFIN ASSOCIATES**
15 Maiden Lane, Covent Garden, London WC2E 7NA
Tel: 0171 836 1020 Fax: 0171 836 1040

**RICHARD LAVER PUBLICITY**
3 Troy Court, High Street, Kensington,
London W8 7NA
Tel: 0171 937 7322 Fax: 0171 937 8670

**THE MARKETING OFFICE**
9 Chiswick High Road, London W4 2ND
Tel: 0181 994 0066 Fax: 0181 994 4499
Email: tmo@vossnet.co.uk

**MCCABE'S**
36 Lexington Street, London W1R 3HR
Tel: 0171 412 2000 Fax: 0171 412 2030 (Marketing)
Fax: 0171 412 2040 (Advertising)
Contact: Penny Mallinson, Elaine McGowan
With offices in London and New York, the company
provides specialist advertising, marketing and design
services to West End and touring productions, London
and regional venues and theatre companies as well as
marketing services for Broadway productions.

**NAMARA COWAN LTD**
45/46 Poland Street, London W1V 3DF
Tel: 0171 434 3871 Fax: 0171 439 6489

**JAMES PARKER ASSOCIATES**
(Jim Parker - Publicity and Marketing)
67 Richmond Park Road, London SW14 8JY
Tel/Fax: 0181 876 1918

**PUBLIC EYE COMMUNICATIONS LTD**
Suite 318, Plaza, 535 Kings Road, Chelsea,
London SW10 0SZ
Tel: 0171 351 1555 Fax: 0171 351 1010
Email: publiceye@ftech.co.uk
Contact: Judy Kneale, Clara Parkes

**RILEY ADVERTISING LTD**
4 Red Lion Court, Fleet Street, London EC4A 3EN
Tel: 0171 353 3223 Fax: 0171 353 2338

**ROYAL NATIONAL THEATRE**
South Bank, London SE1 9PX
Tel: 0171 928 2033 Fax: 0171 620 2416
Senior Press Representative: Fiona Walsh

**ROYAL OPERA HOUSE**
Covent Garden, London WC2E 9DD
Tel: 0171 240 1200 Fax: 0171 212 9502

**IVOR SPENCER**
President of the Guild of Professional Toastmasters
12 Little Bornes, Dulwich, London SE21 8SE
Tel: 0181 670 5585/8424 Fax: 0181 670 0055

**THEATRE DESPATCH LTD**
Azof Hall, Azof Street, London SE10 0EG
Tel: 0181 853 0750 Fax: 0181 293 4861
Email: admin@theatre.org
Theatre Despatch is a flexible and comprehensive
display service including 3,500 leaflet racks, 4,500
other regularly serviced outlets throughout Greater
London, poster distribution, a complete mailing service
including Mailsort, and a database of 60,000 people
and organisations interested in one or more of the arts
and entertainments.

**PETER THOMPSON ASSOCIATES**
134 Great Portland Street, London W1N 5PH
Tel: 0171 436 5991 Fax: 0171 436 0509

**UNDER-COVER**
Dixies, High Street, Ashwell, Hertforshire SG7 5NT
Tel: 01462 743255 Fax: 01462 743171

**SIMON WHITTAM PUBLICITY**
70 Great Russell Street, London WC1B 3BN
Tel: 0802 416420 Fax: 0171 831 3698
Contact: Simon Whittam
Press and PR Company specialising in the promotion
of stage shows and film and TV personalities.

**FAITH WILSON ARTS PUBLICITY**
Unit 31, Waterside, 44-48 Wharf Road,
London N1 7UX
Tel: 0171 250 3600 Fax: 0171 250 3288

**MAUREEN WINGHAM MIPR**
The Old Forge, 2 Bridge Street, Hadleigh, Suffolk
Tel: 01473 828253/828494 Fax: 01473 828064

# Theatre Critics

| | | |
|---|---|---|
| BIRMINGHAM MAIL | FRED NORRIS | 0121 236 3366 |
| BIRMINGHAM POST | TERRY GRIMLEY | 0121 234 5328 |
| DAILY EXPRESS | ROB GORE-LANGTON | 0171 922 7057 |
| DAILY MAIL | MICHAEL COVENEY | 0171 938 6000 |
| DAILY STAR | NIGEL PAULEY | 0171 928 8000 |
| DAILY TELEGRAPH | CHARLES SPENCER | 0171 538 6413 |
| EDINBURGH EVENING NEWS | JOHN GIBSON | 0131 225 2468 |
| FINANCIAL TIMES | MARTIN HOYLE | 0171 873 3662 |
| GLASGOW DAILY RECORD | KATHLEEN MORGAN | 0141 248 7000 |
| GUARDIAN | MICHAEL BILLINGTON | 0171 278 2332 |
| JEWISH CHRONICLE | DAVID NATHAN | 0181 568 8987 |
| ILLUSTRATED LONDON NEWS | MARGARET DAVIS | 0171 805 5555 |
| INDEPENDENT | PAUL TAYLOR | 0171 293 2017 |
| MANCHESTER EVENING NEWS | ALAN HUGH | 0161 832 7200 |
| MORNING STAR | MIKE PARKER | 0171 254 0033 |
| NEWCASTLE EVEN. CHRONICLE | GORDON BARR | 0191 201 6294 |
| OBSERVER | SUSANNAH CLAPP | 0171 278 2332 |
| OXFORD MAIL | HELEN PEACOCK | 01865 244 988 |
| PLAYS & PLAYERS | VARIOUS | 0181 343 8515 |
| SCOTSMAN | JOYCE MCMILLAN | 0131 225 2468 |
| THE STAGE | VARIOUS | 0171 403 1818 |
| THE STANDARD | NICHOLAS DE JONGH | 0171 938 6780 |
| SUNDAY EXPRESS | JOHN LITTLE | 0171 928 8000 |
| SUNDAY TELEGRAPH | JOHN GROSS | 0171 538 7390 |
| SUNDAY TIMES | JOHN PETER | 0171 782 5000 |
| TIME OUT | JANE EDWARDS/ KATE STRATTEN | 0171 813 3000 |
| TIMES | BENEDICT NIGHTINGDALE | 0171 782 5000 |
| VARIETY | DEREK ELLEY | 0171 520 5222 |
| WHATS ON IN LONDON | SAMANTHA MARLOWE | 0171 278 4393 |
| YORKSHIRE POST | LYNDA MURDON | 01430 827577 |

# LOCAL DAILY PRESS

### YORKSHIRE EVENING POST
(LEEDS)
Yorkshire Post Newspapers, Wellington Street, Leeds,
West Yorkshire LS1 1RF
Tel: 0113 243 2701 Fax: 0113 244 3430

### LINCOLNSHIRE ECHO
(LINCOLN)
8 Brayford Wharf East, Lincoln, Lincolnshire LN5 7AT
Tel: 01522 525252 Fax: 01522 545759

### NORTH WEST EVENING MAIL
(BARROW-IN-FURNESS)
Newpapers House, Abbey Road, Barrow-in-Furness,
Cumbria LA14 5QS
Tel: 01229 821835 Fax: 01229 832141

### THE BATH CHRONICLE
(BATH)
Windsor House, Windsor Bridge, Bath BA2 3AU
Tel: 01225 322306 Fax: 01225 322291
Entertainment Editor: Andrew Knight

### BELFAST TELEGRAPH
(BELFAST)
PO Box 25, 124-132 Royal Avenue, Belfast,
County Antrim BT1 1EB
Tel: 01232 321242 Fax: 01232 554504

### IRISH NEWS
(BELFAST)
113-117 Donegall Street, Belfast,
County Antrim BT1 2GE
Tel: 01232 322226 Fax: 01232 337505

### BIRMINGHAM EVENING MAIL - BIRMINGHAM POST
(BIRMINGHAM)
The Birmingham Post & Mail Ltd PO Box 18,
28 Colmore Circus, Queensway, Birmingham,
West Midlands B4 6AX
Tel: 0121 236 3366 Fax: 0121 233 3958

### LANCASHIRE EVENING TELEGRAPH
(BLACKBURN)
Newspaper House, High Street, Blackburn,
Lancashire BB1 1HT
Tel: 01254 678678 Fax: 01254 680429

### THE GAZETTE
(BLACKPOOL)
Blackpool Gazette & Herald Ltd PO Box 20, Preston
New Road, Blackpool, Lancashire FY4 4AU
Tel: 01253 839999 Fax: 01253 831070
Email: BPL-Editorial@upn.co.uk
Entertainments Editor: Robin Duke

### BOLTON EVENING NEWS
(BOLTON)
Newspaper House, 40 Churchgate, Bolton,
Lancashire BL1 1DE
Tel: 01204 522345 Fax: 01204 385103
Chief Theatre Critic: Doreen Crowther

### THE DAILY ECHO
(BOURNEMOUTH)
Southern Newspapers Plc, Richmond Hill,
Bournemouth, Dorset BH2 6HH
Tel: 01202 554601 Fax: 01202 292115

### BRADFORD STAR
(BRADFORD)
Bradford & District Newspaper Co Ltd PO Box 234,
6 Hall Ings, Bradford, West Yorkshire BD1 1JR
Tel 01274 730000 Fax 01274 393685

### TELEGRAPH & ARGUS
(BRADFORD)
Bradford & District Newspaper Co Ltd PO Box 234, 6
Hall Ings, Bradford, West Yorkshire BD1 1JR
Tel 01274 729511 Tel 01274 723634
Theatre Writer: David Behrens

### EVENING ARGUS
(BRIGHTON)
Crowhurst Road, Brighton East Sussex BN1 8AR
Tel: 01273 544544 Fax: 01273 566114

### BURTON MAIL
(BURTON ON TRENT)
65-68 High Street, Burton-on-Trent,
Staffordshire DE14 1LE
Tel: 01283 512345 Fax: 01283 515351

### CAMBRIDGE EVENING NEWS
(CAMBRIDGE)
Cambridge Newspapers Ltd, Winship Road, Milton,
Cambridge CB4 6PP
Tel: 01223 434434 Fax: 01223 434415
Contact: Kay Toon

### SOUTH WALES ECHO
(CARDIFF)
Western Mail & Echo, Thomson House, Havelock
Street, Cardiff, South Glamorgan CF1 1WR
Tel: 01222 223333 Fax: 01222 583624

### GLOUCESTERSHIRE ECHO
(CHELTENHAM)
Cheltenham Newspaper Co., 1 Clarence Parade,
Cheltenham, Gloucestershire GL50 3NZ
Tel: 01242 271900 Fax: 01242 271848

### EVENING GAZETTE
(COLCHESTER)
Essex County Newspapers Ltd, Oriel House, 43-44
North Hill, Colchester, Essex CO1 1TZ
Tel: 01206 761212 Fax: 01206 715386

## COVENTRY EVENING TELEGRAPH
(COVENTRY)
Corporation Street, Coventry, West Midlands CV1 1FP
Tel: 01203 633633 Fax: 01203 550869

## DERBY EVENING TELEGRAPH
(DERBY)
Derby Evening Telegraph Ltd, Northcliffe House,
Meadow Road, Derby, Derbyshire DE1 2DW
Tel: 01332 291111 Fax: 01332 253027

## EVENING NEWS
(EDINBURGH)
The Scotsman Publications, 20 North Bridge,
Edinburgh, Midlothian EH1 1YT
Tel: 0131 225 2468 Fax: 0131 225 7302

## THE SCOTSMAN
(EDINBURGH)
The Scotsman Publications, 20 North Bridge,
Edinburgh, Midlothian EH1 1YT
Tel: 0131 225 2468 Fax: 0131 226 7420

## GUERNSEY EVENING PRESS & STAR
(GUERNSEY)
Braye Road, Vale, Guernsey GY1 3BW
Tel: 01481 45866 Fax: 01481 48972

## EVENING COURIER
(HALIFAX)
Halifax Courier Ltd, PO Box 19, Kings Cross Street,
Halifax, West Yorkshire HX1 2SF
Tel: 01422 365711 Fax: 01422 330021

## HARTLEPOOL MAIL
(HARTLEPOOL)
Northeast Press Ltd, New Clarence House,
Wesley Square, Hartlepool TS24 8BX
Tel: 01429 274441 Fax: 01429 869024

## HULL DAILY MAIL
(HULL)
PO Box 34, Blundells Corner, Beverley Road, Hull,
East Yorkshire HU3 1XS
Tel: 01482 327111 Fax: 01482 584353

## THE EAST ANGLIAN DAILY TIMES
(IPSWICH)
30 Lower Brook Street, Ipswich, Suffolk IP4 1AN
Tel: 01473 230023 Fax: 01473 211391

## JERSEY EVENING POST
(JERSEY)
PO Box 582 Five Oaks, St.Saviour, Jersey JE4 8XQ
Tel: 01534 611611 Fax: 01534 611622
Email: jepdaily@itl.net

## LANCASHIRE EVENING POST
(LANCASHIRE)
Olivers Place, Fulwood, Preston, Lancashire PR2 9ZA
Tel: 01772 254841 Fax: 01772 563288

## DAILY POST
(LIVERPOOL)
Liverpool Daily Post & Echo, PO Box 48,
Old Hall Street, Liverpool, Merseyside L69 3EB
Tel: 0151 227 2000 Fax: 0151 236 4682
Arts Editor: Phillip Key

## MANCHESTER EVENING NEWS
(MANCHESTER)
164 Deansgate, Manchester M60 2RD
Tel: 0161 832 7200 Fax: 0161 832 5351

## CHRONICLE & ECHO
(NORTHAMPTON)
Northampton Mercury Co Ltd., Upper Mounts,
Northampton NN1 3HR
Tel: 01604 231122 Fax: 01604 233000

## NOTTINGHAM EVENING POST
(NOTTINGHAM)
Nottingham Post Group Ltd., PO Box 99,
Forman Street, Nottingham, Nottinghamshire NG1 4AB
Tel: 0115 948 2000 Fax: 0115 964 4000

## EVENING CHRONICLE
(OLDHAM)
Hirst Kidd & Rennie Ltd., PO Box 47, Oldham,
Lancashire OL1 1EQ
Tel: 0161 633 2121 Fax: 0161 627 0905
Editorial Fax: 0161 652 2111
Web Site: www.oldham-chronicle.co.uk
Arts Theatre Correspondent: Paul Genty

## THE NEWS
(PORTSMOUTH)
Portsmouth & Sunderland Newspapers, The News
Centre, Hilsea, Portsmouth, Hampshire PO2 9SX
Tel: 01705 664488 Fax: 01705 673363
Entertainments Editor: Steve Pratt
Theatre Critic: Mike Allen

## READING EVENING POST
(READING)
8 Tessa Road, Reading, Berkshire RG1 8NS
Tel: 0118 957 5833 Fax: 0118 950 3592

## SHEFFIELD TELEGRAPH
(SHEFFIELD)
York Street, Sheffield, South Yorkshire S1 1PU
Tel: 0114 273 8818 Fax: 0114 276 5153

## THE SOUTHERN DAILY ECHO
(SOUTHAMPTON)
Southern Newspapers Plc., Newspaper House,
Test Lane, Redbridge, Southampton SO16 9JX
Tel: 01703 424777 Fax: 01703 424545

## SENTINEL
(STOKE ON TRENT)
Staffordshire Sentinel Newspapers Ltd., Sentinel
House, Etruria, Stoke-on-Trent ST1 5SS
Tel: 01782 602525 Fax: 01782 602616

## SUNDERLAND ECHO
(SUNDERLAND)
Northeast Press Ltd., Echo House, Pennywell
Industrial Estate, Sunderland SR4 9ER
Tel: 0191 534 3011 Fax: 0191 534 5975

## SOUTH WALES EVENING POST
(SWANSEA)
The Swansea Press Ltd., PO Box 14, Adelaide Street,
Swansea SA1 1QT
Tel: 01792 650841 Fax: 01792 655386

## EVENING ADVERTISER
(SWINDON)
Media in Wessex, 100 Victoria Road, Old Town,
Swindon Wiltshire SN1 3BE
Tel: 01793 528144 Fax: 01793 542434

## HERALD EXPRESS
(TORQUAY)
West Country Publications, Harmsworth House, Barton
Hill Road, Torquay, Devon TQ2 8JN
Tel: 01803 676000 Fax: 01803 676799 (advertising)
01803 676299 (editorial)

## YORKSHIRE EVENING PRESS
(YORK)
PO Box 29, 76-86 Walmgate, York North
Yorkshire YO1 1YN
Tel: 01904 653051 Fax: 01904 612853

# LOCAL WEEKLY PRESS

## ADSCENE KENT NEWSPAPERS
12 New Road Avenue, Chatham, Kent ME4 6AT
Tel: 01634 841741 Fax: 01634 400477 Accounts
Department: Westcliff House, West Cliff Gardens,
Folkestone, Kent CT20 1SZ Tel: 01303 850999
Fax: 01303 850618

## BEDFORDSHIRE TIMES GROUP
66 High Street, Bedford, Bedfordshire MK40 1NT
Tel: 01234 363101 Fax: 01234 325721

## BERROWS WORCESTER JOURNAL
Hylton Road, Worcester WR2 5JX
Tel: 01905 748200 Fax: 01905 748213 (advertising)
Fax: 01905 748009 (editorial)

## BOLTON EVENING NEWS
Newspaper House, 40 Churchgate, Bolton,
Lancashire BL1 1DE
Tel: 01204 522345 Fax: 01204 365068

## BRISTOL EVENING NEWS
Temple Way, Bristol BS90 7HD
Tel: 0117 934 3000 Fax: 0117 934 3575

## BUCKS & HERTS NEWSPAPER GROUP
2-4 Exchange Street, Aylesbury,
Buckinghamshire HP20 1UJ

Tel: 01296 244444 Fax: 01296 393451

## CAMBRIDGE EVENING NEWS
(CAMBRIDGE)
Cambridge Newspapers Ltd, Winship Road, Milton,
Cambridge CB4 6PP
Tel: 01223 434434 Fax: 01223 434415
Contact: Kay Toon

## CUMBRIAN NEWSPAPERS
Newspaper House, Dalston Road, Carlisle,
Cumbria CA2 5UA
Tel: 01228 234488 Fax: 01228 594088
Arts Editor: Elizabeth Kay

## EAST LANCASHIRE NEWSPAPERS LTD
Bull Street, Burnley, Lancashire BB11 1DP
Tel: 01282 426161 Fax: 01282 435332
Web Site: www.eastlancsnews.co.uk

## ESSEX COUNTY NEWSPAPERS
Oriel House, 43-44 North Hill, Colchester,
Essex CO1 1TZ
Tel: 01206 715346 Fax: 01206 769523

## FIFE FREE PRESS GROUP
PO Box 3, Kirk Wynd, Kirkcaldy, Fife KY1 1EP
Tel: 01592 261451 Fax: 01592 204180

## GLOUCESTERSHIRE COUNTY GAZETTE SERIES
Reliance House, Long Street, Dursley,
Gloucestershire GL11 4LS
Tel: 01453 544000 Fax: 01453 544577

## GREATER LONDON & ESSEX NEWSPAPERS GROUP
2 Whalebone Lane South, Dagenham,
Essex RM8 1HB
Tel: 0181 517 5577 Fax: 0181 592 7407

## HIGHLAND NEWS GROUP
13 Henderson Road, Inverness, IV1 1SP
Tel: 01463 713709 Fax: 01463 221251

## KENT MESSENGER GROUP NEWSPAPERS
Suite 12, Chancery House, Chancery Lane,
London WC2A 1QX
Tel: 0171 404 6116 Fax: 0171 404 6345

## LINCOLNSHIRE STANDARD PRESS GROUP
Newspaper Centre, Redstone Road, Boston,
Lincolnshire BE21 8EA
Tel: (Head Office) 01205 311433 Fax: (Head Office)
01205 359827

## LONDON NEWSPAPER GROUP
Newspaper House, Winslow Road, London W6 9SF
Tel: 0181 741 1622 Fax: 0181 741 1973
Arts Editor: James Ellis

**NORTH HERTS GAZETTE SERIES**
16-18 Market Place, Hitchin, Hertforshire SG5 1DS
Tel: 01462 422280 Fax: 01462 436384

**NORTH LONDON NEWSPAPERS**
161 Tottenham Lane, London N8 9BU
Tel: 0181 340 6868 Fax: 0181 340 6577

**NORTHEAST PRESS LTD**
PO Box 4, Chapter Row, South Shields,
Tyne and Wear NE33 1BL
Tel: 0191 455 4661 Fax: 0191 456 8270

**OXFORD & COUNTY NEWSPAPERS**
Osney Mead, Oxford, Oxfordshire OX2 0EJ
Tel: 01865 244988 Fax: 01865 243382
Head of Arts and Entertainments: Christopher Gray

**PACKET NEWSPAPERS (CORNWALL) LTD**
Ponsharden, Farnworth, Cornwall TR10 8AP
Tel: 01326 373791 Fax: 01326 373887

**READING & BERKSHIRE NEWSPAPER**
50-56 Portman Road, Reading, Berkshire RG30 1BA
Tel: 0118 950 3030 Fax: 0118 939 1619

**SCOTTISH & UNIVERSAL NEWSPAPERS LTD**
40 Upper Craigs, Stirling, Stirlingshire FK8 2DW
Tel: 01786 448855 Fax: 01786 459470

**SURREY ADVERTISER GROUP**
PO Box 20, Martyr Road, Guildford, Surrey GU1 4LQ
Tel: 01483 571234 Fax: 01483 301271

**SURREY AND SUSSEX NEWSPAPERS**
Trinity House, 51 London Road, Reigate,
Surrey RH2 9PR
Tel: 01737 732000 Fax: 01737 732267 (editorial) Fax:
01737 732001 (advertising)

**SURREY COMET & GUARDIAN**
26 York Street, Twickenham, Middlesex TW1 3LJ
Tel: 0181 744 9977 Fax: 0181 744 1748

**YORKSHIRE POST NEWSPAPERS**
PO Box 168, Wellington Street, Leeds,
West Yorkshire LS1 1RF
Tel: 0113 243 2701 Fax: 0113 244 3430

# MAJOR NEWSPAPERS

**DAILY EXPRESS**
Express Newspapers plc Ludgate House, 245
Blackfriars Road, London SE1 9UX
Tel 0171 928 8000 Fax 0171 633 0244

**DAILY MAIL**
Evening Standard Co Ltd, Northcliffe House, 2 Derry
Street, London W8 5TT

Tel 0171 938 6000 Fax 0171 937 3251/3745

**DAILY MIRROR**
Mirror Group Newspapers, 1 Canada Square,
Canary Wharf, London E14 5AP
Tel: 0171 293 3000 Fax: 0171 293 3405

**DAILY STAR**
Express Newspapers, Ludgate House, 245
Blackfriars Road, London SE1 9UX
Tel: 0171 928 8000 Fax: 0171 633 0244

**DAILY TELEGRAPH**
Telegraph Group Ltd, 1 Canada Square,
London E14 5DT
Tel: 0171 538 5000 Fax: 0171 528 6242

**EVENING STANDARD**
Northcliffe House, 2 Derry Street, London W8 5EE
Tel: 0171 938 6000 Fax: 0171 937 3745

**FINANCIAL TIMES**
1 Southwark Bridge, London SE1 9HL
Tel: 0171 873 3000 Fax: 0171 873 3062

**THE GUARDIAN**
119 Farringdon Road, London EC1R 3ER
Tel: 0171 278 2332 Fax: 0171 837 2114

**JEWISH CHRONICLE**
25 Furnival Street, London EC4A 1JT
Tel: 0171 415 1616 Fax: 0171 405 9040
Theatre Critic: David Nathan

**THE MAIL ON SUNDAY**
Evening Standard Co Ltd, Northcliffe House,
2 Derry Street, London W8 5TS
Tel: 0171 938 6000 Fax: 0171 937 3251/3214/3745

**THE MORNING STAR**
1-3 Ardleigh Road, London N1 4HS
Tel: 0171 254 0033 Fax: 0171 254 5950

**NEWS OF THE WORLD**
News Group Newspapers Ltd, 1 Virginia Street,
London E1 9BD
Tel: 0171 782 4000 Fax: 0171 782 4463

**THE OBSERVER**
119 Farringdon Road, London EC1R 3ER
Tel: 0171 713 4221 Fax: 0171 713 4225

**THE PEOPLE**
Mirror Group Newspapers, 1 Canada Square,
Canary Wharf, London E14 5AP
Tel: 0171 293 3000 Fax: 0171 293 3405

**THE SUN**
PO Box 489, London E1 9BD
Tel: 0171 782 7000 Fax: 0171 782 5605

**THE SUNDAY EXPRESS**
Express Newspapers plc, Ludgate House,
245 Blackfriars Road, London SE1 9UX
Tel: 0171 928 8000 Fax: 0171 633 0244

**SUNDAY SPORT**
Sports Newpapers, 19 Great Ancoats Street,
Manchester M60 4BT
Tel: 0161 236 4466 Fax: 0161236 4535

**THE SUNDAY TELEGRAPH**
Telegraph Group Ltd, 1 Canada Square,
Canary Wharf, London E14 5DT
Tel: 0171 538 5000 Fax: 0171 538 6242

**THE TIMES**
News International Ltd, 1 Virginia Street,
London E1 9BD
Tel: 0171 782 5000 Fax: 0171 782 5988

# BBC LOCAL RADIO

**BBC COVENTRY & WARWICKSHIRE**
25 Warwick Road, Coventry CV1 2WR
Tel: 01203 559911 Fax: 01203 520080
Senior Producer: Conal O'Donnell

**BBC ESSEX**
PO Box 765, Chelmsford, Essex CM2 9XB
Tel: 01245 262393 Fax: 01245 490703
Managing Director: Margaret Hyde

**BBC GLR**
35c Marylebone High Street, London W1A 4LG
Tel: 0171 224 2424 Fax: 0171 487 2908
Manager: Steve Panton

**BBC GMR**
PO Box 951, Oxford Road, Manchester M60 1SD
Tel: 0161 200 2000 Fax: 0161 228 6110
Editor: Karen Hannah

**BBC HEREFORD & WORCESTER**
43 Broad Street, Hereford, Herefordshire HR4 9HH
Tel: 01432 355252 Fax: 01432 356446
Senior Producer: Russell Merryman

**BBC ORKNEY**
Castle Street, Kirkwall, Orkney KW15 1DF
Tel: 01856 873939 Fax: 01856 872908
Senior Producer: John Ferguson

**BBC RADIO BRISTOL**
Whiteladies Road, Bristol BS8 2LR
Tel: 0117 743 2211 Fax: 0117 974 2319
Manager: Michael Hapgood

**BBC RADIO CAMBRIDGESHIRE**
104 Hills Road, PO Box 96, Cambridge,
Cambridgeshire CB2 1LD
Tel: 01223 259696 Fax: 01223 460832
Editor: Nigel Dyson

**BBC RADIO CLEVELAND**
PO Box 95, Newport Road, Broadcasting House,
Middlesborough, Cleveland TS1 5DG
Tel: 01642 225211 Fax: 01642 211356
Editor: David Peel

**BBC RADIO CORNWALL**
Phoenix Wharf, Truro, Cornwall TR1 1UA
Tel: 01872 75421 Fax: 01872 75045
Manager: Leo Devine

**BBC RADIO CUMBRIA**
Annetwell Street, Carlisle, Cumbria CA3 8BB
Tel: 01228 592444 Fax: 01228 511195
Managing Editor: John Watson

**BBC RADIO DERBY**
56 St.Helens Street, PO Box 269, Derby DE1 3HL
Tel: 01332 361111 Fax: 01332 290794
Manager: Mike Dettison

**BBC RADIO DEVON**
PO Box 5, Plymouth, Devon PL3 5YQ
Tel: 01752 260323 Fax: 01752 234990
Manager: Bob Bufton

**BBC RADIO GLOUCESTERSHIRE**
Portland Court, London Road, Gloucester,
Gloucestershire GL1 1SW
Tel: 01452 308585 Fax: 01452 309491
Manager: Jenny Lacey

**BBC RADIO GUERNSEY**
Commerce House, Les Banques, St.Peter Port,
Guernsey GY1 2HS
Tel: 01481 728977 Fax: 01481 713557
Manager: Bob Lloyd Smith

**BBC RADIO HUMBERSIDE**
9 Chapel Street, Hull HU1 3NU
Tel: 01482 323232 Fax: 01482 326038
Email: radio.humberside@bbc.co.uk
Managing Editor: John Lilley
Assistant Editor: Barrie Stephenson

**BBC RADIO JERSEY**
18 Parade Road, St.Hellier, Jersey JE2 3PL
Tel: 01534 87000 Fax: 01534 32569
Manager: Bob Lloyd Smith

**BBC RADIO KENT**
Sun Pier, Medway Street, Chatham, Kent ME4 4EZ
Tel: 01634 830505 Fax: 01634 830573
Manager: David Farwig

**BBC RADIO LANCASHIRE**
Darwen Street, Blackburn, Lancashire BB2 2EA
Tel: 01254 841025/262411 Fax: 01254 680821
Arts Editor: Jacquie Williams, PO Box 339,
Liverpool, L69 3TR
Pager: 01523 437315

**BBC RADIO LEEDS**
Broadcasting House, Woodhouse Lane, Leeds,
West Yorkshire LS2 9PX
Tel: 0113 244 2131 Fax: 0113 242 0652

**BBC RADIO LEICESTER**
Epic House, Charles Street, Leicester, LE1 3SH
Tel: 0116 251 6688 Fax: 0116 2513632
Manager: Liam McCarthy

**BBC RADIO LINCOLNSHIRE**
PO Box 219, Radion Buildings, Newport, Lincoln,
Lincolnshire LN1 3XY
Tel: 01522 511411 Fax: 01522 511058
Manager: David Wilkinson

**BBC RADIO MERSEYSIDE**
55 Paradise Street, Liverpool L1 3BP
Tel: 0151 708 5500 Fax: 0151 794 0988
Managing Editor: Mick Ord

**BBC RADIO NEWCASTLE**
Broadcasting Centre, Newcastle-upon-Tyne,
Tyne and Wear NE99 1RN
Tel: 0191 232 4141 Fax: 0191 232 5082
Managing Editor: Tony Fish

**BBC RADIO NORFOLK**
Norfolk Tower, Surrey Street, Norwich,
Norfolk NR1 3PA
Tel: 01603 617411 Fax: 01603 633692
Manager: Tim Bishop

**BBC RADIO NORTHAMPTON**
Broadcasting House, Abington Street, Northampton,
Northamptonshire NN1 2BH
Tel: 01604 239100 Fax: 01604 230709
Manager: Claire Paul

**BBC RADIO NOTTINGHAM**
York House, Mansfield Road, Nottingham,
Nottinghamshire NG1 3JB
Tel: 0115 955 0500 Fax: 0115 955 0501
Manager: Peter Hagan

**BBC RADIO SCOTLAND**
Broadcasting House, Queen Margaret Drive,
Glasgow G12 8DG
Tel: 0141 338 2000 Fax: 0141 334 0614

**BBC RADIO SCOTLAND (BORDERS)**
High Street, Selkirk, Selkirkshire TD7 4BU
Tel: 01750 21884 Fax: 01750 22400
Producer: Carol Whiteman

**BBC RADIO SHEFFIELD**
Ashdell Grove, 60 Westbourne Road, Sheffield,
South Yorkshire S10 2QU
Tel: 0114 268 6185 Fax: 0114 266 4375
Managing Editor: Barry Stockdale

**BBC RADIO SHROPSHIRE**
2-4 Boscobel Drive, PO Box 397, Shrewsbury,
Shropshire SY1 3TT
Tel: 01743 284484 Fax: 01743 271702
Managing Editor: Barbara Taylor

**BBC RADIO SOLENT**
Broadcasting House, 10 Havelock Road,
Southampton, Hampshire SO14 7PW
Tel: 01703 631311 Fax: 01703 339648
Managing Editor: Chris Van Schaick

**BBC RADIO STOKE**
Cheapside, Stoke-on-Trent, Staffordshire ST1 1JJ
Tel: 01782 208080 Fax: 01782 289115
Managing Editor: Phil Ashworth

**BBC RADIO SUFFOLK**
St.Matthews Street, Ipswich, Suffolk IP1 3EP
Tel: 01473 250000 Fax: 01473 210887
Managing Editor: Ivan Howlett

**BBC RADIO THAMES VALLEY F.M.**
(incorporating BBC Radio Berkshire & Oxford)
269 Banbury Road, Oxford OX2 7DW
Tel: 01645 311444 Fax: 01645 311555
Managing Editor: Steve Eggington

**BBC RADIO ULSTER**
BBC Broadcasting House, Belfast B2 8HQ
Tel: 01232 338000 Fax: 01232 338800

**BBC RADIO WALES & RADIO CYMRU**
Broadcasting House, Llantrisant Road, Llandaff,
Cardiff, South Glamorgan CF5 2YQ
Tel: 01222 572888 Fax: 01222 552973
Senior Producer: Nick Evans

**BBC RADIO WM**
Pebble Mill Road, PO Box 206, Birmingham,
West Midlands B5 7SD
Tel: 0121 414 8484 Fax: 0121 472 3174
Manager: Peter Davies

**BBC RADIO YORK**
20 Bootham Row, York YO3 7BR
Tel: 01904 641351 Fax: 01904 610937
Web Site: radio.york.bbc.co.uk
Acting Editor: Jane Sampson

**BBC SHETLAND**
Brentham House, Fort Road, Lerwick,
Shetland Isles ZE1 0LR
Tel: 01595 694747 Fax: 01595 694307

## BBC SOLWAY
Elmbank, Lovers Walk, Dumfries,
Dumfriesshire DG1 1NZ
Tel: 01387 268008 Fax: 01387 252560
Editor: Willy Johnson

## BBC SOUTHERN COUNTIES RADIO
Broadcasting Centre, Guildford, Surrey GU2 5AP
Tel: 01483 306306 Fax: 01483 304952
Managing Editor: Mark Thomas
Contact for Press Releases: News Editor

## BBC THREE COUNTIES RADIO
PO Box 3cr, Hastings Street, Luton,
Bedfordshire LU1 5XL
Tel: 01582 441000 Fax: 01582 401467
Managing Editor: David Robey

## BBC WILTSHIRE SOUND
Broadcasting House, Prospect Place, Swindon,
Wiltshire SN1 3RW
Tel: 01793 513626 Fax: 01793 513650
Managing Editor: Sandy Milne

## COMMUNITY AND AREA STATIONS BBC HIGHLAND
7 Culduthel Road, Inverness, Invernesshire IV2 4AD
Tel: 01463 720720 Fax: 01463 236125
Managing Editor: Ishbel McLennan

## RADIO FOYLE
8 Northland Road, Londonderry,
County Derry BT48 7JD Northern Ireland
Tel: 01504 262244 Fax: 01504 378666

## RADIO NAN GAIDHEAL
Rosebank, Church Street, Stornoway HS1 2LF
Tel: 01851 705000 Fax: 01851 704633

## RADION NAN GAIDHEAL BBC SCT
Clydsdale Bank Buildings, Somerfield Square, Portree,
Isle of Skye IV51 9EH
Tel: 01478 612005 Fax: 01478 612792

# BBC NATIONAL RADIO

## BBC RADIO 1,2,3,4,5
Broadcasting House, Portland Place,
London W1A 1AA
Tel: 0171 580 4468 Fax: 0171 637 1360

## BBC WORLD SERVICE DRAMA
Room 636, Broadcasting House, London W1A 1AA
Tel: 0171 240 3456 Fax: 0171 497 0287
Email: Gordon.House@bbc.co.uk
Executive Producer: Gordon House

# INDEPENDENT LOCAL RADIO

## 2 TEN FM
PO Box 210, Reading, Berkshire RG31 7RZ
Tel: 01189 254400 Fax: 01189 254456
Programme Controller: Andrew Phillips

## 2CR FM + CLASSIC GOLD 828
5-7 Southcote Road, Bournemouth, Dorset BH1 3LR
Tel: 01202 259259 Fax: 01202 255244

## 96.3 LIBERTY
26-27 Castlereagh Street, London W1H 6DJ
Tel: 0171 963 0963 Fax: 0171 706 0963

## 96.7 BCR
Russell Court, Claremont Street, Belfast BT9 6JX
Northern Ireland
Tel: 01232 438500 Fax: 01232 230505

## 96.9 VIKING FM
Commercial Road, Hull, East Yorkshire HU1 2SG
Tel: 01482 325141 Fax: 01482 587067

## B97 + SUPERGOLD
55 Goldington Road, Bedford, Bedfordshire MK40 3LS
Tel: 01234 272400 Fax: 01234 325137

## BEACON RADIO & RADIO WABC
PO Box 303, 267 Tettenhall Road,
Wolverhampton WV6 0DQ
Tel: 01902 757211 Fax: 01902 838266
New Editor: Tony Attwater

## BRMB FM
PO Box 555, Radio House, Aston Road, Birmingham,
West Midlands B6 4BX
Tel: 0121 359 4481 Fax: 0121 359 1117

## BROADLAND 102
47-49 Colegate, Norwich, Norfolk NR3 1DB
Tel: 01603 630621 Fax: 01603 666252

## CAPITAL FM
30 Leicester Square, London WC2H 7LA
Tel: 0171 766 6000 Fax: 0171 766 6100

## CAPITAL GOLD
30 Leicester Square, London WC2H 7LA
Tel: 0171 766 6000 Fax: 0171 766 6100

## CENTRAL FM
Stirling Enterprise Park, Stirling, Stirlingshire FK7 7YJ
Tel: 01786 451188 Fax: 01786 461883

## CHILTERN FM
Chiltern Road, Dunstable, Bedfordshire LU6 1HQ

Tel: 01582 666001 Fax: 01582 661725
Programme Controller: Trevor James

### CLASSIC FM
Academic House, 24-28 Oval Road, London NW1 7DQ
Tel: 0171 284 3000 Fax: 0171 713 2630

### CLYDE 1FM
Clydebank, Dumbartonshire G81 2RX
Tel: 0141 306 2200 Fax: 0141 306 2301

### CLYDE 2
Clydebank, Dumbartonshire G81 2RX
Tel: 0141 306 2200 Fax: 0141 306 2302

### COOL FM
PO Box 974, Belfast, Co.Antrim BT1 1RT
Tel: 01247 817181 Fax: 01247 814974
Email: music@coolfm.co.uk
Web Site: www.coolfm.co.uk

### DOWNTOWN RADIO
Kiltonga Industrial Estate, Newtownards,
Co.Down BT23 4ES
Tel: 01247 815555 Fax: 01247 818913
Email: programmes@downtown.co.uk
Web Site: www.downtown.co.uk

### ESSEX FM/BREEZE
20 Cliftown Road, Southend-on-Sea SS1 1SX
Tel: 01702 333711 Fax: 01702 345224

### FORTH
13-17 Forth Street, Edinburgh EH1 3LF
Tel: 0131 556 9255 Fax: 0131 558 3277

### FOX FM
Brush House, Pony Road, Cowley, Oxford OX4 2XR
Tel: 01865 871000 Fax: 01865 748721

### GALAXY 101
25 Portland Square, Bristol BS2 8RZ
Tel: 0117 924 0111 Fax: 0117 924 5589
Station Director: Steven Parkinson

### GEM AM
29-31 Castle Gate, Nottingham,
Nottinghamshire NG1 7AP
Tel: 0115 952 7000 Fax: 0115 958 5087

### GREAT NORTH (GNR)
(owned by EMAP Radio plc)
Radio House, Long Rigg,
Newcastle upon Tyne NE99 1BB
Tel: 0191 420 3040 Fax: 0191 488 9222

### GWR FM
PO Box 2000, Bristol BS99 7SN
Tel: 0117 984 3200 Fax: 0117 984 3205

### HEART 106.2
The Chrysalis Group, Chrysalis Building,
13 Bramley Road, London W10 6SP
Tel: 0171 468 1062 Fax: 0171 470 1062

### INVICTA FM
Radio House, John Wilson Business Park, Whitstable,
Kent CT5 3QX
Tel: 01227 772004 Fax: 01227 771558
Web Site: www.invictafm.com

### INVICTA SUPERGOLD
Radio House, John Wilson Business Park, Whitstable,
Kent CT5 3QX
Tel: 01227 772004 Fax: 01227 771558

### JAZZ FM 102.2
26-27 Castlereagh Street, London W1H 6DJ
Tel: 0171 706 4100 Fax: 0171 723 9742

### KCBC AM
PO Box 1584, Robinson Close, Telford Way Industrial
Estate, Kettering, Northamptonshire NN16 8PU
Tel: 01536 412413 Fax: 01536 517390
Programme Controller: Paul Thompson

### KEY 103
The Piazza, Piccadilly Plaza, Manchester M1 4AW
Tel: 0161 236 9913 Fax: 0161 228 1503

### KISS 100
80 Holloway Road, London N7 8JG
Tel: 0171 700 6100 Fax: 0171 700 3979

### LONDON NEWS RADIO
Comprising LBC 1152AM & News Direct 97.3FM
200 Gray's Inn Road, London WC1X 8XZ
Tel: 0171 312 8530 News Direct Fax: 0171 312 8470
LBC Fax: 0171 973 8832

### LUXEMBOURG ( LONDON)
74 Newman Street, London W1P 3LA
Tel: 0171 436 6363 Fax: 0171 436 4017

### MANX
Broadcasting House, PO Box 1368,
Isle of Man IM99 1SW
Tel: 01624 682600 Fax: 01624 682604
Email: postbox@manxradio.com
Web Site: www.manxradio.com
Managing Director: Stewart Watterson
Programme Manager: George Ferguson

### MELODY FM
180 Brompton Road, London SW3 1HF
Tel: 0171 581 1054 Fax: 0171 581 7000
Managing Director: Sheila Porritt

### MERCURY FM & MERCURY EXTRA AM
Broadfield House, Brighton Road, Crawley,
West Sussex RH11 9TT
Tel: 01293 519161 Fax: 01293 403591

**THE NEW 96.3 AIRE FM**
PO Box 2000, 51 Burley Road, Leeds,
West Yorkshire LS3 1LR
Tel: 0113 245 2299 Fax: 0113 242 1830

**PICCADILLY 1152**
Castlequay, Manchester
Tel: 0161 236 9913 Fax: 0161 228 1503
Programme Director: John Dash

**PLYMOUTH SOUND**
Earls Acre, Plymouth, Devon PL3 4HX
Tel: 01752 227272 Fax: 01752 670730

**THE PULSE**
Penine House, Forster Square, Bradford,
West Yorkshire BD1 5NE
Tel: 01274 731521 Fax: 01274 392031

**Q103**
PO Box 103, The Vision Histon, Cambridge CB4 4WW
Tel: 01223 235255 Fax: 01223 233161
Email: CRAIG@Q103.musicradio.com
Programme Controller: Craig Morris

**RADIO BORDERS**
Tweedside Park, Tweedbank, Galashiels,
Selkirkshire TD1 3TD
Tel: 01896 759444 Fax: 01896 759494

**RADIO CITY GOLD**
PO Box 1548, Liverpool L69 7DQ
Tel: 0151 227 5100 Fax: 0151 471 0330

**RAM FM**
Market Place, Derby, Derbyshire DE1 3AA
Tel: 01332 292945 Fax: 01332 292229

**RED ROSE GOLD/ROCK FM**
PO Box 301, St.Pauls Square, Preston,
Lancashire PR1 1YE
Tel: 01772 556301 Fax: 01772 201917

**ROYAL 945FM - LIVERPOOL**
PO Box 845, Liverpool L69 7QB
Tel/Fax: 0151 702125
Contact: Rachel Williams

**SCOT FM**
No 1 Shed, Albert Quay, Leith EH6 7DN
Tel: 0131 554 6677 Fax: 0131 554 2266

**SEVERN SOUND**
Old Talbot House, Southgate Street, Gloucester,
Gloucestershire GL1 2DQ
Tel: 01452 423791 Fax: 01452 529446

**SIBC**
Market Street, Lerwick, Shetland ZE1 0JN
Tel: 01595 695299 Fax: 01595 695696

**SIGNAL CHESHIRE**
Regent House, Heaton Lane, Stockport,
Cheshire SK4 1BX
Tel: 0161 480 5445 Fax: 0161 474 1806

**SIGNAL ONE**
Stoke Road, Stoke-on-Trent, Staffordshire ST4 2SR
Tel: 01782 855866 Fax: 01782 747777
Email: general@signalradio.com
Web Site: www.signalradio.com

**SIGNAL RADIO**
Stoke Road, Stoke-on-Trent, Staffordshire ST4 2SR
Tel: 01782 747047 Fax: 01782 855866
Email: general@signalradio.com
Web Site: www.signalradio.com

**SIGNAL TWO**
Stoke Road, Stoke-on-Trent, Staffordshire ST4 2SR
Tel: 01782 855866 Fax: 01782 747777
Email: general@signalradio.com
Web Site: www.signalradio.com

**SOUND WAVE (96.4)**
Victoria Road, Gowerton, Swansea,
West Glamorgan SA4 3AB
Tel: 01792 430111 Fax: 01792 511965

**SOUTH COAST**
PO Box 2000, Brighton BN41 2SS
Tel: 01273 430111 Fax: 01273 424783

**SOUTH WEST SOUND**
Campbell House, Bankend Road, Brasswells,
Dumfries, Dumfriesshire DG1 4PH
Tel: 01387 250999 Fax: 01387 265629

**SOUTHERN FM**
PO Box 2000, Brighton, East Sussex BN41 2SS
Tel: 01273 430111 Fax: 01273 430098

**SPECTRUM RADIO**
80 Silverthorne Road, Battersea, London SW8 3XA
Tel: 0171 627 4433 Fax: 0171 627 3409

**SUNRISE RADIO**
Sunrise House, 30 Chapel Street, Bradford,
West Yorkshire BD1 5DN
Tel: 01274 735043 Fax: 01274 728534

**SWANSEA SOUND (1170AM)**
Victoria Road, Gowerton, Swansea,
West Glamorgan SA4 3AB
Tel: 01792 511170 Fax: 01792 511171

**TALK RADIO**
76 Oxford Street, London W1N 0TR
Tel: 0171 636 1089 Fax: 0171 636 1053

**TAY**
PO Box 123, Dundee, Angus DD1 9UF

Tel: 01382 200800/593200 Fax: 01382 593252

**TEN 17**
Essex Radios Plc., Latton Bush Business Centre,
Southern Way, Harlow, Essex CM18 7BU
Tel: 01279 432415 Fax: 01279 445289

**TFM**
Radio House, Yale Crescent, Thornaby, Stockton-on-
Tees, Cleveland TS17 6AA
Tel: 01642 615111 Fax: 01642 674402

**TOUCH RADIO**
Radio House, PO Box 99, Cardiff,
South Glamorgan CF1 5YJ
Tel: 0115 952 7000 Fax: 0115 958 5087

**TRENT FM**
29-31 Castle Gate, Nottingham NG1 7AP
Tel: 0115 952 7000 Fax: 0115 958 5087

**VIRGIN RADIO**
1 Golden Square, London W1R 4DJ
Tel: 0171 434 1215 Fax: 0171 434 1197

**WEAR FM**
Forster Building, Sunderland University, Chester Road,
Sunderland, Tyne and Wear SR1 3SD
Tel: 0191 515 2103 Fax: 0191 515 2270

**WEST SOUND**
Radio House, 54 Holmston Road, Ayr,
Ayrshire KA7 3BE
Tel: 01292 283662 Fax: 01292 283665

**WEST SOUND**
Campbell House, Bankend Road, Dumfries,
Dumfriesshire DG1 4TH
Tel: 01387 250999 Fax: 01387 265629

**WYVERN**
5-6 Barbourne Terrace, Worcester,
Worcestershire WR1 3JZ
Tel: 01905 612212 Fax: 01905 612849

# BBC TV STATIONS

**BBC ABERDEEN**
Broadcasting House, Beechgrove Terrace,
Aberdeen AB15 5ZT
Tel: 01224 625233 Fax: 01224 642931

**BBC BRISTOL & BBC WEST**
Broadcasting House, Whiteladies Road,
Bristol BS8 2LR
Tel: 0117 973 2211 Fax: 0117 974 1537

**BBC EAST**
All Saints Green, Norwich, Norfolk NR1 3ND

Tel: 01603 619331 Fax: 01603 667865

**BBC EAST MIDLANDS**
York House, Nottingham, Nottinghamshire NG1 3JB
Tel: 0115 955 0500 Fax: 0115 955 0552

**BBC EDINBURGH**
5 Queen Street, Edinburgh, Midlothian EH2 1JF
Tel: 0131 225 3131 Fax: 0131 469 4220

**BBC MIDLANDS**
British Broadcasting Corp., Pebble Mill Road,
Birmingham, West Midlands B5 7QQ
Tel: 0121 414 8888 Fax: 0121 414 8634

**BBC NORTH**
New Broadcasting House, PO Box 27, Oxford Road,
Manchester M60 1SJ
Tel: 0161 233 2020 Fax: 0161 236 1005

**BBC NORTHERN IRELAND**
Broadcasting House, Ormeau Avenue, Belfast,
Co.Antrim BT2 8HQ Northern Ireland
Tel: 01232 338000 Fax: 01232 338800

**BBC SCOTLAND**
Broadcasting House, Queen Margaret Drive,
Glasgow G12 8DG
Tel: 0141 339 8844 Fax: 0141 334 0614

**BBC SOUTH & EAST**
Elstree Centre, Clarendon Road, Borehamwood,
Hertfordshire WD6 1JF
Tel: 0181 953 6100 Fax: 0181 207 0657

**BBC SOUTH WEST**
Broadcasting House, Seymour Road, Plymouth,
Devon PL3 5BD
Tel: 01752 229201 Fax: 01752 234595

**BBC TELEVISION (LEEDS)**
Television Centre, Woodhouse Lane, Leeds,
West Yorkshire LS2 9PX
Tel: 0113 244 1188 Fax: 0113 243 9387

**BBC TELEVISION (NEWCASTLE)**
Broadcasting Centre, PO Box 2NE, Barrack Road,
Newcastle-upon-Tyne, Tyne and Wear NE99 2NE
Tel: 0191 232 1313 Fax: 0191 221 0112

**BBC TV**
Union House, 65-69 Shepherds Bush Green,
London W12 8TX
Tel: 0181 743 8000 Fax: 0181 740 9680

**BBC TV SOUTH**
Broadcasting House, Havelock Road,
Southampton SO14 7PU
Tel: 01703 226201 Fax: 01703 339931

**BBC WALES**
Broadcasting House, Llantrisant Road, Llandaff,
Cardiff, South Glamorgan CF5 2YQ
Tel: 01222 572888 Fax: 01222 552973

# INDEPENDENT TELEVISION

**ANGLIA TELEVISION LTD**
Anglia House, Agricultural Hall Plain, Norwich,
Norfolk NR1 3JG
Tel: 01603 615151 Fax: 01603 631032

**BORDER TELEVISION LTD**
Television Centre, Brunel Way, Durranhill Industrial
Estate, Carlisle, Cumbria CA1 3NT
Tel: 01228 25401 Fax: 01228 41384

**CARLTON TELEVISION**
101 St.Martin's Lane, London WC2N 4AZ
Tel: 0171 240 4000 Fax: 0171 240 4171

**CENTRAL BROADCASTING**
Central House, Broad Street, Birmingham
West Midlands B1 2JP
Tel: 0121 643 9898 Fax: 0121 634 4957

**CHANNEL FOUR TV CO. LTD.**
124-126 Horseferry Road, London SW1P 2TX
Tel: 0171 396 4444 Fax: 0171 306 8351

**CHANNEL TELEVISION**
Television Centre, La Pouquelaye, St.Hellier, Jersey
Tel: 01534 816816 Fax: 01534 816817

**GRAMPIAN TELEVISION LTD**
Queens Cross, Aberdeen, Aberdeenshire AB9 2XJ
Tel: 01224 846846 Fax: 01224 846800

**GRANADA TELEVISION LTD**
Quay Street, Manchester M60 9EA
Tel: 0161 832 7211 Fax: 0161 827 2029

**HTV WALES TV CENTRE**
Culverhouse Cross, Cardiff CF5 6XJ
Tel: 01222 590590 Fax: 01222 590168

**LWT**
London Television Centre, Upper Ground,
London SE1 9LT
Tel: 0171 620 1620 Fax: 0171 261 3200

**MERIDIAN TV**
TV Centre, Southampton SO14 0PZ
Tel: 01703 222555 Fax: 01703 335050

**MUSIC BOX**
30 Sackville Street, London W1X 1DB

Tel: 0171 287 5700 Fax: 0171 434 3490

**NGTV**
76 Oxford Street, London W1N 0AT
Tel: 0171 412 0400 Fax: 0171 412 0300

**S4C**
Parc Ty Glas, Llanishen, Cardiff,
South Glamorgan CF4 5DU
Tel: 01222 747444 Fax: 01222 754444

**SCOTTISH TELEVISION PLC**
Cowcaddens, Glasgow G2 3PR
Tel: 0141 300 3000 Fax: 0141 300 3030

**TELEWEST COMMUNICATIONS**
Communications House, Factory Lane, Croydon,
Surrey CR9 3RA
Tel: 0181 760 0222 Fax: 0181 681 2340

**THAMES TELEVISION PLC**
Thames Studios, Broom Road, Teddington,
Middlesex TW11 9NT
Tel: 0181 977 3252 Fax: (Press) 0181 614 2417

**TYNE TEES TELEVISION LTD**
The Television Centre, City Road,
Newcastle-upon-Tyne, Tyne and Wear NE1 2AL
Tel: 0191 261 0181 Fax: 0191 261 2302

**ULSTER TELEVISION PLC**
Havelock House, Ormeau Road, Belfast,
Co.Antrim BT7 1EB Northern Ireland
Tel: 01232 328122 Fax: 01232 246695

**VECTOR TV**
Battersea Road, Heaton, Mersey, Stockport,
Cheshire SK4 3EA
Tel: 0161 432 9000 Fax: 0161 443 1325

**WEST COUNTRY TELEVISION LTD**
Western Wood Way, Langage, Plymouth,
Devon PL7 5BG
Tel: 01752 333333 Fax: 01752 333444

**YORKSHIRE TELEVISION LTD**
The Television Centre, Kirkstall Road, Leeds,
West Yorkshire LS3 1JS
Tel: 0113 243 8283 Fax: 0113 244 5107

# SATELLITE & CABLE TV

**CABLE LONDON PLC**
2 Stephen Street, London W1P 1PL
Tel: 0171 911 0555 Fax: 0171 209 8459

**CABLETEL SOUTH WALES LTD**
Cable Tel House, Colchester Avenue, Cardiff,
South Glamorgan CF3 7RR

Tel: 01222 456644 Fax: 01222 456645
Managing Director: Terry Ryan

## CALEDONIAN MEDIA COMMUNICATIONS PLC
Aberdeen Cable Services, Broadcast Satellite
Television, Multichannel Television, 303 King Street,
Aberdeen, Aberdeenshire AB24 5AP
Tel: 01224 646644 Fax: 01224 644601

## CHANNEL ONE
60 Charlotte Street, London W1P2AX
Tel: 0171 209 1234 Fax: 0171 209 1235

## THE CHILDREN'S CHANNEL
9-13 Grape Street, London WC2H 8DR
Tel: 0171 813 7000 Fax: 0171 497 9113

## COVENTRY CABLE
Whitley Village, London Road, Coventry,
West Midlands CV3 4HL
Tel: 01203 505070 Fax: 01203 505445

## THE DISCOVERY CHANNEL
160 Great Portland Street, London W1N 5TB
Tel: 0171 462 3600 Fax: 0171 462 3700

## THE FAMILY CHANNEL
Vinters Park, New Cut Road, Maidstone,
Kent ME14 5NZ
Tel: 01622 691111 Fax: 01622 684456

## GMTV
The London Television Centre, Upper Ground,
London SE1 9LT
Tel: 0171 827 7000 Fax: 0171 827 7001

## JERSEY CABLE LIMITED
3 Colomberle, St.Helier, Jersey JE4 9SY
Tel: 01534 66555 Fax: 01534 66681

## MTV MUSIC TELEVISION EUROPE
17/29 Hawley Crescent, London NW1 8TT
Tel: 0171 284 7777 Fax: 0171 284 7788

## NBC SUPER CHANNEL
4th Floor, 3 Shortlands, Hammersmith,
London W6 8BX
Tel: 0181 600 6100 Fax: 0181 563 9080

## NICKELODEON
15-18 Rathbone Place, London W1P 1DF
Tel: 0171 462 1000 Fax: 0171 462 1030

## THE PARAMOUNT CHANNEL
15-18 Rathbone Place, London W1P 1DF
Tel: 0171 462 1000 Fax: 0171 462 1030

## SCI-FI CHANNEL
77 Charlotte Street, London W1P 2DD

Tel: 0171 805 6100 Fax: 0171 805 6150

## SKY TELEVISION
6 Centaurs Business Park, Grant Way, Isleworth,
Middlesex TW7 5QD
Tel: 0171 705 3000 Fax: 0171 705 3030

## SWINDON CABLE
Newcombe Drive, Hawksworth, Swindon SN2 1TV
Tel: 01793 480482 Fax: 01793 619535

## UNITED ARTISTS COMMUNICATIONS
Communications Centre, 1-5 Factory Lane, Croydon,
Surrey CR9 3RA
Tel: 0181 760 0222 Fax: 0181 681 2340

## WARNER BROS INTERNATIONAL TELEVISION
135 Wardour Street, London W1V 4AP
Tel: 0171 494 3710 Fax: 0171 287 9086

## WESTMINSTER CABLE COMPANY LTD
87-89 Baker Street, London W1M 2LP
Tel: 0171 935 4400 Fax: 0171 935 5789

**THEATRE PUBLISHERS**

**NEWSPAPERS & THEATRICAL MAGAZINES**

**ANNUALS AND DIRECTORIES**

**PERFORMING ARTS BOOKSELLERS**

Publishing

# Theatre Publishers

## ABSOLUTE PRESS
Scarborough House, 29 James Street West,
Bath BA1 2BT
Tel: 01225 316013 Fax: 01225 445836
European classic play texts in translation. Distributors
for Heinmann Education Inc. list of Drama & Drama in
Education Titles. Distributors in UK for Smith & Kraus.
Books for theatre & play list.

## ADDISON WESLEY LONGMAN
Edinburgh Gate, Harlow Essex CM20 2JE
Tel: 01279 623623 Fax: 01279 431059
Education/Drama.

## AMBER LANE PRESS
Cheorl House, Church Street, Charlbury
Oxon OX7 3PR
Tel/Fax: 01608 810024
Plays and books on drama & theatre.

## ANCHORAGE PRESS INC.
UK Agents: Kenyon-Deane, 10 Station Road Ind.
Estate, Colwall, Malvern, Herefordshire WR13 6RN
Tel/Fax: 01684 540154
Plays for young people. Theatre textbooks.

## B.T.BATSFORD LIMITED
4 Fitzhardinge Street, London W1H 0AH
Tel: 0171 486 8484 Fax: 0171 487 4296

## A & C BLACK (PUBLISHERS) LTD
35 Bedford Row, London WC1R 4JH
Tel: 0171 242 0946 Fax: 0171 831 8478
Email: enquiries@acblack.co.uk
Contact: Tesni Hollands
A&C Black publish a wide range of backstage
handbooks, actors guides, audition books, ballet and
dance books, costume and make-up manuals, and
New Mermaid classic plays. They also publish the
Writers' & Artists' Yearbook, and distribute Applause
Bools, New York, in the UK and the rest of Europe.
Their list includes classic plays and filmscripts, theatre
and film biographies and practical texts.
Please write for detailed catalogues.

## BLACKWELL PUBLISHERS
Editorial, Sales & Publicity, 108 Cowley Road,
Oxford OX4 1JF
Tel: 01865 791100 Fax: 01865 791347
Distribution: Marston Book Services Ltd.
PO Box 269, Milton Trading Estate, Abingdon,
Oxon OX14 4YN
Tel: 01235 465500 Fax: 01235 465555
The Blackwell Guide to Musical Theatre on Record.
Author Kurt Ganzl. 229 x 152mm. 350 pages.
0-631-16517-7
Encyclopaedia of Musical Theatre
Author: Kurt Ganzl 0-631-16457 - x 258 x 201mm;
1,536 pages.

## CABBELL PUBLISHING LTD
31 Hartfield Crescent, Wimbledon SW19 3SG
Tel: 0181 395 3808 Fax: 0181 395 3999

## CALDER PUBLICATIONS LTD
179 Kings Cross Road, London WC1X 9BZ
Tel: 0171 833 1300
Playtexts: Modern Plays, Playscripts, Magazines:
Gambit International Theatre Review; Journal of
Beckett Studies. (Back Issues Only).

## CAMBRIDGE UNIVERSITY PRESS
The Edinburgh Building, Shaftesbury Road,
Cambridge CB2 2RU
Tel: 01223 325804 Fax: 01223 315052
Email: schadwick@cup.cam.ac.uk
Web Site: www.cup.cam.ac.uk
Contact: Susan Chadwick
Classic play-texts, books on Theatre studies,
Theatre history and Drama criticism. Major
Shakespeare publisher. Theatre Reference books, and
publications of New Theatre Quarterly, which has
established itself as a leading journal in the field of
theatre studies. It is the oldest press in the world and is
a charitable enterprise.

## CASSELL PLC
Wellington House, 125 Strand, London WC2R 0BB
Tel: 0171 420 5555 Fax: 0171 240 8531
Email: cassellacad@msn.com
Web Site: http://www.cassell.co.uk

## CELEBRITY SERVICE LTD
93/97 Regent Street, London W1R 7TA
Tel: 0171 439 9840 Fax: 0171 494 3500
Contact: Diane Oliver
Publisher of the twice weekly "The Celebrity Bulletin"
which lists arrivals in London and activities of
celebrities world-wide.

## CHATTO & WINDUS/THE HOGARTH PRESS
Random House, 20 Vauxhall Bridge Road,
London SW1V 2SA
Tel: 0171 973 9740 Fax: 0171 233 6117

## I.E. CLARK, INC
European Agents: J. Garnet Miller Ltd, 10 Station Road
Ind Est., Colwall, Malvern, Worcestershire WR13 6RN
Tel/Fax: 01684 540154
US play publishers specialising in young adult
awareness plays (13-21 years).

## DILLONS ARTS BOOKSHOP
8 Long Acre, Covent Garden, London WC2
Tel: 0171 836 1359 Fax: 0171 240 1267
Manager: Heather Haines

## FABER & FABER LTD
3 Queen Square, London WC1N 3AU
Tel: 0171 465 0045 Fax: 0171 465 0034
Whether you are an avid drama buff or an occasional
theatre-goer, Faber's books on theatre studies, plays
and screenplays are sure to be of interest.

## SAMUEL FRENCH LTD
52 Fitzroy Street, Fitzrovia, London W1P 6JR
Tel: 0171 387 9373 Fax: 0171 387 2161
Email: theatre@samuelfrench-london.co.uk
Web Site: samuelfrench-london.co.uk
Managing Director: J Bedding
Editorial Director: A Smith

## GALE RESEARCH INTERNATIONAL LTD/ST JAMES PRESS
PO Box 699, Cheriton House, North Way,
Hampshire SP10 5YE
Tel: 01264 342962 Fax: 01264 342763 Sales &
Marketing: 0118 957 7213

## J. GARNET MILLER LTD
10 Station Road Ind. Est., Colwall, Malvern,
Worcestershire WR13 6RN
Tel/Fax: 01684 565045
Publishers of plays & Theatre Textbooks.
European Agents for I.E. Clark, Inc. US Play publishers
specialising in Young Adult Awareness Plays (13-21
yrs).

## ROBERT HALE LTD
Clerkenwell House, 45-47 Clerkenwell Green,
London EC1R 0HT
Tel: 0171 251 2661 Fax: 0171 490 4958
Biographies, Production handbooks.

## HAMISH HAMILTON LTD
27 Wrights Lane, Kensington, London W8 5TZ
Tel: 0171 416 3100 Fax: 0171 416 3099
Biographies, criticism.

## HARPER COLLINS
77/85 Fulham Palace Road, Hammersmith,
London W6 8JB
Tel: 0181 741 7070 Fax: 0181 307 4440

## HEINEMANN EDUCATIONAL BOOKS LTD
Halley Court, Jordan Hill, Oxford OX2 8EJ
Tel: 01865 311366 Fax: 01865 310043
Heinemann has one of the most comprehensive drama
lists, offering a wide range of titles for performance,
study or general reading for all ages; the list is divided
into four broad sections:
Heinemann Shakespeare is an important series of
hardback editions genuinely accessible to 11-16 year
olds - including activities and questions to help prepare
students for GCSE. Heinemann Advanced
Shakespeare provides the same high standard in texts
for A Level students and is focused on preparing
students for their exams.
Heinemann Plays, offers the best in contemporary
drama as well as a wide range of established classics
suitable for GCSE study.  And there are the popular
Hereford Plays, contemporary classics for 14-16 year
olds.  Also available are Spotlights (School plays for
11-14 year olds), Floodlights (for 14-16 year olds) and
a wide range of books on teaching Drama, Drama
Criticism and the Theatre.

## KENYON-DEANE
Unit 10, Station Road Ind. Est., Colwall, Malvern,
Worcestershire WR13 6RN
Tel/Fax: 01684 540154
Plays & Theatre Textbooks. European Agents for
Anchorage Press, leading American Publishers of
Plays for Young People.

## LOKI BOOKS LTD
38 Chalcot Crescent, London NW1 8YD
Tel/Fax: 0171 722 6718
Email: all@lokibooks.u-net.com
Web Site: www.lokibooks.u-net.com
Contact: Marion Baraitser
Plays by women. Plays for theatre in education. Plays
from international series.

## METHUEN PUBLISHING LTD
215 Vauxhall Bridge Road, London SW1V 1EJ
Tel: 0171 828 2838 Fax: 0171 233 9827
Uk's, major publisher of Theatre books and Playtexts.
Complete catalogue available.

## M.H. PUBLICATIONS
17 West Heath Drive, London NW11 7QG
Tel: 0181 455 4640 Fax: 0181 209 1059
Play publishers including a First Folio Edition for the
International Shakespeare Globe Centre.

## MOORLEY'S PRINT & PUBLISHING LTD
23 Park Road, Ilkeston, Derbyshire DE7 5DA
Phone Day Tel/Fax: 0115 932 0643 (24 hours)
Email: 106545.413@compuserve.com
Religious Playtexts.

## NELSON BLACKIE
Bishopbriggs, Glasgow G64 2NZ
Tel: 0141 772 2311 Fax: 0141 762 0897
Modern play-texts.
Head Office: Thomas Nelson & Sons Ltd,
Nelson House, Mayfield Road, Walton-on-Thames,
Surrey KT12 9PL
Tel: 01932 252211

## NEW PLAYWRIGHT'S NETWORK
PO Box 140, Congleton, Cheshire SW12 3NZ
Tel/Fax: 01782 517791
Modern Playtexts, Drama discount Club. De Novo
Productions.

## NODA PANTOMIMES
NODA House, 1 Crestfield Street, London WC1H 8AU
Tel: 0171 837 5655 Fax: 0171 833 0609
Agents and Publishers for top panto scriptwriters. Over
fifty versions of the popular titles.

## OBERON BOOKS LTD
521 Caledonian Road, London N7 9RH
Tel: 0171 607 3637 Fax: 0171 607 3629
Publishers of Playtexts and theatre books.

## THE ORION PUBLISHING GROUP
Orion House, 5 Upper Street, St. Martin's Lane,
London WC2H 9EA

Tel: 0171 240 3444 Fax: 0171 240 4822
Imprints: Weidenfeld and Nicholson (Biographies, General Illustrated, Fiction).
Orion: Fiction, Biographies, Childrens Books
J. M. Dent (Academic, Childrens).
Everyman Paperbacks

## OXFORD UNIVERSITY PRESS
Great Clarendon Street, Oxford OX2 6DP
Tel: 01865 556767 Fax: 01865 556646

## PCR
PO Box 11, London N1 7JZ
Tel: 0171 566 8282 Fax: 0171 566 8284
Editorial Contact: Bobbi Dunn

## PHAINDON PRESS LIMITED
18 Regents Wharf, All Saints Street, London N1 9PA
Tel: 0171 843 1000 Fax: 0171 843 1010
Publishers of books on the Arts.

## RED GOLD MUSIC
World Fusion Music Label, 87a Queens Road, East Grinstead, West Sussex RH19 1BG
Tel: 01342 300949
Email: egsales@egnet.co.uk
Web Site: www.egnet.co.uk/clients/music/rgm.html
Chairman: Paul Chenour

## RHINEGOLD PUBLISHING LTD
241 Shaftesbury Avenue, London WC2H 8EH
Tel: 0171 333 1721 Fax: 0171 333 1769
Email: sales@rhinegold.co.uk
Web Site: www.rhinegold.co.uk
Publishers of British Performing Arts Yearbook, British Music Yearbook, Music Education Yearbook, Opera Now, Classical Music, Music Teacher, The Singer, Early Music Today, Piano, Museums & Arts Appointments, Arts Marketing.

## RICHMOND HOUSE PUBLISHING COMPANY LTD
Douglas House, 3 Richmond Buildings, London W1V 5AE
Tel: 0171 437 9556 Fax: 0171 287 3463
Email: sales@rhpco.demon.co.uk
Contact: Spencer Block, Gloria Gordon, Lee Rotbart

Leading publishers of theatrical and entertainment directories - The British Theatre Directory, Artistes & Agents, and the Official London Seating Plan Guide (A4 computer plans of major theatres in London).

## ROBSON BOOKS
Bolsover House, 56 Clipstone Street, London W1P 8LE
Tel: 0171 323 1223/637 5937 Fax: 0171 636 0798

## ROUTLEDGE ITP
11 New Fetter Lane, London EC4P 4EE
Tel: 0171 583 9855 Fax: 0171 842 2298
Contacts: Editorial: Talia Rodgers
Marketing: Cynthia Wainwright
Leading British Publisher of books on theatre, dance and performance studies.

## SCHOOLPLAY PRODUCTIONS LTD
15 Inglis Road, Colchester, Essex CO3 3HU
Tel: 01206 540111 Fax: 01206 766944
SchoolPlay Productions is the specialist UK company publishing plays and musicals (scripts, scores and cassettes) for performance by youth groups and schools. A summary catalogue is available on request

## SIMON & SCHUSTER
West Garden Place, Kendal Street, London W2 2AQ
Tel: 0171 316 1900 Fax: 0171 402 0639

## SOCIETY FOR THEATRE RESEARCH
c/o The Theatre Museum, 1e Tavistock Street, London WC2E 7PA
Theatre notebook and Theatre studies and Histories.

## SPECIALIST PUBLICATIONS AND PRINT
151 Wick Road, Bristol BS4 4HH
Tel: 0117 977 9188 Fax: 0117 908 6697
Email: studio@sportspro.co.uk
Design, branding and print for Arts Organisation.

## THAMES AND HUDSON LTD
181a High Holborn, London WC1V 7QX
Tel: 0171 845 5000 Fax: 0171 845 5050
Email: sales@thbooks.demon.co.uk
Web Site: www.thameshudson.co.uk
Promotion Manager: Helen Scott Lidgett
Theatre History and Biography

## VIRGIN PUBLISHING
332 Ladbroke Grove, London W10 5AH
Tel: 0181 968 7554 Fax: 0181 968 0929
List includes stage and screen series of biographies and books on voice from Cicely Berry.

## WARNER/CHAPPELL MUSIC LTD
Griffin House, 161 Hammersmith Road, London W6 8BS
Tel: 0181 563 5800 Fax: 0181 563 5801
Email: warner.chappell@dial.pipex.com
Music publishers and agents for stage rights of musicals.

**WARNER/
CHAPPELL
MUSIC**

**WARNER/
CHAPPELL
PLAYS**

**Music Publishers and Play Publishers
Agents for stage rights**

Warner/Chappell Music Ltd
Warner/Chappell Plays Ltd
Griffin House, 161 Hammersmith Road
London W6 8BS
Tel: (0181) 563 5800   Fax: (0181) 563 5801

A Warner Music Group Company

**WARNER/CHAPPELL PLAYS LTD**
(formerly English Theatre Guild)
Griffin House, 161 Hammersmith Road,
London W6 8BS
Tel: 0181 563 5800 Fax: 0181 563 5801
Email: warner.chappell@dial.pipex.com
Manager: Michael Callahan
Play publishers and Play Agents.

**JOSEF WEINBERGER LTD**
12-14 Mortimer Street, London W1N 7RD
Tel: 0171 580 2827 (4 lines) Fax: 0171 494 3500
Publisher and rightsholder of musicals and agents for
Music Theatre International and the Rodgers &
Hammerstein Theatre Library.

**WORD AND ACTION (DORSET) LTD**
61 West Borough, Wimborne, Dorset BH21 1LX
Tel: 01202 883197/889669 Fax: 01202 881061
Email: wordandaction@wanda.demon.co.uk
Community theatre with twenty-five years language
arts experience. Practitioners of Instant Theatre.
Annual national and international tours. Offers
performances, workshops, business and language
courses and incorporates Wanda Publications Co
founders of the Round Festival.

# Newspapers &
# Theatrical
# Magazines

**AMATEUR STAGE (1946)**
Platform Publications, Hampden House, 2 Weymouth
Street, London W1N 3FD
Tel: 0171 636 4343 Fax: 0171 636 2323
Email: cvtheatre@aol.com
Web Site: www.uktw.co.uk/amstage/editorial.htm
Monthly: £2 per copy.
Subscriptions: £20 p.a. Inland; £28 Europe;
£37 Rest of World.
Editor: Charles Vance
Articles on all aspects of amateur and community
theatre and stagecraft, 32pp A4 - some illustrations.
Latest news from amateur festivals and play
competitions, conferences, courses and other events.
Reports on festivals and productions, etc. Reviews of
books and new published playscripts. London stage
shows and specific amateur productions. Diary of
forthcoming amateur productions.

**ANIMATIONS**
c/o Puppet Centre Trust, Battersea Arts Centre,
Lavender Hill, London SW11 5TN
Tel: 0171 228 5335 Fax: 0171 228 8863
Email: pct@puppetcentre.demon.co.uk
Published six times a year.
Price: £3 per copy; Annual Subscription:

£30 (Organisations), £20 (Individuals).
Review of puppets and related theatre.

## ARTS BUSINESS MAGAZINE

PO Box 957, Cottenham, Cambridge CB4 8AB
Tel: 01954 250600 Fax: 01954 252600
Email: edit@arts-business.co.uk
Web Site: www.arts-business.co.uk
Co-Editors: Brian Whitehead and Liz Hill
Editorial Assistant: Alison Lea
Fortnightly arts management publication

## THE CELEBRITY BULLETIN

Celebrity Service Ltd, 93-97 Regent Street,
London W1R 7TA
Tel: 0171 439 9840 Fax: 0171 494 3500
Editor: Diane Oliver.
Subscription: published twice weekly - Mondays and
Thursday, £60.00 per month; £55.00 per month if paid
by bankers order or per annum.
Information about everyone in the news world-wide,
including London arrivals, International arrivals,
International activities, events and Biographies.

## CONTACTS

7 Leicester Place, London WC2H 7BP
Tel: 0171 437 7631 Fax: 0171 437 5881
Pub: The Spotlight (as Spotlight Casting Directory).
Annually
Price: £10.20 inc. post & packing (UK).
Content: Brief factual contact information (names,
addresses, phone nos) on theatres, management,
agents, commercial concerns, publications,
organisation, critics. TV and radio companies and
stations, film companies and studios, record
companies, training schools and coaches.

## COUNTRY MUSIC ROUND UP

C.M.R.U. Publishing Co., PO Box 111, Waltham,
Grimsby DN37 0YN
Tel: 01472 821707 Fax: 01472 821808
Publisher: John Emptage
Monthly
Price: £1.50 - £18.00 (UK) Subscription.

## DANCE AND DANCERS

83 Clerkenwell Road, London EC1R 5AR
Tel/Fax: 0171 813 1049
Published Monthly
Editor: John Percival

## DANCE RESEARCH

Edinburgh University Press, 22 George Square,
Edinburgh EH8 9LF
Tel: 0131 650 4222 Fax: 0131 662 0053
Contact: Pam O'Connor
Subscription rates Volume 16, 1998 (2 issues).
Institutions: UK & Europe £46; elsewhere US$83
Individuals: UK & Europe £29;  elsewhere US$54
The Journal of the Society for Dance Research covers
a broad spectrum of dance topics, ranging from the
history of European theatrical dance to dance
anthropology and Renaissance spectacle.

## DANCING TIMES

Dancing Times Ltd., Clerkenwell House, 45-47
Clerkenwell Green, London EC1R 0EB
Tel: 0171 250 3006 Fax: 0171 253 6679
Email: DT@dancing-times.co.uk
Web Site: www.dt-ltd.dircon.co.uk
Monthly: 1st week of month.
£2.00 per copy; £28.00 p.a. inland; £32.00 overseas,
surface, £50-4 airmail (depending on destination).
Editor: Mary Clarke
Editorial Adviser: Ivor Guest, M.A.
Ballet, Contemporary dance, Stage dancing, from
general critical, historical and technical angles.
Preliminary arrangements must be made for freelance
articles. Photographs.Book reviews. Calendar of
forthcoming performances, touring dates. News and
reports from festivals, schools, etc.

## DRAMA: ONE FORUM MANY VOICES

National Drama Publications, 6 Cornwell Court, Castle
Dene, South Gosforth, Newcastle-upon-Tyne NE3 1TT
Tel: 0191 284 6520
Issued: Three times a year - January/May/September.
Subs: (incl. P & P) UK £8;
Overseas surface £10; Air Mail £12.
Editor: John Carey.
Magazine of Theatre and Drama in Education.

## ENCORE

240 Tolworth Rise South, Surbiton, Surrey KT5 9NB
Tel/Fax: 0181 330 3707
Independent Trade Monthly for Show Products and
Venues.
Publisher/Editor: Peter G Foot
Monthly.
British theatre and concert hall monthly listings, plus
news on venues, theatre managers, producers,
promoters, societies, agencies, artistes and shows.

## EQUITY JOURNAL

Upper St.Martin's Lane, London WC2H 9EG
Tel: 0171 379 6000 (switchboard) 0171 379 5557
(minicom) Fax: 0171 379 7001
Email: info@equity.org.uk
Four times a year. Free to members. £12.00pa to non-
members.
Journal of British Actors' Equity Association
(Incorporating the Variety Artists' Federation).

## GUIDE TO BEYOND THE WEST END

IMPACT, Culford House, 1-7 Orsman Road,
London N1 5RA
Tel: 0171 729 5962 Fax: 0171 729 5994
The only free arts listings guide to actively promote the
wealth of theatre, dance and visual arts throughout
Greater London's alternative fringe circuit. Listings are
accompanied by a variety of editorial features and
newsbites relating to the innovative world of the arts.
The publication in mirrored on the internet with a
comprehensive website: http://www.theguide.net. All
entries are free.
Copy deadlines ring for details.
For further information contact: Andrew Howarth

## NEW THEATRE QUARTERLY

Cambridge University Press, Edinburgh Building,
Shaftesbury Road, Cambridge CB2 2RU
Tel: 01223 312393 Fax: 01223 325150

### the only magazine for professional arts and cultural managers

Nearly 7,000 named professionals receive ArtsBusiness every fortnight:

- o over 1,000 are chief executives, artistic directors or general managers
- o 1,300 are managers
- o 600 are involved with or directly responsible for marketing
- o 110 are employed in press or PR roles
- o 175 are responsible for education
- o 210 are involved in youth work
- o 110 are involved in membership, fundraising, sponsorship, business development
- o 600 have administrative functions

When it's time for you to recruit your next employee, why use the national press when you could pay less than a quarter of the price and reach the people that count?

**Advertising**
ArtsBusiness, 16 Market Place, Diss, Norfolk IP22 3WF
t: 01379 644200 • f: 01379 650480

**Subscriptions**
ArtsBusiness, PO Box 957, Cottenham, Cambridge CB4 8AB
Credit card hotline 01954 250600 • f: 01954 252600

Editors: Clive Barker and Simon Trussler.
Quarterly: £13 per copy, £28 p.a. for individuals, £49
p.a. for UK institutions.

## OPERA (1950)

Seymour Press Ltd., 86 Newman Street,
London W1P 3LD
Tel: 0171 396 8000
Editor: Rodney Milnes, 1a Mountgrove Road,
London N5 2LU
Tel 0171 359 1037  Fax 0171 354 2700
Published Monthly.
£2.70 per copy; £43.50 p.a. in UK (with index, etc.).
Articles on general subjects relating to opera; reviews
of performances, recordings and books, illus; photos.

## PLAYS INTERNATIONAL (LTD)

33a Lurline Gardens, London SW11 4DD
Tel/Fax: 0171 720 1950
Editor: Peter Roberts
Monthly: £2.80

## PRODUCTION AND CASTING REPORT

PO Box 11, London N1 7JZ
Tel: 0171 566 8282 Fax: 0171 566 8284
Weekly: £25 for 5 weeks
Production and Casting News.

## REPORT

PO Box 100, Broadstairs, Kent CT10 1UJ
Tel: 01843 860885 Fax: 01843 860899
Monthly listings of regional repertory theatre - casting
and audition news.
£10.00 for three months.

## SPEECH AND DRAMA

4 Fane Road, Oxford OX3 0SA
Tel: 01865 728304
Editor: Dr. Paul Ranger.
Subscription rates: £6.50 per annum; £5.00 per annum
for trade; £3.50 per single copy, publication dates:
14th April, 14th October.
Speech and Drama is published twice yearly by the
Society of Teachers of Speech and Drama. It covers
drama, theatre, speech and areas of allied interest,
directed towards educationalists at all levels.
Illustrated.

## THE STAGE INCORPORATING
## TELEVISION TODAY

The Stage Newspaper Ltd., 47 Bermondsey Street,
London Bridge, London SE1 3XT
Tel: 0171 403 1818 Fax: 0171 403 1418 Editorial Fax:
0171 357 9287 Advertising Fax: 0171 378 0480
Editor: Brian Attwood.
Weekly tabloid newspaper: Thursday.
90p per copy.
Covers professional stage (including variety, clubs,
opera, dance, technical etc., professional and student
activity), television and radio; show business news,
reviews and shows, programmes and books;
forthcoming shows and relevant developments; illus;
line and half-tone.

## THEATRE NOTEBOOK (1945)

Society for Theatre Research, c/o The Theatre
Museum, 1e Tavistock Street, London WC2E 7PA
Editors: Trevor Griffiths, Russell Jackson, Marion
O'Connor
Three times a year: February, June, October.
Free to STR members.
Articles on all aspects of theatre research; queries and
answers; book reviews.

## THEATRE RECORD (1981)

305 Whitton Dene, Isleworth, Middlesex TW7 7NE
Tel: 0181 892 6087 Fax: 0181 893 9677
Editor: Ian Herbert.
Bi-monthly.
Price £110 p.a.; US$280 p.a.
Full details of actors and production staff for all new
plays and shows opening in London, with reprints of full
reviews from critics of the major newspapers and
journals (including Guardian, Observer, Time Out, etc.).
Also A-Z of current productions and news of coming
openings in London and outside. Includes Regional
premieres, book reviews and production photographs.
Simply, the most informative theatre journal in Britain

## THEATRE RESEARCH INTERNATIONAL

Oxford University Press, Great Clarendon Street,
Oxford OX2 6DP
Tel: 01865 556767 Fax: 01865 267485
Contact: Sara Blackwell (01865 267112)
Subscription rates: Vol 23, 1998 (3 issues); UK &
Europe £69.00; Elsewhere US$131. Special rates
available for members of the International Federation
for Theatre Research.
Theatre Research International publishes original
articles on theatre history and criticism. It has a broad
focus spotlighting performance, acting and production
techniques, theatre architecture and actor's social
conditions amongst its many subjects. It also contains
an extensive review section.

## TIME OUT

Time Out Magazine Ltd., Universal House,
251 Tottenham Court Road, London W1P 0AB
Tel: 0171 813 3000 Fax: 0171 813 6001
Weekly £1.70 per copy.
Publisher: Tony Elliott.
Editor: Dominic Wells.
Commentary and listings of theatre, arts and
entertainment events in London, including fringe
theatre.

## VARIETY

6 Bell Yard, London WC2A 2JR
Tel: 0171 520 5222 Fax: 0171 520 5217
Weekly - £3.95
The American newspaper for theatre and showbiz.

## WHAT'S ON IN LONDON

180 Pentonville Road, London N1 9LB
Tel: 0171 278 4393 Fax: 0171 837 5838
Editor: Michael Darvell
Theatre Editor: Neil Smith
Advertisement Manager: Paul Lock
Weekly guide to all theatre, cinema, music, arts,
museums, restaurants and eating out and 8-day diary
of events.
Every Wednesday price £1.20.

# Annuals and Directories

The "bible" of the showbusiness and entertainment industry is now in its 27th year of invaluable service to all key decision makers - contains over 15,000 venues and over 10,000 contacts. (£34.95 + £4.95 p&p).

## AMATEUR THEATRE YEARBOOK
Pub. Platform Publications Hampden House, 2 Weymouth Street, London W1N 3ED
Tel: 0171 636 4343 Fax: 0171 636 2323
Email: cvtheatre@aol.com
Subscription rates: 2000 Edition: £16.00, (£18.00 including P&P).
The comprehensive reference source for amateur and community theatre; information listed under the Regional Arts Boards of England and Wales with sections on Scotland and Ireland; Venues, Theatrical Suppliers, Publishers and Publications, Training, National Support Organisations and Individuals offering Skills on all aspects of Theatre.

## ARTISTES & AGENTS (10TH EDITION)
(incorporating the Entertainment Event Organiser)
Richmond House Pub. Co., Douglas House, 3 Richmond Buildings, London W1V 5AE
Tel: 0171 437 9556 Fax: 0171 287 3463
Email: sales@rhpco.demon.co.uk
Published annually in August.
Editor: Lee Rotbart
£28.95 + £3.50 p&p.
The "comprehensive entertainment directory" listing all Showbusiness Agents and who they represent. Artistes & Agents covers all working artistes in all aspects of the industry including the corporate sector - after dinner speakers, sports personalities, actors and actresses as well as the entire music and entertainment Industry. Other sections include TV & Radio, Production, Events Organisers & suppliers, venues, media & Public relations and professional services.

## BRITISH MUSIC YEARBOOK
Rhinegold Publishing Ltd., 241 Shaftesbury Avenue, London WC2H 8EH
Tel: 0171 333 1760 (editorial) 0171 333 1733 (advertising) Fax: 0171 333 1769
Email: bmyb@rhinegold.co.uk
Web Site: www.rhinegold.co.uk
Annually.
Editor: Louise Head
The "bible" of the classical music industry; contact details for national and municipal bodies; trade and professional associations, music clubs and societies; halls and theatres; lunchtime concert venues; agents, promoters; fixers; recording studios; orchestras; bands; ensembles, etc.; individual performers, producers, composers, librettists, music publishers, instrument manufacturers, retailers, education, etc.

## BRITISH THEATRE DIRECTORY 1999
Richmond House Pub. Co., Douglas House, 3 Richmond Buildings, London W1V 5AE
Tel: 0171 437 9556 Fax: 0171 287 3463
Email: sales@rhpco.demon.co.uk
Editor: Spencer Block
Annual: Published January

## DIRECTORY OF PROFESSIONAL PUPPETEERS
c/o Puppet Centre Trust, Battersea Arts Centre, Lavender Hill, London SW11
Tel: 0171 228 5335
Email: pct@puppetcentre.demon.co.uk
Biennial.
Price: £8.50 including P&P.
Director: Loretta Howells
Administrator: Allyson Kirk
Also includes puppet makers, freelance operators and Punch and Judy performers.

## INSTITUTE OF ENTERTAINMENT AND ARTS MANAGEMENT YEARBOOK
9 Bushetts Grove, Merstham, Redhill RH1 3DX
Tel/Fax: 01737 644432
Email: drolph.ieam@virgin.net
Web Site: freespace.virgin/diane_rolph.ieam
Editor: Diane Rolph
An internal publication for members of the institute.

## MCGILLIVRAY'S THEATRE GUIDE
8 Shrubland Road, London E8 4NN
Tel: 0171 254 4490
Editor: David McGillivray.
Annually
Price: £18
Building on the solid foundation of its former alternative theatre directory status, McGillivray's is adding new sections and growing every year. Current sections include: Alternative Theatre (Small and Middle Scale Touring Companies; Community Theatre; Performance Art; Cabaret Artists; Street Entertainment; Dance Companies; Mime; Circus; Young People's Theatre (Children's Theatre; TIE Companies; Young People's Theatre Schemes); Puppet Companies; New York Companies and Venues; Theatre and Cabaret Venues; Arts Councils and Regional Arts Associations; Theatre Organisations; National Festivals, Theatre Training, Services and Suppliers.

## MEDIA CONTACTS: PERFORMING ARTS
Artsinform, Cooper House, 2 Michael Road, London SW6 2AD
Tel: 0171 610 9991 Fax: 0171 610 9992
Email: artsinform.demon.co.uk
Three issues a year.
The media directory for the performing arts with listings of over 1000 arts correspondents in the press, broadcast and electronic media across the U.K. Includes deadlines, editorial schedules and inside advice.

## MUSIC EDUCATION YEARBOOK
Rhinegold Publishing Ltd., 241 Shaftesbury Avenue, London WC2H 8EH
Tel: 0171 333 1761 (editorial) 0171 333 1733 (advertising) Fax: 0171 333 1769
Email: meyb@rhinegold.co.uk
Web Site: www.rhinegold.co.uk
Annually.

Editor: Louise Head
The definitive guide to music education for parents, teachers, students and musicians.

## THE OFFICIAL LONDON SEATING PLAN GUIDE (2ND EDITION)

Richmond House Pub. Co., Douglas House, 3 Richmond Buildings, London W1V 5AE
Tel: 0171 437 9556 Fax: 0171 287 3463
Email: sales@rhpco.demon.co.uk
Editor: Spencer Block
An updated state of the art collection of seating plans for all London's major theatres and concert venues. A4 Format (£14.95 + £1.00 per copy p&p).

## PR PLANNER - UK AND EUROPE

Chess House, 34 Germain Street, Chesham, Buckinghamshire HP5 1SJ
Tel: 01494 797200 Fax: 01494 797217
Email: mi@mediainfo.co.uk
Web Site: www.mediainfo.co.uk

## THE PRESENTERS CONTACT FILE

Presenter Promotions, 123 Corporation Road, Gillingham, Kent ME7 1RG
Tel: 01634 851077 Fax: 01634 316771
Email: presenter-promotions@lineone.net
Contact: Colin Cobb
Directory for presenters and voice artistes looking for work in the UK. Very useful for new entrants into the TV & Radio Industry.

## SHOWCALL

The Stage Newspaper Ltd., Stage House, 47 Bermondsey Street, London Bridge, London SE1 3XT
Tel: 0171 403 1818 Fax: 0171 403 1418 Adveritising
Fax: 0171 378 0480
Annual. Illustrated Directory of artistes etc. for light entertainment bookers.

## SPOTLIGHT CASTING DIRECTORY (1927)

Pub. The Spotlight, 7 Leicester Place, London WC2H 7BP
Tel: 0171 437 7631 Fax: 0171 437 5881
Email: info@spotlightcd.com
Web Site: www.spotlightcd.com
Editor: Christine Barry.
Annual: April (Actors).@ £57
October (Actresses) @ £57
Content: Photographs of actors and actresses with contact information for use by casting directors, etc.

## THE VOICE ANALYSIS

4 Kingly Street, London W1R 5LF
Tel: 0171 734 3393 Fax: 0171 734 3373
Editor: Susan Mactavish.
Subscription rates: £95.00+VAT. Published June. A computer print-out of Actor's voice profiles, denoting age range, accents, languages, tone, class range, etc. and where to contact them.

## THE WHITE BOOK (1997 EDITION)

First Floor, Bank House, 23 Warwick Road, Coventry CV1 2EW
Tel: 01203 559658 Fax: 01203 631185

Editor: Sarah Hutchinson
Annual: January.
Price: £60 inclusive of p&p (to UK destinations).
The International Production Directory.

# Performing Arts Booksellers

## CAMBRIDGE

### PETER WOOD

20 Stonehill Road, Great Shelford, Cambridge CB2 5JL
Tel/Fax: 01223 842419
Holds stock of books and ephemera on theatre. Also cinema, music, opera, television. Comprehensive catalogues issued. Private premises, browsers very welcome by appointment.

## CARLISLE

### ANNE FITZSIMONS

62 Scotby Road, Scotby, Carlisle, Cumbria CA4 8BD
Tel: 01228 513815
Specialist dealer in rare and out of print books, ephemera and memorabilia on all aspects of the performing arts. Regular catalogues issued. Private premises. Postal only, three first class stamps for current catalogue.

## GLASTONBURY

### EDDIE BAXTER-BOOKS (BTD)

The Old Mill House, West Pennard, Somerset BA6 8ND
Tel/Fax: 01749 890369
Mail order out of print and new books, with emphasis on dance bands, jazz, cinema and theatre. Free search facility. No find - No fee.

## LONDON

### BAC BOOKSHOP

Lavender Hill, London SW11 5TF
Tel: 0171 223 6557 Fax: 0171 978 5207
Fiction, women's literature, arts, children's books,. poetry, theatre and plays. Also cards, magazines, etc.

### BOOK BAZAAR

42 Sydney Street, London SW3 6PS
Tel: 0171 352 6810 Fax: 0171 351 5728
Cara Lancaster.
New and secondhand Technical Theatre Books, Lighting, Costume, Scenery, Props, Catalogues issued. Book searches undertaken. Private premises. Visitors welcome by appointment.

## DANCE BOOKS LTD
15 Cecil Court, St.Martin's Lane, London WC2N 4EZ
Tel: 0171 836 2314 Fax: 0171 497 0473
Email: dances@dircon.co.uk
Web Site: www.dancebooks.co.uk
Specialist booksellers and publishers of books on
dance and all forms of human movement.

## DILLONS BOOKSTORE
The Barbican, London EC2Y 8DS
Tel: 0171 382 7007 Fax: 0171 920 9648
General retail outlets on the Mezzanine and Library
level of the Barbican Centre. Fiction, arts related books
and recordings. Opening Times: 11.30 a.m. - 7.30 p.m.
(Level 4 &7)

## SAMUEL FRENCH LTD
52 Fitzroy Street, Fitzrovia, London W1P 6JR
Tel: 0171 387 9373 Fax: 0171 387 2161
Email: theatre@samuelfrench-london.co.uk
Web Site: samuelfrench-london.co.uk
Managing Director: J Bedding
Editorial Director: A Smith

## LOUISE GRANT
65 Parkside Drive, Edgware, Middlesex HA8 8JU
Tel: 0181 958 5862
Theatre programmes, poster, autographs and other
theatrical ephemera (postal only or by appointment).

## GREENROOM BOOKS
11 Bark Lane, Addingham, Ilkley,
West Yorkshire LS29 0RA
Tel: 01943 830497
(Geoff Oldham obtainable on 01943 607662)
Fax 01943 830497
Dealers in secondhand and antiquarian books on the
performing arts. We deal by post only and issue four
catalogues a year. A catalogue will be sent on receipt
of an A5 sae.

## INSTITUTE OF CONTEMPORARY ARTS
## BOOKSHOP
12 Carlton House Terrace, London SW1Y 5AH
Tel: 0171 925 2434 Fax: 0171 873 0051
Stocks books and hard-to-obtain periodicals with
emphasis on contemporary cultural studies, art and
philosophy. Also has a wide range of artists postcards
and ICA exhibition catalogues.

## KIRKDALE BOOKSHOP
272 Kirkdale, Sydenham, London SE26 4RS
Tel: 0181 778 4701
Booksellers: Small stock of both new and secondhand
books on music, the theatre and the cinema.

## OFFSTAGE THEATRE & FILM BOOKSHOP
37 Chalk Farm Road, London NW1 8AJ
Tel: 0171 485 4996 Fax: 0171 916 8046
Theatre and Cinema with media and second-hand
books. Mail Order. Mon. to Sun. 10am - 6pm.

## THE OLD EPHEMERA & NEWSPAPER
## SHOP
37 Kinnerton Street, London SW1X 8ED
Tel: 0171 235 7788
Large stock of playbills, programmes, prints, autograph
letters relating to Performing Arts generally. Also
magazines and newspapers.

## DAVID DRUMMOND AT PLEASURES OF
## PAST TIMES
11 Cecil Court, (St.Martin's Lane), London WC2N 4EZ
Tel: 0171 836 1142
Out of print theatre books and ephemera of performing
arts. Hire facilities and research undertaken for
principals of accredited bodies (notice required).
Hours: Weekdays 11.00am - 2.30 pm; 3.30 - 5.45pm
and by arrangement.

## ROYAL NATIONAL THEATRE BOOKSHOP
Royal National Theatre, South Bank, London SE1 9PX
Tel: 0171 452 3456/8 Fax: 0171 452 3457
Ansaphone: 0171 452 3460
Email: ntbook@dircon.co.uk
Web Site: www.nt-online.org
Bookshop open 10.00am - 10.45pm Monday -
Saturday (check times on Bank Holidays). Olivier +
Cottesloe bookstalls open at performance times.
Shops carry a wide range of playtexts, books on all
aspects of the stage, theatrical biographies/auto
biographies, posters, cards, videos, audio cassettes,
CDs, clothing and merchandise. For current stock lists
please send s.a.e. Worldwide mail order service
available.

## SWISS COTTAGE BOOKS
4 Canfield Gardens, London NW6 3BS
Tel: 0171 625 4632 Fax: 0171 624 9084
Bookshop stocking a range of plays and books on
theatre.

## JOSEF WEINBERGER LTD
12-14 Mortimer Street, London W1N 7RD
Tel: 0171 580 2827 (4 lines) Fax: 0171 494 3500
Publisher and rightsholder of musicals and agents for
Music Theatre International and the Rodgers &
Hammerstein Theatre Library.

# NEWMARKET

## C.D. PARAMOR
25 St.Mary's Square, Newmarket, Suffolk CB8 0HZ
Tel/Fax: 01638 664416
Bookseller specialising in books in the performing arts.
Both new and out-of-print and antiquarian. Free search
service for elusive material undertaken. Visitors
welcome by appointment. Catalogues issued.

# OXFORDSHIRE

## BICESTER
63 Kennedy Road, Bicester, Oxfordshire OX6 8BE
Tel/Fax: 01869 245793

Directors: Ray and Joan DaSilva
Book relating to all aspects of puppet theatre

# SOUTHAMPTON

### A.E.COX
21 Cecil Road, Itchen, Southampton SO2 7HX
Tel: 01703 447989
Dealer in antiquarian and modern out-of-print books
and ephemera covering all Performing Arts. Catalogue
"Stage and Screen' is published four times yearly.

# STRATFORD

### THE RSC COLLECTION
Royal Shakespeare Theatre, Stratford-upon-Avon,
Warwickshire CV37 6BB
Tel: 01789 296655
Open Mon - Sat 9.15 am - 9 pm. Sunday 12.00 - 5pm.
(Nov - Mar 11am. - 4pm.)
Exhibition of theatre material; theatre tours; Sales -
wide variety of material including RSC publications and
books covering all aspects of theatre.

### RSC SHOPS
Royal Shakespeare Theatre, Stratford-upon-Avon,
Warwickshire CV37 6BB
Tel: 01789 412601 Fax: 01789 412639
Web Site: www.rsc.org.uk
Hours of opening: 9.15am - 9.00pm.
Play texts and theatre books relating to Shakespeare
and RSC productions and general theatre interest
books. Souvenirs, posters, programmes and gifts.
Mail Order available.

### ROBERT VAUGHAN ANTIQUARIAN BOOKSELLERS
20 Chapel Street, Stratford-upon-Avon,
Warwickshire CV37 6EP
Tel: 01789 205312
Antiquarian booksellers, specialising in rare and out of
print books on Shakespeare and the performing arts.
Members of the Antiquarian Booksellers Association
(International).

# Training and Education

# Members of the Conference of Drama Schools

## THE ARTS EDUCATIONAL LONDON SCHOOLS
Cone Ripman House, 14 Bath Road, Chiswick,
London W4 1LY
Tel: 0181 987 6666 Fax: 0181 987 6699
Administration/Courses:
Dean: Peter Kyle
Director of the Drama School: David Robson
3-year full-time drama course for students training to
work in professional theatre.
Director of the Acting Company: Adrian James
This 1-year course is for mature students and actors
seeking a renewed focus in their work.
Director of Dance School: Ian Watt-Smith
3-year full time course for mature students in dance,
drama and singing.

## ARTS EDUCATIONAL SCHOOLS LONDON
Cone Ripman House, 14 Bath Road, Chiswick,
London W4 1LY
Tel: 0181 987 6666 Fax: 0181 987 6699/987 6656
Email: drama@artsed.co.uk
Web Site: http://www.artsed.co.uk/drama
Dean: Iain Reid
Director of the School of Acting: Maggie Kinloch
3 year full time course (18+) offering comprehensive
training for students seeking to pursue careers in act-
ing. Stanislavski based - major emphasis on performance and individual development.
Director of the acting company: Adrian James
Intensive 1 year postgraduate course (21+) for mature
students: actors seeking a renewed focus; singers
needing to improve their acting; those whose evoca-
tion manifests itself later in life.
Director of the School of Musical Theatre:
Ian Watt-Smith
3 year full time course (16+) with a flexible new
approach, providing unrivalled training in dance, acting
and singing by leading professionals. Options for
intensive work on specialisms. A'level options.
Postgraduate Musical Theatre Course: A concentrated
1 year course (21+) of intensive training in dance, acting and singing - full time integrated performance
study.
All courses accredited by the NCDT.

## BIRMINGHAM SCHOOL OF SPEECH AND DRAMA
45 Church Road, Edgbaston,
Birmingham B1 1BN
Tel: 0121 454 3424 Fax: 0121 456 4496 99 John
Bright Street, Birmingham B1 1BN Tel: 0121 643 4376
Fax: 0121 633 0476
Administration/Courses:
Principal: Professor Patricia A Yardley
3 year full-time training for the professional theatre
(accredited by N.C.D.T.)
2 year full-time training for the teaching of speech and
drama.

One year Post Graduate/Mature student course for the
professional theatre. Two year Stage Management
Course.
One year Post Graduate/Mature Student Stage
Management course.
Prospectus on application to the secretary.

## BRISTOL OLD VIC THEATRE SCHOOL
2 Downside Road, Clifton,
Bristol BS8 2XF
Tel: 0117 973 3535 Fax: 0117 923 9371
Administration/Courses:
Principal: Christopher Denys
2&3 year full-time acting courses.
1 year full-time postgraduate acting course.
2 year stage management and technical courses.
1 year stage design course.
1 year wardrobe course.

## ROSE BRUFORD COLLEGE
Lamborey Park, Burnt Oak Lane,
Sidcup, Kent DA15 9DF
Tel: 0181 300 3024 Fax: 0181 308 0542
Email: admin@bruford.ac.uk
Web Site: http://www.bruford.ac.uk
Administration/Courses:
Principal: Professor Robert Ely
Courses: BA(Hons) Degrees in Acting, Actor Musician.
Directing, Lighting Design, Stage Management,
Costume Production, Scenic Construction and
Properties, Theatre Design, Music Technology, Sounds
Image Design.
By Distance Learning: Opera Studies, Theatre
Studies, MA Theatre & Performance Studies. MA
Dramatic Writing & MA Theatre Practices.
All courses validated by the University of Manchester.

## THE CENTRAL SCHOOL OF SPEECH AND DRAMA
The Embassy Theatre, 64 Eton Avenue, Swiss
Cottage, London NW3 3HY
Tel: 0171 722 8183 Fax: 0171 722 4132
Administration:
Principal: Professor Robert S.Fowler, FRSA
FULL TIME COURSES:
Performance Related:
Acting - BA - NCDT - 3 years
Performance Studies - MA/PG Dip - 1 year
Voice Studies - PG Dip 1 year
Production Related:
Art & Design - BTec Foundation Course - 1 year
Design Interpretation (Scenic Art/ Scenic Constuction/
Prop Making/ Costume Construction)
DipHE - 2 years
Stage Management and Technical Arts - DipHE -
2 years
Theatre Studies (Design) (Puppetry) - BA(Hons)
3 years.
Advanced Theatre Practice (Set/ Costume/ Lighting/
Sound Design/ Puppetry/ Directing/ Writing/
Dramaturgy/ Performance). PGDip 1 year.
PGCE in Media Education with English, 1 year
Education:
Drama & Education - BA(Hons)
Postgraduate Certificate in Education Drama (PGCE) -
1year
PGCE in Media Education in English - 1 year
Therapy:

# The Complete Performer

## SCHOOL OF ACTING
### Director: Maggie Kinloch

Arts Educational London Schools
14 Bath Road
Chiswick, London W4 1LY
Tel: 0181 987 6666 Fax: 0181 987 6656
e-mail:   drama@artsed.co.uk
web:      http://artsed.drama.ac.uk

## 3 Yr Diploma Course
### an NCDT Accredited Course

A 3-year Diploma Course offering the full range of acting
skills to students aged 18 or more. The emphasis is on
the actor in performance and training is Stanislavski based.
Classes and tutorial work include: voice and speech,
movement and dance, acting techniques, mask, combat,
theatre history and broadcasting skills.

## the**ACTING** company

### Director: Adrian James

A highly intensive one-year post-graduate course offering
a fully integrated ensemble training for mature students with
a degree or equivalent professional experience. The course
includes a summer repertory season in a London venue.

### an NCDT Accredited Course

Drama and Movement Therapy - CSSD/Sesame
PG/Dip - 1 year.
PART TIME COURSES:
Performance Related:
Shakespeare summer course
Actors' Pieces summer course
Movement for Performance summer course
Introduction to Acting - 3 modules each over 8 weeks.
Alternative/New Stand-Up Comedy - over 12 weeks.
Writing for the Stage over 8 weeks.
MA Voice Studies.
Production Related:
Computer-Aided Design - Advanced Cert - 1 year
(modular).
Painting - 2 years - MA/PGDip.
MA in Advanced Theatre Practice, 1 year.
Education:
Drama Education - Advanced Cert - modular
Media Education - Advanced Cert - modular
Arts Education (Drama) - MA - 2 years
Theatre and Education - Post Experience Diploma -
distance learning.
PGCE in Drama + PGCE in Media Education with
English.
The school also offers a variety of Evening Classes
and Summer Schools; Professional Updating courses
and External Assessments. The school can provide
courses for amateur theatre by mutual arrangement.

### THE CENTRAL SCHOOL OF SPEECH AND DRAMA
The Embassy Theatre, 64 Eton Avenue,
Swiss Cottage, London NW3 3HY
Tel: 0171 722 8183 Fax: 0171 722 4132
Administration:
Principal: Professor Robert S.Fowler, FRSA

FULL TIME COURSES:
Performance Related:
Acting - BA - NCDT - 3 years
Performance Studies - MA/PG Dip - 1 year
Voice Studies - PG Dip 1 year
Production Related:
Art & Design - BTec Foundation Course - 1 year
Design Interpretation (Scenic Art/ Scenic Constuction/
Prop Making/ Costume Construction)
DipHE - 2 years
Stage Management and Technical Arts - DipHE - 2
years
Theatre Studies (Design) (Puppetry) - BA(Hons) 3
years.
Advanced Theatre Practice (Set/ Costume/ Lighting/
Sound Design/ Puppetry/ Directing/ Writing/
Dramaturgy/ Performance). PGDip 1 year.
PGCE in Media Education with English, 1 year
Education:
Drama & Education - BA(Hons)
Postgraduate Certificate in Education Drama (PGCE) -
1year
PGCE in Media Education in English - 1 year
Therapy:
Drama and Movement Therapy - CSSD/Sesame
PG/Dip - 1 year.
PART TIME COURSES:
Performance Related:
Shakespeare summer course
Actors' Pieces summer course
Movement for Performance summer course
Introduction to Acting - 3 modules each over 8 weeks.
Alternative/New Stand-Up Comedy - over 12 weeks.
Writing for the Stage over 8 weeks.
MA Voice Studies.
Production Related:

Computer-Aided Design - Advanced Cert - 1 year (modular).
Painting - 2 years - MA/PGDip.
MA in Advanced Theatre Practice, 1 year.
Education:
Drama Education - Advanced Cert - modular
Media Education - Advanced Cert - modular
Arts Education (Drama) - MA - 2 years
Theatre and Education - Post Experience Diploma - distance learning.
PGCE in Drama + PGCE in Media Education with English.
The school also offers a variety of Evening Classes and Summer Schools; Professional Updating courses and External Assessments. The school can provide courses for amateur theatre by mutual arrangement.

## CYGNET TRAINING THEATRE
New Theatre, Friars Gate,
Exeter EX2 4AZ
Tel: 01392 277189
Administration/Courses:
Principal: Monica Shallis
Three year full-time professional acting course.
Options: Acting with Directing
Acting with Music
Acting with Stage Management
Training in the context of a working theatre company with widespread touring.

## DRAMA CENTRE LONDON
176 Prince of Wales Road,
London NW5 3PT
Tel: 0171 267 1177 Fax: 0171 485 7129
Email: info@dcl.drama.ac.uk
Web Site: http://dcl.drama.ac.uk
Principal: Christopher Fettes
3 year full-time BA(Hons) Acting and Acting Diploma Course.
Accredited by the National Council for Drama Training.
2 year full-time professional instructors course.
BA(Hons) Acting Course validated by the University of Central Lancashire.

## EAST 15 ACTING SCHOOL
Corbett Theatre, Hatfields, Rectory Lane,
Loughton Essex IG10 3RU
Tel: 0181 508 5983 Fax: 0181 508 7521
Administration/Courses:
Founder and Artistic Director: Margaret Walker
Full Time:
3 year Acting BA Course
1 year Postgraduate Course
1 week Summer drama workshops at Corbett Theatre from mid-July annually, phone for details

## GUILDFORD SCHOOL OF ACTING
Millmead Terrace,
Guildford, Surrey GU2 5AT
Tel: 01483 560701 Fax: 01483 535431
Administration/Courses:
Principal: Gordon McDougall
Diploma Courses:
Three year degree course, validated by University of Surrey, Acting and Musical Pathways.
Three year performance course: Acting and Musical Theatre options.
One year acting course.

Two year stage management course: One year option for graduates and mature students.

## GUILDHALL SCHOOL OF MUSIC AND DRAMA
Barbican,
London EC2 8DT
Tel: 0171 628 2571 Fax: 0171 256 9438
Web Site: www.gsmd.ac.uk
Administration/Courses:
Principal: Ian Horsbrugh
Director of Drama: Peter Clough
Director of Technical Theatre Studies: Sue Thornton
9 term professional acting course leading to BA(Hons) Degree in acting. 9 term Stage Management course leading to a BA(Hons) Degree in Stage Management & Technical Theatre.
Part-time tuition available in speech and drama.
Junior drama class for 13-18 year olds on Saturdays.

## LAMDA (LONDON ACADEMY OF MUSIC AND DRAMATIC ART)
Tower House, 226 Cromwell Road,
London SW5 0SR
Tel: 0171 373 9883 Fax: 0171 370 4739
Administration:
Principal: Peter James
Assistant Principal:Colin Cook
Administration: Anthony Sprackling
Director Stage Management and Technical Courses: Sarah Rowe
Admissions: Jo Butterworth
Courses: 3 year Acting Course (9 Terms)
1 year Classical Acting Course (3 Terms)
2 year Stage Management Technical Theatre Course (6 Terms)
Postgraduate one year Diploma Course.
Musical Director & Repetiteur (1 place)
Designers (2 Places)
Director (2 places)
Carpentry (1 place)
Movement Instruction (1 Place)
4 week Shakespeare Summer Workshop.

## MANCHESTER METROPOLITAN UNIVERSITY
Capitol Building, School Lane, Didsbury,
Manchester M20 6HT
Tel: 0161 247 2000 extn: 7123 Fax: 0161 448 0135
Administration/Courses:
Head of School: Niamh Dowling
3 year Acting Course leading to Ba(Hons) Theatre Arts (Acting).

## MOUNTVIEW THEATRE SCHOOL
104 Crouch Hill,
London N8 9EA
Tel: 0181 340 5885 Fax: 0181 348 1727
Email: enquiries@mountview.ac.uk
Web Site: http://www.mountview.ac.uk
Administration:
Principal: Paul Clements
Deputy Principal: Jude Tisdall
Courses: Full-time Courses:
3 year BA (Hons) Acting & Musical Theatre*
1 year (4 term) Postgraduate Acting & Musical Theatre.*
2 year BA (Hons) Technical Theatre*

1 year Postgraduate Technical Theatre
1 year (4 term) Directors course.
*Courses accredited by the NCDT.
Part-time courses:
Adult evening foundation courses in Acting, Acting for the screen and Musical Theatre.
2 week Summer schools in Acting, Acting for the Screen and Musical Theatre.
Courses and holiday workshops for children and teenagers.

## THE OXFORD SCHOOL OF DRAMA
Sansomes Farm Studios, Woodstock,
Oxford OX20 1ER
Tel: 01993 812883 Fax: 01993 811220
Email: info@oxford.drama.ac.uk
Web Site: oxford.drama.ac.uk
Courses:
One and Three Year Acting Courses. All courses include: Voice, Movement and Text interpretation. Also Summer Courses and Six Month Foundation course. Member of C.D.S. Three year course accredited by NCDT.

## ROYAL ACADEMY OF DRAMATIC ART
18-22 Chenies Street,
London WC1E 7EX
Tel: 0171 636 7076 Fax: 0171 323 3865
Administration/Courses:
Principal: Nicholas Barter M.A.
9 term (3 year) full time acting course.
6 term (2 year) full-time stage management and theatre production course.
4 term full-time stage electrics course.
4 term full-time scenic construction course.
4 term full-time property making course.
4 term full-time scenic painting course.

## ROYAL SCOTTISH ACADEMY OF MUSIC AND DRAMA
100 Renfrew Street,
Glasgow G2 3DB
Tel: 0141 332 4101 Fax: 0141 353 0289
Administration/Courses:
Principal: Philip Ledger CBE
Director of School of Drama: Vladimir Mirodan
3 year full-time course leading to BA (Dramatic Studies) with fourth year Honous option.
3 year full-time stage course leading to BA (Stage Management Studies) (Subject to validation).

## WEBBER DOUGLAS ACADEMY OF DRAMATIC ART
39 Clareville Street,
London SW7 5AP
Tel: 0171 370 4154 Fax: 0171 373 5639
Administration/Courses:
Principal: R.Jago
3 year acting course (8 terms)
2 year acting course (6 terms)
1 year postgraduate course.
Summer school July/August.

## WELSH COLLEGE OF MUSIC AND DRAMA
Castle Grounds, Cathays Park,
Cardiff CF1 3ER
Tel: 01222 342854 Fax: 01222 237639

Web Site: www.wcmd.ac.uk
Administration/Courses:
Principal: E. Fivet MA FRCM FRSA
Assistant Principal of Drama: David Edwards
Drama trains students for the progessional theatre as Directors, Actors, Designers or Stage Managers. The School also contributes to the training of specialist Drama teachers for work in scondary schools.
The College's principle concern is to provide each individual student with a throrough professional training which will enable him/her to achieve his/her full potential as an artist and craftsman. The College's courses aim to equip students with the  appropriate knowledge, skills and techniques for a career in Theatre and Drama while at the same time stimulating personal enthusiasm, creativity and flair. The College offers the following courses:
Three year
BA Theatre Studies - Acting Option
BA Theatre Studies - Design Option
BA Theatre Studies - Stage Management Option
One year
Advanced Diploma Course in Drama - Acting Option
Advanced Diploma Course in Drama - Directing Option
Advanced Diploma Course in Drama - Design Option
Advanced Diploma Course in Drama - Stage Management Option.
(The School also contributes all Subject Selected modules to the BA in Theatre & Media Drama offered by the University of Glamorgan. Applications for admission to these courses should be made to the institution concerned).
The School has purpose-built teaching spaces and workshops, studio and rehearsal facilities. The principal performance areas are the Bute Theatre and Caird Studio.

# Other Full Time Colleges and Stage Schools

## 344 DANCE CENTRE
Alexandra Park, Fishponds, Bristol BS16 2BG
Tel: 0117 965 5660
Administration/Courses:
Principal: Kathy Plaster L.I.S.T.D
Full time professional dance, musical theatre and teaching training course.
Ballet: ISTD Imperial and RAD, Jazz, Modern, Tap, National, Contemporary RAD & ISTD Major and Teaching exams., ISTD History & Anatomy Drama (LAMDA exams), Singing, Stage Management, A Level Dance.

## THE ACADEMY DRAMA SCHOOL
The Andrew Sketchley Theatre, 189 Whitechapel Road, London E1 1DN
Tel: 0171 377 8735/624 5400
Email: academy@eada.demon.co.uk
Web Site: www.eada.demon.co.uk/
A full-time drama training held entirely in the evening and at weekends. Also full and part-time day and evening courses.

## ACADEMY OF LIVE AND RECORDED ARTS
Royal Victoria Building, Trinity Road, London SW18 3SX
Tel: 0181 870 6475 Fax: 0181 875 0789
Administration/Courses:
Principal: Sorrel Carson
3 year full-time Actors Course*
1 year post-graduate Course
1 year stage management course.
Total training in the performing arts - Film, TV, Theatre
*Accredited by N.C.D.T.
ALRA Associates evening. Weekend and Summer School classes for Television.

## THE ARDEN SCHOOL OF THEATRE
Sale Road, Northenden, Manchester M23 0DD
Tel/Fax: 0161 957 1715
Email: qst@manchester-city-coll.ac.uk
Contact: Barbara Howorth

## ARTS EDUCATIONAL SCHOOL
Tring Park, Tring, Hertfordshire HP23 5LX
Tel: 01442 824255 Fax: 01442 891069
Principal: Mrs J Billing
Full time education in drama, dance and music
Age 8-18

## THE ARTS INSTITUTE AT BOURNEMOUTH
Wallisdown, Poole, Dorset BH12 5HH
Tel: 01202 363279 Fax: 01202 363335
Email: artsandevents@arts-inst-bournemouth.ac.uk
Administration/Courses:
Course Director: Richard Wright
BTEC Higher National Diploma in Arts and Event Administration - a 2 year full-time course preparing students for careers in all aspects of Arts and Event Administration, with the emphasis on practical work.

## ARTTS INTERNATIONAL
Highfield Grange, Bubwith, North Yorkshire YO8 6DP
Tel: 01757 288088 Fax: 01757 288253
Email: artts@pavilion.co.uk
Web Site: http://www.pavilion.co.uk/artts
Contact: Duncan Lewis - Associate Director
Residential skill centre, offering intensive multi-media, multi-skilling courses in theatre, video/film, television and radio. One year diploma course.
Ten week foundation skills course and two week summer short course offered.

## ASIAN MUSIC AND ARTS ACADEMY
10 Dudley Road, Southall, Middlesex UB2 5AR
Tel: 0181 574 1900
Contact: Mr Banga

## DOREEN BIRD COLLEGE OF PERFORMING ARTS
Birkbeck Centre, Birkbeck Road, Sidcup, Kent DA14 4DE
Tel: 0181 300 6004/0181 300 3031
Principal: Miss Doreen Bird
3 year course for the theatre, ballet and specialised teaching. Age 16+.

## BIRMINGHAM THEATRE SCHOOL
Old Repertory Theatre, Station Street, Birmingham B5 4DY
All enquiries ring: 0121 643 3300
Courses:
1 year acting diploma course - 18+
2 year acting foundation course - 16+
1 year open access theatre training course (Jan Start)
1 year postgraduate acting course

## CENTRAL SAINT MARTINS COLLEGE OF ART & DESIGN
Southampton Row, London WC1B 4AP
Tel: 0171 514 7000 Fax: 0171 514 7024
Administration/Courses:
BA(Hons) Theatre Design, 3 years full-time course.
Course Director: Dermot Hayes
MA in European Scenography, 1 year full time course.
Director: Pamela Howard

## CENTRAL SCHOOL OF BALLET
10 Herbal Hill, Clerkenwell Road, London EC1R 5EJ
Tel: 0171 837 6332 Fax: 0171 833 5571
Administration/Courses:
Director: Ann Stannard, Founding Director:
Christopher Gable
Course: Three year, full time diploma course. Students accepted from 16.
CSB has the most comprehensive dance course in Britain today - with Classical ballet at its core, numerous other disciplines are taught - Contemporary, Jazz and Characcter dance, Voice and Singing, Choreography and Drama, with the aim of training the complete dancer. In addition, all senior students are encouraged to continue with academic studies to A'level standard.
Ballet Central, the school's touring company and spring board company for Northern Ballet Theatre, is a unique opportunity for third year graduating students to experience the demands and the realities, not forgetting the rewards of the professional theatre.

## THE CENTRE FOR CONTEMPORARY CIRCUS AND PHYSICAL PERFORMANCE
Circomedia, Kingswood Foundation, Britannia Road, Kingswood, Bristol BS15 8DB
Tel/Fax: 0117 947 7288
Email: info@circomedia.demon.co.uk
Web Site: http://www.circomedia.demon.co.uk
Administration/Courses:
Administrator: Kim Lawrence
Courses:
1 year foundation course in Circus skills and Physical theatre
3 months introductory course
Professional classes in Flying, Trapeze, Corde Lisse, Swinging Trapeze
Summer School
Outreach and Corporate Work
Trapeze Project for Disadvantaged Young People

## CHICHESTER COLLEGE OF ARTS
Westgate Fields, Chichester, West Sussex PO19 1SB
Tel: 01243 786321 Fax: 01243 527884
Administration/Courses:
Head of Department: M G Seath
Studio Theatre (seats 100, retractable) to form large studio or exhibition area.

Workshop, Dressing Rooms
2 dance studios - sprung floors, mirrors
5 drama studios - showers, toilets
Lighting and sound control room, recording facilities.
Administration and Box office, coffee bar area.

### CITY OF LEEDS COLLEGE OF MUSIC
3 Quarry Hill, St.Peter's Square, Leeds LS2 7PD
Tel: 0113 222 3400 Fax: 0113 243 8798
Administration/Courses:
Principal: D. Hoult Mus.B, MPhil, GRSM, ARMCM.
Vocal studies and performance experience for full-time
students (2 and 3 year courses) and part-time course
students.

### CITY OF LIVERPOOL COMMUNITY COLLEGE
Greenbank Centre, Mossley Avenue,
Liverpool L18 1JB
Tel: 0151 733 5511 Theatre Dept. Direct Line:
0151 734 2622 General Fax: 0151 734 2525
Administration/Courses:
Head of Theatre Arts: John Williams
B.Tec/HND in community theatre.
B.Tec/HND in community dance.
B.Tec/HND in music.
B.Tec/First Diploma in Dance and Drama
B.Tec National Diploma in Performing Arts - Dance
B.Tec National Diploma in Performing Arts - Acting
Foundation Course in Performing Arts

### COLLEGE OF THE ROYAL ACADEMY OF DANCING
36 Battersea Square, London SW11 3RA
Tel: 0171 223 0091 Fax: 0171 326 8040
Administration/Courses:
Principal: Dr Susan Danby, LRAD, ARAD
3 year ballet BA(Hons) Degree course in the Art and
Teaching of Ballet.
Distance learning BPhil Hons Degree on Ballet and
contextual studies.

### COURT THEATRE TRAINING COMPANY
The Courtyard, 10 York Way, Kings Cross,
London N1 9AA
Tel/Fax: 0171 833 0870
Artistic Director: June Abbott
Courses:
2 year actors in training: Full time, Thurs-Sun 9.25am-
10pm
1 year theatre design: Full time, Thurs-Sun 9.25am-
10pm
1 or 2 year director's course: Full time, Thurs-Sun
9.25am-10pm
1 year stage management
1 year (4 terms) postgraduate acting - full time Mon-Fri
(9.25am-6pm)
All courses are full time Monday to Friday 09.30 to
18.00.

### CROYDON COLLEGE
School of Art & Design, Fairfield, Croydon CR9 1DX
Tel: 0181 686 5700 Fax: 0181 760 5944
BTEC HND in Design (Theatre Studies)

## KATHLEEN DAVIS STAGE SCHOOL AND EMPIRE THEATRE COLLEGE

Empire Dance Studios, Empire Theatre,
High Street West, Sunderland SR1 3EX
Tel: 0191 522 0365
Juveniles for professional shows, choreography and own dance group.

## DRAMA STUDIO LONDON

Grange Court, 1 Grange Road, London W5 5QN
Tel: 0181 579 3897 Fax: 0181 566 2035
Email: admin@dramastl.demon.co.uk
Administration/Courses:
Executive Director: Peter Layton
1 year full time Postgraduate acting course.
(Accredited by National Council for Drama Training).
1 year full time Director's Course.
Age 21+.

## FI STEPS

6 Cook Road, Horsham, West Sussex RH12 5GG
Tel/Fax: 01403 248626
Principal: Fiona Whyte
Musical Director: Pam Alexander
Secretary: Wendy Irwin
No examination. Concentrating on performance.

## GAIETY SCHOOL OF ACTING

Meeting House Square, Temple Bar, Dublin 2 Eire
Tel: 00 353 1 679 9277 Fax: 00 353 1 679 9568
Email: gaietyschool@indigo.ie
Director: Joe Dowling
Executive Director: Patrick Sutton
2 year Full time intensive Acting Programme*
1 year Post Training Performance Company*
1 year Part Time Foundation Course (Evenings)
1 year Part Time Performance Course
10 week introduction to Drama Course (Evenings)
Practical Playwriting Course (Evenings)
Drama weekends
Young Gaiety 6-16 years (Saturdays)
Youth Theatre 16-19 years
Part Time Performance course for adults
Summer Schools for Adults and Children
Irish International Theatre Summer School
*Entry by audition - Dublin, London & New York.
For further details contact Administration.

## HACKNEY COMMUNITY COLLEGE

Woodbery Down, Woodbery Grove, London N4 2SH
Tel: 0181 809 7737 Fax: 0181 802 5122
Certificate in Technical Theatre
An excellent course for those who wish to learn new skills or to validate skills previously learnt about backstage duties and responsibilities.  Other courses on offer:
BTEC National in Performing Arts
Dance Foundation
Dance Courses
Music Courses
Age 16+

## THE HERTFORDSHIRE THEATRE SCHOOL

Queen Street House, 40 Queen Street, Hitchin,
Hertfordshire SG4 9TS
Tel: 01462 421416

Administration/Courses:
Co-Principals: John Gardiner and Kirk Foster
Contact: Annie Wilkinson
Full-time 3 year course in Acting and Musical Theatre.
Full-time 1 year post-graduate course in Acting and Musical Theatre.
Age 18+

## HOXTON MUSIC HALL THEATRE AND ARTS CENTRE

130 Hoxton Street, London N1 6SH
Tel: 0171 739 5431 Fax: 0171 729 3815
Courses:
Full and part time one year courses in Community Theatre accredited by Middlesex University. Modules in devising, acting, theatre in education, music and songwriting, working with text etc.
Full and part time one year courses in Theatre Technicals and Stagecraft. Modules in costume, theatre management, lighting, sound, stagecraft and music technology etc.
These are access to Higher Education Courses, attendance of which guarantees the student an interview for relevant courses at Middlesex University.
Our full time courses have been specially designed not to affect the benefit entitlement of Students.

## ITALIA CONTI ACADEMY OF THEATRE ARTS

Italia House, 23 Goswell Road, London EC1M 7AJ
Tel: 0171 608 0044 Fax: 0171 253 1430
Administration/Courses:
Principal: Ms Anne Sheward
Junior and student courses in performing arts, dance, drama and singing including GCSE.
Age 9+ full-time education. Weekend associate classes: Age 3 to adult in all.
Student courses 16+ (1 and 3 year full-time). Diploma & B.A Hons Degree

## KENT INSTITUTE OF ART & DESIGN AT MAIDSTONE

Oakwood Park, Oakwood Road, Maidstone,
Kent ME16 8AG
Tel: 01622 757286 Fax: 01622 692003
Administration/Courses:
Director: Vaughan Grylls, Higher DFA (Lond) FRSA
MA Time-based Media with Electronic Imaging.
B.A.(Hons) Visual Communication (3 years) with pathways in Graphic Design, Illustration, Combined Studies, Time-Based-Media (Film & Video)+ Photography. BTEC HND in Graphic Design and Illustration.

## KINGSWAY COLLEGE

Regents Park Centre, Longford Street,
London NW1 3HB
Tel: 0171 306 5954 Fax: 0171 306 5950
Administration/Courses:
Artistic Director: Zizi Conroy
Kingsway College's Performing Arts Centre offers a range of courses from BTEC National Dance and Drama to nightly acting classes. NVQ based courses in Stagecraft/Costume and Arts administration also available, as well as independent dance and drama classes.

## LABAN CENTRE LONDON

Laurie Grove, London SE14 6NH
Tel: 0181 692 4070 Fax: 0181 694 8749
Email: info@laban.co.uk
Web Site: www.laban.co.uk
Administration/Courses:
Principal and Chief Executive: Dr Marion North, PhD, Darts
BA (Hons) or Diploma Dance Theatre - 3 years f/t
Professional Diploma in Dance Studies - f/t or p/t
Professional Diploma in Community Dance Studies - f/t or p/t
Specialist Diploma: Dance Notating - 40 weeks, 2 half days per week
Specialist Diploma: Teaching Studies in Contemprary Dance - p/t
Independent Study - 1 year f/t or 2 years p/t
MA Dance Studies - 1 year f/t, 2 or 3 years p/t
MA Dance Movement Therapy - 2 years f/t or 3 or 4 years p/t
Postgraduate Diploma Dance Movement Therapy - 2 years f/t or 3 or 4 years p/t
MA Community Dance Studies - 2 years p/t
Graduate Diploma in Performance - 1 year f/t
Graduate Diploma in Visual Design for Dance - 15 week course, 1 day per week
MPhil or PhD Research Degrees - f/t or p/t
Enquiries: Dr Marion North

## LAINE THEATRE ARTS

The Studios, East Street, Epsom, Surrey KT17 1HH
Tel: 01372 724648 Fax: 01372 723775
Web Site: www.lainetheatrearts.co.uk
Principal: Betty Laine

## THE LONDON ACADEMY OF PERFORMING ARTS

St.Matthew's Church, St.Petersburg Place, London W2 4LA
Tel: 0171 727 0220 Fax: 0171 727 0330
Administrative Director: Parsonage Kelly
Administration/Courses:
The Academy offers the following courses:
1. 2 Year Diploma in Classical Acting
2. 2 Year Post Graduate Diploma in Acting (Musical Theatre Option).
3. 1 Year Graduate Diploma in Acting
4. 1 Year Stage Management Course.
5. 1 Year Post Graduate Musical Theatre Course
6. Twelve week full-time Classical Acting Semesters.
7. Four week full-time Summer Shakespearean Acting Course (beginners and advanced

## LONDON AND INTERNATIONAL SCHOOL OF ACTING (L.I.S.A)

1 Chippenham Mews, Marylands Road, London W9 2AN
Tel: 0171 727 2342 Fax: 0171 221 7210
Courses:
One year Post-grad Course. Two years intensive Course, 4 x 10 weeks pa. Six Month intensive course.

## LONDON CENTRE OF THEATRE STUDIES

12-18 Hoxton Street, London N1 6NG
Tel:/Fax: 0171 739 5866

The full time and part time acting courses realistically prepare actors for employment in the profession. Excellence is achieved by helping students develop their self confidence and realise their talent potential.

## LONDON CONTEMPORARY DANCE SCHOOL

The Place, 17 Dukes Road, London WC1H 9AB
Tel: 0171 387 0152 Fax: 0171 383 4851
Email: LCDS@mailbox.ulcc.ac.uk
Web Site: www.theplace.org.uk
Administration/Courses:
Director: Veronica Lewis MBE
Full-time certificate and degree courses in Contemporary Dance & Choreography. Evening classes. Vacation courses.

## LONDON STUDIO CENTRE

42-50 York Way, London N1 9AB
Tel: 0171 837 7741 Fax: 0171 837 3248
Administration/Courses:
Director: Nicholas Espinosa
3 year Theatre Dance Course, accredited by the Council for Dance Education and Training (UK): Leading to a London Studio Centre Diploma - entry at 16+ by audition, no academic qualifications needed. Or a BA Honours degree (validated by Middlesex University), 18+ with two A-levels (or equivalent) entry by audition.

## NATIONAL FILM & TELEVISION SCHOOL

Beaconsfield Studios, Station Road, Beaconsfield, Buckinghamshire HP9 1LG
Tel: 01494 671234 Fax: 01494 674042
Email: ajones@nftsfilm-tv.ac.uk
Contact: Central Administration
Professional training programme in film and television specialising in - Animation Direction, Cinematography, Documentary Direction, Editing, Fiction Direction, Producing, Screen Design, Screen Music (2 years), Screen Sound, Screenwriting (2 years). All three years unless otherwise stated.

## OLDHAM COLLEGE

School of Visual & Performing Arts, Rochdale Road, Oldham, Lancashire OL9 6AA
Tel: 0161 624 5214 Fax: 0161 626 9059
Web Site: www.oldham.ac.uk
Courses:
National diploma courses in acting, dance, popular music, stage management, media, theatre lighting and sound audio engineering, television and video.  Higher national diploma courses in acting, dance, arts administration, theatre lighting and sound design, stage management.

## PERFORMERS DANCE COLLEGE

2-4 Chase Road, Corringham, Essex SS17 7QH
Tel: 01375 672053 Fax: 01375 672353
Full time Theatre dance training.

## THE POOR SCHOOL

242 Pentonville Road, London N1 9JY
Tel: 0171 837 6030
Full-time drama training scheduled in the evenings and at weekends and charged for at cost.

Reg.Charity No. 299619

## QUEEN MARGARET COLLEGE DRAMA DEPARTMENT
Clerwood Terrace, Edinburgh EH12 8TS
Tel/Fax Department: 0131 317 3542
BO: 0131 317 3247
Courses:
BA/BA(Hons) Acting, Drama Studies, Stage Management & Theatre Production and Combined Studies (Theatre Studies).

## RAVENSCOURT THEATRE SCHOOL
Head Office: Tandy House, 30-40 Dalling Road, Hammersmith, London W6 0JB
Tel: 0181 741 0707 (4 lines) Fax: 0181 741 1786

## REDROOFS THEATRE SCHOOL
Littlewick Green, Maidenhead, Berkshire SL6 3QY
Tel: 01628 822982 Fax: 01628 822461
Courses:
Full-time professional training for students over 16.
Full-time professional training for children 7-16 with general education.

## RETFORD INTERNATIONAL COLLEGE
(Stage and Character/Special Effects)
25-27 Bridgegate, Retford, Nottinghamshire DN22 7UX
Tel: 01777 707371 Fax: 01777 860374
Courses in basic make-up, photographic, television, competitive make-up, film and stage make-up, special effects, hair design and wig making. CIDESCO diploma in artistic make-up. City and guilds wig making certificate. ITEC diploma in Stage & Character make-up. Beauty therapy and hairdressing also available. Grant maintained. No academic fees payable.

## RICHMOND DRAMA SCHOOL
Parkshot Centre, Parkshot, Richmond, Surrey TW9 2RE
Tel: 0181 940 0170 ext.325 Fax: 0181 332 6560
Courses:
Full time drama school (one year course).
Diploma validated by OCR (Oxford, Cambridge and Royal Society of the Arts).
Nationally recognised Access course.

## ROYAL ACADEMY OF MUSIC
Marylebone Road, London NW1 5HT
Tel: 0171 873 7383 Fax: 0171 873 7384
Administration/Courses:
Principal: Curtis Price
Director of Opera: Michael Rosewell
Professor of Music Theatre: Mary Hammond
Head of Vocal Studies: Mark Wildman
Special course for senior and advanced singing students.

## ROYAL BALLET SCHOOL
Seniors: Darrens Court, 155 Talgarth Road, London W14 9DE
Tel: 0181 748 6335 Fax: 0181 563 0649 Juniors: White Lodge, Richmond Park, Surrey TW10 5HR Tel: 0181 876 5547 Fax: 0181 392 2833

Administration/Courses:
Director: Dame Merle Park, OBE
Assistant Director (Development, Academic & Administration) B. Mus: Nigel Grant
Academic Principal: Mr John Mitchell.
Classical ballet training, juniors 11-16; seniors, 16 plus; Teachers Course offered; Junior associate scheme (age 8+).

## ROYAL COLLEGE OF MUSIC
Prince Consort Road, London SW7 2BS
Tel: 0171 589 3643 Fax: 0171 589 7740
Email: pbritten@rcm.ac.uk
Web Site: www.rcm.ac.uk
Administration/Courses:
Director: Dr Janet Rittaman.
The Bursar: Michael Morgan
Director of Opera: Michael Rosewell
Full Opera Course for post-graduate students.

## BARBARA SPEAKE STAGE SCHOOL
East Acton Lane, London W3 7EG
Tel: 0181 743 1306 Fax: 0181 740 6542
Email: cpuk@aol.com
Ages 4-16
Full-time education

## UNITED KINGDOM DANCE & DRAMA FEDERATION
2 Woodlands Street, Tunstall, Staffordshire ST6 6AP
Tel: 01782 823472 Fax: 01782 823472
Dance education to teacher standards. Training for professional dance careers. Teacher membership welcome.

## WIMBLEDON SCHOOL OF ART
Merton Hall Road, Wimbledon, London SW19 3QA
Tel: 0181 408 5000 Fax: 0181 408 5050
Administration/Courses:
Principal: Prof. Roderick Brigg
Courses: All Higher Education courses are validated by University of Surrey.
BA(Hons) Theatre Design (with areas of specialisation including Technical Interpretation/Desing and Costume Interpretation/Design). 3 years Full time
MA in Theatre Design/scenography - 2 years p-t.
Dip HE/BA (Hons)  2/3 years full-time.

## SYLVIA YOUNG THEATRE SCHOOL
Rossmore Road, Marylebone, London NW1 6NJ
Tel: 0171 402 0673 Fax: 0171 723 1040
Part time stage training/Saturday classes/Summerschool.

# Part Time Colleges and Stage Schools

## ALTERNATIVE DRAMA SCHOOL
20 Waldergrave Road, London SE19 2AJ
Tel: 0181 653 7854 Fax: 0181 768 0189
Courses:

Full-time training (eves. Weekend) for the profession by professionals. One of the longest established of its kind. Entry by interview. Small deposit, then pay as you go.
Courses: 2 Year Intensive Acting course - £50 per wk.
4 Week Summer Acting Courses - £160.

## ANGELA ALLPORT SCHOOLS

Barling Magna Dance Studios, 398 Little Wakering Road, Barling, Essex SS3 0LN
Tel: 01702 217281
Courses:
Teaching children/students from 2 years classical ballet - I.S.T.D. exams, grades to majors, R.A.D. Ballet majors. Modern theatre exams, Tap exams, Jazz, Character, Singing, Drama - Adult classes. Choreography.

## ANGLIA SUMMER SCHOOLS

15 Inglis Road, Colchester, Essex CO3 3HU
Tel: 01206 540111 Fax: 01206 766944
Residential Theatre Performance Courses for 8 to 19 year olds, divided by age groups, during Easter (nine day) and Summer (six and thirteen day) Holidays. Immersed in every aspect of stagework - acting, singing, dancing lighting, stage management, make up, auditions - each course ends with a performance of a show created during the holiday

## JOAN BARNES THEATRE SCHOOL AND THEATRE

20 Green Street, Hazlemere, High Wycombe, Buckinghamshire HP15 7RB
Tel: 01494 523193
Courses:
Part time comprehensive tuition.
All ages: 3 years to adult
Also Summer School - August

## B.L.A. ACADEMY OF THEATRE ARTS

Performance House, 20 Passey Place,
London SE9 5DQ
Tel: 0181 850 9888 Fax: 0181 850 9944
Principals: Miss Susan Hussey &
Mrs Maureen P. Hussey
Headmaster: Mr Peter Monard
Full time & part time Theatre School of Performing Arts. Academic, full time up to GCSE age 7 to 16 years. Student course of Performing Arts age 16+. Saturday schools, evening classes and summer schools. Call for details.

## BRIGHT SPARKS THEATRE SCHOOL & AGENCY

16 Wellfield Road, Streatham, London SW16 2BP
Tel: 0181 769 3500 Fax: 0181 677 8659
Full time Day school for children from 3-16 years combining Theatre Arts with Education following the National Curriculum to GCSE level.
Part time classes in the week and Saturdays in Drama Musical Theatre singing and dancing.

## BRIGHTON DRAMA CENTRE

Office: 79 Sherwood Road, Seaford,
East Sussex BN25 3ED
Tel: 01323 897949 (24 hours) Fax: 01323 897972

Courses:
Acting workshops and tuition for the wide Brighton & Hove area - teenagers and young adults. Evening and holiday courses. Private lessons at anytime.

## BURTON TECHNICAL COLLEGE ROLLESTON

Station Road, Rolleston-upon-Dove, Burton-on-Trent, Staffordshire DE13 9AB
Tel: 01283 812333 Fax: 01283 520297
Administration/Courses:
Senior Course Tutor: Neil Willis.
Junior Youth Theatre: Age 7+.
Senior Youth Theatre: Age 16+.
First Diploma in Performing Arts (1 year).
National Diploma in Performing Arts (2 years f-t).
A-Levels in Theatre Studies, Film, Dance and Music.

## CHADSWORTH STAGE SCHOOL (CLAYGATE)

21 Hinchley Drive, Esher, Surrey KT10 0VZ
Tel: 0181 398 8104
Principal: Michelle Mackrell
Age: 2-18

## THE CLASSICAL ACADEMY FOR THE PERFORMING ARTS

PO Box 2973, London NW7 3JZ
Tel: 0181 951 3397
Adminstration/Courses:
Professor: M. H. Callender-Waldron.
The Academy offers:
A seven week introductory course for age 5-65 years, a one year follow up comprehensive part-time drama course for all age groups, a three year performing arts course, Dance (Ballet, Tap, Modern, Spanish Flamenco) to all levels, Singing and Dance Courses for different grades of varying intensity and duration, and teacher training courses for Dance and Drama.
Film Studies (inc. writing & directing) also available.

## GAIETY SCHOOL OF ACTING

Meeting House Square, Temple Bar, Dublin 2 Eire
Tel: 00 353 1 679 9277 Fax: 00 353 1 679 9568
Email: gaietyschool@indigo.ie
Director: Joe Dowling
Executive Director: Patrick Sutton
2 year Full time intensive Acting Programme*
1 year Post Training Performance Company*
1 year Part Time Foundation Course (Evenings)
1 year Part Time Performance Course
10 week introduction to Drama Course (Evenings)
Practical Playwriting Course (Evenings)
Drama weekends
Young Gaiety 6-16 years (Saturdays)
Youth Theatre 16-19 years
Part Time Performance course for adults
Summer Schools for Adults and Children
Irish International Theatre Summer School
*Entry by audition - Dublin, London & New York.
For further details contact Administration.

## GREASEPAINT: SCHOOL OF STAGE, TV, FILM MAKE-UP

Studio: 143 Northfield Avenue, Ealing,
London W13 9QT

Tel: 0181 840 6000 Fax: 0181 840 3983
Email: info@greasepaint.co.uk
Web Site: http://www.greasepaint.co.uk
Courses:
Intensive 3 month courses (January, April, September),
comprising 6 weeks Make-up, 3 weeks Prosthetics and
3 weeks Hairdressing. Workshops of varying lengths
and Fashion make-up courses also available.

### JENNIFER HALEY STAGE SCHOOL
Toad Hall, 67 Poppleton Road, Whips,
London E11 1LP
Tel: 0181 989 0060/8364
Training in dance drama and singing for both children
and adults (part-time).

### PATRICIA HAMMOND THEATRE SCHOOL
52a Green Lane, Belmont Parade, Chiselhurst,
Kent BR7 6AQ
Tel: 0181 467 9532

### THE HARLEQUIN THEATRE SCHOOL & AGENCY
Suite One, Excelsior House, 3/5 Balfour Road, Ilford,
Essex IG1 4HP
Tel: 0181 478 1848 Fax: 0181 553 1880

### THE DESMOND JONES SCHOOL OF MIME AND PHYSICAL THEATRE
Administration: 20 Thornton Avenue,
London W14 1QG
Tel: 0181 747 3537 School: 450a Uxbridge Road,
London W12

### LONDON CENTRE OF THEATRE STUDIES
12-18 Hoxton Street, London N1 6NG
Tel:/Fax: 0171 739 5866
The full time and part time acting courses realistically
prepare actors for employment in the profession.
Excellence is achieved by helping students develop
their self confidence and realise their talent potential

### MATINEE STAGE SCHOOL
168 Parrock Street, Gravesend, Kent DA12 1ER
Tel: 01474 332200 Fax: 01474 534081
Email: matineess@aol.com
Principal: Mrs.Gill Sage
Administrator: Mr Chris Sage
Part-time stage school with weekly fees plus full time
course for 16+. All aspects of profession covered.

### MORLEY COLLEGE THEATRE SCHOOL
61 Westminster Bridge Road, London SW1 7HT
Tel: 0171 928 8501 Fax: 0171 928 4074
Part-time classes for age 18+.
Director: Brian Croucher

### JACKIE PALMER STAGE SCHOOL
39 Daws Hill Lane, High Wycombe, Buckinghamshire
Tel: 01494 520978 or 01494 525938
Fax: 01494 510479
Age 3-18 years
Evenings and Weekends

### THE QUESTORS THEATRE
Matlock Lane, Ealing, London W5 5BQ
Tel: 0181 567 0011
Administration/Courses:
Director of Studies: David Emmet.
Intensive 2 year part-time training course in acting:
weekends and evenings - age 18 plus.
1 year introductory course: Saturdays - age 17-20.
Young People's groups: weekday evenings and
Saturdays - age 5-17.

### REDROOFS THEATRE SCHOOL
Littlewick Green, Maidenhead, Berkshire SL6 3QY
Tel: 01628 822982 Fax: 01628 822461
Courses:
Full-time professional training for students over 16.
Full-time professional training for children 7-16 with
general education.

### THE RETFORD INTERNATIONAL COLLEGE
25-27 Bridgegate, Retford, Nottinghamshire DN22 7UX
Tel: 01777 707371 Fax: 01777 860374
Courses:
Courses in basic make-up, photographic, television,
mannequin and competitive make-up, film and stage
make-up, special effects, hair design and wig making,
CIDESCO diploma in artistic make-up. City & Guilds
wigmaking certificate. ITEC diploma in Stage and
Character make-up. ITEC diploma in advanced wig
making. Courses are free for the majority of students.

### ROSHE SCHOOL
Holland House, Woodcock Hill, East Grinstead, West
Sussex RH19 2RE
Tel: 01342 326784 Fax: 01342 328098
Administration/Courses:
Principal: Rosemary Wood, A.R.A.D., F.I.S.T.D.
Part time training in all aspects of Drama, Dance and
singing 3 years to adult.
Evening dance college for students wishing to take the
I.S.T.D. Associate teaching qualification in Ballet and
Modern. Established 40 years.
"The Part-time school with a full-time commitment".

### ANNA SCHER THEATRE LTD
70-72 Barnsbury Road, London N1 0ES
Tel: 0171 278 2101 Fax: 0171 833 9467
Aftenoons & Evenings.
9-21+.

### SYLVIA YOUNG THEATRE SCHOOL
Rossmore Road, Marylebone, London NW1 6NJ
Tel: 0171 402 0673 Fax: 0171 723 1040
Part time stage training/Saturday
classes/Summerschool.

# Universities

### UNIVERSITY OF BIRMINGHAM
Drama & Theatre Arts Dept. Edgbaston, Birmingham
B15 2TT
Tel/Fax: 0121 414 5998
Courses:

3 year full-time course in drama and theatre Arts leading to B.A. (Hons) degree. 3 year full-time course Dance and Theatre Arts leading to B.A. (Hons) degree. 1 year full time course leading to M.A. in Playwriting Studies.
Postgraduate research degrees leading to M.A. M.Phil or Ph.D. in Drama or Dance.

## UNIVERSITY OF BRIGHTON
Hillbrow, Denton Road, Eastbourne,
East Sussex BN20 7SR
Tel: 01273 600900
Fax: 01273 643704
Administration/Courses:
Contact: Dr Richard Royce
4-year B.A. QTS in P.E. with Dance.
1 -year Post-graduate course in Dance.
1-year Post-graduate course in P.E. (including Dance).

## UNIVERSITY OF BRISTOL
Drama Department: Theatre, Film, Television
Cantocks Close, Woodland Road, Bristol BS8 1UP
Tel: 0117 928 7833
Fax: 0117 928 8251
Email: mark.sinfield@bris.ac.uk
www.bris.ac.uk/depts/drama
Administration/Courses:
Head of Drama Department: Martin White.
3 year full-time course in Drama leading to B.A. (Hons) degree.
3 year joint courses in Drama and English or a Modern language. The Modern Language Course involves a fourth year of study abroad.
2 year (minimum) postgraduate studies leading to M.Litt or PhD by dissertation.
1 year postgraduate course leading to MA in Early English Drama in Action.
1 year postgraduate course leading to MA in Television Studies.
2 year part-time postgraduate courses leading to MA in Early English Drama in Action.
1 year postgraduate course leading to MA in Film and Television, Production.

## UNIVERSITY OF CENTRAL ENGLAND IN BIRMINGHAM
School of Theatre Design, Corporation Street,
Birmingham B4 7DX
Tel: 0121 331 5820
Fax: 0121 331 5821
Faculty of Education:
Westbourne Road, Edgbaston, Birmingham B15 3TN
Tel: 0121 331 6101 Fax: 0121 331 6147
Administration:
Head of Theatre Design: Michael Clarke.
Education Course Directors: David Davis/Brian Watkins.
Courses:
3 year full-time Theatre Design course leading to BA (Hons.).
Specialist Drama in Education course leading to the Post Graduate Certificate in Education.
MA course in Drama in Education, full-time or part-time.
Birmingham Institute of Art & Design

## CITY UNIVERSITY
Dept. of Arts Policy & Mgmt. Level 7, Frobisher Crescent, Barbican Centre, Silk Street,
London EC2Y 8HB
Tel: 0171 477 8753
Fax: 0171 477 8887
Courses:
Diploma in Arts Administration: one year course.
MA Courses: Arts Management, Museum & Gallery Management, and Arts Criticism. 1 day a week for two years or 2 days a week for 1 year. Research: facilities exist for students to undertake research degrees of MPhil and PhD. Further details: send 12" x 9" sae to above address.

## DE MONTFORT UNIVERSITY
Dept. of Performing Arts, Crown Building, Newarke Street, Leicester LE1 9BH
Tel: 0116 250 6185
Fax: 0116 250 6188
Head: Michael Huxley
3 year full-time Theatre, Dance, Performing Arts.
MA in Performance Studies.

## DURHAM UNIVERSITY
School of Education, Leaszes Road,
Durham City DH1 1TA
Tel: 0191 374 2000
Fax: 0191 374 3506
Administration/Courses:
Head of Department: Professor D M Galloway
Ph.D. Full-time or part-time.
MA or MED by research (full time or part time)

## UNIVERSITY OF ESSEX
Wivenhoe Park, Colchester, Essex CO4 3SQ
Tel: 01206 873333
Fax: 01206 873598
Administration/Courses:
Course Director: Roger Howard.
Full-time undergraduate B.A. Hons. Literature scheme can include courses in modern and Renaissance drama. One-year postgraduate scheme leading to M.A. Literature (Drama) by instruction and dissertation: chiefly modern European drama with attention to current British theatre writing, but also 17th Century

## UNIVERSITY OF EXETER
School of Drama & Music, Department of Drama,
Thornlea, New North Road, Exeter EX4 4JZ
Tel: 01392 264580
Fax: 01392 264594
Email: L.G.Buchanan@ex.ac.uk
http://www.ex.ac.uk/drama/
Administration:
Head of School of Drama & Music: Christopher McCulough
Courses:
3 year full-time drama course !eading to single Honours Degree. Also available with English or a Modern Language as a combined Honours Degree.
NB: Courses include practical training in performance and technical theatre.
MA courses in Theatre Practice, Applied Drama and an MA/MFA course in Staging Shakespeare. Two and three year registration for MPhil and PHd welcomed.
NB: Research into many aspects of Drama and Theatre in education.

## UNIVERSITY OF GLASGOW
Dept. of Theatre, Film and Television Studies,
Gilmorehill Centre for Theatre, Film and Television,
University Avenue, Glasgow G12 8QQ Scotland
Tel: 0141 339 8855 extn. 3809
Email: tftsoffice@arts.gla.ac.uk
http://www.arts.gla.ac.uk/tfts
Administration/Courses:
Professor of Drama: Jan McDonald.
3 year full-time course in theatre studies with other
options including film and television studies leading to
M.A. general degree.
4 year full-time course in theatre studies with a joint
subject and other options including film and television
studies leading to M.A. (Hons) degree.
Postgraduate courses leading to M.Litt., M.Phil or
Ph.D.
N.B. Courses include some practical work

## UNIVERSITY OF HERTFORDSHIRE
School of Humanities and Education, Wall Hall,
Aldenham, Watford, Hertfordshire WD2 8AT
Tel: 01707 284800
Fax: 01707 284870 (General Office)
3 year course, BA Degree in Performing Arts.

## UNIVERSITY OF HUDDERSFIELD
Queensgate, Huddersfield, West Yorkshire HD1 3DH
Division of Theatre Studies, School of Music &
Humanities
St. Peters Building,
St. Peters Street, Huddersfield, West Yorkshire HD1
1RA Tel: 01484 422288 Fax: 01484 478428
Email: s.j.nicholson@hud.ac.uk
Administration/Courses:
Head of Theatre Studies: Dr. Steve Nicholson
3 years full-time Theatre Studies.
3 years full-time Theatre Studies and Media
B.A.(Hons)
3 years full-time Theatre Studies with Music
Also opportunities for postgraduate study for the
degrees of M.Phil and Phd.

## HULL UNIVERSITY
Drama Department, Gulbenkian Centre, Hull HU6 7RX
Tel: 01482 466210
Email: a.s.meech@drama.hull.ac.uk
www.hull.ac.uk/drama/
Administration./Courses:
Head of Department: A.J. Meech
3 year full-time drama course leading to B.A. Single
Honours Degree.
3 year full-time course in drama with American Studies
or English or modern languages, or Music, or
Theology leading to B.A. Joint Honours Degree.
1 year full-time course in Theatre Production leading to
M.A. by assessment, examination and dissertation.
Postgraduate research leading to M.Phil. or Ph.D. in
dramatic literature or theatre history by dissertation.
N.B. Single Honours and MA courses include some
practical training.

## UNIVERSITY OF KENT AT CANTERBURY
Eliot College, The University, Canterbury, Kent CT2
7NS
Tel: 01227 764000 extn. 7567 (drama dept.)
Fax: 01227 827464
Courses:

4 year Single Honours Course with final year devoted
to directing, devising or theatre administration.
3 year Combined Honours Course and 3 year Visual
and Performed Arts Course. Postgraduate research
leading to M.A. and Ph.D. by dissertation.
N.B. Single Honours and Combined Honours Courses
include practical training. Board of Drama and Theatre
Studies has new Drama Studio building, Studio
Theatre and access to Audio-visual Studio and the
Gulbenkian Theatre.

## KINGSTON UNIVERSITY
Faculty of Education, Kingston Hill Theatre, Kingston
Hill, Kingston, Surrey KT2 7LB
Tel: 0181 547 2000
Fax: 0181 546 7116
Administration/Courses:
Tutor: Bernie Farrell.
English and Drama as part of 4 year full-time
Education course leading to B.Ed.(Hons), includes
educational drama and T.I.E. work.
Also education drama in professional studies compo-
nent in above course.

## UNIVERSITY OF LANCASTER
University House, Lancaster, Lancashire LA1 4YW
Tel: 01524 592028
Fax: 01524 846243
Courses:
Single Major; Combined B.A. (Hons) Degree in
Theatre Studies and English/French/German
Educational Studies.
1 year course in Theatre Studies leading to M.A.
degree.

## LEEDS METROPOLITAN UNIVERSITY
Faculty of Cultural and Education Studies, Beckett
Park, Leeds LS6 3QS
Tel: 0113 283 2600 extn. 3634
Fax: 0113 283 3163
Administration/Courses:
Lecturers in Drama: John Mee and Richard Perkin.
Drama components in courses in Teacher Education,
Playwork, Youth and community studies. English and
Drama course leading to B.Ed(Hons) degree.
1 year part-time course in Professional Studies in
Education (Drama in Education).

## UNIVERSITY OF LEEDS
Leeds LS2 9JT
Tel: 0113 233 4720
Fax: 0113 233 4774
Administration/Courses:
Professor of Drama and Theatre Studies and Director
of the Workshop Theatre: Martin J. Banham.
Full-time postgraduate course in Theatre Studies lead-
ing to M.A. Degree (Degree by instruction); also post-
graduate research in Drama and/or Theatre Studies
leading to Degrees of M.Phil or Ph.D. Undergraduate
course in B.A. English Lit. and Theatre Studies (Hons).

## UNIVERSITY OF LONDON - GOLDSMITHS COLLEGE
Drama Department, New Cross, London SE14 6NW
Tel: 0171 919 7414
Fax: 0171 919 7413
Administration/Courses:

Head of Department: Prof. Simon Shepherd
3 year course in Drama and Theatre Arts leading to a BA (Single Hons) Degree.
3 year course in English and Theatre Arts leading to a BA (Interdisciplinary) Degree.
2 year part-time postgraduate course leading to a MA in Drama: (Process of Production).
1 year full-time postgraduate course leading to a MA in Theatre Arts.
Postgraduate research leading to M.Phil. or Ph.D. by thesis. The Drama Department's work takes place in three independently equipped Studios and in the George Wood Theatre (an adaptable 250-seat theatre). The Drama Department also has its own Design, Wardrobe and Workshop facilities.

## LOUGHBOROUGH UNIVERSITY OF TECHNOLOGY
English & Drama Dept SCUDD, Loughborough, Leicestershire LE11 3TU
Tel: 01509 263171
Fax: 01509 869994
Courses:
3 year full-time single or combined honours (with English as a minor) course leading to B.A. (Hons) degree. The course is weighted equally between Textual studies and practical investigation and performance including the use of sound and TV apparatus in well equipped theatre workshops.
Postgraduate work (full and part-time) leading to M.A. Theatre and The Representation of Gender, and higher degrees by research, M.Phil or Ph.D.

## MANCHESTER METROPOLITAN UNIVERSITY
Didsbury School of Education, Faculty of Community Studies & Education, Wimslow Road, Didsbury, Manchester M20 2RR
Tel: 0161 247 2020
Fax: 0161 247 6392
Department of Communication Media,
Capitol Building, School Lane, Didsbury, Manchester M20 1HT Tel: 0161 247 7123 Fax: 01691 448 0135
Administration/Courses:
Subject Leader for Drama: John Raiwer
Tel: 0161 247 2336
Drama can be studied as 1st or 2nd subject in a year full time course leading to 4 year B Ed (Hons) Degree. Drama as main course in secondary level studies leading to the postgraduate certificate in education.
School of Theatre Course Leader: Niamh Dowling. Communication media Dept. 3 year full time Acting course for intended professionals leading to BA(Hons) in Theatre Arts (Acting).

## UNIVERSITY OF MANCHESTER
Drama Department, Oxford Road,
Manchester M13 9PL
Tel: 0161 275 3347
Fax: 0161 275 3349
Administration/Courses:
Head of Department: Professor Kenneth Richards
3 year full-time course in drama leading to B.A. (Hons) degree.
3 year full-time combined studies (including drama) course leading to B.A. (Hons) degree.
4 year full-time course in drama plus English or French leading to B.A. (Hons) degree.

3 year full-time course in drama plus Italian, German or English leading to B.A. (Hons) degree.
1 year full-time diploma course in drama.
M.Phil. and Ph.D. research by thesis. Taught M.A. course in preparation.
N.B. Courses include some practical work, except combined studies and research by thesis.

## MIDDLESEX UNIVERSITY
School of Drama, Trent Park, Bramley Road, Oakwood, London N14 4YZ
Tel: 0181 362 5000
Fax: 0181 441 4672
Ivy House Campus, North End Road,
London NW11 7HU Tel: 0181 362 5000
Fax: 0181 201 9923
Adminstration/Courses:
Head of School: Professor Leon Rubin, M.A.
BA (Hons) Performing Arts: Programme Leader John Topping. Drama available as a major study in performing arts course in conjunction with work in dance, music and other related subjects leading to BA/BA (Hons) degree. Sited at Trent Park.
BA (Hons) Drama and Theatre Studies: Programme Leader Arthur Husk. 3 year full-time course situated at Ivy House.
BA (Hons) Acting: Programme Leader Jane Harrison. Degree designed for the professional actor.
BA (Hons) Theatre Technical Arts: Programme Leader Richard Berry. Degree focusing on all technical theatre aspects: sound, lighting, stage management etc
PGCE Drama: 1 year full-time course. Programme Leader: Kenneth Taylor. Situated at Trent Park.
MA Performing Arts: Programme Leader Patrick Campbell. 2 year part-time course. Drama available as a major study in an interdisciplinary programme involving post graduate students in Music and Dance as well.
MA/MFA Theatre Directing: 1 or 2 year programme redesigned to prepare the professional theatre director. This degree is very practical in content.
Enquiries for all courses should be addressed to: Admissions, Middlesex University, Bounds Green Road, London N11. Tel 0181 362 5400
Fax 0181 362 5733.

## UNIVERSITY OF NORTH LONDON
School of Literary and Media Studies, Faculty of Humanites & Teacher Education, 166 Holloway Road, London N7 8DB
Tel: 0171 607 2789/753 5111
Fax: 0171 753 3159
Courses:
2 year part-time evening postgraduate course in Modern Drama Studies leading to an M.A. degree.
3 year full-time honours degree in Theatre Studies and another subject.

## UNIVERSITY OF NORTHUMBRIA AT NEWCASTLE
Faculty of Arts and Design, Dept of Visual and Performing Arts: Lipman Building, University of Northumbria, Newcastle-upon-Tyne NE1 8ST
Tel: 0191 227 3920
Fax: 0191 227 3632
Administration/Courses:
Contact: Sharon Patterson
BA(Hons) Drama

Three-year full-time course, with emphasis on the-atre/drama in the community.
BA (Hons) Performance.
Contact: Dr.Warwick Dobson
Three year full time course aims to produce multi-skilled performers who meet the demands of current professional practice.

## NOTTINGHAM TRENT UNIVERSITY

Theatre Design, Burton Street, Nottingham NG1 4BU
Tel: 0115 941 8418
Fax: 0115 948 6595
Administration/Course:
Head of Theatre Design: Judith Park MA
BA(Hons). 3 year full-time course in Theatre Design.

## UNIVERSITY OF PLYMOUTH

Exmouth Campus, Faculty of Arts & Education,
Theatre & Performance Studies, Exmouth,
Devon EX8 2AT
Tel: 01395 255309
Courses:
BA(Hons) Theatre
BA(Hons) Drama

## QUEEN MARY AND WESTFIELD COLLEGE

University of London
327 Mile End Road, London E1 4NS
Tel: 0171 975 5555
Fax: 0171 975 5500
Director of Drama: James Redmond.
3 or 4 year course in drama with either: English,
French, German, Hispanic Studies or Russian, leading
to a B.A. Degree. The practical Drama is taught by
The Central School of Speech and Drama.

## READING UNIVERSITY

Dept of Film and Drama, Bulmershe Court, Woodlands
Avenue, Earley, Reading, Berkshire RG6 1HY
Tel: 0118 931 8878
Fax: 0118 931 8873
Email: e.a.silvester@reading.ac.uk
http://www.reading.ac.uk/AcaDepts/LC/FD/home.html
Courses:
B.A. Single Subject Film + Drama.
B.A. Combined Subject Film + Drama with one of:
English, German, Italian.
PGCE Drama with Contextual Studies.
MA Film and Drama
BA in THeatre Arts, Education and Deaf Studies.

## ROYAL HOLLOWAY, UNIVERSITY OF LONDON

Department of Drama, Theatre and Media Arts, Egham
Hill, Egham, Surrey TW20 0EX
Drama Tel: 01784 443922 Drama Fax: 01784 431018
Media Arts Tel: 01784 443734
Media Arts Fax: 01784 443832
Email: Drama@rhbnc.ac.uk / MediaArts@rhbnc.ac.uk
Administration/Courses:
Head of Department: Professor Jacky Bratton.
3 year course in drama and theatre studies leading to
B.A. (Hons).
3 year combined Hons. course in drama and theatre
studies, plus one other subject (English; German;
French; Classics; Music).
3 year course in media arts leading to B.A. (Hons).

3 year course in Science and the Media leading to
Bsc(Hons). Media Arts plus one other subject
(Biological Sciences; Geology; Physics).
M.A. in Drama and Theatre Studies, one year full time,
two years part time. Taught course.
MA in Media Arts, one year full time, two years part
time. Taught course.
M.Phil. by research. Thesis may be submitted after 2
years.
Ph.D. Thesis normally submitted after 3 years.

## SLADE SCHOOL OF FINE ART

University College London, Gower Street,
London WC1E 6BT
Tel: 0171 504 2313
Fax: 0171 380 7801
Administration/Course:
Slade Professor: Bernard Cohen
Head of Theatre Design course: Philip Prowse
MA, MFA and Graduate Diploma in Fine Art

## UNIVERSITY OF SUNDERLAND

School of Arts, Design & Communications, Ashburne
House, Ryhope Road, Sunderland
Tel: 0191 515 2110
Fax: 0191 515 2132
Administration/Courses:
Head of School Arts, Design & Communications:
Professor Flavia Swann
3 year full-time B.A. English Studies.
Practical drama course option. 3 year full-time BA
(Hons) Creative Arts Studies including a
Drama/Theatre option.

## UNIVERSITY OF ULSTER

Cromore Road, Coleraine, County Londonderry BT52
1SA Northern Ireland
Tel: 01265 44141
Fax: 01265 40908
School of Media & Performing Arts:
Tel: 01265 324196 Fax: 01265 324964
Administration/Courses:
Theatre Studies Course Director: Prof. Gerry McCarthy
3 Year FT BA Hons Theatre Studies
3 Year FT BA Hons Humanities Combined with
Theatre Studies as Major/Minor/Joint option
All programmes are modularised and students may
take single modules as part of a programme of accred-ited courses. This allows students access to part-time
modes of study.
Specialism offered within the course includes:
performance, performance theory, playwrighting, arts
management and community drama. Currently the pro-gramme has a modern and contemporary emphasis
built around a selection of core Theory and Practice
modules. Students are encouraged progressively to
develop and apply their own interests and specialisms;
and to pursue the kind of balance between practical,
group based methods and individual study and
research best matching their abilities.
There is also a postgraduate research centre, based
on the Theatre Ireland Database, with a specialism in
Irish Theatre. Applicants should write/phone/fax for
further information.

## UNIVERSITY OF WALES INSTITUTE CARDIFF (UWIC)

Faculty of Education, Cyncoed Road, Cardiff CF2 6XD
Tel: 01222 551111

Fax: 01222 506589
Courses:
B.A. Education (Hons): Secondary Drama.
2 Year B.Ed in Music Secondary.

## UNIVERSITY OF WARWICK
School of Theatre Studies, Coventry CV4 7AL
Tel: 01203 523020
Email: tsraj@warwick.ac.uk
www.warwick.ac.uk/fac/arts/Theatre_S/
Administration/Courses:
Chairman: Professor D. Thomas.
3 year Single Honours Course in Theatre and
Performance Studies. 3 year degree course in hon-
ours, Theatre Studies combined with English and
Italian.
Postgraduate research into Theatre Studies leading to
M.A., M.Phil., Ph.D.
Taught M.A. course (full and part-time) in European
Cultural Policy and Administration.

## UNIVERSITY OF WOLVERHAMPTON
School of Humanities and Social Sciences - Drama,
Castle View, Dudley DY1 3HR
Tel: 01902 323400
Fax: 01902 323379
Administration/Courses:
Head of Drama Division: James Stredder.
Theatre studies modules available as a specialist,
major, joint or minor subject on B.A. and B.A.(Hons)
Modular Degree and Diploma Scheme (3 years full-
time).
Arena Arts (administered by the Drama Division)
promotes a full programme of performances by profes-
sional companies in the Arena Theatre in association
with West Midlands Arts. Other relevant subjects avail-
able with Drama, include Media & Communications,
History of Art and Design, English, Dance and Music.

# Colleges and Institutes of Higher Education

## BISHOP GROSSETESTE UNIVERSITY COLLEGE, LINCOLN
Department of Drama
Tel: 01522 527347 Fax: 01522 530243
Email: registry@bgc.ac.uk
Web Site: www.bgc.ac.uk
BA(Hons) Arts in the Community (Drama)
BA(Hons) Teaching Studies & Drama with QTS

## BRETTON HALL, COLLEGE OF THE UNIVERSITY OF LEEDS
School of Dance & Theatre, West Bretton, Wakefield,
West Yorkshire WF4 4LG
Tel: 01924 830261 Fax: 01924 830521
Contact: Paul Cowen
Bretton Hall is the country`s leading college for the arts
and education.
Powerhouse 1 is our touring venue.

Courses:
BA Hons in: Theatre (Acting), Theatre (Devising),
Theatre (Broadcast Media), Theatre (Design &
Technology), Performing Arts and Performance
management.

## UNIVERSITY COLLEGE CHESTER
Dept of Drama & Theatre Cheyney Road,
Chester CH1 4BJ
Tel: 01244 375444 Fax: 01244 373379
B.A.(Hons), B.Ed.(Hons) in Drama and Theatre
P.G.C.E. in Secondary Drama.

## DARTINGTON COLLEGE OF ARTS
Higher Close Dartington, Totnes, Devon TQ9 6EJ
Tel: 01803 862224 Fax: 01803 506589
Courses:
B.A.(Hons) Theatre.; B.A.(Hons) Theatre with Arts
Management; B.A. (Hons) Performance Writing; B.A.
(Hons) Visual Performance; B.A. (Hons) Music. All
have interdisciplinary elements. Also offered: B.A.
(Hons) Arts Management or Arts Management com-
bined with any of the above.

## EDGE HILL UNIVERSITY COLLEGE
Drama Dept., St.Helen's Road, Ormskirk L39 4QP
Tel: 01695 575171 Fax: 01695 579997
Courses:
B.A.(Hons) Drama available as an honours subject
combined with one other major subject.
B.A. (Hons) with Qualified Teacher Status Drama with-
in English.
Post Graduate Certificate of Education.

## HOMERTON COLLEGE
Hills Road, Cambridge CB2 2PH
Tel: 01223 507111 Fax: 01223 507120
BA(Hons) English with Drama & Education
B.Ed.(Hons) Drama & Education

## KING ALFRED'S COLLEGE
Sparkford Road, Winchester, Hampshire SO22 4NR
Tel: 01962 841515 Fax: 01962 842280
Email: S.Hawes@wkac.ac.uk
Web Site: http://www.wkac.ac.uk
Head of School, Community and Performing Arts:
Stephen Hawes
Courses:
BA(Hons): Drama, Theatre and TV Studies; Drama
Studies; Performing Arts; Dance Studies

BA/BSc Combined Hons: Drama Studies; Dance Studies
BA Ed (Hons)/QTS Primary with Special Subject English with Drama.
MA Theatre for Development.

## LEWES TERTIARY COLLEGE
Mountfield Road, Lewes, East Sussex BN7 2XH
Tel: 01273 483188 Fax: 01273 478561
Administration/Courses:
Principal: H. Ball, BSc., M.A.
Full time GNVQ in performing Arts.  Full time Music preparatory course.  A-Level theatre studies and dance. Large hall with sprung dance floor plus three performance areas and gymnasium. TV studio.  Full technical support.

## LIVERPOOL HOPE UNIVERSITY COLLEGE
Dept of Drama & Theatre Studies, Hope Park, Liverpool L16 9JD
Tel: 0151 291 3451 Fax: 0151 291 3161
BA(Hons) Combined Studies

## LIVERPOOL INSTITUTE FOR PERFORMING ARTS
Mount Street, Liverpool L1 9HF
Tel: 0151 330 3000 Fax: 0151 330 3232
Email: reception@lipa.ac.uk
Web Site: www.lipa.ac.uk
Administration/Courses:
Admissions Officer: Rashid Iqbal
3 year full-time degree in Performing Arts, with the following routes: Acting; Dance, Performance Design; Community Arts (Acting or Music); Music; and Enterprise Management.
3 year full-time BA (Hons) Sound Technology.
Two 1 year Diplomas in Pop Music and Sound Technology and in Performance and Production Technology.

## LIVERPOOL JOHN MOORES UNIVERSITY
Drama Section, Dean Walters, St.James Road, Liverpool L1 7BR
Administration/Courses:
Head of Drama: David Llewellyn,
Tel 0151 231 5068
Fax 0151 231 5049
Programme Administrator: Connie Hancock
Tel 0151 231 5068
Fax 0151 231 5049
B.A.(Hons) Drama; M.A.Drama

## MANCHESTER METROPOLITAN UNIVERSITY: CREWE & ALSAGER FACULTY
Dept. of Contemporary Arts, The Alsager Arts Centre, Alsager Campus, Hassall Road, Alsager ST7 2HL
Tel: 0161 247 5302/3 Fax: 0161 247 6377
Email: n.k.mackenzie@mmu.ac.uk
Web Site: http://come.to/aac
Administration/Courses:
B.A. (Creative Arts),  B.A. Combined studies.
For information and admissions contact: Admissions Office, Crewe & Alsager Faculty, Crewe Green Road, Crewe.

## NENE COLLEGE
Park Campus, Broughton Green Road, Northampton NN2 7AL
Tel: 01604 735500 Fax: 01604 720636
Administration/Courses:
BA(Hons) Performance Studies, Drama, Language Arts
MA Theatre Studies.

## COLLEGE OF RIPON AND YORK ST.JOHN
Department of Drama, Film & Television, Lord Mayor's Walk, York YO3 7EX
Tel: 01904 656771 Fax: 01904 612512
B.A. and Post Graduate Diploma in Drama Therapy.
Also available: Creative Art in Groupwork Postgraduate Diploma.

## ROEHAMPTON INSTITUTE
Drama & Theatre Studies Dept, Jubilee Building, Digby Stewart College, Roehampton Lane, London SW15 5PH
Tel: 0181 392 3230 Fax: 0181 392 3289
Courses:
BA, BSc, BA with QTS, MA, PGCE, Dips, Certs.
Degrees awarded by University of Surrey. Subjects include drama, dance, music. Dips and Certs in arts admin, drama therapy, music therapy, dance movement therapy, music teaching, etc. Many programmes available full and part-time.

## ST MARY'S UNIVERSITY COLLEGE
University of Surrey Dept. of Performing Arts
Strawberry Hill, Twickenham, Middlesex
Tel: 0181 240 4000 Fax: 0181 240 4255
Adminstration/Courses:
Head of Department: Mr. G. Boynton.
3 year Joint Hons. Modular Degree programme in Drama/Theatre Studies and another subject, e.g. English, Sociology, Classics. 4 year BA QTS Drama Educational Studies. Degrees validated by the University of Surrey.  Also a single Hons course in drama

## TRINITY COLLEGE, CARMARTHEN
Department of Theatre Studies, College Road, Carmarthen, SA31 3EP Wales
Tel: 01267 676767 Fax: 01267 676766
Email: k.matherick@trinity-cm.ac.uk
Courses:
B.A.(Hons) Humanities, Honours (Theatre Studies major option).
B.A.(Hons) Theatre Studies.
BA(Hons) Theatre Design and Production

## UNIVERSITY COLLEGE SCARBOROUGH
The North Riding College, Filey Road, Scarborough, North Yorkshire YO11 3AZ
Tel 01723 362392 Fax 01723 370815
Email: ericp@ucscarb.ac.uk
Web Site: http://www.ucscarb.ac.uk
Administration/Courses:
Head of External Relations: Eric Prince
BA (Hons): Theatre Studies (Combined Hons in Arts) and Dance (combined Hons in Arts.)

**UNIVERSITY COLLEGE WARRINGTON**
School of Media & Theatre, Padgate Campus,
Warrington WA2 0DB
Tel: 01925 494494 Fax: 01925 816077
BA(Hons) in Performing Arts with Business and
Management.

# Coaches

**JEAN ANSCOMBE LGSM**
63 Four Elms Court, Newport Road, Cardiff CF2 1AU
Tel: 01222 487250

**AUDITION SUCCESS**
Suite 2, 845 Finchley Road, London NW11 8NA
Tel: 0181 209 1660
Email: philrosch@aol.com
Web Site: http://www.yell.co.uk/sites/audition-success/
Contact: Philip Rosch, BA (Hons); LAMDA Gold Medal
(Hons)
Acting tuition.

**BRIGE BIDELL**
213 Rotherhithe New Road, London SE16 2BA
Tel: 0171 231 3827
Specialist in voice and mask work.

**KENNETH CAMPBELL**
Parkhills, 6 Clevelands Park, Northam, Bideford,
Devon EX39 3QH
Tel: 01237 425217

**JANET EDWARDS (MUSIC INTERNATIONAL
LTD)**
425 Northwood Hill, Hornsey Lane, Highgate,
London N6
Tel: 0181 341 0032

**NINA FINBURGH**
1 Buckingham Mansions, West End Lane,
London NW6 1LR
Tel: 0171 435 9484

**GENINE GRAHAM FGSM, LRAM**
LGSM Speech and Drama
Flat A, 21 Harrington Road, London SW7
Tel: 0171 584 1493

**JOHN HESTER**
(Member of the Society of Teachers of
Speech & Drama)
105 Stoneleigh Park Road, Epsom, Surrey KT19 0RF
Tel/Fax: 0181 393 5705
Deals with Epsom/Sutton area.
Teaching all aspects of acting, voice and public speak-
ing. Also an actor and director, specialising in audition
preparation.

**BRIAN LIDSTONE D.G.G.B.**
London & International School of Acting

138 Westbourne Grove, London W11 2RR
Tel: 0171 727 2342
Fax: 0171 221 7210

**LESLIE ORTON L.R.A.M., L.L.A.M., A.N.E.A.**
141 Ladybrook Lane, Mansfield,
Nottinghamshire NG18 5JH
Tel: 01623 26082

**TERRY POWELL A.C.P., L.N.E.A., CERT ED.
LONDON UNIVERSITY**
35 Schofield Avenue, Witney, Oxfordshire OX8 5JR
Tel: 01993 704820
Email: terrypowell@btinternet.com
Member of the Society of Teachers of
Speech and Drama.
Teaching all aspets of acting, speech and drama, audi-
tion preparation including workshops and lectures

**SANDRA SINGER P.R.**
21 Cotswold Road, Westcliff-on-Sea, Essex SS0 8AA
Tel: 01702 331616
Fax: 01702 339393
Senior Personnel: Sandra Singer
Specialising in Casting, Promotiona/Entertainment,
also Costume Characters.

**TANI MORENA SPANISH DANCE TUITION
FLAMENCO AND CLASSICAL**
81 Fordwych Road, London NW2
Tel: 0181 452 0407
Classes in Central London.

**MAVIS WALKER**
4 St.Albans Studios, St.Albans Grove, South End Row,
London W8 5BT
Tel: 0171 937 6495

**JACOB J WOODD**
Holland House, Woodcock Hill, East Grinstead, West
Sussex RH19 2RE
Tel: 01342 326784
Fax: 01342 326795

# Drama Advisers

## ABERDEENSHIRE

**ANNE DARLING**
Education Officer, E.R. + D Team, Aberdeenshire
Education Dept, Summerhill Education Centre,
Stronsay Drive, Aberdeen, Aberdeenshire AB15 6JA
Scotland
Tel: 01224 208662 Fax: 01224 208671

# BERKSHIRE

**MRS MARIGOLD ASHWELL**
Inspector/Adviser for Drama, Department of Education,
Shire Hall, Shinfield Park, Reading RG2 9XE
Tel: 0118 923 3547 Fax: 0118 975 0360

# BRISTOL

**MARY HARLOW**
Bristol Education Centre, Sheridan Road, Horfield,
Bristol BS7 0PU
Tel: 0117 931 1111 Fax: 0117 931 1619

# CHESHIRE

**SIMON TAYLOR**
Drama Adviser, Hadfield House, St.Mary's Hill,
Chester CH1 1SQ
Tel: 01244 603350 Fax: 01244 603813

# DERBYSHIRE

**JOHN MOORE**
Drama Adviser, Area Education Office, Chatsworth
Hall, Chesterfield Road, Matlock, Derbyshire DE4 3FW
Tel: 01629 580000 Fax: 01629 585466

# DEVON

**JACKIE TAYLOR**
Devon Curriculum Advice, Falcon Road, Sowton,
Exeter EX2 7LB
Tel: 01392 384846 Fax: 01392 384880

# EDINBURGH

**JOHN A TURNER**
Adviser for Aesthetic Subjects City of Edinburgh
Council, Wellington Court, 10 Waterloo Place,
Edinburgh EH1 3EG
Tel: 0131 469 3043 Fax: 0131 469 3311

# HARROW

**TANYA WHITE**
General Education Adviser, PO Box 22, Civic Centre,
Harrow, Middlesex HA1 2UW
Tel: 0181 863 5611 extn. 2601 Tel: 0181 427 0810

# HERTFORDSHIRE

**GILLIAN CAWLEY AND PAULINE SCOTT**
English and Drama Advisers, The Education Centre,
Butterfield Road, Wheathampstead,
Hertfordshire AL4 8PY
Tel: 01582 830311 Fax: 01582 830312

# KENT

**DAVID TOWNSEND**
Lead Consultant for English (Term times only), Clover
House, John Wilson Business Park, Thanet Way,
Whitstable, Kent CT5 3QZ
Tel: 01227 772992 Fax: 01227 772290

# LEEDS

**PAUL KAISERMAN**
Drama Adviser, Advisory and Inspection Service, 10th
Floor, Merrion House, Merrion Centre, Leeds LS2 8DT
Tel: 0113 247 5678 Fax: 0113 247 5671

# LEICESTERSHIRE

**KATE HUTCHON**
The County Drama & Dance Adviser, Leicestershire
Arts in Education, Head of Performing Arts,
The Knighton Field Centre, Herrick Road, LE2 6DH
Tel: 0116 270 0850 Fax: 0116 270 4928

# MERTON

**CLIVE TUNNICLIFFE**
Adviser for English, Civic Centre, London Road,
Morden, Surrey SM4 5DX
Tel: 0181 545 3307 Fax: 0181 545 3260

# NORTH EAST

**GEOFF DAVIES AND ROGER HANCOCK**
The Brewery, Castle Eden, County Durham TS27 4SX
Tel: 01429 837257 Fax: 01429 837153
Drama and Management Consultants: Action in
Management (for Businesses) Action in Role (for
Schools).

# NORTHAMPTONSHIRE

**TONY DRANE**
General Education Inspector for English, Drama and
Media Studies NIAS, Education Department, PO Box
216, John Dryden House, 8-10 The Lakes, Northants
NN4 7DD

Tel: 01604 236248 Fax: 01604 236240

# NORTHUMBERLAND & NORTH TYNESIDE

**CATHERINE REEVES**
Hepscott Educational Development Centre, Hepscott
Park, Stannington, Morpeth,
Northumberland NE61 6NF
Tel: 01670 533000 Direct Tel: 01670 533519 Fax:
01670 533591
General Adviser with Special responsibility for English,
Drama and Media Education.

# OXFORDSHIRE

**CHRISTINE LAWSON**
Inspector for English, Oxfordshire Schools
Inspectorate, The Cricket Road Centre, Cricket Road,
Oxford OX4 3DW
Tel: 01865 711477 Fax: 01865 778591

# REDBRIDGE

**JOSANNE BALCOMBE**
Head of Drama Centre, Churchfields, South Woodford,
London E18 2RB
Tel: 0181 504 5451 Fax: 0181 505 6669
Email: rdc@leonet.co.uk

# SHROPSHIRE

**NEIL RATHMELL**
Arts Adviser, Shropshire Lea, Arts & Media Centre, 5
Belmont, Shrewsbury SY1 1TE
Tel: 01743 243755 Fax: 01743 344773
Email: neil.rathmell@btinternet

# STRATHCLYDE

**RONNIE A.F. MACKLE**
Glasgow City Council, Charing Cross Complex, House
1, 20 India Street, Glasgow G2 4PF
Tel: 0141 287 8182 Fax: 0141 287 8212

# SUFFOLK

**JOSS LEADER**
Advisory Teacher to Drama, Northgate Arts Centre,
Sidegate Lane West, Ipswich IP4 3DF
Tel: 01473 281866 Fax: 01473 286068

# SUSSEX, EAST

**MICHAEL WELLER**
Adviser in English & Drama, Education Offices, County
Hall, St.Anne's Crescent, Lewes BN7 1SG
Tel: 01273 481737 Fax: 01273 481902

# SUSSEX, WEST

**ANNE FENTON**
General Adviser (Drama), North-Eastern Area
Professional Centre, Furnace Drive, Furnace Green,
Crawley, West Sussex RH10 6JB
Tel: 01293 615837 Fax: 01293 533359

# TRAFFORD

**GARTH JONES**
Drama Adviser, Education Offices, Trafford
Metropolitan Borough Council, PO Box 19, Sale,
Cheshire M33 7YR
Tel: 0161 912 3143 Fax: 0161 912 3075

# WALTHAM FOREST

**SCILLA FUREY**
Acting Principal Adviser, Education Centre, Queen's
Road, Walthamstow, London E17 8QS
Tel: 0181 521 3311 Fax: 0181 509 9668

# WILTSHIRE

**ROGER DAY M.A., ADV.DIPED, FRSA**
Independent Drama Adviser, The Barn, Wedhampton,
Devizes, Wiltshire FN10 3QE
Tel: 01380 840128 Fax: 01380 840128

**SOCIETIES AND ORGANISATIONS**

**SOCIETY OF THEATRE CONSULTANTS**

**ARTS COUNCILS & REGIONAL ARTS BOARDS**

**NATIONAL TOURIST BOARDS**

# Societies & Organisations

## ABINGDON OPERATIC SOCIETY
Correspondence Address: 20 Draycott Road,
Southmoor, Near Abingdon, Oxon OX13 5BY
Tel: 01865 820849
Production Co-ordinator: P.A.Hockley

## ACTOR'S BENEVOLENT FUND
6 Adam Street, London WC2N 6AA
Tel: 0171 836 6378
Patrons: H.M. The Queen
President: Penelope Keith, O.B.E.
Secretary: Mrs. R. Stevens.
The foremost representative Charity of the Theatrical
Profession in Great Britain. Founded in 1882 by Henry
Irving, Charles Wyndham, Squire Bancroft, W. H.
Kendal, John Hare, Wilson Barrett and John L. Toole,
all of whom started this much-needed movement for
the calling they loved - unostentatiously and in the
simplest and most self-effacing spirit. The purpose of
the founders is nobly fulfilled, and their names are held
in honoured memory.
The objects of the Fund are to help, by Allowances,
Grants and Loans, elderly or distressed actors and
actresses, managers, stage managers, business
managers and their wives; also choristers whose
efforts are entirely devoted to theatrical work. The Fund
disbursed, during the past year, the sum of £187, 539
by way of regular weekly allowances, loans and grants,
to distressed members of the profession.

## ACTOR'S CHARITABLE TRUST
Reg Charity No. 206809
Suite 255/256, Africa House, 64/78 Kingsway,
London WC2B 6BD
Tel: 0171 242 0111 Fax: 0171 242 0234
President: Lord Attenborough, C.B.E.
Hon. Treasurer: Roger Brierley, F.C.A.
Chairpeople: Angela Thorne and Simon Williams.
General Secretary: Brian Batchelor, MA
Founded in 1896, the Trust gives financial aid to the
children of actors and actresses during family crisis,
and administers Denville Hall - The residential and
nursing home for elderly members of the theatrical
profession.

## ACTORS' CHURCH UNION
St. Paul's Church, Bedford Street, Covent Garden,
London WC2E 9ED
Tel: 0171 836 5221
Senior Chaplain: Canon Bill Hall
Hon. Treasurers: David Chivers and John de Lannoy.
Founded in 1899, members and associates serve the
profession through their interest, their action - often in
association with other related bodies - and their
prayers. Additionally, more than 200 honorary
chaplains serve all members of the profession in
theatres, studios, and schools at home and overseas.
As well as spiritual counsel and practical advice,
material help is given when possible. Through the
Children's Charity, for example, funds are available for
theatrical parents facing difficulties with the costs of
their children's education.

## THE AGENTS' ASSOCIATION (GREAT BRITAIN)
54 Keyes House, Dolphin Square, London SW1V 3NA
Tel: 0171 834 0515 Fax: 0171 821 0261
Email: association@agents-uk.com
Web Site: http://www.agents-uk.com
President: John Baxendale
Past Presidents: Jef Hanlon, Kenneth Earle, George
Elrick FRSA, Philip Hindin, B G MacG (Bunny) Lewis
MC, Tony Lewis, Peter McLeod, Peter Prichard OBE
Vice Presidents: Jenny Dunster, Michael Gelardi, Bob
James, Ralph Phillips, David Winslett, Paul Fenn
The Agents' Association Ltd, founded in 1927, has in
its membership not only the principal agencies of Great
Britain but a wide cross-section of entertainment
agents thoughout the country.
Its functions are primarily for the benefit of members,
but activities cover the entertainment agency business
in particular and the whole of the entertainment
industry in general. In major matters connected with the
latter it acts in co-ordination with leading organisations
both inside and outside the industry.
A full time office with staff operates from London and
an executive council of management meets regularly to
run the affairs of the association. Elected
representatives and branches cover the entire United
Kingdom and all members are governed by strict rules
and regulations. Applications for membership are
welcomed from licensed entertainment agents and
should be addressed to the General Secretary.

## APPLAUSE THEATRE CLUB
The Applause Building, 68 Long Acre,
London WC2E 9JQ
Tel: 0171 312 1991 Fax: 0171 312 8090
Patron: Sir Peter Hall.
Subscription to the Applause Theatre Club offers arts
lovers many special benefits, including:
Monthly magazine - keeping you up to date with the
latest news and gossip in the West End along with
special offers and discounts.
Priority Booking - An exclusive telephone number with
ticket allocations for sell-out shows.
Discounts - Special offers for tickets and Club nights,
rail travel, flights and holiday deals.
Social Events - attend: play readings, theatre suppers,
backstage tours and private viewings of exhibitions and
art galleries. Along with "meet the cast" evenings and
First Nights.
All brought to you in twelve issues a year at £25.00
annual membership.

## APT
The British Centre of ASSITEJ, c/o Oily Cart Theatre,
Smallwood School Annexe, Smallwood Road, Tooting,
London SW17 0TW
Tel: 0181 672 6329 Fax: 0181 672 0792
Email: oilycar@premier.co.uk
Web Site: www.designer.co.uk/apt
Director: Sarah Argent
APT aims to promote and develop the work of
professional theatre organisations and individuals
working for and/or with children and young people.
APT's Policy Is:
To advocate and advance good practice and standards
of excellence within the field of Theatre for Children
and Young people.

To promote a greater knowledge and understanding of the field among funders, educationalists and the general public.
APT is the British Centre of ASSITEJ (International Association of Theatre for Children and Young People) and works with like-minded organisations and individuals in over 50 countries worldwide.

## ARTS AND ENTERTAINMENT TRAINING COUNCIL
3 St. Peter's Building, York Street, Leeds LS9 8AJ
Tel: 01274 738800
Chief Executive: Alan Humberstone
Project Officer: Carla Booth
Office Manager: Clare Clarkson
Responsible for identifying nationally applicable occupational standards for most areas of employment in the arts and entertainment fields and encouraging their use to improve practice: developing and adminstering a new framework of National and Scottish Vocational Qualifications: taking a strategic and advocacy role on matters relating to national arts training policy and development.

## THE ARTS DAY TRUST
3 Earl Road, East Sheen, London SW14 7JH
Tel: 0181 876 2161 Fax: 0181 878 4403
To co-ordinate arts activities, including Drama, Opera, the Lyric Theatre and dance, around the country each year to form an annual day for the arts - 24 June. "National Arts Day" was established on 24 June 1982.

## ARTS THEATRE
6-7 Great Newport Street, London WC2
Tel: 0171 379 3280

## ARTSLINE
54 Chalton Street, London NW1 1HS
Tel: 0171 388 2227 Fax: 0171 383 2653
Email: artsline@dircon.co.uk
Web Site: www.dircon.co.uk/artsline
Director: Roger Robinson
Development Officer: Pauline Guthrie/Liz Porter
Publications and Promotions Officer: Suzanne Bull
Ethnic Arts Officer: Meena Jafarey
Information service for disabled people about access to the arts and entertainments in London. Phone line open Mon-Fri 9.30am-5.30pm.

## ASSOCIATION FOR BUSINESS SPONSORSHIP OF THE ARTS (ABSA)
Nutmeg House, 60 Gainsford Street, Butler's Wharf, London SE1 2NY
Tel: 0171 378 8143 Fax: 0171 407 7527
Email: absa@absa.org.uk
Web Site: www.absa.org.uk
Chief Executive: Colin Tweedy.
ABSA is an independent National Association for Businesses interested or involved in supporting the arts and exists to promote and encourage partner-ships between the private sector and the arts for their mutual benefit and that of the community at large.
ABSA administers the Pairing Scheme on behalf of the Government and also runs the initiative Business in the Arts. ABSA also co-ordinates the ABSA development forum (ADF) which is a network of arts development professionals.

## ASSOCIATION OF BRITISH THEATRE TECHNICIANS
47 Bermondsey Street, London SE1 3XT
Tel: 0171 403 3778 Fax: 0171 378 6170
Chairman: David Wilmore
Vice-Chairman: Roger Fox
Hon. Secretary: Barry Pritchard; Hon Treasurer: Colin Simon
Administrator: Jenny Straker.
An Association formed in 1961 to provide a forum for discussion among technicians in the presentation industry, to collect and disseminate information of a technical nature to arrange in-service training, to influence draft standards and regulations affecting the industry and to advise and assist all those involved in the planning and construction or reconstruction of new and existing theatres. The Association is a member of the Theatres Advisory Council and acts as technical advisor to the Council. Associate Membership is open to all who are interested in technical aspects of the Presentation Industry; Corporate Membership is awarded to experienced professional technicians.

## ASSOCIATION OF CIRCUS PROPRIETERS OF GREAT BRITAIN
PO Box 131, Blackburn, Lancashire BB1 9DT
Tel: 01254 672222 Fax: 01254 681723
Secretary: Malcolm Clay
The Association was formed to enable all the circus proprietors of standing to get together to regulate the business relations between its members, to maintain the status of circus and the standard of entertainment provided by them, to ensure that performing animals were well looked after and maintain certain minimum standards of health and welfare and to settle disputes between members and to conduct negotiations and make agreements on behalf of members with other interested organisations or government bodies. The Association operates a compulsory veterinary inspection scheme.
The Association is able to supply animals, circus acts and equipment as well as film and publicity facilities.

## ASSOCIATION OF LIGHTING DESIGNERS
PO Box 95, Worcester Park, Surrey KT4 8WA
Tel/Fax: 0181 330 6577
Email: office@ald.org.uk
Web Site: www.ald.org.uk
The Association was formed to provide a forum devoted to the development of the art and craft of stage lighting. Membership open to all those professionally engaged in stage lighting. Associate membership open to amateurs and students.

## ASSOCIATION OF METROPOLITAN AUTHORITIES
35 Great Smith Street, London SW1P 3BJ
Tel: 0171 222 8100

## BECTU
Broadcasting Entertainment Cinematography & Theatre Union
111 Wardour Street, London W1V 4AY
Tel: 0171 437 8506 Fax: 0171 437 8268
Email: bectu@geo2.poptel.org.uk
General Secretary: Roger Bolton
Deputy General Secretary: Willy Donaghy

Journal Editor: Janice Turner
Trade union for backstage, technical, front-of-house, administrative and support workers in theatre and arts centres.
Publishes the Stage Screen & Radio journal (10 issues annually).

## THE BENESH INSTITUTE
Benesh Movement Notation
12 Lisson Grove, London NW1 6TS
Tel: 0171 258 3041 Fax: 0171 724 6434

## THE BRITISH ACADEMY OF SONGWRITERS, COMPOSERS & AUTHORS
(incorporating the Songwriters' Guild of GB)
34 Hanway Street, London W1P 9DE
Tel: 0171 436 2261
B.A.S.C.A. (the Songwriters' Guild, founded in July 1947), is recognised by Parliament, the Press and all official bodies connected with the music industry as the organisation representing the interests of British composers and songwriters. Provides legal and business advice, conducts national and international campaigns on behalf of members.
Voting membership of the Academy is confined to members of the Performing Right Society or its equivalent.
Administrators of the Ivor Novello Awards and Song for Europe.

## BRITISH ACTORS EQUITY ASSOCIATION
Incoporating the Variety Artistes' Federation
Guild House, Upper St.Martin's Lane, London WC2H 9EG
Tel: 0171 379 6000 Fax: 0171 379 7001
Email: info@equity.org.uk
Scottish Office:
Equity, 114 Union Street, Glasgow, G1 3QQ
Tel: 0141 248 2472
North West Office:
Equity, Conavon Court, 12 Blackfriars Street, Salford, M3 5BQ
Tel: 0161 832 3183
North East Office:
Equity, PO Box 1254, Sheffield, S10 3XY
Tel: 0114 230 5294
Wales and South West Office:
Equity, Transport House, 1 Cathedral Road, Cardiff, CF1 9SD
Tel: 01222 397971
Midlands Office:
Equity, PO Box 1221, Warwick, CV34 5EF
Tel: 01926 408638
Equity was formed in 1930 and its early members soon established the basic proposition which has held the Union together ever since - that only with complete organisation can Equity achieve solutions to the problems of casual employment and short-term engagements.
Although the membership was originally from the acting profession, this has progressively broadened to include stage management, theatre designers and directors, dancers, opera singers and many others in the entertainment industry. This process was assisted by the creation of the Variety Artistes' Federation in 1967. Standard Contracts laying down minimum terms and conditions have been negotiated with individual employers, or employer's associations in virtually every section of entertainment.

Equity is affiliated to the International Federation of Actors, the TUC and Scottish TUC, the Federation of Entertainment Unions, the Theatres' Advisory Council, the Radio and Television Safeguards Committee, the National Council for Drama Training and the Council for Dance Education and Training, ITI, WCA, British Copyright Council, NCCL, AMNESTY, Save London's Theatres Campaign, Performers Alliance.

## BRITISH ARTS FESTIVAL ASSOCIATION
3rd Floor, Whitechapel Library, 77 Whitechapel High Street, London E1 7QX
Tel: 0171 247 4667 Fax: 0171 247 5010
Web Site: www.artsfestivals.co.uk
Co-ordinator: Gwyn Rhydderch.
Association of over 50 of the major Arts Festivals in Britain for joint publicity and information. Produces free Arts Festivals listing annually.

## BRITISH ASSOCIATION OF CHOREOGRAPHERS
16 Durham Road, London N2 9DN
Tel: 0181 444 9437
Administrator: Fionna McPhee
Aims and objects of BAC: BAC is an independant, non unionised and non profit making body established to raise the professional profile of choreographers. BAC also seeks to lobby for improved conditions for choreographers and to liaise with the Choreographers' Committee of Equity on the introduction of standard agreements in all sectors of the media; to advise and assist members in all matters relating to professional practise; to offer training workshops, master classes and observer schemes; and to provide platforms where choreographers can meet and liaise with each other and with artists in other performance related disciplines.

## THE BRITISH BALLET ORGANIZATION
Woolborough House, 39 Lonsdale Road, London SW13 9JP
Tel: 0181 748 1241 Fax: 0181 748 1301
Examining and Teaching Society.
Exams in Ballet, Tap, Jazz and Modern.

## BRITISH COUNCIL
11 Portland Place, London W1N 4EJ
Tel: 0171 389 3080 Fax: 0171 389 3088
Web Site: www.britcoun.org/arts/theatredance
Head of Arts Group: Simon Gammell
Director of Performing Arts: John Keefer
Deputy Director of Performing Arts: Sally Cowling
Head of Music: Julia Rose
Head of Drama and Dance: Simon Gammell
All correspondence to Music, Drama and Dance Units (Performing Arts Department) for the attention of: Sara Hitchens
The British Council was founded in 1934. Its aim is to promote an enduring understanding of Britain in other countries through cultural, educational and technical co-operation. It maintains staff in over 100 countries, and from 13 offices in Britain advises and assists visitors and students from overseas.

The Council supports tours overseas by British theatre, dance and opera companies and individual recitalists, and by orchestras and individual musicians, facilitating performances in most parts of the world, particularly those where opportunities for British artists would otherwise be rare.

## THE BRITISH FEDERATION OF FESTIVALS
Festivals House, 198 Park Lane, Macclesfield, Cheshire SK11 6UD
Tel: 01625 428297 Fax: 01625 503229
Email: festival@compuserve.com
Web Site:
www.ourworld.compuserve.com/homepages/festivals
HQ of the amateur festival movement with 330 festival members and 400 professional adjudicator members.

## BRITISH FILM INSTITUTE
21 Stephen Street, London W1P 2LN
Tel: 0171 255 1444 Fax: 0171 436 7950
Director: Wilf Stevenson

## BRITISH LIBRARY NATIONAL SOUND ARCHIVE
96 Euston Road, London NW1 2DB
Tel: 0171 412 7440 Fax: 0171 412 7441
Email: nsa@bl.uk
Web Site: http://www.bl.uk/collections/sound-archive
The National Sound Archive holds more than 1 million discs, 170,000 tapes and a growing number of videos. In addition to commercially published recordings there is a wide range of BBC and other broadcast material, and many unique unpublished recordings. Subjects covered include all kinds of music, wildlife sounds. The spoken word collections are extensive, embracing documentary recordings, oral history, language and dialect recordings, and poetry and drama. Productions at the Royal National Theatre and RSC have been recorded since 1964, and coverage has extended more recently to the Royal Court (since 1971) and many fringe and provincial venues.
The recorded Sound information service answers enquiries about the sound and video collections. There are extensive holdings of books, periodicals, record company catalogues and discographies. The Listening & Viewing Service provides access to the NSA's collections of sound and video. Users need to hold a valid British Library reader's pass. Opening times are as for the British Library's reading rooms:
09.30 to 18.00 Monday and Thursday
09.30 to 20.00 Tuesday and Wednesday
09.30 to 17.00 Friday and Saturday
(correct as of December 1998)

## BRITISH MUSIC HALL SOCIETY
c/o The Honorary Secretary, 82 Ferniea Road, London SW12 9RW
President: Roy Hudd
Vice-Presidents: Mary Sparks, Cyril Wilds, Jack Seaton, Wyn Calvin MBE.
Chairman: John Roscoe
Vice-Chairman: Daphne Bailey
Hon. Secretary: Daphne Masterton
Treasurer: Lawrence Cheadle
Membership Secretary: Wendy Lunn
Minutes Secretary: Mary Jane Burcher
Life Patrons: George Elrick, FRSA., Ernie Wise, OBE

The aims of the Society are to preserve theatre and miscellania, including properties, photos, etc., to keep alive the tradition of this particularly British institution and to actively support this entertainment wherever and whenever produced. They have members all over the world, and many public figures are in membership.

## BRITISH MUSIC INFORMATION CENTRE
10 Stratford Place, London W1N 9AE
Tel: 0171 499 8567 Fax: 0171 499 4795
Manager: Tom Morgan
A reference library of contemporary British Classical Music, Scores, Tapes and Records. Open to the public Monday to Friday 12 noon - 5 pm.

## BRITISH RESORTS ASSOCIATION
8 Post Office Avenue, Southport PR9 0US
Tel: 0151 934 2286 Fax: 0151 934 2287
Honorary Secretary: Mr G Haywood, LL.B., A.C.I.S and Barrister
Hon. Treasurer: Mr P Corthorn
Director: Peter Hampson.
The only Association currently open to all Local Authorities (regardless of type), Tourist Boards and simlar organisations with common aims within the United Kingdom, Isle of Man and Channel Islands, who have strong commitment to the promotion and development of inland and coastal resort tourism.

## THE CELEBRITIES GUILD OF GREAT BRITAIN
Knight House, 29-31 East Barnet Road, New Barnet, Hertfordshire EN4 8RN
Tel: 0181 449 1234/1515 Fax: 0181 449 4994
Founder: Ella Glazer (1997)
Patrons: Victor Hochhauser, David Jacobs CBE DL, Greville Janner QC MP, Anthony Shaffer, Janet Suzman, Frankie Vaughan CBE DL.
Trustees: Michael Freedland, Ella Glazer, Robert Rietti, Bernard Spear.
The Celebrities Guild is a registered charity organising events to raise funds to buy equipment for people who are disabled, with the help of many famous people.

## CENTRAL COUNCIL FOR AMATEUR THEATRE
5 Ryehill Road, Harlow, Essex CM18 7JE
Tel: 01279 423821
Nerys Jeffries, Administrative Secretary, Drama Association of Wales, The Library, Singleton Road, Splott, Cardiff, CF2 2ET
Tel 01222 452200
Fax 01222 452277
CCAT was formed in 1976 when a number of amateur theatre organisations agreed to co-operate to pursue common objectives and concerns. The role of CCAT is essentially to seek to influence national policies which affect resources for amateur theatre. This role is realised through representation on bodies such as the Theatres Advisory Council and the Voluntary Arts Network and through specific projects.

CCAT has concerned itself principally with contributions to national surveys of arts activity often in conjunction with bodies such as the Policy Studies Institute seeking to continually emphasise and promote the importance of the amateur theatre movement. It has lobbied strongly against the negative aspects of compulsory competitive tending, against cuts in local authority funding and theatre closures and has sought to influence and clarify legislation relating to the use of performing venues.

CCAT's present priorities are concerned with creating an accessible archive for new writing and improving communication between playwrights and amateur groups, contributing at regional and national level to the Arts Council review of drama policy and funding and providing guidance and information to stimulate the growth of promotion of professional touring companies by amateur theatre venues.

### CENTRE FOR CREATIVE COMMUNITIES

118 Commercial Street, London E1 6NF
Tel: 0171 247 5385 Fax: 0171 247 5256
Email: baaa@easynet.co.uk
Web Site: www.creativecommunities.org.uk
Executive Director: Jennifer Williams.
Promotes utilisation of the arts and education in Community Development. Maintains a reference library. Does not run programmes or give funds.

### CHAPMAN GUY ASSOCIATES

1-2 Henrietta Street, Covent Garden,
London WC2E 8PS
Tel: 0171 379 7474 Fax: 0171 379 8484
Email: chapman@dircon.co.uk
Director: Guy Chapman
Services: To offer a comprehensive Marketing, Press, Project, Tour and General Management service across all art forms and charities.

### THE CITY OF LONDON FESTIVAL

Bishopsgate Hall, 230 Bishopsgate,
London EC2M 4QD
Tel: 0171 377 0540 Fax: 0171 377 1972
Web Site: www.coty-of-london-festival.org.uk
Festival Director: Michal MacLeod

### THE CLUB FOR ACTS AND ACTORS

Incorporating the Concert Artistes Association
20 Bedford Street, Strand, London WC2E 9HP
Tel: 0171 836 3172 (office) Fax: 0171 836 2884 (club)
President: Ruth Madoc
Secretary: Barbara Daniels.
The Club for Acts and Actors.

This is an association of artistes in all branches of entertainment, and was founded in 1897. The objects of the Association are the safeguarding of artistes' interests; the promotion of good fellowship and cooperation amongst its members, the fostering of public interest in entertainment; the provision of opportunities for artistes to perform and to meet those who are likely to be helpful to them in their profession. Amongst the privileges and benefits of membership are the facilities of a central West End Club as headquarters, 20 Bedford Street, Strand, London WC2; benevolent grants, sickness grants; a classified list of members for the use and guidance of members, agents and entertainment providers; dressing room accommodation; introduction by the Committee to special medical consultants.

### COMBINED SERVICES ENTERTAINMENT/SSVC

Chalfont Grove, Narcot Lane, Gerrards Cross,
Buckinghamshire SL9 8TN
Tel: 01494 878363/2/1/0 & 878359 Fax: 01494 872827
Head of Live Entertainment: Richard Astbury
Business Manager Corporate: Tom Spencer
Technical Manager: Alan `Heath` Davis

### THE COMBINED THEATRICAL CHARITIES APPEAL

PO Box 22721, London N22 5WQ
Tel: 0181 889 7570 Fax: 0181 889 4495
The Council exists to co-ordinate the work of the member Charities and attract donations and legacies for their benefit. In addition, to centralising appeals for funds which can in turn be applied where most needed The member charities are The Actors' Benevolent Fund, The Actors' Charitable Trust, The Actors' Church Union, Denville Hall, The Royal Theatrical Fund, The Equity Trust Fund, The Evelyn Norris Trust, King George's Fund for Actors and Actresses, The Theatrical Ladies' Guild.
within the Charities.
Each Charity remains individual and autonomous but co-operates with others in providing the best possible service to those members of the theatrical profession - from stage doorkeeper to director from actress to wardrobe mistress - who are in need of aid.

### COMMUNITY MATTERS

(Nee: National Federation of Community Organisations)
8/9 Upper Street, Islington, London N1 0PQ
Tel: 0171 226 0189

### THE COMPOSERS' GUILD OF GREAT BRITAIN

The Penthouse, 4 Brook Street, Mayfair,
London W1Y 1AA
Tel: 0171 629 0886 Fax: 0171 629 0993
Chairman: Martin Dalby
General Secretary: Naomi Moskovic
The Guild exists to help its members with advice, information and guidance on professional aspects of composing. Membership is open to composers of British nationality, including the Commonwealth, and to those of other nationalities resident in the UK.
Publications include: Composer News and First Performances.

# Entertainment Artistes' Benevolent Fund

**(formerly Variety Artistes' Benevolent Fund)**
Founded 1908

## BRINSWORTH HOUSE

**72 Staines Road, Twickenham TW2 5AL**
Administration Enquiries: **0181 898 8164 (3 lines)**
Brinsworth Enquiries Only: **0181 894 1351**
Fax: **0181 894 0093**
**Life President: Laurie Mansfield**
**Chairman: Peter Prichard, OBE; Vice Chairman: Phillip Hindin**
**Treasurer: Ray Donn; Executive Administrator: Peter Elliott**

On April 8th 1990 Her Majesty Queen Elizabeth The Queen Mother opened the Leslie Grade Wing which had been built on to Brinsworth House, enabling any resident needing nursing care to stay at 'home' rather than having to leave us and go into hospital. This addition to the home than having to go into hospital. This addition to the home cost £500,000 and was made possible by donations from the profession, with the bulk coming from the Grand Order of Water Rats and the Grade family. This, of course, has increased the running costs of Brinsworth, which now is in the region of £1,000,000 p.a. Additionally the Fund spent £200,000 on outside aid to members of the profession who, through no faultof their own have fallen on hard times, meeting their ever increasing gas, electricity, fuel bills and all that makes life easier. All of this we are happy to do but we do need your support.

# Help us to run Brinsworth - it is your own charity

## CONCERT PROMOTERS ASSOCIATION

4th Floor, Avon House, 360-366 Oxford Street,
London W1N 9HA
Tel: 0171 491 9365 Fax: 0171 414082
Please address all correspondence to the Company
Secretary, C.P.A. at the above address.

## CONFERENCE OF DRAMA SCHOOLS

c/o Central School of Speech and Drama, Embassy
Theatre, 64 Eton Avenue, London NW3 3HY
Tel: 0171 722 8183 Fax: 0171 722 4132
Principal: Robert Fowler

## CONSORTIUM FOR DRAMA & MEDIA IN HIGHER EDUCATION

c/o BUFVC, 56 Greek Street, London W1V 5LR
Tel: 0171 734 3687 Fax: 0171 287 3914
Contact: Dr. Nicholas Arnold
Operates as a consortium of University Theatre
departments nationally and internationally whose aim is
to support production and dissemination of AV and IT
in theatre performance for researchers and students, to
compile and organise databases, and to further
consideration and financial support for reading and
disseminating reference info for theatre performance.

## COUNCIL FOR DANCE EDUCATION AND TRAINING (UK)

Riverside Studios, Crisp Road, Hammersmith,
London W6 9RL
Tel: 0181 741 5084 Fax: 0181 748 4604
Director: Victoria Todd

## DANCE COMPANIES RESETTLEMENT FUND DANCERS TRUST

Rooms 222-227 Africa House, Kingsway,
London WC2B 6BG
Tel: 0171 404 6141 Fax: 0171 242 3331
Executive Director: Linda Yates

## DEPARTMENT OF NATIONAL HERITAGE

2-4 Cockspur Street, London SW1Y 5DH
Tel: 0171 211 6000 Fax: 0171 211 6210

## THE DIRECTORS GUILD OF GREAT BRITAIN

15-19 Great Titchfield Street, London W1P 7FB
Tel: 0171 436 8626 Fax: 0171 436 8646
Email: guild@dggb.co.uk
Web Site: www.dggb.co.uk
Chief Executive: Malcolm Moore
Director of Events and Development: Emma Lucia
Administrator: Sarah Wain
Membership Secretary: Kate Hillman
Union and crafts guild for directors in all media.
Publishes "Direct Magazine".

## DRAMA ASSOCIATION OF WALES/CYMDEITHAS DRAMA CYMRU

The Old Library, Singleton Road, Splott,
Cardiff CF2 2ET
Tel: 01222 452200 Fax: 01222 452277
Director: Aled Rhys-Jones
Administrator: Gary Thomas

At the heart of the Drama Association of Wales
member services is the largest specialist Drama
Lending Library in the World! There are over 250,000
volumes of plays, biographies, critical works and
technical theatre books in the DAW Library which
includes the entire Playsets and Lending Collections of
the former British Theatre Association. Both National
and International members are served by post from
Cardiff.
DAW offers a tremendous range of services to
Community Drama. Script & Drape Hire, an extensive
training programme, New Writing and Youth Theatre.
Its members include amateur and professional
practitioners, educationalists and playwrights.

## EDINBURGH FESTIVAL SOCIETY

Edinburgh International Festival, 21 Market Street,
Edinburgh EH1 1BW
Tel: 0131 473 2001 Fax: 0131 473 2002

## ENGLISH FOLK DANCE AND SONG SOCIETY

Cecil Sharp House, 2 Regents Park Road,
London NW1 7AY
Tel: 0171 485 2206 Fax: 0171 284 0534 Tel/Fax
Library: 0171 284 0523
Education &Teacher Training Officer: Diana Jewitt
Librarian: Malcolm Taylor
Administration Manager: Terry Stodell

## ENGLISH REGIONAL ARTS BOARDS

5 City Road, Winchester, Hampshire SO23 8SD
Tel: 01962 851063 Fax: 01962 842033
Email: info.erab@artsfb.org.uk
Chief Executive: Christopher Gordon
Administrator: Carolyn Nixson

## ENTERTAINMENT ARTISTES' BENEVOLENT FUND

Brinsworth House, 72 Staines Road,
Twickenham TW2 5AL
Tel: Admin Enquiries: 0181 898 8164 Brinsworth
Enquiries Only: 0181 894 1351 Residents Only: 0181
894 2894 & 9134
Patrons: H. M. The Queen, H. M. Queen  Elizabeth The
Queen Mother
Life President: Laurie Mansfield
Hon. Chairman: Peter Prichard OBE
Hon. Vice Chairman: Philip Hindin
Hon. Treasurer: Ray Donn
Executive Administrator: Peter Elliott.

## EURO THEATER CENTRAL BONN

Gisela Pflugradt-Marteau, PO Box 7245, D-53072
Bonn 1 Germany
Tel: Box Office: 0228 652951 Tel: Office: 0228 637026
Email: eurotheater@t-online.de

## FILM ARTISTES' ASSOCIATION

111 Wardour Street, London W1V 4AY
Tel: 0171 437 8506 Fax: 0171 437 8268

## FRIENDS OF SHAKESPEARE'S GLOBE

PO Box 70, Southwark, London SE1 9EN

## THE GILBERT AND SULLIVAN SOCIETY

c/o Margaret Bowden 1 Nethercourt Avenue, Finchley,
London N3 1PS

## GRAND ORDER OF WATER RATS

328 Gray's Inn Road, London WC1X 8BZ
Tel: 0171 278 3248 Fax: 0171 278 1765
Administrator: John Adrian
King Rat (1999): Gordon Kaye
The Grand Order of Water Rats was formed in 1889.
The Membership, which is limited to 200, is only open
to members of the Variety profession, and their
activities are social and benevolent. Companion Rats
are gentlemen distinguished in their profession, who
also make a significant contribution to Charitable work.
The Royal Companions are H.R.H. The Duke of
Edinburgh, H.R.H. The Prince of Wales and H.R.H.
Prince Michael of Kent.

## GUILD OF DRAMA ADJUDICATIONS

c/o Judith Claxton 14 Elmwood, Welwyn Garden City,
Hertfordshire AL8 6LE
Tel/Fax: 01707 326488 (Hon Secretary)

## GUILD OF INTERNATIONAL PROFESSIONAL TOASTMASTERS

Life President: Ivor Spencer
12 Little Bornes, Dulwich, London SE21 8SE
Tel: 0181 670 5585/8424 Fax: 0181 670 0055
Car Tel: 0860 313835
The Guild Members officiate at functions all over the
United Kingdom and undertake engagements abroad.
They are expert organisers who arrange authentic
British Banquets with the traditional ceremonies
(Loving Cup, Baron of Beef, etc.) anywhere in the
world. The Guild Toastmasters are experts at
officiating on Royal occasions.
Conferences and Banquets from 12 to 10,000 guests
organised.

## THE GUILD OF INTERNATIONAL SONGWRITERS & COMPOSERS

Sovereign House, 12 Trewartha Road, Praa Sands,
Penzance, Cornwall TR20 9ST
Tel: 01736 762826 Fax: 01736 763328
Email: songmag@aol.com
Web Site: http://www.icn.co.uk/gisc.html

## IMPERIAL SOCIETY OF TEACHERS OF DANCING

Imperial House, 22/26 Paul Street, London EC2A 4QE
Tel: 0171 377 1577 Fax: 0171 247 8979
Email: marketing@istd.org
Web Site: http://www.istd.org
Chief Executive: Michael J Browne
Chair: Joyce Percy

## INCORPORATED SOCIETY OF MUSICIANS

10 Stratford Place, London W1N 9AE
Tel: 0171 629 4413 Fax: 0171 408 1538
Email: membership@ism.org
Web Site: www.ism.org
Chief Executive: Neil Hoyle
Head of Professional Policy: Elizabeth Poulsen
Head of Legal & General Services: Andrew Cosgrove

Head of Finance & Systems: Ralph Seed
The ISM is the UK's professional body for all
musicians-performers, composers and teachers-
supplying its members with a comprehensive range of
advisory, support and information services.

## INDEPENDENT THEATRE COUNCIL (ITC)

12 The Leathermarket, Weston Street,
London SE1 3ER
Tel: 0171 403 1727 Fax: 0171 403 1745
Email: itc@dircon.co.uk
Director: Nicola Thorold
Mempership: Annabel Arndt
The Independent Theatre Council (ITC) is the
representative body and the Managers' Association for
small to middle scale performing arts organisations.
ITC's policy is to strengthen, protect and develop the
field of work by encouraging by good management
parctice.
As the Managers' Association, ITC, on behalf of the
membership, negotiates and administers contracts of
employment with Equity, MSF, TWU and WGGB and
other unions.
ITC Administration provides an advisory service to
members on all matters related to theatre management
and runs a Training Programme of short courses and
seminars.
As the representative body for small to middle scale
theatre, ITC speaks for the area of work at
conferences and public functions. ITC campaigns for
increased recognition and funding for the field and will
initiate support or opposition to any legislation or action
that may affect the interest of the membership.
ITC has a fast growing membership and the figure
currently exceeds 400. Membership is open to touring
and building-based companies and non-producing
venues.
The membership covers a wide range of national and
regional touring companies; arts centres; producing
venues; Theatre in Education teams; Community,
Children's and Young People's Theatre; Mime, Dance
and Puppet companies; Opera and Music Theatre.
Individual and Associate membership is also available.

## INSTITUTE OF CONTEMPORARY ARTS

12 Carlton House Terrace, London SW1Y 5AH
Tel: 0171 9300493 Fax: 0171 873 0051

## INSTITUTE OF ENTERTAINMENT AND ARTS MANAGEMENT

9 Bushetts Grove, Merstham, Redhill, Surrey RH1 3DX
Tel/Fax: 01737 644432
Email: drolph.ieam@virgin.net
Web Site: freespace.virgin/diane_rolph.ieam
Administrator: Diane Rolph
IEAM is the industry-wide professional institute
representing managers and managements throughout
the local government, commercial and subsidised
sectors of the arts, entertainment and related leisure
interests. It holds seminars on a national and regional
basis and publishes a monthly newsletter. Membership
of the institute is available to suitably experienced
applicants. Other classes of membership (Student and
Corporate) are available on application.

## INSTITUTE OF LEISURE & AMENITY MANAGEMENT

Lower Basildon, Reading, Berkshire RG8 9NE
Tel: 01491 874800 Fax: 01491 874801
Email: npo@ilam.co.uk
Web Site: www.ilam.co.uk
President: 96/97 Peter Morrall, 97/98 Alan Barber, 98/99 Gordon Bates
Director: Alan Smith
The Institute of Leisure and Amenity Management came into being on January 1st 1983 as a result of the merger of four professional organisations engaged in Leisure and Amenity Management, one of which was the Institute of Municipal Entertainments (IME).
ILAM has continued IME's role in offering qualifications to arts and entertainments professionals which have developed alongside the evolving vocational qualifications and which take account of prior academic or vocational achievements. ILAM actively represents arts and entertainments professionals in consultation and negotiation with Government and national agencies. The Panel's aims are to promote good practice within the specialisms; improve and facilitate communications with other bodies; promote and support ILAM Members' awareness and involvement with issues affecting management of cultural activities, including education and training; to produce and distribute information in appropriate format to achieve the aims and objectives outlined above.
All enquiries should be addressed to the Director, ILAM, ILAM House, Lower Basildon, Reading, Berkshire, RG8 9NE.

## INTER-ACTION

HMS President (1918), Victoria Embankment, Near Blackfriars Bridge, London EC4Y 0HJ
Tel: 0171 583 2652 Fax: 0171 583 2840
Community Resource, Education and Social Enterprise centre. Rehearsal space available.

## INTERNATIONAL FEDERATION FOR THEATRE RESEARCH

Eliot College, The University, Canterbury, Kent CT2 7NS
Tel: 01227 764000 Fax: 01227 827464
Email: M.J.Anderson@ukc.ac.uk
Web Site: www.arts.gla.ac.uk/t&ts/iftr/home.html
Joint Secretary General: Michael Anderson.
The IFTR exists to promote collaboration and the exchange of information between individuals and organisations concerned with theatre research around the world. It organises international conferences and synopsia and has established working groups for specific research projects.
Publishes the Theatre Research International.

## INTERNATIONAL SHAKESPEARE ASSOCIATION

c/o Dr Susan Brock Shakespeare Centre, Henley Street, Stratford-upon-Avon, Warwickshire CV37 6QW
Tel: 01789 201802 Fax: 01789 294911
Email: isa@intershake.demon.co.uk
Executive Secretary and Treasurer: Dr Susan Brock

## INTERNATIONAL THEATRE EXCHANGE

(UK Centre IATA)

19 Abbey Park Road, Great Grimsby DN32 0HJ
Tel: 01472 343424
Secretariat: Marjorie Havard

## INTERNATIONAL THEATRE INSTITUTE

ITI @ Goldsmiths College, University of London, Lewisham Way, New Cross, London SE14 6NW
Tel: 0171 919 7276 Fax: 0171 919 7277
Email: iti@gold.ac.uk
Chairman: Neville Shulman, O.B.E.
Administrator: Lynne Kendrick

## IRISH ACTORS' EQUITY GROUP

of the Services Industrial Professional Technical Union
9th Floor, Liberty Hall, Dublin 1 Eire
Tel: 00 353 1 874 0081 Fax: 00 353 1 874 3691
President: Robert Carrickford
Vice-President: Ian Montague
Group Secretary: Gerard Browne.
Irish Actors' Equity Group is modelled on British and American Equity lines. Actors' Equity is now a member of the Culture division of the Services Industrial Professional Technical Union. The Group which is a registered Trade Union with a negotiation licence, has been established to protect the rights of Irish Actors, to organise and improve the conditions of those engaged in the acting profession, to propose legislation favourable to the interest of the group. Besides functioning as a properly constituted Trade Union, similar to that of British Actors' Equity, the Group supplies players and crowd artists for Films. The Group's rules and regulations for film Companies on location in Ireland have been agreed to by the British Film Producers Association Ltd. A reciprocal arrangement with British Actors' Equity allows a free exchange of artistes between the two countries.

## THE IRVING SOCIETY

69 Harcourt Street, Newark-on-Trent, Nottinghamshire NG24 1RG
Tel: 01636 702801
Chairman: Michael Sharvell-Martin
Secretary: Brien Chitty
The Irving Society seeks to celebrate the Theatre in the Age of Sir Henry Irving, the Victorian actor/manager. The society meets February, April, June and issues a newsletter, First Knight twice a year.

## THE LIGHTING ASSOCIATION

Stafford Park 7, Telford, Shropshire TF3 3BQ
Tel: 01952 290905 Fax: 01952 290906

## THE LITTLE THEATRE GUILD OF GREAT BRITAIN

181 Brampton Road, Carlisle CA3 9AX
Southport Dramatic Club, 55 York Road, Southport, Lancashire PR8 2AY Tel/Fax: 01704 560607
Web Site: www.uktw.co.uk/clubs/itg.htm
Secretary: Mrs Barbara C Watson
Chairman: Mrs Margaret Mann
Treasurer: Patricia Clough, Bingley Little Theatre.
P.r.o: Marjorie Havard, 19 Abbey Park Road, Grimsby DN32 0HJ
Tel 01472 343424

Objects: The Little Theatre Guild of Great Britain was inaugurated in May 1946, with the following objects: "To promote close co-operation between the Little Theatres constituting its membership, to act as co-ordinating and representative body on behalf of the Little Theatres and generally to maintain and further the highest standards in the art of theatres as practised by existing Little Theatres and to assist in and encourage the establishment of other Little Theatres. The Guild is strictly non-political and non-sectarian." Membership: Membership is confined to independant organisations which control (usually by actual ownership) their own established theatres and which have satisfied the Guild as to their non-commercial character, general aims and artistic standards. Applications must be sponsored by two long-standing members of the Guild, who have seen their work and are willing to recommend admission

## LONDON SCREENWRITERS WORKSHOP

114 Whitfield Street, London W1P 5RW
Tel/Fax: 0171 387 5511
Web Site: www.lsw.org.uk
Forum for writers and novice aspiring writers for contact, information and tuition. Script reading service.

## LONDON THEATRE COUNCIL

32 Rose Street, London WC2E 9ET
Tel: 0171 557 6700 Fax: 0171 557 6799 Guild House, Upper St Martin's Lane, London WC2H 9EG Tel: 0171 379 6000 Fax: 0171 379 7001
Communications re Managers should be addressed to Rupert Rhymes and communications re Artistes should be addressed to Ian McGarry.
Chairman: Harvey McGregor, QC.
The Council represents SOLT (The Society of London Theatre) and Equity (British Actors' Equity Association). Its purpose is to mediate between managers and the artists employed by them in the West End of London. It does so primarily through the use of standard contracts of employment but the Council also facilitates the settlement of any disputes arising from these contracts.

## THE MAGIC CIRCLE

Theatre, Clubroom, Museum & Library, The Victory Services Club, 63/79 Seymour Street, London W2 2HF
Tel: 0171 723 4474
President: David Berglas
Secretary: Chris Pratt
13 Calder Avenue, Brookmans Park, Herts AL9 7AH
The Magic Circle is an Association aimed at the promotion of magic as an art and the establishment of a centre where magicians can meet.

## THE RAYMOND MANDER & JOE MITCHENSON THEATRE COLLECTION

The Mansion, Beckenham Place Park, Beckenham, Kent BR3 2BP
Tel: 0181 658 7725 Fax: 0181 663 0313
Director: Richard Mangan.

Special permission for inspection by appointment. The collection was founded in 1939 with the aim of covering all aspects of the theatre, opera and ballet. A veritable museum, it contains engravings, paintings, souvenirs, photographs, china figures, files of programmes of the London and provincial theatres, and a library of several thousand books. It is now used extensively by authors, designers, publishers, BBC, and television producers. The Collection was made into a Charitable Trust in 1977. The Founders themselves wrote nineteen books on theatrical and operatic subjects.

## THE MASSENET SOCIETY

Flat 2, 79 Linden Gardens, London W2 4EU
Tel: 0171 229 7060
Founder/Director: Miss Stella J Wright

## MECHANICAL COPYRIGHT PROTECTION SOCIETY LTD

Elgar House, 41 Streatham High Road, London SW16 1ER
Tel: 0181 769 4400 Fax: 0181 769 8792
Telex: 946792 MCPS G
The Society was formed in 1910 for the purpose of licensing on behalf of music copyright owners, the recording of their works for all purposes and the collection and distribution of the resulting fees and royalties.
Through reciprocal agreements with the majority of other mechanical collection organisations the interests of the Society's own Members are represented in most countries of the world where copyright is respected. Likewise MCPS represents the mechanical right interests, in its own territory, of virtually all composer, author and publisher members of foreign Societies and Agencies. Copyright clearance and licence may be obtained from the Society to cover the recording on disc, tape, sound, film track, video, etc. of works in its repertoire on application to the above address.

## MID WALES ENTERTAINMENT CIRCUIT

The Guildhall, Brecon, Powys
Tel: 01874 622884
Contact: Andrew Lamont.
Member venues: Theatr Hafren, Newtown; Aberystwyth Arts Centre; Wyeside Arts Centre, Builth Wells; Theatr Ardudwy, Harlech; Theatr Felinfach, Nr. Lampeter; Guildhall, Brecon; Grand Pavilion and Albert Hall, Llandrindodd Wells; Theatr Mwldan, Cardigan.
Policy: As the major promoter of popular entertainment in the region, it brings together the above theatres in an effort to minimise costs and simplify administration by controlling all tours centrally. Formed in 1982, it has proved an attractive proposition for performers since travelling within a confined area on consecutive days in beautiful surroundings gives rise to more comfortable working conditions.

## THE MUSIC CLUB OF LONDON

78 Bedford Court Mansions, Bedford Avenue, London WC1B 3AE
Tel/Fax: 0171 636 2946
COntact: Mr Coleman

## MUSICIANS BENEVOLENT FUND

16 Ogle Street, London W1P 8JB

Tel: 0171 636 4481 Fax: 0171 637 4307
Secretary: Helen Faulkner.
Head of Casework: Sara Dixon
Administrator of Public Affairs: Michael White

## MUSICIANS SOCIAL AND BENEVOLENT COUNCIL

100a Weston Park, London N8 9PP
Tel: 0181 348 9358
The council assists musicians in sickness and distress.
Income is derived from contributions by orchestras,
donations and legacies.
Funds urgently needed.

## MUSICIANS' UNION

National Office: 60/62 Clapham Road,
London SW9 0JJ
Tel: 0171 582 5566 Fax: 0171 582 9805
Email: info@musicianunion.org.uk
Web Site: www.musicianunion.org.uk
General Secretary: Dennis Scard
Assistant General Secretaries: Bob Wearn, Joan
Smith, Andy Knight.
The Musicians' Union is the principal organisation of
musicians in Britain. It is a trade union affiliated to the
TUC and the Labour Party, the Radio and Television
Safeguards Committees, the Theatres' Advisory
Council, the Federation of Entertainment Unions, and
the National Music Council. As a trade union its
principal object is the regulation and improvement of
salaries, fees and working conditions of its members.
Agreements have been made with the BBC,
commercial TV programme contractors, gramophone
and other recording companies, symphony orchestra
managements, theatre and music hall proprietors and
their association and holiday camps.
The Union has over 80,000 members, and branches
have been established in over 80 towns. It occupies a
leading position in the International Federation of
Musicians.
The National Office, and most branches, maintain
benevolent funds for the relief of distress.

## NATIONAL ASSOCIATION FOR THE TEACHING OF DRAMA

30 Heathdene Road, Streatham, London SW16 3PD
Tel: 0181 679 3661
President: Dorothy Heathcote.
Hon. Secretary: Maggie McNeill.
The National Association for the Teaching of Drama
(NATD) was formed in 1977 and represents the
classroom teacher of drama. The primary objectives of
NATD are to encourage the formation of associations
of drama teachers thus improving the status and the
development of drama in education at local level; to
represent the concerns of local associations,
disseminate information and articulate the case for the
development of drama in education.

## NATIONAL ASSOCIATION OF TEACHERS IN FURTHER & HIGHER EDUCATION

27 Brittania Street, London WC1X 9JP
Tel: 0171 837 3636 Fax: 0171 837 4403

## NATIONAL ASSOCIATION OF YOUTH THEATRES

Unit 1304, The Custard Factory, Gibb Street, Digbeth,
Birmingham B9 4AA
Tel: 0121 608 2111 Fax: 0121 608 2333
Email: nayt@11pmail.demon.co.uk
Web Site: http://www.nayt.org.uk
Contact: Lynne Carney, Director

## NATIONAL CAMPAIGN FOR THE ARTS

Francis House, Francis Street, London SW1P 1DE
Tel: 0171 828 4448 Fax: 0171 931 9959
President: Melvyn Bragg
Director: Jennifer Edwards.
The NCA was formed in 1984 by artists and
administrators who decided that the arts needed an
independent voice in politics and the media. Today, it is
well-known in Westminster, Whitehall and Fleet St. The
NCA specialises in research and information services,
lobbying and campaigning. It provides up-to-the-minute
facts and figures for politicians, journalists and anyone
else who needs to know what is happening in the arts.
NCA news, the quarterly magazine, combines in-house
research with the articles by leading figures in the world
of the arts and politics.
The national campaign for the Arts is independent of
any political party or government agency and is funded
solely by membership subscriptions and donations
from nearly 2,000 Arts organisations and individuals.
The NCA agenda:
1.Recognition of the Arts' true value to the nation.
2.A higher priority for the arts on the political agenda.
3.A significant increase in central and local government funding.
4.A secure place for the arts in schools.
5.Policies to advance equal opportunities, regional
and local facilities and fiscal incentives.
For further information about membership contact
office.

## NATIONAL COUNCIL FOR DRAMA TRAINING (NCDT)

5 Tavistock Place, London WC1H 9SN
Tel/Fax: 0171 387 3650
Chairman: Peter Plouviez.
Executive Secretary: Adele Bailey
The NCDT was established in 1976 with the object of
encouraging the highest possible standards of
vocational education and training for drama in the
United Kingdom and to provide a forum within which
the different sides of the profession can discuss
matters of common interest in relation to such training.
The Council is an independent body, registered as a
charity, and is financed by its member organisations -
Equity, TMA, SOLT, BBC,the Conference of Drama
Schools, Channel Four Television and donations from
a number of the independent television companies.

## NATIONAL ENTERTAINMENT AGENTS COUNCIL

PO Box 112, Seaford, East Sussex BN25 2DQ
Tel: 01323 492488 Fax: 01323 492234
Email: chrisbray@neac.org.uk
Web Site: www.neac.org.uk
Chairman: Alan Pope
Vice Chairmen: Keith Harmon, David Blackburn
General Secretary: Chris Bray
Treasurer: Vic Graves

Hon. President: Derek Wells.
An active Trade Organisation for Entertainment Agents. Broadly speaking, the N.E.A.C. is to Entertainment Agents what ABTA is to Travel Agents. The Council is open to all Agents who are prepared to adhere to the Code Of Conduct, which is nationally recognised and adhere to the highest standards of ethical behaviour. Members receive or have access to Legal and Technical Advice and Support, regular Newsletters, Branch and National Meetings, Showcases, Inter Trading and many other benefits, all regulated under the Rules of the Council and the Code Of Conduct. The Council has a Disciplinary Procedure to hear and resolve any complaints against its members.

## NATIONAL OPERATIC AND DRAMATIC ASSOCIATION

NODA House, 1 Crestfield Street, London WC1H 8AU
Tel: 0171 837 5655 Fax: 0171 833 0609
Chief Executive: Mark Thorburn
A registered charity established in 1899, NODA is the largest umbrella body for AMATEUR THEATRE in the UK. Elected Councillors and Regional Representatives support its members at local level. Benefits include a quarterly national magazine, area magazines and directories, summer school, advisory and emergency services and a computerised mailing list. Insurance, Pantomime scripts, make-up and music, theatre tickets, theatre books at discounts to members are also available via its trading company, NODA Ltd.

## THE NATIONAL OUTDOOR EVENTS ASSOCIATION

7 Hamilton Way, Wallington, Surrey SM6 9NJ
Tel: 0181 669 8121 Fax: 0181 647 1128
Email: secretary@noea.org.uk
Web Site: www.noea.org.uk
Honorary President: Tony Speller
President: Alan J Bell
General Secretary: John Barton.
Founded in 1979, the Association exists to promote standards, status and interests of the world of Outdoor Events and is the forum for civic authorities, show organisers and suppliers of equipment and services in general.
The Association provides a comprehensive range of relevant services aimed at creating business opportunities, developing skills and improving the quality of events. A series of Regional Clinics is held during the closed season and has published the first ever comprehensive Code of Practice for Outdoor Events. Copies may be ordered from the Association and has become recognised as a major source of reference for the Outdoor Events Industry.
NOEA works closely with 'Access All Areas' the journal for the Events Industry. NOEA publishes an annual directory of Members and copies may be obtained upon application.

## NATIONAL YOUTH MUSIC THEATRE

5th Floor, The Palace Theatre, Shaftesbury Avenue, London W1V 8AY
Tel: 0171 734 7478 Fax: 0171 734 7515
Artistic Director: Jeremy James Taylor.
General Manager: Felicity Bunt

Music theatre productions and workshops for 11-19 year old actor, singer, dancers and instrumentalists. UK tours including the Edinburgh Festival. International tours have included Canada, USA and Japan. Open national auditions every autumn.

## NATIONAL YOUTH THEATRE OF GREAT BRITAIN

443-445 Holloway Road, London N7 6LW
Tel: 0171 281 3863 Fax: 0171 281 8246
Email: info@nyt.org.uk
Web Site: http://www.nyt.org.uk
Director: Edward Wilson
General Manager: Mig Kimpton

## NEW PLAYWRIGHTS TRUST

Interchange Studios, Dalby Street, London NW5 3NQ
Tel: 0171 284 2818 Fax: 0171 482 5292
Email: npt@easynet.co.uk
Executive Director: Jonathan Meth
NPT is a national research and development organisation for new writing for all forms of live and recorded performance. The Trust aims to encourage new writing and promote the work of writers currently under-represented, believing the continuing emergence of vital and challenging writing to be essential to the future of the industry.
NPT publishes a range of information pertinent to writers on all aspects of development and production in the form of guides and a six-weekly journal which includes articles and reviews on aesthetic and practical issues.
NPT also runs a script-reading service and a link service between writers and producers, organises debates and seminars and undertakes research projects.

## PERFORMING RIGHT SOCIETY (PRS)

29/33 Berners Street, London W1P 4AA
Tel: 0171 580 5544 Fax: 0171 306 4050
Chairman: Andrew Potter
Chief Executive: John Hutchinson
PRS is an association of composers, authors and publishers of music which exists to collect royalties for the non-dramatic public performance and broadcasting of their copyright works. PRS is affiliated to similar societies throughout the world. A PRS licence is required for the use of its international repertoire in concert and variety, as overture, entr'acte or exit music, or for any other form of live or mechanical performance (excluding operas, operettas, music plays, specially written music for plays, revues or pantomimes (apart from interpolations therein of independent items), and ballets). Further information from Alan Scott-Neve, Local Authorities and Theatres.

## PHONOGRAPHIC PERFORMANCE LTD

1 Upper James Street London W1R 3HG
Tel: 0171 534 1000 Fax: 0171 534 1111
PPL is a non profit making company set up by the record industry in 1934 to grant licences to anyone who wants to play records, tapes or CD's in public. PPL looks after the rights of over 12,000 different record labels. This means that 95% of commercially available recordings in the UK need a PPL licence when they are broadcast or played in public. The revenue generated from PPL's licence fees is distributed to record companies and their performers.

## PROVINCIAL THEATRE COUNCIL

32 Rose Street, London WC2E 9ET
Tel: 0171 557 6700 Fax: 0171 557 6799 Guild House,
Upper St. Martin's Lane, London WC2H 9EG Tel: 0171
379 6000 Fax: 0171 379 7001
Communications re Managers should be addressed to
Rupert Rhymes (Joint Secretary) and communications
re Artistes should be addressed to Ian McGarry (Joint
Secretary).
Chairman: Harvey McGregor, QC.
The Council represents TMA (Theatrical Management
Association) and Equity (British Actors' Equity
Association). Its purpose is to mediate between
managers and the artists employed by them in the UK
theatre, outside the West End of London. It does so
primarily through the use of standard contracts of
employment but the Council also facilitates the
settlement of any disputes arising from these
contracts.

## PUPPET CENTRE TRUST

The Puppet Centre, Battersea Arts Centre, Lavender
Hill, London SW11 5TN
Tel: 0171 228 5335 Fax: 0171 228 8863
Email: pct@puppetcentre.demon.co.uk
Director: Loretta Howells
Administrator: Allyson Kirk
Resource centre devoted to promoting the arts of
promoting the arts of animation and puppetry. Small
museum display. Open to general public 2pm-6pm
Monday to Friday, admission free.

## RADIUS

(The Religious Drama Society of Great Britain) - an
interdenominational body
RADIUS, Christ Church & Upton Chapel,
1a Kennington Road, London SE1 7QP
Tel: 0171 401 2422
Patrons: Dr George Carey, the Archbishop of
Canterbury, Dame Judi Dench.
President: The Rt. Revd. Peter Firth.
Radius exists to encourage drama which illuminates
the human condition. Its work is directed towards
improving the standard of writing, production acting of
plays and for Christian education and outreach. It
offers advice, the use of a unique library, a Summer
School, Training Days, and a quarterly magazine.

## RENAISSANCE THEATRE TRUST COMPANY

1st Floor, Ulverston Library, Kings Road,
Ulverston LA12 0BT
Tel: 01229 582299
Contact: Deborah Barrington-Hunt
Event promotion (medium/smaller scale) in South
Lakeland.

## ROY CASTLE LUNG CANCER FOUNDATION

200 London Road, Liverpool L3 9TA
Tel: 0151 794 8800 Fax: 0151 794 8888
Email: williamsc@roycastle.liv.ac.uk
Web Site: www.roycastle.org
Celebrity and Special Events Manager: Cheryl
Williams

## ROYAL THEATRICAL FUND (EST. 1839)

(incorporated by Royal Charters 1853 & 1974)
11 Garrick Street, London WC2E 9AR
Tel: 0171 836 3322
Patron: Her Majesty The Queen
President: Sir Donald Sinden, CBE, FRSA
Secretary: Mrs R. M. Foster
Registered Charity No. 222080.

## RSA

The Royal Society for the Encouragement of Arts,
Manufacturers & Commerce
8 John Adam Street, London WC2H 9EG
Tel: 0171 930 5115 Fax: 0171 839 5805

## SAVE LONDON'S THEATRES CAMPAIGN

Guild House, Upper St.Martin's Lane,
London WC2H 9EG
Tel: 0171 379 6000 Fax: 0171 379 7001
Life President: Graeme Cruickshank
Chairman: John Levitt
The Save London's Theatre Campaign also
administers the Pat Forster Memorial Fund and annual
Lecture, Administrator - Graeme Cruickshank.

## SCOTTISH CIVIC ENTERTAINMENT ASSOCIATION

c/o Monklands District Council Leisure & Recreation
Dept., 101 Bank Street, Coatbridge
Tel: 01236 812222
Secretary: Aileen Armstrong

## SCOTTISH YOUTH THEATRE

6th Floor, Gordon Chambers, 90 Mitchell Street,
Glasgow, G1 3NQ
Tel: 0141 221 5127 Fax: 0141 221 9123
Email: sy001@post.almac.co.uk
Organisation offering young people (3-25 years) the
chance to take part in most aspects of performance
art, working with theatre professionals as a means to
encourage social, artistic and self-development.

## THE SESAME INSTITUTE (UK)

Christchurch, 27 Blackfriars Road, London SE1 8NY
Tel/Messages: 0171 633 9690
Email: sesameinstituteuk@btinternet.com
Drama and Movement in Therapy.
Full time training - Central/Sesame. Short courses.
Sesame Practitioners provided.
General Enquiries - The Sesame Institute.
Full time training - The Central School of Speech &
Drama, London (Tel 0171 722 8183).

## THE SHAKESPEARE CENTRE

Henley Street, Stratford-upon-Avon,
Warwickshire CV37 6QW
Tel: 01789 204016 Fax: 01789 296083
Headquarters of the Shakespeare Birthplace Trust.
Facilities include research library on Shakespeare's
life, work and times, incorporating the collections of the
Royal Shakespeare Theatre; Educational courses;
Poetry Festival, etc. Enquiries to Director: Roger
Pringle, MA.

## THE SHAW SOCIETY
51 Farmfield Road, Bromley, Kent BR1 4NF
Tel: 0181 697 3619
Secretary: Barbara Smoker

## THE SOCIETY FOR THEATRE RESEARCH
c/o The Theatre Museum, 1e Tavistock Street,
London WC2E 7PA
Email: e.cottis@btinternet.com
Web Site: http://www.unl.ac.uk/str
President: Prof. Glynne Wickham
Vice-Presidents: Jack Reading, George Rowell,
George Speaight.
Chairman: Pieter van der Merwe
Hon. Secretaries: Eileen Cottis, Frances Dann;
Treasurer: Barry Sheppard.
The Society aims to link those interested in the history
and technique of the theatre in the United Kingdom and
encourage further research into these subjects. It
publishes the journal 'Theatre Notebook' and one or
more annual volumes as well as holding lectures and
other events and disburses up to £4,000 annually in
grants towards research. It also presents an annual
Theatre Book Prize, currently of £400.

## THE SOCIETY OF AUTHORS LTD
84 Drayton Gardens, London SW10 9SB
Tel: 0171 373 6642 Fax: 0171 373 5768

## SOCIETY OF BRITISH FIGHT DIRECTORS
56 Goldhurst Terrace, London NW6 3HT
Tel: 0171 624 1837

## SOCIETY OF BRITISH THEATRE DESIGNERS
47 Bermondsey Street, London SE1 3XT
Tel: 0171 403 3778 Fax: 0171 378 6170
Chairman: Christopher Richardson;
Secretary: Jenny Straker, A.B.T.T.
The Society exists to enhance the interests and status
of the theatre design profession, covering sets,
costumes and lighting.
Organises exhibitions and debates on current issues
affecting Theatre Design.

## SOCIETY OF LEISURE CONSULTANTS AND PUBLISHERS
1 Sandringham Close, Sandringham Park, Tarleton,
Lancashire PR4 6UX
Tel: 01772 816046
Director: J. B. A. Sharples
Represents consultants and publishers in the field of
entertainment and the arts management, recreation,
catering, tourism, marketing, public relations, recruiting,
advertising, and the leisure industry and related
interests.

## THE SOCIETY OF LONDON THEATRE
32 Rose Street, London WC2E 9ET
Tel: 0171 557 6700 Fax: 0171 557 6799
Web Site: www.officiallondontheatre.co.uk
President: Andre Ptaszynski
Chief Executive: Rupert Rhymes.

Employers' organisation for West End theatres and
producers. Providing industrial relations, legal services,
and collective marketing and advocacy for the industry.
Organisers of the annual Laurence Olivier Awards.
Publishers of the official London Theatre Guide.
Promoters of Theatre Tokens.

## THE SOCIETY OF THEATRE CONSULTANTS
47 Bermondsey Street, London SE1 3XT
Tel: 0171 403 3778 Fax: 0171 378 6170
Chairman: Martin Carr
Hon. Secretary: Chris Baldwin
Hon. Treasurer: Anne Minors
Permanent Secretary: Jenny Straker
A Professional Society whose members advise on the
feasibility, management planning and detail design of
Theatres, Concert Halls, Conference Centres, Arts
Centres, etc.

## STAGE MANAGEMENT ASSOCIATION
Southbank House, Black Prince Road,
London SE1 7SJ
Tel: 0171 587 1514
Chairman: Peter Theobold
Hon. Secretary: John Lonergan
Membership: Open to anyone working professionally in
stage management in the UK.
Objects of the Association: To look after the interests
and speak on behalf of Stage Management. Members'
Meetings: Held regularly in London.
Employment: A list of members available for new
engagements is circulated to managements each
month on request.

## STANDING CONFERENCE OF UNIVERSITY OF DRAMA DEPARTMENTS
Theatre Workshop, Dept. of English Literature,
University of Sheffield, Sheffield S10 2ST
Tel: 0114 282 6273 Fax: 0114 282 4246
Email: P.E.Roberts@Sheffield.ac.uk
Web Site: www.ntu.ac.uk/scudd
Chairman: Philip Roberts
Secretary: Richard Boon, School of English, University
of Leeds, Leeds LS2 9JT
Tel 0113 233 4720  Fax 0113 233 4774
e-mail boon@english.novell.leeds.ac.uk

## THEATRE INFORMATION GROUP
2 Carlton Road, East Sheen, London SW14 7RJ
Tel: 0171 837 0113 Fax: 0181 878 6392
UK Membership Secretary, Treasurer: Angela Douglas

## THEATRE INVESTMENT FUND LTD
The Palace Theatre, Shaftesbury Avenue,
London W1V 8AY
Tel: 0171 287 2144 Fax: 0171 287 0565
Chief Executive: Nick Salmon
Chairman: John Whitney
Vice-Chairman: Bob Swash
Reg.Charity No.271349

## THEATRE MUSEUM
The National Museum of the Performing Arts
1e Tavistock Street, London WC2E 7PA
Tel: 0171 836 7891 Fax: 0171 836 5148

Head of Museum: Margaret Benton
The Theatre Museum exists to provide the national record of stage performance in Britain and to increase the public understanding and enjoyment of the performing arts through the expert interpretation of its collections. In its main premises in Covent Garden, the Museum houses permanent displays and special exhibitions drawn from its unrivalled collections, together with a souvenir shop and box office for West End shows. It runs a popular events and education programme. A study room is also available for research; please call 0171 836 7891 for an appointment. Both the Paintings Gallery and Studio Theatre are available for corporate hire. The public entrance is in Russell Street and admission charges are: adults £3.50, students, OAPs, UB40 holders and children aged 5 to 14 £2, children under 5 and Friends of the V&A free.

## THE THEATREGOERS' CLUB OF GREAT BRITAIN

Harling House, 47-51 Great Suffolk Street, London SE1 0BS
Tel: 0171 450 4040 Fax: 0171 450 4041
President: Susan Hampshire
Vice President: Gary Wilmot
Chairman: Sir Eddie Kulukundis OBE,
The largest theatre Club in the UK, established in 1978. Members enjoy a wide selection of West End and regional theatre, with luxury coach travel.

## THEATRES ADVISORY COUNCIL

47 Bermondsey Street, London SE1 3XT
Tel: 0171 403 3778 Fax: 0171 378 6170
President: Lord Jenkins of Putney
Vice-Presidents: Lord St. John of Fawsley, Lord Donoghue
Chairman: Lord Birkett
Vice-Chairmen: Peter Finch, Neville Hunnings, Charles Vance
Hon. Secretary: Martin Carr
Hon. Treasurer: Neville Shulman.
The Theatres Advisory Council is a federation of theatre organisations, its membership consisting of twenty-two national bodies representative of all theatre interests. Founded in 1963 with initially the primary aim of ensuring the preservation of theatre buildings, its unique composition, including unions, managerial associations and advisory bodies, has enabled the Theatres Advisory Council to act as spokesman for the whole theatre industry on issues which are of concern to all sides of the theatre.
It's main objects are now to provide a forum for the discussion examination and solution of problems affecting the performing arts, excluding those directly related to industrial relations; to make such representations on behalf of the theatre to governmental and other bodies as members may collectively determine and to endeavour to keep the Press and public informed; to give advice regarding new projects for places of performance; and to co-operate with the Theatres Trust regarding places of performance which are thought to be endangered. The Council has close links with the local authority associations.

## THE THEATRES TRUST

22 Charing Cross Road, London WC2H 0HR

Tel: 0171 836 8591 Fax: 0171 836 3302
Email: tttetheatrestrust.org.uk
Life Presidents: Lord Jenkins of Putney
Chairman: Sir John Drummond
Director: Peter Longman
Consultant: John Earl
The Trust was set up by Parliament in 1976 to promote the better protection of theatres for the benefit of the nation. Its 15 Trustees are appointed by the Secretary of State for Culture, Media and Sport. Following a separate Act of Parliament for Scotland in 1978 and an administrative agreement covering Northern Ireland, the Trust's remit now extends over the whole of the United Kingdom. Local Authorities are required by Government order to consult the Trust when considering planning applications affecting land on which there is a theatre.
However, the Trust's work extends far more widely and covers other planning issues, advice on theatre buildings to grant-making bodies, including the Lottery distribtors, and in relevant matters helping theatre managerments and preservation bodies. The Trust also owns three theatre freeholds, from which it derives much of its income. Other income comes from advisory work, donations, subscriptions to its Friends organisation and an annual grant from the Department of Culture, Media and Sport. The Trust works closely with an associated Charitable Fund sharing the same Trustees, staff and offices.

## THE THEATRICAL LADIES GUILD

PO Box 22721, London N22 5WQ
Tel: 0181 889 7570 Fax: 0181 889 4495
Email: tlg@compuserve.com
The Theatrical Ladies' Guild of Charity was founded in 1892 by a group of distinguished actresses to help their dressers and their families and back stage staff. The Guild is prepared to help anyone, male or female, who has worked in the theatrical profession, including stage and wardrobe staff, front of house staff, as well as the acting profession.
Financial help is given by way of small regular grants, help with nursing fees, in homes and privately.
General help is also given and assistance can be given to all ages.
Registered charity no. 206669.

## THEATRICAL MANAGEMENT ASSOCIATION

32 Rose Street, London WC2E 9ET
Tel: 0171 557 6700 Fax: 0171 557 6799
President: Barbara Matthews
Chief Executive: Rupert Rhymes.
TMA is the UK's national trade association for theatre managers, producers, venues and arts professionals. Services for its members include industrial relations and legal advice, information services, a quarterly magazine Prompt, and the annual Barclays Theatre Awards. Information about membership is available from the address above.

## TTA (THEATRICAL TRADERS ASSOCIATION)

c/o Cricket Street, Denton, Manchester M34 3DR
Tel 0161 335 0220
Chairman: Bob Howarth

Membership of all firms serving the entertainment industry who mainly specialise in supplying amateur organisations.

## U.K.D.D.F. (UK DANCE & DRAMA FEDERATION)

2 Woodland Street, Tunstall, Stoke-on-Trent, Staffordshire ST6 6AP
Tel: 01782 823472/267276 Fax: 01782 823472
Education to teacher standards. Training for professional dance careers. Qualified staff and regular guest teachers.

## UNIMA - BRITISH CENTRE

(Union Internationale de la Marionnette)
Cross Border Arts, Wysing Arts Centre, Fox Road, Bourn, Cambridge CB3 7TX
Tel: 01954 718181 Fax: 01954 718333
Email: lorraine@cba.eastern-arts.co.uk
British arm of international association affiliated to UNESCO serving to unite people around the world who contribute to the development of Puppet Theatre. BrUNIMA is a membership organisation of professional and amateur puppeteers with a team of Professional Consultants in most aspects of puppetry. Organises events for puppeteers, usually with an international focus. Publishes BrUNIMA Bulletin 3 times a year, and occasional publications.

## THE UNIVERSITY OF BRISTOL THEATRE COLLECTION

Department of Drama, Cantocks Close, Bristol BS8 1UP
Tel: 0117 928 7836 Fax: 0117 928 7832
Email: s.j.morris@bris.ac.uk
Web Site: http://www.bris.ac.uk/Depts/Drama
Keeper: Sarah Morris
Assistant Keeper: Frances Clayton
The Theatre Collection covers most areas of theatre research and history. It is rich in primary source material, including playbills, photographs, prints, and original scenery and costume designs. Its holdings include the London Bristol Old Vic archives, The Herbery Beerbohm Tree collection, the Alan Tagg collection and the Women`s Theatre Collection. There is also an extensive reference library and collection of journals, plus an enquiry service.
Visiting hours are from Mondays to Fridays, 9.15am to 4.45pm. Appointment reccommended.

## THE VARIETY & LIGHT ENTERTAINMENT COUNCIL

54 Keyes House, Dolphin Square, London SW1V 3NA
Tel: 0171 834 0515 Fax: 0171 821 0261
Guild House Upper St.Martin's Lane, London, WC2H 9EG Tel: 0171 379 6000 Fax: 0171 379 7001
Joint Secretaries: Kenneth Earle (Dolphin Square) Peter Finch (Guild House)
The V.L.E.C. exists to promote and regulate good relations between Managers, Agents and Artistes engaged in the Variety and Allied entertainment business. In particular the Council maintains machinery for the adoption and operation of Standard Contract for all Live Entertainment and the settlement of disputes arising therefrom.

The constitution of the Council includes The Agents' Association (Great Britain), the Association of Circus Proprietors, British Actors' Equity Asociation, the Institute of Leisure & Amenity Management, the National Association of Licensed House Managers, Society of London Theatres and the Theatrical Management Association.

## VARIETY CLUB CHILDREN'S CHARITY LTD

326 High Holborn, London WC1V 7AW
Tel: 0171 611 3888 Fax: 0171 611 3892

## WOMEN & THEATRE (B'HAM) LTD

Friends Institute, 220 Moseley Road, Highgate, Birmingham B12 0DG
Tel: 0121 440 4203 Fax: 0121 446 4280
Email: womenandtheatre@btinternet.com
Administrator: Victoria Firth
Women and theatre is a producing theatre company who tour nationally. The company is well know for its work around health and social core.

## WRITERS GUILD OF GREAT BRITAIN

430 Edgware Road, London W2 1EH
Tel: 0171 723 8074 Fax: 0171 706 2413
Co-chairs: John Scotney, Julia Jones
General Secretary: Alison V Gray

# Society of Theatre Consultants

## IAN B ALBERY

Wyndham Ltd., 54 Cavell Street, London E1 2HP
Tel: 0171 790 2007 Fax: 0171 790 6634

## PETER ANGIER

Carr & Angier, The Old Malthouse, Clarence Street, Bath BA1 5NS
Tel: 01225 446664 Fax: 01225 446654
Email: mail@carrandangier.co.uk

## CHRIS BALDWIN

ACT Consultant Services, The Old Wood Mill, Church Lane, Madingley, Cambridge CB3 8AF
Tel: 01954 210766 Fax: 01954 211466
Consulting services for buildings used for the performing arts including spacial planning, circulation and technical facilities, and also design development consultation, through traditional or lottery-funded methods, for medium and small scale arts projects.

## RICHARD BRETT

Technical Planning Int'l, The Stagehouse, Palace Road, Kingston, Surrey KT1 2LG
Tel: 0181 549 6535 Fax: 0181 549 6545
Email: rechplan@compuserve.com

## MARTIN CARR

Carr & Angier, The Old Malthouse, Clarence Street, Bath BA1 5NS
Tel: 01225 446664 Fax: 01225 446654

Email: mail@carrandangier.co.uk

**RAY CARTER**
Next Stage, Judds Farm, Winsor Lane, Winsor,
Southampton SO40 2HG
Tel: 01703 812011 Fax: 01703 812213
Email: 106177.3466@compuserve.com

**PAUL S COVELL**
Setllands, Sackmore Lane, Marnhull,
Dorset DT10 1PN
Tel/Fax: 01258 820249

**LOUIS K FLEMING**
Theatre Projects Consultants, 3 Apollo Studios,
Charlton Kings Road, London NW5 2SW
Tel: 0171 482 4224 Fax: 0171 284 0636

**JEREMY GODDEN**
Theatre Projects Consultants, 3 Apollo Studios,
Charlton Kings Road, London NW5 2SW
Tel: 0171 482 4224 Fax: 0171 284 0636

**LEONARD GREENWOOD**
Theatre Projects Consultants, 3 Apollo Studios,
Charlton Kings Road, London NW5 2SW
Tel: 0171 482 4224 Fax: 0171 284 0636
Email: pg@tpc-lon.com

**MICHAEL HOLDEN**
Michael Holden Associates, 17 West Heath Drive,
London NW11 7QG
Tel: 0181 455 4640 Fax: 0181 209 1059

**DENIS IRVING**
Entertech Ply Ltd., PO Box 168, Terang, Victoria 3264
Australia
Tel: +61 3 5592 2033 Fax: +61 3 5592 2043
Entertech is the leading consultance in Australia
working exclusively on the planning, detailed design
and technical equipment specification of new or re-
furbished venues for live performance.

**DAVID JACKSON**
David Jackson & Associates, Crowlin Cottage, Little
London Road, Cross in Hand, Near Heathfield, East
Sussex TN21 0LT
Tel: 01435 868808 Fax: 01435 868889

**IAIN MACKINTOSH**
Theatre Projects Consultants, 3 Apollo Studios,
Charlton Kings Road, London, NW5 2SW
Tel: 0171 482 4224 Fax: 0171 284 0636

**KEITH MCLAREN**
Carr & Angier, The Old Malthouse, Clarence Street,
Bath BA1 5NS
Tel: 01225 446664 Fax: 01225 446654
Email: mail@carrandangier.co.uk

**ANNE MINORS**
26 Wimbledon Park Road, London SW18 1LT

Tel/Fax: 0181 874 3640

**CHRISTOPHER RICHARDSON**
Theatre Futures, Onnibus, 41 North Road,
London N7 4DP
Tel: 0171 700 6877 Fax: 0171 700 6876

**ALAN G RUSSELL**
Theatre Projects Consultants, 3 Apollo Studios,
Charlton Kings Road, London NW5 2SW
Tel: 0171 482 4224 Fax: 0171 284 0636
Email: arussell@tpc-lon.com

**DAVID STAPLES**
Theatre Projects Consultants, 3 Apollo Studios,
Charlton Kings Road, London NW5 2SW
Tel: 0171 482 4224 Fax: 0171 284 0636
Email: dstaples@tpc-lon.com

**ANDRE TAMMES**
Lighting Design Partnership, 3 John's Place, Leith,
Edinburgh EH6 7EL
Tel: 0131 553 6633 Fax: 0131 553 3457
Email: edinburgh@ldp.net

**DAVID TAYLOR**
c/o Theatre Projects Cons. Inc London 871,
Ethan Allen Highway, Ridgefield, CT.06877-2801 USA
Email: taylorusa@worldnet.att.net

**JOHN WYCKHAM**
John Wyckham Associates, The Old Malthouse,
Clarence Street, Bath BA1 5NS
Tel: 01225 338300 Fax: 01225 338363

# Arts Councils and Regional Arts Boards

**THE ARTS COUNCIL OF ENGLAND**
14 Great Peter Street, London SW1P 3NQ
Tel: 0171 333 0100 Fax: 0171 973 6590
Web Site: http://www.artscouncil.org.uk
Chief Executive: Peter Hewitt
Deputy Chief Executive: Graham Devlin
Executive Director Planning and Resources:
Graham Long
Executive Director of Communications: Phil Murphy
Director of Combined Arts (Acting): Ferran Bronac
Director of Dance: Hilary Carty
Director of Drama: Anna Stapleton
Director of Education and Training: Pauline Tambling
Director of Finance and Resources: Nigel Copeland
Director of Literature: Gary McKeone
Director of Lottery Film: Carolyn Lambert
Lottery Operations Director: Moss Cooper
Lottery Projects Director: Nicole Penn-Symons
Director of Music: Kathryn McDowell
Corporate Policy Director: Graham Hitchen
Regional Director: Julia Crookenden

Director of Touring: Kate Devey
Director of Visual Arts: Marjorie Allthorpe-Guyton

## ARTS COUNCIL OF NORTHERN IRELAND
NAC Neice House, 77 Malone Road, Belfast BT9 6AQ
Tel: 01232 385200 Fax: 01232 661715
Chairman: Brian Walker
Chief Executive: Brian Ferran;
Performing Arts Director: Philip Hammond

## ARTS COUNCIL OF WALES
9 Museum Place, Cardiff CF1 3NX
Tel: 01222 376500 Fax: 01222 221447
Email: information@ccc.acw.org.uk
Web Site: www.ccc-acw.org.uk
Chief Executive: Joanna Weston
The Arts Council of Wales is the national organisation
with specific responsibility for the funding and
development of the arts in Wales. Most of its funds
come from the Welsh office but it also receives funds
from local authorities, the Crafts council and other
sources. It also distributes National Lottery funds to the
Arts in Wales.
For a guide to schemes and grants available please
contact ACW at the above address.

## EAST MIDLANDS ARTS BOARD
Mountfields House, Epinal Way, Loughborough
Leicestershire LE11 0QE
Tel: 01509 218292 Fax: 01509 262214
Email: info@em-arts.co.uk
Web Site: www.arts.org.uk
Chief Executive: John Buston; Head of Management
Services: Bharat Pandya; Head of Performing Arts
(with responsibility for Drama): Helen Flach; Drama
Development Officer: Michaela Waldram; Head of
Combined Arts & Planning: Philip Thompson; Music
Officer: Karl Chapman; Film Officer: Caroline Pick;
Literature Officer: Sue Stewart; Customer Services and
Information Officer: Deborah Duggan.
East Midlands Arts is one of ten regional Arts Boards
that cover the whole of England. The area of benefit
includes Derbyshire, Rutland, Leicestershire,
Nottinghamshire and Northamptonshire serving a
population of nearly four million people. The Board
represents a wide range of expertise in the arts,
management, finance, marketing and local
government. Its members work to enhance arts
education, develop the cultural industries and promote
excellence in artistic endeavour.

## EASTERN ARTS BOARD
Cherry Hinton Hall, Cherry Hinton Road,
Cambridge CB1 4DW
Tel: 01223 215355 Fax: 01223 248075

Chief Executive: Lou Stein; Director of Business &
Resources: Lesley Thompson; Director of Performing
Arts: Sue Grace; Director of Planning and
Development: Fred Brookes; Director of Visual and
Media Arts: Rosemary Greenlees; Education Officer:
Karen Dust; Information and Technology Officer: Kofi
Owusu; Finance and Business Services Officer: Julia
Money Dance and Mime Officer: Nikki Crane; Drama
Officer: Alan Orme; Music Officer: Kaye Tyrrell,
Literature Officer: Emma Drew; Cinema &
Broadcasting Officer: Martin Ayres; Photography and
Multimedia Officer: Alastair Haines; Crafts Officer:
Alison McFarlane; Visual Arts Officer: Niki Braithwaite;
Training Officer: Katharine Orme.
Bedfordshire, Cambridgeshire, Essex, Hertfordshire,
Lincolnshire, Norfolk, Suffolk.
Financial support is received from local authorities, the
Arts Council of Great Britain, membership
subscriptions and private donations.
The Board's mission is to develop a wide range of arts
activities of the highest quality, to stimulate and extend
involvement in the arts among all sections of the
regional community. The Board gives financial
assistance for artistic activities; provides services for
artistic bodies and initiates projects where they are
needed.

## LONDON ARTS BOARD
Elme House, 133 Long Acre, London WC2E 9AF
Tel: 0171 240 1313 Fax: 0171 240 4580
Chief Executive: Sue Robertson; Deputy Chief
Executive: John Sharples; Director of Arts: John
Kieffer. Director of Finance: Jack Haslam; Principal
Drama Officer: Sue Timothy.
Established October 1, 1992 London Arts Board, both
on its own and in partnership with others, promotes
and supports artistic excellence and innovation
throughout London; develops access to the arts for the
enjoyment, education and benefit of all who live and
work in, or visit, London; celebrates the richness of
London's cultural diversity; seeks to enhance London's
quality of life, reputation and economy.
Restrictions: London Arts Board does not give grants
to individual students.
Beneficial Area: 32 boroughs of London and the
Corporation of London.
Finances: 1994/95 income: £10.8 million; expenditure
(grants) £9.4 million; operating costs £1.4 million. Type
of Grant: Annual grants to client list totalling £6.56
million 1993/94. One-off funding programmes for
projects throughout year, in the arts totalling
£1.6million, in education £446,000. Strategic
development grants total £1.8million.
Type of Beneficiary: Arts organisations, artists, local
authoriites, local education authorities.
Submission of: applications made to specific funding
programmes with set deadlines. There are general
criteria which relate to all applications and include:
artistic, strategic and managerial effectiveness, and
financial requirements.
Reports: approximately 4 newsletters per annum.

## NORTH WEST ARTS BOARD
Manchester House, 22 Bridge Street,
Manchester M3 3AB
Tel: 0161 834 6644 Fax: 0161 834 6969
Email: nwarts-info@mcr1.poptel.org.uk
Web Site: www.arts.org.uk/
Chief Executive: Sue Harrison

North West Arts Board is the regional arts board serving Cheshire, Greater Manchester, Lancashire, Merseyside and the High Peak of Derbyshire. It is an arts funding and development agency providing grants, advice and information on a wide range of arts and cultural activity amongst arts organisations, local communities, voluntary groups and artists across the north west region.

## NORTHERN ARTS

9/10 Osborne Terrace, Jesmond,
Newcastle-upon-Tyne, NE2 1NZ
Tel: 0191 281 6334 Direct Line: 0191 281 2866 ext.
130 Fax: 0191 281 3276
Email: bdm@norab.demon.co.uk
Chief Executive: Andrew Dixon; Head of Performing Arts: Brian Debnam; Performing Arts Officers: Mark Monument, Mark Mulqueen; Administrator: Ursula Heron;  Secretary: Gillian Roe.
Covers Teeside, Cumbria, County Durham, Tyne and Wear and Northumberland.
Northern Arts' principal objective is to promote the arts in the north.
Major Drama includes the RSC's Newcastle residency, the International Season at the Newcastle Playhouse and many specialist festivals.
The Board also welcomes tours by large and small scale companies from Britain and abroad. Details of the region's venues and promoters can be obtained from the Performing Arts Department. Northern Arts is strongly supportive of indigenous work, supporting a major producing company, Northern Stage, and many small and medium scale touring companies.
In addition, new playwriting is actively supported through the New Writing North.

## THE SCOTTISH ARTS COUNCIL

12 Manor Place, Edinburgh EH3 7DD
Tel: 0131 226 6051 Fax: 0131 225 9833
Director: Ms. Seona Reid; Director of Finance & Administration: Graham Berry; Drama and Dance Director: David Taylor; Arts Director: Susan Daniel-McElroy; Music Director: Matthew Rooke; Literature Director: Jenny Brown; Combined Arts Director: John Murphy: Director of Planning & Development (Depute Director): Barclay Price; Lottery Director: David Bonnar.

## SOUTH EAST ARTS BOARD

Union House, Eridge Road, Tunbridge Wells,
Kent TN4 8HF
Tel: 01892 507200 Fax: 01892 549383
Email: info@seab.co.uk
Web Site: www.arts.org.uk
Chief Executive: Felicity Harvest; Executive Assistant: Jean Pain; Finance and Admin. Officer: Andrew Crawford; Director of Visual and Media Arts: Margaret O'Brien; Local Authority Planning Officer: Clarissa Roberts; Director of Performing Arts: Debra Reay; Media Officer: Tim Cornish; Research and Information Officer: Jill Hogan.
South East Arts (SEA) is the regional arts development agency for Kent, Surrey, East Sussex, West Sussex and the unitary authorities of Brighton & Hove and Medway.
We are one of ten regional arts boards in England and part of the national arts funding system along with the Arts Council of England, British Film Institute and Crafts Council.

SEA is a company limited by guarantee and a registered charity; managed by a board of 18 members drawn from the arts community, business sector and local authorities. SEA has 31 staff members consisting of senior management, specialist artform and non artform officers and administrators.
SEA,s mission is to develop, support, lobby for and promote the arts of the highest quality and widest range for the benefit of people living, working, being educated in or visiting the south east of England. We offer funding, advice, information and other services and collaborate with a range of strategic partners throughout the region.

## SOUTH WEST ARTS

Bradninch Place, Gandy Street, Exeter EX4 3LS
Tel: 01392 218188 Fax: 01392 413554
Email: info@swa.co.uk
Web Site: www.swa.co.uk
Chief Executive: Nick Capaldi
South West Arts was the first Regional Arts Association to be formed. In 1971 it was reconstituted to incorporate the local authorities in the region. In Oct. 1991 the association was incorporated as Arts Board South West Ltd (still trading as South West Arts).
The largest number of organisations aided by the board are arts centres, associations and clubs, most of them on a fairly small scale as the region has few large centres of population. Major projects, however, include the Beaford Centre, an area arts centre covering 1000 square miles of rural north Devon.
In theatre the Association funds the Gloucestershire Everyman, the work of several indigenous groups, and visiting companies to the region. In music the Association helps, in combination with Southern Arts, to promote the Bournemouth Symphony Orchestra and Bournemouth Sinfonietta, and a contemporary music and dance programme under the auspices of the Arnolfini (and other) organisations. In literature the main clients are the Cheltenham Festival of Literature. The visual arts and crafts department supports artists and craftsmen.
Details of all schemes and policies are available from the information service.

## SOUTHERN ARTS

13 St.Clement Street, Winchester,
Hampshire SO23 9DQ
Tel: 01962 855099 Fax: 01962 861186
Chair: David Reid; Chief Executive: Robert Hutchinson; Executive Assistant: Vacant; Management Services Unit:
Director of Finance and Management Service: Viv Nixson; Finance Officer: Valerie Brighton;
Planning Unit:
Director - Planning & Co-ordination: Stephen Boyce; Information & Marketing Officer: Paul Clough; Information & Marketing Assistant: Jeannette Smith; Local Authorities Liaison Officer: Richard Russell; Education and Planning Officer: Jane Bryant; Planning Assistant: Jason Knight.
Arts Unit:

Director of Arts: Sarah Maxfield; Performing Arts: Theatre Officer: Sheena Wrigley; Local Arts Development Officer: Joanna Day; Theatre and Local Arts Development Assistant: Claire Poupart; Dance Officer: Sally Abbott; Music Officer: Michael Marx; Music and Dance Assistant: Jane Attwood; Visual Arts and Crafts: Visual Arts Officer: Philip Smith; Crafts Officer: David Kay; Crafts and Visual Arts Assistant: Sandy White; Published and Broadcast Arts: Literature Officer: Keiren Phelan; Film, Video and Broadcasting Officer: Jane Gerson; Literature and Film, Video and Broadcasting Assistant: Phillippa Baker
Southern Arts is the arts development agency for Berkshire, Buckinghamshire, Hampshire, Isle of Wight, Oxfordshire, Wiltshire and South East Dorset. It works in partnership with local authorities and other regional agencies and aims to place the arts at the heart of the region's cultural, social, economic and educational life.

**WEST MIDLANDS ARTS**
82 Granville Street, Birmingham B1 2LH
Tel: 0121 631 3121 Fax: 0121 643 7239
Chief Executive: Sally Luton; Director of Performing and Combined Arts: Tony Davis; Director of Visual Arts, Craft and Media: Caroline Foxhall; Director of Planning: Beverley Parker; Director of Management Services: Sharon Palmer; Executive Officer: Martin Turner; Performing Arts Officer (Music): Val Birchall; Performing Arts Officer (Drama): Kate Organ; Performing Arts Officer (Dance &Mime): Anouk Perinpanayagam; Combined Arts Officer: Stephanie Edmonds; Visual Arts Officer: Mark Dey; Media Officer (Photography & Digital Media): Jennie Hayes; Media Officer (Film & Video): Laurie Hayward; Visual Arts Officer (Public Art Commissions): Emma Larkinson; Visual Arts Officer (Crafts): Penny Smith; Media Officer (Literature): Adrian Johnson; Planning Officer (East): Karen Kirkman; Planning Officer (West): Anne Gallacher; Planning Officer (Central): To be appointed; Senior Lottery Officer: Philip Thompson; Business Development & Training Officer: Dominic Bourton.
West Midlands Arts is the Regional Arts Board for the West Midlands: the counties of Hereford and Worcester, Staffordshire, Warwickshire and Shropshire, and the metropolitan districts of Birmingham, Coventry, Dudley, Sandwell, Solihull, Walsall and Wolverhampton. West Midlands Arts provides funding, advice, information and planning to help develop the arts, crafts and media of the region. The main theatres in the region are the Birmingham Repertory, Birmingham Hippodrome, Birmingham Alexandra, MAC (Midlands Arts Centre), Coventry Belgrade, Shakespeare Memorial Theatre, New Victoria Theatre Stoke-on-Trent, Worcester Swan, Malvern Festival Theatre, Warwick Arts Centre and Wolverhampton Grand.
There are also Arts Centres and Civic Halls with well-equipped stages at Bedworth, Lichfield, Burslem, Whitchurch, Telford, Shrewsbury, Tamworth, Solihull, Leamington, Nuneaton, Ellesmere, Bridgnorth, Evesham, Redditch, Stafford, Burton and Hereford. The policy towards drama includes grants to professional theatres to enable them to extend the range of their activities, promotion of touring, contact with new audiences, and support towards participatory projects.

**YORKSHIRE AND HUMBERSIDE ARTS**
21 Bond Street, Dewsbury, West Yorkshire WF13 1AX

Tel: 01924 455555 Fax: 01924 466522
Email: yharts-info@geo2.poptel.org.uk
Web Site: www.arts.org.uk
Chief Executive: Roger Lancaster; Director of Performing Arts: Jim Beirne; Director of Visual Arts: Vacant; Director of Planning: Andy Carver; Director of Management Services: Alan Wallace; Communications Officers: Jill Foggin/Sally Brown; PA to the Directorate: Mavis Schindler; Head of Administration: Mavis Lowe; Drama Officer: Shea Connolly; Music Officer: Glyn Foley; Dance Officer: Mileva Drljaca; Visual Arts& Crafts Officer: Jennifer Hallam; Film & Broadcasting Officer: Terry Morden; Literature Officer: Steve Dearden; Director of Visual Arts: Nima-Poovaya-Smith.
Yorkshire & Humberside Arts serves the metropolitan districts of South and West Yorkshire; the unitary authorities of York, Hull, East Riding, North Lincolnshire, North East Lincolnshire; and the county of North Yorkshire.

# National Tourist Boards

**CUMBRIA TOURIST BOARD**
Ashleigh, Holly Road, Windermere, Cumbria LA23 2AQ
Tel: 015394 44444 Fax: 015394 44041

**EAST MIDLANDS TOURIST BOARD**
Exchequergate, Lincoln LN2 1PZ
Tel: 01522 531521 Fax: 01522 532501

**EAST OF ENGLAND TOURIST BOARD**
Toppesfield Hall, Hadleigh, Suffolk IP7 5DN
Tel: 01473 822922 Fax: 01473 823063
Email: eastofenglandtouristboard@compuserve.com
Web Site: www.visitbritain.com

**ENGLISH TOURIST BOARD**
Thames Tower, Black's Road, London W6 9EL
Tel: 0181 846 9000 Fax: 0181 563 0302

**HEART OF ENGLAND TOURIST BOARD**
Larkhill Road, Worcester WR5 2EF
Tel: 01905 761100 Fax: 01905 763450
Email: JennyC@bta.org.uk
Web Site: www/visitbritain/HETB

**ISLE OF MAN DEPARTMENT OF TOURISM & LEISURE**
See Terminal Buildings, Douglas, Isle of Man IM1 2RG
Tel: 01624 686801 (General Enquiries) Fax: 01624 686800 Tel: 01624 686868 (Brochure Line) Tourist Information: 01624 686766
Email: tourism@gov.im
Web Site: www.gov.im/tourism

**JERSEY TOURIST INFORMATION OFFICE**
38 Dover Street, London W1X 3RB
Tel: 0171 493 5278 Fax: 0171 491 1565

**LONDON TOURIST BOARD AND
CONVENTION BUREAU**
6th Floor, Glen House, Stag Place, London SW1E 5LT
Tel: 0171 932 2000
Web Site: www.londontown.com
Pre-recorded telephone answer service available on
0839 123456 and charged at 49p a minute at all times.


**NORTH WEST TOURIST BOARD**
Swan House, Swan Meadow Road, Wigan Pier,
Wigan WN3 5BB
Tel: 01942 821222 Fax: 01942 820002
Email: info@nwtb.u-net.com
Web Site: visitbritain.com-west-england


**NORTHERN IRELAND TOURIST BOARD**
St.Anne's Court, 59 North Street, Belfast BT1 1NB
Tel: 01232 231221 Fax: 01232 240960 24 Haymarket,
London SW1Y 4DG
Tel: 0171 766 9920  Fax: 0171 766 9929
Web Site: www.nitb.com


**NORTHUMBRIA TOURIST BOARD**
Aykley Heads, Durham DH1 5UX
Tel: 0191 375 3000 Fax: 0191 386 0899
Email: enquiries@ntb.org.uk
Web Site: northumbria-tourist-board.org.uk/


**SCOTTISH TOURIST BOARD**
23 Ravelston Terrace, Edinburgh EH4 3EU
Tel: 0131 332 2433 Fax: 0131 343 1513 19 Cockspur
Street, London SW1Y 5BL Tel: 0171 930 8661
Fax: 0171 930 1817


**SOUTH EAST ENGLAND TOURIST BOARD**
The Old Brew House, Warwick Park, Tunbridge Wells,
Kent TN2 5TU
Tel: 01892 540766 Fax: 01892 511008


**SOUTHERN TOURIST BOARD**
40 Chamberlayne Road, Eastleigh,
Hampshire SO50 5JH
Tel: 01703 620006 Fax: 01703 320010


**WALES TOURIST BOARD**
Brunel House, 2 Fitzalan Road, Cardiff CF2 1UY
Tel: 01222 499909 Fax: 01222 485031
Web Site: www.visitwales.com
Wales Information Desk,
Britain Visitor Centre,
1 Regent Street, London SW14 4XT
Tel: 0171 808 3838  Fax: 0171 808 3830
email: WalesDest@tourism.wales.gov.uk


**WEST COUNTRY TOURIST BOARD**
60 St.David's Hill, Exeter EX4 4SY
Tel: 01392 425426 Fax: 01392 420891


**YORKSHIRE AND HUMBERSIDE TOURIST
BOARD**
312 Tadcaster Road, York, North Yorkshire YO2 2HF
Tel: 01904 707961 Fax: 01904 701414

1. ACCESS EQUIPMENT
2. ACCOUNTANCY & FINANCIAL SERVICES
3. ANIMAL HIRE
4. ARCHITECTS
5. BILL POSTERS & HOARDING SITES
6. BOX OFFICE SERVICES & TICKET AGENTS
7. CAR & COACH HIRE
8. CASTING
9. CATERING & CONFECTIONERY
10. CIRCUS EQUIPMENT & JUGGLING SUPPLIES
11. CLEANING & HYGIENE
12. COIN COUNTING & CASH REGISTERS
13. COMPUTER SYSTEMS & ELECTRONIC PUBLICITY
14. COOLING AND HEATING SYSTEM HIRE
15. COSTUME (CLEANING)
16. COSTUME (HIRE & SALE)
17. CRECHE FACILITIES
18. DESIGN, PRINTING & PUBLICITY
19. DRAPES, FURNISHINGS & FABRICS
20. EFFECTS & FIREWORKS
21. EMERGENCY SERVICES
22. EVENT & CONFERENCE ORGANISERS
23. FILM, VIDEO & AUDIO VISUAL
24. FIRE & SAFETY
25. FLIGHT CASES & PACKING CHESTS
26. FLIGHT CASE LABELS
27. FLOORS & FLOOR COVERING
28. FLORAL DECORATIONS & PLANT HIRE
29. FLYING BALLET
30. HOSPITALITY AGENTS
31. HOTEL BOOKING SERVICES
32. INSURANCE
33. LEAFLET DISTRIBUTORS
34. LEGAL & PROFESSIONAL SERVICES
35. LIGHTING AND LIGHTING EQUIPMENT SUPPLIERS
36. LIGHTING FIBRE OPTICS
37. MAGICAL EQUIPMENT & VARIETY
38. MAKE-UP & WIGS
39. MANAGEMENT CONSULTANTS
40. MARKET RESEARCH
41. MARQUEE HIRE & OUTDOOR EVENTS
42. MERCHANDISING & ADVERTISING SERVICES
43. MUSICAL EQUIPMENT & SERVICES
44. PASSES AND SECURITY ID
45. PHOTOGRAPHY
46. PIANO HIRE
47. PLASTICS SPECIALISTS
48. PROPS (HIRE & SALE)
49. RADIOS & MOBILE PHONES
50. RECORDING
51. REHEARSAL ROOMS
52. RIGGING
53. SCENERY (BUILDERS, PAINTERS & HIRERS)
54 . SCENERY SUPPLIERS
55. SCRIPTS
56. SEATS & SEATING
57. SECURITY SERVICES
58. SHIPPING
59. SOUND & SOUND EQUIPMENT SUPPLIERS
60. SPONSORSHIP CONSULTANTS
61. STAGE & SCENIC ENGINEERING
62. STORAGE
63. TECHNICAL STAFF
64. THEATRE CONSTRUCTION, MANAGEMENT & RENOVATION
65. TRANSLATION SERVICES
66. TRANSPORT & TRAVEL
67. WARDROBE
68. WEAPONS & ARMOUR
69. MISCELLANEOUS

**Suppliers & Services**

# SUPPLIERS AND SERVICES

## 1

# ACCESS EQUIPMENT

**ACCESS INTERNATIONAL LTD**
South Way, Walworth Industrial Estate, Andover,
Hampshire, SP10 5AD
Tel 01264 324014
Fax 01264 358730
Aluminium access products

**FLINT HIRE AND SUPPLY LTD**
Queens Row, London SE17 2PX
Tel 0171 703 9786
Fax 0171 708 4189
Hire and Sales Manager: Danny Hill
Hire and sales of Zargees ladders, Tallesopes, Power
lifts, cherry pickers and Access towers. Megadek hire

**KWIKFORM UK LTD**
192 Waterloo Road, Hay MIlls, Birmingham B25 8LE
Tel 0121 275 0200
Fax 0121 275 0300

**INSTANT ZIP-UP LTD**
Access House, Halesfield 17, Telford,
Shropshire TF7 4PW
Tel 01952 685200
Fax 01952 685255
e-mail access@instantzip-up.com
Instant Zip-Up are one of the leading access specialists
in the UK, with over 40 years of experience. The
Instant Tallescope aluminium work platform is one of a
range of access products extensively used in theatres
throughout the country.

**LIGHT ALLOY LIMITED**
Dales Road, Ipswich, Suffolk IP1 4JR
Tel 01473 740445
Fax 01473 240002
Aluminium alloy containers and trolleys for storage and
transport, widest range of access equipment in UK.

**LITE SCAFFOLDING LTD**
Clark View, Off Easy Road, Leeds LS9 8QU.
Tel 0113 293 9696
Established manufacturers of aluminium staging
systems. Comprehensive range of access towers. Will
also make to order custom built structures for stage
sets. Manufacturers of Astralite.

**MARLER HALEY EXPOSYSTEMS LTD**
Little End Road, Eaton Socon, St Neots,
Cambridgeshire PE19 3SN.
Tel 01480 218588
Fax 01480 477032
Pedestrian and Crowd Control - Guideline systems.
Freestanding foyer displays - Infoframes - 3 sided
moving message displays - Rotagraphics.

**THE PERFORMING PLATFORM COMPANY**
Unit1C, Pury Hill, Alderton, Towcester, Northants
NN12 7LS
Tel 01604 631296
Fax 01604 624582
Hire or Sale. Specialists in temporary staging for tiered,
shaped and multi-level performance modular systems.
New 'State of the Art' quickly installed revolving stages.
Manual or fully programmed.

## 2

# ACCOUNTANCY & FINANCIAL ADMINISTRATION

**ADDIS & CO**
Emery House, 192 Heaton Moor Road, Stockport,
Cheshire SK4 4DU
Tel 0161 432 3307  Fax 0161 432 3376
Certified Accountants.

**LAWRENCE BLACKMORE**
Suite 5, 26 Charing Cross Road, London WC2H 0DG
Tel 0171 240 1817
Fax 0171 836 3156
Theatre Production Accountant. Production and
running cost estimation, budgeting and general
evaluation of theatrical ventures. Financial and
management accounting systems analysis and
organisation.

**BOWKER, ORFORD AND CO**
15/19 Cavendish Place, London W1M 0DD
Tel 0171 636 6391  Fax 0171 580 3909
Contact: J. Ponton

**BREBNER, ALLEN & TRAPP**
The Quadrangle, 180 Wardour Street,
London W1V 4LB
Tel 0171 734 2244
Fax 0171 287 5315
e-mail partners@brebner.co.uk
Contacts: Simon Cryer, Jose Goumal, Joe O'Sullivan
and Michael Burton are the contacts for our Media
related services. These cover all aspects of financial
and taxation advise and support both at production and
individual level.

**DALES EVANS & CO LTD**
(Chartered Accountants)
96/98 Baker Street, London W1M 1LA
Tel 0171 935 5133
Fax 0171 486 6437
Contact: Lester Dales

**DATAWEST COMPUTER SERVICES**
East Way, Lee Mill Business Park, Ivybridge, Devon
PL21 9GE.
Tel 01752 897171
Contact: John Arnold

Pineapple Software for Theatres and Leisure Venues features a House Diary which can be linked to a simple profit and loss record, with invoicing, for each event. The Facility Management module controls the allocation of resources necessary for each event. The Production/Commitment Accounting system streamlines procedures and ensures tight financial control of actual and committed expenditure. Incorporating a flexibile payroll, purchase orders and budgets with a fully integrated financial ledger system Pineapple Software provides a flexibile and easy-to-use management system. Installations throughout the UK.

**DELOITTE & TOUCHE**
Hill House, 1 Little New Street, London EC4A 3TR
Tel 0171 936 3000
Fax 0171 583 8517
Contact: Charles Bradbrook or Robert Reed
Taxation and accounting services. We have wide experience of West End and overseas theatrical production, international licencing, VAT and witholding tax planning.

**GOODMAN JONES**
(Chartered Accountants)
29/30 Fitzroy Square, London W1P 6LQ
Tel 0171 388 2444
Fax 0171 388 6736

**MARTIN GREENE RAVDEN**
55 Loudoun Road, St. John's Wood, London NW8 0DL
Tel 0171 625 4545
Fax 0171 625 5265
Contact: David Ravden
Chartered Accountants and Business Managers - Audit, Accountancy and Tax Compliance, Business Management, Tour Accounting, Withholding Tax Clearances, Royalty Examinations, Litigation Support.

**NYMAN LIBSON PAUL**
Chartered Accountants
Regina House, 124 Finchley Road, London NW3 5JS
Tel 0171 794 5611
Fax 0171 431 1109
Contact: Paul Taiano
Established for over 60 years with specialist knowledge of the Theatre and Entertainment industries, providing accountancy, audit, and taxation services for companies and individuals. Specialist tax services for UK and overseas clients.

**PANNELL KERR FORSTER ASSOCIATES**
New Garden House, 78 Hatton Garden, London EC1N 8JA
Tel 0171 831 7393
Fax 0171 405 6736
Contact: Brian Tash or Edward Middleton.
Consulting services to the leisure, arts and entertainment industry. Operational management and marketing analysis, financial review and funding, working, where necessary, in close association with technical specialists in other professional disciplines. Advice in the development of computer based accounting and front of house systems.

# 3
# ANIMAL HIRE

**ADS ANIMAL HIRE**
Reform Road, Maidenhead, Berkshire.
Tel 01628 39758
Gun dogs trained and supplied. White ponies for theatre and fetes.

**ANIMAL AMBASSADORS**
Litchfield House, 20 Croft Way, Woodcote, Reading, Berkshire RG8 ORS
Tel/Fax 01491 681202
Mobile 0831 558594
Contact: Kay Weston

**ANIMAL ARK**
Studio, 29 Somerset Road, Brentford TW8 8BT
Tel 0181 560 3029
Fax 0181 560 5762
Specialist animal consultants. Any animal for film, television and advertising industries. Events, kids TV and Exhibitions. Animal props - natural history items D.O.E. licensed, props and models made.
Contact: David Manning or Jenny Seymour.

**ANIMALS GALORE**
208 Smallfield Road, Horley, Surrey
Tel 01342 842400
Website: www.animalsgalore.demon.co.uk
Mrs Cindy Newman
Suppliers of animals for Theatre, Films, Television, Still Photography etc.

**A-Z ANIMALS**
Arts Exchange, Mel Green, Congleton, Cheshire CW12 4AB
Tel 01932 865412
Fax 01932 866369
Contact: Jerry Cott
Animal filming and photographic consultants. Supplying and supervising animals for film and photography. ACTA member.

**ANIMAL WORLD**
19 Greaves Road, High Wycombe, Bucks HP13 7JU
Tel 01494 442756
Fax 01494 441385
Contact: Trevor Smith
Animal Acts/supply.

**CHIPPERFIELDS CIRCUS**
Tel 01608 643885
Fax 01608 645370
Contact: R. Chipperfield

**EXOTIC & PERFORMING ANIMALS**
Chapel House, Chapel Street, Congleton, Cheshire CW12 4AB
Tel 01260 276627
Fax 01260 270777
Suppliers of exotic and domestic animals for TV, Films, Promotions and Publicity. Panto Ponies and Cinderella Coaches etc. Speciality Acts, reindeer and sleigh, indoor and outdoor tiered seating hire.

**MIRAGE INTERNATIONAL**
New Copse Farm, Bentworth, Alton GU34 5NP.
Tel 01420 564439.
Mobile 0427 522391
Email: rat@mirageuk.freeserve.co.uk
Contact: CJ Peters or Gina Croft

Specialising in mice, rats, dogs, minature horses.
Regular work for TV including Big Breakfast
and Danny Baker, Noel Edmonds, Through the Lace
Curtains, Central TV and Anglia.
Film work including Dabrowski and Tales From the
Crypt.

# 4

# ARCHITECTS

## ALL CLEAR DESIGNS LIMITED
3rd Floor, Cooper House, 2 Michael Road, London
SW6 2ER
Tel 0171 384 2950/2951
Fax 0171 384 2951
email: allclear@easynet.co.uk
James Holmes-Siedle, Director
Specialists in making buildings accessible for disabled
people.  Architectural services include access audits,
feasibility studies and construction.  Experience with
theatres and listed buildings.  Assistance with advice
with funding included.

## BENTON & COMPANY ARCHITECTS
33 Northgate, Sleaford, Lincolnshire NG34 7BX.
Tel 01529 304524
Fax 01529 306981
Previous nationwide involvement on diverse arts
provisions large and small. Sympathetic adaptation of
historic building a speciality. If you currently have a
proposal under consideration and need to see an
imaginative way forward contact Tim Benton for an
informal discussion.

## BURRELL FOLEY FISCHER
York Central, 70-78 York Way, London N1 9AG
Tel 0171 836 5097
Fax 0171 379 6619
Contact: Mark Foley
Burrell Foley Fischer have some 18 years experience of
designing specialist facilities for a wide range of arts
organisations ranging from small fringe venues through
to major theatres, concert halls and opera houses in the
U.K. and abroad.
Our experience also includes cinema and educational
and training facilities, media centres and gallery design.
Through the other work of the practice we are also able
to offer advice on the design of ancillary facilities and
Urban Design expertise where the project is of a greater
size, scope and complexity.
As well as advising small scale venues, our past and

current clients include many of the major national and
international performing companies and organisations
including the Almeida Theatre, The Riverside Studios,
The Royal Ballet, South Bank Arts Centre. The Sports
Council, and The Arts Council of England. We can offer
specialist advice on the design of dance facilities.

## CREFFIELDS (TIMBER & BOARDS ) LTD
Unit 6, Marcus Close, Tilehurst, Reading, Berkshire
RG30 4EA
Tel 01734 453533
Fax 01734 453633
Creffield s is one of the UK's leading suppliers of
flame proofed sheets and soft woods for the
exhibition and theatre trades.
Large stocks are held allowing for urgent orders
delivered promptly .

## JOHN ROWE-PARR ASSOCIATES LTD
Chartered Architects, Interior Designers, Theatre
Consultants, 161 Rosebery Avenue, London
EC1R 4QX
Tel 0171 278 8488
Fax 0171 278 4388
Our professional expertise has been well established
over 15 years and we are now the leading consultancy
practice specialising in the restoration of historic and
new theatres throughout the UK.
Working exclusively on demanding and tight program
management projects we provide skills beyond the
normal role of architectural design including site
feasability studies and lottery funding applications.

# 5

# BILL POSTERS & HOARDING SITES

## ADSHEL LTD
33 Golden Square, London W1R 3PA.
Tel 0171 287 6100
Fax 0171 287 9149

## AIRPORT ADVERTISING (EUROPE) LTD
Hale Top House, Thorley Lane, Manchester Airport
M90 5UG.
Tel 0161 489 3098
Fax 0161 489 3814

**C P POSTER ADVERTISING LTD**
Prospect House, The Broadway, Farnham Common,
Berks SL2 3PQ
Tel 01753 647277
Fax 01753 647281

**CREATIVE SIGNWORK**
209A Fernside Avenue, Hanworth Park, Middlesex
TW13 7BQ
Tel 0181 751 1009
Contact: Brynette Tagg

**HP PROMOTION**
6/8 Verney Road, Rotherhithe, London SE16 3DH.
Tel 0171 394 9644
Fax 0171 394 9664
Contact: Malcolm Jacob

**K&J POSTERS**
64 Woodlands Road, Liverpool L17
Tel 0151 707 2498
Mobile 0831 529 730
Contact: Jamie Farrell

**MAIDEN OUTDOOR**
128 Buckingham Palace Road, London SW1W 9SA
Tel 0171 838 4000
Fax 0171 838 4002

**NATIONAL SOLUS SITES LTD**
Astra House, Arklow Road, London, SE14 6EB
Tel 0181 694 2134
Fax 0181 694 9780

**NEWSIGNS**
Loveridge Road, Kilburn, London NW6 2DS
Tel 0171 328 9251
Fax 0171 624 7465
Mobile 0860 258074

**SLATER & WALKER PDS LTD**
Unit 1, Trojan Business Centre, Cobbold Road, London
NW10 9ST.
Tel 0181 451 6302
Fax 0181 451 6083

**STREETWISE ADVERTISING (POSTERS)**
Unit 6, Effra Road, Brixton, London SW2 1BZ.
Tel 0171 924 0199
Mobile 0973 199274
Flyposting company which specialises in outdoor
poster advertising for theatres, concert promoters
magazines and record companies etc. Also handles
official four sheet poster boards.

**THEATRESEARCH**
The Lodge, Braisty Woods, Summerbridge, North
Yorkshire HG3 4DN
Tel 01423 780497
Email david@theatresearch.freeserve.co.uk
Contact: David Wilmore, Ric Green
Theatresearch specialises in the restoration of historic
theatres, providing theatre consultancy services for
planning, design, technical equipment, historic
research/archives and project management.
Theatresearch also undertakes consultancy work for
film and TV companies working on location in theatres,
providing project management, script advice and
historic information for period productions, and
documentaries.

**6**

# BOX OFFICE SERVICES & TICKET AGENTS

**ABBEY BOX OFFICE LTD**
75 Wilton Road, London SW1V 1DE
Tel 0171 233 6900
Fax 0171 233 6384

**ABBEY DATA SYSTEMS LIMITED**
Aptdo De Correos 144, La Cala De Mijas, 29649 Mijas Costa, Malaga, Spain
Tel/Fax 00 34 5249 2111
Mobile 00 34 0955 7400
Suppliers of CREST range of computerised Box Office Systems which are now processing the reservations for over 40 Theatre and Halls in U.K. and Europe. CREST prints tickets at time of booking and provides comprehensive Management information. Systems are also supplied for Night-club table reservations.

**ALBEMARLE OF LONDON**
74 Mortimer Street, London W1N 8HL
Tel 0171 637 9041
Fax 0171 631 0375
e-mail sales@albemarlelondon.demon.co.uk
Website www.demon.co.uk/albemarlelondon2

**ALUSET SECURITY TICKETS**
15 Station Street, Whetstone, Leicester LE8 6JS.
Tel 0116 275 1600

Fax 0116 275 1573
As the leading ticket printer Aluset supply a complete range of tickets from simple continuous stationery to highly secure stadium tickets.
Our thermal tickets are used successfully in all types of printers including BOCA, Gazelle, TOR, Star. We believe our quality will improve your image.

**APPLAUSE LTD**
The Applause Building, 68 Long Acre, London WC2E 9JQ
Tel 0171 878 2090
Fax 0171 911 3490
Group and individual reservations, London. Box-office and telephone room operation.

**BANKHOUSE LEISURE & INCENTIVE BREAKS LTD**
Riverside House, Apsley Manna, Wakefield Road, Huddersfield HD1 3AF
Tel 01484 435353
Fax 01484 423351
London Theatre Weekend Breaks. Tickets, Travel and The Finest Hotel Choice for any major show/event.

**BLUE CHIP TRAVEL**
15 Hill Street, Edinburgh EH2 3JP
Tel 0131 226 6157
Fax 0131 220 1299
Blue Chip Travel specialise in concert, theatre and special event packages.
All holidays include overnight accommodation in 3 or 4 star accommodation, guided tours, return coach travel between your local area and destination and, of course, concert or theatre tickets.

**BOCS (Box Office Computer System)**
68 Long Acre, London WC2E 9JQ
Tel 0171 872 9977
Fax 0171 872 9378

**bocs,** world leaders in ticketing and marketing technology, is reknowned for providing total solutions, offering fully integrated ticketing, marketing, membership, fundraising, subscriptions and facitities management.
**bocs** is continually acclaimed for its ease of use, vast functionality and unique networking ability.  Last year **bocs** helped hundreds of organisations to sell over 75 million tickets worldwide including: the South Bank Centre; Royal National Theatre and the Barbican Centre in London; Apollo Leisure Group; Athens Concert Hall; Sheffield Theatres; the Musical S.R.O.'s nationwide network in the Czech Republic and the Sydney Opera House.

**HENRY BOOTH & COMPANY**
Stockholm Road, Sutton Fields, Hull HU7 OXY
Tel 01482 826343
Fax 01482 839767
Website www.henrybooth.co.uk
Contact: Mark Sneddon - General Sales Manager
e-mail marks@henrybooth.co.uk
For all your ticket requirements contact Henry Booth, manufacturers of all types of tickets for all systems including BOCA, CATS, Databox, DDS, Hebos/Arena, PASS, Quota, TOR & VGS using BOCA, Gazelle, Star, TOR & UBI Printers.

**THE BOX OFFICE**
87 Spenser Road, Bedford, MK40 2BE
Tel 01234 355487/355488
Fax 01234 355486
Concert and West End theatre ticket agents specialising in Hotel Breaks featuring 3-5 star delux hotels and VIP packages in Central London at very competitive prices.

**DATACULTURE LTD**
Midsummer House, Midsummer Boulevard, Central Milton Keynes, MK9 3BN
Tel 01908 232404
Fax 01908 232414
Email: sales@dataculture.com
Website: http://www.dataculture.com
Contact: Jonathan Hyams, Charles Davies, Roger Tomlinson
Creators of Databox, the acclaimed Windows based ticketing and marketing software system which is now in use at over 200 different venues throughout the UK and abroad. Specialist computer solutions for the arts. Training and consultancy services. Evaluation disks/CD ROM available.

**GLOBAL TICKETS, EDWARDS AND EDWARDS**
PO Box 2177, London W1A 2WS
Tel 0171 734 4555
Fax 0171 734 0220
Visa and Access accepted.
Mon 10-6.30; Tues-Fri 10-6.30; Sat 10-6.

**FENCHURCH BOOKING AGENCY LTD**
94 Southwark Street, London SE1 0TF
Tel 0171 928 8585/4256
Fax 0171 928 8407
email: Fenchurch@theatreticket.co.uk
Contact: Melvyn Blackholler.
Officially Accredited London Theatre Ticket Agency. Recognised by the Society of London Theatre (SOLT) and a founder memeber of the Ticket Agents Association.
We book Dance, Theatre, Opera, Sport, Rock and Classical Concert Tickets.
All credit cards accepted.

**Fenchurch Booking Agency Ltd**
94 Southwark Street SE1 0TF
We book Dance, Theatre, Opera,
Sport, Rock and Concert Tickets.

**Tel: 0171-928 8585**

**Fax: 0171-928 8407**

Email:
fenchurch@theatreticket.co.uk

**FIRST CALL GROUP PLC**
First Call, Keith Prowse, Wembley Box Office, BOCS
(Box Office Computer Systems),
73-75 Endell Street, London WC2H 9AJ
Tel 0171 836 9001
Fax 0171 240 0049
Contact: Karl Sydow
Credit card telephone booking service, open 24 hours
a day, 7 days a week for theatre, exhibition, sport and
concert tickets. The First Call Group offers complete
ticketing and marketing support including group and
specialist sales, and a network of over 1,000 sub-
agents.

**GALATHEA SYSTEMS LTD**
54-62 Regent Street, London W1R 5PJ
Tel 0171 734 2299
Fax 0171 287 6728
Website: www.galathea.co.uk
Contact: Bruce Moore (Marketing Co-ordinator)
[bruce@globaltickets.com)
Galathea's ENTA - the UK WindowsNT(C) market
leading event management system used for paid
admissions, access control, marketing and financial
reporting. Major clients include Stoll Moss Theatres,
Sadler's Wells Theatre, Westminster Abbey, the British
Film Institute, Edinburgh Military Tattoo, the Millennium
Dome and Edinburgh International Festival.
Management: General Manager - Richard Leggatt,
Sales and Marketing Manager - Suzannah Zody

**GMS SECURITY TICKETS**
**KALAMAZOO SYSTEM PRINT PLC**
Northfields, Birmingham B31 2NY
Tel 0121 256 2238
Fax 0121 256 2228
High quality security tickets for any event.
Watermarked paper, holograms, foiling, badges.

GMS are also leading suppliers of continuous box
office tickets/paper including Thermal Imaging.

**GROUP LINE & GROUP SALES BOX OFFICE UK**
22-24 Torrington Place, London WC1E 7HF
Tel 0171 436 5588/0171 580 6793
Fax 0171 436 6287/0171 436 4182
Come to us first for all your West End Theatre trips, we
are the official group sales organisation for London's
biggest hits. A completely free service providing group
reductions, advice and sale or return payment scheme.
No booking fees.

**HARLANDS LIMITED**
Numbered Products Division, Land of Green Ginger
House, Springfieldway, Anlaby HU10 6RN
Tel 01482 574408
Fax 01482 574945
Tickets - dated and undated booking tickets. Admission
and Cloakroom tickets for all sporting functions, shows,
festivals and arenas.

**JUST TICKETS**
Unit 2, Empstead Works, Greys Road, Henley-on-
Thames, Oxon RG9 2EF
Tel 01491 413150
Fax 01491 413152
Email: sales@just-tkts.demon.co.uk
Website: www.just-tkts.demon.co.uk
Management Contact: Jim Birney
Computer printed perforated tickets. General
admission and reserved tickets for all professional and
leisure events and venues. 2/3/4 part Vertical tickets;
2-3 & 4 inch deep x 2/3/4 parts Horizontal Tickets.
Quick, easy and inexpensive. Roll and Draw/Lottery
tickets also available. Box Office Systems stationary
supplier. Price list, sample tickets and order forms
available.

**LASHMARS THEATRE TICKETS**
80 Duke Street, Grosvenor Square,
London W1M 5DQ
Tel 0171 493 4731
Fax 0171 493 1748
e-mail lashmars@londontheatre.co.uk
Financial Director: Carol Lashmars
Sales Director: Chris Lashmars
All major credit cards accepted.
Mon/Sat 9 a.m. - 8 p.m.

**LONDON THEATRE BOOKINGS**
96 Shaftesbury Avenue, London W1V 7DH
Tel 0171 439 3371
Fax 0171 494 0267
Open Mon/Sat 10 a.m. - 7 p.m.

**LONDON TICKET BUREAU**
4 Queensway, London W2 3RX
Tel 0171 792 4848

**THE METRIC GROUP LTD**
Love Lane, Cirencester, Gloucestershire GL7 1YG
Tel 01285 651441
Fax 01285 653944
Ticket machines.

**PERFORMANCE TICKET PRINTERS**
FREEPOST, Brownlow Heath, Congleton, Cheshire
CW12 4AT
Tel 01260 276164
Fax 01260 270984
email: tickets@timewell.demon.co.uk
Contact: Keith Arnold
Computer printed theatre tickets. Quick, easy and
inexpensive.

**PREMIER ROLLS (SOUTH) LTD**
99 Leggatts Way, Watford WD2 6BQ
Tel 01923 677333
Fax 01923 674111
Email: mel@premrolls.co.uk
Contact: J.M.Gibbs

**PROMPT DATA LTD**
(TheatrePack - LeisurePack)
8 Chipperfield Road, Bovingdon, Hemel Hempstead,
Hertfordshire HP3 0JN
Tel/Fax 01442 834771
Contact: Vincent Lundy
)Dublin) Tel 00 353 8 454277
Now on release TheatrePack V, the computerised booking
system offering fully integrated ticketing and marketing
controls. Also available LeisurePack V for the modern
leisure complex.
Prompt Data offer computerised Box Office solutions with
facilities to handle all functions of the conventional box
office. The system provides the full range of booking
facilities, from advanced reservation to season ticket,
reflecting over sixteen years of experience in the supply of
theatre and leisure management systems. All solutions can
be integrated with office administration and financial
systems.

**PUBLICITY & DISPLAY LTD**
Douglas Drive, Godalming, Surrey GU7 1HJ
Tel 01483 428326
Fax 01483 424566
e-mail print@p-and-d.com
Design/print of posters, passes, leaflets, tickets and
stickers for the entertainment industry.
Mon-Thur: 9-5:30; Fri 9-5.

**RAKES TICKET AGENCY**
188 Shaftesbury Avenue, London WC2H 8JN
Tel 0171 240 2245
Fax 0171 497 2201

**SECPRINT LTD**
Unit 2, Alexandria Centre, Rall Mill Way, Parkgate,
Rotherham S62 6JQ
Tel 01709 780008
Fax 01709 780909

**SELECT TICKETING SYSTEMS LTD**
Citygate, 17 Victoria Street, St. Albans, Herts AL1 3JJ.
Tel 01727 834303
Fax 01727 859515
Suppliers of PASS, the World`s leading box office
system. PASS is now installed in over 2,000 venues
worldwide. Call us for all computerised ticketing,

marketing and fund development requirements. PASS is available to supervise any type of ticketed event at any venue, from the smallest studio theatre to the largest rock stadium.

**STARGREEN BOX OFFICE**
20 Argyll Street, London W1V 1AA
Tel 0171 734 8932
Fax 0171 734 8006

**SYNCHRO SYSTEMS LIMITED**
International House, Stubbs Gate, Newcastle Under Lyme ST5 1LU
Tel 01782 741999
Fax 01782 741986
Sales Consultant: Martin Goodwin
Sales Co-ordinator: Pauline McMahon
Suppliers of fast computerised booking, ticketing and comprehensive management information systems to theatre and concert venues.

**TICKETING SERVICES**
233 Cowgate, Edinburgh, EH1 1JQ
Tel 0131 622 2220
Fax 0131 622 2221
Email: info@tic8.com
Contact: Tony Davey, Ann Russell
Scottish and North of England distributor for the Wembley Ticketing System, the leading ticketing, marketing and event management system for all types of venue and event. Clients range from small venues to city-wide and national networks.

**TICKETLINE (UK) LTD**
47 Westgate Street, Cardiff CF1 1EH.
Tel 01222 230130
Fax 01222 230196
Pop Concert and Theatre Ticket Agency and Concert Promoter.

**TICKETMASTER UK LIMITED**
48 Leicester Square, London WC2H 7LR.
Admin Tel 0171 344 4000
24 Hour Credit Card Booking Tel 0171 344 4444
Fax: 0171 915 0411
Management: Managing Director Jules Boardman
Sales Director: Nick Blackburn
Director of Marketing: Kate Hampton
The World's leading computerised entertainment ticket retailer providing computerisation, retailing and marketing services for theatres and other venues plus a wide range of events including classical music, rock and pop, jazz and festivals of all kinds. 24 hour credit card booking; group booking services; computerised outlet network.

**TICKETS 24/7 LIMITED**
PO Box 23134, Edinburgh, EH1 1WP
Tel 0870 730 0247 (Call Centre) 0131 622 2220
(Admin) Fax 0131 622 2221(Admin)
Email: info@tic8.com
Contact: Tony Davey, David Boyd, Trish McGuiness
Tickets 24/7 offers a dedicated ticket sales call centre services utilising state of the art integrated telephony and ticketing systems providing maximum efficiency and high volume capacity. The call centre service is backed up by a network of high street outlets.

**TOM'S TICKETS (TRURO)**
Unit 2c Industrial Estate, Grampound Road, Truro, Cornwall TR2 4TB
Tel/Fax 01726 884004
Contact: Tom or Lyndal Bale
Security ticket printers, stock sizes, colours, logos, reserved, numbered; Roll tickets, draw tickets,

cloakroom tickets, vouchers.
Unbeatable turnaround. Try Us!

**TOR SYSTEMS LTD**
58 Longton Road,Trentham, Stoke on Trent, ST4 8YZ .
Tel 01782 644755
Fax 01782 644346
Computerised ticketing and admission systems TOR High Speed Silent Ticket Printers

**WAY AHEAD**
The Hollows, St James Street, Nottingham NG1 6FJ
Tel 0115 934 2019
Contact: Martin Brown

**THE WEMBLEY TICKETING SYSTEM (Wembley International )**
Wembley Stadium, Wembley, Middx HA9 0DW
Tel 0181 902 8833
Fax 0181 900 1047
Email: KetanM@wembley.co.uk
Sales & Marketing Manager: Ketan Mistry
WTS is the leading ticketing, marketing and event management system for all types of venues ranging from single theatres to city wide networks. Developed over 10 years it utilises the most modern system architectures, with a full Windows 95/NT graphic user interface allowing extensive functionality and is integratable with other modern systems. National, city or wide area networking, and the option to use retail ticketing and information services through an integrated Call Centre ar the key features.

# 7
# CAR & COACH HIRE

**ACI LIMOUSINES**
57-59 Coburg Road, Wood Green, London N22 6UB
Tel 0181 889 8889
Fax 0181 889 7500
Contact: D Portner
ACI Limousines fleet of American Stretch Limousines offer the finest Limousine service available; quality service, luxurious vehicles. Limousines are fitted with TV, VCP, stereo, air conditioning bar with crystal glassware.

**AZTEC BIRD LTD**
Low Mills, Guiseley, Leeds LS20 9LU
Tel 0113 250 7385
Fax 0113 250 8204

**BERRYHURST**
Keltan House, 1 Sail Street, Lambeth, London SE11 6NQ.
Tel 0171 582 0244
Fax 0171 793 0297
Telex 25741

**(JAVAWARD LTD trading as) BEST TOURS**
10 Priory Gardens, Hanger Lane, Ealing, London W5 1DX
Tel 0181 997 9094
Fax 0181 991 0411

**CAREY CAMELOT**
11-15 Headfort Place, London SW1X 7DE
Tel 0171 235 0234
Fax 0171 823 1278

Telex 8953647 CAMBAR
Rolls Royce, Daimler, Toyota Previa, Mercedes,
Jaguar, Ford, Luggage Vans.

**FANTASY AMERICAN LIMOUSINES**
87 Victoria Street, Larkhall, Lanarkshire ML9 2BL
Tel/Fax 01698 887574
Contact: Peter McGreskin
American Streched Limousine Hire.

**HUXFORD CHAUFFEUR SERVICES**
6 Burrell Street, London SE1 OUN.
Tel 0181 743 1199
Fax 0181 928 6150

**LEINSTER PRIVATE HIRE (1987) LTD**
9a Craven Terrace, London W2 3QD.
Tel 0171 262 7281
Fax 0171 724 0331
Private car hire and courier service.

**LONDON PULLMAN COACHES**
7 Lexington Way, Barnet, Herts EN5 2SN
Tel 0181 440 4322
Fax 0181 440 6446
Email: londonpullman@compuserve.com
Contact: John and Monica Watson
49/53 seater & 74 seater executive coaches with
drivers conversant with venue "get-ins" in the UK and
abroad.

**LIMCO EXECUTIVE LIMOUSINE SERVICE**
Birch Farm, White Stubbs Lane, Broxbourne, Herts
EN10 7QA
Tel 01992 479555
Fax 01992 499888
The UK's largest American Stretched Limousine
Company. Luxurious Limousines for any
occasion/event. Fully experienced in film and
television work; corporate hospitality etc. Highly
professional service.

**SCAN COACH COMPANY**
Stanstob District Centre, Start Hill, Bishopstortford,
Hertfordshire CM22 7DG
Tel 0181 453 0922
Fax 0181 961 9336

**STARDES LTD**
Ashes Buildings, Old Lane, Holbrook Industrial Estate,
Halfway, Sheffield S19 5GZ
Tel 0114 251 0051
Fax 0114 510 5555
Executive Car and Minibus, Truck and Van Rental,
Concert Tour Transportation, Walk ramps.
Transportation Consultants

**TRISTAR CARS LIMITED**
Galleymead Road, Colmbrook, Berks SL3 OEN.
Tel 01753 790100
Fax 01753 790301

**VISION**
Lawford House, Albert Place, London N3 1QA
Tel 0181 482 4242
Fax 0181 482 9692
Chauffeur and Coach Hire (ex Space Cruisers, self-
drive). Band Coaches, Mobile Phone Hire.

**WHEALS FAR-GO**
Unit 5, 13-15 Sunbeam Rd, London NW10 6JP
Tel 0171 727 3828
Fax 0181 965 0699

**WRIGHT BROS. (COACHES) LTD**
West Road Garage, Blucher, Newcastle-upon-Tyne
NE15
Tel 0191 267 4676

**Y-NOT**
37 Friars Street, Sudbury, Suffolk CO10 6AG
Tel 01787 312405
Fax 01787 313665

# 8
# CASTING

**ACTORS LIST**
3rd Floor, Half Moon Chambers, Chapel Walks,
Manchester M2 1HN
Tel 0161 833 1605
Fax 0161 832 5219
Contact: Debbie Pine
Represent professional actors and actresses.

**FACADE**
43A Garthorne Road, London SE23 1EP
Tel 0181 699 8655
Managing Partner: Richard Andrews
Creation, promotion and production of new musicals.
Casting, Budgeting and General Management services.

**HUBBARD CASTING**
1 Old Compton Street, London W1V 5PH.
Tel 0171 494 3191
Fax 0171 437 0559.

**NIDGES CASTING AGENCY**
3rd Floor, Half Moon Chambers, Chapel Walks,
Manchester M2 1HN
Tel 0161 832 8259
Fax 0161 832 5219
Casting agency for TV, films and theatre.

**PCR**
Production & Casting Report
Editorial Address: PO Box 11, London N1 7JZ
Tel 0171 566 8282
Fax 0171 566 8284
Subscription Address: PO Box 100, Broadstairs,
Kent CT10 1UJ
Tel 01843 860885
Casting leads in TV, theatre, films, commercials.

**SANDRA SINGER ASSOCIATES**
21 Cotswold Road, Westcliff on Sea, Essex SS0 8AA
Tel 01702 331616
Fax 01702 339393
Musical theatre specialists.

# 9
# CATERING &
# CONFECTIONERY

**BIRDS EYE WALLS LTD**
Station Avenue, Walton-on-Thames, Surrey KT12 1NT
Tel 01932 263000
Direct line 01932 263452

Main Fax 01932 263152
Direct Fax 01932 263668
Sales Fax 01932 263668
Business Development Manager: Tim Lord
Walls Ice Cream Enquiries: Jenny Steel

**BOOKER FITCH FOOD SERVICES**
78 Silverthorn Road, Battersea, London SW8 3HJ
Tel 0171 720 1660
Fax 0171 720 8522

**CAMBRIDGE HOUSE**
128 Park Road, Camberley, Surrey GU15 2LW
Tel 01276 670000
Fax 01276 670010
Operation and management of kiosks within theatres.
Supply of branded confectionery and drinks.

**CATERING DISPOSABLES LTD**
Unit 14, Dominion Works, North Drive, Hounslow,
Middlesex TW3 1PP
Tel 0181 570 2428
Fax 0181 569 5039
Comprehensive disposable range.

**THE CHEVALIER CATERING CO. LTD**
Studio 5, Garnet Close, Greycaine Road, Watford,
Herts WD2 4JN
Tel 01923 211703
Fax 01923 211704

**DALEBROOK SUPPLIES LTD**
1 Croft Way, Witham, Essex CM8 2EG
Tel 01376 510101
Fax 01376 510133
Website www.dalebrook.com/

**EAT TO THE BEAT LTD**
Studio 5, Garnet Close, Greycaine Road, Watford,
Herts WD2 4JN
Tel 01923 211702/3
Fax 01923 211704

**LINDLEY CATERING INVESTMENTS LTD**
21 London Road, Newcastle, Staffordshire ST5 1LQ.
Tel 01782 622237
Fax 01782 617619
Provision of catering and licensed bars within theatres,
leisure and sporting venues for public, executive and
corporate hospitality.
A complete service offered to include operational and
design facilities provided with over 25 years worth of
experience.

**LONDON'S FLYING CHEF**
50 Westminster Bridge Road, London SE1 7QY
Tel 0171 721 7460/1
Fax 0171 721 7462

**NESTLE ICE CREAM**
Nestle Lyons Maid, Haxby Road, York Y91 1XY
Tel 01904 602345
Fax 01904 604808

**ORCHIDS**
**(EXCLUSIVE HOSPITALITY SERVICE FOR
THEATRES)**
197-199 Main Street, Wilsden, Bradford BD15 0HR
Tel 01535 273292
Fax 01535 273818
Contact: Stuart Peacock, Chairman
Specialist catering and licensed bars exclusively for
theatres. Part of Caterleisure Limited.

Twenty years experience of high quality service
anywhere in the UK.

**PERSONALIZED PRODUCTIONS LTD**
Butts Road, Alton, Hampshire GU34 1EJ
Tel 01420 84181
Fax 01420 543047
Manufacturers of handmade fine quality chocolates.
Wide range of very attractive boxes of varying shapes
and designs.
We are able to personalise the majority of boxes with
Theatre names and logos of a particular production.

**SAUCERY**
Watchcott, Nordan, Leominster HFDS, HR6 OAJ
Tel 01568 614221
Fax 01568 610256
Completely mobile catering, any occasion for all
requirements.
Video, concert, locations etc.
Crew meals, hospitality, special diets, cooked on site to
order, fully trained chefs.

# 10

# CIRCUS EQUIPMENT & JUGGLING SUPPLIES

**CIRCUS ARTISTES WORLDWIDE**
The Arts Exchange, Mill Green, Congleton,
Cheshire CW12 1JG
Tel 01260 276627
Hire of marquees, big tops and tiered seating. Also
furniture hire, chairs, floors and tables plus all
specialised circus equipment.

**HOWORTH WRIGHTSON LTD**
The Prop House, Unit 2, Cricket Street, Denton,
Manchester M34 3DR
Tel 0161 335 0220

**QUICKSILVER UK LTD**
Broom Grove Lane, Denton, Manchester M34 3DU.
Tel 0161 320 7232
Fax 0161 320 3928
Full range of Circus & Juggling Equipment including
stilts, trapezes & tightropes. Training also available.

# 11

# CLEANING & HYGIENE

**BRITISH NOVA WORKS LTD**
57-61 Lea Road, Southall, Middlesex UB2 5QB
Tel 0181 574 6531

Fax 0181 571 7572
Manufacturers of "Novafrost" which freezes chewing
gum to make it easily removable from carpets,
upholstery, etc.

**CIMEX INTERNATIONAL**
Somerford Road, Christchurch, Dorset BH23 3PS
Tel 01202 499699
Fax 01202 499465
Suppliers of a wide range of floor cleaning
equipment, materials, janitorial products, detergent,
polishes, seals and Matador Entrance Matting.

**CLEANRITE**
112 Besley Street, Streatham, London
SW16 6BD.
Tel 0181 769 9834
Fax 0181 677 2553
Dry Cleaning: tabs, curtains, cycloramas, theatrical
robes. Also flameproofing and on-site carpet and
upholstery cleaning.

**DIRECTA (UK) LIMITED**
Cold Norton, Essex CM3 6UA
Tel 01621 828882
Fax 01621 828072
Five good reasons to buy from Directa:
Σ Cometitive Prices
Σ Speedy Nationwide Delivery
Σ Free Technical Advice
Σ Strict Quality Control
Σ BSN 9002
No quibble guarantee, the customers are always right.

**RENTOKIL LTD**
Hygiene Division, Felcourt, East Grinstead, West
Sussex RH19 2JY
Tel 01342 833022
Fax 01342 326229
Washroom Hygiene and Preventive Maintenance.
Drains Maintenance. Catering Hygiene.
Kitchen Deep Cleaning. Electrostatic Air Cleaners.

# 12
# COIN COUNTING
# &
# CASH REGISTERS

**DE LA RUE SYSTEMS (UK)**
Pool House, Horizon West, Hambridge Road, Newbury
Berkshire RG14 5XF.
Tel 01635 550300
Fax 01635 522015
Sales and Servicing of Cash Handling Equipment: Coin
Counting/Sorting Machines, Note Counters, Systems.
Service support network.

**ELECTRONIC CASH REGISTERS LTD**
ECR House, Colindale Business Park, Carlisle Road,
London NW9 OHN.
Tel 0181 205 7766
Fax 0181 205 1493
Sales and rentals of cash registers.

**OMAL INTERNATIONAL**
Volumatic Ltd, Taurus, Endemere Road,
Coventry CV6 5PY

Tel 01203 684 2177
Suppliers of cash counting equipment, retail solutions
and security equipment.

**OMRON SYSTEMS  (UK) LTD**
Victory House, Cox Lane, Chessington, Surrey
KT9 1SG
Tel 0181 974 2166
Fax 0181 974 1864
Electronic Cash Registers and Point of Sale Systems.

# 13
# COMPUTER
# SYSTEMS AND
# ELECTRONIC
# PUBLICITY

**ANSWERING LIMITED**
11 Rosemont Road, London NW3 6NG
Tel 0171 431 2277 (24 hours)
Fax 0171 435 0801
Personally staffed telephone answering service to
receive your calls 24 hrs a day. Also includes a
facsimile, diary and direct response service.

**BLACK TAB SOFTWARE LTD**
47 Hillreach, London SE18 4AL
Tel/Fax 0171 223 7855

**HENRY BOOTH & COMPANY**
Stockholm Road, Sutton Fields, Hull HU7 OXY.
Tel 01482 826343
Fax 01482 839767
Contact: John Nicholson
For all your ticket requirements contact Henry Booth, manufacturers of all types of tickets for all systems including BOCA, PASS, SYNCHRO, DATABOX, TOR etc. See our main ad.

**BUDDY SOUND & LIGHT LTD**
Unit 1 Parkside Centre, Potters Way,
Temple Farm Industrial Estate, Southend-on-Sea.
SS2 5SJ
Tel 01702 615042
Fax 01702 469017

**CANFORD AUDIO PLC**
Crowther Road, Washington, Tyne & Wear
NE38 0BW
Tel 0191 417 0057
Fax 0191 416 0392
e-mail rs@canford.co.uk
Website www.canford.co.uk

**CREATIVE SYSTEMS TECHNOLOGY**
Sophia House, 28 Cathedral Road, Cardiff, South Glamorgan, Wales CF1 9LJ
Tel 01222 660142
Fax 01222 664891
Contact: Martin Howell
CST provide cost effective solutions whatever your needs. Lighting/Special Effects Design, Remote Control/Motor controlled systems, software management, security & tagging systems, together with an after sales service next to none.

**DATAWEST COMPUTER SERVICES**
East Way, Lee Mill Business Park, Ivybridge, Devon
PL21 9GE
Tel 01752 897171
Contact: John Arnold
Pineapple Software for Theatres and Leisure Venues features a House Diary which can be linked to a simple profit and loss record, with invoicing, for each event. The Facility Management module controls the allocation of resources necessary for each event. The Production/Commitment Accounting system streamlines procedures and ensures tight financial control of actual and committed expenditure. Incorporating a flexibile payroll, purchase orders and budgets with a fully integrated financial ledger system Pineapple Software provides a flexibile and easy-to-use management system.
Installations throughout the UK.

**DRV PUBLIC ADDRESS CONSULTANTS**
Lower Tregenna, St. Columb Minor, Newquay, Cornwall TR8 4HS
Tel 01637 875824
Fax 01637 876082
Hire, sale, installation, servicing of all types of audio visual and stage engineering equipment.

**DRAKE ELECTRONICS**
The Hydeway, Welwyn Garden City, Hertfordshire
AL7 3UQ.
Tel 01707 333866
Fax 01707 371266
Chairman & Managing Director: Alan Brill
Marketing Director: Barry Goldsmith
General Manager: Colin Fox
Wired intercom systems for stage management and television applications in Theatres, Arts/Leisure

Centres and Broadcast Centres. HANDI-COM Belt Packs, Power Supply, Master Stations with up to 6 ring channels and switched paging outputs for Stage Manager.
Also EASI-COM for larger zoned and intercom positions, with in-built HANDI-COM interfaces and Power Supply. All normal television interfaces also available.

**ROY KIRKPATRICK SOUND ENGINEERING**
29 Burgamot Lane, Comberbach, Northwich, Cheshire
CW9 6BU
Tel/Fax 01606 891939
Professional sound and communication systems and equipment. Sales, installation, hire and system design. Also Magnetic Induction Loop Systems.

**L.E.D SYSTEMS LTD**
Aldon House, Aldon Road, Poulton Industrial Estate, Poulton-Le-Fylde, Lancs FY6 8JL.
Tel 01253 892299
Fax 01253 892195
e-mail ledsys@provider.co.uk
Website www.electronic-displays.com
Contact: Adrian Reed/Chris Hope
Electronic displays, internal, external graphic screens, Game show score boards, custom built matrix displays. Sales, rentals service, design.

**MOTOROLA LTD**
Jays Close, Viables Industrial Estate, Basingstoke, Hampshire RG22 4PD.
Tel 01256 358211
Fax 01256 3469838
Motorola Hire, offered through Customer Access, provides an efficient and reliable service including:-
Competitive rates, full equipment range, accessories (at no extra cost), delivery/collection service, licensing, free telephone service.

**MULTIREMOTE LTD**
2, Hanborough Business Park, Long Hanborough, Oxford OX8 8LH.
Tel 01993 883990
Fax 01993 883909
Suppliers of intercom systems (RTS) and digital multicores (BEC Technologies) and other audio equipment for theatre and venue applications.

**M & R COMMUNICATIONS**
7 Bell Industrial Estate, 50 Cunnington Street, Chiswick, London W4 5HB
Tel 0181 995 4714
Fax 0181 995 5136
Infra-red and radio interpretation systems for foreign language productions.

**READYCALL**
1 Stanley Road, Bromley, Kent BR2 9JE
Tel 0181 460 6006
Fax 0181 460 9899
Contact: Ros Williams or Darroll Moore
Professional Telemarketing and Media Response Teams.

**RESOURCES CENTRE LIMITED**
Cambridge House, 128 Park Road, Camberley, Surrey
GU15 2LW
Tel 01276 670000
Fax 01276 670010
Hire and Supply of P.A. Systems. Supply of Operating Technicians.

**SPRINGFIELD PUBLISHING LTD**
Springfield House, Llanfynydd, Nr Wrexham LL11 5HW
Tel 01352 770049
Fax 01352 770816
Contact: Sales
Suppliers of economic software solutions including the renowned Ticketbase, Tourbase and Fundbase. We have a reputation for fast and friendly service. We can help you to identify what your needs really are and save you money in the process.

**STAGE ELECTRICS**
Victoria Road, Avon, Avonmouth, Bristol BS11 9DB
Tel 0117 982 7282
Fax 0117 982 2180
Cofton Road, Marsh Barton, Exeter EX2 HQW
Tel 01392 255868
Fax 01392 410592
2 Parkway Industrial Estate, Plymouth PL6 8LH
Tel 01752 269444
Fax 01752 228283
Dartmouth Road, Smethwick, West Midlands B66 1AX
Tel 0121 525 4545
Fax 0121 525 2413

**UK THEATRE WEB**
New House, High Street, Fernham, Oxon SN7 7NY
Tel/Fax 01367 820827
Contact: Rob Iles
The UK Theatre Web provides information about the UK theatre, opera and ballet scene to users all over the world via the Internet. UK Theatre Web is the premier index and information site for UK performing arts. In addition to promotional activities in UK Theatre Web provides free listings, tours and performances via "What's On Stage".

# 14
# COOLING AND HEATING SYSTEMS HIRE

**AGGREKO LTD**
Central Avenue, Lea Mill Industrial Estate, Plymouth PL21 9PE
Tel 01752 892444
Fax 01752 892141

**ARCOTHERM LTD**
Croft Street, Burslem, Stoke on Trent, Staffordshire ST6 3BQ
Tel 01782 838676
Fax 01782 811064

**SHERIFF PLANT HIRE LTD**
523 Eccles New Road, Salford, Manchester M5 2DN
Tel 0161 736 3814
Fax 0161 736 6074

# 15
# COSTUME CLEANING

**CELEBRITY CLEANERS**
102 Wardour Street, London W1V 3LD
Tel 0171 437 5324 (24 hours)
Fax 0171 434 2138
Contact: Robert Shooman or Sylvia Willingham
Specialist Dry Cleaners to the Theatre Profession and Theatrical Costumiers. Situated in the heart of Theatreland.

**UPSTAGE THEATRICAL DRYCLEANERS**
Unit 8, Acorn Production Centre, 105 Blundell Street, Islington, London N7 9DW
Tel/Fax 0171 609 9119

# 16

# COSTUME HIRE & SALE

**ADS COSTUME HIRE**
Reform Road, Maidenhead, Berkshire SL6 8BT
Tel 01628 29346
Fax 01628 777101

A variety of costumes, adults and children. Police, victorian, ball gowns, music hall etc.

**ANGEL'S & BERMANS**
**Main Costume Store:** 40 Camden Street, London NW1 0EN
Tel 0171 387 0999
Fax 0171 383 5603
Chairman: Tim Angel
Production Director: Richard Green
**Revue and Pantomime Costumes:**
119 Shaftesbury Avenue, London WC2H 8AE
Tel 0171 836 5678
Fax 0171 240 9527
Contact: Emma Angel
**Angels & Bermans (Paris)**
196 Boulevard Voltaire, 75011 Paris, France
Tel 00 33 1 43 67 43 92
Fax 00 33 1 43 67 16 16
Contact: Kristyn Ohanian

**ANNIES**
108 London Road, Bognor Regis, West Sussex PO21 1BD
Tel 01243 866661
Fax 01243 841027
Makers and designers of costumes to the entertainment industry specialising in animal skins and large promotional items, but also renowned for dancers and solo artistes, prompt service and reasonable prices is our forte.

**ARTISTE'S THEATRE SHOP**
23 City Road, Chester, CH1 3AE
Tel 01244 320271
Retail sales ballet shoes and requisites - Theatrical make up and costume hire.

**BABOUCHA SHOES**
218 High Street, Barnet, Herts EN5 5SZ
Tel 0181 441 3788
Fax 0181 441 3788
Theatrical and fashion shoe makers. Footwear for all
occasions. Period, panto, Victorian etc. Also matching
belts and bags, made in almost any leather or fabric

**THE BALLERINA**
1st Floor, 7 Welford Road, Leicester LE2 7AD
Tel/Fax 0116 2544206
Retailer of Ballet, Tap, Jazz, Pointe shoes etc.
Leotards, Catsuits, Ballet 'T' Shirts, Tights, Cycle
Shorts and Aerobic wear. Sequins, Tiara's, Boas, Hats
& Masks. Theatrical & Water Make-Up. Ballroom
Shoes, Wedding Shoes. Shoe Dyeing Service.
Nationwide Mail Order.

**BIRMINGHAM COSTUME HIRE**
Suites 209-210 Jubilee Centre, 130 Pershore Street,
Birmingham B5 6ND
Tel 0121 622 3158
Fax 0121 622 2758
Contact: Lynn Smith, Paul Spilsbury
Over 10,000 professional costumes, original period
clothing and uniforms plus accessories.

**BLACK LION COSTUMES**
Unit 8, Wallbridge Mills, Wallbridge, Frome BA11 5SX
Tel/Fax 01373 472786
Contact: Heather Kiernan
Over 5,000 square feet of costumes. Authentic, all
periods. Good range of uniforms, footware, armour
accessories etc. We specialise in masks, made to any
specification. Sensible prices. Viewing by appointment
only.

**BRISTOL COSTUME SERVICES**
**(Incorporating Bristol Old Vic Costume Hire)**
The Drill Hall, Old Market Street, Bristol BS2 OEJ
Tel 0117 940 5750
Fax 0117 940 5751
Contact: Catriona Tyson
A large selection of costumes from Roman to the
Present Day. Costume & Design Staff for television and
film.

**CARNIVAL STORE**
95 Hammersmith Road, London W14 OQH
Tel 0171 603 7824
Animal costumes on hire or made to order.

**CAVALCADE COSTUMES**
57 Pelham Road, London SW19 1NW
Tel 0181 540 3513 (24 hours)

Fax 0181 540 2243
Experienced makers of costumes, masks and props to
West End standard, and also have extensive stocks of
costumes for hire, including period and light
entertainment costumes and complete sets of
pantomimes and musicals. Single outfits available.

### CHRIS'S CREATURES
The Gables, Dragons Green, Shipley, Horsham,
W.Sussex RH13 7JD
Te/Faxl 01403 741068 Tel 01403 741386
Mobile 07771 542823
Contact: Chris or Dave Barker
The company specialises in large animals with moving
parts (ie. jaw, eye, ear movements). Clients include -
BBCTV, National Trust, Hammonds, Butlins.

### MIKE & ROSI COMPTON
11 Woodstock Road, Croydon, Surrey CR0 1JS
Tel 0181 680 4364
Fax 0181 681 3126
We make props, special effects, costumes and
models, we specialise in the unusual, but can do
almost anything! No hiring.

### COSPROP LTD
26/28 Rochester Place, London NW1 9JR
Tel 0171 485 6731
Fax 0171 485 5942
Costumes and props for hire, 1700 - 1955.

### COSTUME CALL
158 Munster Road, London SW6 5RA
Tel 0171 371 7211

### COSTUME HIRE
The Company of Ten, Abbey Theatre, Westminster
Lodge, Holywell Hill, St Albans AL1 2DL.
Pam Curtis: 01727 863818
Annie Walkington: 01727 858307

### THE COSTUME STUDIO
Montgomery House, 159-161 Balls Pond Road,
Islington, London N1 4BG
Tel 0171 388 4481
Fax 0171 837 6576
Email: costume.studio@easynet.co.uk
Website: www.thecostumestudioltd.co.uk
Contact: Richard Dudley & Rupert Clive
A huge selection of historical period and repro clothing,
accessories, footwear and wigs for hire. Design and
manufacturing also available. Quotes given.

### CRESCENDO COSTUMES LTD
Crown House, 6/8 Crown Street, Reading,
Berks RG21 2SE
Tel 0118 939 3907
Fax 0118 956 1269
Contact: Jan Marketis, Kelvyn Marketis, Sarah Williams

### TREVOR CRESSWELL
9 Kenmor Avenue, Bury, Lancs BL8 2DY
Tel 0161 764 5362
Theatrical Costumes designed and made to measure
for shows, Cabaret, Circus, Television and Historical
etc.

### DAMODES
Unit 11, Bayford Business Centre, Bayford Street,
Hackney, London E8 3SE
Tel 0181 986 8550
Contact: Dave Wilson, Kevin Matthews, Norman
Nygate

All types of uniforms supplied: Police, Fire,
Paramedics, Military, etc.

### DAUPHINE'S OF BRISTOL
32-34 Clouds Hill, St. George, Bristol BS5 7LA
Tel/Fax 0117 955 1700
Costumes, wigs for purchase or hire. Make-up
department. Theatrical materials, hats, masks, carnival
items catalogues available. Promotion costumes a
speciality.
Open Mon-Sat.

### EMPORIUM
330-332 Creek Road, Greenwich, London SE10
Tel 0181 305 1670
Fax 0181 858 0249
Contact: Jonathan Hale
Suppliers of mens and ladies costume, textiles and
accessories, 1930's - 1970's. Large stocks of leather
jackets, hats, dresses, tops, coats and suits etc. New
stock constantly arriving.

### FAMEGLORE LTD
2 Archangel Way, Dunston Park, Thatchham,
Berkshire RG18 4EB
Tel 01635 523363
Fax 01635 872845
Contact: G. Harrison

### FUNN STOCKINGS LTD
PO Box 102, Steyning, West Sussex BN44 3DS
Tel/Fax 01903 892841
Contact: Catherine Coleman

### GAIETY CARNIVAL NOVELTIES
233 Mitcham Road, London SW17
Tel 0181 672 5584
Magic, Fancy Dress, Masks, Wigs, Make-up, Party
Hats, Balloons, Bunting, Fireworks, etc.

### CHARLES HALEY PRODUCTIONS
67 Poppleton Road, Whipps Cross, London E11 1LT
Tel 0181 989 8364
Contact: Phillip Charles, Jennifer Haley.
Costumes, Scenery, Scripts for pantomime, revue and
summer seasons.

### HAYMARKET THEATRE
Belgrave Gate, Leicester LE1 3YQ
Tel 0116 253 0021
Fax 0116 251 3310
Large selection of costumes for hire. Individual
costumes or complete shows available.

### HEALD GREEN THEATRE COMPANY
Heald Green Theatre, Cheadle Royal, Wilmslow Road,
Cheadle, Cheshire SK8 3DG
Tel 0161 428 9704

### HIREARCHY CLASSIC AND CONTEMPORARY COSTUME
45-47 Palmerston Road, Boscombe, Bournemouth
Tel 01202 394465
Specialising in the hire of ladies and gents costumes
from medieval to present day. Also accessories, make-
up, wigs, militaria, jewellery, textiles and luggage.

### W. A HOMBURG LIMITED
King House, 17 Regent Street, Leeds LS2 7UZ
Tel 0113 245 8425
Fax 0113 243 0635
Theatrical Costumier to amateur Operatic and
Dramatic Societies Nationwide.

**KG COSTUMES**
396 West Bromwich Road, Walsall WS5 4NU
Tel 07971 395367
Contact: Mr A G Brown
Costumes made. From sequins to feathers.

**LAURENCE CORNER**
62/64 Hampstead Road, London NW1 2NU
Tel 0171 813 1010
Fax 0171 813 1413
Military Government surplus and alternative clothing, uniforms, headwear and accessories, nets and parachutes, theatrical clothes and accessories and props. Hire and Sale.

**JANET LEWIS ENTERPRISES**
85 Brockley Grove, Brockley, London SE4 1DZ
Tel 0181 691 2806
Professional ballet costumes and sets for hire. Ballet floor also available.

**LYNDON THEATRICAL COSTUME WAREHOUSE**
42 High Street, West Mersea, Nr. Colchester, Essex CO5 8JX
Tel 01206 384471
Fax 01206 386134
Proprietor: Mrs Liz Clements. ARAD
Manager: Miss E Clements
Warehouse Mistress: Mrs Sue Chadwick
Over 15,000 costumes for theatre, promotions, etc.

**MODERN AGE VINTAGE CLOTHING**
65 Chalk Farm Road, London NW1
Tel 0171 482 3787
Mens & Womens Clothing from 1950's to 1970's. To buy or hire. Open 7 days a week 10.30 to 6.00pm.
Contact: Basil Anastasi

**MOVIETONE FROCKS COSTUMIERS**
Lower Ground Floor, Linton House,
39-51 Highgate Road, London NW5 1RS
Tel 0171 482 1066/0181 459 4157 (after 6pm)
Hire of ladieswear and accessories (day and evening) from 1920s to 1970s from Britain and USA. Over 20,000 items.
By appointment only - contact Julia Dollimore

**NORTH WEST COSTUME HIRE**
136 Oxton Road, Birkenhead, Merseyside
Tel 0151 653 4090
Proprietors: Wendy Lee & Robert A Forrester
Costume Hire: period plays, Gilbert & Sullivan, pantomime, stage animals, fancy dress.

**PANTO BOX**
(Formerly Theatre Zoo Ltd)
51 Chapel Road, Dersingham, Norfolk PE31 6PJ
Tel 0171 836 3150/0171 627 1772
For appointments only.
Hire of animal costumes, stage make-up, masks, diamonte jewellery.

**LUKE PASCOE THEATRE COSTUME**
56 Brookhill Road, London SE18 6PU
Tel 0181 855 6654
The making of historical and modern costume male and female, to order for Theatre, Television, Film, Promotions and Advertising.
Strictly no hire.

*Thousands of complete period costumes to choose from*

**RSC**
ROYAL
SHAKESPEARE
COMPANY

# RSC COSTUME HIRE
RSC Hire Wardrobe, Timothy's Bridge Road
Stratford-upon-Avon, Warwickshire CV37 9UY
Tel: 01789 205920

**PERTH THEATRE**
185 High Street, Perth PH1 5UW
Tel 01738 472703
Fax 01738 624576
Contact: Jennifer Melville

**POLLEX PROPS**
Leac Na Ban, Tayvallich, Lochgilphead PA31 8PF
Tel/Fax 01546 870310
Props, special effects, special costumes for theatre, television and advertising. No hiring.

**PROPS GALORE**
15/17 Brunel Road, London W3 7XR
Tel 0181 746 1222
Fax 0181 749 8372
e-mail props@farley.co.uk
Specialists in the hire of period textiles, jewellery and accessories.

**REGAN'S CARNIVAL WAREHOUSE**
Carnival House, 12 Sundridge Parade, Plaistow Lane, Bromley, Kent BR1 4DT
Tel 0181 460 1223
Fax 0181 313 0554
Importers, manufacturers, wholesalers and retailers of Carnival, Theatrical and Party novelties.

**ROYAL EXCHANGE THEATRE HIRE SERVICE**
3rd Floor, 391 Corn Exchange, Hanging Ditch, Manchester M4 3HW
Tel/Fax 0161 834 2333
Contact: Annie Brown
Costume and Prop hire service.

**ROYAL LYCEUM THEATRE COMPANY**
29 Roseburn Street, Edinburgh

Tel/Fax 0131 337 1997
An extensive selection of costumes - period and modern, ladies and mens, single items and complete outfits.

**ROYAL SHAKESPEARE COMPANY**
(Costume Hire Dept)
Timothy's Bridge Road, Stratford-Upon-Avon,
Warwicks CV37 9UY
Tel/Fax 01789 205920
Contact: Alison Mitchell
Period costume hire at reasonable rates. Large range available including Medieval, Shakespearan and Eighteenth Century. Viewing by appointment.

**STAGE DOOR SUPPLIES**
198 Bakers Street, Enfield  EN1 3JY
Tel 0181 367 7337
Fax 0181 367 7557

**STAGESTRUCK**
41 Brushfield Street, Spitalfields, London E1 6AA
Tel 0171 375 1580
Fax 0171 247 5981
Custume Hire, Fancy Dress, Make Up, Masks, Theatre Books and more.

**TAVISTOCK REP. CO.**
Tower Theatre, Canonbury Place, London N1
Tel 0171 226 5111

**THEATRE GEAR**
37a Church Road, Tunbridge Wells, Kent
Tel 01892 525127
Costume Hire - Pantomime, Stage Animals, Fancy Dress. Also Design and Manufacture.

**THEATRE ZOO LTD**
(See Panto Box)

**THEATRICAL COSTUME HOUSE (Westcliff) LIMITED**
83 Brunswick Road, Southend-on-Sea, Essex SS1 2UL
Tel 01702 461573
Theatrical Costumiers of the highest quality.
Pantomime, Summer Season, Musicals, Repertory.

**TORBAY COSTUME HIRE COMPANY**
31 Market Street, Torquay, Devon TQ1 3AW
Tel 01803 211930 Lionel Digby
Fax 01803 293554
Theatrical costume hire for stage plays, television and films. Military Uniforms Specialists.

**TRAFFORD & PARNELL PRODUCTIONS**
85 Marton Drive, Blackpool FY4 3EJ
Tel 01253 766928 or 0860 273341

**TRENDS COSTUMIERS (LONDON) LTD**
54 Lisson Street, London NW1 6ST
Tel 0171 723 8001
Fax 0171 258 3591

**TUNICS LIMITED**
343a Finchley Road, London NW3 6DE
Tel 0171 435 5409
Fax 0171 433 3090
Ballet wear manufacturers. Leotards, tights, etc.
Manufacturers to the Royal Academy of Dancing and Imperial Society of Teachers of Dance.

**UPSTAGE THEATRICAL SUPPLIES**
Unit 5-9, 23 Abingdon Street, Blackpool FY1 1DG
Tel 01253 292321
Contact: Gabriella Gratrix - Head of Wardrobe
Superb design and creation of lavish revue costumes (headdresses, harnesses, etc). Animal skins, full scale illusion, construction, sets and props.

**M & L WARREN**
32 Station Road, Purton, Wilts
Tel 01793 771453
Costumes available for hire and purchase. Also personal props i.e. spectacles, bags, walking sticks, pipes etc.

**WHALEYS BRADFORD LTD**
Harris Court, Great Horton, Bradford, West Yorks
BD7 4EQ
Tel 01274 576718
Fax 01274 521309
Natural fabric suppliers.  Dress and Furnishings, Scenery fabric suppliers, curtain manufacturers.

# 17
# CRECHE FACILITIES

**2 TO 9 CLUB**
Thorton Lodge, 6 West Lane, Bradford, Yorkshire
BD13 3HX.
Tel 01274 834358.

**CHILDSPLAY EVENT SERVICES**
Briar House, The Briars, Caldbec Hill, Battle, East Sussex TN33 OJR.
Tel 01424 775450  Fax 01424 775450
Mobile: 0850 311202
Childrens event organisers. Specialist hire services.
Booking agents, childrens entertainers.

**CRECHE ON THE MOVE**
273 Eversholt Street, London NW1 1BA.
Tel 0171 383 7509  Fax 0171 387 9086

**NIPPERBOUT ACTIVE CHILDCARE & CHILDRENS ENTERTAINMENT**
84 Clonmell Road, London N17 6JU.
Tel 0181 801 0148

**ONCE UPON A TIME**
123 Woodville Road, Croydon, Surrey CR7 8LP.
Tel 0181 653 2552.

# 18
# DESIGN, PRINTING & PUBLICITY

**ALUSET SECURITY TICKETS**
15 Station Street, Whetstone, Leicester LE8 6JS
Tel 0116 275 1600
Fax 0116 275 1573
As the leading ticket printer Aluset supply a complete range of tickets from simple continuous stationery to highly secure stadium tickets.
Our thermal tickets are used successfully in all types of printers including BOCA, Gazelle, TOR, Star. We believe our quality will improve your image.

**ARTS CONTACT**
99 High Street, Morley, Leeds LS27 0DE
Tel 0113 252 7356  /0831 166692 /0860 374723
Directors: Shiela Thorpe, Tony Hyslop
A unique creative bulk distribution service for Arts publicity print, for any Arts event, anywhere in the U.K.

**BATTLEY BROTHERS LIMITED**
37 Old Town, Clapham, London SW4 0JN
Tel 0171 622 3401
Fax 0171 627 0283
ISDN 0171 627 2632
Specialist theatre printers, e.g. programmes, souvenir brochures and publicity for the RNT, ENO, RSC, BBC, RPO etc.
Comprehensive quality service.  Studio, DTP, repro, sheet-fed litho up to 5 colour perfector, finishing and despatch.

**BERFORT REPRODUCTIONS**
8 London Road, St. Leonards-on-Sea, Sussex
Tel 01424 722733
Fax 01424 721777
For all photo publicity cards and show business printing.

**DESIGN IT**
Mill House, Dean Clough, Halifax HX3 5AX
Tel 01422 369441
Fax 01422 343177
e-mail pinder@orbitnewmedia.co.uk
Website www.orbitnewmedia.co.uk
Specialists in the design & production of promotional literature, advertising for the arts & theatres.

**EUROTECH LTD**
4 West Halkin Street, London SW1
Tel 0171 235 8273
Fax 0171 245 5770
Managing Director: G. N. Woolnough
Eurotech manfuacture at our works near Henley on Thames, flags, banners, awnings, canopies and exhibition units of all types.  We can apply decorative or descriptive designs by silk screen printing, sign writing or applique work.

**FINAL SCORE**
Cecilia Cottage, 47 Brighton Road, Horsham, West Sussex RH13 6EZ
Tel 01403 264798
e-mail finalscore@mistral.co.uk
Personnel: Michael & Helen McCabe
Music Typesetting and Printing.

**G AND M ORGAN LTD**
Webbsbrook Printing Works, Wrington,

North Somerset BS18 7QH
Tel 01934 862219 - 2 Lines
Fax 01934 863216
Ticket books, theatre posters, programmes and box office cards, leaflets, full artwork facilities available.

**HAMILTON BROOKE**
Rouge Rue, St Peter Port, Guernsey, C.I., GY1 1ZA
Tel 01481 714437
Fax 01481 714439
Website: http://www.hbgroup.com.
Contact: Ged Kelly
AS suppliers of design and print to one of the UK`s largest promoters of pantomime and summer shows, as well as smaller promoters, we produce rosters, handbills, showcards and programmes.

**HARDSELL LIMITED**
The Exchange, Loga Weston Road, London SE1 3QB
Tel 0171 403 4037
Fax 0171 403 5381
A specialist arts and entertainments full service agency, providing media planning & buying, marketing, PR, sales promotion and in-house design and printing services.

**HASTINGS PRINTING CO LTD**
Drury Lane, St Leonards-on-Sea, East Sussex TN38 9BJ
Tel 01424 720477
Fax 01424 443693/434086
Contact: Gilbert Ticehurst
Design and printing specialising in the Entertainment Industry, including brochures, leaflets and posters.

**JOHN GOOD HOLBROOK LTD**
Progress Way, Binley, Coventry CV3 2NT
Tel 01203 652800
Fax 01203 652425
e-mail @jghcov@globalnet.co.uk
4 Elm Place, Old Witney Road, Eynsham, Oxford OX8 1PU
Tel 01865 883967
Fax 01865 883809
e-mail jghox@globalnet.co.uk
Managing Director: Caroline Good
Specialist suppliers of quality design and printing services to the theatre and music industry, providing in-house editorial, design and print for programmes and promotional material to a wide range of theatres, concert halls, touring companies and promoters.

**KALL KWIK PRINTING**
19 St.Giles High Street, London WC2H 8LN.
Tel 0171 836 9409
Fax 0171 240 6798

All types of printing and copying.  Scripts copied and
bound.  Programmes and inserts.  Presentation
documents, CV's, booklet making service.

**MIDLANDS ARTS MARKETING**
4 Russell Place, Nottingham NG1 5HJ.
Tel 0115 948 3344
Fax 0115 948 3343
Our objective is to increase the number of people who
attend, enjoy and participate in the arts.
We offer a full range of marketing services to regional
and touring clients.

**N.E. PRINT LTD**
1 Stephens Road, St.Ives, Cambridgeshire PE17 4WJ
Tel 01480 492851
Fax 01480 493417
Contact: Peter Randall
Manufacturers of flight case labels, equipment labels,
touring labels, cable and cable coding labels, printed
vinyl tapes and floor graphics.

**PERFORMANCE TICKET PRINTERS**
FREEPOST, Brownlow Heath, Congleton, Cheshire
CW12 4AT
Tel 01260 276164
Fax 01260 270984
email: tickets@timewell.demon.co.uk
High quality inexpensive concert and theatre tickets:
computer printed to your design and seating plan,
perforated, bound and delivered to your door. Also
programmes, posters, handbills and car stickers. Ideal
for fringe theatre companies, producing venues,
community arts and festivals.
For brochure, samples, prices and order form, contact
Keith Arnold.

**PRINTERS INC & DESIGN LTD**
Nobel House, Nobel Road. Eley Estate, London
N18 3BH
Tel 0181 807 5111
Fax 0181 345 5922
Specialists in the design and printing of brochures,
programmes and leaflets.

**PRINTING ADMINISTRATION LTD**
Unit E, Lombard Business Park, 20/26 Purley Way,
Croydon CR0 3JP
Tel 0181 683 3245
Fax 0181 684 0254
Printers of brochures, programmes and leaflets.

**PROSCENIUM THEATRE PUBLICATIONS LTD**
151 Wick Road, Bristol BS4 4HH.
Production & Studio

Tel 0117 925 5030
Fax 0117 925 5035
Advertising:
Tel 0117 925 5393
Fax 0117 929 3902
Editorial:
Tel 0117 925 5070
Theatre programme publishers.  Full design/print
buying facility for all theatrical publicity.

**PUBLICITY & DISPLAY LTD**
Douglas Drive, Godalming, Surrey GU7 1HJ
Tel 01483 428326
Fax 01483 424566
Design/print of posters, passes, leaflets, tickets and
stickers for the entertainment industry.

**PURE DESIGN**
Victoria House, Cooper Street, Green Lane, Hull
HU2 OHG
Tel 01482 210785
Fax 01482 229637
Contact: Tony Whitley
Pure Design is a highly experienced, independant,
consultancy dedicated to producing creative design &
print of the highest possible quality for Theatre and the
Arts on time and in budget.

**REAL PUBLICITY**
The Maltings, Brewery Road, Hoddesdon,
Herts EN11 8HF
Tel 01992 470907
Fax 01992 470516
Contact: Johnny Mans, Philip Crowe.

**SCHWARTZ ORGANISATION LTD**
92 Whitepost Lane, Hackney, London E9 5EN
Tel 0181 986 7429
Fax 0181 986 1125
Brochure, box office cards, leaflets and posters.

**SECPRINT**
Unit 2, Alexandra Centre, Rail Mill Way, Parkgate,
Rotherham S62 6JQ
Tel 01709 780008
Fax 01709 780909

**JOHN SPENCER POSTERS**
11 Stamford Arcade, Ashton-under-Lyne, Lancs
OL6 6JY
Tel 0161 330 4666

**TECHNICAL INSIGHT**
Studio 6, 75 Filmer Road, London SW6 7JF
Tel 0171 371 0875
Fax 0171 736 0051
Theatre Consultant: David Self, BA, BArch(Hons) RIBA
Architectural practice: full service from inception to
design. Newly built and refurbishment. Theatre
consultancy: design, advice and reports, surveys,
maintenance and development.

**TECHNOPRINT**
Rods Mills Lane, Morley, Leeds  LS27 9BD
Tel 0113 253 3920
Fax 0113 253 1881
Managing Director: J.M.Snee
Long-standing suppliers of quality leaflets, posters,
programmes, `what`s-on` guides etc. Typesetting,
design, scanning, repro, printing and finishing in-house.
PC and MAC disks accepted. Competitive prices.
Friendly knowledgeable staff.

**THEATRE DESPATCH LIMITED**
Azof Hall, Azof Street, London SE10  OEG
Tel 0181 853 0750
Fax 0181 293 4861
Email: admin@theatre.org
Administrator: Philip Ormond.
Theatre Despatch is a flexible and comprehensive
distribution service including 1,500 leaflet racks, 4,500
other regularly serviced outlets throughout Greater
London, poster distribution, a complete mailing service
including Mailsort, and a database of 60,000 people
and organisations interested in one or more of the arts
and entertainments.

**3D-4D HOLOGRAPHICS**
23-25 Great Sutton Street, London EC1V 0DN
Tel 0171 250 3545
Fax 0171 250 3566
Flexible holographic designs for posters, invitations
and much more.

**TOM'S TICKETS (TRURO)**
Unit 2c Industrial Estate, Grampound Road, Truro,
Cornwall TR2 4TB
Tel 01726 884004
Fax 01726 884004
Contact: Tom or Lyndal Bale
Security ticket printers, stock sizes, colours, logos,
reserved, numbered; Roll tickets, draw tickets,
cloakroom tickets, vouchers. Unbeatable turnaround.
Try Us!

**TURNERGRAPHIC LTD**
Communications House, Winchester Road,
Basingstoke, Hampshire RG22 4AA
Tel 01256 59252
Fax 01256 51501

**ZINCPARK LTD**
Kaymar Industrial Estate, Trout Street, Preston,
Lancashire PR1 4AL
Tel 01772 562211
Fax 01772 257813
Silkscreen printer.

# 19
# DRAPES, FURNISHINGS & FABRICS

**303 HIRE COMPANY LTD**
12/16 Brunel Road, London W3 7XR
Tel 0181 743 7616
Fax 0181 749 9435
The largest hirer of drapes and soft furnishings, we
can also manufacture to requirements.

**ACRE JEAN LTD**
Unit 7, The Kimber Centre, 54 Kimber Road, London
SW18 4PP.
Tel 0181 877 3211
Fax 0181 877 3213
Email: simon.fryer@acrejean.com
Website: www.acrejean.com
Contact: Simon Fryer
Specialists in the hire, manufacture and installation of
drapes for acoustic, masking and presentation

purposes.  Acre Jean Ltd has been in business for
twelve years serving the entertainment,
conference,television and film industries.
We have installed  drapes for pop shows on a
regular basis at Wembley Arena, Wembley Stadium
and Earls Court and our clients include the leading
promoters in the popular  music industry.
We have also provided drapes to conference centres,
exhibition halls, leisure centres and studios across the
length and breadth of Great Britain and abroad.  Our
constantly expanding stock now includes Wool Serge
in black, Chromakey blue, Chromakey green and grey;
Sharkstooth Gauze in black, white and grey; Velvet in
black, royal blue, plum red, admiral red, midas gold,
leaf green, pewter grey and rose pink.  Also white filled
cloth and star cloths.
See advert on preceeding page.

**AUDITORIA SERVICES LTD**
Denby Way, Hellaby Ind. Estate, Hellaby, Rotheram
S66 8HR
Tel 01709 543345
Fax 01709 700771
Manufacturers of theatre and cinema seating,
retractable platforms and stages, bleacher seating,
stage equipment and curtains.

**MAISON HENRY BERTRAND LTD**
11 Melton Street, London NW1 2EA
Tel 0171 383 3868
Fax 0171 383 4797
Suppliers of fine silks to theatrical costumiers and TV.

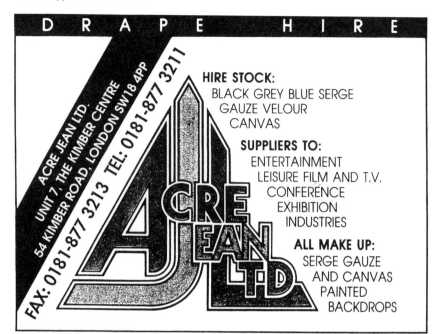

**BLACKOUT**
208 Durnsford Road, London SW19 8DR
Tel 0181 944 8840
Fax 0181 944 8850
e-mail mail@blackout-ltd.com
Contact: Steve Tuck or Tom Lambert
Blackout specialises in the manufacture for hire and
sale of high quality flameproof drapes and star cloths.
We offer full consultancy, installation rigging, 24 hr
backup service and can be relied upon to make any
project happen. We also provide painted cloths to any
size and artistic specification.

**J W BOLLOM & CO LTD**
PO Box 78, Croydon Road, Beckenham, Kent BR3 4BL
Tel 0181 658 2299
Fax 0181 658 8672
15 Theobalds Road WC1 8SN
Tel 0171 242 0313
Fax 0171 831 2457
314/316 Old Brompton Road, London SW5 9JH.

Tel 0171 370 3252
Fax 0171 370 3253
Unit 7, King William Enterprise Park, Salford M5 2UP
Tel 0161 876 4898
Fax 0161 876 5104
Unit 2, Windmill Industrial Estate, Birmingham Road,
Allesley, Coventry CV5 9QE
Tel 01203 405151
Fax 01203 404 978
Moreton Hall Industrial Estate, Easlea Road, Bury St.
Edmunds IP32 7BY
Tel 01284 765252
Fax 01284 765253
121 South Liberty Lane, Ashton Vale, Bristol BS3 2SZ
Tel 0117 966 5151
Fax 0117 966 7180
Flame retardant paints, solutions and coatings for
upgrading existing materials and substrates to meet fire
regulations.

**BRITISH FURTEX FABRICS LTD**
Luddendenfoot, Halifax HX2 6AQ
Tel 01422 882161
Fax 01422 882516

**CAMEO CURTAINS**
1B Hob Hey Lane, Culcheth, Warrington,
Cheshire WA3 4NH
Tel 01925 765308
Fax 01925 765308
Contact: Frank Atherton and M Benbow
Manufacturers of Quality stage and auditorium drapes,
rostra, blinds, blackout curtains, gauzes and canvas.
Also repairs, cleaning and reflameproofing service.

**CAPE SCENIC SERVICE**
34 Queens Row, London SE17 2PX
Tel 0171 252 7418
Fax 0171 277 1701
Directors: Dorothy Cape, P. Everett
Manufacturers of curtains, banners, canvases, etc. to
theatre, exhibition, trade shows, museums.

**CCT LIGHTING LTD**
London Office: 4 Tudor Court, Brighton Road, Sutton,
Surrey SM2 5AE.
Tel 0181 770 3636
Fax 0181 643 9848
Factory: Hindle House, Traffic Street, Nottingham
Notts. NG2 1NE
Tel 0115 986 2722
Fax 0115 986 2546
Directors: David P Manners, Donald D Hindle, George Chapman
CCT Lighting manufacture flameproofed velour and
Bolton Twill curtains in a wide range of colours, quoted
to specification. Also distributed are the entire Rosco
range of products including scenic and projection
materials.
(Main function: Manufacture of Lighting and
accessories)

**CLYDE CANVAS**
50 Lindsay Road, Edinburgh EH6 6NW
Tel 0131 554 1331
Fax 0131 553 7655
Marquee and clearspan structure hire, furniture hire,
textile repair, (stage cloths etc.).

**N & I COSTELLO**
225 Red Lion Road, Tolworth, Surbiton, Surrey KT6 7RF
Tel 0181 397 7830
Fax 0181 391 1633
Shimmer Slash Curtains, metallic or non-metallic up to
48' length.

**KEN CREASEY LTD**
34 Queens Row, London SE17 2PX
Tel 0171 277 1645
Fax 0171 277 1701
Specialist curtain maker for Stage, Cinema, Contract,
Exhibition, Draperies, and Fabric requirements for.

**C.I. DAVIS & CO LTD**
94/96 Seymour Place, London W1H 5DG
Tel 0171 723 7735/0895
Fax 0171 723 4697
Suppliers of plain silk fabrics and lining materials
(acetate).

**DAVMERRY LTD**
Propress House, 33/35 Battersea Bridge Road,
London SW11 3BA
Tel 0171 228 8467

Fax 0171 924 2549

**DONMAR LTD**
2 Tudor Abbey Road, London N10 2UY
Tel 0181 453 6004
Black drapes in velour, wool serge or bolton - legs,
borders, tabs etc. Cycloramas, Slash Curtains & Rosco
designer materials and HARLEQUIN dance flooring.
CHROMAKEY and specialist drapes for video. Site
measuring and custom made service.
Flame retardant fabrics and dyeing to order. Curtain
tracks, drapes and rigging installations anywhere in the
U.K.

**EMPEE SILK FABRICS LTD**
42/44 Brick Lane, London E1 6RF
Also at 46/48 Fashion Street, London E1 6PX
Tel 0171 247 1094
Fax 0171 375 2869

## Gerriets Great Britain Ltd
### Tel 0171 232 2262
### Fax 0171 237 4916
### Curtains, Backcloths, Floor Coverings and Special Effect Materials for the Theatre and Entertainment Industries

e-mail empeesilks@bsnet.co.uk
Wholesalers of a huge range of dress and theatrical fabrics including satins, nets, velvets, cottons, wools, corduroys and many more. We sell stocks and clearance lines off very low prices.

**ENTERTAINMENT SEATING LTD**
The Windmill Centre, Hamilton Street, Saltcoats,
Ayrshire KA21 5DY
Tel 01294 469783/602554
Fax 01294 467093
Auditorium, theatre and cinema seating specialists.
Reconditioning service, including on site. Also carpets and drapes.

**FUTURIST LIGHT & SOUND LTD**
Hoyle Head Mills, New Street, Earlsheaton,
Dewsbury, West Yorks WF12 8JJ
Tel 01924 468183
Fax 01924 458667
Management: Group Managing Director: Michael A
Lister; Financial Director: Dawn Lister; Rental and
Projects Manager: Steve Farnsworth; Productions
Manager: Andrew Waddington; Business Development
Manager: Frank Fallows.
Over 200 star cloths for sale and hire. As well as a full
compliment of drapes, tie backs, legs, borders, tabs
and gauzes.

**GERRIETS OF GREAT BRITAIN LTD**
Unit J412, Tower Bridge Business Complex.,
Drummond Road, London SE16 4EF
Tel 0171 232 2262
Fax 0171 237 4916
Supply and manufacture of theatrical and display
plastics, textiles and finished soft goods.

**REX HOWARD (DRAPES) LTD**
Acton Park Industrial Estate, Eastman Road, The Vale,
London W3 7QS
Tel 0181 740 5881
Fax 0181 740 5994
Stage Drapes of every description, gauzes, flame-proof
textile materials for sale and hire.

**J&C JOEL LTD**
Corporation Mill, Corporation Street, Sowerby Bridge,
Halifax HX6 2QQ.
Tel 01422 833835
Fax 01422 835157/839642
e-mail mail@joel.demon.co.uk
Theatrical drape manufacturers. Specialists in flame
retardant fabrics.

**LANCELYN THEATRE SUPPLIES**
Electric Avenue, Ferry Hinksey Road, Oxford OX2 0BY
Tel 01865 722468
Fax 01865 728791
Made to measure curtains, supply and fix, repair and
cleaning.

**J D McDOUGALL LIMITED**
4 McGrath Road, Stratford London E15 4JP
Tel 0181 534 2921
Fax 0181 519 8423
Email: sales@mcdougall.co.uk
Director: I McDougall (Man)
Stage Drapes, Vision Gauzes, Backcloths, Cyclorama
cloths, Flame-proof textile materials for Scenery
Construction and Stage Effects.

**NEVTEX INTERLOOP LTD**
PO Box 87, 29 Stoney Street, Nottingham NG1 1LR
Tel 0115 959 8781
Fax 0115 950 2687
e-mail sales@nevtex.co.uk

Website www.nevtex.co.uk
Wolesale & mail order of nevtex: fabrics, feathers & dresses. Trimmings to the theatrical & dance costumier.

**P & G STAGE DRAPERIES**
67 Ayres Road, Old Trafford, Manchester M16 9NH
Tel 0161 226 5858
Fax 0161 232 9510
860 Coronation Road, Park Royal London NW10 7PS
Tel 0181 961 8812
Fax 0181 961 6348
Contact: Ian Ferguson
Manufacture and supply of Tabs, Legs, Cycloramas, Festoons, Borders, Nets, Gauzes and Astrocloths.

**PAT TEXTILES**
231 The Broadway, Bexley Heath, Kent DA6 7EJ
Tel 0181 301 4179
Open Monday - Saturday 9 a.m. - 5.30 p.m.

## DRAPES FOR YOUR THEATRE

RUSSELL & CHAPPLE LTD.
11 Garman Road, London N17 0UR
Tel: 0181 885 4209   Fax: 0181 885 2462

**PROPRESS STEAMERS & IRONS**
33-35 Battersea Bridge Road, London SW11 3BA
Tel 0171 228 8467
Fax 0171 924 2549
Portable steamers.

**RUSSELL & CHAPPLE LTD**
23 Monmouth Street, London WC2H 9DE
Tel 0171 836 7521
Fax 0171 497 0554
Made to order Drapes, Backcloths, etc. Suppliers of Flameproof Textile Materials.

**STAGE ELECTRICS**
Victoria Road, Avonmouth, Bristol BS11 9DB
Tel 0117 982 7282
Fax 0117 982 2180
Cofton Road, Marsh Barton, Exeter EX2 8QW
Tel 01392 255868
Fax 01392 410592
Parkway Industrial Estate, Plymouth PL6 8LH
Tel 01752 269444
Fax 01752 228283
Dartmouth Road, Smethwick, West Midlands B66 1AX
Tel 0121 525 4545
Fax 0121 525 2413
Hire, Sales, Installation and Service. Production services for lighting designers, theatre and commercial events.

**STAGE NORTH**
Unit 4 & 5, Woodham Road, Aycliffe Industrial Estate, Co. Durham DL5 6HT
Tel 01325 314946
Fax 01325 311261
Sale of Stage Drapes and Dressing, Made-Up or Cut Pieces, Flame-Proofing Chemicals.

**STAGE SERVICES**
Stage House, Prince William Rd, Belton Park,
Loughborough LE11 5UG
Tel 01509 218857
Fax 01509 265730
Sales, Hire and Installation of Lighting, Sound and
Staging equipment by ADB, CCT, LSD, Electro Control
Systems, Zero 88, AKG, Allen & Heath, Audio Technica,
Tascam, C Audio, JBL, Quad, Sennheiser, Denon,
Trantec, Stage Systems and others. Stage make-up by
Grimas, counter sales, mail order and workshops. Sales
and Hire of optical and pyrotechnic effects by DHA, Le
Maitre and Theatrical Pyrotechnics. Drapes made to
order. Full range of electrical and rigging accessories,
consumables and sales of colour filter by Rosco and Lee.

**STAGESETS (London)**
Unit L, Delta Wharf, Tunnel Avenue, Greenwich
London SE10 0QH
Tel 0181 853 2370
Fax 0181 853 5683
Scenery/Drapes - Backdrops, Gauzes, Furniture.

**THEATRE PICK UPS**
PO Box 232, London WC2B 5SY.
Tel 0115 969 3306
Curtains and tab hire for the stage and studio,
including, black serge, velour, house tabs etc.
Traditional red plush seats available with proscenium
and footlights for TV and films other theatre related
items available.

**MICK TOMLIN DRAPES**
109 Folly Road, Mildenhall, Suffolk IP28 7BT.
Tel 01638 713408
Fax 01638 711077
Drapes of every description, all materials for the
theatre. Stage equipment specialists.

**TRIPLE E LIMITED**
5 Admiral Road, Hyson Industrial Estate
London SE16 3PA
Tel 0171 237 6354
Fax 0171 237 7650
Email: info@tab.com
Designers, manufacturers and distributors of
curtain/scenery tracks and specialist stage hardware.

**VARIA TEXTILES LTD**
197 Kings Rd, Kingston-on-Thames, Surrey KT2 6JH
Tel 0181 549 8590
Fax 0181 549 8290
Contact: Karl Leuthenmayr
We have in stock a complete range of fire resistant
products. We also arrange for fabric to be made up.
Please ask for a quatation.

**VENYFLEX CO**
1 Holly Road, Hampton Hill, Middlesex TW12 1QF
Tel 0181 977 3780
Fax 0181 977 9070
Hire drapes and manufacture blinds.

**WHALEYS BRADFORD LTD**
Harris Court, Great Horton, Bradford, West Yorkshire
BD7 4EQ
Tel 01274 576718
Fax 01274 521309
Fabric suppliers, dress and furnishing, scenery fabrics.
Curtain manufacturers.

# 20
# EFFECTS AND FIREWORKS

**3.D. CREATIONS**
9 Keppel Road, Gorleston, Gt. Yarmouth, Norfolk
Tel 01493 657093 (Studio)  01493 652055 (Workshop)
Fax 01493 443124
Mobile 0860 707287
We can provide all your scenic needs for theatre,
television and film. Scenery and prop design and
construction specialists. Prop makers, set designers,
sculptors, scenic artists we are always prepared to
undertake work of the unusual. Location work
undertaken.

**AJS THEATRE LIGHTING & STAGE SUPPLIES
LIMITED**
Units 25 & 26, Hightown Trading Estate, Crow Arch
Lane, Ringwood, Hampshire BH24 1ND
Tel 01425 481100
Fax 01425 471398
email: enquiries@ajs.co.uk
Website: http://www.demon.co.uk/ajs
Contact: Ian Cross, Technical Sales
Wholesalers and retailers of Pyrotechnic devices for
stage use, also fog machines, mirror balls, smoke
generators and other disco effects. Hirers & Distributors
of products by Le Maitre, Martin, Pulsar, Rosco, The Smoke
Company, JEM, Clay-paky, DHA.

**ANGLO PACIFIC INTERNATIONAL PLC**
Unit 1, Bush Industrial Estate, Standard 12d, London
NW10 6DF.
Tel 0181 965 1955
Fax 0181 965 4954
Ocean freight, air freight, trucking, full carnet services,
forwarders to the performing arts.

**ANY EFFECTS**
64 Weir Road, Wimbledon, London SW19 8UG.
Tel 0181 944 0099
Fax 0181 944 6989
Complete effects services for 15 years. Specialising in
pyrotechnics, mechanical effects, stunt preparation,
atmospheric and model making with comprehensive
breakaway (shatterglass) department.
Films & TV: London`s Burning, Bugs, The Knock,
Soldier Soldier, Thieftakers. Approved BECTU SFX
Supervisor.

**ATOMIC LASERS**
Unit 2, Station Yard Industrial Estate, Wilbraham Road,
Fulbourn, Cambs CB1 5ET
Tel 01223 882111
Fax 01223 881824
Contact: Andy Creighton
Laser effects specialists for over 10 years. Hire of full
colour, multiple output, 'laserium' quality projections,
precision beam targeting systems, fibre-optics,
screens, smoke generation and dazzling stage effects.

**BROCKS EXPLOSIVES LIMITED**
Sanquhar, Dumfriesshire DG4 6JP
Tel 01659 50531
Fax 01659 50526
Suppliers of all types of special effects.

**CCT LIGHTING LTD**
London Office: 4 Tudor Court, Brighton Road, Sutton,
Surrey SM2 5AE
Tel 0181 770 3636
Fax 0181 643 9848
Factory: Hindle House, Traffic Street, Nottingham NG2
1NE
Tel 0115 986 2722
Fax 0115 986 2546
Suppliers of high power effects projection for general
moving effects and profile spotlights for the projection
of fixed and moving gobos. CCT Lighting are also
distributors of the entire Rosco range including fog
systems, gels, scenic paints and materials.
All products are available for sale or hire through a UK
dealer network, or direct.

**CINEBUILD LTD**
Studio House, Rita Road, Vauxhall,
London SW8 1JU
Tel 0171 582 8750
Fax 0171 793 0467
Lighting and Special Effects and breakaway glass, all
types of designs of snow, frost, cobweb sprays,
pyrotechnics and special effects of all kinds, wind and
smoke machines.

**MIKE & ROSI COMPTON**
11 Woodstock Road, Croydon, Surrey CR0 1JS
Tel 0181 680 4364
Fax 0181 681 3126
We make props, special effects, costumes and models,
we specialise in the unusual but can do almost
anything! No hiring

**CONCEPT ENGINEERING LIMITED**
7 Woodlands Business Park, Woodlands Park
Avenue, Maidenhead, Berks SL6 3UA
Tel 01628 882555
Fax 01628 826261
Email: info@concept-smoke.co.uk
Website: www.concept-smoke.uk
Smoke, Fog, Cobwebs, Snow, Scissor Lifts, Turntables, etc.

**THE DEFINITIVE SPECIAL PROJECTS LTD**
PO Box 169, Stevenage, SG2 7SG
Hatfield, Herts AL9 7NT
Tel 01438 869005
Fax: 01438 869006
Laser and special effects.

**DIRECTA UK LIMITED**
Cold Norton, Essex CM3 6UA.
Tel 01621 828882
Fax 01621 828072
Whether you need to shift props with ease or simply
surround it all in fog. Directa has the answer. For a
free catalogue phone 01621 828882.

**DONMAR LTD**
Donmar House, 54 Cavell Street, Whitechapel,
London E1 2HP
Tel 0171 790 1166
Fax 0171 790 6634
Le Maitre main distributors London & South East
England for pyrotechnics, smoke, dry ice and other
effects. Also sales and hire of stage lighting,  optical
effects, snow & bubble machines etc. Sales of
breakaway bottles and blood. UV and fluorescent
paints and tapes.  Cobweb, snow, dulling, breaking
down and other arerosol sprays. Flame retardant
solutions.

**EMERGENCY EXIT ARTS**
PO Box 570, London SE10  OEE
Tel 0181 453 6004
Fax 0181 858 2025
Email: info@ea.org.uk
Website: www.ea.org.uk
Complete events planned and implemented, pyrotechnic
displays, touring pyrotechnic performance and processions,
installations, effigies and decorations.

**EMERGENCY HOUSE**
Manchester Road, Marsden, Huddersfield,
W Yorkshire HD7 6EY
Tel 01484 846999
Fax 01484 845061
Full range of visual effects.
Contact Evan Green-Hughes or Vicki Howard.

**ENTERPRISES UNLIMITED**
Unit 6, Cowbridge Business Park, Cowbridge, Boston,
Lincolnshire PE22 7AX
Tel 01205 310440
Fax 01205 310450
All special effects equipment hire and services.
Manufacturers of the 'Snowboy' for realistic, quick
clearing snow effects.

**E.S.P. (U.K.) LTD**
(Events, Services & Productions)
The Arches, Unit 5, Furmston Court, Letchworth,
Hertfordshire SG6 1EX
Tel 01462 482411
Fax 01462 673856
e-mail 101637.2016@compuserve.com
Contact: Ann Brodhurst, David Stressing

Specialise in lighting sales and hire of equipment, special effects including our unique Snow Effect Machine, set construction and design etc., for theatre, opera, tours, T.V., films and concerts. For your theatrical needs or supplies, please contact us.

**EUROSOUND (UK) LTD**
Unit 1, Intake Lane, Woolley, Wakefield WF4 2LG
Tel 01484 866066
Fax 01484 866299

**FLAMEBAR LTD**
Chestnut Industrial Estate, Bassingham, Lincs
LN5 9LL.
Tel 01522 788818
Fax 01522 788890
Aerosol special effects Kobweb, artificial cobwebs, Snocene decorative snow and Kolsnow falling snow. Frost, flame retardant aerosol adhesives. Cobweb drill attachments with cobweb solution and cleaner. Fire barrier gel. Flame retardant sawdust and chippings. Stockists in London and around UK.

**FUTURIST LIGHT AND SOUND LTD**
Hoyle Head Mill, New Street, Earlsheaton, Dewsbury, Nr. Leeds, West Yorkshire  WF12 8JJ
Tel 01924 468183
Fax 01924 458667
email: Sales@Futurist.Co.UK
London Office: Futurist Special Projects & Productions, 294 Earls Court Road, Kensington, London SW5 9BB
Tel 0171 370 4012
Fax 0171 370 5481
email: Projects@Futurist.Co.UK
Managing Director: Michael A Lister
Production Manager: Vin Holme, 01924 455665
Projects Manager: Jonathan Walters
Full stocking range of Le-Maitre Pyrotechnics, smoke and fog machines and fluids, JEM smoke machines and accessories. Plus full range of Rosco paints, filters and special effect curtains.

**GRADAV THEATRE SERVICES LTD**
613-615 Green Lanes, Palmers Green, London
N13 4EP
Tel 0181 886 1300
Fax 0181 882 6517
Sales of DHA gobos, gobo rotators and animation dics. Le Maitre pyrotechnics.
Smoke Factory smoke guns. Kobweb spray and artificial snow.

**HAYES SOUND & LIGHTING (HSL-HIRE) LTD**
Unit 7, Cunliffe Road, Whitebirk Industrial Estate, Blackburn, Lancashire BB1 5UA
Tel 01254 698808
Fax 01254 698835
Contact: Simon Stuart
Every client is special, each commission totally unique, our in house event management process ensuring that your project is carefully monitored, from the taking of your detailed instructions, through design and planning, and ultimately the installation and staging of the event itself.

**HOWORTH WRIGHTSON LTD**
The Prop House, Unit 2, Cricket Street, Denton, Manchester M34 3DR
Tel 0161 335 0220
Fax 0161 320 3928
Stockists of all major manufacturers for fireworks, theatrical pyrotechnic effects and specialist suppliers of electronic control systems and pyro effects for magicians.

**JEM SMOKE PLC**
Vale Road Industrial Estate, Boston Road, Spilsby, Lincs
Tel 01790 754050
Fax 01790 754051
e-mail smoke@jem.prestel.co.uk
Contact: Jon Petts
JEM manufacture one of the most comprehensive ranges of effects generators including Smoke Machines, Haze Machines and Heavy Fog Machines. JEM guarantees all its products for 5 years and is presently developing a range of silent operation products specifically for Theatres and TV Studios.

**KIMBOLTON FIREWORKS LIMITED**
7 High Street, Kimbolton, Cambs PE18 0HB
Tel 01480 860988
Display fireworks for outside use.

**LANCELYN THEATRE SUPPLIES**
Electric Avenue, Ferry Hinksey Road, Oxford OX2 0BY
Tel 01865 722468
Fax 01865 728791
Jem and Le Maitre distributors, complete range in stock, detonation systems for hire (see Lighting Hire).

**LANCELYN LIGHTING (NORTHWEST)**
Poulton Road, Bebington, Merseyside L63 9LN
Tel 0151 334 8991 (24 hrs)
Fax 0151 334 4047
Contact: Bob Baxter
Optical & special effects, Pyrotechnics supplied and delivered. See entry under Lighting.

**LASER CREATIONS INTERNATIONAL LTD**
55 Merthyr Terrace, Barnes, London SW13 9DL

Tel 0181 741 5747
Fax 0181 748 9879
e-mail lci-uk@compuserve.com
Contact: Roland Connor
Originally famous for its laser spectaculars, LCI has extended its portfolio to include water screens, dancing waters, laser video projection, pyrotechnics and other special effects.

**LASER MAGIC**
LM House, 2 Church Street, Seaford,
East Sussex BN25 1HD
Tel 01323 890752
Fax 01323 898311
Mobile: 0836 252885
email: compuserve 100563.32
Website www.lasermagic.com
Laser Displays and Special Effects.

**LIGHT WORKS LIMITED**
2a Greenwood Road, London E8 1AB
Tel 0171 249 3627
Fax 0171 254 0306

**LE MAITRE SALES LTD**
6 Forval Close, Wandle Way, Mitcham, Surrey
CR4 4NE.
Tel 0181 646 2222
Fax 0181 646 1955
Contacts: Dave Winfield and Steve Ramos
Directors: Harold Berlinski, Richard Wilson, Colin Lane.
Manufacturers of dry ice machines, smoke machines, coloured smoke cartridges, flash puffs, coloured fire, cartridges, maroons, firing systems and related products.  Firework manufacturers, stockists and operators.

**MG GAS PRODUCTS LIMITED**
Cedar House, 39 London Road, Reigate, Surrey
RH2 9QE.
Tel 01737 241133
Fax 01737 241842
Suppliers of 'Cardice' solid carbon dioxide as pellets, blocks and slices for for effects amongst others.
Available from Regional Depots.  Contact above address for details.

**MIDNIGHT SALES LTD**
Unit 1, Chelsea Bridge Business Centre,
326 Queenstown Road, London SW8 4NP
Tel 0171 498 7272
Fax 0171 498 8845
Sales Manager: Damion Dowling

**MTFX**
The Cottage, New Road, Olveston, Bristol BS35 4DX
Tel 01454 615723
Fax 01454 615724
Contact: Mark Turner
MTFX provides imaginative and unusual special effects for the Theatre Industry using skills in pyrotechnics, pneumatics, electronics, lighting and sound.

**OPTIKINETICS LIMITED**
38 Cromwell Road, Luton LU3 1DN
Tel 01582 411413
Fax 01582 400613
e-mail optiuk@optikinetics.com
website www.optikinetics.com
Contact: Neil Rice

**PAINS FIREWORKS**
Romsey Rd, Whiteparish, Salisbury, Wilts SP5 2SD
Tel 01794 884040
Fax 01794 884015
Theatrical & Conference Effects. Firework Displays.

**PHOENIX FIREWORK DISPLAYS**
Pinden End Farm, Pinden, Dartford, Kent DA2 8EA
Tel 01474 702956
Fax 01474 704017
Mobile 0836 753695
Contact: Ian Craig

**QUICKSILVER UK LTD**
Broom Grove Lane, Denton, Manchester M34 3DU.
Tel 0161 320 7232
Contact: Darren Wallis
Suppliers of pyrotechnic effects and fireworks for all types of indoor and outdoor effects.  Specialists in production of smoke effects. Too many products to list.
Too many brands to name.

**ROSCOLAB LIMITED**
Blanchard Works, Kangley Bridge Road, Sydenham
London SE26 5AQ
Tel 0181 659 2300
Fax 0181 659 3153
Shrink mirrors, breakaways. Rear & front projection screens, scenic materials, scenic paint systems.
Lighting colour media including diffusion.
Comprehensive range of gobos.

**SGB WORLD SERVICE**
Empire House, 12 Rutland Street, Hanley,
Stoke on Trent ST1 5JG
Tel 01782 279309
Fax 01782 279309
e-mail email@sgbworldservice.co.uk

Website www.sgbwordservice.com
Contact:Mr S. Boote
See our main advert in Lighting & Lighting Equipment
Suppliers.

### SANDLING FIREWORKS
32 Denmark Road,  Gloucester GL1 3JQ.
Tel 01452 410453
Fax 01452 522848
Importers and manufacturers of fireworks
professionally fired displays and suppliers of D.I.Y. kits
(retail and trade).

### THE SEARCHLIGHT CO
The Smithy, 9 Alms Hill, Bourn, Cambridge CB3 7SH
Tel 01954 718118
Fax 01954 719066
e-mail enquires@searchlight.co.uk
Website www.searchlight.co.uk

### SHELL SHOCK FIREWORK COMPANY
South Manor Farm, Bramfield, Nr. Heisworth,
Suffolk IP19 9AQ
Tel/Fax: 01986 784469
Specialist firework display team in UK and
Internationally.  Also provide pyro and effects
Importers of high quality material from Spain, Malta,
etc.

### SNOW BUSINESS
56 Northfield Road, Tetbury, Glos. GL8 8HQ
Tel/Fax 01666 502857
Email snow@snow-business.com
Contact: David G Crownshaw
Snow and winter effects.

### SOUND ELECTRONICS (NEWCASTLE) LTD
Industry Road, Heaton, Newcastle-upon-Tyne
NE6 5XB
Tel 0191 265 2500
Fax 0191 265 8595
Sales, hire, design, install. Stockist for Le-Maitre, Jem,
Rosco, Abstract, Martin, Effects Company, Coemar.

### STAGE ELECTRICS
Victoria Road, Avonmouth, Bristol BS11 9DB
Tel 0117 982 7282
Fax 0117 982 2180
e-mail hire@stage-electrics.co.uk
e-mail sales@stage-electrics.co.uk
Website www.stage-electrics.demon.co.uk
Cofton Road, Marsh Barton, Exeter EX2 8QW
Tel 01392 255868
Fax 01392 410592
Parkway Industrial Estate, Plymouth PL6 8LH
Tel 01752 269444
Fax 01752 228283
Dartmouth Road, Smethwick, West Midlands B66 1AX
Tel 0121 525 4545
Fax 0121 525 2413
"Hire, Sales, Installation and Service.  Production
services for lighting designers, theatre and commercial
events".

### STAGE NORTH
The Chimes, Low Green, County Durham, DL5 4TR
Tel 01325 314946
Fax 01325 311261
Hire and Sales of Optical and Special Effects
Equipment.

### STAGE SERVICES
Stage House, Prince William Rd, Belton Park,
Loughborough LE11 0GN
Tel 01509 218857
Fax 01509 265730
Sales, Hire and Installation of Lighting, Sound and
Staging equipment by  ADB, CCT, LSD, Electro
Control Systems, Zero 88, AKG, Allen & Heath, Audio
Technica, Tascam, C Audio, JBL, Quad, Sennheiser,
Denon, Trantec, Stage Systems and others. Stage
make-up by Grimas, counter sales, mail order and
workshops. Sales and Hire of optical and Pyrotechnic
effects by DHA, Le Maitre & Theatrical Pyrotechnics.
Drapes made to order. Full range of electrical and
rigging accessories, consumables and sales of colour
filter by Rosco and Lee.

### STAGE TWO LIMITED
Unit J, Penfold Trading Estate, Imperial Way, Watford,
Herts WD2 4YY
Tel 01923 244822
Fax 01923 255048
Hire or Sale of sound, lighting and special effects or all
applications.
Hire Manager: Richard Ford
Special effects Falsh Pots, Maroons, Bullet Hits.
Supplier of soecial effects for stage, films and TV.

### STRAND LIGHTING LTD
North Hyde House, North Hyde Wharf, Hayes Road,
Heston, Middlesex
Tel 0181 571 3588
Fax 0181 571 3305

### THEATRE DIRECT
Unit 2, Kirkwood Road, Kings Hedges, Cambridge
CB4 2PH
Tel 01223 423010
Fax 01223 425010
Contact: James Irvine
Hire sales and service of lighting, sound and staging -
Strand Lighting main dealer.

### THEATRICAL PYROTECHNICS LTD
The Loop, Manston Airport, Ramsgate, Kent
CT12 5DE
Tel 01843 823545
Fax 01843 822655
Contact: Sue Sturges or Malcolm Armstrong
Special effects manufacturers. Flash Pots, Maroons,
Bullet Hits, Battle items. Manufacturer and supplier of
special effects for stage, films and television.

### TRAFALGAR LIGHTING LTD
9 Northway, London N9 0AD
Tel 0181 887 0082
Fax 0181 887 0072
Sales and hire, CCT, Rank Strand, Green Ginger,
Pulsar, Lamps, Special effects hire, dealers in used
equipment.

### TRAVELLING LIGHT (Birmingham) LTD
Unit 34, Boulton Industrial Centre, Icknield Street,
Hockley, Birmingham B18 5AU
Tel 0121 523 3297
Fax 0121 551 2360

### M & L WARREN
32 Station Road, Purton, Wiltshire
Tel 01793 771453
Smoke, fog, cobwebs, rain, snow, wind. Available for
hire with or without operator. Also fire effects and
pyrotechnics with operator only.

**WATER SCULPTURES**
St. Georges Studios, St. Georges Quay, Lancaster
LA1 5QJ
Tel 01524 64430
Fax 01524 60454
Prop: Byll Elliot
Specialists in the Design and Installation of all types of
Water feature, from rain effects to Waterfalls. Many
years of experience in Theatre.

**ZEBEDEE MUSIC SERVICES**
294 Newton Road, Rushden, Northants NN10 OSY
Tel/Fax 01933 350150 (Fax only 11am - 11pm)
Contact: Sheila Lorraine

# 21
# EMERGENCY SERVICES

**AMBULANCE SERVICES**
124 Hillcross Avenue, Morden, Surrey SM4 4EG
Tel 0181 543 5489
Fax 0181 395 6347
Mobile 0831 220299

**AMBULINK INTERNATIONAL**
Po Box 112, Eastwood, Nottingham NG16 1FA
Tel 0115 938 2925
Fax 0115 938 2934

**MEDICALL LTD**
29 Manchester Street, London W1M 5PF
Freephone: 0800 136106
Tel 0181 673 5314
Fax 0171 486 5622

**MIDLAND FIRE PROTECTION SERVICES**
256 Foleshill Road, Coventry CV6 5AY
Tel 01203 685252
Fax: 01203 637575
Freephone: 0500 655352

**OUTDOOR PURSUITS CO-OP**
(Sells equipment only.)
24 Radford Street, Stone, Staffs ST15 8DA
Tel 01785 818500
Fax 01785 817658

**ST JOHN AMBULANCE**
1 Grosvenor Crescent, London SW1X 7EF
Tel 0171 235 5231
Fax 0171 235 0796

# 22
# EVENT & CONFERENCE ORGANISERS

**EVENTSWORK**
Douglas House, 3 Richmond Buildings, Dean Street,
London W1V 5AE

Tel: 0171 434 2100
Fax: 0171 434 0200
Email: dbaa@derekblock.demon.co.uk

# 23
# FILM, VIDEO & AUDIO VISUAL

**BCS DISCO VIDEOS**
Grantham House, Macclesfield, Cheshire  SK10 3NP
Tel 01625 615379
Fax 01625 429667
Computer graphic specialists for the music industry.
Video light shows for live performance or video
production. Main agents for VIDEO DJ effects
equipment. Sales, hire or leasing.

**BLACK LIGHT**
18 West Harbour Road, Granton, Edinburgh, EH5 1PN
Tel 0131 551 2337
Fax 0131 552 0370
Main Mobile: 0836 586262

**BLACK TOWER STUDIOS**
15 Bracondale, Norwich, Norfolk NR1 2AL
Tel 01603 616661
Fax 01603 616668

**DONMAR LTD**
54 Cavell Street, Whitechapel, London E1 2HP
Tel 0171 790 1166
Fax 0171 790 6634
Full range of Arrilite, Redhead & Blonde kits (240V &
120V also 30V battery) accessories, filters, spuns,
diffusions, colour correction (Lee Filters/Rosco). Fixed
& portable front and rear projection screens. Curtain
tracks, rigging and specialist drapes (CHROMAKEY)
for video studios. Studio lighting installations.

**DTL BROADCAST LIMITED**
Johnson's Estate, Silverdale Road, Hayes, Middx UB3 3BA
Tel 0181 813 5200
Fax 0181 813 5022
email: 101534.3607@compuserve.com

**ELECTROSONIC LTD**
Hawley Mill, Hawley Road, Dartford, Kent DA2 7SY
Tel 01322 222211
Fax 01322 282282
Manufacture and supply of audio visual and video
control equipment from single screen up to multi-media
spectaculars.

**EXPERTISE INTERNATIONAL**
Threeways House, 40/44 Clipstone Street, London W1P 8JX
Tel 0171 323 3224
Fax 0171 636 7114
Film and video production, projection and technical
consultancy.

**FIRST FIELD**
Unit C5, 3 Bradbury Street, London N16 8JN 3PS.
Tel 0171 690 4990
Fax 0171 690 4494
Video production company.

**FUTURIST LIGHT & SOUND LTD**
Hoyle Head Mills, New Street, Earlsheaton,
Dewsbury, West Yorks WF12 8JJ

Tel 01924 468183
Fax 01924 458667
Full range of video and TV studio lighting and effects, filter and gels, screens and audio equipment for sale, lease and rental.

## GEARHOUSE
69 Dartmouth Middleway, Birmingham B7 4UA
Tel 0121 333 3333
Fax 0121 333 3347
Conference, exhibition and presentation equipment hire. Audio visual sound and lighting.

## GRAY AUDIO VISUAL
34/36 Bickerton Road, London N19 5JS
Tel 0171 263 9561
Fax 0171 272 0146
Audio Visual Rental and Production.

## HARKNESS HALL LTD
The Gate Studios, Station Road, Borehamwood, Hertfordshire WD6 1DQ
Tel 0181 953 3611/9371
Fax 0181 207 3657
e-mail sales@harknesshall.com
Contact: Jane Delaney, Adele Hitching & Emma Davis
Electric & manual roller screens with front or rear projection surfaces up to 48ft (14.6m) wide. A comprehensive range of cinema screens systems, frames & masking systems, curtain systems, AV screens, portable folding frame screens and a wide variety of specials. Design, survey, installation and maintenance services available.
Catalogues and brochures available on request.

## JVC PROFESSIONAL PRODUCTS (UK) LTD
Ullswater House, Kendal Avenue, London W3 OXA.
Tel 0181 896 6000
Fax 0181 896 6060
Professional Video Manufacturer.

## LINE-UP P.M.C.
9A Tankerville Place, Newcastle Upon Tyne NE2 3AT
Tel 0191 281 6449
Fax 0191 212 0913
Rental of audio-visual/presentation equipment.
Contact: Chris Murtagh.

## MARQUEE AUDIO LTD.
Shepperton Film Studios, Studios Road, Shepperton, Middlesex TW17 OQD
Tel 01932 566777
Fax 01932 565861
Email: marquee.audio@dial.com
Contact: Spencer Brooks
Professional audio sales, design and installation.

## NSR Ltd
Lower Priory Farm, Clamp Hill, Stanmore, Middx HA7 3JJ
Tel 0181 954 7677
Fax 0181 954 9329
Managing Director: Mr R.A. Walker

## PICCADILLY AUDIO VISUAL
Sandpitts Industrial Estate, Sommerhill, Birmingham B1 2PD
Tel 0121 236 3360
Fax 0121 236 7582
Suppliers of monitors, large screen video projectors and screens, videowalls, cameras and most formats of video players/recorders for hire short/long term.

## PROJECTION AND DISPLAY SERVICES LTD
Newton Works, Stanlake Mews, Stanlake Villas, London W12 7HS
Tel 0181 749 2201
Fax 0181 740 8481
Rental of Audio Visual Equipment.

## RESOURCES CENTRE LIMITED
Cambridge House, 128 Park Road, Camberley, Surrey GU15 2LW
Tel 01276 670000
Fax 01276 670010
Comprehensive audio visual and video service. Provision of technical operators and engineers, and all audio visual resource equipment. Production of audio visual programming.

## THE SCREEN COMPANY
182 High Street, Cottenham, Cambridge CB4 4RX
Tel 01954 250139
Fax 01954 252005
Projection Screens and similar equipment.

## SLX STUDIO FACILITIES
Victoria Road, Avonmouth, Bristol BS11 9DB
Tel 0117 982 6260
Fax 0117 982 7778
Studio Hire & Facilities.

## STAGE ELECTRICS
Victoria Road, Avonmouth, Bristol BS11 9DB
Tel 0117 982 7282
Fax 0117 982 2180
Cofton Road, Marsh Barton, Exeter EX2 8QW
Tel 01392 255868
Fax 01392 410592
2 Parkway Industrial Estate, Plymouth PL5 8LH
Tel 01752 269444
Fax 01752 228283
Dartmouth Road, Smethwick, West Midlands B66 1AX
Tel 0121 525 4545
Fax 0121 525 2413
Hire, sales, installation and service. Production services for lighting designers, theatre and commercial events.
e-mail hire@stage-electrics.co.uk
e-mail sales@stage-electrics.co.uk
website www.stage-electrics.demon.co.uk

## STAGETEC
383 Sykes Road Trading Industrial Estate, Slough SL1 4SP
Tel 0121 236 2102
Stagetec provide a complete design, supply, installation and maintenance service for a comprehensive range of sound, lighting and staging products. They are also UK distributor for the world renowned range of Compulite's lighting controls desks, dimmers and scrollers aswell as FLY's intelligent lights.

## TMB ASSOCIATES
The Old Brick Yard, Estbourne Road, Brentford, Middx TW8 9PG
Tel 0181 560 9652
Fax 0181 560 1064
e-mailmt@tmb.com
Website www.tmb.com
Contact: Mark Thompson
Value added distributor of production lighting equipment and sound and lighting cabling. The range covers all major US and European production lighting and hardware including all touring all touring expandable supplies.

## TRANTEC
## BBM ELECTRONICS GROUP LIMITED.
Kestrel House, Garth Road, Morden, Surrey SM4 4LP

Tel 0181 330 3111
Fax 0181 330 3222
e-mail enquiries@trantec.co.uk
Website www.trantec.co.uk
Contact: Chris Gilbert
Trantec offer a full range of both VHF and UHF radio microphones for all theatrical performances. All Trantec products are designed and manufactured in the UK and are fully DTI approved.

**TSL AV LTD**
Studio 9, 75 Filmer Road, London SW6 7JF
Tel 0171 371 5020
Fax 0171 371 0503
Managing Director: Matthew Griffiths
AV equipment hire. Conference Production services.

# 24
# FIRE & SAFETY

**ANTIFYRE LTD**
Unit 16, River Road Business Park, 33 River Road, Barking, Essex IG11 0DA
Tel 0181 591 3433
Fax 0181 591 2113

**ARNOLD LAVER (FLAMEPROOFED BOARDS) LTD**
Station Road, Theale, Reading, Berkshire RG7 4AA
Tel 0118 930 4777
Fax 0118 930 4888
Specialist suppliers of Flame Retardent Plywood Chipboard, MDF, Hardboard & Softwood to Class '1' and Class '0'.

**BLACKOUT**
208 Durnsford Road, London SW19 8DR
Tel 0181 944 8840
Fax 0181 944 8850
e-mail mail@blackout-ltd.com
BLACKOUT specialises in the manufacture, for hire or sale, of high quality, flame- proof drapes and starcloths for conferences, trade shows, film, television or photographic studios, theatres and concert productions. We can also provide scenic backdrops to any size, painted to specific specifications.

**J W BOLLOM & CO LTD**
PO Box 78, Croydon Road, Beckenham, Kent BR3 4BL
Tel 0181 658 2299
Fax 0181 658 8672
15 Theobalds Road, London WC1 8SN
Tel 0171 242 0313
Fax 0171 831 2457
314/316 Old Brompton Road, London SW5
Tel 0171 370 3252
Fax 0171 370 3253
Unit 7, King William Enterprise Park, Salford M5 2UP
Tel 0161 876 4898
Fax 0161 876 5104
Unit 2, Windmill Industrial Estate, Birmingham Road, Allesley, Coventry CV5 9QE
Tel 01203 405151
Fax 01203 404978
Moreton Hall Industrial Estate, Easlea Road, Bury St. Edmunds, IP32 7BY
Tel 01284 765252
Fax 01284 765253
121 South Liberty Lane, Ashton Vale, Bristol BS3 2SZ
Tel 0117 966 5151

Fax 0117 966 7180
Flame retardant paints, solutions and coatings for upgrading existing materials and substrates to meet fire regulations.
Manufacturers and Distributors of flame retardant paints and solutions for fabrics.

**BRISTOL (UK) LTD**
12 The Arches, Maygrove Road, London NW6 2DS.
Tel 0171 624 4370
Fax 0171 372 5242
Manufactures of flame retardant paints and intumescent coatings for all scenic applications.  Complete product range is water based and non-toxic.

**CHUBB FIRE LTD**
Chubb House, Sunbury-on-Thames, Middx TW16 7SL
Tel 01932 785588
Fax 01932 765630
Portable and fixed fire protection systems and equipment.

**CLEANRITE**
112 Besley Street, Streatham, London SW16 6BD.
Tel 0181 769 9834/0181 549 7346
Fax 0181 677 2553
Flame retardant curtain processing to BS5867 Part 2.

**DONMAR LTD**
54 Cavell Street, Whitechapel, London E1 2HP
Tel 0171 790 1166
Fax 0171 790 6634
Flamebar flame retardent solutions for natural and man made materials. Poliac flame retardent lacquer. Flame resistant scenic and drape materials with on site measuring, making and installation service. Electrical Installation and Portable Appliance Testing and Certification for licensing and Health and Safety.

**ERSKINE SYSTEMS LTD**
(Division of Dale Power Systems Plc)
Salter Road, Eastfield, Scarborough, Yorkshire YO11 3DU
Tel 01723 583511
Fax 01723 581231
Emergency lighting systems manufacturers.

**FLAMEBAR LTD.**
Chestnut Industrial Estate, Bassingham, Lincs. LN5 9LL
Tel 01522 788818
Fax 01522 788890
Flame retarding solutions to British Standard levals for fabrics, wood, cardboard, paper, canvas, emulsion paint and scenery. Flamebar PE6, Flamebar N5, Flamebar S3 and Flamebar ACE6  for artificial and dried plants. Poliac flame retardant clear lacquer for canvas, wood etc. Flame retardant adhesives. Suppliers to the industry for 25 years. Stockists in London and around U.K. Contact Flamebar for details or data sheets. Also flame retarding carried out on site.

**THE GENERAL FIRE APPLIANCE COMPANY LTD**
Wistons Lane, Elland, West Yorkshire HX5 9DS
Tel 01422 377521
Fax 01422 377524
Fire Fighting Equipment.

**J&C JOEL LTD**
Corporation Mill, Corporation Street, Sowerby Bridge, Halifax HX6 2QQ
Tel 01422 833835
Fax 01422 835157/839642
e-mail mail@joel.demon.co.uk

Distributor and supplier of fittings and hardware for flight cases and loudspeaker cabinets. Own brand stands for lighting, sound and musical instruments.
Sole distributor of Klotz Cables and Stage Boxes, Amphenol Audio Connectors, Palmer Professional Audio Tools and Power Amplifiers.

Unit 3, The Cordwainers
Temple Farm Industrial Estate, Sutton Road,
Southend-on-Sea, Essex, SS2 5RU.
Tel: 01702 613922 Fax: 01702 617168 E-Mail: mail@adamhall.co.uk

Theatrical drape manufacturers. Specialists in flame retardant fabrics.

### KINGDOM INDUSTRIAL SUPPLIES LIMITED
6/10 Bancrofts Road, Eastern Industrial Estate, South Woodham Ferrers, Essex CM3 5UQ
Tel 01245 322177
Fax: Sales: 01245 325878
Fax: Administration 01245 328936
e-mail sales@kingdomgroup.demon.co.uk
Website www.kingdomgroup.demon.co.uk
Contact: Debby Harding - Technical Manager
Suppliers of safety signage, protective clothing equipment and allied industrial consumables.

### PERROTTS LTD
Macauley Street, Leeds LS9 7SN
Tel 0113 243 3801
Fax 0113 243 5608
Directors: S Haskel, W B Tate, A V Bradfield
Cleaners & Flame-proofers of piece goods and made up curtains.

### PHOTAIN CONTROLS PLC
Rosseter Estate, Ford Aerodrome, Arundel, West Sussex BN18 0BE
Tel 01903 721531
Fax 01903 726795
Telex 87325
Smoke detection systems. Multiplexed data management systems.

### RACAL HEALTH & SAFETY
12-16 Bristol Road, Greenford, Middlesex UB6 8XT
Tel 0990 168118
Fax 0181 832 8799
Contact: Audrey Cooper
Safety Equipment suppliers.

### SAUNDERS-ROE DEVELOPMENTS LTD
Millington Road, Hayes, Middlesex
Tel 0181 573 3800
Fax 0181 561 3436
Makers of "Betalight" self powered safety signs.

### STAGE ELECTRICS
Victoria Road, Avonmouth, Bristol BS11 9DB
Tel 0117 982 7282
Fax 0117 982 2180
Cofton Road, Marsh Barton, Exeter EX2 8QW
Tel 01392 255868
Fax 01392 410592
Parkway Industrial Estate, Plymouth PL6 8LH
Tel 01752 269444
Fax 01752 228283
Dartmouth Road, Smethwick, West Midlands B66 1AX

Tel 0121 525 4545
Fax 0121 525 2413
"Hire, Sales, Installation and Service. Production services for lighting designers, theatre and commercial events".
e-mail hire@stage-electrics.co.uk
e-mail sales@stage-electrics.co.uk
website www.stage-electrics.demon.co.uk

### STOCKSIGNS LTD
Ormside Way, Redhill, Surrey RH1 2LG
Tel 01737 764764
Fax 01737 763763
All types of signs from stock or specially made to order. Safety signs are the main business. Please ask for free quotation.

### THORN SECURITY LIMITED
Security House, The Summit, Hanworth Road, Sunbury-on-Thames, Middlesex TW16 5DB.
Tel 01932 743333
Fax 01932 743155
Fire protection, intruder detection and alarm CCTV, access control and building management systems.

### UK FIRE INTERNATIONAL LTD
The Safety Centre, Mountergate, Norwich NR1 1PY
Tel 01603 727000
Fax 01603 727072
Fire extinguisher manufacturer/supplier. Also fire alarms, emergency lighting, security equipment, including CCTV
5 Regional branches: Bournemouth, Chelmsford, Corby, Milford Haven, Peterlee.

### WALK-OVERS LTD
PO Box 322, Thatcham, Berkshire RG19 3ZH
Tel 01635 865774
Fax 01635 874858
Contact: Barbara Carmichael
Manufacture of safety cable ramps for prevention of accidents and cable damage. 3 sizes available for all lighting and sound cable.

## 25
# FLIGHT CASES & PACKING CHESTS

### ADDA SUPER CASES LIMITED
P.O. Box 366, Cambridge, CB4 5AX
Tel 01223 233101
Fax 01223 233080
Directors: Monica Saunders, Cheryl Bereznyckyj
ADDA have been supplying cases to the entertainment industry for 20 years. Cases can be made to order in either fibre, polypropylene or aluminium. Alternatively, you can choose from their extensive range held in stock.

### ANGLO PACIFIC INTERNATIONAL PLC
Unit 1 Bush Industrial Estate, Standard Road, London NW10 6DF.
Tel 0181 965 1955
Fax 0181 965 4954
Ocean Freight, Air Freight, Trucking, Full Carnet Services, Forwarders to the performing arts.

**CONTRACT AUDIO VISUAL**
Unit F2, Bath Road Trading Estate, Stroud,
Gloucestershire GL5 3QF
Tel 01453 751865
Fax 01453 751866
e-mail sales@cav.co.uk

**CP CASES LTD**
The Dock Office, Trafford, Saifod Quays M5 2XB
Tel 0161 873 8181
Fax 0161 876 6599
e-mail sales@cpcases.com
Website www.cpcases.com/cpcases
Marketing: Karl Haw
Sales Contact: David Hindle
Unit 11, Worton Hall Industrial Estate, Worton Road,
Isleworth, Middx TW7 6ER.
Tel 0181 568 1881
Fax 0181 568 1141
Specialists in the design and manufacture of protective
cases for sensitive and valuable equipment used in the
lighting and sound industry.
Also flight cases, packway cases, 19" rack cases and
19" accessories, collapsible equipment trolleys and
protective bags and covers.

**JAMES CARTONS AND TEA CHESTS**
209a Fernside Avenue, Hanworth Park, Middlesex
TW13 7BQ
Tel 0181 751 1009
Fax 0181 384 7608
Hire and sale of new and once used printed and plain
tea chests and cartons.

**FUTURIST LIGHT & SOUND LTD**
Hoyle Head Mills, New Street, Earlsheaton,
Dewsbury, West Yorks WF12 8JJ

Tel 01924 468183
Fax 01924 458667
Full range of standard fligfht cases and special
bespoke design and manufacture service.

**ADAM HALL LTD**
Unit 3, The Cordwainers, Temple Farm Industrial
Estate, Sutton Road, Southend on Sea, Essex
SS2 5RU
Tel 01702 613922
Fax 01702 617168
Email: mail@adamhall.co.uk
Distributor and supplier of fittings and hardware for
flight cases and loudspeaker cabinets. Own brand
stands for lighting, sound and musical instruments.
Sole distributor of Klotz cables and Stage Boxes,
Amphenol Audio Connectors, Palmer Professional
Audio Tools and Power Amplifiers.

**JOHN HENRY ENTERPRISES**
16/24 Brewery Road, London N7 9NH
Tel 0171 609 9181
Fax 0171 700 7040
Contact: Pepin Clout or Will Wright

**OAKLEIGH CASES LTD**
10 Summit Centre, Summit Road,
Potters Bar EN6 3QW
Tel 01707 655011
Fax 01707 646447
Designers and manufacturers of a full range of flight
cases for Lighting and Audio Visual Equipment, props,
wigs and all things theatrical.

**SSE HIRE LTD**
201 Coventry Road, Birmingham B10 0RA
Tel 0121 766 7170
Fax 0121 766 8217
Contact: Leon Newman
Manufacture of professional flightcases for any item
from a microphone to a grand piano.
Range of finishes available.

**26**

# FLIGHT CASE LABELS

**N.E. PRINT LTD**
1 Stephens Road, St.Ives, Cambridgeshire PE17 4WJ
Tel 01480 492851
Fax 01480 493417
Contact: Peter Randall
Manufacturers of flight case labels, equipment labels,
touring labels, cable and cable coding labels, printed
vinyl tapes and floor graphics.

**27**
# FLOORS & FLOOR COVERING

**BIGGS FURNISHERS (LONDON) LTD**
2/4 Southgate Road, Islington, London N1 3JJ
Tel 0171 254 4385
Fax 0171 241 2164
Any make of British carpet and most makes of furniture
and fabrics supplied. Personal attention, reliable
service and competitive prices.

**BRISTOL U.K.**
12 The Arches, Maygrove Road, London NW6 2DS
Tel 0171 624 4370
Fax 0171 372 5242

**CREFFIELDS (TIMBER & BOARDS ) LTD**
Unit 6, Marcus Close, Tilehurst, Reading, Berkshire
RG30 4EA

Tel 01734 453533
Fax 01734 453633
email: creffields@patrol.i-way.co.uk
Contact: Nigel Creffield
Creffields is one of the UK's leading suppliers of flame retardant timber and boards for the theatre, TV and film. Large stocks are held allowing for urgent orders delivered promptly.

**DIRECTA (UK) LIMITED**
Cold Norton, Essex CM3 6UA
Tel 01621 828882
Fax 01621 828072
Tapes for instant repair, tapes for reliable laying, Vinyl Studio Flooring and much much more. Call Directa for a FREE catalogue 01621 828882

**ENTERTAINMENT SEATING LTD**
The Windmill Centre, Hamilton Street, Saltcoats, Ayrshire KA21 5DY
Tel 01294 469783/602554
Fax 01294 467093
Auditorium, theatre and cinema seating specialists. Reconditioning service, including on site. Also carpets and drapes.

**FORBO-NAIRN LTD**
PO Box 1, Kirkcaldy, Fife KY1 2SB
Tel Head Office-01592 643111
Sales 01592 643777
Fax 01592 643999
Manufacturer of linoleum, contract vinyl and cushioned vinyl floor coverings.

**FUTURIST LIGHT & SOUND LTD**
Hoyle Head Mills, New Street, Earlsheaton, Dewsbury, West Yorks WF12 8JJ
Tel 01924 468183
Fax 01924 458667
Full range stocked of all types of studio and dance studio and stage flooring and tiles.

**GILT EDGE CARPETS LTD**
255 New Kings Road, London SW6 4RB
Tel 0171 731 2588
Fax 0171 736 3042
Carpet suppliers and layers. Also Hardwood flooring.

**HARLEQUIN (British Harlequin plc)**
Bankside House, Vale Road, Tonbridge, Kent TN9 1SJ
Tel 01732 367666
Fax 01732 367755
Harlequin supplies a comprehensive range of stage and studio floorings for all stage applications - dance, drama, opera, exhibitions, shows, touring rock bands, concerts. We lay hardwood and sprung floors for stage and studios. Also special dance tapes, gaffer and cleaning materials.

**LE MARK TVS**
Unit 24, Stephenson Road, St. Ives, Huntingdon, Cambridgeshire PE17 4WJ
Tel 01480 494540
Fax 01480 494206
Director: Stuart Gibbons
UK Sales Director: Linda Gibbons
Sales Advisor: Nicola Jones
Suppliers and approved distributors of self-adhesive single and double sided tapes. Also 'studio flooring' with removable or permanent adhesive grades. Please Note: Le Mark TVS division for T.V. & Theatre industry.

**MALTBURY LTD**
Arch 651, Tower Bridge Business Complex, Clements Road, London SE16 4DG
Tel 0171 252 3700
Fax 0171 252 3710
Contact: Philip Sparkes
The Steeldeck specialist. Platforms and seating tiers for hire (wet or dry) and sale. Largest rental stock in UK. New decks in stock in major sizes. Agents nationwide.

**MARQUEES OVER LONDON**
Unit 15, Ferrier Street Industrial Estate, Old York Road, Wandsworth, London SW18 1SR.
Tel 0181 875 1966
Fax 0181 875 9008
Dance floor hire.

**N.E. PRINT LTD**
1 Stephens Road, St.Ives, Cambridgeshire PE17 4WJ
Tel 01480 492851
Fax 01480 493417
Contact: Peter Randall
Manufacturers of 'Floor Graphics', 'Printed Vinyl Tapes' and 'Studio Flooring Labels'.

**P&O EXHIBITION SERVICES LTD**
Unit 1, N.E.C., Birmingham B40 1PJ
Tel 0121 780 2011
Fax 0121 782 2880
Hire of furniture, floorcoverings and floral.

**ENA SHAW LTD**
22-26 Duke Street, St. Helen's Merseyside WA10 2JR
Tel 01744 731333
Fax 01744 451613
All types of carpets and floorcoverings, curtains and stage curtains supplied and fitted.

**STAGE ELECTRICS**
Victoria Road, Avonmouth, Bristol BS11 9DB
Tel 0117 982 7282
Fax 0117 982 2180
Cofton Road, Marsh Barton, Exeter EX2 8QW
Tel 01392 255868
Fax 01392 410592
Parkway Industrial Estate, Plymouth PL6 8LH
Tel 01752 269444
Fax 01752 228283
Dartmouth Road, Smethwick, West Midlands B66 1AX
Tel 0121 525 4545
Fax 0121 525 2413
Hire, Sales, Installation and Service.  Production
services for lighting designers, theatre and commercial
events.
e-mail hire@stage-electrics.co.uk
e-mail sales@stage-electrics.co.uk
Website www.stage-electrics.demon.co.uk

**VARIA TEXTILE LTD**
197 Kings Rd, Kingston-on-Thames, Surrey KT2 5JH
Tel 0181 549 8590
Fax 0181 549 8290
Contact: Karl Leuthenmayr
We have in stock a complete range of fire resistant
products. We also arrange for fabric to be made up.
Please ask for a quatation.

**VIGERS HARDWOOD FLOORING SYSTEMS**
Beechfield Walk, Sewardstone Road, Waltham Abbey,
Essex EN9 1AG
Tel 01992 711133
Fax 01992 717744

**WALK-OVERS LTD**
PO Box 322, Thatcham, Berkshire RG19 3ZH
Tel 01635 865774
Fax 01635 874858
Contact: Barbara Carmichael
Manufacturer of safety cable ramps for prevention of
accidents and cable damage, 3 sizes available for all
lighting and sound cables

# 28

# FLORAL DISPLAYS & PLANT HIRE

**ABOUT PLANTS**
8 Cedar Avenue, Blackwater, Camberley, Surrey
GU17 OJF.
Tel 01276 32460

**A E SAWDEN**
59 Southcote Avenue, Feltham, Middlesex TW13 4EQ.
Tel 0181 890 6699

**BAKERS FARM NURSERY**
Craigwell Avenue, Feltham, Middx TW13 7JR
Tel/Fax 0181 890 2144

**CHATTELS DRIED FLOWERS**
53 Chalk Farm Road, London NW1 8AN
Tel 0171 267 0877

**DANN ZWART DISPLAY**
Lower Ground Floor, 145 Tottenham Court Road,
London W1P 9LL.
Tel 0171 388 7488
Fax 0171 388 7499

**DIRECT FLOWER**
69 Ramley Road, Pennington, Lymington, Hampshire
SO41 8GY.
Tel 01590 670670
Fax 01590 670671

**DORSET GARDENS**
3 Ranelagh Avenue, London SW6
Tel 0171 736 2863

**FLOWERS UNLIMITED**
The Arches, 64  Patcham Terrace, London SW8 4BP
Tel 0800 783 7780
Mobile 0850 568678

**GARDENIA OF LONDON**
337 Upper Richmond Road West, London SW14 8QR
Tel 0181 878 1303
Fax 0181 878 7914

**GDC (GOOD DESIGN CORPORATION)**
1 St Rule Street, Battersea, London SW8 3ED
Tel 0171 498 8800
Fax 0171 498 9900
Event decorators.

**HANGING GARDEN**
c/o MJS Garden Centre, Wildmoor Lane, Sherfield on
Loddon, Basingstoke, Hampshire RG27 OJD.
Tel 01256 880647
Fax 01256 880651

**IMAGES**
Lingfield Lodge Farmhouse, Marsh Green,
Edenbridge, Kent TN8 5QS.
Tel 01732 864113
Fax 01732 866403

**IMPRESSIVE DISPLAYS**
17-19 The Parade, Oadby, Leicester LE2 5BB.
Tel 0116 271 2443
Fax 0116 271 0914

**PALM BROKERS LTD**
Cenacle Nursery, Taplow Common Road, Burnham,
Bucks SL1 8NW.
Tel 01628 663734
Fax 01628 661047

**PEEBLES EXHIBITION FLORIST LTD**
Fillongley Mill Farm, Tamworth Road, Fillongley,
Coventry CV7 8DZ.
Tel 01676 542234
Fax 01676 42456

**PETAL PARTNERS**
Highlands, 51a Brook Drive, Corsham,
Wiltshire SN13 9AX
Tel 01249 712020
Fax 01249 701313

**SANDRA IN ST MARYS DESIGNER FLORIST**
2 St Marys Street, Lincoln LN5 7EQ
Tel 01522 510688

**SERCO LTD**
254 Kings Drive,  Eastbourne, East Sussex BN21 2XE
Tel/Fax 01323 502883

**SILWOOD PARK NURSERIES**
Cheapside Road, Ascot, Berkshire SL5 7QY.
Tel 01344 21354
Fax 01344 872740

**STROUDS OF LONDON**
Rochester Square, Off Camden Road, London
NW1 9SD.
Tel 0171  485 5514
Fax 0171 267 2166

# 29
# FLYING BALLET & FLYING EFFECTS

**EUGENES FLYING EFFECTS**
71 Boltons Lane, Pyrford, Woking, Surrey.
Tel 01932 341616
We can fly people and props.  Recent work
MacDonalds Ad., Drop the Dead Donkey 4.

**FLYING BY FOY LTD**
Unit 4, Borehamwood Enterprise Centre, Theobald
Street, Borehamwood, Herts WD6 4RQ
Tel 0181 236 0234
Fax 0181 236 0235
Mobile 0468 436977
High quality Flying Effects for stage, TV, Film, Video
and Promotions etc.

**HI-FLI LTD**
4 Boland Drive, Manchester  M14 6DS
Tel/Fax 0161 224 6082
Personnel and prop flying effects. Rigs available for
most venues and budgets.

# 30
# HOSPITALITY AGENTS

**ABBEY LEISURE**
75 Wilton Road, London SW1V 1DE
Tel 0171 222 3356
Fax 0171 233 6384
Contact: Mark Aljoe

**MIKE BURTON CORPORATE HOSPITALITY**
Bastion House, Brunswick Road, Gloucester
GL1 1JJ
Tel 01452 419666
Fax 01452 309146
Hospitality Manager: Sue Stanlake

**CAVENDISH HOSPITALITY**
161-169 Uxbridge Road, London W13 9AU
Tel 0181 567 3530
Fax 0181 579 5237
Contact: Jim Bignal

**HUDSON HAYS HOSPITALITY LTD**
Unit 21, Hays Galleria, Tooley Street, London
SE1 2HD
Tel 0171 378 9090
Fax 0171 929 5483
Contact: Michael Quinn

**KEITH PROWSE HOSPITALITY**
Engineers WayWembley Stadium, Wembley,
Middlesex  HA9 0DT
Tel 0181 795 1111
Fax 0181 795 1188

**PALL MALL CORPORATE HOSPITALITY**
Sabadell House, 120 Pall Mall, London  SW1Y 5EA
Tel 0171 925 2222
Fax 0171 930 2008
Hospitality Managers: Joe Batey, Paul Berk

**UNIVERSAL EVENTS**
41 Loxley Road, Wandsworth, London SW18 3LL
Tel 0181 874 1234
Fax 0181 877 3829
Contact: Mardi Bland

# 31
# HOTEL BOOKING SERVICES

**THE APARTMENT SERVICE**
5-6 Francis Grove, Wimbledon, London SW19 4DT
Tel 0181 944 6744
Fax 0181 944 6744

**BRITANNIA HOTELS LTD**
35 Portland Street, Manchester M1 3LA
Tel 0161 228 2288
Fax 0161 236 9154

**BROMPTON TRAVEL LTD**
64-66 Richmond Road, Kingston Upon Thames, Surrey
KT2 5EH
Tel 0181 549 3334
Fax 0181 547 1160

**HOTEL BOOKING SERVICES LTD**
4 New Burlington Place, London W1X 1FB
Tel 0171 437 5052
Fax 0171 734 2124

**HOTELINE**
City Business Centre, Hyde Street, Winchester,
Hampshire SO23 7TA
Tel 01962 844004
Fax 01962 860974

**HOTELINK (UK) LTD**
Silver House, Church Lane, Lower Fyfield,
Marlborough, Wiltshire SN8 1PY
Tel 01672 861111
Fax 01672 861100

# 32
# INSURANCE

**ADAM BROTHERS CONTINGENCY LTD**
(LLOYDS BROKERS)
12 Camomile Street, London EC3A 7PN.
Tel 0171 638 3211
Fax 0171 374 0726
Contact: Mr Norris
Non-appearance insurance for Theatrical and Concert
Managements, Producers, Artistes and Agents.
Cancellation/Abandonment Insurance for all types of
events. "It is better to have insurance for 100 years
and not need it - than to need it for one day and not
have it."

**ARTHUR DOODSON (BROKERS) LTD**
219-225 Slade Lane, Levenshulme, Manchester
M19 2EX.
Tel 0161  225 9060
Fax 0161 224 6150
Specialists in entertainment insurance.

**DELOITTE & TOUCHE**
Hill House, 1 Little New Street, London EC4A 3TR
Tel 0171 936 3000
Fax 0171 583 8517
Contact: Charles Bradbrook/Robert Reed
Taxation and accounting services. We have wide
experience of West End and overseas theatrical
production, international licencing, VAT and witholding
tax planning.

**GALAXY 7 POLICIES**
21 Market Place, Abbey Gate, Nuneaton, Warks
CV11 5UH.
Tel 01203 326128
For all musical instrumental insurance.

**GORDON & CO**
4-43 London Fruit Exchange, Brushfield Street, London
E1 6EU
Tel: 0171 247 0841
Fax 0171 3751286
Director: Robert Israel
General Insurance for Theatrical Managements. Non

appearance and all types of Personal Insurance.

**HANOVER PARK GROUP PLC**
Greystoke House, 80-86 Westow Street, London
SE19 3AQ
Tel 0181 771 8844
Fax 0181 771 1697

**HEATH SCOTLAND**
97-99 West Regent Street, Glasgow G2 2BA.
Tel 0141 331 2660
Fax 0141 332 5103
A division of the worldwide Heath Group specialising in
theatre and related insurance throughout the U.K.
including cancellation cover.
Contact: Michael Russell ACII.

**G.M. IMBER LTD**
Grange House, Grange Walk, London SE1 3DT
Tel 0171 231 5005
Fax 0171 252 3656
Director: George M. Imber

**INSUREX EXPO-SURE**
The Pantiles House, 2 Nevill Street, Royal Tunbridge
Wells, Kent TN2 5TT
Tel 01892 511500
Fax 01892 510016
Sales Director: Stephen Warner

**KEEVIL MCINTOSH GIBSON LIMITED**
Shepheards Hurst, Green Lane, Outwood, Surrey
RH1 5QS.
Tel 01342 844000
Fax 01342 844554
Contacts: Patrick McIntosh, Norman Hughes.
Specialists in all insurance for Managements (including
non-appearance) and for all personal insurance for
members of the Entertainment profession, including
Life Mortgages and Pensions.

**LAYTON BLACKHAM INSURANCE BROKERS**
51 Lincoln's Inn Fields, London WC2A 3LZ
Tel 0171 404 6363
Fax 0171 242 8306

**NYMAN LIBSON PAUL**
Chartered Accountants
124 Finchley Road, London NW3 5JS.
Tel 0171 794 5611
Fax 0171 431 1109
Financial success in the entertainment industry
depends on people, not just balance sheets.  Our
expertise is widely recognised with services including
corporate and personal tax, auditing and accounts
preparation.

**ROBERTSON TAYLOR INSURANCE BROKERS LTD**
Lloyds Brokers, Members of BIIBA
33 Harbour Exchange Square, London E14 9GG
Tel 0171 538 9840
Fax 0171 538 9919
Contacts: John Silcock, Susan Payne
55 Fulham High Street, London SW6 3JJ.
Tel 0171 731 1454
Fax 0171 736 4803
Contacts: Willie Robertson, Martin Goebbels
Specialist insurance Brokers to the Entertainment
Industry, including first class insurance and risk
management advice to all aspects of Music, Theatre,
TV, Film, Video, Conference, Exhibitions and Sports.

**THEATRES MUTUAL**
Eagle Star Insurance, 22 Arlington Street, London

SW1A 1RW
Tel 0171 929 1111
Fax 0171 409 1784
Underwriter: Adrian Bell
Specialists in insurance for theatres and theatrical
productions both amateur and professional.

### WALTON & PARKINSON LIMITED
20 St.Dunstan's Hill, London EC3R 8PP
Tel 0171 929 4747
Fax 0171 929 4884
e-mail: GB8BFH3J@IBMMAIL.com
Contact: Richard Walton and Cliff Parkinson
Specialist insurance brokers to theatre owners,
producers and suppliers with competitive schemes for
all aspects of theatre, including non-appearance,
cancellation and other contingency risks, hazardous
work, and productions themselves.

### WOODHAM GROUP LTD
17 Fircrost Close, Woking, Surrey GU22 7OZ
Tel 01483 770787
Fax 01483 750302

## 33
# LEAFLET DISTRIBUTORS

### ARTS CONTACT
99 High Street, Morley, Leeds LS27 ODE
Tel 0113 252 7356
Tel 0831 166692/0860 374723
A unique creative bulk distribution service for Arts
publicity print, for any arts event, anywhere in the U.K.

### ARTS MARKETING HAMPSHIRE
Mottisfont Court, High Street, Winchester, Hants
SO23 8ZD.
Tel 01962 865383
Fax 01962 841644
Regional marketing agency for arts in Hampshire,
offeringsupport for audience development projects;
market research; marketing consultancy; tactical
services - mailing, print distribution, audience profiling,
database mapping, telesales, listings magazine, www
listings, press contacts listings.

### BROCHURE DISPLAY LTD
Century Point, Halifax Road, Cressex, High Wycombe,
Bucks, HP12 3SL
Tel 01494 888500
Fax 01494 436914
Display and distribution of brochures for the
entertainment and leisure industry.  Targeted
audiences and weekly merchandising to ensure cost
effective control of advertising print.

### IMPACT DISTRIBUTION SERVICES
Culford House, 1-7 Orsman Road, London N1 5RA
Tel 0171 729 5978
Fax 0171 729 5994
e-mail admin@impact.uk.com
Website www.impact.uk.com
Contact: Zol Hoffmann
The organisation for leaflet and poster distribution
within the arts.  We offer direct and flexible services to
the venues and places you want to be seen in. Make

your mark and target with Impact.

### THEATRE DESPATCH LTD
Azof Hall, Azof Street, London SE10 OEG.
Tel 0181 853 0750
Fax 0181 293 4861
Theatre Despatch is a flexible and comprehensive
distribution service including 1,500 leaflet racks, 4,500
other regularly serviced outlets throughout Greater
London, poster distribution, a complete mailing service
including Mailsort, and a database of 60,000 people
and organisations interested in one or more of the arts
and entertainments.

## 34
# LEGAL SERVICES

### ADAM BROTHERS CONTINGENCY LTD
(LLOYDS BROKERS)
12 Camomile Street, London EC3A 7BP
Tel 0171 638 3211
Fax 0171 374 0726
Contact: Mr Norris
Non-appearance Insurance for Theatrical and Concert
Managements, Producers, Artistes and Agents.
Cancellation/Abandonment Insurance for all types of
events. "It is better to have insurance for 100 years and not
need it - than to need it for one day and not have it."

### ADDIS & CO
Emery House, 192 Heaton Moor Road, Stockport,
Cheshire SK4 4DU
Tel 0161 432 3307
Fax 0161 432 3376
Certified Accountants.

### ALL CLEAR DESIGNS LIMITED
3rd Floor, Cooper House, 2 Michael Road,
London SW6 2ER
Tel 0171 384 2950/2951
Fax 0171 384 2951
email: allclear@easynet.co.uk
Director: James Holmes-Siedle
Specialists in making buildings accessible for disabled
people.  Architectural services include access audits,
feasibility studies and construction.  Experience with
theatres and listed buildings.  Assistance with advice
with funding included.

### BENTON & COMPANY ARCHITECTS
33 Northgate, Sleaford, Lincolnshire NG34 7BX.
Tel 01529 304 524
Fax 01529 306981
Unravel the mysteries of Building for the Arts by
contacting Benton & Company Architects of Sleaford,
Lincolnshire, who normally make no charge for an
initial visit.  they offer a nationwide, prompt,  proficient,
pertinent and personal service.

### LAWRENCE BLACKMORE
Suite 5, 26 Charing Cross Road, London  WC2H 0DG
Tel 0171 240 1817
Fax 0171 836 3156
Theatre Production Accountant. Production and
running cost estimation, budgeting and general
evaluation of theatrical ventures. Financial and
management accounting systems analysis and
organisation.

# HARBOTTLE & LEWIS

*Contact: Alice Rayman*

Hanover House, 14 Hanover Square
London, W1R 0BE
t. 0171 667 5000  f. 0171 667 5100

dx. 44617 Mayfair
hal@harbottle.co.uk
http://www.harbottle.co.uk

**ROBERT CARTER**
8, West Street, Covent Garden, London EC2H 9NG
Tel 0171 836 2785
Fax 0171 836 2786
Email cartelaw@ecna.org
Solicitor - Copywirght, Media and Entertainment Law.

**CAMPBELL HOOPER**
35 Old Queen Street, London SW1H 9JD
Tel 0171 222 9070
Fax 0171 222 5591
email: dmw@campbell-hooper.co.uk
Contacts: David Wills, Michael Oliver
With extensive experience in all areas of the
entertainment industry, we deal with all aspects of
theatre production and financing, in the West End and out-of-
town, and with overseas production and licensing.

**CARR & ANGIER**
The Old Malthouse, Clarence Street, Bath BA1 5NS
Tel 01225 446664
Fax 01225 446654
Consultancy services for the arts, entertainment and
conference industries. Feasibility studies, planning and
technical systems design for new and refurbishment
projects.

**CLINTONS SOLICITORS**
55 Drury Lane, London WC2B 5SQ
Tel 0171 379 6080
Fax 0171 240 9310
Contact: John Cohen and James Jones
We are solicitors specialising in the Entertainment
Industry and we have wide experience of all matters
relating to theatre, acting for producers, writers,
composers, designers, directors and performers.

**ARTHUR DOODSON (BROKERS) LTD**
219 - 225 Slade Lane, Levenshulme, Manchester
M19 2EX
Tel 0161 225 9060
Fax 0161 224 6150
Specialists in Entertainment Insurance.

**MURRAY EDWARDS AND ASSOCIATES**
Barracks Studios, 19 Barracks Square, Newcastle
Staffordshire ST5 1LG.
Tel/Fax: 01782 712732
Contact: Murray Edwards
Management consultancy: feasibility studies, marketing
analyses, financial appraisals, management review in
all aspects of the Arts and Entertainment Industry.

**JUDY FARQUHARSON LTD**
47 New Bond Street, London W1Y 9HA
Tel 0171 493 8824

Fax 0171 493 7161
A professional and confidential service of recruitment
advice and candidate selection, In addition to providing
high calibre permanent P.A.s, our temporary division can
assist you with first class temporary marketing, public
relations, market research, publishing and publications
staff.

**GALAXY 7 POLICIES**
21 Market Place, Abbey Gate, Nuneaton, Warks
CV11 5UH.
Tel 01203 326128
For all Musical Instrument Insurance.

**GENTLE JAYES SOLICITORS**
26 Grosvenor Street, London W1X OBD
Tel 0171 629 3304
Fax 0171 493 0246

**GODDARD & SMITH**
Head Office: 22 King Street, St. James's, London
SW1Y 6QZ
Tel 0171 930 7321
Fax 0171 930 7617
Main Personnel: Michael Biddle BSc FRICS;  Roger A.
Harper FRICS; Simon King.
Specialist Property Advisers to the Entertainment
Industry.

**HARBOTTLE & LEWIS SOLICITORS**
Hanover House, 14 Hanover Square,
London W1R 0BE
Tel 0171 667 5000
Fax 0171 667 5100
e-mail hal@harbottle.co.uk
Website www.harbottle.co.uk
Contact: Alice Rayman
The leading Media and Entertainment practice which
provides legal services to all areas of the UK Theatre,
both nationally and internationally.

**HARRISON CURTIS**
40 Great Portland Street, London W1N 5AH
Tel 0171 637 3333
Fax 0171 637 3334
Email mail@harrisoncurtis.co.uk
Contact Lawrence Harrison, Tim Curtis, Fiona King
Specialist entertainment and media lawyers. Large
theatre practice.

**HART-JACKSON & HALL**
3A Ridley Place, Newcastle-upon-Tyne NE1 8JQ
Tel 0191 232 7411
Fax 0191 232 0429
All aspects of Legal Work for The Entertainment

Industry.

**MICHAEL HOLDEN ASSOCIATES**
17 West Heath Drive, London NW11 7QG
Tel 0181 455 4640
Fax 0181 209 1059
Theatre Consultants, designers of new buildings or the
adaption and refurbishment of existing buildings.
Management Consultants experienced in the formation
of Trusts and other management structures.

**LASSETTER WILLIAMS**
Isgaerwen, Pentrellyncymer, Corwen  LL21 9TU
Tel/Fax 01490 420254
Partner: Michael Williams
Project management (new builidngs and
refurbishments), events management, feasibility
studies, lottery applications.

**KEEVIL MCINTOSH GIBSON LIMITED**
Shepheards Hurst, Green Lane, Outwood, Surrey,
RH1 5QS
Tel 01342 844000
Fax 01342 844554
Contact: Patrick McIntosh or Norman Hughes
Specialists in all insurance for Managements (including
non-appearance) and for all personal insurance for
members of the Entertainment profession, including
Life Mortgages and Pensions.

**MARKETSENSE**
41 Mansfield Street, Chester Green, Derby DE1 3RJ
Tel 01332 291264
Contacts: Robert Corder or Patricia Corder
Sponsorship Event Management.  Organisational
structures, marketing strategy, and  project
management.  Fundraising.

**MARTIN GREENE RAVDEN**
55 Loudoun Road, St. John's Wood, London NW8 0DL
Tel 0171 625 4545
Fax 0171 625 5265
Contact: David Ravden
Chartered Accountants and Business Managers -
Audit, Accountancy and Tax Compliance, Business
Management, Tour Accounting, Withholding Tax
Clearances, Royalty Examinations, Litigation Support.

**TODD MURRAY WS**
66 Queen Street, Edinburgh EH2 4NE
Tel 0131 226 4771
Fax 0131 467 7280
Email richard.findlay@todsmurray.co.uk
Contact: Richard Findlay, David Smith

**MUSICIANS BENEVOLENT FUND**
16 Ogle Street, London W1P 8JB.
Tel 0171 636 4481
Fax 0171 637 4307
The MBF gives help to professional musicians and
their dependants when illness, accident or old age
deprives them of their means of livelihood and its main
activity is providing advice and financial assistance.

**PANNELL KERR FORSTER**
New Garden House, 78 Hatton Garden,
London EC1N 8JA
Tel 0171 831 7393
Fax 0171 405 6736
e-mail Hotels@uk.pkf.com
Consulting services to the leisure, arts and
entertainment industry. Operational management and

marketing analysis, financial review and funding,
working, where necessary, in close association with
technical specialists in other professional disciplines.
Advice in the development of computer based
accounting and front of house systems. Audit,
accounting and taxation services.

**ROBERTSON TAYLOR INSURANCE BROKERS
LTD**
(International Lloyds Brokers, Members of BIIBA)
33 Harbour Exchange Square, London E14 9GG
Tel 0171 538 9840
Fax 0171 538 9919
Contacts: John Silcock, Susan Lee
55 Fulham High Street, London SW6 3JJ
Tel 0171 731 1454
Fax 0171 736 4803
Contacts: Willie Robertson, Martin Goebbels
Specialist Insurance Brokers to the Entertainment
Industry, including first class insurance and risk
management advice to all aspects of: Music, Theatre,
TV, Film, Video, Conference, Exhibitions and Sports.

**SIMKINS PARTNERSHIP, THE**
45-51 Whitfield Street, London W1P 6AA
Tel 0171 631 1050
Fax 0171 436 2744
Contact: Lawrence Harrison, David Franks or Tim
Curtis.
As one of the leading theatre practices in London we
advise on investment and all aspects of theatrical
production. Our experience includes worldwide
licensing as well as a wide range of West End,
Broadway and out of town productions and tours.

**TARLO LYONS SOLICITORS**
Watchmaker Court, 33 St. John's Lane,
London EC1M 4DB.
Tel 0171 405 2000
Fax 0171 814 9421
Tarlo Lyons is a broad-based commercial law firm, but
with a specialist niche practice in entertainment.
Partner D. Michael Rose has been solicitor to among
others, Cameron Mackintosh and his group of
companies since 1977.

**TECHNICAL PLANNING INTERNATIONAL**
The Stagehouse, Palace Road, Kingston, Surrey
KT1 2LG
Tel 0181 549 6535
Fax 0181 549 6545
Email: techplan@csi.com
Planning, space and equipment design services for
theatres, conference venues and concert halls. Design
of rigging, lighting, audio-visual and video
systems and equipment.

**THEATRES MUTUAL**
Eagle Star Insurance, 22 Arlington Street, London
SW1A 1RW
Tel 0171 929 1111
Fax 0171 409 1784
Underwriter: Adrian Bell
Specialists in insurance for theatres and theatrical
productions both amateur and professional.

**PEGGY THOMPSON**
296 Sandycombe Road, Kew, Richmond, Surrey
TW9 3NG
Tel 0181 332 1003
Fax 0181 332 1127
Business Management, Accounts Administration.

**TODS MURRAY**
66 Queen Street, Edinburgh EH2 4NE
Tel 0131 226 4771
Fax 0131 467 7280
e-mail: Richard.Findlay@todsmurray.co.uk
Contact: Richard Findlay, David Smith

**WOODHAM GROUP LTD**
Insurance Brokers
1 Goldsworth Road, Woking, Surrey GU21 1JU
Tel 01483 770787
Fax 01483 750302

# 35
# LIGHTING AND LIGHTING EQUIPMENT SUPPLIERS

**A1 LIGHTING LTD**
Unit 27, The Towers, Hill Top Road, Leeds,
West Yorkshire LS12 3SQ
Tel 0113 263 3777
Fax 0113 263 3770
Contact: Adrian Lee (Director)
Distributor of all theatre and front of house lamps, from
GE lighting,. Philips, Osram, Crompton and Sylvania.
Competitively priced, high quality service.

**A. C. LIGHTING LTD**
Unit 3, Spearmast Industrial Park, Lane End Road,
Sands, High Wycombe, Bucks HP12 4JG
Tel 01494 446000
Fax 01494 461024
email sales@aclighting.co.uk
Website www.aclighting.co.uk

**ACTION LIGHTING NORTH**
46 Kansas Avenue, Salford, Manchester M5 2GL
Tel 0161 876 0576
Fax 0161 876 0517

**AJS THEATRE LIGHTING & STAGE SUPPLIES LTD**
Hightown Industrial Estate, Crow Arch Lane,
Ringwood, Hampshire BH24 1ND.
Tel 01425 470888
Fax 01425 471398
email: sales@ajs.co.uk
Website: http://www.demon.co.uk/ajs
Managing Director: Adrian Sant
General Manager: Simon Sketchley
Sales Manager: Mark Morley 01425 480698
Selecon Sales Manager: Graham Fathers
01730 829732
Midlands Consultant: John Grisswell 01283 585168
S. E. Consultant: Mark Horseman 01424 720747
S. W. Consultant: Chris Coates 01425 480698
Sole UK importers and distributors: for Selecon.
Supply, installation and hire of CCT, Clay Paky,
Electrosonic, Helvar, Lee, Le Maitre, Optikinetics,
Martin Professional, Pulsar, Rosco, Zero 88.

**ANYTRONICS LIMITED**
Units 5 & 6 Hillside Industrial Estate, London Road,
Horndean, Hampshire PO8 0BL
Tel 01705 599410
Fax 01705 598723

Manufacturers of a range of high powered strobes,
modular lighting control systems plus a universal range
of switching/dimming power packs.

**ARENA CABLES**
Unit 5, Raynham Close, Raynham Road Industrial
Estate, Bishops Stortford, Herts CM23 5PJ.
Tel 01279 505531
Fax 01279 505534
Arena Cables is one of the countries leading suppliers
of cables and accessories for the lighting and sound
industries.

**ARIES**
Unit 2, Barrowmore Estate, Great Barrow, Chester
CH3 7JS
Tel/Fax 01829 741262
Design and manufacture of special lighting control
equipment, low voltage, Tivoli type and light curtains,
low voltage neon projects.

**ARK LIGHT (Theatre Lantern Restoration)**
Unit 163, Brunting Thorpe Industrial Estate, Nr. Lutterworth,
Leicestershire LE17 5QZ.
Tel 0116 247.8336
Fax 0116 247 8070
Mobile 0585 102922
Theatre, Film, Television lighting restored to their
original condition. Strand lanterns wanted - lanterns for
sale. We can also supply T/H conversion kits, silicon
cable, strand spares, colour frames, servicing and
preventative maintenance contracts. New lanterns of
any manufacture re-coloured to any BS or RAL number
to match architectural specifications.
Sales literature available.
Manager: Joanne Lake.

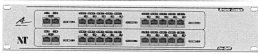

**ARTISTIC LICENCE (UK) LTD**
B1 + B3 Livingstone Court, Peel Road, Harrow, Middlesex HA3 7QT.
Tel 0181 863 4515
Fax 0181 863 4515
e-mail ARTISTIC@compuserve.com
Website www.ArtisticLicence.com
Contact: Tracy Patterson
Artistic Licence specialise in the custom design and manufacture of sophisticated stage lighting and motion control equipment.
Standard products include: Protocol Conversion, DMX & MIDI Test Equipment, PC Based Virtual Lighing control.

**ARRI (GB) LTD**
1-3 Airlinks, Spitfire Way, Heston, Middlesex TW5 9NR
Tel 0181 848 8881
Fax 0181 561 1312
Sales Director: Nick Shapley
Lighting Product Manager: Barrie Guy

**AVOLITES LTD**
184 Park Avenue, London NW10 7XL
Tel 0181 965 8522
Fax 0181 965 0290
Email: *username*@avolites.com
Website: www.avolites.com
Manufacture and sale of highest quality dimming systems memory and manual lighting control consoles. Dry hire department for all AVO products, including moving light's consoles.

**BENNETT & FOUNTAIN LTD**
Unit 9, Abercorn Commercial Centre, Manor Farm Road, Alperton, Middx HA0 1GF
Tel 0181 902 8821
Fax 0181 903 4963
Suppliers of lighting equipment. Commercial and domestic.

**BLACK LIGHT**
18 West Harbour Road, Granton, Edinburgh EH5 1PN
Tel 0131 551 2337
Fax 0131 552 0370
Email: mail@blackminuslight.com
Website: www.blackminuslight.com
Sales and hire of theatre lighting and staging equipment.

**CAITHNESS STAGE AND LIGHTING LTD**
3 Wellington Street, Paisley PA3 2JQ
Tel 0141 887 0949
Fax 0141 887 1175
Design, supply, installation and servicing of stage equipment and stage lighting. Also hire department. Dealers Zero 88 equipment.

**C.C.T. LIGHTING LTD**
London Office: 4 Tudor Court, Brighton Road, Sutton, Surrey SM2 5AE
Tel 0181 770 3636
Fax 0181 643 9848
Sales Administrator (London): Richard Lovejoy
Factory: Hindle House, Traffic Street, Nottingham NG2 1NE
Tel 0115 986 2722
Fax 0115 986 2546
Directors: Donald D. Hindle, David P Manners, George Chapman
C.C.T. Lighting introduced 'Freedom' a new line of profile spotlights in September 1995. This range includes 4 fixed and 4 variable beam tungsten

luminaires at 600w and 800w with light output near to current 1200w and 2000w profiles. An individual DMX dimmer, if required, is available to clip into the underside of the luminaire.

The familiar CCT brand names continue to run alongside this new range. All CCT products are available for sale or hire. UK distribution - direct or through distributors. Dealer list availble.

## CELCO
The Live Entertainment Division of Electrosonic Ltd, Hawley Mill, Hawley Road, Dartford, Kent
DA2 7SY
Tel 01322 282218
Fax 01322 282292
email: sales@celco.co.uk
Manufacturers of the finest Lighting Control Systems in the world.
Electrosonic, Hawley Mill, Hawley Road, Dartford, Kent
DA2 7SY
Tel 01322 222211
Fax 01322 282282
Manufacturers of dimming systems for house and auditorium lighting.

## CENTRAL THEATRE SUPPLIES
1186 Stratford Road, Birmingham B28 8AB
Tel 0121 778 6400
Fax 0121 702 2046
Birmingham based Central Theatre Supplies have a large hire department supplying professional stage lighting, control systems and effects. We sell products from many leading manufacturers. Consumables are always in stock.

## CEREBRUM LIGHTING LIMITED
Units 4 & 5, Shannon Commercial Centre, Beverley Way, New Malden, Surrey KT3 4PT
Tel 0181 949 3171 (6 Lines)
Fax (UK Sales) 0181 395 6111
Fax (Export Sales) 0181 949 3649
World wide wholesalers and Distributors to the TV, Theatre and Stage Lghting industry for over 25 years. Main distributors or stockists of Avolites, Axon, Anytronics, CCT, Celco, DHA, Jands, Jem, Le Maitre, Light Processor, Litestructures, Maris Ensing, Metro Audio, Mode Electronics, Multiform, Optikinetics, Powerdrive, Pulsar, Rainbow, Rosco, Strand, TFL, Thomas and Zero 88.
Trade counter open daily 9am - 5:30pm, Mon-Fri for sales and order collection.

## COMMERCIAL ELECTRONICS (JERSEY) LTD
Unit 4, Springside, Rue de la Monnaie, Trinity, Jersey JE3 5DG
Tel 01534 865858
Fax 01534 863759
Mobile 0979 720650
Sales Manager: David Wilson
Service Manager: Cristin Bouchet
Strand Lighting main dealers and service agents for the Channel Islands. Full lighting, Audio-Visual and Sound Hire facilities. Lamps, colour/diffusion medium, gaffa tape and other accessories always in stock. Dealers for Strand Lighting, Bose, AKG, Studiomaster.

## CONTRACT AUDIO VISUAL
Unit F2, Bath Road Trading Estate, Stroud, Gloucestershire GL5 3QF
Tel 01453 751865
Fax 01453 751866
e-mail sales@cav.co.uk

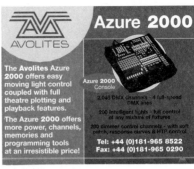

## CP SOUND
20 Crosslands, Chertsey South, Surrey KT16 9QY
Tel 01932 874354
Fax 01932 874355
Mobile 0836 216632
Sale, design and installation of professional sound, lighting and video equipment.

## CRD STAGEHIRE
23 Connaught Road, Seaford, East Sussex BN25 2PT
Tel 01323 895850
Theatrical equipment suppliers, lighting and effects hire service.

## CTL (Control Technology) LIMITED
Unit 2, Britannia Business Park, Quarry Wood, Aylesford, Maidstone, Kent ME20 7NT
Tel 01622 719151/2
Fax 01622 716425
Managing Director: Robert J. Owen
Design, supply, install and commission Sound systems, S.M., Communication Systems, Lighting Systems and Audio Visual Systems.

## CREATIVE SYSTEMS TECHNOLOGY
Sophia House, 28 Cathedral Road, Cardiff, South Glamorgan, Wales CF1 9LJ
Tel 01222 660142
Fax 01222 664891
Contact: Martin Howell
CST provide cost effective solutions whatever your needs. Lighting/Special Effects Design, Remote Control/Motor controlled systems, software management, security & tagging systems, together with an after sales service next to none.

## DAWSON-KEITH LTD
7th Floor, Enterprise House, Isambard Road, PO1 2RX
Tel 01705 882400
Stand-by generator manufacturers.

## DAYLIGHT DESIGNS (UK) LTD
Unit 163, Bruntingthorpe Industrial Estate, Nr. Lutterworth, Leicestershire LE17 5QZ
Tel 0116 247 8336
Fax 0116 247 8070
Email: daylight@easynet.co.uk
Website: www.daylightdesigns.co.uk
Contact: Peter Martindale and Ian Lake
MSR conversions to follow spots. Design, prototyping and supply of bespoke luminaires. Recolouring and refurbishment of luminaires. Supply our own design of barn doors and colour frames. Spares for older luminaires.

**DC LIGHTING LTD**
Unit 11, Harrier Park, Southmead Industrial Estate,
Didcot, Oxon OX11 7PL
Tel 01235 511003
Fax 01235 511004
D C Lighting Ltd carries a full range of branded Studio,
Theatre, Video and Photographic lamps. We can also
supply lanterns, cable, plugs, gel etc and offer a
friendly and efficient service. Account or credit card
facilities available.

**D E W**
222-228 Maybank Road, South Woodford, London
E18 1ET
Tel 0181 504 5832
Fax 0181 505 4845
Manufacturers and suppliers of a full range of standard
and customised lighting control systems for
professional and amateur theatre, television and video

studios and architectural application, including switch
patch and distribution panels.

**DHA LIGHTING LIMITED**
284-302 Waterloo Road, London SE1 8RQ
Tel 0171 771 2900
Fax 0171 771 2901
ISDN: 0171 401 9202
Email: custom.gobo@dhalighting.co.uk
General Manager: Diane Grant
Designers and manufacturers of Digital Light Curtains,
digital beamlights, moving effects, fibre optics, slides
and, of course, custom gobos and a wide range of
stock gobos.

**DONMAR LTD**
Donmar House, 54 Cavell Street, Whitechapel,
London E1 2HP
Tel 0171 790 1166 (Sales & Hire)
Tel 0171 790 6624 (Installation and Service)
Fax 0171 790 6634
Sales & service agents: ARRI, CCT, Pulsar, Strand
Lighting & Zero 88. Sales & hire of all theatre lighting
equipment, sale of Lee & Rosco filters and all
consumable items. Installation of complete stage &
studio lighting systems manufacture of custom internally
wired bars, control panel & socket boxes. Electrical
installation and PAT testing with certification (NICEIC)
Emergency out of hours service (Monday to Friday 1800 to
2300 and Saturday 0900 to 2300)
Tel: 0171 790 6624.

**DRAX LIGHTING AND SPECIAL EFFECTS**
Unit D9, Ivinghoe Industrial Estate, Houghton Regis,
Dunstable LU5 5BQ
Tel 01582 475614
Fax 01582 475669
Contact: Richard Foster
Suppliers of lighting, sound, effects and power
distribution. Hire with or without crew, long or short
term. Sales of equipment and consumables. Call now
for information or assistance.

**DRV**
Lower Tregenna, St. Columb Minor, Newquay,
Cornwall TR8 4HS
Tel 01637 875824
Fax 01637 876082
Contact: Roger Vinton
Provide design, supply, installation and maintenance
services for all types of audio and lighting systems.
The company specialises in custom software based
control systems for all types of facility.

**HOWARD EATON LIGHTING LTD.**
Winterlands, Resting Oak Hill, Cooksbridge, Lewes,
East Sussex BN8 4PR
Tel 01273 400670
Fax 01273 401052
Manufacture, supply, installation and service of Special
Effects, Custom Lighting, DMX Networks, Digital
Dimming, Cue Lights & S.M. Desks, Chain Hoist
Controls, Radio Controlled Lighting, Plugboxes &
Facility Panels. Hire of Genie Personnel Lifts.

**PHILIP L EDWARDS (Theatre Lighting)**
5 Highwood Close, Glossop, Derbyshire SK13 6PH
Tel/Fax 01457 862811 (24 hours)
Comprehensive Lighting Hire, Sales and Design
Service. Stockists of Filters. Spares and Pyrotechnics.
Brochure on request.

**ENTEC SOUND & LIGHT**
517 Yeading Lane, Northolt, Middx UB5 6LN
Tel 0181 842 4004
Fax 0181 842 3310
e-mail sound&light@entec.ftech.co.uk
Hire/Sale of Theatre, Film and Concert Lighting. Control equipment including Diamond, Sapphire and Whole Hog. Profiles, Fresnels, HMIs, Followspots and over 100 moving lights. All your trussing, motor and rigging needs.

**ENTERTAINMENT LIGHTING CO LTD**
49 The Broadway, Cheam, Surrey SM3 8BL
Tel/Fax 0181 643 9084
Contact: Michael Hawkes, Yvonne Hawkes
We also offer A1 Projection lamps, photographic lamps, halogen lamps, low energy lamps, sodium & metal halide lamps - 24 hour delivery service.

**E.S.P. (U.K.) LTD**
(Events, Services & Productions)
The Arches, Unit 5, Furmston Court, Letchworth, Herts SG6 1EX
Tel 01462 482411
Fax 01462 673856
e-mail 101637.2016@compuserve.com
Contacts: Ann Broadhurst and David Streeing
Distributors for RVE range of dimming equipment and colour changers, and MOBIL TECH range of trussing, hoists and stands. We also manufacture stage sets, props, projection screens, lighting accessories and special effects, including a unique snow machine.

**EUROSOUND (UK) LTD**
Unit12, Station Court Road, Clayton, Huddersfield
Tel 01484 866066
Fax 01484 866299
Sound and Lighting Hire Specialists.

**FINELINE LASER & LIGHTING SERVICES**
The Old Quarry, Clevedon Road, Failand, Bristol BS8 3TU
Tel 01275 395000
Fax 01275 395001
Email: hire@fineline.com.uk
Website: fineline.com.uk
Contact: Marcus Goddard

**FRANCIS SEARCHLIGHTS (1990) LTD**
Union Road, Bolton, BL2 2HJ
Tel 01204 527196
Fax 01204 361567
Sales and Marketing Manager: IT Needham

**FUTURIST LIGHT & SOUND LTD**
Hoyle Head Mills, New Street, Earlsheaton, Dewsbury, West Yorks WF12 8JJ
National Call Hotline 0990 168259
Tel 01924 468183
Fax 01924 458667
London Tel 0171 370 4012
London Fax 0171 370 5481
Sales, lease, long and short term rental of stage lighting, indoor and outdoor event lighting. Full compliment of over 200 star cloths for hire and sale. A new lighting book library containing over 200 professional books on stage craft, sound and lighting as well as a full range of pro-video.

**GE LIGHTING LTD**
Conquest House, 42-44 Wood Street, Kingston upon Thames, Surrey KT1 1UZ
Tel 0181 727 4222
Fax 0181 727 4231
Contact: Clive Salmon- Director Lighting Sales, Europe
Clive Connor, Manager, UK Sales.
The enormous variety of lamps now manufactured by GE

 DHA Lighting Ltd has been established for over 25 years and thus offers the best expertise when it comes to image projection and animation.
For a demonstration or more details on any of DHA's products, please call the contacts below or ask for a full product catalogue (also available on the DHA website):

Digital Beamlight 2 & Digital Light Curtain
As used thoughout the world on rock and roll and theatre productions, DHA's moving lights offer low maintenance with high performance.
Contact: Diane in Sales

Catalogue Gobo Designs & Holders
DHA now offers over 800 readily available designs in 12 sizes. Most are held in stock and can be despatched by return.
Contact: Martin or Nicola in Sales

Custom Metal Gobos
With over 40,000 custom gobos to their credit the DHA graphics team is highly experienced in adapting almost any image for gobo manufacture.
Contact: Caroline or Karen in Graphics

Custom Colour or Monochrome Glass Gobos
If your image is not suitable for metal etching it can be made to high resolution on coloured dichroic or monochrome glass. All jobs are individually quoted and advice given on possible combinations.
Contact: Vicky or Hellen in Graphics

OEM Gobo Service
DHA offers special terms and services when it comes to etching gobos and gobo wheels for equipment manufacturers.
Contact: Julie in Sales

Animated Effects
To compliment their gobos, DHA offers a comprehensive range of animated effects units available to special order. All are detailed in the DHA catalogue.
Contact: Louise in Sales

Projection Slides
To complete the projection range, DHA make projection slides in all formats and offers a specialised service in single and double plane distortion.
Contact: Wyatt in Graphics

**CL Irvine Contracts Ltd**

**Unit 8
Parsons Green Depot
Parsons Green Lane
Fulham
London - SW6 4HS**

FORMERLY SHOW CONTRACTS LTD.

# Lighting, Sound, Audio Visual
# Grids and tracks installation
# Inspection and testing
# FOR
# THEATRE AND STUDIO

National Inspection Council for
Electrical Installation Contracting

NICEIC

APPROVED   CONTRACTOR

Tel 0171-384 2913  Fax 0171-384 2914

---

Lighting Ltd has been developed to the current high level of sophistication as the result of extensive and continuing research in many branches of Physics. GE has never been content to merely match the performance of its competitors - always the research has continued which has made GE the leading light source manufacturers in the world.
Products: High voltage stage and studio quartz and discharge lamps.

**GEARHOUSE**
69 Dartmouth Middleway, Birmingham, B7 4VA
Tel 0121 333 3333
Conference, exhibition and presentation equipment hire. Audio visual sound and lighting.

**GLANTRE ENGINEERING LIMITED**
20 Richfield Avenue, Reading, Berks RG1 8EQ.
Tel 0118 964 0000
Fax 0118 964 0064
email: info@glantre.com
Managing Director: Derek Gilbert
Contracts Director: Gareth Davies
Financial Director: Francis Wells
Technical Director: Vic Dobbs
Specialist contractors providing complete theatre electrical installation services including stage lighting, control systems and dimmers. Also custom built working light systems, socket boxes, internally wired barrels, lighting suspensions and power distribution. Wiring installations carried out in accordance with 16th edition of IEE regulations. Glantre is a member of the Electrical Contractor's Association.

**GRADAV THEATRE SERVICES LTD**
613-615 Green Lanes, Palmers Green, London
N13 4EP
Tel 0181 886 1300

Fax 0181 882 6517 (Hire)
Sales of lighting equipment. Stockists of DHA gobos. Lee Filters. Main dealers for Zero 88 and Doughty Engineering.

**HAYES SOUND & LIGHTING (HSL-HIRE) LTD**
Unit 7, Cunliffe Road, Whitebirk Industrial Estate, Blackburn, Lancashire BB1 5UA
Tel 01254 698808
Fax 01254 698835
Contact: Simon Stuart
Every client is special, each commission totally unique, our in house event management process ensuring that your project is carefully monitored, from the taking of your detailed instructions, through design and planning, and ultimately the installation and staging of the event itself.

**S.A. HOLDEN**
The Rising Sun, Machen, Newport, Gwent NP1 8RO
Sales/Service of Lighting equipment and special effects.

**C.L. IRVINE CONTRACTS LTD**
Unit 8, Parsons Green Depot, Parsons Green Lane, Fulham, London SW6 4HS
Tel 0171 384 2913
Fax 0171 384 2914
Contact: Charlie Irvine, Jon Flanagan, Eddie Souster or Fred Williams
Supply and installation of lighting, sound and audio-visual systems for Theatre, Studio and Lecture Theatres.

**CHRIS JAMES & CO LTD**
Lighting Filters, 43 Colville Road, Acton, London W3 8BL.
Tel 0181 896 1772

Fax 0181 896 1773
A comprehensive range of over 150 effects, colour
correction and diffusion filters and a 'live' performance
range of 50 high temperature filters and sundries
including reflectors, scrim, blackwrap and blackout film,
etc.

### JBE STAGE LIGHTING & EQUIPMENT COMPANY
7 Rose Way, Purdeys, Rochford, Essex SS4 1LY
Tel 01702 545826
Hire and Sales of Stage Lighting Equipment, Optical
Effects, Control Desks, Dimmers, UV Lighting, Rigging,
Stands, Cables, Props, Pyrotechnic Effects, Smoke
Machines, Make-Up, Scenic Paints, Replacement
Lamps, Color Filters. Stockist of Strand, CCT, Pulsar,
Teatro & Arri Lighting and Controls. Main Dealer &
Stockist of Rosco Supergel and Scenic Products - Le
Maitre Pyrotechnics.

### J.P.L. SERVICES
15 High Street Rampton, Cambridge CB4 8QE
Tel 01954 250851
Fax 01954 250543
Lighting equipment for hire. Super quiet generators.
Contract work with fit up crews for indoor/outdoor
presentations, festivals, marquees etc.

### LANCELYN THEATRE SUPPLIES
Office and Sales, Electric Avenue, Ferry Hinksey
Road, Oxford L63 9LN
Tel 01865 722468
Fax 01865 728791
Hire and sales of stage lighting and control equipment,
rigging, optical and special effects. Outdoor seating,
rigging, sound and lighting equipment for theatre,
display or son-et-Lumiere. Delivery service.

### LANCELYN THEATRE SUPPLIES (Northwest)
Poulton Road, Bebington, Merseyside L63 9LN
Tel 0151 334 8991 (24 hrs)
Fax 0151 334 4047
Contracts 0151 334 3000
Hire of stage lighting and control, rigging, optical and
special effects.
Delivery service.

### LASER CREATIONS INTERNATIONAL LTD (LCI)
55 Merthyr Terrace, Barnes, London SW13 9DL
Tel 0181 741 5747
Fax 0181 748 9879
Managing Director: Marlyn Weeks
Marketing Manager: Lindsay Egmore-Frost
Laser special effects, specialising in high quality multi-
coloured 3D graphics and animations plus laser fed
fibre optics. Laser video projection.

### LASER MAGIC
LM House, 2 Church Street, Seaford, East Sussex
BN25 1HD
Tel 01323 890752
Fax 01323 898311
Mobile 0836 252885
email: Compuserve 100563,325
Specialists in Hi-Tec promotions for the A.V. industry,
Entertainment industry and theatrical industry. Special
effects include water effects, pyros, lasers, lighting,
sound, videowall and productions.

### LASERPOINT COMMUNICATIONS LTD
44 Clifton Road, Cambridge CB1 7ED
Tel 01223 212331
Fax 01223 214085
Design, manufacture and sales of Laser and Videowall

# H.S.L (Hire) Ltd

## Lowest Prices Around

### LIGHTING & SOUND HIRE

CONFERENCE PRESENTATIONS
THEATRE TOURS
OUTDOOR EVENTS
FILM AND TELEVISION

**FOR THE BEST IN LIGHTING & SOUND EQUIPMENT TECHNOLGY**

### EQUIPMENT
### SALES & INSTALLATION

- THEATRES
- TELEVISION
- EDUCATION
- CONFERENCE VENUES

### New for 1999-2000

MAC 250 / 300 / 500 /600
CITY COLOURS - ND YAG 80w

Hire Tel: +44 (0) 1254-698808

Every client is special, each commission totally unique, our in house event management process ensuring that your project is carefully monitored from the taking of your detailed instructions, through design and planning, and ultimately tthe installation and staging of the event itself.

### Services

Event Management
Themed Decor
Set Design
Staging

**H.S.L.( Hire ) Ltd**
Unit 7, Cunliffe Road,
Whitebirk Industrial Estate
Blackburn,Lancashire,
BB1 5UA, England.

# H.S.L (Hire) Ltd

## Lowest Prices Around

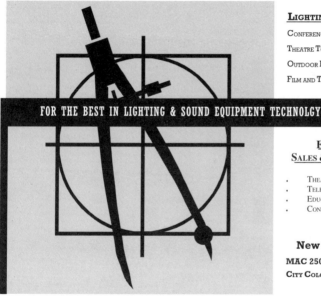

### LIGHTING & SOUND HIRE

CONFERENCE PRESENTATIONS
THEATRE TOURS
OUTDOOR EVENTS
FILM AND TELEVISION

**FOR THE BEST IN LIGHTING & SOUND EQUIPMENT TECHNOLGY**

### EQUIPMENT
### SALES & INSTALLATION

- THEATRES
- TELEVISION
- EDUCATION
- CONFERENCE VENUES

### New for 1999-2000

MAC 250 / 300 / 500 /600
CITY COLOURS - **ND YAG 80w**

Hire Tel: +44 (0) 1254-698808

Every client is special, each commission totally unique, our in house event management process ensuring that your project is carefully monitored from the taking of your detailed instructions, through design and planning, and ultimately tthe installation and staging of the event itself.

**Services**

Event Management
Themed Decor
Set Design
Staging

**H.S.L.( Hire ) Ltd**
Unit 7, Cunliffe Road,
Whitebirk Industrial Estate
Blackburn,Lancashire,
BB1 5UA, England.

systems including a range of fibre optic or direct fed Laser controllers and effects systems producing animation and special effects and a range of videowall electronics capable of high resolution videowall effects up to 20x20 monitors.

## JIM LAWS LIGHTING
West End Lodge, Wrentham, Beccles, Suffolk NR34 7NH
Tel 01502 675264
Fax 01502 675565
Period Entertainment Lighting, Hire and Sales, Lighting Design Service.

## LEE FILTERS
Central Way, Walworth Industrial Estate, Andover, Hampshire SP10 5AN
Tel 01264 366245
Fax 01264 355058
Website: www.leefilters.com
Manufacturers of light filter in both polyester and polycarbonate. Flame Retardant to BS5750 when stated. Also, manufacturers of Photographic Colour Correction and colour Printing Filters and optical Resin Camera Filters.

## LEE LIGHTING LTD
Manchester Road, Kearsley, Bolton BL4 8RL
Tel 01204 794000
Fax 01204 57187

## LIGHT ENGINEERING
64 Eden Road, London E17 9JY
Tel 0181 520 2336 (4 lines)
Fax 0181 509 1332
Contact: Cliff Wilding and Tracey Martin
Manufacture, supply and distribution of lighting, lamps, gell, cable, connectors, safety chains, UV products, effects etc.

## LIGHT PROCESSOR
11 Fairway Drive, Fairway Trading Estate, Greenford, Middlesex UB6 8PW.
Tel 0181 575 2288
Fax 0181 575 8678
Info Fax 0181 575 5510
Web: http://www.lightprocessor.co.uk
Light Processor have a long history of supplying cost-effective, high quality lighting control equipment, including desks, dimmers and DMX accessories to all areas of the lighting industry.
The Q Commander multipurpose console is the latest piece of equipment from Light Processor with the usual array of technical excellence, reliability, power and affordability. This product is ideal for theatre applications and is packed with features, innovations and ideas for the future.

## LIGHTFACTOR SALES LTD
11 Fairway Drive, Fairway Trading Estate, Greenford, Middlesex UB6 8PW
Tel 0181 575 5566
Fax 0181 575 8678
Info Fax 0181 575 5510
Marketing Co-ordinator: Louise Stickland
Lightfactor offer a comprehensive range of state-of-the-art lighting equipment for the theatre environment. The Cyberlight and the new Studio Colour wash luminaire in particular are fast proving to be the most versatile and reliable moving mirror fixtures on the market today.

## LIGHT & SOUND DESIGN LTD
201 Coventry Road, Birmingham B10 0RA
Tel 0121 766 6400
Fax 0121 766 6150

Contact: Robert Wain
Lighting hire including `Icon` moving light and show control system.

## LIGHTING TECHNOLOGY
2 Tudor Estate, Abbey Road, Park Royal, London NW10 7UY
Tel 0181 965 6800
Fax 0181 965 0950
e-mail sales@lighing-tech.com
Website www.lighting-tech.com

## LIGHT WORKS LIMITED
2A Greenwood Road, London E8 1AB
Tel 0171 249 3627
Fax 0171 254 0306

## M&M GROUP
Studio 12, Cameron House, 12 Castlehaven Road, London NW1 8QW
Tel 0171 284 2504
Fax 0171 284 2503
Distributor for Rainbow Colour Changers; The Smoke Factory of Hanover; Electronic Theatre Controls - Lighting Control Equipment & Luminaires; MA Lighting; Microscroller; Diffusion; Selecon Lighting; Blakes Pyrotechnics.

## MAINSTAGE LIGHTING
Head Office: Sharps Mill, Whitecross, Lancaster LA1 4XG
Tel 01524 844099
Fax 01524 841808

## MALDWYN BOWDEN INTERNATIONAL LTD
168 Edward Street, Brighton BN2 2JB
Tel 01273 607384
Fax 01273 694408
Maldwyn Bowden International design, supply and install lighting systems for theatres and clubs and can also provide equipment on hire.

## THE MANCHESTER LIGHT AND STAGE CO.
Depo: 76-78 North Western Street, Hardwick, Manchester M12 6DY
Tel 0161 445 6876
Fax 0161 445 7574
Contact: Bruce Mitchell
Lighting Hire and Sales "Steeldeck" Hire and Sales - Marquee Hire, Event Management - Site Electrics. Catwalks, outdoor roofs & stages.

## BOB MASSEY ASSOCIATES (STAGE CONSULTANTS)
9 Worrall Avenue, Arnold, Nottingham NG5 7GN
Tel 0115 967 3969
Technical theatre consultancy, lottery applications, advice, design and planning service including technical theatre courses for all lighting, engineering, curtain and communication projects.

## METEORLITES PRODUCTIONS LTD
Millenium Studios, Elstree Way, Borehamwood, Herts WD6 1BF
Tel 0181 207 5111
Fax 0181 207 3655
Concert, stage and television lighting.

## MICO LIGHTING LTD
Trydale Lane, Pudsey, Leeds LS28 9LD
Tel 0113 256 7113
Fax 0113 257 2358
Sales Manager: P. Bainbridge

Sales Office Manager: S. Hodson
Specialist in all types of lighting.

## MIDLAND THEATRE SERVICES LTD
Dartmouth Road, Smethwick, Birmingham B66 1AX
Tel 0121 525 4545
Fax 0121 525 2413
Theatre lighting and sound consultants. Equipment
available for sale and hire. Main dealer for Strand
Lighting in the Midlands. Open 9.00a.m. to 6.00p.m.
Monday-Friday. 9.30a.m. to 12.30p.m. Saturday.

## MIDNIGHT DESIGN LTD
100 Garrat Lane, Wandsworth, London SW18 4DJ
Tel 0181 871 4077
Directors: Michael Townsend, Dave Bryant, Steve Clark.
Lighting design and production to the concert, theatre,
conference, television, video and exhibition industries.
They are specialists in effects lighting and computerised
control systems.

## MULTIFORM LIGHTING
Bell Lane, Uckfield, East Sussex TN22 1QL
Tel 01825 763348
Fax 01825 763310
Contact: Iain Price-Smith, Managing Director.
Designers and manufacturers of lighting control boards
and dimmer packs & stroboscopes.
The company also manufacturers DMX Decoders,
Encoders and Soft Patches. Recently introduced in a
range of Smoke Machines for theatrical use.

## NORTHERN LIGHT
Assembly Street, Leith, Edinburgh EH6 7RG
Tel 0131 553 2383
Fax 0131 553 3296
Glasgow Sales: 79 Loanbank Quadrant, Glasgow
G51 3HZ
Tel 0141 440 1771
Fax 0141 445 4406
Proprietor: Lord Rosebery
Management: John Allen, Michael Smyth,
Stockists for Strand Lighting. Hall Stage Products,
Roscolab UK and Le Maitre Pyrotechnics. Stage
Lighting Hire and Sales, Production Lighting Design,
manufacturers of stage drapes, socket outlet boxes,
facilities panels, working light control systems and
sound and communication systems to consultants'
specifications, specialist Electrical Contracting.

## NORTHERN STAGE SERVICES LTD
Trent Industrial Estate, Duchess Street,
Shaw, Oldham OL2 7UT
Tel 01706 849469
Fax 01706 840138
Specialists in stage lighting, sound and curtain
equipment.

## NOVALIGHT (INTERNATIONAL) LTD
15 Old Market Street, Thetford, Norfolk IP24 2EQ.
Tel 01842 762209
Fax 01842 753746
Sales Director: Jon Reay-Young.
Specialists in tungsten-halogen, cold cathode, dichroic
and low voltage lighting and control systems, uniquely
providing 0-100° dimming control of linear and compact
fluorescents.

## ONE STAGE PRODUCTIONS LTD
83 Leamington Crescent, Harrow, Middlesex HA2 9HH
Tel/Fax 0181 864 7362
Email: john@one-stage.co.uk
Website: http://www.one-stage.co.uk

Contact: John Ryan, Jody Ryan, Nic Bridgewater
With a strong team of IT and Audio design staff we
offer a friendly and professional service as suppliers of
market leading equipment suitable for theatre,
conferencing, exhibitions, broadcasting and touring.
We also have an experienced team working in project
and tour management.

## OPTIKINETICS LTD
38 Cromwell Road, Luton LU3 1DN
Tel 01582 411413
Fax 01582 400613
Contact: Neil Rice
Manufacture effects lighting equipment and Trilite
Aluminium Structural system.

## P.A. MUSIC
172 High Road, London N2 9AS
Tel 0181 883 4350
Fax 0181 883 5117
Contact: Mr A. Allan
P.A. Music is a small and flexible company involved in
the supply and hire of lighting and sound equipment to
the leisure/entertainment and conference industries.
We also produce high quality flight cases custom made
to our customers' requirements.

## PHOSPHENE
The Event Shop, Milton Road South, Stowmarket
Suffolk IP14 1EZ
Tel 01449 770011 and 01449 678200 (24 hrs)
Hire and sales of lamps, lanterns and control
equipment. Thomas, Theatro, Zero 88 etc. Production
design, rigging-crew & operators. 'One-nighter' rigging
for unusual venues and churches. Product launches
and fashion shows. Repair & servicing of most makes.

# *LEE* Filters

## *The Professional Choice*

It doesn't matter whether you need to light an Oscar winning performance, or create the right setting on an empty theatre stage, whenever you choose Lee Filters you are assured of achieving just the right effect.

Based in Andover in Hampshire, the company draws on 30 years experience to develop lighting filters and gobos which meet the highest standards set by the theatre world.

All the information you need about the wide range of lighting filters is contained in a choice of free of charge swatch books. These include Editions in both chromatic and number order, whilst the Pocket Edition includes a section which identifies the Lee Filters' equivalents of other manufacturer's products. Also available to buy, is a comprehensive, large format Master Edition.

The broad range of gobos is featured in a full colour Pattern Selector catalogue and a handy pocket guide, and all gobos are available in the industry standard sizes of A, B and M. Lee Filters can also offer a custom-made service, making gobos to your designs.

Lee Filters give you the freedom to create all that you need with one of the widest choices of lighting filters, and a range of gobos that is limited only by your own imagination.

**Lee Filters, Central Way, Walworth Industrial Estate, Andover, Hampshire SP10 5AN, England.**

*Tel: +44 (0)1264 366245  Fax: +44 (0)1264 355058*

*www.leefilters.com*

**PKE LIGHTING**
Unit B4-5, Moss Industrial Estate, St Helens Road,
Leigh WN7 3PT
Tel 01942 678424
Fax 01942 678423

**PLAYLIGHT HIRE LIMITED**
67 Ayres Road, Old Trafford, Manchester M16 9NH.
Tel 0161 226 5858
Fax 0161 232 9510
Contact: Chris Wroe (Hire)
860 Coronation Road, Park Royal, London NW10 7PS
Tel 0181 965 8188
Fax 0181 961 6348
Email: hire.london@playlight.co.uk
Hire - Strand Lighting, CCT. Clay Paky Golden Scan
HPEs, Golden Scan 3s and Mini Scans, Arri lighting
control desk, MA Scancommanders, Starcloths.
Sales - Strand Lighting Main Distributor, Zero 88,
Pulsar, Martin. Playlight also supplies sound
equipment, PA and voice alarm systems, rigging and
stage electrical installation. Fibre optic starcloths and
low voltage peacloths are also manufactured in-house.

**PREFERRED ELECTRICAL WHOLESALE**
18 Lettice Street, Fulham, London SW6 4EH
Tel 0171 731 0805/6
Fax 0171 731 0623

**PRIMARC LTD**
Lamps & Lighting: Unit 8, Wycombe Road, Wembley,
Middlesex HA0 1HR
Tel 0181 900 8535
Fax 0181 900 2232
Marketing: 121 Loverock Road, Reading, Berkshire
RG30 1DZ
Tel 0118 959 6777
Fax 0118 950 5964
Theatre and Studio lighting suppliers.
Primarc have been established for 30 years and are
one of the largest suppliers of stage and studio bulbs
and filters in the country. We also understand the
need for quick delivery.

**PULSAR LIGHT OF CAMBRIDGE LTD**
Henley Road, Cambridge CB1 3EA
Tel 01223 366798
Fax 01223 460708
Stage Lighting Systems.

**PYRAMID LIGHTING AND SOUND SERVICES**
28 Railway Approach, East Grinstead, West Sussex
RH19 1BP
Tel 01342 314328
Fax 01342 410727
Sound and lighting hire and installations.

**QUANTUM LIGHTING & EFFECTS DESIGN**
2 Orchard Road, Erdington, Birmingham B24 9JL
Tel 0121 382 4149
Fax 0121 382 5159
Lighting design and hire for the Trade Show, Conference
and Theatre industries.

**R B LIGHTING LTD**
Unit 10, Teddington Business Park, Station Road,
Teddington, Middlesex TW11 9BQ
Tel 0181 977 9665
Fax 0181 977 5687
Wholesale suppliers of all theatre, studio and display lamps.
Spare parts service for all current and obsolete lanterns.
Colour supply and cutting service. CCT, Rosco & DHA main
dealers. Immediate dispatch.

**R & G GROUP THEATRE SERVICES**
19-21 Forest Vale Industrial Estate, Cinderford,
Gloucestershire GL14 2PQ
Tel 01594 823197
Fax 01594 826045
Email: rggroup@btinternet.com
Managing Director: Greg Moger
Manufacturers and suppliers of theatre lighting control
systems, luminaires, patch panels, lighting bars and turnkey
projects. Installation by our team to 16th edition I.E.E regs.
N.I.C.E.I.C. approved contractors. Agents for Imax - Hall
Stage - Zero 88.

**RENTALIGHT**
7 Rose Way, Purdeys, Rochford, Essex SS4 1LY
Tel 01702 545826
Hire of Film, T.V. and Video Lighting Equipment.

**RESOURCES CENTRE LTD**
Cambridge House, 128 Park Road, Camberley,
Surrey GU15 2LW
Tel 01276 670000
Fax 01276 670010
Hire & Supply of all theatrical lighting effects.
Supply of colour gel and accessories. Supply of specialist
lamps.

**ROSCOLAB LTD**
Blanchard Works, Kangley Bridge Road, Sydenham,
London SE26 5AQ
Tel 0181 659 2300
Fax 0181 659 3153
Suppliers of a wide range of products, including
lighting filters, scenic paints, stage filters, stage
flooring, screens and fog machines for special

effects.

**SAV LTD**
Party House, Mowbray Drive, Blackpool, Lancs
FY3 7JR
Tel 01253 302602
Fax 01253 301000

**SELECON UK**
Units 25 & 26, Hightown Industrial Estate, Crow Arch
Lane, Ringwood, Hampshire BH24 1ND.
Tel 01425 470888
Fax 01425 471398
email: selecon@ajs.co.uk
Website: http://www.demon.uk.co/ajs
Contact: Selecon Sales Manager: Graham Fathers
Tel/Fax 01730 829732
or Adrian Sant/Ian Cross 01425 470888
Bespoke Theatrical and Architectural luminaries.

**SERIOUS STRUCTURES LTD**
Bourne Farm, Pilton, Somerset BA4 4NX
Tel 01749 890320
Fax 01749 890531
Contact: Steven Corfield

**SGB WORLD SERVICE**
Empire House, 12 Rutland Street, Hanley,
Stoke on Trent ST1 5JG
Tel 01782 279309
Fax 01782 279309
e-mail email@sgbworldservice.co.uk
Website www.sgbwordservice.com
Contact:Mr S. Boote
See our main advert in Lighting & Lighting Equipment
Suppliers.

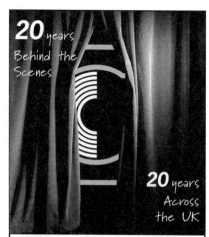

Bristol (0117) 982 7282  Birmingham (0121) 525 4545
Exeter (01392) 255868  Plymouth (01752) 269444

# Lighting • Sound • Staging
# Hire • Sales • Service

**SLOANE ELECTRICAL & MECHANICAL LTD**
Pandora House, 41-45 Lind Road, Sutton, Surrey
SM1 4PP
Tel 0181 643 9462
Fax 0181 643 8172

**SOUND ELECTRONICS (NEWCASTLE) LTD**
Industry Road, Heaton, Newcastle-upon-Tyne NE6 5XB
Tel 0191 265 2500
Fax 0191 265 8595
Sales, hire, design, install. Stockist for Strand, Pulsar, Zero
88, Optikinetics, Mode.

**SPARKS THEATRICAL HIRE**
64a Evelyn Street, Surrey Quays, London SE8 5DD
Tel 0181 469 3171
Fax 0181 469 3181
Contact: Paul Anderson (Director)

**SPECIALIST LAMP DISTRIBUTORS**
10 Sovereign Enterprise Park, King William Street,
Salford, Manchester M5 2UP
Tel 0161 873 7822
Fax 0161 873 8089
Distributors of replacement lamps for stage, studio,
concert and display purposes - nationwide overnight
service.

**SPECIALIST THEATRE SERVICES**
Unit 10, Parkway Court, Glaisdale Parkway,
Nottingham NG8 4GN
Tel 0115 985 4062
Sales and hire of Theatre and Studio Lighting, lighting
control and dimming, curtains & tracking and rigging
equipment. Sales counter open with stocks of scenery
paints, lamps, filters, pyrotechnics etc.

**STAGE CONTROL**
Station Parade, Whitchurch Lane, Edgware,
Middlesex HA8 6RW
Tel 0181 952 8982
Fax 0181 951 4178
Stockists of Lee Filters, CCT lanterns, Zero 88
dimmers and control desks. main dealers of Le Maitre
smoke machines and TP communications equipment.
We also have a Hire Department.

**STAGE DOOR SUPPLIES**
198 Bakers Street, Enfield EN1 3JY
Tel 0181 367 7337
Fax 0181 367 7557
Lighting equipment for hire and sale.

**STAGE ELECTRICS**
Victoria Road, Avonmouth, Bristol BS11 9DB
Tel 0117 982 7282
Fax 0117 982 2180
e-mail hire@stage-electrics.co.uk
e-mail sales@stage-electrics.co.uk
Website www.stage-electrics.demon.co.uk
Cofton Road, Marsh Barton, Exeter EX2 8QW
Tel 01392 255868
Fax 01392 410592
Parkway Industrial Estate, Plymouth PL6 8LH
Tel 01752 269444
Fax 01752 228283
Dartmouth Road, Smethwick, West Midlands B66 1AX
Tel 0121 525 4545
Fax 0121 525 2413
Contacts: Hire, Adrian Searle; Sales, Jane Evans;
Production, Richard Cross.
Hire, sales, installation, and service of sound
equipment for theatre, conference, concert, festival and
commercial presentations. Project management,
designers and engineers.

**STAGE SERVICES**
Stage House, Prince William Road, Loughborough,
Leicestershire LE11 0GN
Tel 01509 218857
Fax:01519 265730
Contact: Mr Ray Dolby
Specialist consultants and suppliers for sales, installations and
hires of lighting, sound, theatre and stage equipment.
Full range of consumables and accessories on sale in our
stage shop or by mail order.

**STAGETEC**
383 Sykes Road Trading Estate, Slough, Berkshire SL1 4TJ
Tel 01753 553522
Fax 01753 553122
Stagetec provide a complete design, supply, installation and
maintenance service for a comprehensive range of sound,
lighting and staging products.
They are also UK distributor for the world renowned range of
Compulite's lighting controls desks, dimmers and scrollers as
well as FLY's intelligent lights.

**STAGE TECHNIQUES**
Unit One, Cotton Drive, Dalehouse Lane Industrial
Estate, Kenilworth, Warwickshire CV8 2EB
Tel 01926 864800
Fax 01929 864964
email: stagetec@dircon.co.uk
Contact: S. Griffiths
Conference, Theatre, Television, Outdoor Events,
Steeldeck Hire.

**STAGE TWO LTD**
Unit J, Penfold Trading Estate, Imperial Way, Watford,

Herts WD2 4YY
Tel 01923 244822
Fax 01923 255048
Hires Manager: Richard Ford
Hire or sale of lighting, sound and special effects of all applications.

**THEATRE DIRECT**
Unit 2, Kirkwood Road, Kings Hedges, Cambridge
CB4 2PH
Tel 01223 423010
Fax 01223 425010
Contact: Hire - James Irvine
Hire sales and service of lighting, sound and staging - Strand lighting main dealer and approved service centre.

**THEATRE PACE**
7 Rose Way, Purdeys, Rochford, Essex SS4 1LY
Tel 01702 545826
Hire of Lighting and Special Effects for Fashion Shows, Product Launches, Conferences.

**THEATRE PROJECTS**
20-22 Fairway Drive, Greenford, Middlesex UB6 8PW.
Tel 0181 575 5555
Fax 0181 575 0105
Email: info@london.vlps.com
Website: www.vlps.com
Contacts: David March, Peter Marshall
Renowned for the world-wide rental of lighting and all associated equipment., the company has its own in-house design teams and first class crews and CAD 3D facilities. It supplies equipment and services to West End and touring theatre, product launches, international events and exhibitions.
Theatre Projects has exclusive UK representation for the spectacular Sky-Tracker and also manufactures Sky-Arts automated searchlight systems.

**RAY THOMPSON LTD**
8 Lorne Street, Belfast BT9 7DU
Tel 01232 664411
Fax 01232 664831
Manufacturers agents for Strand Lighting - A S Green - Lighting, portable stages.

**T.I.S. LIGHTING LTD**
Unit 3, St. Margaret's Business Centre, Drummond Place, Moor Mead Road, Twickenham, Middlesex TW1 1JN
Tel 0181 891 4755
Fax 0181 744 2458
Equipment rental, lighting design and engineers for conference, trade shows, theatre, ballet, outdoor events and festivals.

**TMB ASSOCIATES**
The Old Brick Yard, Estbourne Road, Brentford, Middx TW8 9PG
Tel 0181 560 9652
Fax 0181 560 1064
e-mailt@tmb.com
Website www.tmb.com
Contact: Mark Thompson
Value added distributor of production lighting equipment and sound and lighting cabling. The range covers all major US and European production lighting and hardware including all touring all touring expandable supplies.

**TOTAL FABRICATIONS LIMITED**
Units 3 & 4, Kingston Industrial Estate, 81-86 Glover Street, Birmingham B9 4EN

Unit 3 St. Margarets Business Centre  Drummond Place
Moor Mead Road  Twickenham  Middlesex TW1 1JN
**Tel: 0181-891 4755  Fax: 0181-744 2458**

Tel 0121 772 5234
Fax 0121 772 5231
e-mail info@totalfabs.com
Website www.totalfabs.com
Contact: Adrian Black
Manufacturer of standard and custom aluminium trusses, roof structures, fixtures and associated equipment including motor controllers and full range of Verlinde products catering for broad spectrum of applications

**TRAFALGAR LIGHTING LTD**
9 Northway, London N9 0AD
Tel 0181 887 0082
Fax 0181 887 0072
Sales and hire, CCT, Rank Strand, Pulsar, Lamps. Special effects hire, dealers in used equipment.

**TRAVELLING LIGHT (Birmingham) LTD**
Unit 34, Boulton Industrial Centre, Icknield Street, Hockley, Birmingham B18 5AU
Tel 0121 523 3297
Supply, Hire and Installation of Entertainments and Commercial Lighting Equipment. Television and Film Lighting.

**TUSK SHOWHIRE**
23 Collum Lane, Ashby, Scunthorpe,
North Lincs DN16 2SZ
Tel 01724 859541
Fax 01724 851100
Contact: Stephen R. Ellerington
Suppliers of high quality generic or intelligent lighting and concert sound equipment. Comprehensive lighting stock including CCT, Thomas, HES Cyberlights, Avolites and Anytronics.

**JOHN TWINE LIGHTING HIRE**
2B & 2C, Bath Riverside Business Park, Riverside Road, Bath, North Somerset BA2 3DW
Tel 01225 311964
Fax 01225 445454
Contact: Rob Sangwell
John Twine Lighting Hire was established over 14 years ago and has a reputation for supplying good quality, well maintained equipment and support services to both professional and amateur companies.

**VALIANT LAMPS LTD**
20 Lettice Street, Fulham, London SW6 4EH
Tel 0171 736 8115
Fax 0171 731 3339
In depth stocking of all types of stage and studio lamps and all other ancillary requirements..

**VARI-LITE EUROPE LTD**
20-22 Fairway Drive, Greenford, Middx UB6 8PW
Tel 0181 575 6666
Fax 0181 575 0424
Email: info@london.vlps.com
Website: www.vlps.com
Contacts: David March, Carol Croft, Coral Cooper,
Steve Connolly and Edward Pagett
VLPS London offers a fully integrated service which
provides on rental its award - winning proprietary brand
of automated lighting together with conventional
lighting and first class crew. For the whole spectrum of
entertainment markets. As part of the VLPS network
clients can take advantage of our specialised training
courses, the Vari imaging gobo service, and the
permanent installation programme.

**VITA LIGHTING LTD**
Unit 4, Sutherland Court, Moorpark Industrial Estate,
Tolpits Lane, Watford, Herts WD1 8SP
Tel 01923 896476
Fax 01923 897741
Managing Director: G.C. Grist
Specialist lighting manufacturers design and
consultancy service.

**WALK-OVERS LTD**
14 Windermere Way, Thatcham, Berks  RG19 3UL
Tel 01635 865774
Fax 01635 874858
Contact: Peter Hart
Manufacturers of safety cable ramps for prevention of
accidents and cable damage. 3 sizes available for all
lighting and sound cables.

**WHITE LIGHT (Electrics) LTD**
57 Filmer Road, London SW6 7JF
Tel 0171 731 3291
Fax 0171 371 0806
email: 100637.3040@compuserve.com
Website www.whitelight.htd.uk
A complete range of lighting and control equipment for sale
and hire. Specialists in effects, installation, maintenance and
refurbishing of electrical lighting equipment. Main UK sales
stockist of Strand Lighting, CCT lighting equipment, Rosco,
DHA, Le Maitre, Arri, Lee, etc.

**WHITE LIGHT NORTH LTD**
Corporation Street, Sowerby Bridge, West Yorks
HX6 2QQ.
Tel 01422 839651
Fax 01422 839773
e-mail whitelight.north@dial.pipex.com
Director: J.M. Anderton

**WYBRON U.S. LIGHTS LTD**
19 Buckingham Avenue, Slough, Berkshire SL1 4QB
Tel 01753 533001
Fax 01753 533005
Sales and distribution of quality lighting equipment and
accessories made in the USA.
Contact: Daryl Vaughan and Judy Jones.

**XANADU THEATRES**
Mears Yard, Wintersells Road, Byfleet, Surrey
KT14 7AZ
Tel 019323 51996

**ZEBEDEE MUSIC SERVICES**
294 Newton Road, Rushden, Northants NN10 OSY
Tel/Fax 01933 350150 (Fax only 11am-11pm)
Contact: Sheila Lorraine
**ZERO 88 (Zero 88 Lighting Ltd)**
Usk House, Lakeside Close, Llantarnam Park,
Cwmbran NP44 3HD
Tel 01633 838088
Fax 01633 867880
Sales Director: Freddy Lloyd
Sales Manager: Paul Fowler
Specialists for over 25 years in lighting control, Zero 88
offer a complete range of desk, dimmers, controllers
and luminaires to suit most applications. From simple
units to sophisticated memory desks, the Zero 88
range has been developed to serve the education,
amateur/professional theatre, rental and architectural
markets, with over 65% of production exported world
wide. Zero 88 support an extensive distributor network
both in the UK and all main overseas markets. Multi
language literature available.
Large, fully equipped demonstration studio and training
centre available.

# 36
# LIGHTING FIBRE OPTICS

**CREATIVE SYSTEMS TECHNOLOGY**
Sophia House, 28 Cathedral Road, Cardiff, South
Glamorgan, Wales CF1 9LJ
Tel 01222 660142
Fax 01222 664891
Contact: Martin Howell
CST provide cost effective solutions whatever your
needs.  Lighting/Special Effects Design, Remote
Control/Motor controlled systems, software

management, security & tagging systems, together with an after sales service next to none.

### DHA LIGHTING LIMITED
284-302 Waterloo Road, London SE1 8RQ
Tel 0171 771 2900
Fax 0171 771 2901
ISDN: 0171 401 9202
Email: custom.gobo@dhalighting.co.uk
General Manager: Diane Grant
Manufacturers of gobos and slides, moving effects and fibre optics. Also available are moving light curtain systems including the new Digital Light Curtains and Digital Beamlights.

### EUROSOUND (UK) LTD
Unit 1, Intake Lane, Woolley, Wakefield WF4 2LG
Tel 01484 866066
Fax 01484 866299
Sound and Lighting Hire Specialists.

### LASER CREATIONS INTERNATIONAL LTD
55 Merthyr Terrace, Barnes, London SW13 9DL.
Tel 0181 741 5747
Fax 0181 748 9879
Laser special effects, specialising in high quality multi-coloured 3D graphics and animations plus laser fed fibre optics. Laser video projection.

### LASERPOINT COMMUNICATIONS LTD
44 Clifton Road, Cambridge CB1 4FD.
Tel 01223 212331
Fax 01223 214085
Design, manufacture, sales and rental of laser and videowall systems including a range of fibre optic or direct fed laser controllers and effects systems producing animation and special effects and a range of videowall electronics capable of high resolution videowall effects.

### GRAHAM J McLUSKY
55 High Street, Metheringham, Lincoln LN4 3DZ
Tel 01526 322606
Fax 01526 320356

### PAR OPTI PROJECTS LTD
67 Stirling Road, London W3 8DJ
Tel 0181 896 2588
Fax 0181 896 2599
Email: 74443.1634@compuserve.com
Contact: Mary Conolon or Paul Raymond
Par Opti manufacture and distribute all fibre optic lighting materials: Parglas cables, harnesses and conduits, Parflex polymers, light sources, theatre curtain washers, spot ball and bullet lenses, side-emitting fractured fibres, ceiling fittings and large bore fibre optics.
Distribution direct and through specialists worldwide.

### PLAYLIGHT HIRE LIMITED
67 Ayres Road, Old Trafford, Manchester M16 9NH.
Tel 0161 226 5858   Fax 0161 232 9510
Contact: Chris Wroe (Hire)
860 Coronation Road, Park Royal, London NW10 7PS
Tel 0181 965 8188  Fax 0181 961 6348
Playlight manufactures the Astrocloths range of background effects cloths. Choose from fibre optic or peabulb, static or moving effects. Choice of standard and DMX controllable light sources. Looms and light sources are also supplied for use in rigid displays and ceilings. In addition the company supplies side emitting and endglow fibres which are ideally suited to promotional display, internal and external signage.

### UNIVERSAL FIBRE OPTICS
Optical Goods Manufacturers, Gallowesknowes, Lennel Road, Coldstream, Berwickshire, Scotland TD12 4EP.
Tel 01890 883416
Fax 01890 883062
Manufacturers of a complete range of quality fibre optic lighting and display systems for theatres. Light sources and harnesses manufactured to customers requirements. Also wide range of lenses and fittings.

## 37
# MAGICAL EQUIPMENT & VARIETY

### ARNO PUPPET THEATRE
3a Ridgway, Wimbledon Village, London SW19 4SB
Tel 0181 946 3534
Puppets for hire - manipulators available for marionettes, rod, glove and shaddow puppets.

### GEOFF CHIPPENDALE
52 Hillcrest Road, Biggin Hill, Westerham, Kent TN16 3TY
Tel 01959 575817
International magician.

### INTERNATIONAL MAGIC
89 Clerkenwell Road, London EC1R 5BX
Tel 0171 405 7324
Fax 0171 831 2927
magic@comp.com
Suppliers of magic props, jokes and accessories.
### MAGIC AND ILLUSION HIRE
World of Illusion, Garden House, 4 Sunnyside, Wimbledon, London SW19 4SL
Tel 0181 946 9478
Fax 0181 946 0228
We offer the world's greatest illusions for hire and sale, together with Peter Petroff's own incomparable shows and his 'Magical Creation Service' and, in 1996, we created major illusions for TV, theatre films, and theme park shows.

### THE MAGIC MANICS
'Wood Rising', Kewferry Drive, Northwood, Middx HA6 2NT
Tel 01923 835 618

## PROF. PATTEN'S PUNCH & JUDY
14 The Crest, Goffs Oak, Herts EN7 5NP
Tel 01707 873262
Punch and Judy for Films, TV, Commercials, old time
street scenes. Sales Promotion. Magic and
Ventriloquism adviser Dennis Patten.

## TREASURE TROVE PUPPET COMPANY
The Old Chapel, Glyndwr Road, Gwernymynydd, Near
Mold, Flintshire CH7 5LW.
Tel 01352 750 838
Directors: Stephen Sharples
Hirers and makers of carved puppets, marionettes,
rods, and glove. Puppet manipulators available.

## UPSTAGE THEATRICAL SUPPLIES
Unit 5-9, 23 Abingdon Street, Blackpool FY1 1DG
Tel 01253 292321
Contact: Gabriella Gratrix - Head of Wardrobe
Full scale illusion construction sets and props.

## VENTRILOQUIST'S DUMMIES
Dennis Patten, 14 The Crest, Goffs Oak, Herts
EN7 5NP
Tel 01707 873262
Hire and advice.

# 38
# MAKE-UP & WIGS

## AJS THEATRE LIGHTING & STAGE SUPPLIES LTD
Units 25 & 26, Hightown Trading Estate, Crow Arch
Lane, Ringwood, Hants BH24 1ND
Tel 01425 470888
Fax 01425 471398
email: sales@ajs.co.uk
Internet 100074.1142@Compuserve.Com
Website: http://www.demon.co.uk/ajs
Wholesale & retailers of Leichner, Ben Nye & Kryolan
make-up products.

## ANGELS WIGS
40 Camden Street, London NW1 0EN
Tel 0171 387 0999
Fax 0171 383 5603
Contact: Mark Rhodes

## ARTISTES THEATRE SHOP
23 City Road, Chester CH1 3AE.
Tel 01244 320271
Full range of theatrical make-up.

## THE BALLERINA
3rd Floor, 7 Walford Road, Leicester
Tel 0116 254 4206
Retailer of dance shoes and dancewear, theatrical
make-up, wedding shoes, theatrical fabrics, sequins
and trims, aerobic wear, and ballroom shoes.

## BANBURY POSTICHE LTD
Little Bourton House, Southam Road, Banbury
OX16 7SR
Tel 01295 750606
Fax 01295 750058
Contact: Max Spingall
The UK's leading supplier of wigmaking materials. Over
60 years of wigmaking expertise, specialising in
custom made european hair wigs. Acrylic fashion wigs,

and Mane Connection Human Hair system.

## DAUPHINE'S OF BRISTOL
Orchard Road, St George, Bristol BS5 7HS
Tel/Fax 0117 955 1700
Leichner, Kryolan  Brandel Grimas, Make-up Agents.
Also specialists in wigs and hair-pieces. Costume
Department. Costumes made to order. For sale or hire.
Catalogue available. Open Monday - Saturday 9.00 -
5.00.

## DEREK EASTON (Hair & Wigs)
Studio on 2nd Avenue: Kingsway Court,
Second Avenue, Hove, East Sussex BN3 2LR
Tel 01273 770069
Mobile 0468 166733
Wigs for sale and hire, any style and colour. Hairdressing.

## FANTASY FACES - THEATRE MAKE-UP
90 Market Street, Ashby-de-la-Zouch, Leics LE65 1AP
Freephone 0800 371266
Freefax 0800 371643
Tel 01530 413998
Fax 0800 371643
e-mail 101746.2275@compuserve.com
Proprietor: David V. Cooper BSc (Hons)

## CHARLES H FOX LIMITED
22 Tavistock Street, London WC2E 7PY
Tel 0171 240 3111
Fax 0171 379 3410
Directors: W. Langer, A. Lee
Contact: Suzanne Fletcher
Charles Fox Ltd has recently undergone a major
facelift. We have extended our opening hours for your
convenience as well as supplying a massive range of
theatrical and television make-up.

## FUTURIST LIGHT & SOUND LTD
Hoyle Head Mills, New Street, Earlsheaton,
Dewsbury, West Yorks WF12 8JJ
National Call Hotline 0990 168259
Tel 01924 468183
Fax 01924 458667
Full range of Grimas professional theatrical make up as
well as Grimas make up workshops and training
services.

## HAIR DEVELOPMENT LTD
247 Mile End Road, London E1 4BJ.
Tel 0171 790 3996/4567
Fax 0171 790 3621
Supplying wigs for theatrical & everyday use. Also the
worlds finest mens toupees & hairpieces.

## HAIRAISERS LTD
9-11 Sunbeam Road, Park Royal, London NW10 6JP
Tel 0181 965 2500
Fax 0181 963 1600
Wigs available in 80 different styles, 38 colours. Also in
carnival colours. Glitter wigs, beards and moustaches.
Lace from stock wigs 300 different styles

## HOUSE OF HORROR
43 Bullring, Birmingham City Centre B5 5DB
Tel/Fax 0121 643 0025
Website: www.houseofhorror.co.uk
Contact: Stu Jones
Horror shop specialising in latex masks, props,
theatrical makeup and prosthetics.

## JBE STAGE LIGHTING & EQUIPMENT COMPANY
7 Rose Way, Purdeys, Rochford, Essex SS4 1LY

Tel: 01702 545826
Stockist and suppliers of stage and film make-up.
Specialist in supply prosthetics, stockists of Leichner,
Kryolan, Grimas, Ben Nye, etc.

### LANCELYN THEATRE SUPPLIES
Electric Avenue, Ferry Hinksey Road, Oxford OX2 0BY
Tel 01865 722468
Fax 01865 728791
Postal Service for Stage Make-Up, wigs, beards,
masks & sundries.

### LANCELYN THEATRE SUPPLIES (NORTHWEST)
Poulton Road, Bebington, Merseyside
Tel 0151 334 8991
Fax 0151 334 4047
Stage make-up, wigs, beards, masks and sundries.

### THE MAKE-UP CENTRE
5 Dixon Street, Glasgow G1 4AL.
Tel 0141 248 1882
Fax 0141 248 5854
Scotland's largest stockist of Kryolan theatrical make-
up. Professional make-up artists available for
consultations, demonstrations, classes and workshops.
Mail order and budgeting service.
10% discount for professional/amateur groups and
performers.

### PLAYLIGHT HIRE LIMITED
860 Coronation Road, Park Royal, London NW10 7PS
Sales 0181 961 8812
Fax 0181 961 6348
Contact: Ian Ferguson
Stock manuals supplied by mail order or to personal
callers. Trained staff to advise you.

### SCREENFACE
24 Powis Terrace, London W11 1JH
Tel 0171 221 8289
Fax 0171 792 9357
Screenface has been supplying film, television and
theatre companies for 10 years and carries the largest
range of professional make-up, make-up cases and
location mirrors in the UK.

### SHOWBIZ
11 Acorn Workshops, Empress Road, Southampton
S014 0JY.
Tel/Fax 01703 336341
Wigmakers for stage, television, films. Hire, sale or
make-to-hire service.

### SOUND ELECTRONICS (NEWCASTLE) LIMITED
Industry Road, Heaton, Newcastle-upon-Tyne
NE6 5XB
Tel 0191 265 2500
Fax 0191 265 8595
Stockists for Ben Nye, Leichner, Kryolan, Rosco.
Special effects stockist.

### STAGE DOOR SUPPLIES
198 Bakers Street, Enfield EN1 3JY
Tel 0181 367 7337
Fax 0181 367 7557
Make up by Leichner and Kryolan.

### WIG CREATIONS
40 Camden Street, London
Tel 0171 402 4488
Fax 0171 706 4806
Suppliers of hand-made wigs, beards, moustaches,

etc. to theatre, films and television.

### WIG SPECIALITIES LIMITED
173 Seymour Place, London W1H 5TP
Tel 0171 262 6565
Tel/Fax 0171 723 1566
Managing Director: Carol Waug

### THE WORKSHOP
2 Shipley Cottages, Bridgnorth Road, Shipley, Nr
Pattingham, Nr Wolverhampton WV6 7EH.
Ex-directory.
Promotional costumes and masks. Latex make-up and
prosthetics, custom made masks, heads and body
parts, animals and character costumes, puppets,
models and certain props, monster maker and make-
up. All made to order.

# 39
# MANAGEMENT CONSULTANTS

### DAVID ALLTHORPE MANAGEMENT SERVICES
21 Launcelyn Close, North Baddesley, Romsey,
Hampshire SO52 9NP.
Tel 01703 737505.
Administration, Market Research, Marketing and
Promotion, Staffing/Vacancy Consultancy, Festival and
Event Management/Direction.

### ARTS INTELLIGENCE LTD
PO Box 957, Cottenham, Cambridge, CB4 8AB
Email brian-whitehead@email.msn.com
Contact: Brian Whitehead, Liz Hill, Alison Lea
General management and marketing.

### BIG LITTLE THEATRE PRODUCTIONS LIMITED
Victoria Chambers, Firvale Road,
Bournemouth BH1 2JN
Tel 01202 298298
e-mail magictouch@biglittle.co.uk
Website www.biglittle.co.uk

### LAWRENCE BLACKMORE
Flat 5, 26 Charing Cross Road, London WC2H 0DG
Tel/Fax 0171 240 1817
Theatre Production Accountant. Production and
running cost estimation, budgeting and general
evaluation of theatrical ventures. Financial and
management accounting systems analysis.

### GARRY BROWN ASSOCIATES (INT.) LTD
27 Downs Side, Cheam, Surrey SM2 7EH
Tel 0181 643 3991/8375
Fax 0181 770 7241
e-mail gbaltd@compuserve.com
Leisure/Entertainments Consultants.

### CARR & ANGIER
The Old Malthouse, Clarence Street, Bath BA1 5NS.
Tel 01225 446 664
Fax 01225 446 654
Full consultancy service for the Theatre Concert and
Conference Industries.

### CHAPMAN DUNCAN ASSOCIATES
10-14 Macklin Street, Covent Garden, London
WC2B 5NF

Tel 0171 242 1882
Fax 0171 242 1855
Contact: Guy Chapman, Andrew Toole or Sebastian Warrack.
Offering a comprehensive marketing, press, project, tour & general management service across all forms and charities.

**COLE KITCHENN LTD.**
Nederlander House, 7 Great Russell Street,
London WC1B 3NH
Tel 0171 580 2772
Fax 0171 580 2992
Producing General Mangement, Casting and Theatrical Consultancy.

**JULIAN COURTENAY THEATRE PLANNING**
Savoy Theatre, Strand, London WC2 OET
Tel 0171 836 8117
Fax 0171 379 7322
Consultancy advice for national lottery fund applications, business plans, technical consultancy, project co-ordination and supervision.

**DHA LIGHTING LTD**
284-302 Waterloo Road, London SE1 8RQ
Tel 0171 771 2900
Fax 0171 771 2901
ISDN: 0171 401 9202
Email: custom.gobo@dhalighting.co.uk
General Manager: Diane Grant
Lighting Design Consultants.

**DONMAR LTD**
Donmar House, 54 Cavell Street, Whitechapel,
London E1 2HP
Tel 0171 790 1166
Fax 0171 790 6634
Directors: Ian Albery & Fiona MacLean.
Theatre consultancy, Lighting & Stage equipment planning and specifications. UK and overseas.

**MURRAY EDWARDS AND ASSOCIATES**
Barracks Studios, 19 Barracks Square, Newcastle
Staffordshire ST5 1LG
Tel/Fax 01782 712732
Contact: Murray Edwards
Management consultancy and services; project and event management, tour booking and management, corporate development.

**JACKIE ELLIMAN (ORGANISATION FOR ARTS & MEDIA)**
5 Dryden Street, London WC2E 9NW
Tel 0171 829 8465
Fax 0171 240 5600
Administrative services for the arts - marketing project management, events management, setting up training courses, tour booking.

**MICHAEL HOLDEN ASSOCIATES**
17 West Heath Drive, London NW11 7QG
Tel 0181 455 4640
Fax 0181 209 1059
Theatre Consultants, management consultants in the arts and entertainment industry. Experienced in the formation of trusts and other management structures.

**DAVID JACKSON & ASSOCIATES**
Crowlin Cottage, Little London Road, Cross in Hand, Nr Heathfield, East Sussex TN21 OLT
Tel 01435 868808
Fax 01435 868889
Website: deejaay5.compusound.com
Theatre services, customere care, audience

development studies, business plans.

**MARKETSENSE**
41 Mansfield Street, Chester Green, Derby DE1 3RJ
Tel 01332 291264
Contact: Robert Corder or Patricia Reynolds
Fundraising, sponsorship.  Marketing development. Structures & organisational management.

**MARTIN GABRIEL PROMOTIONS**
The Arts Centre, Vane Terrace, Darlington,
Co.Durham DL3 7AX
Tel/Fax 01325 467272
Mobile 0973 444664
Contact: Martin Roberts
We offer a telemarketing and promotional service for performing company's to help you promote and integrate live theatre into the community and education sectors. All our services can be tailored for your company's individual needs, putting you in control of the costs.
See our advert in the Arts Centres section.

**MIDLAND THEATRE SERVICES LTD**
Junction 1, Industrial Estate, Dartmouth Road,
Dartmouth, Smethwick, Birmingham B66 1AX
Tel 0121 525 4545
Fax 0121 525 2413
Theatre lighting and sound consultants. Equipment available for sale and hire. Main dealer for Strand Lighting in the Midlands. Open 9.00a.m. to 6.00p.m., Monday-Friday, Saturday 9.30a.m. to 12.30p.m.

**MODELBOX LTD**
Studio 9, 75 Filmer Road, London SW6 7JF.
Tel 0171 371 0110
Fax 0171 371 0503
Pre-production planning services to the Theatre, Conference, Exhibition and Music Industries. Production problems are solved before they happen by the use of Advanced Digital Technology. Modelbox also runs a networked system of computer workstations coupled with a powerful Renderfarm for rapid processing of information. All animation is mastered to PAL broadcast standard and if required edited on our BetaCam edit suite.

**POWELL ALLEN ASSOCIATES**
35 Schofield Avenue, Witney, Oxfordshire OX8 5JR
Tel 01993 704820
Consultancy offering design, scenic construction, painting, lighting and sound for theatrical and leisure projects at the most competitive and cost efffective prices.

**BERNARD REECE MARTIN**
89 Oban Drive 3/2, North Kelvinside,
Glasgow G20 6AB
Tel/Fax 0141 946 6359
e-mail bernardreecemartin@compuserve.co.uk
Longest established Theatre Marketing specialist in the North.

**SLOANE PROJECT MANAGEMENT**
Pandora House, 41-45 Lind Road, Sutton, Surrey
SM1 4PP
Tel 0181 643 9662
Fax 0181 643 8172

**TECHNICAL INSIGHT**
Studio 6, 75 Filmer Road, London SW6 7JF.
Tel 0171 371 0875
Fax 0171 736 0051
Main personnel: David Self BA, BArch(Hons) RIBA, Theatre Consultant.

Architectural practice: full service from inception to design. New build and refurbishment. Theatre consultancy: design, advice and reports, surveys, maintenance and development.

**THE TECHNICAL OFFICE**
23 Gibson Square, Islington, London N1 0RD
Tel/Fax 0171 226 3412
Mobile 0973 549 137
Production & Technical Management, National & International Tours & West End.

**THEATRE DEVELOPMENTS LIMITED**
55 High Street, Tring, Herts  HP23 5AG
Tel 01442 890999
Fax 01442 890258
Design & technical consultancy in the building or refurbishment of theatres, cinemas, studios, conference centres, boardrooms, training centres, etc.

**THEATRE PROJECTS CONSULTANTS**
3 Apollo Studios, Charlton Kings Road, London NW5 2SW
Tel 0171 482 4224
Fax 0171 284 0636
Theatre and leisure consulting service.

**TOP DRAW ARTISTS**
Cary Point, Babbacombe Downs, Torquay TQ1 3LU
Tel 01803 322233
Fax 01803 322244
Theatre consultants and artiste management.

**UNCLE BRIAN LTD**
The Wood Cottage, Brompton by Sawdon, Scarborough YO13 9DD
Tel 01723 859497
Fax 01723 859497
Mobile: 0850 615554
Contact: David Reid

# 40

# MARKET RESEARCH

**BOSTOCK MARKETING**
7 Holt Court North, Heneage Street  West, Aston Science Park, Birmingham B7 4AX
Tel 0121 333 6006
Fax 0121 333 6800

**GALLUP ORGANIZATION LTD**
Apex Tower, 7 High Street, New Malden, Surrey KT3 4DG
Tel 0181 336 6400
Fax 0181 336 6455

**MARKET & OPINION RESEARCH INTERNATIONAL (MORI)**
32 Old Queen Street, London SW1H 9HP
Tel 0171 222 0232
Fax 0171 222 1653

**MPS INTERNATIONAL LTD**
Peerland House, 207 Desborough Road, High Wycombe, Bucks HP11 2QL
Tel 01494 452600
Fax 01494 449122

**MARKETSCAN**
8 Dukes Court, Chichester, West Sussex PO19 2FX
Tel 01243 786711
Fax 01243 779671

**NOP RESEARCH GROUP**
Tower House, Southampton Street, London WC2E 7HN
Tel 0171 890 9000

# 41
# MARQUEE HIRE & OUTDOOR EVENTS

**ALBION WOODS**
The Dowding Mill, Slaughterford, Chippenham SN14 8RG
Tel 01225 743790
Fax 01225 743348

**BLACK & EDGINGTON STRUCTURES**
30 Marshgate Lane, Stratford, London E15 2NH
Tel 0181 534 8085
Fax 0181 534 4134
Hire of marquee and all temporary structures.

**CBC MARQUEES LTD**
Blackswarth Road, Bristol BS5 8AD
Tel 0117 977 2400
Fax 0117 972 3012
Hire of marquees, pavilions, interior linings and dance floors, catering equipment.

**DOCKLANDS RACING LTD**
Gate 14, Galleons Reach, Royal Albert Dock Basin (off Woolwich Manner Way), London E16 2NJ
Tel 0171 252 2345
Fax 0171 476 3456

**EUROTECH LTD**
4 West Halkin Street, London SW1.
Tel 0171 235 8273
Fax 0171 235 5770
Managing Director: G. N. Woolnough
Eurotech manufacture at our works near Henley on Thames flags, banners, awnings, canopies and exhibition units of all types.  We can apply decorative or descriptive designs by silk screen printing, sign writing or applique work.

**EVENT SERVICES LTD**
The Old Foundry, Brow Mills Industrial Estate, Brighouse Road, Hippeholme, Halifax, HX3 8EF
Tel 01422 204114
Fax 01422 204431
Outdoor event equipment hire company. Wide range of equipment including crowd barriers, mobile grandstands, marquees, security fence, mobile stages etc.

**FAST STRUCTURES**
235 High Street, Henley-in-Arden, Solihull, West Midlands B95 5BG
Tel 01564 794001
Fax 01564 794752
e-mail relton@waverider.co.uk

**FUTURIST LIGHT & SOUND LTD**
Hoyle Head Mills, New Street, Earlsheaton,
Dewsbury, West Yorks WF12 8JJ
National Call Hotline 0990 168259
Tel 01924 468183
Fax 01924 458667
Full range of marquee services and outdoor event
management and conference services.

**GO LEISURE LTD**
The Arts Exchange, Mill Green, Congleton, Cheshire
CW12 1JG.
Tel 01260 276627.

**HAYES SOUND & LIGHTING (HSL-HIRE) LTD**
Unit 7, Cunliffe Road, Whitebirk Industrial Estate,
Blackburn, Lancashire BB1 5UA
Tel 01254 698808
Fax 01254 698835
Contact: Simon Stuart
Every client is special, each commission totally unique,
our in house event management process ensuring that
your project is carefully monitored, from the taking of
your detailed instructions, through design and
planning, and ultimately the installation and staging of
the event itself.

**LANCELYN THEATRE SUPPLIES**
Office and Sales, Electric Avenue, Ferry Hinksey
Road, Oxford OX2 0BY
Tel 01865 722468
Fax 01865 728791
Hire of stage lighting and control equipment, rigging,
optical and special effects. Outdoor seating, rigging,
sound and lighting equipment for theatre, display or
son-et-Lumiere. Delivery service.

**LIGHT & SOUND DESIGN LTD**
201 Coventry Road, Birmingham B10 0RA
Tel 0121 766 6400
Fax 0121 766 6150
Contact: Robert Wain
Lighting hire including `Icon` moving light and show
control system.

**LONDON CANVAS CO.**
11 Waterside, Pear Tree, Milton Keynes MK6 3DE.
Tel 01908 661017/ 01831 884146
Contact: Dawn Rainbow
Big Top tent and marquee hire including staging,
lighting & sound equipment.

**LONDON STAGING**
217 Blackstock Road, London N5 2LL
Tel 0171 354 1911
Fax 0171 226 2311
Specialists in weatherproof stages for outdoor events.
Also full technical production and event management
service available.

**THE MANCHESTER LIGHTING AND STAGE CO.**
77 Central Road, Manchester M20 4YD
Tel 0161 445 6876
Fax 0161 445 7574
Contact: Bruce Mitchell
Lighting Hire and Sales "Steeldeck" Hire and Sales -
Marquee Hire, Event Management - Site Electrics.
Catwalks, outdoor roofs & stages.

**MARQUEES OVER LONDON**
Unit 15, Ferrier Street Industrial Estate, Old York
Road, Wandsworth, London SW18 1SR
Tel 0181 875 1966

Fax 0181 875 9008
Hire of marquees.

**MASTERS**
Pilgrims Way, Dunton Green, Sevenoaks, Kent
TN13 2TL
Tel 01732 740370
Fax 01732 462854
Tent hire and mobile exhibitions. General display
contractors. Marquees, exhibition stands,
conferences, mobile exhibitions and general display
contractors.

**OWEN BROWN (MARQUEES) LTD**
Station Road, Castle Donington, Derby DE74 2NL.
Tel 01332 850000
Fax 01332 850005
e-mail enq@owen-brown.co.uk
Website www.owen-brown.co.uk
Contact: Mr Keith Iliffe, Sales; Ms Elaine Bywater,
Marketing

**PURVIS MARQUEE HIRE**
50 Lindsay Road, Edinburgh EH6 6NW.
Tel 0131 554 1331
Fax 0131 553 7655
Marquee and clearspan structure hire, furniture hire,
textile repair (stage cloths etc).

**RAINBOW BOUNCERS**
11 Waterside, Pear Tree, Milton Keynes MK6 3DE.
Tel 01908 661017.
Inflatables and ball ponds for hire indoor or out.
Delivery or own pickup.

**STAGE ELECTRICS**
Victoria Road, Avonmouth, Bristol BS11 9DB
Tel 0117 982 7282
Fax 0117 982 2180
e-mail hire@stage-electrics.co.uk
e-mail sales@stage-electrics.co.uk
Website www.stage-electrics.demon.co.uk
Cofton Road, Marsh Barton, Exeter EX2 8QW
Tel 01392 255868
Fax 01392 410592
Parkway Industrial Estate, Plymouth PL6 8LH
Tel 01752 269444
Fax 01752 228283
Dartmouth Road, Smethwick, West Midlands B66 1AX
Tel 0121 525 4545
Fax 0121 525 2413
Hire, sales, installation and service of lighting
equipment for theatre, conference, concert, festival
and commercial presentations. Project management,
designers and engineers.

**STAGE TECHNIQUES**
Unit One, Cotton Drive, Dalehouse Lane Industrial
Estate, Kenilworth, Warwickshire CV8 2EB.
Tel 01926 864800
Fax 01926 864964
Suppliers of Steeldeck stage systems & scenery
construction.

**STAR HIRE**
Milton Road, Thurleigh, Bedford MK44 2DG.
Tel 01234 772233
Fax 01234 772272
Hire of technical services to the entertainment industry
including stage construction and sound services, for both
indoor and outdoor events.

**TRIPLE E LTD**
5 Admiral, Hyson Industrial Estate, Hyson Road,
London SE12 3PA
Tel 0171 237 6354
Fax 0171 237 7650
Email: info@tabtrack.com
Website: www.tabtrack.com
Triple E are the designers, manufacturers and
suppliers of the unique Unitrack system from simple
corded tracks to multi-motor computer controlled
systems. We both sell and install curtain and scenery
track systems. We also hire flight cased tracks and
motor systems. We have a track for every purpose
within the entertainment industry and can supply worldwide either direct or through our distributors.

**TUBULAR BARRIERS LTD**
30-34 Weir Road, London SW19 8UG
Tel 0181 879 8807
Fax 0181 879 8808
Hire of crowd control barriers.

# 42
# MERCHANDISING & ADVERTISING SERVICES

**AEROSIGNS**
130-136 Maidstone Road, Sidcup, Kent DA14 5HS
Tel 0181 302 4921
Fax 0181 302 3971
Banners, flags, signs & display services.

**ARTS CONTACT**
99 High Street, Morley, Leeds LS27 0DE
Tel 0113 252 7356
Mobile 0831 166692/0860 374723
Directors: Sheila Thorpe and Tony Hyslop
A unique creative bulk distribution service for Arts
publicity print, for any Arts event, anywhere in the U.K.

**ARTS MARKETING HAMPSHIRE**
Mottisfont Court, High Street, Winchester, Hants S023 8ZD.
Tel 01962 865383
Fax 01962 841644
Regional Marketing Agency for Central Southern
England, offering strategic services, research &
consultancy to all arts organisations in the area.

**BCL MERCHANDISING LTD**
Suite 108, 222 Kensal Road, London W10 5BN.
Tel 0181 964 3311
Fax 0181 964 3003

**BRANCH LINES**
Milton House, 16 Picts Lane, Princes Risborough,
Buckinghamshire HP27 9DX
Tel 01844 274224
Fax 01844 274182
Contact: Fay Branch

**BRAVADO**
12 Deer Park Road, London, SW19 3TU
Tel 0181 540 8211
Fax 0181 542 1807
On site services.

**BROCHURE DISPLAY LTD**
Units 1+2, Wye Industrial Estate, London Road, High
Wycombe, Buckinghamshire HP11 1LH
Tel 01494 444967
Fax 01494 451026
Display and distribution of brochures for the
entertainment and leisure industry. Targeted audiences
and weekly merchandising to ensure cost effective
control of advertising print.

**CAXTON NAME PLATE MFG. CO. LTD**
Kew Green, Richmond, Surrey TW9 3AR
Tel 0181 940 0041
Fax 0181 940 0642
Badges of all types.

**CHESTER HOPKINS INT.**
24 Fulham Palace Road, Hammersmith, London
W6 9PH.
Tel 0181 741 9910

**COPROM**
Company Promotions House, 32 Back Lane, Ham,
Richmond, Surrey TW10 7LF
Tel 0181 332 3022
Fax 0181 332 2718
Director: Stephen Matthews
Sorting company for merchandising and promotions.

**DALES CLEANING**
2 Swinfield Hillside, Folly Fort Harrogate, North Yorks
HG3 1EE.
Tel 01423 567171
Fax 01423 531020
Suppliers and embroiderers of Casual Leisurewear,
Sweat-Shirts, Polo Shirts etc. Colour brochure on
request.

**DANILO**
Unit 8, Indescon Court, Mill Harbour, London E14 9TN
Tel 0171 538 5557
Fax 0171 537 2677

**DESIGN IT**
Mill House, Dean Clough, Halifax HX3 5AX
Tel 01422 369441
Fax 01422 343177
Email: pinder@orbitnewmedia.co.uk
Website: www.orbitnewmedia.co.uk
Contact: Martin Pinder
Specialists in the design and production of promotional
literature, advertising for the arts and theatres.

**DEWYNTERS PLC**
48 Leicester Square, London WC2H 7QD
Tel 0171 321 0488
Fax 0171 321 0104
Advertising, Design, Marketing, Publishing and
Merchandising.

**EMC ADVERTISING GIFTS**
Derwent House, 1064 High Street, Whetstone,
London N20 0YY
Tel 0181 446 8411
Fax 0181 445 9347
Advertising and promotional gifts.

**EVENT MERCHANDISING LTD**
Unit 11, The Edge, Humber Road, London NW2 6EW
Tel 0181 208 1166
Fax 0181 208 4477
Promotional Merchandising Company. T/Shirts,
Sweatshirts, Jackets, Tour Merchandise etc.

**FAST**
235 High Street, Henley in Arden, Solihull
West Midlands B95 5BG
Tel 01564 794001
Fax 01564 794752
e-mail retton@waverider.co.uk

**THOMAS FATTORINI LTD**
Regent Street Works, Birmingham B1 3HQ
Tel 0121 236 1307
Fax 0121 200 1568
Conference and exhibition badge specialists.

**GALAXY EVENTS**
Holts Cottage, Honington, Shipston-on-Stour,
Warwickshire CV36 5AA
Tel/Fax 01608 661657
A complete merchandising and promotional package
for all Pantomimes, Shows, Musical events and
Shopping centre attractions with print and design
service. SALE OR RETURN CREDIT available on
badges, key rings and other promotional novelties, exc.
fairy wands.

**HAMILTON BROOKE**
Rouge Rue, St Peter Port, Guernsey, C.I., GY1 1ZA
Tel 01481 714437
Fax 01481 714439
Website: http://www.hbgroup.com.
Contact: Ged Kelly
AS suppliers of design and print to one of the UK`s
largest promoters of pantomime and summer shows,
as well as smaller promoters, we produce rosters,
handbills, showcards and programmes.

**HARDSELL LIMITED**
52 Thrale Street, London SE1 9HW
Tel 0171 403 4037
Fax 0171 403 5381
A specialist arts and entertainments full service agency,
providing media planning & buying, marketing, PR, sales
promotion and in-house design and printing services.

**HARIDSTY ROLLS CO.**
PO Box 77, Harrogate, HG3 2ZJ
Tel 01423 567171
Fax 01423 531020
Promotional products of all types including 'Paper
Shaders' (Paper advertising caps), Badges, Beermats, Stickers,
Mugs, Balloons, T-Shirts, etc. Free Colour Brochure upon
request.

**HAYMARKET ADVERTISING LTD**
41 Great Windmill Street, London W1V 7PA
Tel 0171 437 7206
Fax 0171 734 4835
Advertising agency specialising in Theatre and Leisure Industry.

**KEENPAC LTD**
Centurion Way, Meridian Business Park, Leics.
LE3 2WH
Tel 0116 289 0900
Fax 0116 289 3757

**THE KITE & BALLOON COMPANY**
The Old Church, 160 Eardley Road, Streatham,
London SW16 5TG
Tel 0181 679 8844
Fax 0181 679 7792

**LONDON EMBLEM PLC**
Emblem House, Blenheim Road, Longmead
Industrial Estate, Epsom, Surrey KT19 9AP
Tel 01372 745433

Fax 01372745462

**McCABE'S**
36 Lexington Street, London W1R 3HR
Tel 0171 412 2000
Fax 0171 412 2030
Contact: Penny Mallinson, Elaine McGowan, Rebekah
Macleary or Michael McCabe
With offices in London and New York, the company
provides specialist advertising, marketing and design
services to West End and touring productions, London
and regional venues and theatre companies as well as
marketing services for Broadway productions.

**M & T J LTD**
89-91 Norwood Road, London SE24 9AW
Tel 0181 671 3211
Fax 0181 671 3218
Printers of programmes, leaflets and posters.

**THE RAYMOND MANDER AND JOE MITCHENSON
THEATRE COLLECTION**
The Mansion, Beckenham Place Park, Beckenham, Kent
BR3 2BP
Tel 0181 658 7725
Fax 0181 663 0313
Administrator: Richard Mangan
Suppliers of information and photographs relating to
most aspects of theatre.

**THE MARKETING OFFICE LTD**
9 Chiswick High Road, London W4 2ND
Tel 0181 994 0066
Fax 0181 994 4499
Marketing specialists, advertising, print, design,
merchandise, PR.

**MARLER HALEY EXPOSYSTEMS LIMITED**
Little End Road, Eaton Socon, St. Neots,
Cambridgeshire PE19 3SN.
Tel 01480 218588
Fax 01480 477032
Information Boards, Infoframes, Wallboards, Expoloops
and accessories. Moving poster signs, Rotagraphics 3,
portable walls, Gearedge.

**METRO MERCHANDISING LTD**
"The Warehouse", 60 Queen Street, Desborough,
Northants NN14 2RE.
Tel 01536 763100
Fax 01536 763200
Suppliers of promotional and corporate leisurewear and
gifts. Competitive prices – quality merchandise – fast
turnaround. Ring for a quotation or advice on your
requirements.

**MOVITEX SIGNS LTD**
Unit 6, Abbey Mead Industrial Park, Brooker Road,
Waltham Abbey, Essex EN9 1HU.
Tel 01992 719662
Fax 01992 710101
Every kind of sign internal or external.

**NEXO DISPLAY SYSTEMS LTD**
5 Over Minnis, New Ash Green, Kent DA3 8JA
Tel 01474 873512/874991
Fax 01474 879551
Aluminium connectors which clamp together display
panels from 3-25mm thick at any angle using only an
allen key plus a wide range of display lighting.

**NICE MAN EUROPE**
Amsua House, 717a North Circluar Road,

London NW2 7AB
Tel 0171 973 8585
Fax 0171 973 8588

**OCTOPUS ASSOCIATES LTD**
Culford House, 1-7 Orsman Road, London N1 5RA
Tel 0171 729 5962
Fax 0171 729 5994
email: info@theguide.net
Website: http://www.theguide.net
Specialising in the promotion of all forms of Arts and
Entertainment on the Internet. We can provide
everything from Home pages within our major events
listings site to larger stand-alone web sites.

**PADBLOCKS LTD**
Denmark Street, Wokingham, Berks RG40 2BA.
Tel 01734 781499
Fax 01734 771530
Manufacturers of Notepads and Jigsaw Puzzles for
Advertising and Retail.

**PHOSPHENE**
Milton Road South, Stowmarket, Suffolk IP14 1EZ
Tel 01449 678200 & 770011
Badges and Balloons designed and printed. Short runs
a speciality. Balloon displays for product launches,
fashion-shows etc.

**PRIMESIGHT LTD**
14 - 15 Lower Grosvenor Place, Victoria, London
SW1W 0EX
Tel 0171 834 9801
Fax 0171 630 9531
Advertising in airports and air terminals in UK.

**PURE DESIGN**
Victoria House, Cooper Street, Green Lane, Hull HU2 0HG.
Tel 01482 210785
Fax 01482 229637
Pure design is an independent consultancy with vast
experience in producing creative publicity for theatre
and the arts. Apply now for your free set of limited
edition 'pure images' postcards.

**RANK RHINO**
Unit 16, Commercial Road, Edmonton, London
N18 1TP
Tel 0181 803 2584
Fax 0181 807 1139
Screenprinted and Embroidered Leisurewear.

**R M DISPLAY SYSTEMS**
Unit 17, Potters Industrial Park, Coxmoor Close,
Church Crookham, Hants GU13 0EU
Tel 01252 815375
Fax 01252 811486
Portable, modular exhibition display systems and
changeable signs.

**JOHN RUSSELL RECORD ENTERPRISES**
PO Box 71, Lancing, West Sussex BN15 0PE
Tel 01903 753361
Contact: John Russell-Lancing
We supply and sell CDs and cassettes direct to the
public at concert venues.

**SCREENSERVICES**
40 Millmark Grove, London SE14 6RQ
Tel 0181 692 4806
Fax 0181 694 0848
Merchandise related to theatre, music and dance from
the low-cost printed pencils and badges through T-

shirts and other garments, jewellery, bags, umbrellas,
stuffed toys to silk scarves. Small quantities available
on many items. Design service to use a logo effectively
or produce an image for a particular show or season.

**STO-ROSE LIMITED**
'Fantasia" House, Bambers Green, Takeley,
Hertfordshire CM22 6PF
Tel 01279 871444
Fax 01279 871340

**STREETWISE ADVERTISING (POSTERS)**
Unit 6, 49 Effra Road, Brixton, London SW2 1BZ.
Tel 0171 924 0199
Fax 0171 738 4559
Mobile 0973 199274
We are a flyposting company which specialise in
outdoor poster advertising for theatres, concert
promoters magazines and record companies etc.
(We also handle official four sheet poster boards).

**THEATRE DESPATCH LIMITED**
Azof Hall, Azof Street, London SE10 0EG
Tel 0181 853 0750
Fax 0181 293 4861
Administrator: Philip Ormond.
Theatre Despatch is a flexible and comprehensive
distribution service including 1,500 leaflet racks, 4,500
other regularly serviced outlets throughout Greater
London, poster distribution, a complete mailing service
including Mailsort, and a database of 45,000 people
and organisations interested in one or more of the arts
and entertainments.

**TOP DRAW PUBLICITY**
Cary Point, Babbacombe Downs, Torquay TQ1 3LU
Tel 01803 322233
Fax 01803 322244
Marketing of shows and concerts. Producers of theatre
programmes.

**TOTNOLL PROMOTIONS**
Eagle House, Eagle Wharf Road, London N1 7EH
Tel 0171 253 4221
Fax 0171 251 2984

**TOYE, KENNING AND SPENCER LTD**
Regalia House, Newtown Road, Bedworth CV12 8QR.
Tel 01203 315634
Fax 01203 643 018
Civil & Military regalia.

**THE TRADEWINDS MERCHANDISING CO. LTD**
50-56 Wharf Road, Islington, London N1 7SF
Tel 0171 253 4138
Fax 0171 251 4845
Printers and embroiderers of T-Shirts, S-Shirts, Polo
Shirts, Baseball Caps and Jogging Suits.

**UK THEATRE WEB**
New House, High Street, Fernham, Oxon SN7 7NY
Tel/Fax 01367 820827
Website: http://www.uktw.co.uk
Contact: Robert Iles
The UK Theatre Web provides information about the
UK theatre, opera and ballet scene to users all over the
world via the Internet. UK Theatre Web is the premier
index and information site for UK performing arts. In
addition to promotional activities in UK Theatre Web
provides listings of tours and performances to What's
on Stage.

**UNIVERSAL BUTTON CO. LTD**
10/12 Witan Street, Bethnal Green, London E2 6JX
Tel 0171 739 5750/8309
Fax 0171 739 1961
Button Badge Specialists.

**WCM & A LTD**
Kyre Park, Tenbury Wells, Worcs WR15 8RP.
Tel 01885 410247
Fax 01885 410398

**WORLD CLASSICS**
Unit 9, Deane House, 27 Greenwood Place,
Kentish Town, London NW5 1LB
Tel 0171 267 0132
Fax 0171 284 1963

# 43
# MUSICAL EQUIPMENT & SERVICES

**ARDIVAL HARPS**
Orchard House, Caste Leod, Strathpeffer, Ross &
Cromarty IV14 9AA
Tel 01997 421013
Fax 01997 421260
Sale and hire of Harps.

**MICK ASH ORGANISATION**
10 Woodside Park, Juggins Lane, Earlswood B94 5LN
Tel 01564 702482
Fax 01564 703 967
Hire Pianos and musical instruments.

**ARTHUR DAKIN ORGANISATION**
Musical Advisor Orchestral Management
The Old Post House, Hammond Street, Mappowder,
Dorset DT10 2EH
Hiring music stands and lights.

**AUDIOHIRE**
The Linen House, Unit 2, 253 Kilburn Lane, London
W10 HBQ
Tel 0181 960 4466
Fax 0181 969 2162
Contact: James Drew-Edwards
Hire of Sound Equipment; Synthesizers, Samplers,
Recording Equipment, Desks, Noise Reduction,
Microphones, Backline, PA, Drum Machines, Fx, etc etc.

**BLACK CAT MUSIC**
Bankside House, Vale Road, Tonbridge, Kent TN9 1SJ
Tel 01732 367123
Fax 01732 367755
Website www.wengercorp.com
Black cat Music supplies an extensive range of hard-
to-find, everyday, and total unique music equipment
from music stands and chairs to sound-proofed rooms.

**FINAL SCORE**
Cecilia Cottage, 47 Brighton Road, Horsham,
West Sussex, RH3 6EZ
Tel 01403 264798
Composers and Publishers.

**ADAM HALL LTD**
Unit 3, The Cordwainers, Temple Farm Industrial
Estate, Sutton Road, Southend on Sea, Essex
SS2 5RU
Tel 01702 613922
Fax 01702 617168
Email: mail@adamhall.co.uk
Distributor and supplier of fittings and hardware for
flight cases and loudspeaker cabinets. Own brand
stands for lighting, sound and musical instruments.
Sole distributor of Klotz cables and Stage Boxes,
Amphenol Audio Connectors, Palmer Professional
Audio Tools and Power Amplifiers.

**HAYES SOUND & LIGHTING (HSL-HIRE) LTD**
Unit 7, Cunliffe Road, Whitebirk Industrial Estate,
Blackburn, Lancashire BB1 5UA
Tel 01254 698808
Fax 01254 698835
Contact: Simon Stuart
Every client is special, each commission totally unique,
our in house event management process ensuring that
your project is carefully monitored, from the taking of
your detailed instructions, through design and
planning, and ultimately the installation and staging of
the event itself.

**JOHN HENRY ENTERPRISES**
16/24 Brewery Road, London N7 9NH
Tel 0171 609 9181
Fax 0171 700 7040
JHE can provide you with PA/sound reinforcement;
backline equipment; staging and risers; flightcases;
music stands etc. Recent clients have included a
tribute to the Blues Brothers; Shirley Bassey; Michael
Ball etc.

**HINTON INSTRUMENTS**
Oldford, Frome, Somerset BA11 2NN
Tel 01373 451927
Fax 01373 452773
e-mail enquiries@hinton.demon.co.uk
Website www.hinton.demon.co.uk

**HOWORTH WRIGHTSTON LTD**
The Prop House, Unit 2, Cricket Street, Denton,
Manchester M34 3DR.
Tel 0161 335 0220
Fax 0161 320 3928
Manufacturers, retailers and hirers of orchestra stands
and light fittings.

**IMPACT PERCUSSION LTD**
120-122 Bermondsey Street, London SE1 3TX
Tel 0171 403 5900
Fax 0171 403 5910
Hire, retail and repair of percussion instruments
and props.

**MUSIC PLUS**
78 Croydon Road, Reigate, Surrey RH2 ONH.
Tel 01737 226670
Fax 01737 225600
Musicians, composers, programmers and orchestral
management for theatre productions.

**MUSIC ROOM**
The Old Library, 116/118 New Cross Road, London
SE14 5BA.
Tel 0171 252 8271
Fax 0171 252 8252
Sound and musical equipment, hire and sales, 7 days
a week.

**QUICKSILVER UK LTD**
Broom Grove Lane, Denton, Manchester M34 3DU.
Tel 0161 320 7232
Fax 0161 320 3928
Music stand distributers.

**R.A.T. (MUSIC STANDS) LTD**
16 Melville Road, London SW13 9RJ
Tel 0181 741 4804
Fax 0181 741 8949
Manufacturers of purpose designed music stands for orchestra pit, television, concert, school and home use.

**RED GOLD MUSIC LTD**
The World Flute Music Label, 87a Queens Road, East Grinstead, West Sussex RH19 1BG
Tel 01342 300949
Fax 01342 410846
e-mail egsales@egnet.co.uk
Website www.egnet.co.uk/clients/music.rgm.html

**JAQUES SAMUEL PIANOS LTD**
142 Edgware Road, London W2 2DZ
Tel 0171 723 8818
Fax 0171 224 8692
Contact: Terry Lewis
Piano Hire, Tuning Services and Refurbishment Services

**SENSIBLE MUSIC**
Unit 10, Acorn Production Centre, 105 Blundell Street, London N7 9BN
Tel 0171 700 6655
Fax 0171 609 9478
Musical instrument and equipment, hire and sale.

**STEINWAY & SONS**
44 Marylebone Lane, London W1
Tel 0171 487 3391
Fax 0171 935 0466
Piano Retailer. Concert and Tuning Services.

**SWANS MUSIC LTD**
3 Plymouth Court, 166 Plymouth Grove, Manchester M13 0AF.
Tel 0161 273 3232
Fax 0161 274 4111
Email: swansmusicltd@btinternet.com
Contact Bill Swan.
Swans specialise in hiring and servicing all types of pianos. Other instruments also available. Recent credits include Copacobana/In Suspicious Circumstances/Cracker/Choir Girl of the Year/This Morning.

**SYNWAVE PRODUCTIONS**
78 Mount Road, Hastings, East Sussex.
Tel 01424 439465/435790
Fax 01424 439465
Pager 0839 422374·
Music arrangement and orchestration, song composition, pre-production, midi programming and computer services.

**PETER WEBBER HIRE**
110-112 Disreali Road, Putney, London SW15 2DX
Tel 0181 870 1335
Fax 0181 877 1036

# 44
# PASSES AND SECURITY ID

**COVENT GARDEN LAMINATES**
25 Shelton Street, London WC2H 9HT
Tel 0171 836 7695
Fax 0171 836 6562

**ID&C LTD**
MSR International, MSR House, 16 Sandown Grove,
Tunbridge Wells, Kent TN2 4RW
Tel 01892 822660
Fax 01892 823627
ID wristbands a speciality.

**KAHN DISPLAYS LTD**
Units 5+6, Nobel Road, Eley Estate, London
N18 3BH
Tel 0181 803 0800
Fax 0181 803 0412

**PUBLICITY AND DISPLAY LTD**
Douglas Drive, Godalming, Surrey GU7 1HJ
Tel 01483 428326
Fax 01483 424566

**3D-4D HOLOGRAPHICS**
Panther House, 38 Mount Pleasant, London
WC1X 0AP
Tel 0171 837 5767
Fax 0171 713 1994

# 45
# PHOTOGRAPHY

**AMBIENT PHOTOGRAPHY**
Claire McNamee, 1 Primrose Terrace, Hebden
Bridge, W.Yorks HX7 6HN
Tel 01422 844747
Providing a fast reliable service in publicity
photographs for actresses/actors, musicians and
theatres.

**CHRIS ARTHUR**
64 Gloucester Road, Kingston-upon-Thames,
Surrey KT1 3RB
Tel 0181 546 4066

**JOE BANGAY PHOTOGRAPHY**
River House, Riverwoods, Marlow, Bucks
Tel 01628 486193
Fax 01628 890239
Mobile 0860 812529
Casting, portrait and styling photography with
established make up/hair team. Distribution of press
material. Showbiz and Pop library from 1968 to the
present. Theatre and Film Production Photography.
Stage, location, studio photography in the theatre, films
and rock/pop music.

**DONALD COOPER**
P.O. Box 65, Milton Keynes MK5 7YT
Tel 01908 262324
Fax 01908 262082

Mobile 0976 352438

**HADDON DAVIES PHOTOGRAPHY**
Unit 37a, Monument Industrial Park, Chalgrove,
Oxford OX44 7RW
Tel 01865 891900
Production and commercial photography.

**DENBRY REPROS LIMITED**
27 John Adam Street, London WC2N 6HX
Tel 0171 930 1372/0171 839 6496
Fax 0171 925 0183
Top quality photographic reproductions and
composites. Speedy service. Competitive prices.
Mastercard, Switch and VISA accepted.

**DENMAN REPROS**
Commerce Chambers, Elite Buildings, Parliament
Street, Nottingham NG1 2BP
Tel 0115 947 3257
Fax 0115 948 3371

**DOMINIC PHOTOGRAPHY**
4B Moore Park Road, London SW6 2JT
Tel 0171 381 0007
Fax 0171 381 0008
Contact: Zoe Dominic F.R.P.S., Catherine Ashmore,
Photography of Theatre, Opera, Dance and Musicals
for publicity and FOH studio portraiture.

**HAMILTON BROOKE**
Rouge Rue, St Peter Port, Guernsey, C.I., GY1 1ZA
Tel 01481 714437
Fax 01481 714439
Website: http://www.hbgroup.com.
Contact: Ged Kelly
AS suppliers of design and print to one of the UK`s
largest promoters of pantomime and summer shows,
as well as smaller promoters, we produce rosters,
handbills, showcards and programmes.

**JOHN HAYNES**
32 Priory Terrace, London NW6 4DH
Tel 0171 624 2981
Fax 0171 209 3954

**IMAGE PHOTOGRAPHIC**
56 Shepherds Bush Road, London W6 7PH
Tel 0171 602 1190
Fax 0171 602 6219

**VIC JOLLEY PHOTOGRAPHY**
9 Fleet Street, Pemberton, Wigan, Lancs WN5 ODS
Tel 01942 212472

**CAROLE LATIMER**
113 Ledbury Road, London W11
Tel 0171 727 9371
Fax 0171 229 9306

**LEE FILTERS**
Central Way, Walworth Industrial Estate, Andover,
Hants SP10 5AN
Tel 01264 366245
Fax 01264 355058
Contact: Paul Topliss
Manufacturers of lighting filter in both polyester and
polycarbonate. Flame retardant to BS5750 when
stated. Also manufactures of photographic colour
correction and colour printing filters, and optical resin
camera filters. Suppliers of gobos.

**DONALD MCLEMAN**
4a Kelvedon Road, Fulham, London SW6 5BW
Tel 0171 736 1101

Pager 0941 169369
Quality studio and location portraiture, for actors and all other performers.

**RAFAEL**
5 Dalrymple Road, London SE4 2BQ
Tel 0181 694 8517
Portraits, FOH, Live Performances. Exclusive to the Profession. Personal service all arranged by the Director. Rafael also has a back catalogue of photos of stars from 1950s and 60s and is able to suppply copies of these photos.

**REDFERNS**
7 Bramley Road, London W10 6SZ
Tel 0171 792 9914
Fax 0171 792 0921
Music and entertainment picture library with photographers specialising in performance photography.

**RETROGRAPH NOSTALGIA ARCHIVE LTD**
164 Kensington Park Road, London W11 2ER.
Tel 0171 727 9878
Fax 0171 229 3395
Contact: Jilliana Ranicar-Breese.
Vintage posters, advertising, labels and packaging 1860-1960 for wall hangings, backgrounds, back projections, montages, paper action props, mockups, dummies. Transparencies or colour lasers supplied. Picture research service. Free brochure available on request.

**SET REACTION**
Units 7/9, Victoria Road, Avonmouth, Bristol BS11 9DB

Tel 0117 982 6260
Fax 0117 982 7778
Studio hire and facilities.

**BARRY M SHAPCOTT LMPA, LBIPP, LRPS**
65 Hopton Road, Streatham, London SW16 2EL
Tel 0181 769 2786
Fax 0181 696 9664
Mobile 0410 026123
Enquiries welcome for all forms of Photography.
Professional studio and location portfolios a speciality.

**"STILLS"**
373 Footscray Road, London SE9 2DR.
Tel 0181 859 0598/0181 640 7897
e-mail 101320.2653@compuserve.com
Contact: Bill Stirling
Photography and photo processing.

**VISUALEYES PHOTOGRAPHIC SERVICES**
24 West Street, Covent Garden, London WC2H 9NA
Tel 0171 836 3004
Fax 0171 240 0050
Comprehensive photographic services. Specialists in the bulk reproduction of photographs for Press, Public Relations and Theatrical use.

**ROBERT WORKMAN**
32 West Kensington Mansions, Beaumont Crescent, London W14 9PF.
Tel 0171 385 5442
Photography of Theatre, Opera and Ballet Productions.
Photography for Theatre Posters and casting portraits of actors and singers.

## 46
# PIANO HIRE

**JAQUES SAMUEL PIANOS LTD**
142 Edgware Road, London W2 2DZ
Tel 0171 723 8818
Fax 0171 224 8692
Contact: Terry Lewis
Piano Hire, Tuning Services and Refurbishment
Services

## 47
# PLASTIC SPECIALISTS

**TALBOT DESIGNS LTD**
225 Long Lane, Finchley, London N3 2RL
Tel 0181 346 8515
Fax 0181 349 0294
Email: sales@talbotdesigns.co.uk
Website: www.talbotdesigns.co.uk
Contact: Richard Woolff
Over the past 20 years have supplied most of the
notable theatre productions with plastic flooring,
scenery, special effects, hand held props and any
plastic requirements.

## 48
# PROPS HIRE & SALE

**3-D CREATIONS**
9 Keppel Road, Gorleston, Gt. Yarmouth,
Norfolk NR31 6SN
Studio Tel 01493 657093
Workshop Tel 01493 652055
Fax 01493 443124
Mobile 0860 707287
We can provide all your scenic needs for theatre,
television and film. Scenery and prop design and
construction specialists.
Prop makers, set designers, sculptors, scenic artists
we are always prepared to undertake work of the
unusual. Location work undertaken.

**A + M HIRE LTD**
The Royals, Victoria Road, London NW10 6ND.
Tel 0181 233 1500
Fax 0181 233 1550
e-mail hire@amhire.com
The distinguished supplier for period or modern
furniture and dressings.
Established for over 15 years.

**ANIMAL ARK**
The Studio, 29 Somerset Road, Brentford, Middlesex
TW8 8BT
Tel 0181 560 3029
Mobile 0973 242 715
Contact: David Manning.

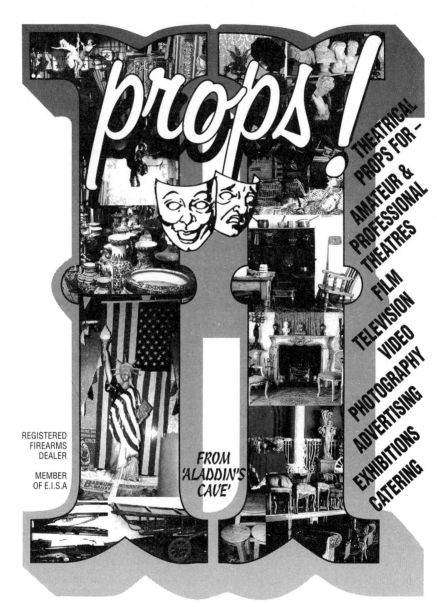

props!

THEATRICAL PROPS FOR –

AMATEUR & PROFESSIONAL THEATRES

FILM

TELEVISION

VIDEO

PHOTOGRAPHY

ADVERTISING

EXHIBITIONS

CATERING

REGISTERED FIREARMS DEALER

MEMBER OF E.I.S.A

FROM 'ALADDIN'S CAVE'

# HOWORTH WRIGHTSON LTD

The Prop House, Unit 2, Cricket Street, Denton, Manchester M34 3DR.   Tel: 0161-335 0220   Fax: 0161-320 3928

The supply and handling of animals and animal props to the film, TV and advertising industries.

**BAPTY & CO LIMITED**
703 Harrow Road, London NW10 5NY
Tel 0181 969 6671
Fax 0181 960 1106
Hirers of fighting weapons of all types and periods and associated props.

**BLACK & EDGINGTON FLAGS**
Orpington Trading Estate, Sevenoaks Way,
Orpington, Kent BR5 3SR
Tel 01689 839389
Fax 01689 870236
Contact: Louise Meredith or Nick Farley

**BRITISH TURNTABLE CO**
Emblem Street, Bolton BL3 5BW
Manchester Depot
Tel 01204 525626
Fax 01204 382407
Email: info@turntable.co.uk
Website: www.british.turntable.co.uk
London Depot
Tel 01992 574602
Fax 01992 560385
British Turntable Company, leaders in creating dramatic movement, offer a range of low profile, self-assembly revolving stages, in diameters ranging from 2m to 8m.  Highly portable, these revolves can be assembled by two men in as little as half an hour*, can be supplied for manual or powered operation and include options such as variable speed, indexing and/or static centre.
This range is in addition to the extremely comprehensive range of revolves available for hire up to 25 tonne capacity and which include units suitable for outdoor location applications.
Competitively priced, all units are available for hire from depots throughout the UK.
*Assembly time based on a 6m standard revolve on sound, level surface.

**CARDIFF THEATRICAL SERVICES LTD**
Unit 1, The 125 Business Park, off Tyndall Street,
Cardiff CF1 5BP
Tel 01222 499977
Fax 01222 481275
Telex: 497858
Scenery Builders, Scenic Artists, Property Markers.

**CINEBUILD EUROPE**
Studio House, Rita Road, Vauxhall, London SW8 1JU
Tel 0171 582 8750
Fax 0171 793 0467
We supply all types of breakaway glass for television and film, plus sales and hire of special effects - snow, mist, rain, cobwebs and dust.

**PAUL COLBECK**
Unit 43, Metropolitan Workshops, Enfield Road,
London N1 5AZ
Tel 0171 249 7540
Mobile 0973 704389
Props and models made to order for TV, stage and films. Scenic sculpting.

**THE COMPANY OF TEN**
Abbey Theatre, Westminster Lodge, Holywell Hill,
St. Albans AL1 2DL
Tel 01727 847472

Fax 01727 812742
Manager: David Griffiths
Property Mistress: Judith Goodban
Tel 01727 856730

**MIKE & ROSI COMPTON**
11 Woodstock Road, Croydon, Surrey CR0 1JS
Tel 0181 680 4364
Fax 0181 681 3126
We make props, special effects, costumes and models. We specialise in the unusual, but can do almost anything! No hiring.

**PETER EVANS STUDIOS LTD**
1 Frederick Street, Luton, Beds LU2 7QW
Tel 01582 25730
Fax 01582 481329
Directors: P Evans, I Adams, R Evans.
Makers of properties and scenic embellishments in rubber, GRP, polystyrene, etc. Supplier of a large range of columns, urns, cornices, friezes, balustrades, brickwork, etc. in vacuum formed PVC, ABS or GRP. Also vacuum forming done from your own patterns or patterns specially made. Catalogue available.

**FARLEY**
1-17 Brunel Road, East Acton, London W3 7XR
Tel 0181 749 9925
Fax 0181 749 8372
e-mail props@farley.co.uk
Specialists in fine furniture.

**FUTURIST LIGHT & SOUND LTD**
Hoyle Head Mills, New Street, Earlsheaton,
Dewsbury, West Yorks WF12 8JJ
National Call Hotline 0990 168259
Tel 01924 468183
Fax 01924 458667
Various studio and stage props for hire and sale plus design and create services.

**GIMBERTS**
Phoenix House, Whitworth Street, Openshaw,
Manchester M11 2GR
Tel 0161 223 6660
Fax 0161 223 6630
Modern and contemporary furniture, refrigerators, modern kitchen units, antique, period and traditional furniture and furnishings.

**GO LEISURE LTD**
The Arts Exchange, Mill Green, Congleton, Cheshire
CW12 1JG.
Tel 01260 276627
Hire of furniture, chairs, floors and tables plus all specialised circus equipment.

**GOOD DESIGN CORPORATION LTD**
1 St Rule Street, London SW8 3ED
Tel 0171 498 8800
Fax 0171 498 9900
A large selection of props and plants. Catalogue available.

**GREENERY LTD**
Bridge Farm, Hospital Bridge Road, Whitton,
Twickenhan TW2 6LH
Tel 0181 893 8992
General garden props of all kinds, floral decor, plants and garden decorations for hire.

**RICHARD HEWER PROPERTY MAKER**
7 Sion Lane, Clifton, Bristol BS8 4BE.
Tel/Fax 0117 9738 760
Property maker, no hiring, working across the broad

# Period Props & Lighting Limited

*(Formerly Mostly Lighting (JMB) Ltd and Mostly Metal Ltd)*

**17/23 Stirling Road, Acton, London  W3 8DJ**
**Telephone:  0181-992 6901   Facsimile:  0181-993 4637**

**For the widest range of period and antique lighting, including:**

Gas Lamps, Oil Lamps, Victorian Street Lamps & Posts, Crystal & Brass Chandeliers, Wrought Iron & Silver Candelabras, Wall Brackets & Sconces, Candlesticks, Table Lamps, Standard Lamps & Shades.

**Also:** Fire Surrounds & Inserts, Grates, Fenders, Fire Irons, Stoves, Coal Buckets, Jardiniers & Stands, Screens, Office Equipment, Baths & Bathroom Fittings, Door Furniture, Books, Mirrors, Clocks & Watches, Photo Frames, Pictures, Stationery Boxes etc. Pub Fittings. Objets D'Art, Kitchen Equipment, Enamel Signs, Bronzes, Desks & Dressings, Smokers Items, Smalls, Gramophones, Medical Items, Pewter, Carpet Bags & Luggage, Oak Furniture etc. etc. etc...

**Our opening hours are:**  8.30 am – 5.30pm Monday to Thursday; 8.30 am – 5.00 pm Fridays and we look forward to welcoming you.

We are sure you will agree that we are well worth a visit.

spectrum of theatre, television, film and natural history. Working in all manner of materials.

### HOWARTH WRIGHTSON LTD T/A HWL
Cricket Street, Denton, Manchester M34 3DR
Tel 0161 335 0220
Email: hwl@quicksilver-uk.demon.co.uk
Contact: Bob Howarth
Hirers of all types of furniture, set dressing, decorative lighting, pictures, hand props etc. Also specialist hirers of weapons and blank firing guns.

### IMPACT PERCUSSION
120-122 Bermondsey Street, London SE1 3TX.
Tel 0171 403 5900
Fax 0171 403 5910
Hire, Retail and Repair of percussion instruments and props.

### JACK 'N' JILL ANIMATIONS
39 High Street, Worle, Weston-Super-Mare,
North Somerset BS22 0EG
Tel 01934 513760
Makers of extraordinary figures, and props. Unusual costumes. Punch & Judy figures and props for childrens entertainers.

### JAMES CARTONS AND TEA CHESTS
209a Fernside Avenue, Hanworth Park, Middlesex TW13 7BQ
Tel 0181 751 1009
Fax 0181 384 7608
Hire and sale of new and once used printed and plain tea chests and cartons.

### JBE STAGE LIGHTING & EQUIPMENT COMPANY
7 Rose Way, Purdeys, Rochford, Essex SS4 1LY.
Tel 01702 545826
Large range of properties for hire includuing Oil lamps, candles, gas lamps, lamposts, brass holn gramophones, period telephones, wireless sets, press cameras, tripod cameras, flash trays, sweeney todd razors, guns, fires, wooden barrels and buckets etc. Please ask for props list.

### KENT HIRE
The Street, Horton Kirby, Dartford, Kent DA4 9BY.
Tel 01322 864919
Fax 01322 864822
Military costumes and props from 1900 to the present day.

### LAURENCE CORNER
62/64 Hampstead Road, London NW1 2NU
Tel 0171 813 1010
Fax 0171 813 1413
Government surplus, alternative clothing, uniforms, headwear, accessories, nets, parachutes, theatrical clothes and accessories and props. Hire or sale.

### JIM LAWS LIGHTING
West End Lodge, Wrentham, Beccles, Suffolk NR34 7NH
Tel 01502 675264
Fax 01502 675565
Period entertainment lighting, hire and sales, lighting design service.

### LEWIS AND KAYE (HIRE) LTD
3B Brassie Avenue, London W3 7DE
Tel 0181 749 2121
Fax 0181 749 9455
Hire of props (silver, glass, china, objects d'art) to TV, films, theatres, photographers.

### ELAINE MCLENACHAN
3/1, 54 Earl Street, Glasgow G14 0DJ
Tel 0141 954 6597
Mobile 0802 236853
All props - carving, modelling, casting, upholstery, costume props, soft furnishings etc. Also prop buying experience, in theatre, film & TV.

### MILTON & PARNELL
### (FORMERLY TRAFFORD & PARNELL PRODUCTIONS)
85 Marton Drive, Blackpool FY4 3EU
Tel 01253 766928 or 0860 273341

### NEWMAN HIRE COMPANY
16 The Vale, Acton, London  W3
Tel 0181 749 1501
Fax 0181 749 3513
Hirers of Properties to TV, Film and Stage.

### PERIOD PROPS & LIGHTING LTD
17-23 Stirling Road, Acton, London W3 8DJ.
Tel 0181 992 6901
Fax 0181 993 4637
Period Props and Lighting Ltd supply props and lighting to the Film, Television and Entertainment Industry ranging from crystal and brass chandeliers to fire surrounds, grandfather clocks and door furniture. They continue to add to their  very comprehensive stocks and are well worth a visit to their premises in Stirling Road, Acton.

### KEN PAUL
22-24 England's Lane, London NW3 4TG
Tel 0171 722 5477/0171 722 7553
Fax 0171 722 7553
Antique Prop. Hire.

### PHELPS LTD
133-135 St. Margarets Road, East Twickenham,
Middlesex TW1 1RG
Tel 0181 892 1778
Fax 0181 892 3661
Antique furniture for hire.

### PHOENIX HIRE LTD incorp. CAMDEN FURNITURE HIRE, OLD TIMES, THE PROP HOUSE & TREVOR HOWSAM
55 Chase Road, London NW10 6LU.
Tel 0181 961 6161
Fax 0181 961 6162
Largest suppliers of period and 20th century furniture, drapes, carpets and decorative objects.

### PICTURES SEVEN STARS CORNER
Paddenswick Road, London W6 OUB
Tel 0181 749 2433
Fax 0181 740 5846
Paintings and works of art.

### PREWETT MILLER - FLOREAT (LONDON)
53 Connaught Street, London W2 2BB
Tel 0171 723 4683
fax 0171 723 6998
Director: J W M Miller
Hire of plants, etc. and floral displays of every description.

### PROPS GALORE
15-17 Brunel Road, Acton W3 7XR
Tel 0181 746 1222
Fax 0181 749 8372
Specialists in the hire of Period textiles, jewellery and accessories.

**NICK REDGRAVE PROPS SCULPTURE**
62-68 Rosebery Avenue, London EC1
Tel 0171 837 8617
Fax 0171 278 8685
Mobile 0385 783593
Props made for stage, TV, films.

**REEVES 'RENT-A-PLANT' SERVICE**
143 Lower Richmond Road, London SW15 1EZ
Tel 0181 788 7089
Floral hire contractor, artificial trees, plants, flowers
available for hire at short notice.  Also real plants with
maintenance for foyers, concert halls etc.

**RETROGRAPH NOSTALGIA ARCHIVE LTD**
164 Kensington Park Road, London W11 2ER.
Tel 0171 727 9878
Fax 0171 229 3395
Contact: Jilliana Ranicar-Breese.
Vintage posters, advertising, labels and packaging
1880-1960 suitable for wall hangings, backgrounds,
back projections, montages, paper action  props,
mockups, dummies.  Transparencies or colour lasers
supplied. Picture research services.

**JANE RUMBLE**
121 Elmstead Avenue, Wembley, Middx HA9 8NT.
Tel 0181 904 6462
Designer, props made to commission only.  Not for
hire, replica paintings, animals, puppets made in resin,
latex, polystyrene, maché.

**SCENE TWO HIRE/H.J.SPILLER/(HIRE) LTD**
18-20 Brunel Road, East Acton W3 7XR
Tel 0181 743 8747
Kitchens, modern and period furniture and
accessories.

**ADRIAN SNELL PRODUCTION SERVICES**
Unit 6, 171 Church Hill Road, Thurmaston, Leicester
LE4 8DH
Tel 0116 260 0901
Fax 0116 260 0933
Contact: Adrian Snell
Our large modern workshops offer a complete
construction service, including engineering, steel
fabrication and all other forms of construction, scenic
art techniques, sculpture, props.  We offer full support
for all projects.

**H. J. SPILLER (HIRE) LTD**
10 Brunel Road, Acton, London W3 7XR
Tel 0181 743 8747
Fax 0181 749 8372
e-mail props@farley.co.uk
Picture and gilt frame hire.

**STUDIO AND TV HIRE**
3 Ariel Way, Wood Lane, London W12
Tel 0181 749 3445
Fax 0181 740 9662
Largest selection of period and modern props in
Britain: 1/2 million props in 20,000 sq ft warehouse.
Special reduced value for theatres.

**SUPERHIRE**
1-4 Bethune Road, North Acton, London NW10 6NJ
Tel 0181 965 9909
Fax 0181 965 8107
Comprehensive modern props, including all types of
furniture, carpets, office dressing and smalls.

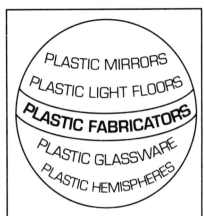 
**TALBOT DESIGNS LTD**
225 Long Lane, London N3 2RL
Tel 0181 346 8515
Fax 0181 349 0294
Email: sales@talbotdesigns.co.uk
Website: www.talbotdesigns.co.uk
Contact: Richard Woolff
Plastic fabricator - supplier and manufacturer of plastic
sheet rod tubes, scenery and props. One way and two
way mirrors.

**THE TRADING POST LIMITED**
Witley Gardens, Norwood Road, Middlesex UB2 4ES
Tel 0181 574 7017
Fax 0181 571 7633
Props hire to Film Business.

**TRAFFORD & PARNELL PRODUCTIONS**
**See MILTON & PARNELL**

**TREASURE TROVE PUPPET COMPANY**
The Old Chapel, Glyndwr Road, Gwernymynydd,
near Mold, Flintshire CH7 5LW.
Tel 01352 750838
Directors: Stephen Sharples
Hirers and makers of carved puppets, marionettes,
rods and glove. Puppet manipulators available.

**TURK FILM SERVICES LTD**
Town End Pier, 68 High Street, Kingston-Upon-
Thames, Surrey KT1 1HR
Tel 0181 546 2434
Fax 0181 546 5775
Hirers of: Marine and boat props, ships, locations and
action sequences.

**M & L WARREN**
32 Station Road, Purton, Wilts
Tel 01793 771453
Thousands of props available for hire. Props made to
your own requirements. Also prop search facilities for
those unusual items
.
**PETER WEBBER HIRE**
110-112 Disraeli Road, Putney, London SW15 2DX.
Tel 0181 870 1335
Fax 0181 877 1036

**THE WORKSHOP**
2 Shipley Cottages, Bridgnorth Road, Shipley, Nr
Pattingham, Nr Wolverhampton, WV6 7EH
Tel: Ex-directory.
Promotional costumes and masks. Latex make up and
prosthetics, custom made masks, heads and body
parts, animals and character costumes, puppets,
models and certain props, monster maker and make-
up. All made to order.

**CHRISTOPHER WRAY'S LIGHTING EMPORIUM LTD**
600 Kings Road, London SW6 2DX
Tel: 0171 736 8434 (5 lines)
Fax: 0171 731 3507
The largest selection of Decorative Lighting, periods 1880's -
1930 in Great Britain. Hire department now open. Spare parts
and glass shades etc., for all Victorian, Edwardian lighting.
Special low rates for long hire. Deocrative ceiling fans.
Showrooms in Caversham, Belfast, Bromley, Bristol,
Bournemouth, Birmingham, Dublin, Glasgow, Manchester,
Nottingham, Norwich, London - Covent Garden, Leeds,
Newcastle, Exeter, Enfield. Offer full hire facilities.

# 49

# RADIO AND MOBILE TELEPHONE SYSTEMS

**AIRCELL COMMUNICATIONS**
Unit 27, The River Road Business Park, 23 River
Road, Barking IG11 0EA
Tel 0181 591 3669

**ARE COMMUNICATIONS**
6 Royal Parade, Hanger Lane, Ealing, London
W5A 1ET
Tel 0181 997 4476
Fax 0181 991 2565

**ASM COMMUNICATIONS**
Ingoldfield Lane, Newtown, Wickham, Hampshire
PO17 6LF
Tel 01329 832156
Fax 01329 832157
Mobile 0831 563973

**ASSOCIATED COMMUNICATIONS**
Communications House, 96-97 King William Street,
Stourbridge, West Midlands DY8 4EY
Tel 01384 440736

**AUDIOLINK RADIO COMMUNICATIONS**
Link House, Heather Park Drive, Wembley, Middlesex
HAO 1SS
Tel 0181 900 2311
Fax 0181 900 1977

**BETTER SOUND LTD**
33 Endell Street, London WC2H 9BA
Tel 0171 836 0033
Fax 0171 497 9285
**BT CORPORATE RELATIONS**
4th Floor, Room 410, Telecom House, 91 London
Road, Manchester M60 1HQ
Tel 0161 600 2190
Fax 0161 236 8100

**CALLSAVER LTD**
20 Caledonian Road, Kings Cross, London N1 9DU
Tel 0171 278 5187
Fax 0171 278 7216
Website www.com.callsaveruk

**COMHIRE COMMUNICATIONS PLC**
Communications House, Disraeli Road, Park Royal,
London NW10 7HX
Tel 0181 961 9686
Mobile 0973 723315

**COMMUNICATION SPARES (UK)**
Empress House, 42 Empress Parade, Chingford Road,
London E4 8SL
Tel 0181 531 1909
Fax 0181 531 0008

**CRAVEN & FINDLAY LTD**
Units 8-10 Adler Industrial Estate, Betam Road, Hayes,
Middx UB3 1ST
Tel 0181 573 1177
Fax 0181 561 8334

**DIRECT TELECOM SERVICES LTD**
Harley Works, Paxton Hill, St Neots, Cambridge
PE19 4RA
Tel 01480 407740
Fax 01480 407767

**ECHO CELLULAR RENTAL**
81 Waltham Street, London SW3 28P
Tel 0171 706 1000
Fax 0171 486 0093
e-mail ncs@echocomms.co.uk
Website echocomms.co.uk
Contact: Clare Jennings

**FIRST EUROPEAN**
39 Lonsdale Road, London SW13 9JP
Tel 0171 221 9555

**GBS - GENERAL BATTERY SUPPLIES**
2 Electric House, Seven Kings Road, Ilford, Essex
IG3 8BY
Tel 0181 599 2920
Fax 0181 599 8186
Radio Mike and General Battery Suppliers.

**HAND HELD AUDIO**
Unit 2, 12-48 Northumberland Park, London N17 0TX
Tel 0181 880 3243
Fax 0181 365 1131
Contact: Mick Shepherd
Radio systems specialists. We sell, rent and service
radio microphones and `in-ear` monitor systems.

**HUGO RADICOM**
6 Waterside Drive, Langley Business Park, Slough
Berks SL3 6EZ
Tel 01753 542828
Fax 01753 543131

**LOCATION SOUND**
Head Office: 57 Fallodon Way, Harleaze, Bristol
BS9 4HT
Tel/Fax 0117 962 4411
Mobile 0468 477994
13 King's Walk, Highridge Green, Bristol BS13 8BB
Tel/Fax 0117 964 4038
Mobile 0836 725743

**LONDON COMMUNICATIONS PLC**
134 Gloucester Avenue, Regents Park, London
NW1 8JA
Tel 0171 586 9851
Fax 0171 722 0966

**LONDON COMMUNICATIONS PLC**
22 Craven Court, Winwick Quay, Warrington
WA2 8QU
Tel 01925 413740
Fax 01925 414577

**LONDON PAGER LIMITED**
21-22 Parkway Newbury, Berks RG14 1EE

**MOTOROLA LTD**
Victory House, Barley Way, Fleet, Hants GU13 8US
Tel 01252 801801
Fax 01252 801800
Contact: Kevin Lawless
The Motorola Radio Parts and Services Group is
responsible for the supply and support of accessories,
batteries, test & parts equipment and customer service
throughout Europe, the Middle East and Africa.

**NATIONAL RADIO BANK**
Pinfold Road, Bourne, Lincolnshire PE10 9HT
Tel 01778 393938
Fax 01778 421603
Contact: Mike Bailey (Hire Manager)
International two way radio hire specialists.
See our advert on page 10.

**NATIONAL SOUND REPRODUCERS LTD**
Lower Priory Farm, Clamp Hill, Stanmore, Middlesex
HA7 3JJ
Tel 0181 954 7677
Fax 0181 954 9329

**OSBORNE SOUND EQUIPMENT LTD**
9 Meard Street, Soho, London W1V 3HQ
Tel 0171 437 6170
Fax 0171 439 4807

**RADIO LINKS COMMUNICATIONS LTD**
Eaton House, Great North Road, Eaton Socon, St
Neots, Cambridge PE19 3EG
Tel 01480 217220
Fax 01480 406667

**RAYCOM**
Technology House, Tything Road, Alcester,
Warwickshire B49 6EP
Tel 01789 400600
Fax 01789 400630
Mobile 0836 282228

**RELCOM COMMUNICATIONS LTD**
12 Alliance Court, Alliance Road, London W3 0RB

Tel 0181 896 8300
Fax 0181 741 4274

**SECURICOR RADIOCOMS LTD**
170a Oval Road, East Croydon, Surrey CR0 6BN
Tel 0181 680 1585
Fax 0181 686 9433

**SHOW HIRE**
Unit 4, Station Yard Industrial Estate, Station Lane,
Milford, Godalming, Surrey GU8 5AD
Tel 01483 414337
Fax 01483 426926
Radio communications and public address systems
hire and sale.

**SKARDA INTERNATIONAL COMMUNICATIONS**
7 Portland Mews, London W1V 3FL
Tel 0171 734 7776
Fax 0171 734 1360
Mobile 0836 200700

**SOLENT SOUNDS SYSTEMS**
7 Mitchell Point, Ensign Park, Hamble, Southampton
SO31 4RF
Tel 01703 456700
Fax 01703 456789

**VIRGIN TELECOM LTD**
760 Great Cambridge Road, Enfield, Middx. EN1 3RN
Tel 0181 364 5888
Fax 0181 364 5539
Website: www.virgin-tle.com
Contact: David King
Business Activities:We offer sales, rental and
installation for mobile, office and satellite telephone
systems, faxes and pagers. We represent all four
mobile networks and all the major manufacturers.

**VODAPHONE HIGHER SOLUTIONS**
69a High Street, Ruislip, Middlesex HA4 8SB
Tel 0171 229 4648
Fax 0171 792 0423
Managing Dirctor: Susie James

**VOICE & DATA COMMUNICATIONS**
Communications House, 21/23 Timbreu Street,
Trowbridge, Wiltshire BA14 8PP
Tel: 01225 764444
Fax: 01225 761999
e-mail vdc@enterprise.net

**MIKE WEAVER COMMUNICATIONS LTD**
Unit 17, Redland Close, Alderman's Green Industrial
Estate, Coventry CV2 2NP
Tel 01203 638767
Fax 01203 602609

# 50
# RECORDING

**AGM DIGITAL ARTS LTD**
14-16 Deacons Lane, Ely, Cambridgeshire CB7 4PS.
Tel 01353 665588
Fax 01353 667637
Manufacture of digital audio equipment and digital
recording services.

**AIR STUDIOS**
Lyndhurst Hall, Lyndhurst Road, Hampstead, London
NW3 5NG

Tel 0171 794 0660
Fax 0171 794 8518

**BIG BEAR MUSIC GROUP**
PO Box 944, Edgbaston, Birmingham B16 8UT
Tel 0121 454 7020
Fax 0121 454 9996
Managing Director: Jim Simpson
A&R: Wilma Vance
Marketing: John Keetley
Press/PR: Clare Jepson-Homer
Record label.

**THE CANDLE MUSIC COMPANY**
44 Southern Row, London W10 5AN
Tel 0181 960 0111
Fax 0181 968 7008
Composing and recording original and non-original
music for film, TV, radio, audio-visual and theatre.

**IMAGE DIGGERS**
618b Finchley Road, London NW11 7RR
Tel/Fax 0181 455 4564
Picture, Slide & Tape Hire.

**R G JONES RECORDING STUDIOS**
Beulah Road, Wimbledon, London SW19 3SB.
Tel 0181 540 9883
Fax 0181 542 4368
Studio Manager: Chue
SSL 4000E console with computer automation and
total recall. 32 track digital and 24 track Studer 827
analogue recording facilities.

**OXRECS DIGITAL**
Magdalen Farm Cottage, Standlake, Witney, Oxon
OX8 7RN
Tel/Fax 01865 300347
Manager: Bernard Martin.
Bookings Manager: Joyce Martin
Specialists in location recording for organs, chamber
orchestras and choirs. Typesetting, design service and
digital editing also available for booklets and inlays.

**REDBRIDGE RECORDINGS**
23 Bethell Avenue, Redbridge, Essex IG1 4UX
Tel 0181 518 6342
Fax 0181 518 0286
e-mail 101456.1034@compuserve.com
Specialist location recording - CD's, cassettes, editing
and artwork.

**SILVERWORD RECORDS LTD**
Crickhowell, Powys NP8 1LB
Tel 01873 810142
Fax 01873 811557
Management company, record producers, marketing
company and music publishers.

**TABITHA MUSIC LTD**
2 Southernhay West, Exeter EX1 5JG
Tel 01392 499 889
Fax 01392 498 068
Record producer, music publisher.

**51**

# REHEARSAL ROOMS

## LONDON

**ABBEY COMMUNITY ASSOCIATION**
34 Great Smith Street, Westminster, London SW1 P3U
Tel 0171 222 0303/4
Fax 0171 233 3308

**THE ALBANY CENTRE & THEATRE**
Douglas Way, London SE8 4AG
Tel 0181 691 3277  BO 0181 692 4446
Fax 0181 469 2253

**B.A.C.**
Lavender Hill, Battersea, London SW11 5TF
Admin 0171 223 6557  BO 0171 223 2223
Fax 0171 978 5207
Theatre Manager: Catherine Thornborrow

**BBC TELEVISION REHEARSAL ROOMS**
Victoria Road, North Acton, London W3 6UL
Tel 0181 576 1831
Fax 0181 749 8717

**BLUESTONE STUDIOS**
Hebron Whitland, West Wales
Tel 01994 419425
Fax 01994 419425 (Phone first)
Contact: Noreen F Vaughan
Luxury residential rehearsal and location recording 3,000
sq ft of acoustically controlled space. Full leisure facilities
licenced, wonderful setting in national park.

**CAMDEN ROUND HOUSE**
Chalk Farm Road, Camden, London NW1
For Bookings Contact: Go Leisure Ltd, The Arts
Exchange, Mill Green, Congleton, Cheshire CW12 1JG
Tel 01260 276627

**CECIL SHARP HOUSE**
2 Regent's Park Road, London NW1 7AY
Tel 0171 485 2206
Fax 0171 284 0534
Main Hall - 500 Capacity.
2 Smaller Halls - 140 Capacity & 60 Capacity.
2 First Floor Rooms - 30/40 Capacity each.

**COURTYARD THEATRE**
10 York Way, King's Cross, London N1 9AA
Tel/Fax 0171 833 0870
Wood Studio 22ft x 18ft wood floor
Dance Studio 34ft x 14ft maple sprung floor, mirrors on
one wall, upright piano
Triangle Studio 15ft x 10ft seating for 15. 6 channel
manual lighting board, lanterns, cassette player/sound
may be available if required.

**CROWN COURT CHURCH HALL**
Theatre Director, Fortune Theatre, Russell Street,
London WC2B 5HH
Tel 0171 836 6260
Fax 0171 379 7493

**DANCE ATTIC STUDIOS**
Old Fulham Baths, 368 North End Road, Fulham,
London SW6 1LY.
Tel 0171 610 2055
Fax 0171 610 0995

**DANCE WORKS**
16 Balderton Street, London W1Y 1TF
Tel 0171 629 6183
Fax 0171 499 9087

**THE DRILL HALL**
16 Chenies Street, London WC1E 7EX
Tel 0171 631 1353
Fax 0171 631 4468
Three rehearsal rooms.

**HAMPSTEAD THEATRE**
Swiss Cottage Centre, London NW3 3EX
Tel 0171 722 1189

**JOHN HENRY ENTERPRISES**
16/24 Brewery Road, London N7 9NH
Tel 0171 609 9181 (8 lines)
Fax 0171 700 7040
Music rehearsal studios, PA and backline rental.

**HOLBORN CENTRE FOR THE PERFORMING ARTS**
Three Cups Yard, Sandland Street, London WC1R 4PZ
Tel 0171 306 5954
Fax 0171 306 5820
Over 7,000 square feet of rehearsal, workshop and
meeting spaces available for hire. Dance floors, sound
and lighting rigs, a café and central location make
Holborn one of the best places in town!

**INSTITUTE OF INDIAN CULTURE**
Bhavan, 4a Castletown Road, London W14 9HQ
Tel 0171 381 3086/4608
Fax 0171 381 8758
Website www.sakti.com/bhavan
Executive Director: Dr. M. N. Nandakumara
Theatre Capacity: 250 seats
Rehearsal Rooms Cap: Room 1: 20; Room 2: 30.
I
**NTERCHANGE STUDIOS**
Dalby Street, London NW5 3NQ
Tel 0171 267 9421
Fax 0171 482 5292

**INTERGALACTIC ART**
31 Morecambe Street, London SE17 1DX
Tel 0171 701 9323
Fax 0171 252 7141
e-mail ro@intergalaticart.demon.co.uk

**ITALIA CONTI ACADEMY OF THEATRE ARTS
LIMITED**
Italia Conti House, 23 Goswell Road, London EC1 7AJ
Tel 0171 608 0044
Fax 0171 253 1430

**JACKSONS LANE COMMUNITY CENTRE**
269A Archway Road, Highgate, London N6 5AA
Admin 0181 340 5226 BO 0181 341 4421
Fax 0181 348 2424
Lettings Officer: Anne Gill
Facilities Manager: Nick Reed

**KING`S HEAD THEATRE CLUB**
285 Goswell Road, London EC17NT
Tel 0171 713 0593

# Cecil Sharp House
## 2 Regents Park Rd,London NW1

*Attractive & undisturbed
rehearsal space
available*

* **Three halls with sprung floors**
  * **excellent acoustics**
  * **café and bar facilities**
  * **easily accessible**

### Tel: 0171 485 2206

**BRIAN LIDSTONE PRODUCTION CENTRE**
138 Westbourne Grove, London W11 2RR
Tel 0171 727 2342
Fax 0171 221 7210

**LONDON WELSH TRUST LIMITED**
157/163 Gray's Inn Road, London WC1X 8UE
Tel/Fax 0171 837 3722

**METHOD & MADNESS**
25 Short Street, London SE1 8LJ
Tel 0171 401 9797
Fax 0171 401 9777
Minicom 0171 928 9367
Contact: Sarah Howard

**MOUNTVIEW THEATRE SCHOOL**
Ralph Richardson Studios, 1 Kingfisher Place,
Clarendon Road, Wood Green, London N22 6XF
Tel 0181 881 2201
Fax 0181 348 1727

**NFTS EALING STUDIOS LTD**
Ealing Green, Ealing, London W5 5EP
Tel 0181 567 6655
Fax 0181 758 8658
Email info@ealing-studios.co.uk
Contact: Charlotte Levin
13m x 12m (150sq m), piano, includes en-suite office
with telephone. Use of on-site cafe bar.

**OVAL HOUSE**
52-54 Kennington Oval, London SE11 5SW
Mgt 0171 582 0080 BO 0171 582 7680
Fax 0171 582 0990
For hire contact: Paul Everitt, Theatre Co-ordinator.

**PEOPLE SHOW**
St. James Institute, Pollard Row, London E2 6NB
Tel 0171 729 1841
Fax 0171 739 0203
Three rooms in newly refurbished space with disabled
access, kitchen, Green Room, showers and car-
parking: Main Hall - 38ft X 27ft, White room -21ft X
25ft, Studio 4 - 26ft X 26ft. Also workshop, sound
studio, Hi-8 video suitr for hire.

**PINEAPPLE DANCE STUDIOS**
7 Langley Street, Covent Garden, London WC2H 9JA
Tel 0171 379 8090
Fax 0171 836 0803

**THE PLACE (CONTEMPORARY DANCE TRUST)**
17 Dukes Road, London WC1H 9AB
Tel 0171 387 0161

Fax 0171 383 4851

**THE PLAYGROUND**
Unit J, 44 St. Pauls Crescent, Camden, London
NW1 9TN
Tel 0171 485 7412
Fax 0171 267 6015

**THE POOR SCHOOL**
242 Pentonville Road, Kings Cross, London N1 9JY
Tel 0171 837 6030

**QUESTORS THEATRE**
Mattock Lane, Ealing, London W5 5BQ
Tel 0181 567 5184
Fax 0181 567 8736

**RAMBERT DANCE COMPANY**
94 Chiswick High Road, Chiswick, London W4 1SH
Tel 0181 995 4246
Fax 0181 747 8323
**THE ROYAL BRITISH LEGION (FULHAM) CLUB**
247/249 New Kings Road, Fulham, London SW6 4XG
Tel 736 1856

**ST. MARY NEWINGTON CHURCH HALL**
57 Kennington Park Road, London SE11 4JQ
The Rectory
Tel 0171 735 1894   Bookings 0181 299 3651
Hall 0171 735 2324

**ST. SAVIOUR'S CHURCH HALL**
Warwick Avenue, London W9
Tel 0171 723 1968

**SADLER'S WELLS**
Rosebery Avenue, London EC1R 4TN
Tel 0171 278 6563
Fax 0171 837 0965
4 rehearsal studios, 3 of which have sprung floors.

**SHARED EXPERIENCE THEATRE**
The Soho Laundry, 9 Dufours Place, London W1V 1FE
Tel 0171 434 9248
Fax 0171 287 8763
Two centrally heated studios in the heart of London.
Studio 1 - 62' x 28' - rest room and showers
Studio 2 - 30' x 21' - competitive rates.

**TOYNBEE STUDIOS**
28 Commercial Street, London E1 6LS
5 minutes from Aldgate/Aldgate East and
Whitechapel underground stations.
Tel 0171 247 5102 - Arts & Admin.
Fax 0171 247 5103
300 seat proscenium arch theatre, 2 large rehearsal
studios 15m x 15m / 15m x 8m and several smaller
rooms available for auditions, readings etc.
Offices of varying sizes available for long term rental.

**TRICYCLE THEATRE**
269 Kilburn High Road, London NW6 7JR
Tel 0171 372 6611
Fax 0171 328 0795

**UPSTREAM REHEARSAL HALLS**
St. Andrew's Church, Short Street, London SE1 8LJ
Tel 0171 633 9819

**PETER WEBBER HIRE**
110-112 Disraeli Road, Putney, London SW15 2DX.

Tel 0181 870 1335
Fax 0181 877 1036

**WENDY WISBEY REHEARSAL ROOMS**
2 Rupert Road, London W4 1LX
Tel 0181 994 1210/5378
Fax 0181 994 5378

**WIMBLEDON SCHOOL OF ART**
Merton Hall Road, London SW19 3QA
Tel 0181 540 0231
Fax 0181 543 1750

# REGIONAL

**BARNSLEY**
**CIVIC THEATRE**
Eldon Street, Barnsley, South Yorks S70 2JL
Tel 01226 205128
Fax 01226 285475

**BINGLEY**
**BINGLEY LITTLE THEATRE**
Main Street, Bingley
Tel 01274 564049

**BIRMINGHAM**
**ARCADEIA REHEARSAL STUDIO AND MUSIC
MANAGEMENT**
Unit 8A Western Road Complex, Western Road,
Hockley, Birmingham B18 7QD
Tel 0121 507 0933

**BRADFORD**
**THEATRE IN THE MILL**
Shearbridge Road, University of Bradford, Bradford,
BD7 1DP
Tel 01274 383185
Fax 01274 383187

**CARLISLE**
**STANWIX THEATRE**
Cumbria College of Art & Design, Brampton Road,
Carlisle CA3 9AY
BO 01228 25333
Fax 01228 514491

**DARLINGTON**
**THE ARTS CENTRE**
Vane Terrace, Darlington DL3 7AX
Tel 01325 483271
Extensive facilities available together with on site
residential accommodation, cafeteria and bars.

**DUBLIN**
**BANK OF IRELAND ARTS CENTRE**
Foster Place, Dublin 2, Ireland
Tel 00 353 1 6711488
Fax: 00 353 1 6707556
Contact: Barry O'Kelly
The Bank of Ireland's Arts Centre stages live
performances as well as exhibitions. It has provided
the first major public platform for many young Irish
artistes.

**DYFED**
**BLUESTONE STUDIOS**
Hebron Whitland, West Wales
Tel 01994 419425
Fax 01994 419425 (phone first)
Contact: Noreen F Vaughn

Luxury residential rehearsal and location recording 3,000 sq. ft of acoustically controlled space. Full leisure facilities licenced, wonderful setting in national park.

**GLASGOW**
**TRON THEATRE**
63 Trongate, Glasgow G1 5HB
Tel 0141 552 3748
Fax 0141 552 6657
Website: www.tron.co.uk

**KENDAL**
**BREWERY ARTS CENTRE**
Highgate, Kendal, Cumbria LA9 4HE
Tel 01539 725133
Fax 01539 730257

**LEEDS**
**LEEDS CIVIC THEATRE**
Cookridge Street, Leeds LS2 8BH
and Stansfeld Chambers, Great George Street, Leeds
Tel 0113 245 6343
Fax 0113 247 7747

**LEEDS GRAND THEATRE AND OPERA HOUSE LTD**
46 New Briggate, Leeds LS1 6NZ
Tel 0113 245 6014
Fax 0113 246 5906
General Manager: Warren Smith
House Manager: Anne Baxendale
Assistant House Manager: Yvonne Simpson
Capacity: Grand studios: 200; Grand Hall: 160;
Assembley Room: 200; Board Room, 12; New Stalls
Bar:12.

**THE WEST YORKSHIRE PLAYHOUSE**
Playhouse Square, Quarry Hill, Leeds LS2 7UP
Tel 0113 244 2141
Fax 0113 244 8252

**LEIGHTON BUZZARD**
**LEIGHTON BUZZARD THEATRE**
Lake Street, Leighton Buzzard, Beds LU7 8RX
Admin 01525 850290
Fax 01525 851368

**NEWCASTLE-UPON-TYNE**
**THE LIVE THEATRE**
27 Broad Chare, Newcastle-upon-Tyne NE1 3DQ
Tel 0191 261 2694
BO 0191 232 1232

**NORWICH**
**ST. ANDREW'S & BLACKFRIARS HALLS**
St. Andrew's Plain, Norwich, Norfolk N3 1AU
Tel 01603 628477 or 212132

Fax 01603 762182

**PERTH**
**THE STATION HOTEL**
Leonard Street, Perth PH2 8HE
Tel 01738 624141
Fax 01738 639912

**ROTHERHAM**
**ROTHERHAM ARTS CENTRE**
Central Library and Arts Centre
Walker Place, Rotherham S65 1JH
Manager: Ian Whiteside
Tel 01709 823623/823641
Fax 01709 823638

**SAFFRON WALDEN LIBRARY & ARTS CENTRE**
The Corn Exchange, Market Square, Saffron Walden,
Essex CB10 1ES
Tel 01799 523178
Fax 01799 513642
Arts Director: Janet Crofts
Seating capacity: 180-200

**TONBRIDGE**
**THE ANGEL LEISURE CENTRE**
Angel Lane, Tonbridge, Kent TN9 1SF
Tel 01732 359966

# 52
# RIGGING

**ARROW RIGGING AND TECHNICAL SERVICES**
7-9 Fowler Road, Hainault, Essex IG6 3UT.
Tel 0181 501 5444
Fax 0181 501 5445

**CERTEX LIFTING PRODUCTS AND SERVICES**
Twickenham Trading Estate, Rugby Road,
Twickenham TW1 1DR
Tel 0181 892 5628
Fax 0181 744 1605
Manager: Andy Stock

**FLINT HIRE AND SUPPLY LTD**
Queens Row, London SE17 2PX
Tel 0171 703 9786
Fax 0171 708 4189
Email: sales@flintltd.demon.co.uk
Sales Manager: Alasdair Flint
Sales of wire rope, pulleys, yacht blocks, black polyester rope, slings, tested wire assemblies, Tirfor,

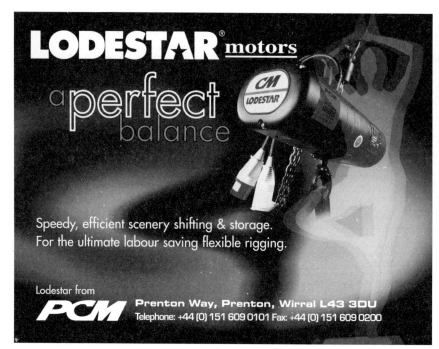
rigging screws, shackles, Crosby products, drop blocks and divertors.

**FUTURIST LIGHT & SOUND LTD**
Hoyle Head Mills, New Street, Earlsheaton,
Dewsbury, West Yorks WF12 8JJ
Tel 01924 468183
Fax 01924 458667
Full selection of staging and rigging for sale, lease and hire including main agents for lite structures and TFL.

**FREEZING STAGES**
Douglas House, 3 Richmond Buildings, London
W1V 5AE
Tel 0171 676 9088
Fax 0171 809 7865
All forms of stages and technical equipment for sale or hire. Indoor and outdoor.

**A. S. GREEN AND CO. (Lancashire) LTD**
Redgate Road, South Lancs Industrial Estate,
Ashton-in-Makerfield, Lancashire WN4 8DT.
Tel 01942 719347
Fax 01942 718219
Rostra, flats, drama shapes, curtains, tracks, lighting, scenery fittings and materials.

**HARKNESS HALL LTD**
The Gate Studios, Station Road, Borehamwood,
Hertfordshire  WD6 1DQ
Tel 0181 953 3611
Fax 0181 207 3657
e-mail info@harknesshall.com
Contacts: Doug Heather & Chris Hitchens
A comprehensive range of curtain tracks systems, drapes, curtains and cycloramas; winches and hoists; grid rigging and suspension gear; PC and PLC control

systems; stage and scenery fittings; stage and studio lighting; design, survey, installation and maintenance services available Electrical and manual roller screens with front and rear projection services up to 48ft (14.6m) wide. Flying frames with or without Moving masking Systems, togethert with a comprehensive range of Portable, Folding Frame Screens. Comprehensive catalogue available FOC.

**OUTBACK RIGGING LTD**
Unit 11, Kendal Court, Kendal Avenue, Park Royal,
London W3 0RP
Tel 0181 993 0066
Fax 0181 752 1753
Contact: Stuart Cooper
Truss, hoists and sundry rigging equipment hire and installation.

**PCM / PFAFF SILVERBLUE LTD**
North Cheshire Trading Estate, Prenton Way, Prenton,
Wirral L43 3DU
Tel 0151 609 0101
Fax 0151 609 0200
Contact: Chris Jolley, John Jones, Tony Dickson
European agents for the Lodestar electric chain hoists - full stock of hoists/spares. Also stock PFAFF Silverblue hoists/winches and work geared screw jacks.

**PLAYLIGHT HIRE LTD**
67 Ayres Road, Old Trafford, Manchester M16 9NH
Tel 0161 226 5858
Fax 0161 232 9510
860 Coronation Road, Park Royal, London NW10 7PS
Tel 0181 965 8188
Fax 0181 961 8591
Playlight also supplies lighting, sound equipment,

stage draperies and stage electrical installation.

**ROPE ASSEMBLIES LTD**
Unit 6, Hallcroft Industrial Estate, Retford,
Notts DN22 7PY
Tel 01777 700714
Fax 01777 860719
Contact: Terry Hitchen
Specialists in wire rope and allied products.
During 1997 Rope Assemblies will be sponsoring
numerous lectures through the UK on Health and
Safety Regulations regarding wire ropes and lifting
tackle.

**STAGE TECHNOLOGIES**
3a Aberdeen Studios, 22 Highbury Grove,
London N5 2DQ
Tel 0171 354 8800
Fax 0171 359 1730
e-mail automation@stagetech.com
Directors: John Hastie and Mark Ager
Business Manager: Nikki Scott

**STAGE TRACK LTD**
Harbour Lane, Garboldisham, Diss, Norfolk IP22 2ST
Tel 01953 688188
Fax 01953 688144
Contact: G. Dashper
Suppliers of various curtain systems, hoists, fire
curtains and associated controls and equipment.

**TRIPLE E LTD**
5 Admiral, Hyson Industrial Estate, Hyson Road,
London SE19 8UG
Tel 0171 237 6354
Fax 0171 237 7650
Contact: David Eddlestein or Phil Sparkes
Triple E are the designers, manufacturers and
suppliers of the unique Unitrack system from simple
corded tracks to multi-motor computer controlled
systems. We both sell and install curtain and scenery
track systems.
We also hire flight cased tracks and motor systems.
We have a track for every purpose within the
entertainment industry and can supply world-wide
either direct or through our distributors.

**UNUSUAL RIGGING LTD**
The Wharf, Bugbrooke, Northants NN7 3QD
Tel 01604 830083
Fax 01604 831144
Email: info@unusual.co.uk
Website: www.unusual.co.uk
Contact: David Mayo
Unusual brings the disciplines of design, rigging,

**9 KEPPEL ROAD, GORLESTON,
NORFOLK NR31 6SN
Telephone: 01493 657093 · 01493 652055**

fabrications and automation to provide an ideal
installation service for the supply, renovation and renewal
of stage engineering and flying systems.

**VERTIGO RIGGING LTD**
Tingley House, 78-82 Brandon Street, London SE17 1AN
Tel 0171 277 2424
Fax 0171 703 3884
Suppliers of Truss, Motors, Rigging Consumables.
Sale and hire.

# 53

# SCENERY (BUILDERS, PAINTERS, HIRERS)

**3-D CREATIONS**
9 Keppel Road, Gorleston, Gt. Yarmouth,
Norfolk NR31 6SN
Studio Tel 01493 657093
Workshop Tel 01493 652055
Fax 01493 443124
Mobile: 0860 707287
Contact: Ian Westbrook
We can provide all your scenic needs for theatre,
television and film. Scenery and prop design and
construction specialists. Prop makers, set designers,
sculptors, scenic artists we are always prepared to
undertake work of the unusual. Location work also.

**ALBEMARLE OF LONDON SCENIC STUDIOS**
74 Mortimer Street, London W1N 8HL

Tel: 0171 631 0135
Scenery builders, scenic artists. Complete pantomimes for hire. Storage space for hire.

**YVONNE ARNAUD THEATRE (SCENERY) LIMITED**
Workshops, Unit 5 The Billings, 3 Walnut Tree Close, Guildford, Surrey GU1 4UL
Tel 01483 300926
Fax 01483 450926
Manager: Graham Bower Wood
Scenery Construction and Metal Fabrication for Theatre, Opera, Exhibitions and Special Events.

**ASETS LTD**
1 Raymond Avenue, Blackpool, Lancashire FY2 0TY
Tel 01253 596030
Fax 01253 596816
Scenery design, building and painting. Conference and exhibition producers, management & technical support.

**BIRMINGHAM REP WORKSHOP**
Centenary Square, Broad Street, Birmingham B1 2EP
Tel 0121 236 6771
Fax 0121 236 7883
Head of Workshop C.M. Blackledge BA Hons Ext 2227
Head of Construction Design C. MacCall Ext 2222
**NICK BLOOM**
2 Deal's Gateway, London SE10 8BU
Tel 0181 691 1409
Fax 0181 691 0936
Construction Services

**BOWER WOOD**
**Production Services and Workshop**
Unit 5 The Billings, 3 Walnut Tree Close, Guildford, Surrey GU1 4UL
Tel 01483 300926
Fax 01483 450926
Website: www.bowerwood.com

Contact: Graham Bower Wood or Nigel Mathias
Scenery Construction & Metal Fabrication for the
Theatre, Opera, Exhibitions & Special Events.

**JOHN CAMPBELL SCENIC STUDIO LTD**
41 Iffley Road, London W6 0PB
Tel 0181 748 7266/2832
Fax 0181 748 1421
Mobile 0976 361240
Scenic artists and prop makers.

**CARDIFF THEATRICAL SERVICES LTD**
Unit 1, The 125 Business Park, off Tyndall Street,
Cardiff CF1 5BP
Tel 01222 499977
Fax 01222 481275
Telex 497858
Scenery & Prop Builders, Engineering Scenic Artists.

**PAUL COLBECK**
Unit 43, Metropolitan Workshops, Enfield Road,
London N1 5AZ
Tel 0171 249 7540
Mobile 0973 704389
Props and models made to order for TV, stage and
films. Scenic sculpting.

**CREFFIELDS (TIMBER & BOARDS ) LTD**
Unit 6, Marcus Close, Tilehurst, Reading, Berkshire
RG30 4EA
Tel 0118 945 3533
Fax 0118 945 3633
Creffields is one of the UK's leading suppliers of flame
proofed sheets and soft woods for the exhibition and
theatre trades. Large stocks are held allowing for
urgent orders delivered promptly.

**DONMAR LTD**
Donmar House, 54 Cavell Street, Whitechapel, London
E1 2HP
Tel 0171 790 1166
Fax 0171 790 6634
Suppliers of Steel Deck, Stage Systems and folding
rostra, scenery kits, full range of Hall Stage
scenery and tab track hardware, custom made black
drapes and house tabs, Rosco designer products and
Supersat, Broadway and Fluorescent paints.
Hire of black drapes. Complete range of flamebar
flame retardant solutions for scenic materials.

**EMERGENCY EXIT ARTS**
PO Box 570, London SE10 OEE
Tel 0181 853 4809
Fax 0181 858 2025
Contact: Les Sharpe, Artistic Director
Complete events planned and implemented. Fantastic
Celebrations of Music, Performance and Fire. Design
of effigies and puppets.
Space Transformation on large scale.
Fireworks.

**FAMEGLORE LTD**
2 Archangel Way, Dunston Park, Thatham, Berkshire
RG18 4EB
Tel 01635 872846
Fax 01635 872845
Contact: G. Harrison

**FLINT HIRE AND SUPPLY LTD**
Queens Row, London SE17 2PX
Tel 0171 703 9786
Fax 0171 708 4189
Email: sales@flintltd.demon.co.uk

Hire of rostra units, winches, drop blocks, stage
weights and braces, tab track, paint frames. All
scenery building hardware and scenic paints supplied.

**FREEZING STAGES**
Douglas House, 3 Richmond Buildings, London
W1V 5AE
Tel 0171 676 9088
Fax 0171 809 7865
All forms of stages and technical equipment for sale or
hire. Indoor and outdoor.

**A. S. GREEN AND CO. (Lancashire) LTD**
Redgate Road, South Lancs Industrial Estate,
Ashton-in-Makerfield, Lancashire WN4 8DT.
Tel 01942 718347
Fax 01942 718219
Rostra, flats, drama shapes, curtains, tracks, lighting,
scenery fittings and materials.

**HOWARTH WRIGHTON LTD T/A HWL**
Cricket Street, Denton, Manchester M34 3DR
Tel 0161 335 0220
Email: hwl@quicksilver-uk.demon.co.uk
Contact: Bob Howarth
Hirers of all types of furniture, set dressing, decorative
lighting, pictures, hand props etc. Also specialist hirers
of weapons and blank firing guns.

**ROBERT KNIGHT LTD**
PO Box 52, London SE17 2QD.
Tel 0171 277 1704
Fax 0171 277 1722
Stage and television scenery contractors and
engineers: workshops in Slough, Berkshire. Wide
range of drapes and equipment available for hire at

# Victor Mara

## SCENIC ARTISTS AND CONTRACTORS

Victor Mara Limited
1-7 Newport Street
Lambeth
London SE11 6AJ

PART OF THE **V**GROUP

Tel: 0171 735 1518    Fax: 0171 735 9163
E Mail: victormara@vgroup.co.uk    www.vgroup.co.uk

Horsley Street, London SE17. Please telephone for list/prices.

**VICTOR MARA LTD**
1/7 Newport Street, Lambeth, London SE11 6AJ
Tel 0171 735 1518
Fax 0171 735 9163
Email: victormara@vgroup.co.uk
Website: www.vgroup.co.uk

**ADRIAN MARCHANT STUDIOS**
Unit C, Roebuck Road, Chessington, Surrey KT9 1EU
Tel 0181 397 5777
Fax 0181 397 6939
Suppliers to TV and Theatres. Stage Sets, Slashed Curtains, P.V.C.'s, Snow, Cobweb Sprays, Bead Strings, poly balls etc.

**MILTON & PARNELL (FORMERLY TRAFFORD & PARNELL PRODUCTIONS)**
85 Marton Drive, Blackpool FY4 3EY
Tel 01253 766928 or 0860 273341

**TERRY MURPHY SCENERY LTD**
Livesey Place, Peckham Park Road, London SE15 6SL
Tel 0171 277 5156
Fax 0171 277 5147
Scenery constructed and painted to specification.

**NEXO DISPLAY SYSTEMS LTD**
Bayley Street, Steely Bridge, SK15 1QQ
Tel 0161 330 9136
Aluminium connectors which clamp together display panels from 3-25mm thick at any angle using only an allen key, plus a wide range of display lighting.

**NORWICH THEATRE ROYAL**
Theatre Street, Norwich, Norfolk NR2 1RL
Tel 01603 623562
Fax 01603 762904
Contact: Arthur Hoare
Pantomime sets, props and costumes for hire. Full workshop services are available at competitive rates for stage, film and exhibition projects.

**OUTBACK RIGGING**
Unit 11, Kendal Court, Western Avenue Trading Estate, Kendal Avenue, London W3 ORP
Tel 0181 993 0066
Fax 0181 752 1753

**DAVID PERRY PRODUCTIONS**
Unit 2, Cadec Trading Estate, Beakes Road, Bearwood, West Midlands B67 5RS
Office 0121 434 3041
Fax 0121 434 3042
Comprehensive service at competitive prices. Set Builders, Engineering, Scenic Artists, Sculptors, Prop Makers, Design, Drapes, Effects for Theatre, Film, TV, Exhibition and Pop Tours.

**THE PENCIL PATCH LTD**
Wittersham Lane, Peasmarsh, Nr. Rye, East Sussex, TW31 6TD
Fax 01797 230 676
Set Design, Model Making, Scenic Construction, Scenic Painting.

**PERTH THEATRE**
185 High Street, Perth PH1 5UW
Tel 01738 472700
Fax 01738 624576

# *Bringing images to life*

## *Backdrops*
## *Scenery*
## *Translights*
## *Tapestry*
## *Murals*

With an annual Pantomime and 10 shows in repertory each year, many sets are available well below cost price. Seasons planned in March for Aug-Dec and August for Jan-May. Co-productions possible.
Contact: Paul McLennan, General Manager.

**PHOSPHENE**
Milton Road South, Stowmarket, Suffolk IP14 1EZ
Tel 01449 678200 & 770011
Partners: C & A Dix
Product launch and theatrical design, full package deals to include LX and sound and merchandising materials available.

**PRODUCTION IMAGINEERS**
PO Box 220, Elvington, York YO41 4YT
Tel 01904 757575
Fax 01904 757576
Email: info@imagineers.co.uk
Website: www.imagineers.co.uk
Contact: Phil Lawson, Phil Green, David Forster
Specialist in theatre, conference & exhibition set design & construction, steel fabrication, scenic painting, lighting design & hire and Themed presentations.

**PROSCENEIUM LTD**
Sladen Wood Mill, Todmorden Road, Littleborough, Rochdale OL15 9EW
Tel 01706 377226
Fax 01706 371953
Theatrical Scenery designed, built and painted for hire or for sale. Large stock of musicals available.

**RETROGRAPH NOSTALGIA ARCHIVE LTD**
164 Kensington Park Road, London W11 2ER
Tel 0171 727 9878/9426 (24 hr. answering machine)
Fax 0171 229 3395
Contact: Jilliana Ranicar-Breese
Worldwide vintage posters, advertising, labels and packaging 1880-1960 for wall hangings, backgrounds, back projections, montages, paper action props, mockups, dummies.
Transparencies or colour lasers supplied.Picture research service.  Specialist in food, drink, fashion, travel, leisure & entertainment.

**ROYAL LYCEUM THEATRE COMPANY**
29 Roseburn Street, Edinburgh
Tel/Fax 0131 337 1997
Scenery builders, painters, propmakers and paint-frame to hire.

**RUTTERS/SCANACHROME**
16 Jacksons Lane, Gt Chesterford, Saffron Walden, Essex CB10 1PD

Tel 01799 531049
Fax 01799 530651
Car 0973 631052
Contact: Paul Rutter
Producers of scenic cloths from simple B/W to elaborate colour onto all textiles with very short lead times.

**S&H TECHNICAL SUPPORT GROUP**
Unit A, The Old Laundry, Chambercombe Road, Ilfracombe, Devon EX34 9PH.
Tel 01271 866832
Fax 01271 865423
Mobile 0850 234151/0385 342537
e-mail shtsg@aol.com
Website www.new-med.co.uk/s+h
Contract Sales: Terry Murtha
Lighting Design: Chris Horrell
Technical Development: Nigel Smith
Hire and sale of Starcloths/controllable LV, miniature lamp lighting designers.  Consultation and design of theatre/studio sets and backdrops.

**SCENIC HAPPENINGS LTD**
PO Box 178, Elvington, York YO4 5YY
Tel 01904 607607
Fax 01904 607608
e-mail scenic@scenichp.demon.co.uk
Website www.scenichp.demon.co.uk
Contact: Martin Witts, David Forster, Phil Lawson or Phil Green
Specialists in all aspects of production management, set design/construction, stage management, orchestral management, lighting design/supply, consultancy, programming, exhibition and conference design/construction/management.

**SLX THEATRE SET HIRE**
Victoria Road, Avonmouth, Bristol BS11 9DB
Tel 0117 982 6260
Fax 0117 982 7778
Set design and construction, scenic artists, stage engineering and complete set hire.

**ADRIAN SNELL PRODUCTION SERVICES**
Unit 6, 171 Church Hill Road, Thurmaston, Leicester LE4 8DH
Tel 0116 260 0901
Fax 0116 260 0933
Our large modern workshops offer a complete construction service, including engineering, steel fabrication and all other forms of construction, scenic art techniques, sculpture, props.  We offer full support for all projects.

**SOUVENIR SCENIC STUDIOS LTD**
64 Verney Road, London SE16 3DH
Tel 0171 237 7557
Fax 0171 237 7626
Contact: Simon Kenny
Specialist scenery construction for theatre, opera and ballet. Large scale props, installations and scenic artists.

**STAGE TECHNIQUES**
Unit One, Cotton Drive, Dalehouse Lane Industrial Estate, Kenilworth, Warwickshire CV8 2EB.
Tel 01926 864800
Fax 01926 864964
Contact: Sean Griffiths
Suppliers of Steeldeck stage systems & scenery construction. Please see display advert.

**STAGESETS (LONDON)**
Unit L, Delta Wharf, Blackwall Industrial Estate, Tunnel Avenue, Greenwich, London SE10 0QH
Tel 0181 853 2370
Fax 0181 853 5683
Scenery/Drapes, rostra, period furniture hire & sales.

**STAGEWORKS LTD**
Units H1, Colchester Industrial Estate, Colchester Avenue, Cardiff CF3 7AP
Tel 01222 462713
Fax 01222 462718
Contacts: Jo Price or Peter Bailey
Set builders, fabrication and engineering, scenic artists, sculpture and GRP work. Transport and storeage facilities. Brochure available. Please see display advert.

**STAGEWRIGHTS**
Mears Yard, Wintersells Road, Byfleet, Surrey KT14 7AZ
Tel 01932 351996
Fax 0932 351996
Scenery Builders.

**STEELDECK**
Barpart House, King's Cross Freight Depot, York Way, London N1 0UZ
Tel 0171 833 2031
Fax 0171 278 3403
Contact: Philip Parsons, Michael Passmore.
Original manufacturers of Steeldeck staging, available for sale, hire and installation.
Scenery builders and steel fabricators.

**STREETER & JESSEL**
Unit B, New Baitick Wharf, Oxestalls Road, Evelyn SE8 5RS
Tel 0181 469 2777
Fax 0181 694 2430
Scenery builders and stage supplies. Free brochure of stage supplies available.

**SUFFOLK SCENERY**
Office: 28 The Street, Brettenham, Suffolk IP7 7QP
Workshop: Pie Hatch Farm, Buxhall, Stowmarket, Suffolk IP14 3DZ
Tel 01449 736679, 0836 216045
Fax 01449 737620
Scenery Manufacturers. Large stock of settings available for hire. Will convert existing sets to your production. UK distributors of Foyal and Atlas Silk Curtain tracks and accessories.

**TEMPLE DECOR**
Unit 9, Albury Close, Loverock, Reading RG30 1BD
Tel 0118 966 4914
Fax 0118 959 4357
Managing Director: T. Carroll

**TRIPLE E LTD**
B3, Tower Bridge Business Complex, Clements Road, London SE16 4EF
Tel 0118 957 3366
Fax 0171 957 3377
Contact: David Eddlestein or Phil Sparkes
Triple E are the designers, manufacturers and suppliers of the unique Unitrack system from simple corded tracks to multi-motor computer controlled systems. We both sell and install curtain and scenery track systems.
We also hire flight cased tracks and motor systems. We have a track for every purpose within the entertainment industry and can supply world-wide either direct or through our distributors.

**VELVETFIELD LTD**
10 Hillfoot Road, Neepsend, Sheffield S3 8AA
Tel 01142 756772
Fax 01142 725174
Scenery construction. Property makers and scene painters.

**WALLSPACE**
2 Peacock Yard, London SE17 3LH.
Tel/Fax 0171 701 7800
Creative Director: Sonia Newell
Innovative Backdrops and Wall-Hangings for people wanting original and exciting environments.
Also props made to commission.

**WELD-FAB STAGE ENGINEERING LTD**
Harbour Lane, Garboldisham, Diss, Norfolk IP22 2ST
Tel 01953 688133
Fax 01953 688144
e-mail weld-fab.stage@paston.co.uk
Contact: Brian Skipp
Design and manufacturers of various stage, studio, television & exhibition equipment for sale or hire. Motorised and fixed scenery, revolving stages, scissor lifts, power flying & counterweight systems.

# 54
# SCENERY (SUPPLIERS)

**ARROWTIP LTD**
31/35 Stannary Street, London SE11 4AA
Tel 0171 735 8848
Fax 0171 735 7325
Expanded polystyrene suppliers.

**BLACKOUT**
208 Durnsford Road, London SW19 8DR
Tel 0181 944 8840
Fax 0181 944 8850
e-mail mail@blackout-ltd.com
Blackout is a company specializing in the manufacture, for hire or sale, of high quality, flame-proof drapes and starcloths for conferences, trade shows, film, television or photographic studios, theatres and concert productions. We can also provide scenic backdrops to any size, painted to specific specifications.

**BEIRSDORF UK LTD**
Tesa Division,
Yeomans Drive, Blakelands, Milton Keynes MK14 5LS
Tel 01908 211333
Fax 01908 211555
Suppliers of adhesive tapes.

**BRISTOL (UK) LTD**
12 The Arches, Maygrove Road, London NW6 2DS
Tel 0171 624 4370
Fax 0171 372 5242
Manufacturers of scenic paints and coatings for
theatre, film and television. Complete product range is
water based and non-toxic. Colour swatch and full
technical data available on request.

**BRODIE & MIDDLETON LTD**
68 Drury Lane, Covent Garden, London WC2B 5SP
Tel 0171 836 3289/3280
Fax 0171 497 8425
Fireproofed Scenic Canvas, Twill, etc. Scenic colours,
Dyes, Glitters and Brushes, Fireproofing solutions.
Curtains, Drapes, Backcloths and Gauzes made to
order. Grimas stage make-up etc.

**BUCK AND RYAN LTD**
101 Tottenham Court Road, London W1 OPDY
Tel 0171 636 7475
Fax 0171 631 0726
Specialist tool suppliers.

**CHRIS JAMES & CO LTD**
43 Colville Road, Acton, London W3 8BL
Tel 0181 896 1772
Fax 0181 896 1773

**N & I COSTELLO (Scenic Supplies)**
142 Raebern Road, Surbiton, Surrey
KT5 9EB
Tel 0181 399 6214
Director: Norman Costello
Suppliers to major TV and Theatres of Curtains, Glitter
and Mirrored PVC Cladding.

**CREFFIELDS (TIMBER & BOARDS) LIMITED**
Unit 6, Marcus Close, Tilehurst, Reading, Berkshire
RG30 4EA.
Tel 0118 945 3533
Fax 0118 945 3633
Specialist suppliers of Flame Retardent Plywood,
Chipboard & Hardboard to Class '1', Class '0' and
French M1. Also Softwoods to Class '1' and Class '0'.

**DIRECTA (UK) LTD**
Cold Norton, Essex CM3 6UA
Tel 01621 828882

Fax 01621 828072
Suppliers of all types of stage marking and gaffer tapes.

**DONMAR LTD**
Donmar House, 54 Cavell Street, Whitechapel,
London E1 2HP
Tel 0171 790 1166
Fax 0171 790 6634
Suppliers of Steeldeck, Stage Systems and folding
rostra, scenery kits.  Winches, flying systems and full
range of Hall Stage scenery and tab track hardware,
custom made black and coloured drapes and house
tabs, Rosco designer products and Supersat,
Broadway fluorescent paints. Complete stage
installations anywhere in the U.K. Hirers of black
drapes.
Complete range of Flamebar flame retardant solutions
for scenic materials.

**PETER EVANS STUDIOS LIMITED**
1 Frederick Street, Luton, Beds LU2 7QW
Tel 01582 25730
Fax 01582 481329
Directors: P Evans, I Adams, R Evans
Makers of props and scenic embellishment in plastic,
polystyrene etc. Suppliers of a large range of columns,
pilasters, urns, friezes balustrades, brickwork etc. in
vacuum formed PVC, ABS or GRP.
Also vacuum forming done from your own patterns or
patterns specially made; maximum pattern sizes
650mm x 700mm, small machine  2400mm x 1200mm
large machine.
Catalogue available.

**THE EXPANDED METAL CO LTD**
PO Box 14, Longhill Industrial Estate, Hartlepool TS25 1PR
Tel 01429 266633
Fax 01429 866795
Manufacturers of all types of expanded metal.

**FLINT HIRE & SUPPLY LTD**
Queens Row, London SE17 2PX
Tel 0171 703 9786
Fax 0171 708 4189
Email: sales@flintltd.demon.co.uk
Sales Manager: Alasdair Flint
Suppliers of powder paints, Rosco, Bolloms and Bristol
paints, tools, compressors, tapes, our own range of
scenery fittings, podgers, truck winches; weights and
braces, wire ropes; and fire retardents. Hire of
Megadeks, paint frames, winches and tab tracks.

**FORWARD STATIONERS**
Forward House, Leyton Industrial Village, Argall
Avenue, London E10 7QP
Tel 0181 558 7110

## Theatrical Chandlers

Flint Hire & Supply is the one stop shop for all theatre hardware. We hold a stock of over 5000 product lines and have access to many more. We can provide the technical theatre practitioner, whether workshop manager, stage manager, master carpenter or production manager with an easy source for the diverse range of goods that the backstage worker requires. Our large illustrated catalogue covers most of our range,

Flints have expanded beyond the theatre industry to supply to TV companies, film companies, commercial presentations, museums and art galleries. Our customers included virtually every theatre in the UK plus many abroad.

We are able to offer bulk discount prices to large user workshops. If you think you fall into this category ask for an appointment and we will specially tailor a price structure to suit your company's needs.

For scenic artists Flints are stockists of Bristol, Rosco, Bolloms, Ardenbrite, Hammerite, shellac, varnishes, Idenden, Polyvine, Whistler brushes, Toupret, Hamiltons, Dutch metal, powder pigments, graphite, marble dust, French enamel varnish, metallic powders, Purdy brushes, graining brushes, Pacific Strong, Slip Nomor, compressors, glitters, Covent Garden Primer and Flints multi purpose water based black primer for steel and plastics. We also have London's best paint frames to hire.

For the carpenter we sell boss plates, grummets, hanging irons, Supadriv and Stylus woodscrews, BZP and black bolts, cement coated nails, loose part backflaps, Triple E hinges, sash cord, Makita cordless drills, Bosch jigsaws, ratchet podgers, PVA resin glues, Tretobond, staples, tapes, castors, hand tools and Megadek staging.

For the rigger we supply Tallescopes, access towers, wire rope, black polyester rope, tab tracks by Halls and Triple E, Doughty fittings, Tirfors, pulleys, snatch blocks, rope clutches, cleats, shackles, wire rope assemblies with test certificates, architectural stainless swaged fittings, hardy hemp, manilla, Zarges ladders and round slings.

We will open credit accounts or we accept Delta, Switch, American Express, Visa and Mastercard telephone orders. We deliver countrywide and orders over £250 nett go free (excludes weights and items over 3.6m long). Flints can also offer a depth of advice not available at other suppliers. If you haven't used our services already, give us a call and find out why our customers keep coming back to us.

## Phone 0171 703 9786 • Fax 0171 708 4189
### Queens Row • London • SE17 2PX

# Just two of our range of over <u>5000</u> specialist products

For your *free* catalogue
Phone
0171 703 9786 or
Fax 0171 708 4189

**FLINT HIRE & SUPPLY**

Est 1981

**Theatrical Chandlers**

**Queens Row • London • SE17 2PX**

Fax 0181 558 5974
Suppliers of stage and marking tape - PVC Electrical
tape, staples and staple tackers.
Double sided cloth tape.

**FUTURIST LIGHT & SOUND LTD**
Hoyle Head Mills, New Street, Earlsheaton,
Dewsbury, West Yorks WF12 8JJ
Tel 01924 468183
Fax 01924 458667
Full compliment of Scenery fixtures, dittings and
acessories, including Rosco scenic paints, foam coat,
flex bond and full comprehensive range of scenery
materials.

**GERRIETS GB LTD**
Unit J412, Tower Bridge Business Complex,
Drummond Road, London SE16 4EF
Tel 0171 232 2262
Fax 0171 237 4916
Supply and manufacture of theatrical and display
plastics, textiles and finished soft goods. Famous in
Europe for forty years.

**G. S. J. (Engineers Supplies) LTD**
86 Acre Lane, London SW2 5QN
Tel 0171 737 1222
Fax 0171 737 6757
Wholesalers of nuts bolts, woodscrews etc.

**HARKNESS HALL LTD**
The Gate Studios, Station Road, Borehamwood,
Hertfordshire WD6 1DQ
Tel 0181 953 3611
Fax 0181 207 3657
e-mail info@harknesshall.com
Contacts: Doug Heather & Chris Hitchens
A comprehensive range of curtain tracks systems,
drapes, curtains and cycloramas; winches and hoists;
grid rigging and suspension gear; PC and PLC control
systems; stage and scenery fittings; stage and studio
lighting; design, survey, installation and maintenance
services available Electrical and manual roller screens
with front and rear projection services up to 48ft
(14.6m) wide. Flying frames with or without Moving
masking Systems, togethert with a comprehensive
range of Portable, Folding Frame Screens.
Comprehensive catalogue available FOC.

**HOWARTH WRIGHTSON LTD T/A HWL**
Cricket Street, Denton, Manchester M34 3DR
Tel 0161 335 0220
Email: hwl@quicksilver-uk.demon.co.uk
Contact: Bob Howarth
Hirers of all types of furniture, set dressing, decorative
lighting, pictures, hand props etc. Also specialist hirers
of weapons and blank firing guns.

**I.S.+ G STEEL STOCKHOLDERS LTD AND
THOMAS TINGLEY LTD**
Laker Industrial Estate, Kenthouse Lane, Beckenham,
Kent BR3 1JT
Tel 0181 778 8881
Fax 0181 659 1643
Suppliers of castors, wheels, bolts, screws, etc,
aluminium sections, fixing and fasteners, steel
sections, bowing equipment, turntables.

**LANCELYN THEATRE SUPPLIES**
Electric Avenue, Ferry Hinksey Road, Oxford OX2 0BY
Tel 01865 722468 Oxford
(North West)

Tel 0151 334 8991
Fax 0151 334 4047
Scenery fittings, pulleys, tape etc.
Delivery service.

**LE MARK TVS**
Unit 24, Stephenson Road, St. Ives, Huntingdon,
Cambridgeshire PE17 4WJ
Tel 01480 494540
Fax 01480 494206
Managing Director: Stuart Gibbons
Sales Director: Linda Gibbons
Administrator: Sally Noble
Le Mark T.V.S. formed to offer a complete range of
self-adhesive tapes, printed labels and cable coding
systems for the lighting, music and television industry.
A complete product advisory service and 'in house'
artwork facilities available. Dealers for: Advance
Tapes, Rotunda, D.R.G. Kwikseal.

**J. D. McDOUGALL LIMITED**
4 McGrath Road, Stratford, London E15 4JP
Tel 0181 534 2921
Fax 0181 519 8423
Email: sales@jdmcdougall.co.uk
Managing Director: Ian McDougall.
Stage Drapes, Vision Gauzes, Backcloths,
Cyclorama Cloths, Flameproofing textiles
materials for Scenery Construction and
Stage Effects.

**MARLOW ROPES LTD**
South Road, Hailsham, East Sussex BN27 3JS
Tel 01323 847234
Fax 01323 440093
e-mail marketing@marlowropes.com
Contact: Mark Durbidge
Ropemakers

**MILTON & PARNELL (FORMERLY
TRAFFORD & PARNELL PRODUCTIONS)**
85 Marton Drive, Blackpool FY4 3EY
Tel 01253 766928 or 0860 273341

**MUDFORD (SHEFFIELD) LTD**
Ropeman Works, 400 Petre Street, Sheffield S4 8LU
Tel 0114 243 3033
Fax 0114 244 4536
Ropemakers and all types of canvas goods.

**JOHN MYLAND LTD**
80 Norwood High Street, West Norwood, London
SE27 9NW
Tel 0181 670 9161
Fax 0181 761 5700
Paint manufacturers and suppliers of removable floor
paint and wood finishes.

**N.E. PRINT LTD**
1 Stephenson Road, St.Ives, Cambridgeshire,
PE17 4WJ
Tel 01480 492851
Fax 01480 493417
Contact: Peter Randall
Manufacturers of flight case labels, equipment labels,
touring labels, cable and cable coding labels, printed
vinyl tapes and floor graphics.

**OAKLEAF REPRODUCTIONS LTD**
Ling Bob Mills, Main Street, Wilsden, Bradford
Yorks BD15 0JP
Tel 01535 272878

Fax 01535 275748
Manufacturers of polyurethane mouldings - ranging from simulated wood beams panelling, embellishments, pillasters, cornice to false book backs. Decorative mirrors, bed heads, four poster beds. Also able to prepare specials to individual requirements. All available to Class 1 BS. 476 Part 7 surface spread of flame to order.

## W R OUTHWAITE AND SON, ROPEMAKERS
Town Foot, Hawes, North Yorkshire DL8 3NT
Tel 01969 667487
Fax 01969 667576
Ropemaking and rope products. Tailor-made service for Barrier Ropes - quick delivery.

## THE PERFORMING PLATFORM COMPANY
Unit 7a, Pury Hill, Alderton, Towcester, Northants NN12 7LS
Tel 01604 631296
Fax 01604 624582
Temporary staging, conference, exhibition, fashion shows. Revolves, trussing, rigging, modular system. Complete Staging Service. Flightcases ("Nutcases').

## PINEWOOD STUDIOS
Pinewood Studios, Pinewood Road, Iver, Bucks SL0 ONH
Contact: Ken Jacobs
Tel 01753 656277
Fax 01753 656844
Vac-formed scenery and construction.

## REVVO CASTOR CO LTD
Somerford Road, Christchurch, Dorset BH23 3PZ
Tel 01202 484211
Fax 01202 477896
e-mail sales@revvo.co.uk
Manufacturers of castors and wheels.

## ROSCO SCENIC MATERIALS
Roscolab Limited, Blanchard Works, Kangley Bridge Road, Sydenham, London SE26 5AQ
Tel 0181 659 2300
Fax 0181 659 3153
14 product groups with hundreds of permutations, Shrink Mirrors. Rear screen projection materials, scenic paints, brushes, matallized scenic design materials. Breakaways, bottles and glasses. Suppliers of a wide range of products, including lighting filters, scenic paints, stage filters, stage flooring, screens and fog machines for special effects.

## RUSSELL & CHAPPLE LTD
23 Monmouth Street, London WC2H 9DE
Tel 0171 836 7521
Fax 0171 497 0554
Made to order drapes, backcloths etc. Suppliers of flameproof textile materials.

## SLX THEATRE SET HIRE
Victoria Road, Avonmouth, Bristol BS11 9DB
Tel 0117 982 6260
Fax 0117 982 7778
Set design and construction, scenic artists, stage engineering and complete set hire.

## ADRIAN SNELL PRODUCTION SERVICES
Unit 6, 171 Church Hill Road, Thurmaston, Leicester LE4 8DH
Tel 0116 260 0901
Fax 0116 260 0933
Our large modern workshops offer a complete construction service, including engineering, steel fabrication and all other forms of construction, scenic art techniques, sculpture, props. We offer full support for all projects.

## STAGE NORTH
Unit 4 & 5, Woodham Road, Aycliffe Industrial Estate, Co. Durham DL5 6HT
Tel 01325 314946
Fax 01325 311261
Hire and Sales of Rigging Equipment, Scenery Fittings.

## STAGEWORKS
Unit H1, Colchester Industrial Estate Colchester Avenue, Cardiff CF3 7AP
Tel 01222 462713
Fax 01222 462718
Scenery Construction and engineering, scenic artists and sculptors, staging hire and scenery supplies.

## STREETER & JESSEL
3 Gasholder Place, The Oval, London SE11 5QR
Tel 0171 793 7070
Fax 0171 793 7373
Scenery builders and stage supplies. Free brochure of stage supplies available.

## TALBOT DESIGNS LTD
225 Long Lane, Finchley, London N3 2RL
Tel 0181 346 8515
Fax 0181 349 0294
Email: sales@talbotdesigns.co.uk
Website: www.talbotdesigns.co.uk
Contact: Richard Woolff
Plastic fabricator - supplier and manufacturer of plastic sheet rod tubes, scenery and props. One way and two way mirrors.

## THEME NIGHT SPECIALISTS
Unit C5, The Seedbed Centre, Avenue Road, Aston, Birmingham, B7 4NT
Tel 0121 359 4925/6
Suppliers of entertainment and scenery to conferences, promotions and the leisure industry.

## THOMAS TINGLEY
See I.S.+G. STEEL STOCKHOLDERS LTD
## A TIRANTI LTD
70 High Street, Theale, Reading, Berks RG7 5AR
Tel 0118 930 2775
Fax 0118 932 3487
27 Warren Street, London W1P 5DG
Tel/Fax 0171 636 8565
Resins, glass fibre, plaster, clay, rubber moulding materials, white metal. Sculptors' Tools, Algmate, Plaster Bondage.

## TRAFFORD & PARNELL PRODUCTIONS
See MILTON & PARNELL)

## TRAVIS PERKINS (Southern Region)
Cobtree House, Forstal Road, Aylesford, Kent ME20 7AG
Tel 01622 710111
Fax 01622 719800
Suppliers of: Timber, Building Materials, Plumbing, Heating, Toolhire.

## TRIMITE LTD
Arundel Road, Uxbridge, Middlesex UB8 2SD.
Tel 01895 251234
Fax 0116 25 6789
Paint manufacturers and suppliers. Suppliers of fixative & bonding solution. (Formerly Hamerfix bonding &

texturising agent).

### TRIPLE E LIMITED
B3, Tower Bridge Business Complex, Clements
Road, London SE16 4EF
Tel 0171 237 6354
Fax 0171 237 7650
Manufacturers of the UNITRACK system for curtains
and scenery, manual or Linear Induction Motor
powered. UNITRACK HIRE service, plus a range of
specialist stage hardware. Catalogue available on
request.

### VARIA TEXTILES LIMITED
197 Kings Road, Kingston-on-Thames, Surrey KT2 6JH
Tel 0181 549 8590
Fax 0181 549 8290

### WHALEYS BRADFORD LTD
Harris Court , Great Horton Road, Bradford, West
Yorks BD7 4EQ.
Tel 01274 576718
Fax 01274 521309
Natural fabric suppliers, dress and furnishing scenery
fabrics suppliers curtain manufacturers.

### WOLFIN TEXTILES LIMITED
64 Great Titchfield Street, London W1P 7AE
Tel 0171 580 4724/0171 636 4949
Fax 0171 580 4724
All basic materials for Stage, Screen and TV.
Costume interlinings, scenery canvas, calico, duck,
blackout hessian.

# 55
# SCRIPTS

### GO LEISURE LTD
The Arts Exchange, Mill Green, Congleton, Cheshire
CW12 1JG
Tel 01260 276627
Contact: John Machin
Comedy TV scripting

### PHIL COLLINGE & ANDY LORD
156 Daventry Road, Rochdale, Lancashire OL11 2JE
Tel 01706 712933
Contact: Phil Collings and Andy Lord
All aspects of comedy script writing - sketches, sit-
com, stand-up and routines. UK and European
markets. Stage, screen and radio catered for.

### GROOVY MOVIES LTD
The Dower House, Rocky Lane, Reigate,
Surrey RH2 0TA
Tel 01737 643731
Contact: Yeti & Mister Bunny
Comedy Writing (Video and TV Production)

### ROBERT LAMBOLLE SERVICES
618b Finchley Road, London NW11 7RR
Tel: 0171 387 5511
Script and screenplay manuscript evaluation/
editing/advice.

### LONDON SCREENWRITERS WORKSHOP
Holborn Centre for Performing Arts, Three Fandland

Street, Holborn, London WC1R 1PZ
Tel/Fax 0171 242 2134
Forum for writers and novice aspiring writers for
contact, information and tuition. Script reading service.

### PARAGRAPH PRODUCTIONS LTD
Pinewood Studios, Iver Heath, Bucks SL0 0NH
Tel 01753 655344
Fax 01753 655944
Directors: Victoria Eskridge, Charles Savage.

### SILVERWORD PRODUCTIONS
Crickhowell, Powys NP8 1LB
Tel 01873 810142
Fax 01873 811557
Management company, record producers, marketing
company and music publishers. Script writers.

# 56
# SEATS &
# SEATING

### ARENA SEATING LTD
Arena House, Station Road, Hermitage, Berkshire
RG18 9TN
Tel 01635 201710
Fax 01635 200135
Hire and sale of Grandstands.

### AUDIENCE SYSTEMS LTD
Washington Road, West Wilts Trading Estate,
Westbury, Wiltshire BA13 4JP
Tel 01373 865050
Fax 01373 827545
e-mail audience.systems@virgin.net
Contact: David Black (Sales Director)
Audience Systems has been at the forefront of the
public seating industry for nearly twenty five years, The
Royal Albert Hall, Bridgewater Hall, Waterfront Hall,
Glydebourne Opera House, Nynex Arena, National
Indoor Arena, BBC TV and ITV are just some of our
high profile customers. Experts in the design and
manufacture of auditorium and multi-purpose seating
systems for over 25 year'.

### AUDITORIA SERVICES LTD
Unit 2, Denby Industrial Estate, Hellaby, Rotherham
S66 8HR.
Tel 01709 543345
Fax 01709 700771
Contact: David J. Jones
Manufacturers of a comprehensive range of
`retractable seating` suitable for studio & theatre type
situations, from the most basic chair to luxury theatre
chairs.

### BOURNEMOUTH UPHOLSTRY CENTRE
890 Wimbourne Road, Moordown, Bournemouth,
Dorset BH9 2DR
Tel 01202 516949
Re-upholsterers of theatre seating and contract
furniture. Seats can be re-furbished in small sections,
weekly or monthly, to spread the cost.

### BROCKLEY UPHOLSTERY LTD
182 Dartmouth Road, London SE26 4QZ
Tel 0181 699 7433
Fax 0181 699 9655
Contact: James Hooper

Manufacturers of Theatre and Cinema auditorium seating with full installation service. Quality reupholstery of existing seating by craftsmen.

**CPS SEATING & STAGING**
Station Yard, Station Road, Bawtry, Doncaster
DN10 6QD
Tel 01302 711183
For Hire contact: John Hughes
For Sales contact: Les Hughes
Adaptable seating and staging systems. Including demountable staging for hire or sale.

**ENTERTAINMENT SEATING LTD**
The Windmill Centre, Hamilton Street, Saltcoats, Ayrshire, KA21 5DY
Tel 01294 469783
Auditorium, theatre and cinema seating specialists. Reconditioning service, including on site. Also carpets and drapes.

**FASTSTAND**
235 High Street, Henley in Arden, Solihull, West Midlands. B95 5BG
Tel 01564 794001
Fax 01564 794752

**GO ENTERTAINMENTS LTD**
Chapel House, Chapel Street, Congleton, Cheshire CW12 4AB
Tel 01260 276627
Suppliers of exotic and domestic animals for TV, Films, Promotions and Publicity, Panto Ponies and Cinderella Coaches etc. Speciality Acts, reindeer and sleigh, indoor and outdoor tiered seating hire. Big Tops, Marquees, entertainment agency, circus acts

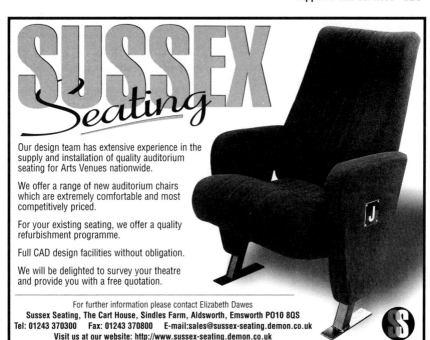
**HILLE AUDITORIUM SEATING LTD**
Church Lane, Lowton, Warrington, Cheshire
WA3 2PN
Tel 01942 728567
Fax 01942 722523
Contact: Anthony Hall
Hille Ltd are volume seating suppliers to the Cinema & Theatre world. Also available are drapes & curtains etc.

**HUSSEY SEATING SYSTEMS
(Europe) LTD**
37 Arkwright Road, Astmoor Industrial Estate,
Runcorn, Cheshire WA7 1NU
Tel 01928 575751
Fax 01928 575767
Manufacturers of cinema, auditorium and conference hall seating, specialist design work undertaken to suit clients requirements.
Telescopic platforms with a comprehensive range of integral seating options.
Full CAD design facilities - consultation without obligation.

**IRWIN SEATING EUROPE**
8 Monmouth Paddock, Norton St.Philip, Bath,
Somerset BA3 6LA
Tel 01373 834557
Fax 01373 834 695
Email sales@irwinseatingeu.prestel.co.uk
Website: ww.irwinseatingeurope.com
The world's leading manufacture of theatre and cinema seating with over 90 years of experience in providing customer satisfaction.

**KIRWIN & SIMPSON**
3B Denver Estate, Ferry Lane, Rainham,
Essex RM13 9BU
Tel 01708 558855
Fax 01708 525987
Enquiries: Andrew Simpson
Specialist re-upholsterers of auditorium seating, manufacturers of new chairs, bar and banquet furniture.

**LANCELYN THEATRE SUPPLIES**
Electric Avenue, Ferry Hinksey Road, Oxford OX2 0BY
Tel 01865 722522
Fax 01865 728791
Outdoor seating stands for hire. See also under Lighting.

**MALTBURY LTD**
Arch 651, Tower Bridge Business Complex, Clements
Road, London SE16 4DG
Tel 0171 252 3700
Fax 0171 252 3710
Contact: Philip Sparkes
The Steeldeck specialist. Platforms and seating tiers for hire (wet or dry) and sale. Largest rental stock in UK. New decks in stock in major sizes. Agents nationwide.

**MARQUEES OVER LONDON**
Unit D, 24-26 New Covent Grd. Market Sw8 5LL
Tel 0171 622 1988
Furniture hire.

**A J OWEN & CO**
The Malt Kiln Warehouse, Whitcliffe Road,
Cleckheaton, W.Yorks BD19 3DR
Tel 01274 879868
Seating Contractors. (Theatre and Auditorium)

**P+O EXHIBITION SERVICES**
Unit 1, NEC, Birmingham B40 1PJ
Tel 0121 780 2011
Fax 0121 782 2880

**PEER TANSAD LTD**
Lapdown House, Tormarton, Badminton,
Avon GL9 1JG
Tel 01454 218360
Fax 01454 218360
Designers and manufacturers of theatre air conditioned
seating, and refurbishing to the highest standards
existing theatres.

**SANDLER SEATING**
58-64 Three Colts Lane, London E2 6JR
Tel 0171 729 4777
Fax 0171 729 2843
Large range of portable folding seating for multi-
purpose halls.

**SUSSEX SEATING**
The Cart House, Sindles Farm, Aldsworth, Emsworth
PO10 8QS
Tel 01243 370300
Fax 01243 370800
Email: sales@sussex-seating.demon.co.uk
Website: www.sussex-seating.demon.co.uk
Contact: Elizabeth F Dawes (Sales Manager)
Designers and manufacturers of auditorium, theatre
and cinema seating. Re-upholstery of existing chairs
also available. Full installation service. Also available
are drapes and curtains.

# 57
# SECURITY

**ALL PURPOSE SECURITY**
4th Floor, Dexion House, 2-4 Empire Way, Wembley,
Middlesex HA9 0ES
Tel 0181 795 1991/0181 902 1485 Ext 245
Fax 0181 9009844
Sales and Marketing Manager: Pat Carr
A specialist supplier of cost effective and professional
security staff in security and stewarding services, V.I.P.
protection services and sit guarding services.

**BURNS INTERNATIONAL SECURITY SERVICES
(UK) LTD**
100 Warwick Road, Ealing, London W5 5PT
Tel 0181 567 3663
Fax 0181 567 3858
Manned Security Services.

**MIKE JACKSON LOCATION SECURITY**
21a Bellevue Road, Wandsworth Common, London
SW17 7EB
Tel/Fax 0181 767 3888
Security services, specialists in entertainment security,
personal and for promotional events.

**RENTOKIL SECURITY SERVICES LTD**
23-29 Emerald Street, London WC1N 3QL
Tel 0171 831 7551
Fax 0171 405 4928
Security guards, exhibition, attendants, mobile
patrolmen and key holding services.

**SAFE EVENT**
235/9 High Road, Wood Green, London N22 4HF
Tel 0181 889 5999
Fax 0181 889 5261
Mobile 0956 620491 (24hr)
We specialise in all kinds of event work.

**SECURITY AND PROTECTION**
40 Dean Street, London W1V 5AP
Tel 0956 226826
Consultant: Ludovic Lesdalon

**SECUREWEST**
117 Fore Street, Kingsbridge, Devon TQ7 1AL
Tel 01548 856302
Fax 01548 856637

**STARGARD SECURITY SERVICES**
22 Kingsley Park Terrace, Northampton NN2 7HG
Tel 01604 722211
Fax 01604 710120
Pager 0839 470694
e-mail vic@stargard@demon.co.uk
Artistes personal security, merchandise/copyright
infringement venue, tour security, gate audits,
consultancy, full UK and Europe cover associates
worldwide.

**SUBAN SECURITY SERVICES**
40 Seely Road, Tooting, London SW1Y 9QS
Tel 0860 603044/07050 135463
Fax 0181 953 5734

**TOPGUARDING SECURITY**
169 High Road, Loughton, Essex IG10 4LF
Tel 0181 502 5599
Fax 0181 502 5512

# 58
# SHIPPING

**AIR SEA TRANSPORT INTERNATIONAL LTD**
Unit 1, Brunel Business Court, Brunel Way, Thetford,
Norfolk IP24 1HP
Tel 01842 755635
Fax 01842 765448
Mobile 0831 571862
e-mail astisales@aol.com
Contact: Steve Bradley – Henry Bradley
Providing a Comprehensive Service Worldwide!
Airfreight – Ocean Freight – Trucking – Storage –
Packing.
From full scale Symphony Orchestra – to Ballet and Dance
Companies, to small touring Theatrical Companies.

**ANGLO PACIFIC INTERNATIONAL PLC**
Units 1, Bush Industrial Estate, Standard Road,
London NW10 6DF
Tel 0181 965 1955
Fax 0181 965 4954
Telex 8954466 ANGPAC G
Email: info@anglopacific.co.uk
Website: www.anglopacific.demon.co.uk
Ocean Freight, Air Freight, Trucking, Full Carnet
Services, Forwarders, to the Performing Arts.

**BRUNELS THEATRICAL SERVICES**
Unit 4, Crown Industrial Estate, Crown Road, Warmly,
Bristol BS15 8JB
Tel 0117 907 7855
Fax 0117 907 7856

# Anglo Pacific.
# Forwarders to the Performing Arts.

Trucking. Airfreight. Ocean Freight. Storage.
Complete Carnet Service.

## 0181 838 8084

Anglo Pacific International plc, Unit 1, Bush Industrial Estate, Standard Road, London NW10 6DF. Fax 0181 965 4954

Contact: Shane Hippisley
A 24 hour professional service throughout the UK and Europe. We specialise in all forms of transport to film, TV and theatrical companies including Green Room and Storage. Competitive rates tailor made to suit your needs. Our large fleet of vehicles ranges from transit vans to Supercube Airride step framed trailers.

**DAP INTERNATIONAL**
209 Manor Road, Erith, Kent DA8 2AD
Tel 0181 310 3003
Fax 01322 332518
Export packing, shipping, forwarding, transportation, storage and warehousing.

**EXPRESS EXPORT SERVICES LIMITED**
Arlette House, 143 Wardour Street, London W1
Tel 0171 734 8356
Fax 0171 734 3729

Shipper of costumes, props, stages and all other associated goods to the theatrical industry, by air, sea or overland truck to all parts of the world. Also specialise is offering discount airfare tickets worldwide.

**ROCK-IT CARGO LTD**
Delta Way, Egham Surrey, TW20 8RX
Tel 01784 431301
Fax 01784 471052
Email: Info@Rock-it.co.uk
Contact: Mark Cahill, Jackie Jupp, Alan Durrant
Rock-It Cargo is the world's leading and most experienced freight and logistics specialist for the performing arts and touring productions. Air freight, ocean freight, charter, trucking, carnets & packing. Global door to door services.

**TRANS EURO WORLDWIDE MOVERS**
Commercial Division, Drury Way, London NW10 0JN
Tel 0181 784 0100

Fax 0181 459 7121
Email: rachel.james@transeuro.com
Website: www.transeuro.com
Contact:: Rachel James or Mike Smith
As a quick reminder, our expertise lies in the planning and preparation of transport for UK, European and Worldwide Events, using our vehicle fleet and worldwide air and seas freight forwarding. See our ad and call today for a no obligations quote.

**WILSON & CO (UK) LTD**
Unit 5 & 6, Parkway Trading Estate, Cranford Lane, Hounslow Middx. TW5 9QA
Tel 0181 814 7000
A complete worldwide service for passengers and cargo. Embassy have over 30 years experience in the logistics of overseas touring and as part of Bilspedition Sweden are able to provide favourable rates to and from all parts of the world.

# 59
# SOUND & SOUND EQUIPMENT SUPPLIERS

**ACCUSOUND MICROPHONE SYSTEMS**
19 Bitteswell Road, Lutterworth, Leics LE17 4EL
Tel 01455 552306
Fax 01455 559448
e-mail griff@accusound.com
Website www.accusound.com
Contact: Griff Jones

**ADVANCED SOUND AND LIGHTING LTD**
15 Baiderstone Close, Heasandford Industrial Estate, Burnly BB10 2TA
Tel 01282 839400
Fax 01282 839040
Contact: Michelle Almond

**AGM COMMUNICATIONS LTD**
14–16 Deacons Lane, Ely, Cambridgeshire CB7 4PS
Tel 01353 665588
Fax 01353 667637
Contact: Anthony Morris
Manufacturer of Digital Audio Equipment, Digital Recording Services – Audio.

**AIRO (Acoustical Investigation & Research Organisation Ltd)**
Duxons Turn, Maylands Avenue, Hemel Hempstead, Herts HP2 4SB
Tel 01442 247146
Fax 01442 256749
Acoustic consultants offering specialist sound system design service.

**AJS THEATRE LIGHTING & STAGE SUPPLIES LTD**
Hightown Industrial Estate, Crow Arch Lane, Ringwood, Hampshire BH24 1ND
Tel 01425 470888
Fax 01425 471398
email: sales@ajs.co.uk
Website: http://www.demon.co.uk/ajs
Managing.Director: Adrian Sant
General Manager: Simon Sketchley
Sales Manager: Mark Morley 01425 480698

Selecon Sales Man.: Graham Fathers 01730 829732
S.E. Consultant: Mark Horseman 01424 720747
S.W. Consultant: Chris Coates 01425 480698
Midlands Consultant: John Grisswell 01283 585168
Supply, Installation & Hire of AKG, Allen & Health, Beyer, C-Audio, Denon, Fostex, Harman, JBL, Peavey, Revox, Tascam/Teac, Tecpro, 3G, Trantec, Yamaha etc.

**ALLEN & HEATH**
Kernick Industrial Estate, Penryn, Falmouth, Cornwall TR10 9LU
Tel 01326 372070
Fax 01326 377097
e-mail sales@allen-heath.com
Website www.allen-heath.com
Sales & Marketing Director: Bob Goleniowski
Manufacturers of professional sound mixing consoles for theatres, live sound and studios.

**AMEK SYSTEMS AND CONTROLS LTD**
New Islington Mill, Regent Trading Estate, Oldfield Road, Salford M5 4DE
Tel 0161 834 6747
Fax 0161 834 0593
Telex 688127
Amek Systems and Controls Ltd ranks among the world's leading designers and manufacturers of professional quality audio mixing consoles. The firm also has a division which manufactures very high power custom loudspeaker systems, audio cabling systems, and flightcases for use in transportation of delicate equipment.

**APPLE SOUND**
Unit 3, Cambrian Business Park, Queens Lane, Mold, Flintshire CH7 1NJ
Tel 01352 700433
Fax 01352 758336

**AQUARIUS PROMOTIONS**
27 Brampton Close, Cheshunt, Herts EN7 6HZ
Tel 01992 629970
Fax 01992 633488
Hire of P.A. systems.

**AUDIO & ACOUSTICS LTD**
United House, North Road, London N7 9DP
Tel 0171 700 2900
Fax 0171 700 6900
Sound system design and acoustic consultancy.
Sound equipment installation and hire.

**AUDIO FORUM LTD**
147 Westbury Leigh, Westbury, Wiltshire BA13 3SU
Tel/Fax 07071 222771
Contact: Mike Reeves, Rupert Graves
Distributor of Audio products in the UK & Ireland.

**AUDIOHIRE**
The Linen House, Unit 2, 253 Kilburn Lane, London W10 HBQ
Tel 0181 960 4466
Fax 0181 969 2162
Contact: James Drew-Edwards
Hire of Sound Equipment; Synthesizers, Samplers, Recording Equipment, Desks, Noise Reduction, Microphones, Backline, PA, Drum Machines, Fx, etc etc.

**AUTOGRAPH SALES LTD**
102 Grafton Road, London NW5 4BA
Tel 0171 485 3749
Fax 0171 485 0681

Pro-audio sales and installation company. Suppliers of Meyer Loudspeakers, ATM Flyware, Clear-Com intercom systems, Lab Gruppen amplifiers, Micron radio mics, BSS and Klark Teknik signal processors.

### AUTOGRAPH SOUND RECORDING LTD
2 Spring Place, London NW5 3BA
Tel 0171 485 4515
e-mail hier@autograph.co.uk
www.autograph.co.uk
Managing Director: Andrew Bruce
Hire Director: Terry Saunders
Technical Director: Phil Leaver
Service Director: Tony Robinson
Sound Designer: Bobby Aitken
Sound Designer: Matt McKenzie
Sound Designer: Terry Jardine
For 25 years Autograph Sound Recording have sound designed & supplied professional audio equipment to the worlds most prestigious musical & dramatic theatre productions.

### BEYMA UK LTD
Unit 10, Acton Vale Industrial Park, Cowley Road, London W3 7QE
Tel 0181 749 7887
Fax 0181 743 1925
Contact: Paul Sayer
Manufacturers and distributers of chassis loudspeakers.

### BLACK TOWER STUDIOS
15 Bracon Dale, Norwich, Norfolk NR1 2AL
Tel 01603 616661
Fax 01603 616668

### BRÄHLER ICS UK LTD
Unit 2, The Business Centre, Church End, Cambridge CB1 3LB
Tel 01223 411601
Fax 01223 411602
Managing Director: S.M. Sainsbury
Conference equipment. Simultaneous interpretation equipment.

### BUDDY SOUND & LIGHT
Unit 1, Parkside Centre, Potters Way, Temple Farm Industrial Estate, Southend on Sea SS2 5SJ
Tel 01702 615042
Fax 01702 469017
Design, supply, installation and servicing of stage equipment and stage lighting. Also hire department dealers for Zero 88 equipment.

### CAITHNESS STAGE AND LIGHTING LTD
3 Wellington Street, Paisley PA3 2JQ
Tel 0141 887 0949
Fax 0141 887 1175
Design, supply and installation of stage equipment also hire department, stage lighting. Also dealers for Zero 88.

### CANFORD AUDIO PLC
Crowther Road, Washington, Tyne & Wear NE38 0BW
Tel 0191 417 0057
Fax 0191 416 0392
Manufacturers and suppliers of over 9,000 professional audio products. Manufacturers of the Tecpro Communications system. Call for a copy of the Canford Audio Catalogue.

### CAPITAL SOUND
Unit K, Bridges Wharf, off Lombard Road, Battersea, London SW11 3QS

Tel 0171 978 5825
Fax 0171 978 5826
e-mail capital-sound.co.uk
Website www.capital-sound.co.uk
Rental Manager: Martin Connolly
Managing Director: Keith Davis
Rental of professional audio equipment.

### CENTRAL THEATRE SUPPLIES
1186 Stratford Road, Birmingham B28 8AB.
Tel 0121 778 6400
Fax 0121 702 2046
Birmingham based Central Theatre Supplies have a large hire department supplying professional public address and sound re-enforcement systems. We also are dealers for many of the leading sound manufacturers.

### THE CLOUD ONE GROUP LTD
24 Procter Street, Birmingham B7 4AE
Tel 0121 333 7711
Sales, design, installation, consultancy.

### CLYDE ELECTRONICS LTD
2 Rutherford Court, 15 North Avenue, Clydebank Business Park, Clydebank G81 2QP
Tel 0141 952 7950
Fax 0141 941 1224
Contact: Paul Stephens.

### COMPOST P.A. HIRE AND MUSIC SERVICES
11 Page Moss Parade, Huyton, Merseyside L36 2PA
Tel/Fax 0151 708 9171

### CONCERT SYSTEMS
Unit 4D, Stag Industrial Estate, Atlantic Street, Altrincham, Cheshire WA14 5DW
Tel 0161 927 7700
Fax 0161 927 7722
Public address sales, hire and installation.

### C.A.V. (CONTRACT AUDIO VISUAL)
Unit F2, Bath Road Trading Estate, Stroud, Gloucestershire GL5 3QF
Tel 01453 751865
Fax 01453 751866
e-mail sales@cav.co.uk

### CP SOUND
20 Crosslands, Chertsey South, Surrey KT16 9QY
Tel 01932 874354
Fax 01932 874355
Mobile 0836 216632
Sale, design and installation of professional sound,

lighting and video equipment.

### CTL (Control Technology) LTD
Unit 2, Brittania Business Park, Quarry Wood,
Aylesford, Maidstone, Kent ME20 7NT
Tel 01622 719151
Fax 01622 716425
Design Manufacture, Project Management, Installation
and Commissioning of Audio. Audio-Visual, S.M.
Communication and Lighting Systems.

### DESISTI LIGHTING (UK) LTD
15 Old Market Street, Thetford, Norfolk IP24 2EQ
Tel 01842 762209/752909
Fax 01842 753746
Sales Director: Jon Reay-Young
Suppliers of theatre fresnels, PC's, Profiles, floods,
PARS and accessories. Specialists in the control of
QH, Cold Cathode, Neon, Dichroic and Low Voltage
Control Systems.and fluorescent dimming at both
50Hz and 28Hz.

### DENON
Hayden Laboratories Ltd., Chiltern Hill, Chalfont
St. Peter, Bucks SL9 9UG
Tel 01753 888447
Fax 01753 880109

### DONMAR LTD
Donmar House, 54 Cavell Street, Whitechapel,
London E1 2HP
Tel 0171 790 1166
Fax 0171 290 6634
Tecpro intercom systems for theatres and productions
and complete sound installations AV and sound
systems designed, manufactured, installed and
serviced.
Stage management desks and cuelights.

### DRAGON SERVICING
32 Woodstock Road, Carshalton, Surrey SM5 3DZ
Tel 0181 395 6774
e-mail dragonser@aol.com
Website members.aol.com/dragonser/
Servicing and repair of mixing desks and amplifiers,
keyboards and tape machines.

### DRAX LIGHTING AND SPECIAL EFFECTS
Unit D9, Ivinghoe Industrial Estate, Houghton Regis,
Dunstable LU5 5BQ
Tel 01582 475614
Fax 01582 475669
Contact: Richard Foster
Suppliers of lighting, sound, effects and power
distribution. Hire with or without crew, long or short
term. Sales of equipment and consumables. Call now
for information or assistance.

### DRINKLE & MANN
Unit 2, Peel Green Trading Estate, Green Street,
Eccles, Manchester M30 7HF
Tel 0161 707 7588
Fax 0161 707 7599
Sales/Accounts: 0161 789 4140
Wet & dry hire specialists, operators & logistics, sales,
installations & maintenance agents for all leading suppliers.

### DRV
Lower Tregenna, St. Columb Minor, Newquay,
Cornwall TR8 4HS
Tel 01637 875824
Fax 01637 876082
Contact: Roger Vinton
Provide design, supply, installation and maintenance

services for all types of audio and lighting systems.
The company specialises in custom software based
control systems for all types of facility.

### E.D.C. ELKOM DESIGN LTD
Unit 11, Justin Business Park, Sandford Lane,
Wareham , Dorset BH20 4DX
Tel 01929 556050/556061
Fax 01929 551831
Manufacture, Sales and Hire of Professional
Radiomicrophone Systems and associated equipment
for Theatres, Conferences, Recordings & T.V. Studios
O.B.'s etc. Select from the EDC Sirius range of Hand
and Pocket systems - EDC's top of the range Sirius 4
Diversity Receiver is compatible with the various
mics/transmitters and when used with the EDC series
of mic transmitters give Absolute Silent Switching and
is protected from outside interference by the use of
EDC's unique Security Coding Circuit. EDC's Miniature
Portable Minkom system can be worn discreetly for
cueing, talkback, teaching and OB work.
The Minkom receiver can be connected directly into
Camera or VTR and is PP3 operated. In addition
EDC's Mixer PA Amplifiers and Inductive Loop
Amplifiers are available.

### ELECTROSONIC LIMITED
Hawley Mill, Hawley Road, Dartford, Kent DA2 7SY
Tel 01322 222211
Fax 01322 282282
Manufacturers of audio-visual and video wall display
systems.

### E.M.O. SYSTEMS LTD
Durham Road, Ushaw Moor, Durham City  DH7 7LF
Tel 0191 373 0787
Fax 0191 373 3507
e-mail sales@emo.co.uk
Sales manager: Mike Reay
Manufacturers of professional audio and electronic
equipment for the entertainment industry.

### ENTEC SOUND AND LIGHT
517 Yeading Lane, Northolt, Middx UB5 6LN
Tel 0181 842 4004
Fax 0181 842 3310
e-mail sound&light@entec.ftech.co.uk
Professional PA hire for all aspects of the
entertainment industry.  Highest quality equipment
covering all sizes of venue. Experienced operators,
competitive rates, friendly and efficient service.

### EUROSOUND (UK) LTD
Unit 1, Intake Lane, Woolley, Wakefield WF4 2LG
Tel 01484 866066
Fax 01484 866299
Sound and Lighting Hire Specialists.

### FARRAHS LIMITED
Unit 8, Parsons Green Depot,  Parsons Green Lane,
Parsons Green, London SW6 4HS.
Tel 0171 371 7111
Fax 0171 371 7331
Sound equipment rental, installation and sales.

### FORMULA SOUND
Stuart Road, Ashton Road, Bredbury, Stockport,
Cheshire SK6 2SR
Tel 0161 494 5650
Fax 0161 494 5651
e-mail info@formula-sound.com
Website www.formula-sound.com

**FUTURIST LIGHT & SOUND LTD**
Hoyle Head Mills, New Street, Earlsheaton, Dewsbury,
West Yorks WF12 8JJ
Tel 01924 468183
Fax 01924 458667
Full compliment of stage and studio sound equipment for
sales, lease and hire for most major manufacturers of
sound equipment.

**GB AUDIO**
Unit D, 51 Brunswick Road, Edinburgh EH7 5PD
Tel/Fax 0131 661 0022
Hire, sale, installation and servicing of state-of-the-art
sound equipment for concert, festival, theatre,
conference and presentations.

**GEARHOUSE**
69 Dartmouth Middleway, Birmingham B7 4UA
Tel 0121 333 3333
Fax 0121 333 3347
Conference, exhibition and presentation equipment
hire. Audio visual sound and lighting.

**GLANTRE ENGINEERING LTD**
20 Richfield Avenue, Reading, Berkshire, RG1 8EQ
Tel 0118 964 0000
Fax 0118 964 0064
email: info@glantre.com
Directors: Derek Gilbert (Managing)
Gareth Davies (Contracts)
Francis Wells (Financial)
Vic W Dobbs (Technical)
Specialist contractors providing complete theatre
electrical installation services, including stage sound
mixing, effects and reinforcement, ring intercom,
cuelight and paging systems. Also conference
microphone, simultaneous interpretation, public
address and background music. Sound systems are
based on products of leading international
manufacturers such as Soundcraft, Allen & Heath,
Electro-Voice, AKG, Studer-Revox, Phillips, Toa &
Sony. Custom built special panels, racks,
communications modules and socket boxes are
incorporated as required. Wiring, installations are
carried out in accordance with 16th edition of IEE
regulations. Glantre is a member of Electrical
Contractors' Association.

**GRADAV THEATRE SERVICES**
613-615 Green Lanes, Palmers Green, London
N13 4EP
Tel 0181 886 1300
Fax 0181 882 6517
Main dealers of Soundcraft. Sennheiser, Beyer
Dynamic. Good stocks held of cables and Neutrik
connectors. Denon CD & Cassette players.

**CLIVE GREEN & CO LTD**
1 New Street, Luton, Beds LU1 5DX
Tel 01582 404202
Fax 01582 412799
Designer and manufacturer of specialist theatre sound
mixing consoles - used internationally on major
musical and dramatic productions, in both permanent
and touring installations

**ADAM HALL LTD**
Unit 3, The Cordwainers, Temple Farm Industrial
Estate, Sutton Road, Southend on Sea, Essex
SS2 5RU
Tel 01702 613922
Fax 01702 617168
Email: mail@adamhall.co.uk

**J H E**
**group**
John Henry Enterprises
JHE Overseas Ltd • JHE Audio Ltd

**SPECIALIST SUPPLIERS TO THE**
**ENTERTAINMENT INDUSTRY**

16/24 Brewery Road, London N7 9NH
Tel: +44 (0) 609 9181  Fax: +44 (0) 171 700 7040
Email: hiredept@jhe.co.uk
Website: http://www.jhe.co.uk

Distributor and supplier of fittings and hardware for
flight cases and loudspeaker cabinets. Own brand
stands for lighting, sound and musical instruments.
Sole distributor of Klotz cables and Stage Boxes,
Amphenol Audio Connectors, Palmer Professional
Audio Tools and Power Amplifiers.

**HAYES SOUND & LIGHTING (HSL-HIRE) LTD**
Unit 7, Cunliffe Road, Whitebirk Industrial Estate,
Blackburn, Lancashire BB1 5UA
Tel 01254 698808
Fax 01254 698835
Contact: Simon Stuart
Every client is special, each commission totally unique,
our in house event management process ensuring that
your project is carefully monitored, from the taking of
your detailed instructions, through design and
planning, and ultimately the installation and staging of
the event itself.

**JHE AUDIO LTD**
16/24 Brewery Road, London N7 9NH
Tel 0171 609 9181
Fax 0171 700 7040
Email: hiredept@jhe.co.uk
Website: www.jhe.co.uk
Contact: Robert Harding, Pepin Clout.
Suppliers of sound re-inforcement for Theatre, TV and
Live Music.

**HUXTER PRODUCTION SERVICES**
8 Hawthorne Avenue, Haxby, York YO3 3JT
Tel 01904 765 696
Sound/Lighting and Staging services.

**R G JONES SOUND ENGINEERING**
16 Endeavour Way, Wimbledon, London SW19 8UH
Tel 0181 971 3100
Fax 0181 971 3101
Design, hire and sale of professional sound equipment.

**JYG LTD**
D10 The Seedbed Centre, Davidson Way, Romford,
Essex RM7 0AZ
Tel 01708 741613
Fax 01708 741579
Sales Contacts: Garry Clark, Mark Joseph or Andrew
Williams.
JYG are worldwide suppliers, distributors, installers
and designers of a comprehensive range of sound and
lighting equipment and related products for the leisure
industry.

**KELSEY ACOUSTICS LTD**
27 Beethoven Street, London W10 4LG

PROFESSIONAL
SOUND HIRE
◆
SALES
◆
SERVICE
◆
COMMUNICATIONS

Merseyside Audio Consultants
1-2 Attenburys Park, Park Road, Altrincham, Cheshire WA14 5QE

TEL: (0161) 969 8311    FAX: (0161) 962 9423

Tel 0181 964 8000
Fax 0181 964 1010
Specialist audio/lighting connector, cable distributor and installer.

**ROY KIRKPATRICK SOUND ENGINEERING**
29 Burgmont Lane, Comberbach, Nr. Northwich,
Cheshire CW9 6BU
Tel/Fax 01606 891939
Design equipment installation hire of Public Address.
Sound reinforcement and Magnetic Induction Loop
Systems.

**LANCELYN THEATRE SUPPLIES**
Electric Avenue, Ferry Hinksey Road, Oxford OX2 0BY
Sales 01865 722468
Hire 01865 722522
Fax 01865 728791
Equipment for hire and sale.
**LIGHT RELIEF**
Ellar House, Alexandra Industrial Estate, Wentloog
Road, Rumney, Cardiff CF3 8EE
Tel 01633 440426
Supply, installation and hire of theatre lighting, sound
and effects. N.I.C.E.I.C. approved contractor. Stage
lighting & sound consultants.

**LINE-UP P.M.C.**
9A Tankerville Place, Newcastle upon Tyne NE2 3AT
Tel 0191 281 6449
Fax 0191 212 0913

**LINK COMMUNICATIONS**
61 Ipswich Crescent, Great Barr, Birmingham B42 1LY
Tel/Fax 0121 357 8261

**LMC AUDIO SYSTEM LTD**
Unit 10, Acton Vale Industrial Park, Cowley Road,

London W3 7QE
Tel 0181 743 4680
Fax 0181 7499875
e-mail 100617@compuserve.com
Website lmcaudio.co.uk
Contact: Iolo Pierce, Theatre Specialist

**MAC SOUND**
1-2 Attenburys Park, Park Road, Altrincham, Cheshire
WA14 5QE
Tel 0161 969 8311
Fax 0161 962 9423
MAC sound provides a comprehensive hire facility of
quality equipment with an out of hours helpline service.
Contact us for a brochure or a quotation without
obligation.

**MALDWYN BOWDEN INTERNATIONAL LTD**
168 Edward Street, Brighton BN2 2JB
Tel 01273 607384
Fax 01273 694408
Supply, install, hire out, and custom-built audio
equipment for use in theatres from the S.M.'s talkback
desk through to installation of the most advanced
multi-channel sound systems for front-of-house public
address. Hire of mix-down and amplification
equipment, provision of background music, paging
systems, and supply/installation of mood lighting for
theatres/clubs. Supply of engineers and equipment for
mix-downs, hire contracts for productions on tour. Will
integrate own equipment with modified existing
equipment.

**MARK IV PRO AUDIO GROUP**
Klark Teknik Building, Walter Nash Road,
Kidderminster, Worcestershire DY11 7HJ
Tel 01562 741515
Fax 01562 745371
Sales & Distribution of Klark Teknik , Midas, DDA and Electro-
Voice concert sound products.

**MARQUEE AUDIO LTD**
Shepperton Film Studios, Studios Road, Shepperton,
Middlesex TW17 0QD
Tel 01932 566777
Fax 01932 565861
Professional audio sales, design and
installation.

**MEYER SOUND EUROPE LTD**
39-49 Hastings Street, Luton, Bedfordshire LU1 5BE
Tel 01582 728400
Fax 01582 728434
e-mail meyer-europe.com
Meyer Sound designs and manufactures high-
definition sound reinforcement systems and is the
industry standard loudspeaker for the professional
theatre market. Distributed exclusively in the UK by
Autograph Sales Ltd.

**MIDLAND THEATRE SERVICES LTD**
Dertmouth Road, Smethwick, Birmingham B66 1AX.
Tel 0121 525 4545
Fax 0121 525 2413
Main dealers for Audio Technica/Beyer/Bose/HH/Metro
Audio/Sennheiser/Shermann Audio/Tecpro
Sale/Hire/Installation/Special Effects.
Open 9.00a.m. to 6.00p.m. Monday-Friday, Saturday
9.30a.m. to 12.30p.m.

**MIDNIGHT DIRECT LTD**
Unit 1, Chelsea Bridge Business Centre,
326 Queenstown Road, London SW8 4NP
Tel 0171 498 7272
Fax 0171 498 8845
Sales Manager: Damion Dowling
A sales and installation company, supplying the trade
with lighting and effects equipment.

**MUSIC ROOM**
116-118 New Cross Road, New Cross Gate, London
SE14 5BA
Tel 0171 252 8271
Fax 0171 252 8252
Sound systems/musical equipment, hire and sales, 7
days a week. JBC main dealer.

**MUSTANG COMMUNICATIONS LTD**
Eastfield Industrial Estate, Scarborough, North
Yorks YO11 3UT
Tel 01723 582555/01723 582289
Fax 01723 581673
Manufacturer of amplification and loop induction
equipment.

**NATIONAL SOUND REPRODUCERS LIMITED**
Lower Priory Farm, Clamp Hill, Stanmore, Middx
HA7 3JJ
Tel 0181 954 7677
Fax 0181 954 9329
Director: Ronald A Walker
Public Address, Tape Recording, Film, Slide and
Video, Projection, Engineers Hire, Sale and Service.

**ONE STAGE PRODUCTIONS LTD**
83 Leamington Crescent, Harrow, Middlesex HA2 9HH
Tel/Fax 0181 864 7362
Email: john@one-stage.co.uk
Website: http://www.one-stage.co.uk
Contact: John Ryan, Jody Ryan, Nic Bridgewater
With a strong team of IT and Audio design staff we
offer a friendly and professional service as suppliers of
market leading equipment suitable for theatre,
conferencing, exhibitions, broadcasting and touring.
We also have an experienced team working in project
and tour management.

**OUT BOARD ELECTRONIC LIMITED**
Unit D, Copley Hill Farm, Cambridge Road, Babraham,
Cambs CB2 4AF
Tel 01223 837827
Fax 01223 837798
e-mail www.outboard.co.uk
Contact: Robin Whittaker
Manufacturers of automated sound control equipment
for surround sound and level control, products include
TiMax, Octopus, retrofit moving fader automation
systems, QP4 quad panner, mains power distribution
systems and hoist controllers.

**OXRECS DIGITAL**
Magdalen Farm Cottage, Standlake, Witney, Oxon
OX8 7RN
Tel/Fax 01865 300347
Website: www.oxrecs.com
Manager: Bernard Martin
Artistic Director: Joyce Martin
Specialist location recording for organs, chamber
orchestras and choirs. Digital editing, artwork design
and typesetting services also available for inlays and
booklets.

**P.A. MUSIC**
172 High Road, London N2 9AS
Tel 0181 883 4350
Fax 0181 883 5117
Contact: Mr A. Allan
P.A. Music is a small and flexible company involved in
the supply and hire of lighting and sound equipment to
the leisure/entertainment and conference industries.
We also produce high quality flight cases custom made
to our customers' requirements.

**THE P.A. COMPANY LIMITED**
Unit 7, The Ashway Centre, Elm Crescent, Kingston,
KT2 6HH
Tel 0181 546 6640
Fax 0181 547 1469
Hire/sale/installation of all sound equipment 'BOSE'
main agents.

**PHOSPHENE**
Milton Road South, Stowmarket, Suffolk IP14 1EZ
Tel 01449 678200/01449 770011
Contact: Cliff Dix
Sales and Hire of sound equipment, operators
available, extensive experience of mixing with major
name cabaret artists and on touring musicals.
Stage management systems custom designed and
built to order.

**PLAYLIGHT HIRE LIMITED**
67 Ayres Road, Old Trafford, Manchester M16 9NH
Tel 0161 226 5858
Fax 0161 232 9510
Contact: Ed Draycott
Hire: Sennheiser diversity radio mics, Soundcraft
Ramsa and Bose speakers.
Sales: Dealer for Ramsa, Sennheiser, Beyer, Tascam
and Nexo – Playlight also supplies lighting, stage
draperies, rigging, and stage electrical installations
services. Design, supply and installation of voice
evacuation systems.

**PYRAMID LIGHTING AND SOUND SERVICES**
28 Railway Approach, East Grinstead, West Sussex
RH19 1BP
Tel 01342 314328
Fax 01342 410727

**R.C.F. ELECTRONICS (UK) LTD**
2 Blenheim Court, Hurricane Way, Wickford Business
Park, Wickford, Essex SS11 8YT
Tel 01268 570808
Fax 01268 570809
RCF Public Address equipment, RCF loudspeakers
and components, RCF loudspeaker systems.

**RAPER & WAYMAN**
Unit 3, Crusader Estate, 167 Hermitage Road, Manor House, London N4 1LZ
Tel 0181 800 8288
Fax 0181 809 1515
Email randwengineering@dial.pipex.com
Contact: Jon Raper, Peter Kenny
Raper and Wayman are the only UK company approved for the installation and service of acoustic control systems.

**RAYCOM LTD**
16 Tything Road, Ardon Forrest Trading Estate, Alcester B49 6EP
Tel 01789 400255
Fax 01789 400630
Raycom Ltd specialise in the supply and service of radio Talkback and Wireless Microphone Systems to the Broadcast, Entertainment and Music Industry. Raycom Ltd is a division of the Raycom Group of companies and provides Technical Consultancy on an International Basis. Our qualified engineers are available 24 hours a day and are known for being able to solve technical and supply problems very quickly and efficiently, anytime, anyplace. With the combined resources of other Raycom companies we are able to provide all types of communication systems in very short time scales. We are approved ASP/DTI suppliers and can arrange the supply and licensing of Radio Systems at the shortest notice as we have often obtained the necessary licences immediately.

**ROBBOTRONIC CO**
Industrial Estate, 14 Blatchford Close, Horsham, West Sussex RH13 5RG
Tel 01403 210420
Consult/design/supply and install sound re-inforcement and infra-red/audio frequency inductive loop systems.

**ROGERS INTERNATIONAL (UK) LTD**
Unit 3, 310 Commonside East, Mitcham, Surrey CR4 1HX
Tel 0181 640 2172
Fax 0181 685 9496
Producers of the legendary LS3/5a loudspeaker Rogers now combine traditional models with new range loudspeakers. With worldwide distribution Rogers recently won the Las Vegas WCES Audio Exhibitions Award for the legendary AEB-1 model.

**S.A.V. LIMITED**
Party House, Mowbray Drive, Blackpool, Lancashire FY3 7JR
Tel 01253 302602
Fax 01253 301000
Distributors of Professional Sound Lighting and Stage Effects.

**SENNHEISER UK LTD**
3 Century Point, Halifax Road, High Wycombe, Buckinghamshire HP12 3SL
Tel 01494 551551
Fax 01494 551550
Contact: Rob Piddington
Sound communications equipment. Specialists in headphones microphones, radio frequency and infra-red transmission systems, supplying all major national and local theatre productions. Clear technical advice and full service support.

**SGB WORLD SERVICE**
Empire House, 12 Rutland Street, Hanley, Stoke on Trent ST1 5JG
Tel 01782 279309
Fax 01782 279309
e-mail email@sgbworldservice.co.uk
Website www.sgbwordservice.com
Contact:Mr S. Boote
See our main advert in Lighting & Lighting Equipment Suppliers.

**SHERMAN UK**
Units 58-61 Mochdre Enterprise Park, Newtown, Powys SY16 4LE
Tel 01686 622997
Fax 01686 622616
Contact: Ken Hughes
Professinal loudspeaker systems with over 40 models in production. Shermann Systems are used worldwide but designed and built in Britain. Distribution through selected dealers. Demo rigs available.

**JOHN HORNBY SKEWES & CO LTD**
Salem House, Parkinson Approach, Garforth, Leeds LS25 2HR
Tel 01132 865381
Fax 01132 868515
Managing Director: John H. Skewes
Musical Amplification Equipment and Merchandise.

**SOLENT SOUNDS SYSTEMS**
7 Mitchall Point, Ensign Park, Southampton SO31 4RF
Tel 01703 458700
Fax 01703 456789

**SONIFEX LIMITED**
61 Station Road, Irthlingborough, Northants NN9 5QE
Tel 01933 650700
Fax 01933 650726
e-mail sales@sonifex.co.uk
Website www.sonifex.co.uk
Sales contacts: Richard Goodliffe, Jo Barker
Manufacturing: Effects Cartridge Machines, Players and Recorders. Digital FX machines. Hard disk audio recording systems – Digital cart machines.

**SONIX AUDIO LTD**
Studio House, Flowers Hill, Brislington, Bristol BS4 5JJ
Tel 0117 908 5558
Fax 0117 908 5559
Email: sonix@soundgear.demon.co.uk
Website: www.sonixaudio.com
Contact: Nick Hobbs
Sonix are sound equipment Hire, Sales, Design and installation specialists with expertise in touring productions and UHF Radio Microphones. They are also one of the first UK rental companies to offer internet online equipment booking with Europe Wide 24 hour technical support.

**SOUND ALIBI PRODUCTIONS**
92 Hartley Avenue, Woodhouse, Leeds, LS6 2HZ
Tel/Fax 0113 243 0177
Pager 01426 253830
Email andy@manitou.free-online.co.uk
Contact: Andy Wood (partner)
Production company specialising in theatre backing sound and music (also sound effects & web site design) from initial concept to CD master. Friendly, effecient service.

**THE SOUND COMPANY**
2 Lord Hills Road, London W2 6PD
Tel 0171 286 7477

Fax 0171 286 7377
Professional audio equipment hire for all aspects of theatre. Very competitive rates with friendly and efficient service.

**SOUND DEPT**
19 Blacklands Way, Abingdon Business Park, Abingdon OX14 1DY
Tel 01235 555622
Fax 01235 536654
Contact: Steve Smith
Sound Dept. are distributers of professional audio & commercial sound eqipment. They also provide technical support to consultants & contractors. Products represented - Ashley Audio, Astatic Microphones, Biamp Electronics, Carver Amplifications. Community loudspeakers and Sound Advance systems planar loudspeakers.

**SOUND ELECTRONICS (NEWCASTLE) LTD**
Industry Road, Heaton, Newcastle Upon Tyne NE6 5XB
Tel 0191 265 2500
Fax 0191 265 8595
Sales, Hire, Design, Install. Bose Main Dealer. Stockist for Citronic, Beyer, Shure, J.B.L. A.K.G., Trantect, Denon, Allen & Heath, T.O.A., HH, Carlsbro, Scott Audio.

**SSE HIRE LTD**
201 Coventry Road, Birmingham B10 0RA
Tel 0121 766 7170
Fax 0121 766 8217
PA Hire company, also involved in sound installation in large venues and new equipment sales of sound products.
Manufacture of flightcases staging and riser hire.

**STAGE DOOR SUPPLIES**
198 Bakers Street, Enfield EN1 3JY
Tel 0181 367 7337
Fax 0181 367 7557
Sound equipment for hire and sale.

**STAGE ELECTRICS**
Victoria Road, Avonmouth, Bristol BS11 9DB
Tel 0117 982 7282
Fax 0117 982 2180
e-mail hire@stage-electrics.co.uk
e-mail sales@stage-electrics.co.uk
Website www.stage-electrics.demon.co.uk
Cofton Road, Marsh Barton, Exeter EX2 8QW
Tel 01392 255868
Fax 01392 410592
2, Parkway Industrial Estate, Plymouth PL6 8LH
Tel 01752 269444
Fax 01752 228283
Dartmouth Road, Smethwick, West Midlands B66 1AX
Tel 0121 525 4545
Fax 0121 525 2413
Contacts: Hire, Adrian Searle; Sales, Jane Evans; Production, Richard Cross.
Hire, sales, installation, and service of sound equipment for theatre, conference, concert, festival and commercial presentations. Project management, designers and engineers.

**STAGE NORTH**
Unit 4 & 5, Woodham Road, Aycliffe Industrial Estate, Co. Durham DL5 6HT
Tel 01325 314946
Fax 01325 311261
Hire and sales of sound equipment.

**STAGE SERVICES**
Stage House, Prince William Road, Loughborough, Leicester, LE11 0GN.
Tel 01509 218857
Fax 01509 265730
Sales, hire and installation of lighting, sound and staging equipment by ADB, CCT, LSD, Electro Control Systems, Zero 88, AKG, Allen & Heath, Audio Technica, Tascam, C Audio, JBL, Quad, Sennheiser, Denon, Trantec, Stage Systems and others. Stage make-up by Grimas, counter sales, mail order and workshops. Sales and Hire of optical and pyrotechnic effects by DHA, Le Maitre & Theatrical Pyrotechnics. Drapes made to order. Full range of electrical and rigging accessories, consumables and sales of colour filter by Rosco and Lee.

**STAGETEC (UK) LTD**
363 Sykes Road Trading Estate, Slough, Berkshire SL1 4SP
Tel 01753 553522
Fax 01753 553122
Stagetec provide a complete design, supply, installation and maintenance service for a comprehensive range of sound, lighting and staging products. They are also UK distributor for the world renowned range of Compulite's lighting controls desks, dimmers and scrollers aswell as FLY's intelligent lights.

**STAGE TECHNIQUES**
Unit One, Cotton Drive, Dalehouse Lane Industrial Estate, Kenilworth, Warwickshire CV8 2EB
Tel 01926 864800
Fax 01929 864964
email: stagetec@dircon.co.uk
Contact: S. Griffiths
Conference, Theatre, Television, Outdoor Events, Steeldeck Hire.

**STAGE TWO LTD**
Unit J, Penfold Trading Estate, Imperial Way, Watford,
Herts WD2 4YY
Tel 01923 244822
Fax 01923 255048
Hires Manager: Richard Ford
Hire or sale of sound, lighting and special effects of all
applications.

**TSL AV LTD**
Studio 9, 75 Filmer Road, London SW6 7JF.
Tel 0171 371 5020
Fax 0171 371 0503
Managing Director: Matthew Griffiths
A.V. Equipment Hire, Conference Production services.

**TANNOY LTD**
Professional Division, Rosehall Industrial Estate,
Coatbridge, Strathclyde ML5 4TF
Tel 01236 420199
Fax 01236 428230
email: prosales@tannoy.com
Product Manager: D.P.West
Contact: Alan Lochhead
Tannoy`s unique range of high performance point
source systems are designed to offer the ultimate in
sound reinforcement; compact, incredibly powerful, yet
so natural they become invisible to the performance.

**TELE-STAGE ASSOCIATES (UK) LIMITED**
Unit 14, Bunting Road, Moreton Hall Industrial
Estate, Bury St. Edmunds, Suffolk IP32 7BX
Tel 01284 755512
Fax 01284 755516
Email: TRAMKB@compuserve.com

**THEATRE DIRECT**
Unit 2, Kirkwood Road, Kings Hedges, Cambridge
CB4 2PH
Tel 01223 423010
Fax 01223 425010
Contact: James Irvine
Hire sales and service of lighting, sound and staging -
Strand Lighting main dealer.

**TP SOUND/**
**THEATRE PROJECTS SOUND SERVICES LTD**
Unit 100, Centenniel Estate, Herts WD6 37A
Tel 0870 162 1010
Fax 0870 162 1020
Theatre Sound: Dave Perry
Corporate Sound: Richard Rogers
Hire of theatre and conference sound systems with
fully trained technicians and the multi art show control
system.

**TOUCHWOOD AUDIO PRODUCTIONS**
6 Hyde Park Terrace, Leeds LS6 1BJ
Office Tel 0113 243 0177
Studio Tel 0113 278 7180
Specialists in production and recording of theatre
backing tracks, voice-overs and special effects. Digital
editing and large library of original and non-original
source material available.

**TRANTEC**
**BBM ELECTRONICS GROUP LIMITED.**
Kestrel House, Garth Road, Morden, Surrey SM4 4LP
Tel 0181 330 3111
Fax 0181 330 3222
Contact: Chris Gilbert
Trantec offer a full range of both VHF and UHF radio
microphones for all theatrical performances. All Trantec
products are designed and manufactured in the UK and
are fully DTI approved.

**ROY TRUMAN SOUND SERVICES**
Unit 23, Atlas Business Centre, Oxgate Lane, London
NW2 7HU
Tel 0181 208 2468
Fax 0181 208 3320
Sound equipment hire: complete systems or items - more
interested in "good sound" and happy customers than in
sales techniques!

**TURBOSOUND**
Units 5+6, Star Road, Partridge Green, West Sussex
RH13 8RY
Tel 01403 711447
Fax 01403 710155

**VAN DAMME CABLE**
VDC House, 4 Brandon Road, London N7 9AA
Email: sales@vdctrading.com
Website: www.vdctrading.com
Contact: Niall Holden
Manufacturer and distributor of all Van Damme cables
and products.

**VDC TRADING LTD**
VDC House, 4 Brandon Road, London N7 9AA
Email: sales@vdctrading.com
Website: www.vdctrading.com
Contact: Niall Holden
Manufacturer and distributor of audio & video cable and
components. Also distribute the Van Damme range of
cables. Specialise in producing bespoke assemblies for
the recording, presentation and broadcast markets.

**VDM**
VDC House, 4 Brandon Road, London N7 9AA
Email: sales@vdctrading.com
Website: www.vdctrading.com
Contact: Niall Holden
Manufacturer and distributor of the VDM range of multi-
channel audio connectors. The VDM range of connectors
is available from 8 channels to 48 channels.

**VILLA AUDIO LTD**
Bailey's Farm, Chatham Green, Little Waltham, Essex
CM3 3LE.
Tel 01245 361694
Fax 01245 362281
Managing Director: Gareth Jones
Contact: Jeff Clennel
Pro audio rental, Pro audio sales, Pro audio
installations.

**WHITWAMS SOUND**
70 High Street, Winchester, Hampshire SO23 9DE
Tel 01962 865253
Fax 01962 842064
Professional Sound Sales: David Harding (Director)
Consultants, designers, equipment, supply and hire,
installation and commissioning of sound, public
address and communications systems for theatres,
conference centres, local authorities, churches, arts
centres, concerts halls, etc. Member Plasa.

**WIGWAM ACOUSTICS LTD**
The Courtyard, Green Lane, Heywood,
Lancashire OL10 2EX
Tel 01706 363400
Fax 01706 363410
Direct Hire 01706 363800
Sound systems. Hiring everything from a microphone
to a complete touring sound system. Sales and

installation.

**WILLIAM SOUND AND SENNHEISER INFRA-RED SYSTEMS**
**WINTONFIELD SYSTEMS**
Albyn Industrial Estate, Broxburn,
West Lothien, EH5 5PQ
Tel 0131 313 1313
Fax 0131 313 1314
Williams Sound and Sennheiser Infra-Red Systems:
Authorised dealers for providing Infra-Red Sound
Transmission systems for the hard of hearing and/or
Visually impaired patrons (Audio description) in
theatres, concert halls, cinemas, galleries and various
art venues.
Systems with up to 32 channels are available for
simultaneous translation and conferencing
applications.
Also dealers for Door Aid: Door access for disabled.
Scantronic Radio Systems - wireless monitoring and
emergency call systems: eg Disabled Toilet Call
systems.

# 60

# SPONSORSHIP AGENTS & CONSULTANTS

**ADVANTAGE INTERNATIONAL**
Glenn House, Stag Place, London SW1E 5AG
Tel 0171 862 0000

**ESPRIT GROUP**
176 Blackfriars Road, London SE1 8ER
Tel 0171 928 5055
Fax 0171 928 5628

**FOCUS**
19 Biscay Road, London W6 8JW
Tel 0181 748 6006

**KAREN EARL LIMITED**
2-3 Ledbury Mews West, London W11 2AE
Tel 0171 243 0064
Fax 0171 792 1220

**M HUMPHREYS & PARTNERS LTD**
68 South Lambeth Road, Vauxhall, London SW8 1RL
Tel 0171 820 9911
Fax 0171 820 9259

**PRO MOTIONS CONSULTANTS**
27 Oxford Road, Hampton Poyle, Oxford OX5 2QA
Tel 01865 842264
Fax 01865 379962

**SCOPE SPONSORSHIP**
Tower House, 8-14 Southampton Street, Covent
Garden, London WC2E 7HA
Tel 0171 379 3234
Fax 0171 465 8241

# 61

# STAGE & SCENIC ENGINEERING

**ALISTAGE**
Unit 2, Hotspur Industrial Estate, West Road,
Tottenham, London N17 0XJ
Tel 0181 808 5005
Fax 0181 801 9851
Stage systems, raked seating, bandstands, catwalks,
marquees, couplers and fittings, trussing, aluminium
towers, specials.

**AT A STROKE OF MIDNIGHT**
Unit 1, Chelsea Bridge Business Centre,
326 Queenstown Road, London SW8 4NP
Tel 0171 498 7272
Fax 0171 498 8845
Management: Oliver Barnicoat
Designers: Liza Townsend
The staging, set, prop and production management
division of the Midnight group

**BOWER WOOD**
Production Services & Workshop
Unit 5 The Billings, 3 Walnut Tree Close, Guildford,
Surrey, GU1 4UL
Tel 01483 300926
Fax 01483 450926
Website: www.bowerwood.com
Partners: Graham Bower-Wood and Nigel Mathias.
Scenery construction and metal fabrication for the
theatre, Opera, exhibitions and special events.

**BRITISH TURNTABLE CO**
Emblem Street, Bolton BL3 5BW
Manchester Depot
Tel 01204 525626
Fax 01204 382407
Email: info@turntable.co.uk
Website: www.british.turntable.co.uk
London Depot
Tel 01992 574602
Fax 01992 560385
British Turntable Company, leaders in creating
dramatic movement, offer a range of low profile, self-
assembly revolving stages, in diameters ranging from
2m to 8m. Highly portable, these revolves can be
assembled by two men in as little as half an hour*, can
be supplied for manual or powered operation and
include options such as variable speed, indexing
and/or static centre.
This range is in addition to the extremely
comprehensive range of revolves available for hire up
to 25 tonne capacity and which include units suitable
for outdoor location applications.
Competitively priced, all units are available for hire
from depots throughout the UK.
*Assembly time based on a 6m standard revolve on
sound, level surface.

**CONCEPT ENGINEERING**
7 Woodlands Business Park, Woodlands Park,
Maidenhead, Berks. SL6 3UA
Tel 01628 825555
Fax 01628 826261

**CONCEPT STAGING LTD**
Station Garage, Station Road, Foulridge, Colne,

Lancashire BB8 7LB
Tel 01282 841444
Fax 01282 841555
Mobile 0976 733849

**DOUGHTY ENGINEERING LIMITED**
Crow Arch Lane, Ringwood, Hants BH24 1NZ
Tel 01425 478961
Fax 01425 474481

**DRV PUBLIC ADDRESS CONSULTANTS**
Lower Tregenna, St. Columb Minor, Newquay,
Cornwall TR8 4HS
Tel 01637 875824
Fax 01637 876082
Hire, sale, installation, servicing of all types of audio
visual and stage engineering equipment.

**DUO GB LTD**
254 Wellingborough Road, Northampton NN1 4EJ
Tel 01604 230445
Fax 01604 231389

**FLINT HIRE & SUPPLY LTD**
Queens Row, London SE17 2PX
Tel 0171 703 9786
Fax 0171 708 4189
Email: sales@flintltd.demon.co.uk
Contact: Alasdair Flint
Suppliers of high tensile and BZP bolts, sanners,
podgers, Podgalugs (tm), drills, angle grinders, drop
blocks, winches, pulleys, Flints water based multi
primer, wire rope, tested wire assemblies and all
scenic hardware.

**FUTURIST LIGHT & SOUND LTD**
Hoyle Head Mills, New Street, Earlsheaton,

Dewsbury, West Yorks WF12 8JJ
Tel 01924 468183
Fax 01924 458667

**GLANTRE ENGINEERING LIMITED**
20 Richfield Avenue, Reading, Berks RG1 8EQ
Tel 0118 964 0000
Fax 0118 964 0064
email: info@glante.com
Managing Director: Derek Gilbert
Contracts Director: Gareth Davies
Financial Director: Francis Wells
Technical Directors: Vic W Dobbs
Specialist contractors providing complete theatre
installation services including stage suspension sets
(power, counterweight, winch and hemp operated),
safety curtains, stage lifts, revolves, wagons, projection
screens, acoustic doors, tracks, drapes, cycloramas,
rostra, flooring, access equipment and scenery
accessories. Also stage equipment control panels and
electrical wiring installations in accordance with 16th
edition of IEE Regulations.

**A S GREEN & CO (LANCASHIRE) LTD**
Redgate Road, South Lancs Industrial Estate, Ashton-
in-Makerfield, Lancashire WN4 8DT.
Tel 01942 718347
Fax 01942 718219
Email: pmcferran@aol.com

**HALL & DIXON**
182a High Street, Cottenham, Cambridge CB4 4RX
Tel 01954 251655
Fax 01954 252005
Stage equipment, curtains, A.V equipment, contract
furnishings, cinema screens and frames, electrical and
manual operated draw and roller tracking systems.

**HARKNESS HALL LTD**
The Gate Studios, Station Road, Borehamwood,
Hertfordshire  WD6 1DQ
Tel 0181 953 3611
Fax 0181 207 3657
e-mail info@harknesshall.com
Contacts: Doug Heather & Chris Hitchens
A comprehensive range of curtain tracks systems,
drapes, curtains and cycloramas; winches and hoists;
grid rigging and suspension gear; PC and PLC control
systems; stage and scenery fittings; stage and studio
lighting; design, survey, installation and maintenance
services available Electrical and manual roller screens
with front and rear projection services up to 48ft
(14.6m) wide. Flying frames with or without Moving
masking Systems, togethert with a comprehensive
range of Portable, Folding Frame Screens.
Comprehensive catalogue available FOC.

**JOHN HENRY ENTERPRISES**
16/24 Brewery Road, London N7 9NH.
Tel 0171 609 9181
Fax 0171 700 7040
Contact: Pepin Clout or Will Wright
John Henry Enterprises can provide you with a
pa/sound reinforcement; backline equipment; staging
and risers; flightcases; music stands etc. Recent
clients have included a Tribute to the Blues Brothers;
Shirley Bassey; Michael Ball; BBC TV's Later with
Jools Holland, Bob Monkhouse and the National
Lottery Live.

**KING COLE TUBE BENDING CO. LIMITED**
40 Buckland Road, Penmill Trading Estate, Yeovil,
Somerset  BA21 5EJ
Tel 01935 26141
Fax 01935 29756
General Purpose Stage Units.

**ROBERT KNIGHT LTD**
PO Box 52, London SE17 2QD.
Tel 0171 277 1704
Fax 0171 277 1722
Stage and television scenery contractors and
engineers: workshops in Slough, Berkshire. Wide
range of drapes and equipment available for hire at
Horsley Street, London SE17 (please telephone for
list/prices).

**LANCELYN THEATRE SUPPLIES**
Electric Avenue, Ferry Hinksey Road, Oxford
OX2 0BY
Tel 01865 722468
Fax 01865 728791
Portable staging for hire and sale.

**LEITNER GB LIMITED**
254 Wellingborough Road, Northampton NN1 4EJ
Tel 01604 230445
Fax 01604 231389

**MALTBURY LTD**
Arch 651, Tower Bridge Business Complex, Clements
Road, London SE16 4DG
Tel 0171 252 3700
Fax 0171 252 3710
Email: info@maltbury.com
Website: www.maltbury.com
Contact: Philip Sparkes
Hire or buy portable staging from the specialists.
Syeeldeck 7.5 - the strongest, most versatile system
on the market or the new, lighter alternative -
METRODECK. Call us for more details.

**THE MANCHESTER LIGHTING AND STAGE CO.**
77 Central Road, Manchester M20 4YD
Tel 0161 445 6876
Fax 0161 445 7574
Contact: Bruce Mitchell
Lighting Hire and Sales "Steeldeck" Hire and Sales -
Marquee Hire, Event Management - Site Electrics.
Catwalks, outdoor roofs & stages.

**BOB MASSEY ASSOCIATES**
**(Stage Consultants)**
9 Worrall Avenue, Arnold, Nottingham NG5 7GN
Tel 0115 967 3969
Fax 0115 967 3969
e-mail b.massey@virgin.net
Technical theatre consultancy, advice, design and
planning service including lottery applications for all
lighting, engineering, curtain and communication
projects.

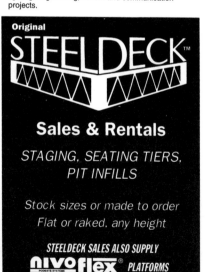
**OUTBACK RIGGING**
Unit 11, Kendal Court, Western Avenue
Trading Estate, Kendal Avenue, London. W3 0RP
Tel 0181 993 0066
Fax 0181 752 1753

**THE PERFORMING PLATFORM COMPANY**
Unit 1C, Pury Hill, Alderton, Towcester,
Northamptonshire NN12 7LS
Tel 01604 31296
Fax 1604 24582
Temporary staging, conference, exhibition, fashion shows.
Revolves, trussing, rigging, modular system. Complete
Staging Service plus Flightcase manufacture ("Nutcases").

**PIT STOP BARRIERS**
Unit B10 Alladin Workspace, Longdrive, Greenford,
Middlesex UB6 8UH
Tel 0181 813 1664
Fax 0181 813 1285
Stage Barriers, Crowd Control Barriers and platform
staging.

**SERIOUS STRUCTURES**
Bourne Farm, Pilton, Somerset, BA4 4NX
Tel 01749 890 320
Fax 01749 890 531
Contact: Steven Corfield

**SET REACTION**
Unit 9, Victoria Road, Avonmouth, Bristol BS11 9DB
Tel 0117 982 6260
Fax 0117 982 7778
Scenic construction.

**SHOWSTAGE**
Unit D1, Cumberland Trading Estate, Cumberland
Road, Loughborough, Leicester LE11 0DF
Tel 01509 249191
Fax 01509 231717
Mobile: 0468 212140
Contact: Frank Cheadle

**SICO EUROPE LIMITED**
Henwood Industrial Estate, Ashford, Kent TN24 8DH
Tel 01233 643311
Fax 01233 645143
Folding, mobile stage units, steps, guardrails, skirt
curtains, backdrops. Also sole UK distributor for
Hussey Audience Tiering ans Seating systems.

**SPACE CONTRACTS LTD**
34 Thornby Avenue, Solihull B91 2BJ
Tel 0121 704 4934
Structural steel in theatres, especially moving stages,

# TeleStage Associates Ltd.

## Unit 14, Bunting Road, Moreton Hall Industrial Estate, Suffolk IP32 7BX. Telephone (01284) 755512. Telefax (01284) 755516. e-mail: tsamkb@compuserve.com

### Manufacturers of stage machinery. Manufacturers of TV studio suspension equipment.

### Supply, design and installation of mechanical stage equipment, stage lighting and audio visual systems.

### Call out, term and preventative maintenance of theatre equipment including supply of spare parts.

## SPECIALIST CONTRACTORS TO THE BRITISH THEATRE INDUSTRY

lifts, etc. Incorporating hydraulic and pneumatic systems.

**SSE HIRE LTD**
201 Coventry Road, Birmingham B10 0RA
Tel 0121 766 7170
Fax 0121 766 8217
Manufacturer and hirer of staging, sets and podia. Range of sets available for hire. Custom items manufactured to specifications supplied.

**STAGE DRIVES & CONTROLS LTD**
Manor Farm, Common Road, Shelfanger, Diss, Norfolk IP22 2DR
Tel 01379 644656
Fax 01379 644684

**STAGE SERVICES**
Stage House, Prince William Road, Loughborough, Leicestershire LE11 0GN
Tel 01509 218857
Fax 01509 265730
Sales, Hire and Installation of LIghting, Sound and Staging Equipment by ADB, CCT, LSD, Electro Control Systems, Zero 88, AKG, Allen and Heath, Audio Technica, Tascam, C Aduio, JBL, Quad, Sennheiser, Deonon, Trantec, Stage Systems and others. Stage make-up by Grimas, counter sales, mail order and workshops. Sales and Hire of optical and pyrotechnic effects by DHA, Le Maitre & Theatrical Pyrotechnics. Drapes made to order. Full range of electrical and rigging accessories, consumables and sales of colour filter by Rosco and Lee.

**STAGE SYSTEMS**
Stage House, Prince William Road, Loughborough, Leicestershire LE11 0GN

Tel 01509 611021
Fax 01509 233146
e-mail stagesystm@aol.com
Website www.stagesystems.co.uk
Demountable staging, tiering and seating systems. For sale or hire. All systems are lightweight, easy to assemble and compact to store.

**STAGE TECHNIQUES LTD**
Unit One, Cotton Drive, Dalehouse Lane Industrial Estate, Kenilworth, Warwickshire CV8 2EB
Tel 01926 864800
Fax 01926 864964
email: stagetec@dircon.co.uk
Contact: S. Griffiths
Scenery construction and Steeldeck hire for Conferences, Theatre, Television and Outdoor Events,

**STAGE TECHNOLOGIES**
3a Aberdeen Studios, 22 Highbury Grove, London N5 2DQ
Tel 0171 354 8800
Fax 0171 359 1730
Contacts: Nikki Scott, John Hastie and Mark Ager.
Stage automation control systems for fixed installations and one-off productions. Manufacturers of winches and control systems for flying and automating trucks and revolves.

**STAGE TRACK LTD**
Harbour Lane, Garboldisham, Diss, Norfolk IP22 2ST
Tel 01953 688188
Fax 01953 688144
Email: sales@stagetrack.co.uk
Website: www.stagetrack.co.uk
Contact: G. Dashper
Suppliers of various curtain systems, hoists, fire

---

# WELD-FAB STAGE ENGINEERING LTD.

## DESIGN & MANUFACTURE OF TRUCKING SCENERY, REVOLVES, LIFTS, ROSTRA FLOORING & TIMBER FINISHING. FOR TELEVISION, THEATRE & EXHIBITION SERVICES. VARIOUS EQUIPMENT AVAILABLE FOR SALE OR HIRE.

### PLEASE CONTACT BRIAN SKIPP FOR DETAILS.

HARBOUR LANE WORKS, GARBOLDISHAM, DISS, NORFOLK IP22 2ST

**Telephone: 01953 688133  Fax: 01953 688144**

**E-mail: weld-fab.stage@paston.co.uk**

---

curtains and associated controls and equipment.

**STAGEWORKS LTD**
Units H1, Colchester Industrial Estate, Colchester Avenue, Cardiff CF3 7AP
Tel 01222 462713
Fax 01222 462718
Contacts: Jo Price or Peter Bailey
Set builders, fabrication and engineering, scenic artists, sculpture and GRP work. Transport and storeage facilities. Brochure available.
Please see display advert.

**STAR HIRE**
Milton Road, Thurleigh, Bedford MK44 2DG
Tel 01234 772233
Fax 01234 772272
Hire of technical services to the entertainment industry for both indoor and outdoor events. Agents in the South of England for Hangar services indoor staging.

**STEELDECK SALES & RENTALS LTD**
Barpart House, King's Cross Freight Depot, York Way, London N1 0UZ
Tel 0171 833 2031
Fax 0171 278 3403
Contact: Philip Parsons, Michael Passmore.
Original manufacturers of Steeldeck staging, available for sale, hire and installation. Steeldeck builds platforms, seating tiers, catwalks and ramps for indoor and outdoor use. Affordable, durable and versatile.

**TELESTAGE ASSOCIATES (UK) LIMITED**
Unit 14, Bunting Road, Moreton Hall Industrial Estate, Bury St. Edmunds, Suffolk IP32 7BX
Tel 01284 755512
Fax 01284 755516
Email: tsamkb@compuserve.com
Website: www.telestage.com
Contact: Mike Bacon

**TOTAL FABRICATIONS LIMITED**
Units 3 & 4, Kingston Industrial Estate, 81-86 Glover Street, Birmingham B9 4EN
Tel 0121 772 5234
Fax 0121 772 5231
e-mail info@totalfabs.com
Website: www.totalfabs.com
Contact: Adrian Black
Manufacturer of standard and custom aluminium trusses, roof structures, fixtures and associated equipment including motor controllers and full range of Verlinde products catering for broad spectrum of applications

**TRIPLE E LTD**
B3, Tower Bridge Business Complex, Clements Road, London SE16 4EF
Tel 0171 237 6354
Fax 0171 237 7650
Contact: David Eddlestein and Phil Sparkes
Triple E are the designers, manufacturers and suppliers of the unique Unitrack system from simple corded tracks to multi-motor computer controlled systems. We both sell and install curtain and scenery track systems. We also hire flight cased tracks and motor systems. We have a track for every purpose within the entertainment industry and can supply world-wide either direct or through our distributors.

**VELVETFIELD LTD**
10 Hillfoot Road, Neepsend, Sheffield S3 8AA
Tel 0114 275 6772
Fax 0114 272 5174
Scenery construction. Property makers. Scenic Artists.

**UNUSUAL RIGGING LTD**
The Wharf, Bugbrooke, Northants NN7 3QD
Tel 01604 830083
Fax 01604 831144
Email: info@unusual.co.uk
Website: www.unusual.co.uk
Contact: David Mayo
Unusual brings the disciplines of design, rigging, fabrications and automation to provide an ideal installation service for the supply, renovation and renewal of stage engineering and flying systems.

**WELD-FAB STAGE ENGINEERING LTD**
Harbour Lane, Garboldisham, Diss, Norfolk IP22 2ST
Tel 01953 688133
Fax 01953 688144
e-mail weld-fab.stage@paston.co.uk
Contact: Brian Skipp
Design and manufacturers of various stage, studio, television & exhibition equipment for sale or hire. Motorised and fixed scenery, revolving stages, scissor lifts, power flying & counterweight systems.

# 62
# STORAGE

**UPSTAGE**
Unit 7-8, Acorn Production Centre, 105 Blundell Street, Islington, London N7 9DW
Tel 0171 609 9119
Fax 0171 609 3400
Secure, Dry Premises; 10 minutes from London's West

End; Collection/delivery nationwide; Easy access; Parking; Stage lit fitting room; Competitive long & short term rates;
See our main ad under Costume (Cleaning).

# 63
# TECHNICAL STAFF

**BIG WORLD PRODUCTIONS**
**SOUND AND LIGHT PRODUCTIONS**
Kerrison Hall, 28 Kerrison Road, London W5 5NW
Tel 0181 579 2748
Fax 0181 840 6482
Mobile 0860 594620

**FM PRODUCTIONS**
134 Widdenham Road, London N7 9SQ
Tel 0171 700 6361
Fax 0171 700 6352
Mobile 0802 250877

**IDEAL PRODUCTION SERVICES**
94 Gordon Road, Nunhead, London SE15 3RP
Tel 0171 564 3384
Fax 0171 564 3147
Mobile 0831 282887
Email m-shayle@dircon.co.uk
Contact: Mark Shayle

**MILL SEA PRODUCTION SERVICES**
7b Angles Road, London SW16 2UU
Tel 0181 677 2370
Fax 0181 677 8690

**STAGE MANAGEMENT**
29 Derby Street, Colne, Lancs BB8 9AA
Tel/Fax 01282 867930
Warehouse Fax 01282 870366
Mobile 0831 437062

**TOUR SUPPORT LTD**
40 High Road, Buckhurst Hill, Essex IG9 5HP
Tel 0181 505 1073
Fax 0181 559 2598

**THE WHATEVER CREW**
226b Paisley Road, West Glasgow G52 3QL
Fax/Tel 0141 882 3781
Contact: Jason McSwan, Dave Triney
Stage crew hire. Running stage security. Backline crew. Drum and guitar tech tours. Load in/out,etc.

# 64
# THEATRE CONSTRUCTION, MANAGEMENT & RENOVATION

**BOVIS CONSTRUCTION LIMITED**
Bovis House, 142 Northolt Road, Harrow, Middlesex HA2 0EE
Tel 0181 422 3488

Fax 0181 864 4055
Contact: Mr Chris Purves
Bovis is a market leader in the provision of consultancy, management and specialist contracting services services for theatre and leisure projects.
Our experience include Glyndebourne Opera House, The Savoy theatre, Sadlers Wells, Edinburgh Festival.

**LASSETTER WILLIAMS**
Isgaerwen, Pentrellyncymer, Corwen LL21 9TU
Tel/Fax 01490 420254
Partner: Michael Williams
Project management (new buildings and refurbishments), events management, feasibility studies, lottery applications.

**THEATRE DEVELOPMENTS LIMITED**
55 High Street, Tring, Herts HP23 5AG
Tel 01442 890999
Fax 01442 890258
e-mail TDL@dial.pipex.com
Design and Consultancy in respect of all professional disciplines for the design and/or refurbishment of Theatres; Cinemas; Studios; Lecture Theatres; Boardrooms; Training Centres etc.

**THEATRESEARCH**
The Lodge, Braisty Woods, Summerbridge, North Yorkshire HG3 4DN
Tel 01423 780497
Email david@theatresearch.freeserve.co.uk
Contact: David Wilmore, Ric Green
Theatresearch specialises in the restoration of historic theatres, providing theatre consultancy services for planning, design, technical equipment, historic research/archives and project management.
Theatresearch also undertakes consultancy work for film and TV companies working on location in theatres, providing project management, script advice and historic information for period productions, and documentaries.

**UNUSUAL RIGGING LTD**
The Wharf, Bugbrooke, Northants NN7 3QD
Tel 01604 830083
Fax 01604 831144
Email: info@unusual.co.uk
Website: www.unusual.co.uk
Contact: David Mayo
Unusual brings the disciplines of design, rigging, fabrications and automation to provide an ideal installation service for the supply, renovation and renewal of stage engineering and flying systems.

# 65
# TRANSLATION SERVICES

**ADVANCED INTERPRETATION SERVICES**
Westminster House, Herschel Centre, Church Street, Slough SL1 1PJ
Tel 01753 553325
Fax 01753 553867

**UPS TRANSLATIONS**
111 Baker Street, London W1M 1FE
Tel 0171 837 8300
Fax 0171 486 3272

**VOICE AND SCRIPT INTERNATIONAL**
132 Cleveland Street, London W1 6AB
Tel 0171 584 7000
Fax 0171 584 5544
Script translation service.

# 66
# TRANSPORT & TRAVEL

**AIR-RIDER**
18 Gisburn Mansions, Tottenham Lane, London
N8 7EB
Tel 0181 341 5871/0836 519902
Trucking

**ANGLO PACIFIC INTERNATIONAL PLC**
Unit 1, Bush Industrial Estate, Standard Road, London
NW10 6DF
Tel 0181 965 1955
Fax 0181 965 4954
Email: info@anglopacific.co.uk
Website: www.anglopacific.demon.co.uk
Ocean Freight, Air Freight, Trucking, Full Carnet
Services, Forwarders to the performing Arts

**BOURNES**
Unit 12B, Mills Road, Quarry Wood Industrial Estate,
Aylesford, Maidstone, Kent ME20 7NA
Tel 01622 791013
Fax 01622 710237
Van Transport & Storage

**BRITANNIA CHAPMANS**
Units N&P, Block 9, Distribution Centre, Paddock
Wood, Tunbridge TN12 6UU
Tel 01892 833313
Fax 01892 834714
Furniture Removals and Storage. Theatrical Scenery
and Works of Art Great Britain and T.I.R. Service to
Europe - Worldwide Shipping.

**BRUNELS THEATRICAL SERVICES**
Unit 4, Crown Industrial Estate, Crown Road, Warmly,
Bristol BS15 2JB
Tel 0117 907 7855
Fax 0117 907 7856
Contact: Shane Hippisley
A 24 hour professional service throughout the UK and
Europe. We specialise in all forms of transport to film,
TV and theatrical companies including Green Room
and Storage. Competitive rates tailor made to suit your
needs. Our large fleet of vehicles ranges from transit
vans to Supercube Airride step framed trailers.

**BULLENS LIMITED**
PO Box 12, Nuffield Rd, Hinckley, Leicestershire
LE10 3DQ
Tel 01455 251152
Fax 01455 251058
Branches covering UK and facilities in Europe. A
comprehensive warehouse and transport service in the
UK and on the continent for theatrical tours. Transport for
scenery, props, electrics, orchestras etc

**COWLEY CARRIERS LTD**
London Road, Wheatley, Oxford OX33 1JG
Tel 01865 872466/01865 872499

Fax 01865 874414

**K W DEVEREUX & SONS**
Daimler Drive, Cowpen Lane Industrial Estate,
Billingham, Cleveland  TS23 4JD
Tel 01642 560854
Fax 01642 565562
Devereux's have been in the theatrical removal
business for over 4 decades and being based in the
centre of the UK are ideal for nationwide tours.

**EXPRESS EXPORT SERVICES LIMITED**
Arlette House, 143 Wardour Street, London W1
Tel 0171 734 8356
Fax 0171 734 3729
Shippers of costumes, props, stages and all other
associated goods to the theatrical industry, by air, sea
or overland truck to all parts of the world.

**FLIGHT DIRECTORS LTD**
Ocean House, Hazelwick Avenue, Crawley, West
Sussex RH10 1NP
Tel 01293 552757
Fax 01293 553321
Private aircraft charter, from a worldwide database we
can locate and negotiate for any aircraft size required.
Small air taxis, private jets up to Boeing 747 can be
supplied.

**GEE TRAVEL (NEW YORK)**
12 Stamford Hill, London N16 6XZ
Tel 0181 806 3434
Fax 0181 800 1082
Branch Address:
60 Cranwich Road, London
N16 5JN
Tel 0181 800 1082
24 hour urgent air tickets telephone service to the
Theatre/Film Industry.
New York Office:
543 Bedford Avenue, Brooklyn 11211
Tel 00 1 718 782 4000
Fax 00 1 718 782 1736

**G&R REMOVALS**
100 Bollo Lane, London W4 5LX
Tel 0181 994 9733
Fax 0181 995 0855

**JETAIR**
4 Charlwood Court, County Oak Way, Crawley, West
Sussex RH11 7XA
Tel 01293 614400
Fax 01293 614499
Telex 87547
Experts in arranging all types of aircraft charter
worldwide. From two seat executive aircraft,
helicopters and luxury jets to large airliners for
passengers or freight.

**LOMAS HELICOPTERS**
Lake Heliport, Abbotsham, Bideford, North Devon
EX39 5BQ
Tel 01237 421054
Fax 01237 424060
Operations Manager: Emma Cocks

**G. H. LUCKING & SONS**
Commerce Road, Brentford, Middlesex TW8 8LX
Tel 0181 569 9030
Fax 0181 569 9847
(Manchester Office) Preston Street, Manchester
Contact London office for further details

**PAUL MATHEW TRANSPORT LTD**
Unit 1, Ferry Road, Littlehampton Marina,
Littlehampton Sussex BN17 5DS.
Tel 01903 730 930
Fax 01903 730630
Email: paul.mathew@btinternet.com
Contact: Paul Mathew
International theatre scenery exhibition & concert movers.

**MOTORVATION**
The Station Buildings, Shoreham Station, Shoreham,
Nr Sevenoaks, Kent TN14 7RT
Tel 01959 525210
Fax 01959 525170
Specialist transport for lighting, scenery and sound equipment for all types of Theatrical Tours.

**PICKFORD REMOVALS LIMITED**
7 Jubilee Road, Burgess Hill, West Sussex RH15 9TL
Tel 01273 730238
Fax 01444 243007
Haulage and Transporting

**RADCLIFFES TRANSPORT SERVICES**
Head Office: Comerce Road, Brentford, TW8 8LX
Tel 0181 687 2344
Fax 0181 568 6086

**REDBURN TRANSFER LTD**
Redburn House, Stockingswater Lane, Enfield,
Middlesex EN3 7PH
Tel 0181 804 0027
Fax 0181 804 8021
Contact: Chris Redburn
Full UK and international trucking service. 45ft and 40ft air ride stepframe trailers, Scania and Volvo tractor units, 16 ton and 3 ton Saviem box trucks and transit vans.
Storage facilities.

**RICHARDSON REMOVAL AND STORAGE CONTRACTORS LIMITED**
Vickers Close, Preston Farm Industrial Estate, Preston Farm Industrial Estate, Stockton on Tees, Cleveland TS18 3TD
Tel 01642 673207
Fax 01642 671080

**EDWIN SHIRLEY TRUCKING LTD**
Marshgate Sidings, Marshgate Lane, London E15 2PB.
Tel 0181 522 1000
Fax 0181 522 1002
Contact: Del Roll
40' and 45' air-ride trailers, staging and warehousing.

Plus 7.5 tonne & 16 tonne trucks.

**SOUTHERN VAN LINES**
41 Crowden Way, Crossway, London SE28 8HE
Tel 0181 310 8512
Fax 0181 312 0148

**STAGE TRUCK**
Unit 3, Green Lane, Hounslow, Middx TW4 6BY.
Tel 0181 569 4444
Fax 0181 569 4194

**STAGEFREIGHT LTD**
Unit B, Gildersome Spur, Leeds LS27 7JZ
Tel 0113 238 0805
Fax 0113 238 0806
Email: showmover@aol.com
Contact: Peter Cresswell
Transport specialists throughout Britain and Europe serving the needs of the Theatre, TV, Conference and Exhibition sectors. Above all reliable.

**STARDES LTD**
Ashes Buildings, Old Lane, Holbrook Industrial Estate, Halfway, Sheffield S19 5GZ
Tel 0114 251 0051
Fax 0114 251 0555
Exec Minibuses, Truck & Van Rental, Concert Tour Transportation, Walkramps, Transportation Consultants.

**THEATRE PICK-UPS**
PO Box 232, London WC2B 5SY
Tel 0115 969 3306
Transport for West End and regional theatre, TV and media, storage available.  General services including tab hire, stage hire, building maintenance, promotion and leaflet distribution.

**TRANS EURO WORLDWIDE MOVERS**
Drury Way, London NW10 0JN
Tel 0181 784 0100
Fax 0181 459 7121
email: rachel.james@transeuro.com
Website www.transeuro.com
Contact: Rachel James or Mike Smith
As a quick reminder, our expertise lies in the planning and preparation of transport for UK, European and Worldwide Evcents, using our vehicle fleet and worldwide air and sea freight forwarding. See our ad and call today for a no obligations quote.

**TRINIFOLD TRAVEL LTD**
West End House, 11 Hills Place, London W1R 2LB

UK &
Worldwide
Tours

Roadshows

Panto's

*Transeuro* ➤
Commercial Division

Call: Mike Smith:
**0181 780 0100**
**0181 459 7121**

Theatre

Road/Air/
Sea Freight

Opera

Storage

Orchestras

Tel 0171 734 5577/413 0400
Fax 0171 839 3690
Telex 896232 HAWKO G

**WAYNE POWELL TRANSPORT SERVICES**
9 Underwood Terrace, Abertridwr, Caerphilly, Mid
Glamorgan CF83 4BQ
Tel 01222 832070
Fax 01222 832300
Contact: Wayne Powell

# 67
# WARDROBE

**ARTIST'S THEATRE SHOP**
23 City Road, Chester CH1 3AE
Tel 01244 320271
Retail sales, ballet shoes and requisites - theatrical
make-up and costume hire.

**THE BALLERINA**
52 London Road, Leicester LE2 0QD
Tel 0116 254 4206
Ballet Shoes, Ballroom and Wedding Shoes.
Regulation Dancewear and all ballet accessories,
aerobic leotards and tights. Theatrical Materials,
Sequins and Trims, Tiaras and Theatrical Make-Up.
Nationwide Mail Order Service.

**BABOUCHA SHOES**
218 High Street, Barnet, Herts EN5 5SZ
Tel 0181 441 3788
Fax 0181 441 3788
Theatrical and fashion shoe makers. Footwear for all
occasions. Period, panto, Victorian etc. Also matching
belts and bags, made in almost any leather or fabric

**BLACK LION COSTUMES**
Unit 8, Wallbridge Mills, Wallbridge, Frome BA11 5SX
Tel 01373 472786
Contact: Heather Kiernan
Over 5,000 square feet of costumes. Authentic, all
periods. Good range of uniforms, footware, armour
accessories etc. We specialise in masks, made to any
specification. Sensible prices. Viewing by appointment
only.

**CELEBRITY CLEANERS**
102 Wardour Street, London W1V 3LD
Tel 0171 437 5324 (24 hours)
Fax 0171 434 2138
Contact: Robert Shooman or Sylvia Willingham
Specialist Dry Cleaners to the Theatre Profession and
Theatrical Costumiers. Situated in the heart
Theatreland.

**THE COMPANY OF TEN**
Abbey Theatre, Westminster Lodge, Holywell Hill, St.
Albans AL1 2DL.
Tel 01727 847472
Fax 01727 812742
Manager: David Griffiths
Wardrobe Mistresses: Pam Curtis, Tel/Fax 01727
863818, and Phyl Swindlehurst, Tel 01727 858307

**CREATIVE BEADCRAFT LTD**
Also trading as Ells & Farrier
Personal Callers Only: 20 Beak Street, London
W1R 3HA
Tel 0171 629 9964
All enquiries/Mail and Telephone Orders: Denmark
Works, Beamond End, Amersham, Bucks HP7 0RX
Tel 01494 715606
Fax 01494 718510
e-mail beads@creativebeadcraft.com
Website www.creativebeadcraft.co.uk
Importers and distributors of beads, imitation pearls,
jewellery findings, diamante, imitation stones,
trimmiings, sequins, feathers.

**C I DAVIS & CO LTD**
94-96 Seymour Place, London W1H 5DG
Tel 0171 723 0895/0171 723 7735
Fax 0171 723 4697
Wholesale silk and Rayon Fabrics.

**EMPEE SILK FABRICS LIMITED**
42-44 Brick Lane, London E1 6RF
Tel 0171 247 1094
Fax 0171 375 2869
Suppliers of Fashion Fabrics to Stage and Dancing
Schools. Cut lengths supplied, minimum 10 yards but
special rates for full pieces.
Also at: 46/48 Atherton Street. All types of fabrics held
in stock.

**A R FABB BROS LTD (Est. 1887)**
29/31 Risborough Road, Maidenhead, Berkshire
SL6 7YT
Tel 01628 22705
Costume gold wire embroiderers, manufacturers in
metal of costume and wardrobe accessories, machine
embroidery. Flags and banners etc.

**FREED OF LONDON LTD**
Wholesale Department: 62-64 Well Street, London
E9 7PX
Tel 0181 985 6121
Fax 0181 985 7187
Retail Shop: 94 St. Martins Lane, London WC2N 4AT
Tel 0171 240 0432

Fax 0171 240 3061
e-mail sales@freed.co.uk

**GAMBA LIMITED**
3 Garrick Street, London WC2E 9AR
Tel 0171 437 0704
Fax 0171 497 0754
Retailing Footwear for Ballet and Theatre, Hosiery,
Garments.

**GANDOLFI GROUP**
Mill Road, Wellingborough, Northants NN8 1PR
Tel 01933 224007 (3 Lines)
Fax 01933 227009
Trade/wholesale, factory production.

**GANDOLFI GROUP**
London Retailer (The Gandolfi Shop):
Dorset House, 150 Marylebone Road,
London NW1 5PP
Tel/Fax 0171 935 6049
Manufacturers, Suppliers and Importers of Dance and
Ballet Footwear, Leotards, Tights etc. Distribution
through Specialist Shops and Selected Retails. "Local
Stockist List" provided against enquirer stating nearest
centres.

**KERSEN TRIMMINGS LIMITED**
449-451 High Road, Willesden, London NW10 2DA
Tel 0181 459 9060
Fax 0181 459 9061
Leading suppliers of Trimmings: Sequins, Beading,
Motives, Lace, Anglais, Guipure, Ribbons, Sequin
Material, Stretch Sequins, Braids, Cotton Zips, Nets,
Marabou, Feather Boas. Always plenty of clearing lines
available.

**MILTON & PARNELL (FORMERLY TRAFFORD &
PARNELL PRODUCTIONS)**
85 Marton Drive, Blackpool FY4 3EY
Tel 01253 766928 or 0860 273341

**NEVILLES TEXTILES**
PO Box 87, 29 Stoney Street, Nottingham NG1 1LR
Tel 0115 959 8781
Fax 0115 950 2687
Merchant stockist of Fluorescent fabrics, Feathers and
Trimmings.

**PROPRESS STEAMERS**
33-35 Battersea Bridge Road, London SW11 3BA
Tel 0171 228 8467
Fax 0171 924 2549

**ADEL ROOTSTEIN DISPLAY MANNEQUINS**
9 Beaumont Avenue, London W14 9LP
Tel 0171 381 1447
Fax 0171 381 3263
Hire of Display Mannequins and Wigs.

**JANE RUMBLE**
121 Elmstead Avenue, Wembley, Middlesex HA9 8NT
Tel 0181 904 6462
Props specially made to order. Not for hire. Crowns,
Masks, Helmets, Jewellery, Leatherwork, Small props,
One-off Animal Outfits. Design service available.

**SILVAN LTD**
21 Blandford Street, London W1H 3AD
Tel 0171 486 5883
Fax 0171 486 5887
Speciality suppliers of Gold and Silver wide and edging
lace also corded and beaded lace. Cotton and Silk

Tulles, Embroidered Tulles suitable for Theatre, Opera
and Ballet.

**STOCKMAN LONDON LTD**
Stockman House, 9 Dallington Street,
London EC1V OBQ
Tel 0171 251 6943
Fax 0171 250 1798
Sales: Gavin Hippard
Dressmakers and tailors dummies, workroom etc.
millinery accessories. Mobile dress rails, hangers etc.

**TIMEFARER FOOTWEAR**
Shoemakers, Gorthleck, Inverness IV1 2YS
Tel 01456 486 696
Hand-made reproduction historical footwear.
Historically accurate construction methods & materials;
all periods, military & civilian, ladies & childrens.

**TRAFFORD & PARNELL PRODUCTIONS**
See MILTON & PARNELL

**UPSTAGE THEATRICAL SUPPLIES**
Unit 5-9, 23 Abingdon Street, Blackpool FY1 1DG
Tel 01253 292321
Contact: Gabriella Gratrix - Head of Wardrobe
Specialists in lavish revue costumes (feathered
headdresses and harnesses). Wardrobe maintenance
service.

**WOLFIN TEXTILES LIMITED**
64 Great Titchfield Street, London W1
Tel 0171 580 4724/636 4949
Fax 0171 580 4724
All basic materials for Stage, Screen and TV. Costume
interlinings, scenery canvas, calico, duck, blackout etc.

# 68

# WEAPONS & ARMOUR

**ARVALON STAGE ARMOURY**
8 Scone Gardens, Edinburgh EH8 7DQ
Tel 0131 661 1123
Contact: C & A Jeffroys
Hire of Weapons, Heraldic Shields, Armour and Allied
Properties for Theatre, Film and Publicity Work

**BAPTY & CO LIMITED**
703 Harrow Road, London NW10
Tel 0181 969 6671
Fax 0181 960 1106
Telex 939099
Hirers of fighting weapons of all types and periods and
associated props.

**ENGLISH FIELD ARTILLERY COMPANY**
John Slough of London, Old Forge, Peterchurch,
Hereford HR2 OSD
Tel 01981 550145
Fax 01981 550506
For sale and hire, cannons, field artillery - blank firing
from central control unit. Open-air concerts - 1812
overture - our speciality. Antique and modern firearms
and military props.
Special effects, controlled explosions.
Consultant on all things military and all aspects of
firearms.

**PETER EVANS STUDIOS LTD**
1 Frederick Street, Luton, Bedfordshire LU2 7QW
Tel 01582 25730
Fax 01582 481329
Makers of suits of armour, Helmets, Shields and
Breast plates in glass fibre and A.B.S.
Catalogue available.

**FIREBRAND**
Leac Na Ban, Tayvallich, Lochgilphead,
Argyll PA31 8PF
Tel/Fax 01546 870310
Contact: Alexander Hamilton
Flambeaux Torch - Supplies in association with "Pollex
Props" - property makers.

**FLAME ENTERPRISE LIMITED**
1st Floor, 31 Market Street, Torquay, Devon TQ1 3AW
Tel 01803 211930
Fax 01803 293554
Armour and Weapons made to order, for hire or sale.

**HOWORTH WRIGHTSON LTD**
The Prop House, Unit 2, Cricket Street, Denton,
Manchester  M34 3DR
Tel 0161 335 0220
Fax 0161 320 3928
Hirers of guns, firearms and weapons. Specialising in
blank firing guns which do not require a firearm
licence. Also retail sales of pyrotechnics effects.

**ADRIAN MARCHANT STUDIOS**
Unit C, Roebuck Road, Chessington, Surrey KT9 1EU
Tel 0181 397 5777
Fax 0181 397 6939
Company of artists and sculptors.  Also suppliers of
Slashed Curtains, Glitter, Poly Balls, Rolls PVC, Snow,
Cobweb Sprays, Bead Strings etc. Also statues,
including full suit of armour.

**RENT-A-SWORD**
180 Frog Grove Lane, Wood Street Village, Guildford,
Surrey GU3 3HD
Tel 01483 234084
Fax 01483 236684
Proprietor: Alan M Meek
Helmets, String Mail, Swords, Daggers, Pole-arms for
hire or sale, suitable for stage fighting. Recommended
by the British Academy of Dramatic Combat.

# 69
# MISCELLANEOUS

**CELEBRITY CLEANERS**
102 Wardour Street, London W1V 3LD
Tel 0171 437 5324 (24 hours)
Fax 0171 434 2138
Contact: Robert Shooman or Sylvia Willingham
Specialist Dry Cleaners to the Theatre Profession and
Theatrical Costumiers. Situated in the heart
Theatreland.

**CREATIVE SYSTEMS TECHNOLOGY**
Sophia House, 28 Cathedral Road, Cardiff, South
Glamorgan, Wales CF1 9LJ
Tel 01222 660142
Fax 01222 664891
Contact: Martin Howell
CST provide cost effective solutions whatever your

needs.  Lighting/Special Effects Design, Remote
Control/Motor controlled systems, software
management, security & tagging systems, together
with an after sales service next to none.

**CREFFIELDS (TIMBER & BOARDS ) LTD**
Unit 6, Marcus Close, Tilehurst, Reading, Berkshire
RG30 4EA
Tel 01734 453533
Fax 01734 453633
email: creffields@patrol.i-way.co.uk
Creffields is one of the UK's leading suppliers of flame
retardant timber and boards for the theatre, TV and
film. Large stocks are held allowing for urgent orders
delivered promptly.

**DIRECTA (UK) LIMITED**
Cold Norton, Essex CM3 6UA
Tel 01621 828882
Fax 01621 828072
Five good reasons to buy from Directa:
$\Sigma$ Cometitive Prices
$\Sigma$ Speedy Nationwide Delivery
$\Sigma$ Free Technical Advice
$\Sigma$ Strict Quality Control
$\Sigma$ BSN 9002
No quibble guarantee, the customers are always right.

**FLINT HIRE & SUPPLY LTD**
Queens Row, London SE17 2PX
Tel 0171 703 9786
Fax 0171 708 4189
Email: sales@flintltd.demon.co.uk
Contact: Alasdair Flint
Suppliers of scenic paints, textures, tools, fixtures,
fittings, adhesives, flame retardents, adhesive tapes
and safety equipment. Hire and sales for Megadek
modular staging, weights, braces, truck winches, 2
scenic paintframes.

**LEE FILTERS**
Central Way, Walworth Industrial Estate, Andover,
Hants SP10 5AN
Tel 01264 366245
Fax 01264 355058
Contact: Paul Topliss
Manufacturers of lighting filter in both polyester and
polycarbonate. Flame retardant to BS5750 when
stated. Also manufactures of photographic colour
correction and colour printing filters, and optical resin
camera filters. Suppliers of gobos.

**THE LONDON OPERA GLASS COMPANY LTD**
3 The Crystal Business Centre, Sandwich Industrial
Estate, Ramsgate Road, Sandwich, Kent CT13 9QX
Tel/Fax 01304 620360
Contact: Les Irvine
Sole manufacturers of opera glasses and opera glass
vending machines in the UK. Offer  a comprehensive
Back-up service in opera glass machines and
customised binoculars.
Customised opera glasses also available.

**QUICKSILVER UK LTD**
Broom Grove Lane, Denton, Manchester M34 3DU
Tel 0161 320 7232
Contact: Darren Wallis
Suppliers of pyrotechnic effects and fireworks for all
types of indoor and outdoor effects.  Specialists in
production of smoke effects. Too many products to list.
Too many brands to name.

**DONNA RUANE ASSOCIATES LTD**
31 Fenhurst Road, Croydon, Surrey, CR0 7DJ
Tel/Fax 0181 654 9282
Email SignAway@compuserve.com
Director: Terry Ruane
We provide sign language interpreters to interpret
theatre shows and for situations where deaf actors
work in Theatre, TV, etc.

**SGB WORLD SERVICE**
Empire House, 12 Rutland Street, Hanley,
Stoke on Trent ST1 5JG
Tel 01782 279309
Fax 01782 279309
e-mail email@sgbworldservice.co.uk
Website www.sgbwordservice.com
Contact:Mr S. Boote
See our main advert in Lighting & Lighting Equipment
Suppliers.

**STAGE TRACK LTD**
Harbour Lane, Garboldisham, Diss, Norfolk IP22 2ST
Tel 01953 688188
Fax 01953 688144
Email: sales@stagetrack.co.uk
Website: www.stagetrack.co.uk
Contact: G. Dashper
Suppliers of various curtain systems, hoists, fire
curtains and associated controls and equipment.

**TMB ASSOCIATES**
The Old Brick Yard, Estbourne Road, Brentford,
Middx TW8 9PG
Tel 0181 560 9652
Fax 0181 560 1064
e-mailmt@tmb.com
Website www.tmb.com
Contact: Mark Thompson
Value added distributor of production lighting equipment
and sound and lighting cabling. The range covers all
major US and European production lighting and hardware
including all touring all touring expandable supplies.

**WELD-FAB STAGE ENGINEERING LTD**
Harbour Lane, Garboldisham, Diss, Norfolk IP22 2ST
Tel 01953 688133
Fax 01953 688144
e-mail weld-fab.stage@paston.co.uk
Contact: Brian Skipp
Design and manufacturers of various stage, studio,
television & exhibition equipment for sale or hire.
Motorised and fixed scenery, revolving stages, scissor
lifts, power flying & counterweight systems.

# ADVERTISERS INDEX

# AWARD-WINNING TOURING MUSICAL PRODUCTION

BILL BEN

*Trevor Paynes*

That The

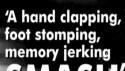

'A hand clapping, foot stomping, memory jerking **SMASH**'

The Daily Mirror

'Crammed full of high energy music and fun **FAB**'

The Express

HAIR

*Exclusive Wor*

## Derek Block

Douglas House
Dean Stree
Tel: 0171 434 21
Email: dbaa@